D0084392

READINGS
★ ON ★ POLITICAL
COMMUNICATION

FREE COPY

READINGS
★ON★ POLITICAL
COMMUNICATION

Edited by

Theodore F. Sheckels
Randolph-Macon College

Janette Kenner Muir
George Mason University

Terry Robertson
University of South Dakota

Lisa M. Gring-Pemble
George Mason University

STRATA PUBLISHING, INC.
State College, Pennsylvania

Strata Publishing, Inc.
State College, Pennsylvania
9 8 7 6 5 4 3 2 1

Copyright © 2007 by Theodore F. Sheckels, Janette Kenner Muir, Terry Robertson, and Lisa M. Gring-Pemble
All rights reserved. Printed and bound in the United States of America. No part of this publication may be reproduced, stored in a data base or retrieval system, or transmitted in any form or by any means (electronic, mechanical, photocopying, scanning, or otherwise) without the prior written permission of the publisher.

Published by:
Strata Publishing, Inc.
P.O. Box 1303
State College, PA 16804
telephone: 814-234-8545
fax: 814-238-7222
web site: http://www.stratapub.com

Text and cover design by WhiteOak Creative.
Cover and interior photograph: Vintage American Patriotic and Political Pins © Comstock/Corbis.
Printed and bound by Malloy Incorporated.

Credits and acknowledgments appear on pages v–vi and on this page by reference.

Library of Congress Cataloging-in-Publication Data

Readings on political communication / edited by Theodore F. Sheckels ... [et al.].
    p. cm.
  Includes bibliographical references and index.
   ISBN 978-1-891136-18-4 (pbk.)
   1. Communication in politics--United States. 2. United States--Politics
and government.   I. Sheckels, Theodore F.

JA85.2.U6R43 2007
320.97301'4--dc22

                                                    2007001778

Credits and Acknowledgments

Dan D. Nimmo and Keith R. Sanders, "The Emergence of Political Communication as a Field," from Dan D. Nimmo and Keith R. Sanders, eds., *Handbook of Political Communication,* pp. 11–36, copyright 1981 by Sage Publications, Inc., Reprinted by Permission of Sage Publications, Inc.

David Zarefsky, "Spectator Politics and the Revival of Public Argument," *Communication Monographs* 59 (December 1992): 411–414. Used by permission of Taylor & Francis, Ltd., http://www.tandf.co.uk/journals.

Robert D. Putnam, "Bowling Alone: America's Declining Social Capital," *Journal of Democracy* Vol. 6, No. 1 (January 1995): 65-78. Used by permission of The Sagalyn Agency and the author.

J. Michael Hogan, "George Gallup and the Rhetoric of Scientific Democracy," *Communication Monographs* 64 (June 1997): 161–179. Used by permission of Taylor & Francis, Ltd., http://www.tandf.co.uk/journals.

Trevor Parry-Giles and Shawn J. Parry-Giles, "Reassessing the State of Political Communication in the United States," *Argumentation and Advocacy* 37 (Winter 2001): 158–170. Used by permission of American Forensic Association.

Judith S. Trent, "Presidential Surfacing: The Ritualistic and Crucial First Act," *Communication Monographs* 45 (November 1978): 281–292. Used by permission of Taylor & Francis, Ltd., http://www.tandf.co.uk/journals.

Michael Gurevitch and Anandam P. Kavoori, "Television Spectacles as Politics," *Communication Monographs* 59 (December 1992): 415–420. Used by permission of Taylor & Francis, Ltd., http://www.tandf.co.uk/journals.

Kathleen E. Kendall, "The Problem of Beginnings in New Hampshire: Control over the Play," Reprinted by permission from *Presidential Campaign Discourse: Strategic Communication Problems* edited by Kathleen E. Kendall, the State University of New York Press © 1995, State University of New York. All rights reserved.

Trevor Parry-Giles and Shawn J. Parry-Giles, "Political Scopophilia, Presidential Campaigning, and the Intimacy of American Politics," *Communication Studies* 47 (Fall 1996): 191–205. Used by permission of Central States Communication Association.

"Effects of Political Information in the 2000 Presidential Campaign: Comparing Traditional Television and Internet Exposure," Lynda Lee Kaid, *American Behavioral Scientist,* Vol. 46, No. 5, 677–691, copyright 2003 by Sage Publications, Reprinted by Permission of Sage Publications, Inc.

Michael Pfau, Henry C. Kenski, Michael Nitz, and John Sorenson, "Efficacy of Inoculation Strategies in Promoting Resistance to Political Attack Messages: Application to Direct Mail," *Communication Monographs* 57 (March 1990): 25–43. Used by permission of Taylor & Francis, Ltd., http://www.tandf.co.uk/journals.

Lynda Lee Kaid and Anne Johnston, "Negative versus Positive Television Advertising in U.S. Presidential Campaigns, 1960–1988," *Journal of Communication* (1991) 41(3): 53–64, by permission of Oxford University Press.

"Tactics of Attack," from Kathleen Hall Jamieson, *Dirty Politics: Deception, Distraction, and Democracy* (New York: Oxford University Press, 1992), 43–63, 293–295. By permission of Oxford University Press, Inc.

Kim Fridkin Kahn, "Gender Differences in Campaign Messages: The Political Advertisements of Men and Women Candidates for U.S. Senate," *Political Research Quarterly,* Vol. 46, No. 3 (September 1993): 481–502. Reprinted by Permission of the University of Utah, Copyright Holder.

Stephen Ansolabehere, Shanto Iyengar, Adam Simon, and Nicholas Valentino, "Does Attack Advertising Demobilize the Electorate?" *American Political Science Review,* Vol. 88, No. 4 (December 1994): 829–838. Copyright © 1994 by the *American Political Science Association.* Reprinted with the permission of Cambridge University Press.

Diana Prentice Carlin, Charles Howard, Susan Stanfield, and Larry Reynolds, "The Effects of Presidential Debate Formats on Clash: A Comparative Analysis," *Argumentation and Advocacy* 27 (Winter 1991): 126–136. Used by permission of American Forensic Association.

John T. Morello, "The 'Look' and Language of Clash: Visual Structuring of Argument in the 1988 Bush-Dukakis Debates," *The Southern Communication Journal,* Vol. 57, No. 3 (1992): 205–218. Used by permission of Southern States Communication Association.

William P. Eveland, Jr., Douglas M. McLeod, and Amy I. Nathanson, "Reporters vs. Undecided Voters: An Analysis of the Questions Asked during the 1992 Presidential Debates," *Communication Quarterly*, Vol. 42, No. 4 (Fall 1994): 390–406. Used by permission of Eastern Communication Association.

The Racine Group, "White Paper on Televised Political Campaign Debates," *Argumentation and Advocacy* 38 (Spring 2002): 199–218. Used by permission of American Forensic Association.

William L. Benoit, Kevin A. Stein, and Glenn J. Hansen, "Newspaper Coverage of Presidential Debates," *Argumentation and Advocacy* 41 (Summer 2004): 17–27. Used by permission of American Forensic Association.

William F. Lewis, "Telling America's Story: Narrative Form and the Reagan Presidency," *Quarterly Journal of Speech* 73 (1987): 280–302. Used by permission of Taylor & Francis, Ltd., http://www.tandf.co.uk/journals.

"Inaugural Addresses," from Karlyn Kohrs Campbell and Kathleen Hall Jamieson, *Deeds Done in Words: Presidential Rhetoric and the Genres of Governance*, © 1990 by The University of Chicago. Used by permission of The University of Chicago Press.

Martin J. Medhurst, "Reconceptualizing Rhetorical History: Eisenhower's Farewell Address," *Quarterly Journal of Speech* 80 (1994): 195–218. Used by permission of Taylor & Francis, Ltd., http://www.tandf.co.uk/journals.

Amos Kiewe, "The Body as Proof: Franklin D. Roosevelt's Preparations for the 1932 Presidential Campaign," *Argumentation and Advocacy* 36 (Fall 1999): 88–100. Used by permission of American Forensic Association.

John M. Murphy, "'Our Mission and Our Moment': George W. Bush and September 11th." This work originally appeared in *Rhetoric and Public Affairs*, Vol. 6, No. 4, 2003, published by Michigan State University Press. Used by permission of the publisher.

Michael Halloran, "Doing Public Business in Public," from Karlyn Kohrs Campbell and Kathleen Hall Jamieson, eds., *Form and Genre: Shaping Rhetorical Action* (Falls Church, VA: Speech Communication Association, 1978): 118–138. Used by permission of National Communication Association.

Marouf Hasian, Jr., Celeste Michelle Condit, and John Louis Lucaites, "The Rhetorical Boundaries of 'the Law': A Consideration of the Rhetorical Culture of Legal Practice and the Case of the 'Separate but Equal' Doctrine," *Quarterly Journal of Speech* 82 (1996): 323–342. Used by permission of Taylor & Francis, Ltd., http://www.tandf.co.uk/journals.

Kirt H. Wilson, "The Contested Space of Prudence in the 1874–1875 Civil Rights Debate," *Quarterly Journal of Speech* 84 (1998): 131–149. Used by permission of Taylor & Francis, Ltd., http://www.tandf.co.uk/journals.

"Carol Moseley-Braun Defies the Confederate Flag" from *When Congress Debates: a Bakhtinian Paradigm*, Theodore F. Sheckels. Copyright © 2000 by Theodore F. Sheckels. Reproduced with permission of Greenwood Publishing Group, Inc., Westport, CT.

Lisa M. Gring-Pemble, "'Are We Going to Now Govern by Anecdote?': Rhetorical Constructions of Welfare Recipients in Congressional Hearings, Debates, and Legislation, 1992–1996," *Quarterly Journal of Speech* 87 (2001): 341–365. Used by permission of Taylor & Francis, Ltd., http://www.tandf.co.uk/journals.

Randall A. Lake, "Temporal Metaphors, Religions, and Arguments," from Bruce E. Gronbeck, ed., *Spheres of Argument: Proceedings of the Sixth SCA/AFA Conference on Argumentation* (Annendale, VA: Speech Communication Association, 1989): 245–254. Used by permission of the National Communication Association.

Karlyn Kohrs Campbell, "Gender and Genre: Loci of Invention and Contradiction in the Earliest Speeches by U.S. Women," *Quarterly Journal of Speech* 81 (1995): 479–495. Used by permission of Taylor & Francis, Ltd., http://www.tandf.co.uk/journals.

Lisa A. Flores, "Creative Discursive Space through a Rhetoric of Difference: Chicana Feminists Craft a Homeland," *Quarterly Journal of Speech* 82 (1996): 142–156. Used by permission of Taylor & Francis, Ltd., http://www.tandf.co.uk/journals.

Lester C. Olson, "On the Margins of Rhetoric: Audre Lorde Transforming Silence into Language and Action," *Quarterly Journal of Speech* 83 (1997): 49–70. Used by permission of Taylor & Francis, Ltd., http://www.tandf.co.uk/journals.

Gary S. Selby, "Mocking the Sacred: Frederick Douglass's 'Slaveholder's Sermon' and the Antebellum Debate over Religion and Slavery," *Quarterly Journal of Speech* 88 (2002): 326–341. Used by permission of Taylor & Francis, Ltd., http://www.tandf.co.uk/journals.

Contents

CHAPTER 7
Voices from the Margins   427

Looking Toward the Future: Additional Readings   504

Preface

As scholars and teachers, we wished for a book that would expose students to the study of political communication and to the depth and diversity of research in this field. When we discussed our ideas with colleagues teaching similar courses, we found that they too wanted their students to read a more comprehensive selection of the important literature of the field, in addition to traditional, groundbreaking works. A recurring theme throughout these conversations was that we needed a collection that would discuss campaign communication, address the growing body of political communication theory, identify important explorations of the legislative and judicial branches of the federal government, and discuss the political discourse of groups that are often marginalized in the political world.

Readings on Political Communication is our attempt to respond to these needs. This book identifies major areas of interest for teachers and scholars of political discourse. It also demonstrates the depth and breadth of scholarship and provocative research in the study of political communication. The book is designed for students, scholars, and researchers who wish to know more about campaign communication, to learn about major trends in this field, and to understand other forms of political communication in governing bodies and people's movements.

There are so many good researchers and so much excellent work in our field, selecting only thirty-five essays was a difficult challenge. In general, our selections were guided by our desire to include essential concepts and scholarship that would also be accessible to students, while still allowing us the flexibility to assign additional books or essays. Within each chapter, we selected essays that would provide someone new to political communication with a sound understanding of what the study of political communication is and does, and that we thought would best advance students' broad understanding of political communication.

Our goal was to reflect the multiple concerns and the multiple research methodologies of the field. To introduce students to the study of political communication, we needed a mix of essays that would present important observations and challenge conventional thinking. We wanted essays that have advanced the study of political communication by refining and revising its research norms, as well as essays that would reflect important historical developments in the scholarship. We also wanted the readings to run the chronological gamut, from groundbreaking pieces of earlier decades to some of the most incisive work of recent years.

Throughout, the book reflects the concerns of the rhetorical critics, media studies scholars, and social scientists who study political communication. It is intended for a variety of political communication courses—from the traditional to the not-so-traditional, from the rhetorical to the social scientific, from courses within the speech communication tradition to those more attentive to how mediated communication affects politics.

★ Organization of the Book

The introduction to *Readings on Political Communication* traces the evolution of political communication as an area of scholarly and classroom study. It highlights several themes that characterize work in that area and that are woven throughout the rest of the book. Each subsequent chapter begins with an introduction that briefly previews the selections and contextualizes them within the field of political communication and within politics.

Chapter 1, "Political Communication Frameworks," provides an overview of several prevailing frameworks for understanding political communication and presents students with a picture of a dynamic field of inquiry. The first and last essays assess the field and suggest how the study of political communication has evolved over several decades. Other essays in this chapter point to changes in perspective that have caused students of political communication to ask new questions.

Chapter 2, "Election Campaigns," is the first of three chapters on election communication. Essays in this chapter discuss the dynamics of campaign communication and explore the phases of a campaign. They also point to changes in campaign communication over the years, particularly those wrought by the media.

Chapter 3, "Election Campaign Advertising," deals more specifically with the televised advertising that has become an important facet of contemporary elections. The essays in this chapter analyze mass media advertising, explore its effects, and deal extensively with the attack ads that have evoked concern about effects on the electorate. These essays also reflect the nature of political advertising research that was particularly robust in the early 1990s.

Chapter 4, "Election Campaign Debates," turns to televised debates—in particular, those debates between or among those who aspire to the presidency. These debates have been criticized by some communication scholars and defended by others. The essays in this chapter reflect the criticism but move beyond it, to an understanding of what the debates do and do not accomplish in a campaign. In addition, the essays offer valuable insights into how media have played a role in what the debates—for good or ill—communicate through the questions that journalists choose to ask, the camera shots that directors choose to use, and the stories that reporters choose to write.

Chapter 5, "The Presidency," moves beyond elections to presidential governance. The essays in this chapter reflect the growing attention to the "rhetorical presidency" that has arisen with increased media coverage. The essays also reflect a change in scholarship, from studying the speech to studying presidential public address in larger contexts and with a greater awareness of the president's physical presence and cadre of speechwriters.

Chapter 6, "The Legislature and the Judiciary," consider essays that range from congressional debates—historical and more recent—to proceedings conducted by committees. The concluding essay examines legal practice rhetorically, with a landmark Supreme Court decision as its illuminating example.

Chapter 7, "Voices from the Margins," focuses on the rhetorical strategies that native North Americans, African Americans, women, and other marginalized groups use to engage in political communication. These voices from the margins often result in important political changes. While previous chapters focus on government, these last essays take students from the hallowed halls of Washington, D.C., to sites they may not immediately associate with politics.

We know there is no single design for political communication courses. Thus, the book is designed to be used in whatever way fits a particular course. An instructor might well proceed chapter by chapter through this anthology. In each chapter, the articles are arranged chronologically, and it might be profitable to have students read them in that order to suggest how research in that area has progressed. Other orders are possible, however, depending on the issues that an instructor wishes to emphasize or the structure of the course. We hope that the book reflects a logic, but also permits a good bit of flexibility.

Finally, "Looking Toward the Future: Additional Readings," provides an annotated list of supplementary articles and book chapters that have contributed significantly to the research community's collective understanding of political communication. We felt that a short, focused list might encourage individual students to locate and read selections of interest to them. These essays may also guide students in further explorations of topics related to their research interests.

★ Acknowledgments

The word "community" was used intentionally in the preceding section. We think it is appropriate to close this preface by talking about the political communication community of scholars and teachers who are passionate—as we are—about political matters and diligent in their application of varied methodologies to the study of those matters. We see ourselves, through this book, providing a service to this community of which we are active members. In our view, political communication was not only ready for a collection of readings such as this one; it needed such a text to introduce students to the breadth of an exciting field. Our goal has been to serve the community by bringing together in a single volume the theory and research that would introduce what we do, as scholars of political communication, to others who might, in turn, embrace the field and join our community.

Throughout the process of compiling this anthology, we were helped by two groups of colleagues. The first group responded to a questionnaire we circulated, asking respondents to rate eighty-eight possible selections as well as point out omissions. These valued colleagues were William L. Benoit, University of Missouri; Celeste Condit, University of Georgia; J. Michael Hogan, The Pennsylvania State University; Kim Kahn, Arizona State University; Kathleen Kendall, University of Maryland; Mitchell S. McKinney, University of Missouri; Richard M. Perloff, Cleveland State University; Michael W. Pfau, University of Oklahoma; Mary E. Stuckey, Georgia State University; and Judith S. Trent, University of Cincinnati. We thank them for their help.

The second group evaluated the proposed book at several stages at the request of our editor. These reviewers offered numerous suggestions about not only the selected readings but many other aspects of the anthology. They were Diana B. Carlin, University of Kansas; Alan Chartock, University of Albany, State University of New York; Jean L. DeHart, Appalachian State University; David Henry, University of Nevada, Las Vegas; Allan Louden, Wake Forest University; Shawn J. Parry-Giles, University of Maryland;

Trevor Parry-Giles, University of Maryland; Sandra J. Sarkela, University of Memphis; J. Cherie Strachan, University of Albany, State University of New York; Patricia Sullivan, State University of New York, New Paltz; and Robert E. Terrill, Indiana University. We also thank them for their valuable advice.

As is typical in publishing a manuscript of this volume, many life changes occur along the way. In the process of putting this together there have been job changes, new babies, home renovations, and family crises. We are grateful to our families and colleagues who have supported us along the way, and who have watched with great patience as we have gone through numerous drafts, final edits, and word counts.

Finally, we would like to acknowledge the guidance, assistance, and sometimes insistence of our editor Kathleen Domenig. As editor and publisher, Kathleen, from the outset of this project, wanted this anthology to be of the highest quality. We, at times, tended to look at the book from our disciplinary perspective. She kept nudging us back to the prospective instructor's and the prospective student's perspective, encouraging us to balance these two slightly different perspectives. For Kathleen's commitment to us and this project, her limitless patience, thoughtful suggestions, and meticulous attention to detail, we are most grateful.

We've made every effort through scanning technology and extensive proofreading to reproduce essays accurately and free of error. We have fixed minor typos and used "[sic]" to indicate when an unusual or unorthodox phrasing might have been used in the original essay. (When "[sic]" appears without italics, it was in the original publication.)

We hope you will find this book to be useful in representing this rich body of knowledge that we know as political communication. May these essays inform and inspire you.

Introduction to Political Communication

How do citizens come to choose one person over another for a political office? What is it about the young passionate conservative or the older, more seasoned liberal that excites political workers so much that they are willing to spend long hours engaged in the campaign process, in the snows of New Hampshire or in the Florida heat? Why do some people care passionately about politics while others do not? How do leaders really persuade people to vote for constitutional amendments or policy changes?

These are just a few of the questions that point to why the intersection of politics and communication is an important area to study. Since ancient Greco-Roman times, when philosophers, poets, and rhetoricians wrote of ways to delight, inspire, and persuade public audiences, political communication has been central to how societies engage in the work of governance. Rhetoricians served as ghostwriters and speechmakers, framing arguments to achieve the best results with their audiences and practicing ways to effectively present those arguments in public settings. Legal suits, celebratory speeches, and policy arguments were prominent forms of political communication.

Since then, rhetoricians and philosophers alike have written about early democracy and its influence on today's political systems, especially in the United States. Writers such as Plato, Aristotle, Cicero, Machiavelli, Thomas Jefferson, Ben Franklin, Alexis de Tocqueville, Thomas Dewey, and Kenneth Burke, among others, have developed ideas about effective citizenship, rhetorical actions, and the forces that shape political systems, structures, and the people that create them.[1] People such as Susan B. Anthony, Franklin D. Roosevelt, Martin Luther King, Jr., and Ronald Reagan were leaders who effectively communicated their passions and concerns and who transformed the face of American politics.

The study of political communication addresses how the world is changed by people who come together for common meaning and causes. Major changes in the world, and in the United States specifically, have come about through groups united for a common goal. Political communication is an important instrument for change: a force that can strengthen society. The founding of this country, constitutional amendments for minority rights, and legislation that promotes a better welfare system are all examples of the power of groups working and communicating together to make America a better place to live.

Political communication scholars also focus on those who compete at the state, national, or local level for power, money, and influence, using persuasive strategies such as speech-making, debates, and advertising. From the presidential candidate to the congressional representative and the school board member, political actors use messages to gain public support and shape political arguments. It is important for scholars and citizens to think about these messages from the standpoint of the specific strategies used and the effectiveness of those strategic choices.

Political communication can be used to delight and unite publics, joining fragmented groups together for common causes and issues. It can also create disarray in the democratic system, leading to "greater cynicism and decreased civic engagement."[2] Given its pervasive nature, it is easy to understand why there are so many different ways to look at political communication. This anthology reflects just a sample of the vast array of literature and thought in this field. The remainder of this introduction will briefly trace some of the major strands of study and provide an overview to help frame your reading of the essays in this anthology.

★ MAJOR APPROACHES TO THE STUDY OF POLITICAL COMMUNICATION

Some of the earliest writing about political communication research can be found in Dan D. Nimmo and Keith Sanders's 1980 *Handbook of Political Communication*. Their focus centered on factors that can influence voting behavior, reflecting a dominant approach to psychology in the 1950s known as behaviorialism. Identifying political communication as "an intervening process" that helps to build the connection between government and citizens was a significant move. It legitimized political communication, establishing it as a viable field that crossed several disciplines such as communication, psychology, sociology, and political science.[3]

Political communication research has grown dramatically since the 1950s. Numerous journals, edited books, conference proceedings, and association interest groups give significant emphasis to the study of this field. A typical Google search turns up dozens of university centers, think tanks, and researchers that approach the study of political communication in widely varied ways. Whether they focus on institutions, major leaders, or the role of media in the political process, students who learn about political communication essentially learn about the power of messages, both verbal and visual, to define and shape our understanding of politics and government.

Researchers use a variety of methods to understand how political communication functions in society. Some approach it from rhetorical frameworks, looking at how messages are shaped for various audiences and situations. Strategic argument development, language choices, and story-telling are some examples of ways that speakers use rhetoric to persuade their audiences.[4] For example, a presidential State of the Union address filled with poignant stories about families affected by war or a speech such as Martin Luther King's "I Have a Dream," with its powerful metaphors, can provide rich material for a rhetorical critic to analyze in terms of the impact the speeches may have on immediate and long-term audiences.

Other researchers approach political communication from the standpoint of how the media interacts with the political process. There is a great deal of interest in how major newspapers and television networks help to shape news about political candidates or presidential actions. Comparisons of media coverage, critiques of text and visual choices, and media biases are issues of great importance to these researchers.[5]

Social scientists look at ways to measure the effectiveness of certain types of political communication, often with an interest in how messages impact voter behavior. Polling results, demographic analyses and various survey instruments attempt to measure the impact of certain messages on voter image and issue formation. For example, following the 2004 presidential campaign, there was significant focus on the turnout of younger voters and the impact it might have had on the election.[6] The numerous maps of "blue and red states" illustrating voter turnout in that election also provided interesting ways to analyze campaign results and to predict where messages might have been targeted differently.

From rhetorical analysis to media critiques and behavioral research, approaches to the study of political communication are varied and complex. The remainder of this chapter will lay the groundwork for major questions to consider when thinking about political communication and reading this collection of essays.

★ SOME QUESTIONS FOR CONSIDERATION

Whether we are studying rhetorical appeals, the role of the media in shaping political understanding, or how people decide to vote—or not to vote, there are certain fundamental questions:

- How do people get elected to office? Whether the election is for U.S. president, congressional representative, or gubernatorial candidate, what major strategies are used to win elections and, in many cases, stay elected?
- What major forms of communication do candidates use once they are elected? In an eloquent presidential address or a passionate congressional debate, what strategies

(logical, emotional, and ethical) tend to be effective in communicating with various audiences?

- How do groups gain access to political leaders and institutions? How do they achieve political change? Historically, what roles do social movements, special interest groups, and political action committees play in bringing about social change?
- What role do the media play in shaping public understanding of candidates, political leaders, and issues? How has that role been affected by new technology that has led to increased access to information and an increasingly interactive political society?
- And, finally, how can we ensure an engaged, vibrant, participating citizenry? What can be done to educate citizens so that they feel compelled to learn about candidates and issues, and to exercise their right to vote?

These questions frame the remainder of the discussion in this introductory section and are pervasive throughout the book. While there are certainly many other ways to study political communication, these questions are often emphasized in political communication research, books, and classrooms.

★ POLITICAL ELECTIONS AND COMMUNICATION STRATEGIES

A vast array of writing explores the world of political campaigns and the quantity and quality of communication that takes place during these multi-year events. The U.S. presidency provides a rich history of colorful characters, campaign stories, public speeches, and symbolic acts as material for analysis, and it is often the focus of political communication study.[7] Presidential campaign discourse such as announcements, "stump speeches," and acceptance speeches provide material for studying why some communication messages work better than others given the audience and the situation. Thus a large part of research focuses on how presidents get elected and the quality of communication leadership they exhibit once in office. Chapter 2 shows some of the ways that the communication strategies of presidential campaigns have been studied.

Another significant area of research is political advertising in election campaigns. From the earliest direct mail to the television advertising and interactive websites, advertising has been an essential aspect of campaigns and of political communication scholarship. Reflecting the evolution of technology, public relations, and campaign management, research considers topics such as the types and functions of ads, the quality of message content, visual impact, and the characteristics of negative (or comparative) advertising.[8] Chapter 3 highlights research about various types of political advertising and the effectiveness of certain persuasive strategies.

Another important area of political campaign research centers on the debates that occur during the primary and general election campaigns. Researchers have studied political debates for decades from the standpoint of presentation, quality of arguments, and media coverage to gain a sense of what messages resonate with voters and what qualities of leadership are most evident in the candidate's debate style.[9] Chapter 4 provides examples of presidential debate research that focuses on how debates are organized and the role television plays in presenting the debates.

Taken together these areas dominate research in political campaign communication. There are, of course, many aspects of campaigns worthy of discussion, such as the stages of a campaign, campaign finance issues, and the management team that supports a candidate.[10] However, the chapters focused on campaign coverage in this anthology reflect major interests in the field of communication.

★ MAJOR FORMS OF COMMUNICATION IN OFFICE

Every nation has rituals—specific events, celebratory moments, days of mourning, symbolic activities—that mark passages of time, changes in leadership, and historical moments when the nation needs to hear a unifying voice. These rituals are necessary to the identity and unity of the nation. Every free country engages in the ritual of public debate and deliberation over policy issues. Many debates center on rights, responsibilities, and freedoms.[11] While elected officials engage in a variety of forms of communication in their public lives, political communication research often focuses on specific speech events and debates.

As the symbolic focal point of United States society, every president has certain public speaking requirements and expectations. In looking at presidential communication over time, researchers have found that clear patterns emerge. In the Inaugural Address, the State of the Union Address, or a eulogy for a world leader, a U.S. president is responsible for enacting the ritual of bringing the country together, especially in a time of strife and uncertainty. Critics who consider the rhetorical styles of many presidents have discussed in depth the president's ability to speak effectively.[12] Researchers have also begun to look more carefully at the presidential spouse's rhetorical roles and functions.[13] Essays in Chapter 5 underscore the rhetorical nature of presidential speeches. From examining Ronald Reagan's use of narrative in his speeches to rethinking how history and myth frame the presidency, the essays in this chapter focus on symbols and themes important to American presidents.

Recent research in political communication also focuses on the legislative and judiciary branches of government and the specific communication expectations that come with them. As Senators grapple with difficult hearings over Iraqi prisoner abuse, as members of Congress engage in eloquence and puffery on the House floor over constitutional amendments, as lawyers argue civil rights cases before the Supreme Court, the role of communication becomes essential for managing these areas of governance and understanding the political realities of the situation. Chapter 6 includes legislative and judicial examples that show the impact political discourse can have in shaping public debate. The focus is often on the type and quality of arguments developed, the kinds of appeals used in presenting the message to different audiences, and the way issues are framed given the historical context. The televised debate of the House Judiciary Committee on impeaching Richard Nixon and the late 1990s legislative hearings on welfare reform provide two rich examples for analysis of legislative and judicial discourse.

★ ACCESS AND POLITICAL CHANGE

Political communication, as exercised by social movements and special interest groups, is an important area of study because it underscores the foundation of democracy and the importance of people joining together with the common goal to achieve positive social change. How social movements are envisioned, created, maintained, and sustained can be considered through the lens of political communication. How groups gain access to their representatives, win the right to vote, gain prominence in electoral politics, and finally are given a legitimate voice in the political process are other important aspects of political change that researchers investigate.[14] Those who have been silenced or marginalized in history (such as women, African Americans, and Native Americans) have, in recent years, given voice to important problems and have been instrumental in developing solutions for change. Political communication study in this area explores how these groups emerge and come to the forefront—their struggles and their triumphs, the stories and strategies that emerge along the way.

Chapter 7 provides examples of groups that have impacted American society—people who have pushed from a marginalized standpoint, riding on the fringes of the political process, attempting to stir the winds of change. Examples of rhetorical strategies in their communication—from Native American protest to anti-slavery arguments—illustrate the particular challenges these groups face and the effectiveness of various strategies in achieving recognition and influence.

Chapter 7 also discusses the evolution of political influence in American society, as seen by the creation and tremendous growth of political action committees and special interest groups.[15] As social movements have grown into legitimate social justice organizations, there has been increased focus on fund-raising and lobbying. Direct mail appeals for groups that pool money to achieve greater societal change have become more important as the costs of political campaigning (whether for office or for issues) increase. Although social movements in the past have changed the world through powerful speeches and marches, in the twenty-first century, societal change will more likely come through emerging technologies that provide the ability to reach global audiences and harness financial resources through the Internet.

★ THE ROLE OF THE MEDIA

The role of the media in shaping public understanding of candidates, political leaders, and national issues is an essential consideration for many people who study political communication. In both the campaign process and in political institutions, there is a deep connection with the media that affects candidates, events, and issues. Without media coverage, politicians do not exist. Without politicians, journalists have little to write about with regard to governance. This mutual dependence influences the education of the public about politics. It can also create a chasm between the average citizen and political leaders.

Studies of the media and politics take many directions. Some researchers look at certain effects of media campaign coverage; others consider how politicians respond to media coverage; still others examine how media coverage can be more effective. The ultimate concern, however, is the role of media in shaping public understanding of political events. Learning when to respond or not to respond to media pressures, how to jockey for media access, and how media coverage is related to interpersonal interactions are all important areas of political communication research.[16]

The media's relationship to the political process is evident throughout this anthology. From the outset, Chapter 1 identifies examples of this integration, with its focus on political communication research, voter responses to politics, and the role of media as critical to understanding the full range of political communication. Chapter 2 looks at the ways political stories are reported in early primary states, such as New Hampshire, and in one essay also considers problems that result from viewing campaign events as television "spectacles." The role of the media in reporting and critiquing political advertisements and political debates is discussed in Chapters 3 and 4. In Chapter 5, the role of television in helping to shape the "rhetorical presidency" is highlighted in Campbell and Jamieson's essay. Regardless of the political context, media will always play some role in shaping the messages that the public receives.

In the context of media use, advances in technology have greatly influenced the ways campaigns are carried out and daily government business is conducted. Internet technology, in particular, has dramatically shifted the ways in which citizens obtain, manage, and process political information. Essays on citizen engagement in Chapter 1 explore changing relationships of participation in an increasingly technological world. As technology advances accelerate, it is important to consider how these new technologies impact the political process and how people get their news. In recent years there has been a dramatic shift in campaign rhetoric from direct mail and television advertising to interactive websites where people can donate money directly and volunteer online. In many ways technology advancements improve government operations and enhance transmission of communication.[17]

Technological advances, particularly in computer-mediated communication, have dramatically changed patterns and channels of political influence and access in local, national, and global politics. Through technology, people across nations can unite for common causes—to stop a war or boycott a large corporation—by accessing Internet websites. These websites provide easy access to political information that can help voters become better educated about leaders and issues. At the same time, technology advances raise serious concerns: the digital divide widens as those with slower computers and weaker signal strengths have fewer opportunities to engage in public deliberation. It also becomes increasingly difficult to distinguish between propaganda and legitimate political communication, a serious concern given the number of potentially dangerous groups that have large web followings. These problems are addressed in Chapter 1.

★ CITIZEN PARTICIPATION AND CIVIC ENGAGEMENT

As people come to understand the importance of political communication and learn about government systems and leaders, they can become cynical about the process and the "manipulation" that seems evident. As you look at the political staging on the House floor, or see an advertisement that is clearly inaccurate and negative, or feel the continual bombardment of persuasive campaign messages, it is easy to lose interest in politics.

The issue of civic engagement and voter behavior has been around for decades. Many political communication researchers have pondered the characteristics of citizen engagement and explored ways to increase citizen participation.[18] The 2000 presidential election underscored the idea that "every vote counts" when problems with paper balloting and election poll access directly affected the outcome of the election and George W. Bush won the electoral vote but not the popular vote. The 2004 election, though not so hotly contested, also raised questions about election results and voting reports. While emphasizing the notion that a few votes can truly make a difference for a candidate, these elections showed how cynicism emerges when inherent flaws in the American voting system are seen.

Issues of voter participation and civic engagement also pervade this anthology. Whether they are treated explicitly, as in Robert Putnam's and David Zarefsky's essays in Chapter 1, or indirectly in discussions on political advertising and debates in Chapters 3 and 4, the fundamental problem of how to engage publics in political issues and activities lies at the heart of why we study political communication.

★ AN OVERVIEW OF THIS COLLECTION

The following chapters begin with aspects of the campaign cycle, then move to a focus on those who serve in elected offices, then to social groups who work for change in society. Chapter 1 includes articles that provide sense of the historical evolution of political communication research, with special consideration for the role of citizens in the political process. Chapter 2 turns to the election process, with articles that discuss key features of presidential elections such as campaign stages and speech-making strategies. Political advertising, as viewed especially in presidential campaigns, is discussed in Chapter 3, with essays that look at topics such as gender differences in campaign messages, and the effects of attack ads. Chapter 4 underscores the importance of structure and format of presidential debates. Articles about people elected to public office are highlighted in Chapter 5 as the presidency is discussed in greater detail from the standpoints of image creation and speech writing. Chapter 6 looks at communication in the legislative and judicial arenas, with specific case studies. Finally, Chapter 7 considers people and groups who have struggled to find a voice in American society, and provides specific examples of challenges and success.

Taken together, the chapters in this book provide a rich body of work on political communication. Multiple methods and disciplines contribute to framing a field of study that is rich in tradition, yet responsive to a changing world. How is it that citizens come to choose one person over another for a political office? Why do some candidates ignite voter passions, while others do not? How do ordinary citizens advocate for important changes in society? Read on, and learn more about this wonderfully complex field we call political communication.

NOTES

[1] For a useful discussion on the history of rhetoric since ancient Greece, see James L. Golden, Goodwin Berquist, and William E. Coleman, *The Rhetoric of Western Thought,* 4th ed. (Dubuque, Iowa: Kendall/Hunt, 1989). Observations about early American citizens and their political activism are described by Alexis de Tocqueville in *Democracy in America,* ed. J. P. Maier, trans. George Lawrence (Garden City, N.Y.: Anchor, 1969), 513–17. Twentieth-century writing by Kenneth Burke is useful for understanding the significance of symbolic action. Burke's work on dramatism and identification are particularly useful concepts to the analysis and understanding of rhetorical messages. A classic piece by Burke is "The Rhetoric of Hitler's 'Battle',"

reprinted in *Readings in Rhetorical Criticism,* 3rd ed., ed. Carl R. Burgchardt (State College, Pa.: Strata, 2005), pp. 188–202.

2 See the essay by Robert D. Putnam included in this volume, " Bowling Alone: America's Declining Social Capital," *Journal of Democracy* 6, no. 1 (1995): 65–78. Putnam addresses the cynicism and lack of citizen engagement prevalent in American society. An earlier focus on citizen apathy and how factors such as the media and political leaders come into play, can be found in E. J. Dionne's work *Why Americans Hate Politics: The Death of the Democratic Process,* (New York: Simon & Schuster, 1991; reprint, 1994).

3 Dan D. Nimmo and Keith R. Sanders, "Introduction: The Emergence of Political Communication as a Field," in *The Handbook of Political Communication* (Beverly Hills, Calif.: Sage, 1981), pp. 12–13. This piece is excerpted in the first chapter of this book.

4 There are many outstanding rhetorical scholars of political communication. A classic volume on the power of rhetorical symbols, updated in the latter half of the twentieth century, is *The Symbolic Uses of Politics: With a New Afterword,* by Murray Edelman (Chicago: University of Illinois Press, 1985). Kathleen Jamieson's work is particularly noteworthy for understanding the power of persuasion in political campaigns. A chapter from her book, *Dirty Politics: Deception, Distraction, and Democracy* (New York: Oxford University Press, 1992) is included in this volume. Martin Medhurst's *Beyond the Rhetorical Presidency* (College Station: Texas A & M University Press, 1996) is an important volume with examples of how presidential rhetoric is used to generate policy and public support. An example of Medhurst's work can also be found in this anthology.

5 A classic discussion on how the media could better handle presidential coverage can be found in an essay by Dan Hahn, "The Media and the Presidency: Ten Propositions," *Communication Quarterly* 35 (1987): 254–266. For other critiques of media coverage, see Rod Hart, *Seducing America: How Television Charms the Modern Voter.* (New York: Oxford University Press, 1994) and Larry J. Sabato, *Feeding Frenzy: How Attack Journalism Transformed American Politics* (New York: Free Press, 1991). David Zarefsky's article on "spectator politics," included here in Chapter 1, also addresses these concerns.

6 The essay on George Gallup in Chapter 1 helps explain how modern polling came to gain both scientific and cultural legitimacy in American society and its specific impact on the democratic process.

For a different perspective on the relationship of the media to voter education and behavior, see D. H. Weaver, "What Voters Learn from Media," *The Annals of the American Academy of Political and Social Science,* 546 (1996): 34–47.

7 Volumes have been written on specific presidential campaigns and the major strategies used to gain citizen approval and win elections. It is also important to note work that has been done on gubernatorial and congressional elections as well. See for example Rita Whillock's *Political Empiricism: Communication Strategies in State and Regional Elections* (New York: Praeger, 1991) to examine the strategies and variables unique to smaller political campaigns, such as budgetary constraints, inexperienced campaign staffs, and low voter support.

8 See for example Montague Kern's work *30-Second Politics: Political Advertising in the 1980s* (New York: Praeger, 1989), or Linda Lee Kaid, Dan D. Nimmo and Keith R. Sanders's early work on political advertising in *New Perspectives on Political Advertising* (Carbondale: Southern Illinois University Press, 1986). Patrick Devlin's work on political advertising (as well as his vast collection of political advertisements) is also noteworthy; see *Political Persuasion in Presidential Campaigns* (New Brunswick, N.J.: Transaction, 1987). During the 2004 presidential campaign, William Benoit's political website: http://presidentialcamp2004.coas.missouri.edu, was an important resource for analyzing political ads.

9 One of the most successful research projects conducted in recent years has been DebateWatch, a voter education program sponsored by the Commission on Presidential Debates (CPD). This program encourages people to watch the presidential debates together, turn off the television, and then engage in discussion about the issues. Absent the media "spin control" that dominates the television networks following a presidential debate, average citizens discuss the issues and develop opinions before the networks can set an agenda. For more information visit the website http://www.debates.org.

10 For a book that addresses many of these aspects see *Political Campaign Communication: Principles and Practices,* 5th ed., by Judith S. Trent and Robert V. Friedenberg (Lanham, Md.: Rowman & Littlefield, 2004). An example of how political campaigns have changed over three decades can be found in *Under the Watchful Eye: Managing Presidential Campaigns in the Television Era,* edited by Mathew D. McCubbins (Washington, D.C.: Congressional Quarterly Press, 1992).

Robert Denton's work on political communication and presidential campaigns has been especially important for looking at specific campaign years and key parts of the campaign that collectively tell the campaign's story. For example, see Denton's edited volume, *The 1996 Campaign: A Communication Perspective*, (New York: Praeger, 1998).

[11] See for example Dan F. Hahn's focus on argument and ideology in *Political Communication: Rhetoric, Government, and Citizens*, 2nd ed. (State College, Pa.: Strata, 2002).

[12] As a way to understand the relationship of rhetoric to the presidency, see an essay in this volume that specifically addresses the meaning of "the Rhetorical Presidency": Campbell and Jamieson's "Inaugural Addresses" from their seminal book, *Deeds Done in Words: Presidential Rhetoric and the Genres of Governance* (Chicago: University of Chicago Press, 1990). For a useful account of a speechwriter's perspective on presidential speech-making and style, see Peggy Noonan's book *What I Saw at the Revolution* (New York: Random House, 1990). Noonan discusses her life as a speechwriter during Ronald Reagan's presidency and George H. W. Bush's 1988 campaign, as well as the importance of helping each president find a voice as a speech maker.

[13] One of the most recent books on First Ladies and their impact on the presidency is *Inventing a Voice: The Rhetoric of American First Ladies of the 20th Century*, Molly Meijer Wertheimer, editor (New York: Rowman & Littlefield, 2004).

[14] For a classic study on specific social movements and their impact on society, see Frances Fox Piven and Richard Cloward's book *Poor People's Movements: Why They Succeed, How They Fail* (New York: Vintage, 1978).

[15] A useful discussion of the growth of political action committees and their impact on presidential campaigns is featured in Trent and Friedenberg, pp. 8–11. A thorough discussion of the history of political action committees and how they function can be found in Larry J. Sabato's classic work, *PAC Power: Inside the World of Political Action Committees* (New York: Norton, 1985).

[16] A useful historical perspective on campaigns and media coverage can be found in Sig Mickelson's book *From Whistle Stop to Sound Bite: Four Decades of Politics and Television* (New York: Praeger, 1989). A more recent treatment of media coverage and politics is David L. Paletz, *The Media in American Politics: Contents and Consequences* (New York: Longman, 1999). For a useful view of the relationship between media and politics, with significant international focus, see Pippa Norris, *A Virtuous Circle: Political Communications in Postindustrial Societies* (Cambridge, U.K.: Cambridge University Press, 2000).

[17] See Gary Selnow, *High-Tech Campaigns: Computer Technology in Political Communication* (Westport, Conn.: Praeger, 1994). Ron Faucheux, "How Campaigns are Using the Internet: An Exclusive Nationwide Survey," *Campaigns and Elections*, 23 (September 1998), addresses developments in technological use using survey data. Doris Graber's *Processing Politics: Learning from Television in the Internet Age* (Chicago: University of Chicago Press, 2001) is also important for understanding the relationship between traditional media (such as television) and the new technologies.

[18] For a useful discussion about civic engagement in American society see Michael Schudson, *The Good Citizen: A History of American Civic Life* (New York: Free Press, 1998).

CHAPTER 1
Political Communication Frameworks

Take one very dynamic political speaker. Add political advisors, media strategists, and advertising consultants. Mix in numerous journalists, commentators, and media analysts. Sprinkle with technological innovations. Start at a low temperature, but turn up the heat as it gets closer to the finish. Serve to multiple audiences and await the reviews.

This recipe for the election of a political leader identifies in simple form much of the major work that goes into developing political campaigns. While campaign development is the most visible aspect of political communication, however, it is only one aspect of the rich and complex field we focus on in this volume. The study of political communication, whether it is approached through disciplinary lenses such as rhetoric, political science, or sociology, or framed by studies of political leaders, social groups, or government structures, is far-reaching and complex. When we consider the impact

of a political leader on the American political landscape, the role of advisors and consultants in helping that leader get elected, or the role of the media in shaping the election, we can learn much about how individuals and groups participate in campaigns, public advocacy and deliberation, or other forms of civic life.

The essays in this chapter frame the significant and substantial political communication research that has developed over the last fifty years. They review the ways researchers and critics have approached this topic and the larger questions that have evolved from that research. They explain why the study of political communication is so rich and varied and why it is difficult to know the impact of any specific message. Two essays, the first and the last, serve as bookends to the chapter: the first essay provides a survey of major research trends from the late 1950s to the 1970s; the last essay considers more recent trends in political communication. The other three essays discuss questions central to the study of politics, such as the decline of civic engagement and deliberation in American society, as well as the relationship between symbolism and "political reality."

The section begins with Dan D. Nimmo and Keith R. Sanders's "The Emergence of Political Communication as a Field," the introduction from their 1981 book *The Handbook of Political Communication*. The authors provide a significant review of major research approaches to political communication before 1980. As scholars began to seriously grapple with understanding political communication, approaches to its study proliferated across several disciplines. This article summarizes key areas of inquiry that helped frame the study of political communication at the time—inquiry that is still relevant in the twenty-first century.

David Zarefsky's 1992 essay, "Spectator Politics and the Revival of Public Argument," focuses on public participation in the political process by examining the media coverage of the 1992 election and the impact this coverage had on public interest. The essay considers how people are persuaded to think about politics, and the cynicism and apathy that can often develop as a result. Addressing ways the media influences how people view and understand politics, Zarefsky lays out five characteristics of the political scene that, he argues, led to a decrease in public participation and citizen interest. Noting the tensions between increased media access and decreased public interest, he points out that, ironically, while media and communication technology permit greater access to politics, political participation is declining and people are increasingly cynical about political action. Zarefsky suggests that "a vibrant concept of argument and public deliberation" is needed to revitalize the public sphere and increase engagement in the political process.

Robert D. Putnam's 1995 essay, "Bowling Alone: America's Declining Social Capital," also notes the problem of decreased public participation in civic life. Putnam notes a steady decline in the vibrant American civil society that Alexis de Tocqueville originally discussed in Democracy in America. Using the framework of "social capital," defined as "the networks, norms and social trust" that develop among people, Putnam discusses an empirical survey of trends in contemporary America and notes a steady decline in civic engagement and citizenship activities. Offering some explanations for eroding social capital and suggesting further lines of inquiry, Putnam's essay provides an important snapshot of contemporary civic life as well as questions that could help restore engagement and trust in public officials.

J. Michael Hogan's 1997 study of pollsters, "George Gallup and the Rhetoric of Scientific Communication in the United States," provides a useful, practical example of the power of symbols in shaping political realities and of one individual's success in elevating the polling process to a level of prominence. Creating the myth that scientific legitimacy was achieved through "the collective wisdom of the people," Gallup was able to achieve a significant status for polling in American culture, still prevalent today, despite limitations such as sampling errors and bias. Hogan's review of Gallup's rhetorical strategies provides both a significant biographical piece and an important critique of the problems associated with the symbolic use of polling in American society. Using the example of the Truman/Dewey presidential election, Hogan explains the impact of polling errors and of the way political campaign results get reported. He also offers a perspective on how the use of polling results to predict election success causes cynicism about politics.

Trevor Parry-Giles and Shawn J. Parry-Giles's 2001 essay, "Reassessing the State of Political Communication in the United States," offers a more optimistic view of political communication and its evolution in the public sphere. The authors list several points of optimism: increased public deliberation on policy issues, a historically high quality of leadership, increased democratization through technology, and the general success of political discourse. They argue that while critics should recognize the inherent problems in political communication, they should "also acknowledge and embrace the essence of politics as 'rhetorical,' with all of the uncertainty and complications and democratization such an acknowledgement entails."

The Emergence of Political Communication as a Field

Dan D. Nimmo and Keith R. Sanders

A mythology surrounds the decade of the 1950s, one to which we in the United States are especially prone. It depicts a nation of paradoxes, defending itself against enemies foreign and domestic (fighting a cold war and Korean war abroad, undergoing a Red scare at home), yet secure in its nuclear superiority, living the golden consensus of the Eisenhower years, and witnessing its youth maturing into the "silent" generation. The paradoxes added up to an overall sense—perhaps a yearning—for order, stability, and consolidation. Viewed from a perspective of three decades hence, the 1950s offer a nostalgic glow of national calm, tranquility, and strength.

But those suffering from intellectual growing pains in the 1950s knew differently. For anyone interested in studying human behavior the times were not placid, nor the spirit serene. Something was happening in the social sciences, something exciting. More than one scholar called it a "revolution" (Truman, 1955, pp. 202–231). Others were to label it a "movement" (Dahl, 1961). Years later there would be reflections about a "paradigm change" (Kuhn, 1962). Whatever its designation, the new mood among social scientists in the 1950s espoused increasingly shared concerns and orientations. The "science" in social science was to be taken seriously. The implications of that were to turn to the physiological and biological sciences for guidelines for effective study of human affairs, to the philosophical stance of logical positivism as an orientation to the appropriate facts for study, and to empiricism for suitable techniques of data-gathering and analysis. The "social" in social science was not so honored, however; in fact, the term "behavioral sciences" seemed best suited to convey the new intent—one focusing on discovering patterns and laws of observable behavior.

Today the behavioral impetus, although not spent, is much abated. Many of its earlier unquestioned assumptions about the nature of scientific inquiry, the distinction between facts and values, the appropriateness of empirical (especially quantitative) techniques, and the social versus individualistic quality of human behavior have been challenged. Readers will find those and other assumptions and such challenges discussed throughout this volume. We take note of that impetus and the intellectual ferment of the 1950s, however, to neither honor nor bury "behavioralism." Instead, we call attention to one other facet of the behavioral climate of that and ensuing decades that left a lasting imprint on scholarly activity and, indeed, makes publication of this volume fitting, timely, and necessary. We refer to the tendency in the behavioral sciences to bring together bodies of knowledge, from whatever academic disciplines and departments they be found, and to merge them into cross-disciplinary fields hitherto investigated as offshoots of more conventional areas of inquiry. It is, of course, a tendency running throughout the development of all of the physical and biological sciences and, to some extent, has been evident in the development of the humanities as well. It dates in the

This essay is excerpted from a chapter in a book by Dan D. Nimmo and Keith R. Sanders, Handbook of Political Communication *(Thousand Oaks, Calif.: Sage, 1981).*

evolution of the behavioral sciences, as Truman notes (1955), at least as far back as 1930, when the first edition of the *Encyclopedia of the Social Sciences* was published.

It is our contention that political communication is such an emerging field. Its piecemeal origins date back several centuries, but a self-consciously cross-disciplinary focus is of more recent vintage. Although we might with, ample justification, trace the lineage of political communication back much earlier, we think it convenient to speak of the emergence of the cross-disciplinary field as beginning in the behavioral thrust of the 1950s. For example, it is in 1956 that we find one of the first attempts to designate something called "political communication" as one of three "intervening processes" (political leadership and group structures being the other two) "by means of which political influences are mobilized and transmitted" between "formal governmental institutions, on the one hand, and citizen voting behavior, on the other hand." The editors of the volume in which that statement appeared (a reader entitled Political Behavior expressly intended to persuade students to employ "the political behavior approach") went on to write: "[A]lthough the body of knowledge emerging about such intervening processes . . . is still gross and tentative, more reliable understanding is being acquired." Unfortunately, however, "political communication research has lagged behind similar work in other substantive fields of social science" (Eulau, Eldersveld, & Janowitz, 1956, p. 175).

As we shall see in the remainder of this introductory essay, and as exemplified in the chapters of this volume, the 1956 statement was instructive and prophetic. First, it designates political communication as a substantive field of social science. Second, however, it was a retarded field. Yet, third, even in the 1950s a body of knowledge about political communication as an intervening process was emerging. Finally, the statement defines the boundaries of the field—that is, as a process intervening between formal governing institutions and citizen voting behavior. In the 1980s political communication is even more a substantive field, but it is certainly no longer retarded, a cross-disciplinary effort at knowledge-building continues to emerge, and the boundaries of political communication have expanded considerably. The sections that follow speak to each of these points.

★ THE CURRENT STATE OF POLITICAL COMMUNICATION

In the quarter-century that has elapsed since research in political communication was criticized for lagging behind other substantive fields of social science, there have been noteworthy advances. These advances include not just research, but extend to political communication as a distinct domain of publication, a teaching area, a professional endeavor, a field with practical and policy applications, and a cross-national enterprise.

Research

In searching for a way to illustrate what the emerging field of political communication was all about in the 1950s, Eulau et al. (1956) relied on the republication of three case studies—one using a post facto experimental design to examine television's effects in the 1952 presidential election; another reporting a field experiment evaluating the effectiveness of propaganda techniques; and the third, a content analysis of political language. As essays in this volume attest, these concerns remain key areas and techniques of inquiry for political communication scholars: Doris Graber echoes the importance of political languages, Lynda Lee Kaid focuses on political advertising, Cliff Zukin examines the role of mass communication in the public opinion process, and Richard Hoffstetter and Roy Miller remind us that content analysis and experimentation are very much a part of contemporary political communication research.

If, however, there was a paucity of research literature in the 1950s to illustrate the nature of political communication, that was to change rapidly. In 1972, for example, Sanders, Hirsch, and Pace compiled over 1000 entries in their comprehensive bibliography of political communication research. Two years later Kaid, Sanders, and Hirsch (1974), limiting themselves to the available research in political *campaign* communication in the United States and other selected nations, listed more than 1500 items in their bibliography. As this *Handbook's* "Guide to the literature" (Appendix A) implies, the available published and unpublished research in political communication now virtually surpasses cataloguing possibilities.

Matching the sheer quantity of research projects undertaken in political communication is an impressive diversification of the generic field. No longer regarded as simply an intervening process between formal governmental institutions and citizen voting behavior, political communication now has a wide variety of facets. Numbered among the substantive areas of the field are studies of political languages, political rhetoric, political advertising and propaganda, political debates, political socialization, election campaigns, public opinion, public policy, political movements, government-news media relations, political imagery, political symbolism, and a growing number of other research specializations. Moreover, as the chapters in this *Handbook* ably illustrate, political communication researchers are increasingly sensitive to the strengths and limitations of a variety of methodological approaches and techniques. Theoretical concerns revolve around such approaches as process, uses and gratifications, information diffusion, agenda-setting, critical theory, constructivist views, and social structure. And researchers apply a plethora of techniques to their tasks—historical, critical, content-analytical, experimental, quasi-experimental, survey, and small-sample designs. The laggard of the social sciences in the 1950s has, as the cigarette advertisement says, "come a long way, baby."

The Publication Domain

One possible indicator that a research field is obtaining a separate identity among the social sciences is the appearance of scholarly publications devoted exclusively to the research and writing of the field's specialists. This *Handbook's* appended "Guide to the literature" offers a set of useful suggestions regarding the published efforts of scholarly specialists; hence, we need not duplicate that effort here. However, it is important to note that the field now possesses its own publication domain. Thus, *Political Communication Review* is a handy tool for

scholars interested in current research trends, listings of unpublished papers, and reviews of both article and book-length research. *Political Communication and Propaganda*, a quarterly journal, is an organ publishing research of both a qualitative and a quantitative nature. Two annual volumes, *Communication Yearbook* and *Mass Communication Review Yearbook*, devote separate sections to political communication research; the former also provides an annual overview of theoretical, methodological, and research developments in the field. Finally, "political communication" has for some time been a key substantive category in publications devoted to abstracting reported research in the communication sciences, as evidenced by *Communicontents* (now no longer published) and by *Communication Abstracts*.

Teaching Political Communication

The emergence of political communication as a distinctive scholarly field encompasses more than the research enterprise. Once rarely found in a university or college catalogue, it is now increasingly commonplace to find listings of both undergraduate and graduate courses in political communication. They are not confined to a single academic department, but appear in the listings for departments of speech communication, mass communication, journalism, political science, sociology, and social psychology. Although generally taught by a specialist within the department in question, a few such courses involve the joint efforts of persons from two or more specializations. Course titles vary: "political communication," "political persuasion," "public opinion," "campaigns and voting," "mass media and politics," "political rhetoric," "political attitudes, opinions, and communication," "the sociology of mass media."

As specialized course offerings in political communication exist, so also do bibliographical guides and textbooks to serve them. For example, the publication of the American Political Science Association devoted to improving the quality of teaching in that discipline, *News for Teachers of Political Science*, has published extensive articles describing the results of a survey of types of courses in political communication offered and materials used (Blanchard & Wolfson, 1980) and course outlines and readings for courses in the mass media and American politics (Pohlmann & Foley, 1978). And clearly marking the arrival of political communication as a growth industry has been the increased competition between rival textbook authors and their respective publishers for a share of the market. The five-year period 1975–1980 witnessed the publication of core texts addressed exclusively to the political communication market (Chaffee, 1975; Kraus & Davis, 1976; Nimmo, 1978; Graber, 1980; Meadow, 1980) and a host of specialized, supplementary works. There seems little question that the textbook-monograph explosion will continue, especially with publishing houses planning specialized "topics" and "series" volumes in the field.

Professional Recognition

Scholarly and professional organizations, which once gave little thought in their planning for annual conferences to providing forums for the discussion of research in political communication, now set aside panels, plenary sessions, workshops, and other meetings for political communication scholars. Rare is the annual meeting of an internationally, nationally, or regionally based scholarly organization—in any of the social sciences—that does not conduct such sessions. Moreover, the International Communication Association provided formal recognition of political communication as a distinctive teaching and research field transcending the boundaries of separate academic disciplines when, in 1973, it accepted the founding of the Political Communication Division within its structure. The Eastern Communication Association did the same.

Policy Implications

As we shall note later, many of the progenitors of what has emerged as the distinctive field of political communication (e.g., rhetorical analysis, propaganda analysis, persuasion studies) provided research findings with policy applications. That heritage of a research enterprise with practical implications remains viable, as many of the chapters in this handbook clearly indicate. One example of many is noteworthy here. Also evolving since the 1950s

has been a distinct profession—that of political campaign management and consulting—whose practitioners apply many of the research theories, methods, and findings to a wide range of electoral and policy-oriented questions, such as the effectiveness of alternative campaign techniques, deriving profiles of citizens' communication habits, addressing problems in fund-raising, and legislative lobbying. Such applications are exemplified by the regularity with which newsletters of professional management and consulting firms (for example, *Campaign Insight*, *Campaigning Reports*, *Campaign Practices Report*) summarize applied political communication research or include sessions incorporating that research in their candidate training seminars.

Cross-National Growth

We have asserted that political communication as a field of inquiry is cross-disciplinary—that is, it combines the interests and skills of scholars from a wide variety of academic disciplines. Similarly, political communication is emerging as a field with a cross-national scope. In his appendix to this volume, "European Research," Richard Fitchen offers a brief sketch of some of the work being undertaken outside the United States. But the emergence of the field extends even wider. A separate volume would be required to summarize the major research and teaching programs now taking place on each continent. The ferment in political communication research of a cross-national nature can be sampled by close attention to Fitchen's contribution as well as to the efforts of Richard Lanigan, and Jay Blumler and Michael Gurevitch.

★ ORIGINS AND BACKGROUNDS OF AN EMERGING FIELD

Granted, then, that as a field of inquiry political communication is in a healthy, thriving, burgeoning state. To understand how it reached that identity, and to grasp the diverse facets of this manifold field, we must look back and trace the beginnings of the various threads of intellectual concern that evolved singly, then in combination, to form the field of political communication. We need not, nor can we in such brief fashion touch upon every line of ancestry, but we will select a few key ones for emphasis.

Interest in the interrelationship of communication and politics is scarcely new. Systematic inquiry began at least as early as the work of the Sophists and the insights provided by Aristotle in his *Politics and Rhetoric*. Moreover, the heritage of political communication must include classics in the arts of persuasion penned by Sun Tzu, St. Thomas Aquinas, Shakespeare, Machiavelli, and many others. And surely no student of American politics can ignore the rhetorical aspects of The Declaration of Independence, *The Federalist Papers*, or the Gettysburg Address.

Rather than pinpoint a precise era for the origins of political communication studies, it is more useful to catalogue a few of the key areas of inquiry that constitute the lineage of the field. For this purpose we select rhetorical analysis, propaganda analysis, attitude change research, voting studies, government-news media studies, functional and systems analyses, and technological change. It is important to bear in mind that in each of these areas, we frequently see investigators from a variety of academic disciplines employing a host of differing theoretical postures, research methods, and techniques. For example, anthropology and sociology stimulated interest in linguistics and symbolism, giving rise to the study of political languages; psychology and social psychology provoked interest in the subjective aspects of communication, attitude change studies, and learning—the bases of research into constructs of political discourse, the effects of mediated political appeals, and political socialization; speech communication has provided historical, critical, and quantitative analyses of messages and their reception, the bases of modern concerns with political rhetoric; political scientists undertook generations of voting studies that formed the received notions of communication's role in electoral campaigns; students of mass communication inquired into the impact of changing communication technology on social life, thus prompting concerns about the role of mass communication in altering political systems; cybernetic and systems analyses previewed the possibilities of treating entire political communities in holistic

terms as communications systems of learning and control; and from philosophy stem existential, phenomenistic, and other schools of thought yielding current emphases on critical theory in political communication. In sum, bound up with the diverse substantive origins of the field are the elements lending a distinctly cross-disciplinary character to political communication inquiry.

Rhetorical Analysis

From the classical writers, of which Aristotle was the most prominent, through the eighteenth-century English triumvirate of Blair (1783/1965), Campbell (1776/1963), and Whately (1828/1963), and into the twentieth century via such works as the three volumes (Brigance, 1943; Hochmuth, 1965) on *The History and Criticism of American Public Address*, much has emerged that is relevant to political communication. Indeed, since the founding of *The Quarterly Journal of Speech* in 1915, there has hardly been an issue that did not contain at least one essay on the history or criticism of public political discourse. More recently, this journal has undertaken to publish quadrennially a collection of essays on the presidential campaigns. The rhetorical tradition has kept alive and well the contributions of the ancients, elaborated and supplemented them, and, along with the behavioral trends of the 1950s, have fostered a cross-disciplinary spirit of inquiry.

Early in their presentation of the methods of rhetorical analysis, Brock and Scott (1980) traced approaches to rhetorical study through distinct perspectives. The first, which they label "traditional," has its roots in Aristotelian analysis, now appearing in neo-Aristotelian form. Brock and Scott note that the traditional perspective focuses on the speaker (source of communication) as the object of inquiry, analyzing how that speaker responds to rhetorical problems posed by the situation. Rhetoric they define as "the human effort to induce cooperation through the use of symbols" (p. 16). Students in this tradition accept the proposition that principles of sound rhetoric are discoverable, have indeed been derived, and are so stable that they transcend discrete episodes of political discourse.

If the traditional mode of rhetorical analysis focuses on the speaker as the essential element of inquiry, the "experiential" perspective, note Brock and Scott, denies any such essential starting point for analysis. Instead, society is regarded as in a state of process, of flux. Any analytical scheme, therefore, is arbitrary in what it examines, what it emphasizes, how it carves up chaos. It is up to the rhetorical analyst to choose among speaker, message, audience, setting, and other phases of that process of discourse. Hence, no fundamental principles of rhetoric can or do exist.

A third perspective on rhetorical analysis, say Brock and Scott, is that of the "new rhetoric." It falls between the traditional and experiential perspectives. Like the latter, it accepts the view that society is in process; but, like the former, it believes that stable relationships can be found in human interaction. The procedure for accomplishing that is via the construction of a framework for the analysis of discourse that assumes that symbols so influence human perceptions of reality that life itself, in any social sense, is symbolic action.

So permanent and prominent a place has rhetorical analysis occupied in the history of studies dealing with the emerging facets of political communication that it is not surprising that the tradition itself has come under investigation and criticism. The approach has been criticized for its lack of theoretical breadth and methodological imagination (Black, 1965/1978). Trent (1975) concluded, after reviewing 54 articles on political communication appearing in national and regional journals in speech communication, that the tradition could best be extended through greater methodological awareness and sophistication. Assessing the changes that had taken place in the field between the publication of his book in 1965 and its republication in 1978, Black (1965/1978, p. ix) concluded: "There is less uniformity in the techniques of rhetorical criticism and in the sorts of subjects deemed appropriate to it, less agreement on its proper role or its ideal condition, more contention, more experiment, more confusion, more vitality."

Propaganda Analysis

At the outbreak of World War I Charles E. Merriam, frequently regarded as the father of modern political science—or at least the chief figure in training a generation of political scientists who were later to found the behavioral movement in that discipline—left his professorial duties to accept responsibility for U.S. public information programs in Italy. Out of that experience grew an interest in public opinion, propaganda, and communication. A young graduate student picked up on that interest and prepared his Ph.D. dissertation on propaganda in the world war. Merriam's former student, Herbert Lasswell, soon became the leading exponent of propaganda analysis, writing a definitive history of propaganda in World War I (1927), exploring and perfecting techniques of content analysis in World War II (Lasswell & Leites, 1949), and collaborating in a volume that clearly marked propaganda analysis a forerunner of political communication studies (Smith, Lasswell, & Casey, 1946).

The interest in propaganda stimulated by the activity surrounding the two world wars produced twin foci of inquiry—on the motives of the communicator and on the key symbols composing message content. The two merged in analysts' growing fascination with what became known as the "techniques of propaganda." In 1937 philanthropist Edward A. Filene provided financing for The Institute of Propaganda Analysis. The institute sponsored, among other things, academic research, secondary school programs in propaganda analysis, and manuals with guidelines for spotting propaganda techniques. The "seven devices of propaganda" (name-calling, glittering generalities, transfer, testimonial, plain-folks appeals, card-stacking, and band-wagon appeals) were staples for textbooks in propaganda and public opinion for decades. So venerable has been the fascination with applying and detecting propaganda techniques that in 1969 a producer of table games, the "Wff 'N Proof" organization, marketed a widely sold game based on the seven devices of propaganda, a game co-created by television actor Lorne Greene (Allen & Greene, 1969).

Today, political communication studies with a propaganda focus continue the long-term emphasis on propagandists' motives and the content of appeals. However, there is much less concern in contemporary research with direct propaganda than with the covert propagandistic content of other messages—for example, news media content and television documentaries. These studies take both an empirical bent (Efron, 1971; Hofstetter, 1976) and a speculative tone (Ellul, 1965; Schiller, 1973). Moreover, as Richard Hofstetter reports, content analysis has become increasingly sophisticated, with techniques developed for measuring manifest and latent content of messages, verbal and nonverbal communication.

Attitude Change Studies

Another progenitor in the evolution of political communication studies also grew out of the period of world war, especially out of the era of World War II. At the time, the Research Branch of the Army's Information and Education Division employed a number of social psychologists to examine soldiers' attitudes and opinions, then apply those findings to the design and implementation of information, orientation, and education programs. One focus was on the effects of mass communication (chiefly military training films) on attitude change, a focus later reported in a volume prepared by Hovland, Lumsdaine, and Sheffield (1949).

Following the war, attitude change studies remained a key facet of communication research. Carl Hovland and his colleagues, through a published series of "Yale Studies in Attitude and Communication," reported numerous experimental findings dealing with the impact of a host of variables on attitude shifts: the credibility of the communicator, fear-arousing appeals, the organization of messages, personality and susceptibility to persuasion, group membership and participation, and the role of social judgment (Hovland, Janis, & Kelly, 1953; Hovland, 1957; Hovland & Janis, 1959; Hovland & Rosenberg, 1960; Sherif & Hovland, 1961). Other investigators aimed at generating theories and models of attitude change, including balance (Heider, 1946), congruity (Osgood, 1960), dissonance (Festinger, 1957), and discrepancy (Sherif, Sherif, & Nebergall, 1965) models.

It did not take long for investigators to extend their inquiries into the attitudinal effects of communication to include political attitudes.

As will be noted, the early voting studies focused in part upon such matters. Yet, by the time of publication in 1960 of a now-classic review and synthesis of research of the effects of mass communication (Klapper), there were still relatively few studies solely addressing the political effects. Less than two decades later, however, that no longer was the case. In 1976, for example, an entire volume appeared which did for politics what Klapper's work had done in a more generic sense earlier (Kraus & Davis, 1976). Whereas Klapper had only 1000 studies on which to base his conclusions about mass communication's impact on behavior generally, Kraus and Davis consulted 3000 sources for effects on political behavior alone. As readers of this *Handbook* will discover, attitude change and effect studies continue to occupy a central role in inquiries into political advertising, political debates, political socialization, elections and voting, and public opinion.

The Voting Studies

Systematic studies of the attitudes and forces surrounding voting behavior date back to the 1920s (Merriam & Gosnell, 1924; Rice, 1928), and communication variables were taken into account at an early stage (Gosnell, 1927). That tradition continued through three generations of voting studies that were to follow: first-generation studies of the Bureau of Applied Social Research (Lazarsfeld, Berelson & Gaudet, 1944; Berelson, Lazarsfeld, & McPhee, 1954); second-generation research led by the studies of the University of Michigan's Survey Research Center (Campbell, Gurin, & Miller, 1954; Campbell, Converse, Miller, & Stokes, 1960, 1966); and more recent, third-generation studies (Blumler & McQuail, 1969; Mendelsohn & O'Keefe, 1976; Miller & Levitin, 1976; Nie, Verba, & Petrocik, 1976; Patterson & McClure, 1976; Patterson, 1980).

First-generation studies, designed in large measure to test the hypothesis that campaign communication did make a difference in voting, revealed that campaign appeals were less likely to convert voters than to activate, crystallize, or reinforce choices already made on the basis of some other factor, such as socioeconomic position, partisan loyalty, religion, or residence.

Second-generation studies also minimize the effects of campaigns in the face of long-term, enduring partisan identifications of voters. More recent, third-generation inquiries yield a complicated interpretation of the relationship between political communication and voting behavior, one that varies depending on what uses voters made of campaign communication, how information diffuses throughout a campaign, the agenda-setting role of the news media, and how people construct their political views. In sum, after starting with a simplistic notion of direct effects of communication on voting (the hypodermic-needle view), then adopting a minimal effects posture, voting studies now appear wed to a phenomenistic conclusion; that is, the influence of communication on voting depends on a number of phenomena operating within the field where such communication appears.

Government and the News Media

The relationship of the press to politics, the news media to government, has long been a mainstay of scholarly curiosity, fascination to and frustration of politicians, and narcissistic interest to journalists. The relationship of government and press evoked particular concern toward the end of the eighteenth century as the power of the latter began to match that of the former. English philosopher-statesman Edmund Burke, believing the press was exercising a usurping and malignant power challenging that of the House of Commons, coined the term "the Fourth Estate" to deplore the shift (Bums, 1971).

In the United States it took longer to recognize the potentially influential role the press could play independently of constitutional and extraconstitutional political institutions. One reason lay in the fact that the institutions themselves employed newspapers as direct mouthpieces of partisan interests. The press in America in the late eighteenth and early nineteenth century was essentially a party press, as witnessed by President Jefferson's providing a patronage slot on the government payroll for the editor of his party's paper. The press as challenger to governing authority would await a later era, that of "yellow journalism," toward the end of the nineteenth century. And it would not

be until the publication of Walter Lippmann's classic *Public Opinion* (1922) that a serious effort to analyze the government-press relationship would be made.

Since the Lippmann era, however, the focus on government-press relations has evolved continuously, intensifying considerably in recent decades. No longer limited to discussions of print journalism, the relationship now examines the political role of all of the organs of the news media. Moreover, scholarly interest resides in specialists of a variety of academic disciplines. Hence, in the 1970s alone, for example, major book-length contributions came from political scientists (Epstein, 1973; Sigal, 1973), sociologists (Gans, 1979; Tunstall, 1970; Tuchman, 1978), and communication scientists (Shaw & McCombs, 1977; Blanchard, 1974). Moreover, apparently attempting to emulate—but not surpass—the example set by Lippmann, numerous working journalists now deem it essential at some point in their careers to assess the relationship of government and news media. The result is a sizable supply of volumes, of which those by Reston (1967), Wicker (1978), and Halberstam (1979) are representative.

Functional and Systems Analyses

During the period of interest in behavioral approaches to the social sciences, one of the areas provoking considerable activity among political scientists was that of the comparative analysis of political systems. Dissatisfied with merely comparing governments (nation to nation, national to subdivision, subdivision to subdivision, etc.) by describing the institutional features of each, students of comparative politics argued that theory-building in political science would be better advanced by a new tact. That was to agree on the key functions performed by politics in any society, discover the sociopolitical structures performing those functions, then compare each structure across various societies and cultures.

In a highly influential work political scientists Gabriel Almond and James Coleman (1960) spelled out the functional requisites on which a comparative analysis of politics should rest: the "common properties of political systems" (pp. 9–58). One such function they identified as "the political communication function." "All of the functions performed in the political system" they noted, "are performed by means of communication." For this reason, they observed, "at first thought, it might appear that there is no political communication function as such, that communication is an aspect of all other functions." What, then, might justify the differentiation? For Almond and Coleman, it was the fact that "in the modern political system differentiated media of communication have arisen which have developed a vocational ethics of 'neutral' or objective communication" (p. 45). Such ethics require that, analytically, the dissemination of information should be treated separately from other functions. Almond and Coleman then pointed out that the separation was not unique only to modern political systems but could also apply to ancient systems—Mercury in the Greek Pantheon; duty messengers in the Old Testament; drummers and runners, medieval criers, heralds, and so on.

Picking up on this structural/functional approach to the study of political communication, a number of works have attempted to identify, isolate, and compare the institutions of political communication across national systems. For example, Fagan (1966) attempts to apply the structural/functional approach to cross-national comparisons of networks of political communication, flows of political images, determinants of communication patterns, and the influence of communication on governmental performance and political change. In a more restrictive effort, Almond and Powell (1966) compare the functions performed by the political communication function in developing nations. The essays in the volume of Nimmo and Mansfield (1981) compare the structures of government and news media relations across several political systems.

Studies derived from the Almond and Coleman model treat political communication in different ways. However, in a major treatise, Deutsch (1963) views all of government and politics as an exercise in communication and control. Deutsch thus applies cybernetics theory to the holistic analysis of political systems, emphasizing concepts of feedback, goals, purposes, learning capacities, autonomy, self-closure, and growth. Provocative though his speculations are, there have been few attempts

to build upon Deutsch's work. Galnoor has made the most explicit effort, first reviewing the contours of a systems approach to political communication (1980) and applying it in the case of the Israeli political system (1981). Other works that make reference to Deutsch's model, however, either direct their attention to side issues, thus losing sight of the main thrust of a cybernetic approach (Meadow, 1980; Merritt, 1972), or base their analyses on Deutsch's earlier, more limited (1953), efforts to analyze national development as a function of trends in social communication (Merritt, 1966).

Although studies arising out of the traditions of the structural/functional and systems analyses approaches to political communication may provide considerable insight in the future, the relative absence of such investigations to date do not warrant treating either area as a separate substantive domain of study at present.

Technological Changes

The evolving interest in political communication derived from the academic spheres outlined above also emerged from a number of miscellaneous developments. It is convenient to label these changes in technology. Three merit special mention—changes in the diffusion of political information, the development of professional campaign techniques, and increased sophistication in research methodology.

Media Technology. As noted above, in the early days of the U.S. republic the press consisted primarily of partisan newspapers. Out of that era evolved periods of story journalism, sensationalist reporting, contemporary newspapers and news magazines, and the more recent emergence of electronic journalism (Nimmo, 1981). Similar trends developed in Great Britain (Johnson, 1981) and in a wide variety of other nations in Europe, North America, and Australia (Nimmo & Mansfield, 1981).

In part at least, the evolution of journalism has been a function of developments in media technology. The changes in print and the advent of sound and then visual media have certainly left marks on politics, an overall impact researchers have examined with keen interest. Few stories (even if apocryphal) so well illustrate the impact as that related of publisher

William Randolph Hearst's fomenting of the Spanish-American War. Witnessing his *New York Journal* locked in a circulation fight with rival Joseph Pulitzer's *New York World*, Hearst sent artist Frederic Remington to Cuba to send back visual accounts of the insurrection against the Spanish. But Remington wired Hearst: "Everything is quiet. There is no trouble here. There will be no war. I wish to return." Hearst, undaunted, responded: "Please remain. You furnish pictures. I will furnish war" (Knightly, 1975, pp. 57–58).

If newspapers had their impact on political events, so did radio, film, and television. Scholars can scarcely ignore the role played by the electronic media in the contemporary history of either democracies or totalitarian systems. Recognizing the advantages provided by radio for mass communication, Franklin D. Roosevelt hired poets and playwrights to help him craft a Lincolnesque image to be disseminated via radio and newsreels (Jones, 1974). In the same era, Joseph Goebbels was explicit in his plans to exploit both sound and film as the media for bringing Adolf Hitler to power, keeping him there, and winning his war (Reimann, 1976).

A spate of voting studies already cited (Mendelsohn & O'Keefe, 1976; Patterson & McClure, 1976; Patterson, 1980) have explored television's impact on one facet of political life. Barber (1980) went on to argue that the evolution of media technology has created and reinforced a fundamental pattern in American electoral politics. He maintains that the media cover presidential elections in 12-year cycles, each election in the cycle evoking a predictable drama. The cycle begins with a political drama of conflict (1900, 1948, 1960, and 1972 are examples) in which campaign coverage emphasizes the divisive, cleavage-ridden side of American politics. Four years later media coverage likens the presidential campaign (1916, 1940, 1964, and 1976 are Barber's key illustrations) to a drama of conscience wherein the good and moral side of politics shows through. The final election in each cycle (for example, 1920, 1932, 1956, 1968) emerges in media coverage as a drama of conciliation—one of bringing the nation together, binding old wounds, and offering a new beginning. Much can be said in praise and criticism of Barber's Polybian thesis, but the key point is that he takes seriously the interlocking relationship of media technology to politics, even hinting that there may be a media determinism inherent in political events. Such a viewpoint goes far to promote the growth of political communication as a field worthy of serious inquiry.

Campaign Techniques. Parallel with evolving technologies of political communication have been adjustments in the techniques of political campaigning. Jensen (1980), after examining the campaign styles of all presidential elections from 1800 through 1980, noted three classifications of campaign styles and techniques, two with variations. The first, most common to campaigns in the era of the party press, was the rally campaign. A rally activates and reinforces party loyalties. Its goal is not to convert partisans but to mobilize one's own and overwhelm the opposition at the polls with sheer numbers. There were two variations: The army rally involved tight, military-like organizations of precinct and ward loyalists, communication to the rank and file via party newspapers (there were 1630 in the U.S. by 1850), and crowd-pleasing oratory; the missionary rally was designed to create a new movement or rebuild an old one through membership in clubs, evangelical appeals, and educational forums. In sum, the rally derived from a network of interpersonal and print communication. After the turn of this century, however, with the development of mass circulation newspapers, radio, film, and television, the *advertising* campaign became the norm. Candidates were mass marketed, brand (party) loyalties counted for less, public relations and advertising techniques came to the fore, and consumer (voter) surveys helped segment and target the market. Jensen notes that the advertising strategy first emerged in 1916; since that time an entire campaigning industry has grown around it (Agranoff, 1976; Nimmo, 1970; Rosenbloom, 1973). Finally, interspersed throughout the rally and advertising have been crusade (and countercrusade) campaigns. Notes Jensen (p. 49), "The dominant characteristic of the crusade is a pervasive moral fervor that animates both the standard bearer and his supporters to extirpate evil from government in the name of the people." Hence, "evil powerholders must be routed; apocalyptic doom is prophesied if the forces of evil prevail; war, social calamities, economic exploitation, or deep injustice all lie just around the corner." Crusades employ the full panoply of campaign media: mass meetings, parades, newsletters, distinctive logos, and mass communication. Conversion, not mobilization, purification, not fabrication, and moral as much as political victory are the goals.

Research Techniques. The influence of changing media technologies on politics and of changing campaign techniques on appeals via the media have both caught the fancy of an emerging community of researchers in political communication. It is doubtful, however, that the various antecedents of the emerging scholarly field would have reached confluence if the researchers themselves had not become increasingly self-conscious about the assumptions underlying their efforts, the methodologies guiding their research, and the techniques providing their evidence. One of the hallmarks of the behavioral period in the social sciences was the effort to apply hitherto neglected (and usually quantifiable) techniques to the analysis of social events. In many respects political communication research ceased to lag behind similar work in "other substantive fields of social science" (the charge made in 1956 by Eulau, Eldersveld, and Janowitz) when it, too, grew more methodologically sophisticated. As we shall see, and as amply illustrated in the chapters of this *Handbook* in the section on "Methods of Study," researchers now employ a wide range of qualitative and quantitative techniques but in an increasingly self-critical manner that looks to considerable methodological refinements in the future (consult the concluding essay in this volume, "Constructing the Realities of a Pluralist Field").

★ FROM DIVERSIFIED ORIGINS TO A PLURALIST BEGINNING

We have described the current status of political communication as an emerging field of inquiry and traced selected aspects of its lineage. However, readers will note that we have not specified the precise substantive content of the field, nor have we defined the field's boundaries. There are reasons for that. One lies in the absence of consensus among political communication scholars regarding content and boundaries. This is not for want of proffered definitions. For example, political communication has been defined as "any exchange of symbols or messages that to a significant extent have been shaped by, or have consequences for, the functioning of political systems" (Meadow, 1980, p. 4); "communicatory activity considered political by virtue of its consequences, actual and potential, that it has for the functioning of the political system" (Fagen, 1966, p. 20); "the role of communication in the political process" (Chaffee, 1975, p. 15); "communication (activity) considered political by virtue of its consequences (actual and potential) which regulate human conduct under conditions of conflict" (Nimmo, 1978, p. 7); communication with actual or potential "effects on the functioning of a political state or other political entity" (Blake & Haroldsen, 1975, p. 44); and the political symbols salient in the elite press (Arora & Lasswell, 1969). To be sure, the bulk of these characterizations agree that there is some body of activity which is "communication" (but scholars do not agree what activity); another body of activity called "politics" (again, there is little agreement on what that activity is); and that when the former activity influences the latter, there is "political communication" (but once again, the nature of that influence is not a matter of concurrence).

There is another reason for avoiding the problem of precise characterization of the scholarly field. If there is a lack of consensus among students of political communication on a definition of subject matter, so also do they disagree on goals. In the spirit of the behavioral era that provided the impetus for the field's emergence, students concur that theory-building is their task; that is, the construction of a body of tested, confirmed, explanatory generalizations. But there are different visions of what shape such theory should take. Deutsch (1963) and his followers strive for a communication *theory of politics,* one that considers all political activity as systems of communication and control. Other researchers, viewing neither all of politics as communication nor all of communication as politics, aim for a *theory of political communication* (Fagen, 1966; Chaffee, 1975). The result would be a functionalist-oriented body of generalizations akin to those derived by scholars seeking a theory of political leadership, a theory of political socialization, a theory of public policy-making, and so on. Finally, there are researchers speculating that communication is political in achieving/disrupting social order; hence communication has key political dimensions—power, influence, authority, control, negotiation, symbolic transaction, and the like. Thus, a *political theory of communication* warrants aspiration (Bell, 1975; Mueller, 1973).

For a field of such disparate origins and recent vintage it is perhaps not surprising to find only superficial agreement on definitions and explicit debate on goals. And this constitutes a third reason for shunning the temptation to attempt a definitive statement of what the field of political communication is, where it is going. Decades ago a lifelong journalist and social scientist pondered the desirability of trying to define government as isolated from other forms of social activity (Bentley, 1908), a problem like trying to separate politics from communication, political communication from other varieties of communicatory activity. Bentley decided the effort was not only in vain but a dangerous exercise:

> One more question remains as to this raw material for the study of government. Ought we not to draw a distinction in advance between it and other varieties of social activity, so that we can have our field of study defined and delimited at the outset? The answer is No. Many a child, making paper toys, has used his scissors too confidently and cut himself off from the materials he needs. This is an error to avoid [p. 199].

To behave like the too-confident child in approaching political communication would be particularly foolish. The field's current immaturity and diverse antecedents make of it a pluralist endeavor that as yet defies neat characterization. As the chapters in this *Handbook* demonstrate, political communication is a field with continuously evolving theoretical approaches, subject matter areas, and methodological stances. As yet there are no fixed boundaries, hardened dogmas, methodological orthodoxies, or conventional truths. The flavor of that pluralist core of the field of political communication, we believe, pervades each of the four major sections of this *Handbook*.

REFERENCES

Agranoff, R. *The management of election campaigns.* Boston: Holbrook Press, 1976.

Allen, R. W., & Greene, L. *The propaganda game.* New Haven. CT: Autotelic Instructional Materials, 1969.

Almond, G. A., & Coleman, J. F. (Eds.). *The politics of developing areas.* Princeton: Princeton University Press, 1960.

Almond, G. A., & Powell, G. B., Jr. *Comparative politics: A developmental approach.* Boston: Little, Brown, 1966.

Arora, S., & Lasswell, H. E. *Political communications: The public language of political elites in India and the United States.* New York: Holt, Rinehart & Winston, 1969.

Barber, J. D. *The pulse of politics.* New York: W. W. Norton, 1980.

Becker, L. B., McCombs, M. E., & McLeod, J. M. The development of political cognitions. In S. Chaffee (Ed.), *Political communication.* Beverly Hills, CA: Sage, 1975.

Bell, D. V. J. *Power, influence, and authority.* New York: Oxford University Press, 1975.

Bentley, A. F. *The process of government.* Chicago: University of Chicago Press, 1908.

Berelson, B., Lazarsfeld, P. & McPhee, W. *Voting.* Chicago: University of Chicago Press, 1954.

Black, E. *Rhetorical criticism, a study in method.* Madison: University of Wisconsin Press, 1978. (Originally published, 1965)

Blair, H. [*Lectures on rhetoric and belles lettres*] (2 vols.) (H. Harding, ed.). Carbondale: Southern Illinois University Press, 1965. (Originally published, 1783).

Blake, R. H., & Haroldsen, E. O. *A taxonomy of concepts in communication.* New York: Hastings House, 1975.

Blanchard, R. O. (Ed.). *Congress and the news media.* New York: Hastings House, 1974.

Blanchard, R. O., & Wolfson, L. Courses on the media, government, and public policy. *News for Teachers of Political Science,* 1980, 25, 14–15.

Blumler, J. G., & McQuail, D. *Television in politics.* Chicago: University of Chicago Press, 1969.

Brigance, W. (Ed.). *A history and criticism of American public address* (2 vols.). New York: McGraw-Hill, 1943.

Brock, B. L., & Scott, R. L. (Eds.). *Methods of rhetorical criticism* (2nd ed.). Detroit: Wayne State University Press, 1980.

Budd, R., & Ruben, B. (Eds.). *Approaches to human communication.* Rochelle Park. NJ: Hayden Book Co., 1972.

Burns, T. *The BBC: Public institution and private world.* London: Macmillan, 1977.

Campbell, A., Converse, P., Miller, W. E., & Stokes, D. *The American voter.* New York: John Wiley, 1960.

Campbell, A., Converse, P., Miller, W. E., & Stokes, D. *Elections and the political order.* New York: John Wiley, 1966.

Campbell, A., Gurin, G., & Miller, W. E. *The voter decides.* New York: Harper & Row, 1954.

Campbell, G. [*The philosophy of rhetoric*] (2 vols.) (L. Bitzer, ed.). Carbondale: Southern Illinois University Press, 1963. (Originally published, 1776)

Chaffee, S. (Ed.). *Political communication.* Beverly Hills, CA: Sage, 1975.

Dahl, R. A. The behavioral approach in political science: An epitaph for a monument to a successful protest. *American Political Science Review,* 1961, 55, 763–772.

Deutsch, K. *Nationalism and social communication.* Cambridge: MIT Press, 1953.

Deutsch, K. *The nerves of government.* New York: Free Press, 1963.

Efron, E. *The news twisters.* Los Angeles: Nash Publishing, 1971.

Ellul, J. *Propaganda.* New York: Alfred A. Knopf, 1965.

Encyclopedia of the social sciences. New York: Macmillan, 1930.

Epstein, E. J. *News from nowhere.* New York: Vintage Books, 1973.

Eulau, H., Eldersveld, S. J., & Janowitz, M. (Eds.). *Political behavior.* New York: Free Press, 1956.

Fagen, R. R. *Politics and communication.* Boston: Little, Brown, 1966.

Festinger, L. *A theory of cognitive dissonance.* Evanston, IL: Row, Peterson, 1957.

Galnoor, I. Political communication and the study of politics. In D. Nimmo (Ed.), *Communication yearbook 4.* New Brunswick, NJ: Transaction Books, 1980.

Galnoor, I. *The Israeli political system.* Beverly Hills, CA: Sage, 1981.

Gans, H. J. *Deciding what's news.* New York: Pantheon, 1979.

Goodin, R. E. *Manipulatory politics.* New Haven, CT: Yale University Press, 1980.

Gosnell, H. F. *Getting out the vote.* Chicago: University of Chicago Press, 1927.

Graber, D. A. *Mass media and American politics.* Washington, DC: Congressional Quarterly Press, 1980.

Halberstam, D. *The powers that be.* New York: Alfred A. Knopf, 1979.

Heider, F. Attitudes and cognitive organization. *Journal of Psychology,* 1946, 21, 107–112.

Hochmuth, M. K. (Ed.). *A history and criticism of American public address.* New York: Russell and Russell, 1965.

Hofstetter, R. *Bias in the news.* Columbus: Ohio State University Press, 1976.

Hovland, C. I. (Ed.). *The order of presentation in persuasion.* New Haven, CT: Yale University Press, 1957.

Hovland, C. I., & Janis, I. L. (Eds.). *Personality and persuasibility.* New Haven, CT: Yale University Press, 1959.

Hovland, C. I., Janis, I. L., & Kelley, H. H. *Communication and persuasion.* New Haven, CT: Yale University Press, 1953.

Hovland, C. I., Lumsdaine, A. A., & Sheffield, F. D. *Experiments on mass communication.* Princeton: Princeton University Press, 1949.

Hovland, C. I., & Rosenberg, M. J. (Eds.). *Attitude organization and change.* New Haven, CT: Yale University Press, 1960.

Jensen, R. Armies, admen and crusaders: Strategies to win elections. *Public Opinion,* 1980, 3, 44–49, 52–53.

Johnson, K. S. Political party and media evolution in the United States and Great Britain. In J. P. McKerns (Ed.), *Communications research symposium* (vol. 4). Knoxville: University of Tennessee, College of Communications, 1981.

Jones, A. H. *Roosevelt's image-brokers.* Port Washington, NY: Kennikat Press, 1974.

Kaid, L. L., Sanders, K. R., & Hirsch, R. O. *Political campaign communication: A bibliography and guide to the literature.* Metuchen, NJ: Scarecrow Press, 1974.

Kaplan, A. *The conduct of inquiry.* San Francisco: Chandler Publishing, 1964.

Klapper, J. T. *The effects of mass communication.* New York: Free Press, 1960.

Knightly, P. *The first casualty.* New York: Harcourt Brace Jovanovitch, 1975.

Kraus, S., &. Davis, D. *The effects of mass communication on political behavior.* University Park: Pennsylvania State University Press, 1976.

Kuhn, T. S. *The structure of scientific revolutions.* Chicago: University of Chicago Press, 1962.

Lasswell, H. D. *Propaganda technique in the world war.* New York: Peter Smith, 1927.

Lasswell, H. D., &. Leites, N. *Language of politics: Studies in quantitative semantics.* Cambridge: MIT Press, 1949.

Lazarsfeld, P., Berelson, B., &. Gaudet, H. *The people's choice.* New York: Duell, Sloan and Pearce, 1944.

Lippmann, W. *Public opinion.* New York: Macmillan, 1922.

McGuire, W. J. Persuasion, resistance, and attitude change. In I. de Sola Pool, W. Schramm, F. Frey, N. Maccoby, & E. B. Parker (Eds.), *Handbook of communication.* Chicago: Rand McNally, 1973.

Meadow, R. B. *Political communication.* Norwood, NJ: ABLEX Publishing, 1980.

Meehan, E. *The theory and method of political analysis.* Homewood, IL: Dorsey Press, 1965.

Mendelsohn, H., &. O'Keefe, G. *The people choose a president.* New York: Praeger, 1976.

Merriam, C. E., &. Gosnell, H. F. *Non-voting.* Chicago: University of Chicago Press, 1924.

Merritt, R. L. *Symbols of American community, 1735–1775.* New Haven, CT: Yale University Press, 1966.

Merritt, R. L. Political science: An approach to human communication. In R. W. Budd & B. D. Ruben (Eds.), *Approaches to human communication.* Rochelle Park, NJ: Hayden Book Co., 1972.

Miller, W. E., &. Levitin, T. E. *Leadership and change.* Cambridge: Winthrop, 1976.

Mueller, C. *The politics of communication.* New York: Oxford University Press, 1973.

Nie, N. H., Verba, S., & Petrocik, J. R. *The changing American voter.* Cambridge: Harvard University Press, 1976.

Nimmo, D. *The political persuaders.* Englewood Cliffs, NJ: Prentice-Hall, 1970.

Nimmo, D. *Political communication and public opinion in America.* Santa Monica, CA: Goodyear, 1978.

Nimmo, D. Mass communication and politics. In S. Long (Ed.), *Handbook of political behavior, vol 4.* New York: Plenum, 1981.

Nimmo, D., &. Mansfield, M. (Eds.). *Government and the news media: Cross-national perspectives.* Waco, TX: Baylor University Press, 1981.

Osgood, C. E. Cognitive dynamics in the conduct of human affairs. *Public Opinion Quarterly,* 1960, 24, 341–365.

Patterson, T. E. *The mass media election.* New York: Praeger, 1980.

Patterson, T. E., &. McClure, R. D. *The unseeing eye.* New York: Putnam, 1976.

Pohlmann, M. D., &. Foley, T. P. Course outline and readings: Mass media and American politics. *News for Teachers of Political Science,* 1978, *19,* 5, 7, 17.

Reimann, V. *Goebbels: The man who created Hitler.* Garden City, NY: Doubleday, 1976.

Reston, J. *The artillery of the press.* New York: Harper &. Row, 1967.

Rice, S. *Quantitative methods in politics.* New York: Alfred A. Knopf, 1928.

Rosenbloom, D. L. *The election men.* New York: Quadrangle, 1973.

Sanders, K. R., Hirsch, R. O., &. Pace, T. *Political communication: A bibliography.* Carbondale: Southern Illinois University, School of Communication, 1972.

Schiller, H. I. *The mind managers.* Boston: Beacon, 1973.

Shaw, D. L., &. McCombs, M. E. *The emergence of American political issues: The agenda-setting function of the press.* St. Paul, MN: West Publishing, 1977.

Sherif, C. W., Sherif, M., &. Nebergall, R. E. *Attitude and attitude change.* Philadelphia: W. B. Saunders, 1965.

Sherif, M., & Hovland, C. I. *Social judgment.* New Haven, CT: Yale University Press, 1961.

Sigal, L. V. *Reporters and officials.* Lexington, MA: D. C. Heath, 1973.

Smith, B. L., Lasswell, H. D., &. Casey, R. D. *Propaganda, communication, and public opinion.* Princeton: Princeton University Press, 1946.

Trent, J. A synthesis of methodologies used in studying political communication. *Central States Speech Journal,* 1975, 26, 278–297.

Truman, D. B. The impact on political science of the revolution in the behavioral sciences. In R. D. Calkins (Ed.), *Research frontier: in politics and government.* Washington, DC: Brookings, 1955.

Tuchman, G. *Making news.* New York: Free Press, 1978.

Tunstall, J. *The Westminster lobby correspondents.* London: Routledge & Kegan Paul, 1970.

Van Dyke, V. *Political science: A philosophical analysis.* Stanford: Stanford University Press, 1960.

Whately, R. [*Elements of rhetoric*] (D. Ehninger, ed.). Carbondale: Southern Illinois University Press, 1963. (Originally published, 1828)

Wicker, T. *On press.* New York: Viking, 1978.

Spectator Politics and the Revival of Public Argument

David Zarefsky

By the time this issue appears, the 1992 election will have been decided. But I write during the weeks between the two national conventions, when the overriding fact is the volatility of our politics. Less than two months ago, Bill Clinton was written off as the probable last-place finisher in a three-way race. Now he leads President Bush by as much as 25 points in the opinion polls after the abrupt withdrawal of Ross Perot who concluded that he could not win. The Republican campaign apparatus, formerly thought to be a well-oiled machine, appears in such disarray that emergency treatment at the hands of Secretary of State James Baker may be required. All this may change by the time you read these words, because American politics this season is nothing if not changeable. Political realities seem to last no longer than the images of the mass media.

This observation may form an appropriate starting point for examining the relationship between media spectacle and the political process. The recent political scene has at least five characteristics which strongly resemble the cognitive mindset of mass media.

1. *Events are transient and volatile.* Fame may last for more than 15 minutes, but not much. Who would have thought that the Persian Gulf war, a tactical success that boosted the President's approval rating to 90 percent and seemed to assure his re-election, would be virtually forgotten? Neither the controversy surrounding American actions before the war, nor the continuing taunts of Saddam Hussein, command much interest. Ross Perot burst upon the political scene with a casual remark on *Larry King Live,* spurted to the top in national polls, suffered a series of minor mishaps and committed a *faux pas* in addressing the NAACP as "you people," saw his support erode, and gave up the race—all within a matter of months. On the Democratic side, Bill Clinton emerged as the early favorite, saw his ratings plummet in the face of questions about his character, heard himself dismissed as "damaged goods," and then effectively redefined himself and survived the onslaught—within a similarly short period of time.

2. *We avoid complex subjects.* Just as television is not a good medium for conveying complex issues without a clear plot or dramatic structure, so American politics has found complexity unbearable and hence avoidable. We are unprepared to discuss in any depth the economic and political transformations caused by the end of the Cold War, substituting instead the slogan of a "new world order" or the assertion, "We've changed the world, now let's change America." At home, too, we evade the complex questions. We want a rich array of social programs but do not want to pay for them, so we elect a President and Congress from different parties, enhance the risk of national gridlock, and then cite that condition as proof of the inefficacy of politics. We've lost interest in the Iran-Contra affair, even though the continuing investigation has profound consequences for American foreign policy and the people who make it. We've allowed slogans and photo opportunities to substitute for policy on issues such as education and the environment. We bore out the wisdom of Haynes Johnson's assessment (1991, p. 448), "In the course of their triumvirate alliance in the eighties, Reagan, television, and America had steered away from complexity. . . . Many Americans displayed a noticeable loss of appetite for real issues and information. They opted for predigested packages, the kind that made no demands."

3. *We simplify what cannot be avoided,* through sound bites and visual images that stand in for a more complex reality. Supreme Court rulings on the difficult issue of abortion are reduced to slogans—"protection of innocent life" vs. "a woman's right to choose." The difficult moral dilemmas of the Vietnam war are reduced to quibbling about whether Dan Quayle or Bill Clinton tried to avoid the draft. Almost all we remember about the Clarence Thomas confirmation controversy is the image of Anita Hill facing an all-male Senate Judiciary Committee.

4. *We magnify the trivial,* obscuring the difference between the mundane and the profound. Olson (1991) suggests that media focus on tangential and trivial subjects in order to fill

a coverage vacuum. American politics seems to have done the same. In 1984, Democratic candidate Walter Mondale echoed a hamburger commercial by asking a primary opponent, "Where's the beef?" Four years later, the Pledge of Allegiance emerged as a major campaign theme, and in the current season the orthographic skills of Vice President Quayle have become a *cause celebre*. Television reduces distances, denying the audience a sense of proportion. So too has our politics.

5. *We have debased political debate.* Arguably one of the most important changes in the last generation, political debates have become an expected element in virtually every campaign. Debates have great potential for focusing the audience's attention, for identifying issues, and for inviting deliberation. Sadly, however, this potential is largely unrealized. The debates have been formatted for television—the confrontation with reporter-questioners adds dramatic conflict and the short time limits respond to audiences' limited attention span. But these same conventions thwart sustained discussion of serious issues; they encourage one-liners and canned mini-speeches.

The focus in political debates is on winning by not losing, or by cleverly scoring a hit against the opponent. The questions are: Were there any major gaffes or blunders? Were there any great one-liners or sound bites? If not, the debates are dismissed as inconsequential. We remember the 1976 debates for Gerald Ford's (prescient?) statement that there was no Soviet domination of Eastern Europe, the 1980 debates for Jimmy Carter's use of his daughter Amy as a consultant on nuclear weapons and for Ronald Reagan's "There you go again," the 1984 debates for Reagan's rejoinder to the age issue, and the 1988 debates for Dukakis's lack of passion and Senator Lloyd Bentsen's retort to Dan Quayle, "You're no Jack Kennedy." This piling up of debating points (in the pejorative sense of that term) is not what public debate on important questions ought to be. And people realize it. The audience for debates has declined, and besides their lack of novelty one reason must be a widespread anticipation that not much will happen—serious issues won't be discussed, the statements of the candidates can't be trusted, and politicians are all the same anyway. Even

worse, as Olson (1991) has observed in a different context, by presenting superficial but balanced conflict, debates encourage viewers to adopt the persona of spectator rather than participant. And if one is looking for spectator sport, there are more exciting options.

These five features of the contemporary scene help to define a crisis in American political communication. At the very time that media and communication technology permit *greater* access to politics, we find instead declining rates of political participation, a declining belief in the efficacy of political action, a declining belief that it makes any difference who is elected, and a vastly diminished belief in the nobility of politics as a profession. There is, as Dionne (1991) noted, a growing sense of alienation from and outright hatred toward the American political system.

When so much is transitory, it is easier to opt out than to maintain anchors for public thought or accepted standards for discourse. Without such standards, however, political rhetoric becomes almost free-floating. Theodore White (1970, p. 518) recognized the problem a generation ago: Without common standards of judgment, "there could be no sense of order, no thongs of discipline to bind individuals to each other, to law, to moralities, to community. . . . Nations need dreams, goals they seek in common, within which the smaller dreams of individuals can guide their personal lives."

Edelman (1988) is right that much of what passes for political action is a constructed spectacle. This Chautauqua asks whether the perversion of politics I've tried to describe is caused by the nature of media portrayals. In large measure that is a chicken-and-egg question. Media alternatives often are available but find no market—how many, after all, chose to watch the political conventions on C-Span? As Entman (1989) implies, it is hard to know which comes first, more "responsible" media or increased voter sophistication. We are asking too much of the media if we assign primary responsibility there.

The problem is not media coverage *per se;* it is that we have conceived of politics in the image of our media, importing conventions of taste and judgment into an arena where they do not so easily fit. We've transformed the active citizen into the political couch potato (without the *e*), made political discourse into a text which masks issues, and made politics into a game in which survival is an end in itself. If a candidate's most important goal for an office is to win election to it, it's not surprising that voters will find the game tedious and without point and that they will decide not to play.

That way, however, lies susceptibility to despotism. It's ironic that Americans flirt with this possibility at the very moment that nations in the East are involving their people, often for the first time, in the experience of citizenship. It's also antithetical to the roots of our own discipline. We followed Aristotle in regarding rhetoric as an offshoot of politics and ethical studies; we saw communication as crucial to the survival of a democratic polity (and frequently in our basic textbooks made just this case for the importance of our field). But too often today, political communication is *assumed* to be inauthentic, to mask the real issues, and to pervert rather than strengthen the exercise of judgment.

The media are convenient scapegoats for this state of affairs, but the causes lie deeper: first, that we depend on news media to play a far greater educational role than they are able to perform, and second, that we have allowed ourselves to conceive of our political system in media terms. We have fashioned a "postmodern public" which has the trappings *but not the substance* of life in the *polis*.

What is missing from our political discourse is a rich and vibrant concept of *argument*, of public deliberation in which "a widening tradition of free speech renders interests articulate, prioritizes actions, and engages active audiences" (Goodnight, 1990, p. 174). In such a space, competing grounds for assent can be identified and justified. Audiences bring their interests and experiences to bear in evaluating claims and warrants, and a folk wisdom emerges from the give-and-take of advocates in controversy—a wisdom, to be sure, that sometimes is in error, but one which is rendered more reliable when participants in public deliberation take their responsibilities seriously and discharge them conscientiously.

It is customary to point to the Lincoln-Douglas debates as the model for what public argument could be and as the index of how far we have fallen. As I have suggested (Zarefsky, 1990), those debates were much different from what we often imagine, and more like contemporary political discourse than we might suppose. Candidates traded unsupported charges and personal attacks, digressed from the issues, and pandered to the audience. But at the core of those debates was a live controversy, discussed through carefully developed arguments which candidates and listeners could compare and evaluate—not sound bites, slogans, or one-liners which squeeze the argument out of the appeal. Even today, even in a media-saturated society, revival of the art of argument is an ideal to which we should aspire.

Instead of cultivating argument, we have truncated the public space, distanced people from politics, emptied "the public" of meaning as a collective noun, and trivialized such means for citizens' expression as responding to public opinion polls, calling "900" numbers, or showing up to cast a ballot on Election Day. Rather than praise or blame the media for our plight, we would be better advised to focus on the larger issue of how to revitalize the public sphere.

REFERENCES

Dionne, E. J. (1991). *Why Americans hate politics.* New York: Simon and Schuster.

Edelman, M. (1988). *Constructing the political spectacle.* Chicago: University of Chicago Press.

Entman, R. M. (1989). *Democracy without citizens: Media and the decay of American politics.* New York: Oxford University Press.

Goodnight, G. T. (1990). The rhetorical tradition, modern communication, and the grounds of justified assent. In David Cratis Williams & Michael David Hazen (Eds.), *Argumentation theory and the rhetoric of assent* (pp. 173–195). Tuscaloosa, AL: University of Alabama Press.

Johnson, H. (1991). *Sleepwalking through history: America in the Reagan years.* New York: Norton.

Olson, K. M. (1991). Constraining open deliberation in times of war: Presidential war justifications for Grenada and the Persian Gulf. *Argumentation and Advocacy,* 28 (2), 64–79.

White, T. H. (1970). *The making of the President 1968.* New York: Pocket Books.

Zarefsky, D. (1990). *Lincoln, Douglas, and slavery: In the crucible of public debate.* Chicago: University of Chicago Press.

Bowling Alone: America's Declining Social Capital*

Robert D. Putnam

Many students of the new democracies that have emerged over the past decade and a half have emphasized the importance of a strong and active civil society to the consolidation of democracy. Especially with regard to the post-communist countries, scholars and democratic activists alike have lamented the absence or obliteration of traditions of independent civic engagement and a widespread tendency toward passive reliance on the state. To those concerned with the weakness of civil societies in the developing or postcommunist world, the advanced Western democracies and above all the United States have typically been taken as models to be emulated. There is striking evidence, however, that the vibrancy of American civil society has notably declined over the past several decades.

Ever since the publication of Alexis de Tocqueville's *Democracy in America,* the United States has played a central role in systematic studies of the links between democracy and civil society. Although this is in part because trends in American life are often regarded as harbingers of social modernization, it is also because America has traditionally been considered unusually "civic" (a reputation that, as we shall later see, has not been entirely unjustified).

When Tocqueville visited the United States in the 1830s, it was the Americans' propensity for civic association that most impressed him as the key to their unprecedented ability to make democracy work. "Americans of all ages, all stations in life, and all types of disposition," he observed, "are forever forming associations. There are not only commercial and industrial associations in which all take part, but others of a thousand different types—religious, moral, serious, futile, very general and very limited, immensely large and very minute.... Nothing, in my view, deserves more attention than the intellectual and moral associations in America."[1]

Recently, American social scientists of a neo-Tocquevillean bent have unearthed a wide range of empirical evidence that the quality of public life and the performance of social institutions (and not only in America) are indeed powerfully influenced by norms and networks of civic engagement. Researchers in such fields as education, urban poverty, unemployment, the control of crime and drug abuse, and even health have discovered that successful outcomes are more likely in civically engaged communities. Similarly, research on the varying economic attainments of different ethnic groups in the United States has demonstrated the importance of social bonds within each group. These results are consistent with research in a wide range of settings that demonstrates the vital importance of social networks for job placement and many other economic outcomes.

Meanwhile, a seemingly unrelated body of research on the sociology of economic development has also focused attention on the role of social networks. Some of this work is situated in the developing countries, and some of it elucidates the peculiarly successful "network capitalism" of East Asia.[2] Even in less exotic Western economies, however, researchers have discovered highly efficient, highly flexible "industrial districts" based on networks of collaboration among workers and small entrepreneurs. Far from being paleoindustrial anachronisms, these dense interpersonal and interorganizational networks undergird ultra-modern industries, from the high tech of Silicon Valley to the high fashion of Benetton.

The norms and networks of civic engagement also powerfully affect the performance of representative government. That, at least, was the central conclusion of my own 20-year, quasi-experimental study of subnational governments in different regions of Italy.[3] Although all these regional governments seemed identical on paper, their levels of effectiveness varied dramatically. Systematic inquiry showed that

The argument in this essay was amplified and to some extent modified in Bowling Alone: The Collapse and Revival of American Community, *by Robert Putnam (New York: Simon & Schuster, 2000).*

the quality of governance was determined by longstanding traditions of civic engagement (or its absence). Voter turnout, newspaper readership, membership in choral societies and football clubs—these were the hallmarks of a successful region. In fact, historical analysis suggested that these networks of organized reciprocity and civic solidarity, far from being an epiphenomenon of socioeconomic modernization, were a precondition for it.

No doubt the mechanisms through which civic engagement and social connectedness produce such results—better schools, faster economic development, lower crime, and more effective government—are multiple and complex. While these briefly recounted findings require further confirmation and perhaps qualification, the parallels across hundreds of empirical studies in a dozen disparate disciplines and subfields are striking. Social scientists in several fields have recently suggested a common framework for understanding these phenomena, a framework that rests on the concept of *social capital*.[4] By analogy with notions of physical capital and human capital—tools and training that enhance individual productivity—"social capital" refers to features of social organization such as networks, norms, and social trust that facilitate coordination and cooperation for mutual benefit.

For a variety of reasons, life is easier in a community blessed with a substantial stock of social capital. In the first place, networks of civic engagement foster sturdy norms of generalized reciprocity and encourage the emergence of social trust. Such networks facilitate coordination and communication, amplify reputations, and thus allow dilemmas of collective action to be resolved. When economic and political negotiation is embedded in dense networks of social interaction, incentives for opportunism are reduced. At the same time, networks of civic engagement embody past success at collaboration, which can serve as a cultural template for future collaboration. Finally, dense networks of interaction probably broaden the participants' sense of self, developing the "I" into the "we," or (in the language of rational-choice theorists) enhancing the participants' "taste" for collective benefits.

I do not intend here to survey (much less contribute to) the development of the theory of social capital. Instead, I use the central premise of that rapidly growing body of work—that social connections and civic engagement pervasively influence our public life, as well as our private prospects as the starting point for an empirical survey of trends in social capital in contemporary America. I concentrate here entirely on the American case, although the developments I portray may in some measure characterize many contemporary societies.

★ WHATEVER HAPPENED TO CIVIC ENGAGEMENT?

We begin with familiar evidence on changing patterns of political participation, not least because it is immediately relevant to issues of democracy in the narrow sense. Consider the well-known decline in turnout in national elections over the last three decades. From a relative high point in the early 1960s, voter turnout had by 1990 declined by nearly a quarter; tens of millions of Americans had forsaken their parents' habitual readiness to engage in the simplest act of citizenship. Broadly similar trends also characterize participation in state and local elections.

It is not just the voting booth that has been increasingly deserted by Americans. A series of identical questions posed by the Roper Organization to national samples ten times each year over the last two decades reveals that since 1973 the number of Americans who report that "in the past year" they have "attended a public meeting on town or school affairs" has fallen by more than a third (from 22 percent in 1973 to 13 percent in 1993). Similar (or even greater) relative declines are evident in responses to questions about attending a political rally or speech, serving on a committee of some local organization, and working for a political party. By almost every measure, Americans' direct engagement in politics and government has fallen steadily and sharply over the last generation, despite the fact that average levels of education—the best individual-level predictor of political participation—have risen sharply throughout this period. Every year over the last decade or two, millions more have withdrawn from the affairs of their communities.

Not coincidentally, Americans have also disengaged psychologically from politics and government over this era. The proportion of Americans who reply that they "trust the government in Washington" only "some of the time" or "almost never" has risen steadily from 30 percent in 1966 to 75 percent in 1992.

These trends are well known, of course, and taken by themselves would seem amenable to a strictly political explanation. Perhaps the long litany of political tragedies and scandals since the 1960s (assassinations, Vietnam, Watergate, Irangate, and so on) has triggered an understandable disgust for politics and government among Americans, and that in turn has motivated their withdrawal. I do not doubt that this common interpretation has some merit, but its limitations become plain when we examine trends in civic engagement of a wider sort.

Our survey of organizational membership among Americans can usefully begin with a glance at the aggregate results of the General Social Survey, a scientifically conducted, national-sample survey that has been repeated 14 times over the last two decades. Church-related groups constitute the most common type of organization joined by Americans; they are especially popular with women. Other types of organizations frequently joined by women include school-service groups (mostly parent-teacher associations), sports groups, professional societies, and literary societies. Among men, sports clubs, labor unions, professional societies, fraternal groups, veterans' groups, and service clubs are all relatively popular.

Religious affiliation is by far the most common associational membership among Americans. Indeed, by many measures America continues to be (even more than in Tocqueville's time) an astonishingly "churched" society. For example, the United States has more houses of worship per capita than any other nation on Earth. Yet religious sentiment in America seems to be becoming somewhat less tied to institutions and more self-defined.

How have these complex crosscurrents played out over the last three or four decades in terms of Americans' engagement with organized religion? The general pattern is clear: The 1960s witnessed a significant drop in reported weekly churchgoing—from roughly 48 percent in the late 1950s to roughly 41 percent in the early 1970s. Since then, it has stagnated or (according to some surveys) declined still further. Meanwhile, data from the General Social Survey show a modest decline in membership in all "church-related groups" over the last 20 years. It would seem, then, that net participation by Americans, both in religious services and in church-related groups, has declined modestly (by perhaps a sixth) since the 1960s.

For many years, labor unions provided one of the most common organizational affiliations among American workers. Yet union membership has been falling for nearly four decades, with the steepest decline occurring between 1975 and 1985. Since the mid-1950s, when union membership peaked, the unionized portion of the nonagricultural work force in America has dropped by more than half, falling from 32.5 percent in 1953 to 15.8 percent in 1992. By now, virtually all of the explosive growth in union membership that was associated with the New Deal has been erased. The solidarity of union halls is now mostly a fading memory of aging men.[5]

The parent-teacher association (PTA) has been an especially important form of civic engagement in twentieth-century America because parental involvement in the educational process represents a particularly productive form of social capital. It is, therefore, dismaying to discover that participation in parent-teacher organizations has dropped drastically over the last generation, from more than 12 million in 1964 to barely 5 million in 1982 before recovering to approximately 7 million now.

Next, we turn to evidence on membership in (and volunteering for) civic and fraternal organizations. These data show some striking patterns. First, membership in traditional women's groups has declined more or less steadily since the mid-1960s. For example, membership in the national Federation of Women's Clubs is down by more than half (59 percent) since 1964, while membership in the League of Women Voters (LWV) is off 42 percent since 1969.[6]

Similar reductions are apparent in the numbers of volunteers for mainline civic organizations, such as the Boy Scouts (off by 26 percent since 1970) and the Red Cross (off by 61 percent since 1970). But what about the possibility that volunteers have simply switched their loyalties to other organizations? Evidence on "regular" (as opposed to occasional or "drop-by") volunteering is available from the Labor Department's Current Population Surveys of 1974 and 1989. These estimates suggest that serious volunteering declined by roughly one-sixth over these 15 years, from 24 percent of adults in 1974 to 20 percent in 1989. The multitudes of Red Cross aides and Boy Scout troop leaders now missing in action have apparently not been offset by equal numbers of new recruits elsewhere.

Fraternal organizations have also witnessed a substantial drop in membership during the 1980s and 1990s. Membership is down significantly in such groups as the Lions (off 12 percent since 1983), the Elks (off 18 percent since 1979), the Shriners (off 27 percent since 1979), the Jaycees (off 44 percent since 1979), and the Masons (down 39 percent since 1959). In sum, after expanding steadily throughout most of this century, many major civic organizations have experienced a sudden, substantial, and nearly simultaneous decline in membership over the last decade or two.

The most whimsical yet discomfiting bit of evidence of social disengagement in contemporary America that I have discovered is this: more Americans are bowling today than ever before, but bowling in organized leagues has plummeted in the last decade or so. Between 1980 and 1993 the total number of bowlers in America increased by 10 percent, while league bowling decreased by 40 percent. (Lest this be thought a wholly trivial example, I should note that nearly 80 million Americans went bowling at least once during 1993, *nearly a third more than voted in the 1994 congressional elections* and roughly the same number as claim to attend church regularly. Even after the 1980s' plunge in league bowling, nearly 3 percent of American adults regularly bowl in leagues.) The rise of solo bowling threatens the livelihood of bowling-lane proprietors because those who bowl as members of leagues consume three times as much beer and pizza as solo bowlers, and the money in bowling is in the beer and pizza, not the balls and shoes. The broader social significance, however, lies in the social interaction and even occasionally civic conversations over beer and pizza that solo bowlers forgo. Whether or not bowling beats balloting in the eyes of most Americans, bowling teams illustrate yet another vanishing form of social capital.

★ COUNTERTRENDS

At this point, however, we must confront a serious counterargument. Perhaps the traditional forms of civic organization whose decay we have been tracing have been replaced by vibrant new organizations. For example, national environmental organizations (like the Sierra Club) and feminist groups (like the National Organization for Women) grew rapidly during the 1970s and 1980s and now count hundreds of thousands of dues-paying members. An even more dramatic example is the American Association of Retired Persons (AARP), which grew exponentially from 400,000 card-carrying members in 1960 to 33 million in 1993, becoming (after the Catholic Church) the largest private organization in the world. The national administrators of these organizations are among the most feared lobbyists in Washington, in large part because of their massive mailing lists of presumably loyal members.

These new mass-membership organizations are plainly of great political importance. From the point of view of social connectedness, however, they are sufficiently different from classic "secondary associations" that we need to invent a new label—perhaps "tertiary associations." For the vast majority of their members, the only act of membership consists in writing a check for dues or perhaps occasionally reading a newsletter. Few ever attend any meetings of such organizations, and most are unlikely ever (knowingly) to encounter any other member. The bond between any two members of the Sierra Club is less like the bond between any two members of a gardening club and more like the bond between any two Red Sox fans (or perhaps any two devoted Honda owners): they root for the same team and they share some of the same interests, but they are unaware of each other's existence. Their ties, in short, are to common symbols, common leaders, and perhaps common ideals, but not to one another. The theory of social capital argues that associational membership should, for example, increase social trust, but this prediction is much less straightforward with regard to membership in tertiary associations. From the point of view of social connectedness, the Environmental Defense Fund and a bowling league are just not in the same category.

If the growth of tertiary organizations represents one potential (but probably not real) counterexample to my thesis, a second countertrend is represented by the growing prominence of nonprofit organizations, especially nonprofit service agencies. This so-called third sector includes everything from Oxfam and the Metropolitan Museum of Art to the Ford Foundation and the Mayo Clinic. In other words, although most secondary associations are nonprofits, most nonprofit agencies are not secondary associations. To identify trends in the size of the nonprofit sector with trends in social connectedness would be another fundamental conceptual mistake.[7]

A third potential countertrend is much more relevant to an assessment of social capital and civic engagement. Some able researchers have argued that the last few decades have witnessed a rapid expansion in "support groups" of various sorts. Robert Wuthnow reports that fully 40 percent of all Americans claim to be "currently involved in [a] small group that meets regularly and provides support or caring for those who participate in it."[8] Many of these groups are religiously affiliated, but many others are not. For example, nearly 5 percent of Wuthnow's national sample claim to participate regularly in a "self-help" group, such as Alcoholics Anonymous, and nearly as many say they belong to book-discussion groups and hobby clubs.

The groups described by Wuthnow's respondents unquestionably represent an important form of social capital, and they need to be accounted for in any serious reckoning of trends in social connectedness. On the other

hand, they do not typically play the same role as traditional civic associations. As Wuthnow emphasizes,

> Small groups may not be fostering community as effectively as many of their proponents would like. Some small groups merely provide occasions for individuals to focus on themselves in the presence of others. The social contract binding members together asserts only the weakest of obligations. Come if you have time. Talk if you feel like it. Respect everyone's opinion. Never criticize. Leave quietly if you become dissatisfied. . . . We can imagine that [these small groups] really substitute for families, neighborhoods, and broader community attachments that may demand lifelong commitments, when, in fact, they do not.[9]

All three of these potential countertrends—tertiary organizations, nonprofit organizations, and support groups—need somehow to be weighed against the erosion of conventional civic organizations. One way of doing so is to consult the General Social Survey.

Within all educational categories, total associational membership declined significantly between 1967 and 1993. Among the college-educated, the average number of group memberships per person fell from 2.8 to 2.0 (a 26-percent decline); among high-school graduates, the number fell from 1.8 to 1.2 (32 percent); and among those with fewer than 12 years of education, the number fell from 1.4 to 1.1 (25 percent). In other words, at *all* educational (and hence social) levels of American society, and counting *all* sorts of group memberships, *the average number of associational memberships has fallen by about a fourth over the last quarter-century.* Without controls for educational levels, the trend is not nearly so clear, but the central point is this: *more Americans than ever before are in social circumstances that foster associational involvement (higher education, middle age, and so on), but nevertheless aggregate associational membership appears to be stagnant or declining.*

Broken down by type of group, the downward trend is most marked for church-related groups, for labor unions, for fraternal and veterans' organizations, and for school-service groups. Conversely, membership in professional associations has risen over these years, although less than might have been predicted, given sharply rising educational and occupational levels. Essentially the same trends are evident for both men and women in the sample. In short, the available survey evidence confirms our earlier conclusion: American social capital in the form of civic associations has significantly eroded over the last generation.

★ GOOD NEIGHBORLINESS AND SOCIAL TRUST

I noted earlier that most readily available quantitative evidence on trends in social connectedness involves formal settings, such as the voting booth, the union hall, or the PTA. One glaring exception is so widely discussed as to require little comment here: the most fundamental form of social capital is the family, and the massive evidence of the loosening of bonds within the family (both extended and nuclear) is well known. This trend, of course, is quite consistent with—and may help to explain—our theme of social decapitalization.

A second aspect of informal social capital on which we happen to have reasonably reliable time-series data involves neighborliness. In each General Social Survey since 1974 respondents have been asked, "How often do you spend a social evening with a neighbor?" The proportion of Americans who socialize with their neighbors more than once a year has slowly but steadily declined over the last two decades, from 72 percent in 1974 to 61 percent in 1993. (On the other hand, socializing with "friends who do not live in your neighborhood" appears to be on the increase, a trend that may reflect the growth of workplace-based social connections.)

Americans are also less trusting. The proportion of Americans saying that most people can be trusted fell by more than a third between 1960, when 58 percent chose that alternative, and 1993, when only 37 percent did. The same trend is apparent in all educational groups; indeed, because social trust is also correlated with education and because educational levels have risen sharply, the overall decrease in social trust is even more apparent if we control for education.

Our discussion of trends in social connectedness and civic engagement has tacitly assumed that all the forms of social capital that we have discussed are themselves coherently correlated across individuals. This is in fact true. Members of associations are much more likely than nonmembers to participate in politics, to spend time with neighbors, to express social trust, and so on.

The close correlation between social trust and associational membership is true not only across time and across individuals, but also across countries. Evidence from the 1991 World Values Survey demonstrates the following:[10]

1) Across the 35 countries in this survey, social trust and civic engagement are strongly correlated; the greater the density of associational membership in a society, the more trusting its citizens. Trust and engagement are two facets of the same underlying factor—social capital.

2) America still ranks relatively high by cross-national standards on both these dimensions of social capital. Even in the 1990s, after several decades' erosion, Americans are more trusting and more engaged than people in most other countries of the world.

3) The trends of the past quarter-century, however, have apparently moved the United States significantly lower in the international rankings of social capital. The recent deterioration in American social capital has been sufficiently great that (if no other country changed its position in the meantime) another quarter-century of change at the same rate would bring the United States, roughly speaking, to the midpoint among all these countries, roughly equivalent to South Korea, Belgium, or Estonia today. Two generations' decline at the same rate would leave the United States at the level of today's Chile, Portugal, and Slovenia.

★ WHY IS U.S. SOCIAL CAPITAL ERODING?

As we have seen, something has happened in America in the last two or three decades to diminish civic engagement and social connectedness. What could that "something" be? Here are several possible explanations, along with some initial evidence on each.

The movement of women into the labor force.
Over these same two or three decades, many millions of American women have moved out of the home into paid employment. This is the primary, though not the sole, reason why the weekly working hours of the average American have increased significantly during these years. It seems highly plausible that this social revolution should have reduced the time and energy available for building social capital. For certain organizations, such as the PTA, the League of Women Voters, the Federation of Women's Clubs, and the Red Cross, this is almost certainly an important part of the story. The sharpest decline in women's civic participation seems to have come in the 1970s; membership in such "women's" organizations as these has been virtually halved since the late 1960s. By contrast, most of the decline in participation in men's organizations occurred about ten years later; the total decline to date has been approximately 25 percent for the typical organization. On the other hand, the survey data imply that the aggregate declines for men are virtually as great as those for women. It is logically possible, of course, that the male declines might represent the knock-on effect of women's liberation, as dishwashing crowded out the lodge, but time-budget studies suggest that most husbands of working wives have assumed only a minor part of the housework. In short, something besides the women's revolution seems to lie behind the erosion of social capital.

Mobility: The "re-potting" hypothesis.
Numerous studies of organizational involvement have shown that residential stability and such related phenomena as homeownership are clearly associated with greater civic engagement. Mobility, like frequent re-potting of plants, tends to disrupt root systems, and it takes time for an uprooted individual to put down new roots. It seems plausible that the automobile, suburbanization, and the movement to the Sun Belt have reduced the social rootedness of the average American, but one fundamental difficulty with this hypothesis is apparent: the best evidence shows that residential stability and homeownership in America have risen modestly since 1965, and are surely higher now

than during the 1950s, when civic engagement and social connectedness by our measures was definitely higher.

Other demographic transformations. A range of additional changes have transformed the American family since the 1960s—fewer marriages, more divorces, fewer children, lower real wages, and so on. Each of these changes might account for some of the slackening of civic engagement, since married, middle-class parents are generally more socially involved than other people. Moreover, the changes in scale that have swept over the American economy in these years—illustrated by the replacement of the corner grocery by the supermarket and now perhaps of the supermarket by electronic shopping at home, or the replacement of community-based enterprises by outposts of distant multinational firms—may perhaps have undermined the material and even physical basis for civic engagement.

The technological transformation of leisure. There is reason to believe that deep-seated technological trends are radically "privatizing" or "individualizing" our use of leisure time and thus disrupting many opportunities for social-capital formation. The most obvious and probably the most powerful instrument of this revolution is television. Time-budget studies in the 1960s showed that the growth in time spent watching television dwarfed all other changes in the way Americans passed their days and nights. Television has made our communities (or, rather, what we experience as our communities) wider and shallower. In the language of economics, electronic technology enables individual tastes to be satisfied more fully, but at the cost of the positive social externalities associated with more primitive forms of entertainment. The same logic applies to the replacement of vaudeville by the movies and now of movies by the VCR. The new "virtual reality" helmets that we will soon don to be entertained in total isolation are merely the latest extension of this trend. Is technology thus driving a wedge between our individual interests and our collective interests? It is a question that seems worth exploring more systematically.

★ WHAT IS TO BE DONE?

The last refuge of a social-scientific scoundrel is to call for more research. Nevertheless, I cannot forbear from suggesting some further lines of inquiry.

• We must sort out the dimensions of social capital, which clearly is not a unidimensional concept, despite language (even in this essay) that implies the contrary. What types of organizations and networks most effectively embody—or generate—social capital, in the sense of mutual reciprocity, the resolution of dilemmas of collective action, and the broadening of social identities? In this essay I have emphasized the density of associational life. In earlier work I stressed the structure of networks, arguing that "horizontal" ties represented more productive social capital than vertical ties.[11]

• Another set of important issues involves macrosociological crosscurrents that might intersect with the trends described here. What will be the impact, for example, of electronic networks on social capital? My hunch is that meeting in an electronic forum is not the equivalent of meeting in a bowling alley—or even in a saloon—but hard empirical research is needed. What about the development of social capital in the workplace? Is it growing in counterpoint to the decline of civic engagement, reflecting some social analogue of the first law of thermodynamics—social capital is neither created nor destroyed, merely redistributed? Or do the trends described in this essay represent a deadweight loss?

• A rounded assessment of changes in American social capital over the last quarter-century needs to count the costs as well as the benefits of community engagement. We must not romanticize small-town, middle-class civic life in the America of the 1950s. In addition to the deleterious trends emphasized in this essay, recent decades have witnessed a substantial decline in intolerance and probably also in overt discrimination, and those beneficent trends may be related in complex ways to the erosion of traditional social capital. Moreover, a balanced accounting of the social-capital books would need to reconcile the insights of this approach with the undoubted insights offered by Mancur Olson and others who stress that closely knit social, economic, and political organizations are prone to inefficient cartelization and to what political economists term "rent seeking" and ordinary men and women call corruption.[12]

• Finally, and perhaps most urgently, we need to explore creatively how public policy impinges on (or might impinge on) social-capital formation. In some well-known instances, public policy has destroyed highly effective social networks and norms. American slum-clearance policy of the 1950s and 1960s, for example, renovated physical capital, but at a very high cost to existing social capital. The consolidation of country post offices and small school districts has promised administrative and financial efficiencies, but full-cost accounting for the effects of these policies on social capital might produce a more negative verdict. On the other hand, such past initiatives as the county agricultural-agent system, community colleges, and tax deductions for charitable contributions illustrate that government can encourage social-capital formation. Even a recent proposal in San Luis Obispo, California, to require that all new houses have front porches illustrates the power of government to influence where and how networks are formed.

The concept of "civil society" has played a central role in the recent global debate about the preconditions for democracy and democratization. In the newer democracies this phrase has properly focused attention on the need to foster a vibrant civic life in soils traditionally inhospitable to self-government. In the established democracies, ironically, growing numbers of citizens are questioning the effectiveness of their public institutions at the very moment when liberal democracy has swept the battlefield, both ideologically and geopolitically. In America, at least, there is reason to suspect that this democratic disarray may be linked to a broad and continuing erosion of civic engagement that began a quarter-century ago. High on our scholarly agenda should be the question of whether a comparable erosion of social capital may be under way in other advanced democracies, perhaps in different institutional and behavioral guises. High on America's agenda should be the question of how to reverse these adverse trends in social connectedness, thus restoring civic engagement and civic trust.

NOTES

[1] Alexis de Tocqueville, *Democracy in America*, ed. J. P. Maier, trans. George Lawrence (Garden City, N.Y.: Anchor Books, 1969), 513–17.

[2] On social networks and economic growth in the developing world, see Milton J. Esman and Norman Uphoff, *Local Organizations: Intermediaries in Rural Development* (Ithaca: Cornell University Press, 1984), esp. 15–42 and 99–180; and Albert O. Hirschman, *Getting Ahead Collectively: Grassroots Experiences in Latin America* (Elmsford, N.Y.: Pergamon Press, 1984), esp. 42–77. On East Asia, see Gustav Papanek, "The New Asian Capitalism: An Economic Portrait," in Peter L. Berger and Hsin-Huang Michael Hsiao, eds., *In Search of an East Asian Development Model* (New Brunswick, N.J.: Transaction, 1987), 27–80; Peter B. Evans, "The State as Problem and Solution: Predation, Embedded Autonomy and Structural Change," in Stephan Haggard and Robert R. Kaufman, eds., *The Politics of Economic Adjustment* (Princeton: Princeton University Press, 1992), 139–81; and Gary G. Hamilton, William Zeile, and Wan-Jin Kim, "Network Structure of East Asian Economies," in Stewart R. Clegg and S. Gordon Redding, eds., *Capitalism in Contrasting Cultures* (Hawthorne, N.Y.: De Gruyter, 1990), 105–29. See also Gary G. Hamilton and Nicole Woolsey Biggart, "Market, Culture, and Authority: A Comparative Analysis of Management and Organization in the Far East," *American Journal of Sociology* (Supplement) 94 (1988): S52–S94; and Susan Greenhalgh, "Families and Networks in Taiwan's Economic Development," in Edwin Winckler and Susan Greenhalgh, eds., *Contending Approaches to the Political Economy of Taiwan* (Armonk, N.Y.: M.E. Sharpe, 1987), 224–45.

[3] Robert D. Putnam, *Making Democracy Work: Civic Traditions in Modern Italy* (Princeton: Princeton University Press, 1993).

[4] James S. Coleman deserves primary credit for developing the "social capital" theoretical framework. See his "Social Capital in the Creation of Human Capital," *American Journal of Sociology* (Supplement) 94 (1988): S95–S120, as well as his *The Foundations of Social Theory* (Cambridge: Harvard University Press, 1990), 300–21. See also Mark Granovetter, "Economic Action and Social Structure: The Problem of Embeddedness," *American Journal of Sociology* 91 (1985): 481–510; Glenn C. Loury, "Why Should We Care About Group Inequality?" *Social Philosophy and Policy* 5 (1987): 249–71; and Robert D. Putnam, "The Prosperous Community: Social Capital and Public Life," *American Prospect* 13 (1993): 35–42. To my knowledge, the first scholar to use the term "social capital" in its current sense was Jane Jacobs, in *The Death and Life of Great American Cities* (New York: Random House, 1961), 138.

[5] Any simplistically political interpretation of the collapse of American unionism would need to confront the fact that the steepest decline began more than six years before the Reagan administration's attack on PATCO. Data from the General Social Survey show a roughly 40-percent decline in reported union membership between 1975 and 1991.

[6] Data for the LWV are available over a longer time span and show an interesting pattern: a sharp slump during the Depression, a strong and sustained rise after World War II that more than tripled membership between 1945 and 1969, and then the post-1969 decline, which has already erased virtually all the postwar gains and continues still. This same historical pattern applies to those men's fraternal organizations for which comparable data are available—steady increases for the first seven decades of the century, interrupted only by the Great Depression, followed by a collapse in the 1970s and 1980s that has already wiped out most of the postwar expansion and continues apace.

[7] Cf. Lester M. Salamon, "The Rise of the Nonprofit Sector," *Foreign Affairs* 73 (July–August 1994): 109–22. See also Salamon, "Partners in Public Service: The Scope and Theory of Government-Nonprofit Relations," in Walter W. Powell, ed., *The Nonprofit Sector: A Research Handbook* (New Haven: Yale University Press, 1987), 99–117. Salamon's empirical evidence does not sustain his broad claims about a global "associational revolution" comparable in significance to the rise of the nation-state several centuries ago.

[8] Robert Wuthnow, *Sharing the Journey: Support Groups and America's New Quest for Community* (New York: The Free Press, 1994), 45.

[9] Ibid., 3–6.

[10] I am grateful to Ronald Inglehart, who directs this unique cross-national project, for sharing these highly useful data with me. See his "The Impact of Culture on Economic Development: Theory, Hypotheses, and Some Empirical Tests" (unpublished manuscript, University of Michigan, 1994).

[11] See my *Making Democracy Work*, esp. ch. 6.

[12] See Mancur Olson, *The Rise and Decline of Nations: Economic Growth, Stagflation, and Social Rigidities* (New Haven: Yale University Press, 1982), 2.

George Gallup and the Rhetoric of Scientific Democracy

J. Michael Hogan

*"Everybody believes in public opinion polls—everyone from the man
on the street all the way up to President Thomas E. Dewey."*

—Goodman Ace (as cited in Field, 1990, p. 37)

Polling has come a long way since 1936. In that fateful year, George Horace Gallup, the father of "scientific" polling, predicted the spectacular failure of the *Literary Digest's* presidential "straw poll." Over the next half century, Gallup's name became virtually synonymous with polling, and today his legacy is an industry of more than 2000 organizations with annual revenues in excess of $4 billion (Walden, 1990, p. xiii). Promoting polling as "the pulse of democracy," George Gallup sold America on a new scientific "instrument" that he promised might "bridge the gap between the people and those who are responsible for making decisions in their name" (Gallup & Rae, 1940, pp. 14–15).

Throughout his life, Gallup preached about polling with "evangelical devotion" (Wheeler, 1976, p. 87). In public speeches, several books, and more than a hundred articles in trade publications, academic journals, and popular magazines,[1] Gallup served as polling's unofficial historian as he mythologized the critical incidents in polling's story of "progress." In addition, he campaigned hard to establish polling's claim to science by statistically documenting its record of accuracy and developing lay explanations of its technical procedures. Above all, Gallup promised that polling could make "democracy work more effectively" (Gallup & Rae, 1940, p. 11). Celebrating the wisdom of the "common man," Gallup dreamed of a final stage in the evolution of the American democratic experiment—an age of scientific democracy, in which "the will of the people" would provide continuous direction to policy makers "on all the major issues of the day["] (Gallup & Rae, 1940, p. 125). For Gallup, polling represented more than an imperfect social science or a profit-making venture. To criticize polling was to criticize "progress," "science," and democracy itself.

Gallup died in 1984, but his American Institute for Public Opinion Research remains an industry leader. Today, the Gallup Poll is syndicated to hundreds of newspapers and conducts "exclusive" polls for CNN, *USA Today, Newsweek,* and other news media. Meanwhile, Gallup's rhetoric of scientific democracy continues to sustain polling's cultural legitimacy by deflecting attention from its most perplexing sources of error and stifling debate over its deleterious effects on the democratic process. With leaders refusing to lead out of deference to the polls, and with references to the polls often supplanting deliberation over the merits of policies, the polls increasingly shape both the agenda and the outcomes of public debate. George Gallup alone did not create our cultural obsession with polls, nor would he have approved of how politicians and journalists often invoke the polls as a substitute for policy analysis. Yet echoes of Gallup still can be heard in the contemporary defense of polling, and he pioneered many of the polling practices that, ironically, now threaten his own dream of a more inclusive and efficient democracy.

Properly conducted and interpreted, polls might well serve democracy as Gallup envisioned by providing at least one (albeit imperfect) measure of public opinion. In recent years, however, polls have become, if anything, even less reliable, and the mission of polling has been changed radically by journalistic imperatives. Instead of guiding policy makers, polls have become "news events" in themselves that not only substitute for substantive information, but also fuel so-called "horse race" journalism. In one sense, Gallup's youthful dream has become a reality. Polls are ubiquitous in American public life. Unfortunately, they rarely serve democracy as Gallup envisioned, and what Michael Wheeler (1967) said about the polls nearly 30 years ago is even truer today: "for every good poll there are dozens, perhaps hundreds, of bad ones" (p. 301).

★ THE HISTORICAL FOLKLORE

As a young entrepreneur in 1935, George Horace Gallup made a remarkable sales pitch to the newspapers of America: a money-back guarantee that he could predict the outcome of the 1936 presidential election more accurately than the famed *Literary Digest* poll. As David Moore (1992) has written, this was "no small gamble." If he failed, Gallup faced financial ruin, and the *Literary Digest*'s record had been impressive. In 1928, it accurately predicted Herbert Hoover's landslide, and four years later it came within a percentage point in predicting FDR's victory over Hoover. Despite confidence in his new "scientific" methods, Gallup remained anxious. He had faith in his figures, but as he confided to friends, there was "always a reasonable doubt" (pp. 31–33).

The story had a happy ending, of course. Gallup proved right, the *Digest* proved wrong, and polling thereafter emulated Gallup's use of "scientific" methods. In large measure, however, the story of 1936 was the product of Gallup's own public relations and ignores one important fact: Gallup also missed the mark badly in 1936. Gallup correctly predicted the winner, but he too significantly underestimated FDR's vote— by nearly seven percentage points.[2]

Telling the story in his coauthored 1940 book, *The Pulse of Democracy*, Gallup actually defended the *Digest* against critics who suspected a Republican conspiracy. The *Digest* poll had not been "rigged" to favor the Republicans, Gallup insisted; the "sincerity and honesty" of the poll's sponsors were "beyond question." So why, then, did the *Digest* "go wrong?" The answer lay "not in a lack of honesty . . . , but rather in the fact that in this business of polling public opinion, sincerity and honesty . . . are not in themselves guarantees against errors and inaccuracies." The "disaster" of the *Literary Digest* poll resulted from its "sampling methods," not from "the morals of its organizers," according to Gallup. Thus emerged the case for his new, more "scientific" methods (Gallup & Rae, 1940, p. 44).

Gallup's "Lessons of 1936" were cleverly misleading. In discussing his own performance (Gallup & Rae, 1940, pp. 44–55), he began by emphasizing more accurate figures that he had released earlier in the 1936 campaign. When he finally, admitted that his final prediction missed the mark by seven percent, he claimed to have "erred on the side of caution" and, of course, he still did better than the Digest poll. Gallup also discussed his own poll in the context of other "scientific" polls that did better: the Crossley poll (less than 6 percent error) and the *Fortune* poll (which came "amazingly close" in predicting the outcome within a percentage point). In mentioning these other "new polls," whose methods also were "based on scientific principles," Gallup took at least some of the credit for those who did better:

> The surprising accuracy of the results obtained by these new polls in 1936, bearing in mind that it was the first real test of scientific sampling in a national election, bears witness to the cogency of the criticisms of the Digest poll, and to the underlying soundness of the alternative methods which were put to the test. (Gallup & Rae, 1940, p. 49)

Gallup thus designated 1936 as the starting point of the modern era in polling and distinguished it from a dark age of straw polling dating back to 1824. Even though some of the new polls "weren't quite as accurate as their sponsors hoped," all proved to be far more accurate than the *Literary Digest* poll, despite their reliance on "only a small fraction of the gigantic sendout employed by *The Digest*" (Gallup, 1940b, p. 23). Gallup marveled at how "in our own day" polling had "developed from a glorified kind of fortune telling to a practical way of learning what the nation thinks." Describing this "first national-election test" as "by no means a final statement of the accuracy of the results which could be obtained by the sampling method," Gallup promised still better things to come (Gallup & Rae, 1940, pp. 5, 55).

Gallup appeared to deliver on that promise over the next decade as he wrote a new chapter in polling's story of "progress" with each new election. Correctly predicting FDR's victories in both 1940 and 1944, Gallup's became America's best-known and most trusted pollster, a man celebrated in a *Time* magazine cover story as the "Babe Ruth of the polling profession," a "big, friendly, teddy bear of a man with a passion for facts and figures" (The black and white beans, 1948, p. 21). A few critics questioned his methods, and some even alleged political biases (see, e.g., Ginzburg, 1944, pp. 737–739), but Gallup (1944) simply dismissed such allegations as "unintelligent, even fantastic." Confident that such an inquiry would put an end to the "misrepresentations and downright falsehoods" and help Americans "become familiar with the technique of polls and their contribution to this government" (p. 795), he even endorsed calls for a congressional investigation of polling.

Then came the "scientific pollsters'" own great disaster, the prediction that Thomas Dewey would defeat Harry Truman by anywhere from five to fifteen percentage points in 1948. When Truman actually won by more than four percentage points, the entire industry came under attack, with Gallup personally taking much of the heat. Initially, an obviously distraught Gallup suggested that bribes and rigged ballot boxes must have altered the outcome and argued, in effect, that the election, not the polls, had turned out wrong (Wheeler, 1967). Soon, however, Gallup joined with a number of social scientists, journalists, and politicians in investigating what went wrong and, in the process, rhetorically transformed the 1948 into a "blessing in disguise."

The Social Science Research Council (SSRC) sponsored the first of two major investigations (Mosteller et al., 1949). Concerned that the pollsters' miscall might have "extensive and unjustified repercussions," not only on polling but "social science research generally," the SSRC appointed a committee to study "the technical procedures and methods of interpretation" that had led the pollsters astray (p. vii). Completing its investigation in just five weeks, the SSRC committee considered possible errors at every step in the polling process, including sample and questionnaire design, interviewing, problems in dealing with "likely" and "undecided" voters, data processing, and the interpretation and presentation of results. In its final report, however, the committee identified two major "causes of error" in 1948: (a) errors of sampling and interviewing and (b) errors involving the pollsters' "failure to assess the future behavior of undecided votes and to detect shifts near the end of the campaign" (pp. 299–300).

The first problem, the SSRC argued, stemmed from the "quota method" then used by all the major pollsters in their national forecasts. In that method, quotas were established for respondents with certain attributes, but interviewers selected specific individuals to be questioned. Aside from the problem of determining relevant "attributes," as the SSRC observed, this method caused two major difficulties: "the composition of the population may not be accurately known for the determination of quotas, and the interviewers may operate . . . as 'biased' selecting devices" (p. 84). The SSRC concluded that "probability" sampling, which the pollsters had considered too costly, would have eliminated at least the problem of interviewer bias in selecting respondents.

The second source of error, according to the SSRC, involved a "central problem" in all social science research: how to predict human behavior. With no good way to assess the future behavior of undecided voters or to detect late trends, the pollsters simply ignored "undecided" voters or allocated them arbitrarily to candidates, which created an error that was significant, but "not precisely measurable." The committee predicted that "the gap between an expression of intent and actual behavior" would continue to be a major source of error in election forecasts and that this had to be "recognized as a baffling and unsolved problem imposing serious limitations on opinion poll predictions" (p. 302).

While cooperating fully with the SSRC committee, Gallup challenged its basic conclusions at a second postmortem held a few weeks later at his alma mater, the University of Iowa (Meier & Saunders, 1949). Suggesting that the SSRC committee "felt that it had to point an accusing finger at the pollsters," Gallup declared: "Hindsight is always twenty-twenty!" Having since read the committee's report, Gallup still had not seen "any evidence to support the contention that our sampling and interviewing methods accounted for any large part of our error." Gallup had a very different view of what had gone wrong: the pollsters, in effect, had been victimized by their own remarkable record, by the public's belief that polling had "reached a stage of absolute perfection" (pp. 178, 203–204).

Gallup himself preferred to view 1948 "against the background of poll performance recorded in the years since 1935," since the "average error in these forecasts—including those made in the presidential election of 1948" —remained "approximately four percentage points." That, he argued at the Iowa Conference, fell within the expected range of error for polling research "at this stage of its development." Even counting 1948, Gallup insisted that the pollsters had established a remarkable record: "I, for one, marvel that elections in this country can be forecast with an average error of only four percentage points" (pp. 177–178, 182).

To the extent that they erred in 1948, Gallup insisted that pollsters had made "mistakes in judgment and not in basic procedures." At the Iowa conference, he identified two such "mistakes": the failure to conduct "a last-minute poll" and the assumption that "undecided" voters "could be ignored and eliminated from the sample." As it turned out, "many voters" apparently had been "lured back into the Democratic fold" in the final days of the campaign, and "many" of the "undecided" voters had, in fact, voted for Truman (pp. 177, 180–181).

Gallup thus turned 1948 into a useful learning experience and, in effect, an argument for more extensive polling. Promising "improvements in every single department" of his operation, Gallup concluded his remarks at the Iowa Conference by again predicting better things to come: "You may think that I am merely a chronic optimist, but I can't help feeling that this bitter experience of November, 1948, has made a lot of people examine the whole business of polling more critically, and I think that is a real gain" (pp. 204–205).

In later years, Gallup routinely referred to 1948 as a "blessing in disguise" (see, e.g., Gallup, 1955–56, p. 237; Gallup, 1972, p. 200). Because it inspired an "agonizing reappraisal," 1948 offered valuable lessons about how to deal with undecided voters, how to screen out nonvoters, how to take account of "intensity and prestige factors," and how to poll "within a couple of days of the election" (Gallup, 1972, pp. 200–01). Gallup never admitted that his sampling errors had failed in 1948,

but over the next several elections he quietly expanded his use of "pin-point" or "precinct" probability sampling. By the 1956 election, he had abandoned "quota" sampling altogether, and had developed new "machinery" for measuring "trends to the very end of a campaign" (see Gallup, 1957–58, pp. 25–26). By the early 1960s, Gallup could boast that he had bested even his most optimistic predictions of the pre-1948 era by achieving an "average error" of only about "one to one-and-a-half percentage points." "There are still problems," Gallup told an interviewer in 1962, "but . . . I doubt if we can improve our accuracy very much . . . obviously we can't do much better than that" (as cited in McDonald, 1962, p. 22).

Today, the *Gallup Poll Monthly* features a "Gallup Poll Accuracy Record" that begins with 1936 and calculates the "average error" of the Gallup polls separately for the pre- and post-1948 periods: 3.6 percentage points between 1936 and 1950, compared with only 1.6 percent between 1952 and 1992 (see *Gallup Poll Monthly*, 1992). The elections of 1936 and 1948 thus serve as defining moments in the history of polling by providing benchmarks for statistical demonstrations of improved accuracy and anecdotal evidence of key developments in polling's story of "progress."

Unfortunately, polling's historical folklore has diverted attention from more fundamental questions about polling's claim to "science." While pollsters undeniably have made technical advances in sampling and statistical procedures they have barely scratched the surface of more basic methodological problems—problems related to what the pollsters euphemistically call "nonsampling error." For more than forty years, George Gallup downplayed these more mysterious and nonquantifiable sources of error by boasting of the industry's record in predicting national elections. In the final analysis, however, Gallup not only misled the public but encouraged his own industry to ignore its most perplexing methodological problems.

★ A RHETORIC OF SCIENCE

While pollsters today generally disclaim the predictive value of polls (see Crespi, 1988), Gallup portrayed election forecasts as important scientific "tests." In *The Pulse of Democracy* (1940), he and Rae wrote: "Pre-election tests are important because they enable surveyors to put this new method of measuring public opinion through its most exacting test" (p. 81). Several years before the 1948 miscall, Gallup told the House Campaign Expenditures Committee (U.S. House, 1945) that although the polls had not achieved "absolute accuracy," their record did "represent a degree of accuracy found in few fields outside the exact or physical sciences" (p. 1254). Even after the 1948 debacle, Gallup called election predictions the "acid test for polling techniques" and boasted of "a record of which we can all be proud." In "no other field," he insisted at the Iowa Conference, "has human behavior been predicted with such a high degree of accuracy" (Meier & Saunders, 1949, pp. 177, 286).

Gallup conceded that election predictions have "no great social value" (Meier & Saunders, 1949, p. 286). They were, Gallup (1972) wrote, "the least socially useful function that the polls perform" (p. 123). So why predict elections? Why risk standing "naked before the whole world" the day after an election? For Gallup, the answer lay not so much in the realm of science as public relations: "It was the demonstrated accuracy of election polls, based upon scientific sampling procedures, that convinced the public and office holders that public opinion on social, political, and economic issues of the day could be gauged" (p. 124).

For half a century, Gallup campaigned tirelessly to establish that polling had indeed passed the "test," a conclusion that in turn rested on two distinct claims: polling's record in predicting elections had, in fact, been good, and this record established the reliability of all other polls. Neither of these claims holds up under scrutiny. Both rested on a misleading— indeed, a deceptive and disingenuous—rhetoric of science.

Gallup invariably employed the same statistical measure to document the accuracy of his election forecasts: the "average deviation" of those forecasts from actual election results, in "percentage points," on an "all party-basis." Yet not only did this measure ignore the impact of the electoral college,[3] it also put the best face on a record that, by most other statistical

measures, was far from impressive. For example, Gallup boasted at the Iowa Conference of the "surprising" fact that, on an "all-party basis," even his 1948 miscall fell within the expected "margin of error" of four percentage points (Meier & Saunders, 1949, p. 178). Yet calculating the "average deviation" on an "all-party-basis" in 1948 meant summing the error in his predictions for each of the two major *and* the two minor-party candidates, then dividing by four. This procedure produced a respectable "average deviation" of only 2.9 "percentage points." Gallup's error in predicting the vote for just the two major candidates was far less impressive: 4.7 percentage points.[4]

Looking at 1948 through yet another statistical lens, an even more dismal performance is revealed. In terms of raw percentages, Gallup overestimated Dewey's vote by about 10 percent and underestimated Truman's vote by approximately the same amount. Similarly, in predicting that third-party candidate Henry Wallace would get 4 percent of the vote, Gallup missed Wallace's actual vote of 2.4 percent by only 1.6 "percentage points." Yet in percentage terms, Gallup missed the mark badly; he overestimated Wallace's vote by 40 percent (Rogers, 1949, pp. 117–118, 124).

Even by Gallup's preferred statistical measure, the pollsters' overall record in predicting presidential elections has been, to say the least, spotty. Between 1952 and 1972, as Wheeler (1976) pointed out, the pollsters predicted only the obvious "landslides," and one could have done just as well simply by picking incumbents to win every election (pp. 39–40). Since Wheeler's study, the pollsters have done even worse. In 1980, they completely missed the Reagan landslide, with most major polls calling the election a toss-up and some even predicting that Carter would win (Shelley & Hwang, 1991, p. 61). In 1984, the pollsters disagreed widely over the magnitude of Reagan's reelection, with figures ranging from Roper's underestimate of 55%-45% to Gordon Black's overestimate of 60%-35% (5% undecided) for *USA Today* (Crespi, 1988, p. 3). Despite further attempts to tighten their procedures in 1988, only one of the five best-known polls predicted the correct vote for both Bush and Dukakis within three percentage points (Shelley & Hwang, 1991, pp. 67–68). And in 1992, the pollsters had their worst year since 1936, as the Gallup Poll overestimated Clinton's vote by 5.8 percentage points. Despite this substantial error, the *Gallup Poll Monthly's* "Accuracy Record" continues to boast of an "average deviation for 28 national elections" of 2.2 "percentage points." Yet, curiously, the "Record" no longer appears in every issue, and it now bears the indignity of an asterisk referring readers to an *apologia* for the 1992 miscall.[5]

The pollsters' election forecasts have been off so frequently in recent years that even some pollsters now question their own industry's claim to "science." Reacting to the polls' poor performance in 1984, for example, Burns Roper lamented: "I'm very concerned. This raises real questions of whether this business is anywhere near a science." Pollster Irwin Harrison went even further: "There's no science in the questions. There's no science in the interviews. And there's more art than science in the results" (as cited in Crespi, 1988, p. 2).

All this would be reason enough to question whether election forecasting has established the reliability of polling. Yet there is another, more important reason for questioning Gallup's "test": presidential election polls bear very little resemblance to the vast majority of polls. Recognizing that "their reputations, and as a consequence their profits, depend on how close they can come to the actual outcome," the pollsters historically have employed much larger samples in their final election polls,[6] and they have tightened other procedures as well to avoid being "proven wrong" by the voters (Wheeler, 1976, pp. 38–39). As a result, final election forecasts are not so much a "test" of their general procedures, but instead unique, special events. Indeed, election polls are not only methodologically different from all other polls; they are, as Wheeler (1976) has pointed out, "the best things that the pollsters do" (p. 43).

Far more suspect are the hundreds, even thousands of *issue* polls conducted each year—the polls Gallup considered most socially useful. Throughout his career, Gallup (1940b) insisted that, technically, issue polls were "relatively simple" compared to election forecasts, since the latter could "go awry" because of any number of factors affecting turnout (p. 25).

Yet the notion that one need not discriminate among respondents in issue polls implies that variations in knowledge and salience have no substantive significance. It suggests no need to distinguish uninformed and perhaps unstable opinions from carefully considered positions, nor the passionately committed from the largely indifferent.

More importantly, issue polls have far more potential than election polls for what the pollsters call "nonsampling error." These sources of error, which range from interviewing problems to flawed interpretive theories, have received far less attention than sampling and statistical techniques in the literature of polling. Yet not only are the effects of such errors often "five or ten times greater" than those of sampling error, as Brady and Orren (1992) have pointed out, but they also are "harder to understand and measure" (p. 68).

A comprehensive review of the various sources of "nonsampling error" is beyond the scope of this essay. Suffice it to say that a growing body of research has documented enormous "response effects" from such "nonsampling" factors as the race, gender, or class of interviewers, the context and timing of surveys, and variations in the order and phrasing of both questions and response options. In addition, researchers recently have called attention to the need for pollsters to develop explicit and more sophisticated interpretive theories. Yet none of these concerns has undermined discernibly the apparent cultural legitimacy of public opinion polling. As may be illustrated by just one example, the problem of question-wording, George Gallup helped shroud such problems in a fog of scientific mystification that only now is beginning to lift.

The "Science" of Question-Wording

Concerned with complex subjective phenomena —beliefs, attitudes, and opinions—rather than a simple choice among candidates, issue polls demand far more attention to question-wording than election polls. Not only must the questions in such polls tap appropriate, relevant opinions and attitudes, they also must mean the same thing to different respondents and inject no bias into the measurement process. In contemporary polling, batteries of questions are often employed to assess not only opinions, but also the awareness and salience of issues, the level and character of existing knowledge, the strength of opinions, and even how opinions might be changed by exposure to information or arguments about an issue. Unfortunately, this only introduces more potential for error into the polling process. Not only does error result from the wording of individual questions, but also from the order in which questions are asked and other factors that affect the context within which respondents interpret particular questions.

Throughout his career, Gallup (1972) paid lip service to problems of question wording by occasionally conceding that question-wording posed "difficult" and "important" problems for polling (p. 77). At the same time, however, he insisted from the outset that variations in question-wording made little difference and that "science" already had solved virtually all problems of question-wording. Devoting barely a dozen pages to question-wording in the 290-page *Pulse of Democracy* (Gallup & Rae, 1940), Gallup declared that his Institute for Public Opinion Research was hard at work perfecting a "neutral vocabulary a public-opinion glossary—within the comprehension of the mass of people" (p. 106). More importantly, he insisted from very early in his career that scientific experiments had shown that variations in question-wording were of "relatively minor importance." Touting his own "split-ballot" technique for testing question wording effects, Gallup noted that his firm often employed two different versions of a question to assess what, "if any," difference question-wording might make. In more than 200 such experiments, Gallup (1940b) reported that "greater-than-expected" differences had been discovered in "only a small fraction" of cases. Where there was "no material alteration in the thought expressed," Gallup concluded, "there will be no material difference in the result, no matter what wording is used" (p. 26).

Despite his protestations, Gallup's own "split-ballot" data often revealed question-wording effects that seemed quite material indeed. In one of his own experiments in 1939, for example, half of the sample was asked, "Do you think the United States will go into the war before it is over?" The other half was asked, "Do you think the United States will succeed in staying out of the war?" Of those asked the first question, 41 percent said "yes" and 33 percent said "no." Of those asked the second, 44 percent said "yes" and 30 percent said "no." In short, a plurality of respondents answered "yes" to both questions. This represented an eleven-point difference in the percentage of people who felt that the U.S. *would* go to war. In all likelihood, the explanation lies in what modern researchers call "response acquiescence," or the inexplicable tendency of people to say "yes" when asked about unfamiliar issues. Gallup, however, ingeniously attributed the finding to the instability of opinion on the issue (Moore, 1992, pp. 325–326).

Other researchers employing Gallup's split-ballot technique likewise discovered significant but mysterious effects from seemingly nonsubstantive variations in question-wording. For example, Rugg (1941) analyzed split-ballot data gathered by Elmo Roper. In a survey on attitudes toward free speech, Roper had asked half his sample whether "the United States should *forbid* speeches against democracy" and the other half whether "the United States should *allow*" such speeches. The difference proved startling: 46 percent opposed "forbidding" such speeches, but only 25 percent favored "allowing" them.

In the late 1940s, Gallup (1947) announced a major breakthrough in the "science" of question-wording—a new "system of question-design" that he insisted answered all of the most "frequently voiced criticisms of public opinion measurement." Impressively jargonized as the "quintamensional approach," this new "system" allegedly allowed the pollster to "exclude from poll results the answers of any and all persons who are uninformed on any given issue" and to probe in greater depth opinions on "almost any type of issue and at all stages of opinion formation." Employing five categories of questions, including "filter" questions to assess knowledge and follow-up questions to probe the motivations and reasoning behind opinions, the "quintamensional approach," as Gallup described it, allowed a number of different dimensions of public opinion to be "intercorrelated, with a consequent wealth of data by which public opinion on any issue of the day can be described" (pp. 385–393).

Throughout his career, Gallup (1972) touted the "quintamensional approach" as among the most "important developments" in the history of polling, a development that made possible the assessment of public opinion even on the most technical or complex of issues (pp. 90–91). In reality, however, it only created new problems in question-wording. The use of "filter questions," for example, created unique and artificial interpretive contexts for questions that came later in the interview process. The whole approach also encouraged the most empirically and philosophically indefensible practice in modern polling: the practice of "informing" respondents about an issue before asking their opinion. When Gallup (1947) first unveiled the "system," he envisioned this very practice as among its most exciting possibilities, as he suggested that pollsters might use "simple and neutral language" to "explain" issues to those identified by the "filter questions" as "uninformed." This would allow pollsters to compare informed and uninformed opinion and, more generally, "to obtain the views of the maximum number of voters" (p. 389). Only a handful of critics have questioned the possibility of providing genuinely "neutral information" (see, e.g., Robinson and Meadow, 1982, pp. 118–120). So too have researchers only recently begun to ask whether pollsters ought to be in the business of predicting what the public *might* think if exposed to selected "information" (see, e.g., Hogan & Smith, 1991, p. 547).

At best, the "quintamensional approach" was a diversion and, at worst, a scientific hoax. A classic case of scientific mystification, it did nothing to solve the real problems in question-wording. It provided virtually no guidance for *how* to word questions; it specified only the *types* of questions to be asked and their order. It did nothing to answer the most fundamental question about the wording of questions: how does one account for the often enormous impact of seemingly nonsubstantive variations in wording?

Meanwhile, additional studies revealed significant question-wording effects, not only from variations in wording, but also from the

number, character, and even order of response options. In 1951, Stanley Payne summarized a number of these studies in *The Art of Asking Questions,* a book whose very title challenged Gallup's efforts to scientize question-wording. Payne documented a wide variety of question-wording effects that ranged from the false portraits created by obviously "loaded" questions (pp. 177–202) to a more subtle and mysterious "recency" effect—that is, a tendency among respondents to choose the last response option in some but not all questions (pp. 129–134). Payne concluded that "improvements in question wording" could "contribute far more to accuracy than further improvements in sampling methods"—"tens" rather than "tenths" of percents (p. 4).

Over the next twenty years, however, research on question-wording all but disappeared from the polling literature—as if Payne's book, with its "concise list of 100 considerations" in asking questions, "represented the final, and comprehensive, word on the subject" (Moore, 1992, p. 328). Gallup played a major role in this neglect of question-wording by continuing to insist well into the 1970s that "thorough pre-testing" assured the reliability of all questions and that, in any case, "split-ballot" experiments had proven that "even a wide variation in question wordings" did not produce "substantially different results if the basic meaning or substance of the question remained the same" (Gallup, 1972, pp. 78, 83).

Question-wording did not become a serious and sustained focus of research until a new "intellectual movement" emerged among academic survey researchers in the 1980s—a movement that broke the conspiracy of silence about question-wording and finally made research on "response effects" a "mainstream pursuit" (Moore, 1992, p. 343). This "movement," led by University of Michigan researcher Howard Schuman and others, began with efforts to summarize and replicate earlier research. The effort to theorize about question-wording was frustrated, however, as explanations for a number of question-wording effects proved elusive. Intrigued by Rugg's 1941 study of attitudes toward free speech, for example, Shuman and Presser (1981) repeated the experiment and found the same effect. Despite the passage of forty years, respondents still were far more likely to agree that the U.S. should "not allow" anti-democratic speeches than to agree that the U.S. should "forbid" such speeches. When they performed the same experiment on the question of "forbidding" or "not allowing" pornographic movies, however, the effect disappeared. In this case, there *was* no statistically significant difference between those who would "forbid" and those who would "not allow" such movies (pp. 276–283).

In addition to variations of ten, twenty, or more percentage points from seemingly nonsubstantive variations in question wording,[7] more recent studies also have shown significant response effects even when questions are not reworded at all, but merely reordered. In studying polls on abortion, for example, Schuman and Presser (1981) attempted to account for a 15 percentage point difference in two surveys employing exactly the same question: "Do you think it should be possible for a pregnant woman to obtain a legal abortion if she is married and does not want any more children?" The researchers noted that the survey revealing less support for abortion rights placed this question *after* another question asking whether it should be possible to get a legal abortion "if there is a strong chance of a serious defect in the baby." Testing the possibility that this question created a different interpretive context for the second question, the researchers conducted a split-ballot experiment in which half the sample was asked both questions, with the "defective fetus" question first, and the other half both questions, but with the order reversed. The difference was substantial, with the "defective fetus" question, when asked first, reducing support for abortion rights in the other question by about 13 percent—the difference between majority support and majority opposition to abortion rights (pp. 36–39).

Expanding into the area of response options, Schuman and Presser (1981) not only confirmed the "recency" effect observed by Payne (1951), but also demonstrated a very substantial effect from offering or not offering "don't know" as a response option. In Schuman and Presser's experiments, explicitly offering the "don't know" option increased the number of people in that category by an average of 22 percent (pp. 113–146). Studies by other researchers revealed that, in the absence of the "don't know" option, many respondents would express opinions even on entirely fictitious policies or programs (see, e.g., Hawkins & Coney, 1981, p. 372).

These and similar findings would seem to confirm what polling pioneer Hadley Cantril observed many years ago in the foreword to Payne's (1951) book: the variables involved in question-wording are "legion"; "they are also subtle and they defy quantification" (p. viii). More recently, Brady and Orren (1992) went further in concluding that "the more one explores the many sources of . . . error [in question wording], the more hopeless the prospect seems of ever preparing a poll questionnaire that is not fatally flawed" (p. 77). Reflecting on the limitations of both open and closed-ended questions, Schuman and Scott (1987) have suggested, quite simply, that no survey question, nor even any set of survey questions, should be taken as a meaningful indicator of either absolute levels or relative orderings of public preferences. Not surprisingly, this sort of conclusion has caused considerable consternation among pollsters and survey researchers. Responding to Schuman and Scott, Eleanor Singer (1988), then President of the American Association for Public Opinion Research, complained that such a view threatened to undermine the "intellectual defense" of survey research—that it was only "a short way" from Schuman and Scott's conclusion to the rationale for survey research and polling "being blown out of the water altogether" (p. 578).

The pollsters nevertheless continue to say little publicly about problems of question-wording. They now insist more strongly than ever that a poll's "margin of error" be reported, but this insistence only sustains the illusion of science and wrongly implies "that sampling is the primary, if not the only, source of possible error in a poll" (Cantril, 1991, p. 119). Even pollster Burns Roper has conceded that reporting the "margin of error" is little more than a diversionary tactic. As Roper (1980) observed, pollsters typically present their findings in the media as "within three percentage points" of what the public actually thinks on some issue, "when, in fact, a differently worded question might—and often does—produce a result that is 25 or 30 points from the reported result" (p. 16).

The Illusion of Science

Gallup's great pet peeve was the tendency of some writers to place quotation marks around the word "scientific" as applied to polling. "If our work is not scientific," Gallup (1957–58) complained to the sympathetic readers of *Public Opinion Quarterly*, "then no one in the field of social science, and few of those in the natural sciences, have a right to use the word." According to Gallup, polling fully qualified as "scientific" even under "the most rigid interpretation" of that word (p. 26). Those who thought otherwise simply did not understand "the nature of the new science of public opinion measurement" (Gallup, 1940b, p. 23). When Professor Lindsay Rogers of Columbia University published a scathing critique of the industry in 1949, for example, Gallup (1949b) characterized him as "the last of the arm-chair philosophers in this field" and declared: "One cannot blame the Professor for his lack of knowledge about polling techniques. He says, quite honestly, that he knows nothing about research procedures—a fact which is abundantly clear in his chapters dealing with these matters" (pp. 179–180). When Congress considered regulating polls in the wake of the 1948 debacle, Gallup (1948c) similarly dismissed critics who raised questions about question-wording as ignorant of "the new procedures that are followed and of the care that is taken to dissect opinion not only with one question but, in the case of complex issues, with a whole battery of questions" (p. 735).

Gallup's claim to "science" also buffered the pollsters against criticism of their interpretive practices. In responding to such criticism, Gallup did not merely claim to interpret his data objectively; indeed, he claimed that, as a scientist, he did not interpret at all! Characterizing polling firms as "fact-finding institutions" whose "responsibility ends with the objective reporting of survey results," Gallup (1960) attributed all complaints about the polls to partisanship or sour grapes. "Obviously," he

argued, the pollsters could not be "charged for the manner in which others may interpret or use poll findings," nor could they be "properly attacked for results which happen to be unpalatable to some people." Such attacks, Gallup concluded, were akin to blaming the mete[o]-rologist for bad weather: "Just as barometers do not make the weather, but merely record it, so do modern polls *reflect*, but not *make* public opinion" (pp. ix–x).

The pollsters continue to maintain a scientific facade by placing heavy emphasis on sampling, data collection, and data processing in their public discussions of methodology. In its monthly journal,[8] for example, the Gallup Poll historically has said little about question-wording and nothing about interpreting data. In the 1980s and 1990s, the *Gallup Poll Monthly* added a statement about question-wording and other sorts of "nonsampling error" to its regular "Note to Our Readers": "In addition to sampling error, readers should bear in mind that question wording and practical difficulties encountered in conducting surveys can introduce error or bias into the findings of opinion polls." At the same time, however, the *Monthly* added two new pages on weighting procedures, sampling tolerances, and the "random digit stratified probability design" used in telephone surveys. The *Monthly* even added tables for calculating the error for subsamples of various sizes (see *Gallup Poll Monthly*, 1992).

Gallup's rhetoric of science thus lives on, not only within the firm he founded but in the entire polling industry's claims of "scientific prowess." Pointing to continued improvements in sampling techniques and a variety of other "new technologies available through computers," pollsters began boasting in the 1970s that their "science" had "truly come of age" (Roll & Cantril, 1980, p. 13). In this respect, pollsters may differ little from economists, psychologists, sociologists, or anthropologists, whose claims to "science" have been demystified in recent years by students of the "rhetoric of inquiry" (see Nelson et al., 1987). Yet pollsters take such claims one step further by boasting that *their* science can "greatly strengthen the democratic process by providing 'the people' yet another way of making their views known, particularly between elections" (Roll & Cantril, 1980, p. 14).

★ PREACHING THE DEMOCRATIC FAITH

In classical democratic theory, public opinion did not equate with some numerical majority, however measured. Only ideas tested in public discourse were considered worthy of the label "public opinion" (MacKuen, 1984, pp. 236–238). Gallup (1948a) subscribed to a different view. He embraced James Bryce's definition of "public opinion" as the *"aggregate* of the views men hold regarding matters that affect or interest the community" (p. 84). Substituting undifferentiated mass opinion for "tested" ideas and thoughts expressed *privately* and *confidentially* for genuinely "public" opinions (see Herbst, 1993, pp. 64–65), Gallup, in effect, redefined public opinion as that which the polls measured.

This redefinition, in turn, raised anew the most fundamental philosophical and empirical questions of democratic theory. Should public opinion, however defined or measured, dictate public policy? Is the public, especially as more broadly defined by polls, sufficiently interested and informed to govern itself? Not surprisingly, George Gallup had answers to these questions. Less surprisingly still, those answers rested largely on the results of his own polling. Enthusiastically preaching the democratic faith, Gallup did not merely celebrate America's democratic heritage and affirm the people's *right* to govern themselves; he flattered the American people by invoking his own polls as proof of their seemingly mystical "collective wisdom."

Gallup did not dwell on the philosophical question of whether public opinion *should* dictate public policy. His answer seemed obvious from how he phrased the question itself: "shall the common people be free to express their basic needs and purposes, or shall they be dominated by a small ruling clique?" (Gallup & Rae, 1940, p. 6). In Gallup's polarized world, there were only "two points of view" on this question, and between them there could be "no compromise" (Gallup & Rae, 1940, p. 8). One either sided with those "who would

place more power in the hands of the people" or those "who are fearful of the people and would limit that power sharply" (Gallup, 1940b, p. 57). In no uncertain terms, Gallup stood with the democrats: "In a democratic society the views of the majority must be regarded as the ultimate tribunal for social and political issues" (Gallup & Rae, 1940, p. 15).

The empirical question remained: were the "common people" capable of governing themselves? Only with the advent of polling, according to Gallup (1940b), had it become possible to answer this question—to ascertain whether the people were "responsible or irresponsible; blindly radical, blindly conservative or somewhere in between; and whether their judgments may or may not make sense when viewed in perspective" (p. 57). Happily, according to Gallup (1948b), "the polls" had shown again and again "a quality of good common sense" in the American people that was "heartening to anyone who believes in the democratic process" (p. 177). In a refrain that echoed throughout his career, Gallup insisted that the people not only proved to be "right" about most issues but typically were "far ahead" of their leaders.

Early in his career, Gallup pointed to attitudes concerning preparedness and World War II as proof of the public's wisdom and foresight. Not only did the public understand far better than their leaders the threat posed by Hitler, but they were willing, even eager, to sacrifice personally to counter that threat. "Instead of balking at increased taxes," Gallup (1940a) wrote, "the American people have been ready to make direct, personal sacrifices in order to build up an army, a navy and an air force—and all this long before Congressmen and other political leaders were ready to recognize the fact" (p. 21). In a radio address, he even described the public as "cheerfully" accepting "the burden of heavy wartime taxation" (Gallup, 1942a, p. 688). Elsewhere, Gallup (1942c) detailed how the American people would be willing to sacrifice 10 percent of each paycheck for defense bonds, to accept "complete government control" over prices and wages, and even to allow the government to dictate "what kind of work" they should do and for "how many hours" (p. 16). Thus, the polls not only confirmed "the sound judgment and foresight of the common people" on "virtually all . . . important war-time issues," but also their willingness to sacrifice personally "to help the country win the war." Indeed, the people were so far "ahead of their political leaders," Gallup (1942b) concluded, "as to raise the real question as to whether the leaders are leading the people or whether the people are leading the leaders" (pp. 440–442).

In the 1950s, Gallup changed his tune somewhat as he lamented the public's failure to appreciate fully the threat posed by communism. "Today for the first time," he wrote in the *New York Times Magazine* in 1951, "I must confess that I am concerned lest lack of information lead the American people to decisions which they will regret" (p. 12). Significantly, however, Gallup blamed a "lack of information," not the people themselves, and he took it upon himself to "inform" both the public and Congress of the need for more vigorous American propaganda to counter the Soviet threat (see U.S. Senate, 1953, pp. 772–793). Gallup thus simultaneously worried about public apathy and sounded his usual refrain that the public was "far ahead" of its leaders. In a speech at Georgetown University, for example, Gallup (1952b) worried that the American people might "delude themselves" into complacency, yet again the public was "years ahead of Congress" its desire "to go all-out to sell our point of view to the world," even if it meant "the expenditure of a billion dollars and more to do the job" (p. 502).

A decade later, Gallup (1968b) focused on electoral reform and declared that never before in history had "the man in the street been so conscious of all the shortcomings and faults in the whole electoral process from beginning to end" (p. 41). Noting that presidential campaigns had "degenerated" into a "phony business," a "matter of showmanship" and "a test of the candidate's stamina" rather than of "his intelligence" (Gallup, 1968a, p. 133), he again claimed that the polls showed the public ahead of its leaders. For "many, many years," Gallup (1968c) told an interviewer, the people had "favored doing away with the Electoral College" and establishing "a nationwide primary." They also favored "shorter campaigns" and "more

serious and shorter conventions." They would "put an absolute top on campaign spending by any candidate or any party," and they would "give each candidate five or six half-hour broadcast periods to present his case—at which time everything else would be ruled off the air." In short, the public supported "a whole series of reforms that would change virtually every step and stage of the business of getting elected." Again, the public not only was "right" about electoral reform but "far, far ahead of the parties and the politicians" (p. 34).

In the twilight of his career, Gallup continued his crusade for electoral reform and also became deeply concerned about public education. Inaugurating an annual Gallup Poll on public attitudes toward education in 1968 (see Elam, 1984), Gallup became a major voice for educational reform. Meanwhile, he continued to chart public opinion on a wide variety of foreign and domestic issues and to celebrate the public's wisdom and foresight on even the most complex and divisive issues of the late 1960s and 1970s. On Vietnam, for example, Gallup (1972) again declared the public to be "far ahead of its leaders" for supporting Vietnamization three years before Nixon even proposed it (p. 17). Even in the post-Watergate climate of political alienation and disenchantment, Gallup's faith in the wisdom of "the people" remained undiminished. At the age of 77, Gallup (1978) sounded the refrain that he first introduced in the 1930s in summarizing what he had learned from "conducting thousands of surveys on almost every conceivable issue for nearly half a century": "One is that the judgment of the American people is extraordinarily sound. Another is that the public is almost always ahead of its leaders" (p. 59).

In preaching the democratic faith, Gallup obviously went beyond merely "reporting" his data. Recalling "very few instances . . . when the public was clearly in the wrong on an issue" (as cited in McDonald, 1962, p. 28), Gallup *judged* the wisdom both of policies and of the public's opinions. Gallup also routinely reflected on the historical significance of findings, discerned causes and trends, and even predicted the future. Most significantly, however, Gallup invoked the moral authority of *vox populi* in a number of his own pet causes. Notwithstanding his professions of scientific objectivity and political independence, it seems more than coincidence that Gallup—the conservative businessman, the close personal friend of Thomas Dewey, the staunch Cold Warrior—almost invariably discovered a public with the "right" political views. In short, George Gallup was no mere "weatherman" of public opinion. To the contrary, he sought to alter the ideological climate of his era with the results of his own polls.

★ THE FAINT "PULSE OF DEMOCRACY"

Academic survey researchers now generally agree that if polls are to be anything more than "entertainment . . . or propaganda for political interests," they must be integrated with "additional sources of information into a fuller, textured, portrait of public opinion" (MacKuen, 1984, p. 245). In other words, individual polls, if they are to be meaningful at all, must be interpreted both in terms of larger historical or social trends, and within the context of public debate and discussion. At a minimum, polls must be compared to related polls if one hopes to speak of trends, shed light upon the impact of question-wording, or explore the salience and logic of the public's opinions. Indeed, recent studies suggest that meaningful conclusions about public opinion can emerge only through comprehensive, comparative analyses of all available opinion data on particular topics or issues (see, e.g., Hogan & Smith, 1991).

George Gallup's legacy discourages such comprehensive and integrative analysis. Establishing polling as a commercial enterprise and aligning it with journalism, Gallup pioneered the institutional arrangements that today not only discourage comparative and in-depth analyses of polling data but have corrupted the mission of polling. Some polls, of course, are commissioned by politicians or special interest groups, which creates an obvious incentive for bias. Less obvious, yet even more troubling, however, is how journalistic imperatives have corrupted even the syndicated media polls.

Early in his career, Gallup offered media syndication as "a pretty realistic guarantee" of polling's honesty and impartiality. As Gallup (1938) summarized that guarantee, the Gallup Poll derived "all its income" from some sixty newspapers "of all shades of opinion"—some "left of center," some "right of center," and some in "the middle of the road." With that arrangement, Gallup asked rhetorically, "how long do you suppose we would last if we were anything but honest?" (p. 138).

"Honesty" is not the issue when considering how journalism has affected the quality and character of public opinion polling. Rather, as Everett Carll Ladd (1980) has argued, there is a "clash of institutional imperatives" between journalism and polling, with contemporary notions of "news" encouraging technically deficient polling. So serious is this "clash," and so different are the requirements of a good news story and sound polling, that the linkage of polling and the press raises serious questions as to whether opinion research does, or even can, enhance the democratic process" (p. 575). Indeed, there is no longer much question about it: as essentially wholly owned subsidiaries of a handful of media conglomerates, polling firms do not, in fact, aspire to "scientific" assessment of public opinion. Instead, they strive to make news.

The highest priority among journalists using polls is "timeliness," yet this creates a built-in incentive for methodological shortcuts: smaller samples, fewer efforts to track down respondents, truncated and unverified interviews, and less data processing. Once the data are collected, moreover, time and space limitations, along with the dictates of a good news story, encourage interpretations that oversimplify and overdramatize the results. As Ladd (1980) pointed out, good news reporting "has focus and arrives at relatively clear and unambiguous conclusions," whereas "good opinion research typically reveals . . . tentativeness, ambivalence, uncertainty, and lack of information or awareness" (p. 577). As Moore (1992) further reminds us, news organizations pay dearly for their "exclusive" polls and thus have a "vested interest" in making the results "sound important" (p. 250). As a result, both journalists and the pollsters themselves look for something more than disinterest or ambivalence in polling data: something new or surprising, something dramatic, a "lesson" to be learned, or some portent of conflict.

Journalistic imperatives have, in a sense, relieved pollsters of the problem of framing good questions. Failing to discern news in the public's relatively stable opinions on persistent political issues, journalists now demand more quirky polls from the pollsters—polls that pursue fresh, often non-political, and occasionally even silly angles on "old news." During the Persian Gulf War, for example, the pollsters typically asked the public not to assess the Bush administration's war policy, but to speculate about the unknowable: "How long do you think the war will last?" And "how many Americans do you think will be killed before the war is over?" The Gallup poll asked Americans not only to speculate about whether America would "win" the war, but even whether they thought "prayers" might be "effective" in resolving "a situation like this one in the Persian Gulf" (*Gallup Poll Monthly*, 1991, pp. 7, 25). As Mueller (1994) has observed, the Persian Gulf War was the "most extensively polled" issue in American history—the "mother of all polling events" (p. xiv). Yet despite asking some 5,000 questions (Ladd & Benson, 1992, p. 29), the "picture of public opinion" that emerged from polling on the Gulf War remained "fuzzy," as Moore (1992) has written, and "the crucial question of whether the public supported or opposed a war with Iraq could not be summarized with a percentage point estimate" (p. 353).

Polls have become "news events" in and of themselves. As a result, they substitute for substantive information about political issues and stifle debate. Indeed, as Herbst (1993) has observed, polls often make political debate seem "superfluous," since "they give the illusion that the public has already spoken in a definitive manner" (p. 166). When debates do occur, they often focus on the polls themselves, with partisans debating not the merits of a policy but the "message" of "the polls" (see, e.g., Hogan, 1994, pp. 119, 137). Such an emphasis, in turn, discourages bold leadership, since it pressures elected representatives to defer to the polls. It may even discourage the public itself from other modes of political expression (such as letter-writing or demonstrations), since it suggests not only that the public already has spoken but that the public "speaks" *only* through the polls.

During election campaigns, polls likewise substitute for substantive information about the records or proposals of candidates. During the 1988 presidential primaries, for example, nearly a third of all election stories on the network news noted poll results, and during the final months of the campaign, a new poll was reported, on average, every other day (Jamieson, 1992, p. 175). More importantly, the polls have redefined campaign "news" itself and have fueled an astonishing increase in so-called "horse race journalism"—an emphasis on the strategic "game" of politics—since the 1960s (see Patterson, 1994, pp. 53–93). Not only does such reporting deprive voters of the information they need to assess candidates, but it may discourage political participation altogether by casting voters as mere "spectators" (See Jamieson, 1992, pp. 186–188).

Despite all the historical "lessons" and "scientific" breakthroughs, we thus remain a long way from George Gallup's vision of a "scientific democracy." Indeed, the public opinion poll not only has failed to become "the most useful instrument of democracy ever devised," as Gallup predicted (Meier & Saunders, 1949, p. 218), but it has had a number of deleterious effects on public discussion and political leadership in America. Properly designed and interpreted, polls might well serve George Gallup's dream of a more inclusive and efficient democracy. In a sad irony of history, however, Gallup's own rhetorical legacy subverted that dream, and the "pulse of democracy" only beats fainter in the age of saturation polling.

ENDNOTES

[1] A survey of Gallup's articles listed in *Reader's Guide to Periodical Literature, the International Index, the Social Science Index,* and the *Humanities Index* reveals 94 published speeches and articles by Gallup and 10 others co-authored by Gallup. That number includes six speeches published in *Vital Speeches of the Day,* along with articles in everything from the most popular, general circulation magazines to obscure scholarly journals. Gallup's articles appeared in *Reader's Digest,* as well as in news

magazines (*Newsweek* and *U.S. News and World Report*), women's magazines (*Good Housekeeping* and *Ladies Home Journal*), business publications (*Business Week* and *Nation's Business*) and journals in education (*Phi Delta Kappa*), philosophy (*American Philosophical Society Proceedings*), government (*National Municipal Review*), and health sciences (*The Journal of Social Hygiene*). He also published regularly in his own industry's flagship journal, *Public Opinion Quarterly,* and he even published one article, ironically, in the *Literary Digest.*

[2] FDR received 60.7 percent of the total vote and 62.5 percent of the major party vote, while Gallup's final poll predicted 53.8 percent of the total and 55.7 percent of the major party vote. See Gallup and Rae (1940, pp. 50, 53).

[3] Rogers (1949) illustrated the significance of this fact in analyzing Gallup's performance in 1948. By wrongly predicting the winner in seven states, Gallup underestimated FDR's electoral vote by more than 33 percent (pp. 118–119).

[4] The figures are as follows: Gallup missed Truman's vote by 5.3 percentage points, Dewey's by 4.1 percentage points, Wallace's by 1.6 percentage points, and Thurmond's by 0.4 percentage points (see Gallup, 1949a, p. 55).

[5] Ross Perot's candidacy, the note explains, "created an additional source of error in estimating the 1992 presidential vote" because it had "no historical precedent." According to the note, the Gallup Poll erred in allocating none of the undecided vote to Perot, which neglected to take into account Perot's "equal status" in the presidential debates and his "record advertising budget" (*Gallup Poll Monthly,* 1992).

[6] The Gallup Poll, in particular, has employed extraordinarily large samples to make election forecasts. In 1944, for example, Gallup employed a national sample of more than 6,000, as compared to only two- to three-thousand in most issue polls. After the 1948 debacle, Gallup told *U.S. News* that the Gallup Poll would interview "in the neighborhood" of 40,000 to 50,000 people in the two months preceding the 1952 election, including some 10,000 interviews in the week just prior to the election (U.S. House, 1945, p. 1239; Gallup, 1952a, p. 61).

[7] To cite just a couple of additional examples, split-sample experiments have shown that while only 19% agreed that too little money was being spent on "welfare," 63% agreed that too little was being spent on "assistance to the poor"; and while only 20% agreed that too little was being spent on "assistance to big cities," 49% agreed too little was being spent

on "solving the problems of big cities" (see Moore, 1992, pp. 343–346).

[8] The Gallup Poll's monthly journal has been published since 1965 under three different titles: the *Gallup Opinion Index,* the *Gallup Report,* and the *Gallup Poll Monthly.*

REFERENCES

Brady, H. E., &. Orren, G. R. (1992). Polling pitfalls: Sources of error in public opinion surveys. In T. E. Mann &. G. R. Orren (Eds.), *Media polls in American politics* (pp. 55–94). Washington, DC: Brookings Institution.

Cantril, A. H. (1991). *The opinion connection: Polling, politics, and the press.* Washington, DC: Congressional Quarterly Press.

Crespi, I. (1988). *Pre-election polling: Sources of accuracy and error.* New York: Russell Sage Foundation.

Elam, S. M. (Ed.). (1984). *Gallup polls of attitudes toward education, 1969–1984: A topical summary.* Bloomington, IN: Phi Delta Kappa.

Field, M. D. (1990). Opinion polling in the United States of America. In M. L. Young (Ed.), *The classics of polling* (pp. 34–45). Metuchen, NJ: Scarecrow Press.

Gallup, G. (1938). Government and the sampling referendum. *Journal of the American Statistical Association, 33,* 131–142.

Gallup, G. (1940a, October). Can we trust the common people? *Good Housekeeping, 111,* 21.

Gallup, G. (1940b, February). Polling public opinion. *Current History, 51,* 23–26, 57.

Gallup, G. (1942a, September 1). Democracy and the common man. *Vital Speeches of the Day, 8,* 687–688.

Gallup, G. (1942b). How important is public opinion in time of war? *Proceedings of the American Philosophical Association, 85,* 440–444.

Gallup, G. (1942c, March 29). The people are ahead of Congress. *New York Times Magazine, 91,* 16, 35.

Gallup, G. (1944, December 30). I don't take sides. *The Nation, 159,* 795–796.

Gallup, G. (1947). The quintamensional plan of question design. *Public Opinion Quarterly, 11,* 385–393.

Gallup, G. (1948a). *A guide to public opinion polls.* Princeton, NJ: Princeton University Press.

Gallup, G. (1948b, January 1). Main street rates the issues. *Vital Speeches of the Day, 14,* 177–179.

Gallup, G. (1948c). On the regulation of polling. *Public Opinion Quarterly, 12,* 733–735.

Gallup, G. (1949a, February 27). The case for the public opinion polls. *New York Times Magazine, 98*, 11, 55, 57.

Gallup, G. (1949b). A reply to "The Pollsters." *Public Opinion Quarterly, 13*, 179–180.

Gallup, G. (1951, November 4). What we don't know can hurt us. *New York Times Magazine, 100*, 12, 50–51.

Gallup, G. (1952a, May 23). Interview with George Gallup: How 55 million vote. *U.S. News and World Report, 32*, 56–64.

Gallup, G. (1952b, June 1). Why we are doing so badly in the ideological war. *Vital Speeches of the Day, 18*, 501–504.

Gallup, G. (1955–56). The absorption rate of ideas. *Public Opinion Quarterly, 19*, 234–242.

Gallup, G. (1957–58). The changing climate for public opinion research. *Public Opinion Quarterly, 21*, 23–27.

Gallup, G. (1960). Foreword. In J. M. Fenton, *In your opinion: The managing editor of the Gallup Poll looks at polls, politics, and the people from 1945 to 1960* (pp. vii–xi). Boston: Little, Brown and Co.

Gallup, G. (1968a, November 18). Gallup: Humphrey "probably" would have won—if the election had come a few days later: Interview with Dr. George Gallup. *U.S. News and World Report, 65*, 132–133.

Gallup, G. (1968b, November 4). How Dr. Gallup sees the campaign homestretch: Interview with a veteran pollster. *U.S. News and World Report, 65*, 40–41.

Gallup, G. (1968c, July 29). Interview with Dr. George Gallup: '68 election size-up. *U.S. News and World Report, 65*, 30–34.

Gallup, G. (1972). *The sophisticated poll watcher's guide*. Princeton, NJ: Princeton Opinion Press.

Gallup, G. (1978, August). Six political reforms most Americans want. *Reader's Digest, 113*, 59–62.

Gallup, G., & Rae, S. F. (1940). *The pulse of democracy: The public opinion poll and how it works*. New York: Simon and Schuster.

Gallup Poll Monthly, No. 304, (1991, January).

Gallup Poll Monthly, No. 326, (1992, November).

Ginzburg, B. (1944, December 16). Dr. Gallup on the mat. *The Nation, 159*, 737–739.

Hawkins, D. I., & Coney, K. A. (1981). Uninformed response error in survey research. *Journal of Marketing Research, 18*, 372.

Herbst, S. (1993). *Numbered voices: How opinion polling has shaped American politics*. Chicago: University of Chicago Press.

Hogan, J. M. (1994). *The nuclear freeze campaign: Rhetoric and foreign policy in the telepolitical age*. East Lansing, MI: Michigan State University Press.

Hogan, J. M., & Smith, T. J., III. (1991). Polling on the issues: Public opinion and the nuclear freeze. *Public Opinion Quarterly, 55*, 534–569.

Jamieson, K. H. (1992). *Dirty politics: Deception, distraction, and democracy*. New York: Oxford University Press.

Ladd, E. C. (1980). Polling and the press: The clash of institutional imperatives. *Public Opinion Quarterly, 44*, 574–584.

Ladd, E. C., & Benson, J. (1992). The growth of news polls in American politics. In T. E. Mann & G. R. Orren (Eds.), *Media polls in American politics* (pp. 19–31). Washington, DC: Brookings Institution.

MacKuen, M. B. (1984). The concept of public opinion. In C. F. Turner & E. Martin (Eds.). *Surveying subjective phenomena* (Vol. 1, pp. 236–45). New York: Russell Sage Foundation.

McDonald, D. (1962). *Opinion polls: Interviews by Donald McDonald with Elmo Roper and George Gallup*. Santa Barbara, CA: The Fund for the Republic.

Meier, N. C., & Saunders, H. W. (Eds.). (1949). *The polls and public opinion*. New York: Henry Holt and Co.

Moore, D. W. (1992). *The superpollsters: How they measure and manipulate public opinion in America*. New York: Four Walls Eight Windows.

Mosteller, F., Hyman, H., McCarthy, P., Marks, E. S., & Truman, D. B. (1949). *The pre-election polls of 1948: Report to the committee on analysis of pre-election polls and forecasts*. New York: Social Science Research Council.

Mueller, J. (1994). *Policy and opinion in the Gulf War*. Chicago: University of Chicago Press.

Nelson, J. S., Megill, A., & McCloskey, D. N. (Eds.). (1987). *The rhetoric of the human sciences: Language and argument in scholarship and public affairs*. Madison, WI: University of Wisconsin Press.

Patterson, T. F. (1994). *Out of order*. New York: Vintage Books.

Payne, S. L. (1951). *The art of asking questions*. Princeton, NJ: Princeton University Press.

Robinson, J. P., & Meadow, R. (1982). *Polls apart*. Cabin John, MD: Seven Locks Press.

Rogers, L. (1949). *The pollsters: Public opinion, politics, and democratic leadership*. New York: Alfred A. Knopf.

Roll, C. W., & Cantril, A. H. (1980). *Polls: Their use and misuse in politics*. Cabin John, MD: Seven Locks Press.

Roper, B. W. (1980). The impact of journalism on polling. In A. H. Cantril (Ed.), *Polling on the issues: Twenty-one perspectives on the role of opinion polls in the making of public policy* (pp. 15–19). Cabin John, MD: Seven Locks Press.

Rugg, W. D. (1941). Experiments in wording questions: II. *Public Opinion Quarterly, 5*, 91–92.

Schuman, H., & Presser, S. (1981). *Questions and answers in attitude surveys: Experiments on question form, wording, and context.* New York: Academic Press.

Schuman, H., & Scott, J. (1987, May 22). Problems in the use of survey questions to measure public opinion. *Science, 236*, 957–959.

Shelley, M. C., & Hwang, H. (1991). The mass media and public opinion polls in the 1988 presidential election: Trends, accuracy, consistency, and events. *American Politics Quarterly, 19*, 59–79.

Singer, E. (1988). Controversies. *Public Opinion Quarterly, 52*, 576–559.

The black and white beans. (1948, May 3). *Time, 51*, 21–23.

U.S. House. (1945). *Campaign expenditures: Hearings before the committee to investigate campaign expenditures . . . seventy-eighth Congress, second session, on H. Res. 551.* (Part 12, December 12, 1944). Washington, DC: Government Printing Office.

U.S. Senate (1953). *Overseas information programs of the United States: Hearings before a subcommittee of the committee on foreign relations . . . eighty-third Congress, first session, on overseas information programs of the United States.* (Part 2, April 1, 1953). Washington, DC: Government Printing Office.

Walden, G. R. (1990). *Public opinion polls and survey research: A selective annotated bibliography of U.S. guides and studies from the 1980s.* New York: Garland Publishing.

Wheeler, M. (1976). *Lies, damn lies, and statistics: The manipulation of public opinion in America.* New York: Dell.

Reassessing the State of Political Communication in the United States

Trevor Parry-Giles and Shawn J. Parry-Giles

Though the metaphors may differ, the same basic commonplace about the nature and quality of contemporary political communication in the United States dominates academic and public commentary. Intellectual leaders repeatedly tell Americans that political communication is baseless, is in crisis, and is lacking in substance. It is diseased, dirty, infected, flawed, poisoned, and/or hopelessly polluted by money and special interests. It appeals to the lowest common denominator, threatens America's standing in the world, and ignores the severity of the problems facing American society.

This cacophony of criticism and cynicism has persisted for much of the 1990s, perhaps in response to a series of events and occurrences over the last twenty years. Each new example, each new spectacle (e.g., Watergate, Ronald Reagan's election to the presidency, Iran/contra, the 1988 presidential election, Clarence Thomas/Anita Hill, Gennifer Flowers, the Clinton impeachment, George W. Bush and cocaine) evidences for the naysaying commentators the truly flawed nature of American political communication. Our nation is perpetually at risk, they maintain, and our democracy imperiled by the character of our political discourse.

We know these commentators because of the power of their criticism and the frequency of their appearance. Jamieson (1992) laments the "Svengalian power" of the mass media and concludes that "Campaign discourse is failing the body politic . . . because it has conventionalized genres of candidate and press discourse that minimize argumentative engagement and ignore the responsibility that all parties should shoulder for the claims they make" (pp. 9, 11). Bennett (1996) warns us about "the governing crisis" where the "media spiral, the marketing syndrome, and the money chase in contemporary politics have undermined the connection between elections and government in the United States" (p. 10). We live in a cynical society, Goldfarb (1991) reveals, where "Leaders use rhetorics which neither they nor their constituents believe, but which both leaders and followers nonetheless use to justify their actions" (p. 1). Salvador (1998), reporting on the findings of the Eisenhower Leadership Group, fears that "democracy is at risk" because citizens are leaving the business of politics and governance to others (p. 3). Kamber (1997) believes that "American politics has been poisoned by harsh personal attacks" and that "democratic debate has been dragged down to the level of tabloid scandal" (p. xiii). And Hart (1994) suggests that our political culture needs a "New Puritanism" that resists television's tendency toward "emotional excess and servile distraction" and its capacity to "seduce America" (p. 163).

Our reading of contemporary political communication is somewhat different and significantly more hopeful. We suggest that American political communication is in many ways quite healthy and we assert that there is much to be optimistic about regarding the state of political communication in the United States. We base this conclusion on four distinctive characteristics of contemporary political discourse. First, American political discourse is often detailed and specific in its focus on policy. Second, this same discourse is generally successful at producing high quality leaders and leadership. Third, American political discourse is increasingly democratized via technology and media. Fourth, the success of political discourse in America has created truly rhetorical politics to the benefit of the American community. In our discussion of each of these dimensions of American political discourse, we examine Bill Clinton as a contemporary example of the optimism about the contemporary political context, highlighting his role in rhetoric's renaissance as a political force. Ultimately, in advancing this view of political discourse in the United States, we hope to offer an alternative direction for political communication research—a direction that eschews cynicism for teleologically hopeful criticism, a direction that embraces progress instead of pessimism.

★ THE UBIQUITY OF POLICY IN POLITICAL COMMUNICATION

One of the most persistent complaints about political communication is that it either ignores or simplifies complex national policy issues (Zarefsky, 1992). This occurs, the critics say, because of television and its obsession with "strategy" rather than "substance," or because of a misplaced focus on character and

personality or because attack politics simplify and distort policy argument and disagreement (Hart, 1994; Jamieson, 1992). The focus on strategy or character is additionally credited with spreading the cynicism about politics (Cappella & Jamieson, 1996). Whatever the reason, many commentators come to the regrettable conclusion that contemporary political communication is devoid of serious policy engagement.

These complaints ignore the practice of political campaigns and legislative debates as they occur in the United States. At the presidential level, campaigns for party nominations begin earlier and earlier every cycle, with candidates storming Iowa, New Hampshire, and the national airwaves months before any votes are cast or caucuses are held. And during their journeys, many contenders address complex and detailed policy questions. Indeed, because campaigns start so early, more speeches are given, and more advertising is produced, much of which concerns policy choices and decisions. Buchanan (1996) cites the results of a Center for Media and Public Affairs content analysis of the 1992 campaign. That study revealed that 72% of speeches, 84% of commercials, and 93% of book chapters presented by the presidential candidates in 1992 focused on substantive issues and concerns (p. 11).

One need only examine the 2000 presidential election campaign to discover the ubiquity of policy debate. On the Republican side, several of the candidates have discussed in detail their policy positions on such diverse matters as tax policy, educational vouchers, relations with China, Medicare and Social Security reform, and agricultural price restoration. For instance, Steve Forbes features detailed position papers and issue statements on his campaign website, including his plans for a flat tax, a personal retirement security system, medical savings accounts, and his "power to parents" plan (Forbes, 1999). Gary Bauer informs voters of his positions on abortion, the military, assisted suicide, property rights, and over fifteen other policy matters (Bauer, 1999). And John McCain tells voters about his views on thirteen different issues, ranging from small business policy to his proposals for campaign finance reform (McCain, 1999). These candidates are typical rather than unique; all of the major GOP candidates host websites containing detailed policy positions and speech transcripts. Their policy positions, though, are not restricted to websites and e-mails. Policy discourse occupies a considerable portion of overall campaign discourse—from stump speeches to fund-raising mail to television advertising. Although policy-based political oratory may not generate extensive media coverage, the texts of such discourse are widely available in sources like *Vital Speeches of the Day*, mainstream journalistic coverage and/or newspaper summaries of candidate policy positions, and again via candidate webpages. Furthermore, there is considerable evidence that voters actually acquire knowledge about policy and issue positions from media coverage (Weaver, 1996).

As for the Democrats, Vice President Al Gore's main focus has been the discussion of policy options and governance platforms, leading to the rather mundane but oft-repeated conclusion that he is boring and stiff. So, while Gore tries to recast his political identity and profile, his campaign website continues to highlight daily policy announcements. On October 12, 1999, for example, the website featured a speech by the Vice President on the need for improved health care for "working families." Included in the summary were a press release, fact sheet, and full speech transcript (Gore, 1999). Even as Gore seeks a more visceral connection with voters by moving his headquarters out of Washington and sporting a new wardrobe, his official campaign communications still privilege policy discourse.

Campaign 2000 is also unique for the large amount of early debates between all of the candidates vying for the two major party nominations. As Bill Schneider reported on CNN, the 1988 primaries (the last election without an incumbent president seeking re-election) only witnessed six debates and there were only three debates in 1992 and 1996 before the New Hampshire primary. The 2000 campaign will feature sixteen debates before the New Hampshire primary—nine for the Republicans and seven for the Democrats. Schneider sees this development positively, citing voters who seem to prefer debates to commercials and highlighting Vice President Gore's attempt

to increase the amount of debates with Senator Bradley before the primaries begin (CNN, 2000).

Furthermore, when candidates ignore policy or refuse to offer specific policy positions, they are castigated by the press and by their opponents. As of January 2000, George W. Bush faces the charge from many quarters that he has yet to offer specific policy positions on several key issues and concerns and that he lacks the specific knowledge of public policy necessary for the presidency (Kelly, 1999; Milbank, 1999). When he was asked by a television interviewer to name four world leaders in various trouble spots around the globe, the Texas Governor could only name one, furthering the perception that Bush lacks policy expertise (Neal, 1999). And his performance in three 1999 GOP primary debates added to the belief that this front-running, heavily financed Republican may lack sufficient knowledge and preparation about complex policy issues.

Another candidate facing charges of policy laxity is Bill Bradley. In fact, the main point of clash between the Democratic candidates in debates and individual speeches concerned a specific policy question—the cost of Bradley's health care proposals. Gore did not attack Bradley's preparedness for the presidency, or his lack of executive experience, but rather highlighted his failure to offer supported and specific policy answers on the likely cost of his health care plan.[1] Gore offered a similar critique in the first debate between the candidates in 2000 at the University of New Hampshire on January 5. Indeed, Gore pointedly refused to comment on Bradley's presidential preparedness, instead noting that Bradley gets "a little out of sorts just when I talk about the substance of policy" (Balz & Harris, 2000, p. A4).

As campaigns progress, the policy discussions persist. Political advertisements, often pejoratively characterized as "negative ads," frequently highlight voting records or policy positions. These ads may simplify, or distort, but voters know that and are guarded in their consumption of such discourse. A study of voter responses to negative advertising from the Thomas C. Sorensen Institute for Political Leadership at the University of Virginia conducted in 1998 and 1999 reveals that voters "make sophisticated appraisals about what does and what does not constitute mudslinging." This same study demonstrates that the voters surveyed, by large majorities, believe that political ads are fair when they highlight an opponent's inconsistencies, voting records, private business practices or ethical problems, and current problems with drugs or alcohol (Freedman, Wood, & Lawton, 1999). Indeed, the view the voters are manipulated by political advertising is elitist and not well supported (Ansolabehere & Iyengar, 1995; Johnson-Cartee & Copeland, 1991).

Voters also consume debates, where policy positions again are the focus of questions and discussion, and where the absence of a policy position or the commission of a policy error can seriously undermine a candidate's credibility. And voters who care deeply about policy, and who want to cast their votes on the basis of policy specifics, are able to access complicated and enumerated information about candidate voting behaviors, policy statements, policy contradictions, and detailed projections that are offered by campaigns, watchdog groups, and the media (e.g., http://www.issues2000.org; http://www.2000Vote.com; http://www.c-span.org/guide/executive/rwh/; http://www.freedomchannel.com).

Rather than over-simplify or ignore policy concerns, the proliferating and ever-present mass media provide ample coverage of policy positions and policy deliberations.[2] On C-Span alone, citizens can watch congressional hearings, follow candidates along the campaign trail to assess their policy stances, see academic symposia on policy concerns, and dialogue with other citizens and moderators concerning policy issues. Indeed, a random day's program content on C-Span reveals considerable policy discussion. The cable network's programs for October 12, 1999, for instance, included its *Washington Journal* series with prominent journalists, a panel on youth violence, a panel on watchdog journalism in presidential politics, and live coverage of House and Senate legislative business on the budget and campaign finance reform (http://www.c-span.org/guide/schedule/highlights.asp). If there is a problem with media coverage of policy, it may be that policy discussion tends to be too event-driven.

That is, rather than discussing long-term policy options or specific plans for future policy enhancements, mass mediated policy discussions deliberate about policy in the wake of an event, as with the discussion of gun control in the aftermath of Columbine High School's shootings. Nonetheless, the dimensions and gradations of policy are frequently aired and discussed for concerned voters. But, as Lee Sigelman has quipped, while you can lead people to *Washington Week in Review*, you can't make them watch (Sigelman, 1992).

The expectations for policy information and policy knowledgability by candidates are indeed on the rise. Bill Clinton and his mastery of policy matters has created an expectation that a presidential contender ought to have the ability to engage intricate policy discussions in a facile and competent manner—a standard that will be tested in the 2000 campaign. Few politicians in recent memory match his ability to discuss wide-ranging policy matters in detail and with deep background knowledge. In the wake of Ronald Reagan's endearing ineptitude and George Bush's perpetual indifference, Clinton's engagement with any and all policy questions marked him as a different type of political leader—one with the competence and the intelligence to fully comprehend the intricacies and nuances of federal policymaking (Maraniss, 1995; Renshon, 1998; Walker, 1996). Indeed, as Burns & Sorenson (1999) reveal, "Clinton impressed friends and foes alike with his knowledge of policy alternatives." They quote a former member of Congress as saying, "'It just blows me away whenever I meet with him [Clinton] to see how thorough his understanding is of a whole range of issues'" (p. 113). This characteristic elevates expectations that candidates like George W. Bush will possess similar knowledge of policy and governance. It might reasonably be argued, moreover, that one of the reasons Clinton maintained steady job approval ratings throughout the scandals, hearings, and trials of 1998 was his ability, on a purely discursive level, to manifest effective job performance through his engagement with policy matters. As he was fond of saying throughout the Lewinsky matter, his goal was simply to "get back to work" on the things that matter most to the American people.

So the policy discussions continue, unabated, ad infinitum, over the droning and omnipresent television airwaves. Policy discussions are a pervasive part of contemporary political communication, fed largely by the presence of 24-hour news outlets, a proliferating Internet, and the election of candidates with policy acumen. As our national problems become more detailed and numerous in the aftermath of the Cold War, the demands those problems place on leaders is larger and more complete—a knowledge that is critical for electoral success.

★ CREATING SUCCESSFUL LEADERS

The capacity to engage layers of policy discussion has emerged as one of the primary leadership traits required of American political candidates. But it is only one part of a larger leadership puzzle constructed by a system of political communication that asks voters to, primarily and fundamentally, make judgments about a candidate's fitness for public office. America's lengthy election season and rigorous campaign process seek to give voters a clear and complete picture of the individuals vying as guardians of the public trust. Occasionally, we make mistakes in our judgments. But, by and large, that system, and our political communication processes, has produced successful leaders who enact effective leadership.

In depicting a model of political thinking at the end of the millennium, Hariman & Beer (1998) return to a "premodern theory of political intelligence known as 'prudence'" (p. 299). A prudence paradigm that reflects contemporary politics requires leaders that "strive to achieve what is good both for the individual and for the community," requires adaptation to "contingent events" through a commitment to "deliberation" that "culminates in character rather than technical knowledge" (p. 301). Certainly, the twentieth century is replete with American presidents who sought what was best for the individual and the community (e.g., FDR's New Deal; LBJ's War on Poverty), who successfully adapted to contingent circumstances (e.g., Wilson and World War I; FDR and Truman to World War II; Bush and the Gulf War), who were committed to deliberation

(e.g., FDR's Fireside chats; Clinton's Town Hall meetings), and who cultivated the importance of character in political life (e.g., Theodore Roosevelt; Coolidge; Ford; Carter).

Scholars of political communication have long recognized the place and importance of character and biography in the discourse that surrounds and defines campaigns and elections (McGee, 1978; Hahn, 1987; Parry-Giles, 1996; Murphy, 1997). Along with the ubiquitous policy debates, elections are also about character and competence—about who voters think will offer the most prudent and effective leadership and the most competent governance. Those decisions are interwoven with policy concerns such that the dichotomy between "image" and "issue" is largely a meaningless one for contemporary political communication (Hahn, 1987).

American politics has always involved discussions of biography and personality, put forth by campaigns in the form of packaged images that distort and display. And there have always been rumors and gossip that swirl around presidential candidates and their confederates. In a speech at the National Press Club, documentary filmmaker Ken Burns reflected on the lessons he learned from producing his film about Thomas Jefferson. One of the lessons Burns identified was that American politics in the 1990s is much more civil and much more dignified than in the early years of the Republic (Burns, 1997). His basis for this claim was his study of the presidential election of 1800, where Jefferson's deism, his tendency to form sexual relationships with women/girls he held in captivity as slaves, and his general character were thoroughly aired and repeatedly maligned in Federalist newspapers. Burns concluded that our contemporary negative campaigns paled in comparison with the campaigns waged by the Founders. The romanticized myth is of America's forebearers engaged in thoughtful and intellectual discussions of the issues of the day with little concern for personality or image; the historical evidence, however, reveals an intensely partisan, highly personalized American political culture (Schudson, 1992, 1998). As Jack Stanton asks Henry Burton in *Primary Colors* (Anonymous, 1996) "You don't think Abraham Lincoln . . . had to tell his little stories and smile his shit-eating, backcountry grin? He did it all just so he'd get the opportunity, one day, to stand in front of the nation and appeal to 'the better angels of our nature'" (p. 364).

This characteristic of campaigns means that much political communication will address issues of biography and character. Some of that material is straightforward and well researched; some of it is salacious, based in rumor or innuendo, and simply irresponsible. But the voting public has demonstrated a resistance to false information and an amazing capacity to decide what information matters to them in their electoral decision-making. Indeed, those commentators most concerned about the media and its "feeding frenzies" (Sabato, 1991; Patterson, 1993; Fallows, 1997) seem to harbor an outdated and elitist conception of mass mediated communication that sees viewers as passive receptacles of any and all information beamed at them. But media consumers are savvy, smart, and skilled. That Bill Clinton survived Gennifer Flowers and George W. Bush has weathered rumors of cocaine use attests to the power of the voting population to separate the important from the immaterial or perhaps to distinguish between rumors and facts.

In spite of historical and contemporary media frenzies, American political culture has produced leaders like Jefferson, Madison, Lincoln, and countless others in Congress and throughout the nation that were generally successful at meeting the nation's challenges. At the presidential level, most of the surveys that measure effective leadership rank the vast majority of American presidents as average, near great, or great (Murray & Blessing, 1994). Those who have populated all branches of the American government have been normally triumphant at weathering significant crises, from the British invasion of 1812, to the Civil War, to the Cold War. When an action by a leader has significantly threatened the nature and integrity of the constitutional system, that leader has been impeached or has resigned. The fact that only one president in the nation's history, brief as that history is, has been forced from office is a general testament to the quality of our campaign processes and our political communication.

Ronald Reagan's election in 1980 heightened the fears of political observers that American political discourse is primarily image-driven and devoid of substance and quality, and they reference each successive election to bolster their claims. The three presidents elected since 1980, though, have presided over the rather remarkable ascendancy of the United States to global prominence and economic prosperity. The United States nicely survived the Cold War and is regarded as the world's dominant military power. American cultural products, for good or ill, are sought after and consumed by much of the globe's population, and this nation is at the forefront of the current global information and technology revolution. In February 2000, the United States will enjoy the longest peacetime economic expansion ever.[3] Indeed, by every pragmatic measure of national success, the twenty years since Ronald Reagan's first election, since the victory of image politics, has been a time of unparalleled growth and opportunity for the United States. There are many factors to account for this success, but one of those factors must be the propensity of the American public to select effective leaders at various levels of government. Dallek (1996) contends, "the global responsibilities a chief executive faces today dwarf those that his counterpart encountered in the 1790s, as does his impact on the economic and social life of the nation" (p. xxi). Scholars of political communication should acknowledge these complexities and accomplishments rather than only pining for a mythologized past and lamenting the failure of contemporary leaders to meet those mythologized standards.

Bill Clinton may be the best testament to the sophistication of the American voter and her/his ability to discern what is important vis-à-vis character and competence from what is trivial. Most polling indicates that, by fairly substantial majorities, the Americans polled approve of Clinton's performance in office (*National Journal*, 1999). There is relative agreement that this president has been successful on several fronts—from economic stewardship and fiscal responsibility to peace efforts in the Middle East, Northern Ireland, the Balkans, and Indonesia. Clinton's ability to provide symbolic leadership at times of national crisis—the Oklahoma City bombing, the shootings at Columbine High School—are also recognized and applauded. At the same time, most polls also demonstrate that the various samples surveyed do not approve of Clinton's morals, his character, or his trustworthiness (*National Journal*, 1999). While we may nostalgically long for a president of high moral rectitude, the political culture appears content to accept a competent leader with moral lapses. The level of voter sophistication represented by the willingness and ability to separate Clinton the president from Clinton the individual is lost on all but a few commentators. Moreover, the beneficial and useful power of political communication to express all facets of an individual leader's character and personality is lost in the maelstrom of criticism usually unleashed upon the political environment with word of a new scandal.

★ THE DEMOCRATIZATION OF POLITICAL COMMUNICATION

Along with technology and new attempts to increase voter registration and participation, the focus on character and leadership endemic to contemporary political communication represents a further democratization of the political process. Political rhetors respond, as they have done for all of American history, to the need for voters to understand and evaluate individuals vying for positions of leadership. Such evaluations, when made solely on policy grounds, are incomplete and the individual citizen may not want to make such decisions by only calculating the differences in policy positions. If anything, the power of contemporary political communication to disseminate both policy information and character/biographical background gives voters additional freedom in making their electoral decisions. And as new techniques and new media are used to communicate these messages to larger and more diverse audiences and thus to enhance and elevate American democracy, the elites complain and bemoan the further denigration of politics in the United States.

Of course, one reason for the criticism of democratized politics is that political office seekers are circumventing the traditional media elites who have determined the nature and state of political campaigns in the past. As candidates reach more voters through non-traditional television outlets (*MTV*, infomercials, talk shows, etc.) and via new technologies, media and political elites are marginalized. Much as the breakdown of the political machines left old-time party bosses bereft of power and influence, new media and information technology mean the end of consolidated political/media power reserved only for a handful of newspapers and television networks.

Several centuries ago, Plato complained loudly about the demise of Athenian civilization at the hands of the sophists. Their art was mere fakery or technique, he concluded, and they posed significant dangers to the community. Modern day Platonists make much the same claim about political communicators—be they politicians or the consultants they hire (Nimmo, 1970; Sabato, 1981). Yet the expansion of news outlets, the increase in political websites, the growth of political campaigns and other political advertising only means that politicians and political operatives are trying to reach out to more voters; more citizens are, thus, receiving political messages. The quality of those messages varies, but their number and their scope represent the increasingly democratized politics of the late 1990s.

Once again, Bill Clinton serves as an exemplar of the democratization of American political discourse. As Benson (1994) reports, "In 1992 the United States presidential campaign came to the Internet," and the Clinton campaign was the first to truly exploit the new medium for political purposes. Voter turnout in 1992 increased from previous elections, due in large part to Clinton's attempts to reach out to segments of the population largely ignored in most political campaigns. Of course, Clinton reached these voters through nontraditional venues like *The Arsenio Hall Show* and *MTV* (see Diamond & Silverman, 1995; Davis & Owen, 1998). Nontraditional formats are now characteristic of American politics, largely as a result of Bill Clinton and his rhetorical abilities. The 1992 campaign was notable for its use of "town hall" formats, for instance, which worked well for Clinton but not for his opponents. This format resurfaced in a 1996 presidential debate and the early primary forums in the 2000 campaign have also been of the "town hall" variety. Once in office, the Clinton administration continued using "town halls" to discuss with citizens questions of economic recovery, race relations, gun violence, and the Hollywood media's moral responsibility. The Clinton administration also spearheaded the development of the White House website and encouraged the increased access by citizens to their elected officials. And, on November 8, 1999, Clinton became the first president to participate in a live Internet conference (Kurtz, 1999).

The political naysayers will charge, in response, that despite more political communication, despite the ubiquity of policy discussion, and despite the increase in media and technology venues, voters are dissatisfied and cynical about politics. And those same critics will point to one clear fact that is, for them, the ultimate indicator of public apathy—low voter turnout. Perhaps the most definitive act of disengaging from the political process, by most commentators' estimation, is low voter turnout. A political system where a small percentage of the population vote is not more democratized, but less, they claim.

Given the ubiquity of political communication, it seems clear that voting rates in elections would be a strong barometer of the quality of political communication. But the fact that voters may choose not to engage or connect with the political process is no indication of the quality or success of political communication. There are inherent difficulties with judging the quality of a given phenomenon (e.g., political communication) by the level of a specific human activity (e.g., voting). Voting is a difficult activity in the United States. It usually requires advanced registration and a journey to the polling place in order to cast the ballot. Because voting is held on a Tuesday, the act of voting requires schedule adjustment and inconvenience. And in some states and localities, the ballot is pages and pages long, filled with referenda, candidates for down-ballot offices, constitutional amendments, etc. The American system of voting is time-consuming, inconvenient, and for some, impossible. Other nations declare a national holiday on Election Day. There are greater degrees of obligation or expectation to vote. In many European countries, where taxation rates are quite high, voting is not only a political decision, but an economic one as well. In still other democracies, where free elections are the result of bloody revolutions or long struggles

for independence, voting has special meaning and is a rite/right of some personal significance. To say that American voter turnout speaks to public cynicism or decaying political communication, thus, is to ignore an entire set of compelling and powerful reasons why Americans may choose not to vote.

Even with all of the impediments to voting in the United States, Americans still vote in fairly large numbers. According to the Federal Election Commission, 76 percent of registered voters went to the polls in 1992 while 65.97 percent of registered voters voted in 1996. A little over half of the voting age population voted in 1992 with that number dropping in 1996. But these numbers have stayed roughly the same, give or take a few percentage points, since 1960, and they are fairly consistent with voter turnout numbers from around the world, despite the myth that voters in other nations take this responsibility more seriously than do Americans (http://www.fec.gov/).

Indeed, low voter turnout validates the liberty and freedom of the American republic and the relative stability of the system. When it matters most to Americans, when the stakes are high and the issues profound, Americans vote in greater numbers. Furthermore, particular campaigns or local races may excite voters and increase turnout, as was the case in the Minnesota gubernatorial campaign of 1998 (http://www.fec.gov/). That excitement and enthusiasm, though, is a direct result of political candidates who engaged in new and interesting forms of discourse designed to energize voters. And when the citizenry becomes engaged, they may seek more active forums for the discussion of their views than the ballot box. Citizen action groups and on-line discussion groups offer voters another means of political expression that may be more personally empowering and meaningful than casting a vote. Even involvement in labor unions or political action committees offers citizens a better opportunity to contribute directly to and influence political debate than does voting (Herbst, 1996). At bottom, democratic action and citizen involvement take many forms in a diverse and complicated system, from working to better a local community center or support a day care facility to involvement with national campaigns or voting in every election.

★ POLITICAL COMMUNICATION AND THE AMERICAN COMMUNITY

Political communication in the United States is filled with policy discourse, generally results in the selection of effective leaders, and is increasingly democratized. And, despite attempts to delegitimize the rhetorical analysis of politics (Edwards, 1996), our political telos and practice are decidedly "rhetorical" as Bill Clinton and the emerging 2000 campaign reveal. Ultimately, this rhetorical system works to the benefit of the American political culture and highlights the role of rhetoric in the political process.

Borrowing from Isocrates and Cicero, Medhurst (1996) defines rather clearly what it means when rhetoric is conceived as a "way of being":

> . . . "rhetorical" refers to a general way
> of existing in the world—approaching the
> world as a rhetorical being who understands
> that few things in life are given or inalterably
> determined; one who understands that most
> things are amenable to choice and to selection
> from among several competing choices;
> one who understands that the ability to use
> symbols carries with it the power both to build
> and to destroy; one that believes that all of
> life is the domain of the rhetorical, not merely
> those formal occasions that call for speech or
> discourse; and one who comprehends that the
> truly important questions in life seldom lend
> themselves to clear-cut answers that can be
> held with absolute certainty. (p. 219)

This way of viewing political communication allows for a more productive and engaged critical standpoint toward this genre of discourse, one that gets past the cynicism so characteristic of most political communication scholarship. Seeing politics as a "rhetorical" phenomenon acknowledges the contingency and uncertainty of the process; a "rhetorical" politics appreciates the messiness of negative politics and contentious public deliberation and the popularization of political discourse.

In the wake of the Clinton presidency, the "rhetorical" is the central focus of political campaigns and is the crucial evaluative test used by observers of these quadrennial events.

Already, the communicative abilities of Al Gore, Bill Bradley, George W. Bush and the rest of the candidates in the 2000 election are a locus of political commentary. As one journalist noted, for instance, Gore's fundamental challenge is "telling his story to the American people" (Connolly, 1999). During an October 1999 National Press Club forum on gender and politics, two journalists reiterated the importance of candidate narratives in an effective campaign; Kathleen Hall Jamieson concluded, "the news media wants that narrative, which presumably helps create a sense of identification between the candidate and audience."

The "rhetorical" focus of political communication may be best represented by the repeated references to the "vision thing." Presidential "vision," Dallek (1996) maintains, requires "a balancing act, an ability to sell the country on a grand purpose . . . that would not carry it too far toward presidential control, national planning, or bold foreign commitments" (p. 2). To that end, George W. Bush speaks of "compassionate conservatism," filling in its contours with tax proposals that are beneficial to the working poor, references to Jesus Christ's influence in his life, and articulations of the need to integrate government and faith-based organizations. Bill Bradley asks Americans to consider the "essence of leadership" as he weaves together proposals for gun registration and universal health care with his own basketball career and his wife's successful struggle with breast cancer. John McCain's "vision" of reform and renewal involves dramatic proposals for campaign finance reform and compelling narratives about the candidate's captivity in Vietnam. And Al Gore offers a moderate's "vision" of an America progressing from the Clinton-Gore successes by moving to other pressing concerns, with the candidate as the fighter for "working families."

These candidates are all responding to the legacy of Bill Clinton and his ability to articulate a vision that had a grand purpose but also insured that government's growth and role was kept in check, and to master the other rhetorical arts so crucial for political success in an age of media proliferation. Jack Valenti, an LBJ advisor and speechwriter, remarked at a May 1999 Smithsonian Institution forum on presidential speechwriting that the "words of the president become even more important with TV." At that same forum, Clinton speechwriter Michael Waldman noted that most presidential words were not recorded in full in the past. Now, Waldman concluded, even what used to be known in White House speechwriting circles as "Rose Garden rubbish" is not only recorded *in toto*, but also is excerpted on the nightly news, forming the centerpiece of many broadcasts. Indeed, Clinton's rhetorical abilities have significantly raised the bar for future presidents and presidential contenders. Clinton's vision of a "Third Way" is so compelling that leaders around the globe (in Germany, Great Britain, and Israel, for instance), with the help of American political consultants, have parlayed that vision into electoral success. As Tony Snow, a Bush speechwriter and Fox News commentator, concluded at the Smithsonian seminar, "future presidents will go to school on Clinton," because of his unique rhetorical skill.

CONCLUSION

As scholars and commentators prepare to assess the 2000 campaign, and as they continue to reflect on the nature of political communication in the United States, they should not automatically assume an elitist fatalism toward political communication practices. Unfortunately, cynicism and sanctimony have become fashionable among journalists, pundits, and public intellectuals. An "antipolitics" bias is decidedly present in the news media (Patterson, 1996), supported and encouraged by the commentary of the academic "experts" regularly consulted by journalists. These appointed guardians of our political culture cling to a normative ideal of political discourse as purely rational, highly detailed, and devoid of emotional clutter and stylistic excess. In so doing, they ignore America's history, where public discussion and political debate have rarely, if ever, been predominantly "rational" (Ryan, 1992; Schudson, 1992, 1998). They forget that a political culture that values biography and character alongside public policy is a successful one. They forget that a political culture that values public choices and embraces the decision by its citizens not to participate is one that is stable and effective. And they neglect to recognize that when a political culture continues to offer its citizens more, not less, political information, advertising,

and oratory, that political culture is more, not less, democratic. Perhaps Condit (1987) put it best, when speaking of public morality: "Our stance, therefore, cannot be joyously optimistic; we can only deny the necessity of pessimism" (p. 88). We would even go further, and suggest that there is considerable evidence for optimism about the state of political communication in the United States.

A less cynical and more hopeful critical approach to political communication would not blithely accept political discourse or praise its quality. It should question, for instance, why political communication in America continues to be dominated by masculine themes and rhetorics of power. It should scrutinize the power of money on the political process and wonder why the far left is generally absent from public discussion while the far right is legitimated. Such criticism would explore why centrism prevails over more extreme views and how new technologies and new media affect political argument. But this criticism would also acknowledge and embrace the essence of politics as "rhetorical," with all of the uncertainty and complications and democratization such an acknowledgement entails.

Perhaps it is the existing puritanical impulses of the American psyche that motivates the incessant carping about political discourse in the United States. Maybe it is this lingering perfectionist, elitist tendency that seeks to drive out the base and popular for that which is arcane and idiosyncratic. But criticism of political discourse that follows this path runs the profound risk of eliminating from our discourse the power of political symbols to create a better, more democratic society for its citizens.

NOTES

[1] Gore's exact response in the first "debate" is instructive for its specificity. He said in the forum, "I put out a health care plan that reaches coverage for almost 90 percent of the American people. It gives coverage to 100 percent of all children. The cost is $146 billion over 10 years, and a prescription drug benefit is provided under Medicare for $118 billion over 10 years. Just today, the respected Emory School of Public Health came out with a nonpartisan analysis of both my plan and Senator Bradley's and they said that his plan costs $1.2 trillion. That is more than the entire surplus over the next 10 years. We have to look

ahead and save some of that surplus for Medicare." Bradley's response was to simply note that experts differ over the cost of the proposals (CNN, 1999).

2 Swanson (1997) argues that there is an evolving "political-media" complex that may yield a more fragmented electorate. He worries that media proliferation creates an electorate that is less informed and more diffuse. An alternative view might see expanded media options as a diffusion of media power, a breakdown of the "political-media" complex, and a democratizing influence beckoning more citizens into the political process by increasing the amount and relevance of political discourse.

3 President Clinton made clear the extent of the economic success in the U.S. when he renominated Alan Greenspan as Chair of the Federal Reserve on January 4, 2000. As Clinton noted, the United States is enjoying "strong economic growth with low inflation and low unemployment. Thanks to the hard work of the American people, we now enjoy the longest peacetime expansion in our history. In February, it will become the longest economic expansion ever. With productivity high, inflation low and real wages rising, it is more than the stock markets which have boomed. This has helped ordinary people all over America. We have a 30-year low in unemployment, a 32-year low in welfare, a 20-year low in poverty rates, the lowest African-American and Hispanic unemployment rates ever recorded, the lowest female unemployment rate in 40 years, the lowest single-parent household poverty in 46 years" (Clinton, 2000).

REFERENCES

Anonymous. (1996). *Primary Colors*. New York: Random House.

Ansolabehere, S., & Iyengar, S. (1995). *Going negative: How attacks ads shrink and polarize the electorate*. New York: The Free Press.

Balz, D. & Harris, J. F. (2000, January 6). Democrats spar over guns, health, ability. *Washington Post*, pp. A1, A4.

Bauer, G. (1999). On the issues. Retrieved October 12, 1999 from the World Wide Web: http:// www.bauer2k.com/html/issuesindex.html

Bennett, W. L. (1996). *The governing crisis: Media, money, and marketing in American elections*. 2d ed. New York: St. Martin's Press.

Benson, T. W. (1994). The first e-mail election: Electronic networking and the Clinton campaign. In S. A. Smith (Ed.) *Bill Clinton on stump, state, and stage: The rhetorical road to the White House* (pp. 315–340). Fayetteville: University of Arkansas Press.

Buchanan, B. (1996). *Renewing presidential politics: Campaigns, media, and the public interest*. Lanham, MD: Rowman & Littlefield.

Burns, J. M., & Sorenson, G. J. (1999). *Dead center: Clinton-Gore leadership and the perils of moderation*. New York: Scribner.

Burns, K. (1997, February 14). National press club luncheon. Retrieved October 27, 1999 from LEXIS-NEXIS Academic Universe database.

Cappella, J. N., & Jamieson, K. H. (1996). News frames, political cynicism, and media cynicism. *The Annals of the American Academy of Political and Social Science, 546*, 71–84.

CNN. (1999, October 27). First in the nation: A New Hampshire town meeting transcript, October 27, 1999. Atlanta, GA: CNN. Retrieved November 2, 1999 from the World Wide Web: http://www.cnn.com/ALLPOLITICS/ stories/1999/10/27/debate/transcript.html

CNN. (2000, January 7). Inside politics. Atlanta, GA: CNN. Retrieved January 10, 2000 from the World Wide Web: http://www.cnn.com/ TRANSCRIPTS/0001/07/ip.00.html

Clinton, B. (2000, January 4). Remarks of the president and Alan Greenspan in announcement of the renomination of Alan Greenspan as chairman of the Federal Reserve Board. Washington, DC: The White House. Retrieved January 6, 2000 from the World Wide Web: http:// www.pub.whitehouse. gov/uri-res/12R?urn:pdi://oma. eop.gov.us/2000/ l/4/7.text.1

Condit, C. M. (1987). Crafting virtue: The rhetorical construction of public morality. *Quarterly Journal of Speech, 73*, 79–97.

Connolly, C. (1999, May 18). For Gore, a more polished stump speech begins to bear fruit. *Washington Post*, p. A5.

Dallek, P. (1996). *Hail to the chief: The making and unmaking of American presidents*. New York: Hyperion.

Davis, R., & Owen, D. (1998). *New media and American politics*. New York: Oxford University Press.

Edwards III, G. C. (1996). Presidential rhetoric: What difference does it make? In M. J. Medhurst (Ed.) *Beyond the rhetorical presidency* (pp. 199–217). College Station: Texas A & M University Press.

Fallows, J. (1997). *Breaking the news: How the media undermine American democracy*. New York: Vintage Books.

Forbes, S. (1999, October 12). Forbes blasts Clinton, Greenspan for threatening the U.S. economy. Alexandria, VA: Forbes 2000. Retrieved October 12, 1999 from the World Wide Web: wysiwyg://66/http://www.forbes2000 . . . ages/ guestin.jsp?page=homepage.jsp

Freedman, P., Wood, W., & Lawton, D. (1999, October/November). Do's and don'ts of negative ads: What voters say. *Campaigns & Elections*, pp. 20–25.

Goldfarb, J. C. (1991). *The cynical society: The culture of politics and the polities of culture in American life.* Chicago: University of Chicago Press.

Gore, A. (1999). The Gore agenda: Improving health care for America's working families. Retrieved October 12, 1999 from the World Wide Web: wyaiwyg://19/http://www.AlGore2000.com/agenda/index.html

Hahn, D. F. (1987). The media and the presidency: Ten propositions. *Communication Quarterly, 35,* 254–266.

Hariman, R., & Beer, F. A. (1998). What would be prudent? Forms of reasoning in world politics. *Rhetoric & Public Affairs, 1,* 299–330.

Hart, R. P. (1994). *Seducing America: How television charms the modern voter.* New York: Oxford University Press.

Herbst, S. (1996). Public expression outside the mainstream. *The Annals of the American Academy of Political and Social Science, 546,* 120–131.

Jamieson, K. H. (1992). *Dirty politics: Deception, distraction, and democracy.* New York: Oxford University Press.

Johnson-Cartee, K. S., & Copeland, G. A. (1991). *Negative political advertising: Coming of age.* Hillsdale, NJ: Lawrence Erlbaum.

Kamber, V. (1997). *Poison politics: Are negative campaigns destroying democracy?* New York: Insight Books.

Kelly, M. (1999, December 1). Not ready for prime time? *Washington Post,* p. A43.

Kurtz, H. (1999, October 30). Clinton to field questions live in first online chat by a president. *Washington Post,* p. A9.

Maraniss, D. (1995). *First in his class: A biography of Bill Clinton.* New York: Simon & Schuster.

McCain, J. (1999). John McCain on the issues. Alexandria, VA: azfasnily.com. Retrieved October 12, 1999 from the World Wide Web: http://www.mccain2000.com/issues/papers.html

McGee, M. C. (1978). "Not men, but measures": The origins and import of an ideological principle. *Quarterly Journal of Speech, 64,* 141–154.

Medhurst, M. J. (1996). Afterword: The ways of rhetoric. In M. J. Medhurst (Ed.) *Beyond the rhetorical presidency* (pp. 218–226). College Station: Texas A & M University Press.

Milbank, D. (1999). Campaign journal: Seen but not heard. *New Republic.* Retrieved October 16, 1999 from the World Wide Web: http://www.tnr.com/magazines/tar/current/milbank110899.html

Murphy, J. M. (1998). Knowing the president: The dialogic evolution of the campaign history. *Quarterly Journal of Speech, 84,* 23–40.

National Journal (1999). *1999 polling on President Clinton's job approval rating and 1999 fav/unfav polling on President Clinton.* Washington, DC: National Journal. Retrieved October 16, 1999 from the World Wide Web: http://www.cloakroom.com/members/p . . . ack/ national/clinton/clintonja.html

Neal, T. (1999, November 5). Bush falters in foreign policy quiz. *Washington Post,* pp. A1, A19.

Nimmo, D. (1970). *The political persuaders: The techniques of modern election campaigns.* Englewood Cliffs, NJ: Prentice-Hall.

Parry-Giles, T. (1996). Character, the Constitution, and the ideological embodiment of "civil rights" in the 1967 nomination of Thurgood Marshall to the Supreme Court. *Quarterly Journal of Speech, 82,* 364–382.

Patterson, T. E. (1993). *Out of order.* New York: Knopf.

Patterson, T. E. (1996). Bad news, bad governance. *The Annals of the American Academy of Political and Social Science, 546,* 97–108.

Renshon, S. A. (1998). *High hopes: The Clinton presidency and the politics of ambition.* New York: Routledge.

Ryan, M. P. (1992). Gender and public access: Women's politics in nineteenth-century America. In C. Calhoun (Ed.) *Habermas and the public sphere* (pp. 259–288). Cambridge, MA: MIT Press.

Sabato, L. J. (1981). *The rise of political consultants: New ways of winning elections.* New York: Basic Books.

Sabato, L. J. (1991). *Feeding frenzy: How attack journalism transformed American politics.* New York: Free Press.

Salvador, M. (1998). Practicing democracy. In M. Salvador and P. M. Sias (Eds.) *The public voice in a democracy at risk* (pp. 3–10). Westport, CT: Praeger.

Schudson, M. (1992). Was there ever a public sphere? If so, when? Reflections on the American case. In C. Calhoun (Ed.) *Habermas and the public sphere* (pp. 143–163). Cambridge, MA: MIT Press.

Schudson, M. (1998). *The good citizen: A history of American civic life.* New York: Free Press.

Sigelman, L. (1992). There you go again: The media and the debasement of American politics. *Communication Monographs, 59,* 407–410.

Swanson, D. L. (1997). The political-media complex at 50. *American Behavioral Scientist, 40,* 1264–1282.

Walker, M. (1996). *The president we deserve: Bill Clinton, his rise, falls, and comebacks.* New York: Crown.

Weaver, D. H. (1996). What voters learn from media. *The Annals of the American Academy of Political and Social Science, 546,* 34–47.

Zarefsky, D. (1992). Spectator politics and the revival of public argument. *Communication Monographs, 59,* 411–414.

CHAPTER 2
Election Campaigns

The electoral process

in the United States provides a lens through which observers may view the history and contemporary structure of American political life. Essays in this chapter guide readers through the fascinating world of elections, campaigns, and candidate strategies. They present useful historical background, including the advent of television, political speeches, and primary "surfacing." They discuss how elections are driven, who votes and who does not, and the development of the modern campaign. Overall, this chapter provides an overview of the political process and how campaigns and candidates use television technology to present their messages.

Judith S. Trent's 1978 work, "Presidential Surfacing: The Ritualistic and Crucial First Act," describes the process by which candidates "surface" as contenders and front-runners. Using the 1978 presidential nomination as a case study, Trent argues that the process must be carefully planned and, most important, intricately timed to capture the attention and

imagination of the electorate. The essay details how the surfacing candidate must live up to the electorate's expectations concerning character and establish additional expectations about the specific campaign. According to Trent, the candidate who understands the dramas that must be played out during the early campaign process inevitably receives the nomination.

Michael Gurevitch and Anandam P. Kavoori's 1992 essay, "Television Spectacles as Politics," investigates voter disenchantment. The authors suggest that television spectacles create rhetorical exigencies and frame issues in ways that create opportunities to open the public sphere and regenerate democracy, but can represent the metamorphosis of the public sphere into a derisory show, a circus for the crowd rather than a forum for engaged citizens. Although politics has always involved display, postmodern political spectacle goes farther, reducing public discourse to irrelevant debates that obscure real social issues and are consumed as entertainment by spectators. Media tend to cover political contests as they would sporting events, trying to convince the public that politics are, indeed, as exciting as the World Series or Super Bowl.

Kathleen E. Kendall's 1995 essay, "The Problems of Beginnings in New Hampshire: Control over the Play," from her edited volume *Presidential Campaign Discourse: Strategic Communication Problems*, investigates the communication strategies and problems that presidential candidates confront, especially during the early primary period. The author discusses the decisions that candidates must make about speeches, interviews, free media, and political ads. Foremost in the work, however, is the news media's propensity to cover the New Hampshire primary as a dramatic conflict and to focus on coverage of candidates' personal traits and on the contest (or horserace) itself rather than on candidates' positions on the issues. The author also notes that subsequent media coverage of the election after the New Hampshire primary tends to dramatically decline, despite the influence of that primary upon the presidential nomination process.

Trevor Parry-Giles and Shawn J. Parry-Giles's 1996 essay, "Political Scopophilia, Presidential Campaigning, and the Intimacy of American Politics," further explores the concept of the angry, disinterested electorate. Scopophilia is defined as excitement or arousal from viewing acts or people or, in this case, a voyeuristic view of politics. There have been several attempts to find the culprits responsible for the decline in voter turnout at the polls. The authors suggest that the tendency for campaigns and television coverage to present a more intimate view of the candidate may create a sense of "scopophiliac shame" with the electorate, which could result in a guilty and angry electorate, disgusted with the process and apathetic towards elections. They suggest that much of the blame for voter disgust might belong in the way candidates present themselves.

Lynda Lee Kaid's 2003 essay, "Effects of Political Information in the 2000 Presidential Campaign: Comparing Traditional Television and Internet Exposure," explores the growing use of the Internet in political campaigns and compares its impact on voters to that of more traditional media. The article suggests that Internet exposure may result in different evaluations of candidates, but may not diminish the electorate's level of political cynicism. The Internet does seem to encourage voters to seek out other sources of information concerning the candidate. This is one of the first studies to compare the effect of television viewing with that of Internet surfing as a means of political communication.

Presidential Surfacing: The Ritualistic and Crucial First Act

Judith S. Trent

"Presidential Fever," for many years a symbolic and compelling drama playing approximately every four years in a few carefully selected theatres throughout the United States, has recently undergone significant change and expansion. Although producers have more than doubled the size of the cast, taken the show on nation-wide tours, and extended the season so that one company opens when another closes, they have also confused the audience so that by opening night they might not recognize that the first act has begun. Actors might even deny their role in the drama, or produce dialogue so inconsistent with behavior that they are no longer credible players.

Examples of the confusion are numerous. In a 1974 Texas production, an actor who had spent almost a year trying to make himself visible by speaking and meeting producers and critics in thirty states called a press conference to announce that he was "flattered by the attention the possibility of my becoming a presidential contender has been given."[1] The same year, this time in Georgia, a bit player from Plains decided he needed national exposure and so became the Chairman of the Democratic National Campaign. He visited thirty states, campaigned for sixty candidates, and then announced that he was a candidate for President because he had discovered that only a non-nationally oriented candidate could bring the American people a government as decent, loving, and compassionate as themselves. Again in 1974, a California actor who had just finished visiting thirty-four states to raise campaign funds and to "audition" his "Presidential appeal," called a press conference to announce that he had not yet decided whether he was interested in the role.[2] And in October, 1975, from a circus tent production staged in a winter-wheat field on his farm in Shirkieville, an Indiana actor who had just finished raising campaign funds in twenty states began his first act by denying any deep interest in the part when he said, "those of you who have known me longest know I never had any burning desire to be President of the United States."[3]

As these examples illustrate, the first act of the drama "Presidential Fever" has become confused and confusing to the audience. Yet the first act is crucial if the players are to be credible and the drama is to be understood. It is precisely because of the importance of the first act to American political theatre that its examination is necessary.

Therefore the purpose of this essay is to explore the process by which people sought to emerge as contenders for the presidential nomination of a major political party in 1976. To accomplish this, I shall examine theoretically "surfacing" in light of recently imposed constraints or changes, and then analyze the probable impact of the changes on the process as it was developed by the 1976 presidential candidates.

★ SURFACING: THEORETICAL ASSUMPTIONS AND RHETORICAL FUNCTIONS

Any attempt to understand "surfacing" must begin by viewing the concept within the total context of a campaign and within the constraints imposed on the 1976 scene by party and federal rules changes. If it can be assumed that contemporary[4] presidential campaigns pass through relatively discrete periods or acts that can be categorized roughly as pre-primary, primary, convention, and general election, "surfacing" occurs in the first act or pre-primary period. This period varies in length, according to candidates' perceptions of their national visibility and credibility, financial backing, and organizational strength. "Surfacing" begins with candidates' initial efforts to create a presidential interest and image for themselves in the public imagination, and extends through a variety of public rhetorical transactions to the New Year's day prior to the first state delegate caucus (in 1976, Iowa's) and/or to the first primary election, traditionally New Hampshire's. Although transactions may vary from candidate to candidate and campaign year to campaign year, predictable rhetorical activities include building state organizations, speaking to many different kinds of public gatherings in an attempt to capture media attention, conducting public opinion polls to assess visibility or to determine potential issues for which stands will later have to be devised, putting together an organizational structure and campaign "blueprint," raising money, and announcing to the media that they are, or could be, or might be, or are flattered to be considered a presidential contender. Thus, "surfacing" is defined in this essay as the series of predictable and specifically timed rhetorical transactions which serve consummatory and instrumental functions during the pre-primary phase of the campaign.

Changes in the Rules

It would be pointless to analyze the surfacing process of a presidential campaign without acknowledging the constraints imposed on it by changes in campaign financing and delegate selection. The new rules became so important to the pre-primary and primary stages of the campaign that any study of the 1976 presidential election must become, in one sense, a study of their probable impact.

The Federal Election Campaign Act of 1974 changed much of the character of surfacing. The Act provided for voluntary income tax check-offs and, beginning January 2, 1976, the United

States Treasury used these funds to provide matching grants to candidates who had raised $5000, in amounts of $250 or less, from citizens in at least twenty states.[5]

Suddenly, "running for President" became a possibility for people who were not wealthy. A month before the New Hampshire primary, twelve people had become serious enough presidential contenders to have received federal matching funds. No previous election year in political history had generated as much participation.

Not only did the finance law aid in changing the political landscape, it also added an important constraint to the drama. No longer could presidential hopefuls rely on the traditional "fat cats" who always financed "favored" candidates. Qualifying for federal funds forced the candidates to establish themselves among small donors in a number of states. This was a handicap for some and an advantage to others, but it was important to all candidates and affected the progression and outcome of the campaign.

Reform rules, adopted by the Democratic Party and, to a lesser extent, by the Republican Party, forced changes in state laws regarding delegate selection which were to have significance almost equal to changes in federal law. Under the rules adopted before the 1976 campaign, the caucus-convention procedure was wide open for participation by everyone, and any candidates who could inspire a following had a chance to win delegates. By changing the process of delegate selection, political reformers aided in reshaping the presidential nominating system. In 1968, more than half of the delegates at the Democratic Nominating Convention had come from thirty-four caucus states, but by 1976 seventy-seven percent of the delegates at the Democratic Convention came from thirty primary states, reducing the strength of delegates from caucus states to 704 of the 3008 delegates. What happened, of course, was that the type of persons who made decisions on presidential nominees was altered, and candidates had to appeal to a new audience. Through 1968, the audience for Democratic candidates had been party leaders and heads of groups which supported the party. By 1976, the audience had changed drastically for the Democrats

(less for the Republicans), and presidential contenders were forced to consider entering and campaigning in many of the thirty primaries. No longer could candidates rely primarily on the once powerful party bosses for the nomination. The impact of this constraint on the first act was considerable.

The Role of Timing

Presidential surfacing is not a hit-or-miss affair. Surfacing activities always have been carefully planned and timed, but the changes in campaign financing and delegate selection resulted in making the element of timing even more important.

The role of "timing in human discourse is determined by exigencies within a so-called 'rhetorical situation,' which can grow, mature and decay through chronological time."[6] Rhetorical timing involves "essentially evolving events, that is, events which progress through time and which demand a series of strategic decisions regarding when to speak, what to say, how to say it and from what posture or stance to deliver the sentiments."[7] Similarly, surfacing refers to factors which interact with other elements in the environment to determine what rhetorical action is needed by what receivers at what place and at what time. Timing is as crucial to the transactions involved in presidential surfacing as it is to other areas of human discourse. Such factors as how long it will take to raise enough money to qualify for federal matching funds, or how long it will take to organize a dedicated corps of volunteer workers in the early caucus and primary states are obviously important to the process.

Equally significant is the relationship of timing to the difficult act of officially emerging or announcing candidacy. Should candidates announce before they have raised money and stirred volunteers in the early primary states? Will candidates who announce too early receive little or no attention from the media and thus the public? Can candidates delay announcement of their intentions until it is too late to compete with public attention focused on earlier and already known contenders by the media? A candidate's first steps onto the presidential stage may be damaged irreparably if these questions are not answered correctly.

Perhaps the importance of timing to the first act is illustrated best by candidates who had a poor sense of timing and entered the stage off-cue. Gerald Ford, for example, might have been spared some of the agonies of the Republican primary election had he not let people believe he was not interested in a term of his own when he took office in August, 1974. It was eleven months later, in July, 1975, that Ford officially announced his candidacy. Throughout late spring and early summer of 1975, Ronald Reagan had been quietly gaining the support around the country that he needed to launch his own campaign. Reagan's support might never have materialized had Ford understood the nuances of timing in the presidential theatre.[8] Or consider the cases of Frank Church and Jerry Brown. Each delayed official entry to the competition until it was almost over. Each made a grand entrance and stole a few scenes, but by the time he announced his candidacy, the first act was already controlled by Jimmy Carter, a contender who seemed to have a better understanding of timing for the 1976 campaign.

The Rhetorical Functions

Not only can surfacing be understood as a series of predictable and specifically timed rhetorical events, but also in terms of the important consummatory (symbolic and ritualistic) and instrumental (pragmatic) functions it must serve.[9] If the first act fails in either its symbolic or pragmatic roles, there may be no second act.

During the campaign, especially the earliest portions, the electorate draws inferences from campaign actions about each candidate's fitness for office. Although there is not a one-to-one relationship between the two, campaign actions are taken as symbolic of actions as President. Americans do not want Presidents who hit their heads on helicopter doors, fall down steps, wear suits with trousers that are too short, or mispronounce words. These are behaviors that cause a candidate to be characterized as "clumsy," "stumbling," "dumb," and "graceless," as Gerald Ford was labeled during the surfacing period of the 1976 campaign.[10]

Certain rituals are expected during the surfacing or pre-primary stage, just as others are expected in later stages of the campaign, because the electorate has preconceptions of how a person becomes a presidential candidate. For example, the candidate is expected to call a press conference, announce intentions, and embark immediately on a campaign swing to the early primary and/or caucus states.[11]

The ritualistic requirements of surfacing are not trivial. Candidates must announce early so that decision-makers have time to consider them; they must begin campaigning immediately after the announcement to demonstrate their commitment, sincerity, and ability to persevere during a long campaign. The importance of the ritualistic requirements is best illustrated when a tradition is broken, as it was in the case of Terry Sanford. He announced his intention to run for President on May 29, 1975, but followed his announcement by continuing in his job at Duke University and neither campaigned nor planned to campaign until January, 1976. Sanford probably received more media coverage when he withdrew from the campaign twenty-three days later than he had as a candidate.[12] He had deviated from the script which dictates that the announcement of candidacy be followed by a campaign trip and his candidacy received little attention.

Surfacing plays three instrumental or pragmatic functions in the opening night drama which are crucial to later stages of the campaign: (1) public expectations about candidates begin to be established; (2) important issues or themes of the campaign begin to emerge; and (3) front runners or serious contenders begin to be determined.

It is during the surfacing period that a candidate must begin living up to the electorate's expectations about honesty, candor, physical and emotional stamina, intelligence, humor, and grace. Obviously, these are in part symbolic, but just as clearly they have instrumental aspects. Not only must candidates live up to prior expectations, but through their rhetoric during the surfacing stage they help establish additional expectations about the specific campaign in which they are engaged. In 1976, the earliest candidates (Carter and Udall) set the standard—candidates had to enter all or a large number of the primaries, and personally campaign in each primary and/or caucus state in which their names had been entered. Candidates who failed to live up to these expectations soon were dropped from the competition.

As the early candidates crisscross the country, they begin to come to grips with the issues which are on people's minds, begin to address themselves to these issues, begin to formulate "solutions" to problems which seem compatible with popular perception, and with the help of the media begin translating these problems or positions into national issues. Thus the rhetorical agenda to which subsequent candidates must in some way adhere begins to be established. If these early concerns are widespread enough, as were the 1976 themes of trust and anti-Washington sentiment, they can become the dominant issues in succeeding stages of the campaign.

The final function the first act provides is beginning the process of selecting front runners and separating serious contenders from the not-so-serious. Developing as a leading candidate involves far more than fulfilling the ritualistic and/or symbolic requirements. Becoming a serious contender during the surfacing period involves visibility, and obtaining visibility requires persuading the national media that one is a viable enough candidate to deserve attention.[13]

Almost from the beginning of the first act, the media influence strongly who will be considered a major candidate, who will be the hero of the political melodrama.[14] Although extensive coverage is guaranteed to the candidates who do well in the first caucus and primary states, visibility during the surfacing period is often the initial reaction of the media to a candidate's past or present self. This was illustrated in 1976 when both Wallace and Humphrey, because of previous roles, were selected by the media as serious candidates and were accorded early, frequent, and fairly extensive attention.

Who candidates are and the office they hold also aid in determining initial visibility. Henry Jackson and Birch Bayh were considered leading contenders during the first act of 1976 because of their positions in the United States Senate. On the other hand, Sargent Shriver, Terry Sanford, Fred Harris, and Jimmy Carter were not thought of as serious candidates by the media because they did not currently hold powerful governmental positions.

Quite apart from persuading the national media that one is a front runner because of past roles and present positions, a candidate now must emerge from the surfacing period as a possible leading contender through successful grass roots organizing and fund raising. Acquiring sufficient money to generate the momentum necessary to do well in the primaries has long been a key factor in presidential campaigns, but with the advent of the 1974 campaign finance law, motivating enough support to raise the money to qualify for federal matching funds became crucial.

These, then, are the necessary functions of the pre-primary period. The difference between a successful and unsuccessful first act may be simply a matter of candidates understanding the generic constraints and demands of the role they seek. Certainly in the 1976 pre-primary period, it was essential for candidates to come to grips with the rhetorical manifestations of the new laws which had been imposed on the scene. Failure to comprehend the specialized nuances of timing and failure to use the period to fulfill the necessary instrumental and consummatory functions resulted in defeat. Only the successful were able to proceed to the second act of the drama.

★ SURFACING: THE 1976 PATTERNS

When the curtain went up for the first act of Campaign '76, the opening night audience was astonished to see not one or two leading characters, but eighteen of them, each wanting to be heard, each scrambling for a share of the spotlight. From beginning to end, the drama turned into a comedy of errors as candidates crisscrossed the country, tripping over each other at shopping malls, health centers, factory gates, and town squares. The contenders debated each other, ignored each other, challenged each other, and as one dropped out of the race another entered. While each candidate tried to occupy center stage, the audience yawned. As one contender told reporters, "it looks to me as if we may give an election and nobody will come."[15]

Presidential surfacing was a fascinating rhetorical phenomenon during the 1976 campaign.

Obviously, it was interesting because of the sheer number who announced their intentions. But less obviously, the first act was interesting because old traditions were broken and because those contenders who were successful appeared to have an understanding of the new generic constraints and functions and their relationship to the entire campaign.

The first, and perhaps initially the most interesting, development during the pre-primary period was the large number of candidates, especially on the Democratic side. Beginning with Morris Udall on November 22, 1974, and concluding with Frank Church on March 18, 1976, fourteen presidential hopefuls surfaced, announced, continued running, or withdrew.[16] Each of the fourteen who surfaced[17] made some kind of an announcement of intentions to a press he had asked to assemble. There were vast differences in the way in which they made their candidacies public, but all conformed to the ritual of announcing intentions long before the nominating conventions.

Ronald Reagan said he was running for President because the nation needed to embark on a new, constructive course, presumably a course which only he and not the current Republican President was able to set. For good measure, Reagan not only gave his announcement speech once, he gave it three times. The first was at the National Press Club in D.C., the second in Manchester, New Hampshire, and the third in Miami. Gerald Ford, on the other hand, apparently viewed the official announcement of his entry into the race as a low-key affair. He called a small group of pool reporters into the Oval Office for five minutes, promised to run an "open and above-board campaign," and introduced his campaign leaders as "outstanding Americans on whose integrity both my supporters and all others can depend."[18] Eight months later, Jerry Brown also saw the official announcement as a "no-speech," mini-media event. The Governor called four newsmen into his office for a rambling chat, and said he would run a "full and serious favorite-son campaign because no clear-cut front-runner had emerged from the early primaries" and because his "new ideas and fresh thoughts deserved a hearing."[19]

Conversely, two of the candidates viewed the announcement ritual as full-fledged media spectaculars, complete with setting and long-time supporters cheering them on. Birch Bayh set up a circus tent on his family farm in Indiana.[20] Frank Church, with his wife at his side, and red, white, and blue streamers fluttering in the wind, stood on the wooden steps of the Boise County Courthouse in Idaho City where his father-in-law had announced his candidacy for governor in 1940, and told the assembled group that "The odds [are never] too great to try. In that spirit the West was won and in that spirit I now declare my candidacy."[21]

Two of the more veteran presidential candidates handled the public statement of intention quite differently. Henry Jackson ran a paid political announcement on national television in which he talked about the neglected agenda in the country that cried out for leadership and demanded something better than stop-gap action when a crisis develops.[22] And Hubert Humphrey called a press conference in the Old Senate Caucus Room to tell the nation tearfully that he would not run, but that he would not suppress a draft.[23]

Of greater interest than the traditional announcement ritual performed by all of the presidential hopefuls were the five changes or breaks from tradition enacted by the contenders. These changes were peculiar to the 1976 campaign and were, in large part, the result of constraints imposed by rule modifications in delegate selection and campaign financing. Taken together, these changes may provide predictive generalizations about future presidential surfacing, and thus demand to be examined.

The first and perhaps most striking phenomenon was that in the 1976 campaign, presidential hopefuls declared their candidacies far earlier than had their predecessors. Of the thirteen who surfaced nationally and announced their entry into the race (Humphrey surfaced but announced he would not be a candidate), two formally announced fifteen months before the first primary, four others declared themselves a year before New Hampshire, and five entered officially within five to six months before the first competition.

Not only did candidates make formal announcements earlier than had been the custom, the vast majority of them had surfaced long before they announced. In other words, as much as two years in advance of the first primary, presidential hopefuls were campaigning all over the country. While previous candidates for President had contacted party leaders and had campaigned for state and/or congressional candidates in advance of New Hampshire, the 1976 contenders were out raising money and speaking at every conceivable public gathering long before the curtain had officially opened.

Carter claimed he had campaigned in 175 cities and towns in forty states six months before the first primary. Wallace raised more than four million dollars by the time he announced. Reagan visited and organized "Citizens for Reagan Committees" in thirty-four states. Udall crisscrossed the country many times before New Hampshire. Bentsen and Jackson raised over one million dollars before they announced. Bayh spoke in twenty states in an effort to raise campaign funds before declaring his candidacy, and even Humphrey, who had said he would not be an active candidate, accepted speaking engagements in a number of primary states.

By the time the congressional campaign of 1974 was over, the presidential campaign had begun. Of course, the change in campaign financing was the primary reason for early national campaigning. Candidates had to be out raising money to qualify for federal matching funds. Perhaps Robert J. Keefe, Henry Jackson's campaign manager, summarized the reason for early and extensive national campaigning best when he said in 1975, "We've built basically our whole campaign concept around the new election law and have concentrated on raising money most of this year."[24]

The third change was more complex. The campaign, from beginning to end, seemed to revolve around disassociation from Washington, which was, in a sense, a response to the scandals of Watergate. Perhaps the clearest manifestation of what the Watergate scandals had done to American faith in the government and the presidency was the insistence of candidates in talking about their personal honesty and integrity. Gerald Ford, for example, in a pre-announcement interview with columnist Joseph Kraft said that his record to date made him "entitled to trust." He also said that "people

know what I've done. They know I'm an honest man."[25] Jimmy Carter seemed to have based the crux of his early campaign on the issue of his personal honesty and integrity.[26]

Not only were candidates campaigning on their honesty, they tried mightily to show that they were not a part of the Washington establishment. As Martin Schram pointed out, "Anti-Washington had become the gospel of Campaign '76."[27] Jimmy Carter, of course, understood long before he announced his candidacy that his status as an "outsider" would be an asset. Fred Harris also contributed to the "populist" rhetoric with his angry shouts against Washington. By the time of New Hampshire, Morris Udall had begun focusing his campaign on the anti-establishment sentiment by using one of the nonpoliticians, former Watergate Special Prosecutor Archibald Cox, who had helped bring down the "crowd of politicians" who had created the crisis of leadership in Washington.[28] And the few early contenders who, because of their prior affiliation with the Washington establishment, could not claim suddenly to be "fresh faces" or "outsiders" suggested that experience in government was the crucial issue of the campaign. Birch Bayh, for example, used television to try and refute the anti-politician sentiment. In one such attempt, Bayh was shown staring straight at the camera, speaking against a stark backdrop and saying:

> To listen to the other candidates, none of them are politicians. Even the ones who've held public office say they're not politicians. Well I'm Birch Bayh—and I'm a politician. It took a good politician to stop Nixon's plan to pack the Supreme Court. And it's going to take a good politician to break up the big oil companies, to get jobs for unemployed workers and hold food prices in line. The question isn't whether you're a politician, but what kind of politician you are. Because it takes a good politician to make a good President.[29]

With this appeal and others like them, candidates such as Bayh, Jackson, and Ford sought to lure voters away from the virtually unprecedented campaign theme that to be experienced in the knowledge and mechanisms of the Federal government was a disadvantage.

The fact that they did not succeed was the painful legacy of Watergate.

The fourth variation from tradition was the attempt of candidates to build state organizations during the surfacing period. Although this strategy was apparent in George McGovern's 1972 campaign, in 1976 many of the candidates worked at state-by-state organization.[30] Jimmy Carter, for example, spent three months campaigning and organizing in New Hampshire prior to the state's primary. As Carter told of his efforts in New Hampshire, he said:

> I would say we had far superior organizational structure to Udall and the rest in New Hampshire. . . . We kind of played it down—we never bragged about it—but it was there. We contacted 95 percent of the Democratic homes in New Hampshire. And it was a tedious person-to-person relationship.[31]

Carter may have been the most successful at early state-by-state organizing, but he was joined in the effort by many of the other contenders. Fred Harris traveled in a Winnebago camper to fourteen states in an effort to raise enough funds and interest in his candidacy to build volunteer organizations in individual states. Before George Wallace even announced his presidential intentions, his county organizations in the non-primary states were thoroughly trained and were attracting "hundreds of precinct-level volunteers."[32] Henry Jackson concentrated on building state organizations and raising money through direct mail appeals and through countless public appearances at Democratic dinners throughout the country. In fact, he even hired a "speech coach" to help him sound "less dull" as he planned and prepared his early campaign strategy for what he believed would be the "key" states.[33] Ronald Reagan spent the summer of 1975 speaking in thirty-four states and organizing volunteer groups throughout the country. Morris Udall realized the importance and did a great deal of early grass-roots organizing. It was just that, early as he was, Jimmy Carter frequently seemed to have been there first, and in a much stronger, more organized position.

Morris Udall was the first candidate to announce for the presidency. But his campaign, from beginning to end, was a series of organizational disasters. In Iowa, for example, Udall, like Carter, was there early and invested heavily in the state in both campaign time and money because he hoped to build the kind of state organization that would give him a head start over his competition. However, the early Udall efforts in Iowa achieved little. His staff was not organized, argued with each other, and even lost a master list of people who had attended Democratic caucuses in the state. Perhaps the following memorandum from Udall's national campaign manager to the candidate and his brother described the situation best:

> To: Mo, Stewart
> From: Jack Quinn
> December 9, 1975
> Re: Areas of immediate Concern
> . . . We've got a reputation, frankly, as the sloppiest campaign in memory. No one knows who is in charge, who can make a quick decision that will stick.
> . . . Moreover, we're genuinely in danger of splitting this campaign into warring factions—anyone who disagrees should give Mankiewicz a call and ask him what happened in 1972 to a campaign which was hopelessly split among headquarters and congressional staff. . . .[34]

The point is that early state-by-state organization by numerous candidates was an important alteration in pre-primary campaigning. Although not all contenders were equally successful, more attempts were made than had been the case in the past. There was, of course, an important reason for the change. The radical shift in delegate selection had made pre-primary state campaigning and organization crucial. The appeal of the primaries was great—delegates could be won in thirty states. And the candidate who campaigned state-by-state organizing support and building local teams of workers had the best chance of winning a large share of the delegates and thus the nomination. Those who had not built state organizations during the surfacing period never came close to capturing the lead from those candidates who had. As Birch Bayh said when he thought back to his defeat in the New Hampshire primary, "I should have been out working like Carter and Udall were doing all summer. I should have been visible."[35]

The fifth surfacing change in 1976 was that Democratic candidates did not depend on endorsements from party, business, and labor leaders. It wasn't that the candidates turned down public endorsements; they simply did not rely on them as successful candidates had done in the past. The 1976 aspirants took their case directly to the people. Birch Bayh, for example, received some early endorsements from labor, but Bayh also campaigned in twenty states. Carter received no endorsements from party leaders until long after the surfacing period. Although Morris Udall sought eagerly the endorsement of Archibald Cox, the Watergate prosecutor was a non-Washington and a non-Democratic establishment figure. The overall strategy for the majority of the 1976 contenders was to appeal to the public at large, not to small groups of party leaders or "kingmakers."

There were some exceptions. A few candidates had strong ties to the traditional power structure of the two major political parties and perceived endorsements from these leaders as instrumental in determining who the nominees would be. This was obviously the strategy of Hubert Humphrey and, to a lesser extent, Sargent Shriver. Humphrey, after all, had received the 1968 nomination without ever entering a primary and was the pre-primary favorite of most party leaders in 1976. Shriver depended on his Kennedy connections for public support. For each of these men, reliance on the more traditional strategy may have been the only option which seemed possible at the time.

But Campaign '76 was not the traditional campaign. Some of the old rituals were there, but it was a new process and endorsements were part of the old system. The delegates would not allow a brokered convention where the party bosses would bestow the nomination on their favorite. Obviously, the Carters, the Browns, the Sanfords, the Reagans could not win in that system. Only by entering primaries and winning delegate support could the "fresh faces" of 1976 be successful. And while only two men ultimately succeeded in capturing the nominations of their parties, the fact that one of them represented a severe break with tradition, the fact that this man was not the candidate of party leaders, and the fact that he had secured the nomination by taking his campaign directly to the electorate provides sufficient support to conclude that public endorsements did not play the role in the 1976 pre-primary campaign they once had.

CONCLUSION

Surfacing was an especially important phenomenon of the 1976 campaign; perhaps more than any other it was affected by the changes in campaign financing and delegate selection. Hence, any rhetorical examination of how the first act was produced in 1976 ultimately becomes a study of the ways in which candidates accepted or did not accept, understood or did not understand the constraints and functions of the drama. New patterns emerged. It was during the first act that candidates could begin to conform to the public's image of a President. It was during the first act that candidates could announce campaigns, begin raising enough money to qualify for federal matching funds and thus force consideration as "serious" presidential contenders. It was during the first act that candidates could not only discover the issues which were on the public mind but could aid in determining the agenda for succeeding stages. And it was during the first act that candidates who understood the importance of timing to campaigning could lay the groundwork for the entire second act.

The new constraints demanded that the old traditions be broken. Some of the contenders never understood this demand and soon disappeared from the scene. A few of the candidates seemed reluctant to part with old traditions and they too were dropped from the production. But as the first act passed to the second and third, it became increasingly evident that one man, the bit player from Plains, who had spent fifteen months understanding the constraints of the drama and the demands of the role he sought, and who had aided in producing a profound change in political theatre, was to win the award of the Academy of American Electorate, President of the United States.

NOTES

[1] Senator Lloyd Bentsen made this statement at a press conference he called following a speech at a

fund-raising dinner in Wichita, Kansas. See: Ray Morgan, "G.O.P. Economics," *Kansas City Star,* October 6, 1974, p. 4-A.

2 Although Ronald Reagan had been interested in the presidency since 1968, he maintained that he had not wanted to run in 1976 because he realized that a challenge to a sitting President might "disembowel" the Republican Party. In an interview in which he explained his decision to challenge Ford, Reagan said, "No one in this country prayed harder than I did that Ford would be so successful there wouldn't be any need for me to make a decision." See: James M. Naughton, "Campaign without a Knockout Punch," *The New York Times Magazine,* June 6, 1976, pp. 15–65.

3 Senator Birch Bayh made this statement in his announcement speech in Indiana. Bayh had made a brief try for the White House in 1971, but dropped out when his wife underwent surgery for cancer. See: "All-American Boy," *Newsweek,* December 29, 1975, pp. 17–18.

4 For a number of reasons, John F. Kennedy's 1960 presidential campaign is often considered the beginning of "modern" presidential campaigning. Certainly, the idea of the pre-primary period and its relationship to the total campaign effort had its real start in the Kennedy campaign. See: Carl P. Leubsdorf, "The Reporter and the Presidential Candidate," *The Annals of the American Academy of Political and Social Science,* 427 (1976), pp. 2–3.

5 Although the Supreme Court later declared several important sections of the act unconstitutional, the thrust of the original 1974 act established the tone for planning and budgeting the campaigns of the early presidential contenders. See: Joseph Napolitan, "Media Costs and Effects in Political Campaigns," *The Annals of the American Academy of Political and Social Science,* 427 (1976), 114–124.

6 Bruce E. Gronbeck, "Rhetorical Timing in Public Communication," *Central States Speech Journal,* 25 (1974), 85.

7 Ibid., p. 86.

8 Naughton.

9 See Bruce E. Gronbeck, "The Functions of Presidential Campaigning," pp. 268–280, for detailed descriptions of these functions.

10 Throughout his tenure as President, Ford had problems with what advisors called his "competency package," his bland style, his preference for "plain language," and his propensity for bumping his head. In fact, the White House was so sensitive to public ridicule of the President that on one campaign trip to Orlando, a "Presidential operative was assigned to make certain a Mickey Mouse character

from Walt Disney World did not get within photographers' range of Ford." See: Naughton, p. 60.

11 Although ritualistic expectations specify certain behaviors they do not appear to specify the content of these behaviors. A candidate must announce his intentions publicly, but how he goes about it is not dictated. A candidate may, of course, make some unwise decisions (announce his candidacy at a time when another contender has all but won the competition or announce his intentions in a manner that does not guarantee much media coverage), but so long as there is no failure to perform the required acts, the candidate has a chance to emerge as a person of "presidential timber."

12 Malcolm G. Scully, "A University President Ends His Run for the White House," *The Chronicle of Higher Education,* February 2, 1976, p. 3.

13 Leubsdorf, pp. 2–7.

14 According to Weaver, "Winners in the early primaries were given the role of front-runner cast as the hero of the play. As television now defines him, the front-runner isn't simply the candidate with the most votes; he is a person who by virtue of his success has the character of a winner. He is 'serene.' Everything goes well for him; his campaign organization works efficiently, his book account is flush, his issues take hold, his opponents go on the defensive and fall by the wayside. As a result, his candidacy has 'momentum,' and in time he has what CBS's Ed Rable called 'the kind of invincibility that assures a candidate the nomination.' In short, the alchemy of television news' melodramatic imperative transforms a winner into a winner-type and victory into evidence of absolute invincibility." Quoted from: Paul H. Weaver, "Captives of Melodrama," *The New York Times Magazine,* August 29, 1976, p. 6.

15 North Carolina Democrat Terry Sanford said this before he pulled out of the presidential race. See: "The Spirit of '76," *Newsweek,* January 12, 1976, p. 16.

16 The twelve Democratic candidates who announced and/or withdrew sometime during the first or early second acts were: (1) Birch Bayh announced February 17, 1975, and withdrew February 10, 1976; (2) Lloyd Bentsen announced February 17, 1975, and withdrew February 10, 1976; (3) Jerry Brown announced March 12, 1976; (4) Jimmy Carter announced December 12, 1974; (5) Frank Church announced March 18, 1976; (6) Fred Harris announced January 11, 1975, and withdrew April 8, 1976; (7) Hubert Humphrey announced he wouldn't be an active candidate April 28, 1976; (8) Henry Jackson announced February 3, 1975, and withdrew May 1, 1976; (9) Terry Sanford announced May 29, 1975, and withdrew January 23, 1976; (10) Sargent Shriver announced in September, 1975,

and withdrew March 22, 1976; (11) Morris Udall announced November 22, 1974; and (12) George Wallace announced in October, 1975.

17 Although there were seventeen candidates for the Democratic or Republican presidential nomination (Eugene McCarthy was running as an Independent), only fourteen of them actually went through the series of timed rhetorical transactions nationally. The three who declared but did not surface nationally were Robert Byrd, Eileen McCormick and Milton Shapp.

18 "Now, F Is For Favorite," *Newsweek,* July 21, 1975, p. 14.

19 R. W. Apple, Jr., "Brown Complicates Democratic Race," *The New York Times,* March 14, 1976, p. 41.

20 *Newsweek,* December 29, 1975.

21 "Enter Frank Cathedral," *Newsweek,* March 29, 1976, p. 20.

22 Jackson's method of announcing his candidacy fell completely within his total surfacing strategy. It was fairly modest, low-key, and within keeping of the image he was trying to maintain—an experienced and conscientious legislator who spent most of his time in Washington doing his job. An interesting early analysis of the surfacing stage of Jackson's campaign is the one by Douglas E. Kneeland, "Jackson Views the Issue As Ability, Not Charisma," *The New York Times,* December 28, 1975, p. 1.

23 This was, of course, a difficult decision for Humphrey. He wanted to be President but he did not want to lose again. Although he was the favorite of party leaders, he would not let his name be placed on state primary ballots because he may have feared losing to Carter who had been campaigning for so long. In addition, we now may hypothesize that Humphrey knew he did not have the health for a real presidential bid.

24 Kneeland.

25 *Newsweek,* July 21, 1975.

26 For an interesting discussion of Carter's "integrity strategy," see: James T. Wooten, "The Well-planned Enigma of Jimmy Carter," *The New York Times Magazine,* June 6, 1976, pp. 16–89.

27 Martin Schram, *Running for President: A Journal of the Carter Campaign* (New York: Pocket Books, 1977), p. 88.

28 Ibid., p. 25.

29 Ibid.

30 McGovern, of course, was the first candidate to use completely the early announcing and early organizing strategy. For an interesting account of the McGovern strategy see: Theodore H. White, *The Making of the President 1972* (New York: Atheneum, 1973), pp. 42–43; 96–133.

31 Schram, p. 24.

32 James T. Wooten, "Wallace's Last Hurrah?" *The New York Times Magazine,* January 11, 1976, pp. 14–56.

33 Kneeland.

34 Schram, p. 16.

35 Speech, Senator Birch Bayh at Miami University, April 20, 1976.

Television Spectacles as Politics

Michael Gurevitch and Anandam P. Kavoori

In the beginning (or is it the end?) was the image. Images of Anita Hill, her face etched in dignity; of Rodney King being pummeled to the ground; of the blue dot over the face of Kennedy-Smith's accuser; of Gennifer Flowers primping on prime time. These images draw us back again and again. They arrest, recreate in our collective memory a range of responses and emotions. Their symbolic function is iconic, their form by now so familiar that we recognize them instantly as "media events" or "spectacles" (Dayan & Katz, 1992).

How do television spectacles resonate in our political and cultural life? One familiar and pervasive school of thought claims that media spectacles (e.g., of the Thomas/Hill kind) pervert the political process. We will contend that while in the immediate, institutional sense, media spectacles may be seen as "disruptive," in the larger culturalist sense, television spectacles, seen as social texts, should be regarded as playing a role in expanding and configuring what Habermas calls "the public sphere," or Dewey's notion of the democratic community. Communication for Dewey was a matter of discursive practices, and democracy was manifested not in institutions but in the principle of associated life. The role of communication was not limited to that of providing information, but was essential for re-creating and converting "society into a great community" (Peters, 1989). Likewise with Habermas' public sphere.

We will discuss how television spectacles work to further or limit such a role. Our aim is to point out television's unique (or near unique) contribution to the formation of a public sphere. We will do this by discussing three different aspects or dimensions of television spectacles, using examples from the Clarence Thomas hearings, the Rodney King incident, and the 1992 presidential campaign.

★ SPECTACLES AND CONVERSATION

A street spectacle draws a crowd of passers by. A television spectacle does more—it generates a national audience. In an age when audiences are increasingly fragmented, television spectacles create a unified mass audience. In doing so, they open up opportunities for public discussion. Television spectacles such as the Clarence Thomas hearings present, as Klumpp and Hollihan (1979) put it, a rhetorical exigency. Society, in their words, "must talk about such events to develop a contextual placement that defines their cultural meaning." (pp. 2–3).

The importance of such spectacles is that they allow for the emergence into public discourse of perspectives, frames of reference that are not usually present. In a sense, television spectacles constitute "faults" (Agar, 1985) on the surface of the commonly accepted common sense. These faults present an opportunity to reveal what Habermas has called elements of "systematically distorted communication," inquiry into the origins of which reveals cultural ideologies.

The Clarence Thomas hearings present just such a "fault" in the terms in which conventional discourse about gender relations has been structured. Sexual harassment is one amongst a range of social issues which for many years have been suppressed from full public discussion. Although in recent years this, and other aspects of sexual behavior, have been more openly discussed, the Clarence Thomas hearings foregrounded the issue of sexual harassment and thrust it into the public sphere in a new and forceful way. The reasons for the newly achieved prominence of this issue may be many and varied, but there is no doubt that a major contributing factor has been the live television coverage of the hearings, which turned them into a nation-wide televised spectacle.

Besides the obvious political significance of the hearings, they had an equally powerful impact on the cultural politics of American society. We would argue, initially, that the hearings were significant in that they highlighted the versatility of the dominant discourse's capacity to ex-nominate (in Barthes' terms) certain discourses (those of feminist origins) and to successfully "hail" and "interpellate" (all Althusser's terms) both members of the dominant group and minority groups (as for example in the position that successful African-Americans are always subjected to negative publicity).

The role of television in such events is crucial, because it is through television that the *discoursal* nature of major political events is played out. Intriguingly, in the case of the Thomas hearings, television largely allowed the members of the Senate Sub-Committee which conducted the hearings to control the nature of the discourse about sexual harassment. Having created a spectacle by focusing on the hearings, the television cameras then let the proceedings run their course—in a sense becoming a transparent medium rather than a "mediating" intervening one. By effacing its role, television allowed the participating Senators to become the "primary definers" of the issue.

While in the Clarence Thomas case the television spectacle "closed off" the development of subordinate discourses about sexual harassment, it needs to be emphasized that it was the spectacle itself that triggered and rendered public discussion possible in the first place. In Foucauldian terms it allowed for "objects" (arguments) to appear in discourse even though they were eventually subverted. And so, paradoxically, while television may have been part of that subversion, it also provided the opportunity for that public debate to take place. In this important sense, then, television spectacles not only do not pervert the political process, but may indeed facilitate it by creating the conditions for individual conversations and public debates, and by helping to wedge open an area for debate which continued into the days and months after the immediate judgment.

And indeed the significance of that debate can now be seen in the real political consequences it has wrought. Already politicians who supported Thomas have lost elections, while others face uphill re-election battles. In many cases, opposing candidates have used a particular Senator's tough handling of Hill to condemn his anti-women attitudes. In addition there has been increasing mobilization by women activist groups across the country, aiming to influence the conduct of the elections campaign. Moreover, the impact of the Thomas hearings has spilled over into debates on abortion, single motherhood, and other issues. Note, for example, Lynn Sherr's (of ABC News) report from the 1992 democratic convention, in which she described how the "spirit of Anita Hill" dominated the Convention's proceedings, and ventured that it will probably continue to do so throughout the '92 campaign. These are the real political consequences of the Thomas/Hill television spectacle. They offer a contemporary illustration of Gabriel Tarde's notion of the linkages between the press, individual conversations, public opinion, and eventual political action (Katz, 1992).

★ SPECTACLES AND THE IMPRESS OF IMAGES

The second dimension of the contribution of television spectacles to the formation of the public sphere has to do with their unique capacity to deploy images as constructors of texts. The Rodney King incident offers a powerful illustration of the ways in which images are central to the societal resonance of television spectacles.

The violence that followed the jury's verdict in the Rodney King case was rooted in a number of critical crises facing American society today—the decay of the inner cities, the poverty and hopelessness of their populations and, indeed, the entire spectrum of race and ethnic relations in American society. Intriguingly, however, what triggered off the near volcanic eruption of these explosive issues was a piece of videotape. Shown over and over again, the videotape, depicting a man being brutally beaten, defined the reality of what took place. John Berger (1973) has argued that certain

artifacts, especially religious ones, have, by repeated viewing, gained only a single referent. In looking at such images, the viewer coalesces in his or her mind the signifier with the signified. Unlike many other popular texts where a multiplicity of signifieds may be attached to any signifier, in the case of the Rodney King videotape the beating has become the single signified. The signifier and the signified have become one, and the consensual decoding of the images on the tape has been that of a racist attack on a defenseless Black man by White police officers (i.e., a lynching). The centrality of the image in the television spectacle functioned to crystallize the debate in these polarized terms and closed it off from any other version.

When the jury decided to acquit the four policemen, they were up against the power of this signified, a signified that controlled the discourse around this event. In the minds of the national audience it seemed almost impossible that there could be any other meanings in the image than the one they had seen.

The power of the image in television spectacles is thus important for the ways in which it crystallizes its meaning. But it is also important in two other, more general ways. First, the repeated showing of the Rodney King videotape speeds up its impact. Years from now what will be remembered will be not only the verdict or the riots that followed it, but significantly the grainy, out of focus image of a man being pummeled and beaten viciously. The image is so powerful that it creates an instant transcendental judgment. Ideas and images resonate and become part of our collective memory through repetition over time, and the power of electronic imagery rests in part in its capacity to speed up this process and to create a history that begins at the moment of its filming. Frank (1992) has argued that by reaching out to single images, we change the way we construct history. The new rules of history, then, are images. Our common understanding of the past—our collective memory—is tied into these immediate and powerful signifieds that recall other, similar ones. These remain unchanging, frozen in time: Rodney King keeps writhing on the ground; "Bull" Connor keeps deploying fire hoses against civil rights protestors; a woman forever weeps over the dead at Kent State.

Also, Armstrong keeps landing on the moon; Martin Luther King keeps telling us of his dream; and John F. Kennedy remains forever young, bronzed, and embodying hope.

A second way of understanding the power of these images is to consider the ways in which they mutate within different television genres. For contemporary audiences already saturated with electronic imagery, Rodney King blurs into Blair Underwood, who faced a similar crisis on *L.A. Law,* and was in turn interviewed by NBC's Tom Brokaw during the post-verdict Los Angeles riots, thereby completing the movement from reality to fiction and then back to "reality" (i.e., "news"). Monica Lisch, the prosecutor in the Kennedy-Smith trial, at once blends with Susan Dey (again *L.A. Law*); and Murphy Brown is brought before a senate subcommittee which investigates senate leaks to the media (a.k.a. leaks about Anita Hill's allegations to an NPR reporter). These connections are being made on a medium that is increasingly blurring the line between news and fiction, and news and advocacy. Fiction-based narrative techniques are being used not only on "news" shows like *Hard Copy, Entertainment Tonight,* and *Prime Time Live,* but also on the more traditional news programs such as *60 Minutes* and *20/20.* Television news, both local and national/international, also increasingly focuses on elements of style. In fact, it is becoming increasingly difficult to separate in any complete way the differences between these different genres. "Hard news" blends into tabloid television and into docu-dramas which in turn blend into dramas based on "real life" stories, and on into fiction and fantasy.

The contemporary citizen/viewer is thus a "voyeur floating in a sea of symbols." In an age in which images are all pervasive, the entry of "issues" into the public sphere becomes a question of the degree and the power of images to reach the largest possible audience, to draw sustenance from the range of genres that saturate the viewer while at the same time contextualize the images in culturally and politically fundamental ways (as the Rodney King image did with race relations). Questions of image, then, are at the core of the role that television spectacles play in creating a "community" (in Dewey's terms) of viewers.

★ SPECTACLES AND THE POPULAR/POLITICAL DISJUNCTION

The third dimension we focus on is the way in which television spectacles create a dynamic between popular and formal political discourse, and in so doing further expand the public sphere. Spectacles have historically been the norm in American presidential campaigns—and the advent of television has increasingly turned the campaigns into one long television spectacle. The 1992 campaign has spawned some significant departures from the old style of campaign communication, primarily the attempts by many of the presidential candidates to break down the barrier between "high" and "popular" political discourse and to reach out to voters through seemingly direct, quasi-intimate appeals. Jerry Brown's 1-800 number ploy, initially regarded as an amusing sideshow, can now be recognized as a breakthrough attempt to open up the campaign to direct participation by blatantly rejecting the traditional, "official" modes of campaign financing. Others have rushed to television's talk shows, call-in programs, electronic town meetings, and the late-night entertainment programs. One pollster summed up the candidates' efforts as an attempt to "play the piano of popular culture."

In our understanding of the role of television spectacles the importance of these developments should not be minimized. Their significance goes beyond the immediate context of this election year (e.g., a recession, public disenchantment with politicians). They could foretell a movement where the instrumentality of popular culture may eventually come to replace (at least in part) the formalized institutional/cultural apparatus of power. We draw briefly on Mikhail Bakhtin's study of Rabelais, the 16th century French satirist, to discuss such a possibility. Bakhtin argued that Rabelais' bawdy narratives had been considered an enigma because they had been "read" incorrectly. The proper meaning of these tales, Bakhtin argued, was to read them as accounts of folk or popular culture, introducing into the (Habermasian) public sphere a set of discourses that were not usually present in the traditional and power-bounded official culture. Bakhtin argues that Rabelais used popular culture because it represented everything that official culture was not, and that Rabelais' basic goal "was to destroy the official picture of things" (Berrong, 1986, p. 11).

The creation of a community (in Dewey's terms) may thus be enhanced when these two usually disparate political cultures—the official and the popular—are brought closer together. In this sense, it is the Donahue show, "Larry King Live," and the numerous talk-cum-call-in shows that begin to approximate a more egalitarian discourse. We might want to consider the democratic possibilities of these shows rather than focus on or bemoan the loss of "traditional" values of journalism (Hallin, forthcoming). At the same time it should be clear, of course, that the populism of these shows is a long way from the "communicative action" envisaged by Habermas. Their importance lies simply in their introduction into the political debate of the language of popular culture. George Lipsitz (1990) has underlined the importance of looking at what language is used, especially in political discourse. How things are framed—whether in the language of officialdom or in the language of direct inquiry—impinges directly on how the public sphere is opened up. By extending the boundaries of linguistic representations, from the aesthetic to the overtly political, Lipsitz argues that "struggles over meaning" are ultimately "struggles over resources."

Ross Perot's (defunct) plan to create an "electronic town hall" is another case in point. Perot was drawing, of course, on the American vision of the "purity" of direct, grass-roots democracy coupled with the enduring myth of the power of technology to solve society's problems. This vision of "government by television," destructive as it is to the principles of representative democracy, has the merit, however, of hugely expanding the public sphere, at least theoretically. The other, darker side of this gleaming coin has to do, of course, with the susceptibility of television spectacles of that kind to the needs of drama, conflict, and other potentially manipulative narratives that tend to simplify and thus pervert the political discussion, rather than enhance its scope.

Overall, the way in which American television has introduced the political into the popular and the popular into the political may have gone further than it has in other western democracies. The image of presidential candidate Bill Clinton playing the trumpet on the *Arsenio Hall Show* may be quintessentially American. The significance of such television spectacles lies precisely in the way they use the popular/official disjunction to open up the public sphere. The options that follow from that point all raise a different set of questions. Whether popular culture can retain its democratizing force or whether it degenerates into what Walter Benjamin (1979) memorably described as "the situation of politics which fascism is rendering aesthetic" remains to be seen.

In summary, then, we have attempted to discuss the ways in which television spectacles resonate in politics. Minimally, we would argue, television spectacles create rhetorical exigencies, frame issues in critical ways through images, and straddle the official/popular divide. In doing so, they create opportunities to open up the public sphere and to regenerate democracy.

At the same time we should also be wary. Television spectacles as interventions are not unmuddled opportunities for democratic change. In the Thomas/Hill case television, we argued, helped to trigger a national debate. In the Rodney King case, we observed how the medium determined and imposed the terms of the discussion, and thereby closed off public debate. In the presidential campaign of 1992, television has thus far been able, for better and/or for worse, to inject the popular into the political and vice versa. In at least these three different ways, television spectacles are a part of the ongoing drama of society as a communicative community, and of democracy.

REFERENCES

Agar, M. (1985). *Speaking of ethnography.* Beverly Hills, CA: Sage.

Benjamin, W. (1979). The work of art in an age of mechanical reproduction. In J. Curran, M. Gurevitch, & J. Woollacott (Eds.), *Mass communication and society* (pp. 384–408). Beverly Hills, CA: Sage.

Berger, J. (1973). *Ways of Seeing.* New York: Viking.

Berrong, R. (1986). *Rabelais and Bakhtin: Popular culture in Gargantua and Pantagruel.* Lincoln, NE: University of Nebraska Press.

Dayan, D., &: Katz, E. (1992). *Media events: The live broadcasting of history.* Cambridge, MA: Harvard University.

Frank, J. (1992). Are there new rules of history: The transcendent of judgments of electronic imagers. *The Washington Post,* May 3, 1992.

Hallin, D. (in press). The passing of the "high modernism" of American journalism. *Journal of Communication.*

Katz, E. (1992). On parenting a paradigm: Gabriel Tarde's agenda for opinion and communication research. *International Journal of Public Opinion Research, 4,* 80–87.

Klumpp, J. F., & Hollihan, T. A. (1979). Debunking the resignation of Earl Butz: Sacrificing an official racist. *The Quarterly Journal of Speech, 65,* 2–3.

Lipsitz, G. (1990). Listening to learn and listening to listen: Popular culture, cultural theory, and American studies. *American Quarterly, 42,* (1), 515–636.

Peters, J. D. (1989). Democracy and American mass communication theory: Dewey, Lippman, Lazersfeld. *Communication, 11,* 199–220.

The Problem of Beginnings in New Hampshire: Control over the Play

Kathleen E. Kendall

The New Hampshire primary: "It's the closest thing we've got to political amniocentesis."

—Dayton Duncan, Booknotes interview,
C-SPAN, March 31, 1991

★ INTRODUCTION AND BACKGROUND

That the New Hampshire primary is a key event in American political campaigns has been well established. It is the first primary in the nation, as mandated by the New Hampshire legislature.[1] This chapter takes an interpretive perspective, based on direct observation of the candidates and media during the primary and on an analysis of the primary's messages. This single primary constructs a critical part of the quadrennial electoral drama, defining the characteristics of the protagonists. The candidates have an unusually broad array of communication strategies available to them in this state. The focus of this chapter is on the initial electoral struggle of the candidates and media to exert control over the discourse of the 1992 New Hampshire presidential primary, and through it, the campaign to follow.

New Hampshire's voter turnout is regularly among the highest in the nation for a primary: 67 percent of registered voters voted in 1992, when the average turnout in primaries was just over 30 percent of registered voters (Baker, 1993). Not only is voter interest and participation high, but "tidal shifts in preference have not been uncommon in the final days before primaries there" (John, 1989, p. 592), placing great pressure on the candidates to respond quickly to change and on the media to make sense of a volatile situation.

From 1952 through 1988 no candidate ever won the presidency without winning there. (Bill Clinton broke this pattern in 1992, coming in second in New Hampshire.) News coverage of this primary is often the heaviest of all the states (Adams, 1987; Lichter, Amundsen, and Noyes, 1988; Kerbel, 1994). Research on the 1992 primaries has established that voters in other states formed candidate perceptions based on network news coverage of the New Hampshire primary, extending its influence far beyond the Northeast (Pfau et al., 1993). And the winner in New Hampshire has regularly made significant gains in the opinion polls (Mayer 1987).

Much prior research has been done on this subject. We know that the candidates go through a frenzy of presidential surfacing in New Hampshire, introducing themselves and attempting to emerge as serious contenders for the nomination of a major party, their final chance before the first primary votes are cast (Trent, 1978; Kendall and Trent, 1989). In an

This essay originally appeared as a chapter in a book edited by Kathleen E. Kendall, Presidential Campaign Discourse: Strategic Communication Problems *(Albany: State University of New York Press, 1995)*

age of television and computers, this frenzy is only heightened. As Meyrowitz says, "action and reaction collapse into a co-constructed reality once possible only in face-to-face communication," with groups reacting "to each other's reactions to each other—in real time" (1992, p. 470). Voters at this early stage are just beginning to focus on the campaign; they tend to be so uninformed and uncertain about who the candidates are and which one they prefer that the candidates have an unparalleled opportunity to influence their knowledge and feelings (Patterson, 1980; Kennamer and Chaffee, 1982; Popkin, 1991).

We know that the majority of media coverage of the primary deals with the horse race, the question of who is winning (Patterson, 1980, 1993; Robinson and Sheehan, 1983), and with the candidates' viability, or "the relative chances of candidates winning the nomination." These questions about winning include the media's "fascination with [the] momentum" of the candidates (Brady and Johnston, 1987, p. 132). Matthews (1978) has established that the early primaries have a winnowing effect, as candidates who have done poorly withdraw from the race because they no longer seem to be viable.

Finally, we know that the voters and media are looking at the candidates' character, for signs that they have the presidential leadership traits to solve the nation's problems (Brady and Johnston, 1987; Bartels, 1988). This focus explains the heavy attention given to such presumed revelations of inner character as Senator Edmund Muskie's crying while defending his wife from an editorial attack in the 1972 New Hampshire primary. Candidates work to convey image traits effectively through their messages, both interpersonally and through the media. But the task is complex and difficult, because images are not only multifaceted and to some extent affected by the particular campaign context, but also co-constructed among the candidates, the media, and the voters. According to Louden (1990), image is "an evaluation negotiated and constructed by candidates and voters in a cooperative venture" (p. 1). Certainly that is true, but the media also play a role in this construction.

Voters have an ideal image of a candidate in their minds, and some of the traits in that profile have reappeared across campaigns: honesty, competence (including experience), empathy, and strength and decisiveness (Nimmo and Savage, 1976; Hellweg and King, 1983; Hellweg, King, and Williams, 1988; Trent et al., 1993). In a study of New Hampshire citizens attending candidate events during the 1992 primary, respondents said the most important candidate characteristics (4 or above on a 5-point scale) were (in this order): honesty, talks about the nation's problems (tied), has solutions to problems, good moral character, calm and cautious, energetic and aggressive leader, forceful public speaker, and experience in office (Trent et al., 1993).

These research findings have been valuable in aiding our understanding of the nature and significance of communication in the early primaries. However, the overall picture may be lost sight of when we focus on these pieces of the whole. The metaphor of the dramatic ritual advocated by Nimmo and Combs (1990) allows us to examine the whole event. They define ritual as "a series of acts that, for the most part, people regularly and faithfully perform time and time again"; a dramatic ritual exists "when the elements of a drama repeatedly relate to one another in a ritualistic fashion" (p. 54). Rituals are much more powerful than ceremonies, because they transform, appealing to the emotions; they "tap, reflect, and intensify deeply held values, ideals, and desires" (p. 69).

The presidential election is such a structured, rule-governed ritual, they argue, consisting of "dramatic confrontations, each side fantasizing an ideal America either lost but to be regained, or one yet to found." In this ritual, the incumbent generally defends the status quo, arguing that his administration has brought gains and there will be more to come. The challenger attacks the *status quo* and argues for changes to bring about a brighter future, presenting himself as the one most capable of effecting these changes. The campaign renews the belief "that the story will have a happy ending (that is, that the contest can be won and greatness can be found or regained)" (pp. 54–55). The dramatic ritual of the campaign places a premium on hope: if it makes a difference who is going to be president, and if the choice is important to voters—a concept underlined by the campaign ritual—then the candidates "must enunciate a rhetorical vision of hope" (p. 68). Examples of such visions have been John F. Kennedy's promise to "get America moving again" and Jimmy Carter's theme of restoring trust and providing a "government as good as its people."

This metaphor of the dramatic ritual seemed particularly appropriate for examining the New Hampshire primary, after my immersion in that primary in 1988 and 1992. My perspective both years was that of a participant observer, a communication professor with media credentials,[2] traveling with the journalists and observing them and the candidates every day. All appeared to be engaged in a quest and a struggle: a quest to find out what the campaign (or play) was going to be about, and a struggle to shape the way the play was written. The concern with surfacing and the horse race and viability and winnowing and character were all there, but the main goal was to grasp and shape the presidential campaign story.

Nimmo and Combs say that "each phase of the presidential election coverage . . . is a minidrama" (p. 55), and identify the primary and caucus phase as one of those minidramas. In this view, New Hampshire would be a small part of the overall minidrama of thirty-eight primaries and thirteen caucuses in 1992. But the view from within the New Hampshire primary seemed bigger than that. At this early point in the campaign, when public opinion was so unformed (Patterson, 1980; Kennamer and Chaffee, 1982; Popkin, 1991), there was an obvious opportunity for a substantial part of the election drama to be constructed. The New Hampshire primary received almost undivided attention from the media and candidates during the February 11–19 period. Never again would there be such a concentrated focus; after New Hampshire, as Renee Loth of the *Boston Globe* wrote (Feb. 19, 1992, p. 1), the presidential campaign would split "like a band of refracted light, flashing attention on the 27 states that will hold primaries or caucuses in the next 30 days." The media focused heavily on the matter of electability, on who could win, not just in New Hampshire, but also in the fall election. In effect, they were trying to foresee the end of the play.

With these impressions of the large scope and influence of New Hampshire in mind,

I examined the efforts of the candidates and media to shape answers to the following questions, which are inherent in the electoral drama, and the evidence of their success:

1. Who were the protagonists, and who were the minor characters in the play? Indicators of such position included endorsements, pictures, press attention, claims of important accomplishments, poll standings, crowd size, and titles.
2. What was the content of the character of the protagonists? Who had the traits of honesty, competence, compassion, and strength most closely approximating the ideal image of a presidential candidate? Character was conveyed through word choice, pictures, and the selection of representative anecdotes supposedly revealing of character.
3. What visions did the protagonists project, and who best projected the vision of hope? Language and pictures were instrumental in creating these visions.

For the candidates, it was vital that the construction of answers to these questions would please the voters, first in New Hampshire, and because New Hampshire influenced national perceptions, voters in the rest of the nation (Pfau et al., 1993). The media, as interpreters of the action to the public, also had to make decisions about these questions. The candidates struggled among themselves to make their answers prevail, and they also struggled with the media. All were well aware of the record of this primary in selecting a winner and dooming most of the candidates to life as a historical footnote. (Note: Other scholars are doing important work focusing upon voter involvement in this process during the primaries. See Kern and Just, 1994; Kern and Just, forthcoming, 1995; West, Kern, and Alger, 1992; Neuman, Just, and Crigler, 1992).

New Hampshire is a small state (in 1992 its population was only 1,110,801; *World Almanac*, 1994). The main way voters learn about the candidates is through mass communication— the candidates' television ads, and newspapers and television news—and the primary emphasis of this study is on those media. But "retail politics" remain vitally important in New Hampshire. Because the bulk of the population is clustered in the southern part of the state, the candidates can easily travel around and be seen by thousands of voters personally. They can meet with influential people who, with a phone call, can secure a vote. The state also has a long history of intense interest in primaries and high voter turnout. Thus, the chapter discusses three other avenues through which the candidates reached smaller numbers of voters and the press: their campaign literature, their published daily schedules, and their speeches.

This chapter focuses on the two front-runners in each party in February 1992: Republicans George Bush and Pat Buchanan, and Democrats Paul Tsongas and Bill Clinton. The information is part of a larger study that will include Democrats Tom Harkin, Bob Kerrey, and Jerry Brown as well.

★ METHODS

In examining the candidates' input into the script, I reviewed the following: one major campaign leaflet from each candidate, secured at the campaign headquarters, as well as Tsongas's larger booklet; the first three or four of their television ads shown in New Hampshire; the video distributed door to door by the Clinton campaign; the candidate schedules distributed by the campaigns; and sample speeches I observed. I based my analysis of the campaign leaflets on the pictures, the language that appeared in bold or large type, and the captions. Important analysis of New Hampshire television advertisements has been done by L. Patrick Devlin (1994), and I relied on that and added analysis of Clinton's video distributed to undecided voters. I read the candidates' schedules to see which groups they spoke to, and counted each person's public campaign appearances.

The discussion of speeches and speech events is based on those I saw myself, including six by Clinton, two each by Tsongas and Buchanan, and one by Bush; a debate involving all five leading Democrats; a Democratic dinner at which three of the Democrats spoke; and a Buchanan whistle-stop tour.

In describing the media's efforts to construct the script, I examined all front-page stories and pictures about the primary in the newspapers (150 stories and 58 pictures), and 25 television news broadcasts in the February 11–19,

1992 period (the primary was on Feb. 18). The national print sources examined were the *New York Times* and *USA Today*. Regional sources were the *Boston Globe* and the *Boston Herald*. Local sources were the *Manchester Union Leader, Concord Monitor* (Feb. 13, 14, 15, and 17 only), and *Nashua Telegraph*. These papers were selected because they were available in the Manchester-Concord-Nashua area where the majority of New Hampshirites live, and where the candidates and journalists clustered. The television broadcasts viewed were from NBC, CBS, and ABC nightly news, complete except for NBC, February 15 and 16. A more exhaustive study would have included coverage by CNN, WMUR (the New Hampshire television station), and several Boston stations.

The units of analysis for television were stories on the New Hampshire campaign. The coding scheme drew on Graber (1987), recording the date, network, anchor and reporter names, and topics covered, and then examined the way the story answered the three research questions. For each story the researcher asked: (1) which candidates were mentioned (to distinguish major and minor characters in the play); (2) what candidate characteristics were described or shown; and (3) what attention, if any, was given to the candidates' visions of the future.

The units of analysis for newspapers were the front-page stories and pictures on the primaries. These first-presented messages were selected because of their attention-getting position, because newspaper readers whether interested in politics or not generally scan the first page, and because this choice brought the volume of material down to a manageable size. The coding scheme followed for the newspaper stories was similar to that used for the televised news stories.

★ THE CANDIDATES' ATTEMPT TO CONSTRUCT THE PLAY

Campaign Literature

The candidates have complete control over the message in their literature, and therefore an examination of the contents was useful to discover how they chose to present themselves. It is not surprising that all the candidates used their literature to claim that they were major characters in the play. They were the stars of their leaflets pictorially: their faces always appeared on the cover, except for that of Tsongas, who appeared waving and smiling once the leaflet was opened. Bush emphasized his importance through the use of title—he was "President George Bush"—while the others chose a less hierarchical and more folksy approach, calling themselves Bill Clinton, Paul Tsongas, and Pat Buchanan.

Three of the four protagonists used their past records to support a claim to a major role, summarizing positions held, legislation initiated, proposals made. The exception to this pattern was Buchanan, whose leaflet made no claims to a past record of accomplishment; instead, it devoted the entire space to attacking the *status quo* and proposing a ten-point plan for change.

Two other strategies candidates used in their literature to convey an impression of viability and legitimacy were endorsements and accounts of how they had won against the odds before.

There was a sameness in the way the Democratic candidates constructed their images in the literature. The ideal image of the president, based on the Democrats' literature, was of a "fighter." Both used that word on the pamphlet cover: Clinton was "Fighting for the Forgotten Middle Class," and Tsongas told "How to fight for America's economic future and win."

The two Republicans displayed little common ground in their efforts to flesh out their images. The Buchanan character, according to his leaflet, was first of all patriotic: he favored "Putting and Keeping America First." The whole leaflet developed this theme, presenting ten steps for achieving these goals. Bush, in contrast, stressed his competence and decisiveness on the topic New Hampshirites were most concerned about: the economy. His pamphlet was "A Plan" for an "Economic Growth Agenda," and the pictures showed him in action, presumably promoting his plan.

A third question about the literature concerns the efforts of each candidate to project a vision of what he would do as president, a fantasy of "an ideal America either lost but to be regained, or one yet to be found" (Nimmo and Combs, 1990, pp. 54–55).

Clinton's pamphlet had a clear, dominant vision, called "Bill Clinton's Plan" to "Put America Back to Work." He offered an economic plan, a health care plan, and a plan to improve education; in each plan he envisioned the positive effects of his proposal. Positive, smiling pictures and language reinforced the vision.

The most original and ambitious print document in the 1992 New Hampshire primary was Tsongas's eighty-five-page booklet, "A Call to Economic Arms." He distributed it widely by mail and in person, autographing and giving away dozens of copies at every public appearance. It argued that America was not prepared to do battle economically in world markets, that there was an economic crisis, and that the nation must take action to reemerge as the world's preeminent economic power. He discussed what must be done in education, the environment, energy, and foreign policy.

The booklet presented the Tsongas vision, stern about recognizing and facing problems, but inspirational in urging that "the spirit of the American people" should be unleashed so we could return to an ideal America, once again securing "our future and the future of our descendants" (p. 85). The weight and scope of the booklet were impressive at a glance, even daunting, and that impression alone may have served Tsongas's purpose. It is not clear how many recipients actually read this lengthy booklet.

The Tsongas campaign leaflet examined was larger and longer than those of other candidates —three 8 1/2 x 11 sheets, front and back—and the most informative. For those who took the time to penetrate the dense text, Tsongas's pamphlet presented a vision of a return to economic greatness, with him at the helm, summarizing the proposals in "A Call to Economic Arms." The tone was hopeful and optimistic, predicting that "America can once again be the world's number one economic power."

The Buchanan leaflet was short and modest in size (the front and back of an 8 1/2 x 11 page), picturing a smiling Buchanan. The vision he projected in his ten-point plan for "Putting and Keeping America First" was one of cutting programs and saying no. He would "phase out foreign aid," "play hardball in trade talks," "cut tax rates," "veto tax hikes," "freeze Federal spending," and "limit terms for politicians." The language was decisive and firm, conveying a no-nonsense, businesslike image. Buchanan predicted that tax cuts would bring America the "most attractive economic climate in the industrial world," with "millions of new jobs." For those already convinced that the status quo in American government was in urgent need of repair, his crisp list might well offer hope. Like Tsongas, he expressed a longing for an ideal America, pledging efforts to regain it: "With God's help, we can hand down to the next generation a country as great and grand and good as the one that our parents gave to us."

Bush's pamphlet, like Tsongas's, was large, covering both sides of three 8 1/2 x 11 sheets, and contained eight pictures. His vision or "Plan to Make New Hampshire and America Move" would "spur economic growth and create jobs for New Hampshire," "provide tax relief for the people of New Hampshire," and "strengthen New Hampshire families." The parts of the plan were highlighted by dark type and generous spacing, and they addressed specific audiences, of businesses and of families longing for tax relief. Bush sounded as though he understood the problems and knew what to do about them. His "Growth Agenda" would "stimulate the economy, help put more money in the pockets of taxpayers, restore consumer confidence, and keep interest rates and inflation down." Any reader would find these to be desirable goals: they described a return to happier times.

However, the credibility of the Bush message in evoking a vision of hope was undermined by two factors. First, the pictures did not reinforce the message effectively: he did not look optimistic. A second problem was that the carefully outlined and extensive vision of the future, while well suited to a challenger, seemed inappropriate for an incumbent entering his fourth year as president. Such a future-oriented agenda might well raise questions such as "Where have you been?"

Candidate Schedules

In contrast to their literature, the candidates' daily schedules (called editors' advisories or press advisories) were targeted to the press. However, they were also published daily in the *Union Leader* (Manchester), thus reaching a much wider audience. The schedule was strictly factual, reporting on the events the candidate would be attending each day. But the selection of groups and subjects addressed and the scope of the campaign effort provided clues to the visions and character traits of the candidates. High numbers of appearances, for example, created an impression of high motivation to win, and of vigor and energy.

Perhaps the most striking finding regarding the schedules was that Tsongas made the fewest public appearances per day. The candidates' average daily number of public and press events was three; for Tsongas it was only two. Such evidence of low activity was not at all in Tsongas's interest. Questions about his health circulated constantly among the press, as he had had cancer and claimed to be fully recovered. But doubts lingered—was he strong enough and well enough to handle the responsibilities of the presidency? The members of the press I talked with interpreted his paucity of appearances as evidence that he had to conserve his strength.

Candidate Speeches

During my week in New Hampshire, I observed sixteen speeches or speech-type events, including debates, dinners, whistle-stop speeches, individual speeches, and rallies. Hundreds of voters a day heard the candidates personally (some of the rallies attracted close to one thousand people). New and personal information, even in small amounts, has been found to carry more weight with voters than abstract information (Popkin, 1991). In a primary in which the difference between the first- and second-place Democrats was only 14,116 votes, and the totals for Kerrey and Harkin differed by only 1,518 votes (*New York Times*, Feb. 20, 1992, p. A21), the thousands who attended speeches, with their networks of friends and family, could have affected the outcome. Speeches are part of the retail politics still thriving in New Hampshire.

In addition to the role speeches played in communicating directly with interested citizens, speeches by these four candidates were also heavily attended by the media. The television networks showed little of the actual speeches to the public, except for C-SPAN (Kendall, 1993). However, reporters observing the speeches had a chance to form personal impressions of the candidates and their abilities, and to see who came to hear the candidate, how the audience responded, and how the candidate dealt with their questions. These impressions often formed the nucleus of stories on television and in the print media.

The speeches provided excellent opportunities for the candidates to "write the play" their own way. First, the candidates had complete control over the content of the speeches, unlike press conferences or interviews, in which the press led with the questions. They had a chance to show their priorities, as when Buchanan explained his support of the voucher system for schools (Concord, Feb. 11), and Tsongas criticized the proposal for a middle-class tax cut, saying he wanted to be the "pathfinder," not "Santa Claus" (Nashua, Feb. 14). They had a chance to show how much (or how little) they knew, backing up their proposals with evidence, or telling the audience about their experience in solving the problem. They could introduce themselves to the press and the voters as people with unique human qualities and feelings, as when Tsongas joked about his lack of charisma, or Clinton showed his teaching skills, explaining the ramifications of the policies he advocated. They could also use the content of their speeches to stress the campaign themes found in leaflets, ads, and interviews.

Second, the candidates cast their speeches in their own language, making stylistic choices for such purposes as conveying their personal characteristics, or inspiring, or ridiculing. Buchanan's speech at Concord (Feb. 11) attempted all these things. He was tough—he would "play hardball" with countries that "give us a hard time"; we shouldn't be "trade wimps," he said. He was patriotic, calling for a "new patriotism": "Not only America first, but America second and third as well." He ridiculed the Democrats, especially Teddy Kennedy, who would sign a bill "if only he can find his pants." "How many fifty-nine-year-olds do you know," he asked, "who still go to Florida for spring break?" He appealed to deeply held values such as "shared sacrifice" (he would roll back the federal pay raise, turn in half of the president's pay, and call for reduction in the salaries of the boards of directors of automobile companies).

He reminded his audience of the principles of the American Revolution; the federal bureaucracy was like the British, he said, spending 25 percent of the GNP. "I hope you will join me in a second American Revolution, and take America back," he concluded.

Vivid words can touch an audience's emotions, making them laugh, and applaud, and nod, and go away full of enthusiasm or anger. Clichés, such as the jokes about Senator Kennedy, a favorite butt of conservative humor, can give audiences a satisfying sense of participation. The candidates' words are at the heart of the campaign ritual, tapping and "intensifying deeply held values" (Nimmo and Combs, 1990, p. 69). Yet they are seldom present in media coverage of the events.

Third, the speeches gave the candidates free media exposure. Except for the cost of travel to the location and press releases distributed in advance, the speech event guaranteed some media attention at a nominal cost.

Fourth, the speeches gave the candidates a chance to make distinctions between themselves and their opponents. As Jamieson (1992) has pointed out, "The longer the statement, the more likely it is to compare and contrast candidates' positions," providing useful information to voters (p. 259). And speeches are long enough to make substantive distinctions. Clinton's speech to the American Association of Retired Persons (Concord, Feb. 13), for example, contrasted his position on health care with that of Bush, and proposed specific reforms, such as uniform billing, the establishment of more group centers, and an emphasis on promoting wellness.

Fifth, speeches gave the candidates a chance to move quickly to meet campaign developments, replying to charges of opponents or media claims immediately. Tsongas responded immediately to a February 13 attack by Harkin on his position on nuclear power (Seabrook); on February 14, Tsongas said, "Tom is playin' fast and loose right now," discussed his support by environmental groups, and proclaimed that if companies violated environmental standards he would "prosecute and prosecute hard" (Nashua). Buchanan built his campaign on attacks against Bush for breaking his promise about "no new taxes", and for being a distant and uncaring figure. Bush's whirlwind campaign day on February 15 could well have been interpreted as a response to Buchanan's attacks, as it was devoted mainly to defending his attempts to revive the economy through a seven-point economic plan. While references to Buchanan were only oblique, his surrogates, such as Senator Warren Rudman, fought off Buchanan's charges with sentences such as, "I've never known a man who suffers when you suffer more than George Bush" (Derry, Feb. 15).

Finally, speeches gave the candidates an opportunity to interact directly with the voters, showing their quickness and adaptability, their knowledge of issues voters inquired about, and, when there were hecklers (as there were with Clinton and Bush), their ability to react well under fire. For example, when Bush was heckled by an ACT-UP AIDS demonstrator shouting, "What about AIDS?", the heckler was quickly removed from the room. But Bush then departed from his text to say, "Understandably, they're upset, but sometimes their tactics hurt their effort. We are going to whip that disease . . . we're doing everything we can." He then cited figures to show the growth of AIDS research funding during his administration (Derry, Feb. 15).

Some of the candidates, especially Clinton and Tsongas, regularly engaged in long, substantive question periods with audiences, using the opportunity to develop their themes and further shape impressions of their character. Reporters I spoke with remarked on Clinton's ability to speak knowledgeably and at length on a wide variety of public policy issues; they were impressed with his competence. Tsongas, with his quick-witted humor, courage to criticize and reject the popular middle-class tax cut idea, and efforts to dissect and analyze complex issues, also won respect and admiration among the press.

Candidate Television Advertisements

The candidates used ads heavily in a traditional way in New Hampshire, to write the script themselves, uncensored by the media. They cast themselves as the experienced incumbents, as attractive alternatives to the *status quo,* or, in the case of Buchanan, battler against the representative of the *status quo,* Bush.

If the quantity of television advertising is used as a criterion, all of the candidates except Brown established themselves as major characters in the play. Brown spent only $60,000, but the others spent between $430,000 (Tsongas) and $1.4 million (Buchanan) on the New Hampshire primary. Clinton was the top spender on campaign ads among the Democrats in New Hampshire, using 18 ads for a cost of $950,000; Bush ran 4 ads, spending $700,000 (Devlin, 1994).

Specific ads by Clinton and Buchanan were notable for their effectiveness in the New Hampshire context: the twelve-minute videotape "American Dream" distributed door-to-door by the Clinton campaign, and Buchanan's "Read My Lips" ads. In addition, Clinton made unusual use of paid television in audience question formats.

During the last weekend before the primary, Clinton distributed twenty thousand free copies of a twelve-minute videotape to undecided households in New Hampshire. The Clinton campaign called recipients and reported that 60 percent to 70 percent had watched the tape (James Carville, comments to press, Feb. 16, 1992). Half of those who watched it reported that they had voted for Clinton (Ceaser and Busch, 1993). This tape made a vigorous effort to construct Clinton as an ideal candidate for New Hampshire. It painted him as a major character in the electoral play, and a character of strong and admirable image traits. But the dominant and most effective emphasis was on his vision of hope for the future.

He spoke constantly of change, of making life better, of the future. Through skillful use of synonyms and repetition, in words full of optimism and determination, he drove the point home. He advocated change (6 repetitions) in the future (4 repetitions), a vision (2 repetitions), a plan (3 repetitions), a dream (3 repetitions). It was a dream for us, for you in the middle class (5); it was your dream and our dream, to work with common purpose (2), to take the responsibility (3) and provide the leadership (6) to "bring this country together again." He would do it with us; we would win again (4), together.

There was tremendous emphasis on winning as a people; Clinton managed to equate *his* winning with *our* winning, taking over the game metaphor that so dominates media coverage of campaigns and changing it from the victory of an individual candidate into the victory of a group, the middle class, and even more specifically, the middle-class voters in New Hampshire, with Clinton as one of them.

In addition to these forms of paid advertising, Clinton also purchased two half hours of time on New Hampshire's largest television station, WMUR, on Thursday and Friday nights, February 13 and 14. He bought the time at the height of the controversy over his draft status during the Vietnam War, and used the first evening for questions from a small studio audience of uncommitted voters, and the second evening for a live call-in show. With these two programs, Clinton dominated television for three nights in a row, for on February 12 he had appeared on "Nightline" with Ted Koppel, discussing his 1969 letter regarding the draft. As a condition of appearing on "Nightline," he had insisted that the entire draft letter be shown on the screen, and Koppel agreed. The letter, which was over 1,200 words long, filled one screen after another, allowing viewers to read it in its entirety. He also paid to have the letter printed in full in the Union Leader the next day, and other papers, including the *Concord Monitor*, the *Boston Globe* (partial transcript), and the *New York Times*, published it as news. The result was a blurring together of advertising and news in which voters were presented with Clinton's own construction of the script. Both the degree of candidate control over the language and the quantity of the language were unusual.

Buchanan's New Hampshire ads such as "Protect" and "Broken Promises" contained much large print about Bush's broken promises, and pictures of Bush, particularly the famous "Read my lips, no new taxes" scene from his 1988 acceptance address. "Can we afford four more years of broken promises?" asked the narrator. "Send Bush a message. Vote for Pat Buchanan for president." Symbolically these bold attacks on the president promoted Buchanan as a major character in the play, the only Republican to take on the president of the United States and offer an alternative. Focus groups reported that the "Read My Lips" ads made the biggest impression of all the ads in the primaries, that they resonated with the voters' anger about Bush; polls confirmed this effect (West, Kern, and Alger, 1992). But Buchanan did little to develop his own character or present a vision of hope. At the end of the ads voters saw Buchanan's smiling face on the screen, and heard his gravelly voice. But they learned nothing about this character in the play, except that he was "not Bush." Unlike his pamphlet, in which he proposed a plan for a presidency of "Putting and Keeping America First," especially through cutting taxes and spending and foreign aid, his television ads devoted themselves mainly to identifying and describing the villain in the play, George Bush. In this he was very successful.

On election day, 53 percent of the Republicans voted for Bush, 37 percent for Buchanan, 10 percent for others. The majority of Buchanan voters in exit polls reported that "they were trying to get through to Bush, not backing the challenger" (Richard Benedetto, *USA Today*, Feb. 13, 1992, p. 1). While Bush was still the clear winner of the primary, the anti-Bush vote was surprisingly large. In constructing himself as the antibush, Buchanan gave the Republicans a way to express their anger at the president. He also won favorable attention for having the courage to fight against the odds, in a context in which even prominent Democrats had refused to compete with Bush. But he was never able to gain this much support in other primaries, though he expressed the hope he would begin to win in the South. Instead, his vote percentages dwindled steadily. The Buchanan team's decision to write the script for his opponent's character and not to develop his own character or vision of the presidency was shortsighted for his own candidacy. There are limits to a candidacy cast simply as "not the incumbent." However, Clinton and Perot picked up some of Buchanan's themes and language and employed them effectively later in the campaign.

The Tsongas ad "Swim," in which he swam the difficult butterfly stroke, has been described as "one of the most memorable ads of the primary campaign year" for its visual uniqueness and skillful creation of a metaphor for Tsongas's whole life (Devlin, 1994, pp. 83–84). The ad emphasized his characteristics of strength and determination, describing his victories over corrupt politicians and cancer, the same fighting spirit portrayed in his literature. However, when the ad appeared around the country in ad watches, it worked against him. Instead of being impressed with his strength, viewers raised questions about his cancer and discussed the importance of health in a presidential candidate (West, Kern, and Alger, 1992).

Bush only ran four ads in New Hampshire, with the goals of showing that he cared about people's economic troubles, presenting his economic plan, demonstrating leadership, and asking for votes on Election Day (Devlin, 1994). As president and clear front-runner of the Republicans, Bush was *de facto* a major character in the play. His ads relied heavily on the incumbency strategies discussed by Trent and Trent in chapter 3 of this book, and in general maintained the themes found in his campaign literature. They ignored Buchanan and his attacks, and portrayed the enemy as the Democratic Congress.

★ THE MEDIA ATTEMPT TO CONSTRUCT THE PLAY

Television News Coverage of the Candidates

Kenneth Burke long ago pointed out the power of naming: "Naming . . . [is an] interpretive act," he said, and thus has the power not only to describe but also to shape events (1965, pp. 176–91). This power is clearly seen in the lead stories of television news, in which certain events are named as most deserving of our attention. In the February 11–19, 1992 period, 60 percent (15 out of 25) of the lead stories on ABC, CBS, and NBC were about the New Hampshire primary; two others were about the primaries in general. There is no doubt that the news professionals saw the dramatic potential of this story, which they selected over all the crimes and disasters of the day.

Network Choices of Major and Minor Characters. Previous research on media coverage of campaigns has found that the media measure candidates through a number of means: "opinion polls, assessments by experienced politicians and observers, the status of each candidate's campaign organization, who is supporting whom, the size of the contenders' financial war chests, even the amount of coverage the media themselves give respective candidates" (Nimmo and Combs, 1990, p. 56). We also know from prior research that the media are likely to convey these impressions with heavy use of metaphors, especially metaphors of violence and sports (Blankenship, 1976). These patterns emerged in this study as well.

Network news coverage of the 1992 New Hampshire primary in the February 11–19 period suggested that there were six individuals and two groups who were major or potentially major characters in the campaign play. The individuals were: Buchanan, Bush, Clinton, Harkin, Kerrey, and Tsongas. The groups were the citizen/voters and "Democratic leaders."

The networks gave these individuals and groups status as major characters by two means: by covering them in the news, and by discussing their viability or electability. Citizen/voters were mentioned explicitly or implicitly in every broadcast, usually as numbers. They were the numbers in the polls. Occasionally they were interviewed, and they were often shown meeting candidates or in crowds gathered to hear candidates. The chart below shows the number of days the candidates were mentioned by the networks.

Number of Days Networks Mentioned Candidate, Feb. 11–19 (Possible total: 25)

Clinton	24
Bush	20
Tsongas	19
Buchanan	17
Kerrey	16
Harkin	15
Democratic leaders	9
Cuomo	7
Brown	6
Nader, Ralph	1
Leynane, James	1

The main reason for this order of attention to the candidates seems to be tangled up in the question of candidate viability or electability, a major finding in previous studies (Patterson, 1980, 1993; Robinson and Sheehan, 1983). Network stories discussed everyone's electability; not a candidate was spared. Here at the very start of the campaign, the news focused on the ending: who would win the election? Who could win the election?

Electability also emerged as the most significant trait in the ideal Democrat sought by the Democratic leaders. As portrayed by the networks, these powerful leaders loomed in the wings; at any moment they might push a new candidate onto the stage, or rush onto the stage themselves (Bentsen and Gephardt were mentioned). They were "fearful," "worried," "uneasy," and "unhappy" about the chances of the announced candidates for election, afraid that no one would work out. Their chorus served to magnify the theme.

Network Descriptions of Character Traits. In addition to developing a lineup of major and minor characters in the play, organized around the theme of electability, the networks sketched the personal traits of each candidate. The following summaries attempt to capture the recurring images of the candidates communicated by the words and pictures used by each network.

Buchanan: Buchanan emerged in the three ABC stories as a potentially strong character, powerful enough to embarrass the president, teasing the president by accusing him of stealing his lines (Feb. 12). He was shown fighting hard for votes, going on an ambitious whistle-stop bus tour of the state, and exuding confidence that he would give the president a "wake-up call" (Feb. 17). In the six CBS stories the image was similar but more developed. Buchanan was described as a strong and aggressive candidate, who attacked Bush for betraying the American middle class (Feb. 14). Shown actively campaigning at rallies, in ads, and during his long bus tour, he was described as having the power to hurt Bush by exposing his flaws (Feb. 17). The question was raised, however, about whether Buchanan had real

power or was just a way for the voters to send a message to Bush (Feb. 14).

NBC's coverage was also quite favorable to Buchanan, emphasizing the energetic fighter who used hard-hitting ads and hammered at Bush (Feb. 14, 17).

Bush: The ABC image of President Bush was decidedly mixed, both positive and negative. In their five stories during this period, they showed him as an out-of-touch elitist, worried and fearful about a Buchanan protest vote, and lacking in charisma. Demonstrators were televised carrying signs saying, "Jobs not socks" and something about yachts. On the other hand, the ABC reports showed Bush in his presidential role, as he said that presidents have important things to do, and that elections are not about charisma. The CBS coverage was more negative. While they portrayed Bush as actively and aggressively working for reelection, and indicated that there was no doubt he would be the winner of the Republican primary, they also portrayed him as a worried, defensive player.

Finally, the NBC coverage portrayed a Bush of uncertain stature, a man who on the one hand was aggressively campaigning and fighting to keep Buchanan in the low numbers, and who was more statesmanlike than Buchanan. On the other hand, this was the same Bush who failed to command strong voter support and who never really caught fire with his audiences. In the end, even when he won the primary, the network raised the question of electability (Feb. 19).

Clinton: The networks constructed an ambivalent characterization of Clinton. On ABC there was the ever-present question of electability; he had fallen from the position of front-runner and the party's hope, and now was fighting to save his candidacy, even "scrambling" (Feb. 15). Party leaders said he had been wounded. But his fighting to save himself was shown as a mighty effort, displaying great energy and inventiveness. As he fought, the network selected words and pictures that emphasized his upbeat style and positive personality traits (Feb. 13, 14).

CBS developed a similar ambivalent picture of Clinton in the February 11–18 period. Their questions about his electability were more prominent than ABC's, as they reported his drop in the polls and gave a visible role to the Democratic leaders who doubted his survivability (Feb. 12, 14). As late as February 17, Dan Rather wondered if Clinton might be politically dead. Members of the public were shown coming to his defense, however, lamenting that there was so much "looking for dirt" (Feb. 11), and casting him as a kind of sympathy-evoking underdog figure. In general, CBS emphasized that he was an active, energetic campaigner.

Once the primary results were known, CBS gave Clinton important national attention and a platform for shaping perceptions of his character in a live interview with Dan Rather on the February 19 news broadcast. Considering that Clinton had come in second to Tsongas in New Hampshire, one could ask why this prime-time interview was not with Tsongas. In answer to Rather's questions, Clinton naturally seized the opportunity to portray himself as a strong, competent, honest, experienced candidate who understood what the people wanted.

NBC cast a pall over all the Democratic candidates in their early (Feb. 11) coverage, suggesting that none of the candidates was strong. They presented a mixed picture of Clinton, raising doubts almost nightly, which contributed to a more negative image than that of ABC or CBS. The question of his honesty received much more attention here than on the other networks, chiefly through the voices of citizens discussing the draft issue and marital infidelity (Feb. 11, 18). NBC questioned his electability by pointing to his fall in the polls (Feb. 11, 12) and suggested that his handling of the draft issue had wounded his chances for victory in the South (Feb. 19). On Election Day, anchor Tom Brokaw wondered if Clinton could survive (Feb. 18), just as Dan Rather had done on CBS (Feb. 17).

But NBC also had positive words and pictures for Clinton. They noted that he had a good campaign organization and was well funded (Feb. 11, 13), and that he was aggressively fighting to save his candidacy (Feb. 12). And they let him speak for himself in a vivid moment of his campaign, when he almost pleaded with New Hampshirites to give him a second chance. If they did, he said he would be there for them "'til the last dog dies" (Feb. 13).

Tsongas: Tsongas's front-runner status in New Hampshire, based on his standing in the polls, made him a major character in the play, and he was mentioned in nineteen of the twenty-four news broadcasts studied between February 11 and 19. But the networks seemed puzzled by Tsongas, trying out one description and then another. The only characteristic they discussed consistently was his lack of electability, expressing doubts that his success in New Hampshire would carry over to the rest of the country.

In spite of their doubts, they had to explain him to the voters, all the more so when he won the Democratic primary, gaining 34 percent of the votes in a field of five, including votes from many Republicans. This character had the following traits. He was witty (ABC and CBS showed him joking about his charisma, and about a T-shirt he had been given [Feb. 11]). He was a nice guy, who defended Clinton when the draft letter story broke (ABC, Feb. 13), in contrast to Harkin. He was knowledgeable and competent about economic issues (he was shown speaking about the economy, and opposing the middle-class tax cut, NBC, Feb. 14; ABC, Feb. 16). He was courageous, adopting an "I'm no Santa Claus" position on the popular middle-class tax cut. And clearly, as front-runner, he was powerful.

None of the candidates fit the image of the ideal presidential candidate, as they were portrayed by the media. But Tsongas, who had not held a major elective office for eight years, who had not been a dominant figure when he was in the Senate, and who rejected the popular middle-class tax break, deviated from the ideal image enough that the networks portrayed him as an unconventional and unlikely candidate. Tsongas fostered the idea himself at a rally the day before the election, saying, "This is so bizarre. This is so bizarre. I am such an unlikely candidate" (author's notes and NBC, Feb. 17). The networks suggested that Tsongas had simply been lucky in New Hampshire, benefiting from Clinton's problems, from a kind of protest vote against the economic *status quo* (CBS, Feb. 18), and from the advantage of his early entry and proximity to New Hampshire (NBC, Feb. 18). He had little money or backing from leading Democrats (ABC, Feb. 18; NBC, Feb. 19), and both are usually necessary for a successful campaign. And lurking in the background was the question of his health: Would his cancer recur? The question was not discussed openly, but suggested obliquely when Richard Threlkeld asked whether the Tsongas campaign had the "stamina" to last through the primaries (CBS, Feb. 19). Never was the campaign described as energetic or aggressive.

These doubts and qualifications seemed geared to prepare the viewer for an early failed candidacy. Tsongas was a major player now, but he would not last long.

Network Coverage of Candidates' Visions of Hope. The candidates' efforts to project a vision of hope for the future, a positive visualization of what the nation would look like under their presidency, received little attention on network television news. A citizen wishing to determine what the candidates intended to do as president would find little evidence there. These messages were usually contained in candidate speeches, and the networks seldom used candidate language from the speeches. In a few cases they reported a candidate's main theme, such as Tsongas's "call to economic arms" (CBS, Feb. 18). Favorite issues or topics of candidates were sometimes mentioned, such as Clinton's proposal for lower middle-class taxes (NBC, Feb. 14), Tsongas's views of what needed to be done for the environment (NBC, Feb. 17), and Buchanan's opposition to the civil rights bill (NBC, Feb. 19). Perhaps the closest they came to presenting any candidate's vision was with Bush, when they let him speak for himself as he announced his candidacy, told of his goal to reduce the size and cost of government, and described his economic recovery plan (CBS and NBC, Feb. 12). But in general the rhetorical visions of hope enunciated by most of the candidates in their speeches, leaflets, and ads received little explicit attention on the network news.

Newspaper Coverage of the Candidates

The Leading Characters as Portrayed in the Papers. As the newspapers wrote the campaign play on their front pages during the February 11–19 period, Clinton, Tsongas, Bush, and Buchanan were the dominant characters, the same names leading the network stories.[3] But there were differences in the way the print media constructed the play. They paid less attention than the networks to the "Democratic leaders" with their gloomy remarks about electability, giving them front-page coverage in only five stories (*USA Today*, Feb. 19; *New York Times*, Feb. 16; *Boston Globe*, Feb. 12 and 18; *Union Leader*, Feb. 18). They made a clearer distinction between major and minor characters than the networks: only four candidates had regular front-page coverage. Television, though it devoted more time to the poll leaders than the others, mentioned and showed six of the seven candidates regularly. The nature of the medium is such that there is no clear front page, middle section or back page on television. When Harkin and Kerrey were shown almost as often as Tsongas and Clinton, for example, that created some equality in prominent coverage, even though Tsongas and Clinton received more time.

In addition, the national press and the regional and local press differed in the four candidates they covered most heavily. In the national papers, Clinton led in frequency of coverage (followed by Bush, Tsongas, and Buchanan), while in the regional and local papers, Bush led in number of stories (followed by Buchanan, Clinton, and Tsongas). On the following page are tables of frequency of front-page textual and pictorial coverage of the candidates during the February 11–19 period. Any mention of a candidate was considered to be coverage of that person, except for straight listing of poll figures.

These figures suggest that the "electability" rule followed in network coverage (electability as measured by the poll standings of the candidates) also governed the papers. For example, the Republican poll standings of February 12, according to the *Boston Globe/WBZ-TV* tracking poll, were: Bush, 50 percent; Buchanan, 29 percent; other, 9 percent; don't know, 12 percent. The Democratic ratings in the same poll were: Tsongas, 26 percent; Clinton, 20 percent; Harkin, 12 percent; Kerrey, 9 percent; Brown, 6 percent; Cuomo, 6 percent;

Frequency of Front-Page Coverage,
February 11–19

National Press	Clinton	15
	Bush	13
	Tsongas	9
	Buchanan	6
	Harkin	2
	Kerrey	2
	Brown	2
	Cuomo	1
Regional Press	Bush	19
	Buchanan	13
	Clinton	12
	Tsongas	10
	Harkin	3
	Kerrey	2
	Cuomo	1
	Brown	0
Local Press	Bush	36
	Buchanan	27
	Clinton	20
	Tsongas	20
	Kerrey	12
	Harkin	11
	Brown	10
	Cuomo	4

Frequency of Front-Page Pictures

National Press	Clinton	4
	Tsongas	3
	Bush	2
	Buchanan	2
Regional Press	Buchanan	4
	Bush	3
	Tsongas	3
Local Press	Bush	6
	Clinton	5
	Tsongas	4
	Kerrey	4
	Buchanan	3
	Harkin	1
	Cuomo	1

other, 3 percent; don't know, 18 percent (*Boston Globe*, Feb. 23, 1992, p. 20). The front-runners received much more coverage than those who were low in the poll standings.

Candidate Characteristics Portrayed in the Newspapers. The newspapers developed the personal characteristics of the cast of characters through their word choice, pictures, and selection of representative anecdotes. This study examined the front-page coverage of the candidates in the 150 stories and 58 pictures of the February 11–19 period, thereby determining which candidate characteristics were given the most prominence. The extensive coverage inside the papers was not examined.

On the simplest level, the coverage was examined to determine whether the candidates were shown as happy and positive, or sad or angry. Each picture was coded as (1) smiling, (2) neither smiling or frowning, or (3) glum or frowning. The assumption was that these expressions communicated an optimistic, positive outlook or pessimistic outlook to the voters. Based on the pictures, the happiest candidates were Buchanan (7 smiling, 2 neutral) and Tsongas (6 smiling, 4 frowning), with a mixed portrayal of Clinton (2 smiling, 5 neutral, 2 frowning). Pictures of Bush were decidedly downbeat on the national and regional levels (none smiling, 5 frowning), with a more positive look on the local level (4 smiling, 2 frowning).

The tone of the language reporters chose to describe the candidates was also analyzed. Stories in which the candidate was described as pleased, winning, getting voter support, or improving his standing were counted as positive; stories in which the candidate was described as worried, slipping, scrambling, under attack, and the like, were counted as negative. Stories in which no clear position emerged, or a mixture of positive and negative factors emerged, were counted as neutral. Because there was only one coder, I will report only the most obvious and clear-cut results.

The tone of coverage for Tsongas was positive in all three levels of newspapers, national, regional, and local (24 positive, 14 neutral, 1 negative). Just as clearly, the tone was predominantly negative for Bush on all three levels (12 positive, 18 neutral, 39 negative). Stories of sour and skeptical voters, and of Democratic leaders who thought the field should be broadened, contributed to a negative tone in general.

Bush: Of particular interest was the treatment of Bush, who received heavily negative coverage. If the New Hampshire primary established the characterizations of the candidates for the whole campaign to follow, the clear image drawn in New Hampshire may well have tarred Bush for the rest of the year. Throughout the primary campaign, the newspapers referred to Bush's campaign as "weak" or "weakening." This generally referred to his standing in the polls. The main reason for his weakness, according to the front-page stories, was that the voters doubted his competence to deal with the recession. Buchanan and the Democrats drove this point home, using "the ravaged economy as a club against President Bush in their campaigns" (Doina Chiacu, AP, *Telegraph*, Feb. 16).

The response of the Bush campaign to Buchanan's attacks and gains in the polls was also portrayed as weak; it was described as "limping" (Joe Battenfeld, *Boston Herald*, Feb. 16), "lackluster" (Michael Kranish, *Boston Globe*, Feb. 11), "frantic" (Walter V. Robinson, *Boston Globe*, Feb. 18), and "nervous" (John Distaso, *Union Leader*, Feb. 12). Stories noted that he had spent little time in New Hampshire, and was scrambling to add a few visits the last week.

The public's response to Bush's campaigning was described as weak too: there was no "real excitement" at his events (Tammy Annis, *Union Leader*, Feb. 17); crowds were small and there was more applause for Barbara Bush and Arnold Schwarzeneger than for Bush (Andrew Rosenthal, *New York Times*, Feb. 17).

Bush was charged with another kind of weakness, which dovetailed an issue with image traits. Buchanan addressed this point when he derided Bush for breaking his no-tax pledge, and for first proposing a middle-class tax exemption for children in his State of the Union Address, then withdrawing it from his budget proposal. The Democrats reinforced this attack in their debate, saying he was "indifferent to the suffering of those hurt by the recession" (Felice Belman, *Concord Monitor*, Feb. 17); Tsongas said that all five Democrats had "a stronger core" than Bush (Richard Benedetto, *USA Today*, Feb. 17). Bush's changes on particular issue positions were thus used to portray him as weak in honesty and empathy.

Bush aides contributed to this aura of weakness by entering into the numbers game with the press, discussing what percentage of the vote Bush needed to avoid being embarrassed by Buchanan. Considering the media's history of turning New Hampshire primary victories into defeats because candidates have not made a certain magic number (Edmund Muskie's 1972 campaign is the best example), one would expect that campaigns would avoid discussing percentages at all costs. When Bush received only 53 percent of the Republican vote and Buchanan 37 percent on Election Day, with 10 percent going to other candidates, the Bush campaign estimates proved too optimistic, and the outcome was portrayed as a stunning defeat for Bush.

One would hardly have known that Bush had won the New Hampshire primary. The beaming Republican "winner" on the February 19 front pages was Buchanan, not Bush. The headlines focused on the blow dealt to Bush: "Bush Jarred in First Primary" (*New York Times*); "Buchanan Grabs 40% in New Hampshire, Shocks Bush" (*USA Today*); "Bush Whacked!" (*Boston Herald*); "GOP Voters Signal Protest on Recession" (*Boston Globe*); "Bush Supporters: Presidency Weakened" (*Union Leader*); "Buchanan Fire Wounds Bush" (*Telegraph*).

Saussure (1916/1959) has argued that pairs of words (such as open/closed) get their meaning from each other; that one term in the pair becomes meaningful because we associate the other term with it. It is in the antithesis of the terms that meaning arises (Corcoran, 1990). The words used to describe the state of the Bush campaign after the New Hampshire primary gained power from just such antithetical meaning. The media called the results a "wake-up call" (Judy Keen, *USA Today*, Feb. 19), implying that Bush had been asleep. A voter remarked that she voted for Buchanan so Bush would "sit up and take notice," implying that he had been lying down (asleep? tired?). "An absent Bush conceded Buchanan gave him a huge scare," said the *Telegraph* (Feb. 19, Kevin Landrigan); the opposites were much more positive, suggesting that a candidate who was present and brave would be a better choice. Finally there came the amazing suggestion that Bush might drop out of the race, introduced both through analogies to other incumbent presidents who had decided not to run after getting the primary results (such as Lyndon Johnson and Harry Truman), and through the loaded sentence, "The president himself has vowed to stay in the race," with the implication of its opposite, "get out of the race" (John Distaso, *Union Leader*, Feb. 13).

Although Saussure never talked about antithesis in relation to pictures, there is such a striking difference in the Bush and Buchanan pictures (and, in fact, between the Bush pictures and those of all the other candidates), that the idea of such opposites leaps to mind. Bush was older than Buchanan, and older than all the Democrats as well. In the pictures he looked worried, puzzled, and angry more than any of the other candidates. Pictures, of course, are much more ambiguous in meaning than words, and leave much to the viewer to fill in. But in a state that was hard hit economically, in a primary campaign requiring that voters choose among many candidates, six out of seven of whom were calling for change, it would be understandable if many voters concluded that this old, tired, worried-looking president should be replaced by someone younger and with more energy and fresh ideas.

There were positive Bush stories, of course. Much of the front-page coverage in the *Concord Monitor* and *Telegraph* (Nashua) was positive, with Bush and his spokespeople quoted frequently. But in general the visual and verbal portrayal by the newspapers was unflattering.

Buchanan: Buchanan was portrayed as the anti-bush; he was defined by what he said against Bush. Though stories often reported that voters were using him as a messenger, as a way "to get through to Bush," rather than seeing him as a serious candidate (Richard Benedetto, *USA Today*, Feb. 19), the frequency of Buchanan stories, pictures, and quotations established him as a major character in the play. He was "the challenger," the "rival."

The dominant qualities emphasized in the Buchanan stories were his energy and strength—energy in fighting against Bush and strength in driving Bush down in the polls. This image was in direct contrast to the weak image of Bush. Words such as "pugnacious" (Adam Nagourney, *USA Today*, Feb. 18), "fired up" (Wayne Woodlief, *Boston Herald*, Feb. 16), "upbeat" (Chris Black and Michael Kranish, *Boston Globe*, Feb. 18), and "aggressive" (Mark Travis, *Concord Monitor*, Feb. 17) characterized coverage on Buchanan.

The Buchanan quotations chosen for these stories were consistent with this fighter image. For example, he said he would "shock the world." by humbling Bush at the polls, that "the Buchanan brigades are going to run into the hollow army of King George and cut through it like butter" (Wayne Woodlief, *Boston Herald*, Feb. 16). The boldness in such statements was particularly striking considering that no major Democrat had been willing to run against Bush due to his popularity after the Persian Gulf War.

The stories also commented on Buchanan's effectiveness in producing changes in voter attitudes and behavior, a major sign of power. For example, his political advertising was reported to be effective: "significant numbers of voters" were repeating his advertising themes (R. W. Apple Jr., *New York Times*, Feb. 15). Polls showed him "closing fast on the president" (Wayne Woodlief, *Boston Herald*, Feb. 14), who was trying to "stave off an embarrassingly strong showing" by Buchanan (Robin Toner, *New York Times*, Feb. 17).

There was little suggestion in all this coverage that Buchanan was competent to be president. In fact, the *Boston Herald*, which endorsed him in a front-page editorial, confessed they did not know much about his leadership abilities, and focused on Bush's weaknesses. They urged a vote for Buchanan "to protest the state of the country" (Feb. 12). Buchanan's presumed incompetence was discussed by Bush, who wondered why anyone would vote for a man with so few qualifications for president, a former television commentator (Michael Kranish and Chris Black, Feb. 17, *Boston Globe*). But as a fighting antibush, running on a platform of change, Buchanan gave Republicans a way to express their dissatisfaction with Bush. Clinton was already adopting this refrain in

New Hampshire and later Ross Perot did the same. In November, both candidates succeeded in converting voters from Bush; 12.2 percent of Clinton's 43.7 percent vote came from 1988 Bush voters; 11.3 percent of Perot's 19 percent vote came from Bush voters (Pomper, 1993, p. 141).

Tsongas: The coverage of Tsongas was generally positive on all levels, with the question of his electability raised occasionally. His dominant trait as portrayed by the newspapers was his front-runner status and his "growing lead" (Judy Keen, *USA Today,* Feb. 12). Many of Tsongas's traits were described in relation to his leadership in the polls. For example, he was shown as confident—that voters would "flock to his message" (Joe Battenfeld and Andrew Miga, *Boston Herald,* Feb. 18). He was "glowing"— about his new status as front-runner (Robin Toner, *New York Times,* Feb. 12). He had credibility—because he had bested Clinton in the primary (Curtis Wilkie, *Boston Globe,* Feb. 19).

The reporters of the *New York Times* and *Boston Globe* gave Tsongas stature as a serious, substantive, knowledgeable candidate in several front-page stories, and the *Boston Herald* did it with an editorial. Robin Toner referred to his "against-the-grain economic message," describing his positions on capital gains and the middle-class tax cut (*New York Times,* Feb. 12); Gwen Ifill described him as a serious, policy-oriented candidate who criticized policy issues instead of attacking fellow Democrats (*New York Times,* Feb. 15). Walter Robinson said he focused on his positions on the economy and the environment, contrasting him with Clinton, who was busy blaming the Republicans for dirty tricks (*Boston Globe,* Feb. 11). The *Boston Herald* editorial praised him for many qualities, including integrity, decency, strength of character, experience, knowledge, and moral leadership, not to mention his pro-business philosophy.

Tsongas was also portrayed as a man amazed by his success; he sounded "almost awed by the status he had achieved" (Robin Toner, *New York Times,* Feb. 16), and "labelled himself a 'most unlikely candidate'" (Walter V. Robinson, *Boston Globe,* Feb. 18). While these reactions gave him an aura of genuine humility, they also conflicted with the image of confidence and did little to rebut the question of his electability. This question was raised in several stories: Would he be able to translate a win in his own backyard into national credibility and the necessary financial support? (Richard Benedetto, *USA Today,* Feb. 19, Michael J. Birkner, *Concord Monitor,* Feb. 17; Tsongas picture text, *USA Today,* Feb. 19).

Clinton: The description of the Clinton character in the primary play was quite mixed in the newspapers. Like Bush, he was slipping in the polls during the February 11–19 period, and the words used to describe his status made him sound desperate and his campaign hopeless. On the other hand, he was fighting to save himself, and, just as with Buchanan, the press expressed its admiration for a tough, energetic fighter. The two events that precipitated his decline in the polls—the Gennifer Flowers story and the draft letter incident—were often alluded to in the coverage, and each carried with it a host of negative associations, about his honesty, faithfulness, courage, and patriotism. The national press gave Clinton more front-page coverage than all the other candidates of either party, while the regional and local press wrote the play a different way, focusing the script on the Bush-Buchanan struggle. But there, too, Clinton received as much or slightly more coverage than Tsongas, the Democratic front-runner.

There seemed to be two main reasons for this heavy coverage. First, the "falling front-runner" stories of Bush and Clinton played right to the reporters' dramatic instincts, for successful dramatic ritual requires both rising and falling action. A front-runner remaining steadily in the lead fails to meet these requirements. This finding is consistent with Nimmo and Combs' (1990) research on the 1988 preprimary campaigns where the front-runners also received the most coverage, and the most negative coverage. A second explanation for the attention to Clinton was that he created a story by fighting, vowing to "fight like hell," and beginning a "blitz" of door-to-door campaigning, rallies, call-in shows, and television ads (Richard Benedetto, *USA Today,* Feb. 17). His words emphasized his determination: "I want these people to see me out there working hard, reaching out to them and fighting until the last dog dies" (Robin Toner, *New York Times*, Feb. 16).

Clinton's image suddenly took a positive turn after he finished second to Tsongas. He had demonstrated his "resilience," said the *Boston Globe* (Curtis Wilkie, Feb. 19). More dramatically, he had been resurrected, as from the dead (Kevin Landrigan, "Clinton claims . . . ," *Telegraph*, Feb. 19). Clinton's own words were, "New Hampshire tonight has made Bill Clinton the comeback kid" (Richard Benedetto, *USA Today*, Feb. 19).

Newspaper Coverage of Candidates' Visions of Hope. The front-page newspaper coverage of the primary gave few insights into the vision of the individual candidates. The emphasis was heavily on electability, poll standings, and the characteristics of the candidates, not the ideal America and plans for the future envisioned by each candidate. Voters who read the front page would have little information on how the candidates' goals differed.

CONCLUSIONS

This chapter has focused on the struggle of the candidates and the media in the New Hampshire primary to construct the script for the presidential campaign drama. The primary is part of a dramatic ritual, a contest among candidates to try to win over the voters through a series of repeated acts, introducing themselves as major characters in the play, establishing the nature of their characters, and projecting their visions of the future. The media participate in the ritual by reconstructing these messages and transmitting them to the citizens, with a heavy overlay of horse race imagery.

Both candidates and the media go to New Hampshire with a sense of urgency. The candidates know, based on the primary's history, that the state has a remarkable record of selecting winners in the general election, and that most of them will be winnowed out of the contest soon after the primary. They play a dual role, as both playwrights and as characters in the play.

The media also have a sense of urgency. They must grasp a complicated story and communicate it to their audiences. The primary season will be long (there were thirty-eight primaries in 1992, occurring over almost four months), and it will require that they know something about many candidates. Like the voters, they, too, are not very familiar with some of the candidates. The outcome of the drama is uncertain, and they must decide how to cover it. Journalists from around the nation and world congregate in New Hampshire to "get a fix on" the contest. The script they construct their through their intensive coverage has the effect of introducing the electoral drama to much of the nation.

The findings of this research reveal that the candidates and media in 1992 sometimes co-constructed the script and sometimes wrote different scripts. Each candidate tried to present himself as a major character in the play while the media were much more selective, relying chiefly on opinion polls to determine who the two front-runners were in each party and emphasizing them. The candidates constructed themselves as characters with many qualities, while the media focused chiefly on electability and winning.

On one image trait most of the candidates and media were in agreement: the presidential candidate must be a "fighter." Demonstrations of fighting against the odds by Clinton and Buchanan received heavy coverage, and Tsongas stressed his fighter image in ads and the booklet "A Call to Economic Arms." Bush and the *status quo* were the main objects of this fighting. The Saussurian concept of symbolic differentiation, in which words gain important meaning from their opposites (Saussure, 1959), played a crucial role in the construction of the primary. On the Republican side, Buchanan and the press portrayed Buchanan as strong, a fighter; Bush was weak, slipping in the polls, afraid. So pervasive was this verbal and visual image that Buchanan, the loser in the primary (by a 53-37 margin), received the triumphant front-page pictures.

On the Democratic side, the question of whether Clinton could survive the scandals, raised frequently by the media and Democratic leaders quoted by the national press, gave a special definition to the concept of strength. Here the issue was whether a campaign would be strong enough to survive, or would prove to be politically dead (Dan Rather, CBS,

Feb. 17; Tom Brokaw, NBC, Feb. 18). The word "survive" suggests that one has continued to live in spite of a dangerous event such as a wreck; the dangerous events were the stories of Clinton's infidelity and draft evasion. In the context of a multi-candidate campaign, a survivor is stronger than those who have not survived; the word takes its meaning combined with its opposite, the dead. The result is hardly the image of a winner. But Clinton's burst of energy to save himself won admiration and positive coverage in the media, more coverage than all the other candidates in the national press. With their coverage of his strength and energy, they created an intriguing mosaic rather than the predictable, moralistic, negative images projected during the controversies over infidelity and the draft.

In addition to their claims to be protagonists and their efforts to project admired personal traits, the candidates also attempted to explain their vision for the future of the nation, their plans and priorities. In these efforts, however, they had to rely chiefly on themselves; the media gave little prominent attention to their goals or the language they used to express them. Unlike stories about winning and losing and fighting, which met the dramatic requisites for television and newspapers and were easily constructed in poll numbers and battle imagery, accounts of the candidates' visions took more discussion and explanation, and lent themselves less readily to dramatic portrayals. Pictures in the media may have conveyed some impressions of the candidates' outlook on a superficial level (optimistic, pessimistic, happy, sad), as a smile is a more hopeful expression than a frown. But little of what the candidates visualized or proposed came through on network television or front-page newspaper stories.

In most states, the media script would be the only script. How else would voters learn about the campaign in New York? Florida? Illinois? Thomas Patterson (1993) has made a persuasive case that the media have replaced the political parties as chief intermediaries between candidates and voters. Now the media, not the parties, he argues, outline the candidates' strengths and weaknesses and guide the voters in their choices. In their guidance, they have portrayed the candidates in a heavily negative

light, souring the public on the process. But the evidence in the New Hampshire primary is somewhat different. There the candidates often found ways around the intermediaries, and got to the voters directly. They communicated in their own language, not the language of the media, in messages of sufficient length that they were able to explain their visions for the future.

Only through remarkably inventive, persistent, and often expensive means could the candidates compensate for the media's neglect of their goals. They reached the voters both interpersonally and through the paid media. Tsongas managed to communicate his message by giving speeches and meeting people in New Hampshire for almost a year before the primary, and through his booklet, *A Call to Economic Arms*. Clinton communicated his vision by giving the longest speeches, with the most extensive question-and-answer periods, having a rally every day the final week, buying two half hours of television for call-in questions, distributing twenty thousand videotapes, and publishing his full draft letter in the newspaper. Over one hundred Arkansan friends also descended on the state, meeting and greeting voters and telling them about "Bill and Hillary." Buchanan campaigned in New Hampshire for over two months (while Bush was absent), giving speeches and meeting voters, and bombarded the state with his advertisements, spending more than all the other candidates. Most of the candidates made heavy use of advertising, some of it to outline their vision of an ideal America. These efforts, rather than the media coverage, allowed the voters to hear the candidates discussing their goals.

In contrast to the other candidates, Bush violated the New Hampshire "rules," spending little time there—only twelve hours until the final week (Michael Kranish, *Boston Globe*, Feb. 11, p. 1). He gave a few short speeches, but chose a largely nonverbal personal style. He passed through malls, shook hands, waved and smiled, providing good pictures but avoiding the microphone. His ads, leaflets, and surrogate speakers carried his message. Yet he won, and decisively. He won in spite of heavily negative media coverage, steady attacks from all the Democrats, and an opponent who campaigned vigorously and conveyed the image of a "fighter." One can only surmise that the reservoir of reputation he had built up as the Republican president in a state that favored Republicans was sufficient to protect him against the onslaught. His winning percentage of the vote was far smaller than his campaign had predicted, however, and smaller than most incumbent presidents had received. The image of weakness and ineptitude constructed of him by Buchanan, the Democrats, and the media haunted him for the next nine months.

Rituals are emotionally satisfying because they engage people in repetitive acts that remind them of deeply held values. A major part of most important rituals is their language, as people repeat the age-old marriage vows, or catechism, or slogans, drawing sustenance and a sense of worth from the words. The dramatic ritual of political campaigns *can* reinforce deeply held values, but without language, the satisfaction from participation is very limited. In many states, the only candidate language citizens hear is in ads, and though ads appeal to the emotions through the language of values and feelings (Kern, 1989), their brevity makes it difficult to develop and sustain political messages in the way a speech or a prolonged discussion can.

In New Hampshire, candidates have found ways to reach the voters with their own political language, expressing their visions and plans for the future, in spite of media obstacles. Perhaps the high voter participation in that state is in part due to the satisfaction of the citizens with a dramatic ritual that engages them so fully through its language.

The words and pictures from New Hampshire, and the votes that give them credence, establish who and how and what kind of characters will perform in the electoral drama. This primary is the critical beginning of the drama, but far more than a chronological beginning. It is a definitional beginning, whose character constructions will dominate the rest of the play.

NOTES

[1] The Iowa caucuses precede the New Hampshire primary, and also claim attention as "first in the nation." They have played pivotal roles in several presidential campaigns, starting in 1976. Their record as predictor of the campaign to come has not been impressive, however. In 1988 the winners there were soon winnowed out in early primaries; in 1992, candidates abandoned the Iowa caucuses to favorite son Senator Tom Harkin.

[2] In February 1988 and 1992, I spent 8–9 days before the primary traveling with the media and attending public events of the candidates in New Hampshire. I received press credentials from WAMC in Albany, New York, a National Public Radio affiliate, and called in several stories during the trip.

[3] The newspapers, like the networks, gave substantial coverage to the citizen/voters, both by reporting their preferences in poll standings, and through interviews and quotations. The "New Hampshire voters" were characterized as "cantankerous," "crotchety," "unpredictable," "savvy," "skeptical," and "difficult to please." On top of that, they were sour about the economy and not happy with the candidates chosen—all in all a tough bunch. More research is needed on their role in the electoral drama.

REFERENCES

Adams, William C. (1987). As New Hampshire goes . . . In Gary R. Orren and Nelson W. Polsby, eds., *Media and momentum: The New Hampshire primary and nomination politics*. Chatham, N.J.: Chatham House, pp. 42–59.

Baker, Ross K. (1993). Sorting out and suiting up: The presidential nominations. In Gerald M. Pomper, ed., *The election of 1992*. Chatham, N.J.: Chatham House, pp. 39–73.

Bartels, Larry M. (1988). *Presidential primaries and the dynamics of public choice*. Princeton, N.J.: Princeton University Press.

Blankenship, Jane (1976). The search for the 1972 Democratic nomination: A metaphorical perspective. In Jane Blankenship and Hermann G. Stelzner, eds., *Rhetoric and communication: Studies in the University of Illinois tradition*. Urbana, Ill.: University of Illinois Press, pp. 230–60.

Boot, William (1989, Jan.–Feb.). Campaign '88: TV overdoses on the inside dope. *Columbia Journalism Review*, 23–29.

Brady, Henry E., and Richard Johnston (1987). What's the primary message: Horse race or issue journalism? In Gary R. Orren and Nelson W. Polsby, eds., *Media and momentum: The New Hampshire primary and nomination politics*. Chatham, N.J.: Chatham House, pp. 127–86.

Buchanan, Pat (1992, Feb.). Putting and keeping America first. Leaflet.

Burke, Kenneth (1965). *Permanence and change: An anatomy of purpose.* Indianapolis, Ind.: Bobbs-Merrill.

Bush, George (1992, Feb.). A plan to make New Hampshire and America move . . . and keep moving. Leaflet.

Castle, David S. (1992, Jan.). Media coverage of presidential primaries. *American Politics Quarterly, 19,* 33–42.

Ceaser, James, and Andrew Busch (1993). *Upside down and inside out: The 1992 elections and American politics.* Boston: Littlefield Adams.

Clinton, Bill (1992a, Feb.). America Dream. Great American Media, Inc. Videotape.

Clinton, Bill (1992b, Feb.). Fighting for the forgotten middle class. Leaflet.

Corcoran, Paul E. (1990). Language and politics. In David Swanson and Dan Nimmo, eds., *New directions in political communication.* Newbury Park, Calif.: Sage, pp. 51–85.

Crouse, Timothy (1972). *The boys on the bus.* New York: Ballantine Books.

Devlin, L. Patrick (1994, Jan.–Mar.). Television advertising in the 1992 New Hampshire presidential primary election. *Political Communication, 11,* 81–99.

Duncan, Dayton (1991a). *Grassroots.* New York: Viking.

Duncan, Dayton (1991b, Mar. 31). Interview on Booknotes, C-SPAN.

Graber, Doris A. (1987). Framing election news broadcasts: News context and its impact on the 1984 presidential election. *Social Science Quarterly, 69,* 552–67.

Hellweg, Susan A., and Stephen W. King (1983). Comparative evaluation of political candidates: Implication for the voter decision-making process. *Central States Speech Journal, 34,* 134–38.

Hellweg, Susan A., Stephen W. King, and Steve E. Williams (1988). Comparative candidate evaluation as a function of election level and candidate incumbency. *Communication Reports, 1,* 76–85.

Jamieson, Kathleen Hall (1992). *Dirty politics: Deception, distraction, and democracy.* New York: Oxford University Press.

John, Kenneth E. (1989). The polls—A report. 1980–1988 New Hampshire presidential primary polls. *Public Opinion Quarterly, 53,* 590–605.

Kendall, Kathleen E. (1993, Nov.–Dec.). Public speaking in the presidential primaries through media eyes. *American Behavioral Scientist, 37,* 240–51.

Kendall, Kathleen E., and Judith S. Trent (1989, Fall). Presidential surfacing in the New Hampshire primary. *Political Communication Review, 14,* 1–29.

Kennamer, J. D., and S. H. Chaffee (1982). Communication of political information during early presidential primaries: Cognition, affect, and uncertainty. In M. Burgoon (Ed.), *Communication Yearbook 5* (pp. 627–650). New Brunswick, N.J.: Transaction.

Kerbel, Matthew Robert (1994). *Edited for television: CNN, ABC, and the 1992 presidential campaign.* Boulder, Colo.: Westview.

Kern, Montague (1989). *30-second politics: Political advertising in the eighties.* New York: Praeger.

Kern, Montague, and Marion Just (1994, April). How voters construct images of political candidates: The role of political advertising and televised news. Research Paper R-10, The Joan Shorenstein Barone Center, Harvard University.

Kern, Montague, and Marion Just (1995, forthcoming, June). The focus group method, political advertising, campaign news and the construction of candidate images. *Political Communication, 12.*

Lichter, S. Robert, Daniel Amundsen, and Richard Noyes (1988). *The Video Campaign: Network Coverage of the 1988 Primaries.* Washington, DC: American Enterprise Institute for Public Policy Research.

Louden, Allan Dean (1990). Image construction in political spot advertising: The Hunt/Helms Senate campaign 1984 (Ph.D. diss., University of Southern California).

Matthews, Donald R. (1978). Winnowing. In James D. Barber, ed., *Race for the presidency.* Englewood Cliffs, N.J.: Prentice Hall, pp. 55–78.

Mayer, William G. (1987). The New Hampshire primary: A historical overview. In Gary R. Orren and Nelson W. Polsby, eds., *Media and momentum: The New Hampshire primary and nomination politics.* Chatham, N.J.: Chatham House, pp. 9–41.

Meyrowitz, Joshua (1992, June). The power of television news. *The World and I, 6*(7), 452–73.

Neuman, W. Russell, Marion R. Just, and Ann N. Crigler (1992). *Common knowledge.* Chicago: University of Chicago Press.

Nimmo, Dan, and Robert L. Savage (1976). *Candidates and their images: Concepts, methods, and findings.* Pacific Palisades, Calif.: Goodyear.

Nimmo, Dan, and James E. Combs (1990). *Mediated political realities.* 2nd ed. New York: Longman.

Orren, Gary R. and Nelson W. Polsby, eds. (1987). *Media and momentum: The New Hampshire primary and nomination politics.* Chatham, N.J.: Chatham House.

Patterson, Thomas E. (1980). *The mass media election: How Americans choose their president.* New York: Praeger.

Patterson, Thomas E. (1993). *Out of order*. New York: Alfred A Knopf.

Pfau, Michael, Tracy Diedrich, Karla M. Larson, and Kim M. Van Winkle (1993, Summer). The influence of communication modalities on voters' perceptions of candidates during presidential primary campaigns. *Journal of Broadcasting and Electronic Media, 37*, 275–92.

Pomper, Gerald M. (1993). *The election of 1992: Reports and Interpretations*. Chatham, N.J.: Chatham House.

Popkin, Samuel L. (1992). Decision making in presidential primaries. In Shanto Iyengar and William J. McGuire, eds., *Explorations in political psychology*. Durham, N.C., and London: Duke University Press, pp. 361–79.

Popkin, Samuel L. (1991). *The reasoning voter: Communication and persuasion in presidential campaigns*. Chicago: University of Chicago Press.

1992 Presidential Primary Commercials. Purdue University Public Affairs Video Archives, # 91-04-30-0000-45660-24630.

Ridout, Christine F. (1991). The role of media coverage of Iowa and New Hampshire in the 1988 Democratic nomination. *American Politics Quarterly, 19*, 43–58.

Robinson, Michael J. and Margaret A. Sheehan (1983). *Over the wire and on tv*. New York: Russell Sage Foundation.

Rosenstiel, Tom (1993). *Strange bedfellows: How television and the presidential candidates changed American politics, 1992*. New York: Hyperion.

Saussure, Ferdinand de (1959). *Course in general linguistics*. Trans. W. Baskin. New York: Philosophical Library. (Original work published 1916).

Trent, Judith S. (1978). Presidential surfacing: The ritualistic and crucial first act. *Communication Monographs, 45*, 281–92.

Trent, Judith S., Paul A. Mongeau, Jimmie D. Trent, Kathleen E. Kendall, and Ronald B. Cushing (1993, Nov.). The ideal candidate: A study of the desired attributes of the public and the media across two presidential campaigns. *American Behavioral Scientist, 37*, 225–39.

Tsongas, Paul E. (n.d.) *A call to economic arms: Forging a new American mandate*. Boston, Mass.: The Tsongas Committee.

Tsongas, Paul (1992, Feb.). How to fight for America's economic future and win. Leaflet.

West, Darrell M., Montague Kern, and Dean Alger (1992, Sept.). Political advertising and ad watches in the 1992 presidential nominating campaign. Paper presented at the American Political Science Association, Chicago, Ill.

Newspapers (Feb. 11–19, 1992):
Boston Globe, Boston Herald, Concord Monitor (Feb. 12, 13, 15, 17), *New York Times, The Telegraph* (Nashua), *Union Leader* (Manchester), *USA Today*

Television news (Feb. 11–19, 1992, 6:30 or 7:00 P.M.)
ABC World News Tonight, CBS Evening News, NBC Nightly News (missing Feb. 15–16)

Political Scopophilia, Presidential Campaigning, and the Intimacy of American Politics

Trevor Parry-Giles and Shawn J. Parry-Giles

A particularly ironic moment in the 1992 presidential campaign occurred just prior to the New York primary, when Bill Clinton appeared on the syndicated talk show *Donahue*. Pressed by the host to address allegations of his extramarital activities, Clinton responded angrily: "We're going to sit here a long time in silence, Phil. I'm not going to answer any more of these questions." As the studio audience cheered, Clinton continued, attacking Donahue with the charge, "You are responsible for the cynicism in this country. You don't want to talk about the real issues" (Jamieson, 1992a, p. 265; see also Germond and

Witcover, 1993; Goldman, DeFrank, Miller, Murr, & Mathews, 1994; Simons, 1994). Ironically, the presidential candidate, in making a rare appearance on a program devoted to the discussion of the personal, sensational, and scandalous, challenged the importance of such concerns for political decision-making. As Clinton insisted, Donahue should instead address the "real issues."

This moment reveals an existing paradox in contemporary political image construction by presidential candidates. Put simply, candidates are forced to construct an image of presidential leadership in an era of televisual intimacy and intrusion. As Jamieson (1988) argues, the "intimate medium of television requires that those who speak comfortably through it project a sense of private self, [and] unself-consciously self-disclose" (p. 81).[1] Candidates who exhibit their intimate selves via television, however, sacrifice the interpersonal distance necessary to appear "presidential." American politics has traditionally valued presidents who project heroic and mythic personas (Bailey, 1966; Edelman, 1988; Fisher, 1982; Hankins, 1983) and those who manage the symbolism of the presidency successfully (Denton, 1982; Hahn 198; Hinckley, 1990; Luke, 1986–1987; Schmuhl, 1992.) Yet the heroism and symbolism of the presidency occur, in part, because of the distance created between presidents and the public; a distance sacrificed by self-disclosure and personal revelation. Thus, while Clinton appeared on "talk" shows in order to reach new television audiences, he simultaneously rejected the intimacy of the "talk" show in order to appear presidential. The paradox that Clinton confronted in the 1992 election plagues all candidates vying for office in this time of televisual, postmodern electioneering (Schram, 1991).

To fully explain this paradox facing contemporary presidential candidates, it is necessary to reach beyond standard political, historical, or ideological parameters of political communication. The choices and strategies of candidates represent a confluence of factors, from the individual and psychological to the social and ideological. An exclusive focus on the collective, ideological bases for electoral choices ignores, in the words of Rushing and Frentz (1991), "the role of the interior world of the psyche in the visualization of a cultural ideal" (p. 403). Analyzing campaign rhetorics of image construction by attending to their psychological origins and consequences allows for a greater appreciation of the multiple dimensions of moral choice and political judgment that might otherwise be missed or misunderstood (Rushing & Frentz, 1991, p. 386).[2]

In this essay we offer an explanation for the intimacy present in American political discourse and examine how presidential contenders construct their images within the intimate parameters of contemporary politics.

Specifically, we isolate the psychoanalytic concept of scopophilia at the foundation of contemporary image construction and we explore the consequences of this impulse for American electoral politics. Through an analysis of the presidential campaign films of the last three successful candidates (Ronald Reagan, George Bush, and Bill Clinton),[3] we conclude that, while there are differences in method and form, contemporary candidates engage in a high degree of personal display to achieve electoral success. Such display recognizes and adapts to the scopophiliac impulse present in contemporary audiences practiced in the art of gazing at mass-mediated messages.

The presidential campaign film is a unique form of campaign rhetoric that functions as the centerpiece of image construction in the presidential election ritual. Dating back to Calvin Coolidge (Morreale, 1993), such films occupy a central place in contemporary political campaigns. Routinely presented at the national nominating conventions, these films formally introduce the candidates to the voting public. Their discourse is often appropriated in subsequent campaign advertising and pre-election features (Morreale, 1993), achieving wide exposure beyond their initial screening at the conventions. Such films are, at bottom, prototypical discourses of image construction that represent and express larger campaign rhetorics, and that define the candidate for the voting public.

★ FREUD, SCOPOPHILIA, AND AMERICAN ELECTIONS

Freud (1905/1957, 1915/1957) theorized that human beings, from early childhood, possess a need to gaze at others, which produces a feeling of pleasure. This impulse is "scopophilia," and Freud observed the instinct to look as a phenomenon of infantile sexuality that develops into a "normal" part of adult sexual behavior. The visual sense works, in this theory, as a part of the sexual identity of the individual. When taken to extremes, however, scopophilia becomes the "perversion" called voyeurism when gazing transforms into a means to suppress rather than to prepare for the sexual aim (Freud, 1905/1957, 1915/1957). Scopophilia also involves, inherently, its opposite—display and exhibition. Within the "normal" sexual aim, the individual who looks must have something or someone who is the recipient of such a gaze, and both looking and displaying functions as pleasurable activities. Voyeurism, Freud maintains, also reverses into its opposite perversion, or exhibitionism, as the voyeur not only derives pleasure exclusively from gazing but also from displaying (1915/1957, pp. 126–127, 129–133).

For Freud (1905/1957, 1915/1957), looking and displaying are both instincts and aberrations. To this extent, he observes that these impulses are present in everyone, but are controlled by social norms, taboos, and rules that prevent their common manifestation as perversions (Freud, 1905/1957, 1915/1957). In Freud's theory, while all humans are instinctually driven to look at others, only some "perverse" individuals employ this instinct as the sole source of sexual gratification.

The Rhetorical Dimensions of Scopophilia

The application of Freud's theories of scopophilia in communication and rhetorical theory is restricted primarily to cinematic and televisual secularity theory, and largely centers on voyeurism as a sexual perversion (Ellis, 1982; Fiske, 1987; Flitterman, 1978/1981; Flitterman-Lewis, 1987; Kuhn, 1982; Metz, 1975, 1976/1981; Mulvey, 1975). Premised on the technological apparatus of cinema (see Cha, 1980), such theories hold that film (and, for some, television) encourages voyeurism in viewers because the viewing experience allows/commands audiences to gaze at characters who are, the fiction maintains, unaware of being watched, giving the spectator control and power over the projected images. This "secret" gazing allows for the objectification of women in particular, and permits an almost sexual gratification on the part of the spectator.

Television and cinema both encourage and invite the scopophiliac *impulse* (as opposed to voyeurism as a perversion) in audiences, not only because of technology, but because of curiosity and possibility. An audience's scopophilia is aroused because television and cinema allow for the possibility of gazing, without guilt, into the private affairs of others, whether they be fictional characters or the subjects of news accounts. As Freud (1901/1955) suggests, there is an epistemophiliac impulse, of which scopophilia is a prime component (see also Rabinowitz 1992, pp. 148–149). Pleasure is derived from knowing (as opposed to the controlling/dominating pleasure emergent from voyeurism), which looking and gazing make possible. Television and cinema technologize that pleasure and extend the scopophilia of the viewers beyond their immediate context.

The focus of communication theories of specularity on the darkness of movie theaters, or the interrupted viewing of television, while useful, may be totalizing (Brummett & Duncan, 1990). Such theories seemingly ignore looking and gazing as pleasurable instincts, privileging instead the aberrant looking of voyeurism. Yet the aberrant voyeur is atypical, and the power of television and film to allow for the possibility of pleasurable looking that is not perverse is a more reliable reflection of material communication practices. Recognizing the power of visual media to stimulate scopophilia more accurately explains the common viewing experience. It is when viewing is taken to extremes, when it becomes perverse, that the guilt and shame of aberrant voyeurism grips the spectator.

Freud's explanation of the pleasures resulting from the scopophiliac impulse offers an alternative perspective on significant trends in contemporary political communication. With the proliferation of television and its increased importance in political campaigning, voters encounter greater opportunities to gaze at political candidates, both literally and figuratively. Television, as a medium, recognizes and capitalizes on the scopophilia present in its audience and the impact on American politics is considerable. To be successful in the world of "electronic electioneering" (Schram, 1991, p. 210), the politician must willingly accommodate this impulse in an audience of voters accustomed to a televisual diet of intimacy and personal display.

Personal revelation and intimacy on the part of presidential candidates, though, may be a risky and counterproductive political strategy. It was Freud (1921/1955) who theorized that leaders are powerful when they are substitutes for the ego-ideal and distant from their subjects (see also Borch-Jacobsen, 1992; Craib, 1990).[4] This distance is part of the symbolic presidency that is central to the political and moral leadership of the office and the institution (Hinckley, 1990). Candidates who "exhibit" their intimate and private selves to the gazing voters sacrifice the interpersonal distance necessary to appear "presidential."

Candidates for the presidency must negotiate their image construction carefully within this more complicated and perilous symbolic environment. They still must strive for a presidential image, and they must utilize and associate the myths and images of the presidency with their candidacy. However, because of the presence of television and the intimate gazing that this medium invites, candidates must exhibit their private and intimate selves to voters in order to appear credible and forthcoming. We now turn to specific instances of presidential image construction in order to illustrate the proclivity of such rhetorics toward the intimate and the personal.

★ INTIMACY, DISCLOSURE, AND THE PRESIDENTIAL CAMPAIGN FILM

Existing analyses of presidential campaign films privilege their mythic qualities, focusing on the association that candidates make between themselves and iconic images of America (Luke, 1986–1987; Morreale, 1991a, 1991b, 1993; Mackey-Kallis, 1991; Simons & Stewart, 1991). As such, Morreale (1993) maintains that campaign films "provide comprehensive, structured storehouses of mythic images of the president, the country, and its citizens" (p. 6). Our analysis, however, explores the emergent and differing levels of intimate revelation present in these campaign rhetorics. Such intimacy may be a calculated campaign strategy or simply an outgrowth of existing pressures from television and voters accustomed to such disclosure. Nevertheless, given the centrality of the campaign film to the construction of candidate image, such discourses are paradigmatic of the intimacy required of candidates in ways that

other campaign discourses (policy speeches, for instance) are not.

Our concern with the intimate levels of disclosure present in these films recognizes the particular ways these image discourses appeal to and utilize the scopophilia present in the contemporary voter. Scopophiliac pleasure comes from the experience of rhetorics that invite and encourage the awareness, the knowledge, of the intimate and the personal in the lives of public characters. There is a political pleasure in the process of learning about leaders and their lives, their histories, and their personalities that is maximized in the contemporary media environment. Moreover, the image strategists appeal to that pleasure as they craft a persona for a candidate seeking office. Nowhere is such strategizing more evident than in the political campaign film.

The films examined here reveal differing strategies taken by successful candidates to both appeal to the scopophiliac impulse of the voter and to adapt to particular situational exigencies of the individual campaign.[5] Ronald Reagan exhibits a more distant "presidential" intimacy to voters in 1984, while George Bush's intimate display centers on his role within the family. Bill Clinton's unprecedented 1992 display of personal exhibitionism in his campaign film demonstrates the powerful forces in American politics that require intimate revelations form candidates. From Reagan's "presidential" intimacy to Clinton's personal disclosures, these campaign films evidence the importance of scopophilia for political discourse and the power of that impulse to influence candidate image construction.

Presidential Intimacy and "A New Beginning"

The most scrutinized and criticized presidential campaign film is Ronald Reagan's 1984 presentation entitled *A New Beginning* (Luke, 1986–1987; Mackey-Kallis, 1991; Morreale, 1991a; Simons & Stewart, 1991). Produced at the cost of nearly one million dollars, *A New Beginning* was the product of the Madison Avenue advertising team that also produced commercials for Pepsi Cola and McDonalds. The film is a lavish and lush text (shot on 35 mm film) of mythic images portraying a prosperous America in the early 1980s. The film reflected the themes of the 1984 Reagan campaign that sought to revive American self-adoration and confidence as embodied in Reagan as leader and incumbent president. Its mythic dimensions are well documented (Morreale, 1991a), but often ignored, partly because of the film's powerful mythology. These mythic dimensions are the specific strategies employed in the film to display Ronald Reagan as a candidate, president, and leader.

A New Beginning offers an intimate look at Ronald Reagan *as president,* inviting the viewer to look at the presidency from the inside. The film fuses the institution of the presidency with Reagan as an individual and suggests a natural connection between the two. This intimacy enhances the leadership of Reagan while simultaneously adapting to the scopophiliac needs of the voting audience. Not only are voters encouraged to feel confident about the leadership of the nation, but they may also gain some pleasure from learning how a president functions in office, from watching as the president reveals his personal reactions to public events. The film preserves the mythos of the presidency while also offering voters a knowledge or understanding of Ronald Reagan as president that satisfies the scopophiliac curiosity demanded of candidates in contemporary campaigning.

The first vehicle for the "presidential intimacy" of *A New Beginning* is the form of direct address used by the producers of the film. The strategy of direct address intensifies the scopophiliac pleasure in voters as it creates an illusion of interpersonality. Viewers are invited to believe that the candidate, or those who speak for him, are actually addressing them, individually, emphasizing the sincerity of the message presented. The illusion of interpersonality is a popular feature of political campaigning, from direct mail that is meant to appear personalized, to 800 telephone numbers designed to encourage voter participation and involvement.

Reagan frequently speaks directly to the audience throughout the film, often revealing his intimate thoughts and feelings at particular points during his first term in office. The only other direct address to the viewer comes from "average" people offering their positive impressions of Ronald Reagan's performance

as president. By reserving the direct address for Reagan and "people-on-the-street," the film suggests a similarity or unity between Reagan and the "average" voter. Reagan emerges as the "people's" president, and the interplay between what Reagan discusses and what the "average" voter concludes manifests the symbiotic relationship between candidate and voter that the film works to create. At one point in the film, for example, an elderly woman is featured discussing Reagan's compassion for older Americans. As she looks into the camera, she reveals, "I know that President Reagan is a caring man, that he cares about old people, and children, and ill people" (Dusenberry, 1984). This statement is immediately followed by Reagan, directly addressing the camera, and assuring voters that his administration does not pose a threat to Social Security. Reagan not only shares the concerns of "average" people, but as president, he works to protect and advance their interests. Moreover, the concerns of Reagan and the voters who address the viewer directly are all political, focusing exclusively on policy matters. The intimacy emergent, then, is a presidential intimacy wherein the candidate is exhibiting only his political self to the voter, revealing only those aspects of him that are of concern to the political process.

The presidential intimacy of the direct address strategy employed in A New Beginning is enhanced by the film's focus on Reagan's feelings and personal thoughts as president during his first term. The film opens with Reagan's 1981 inauguration ceremony. As the ceremony concludes, Reagan is heard discussing his feelings about the inauguration and the presidency in general. Indeed, much of the film concerns Reagan's personal feelings, thoughts, or impressions about various responsibilities or events from his first term as president. He talks about the isolation of the presidency and the importance of the advice he receives from his cabinet. Reagan also discusses in detail his reactions to the assassination attempt in March of 1981. He reveals specific, private conversations that took place between himself and his doctors and recalls a private encounter that occurred when Cardinal Cook came to visit him following the attempt on his life. A particularly revealing disclosure occurs near the end of the film. With an expression of sincerity, Reagan self-discloses to the camera:

> Sitting in the Oval Office, you look around and sometimes you can't help but choke up a little bit because you're surrounded by history that somehow has touched everything in this room. And it occurs to you that every person who ever sat here yearned in the depths of his soul to bring people and nations together in peace. Four times in my life, America's been at war. That's a tragic waste of lives and it makes you realize how desperately the world needs a lasting peace. (Dusenberry, 1984)

Each of these instances in the film reflect a projection of intimacy, as they all concern private or exclusive feelings and encounters. As such, they appeal to the scopophiliac viewer by providing the intimate knowledge that is expected from televisual discourse. The voter is, in effect, beckoned to see and know history from the perspective of Reagan's participation. The film summons, thusly, a feeling of pleasure from voters who now know how their president felt at crucial moments of his presidency.

The intimacy of Reagan's personal feelings and reactions to his first term are accompanied by expressions of "ceremonial" intimacy that are highlighted in *A New Beginning*. The film's producers present to viewers scenes of the president in assorted ceremonial roles, calling forth a scopophiliac pleasure of witnessing, of accessing, remote and distant events that would otherwise be inaccessible. Viewers, for example, witness private interactions between Reagan and American soldiers in Korea, as we hear Reagan express his pride and satisfaction with each particular soldier before a Sunday prayer service. The most significant display of Reagan's "ceremonial" intimacy occurs in the film's portrayal of his 1984 trip to Normandy, commemorating the 40th anniversary of D-Day. As Reagan speaks to gatherings of veterans and their families, the camera repeatedly displays weeping veterans with Reagan's voice recounting their heroism in the background. Ronald and Nancy Reagan are shown walking alone through rows of graves as Nancy places flowers by the cross signifying the grave of Theodore Roosevelt, Jr. Most poignantly, Reagan is displayed delivering a commemorative speech at another battlefield in which he reads the private letters of the daughter of a D-Day veteran. At a particularly emotional passage, Reagan's voice cracks, as the camera displays the weeping daughter.

These instances are private moments, or activities normally enacted in private, which are captured on film and displayed as evidence of Reagan's political leadership and his capacity to act as president. Together, they represent a "ceremonial" intimacy that worked in the film to construct an image for Reagan that was presidential yet intimate enough to provide viewers a look into the candidate's private self and personal emotions. Crucially, these scenes permit curious and gazing voters access to ceremonies and formalities in remote places, and they allow those scopophiliac voters to watch as their president masterfully and emotionally manages these ceremonies with grace, ease, and dignity.

Kellner (1990) charges that the Reagan administration "developed a simulated presidency that carried out largely symbolic politics, devoting much of its time to image production and using television to govern and to sell the figurehead and his conservative policies" (p. 137; see also Johnson, 1991; Luke, 1986–1987; Rogin, 1987). Part of the success of that symbolism came from the Reagan administration's ability to appeal to the scopophilia engendered by television while also preserving the statured aura of the presidency. The 1984 campaign film successfully presented images of the American presidency as heroic and steadfast—a synecdoche for the image of America that Reagan seemingly sought to embody. More significantly, though, these images also allowed the viewer/voter to glimpse, to actually see, the private and intimate moments of the Reagan presidency. As such, the film utilizes a guarded revelation strategy and allows the gaze of the viewer to see only the private Reagan *as president*, not the private Reagan as individual. The intimacy that is powerfully evident in *A New Beginning* heralds the influence of television in presidential politics and the dilemma facing candidates struggling to appear both forthcoming and presidential. *A New Beginning* demonstrates how that dilemma is successfully managed for maximum effect by presenting a candidate with whom average voters could identify (because of the knowledge gained by looking at Reagan in his private moments as president) and still regard as a hero and a leader. Despite Reagan's success with *A New Beginning,* however, Bush campaign officials in 1988 presented a new form of intimate display, brought about in part by different campaign circumstances.

Familial Intimacy with George and Barbara Bush

The untitled 1988 Bush presidential campaign film mirrors *A New Beginning* in its production values and lushness. Also shot on 35 mm film, the Bush film was produced by Roger Ailes, with much of the production responsibility divested to Clay Rossen, an Ailes assistant (Morreale, 1993). The film, and all of Bush's advertising in the 1988 campaign, sought to overcome existing and damaging perceptions of the candidate as weak and ineffective—the so-called "wimp" factor (Devlin, 1989).

As with *A New Beginning,* the 1988 Bush film is mythic in its portrayal of American life and the candidate. As a non-incumbent, Bush relied on what he possessed, his large family, in the crafting of his image. The strategy generated a sixty-second political commercial (drawn from the campaign film) entitled "Family/Children" that the campaign's media director claimed was very effective, giving viewers "a little chill at the end" (Devlin, 1989, p. 393). The campaign film, and other campaign rhetorics derived from it, utilize, therefore, an intimacy that comes not from the institution of the presidency, but from the Bush family. Significantly, this strategic choice also appeals to the scopophiliac impulse as it allows the viewer into the Bush family, to see it as it functions naturally and normally, and to feel a pleasure from the knowledge gained in the process of viewing.

The Bush film features the direct address of only three individuals—George Bush, Barbara Bush and Ronald Reagan. Gone are the testimonials from "average" Americans attesting to the qualifications of the candidate. Instead, the Bush film features intimate testimonials from the candidate himself and from his wife. This form of direct address represents an increased level of intimacy in the Bush film, as both George and Barbara Bush disclose personal and private feelings, thoughts, and reactions to the events that comprise their lives. The viewer is provided intimate knowledge of the Bush family via this direct address as both Bushes retell their history together, in a manner similar to the way children are told of the lives of their parents and grandparents. The film is largely biographical, and the direct address from George and Barbara Bush enhance the intimacy of what might have been an otherwise routine biographical narrative. As the viewer looks upon the events and happenings of the life of George Bush, both the candidate and his spouse enhance the epistemophiliac effect by adding personal insights and reflections. Unlike *A New Beginning,* the 1988 Bush film is less institutional in its focus and more disclosive of the Bush persona as a "fatherly" or paternal candidate.

The film, in utilizing a family motif, forms a metaphoric link between the extended Bush family and the United States, suggesting that Bush function as the patriarch of both. It begins with a small girl running through a grassy meadow. Quite suddenly, this image is interrupted with the sounds of gunfire and bombs as a date on the screen reads "December 1941." A narrator discusses the perils of World War II as familiar images of military aircraft and sinking battleships represent the bombing of Pearl Harbor. The film proceeds to tell the story of George Bush's famous World War II bombing mission.

The use of Bush's war experience is significant for its characterization of the candidate's war attitudes and as a means of appealing to the scopophiliac demands of the contemporary political environment. George Bush tells of the facts of the bombing mission. He recounts smelling smoke as enemy fire hit his airplane. Bush also relates how he finished the mission, unloading his payload. Even with his bomber in flames, he confronted imminent danger or death. As Bush speaks, actual footage is shown, creating an almost "you are there" feel to the narrative, allowing the viewer to see the mission as it unfolds.

The film subsequently features Barbara Bush, reflecting on George's war experiences and the impact of those experiences on her husband. She reveals that George Bush's war experience "made him more serious, more caring, more against war, more, uh, certain that we should never be caught unprepared again" (Ailes, 1988). With these comments, Barbara Bush manifests the stereotypically feminine role of emotional guardian and facilitator. Barbara Bush is the voice who reveals George Bush's emotional reaction to the war and its overall impact on his life. Thus, not only does the viewer glimpse this defining event of Bush's life, but the experience is further personalized by Barbara Bush's testimony to her husband's affective reactions. Moreover, the separate roles that both Barbara and George Bush play in telling this particular biographical incident represent a familial model replete with complementary gender roles. The male figure (the father) is the purveyor of the family historical facts while the female figure (the mother) offers the emotion, the telling insights and intimate details, that give that history meaning.

The familial intimacy of the Bush campaign film is most apparent at the end of the biographical narrative where the metaphoric link between family and country is most profoundly drawn. After presenting the viewer with a visual resume of Bush's career that substantiates the narrative's claim that "no one in this century is better prepared to be President of the United States," the film again features the young girl from the beginning running through the meadow. She runs to the arms of her grandfather, George Bush, as he hoists her in the air before kissing her cheek. The film presents several scenes featuring the Bush family on a picnic and at play. Barbara Bush remarks:

I wish people could *see* George as I *see* him, as thousands of people *see* him. And, you know, I always loved the time someone said to George, "How can you run for President? You don't have any constituency." And George said, "Well, you know, I've got a great big family and thousands of friends." And, uh, that's what he has. (Ailes, 1988, emphasis added)

The film concludes with George Bush again holding his granddaughter in the air as they both smile and the music fades. Powerfully, the film allows the voter to *see* George as Barbara *sees* him. It is the film that permits such access, such intimacy, into the Bush family, and by extension, into the Bush character.

Edelman (1988) speculates that the "idea of leadership offers the security and also the sternness associated with the father" (p. 39) and the Bush campaign film from 1988 capitalizes on this linkage between political leadership and the family. As Morreale (1993) notes, the viewer of this film "becomes a member of his [Bush's] clan, privy to the knowledge of the 'real' George Bush relaxing at home" (p. 152). The viewer is provided intimate access to the Bush family and to the patriarch's thoughts and feelings, though such reactions come from the feminine voice in the film—Barbara Bush. The intimacy of this film works to fuse together a sense of family with politics and leadership in order to justify the candidacy of George Bush. By providing the voter glimpses of the successful and happy Bush family, and by linking his leadership of the family to his leadership of the country, the film activates a powerful ideological structure of meaning deeply embedded within American culture. Moreover, this structure is possible because of the film's visual portrayal of the Bush family and its invitation of viewer participation and intimate access to that family. While Reagan's film centered on presidential intimacy, and Bush's on familial intimacy, the Clinton campaign devised an even more personal view into the candidate's constructed character.

Personal Intimacy and "The Man from Hope"

Bennett (1995) reports that during the 1992 election campaign, the Clinton camp confronted their candidate's image problems with a strategy designed to "replace his checkered image with a human persona that was vulnerable, humble, and accessible to ordinary people" (p. 108; see also Goldman et al., 1994). Their plan is reflected in the campaign film offered to voters at the 1992 Democratic convention entitled *The Man from Hope*. The film was produced by Harry Thomason and Linda Bloodworth-Thomason, noted friends of the Clintons and producers of several successful television comedies. The film was, reportedly, received well by critics and pundits (Rosteck, 1994) and both Bill and Hillary Clinton were moved to tears by its narrative (Goldman et al., 1994, p. 287).

The Man from Hope is dominated by personal reflections and revelations from a variety of individuals close to the candidate, as well as Clinton himself. Where the Reagan and Bush films featured direct address from relatively few people, the Clinton film presents the ruminations of the entire Clinton family, from his mother to his daughter. Their stories are uniformly about Bill Clinton's upbringing, his personal family life, and his character. The film is devoid of any discussion of politics, offices held by the candidate, or any accomplishments achieved by Clinton as Arkansas' governor. The entire structure of the film is consistent with the campaign's goal of (re)introducing Bill Clinton to the voting public.

The level of intimate revelation in the film is extremely high, reflecting the progression of this genre of political discourse toward the truly scopophiliac. The film begins with Clinton (dressed casually, lit softly, and seated in a comfortable room at the Arkansas Governor's Mansion) telling of his upbringing in Arkansas, his adolescence, his experiences in college and law school, and his early years as a husband and father. As he speaks of his childhood, Clinton recalls vivid memories of his mother leaving him with his grandparents to pursue a nursing career. He reveals a memory of a visit to his mother when she "kneeled at the side of the [train] track and cried cause she felt so bad that I was leaving" (Thomason & Bloodworth-Thomason, 1992). Clinton also speaks, as does his mother, of an incident when he confronted his alcoholic stepfather, at age fourteen, about the domestic violence present in the home. The candidate concludes this memory by reflecting:

> I never stopped loving my stepfather, or thinking he was a really good person. I wish I'd known more about human psychology as a child than I did because I came to realize that he was a good person and that the problem was not that he didn't love my mother or me or my brother. The problem was that he didn't think enough of himself. (Thomason & Bloodworth-Thomason, 1992)

Roger Clinton reveals further personal information about his brother's religious foundations and he details memories of Bill Clinton reciting Martin Luther King's "I Have a Dream" speech from memory. The viewer is offered, through these recollections, a personal portrait of the candidate's upbringing and his childhood. Our impulsive need to see and to know is also enhanced by old photographs and the direct address of the candidate and his family.

The film's narrative progresses to Clinton's adult family life, and it features prominently the memories of Hillary Clinton. She speaks of her courtship and marriage to Bill Clinton while at the Yale University Law School. The candidate reveals his amazement and gratitude at the birth of his daughter. He recounts how, "I remember how scrunched up she was when she came out. I still, uh, remember how profoundly grateful I was that, you know, Hillary was okay and that I had lived to see it. I mean, I was very aware at that moment that that's something my father hadn't done" (Thomason & Bloodworth-Thomason, 1992). In a particularly intimate revelation, Clinton speaks of watching the *60 Minutes* interview with Chelsea in which he and Hillary discussed the difficulties in their marriage, and that "It was pretty painful, you know, to have your child watch that." The candidate reveals that when asked what she thought of the interview, Chelsea responded "I'm glad you're my parents." Bill Clinton, as he tells this story, is near tears, and concludes that he knew after that moment that whatever happened with the election, "it would be alright" (Thomason & Bloodworth-Thomason, 1992).

The final montage of visual scenes at the conclusion of *The Man from Hope* demonstrate most dramatically the personal and intimate nature of this particular rhetoric of image construction. As Clinton, in voice over, discusses the nature of his campaign and its goals for the country, the visual images show scenes of home videos of Chelsea in a party dress and of Bill and Chelsea Clinton dancing. The viewer also sees home videos of the Clintons fishing and of Bill and Hillary Clinton dancing at a campaign rally, sharing a whispered conversation. All of the pictures are very personal, intimate moments that would normally be reserved for private screening. They are used here, though, to demonstrate the vulnerability and humility of the candidate, as is the entirety of the film's scripted content. And they dramatically illustrate how such discourse can capitalize on and exploit the scopophiliac impulses of a voting public accustomed to personal revelation and self-disclosure.

The intimacy of *The Man from Hope* emerges from the character and persona of the candidate, and represents a significant departure from the presidential and familial intimacy of the Reagan and Bush films. The entire Clinton campaign, Bennett (1995) suggests, provided a "daily intimacy" that began with the convention film, and that offered voters a "fantasy of renewal and hope" (p. 101). That fantasy is made real by the exhibitionist nature of the campaign film that appeals to the scopophilia at work in the viewing, voting public. Many of the Clinton family secrets are revealed and the viewer is asked to "feel his pain" as Clinton demonstrates his strength of character in conquering that pain. The film lets the viewer experience the pleasure of knowing the candidate and invites the viewer into his personal life and private matters, both through the revelations offered in the film and through the display of private photographs and home video. Clinton represents, fundamentally, the American Dream of conquering adversity and achieving success. *The Man from Hope* lets the viewer see that dream's enactment in Clinton's life and to gain pleasure from the knowledge that Bill Clinton represents that dream for all of America.

CONCLUSION

The power and presence of television in American elections invites and encourages a political scopophilia in the American community that promises to further alter the political process. In the eight years from 1984 to 1992, successful presidential candidates adopted differing strategies of personal display and intimate self-disclosure in order to achieve electoral triumph. Such intimacy alters not only the candidate and the governmental institutions staffed via elections, but it also transforms the voter and the American political culture. Recognizing the psychological dimensions to this transformation of American political life enhances the understanding of important communicative phenomena in American political life.

One consequence of television and the scopophilia that it invites from voters is a "politics of intimacy" with profound influences on the American community. Conservative and nostalgic pundits and scholars bemoan the perceived shift in discourse away from policy concerns to questions of image and personality (Bennett, 1992; Jamieson, 1992a; Patterson, 1993). For example, Jasinski (1993) argues that a politics of intimacy "shifts emphasis away from the 'what' of human interaction . . . and refocuses attention on the topic 'who' (embodied in quests for the 'essence' or ultimate motive of the person)" (p. 469).[6] And Hart (1994) argues that the intimacy encouraged and cultivated by television is illusory and potentially spurious for the American political culture. Yet, as candidates reveal or exhibit more of themselves to the voting public, the intimate knowledge possessed by the voters becomes more centrally the focus of the political/symbolic cultural environment. The intrusion of television mitigates the possibility for mystification or impression management, and the television camera "minimizes the distance between audience and performer [politician]," such that political leaders lose control of their own image construction (Meyrowitz, 1985, pp. 271–272; see also Barilleaux, 1988; Schmuhl, 1992; Schram, 1991).

The shift to a "politics of intimacy," though, is at least partly the result of the increased levels of knowledge possessed about political leaders and their problems, and may yield a positive reordering of American political culture. Such knowledge is a source of pleasure, and campaign rhetorics provide such knowledge with discourses that appeal to the scopophiliac and epistemophiliac impulses that characterize the contemporary voter. The more that voters *see* and *know* of a candidate's character and private life, the more confident voters can be of their ability to pass judgment on the candidate's suitability for office and the candidate's ability to confront the public issues of importance.

The scopophilia encouraged by television may actually be the inevitable reflection of McGee's (1978) admonition that "Human beings make up a government, not 'measures' or 'issues'" (p. 154).

The outcome of the rehumanization of the presidential "hero" may be a positive reordering of presidential politics for a changing and evolving political culture. The erosion of existing, traditional conceptions of presidential leadership may signal an end to leadership based in manipulation, power, and control. As voters learn more and more about their candidates (and presidents), and the distance between leader and those led is diminished, the political climate might possibly allow for leaders to express emotion, to waver and ponder complexity and uncertainty in policy, and to really "feel the pain" of an American electorate unsure of its nation's future.

Such shifts in the demarcation of "presidentiality" are difficult, and perhaps uncomfortable, for a political culture that is tied to conceptions of presidential leadership based in power, control, and force. Indeed, the negative reactions of pundits and scholars to increased intimacy in politics may reflect a sexism that fears the demasculinization of the presidency. Presidents are supposed to fit within traditional, stereotypical, masculine roles that value strength, power, violence, and aggressiveness. As the political culture also is beginning to reward and value intimate self-disclosure from presidential candidates, it confronts candidates who are contemplative, potentially reflecting their vulnerability and sensitivity. As such, that culture may come to fear the potential and increased "feminization" of the presidency.[7]

Despite potential benefits from increased intimacy, a televisual politics of intimacy may create a sense of "scopophiliac shame" within the public realm. There is, in the contemporary political environment, the sense that political campaigning no longer invites voters to scrutinize candidates, but that it asks them to become aberrant voyeurs of the private lives of those vying for high public office. The consequence is a backlash expressed graphically by the *Donahue* audience that booed and hissed their host when he was scolded by candidate Clinton for repeatedly probing into personal matters. This backlash is also manifested in reactions by voters to negative political advertising. Negative advertising employs a variety of tactics (Jamieson, 1992a) that work to invite voter scrutiny of secret, private concerns, thus exploiting the gazing impulse in voters. Yet voters routinely register their dislike for such advertising, even though it is often extremely effective. Put simply, though they disdain prying into the private and the intimate, voters seem unable to prevent such "gazing" from influencing voting. Shame is the ultimate outcome, resulting in a guilty and angry electorate expressing widespread disenchantment and disgust with the political process and yielding a gradual erosion in the uniquely American concept of a self-governing community (Dionne, 1991).

The psychological explanation of political strategy and behavior expresses quite clearly the tension experienced by voters in the contemporary postmodern political culture. On the one hand, voters long nostalgically for a mythic leadership that never really existed, but that is powerful and symbolically meaningful in the electoral choices people make. Such leadership is remote, paternal, and largely inaccessible. On the other hand, voters are accustomed to a televisual culture that exploits and manipulates both the scopophilia and its accompanying epistemophilia for profit and ratings. Quite expectantly, that culture encroaches upon political behavior and motive, providing both pleasure and shame to a citizenry possessing large levels of intimate knowledge about political leaders. Confusion results, as voters crave distant, heroic leadership while responding to strategies that manipulate the intimacy of contemporary politics. Such confusion is an outgrowth, though, of a dynamic, evolving political culture, questioning its ideological assumptions, and challenging its political practices. The fruitful response to such confusion is continued critique, by all concerned with politics, of the ever-changing rhetorics that manifest American democratic governance.

NOTES

[1] The intimacy of television, Jamieson (1988) maintains, forces candidates to adopt an "effeminate" style of communication that is more personal and inductive in order to achieve

electoral success. The "feminine" style is the focus of Campbell (1989), Dow and Tonn (1993), and Blankenship and Robson (1995) as they seek to articulate the presence and power of such a discursive style in historical and contemporary American public address. More recently, Jamieson (1995) argues that the presence of an effeminate style favors women striving for leadership and political influence. This style, she maintains, offers an escape from the double bind that traps women between silence and shame. There is, of course, nothing inherently feminine about a style of communication that is more personal or intimate, and the use of these labels may potentially misread and stereotype the nature of existing political discourse. A reassessment of the "feminine style" and its applicability to contemporary presidential image construction is offered by Parry-Giles and Parry-Giles (1996).

2 Psychoanalytic theory and Freud's work are occasionally used to inform rhetorical criticism or as the starting point for the development of new strands of rhetorical theory (Frentz & Rushing, 1993; Hyde, 1980; Makay, 1980; O'Leary & Wright, 1995; Payne, 1989; Pettigrew, 1977; Rushing & Frentz, 1991; Terrill, 1993). In addition, the rhetorical nature of psychoanalysis and the therapeutic process is the source of some anxiety to those who cling to psychoanalysis as a scientific process. Spence (1994) predicts that unless the power of rhetoric is diminished, "the fate of psychoanalysis as a creative enterprise would seem in jeopardy" (p. 4). Nevertheless, the link between psychoanalysis and rhetoric is a powerful one, and it may well be the case that psychoanalysis is impossible without the tools and practices of rhetoric (Borch-Jacobsen, 1992).

3 These films are chosen for two reasons. First, they represent different strategies of display by presidential candidates as they appeal to the scopophilia present in voter's mass media consumption. As such, they offer the potential for a richer and more comprehensive analysis of the management of intimacy in presidential campaigning. Second, they are the films of the last three successful candidates for president. With the extension of the image construction from these films to other campaign rhetorics, it is useful to examine those efforts that are successful and achieve electoral validation.

4 In his analysis of group psychology, Freud (1921/1955) examines the power of leaders in primitive societies and links that power to the influence of hypnotists. As he reveals, "it is precisely the sight of the chieftain that is dangerous and unbearable for primitive people, just as later that of the Godhead is for mortals" (p. 125). Leaders are successful when they are "of a masterful nature, absolutely narcissistic, self-confident and independent" (p. 124).

5 Other presidential campaign films portray candidates intimately, though most of the biographical or resume films tend to focus on leadership qualities and sanitized biographical narratives. Morreale (1993) provides a complete history of presidential campaign films, and she isolates 1984 as a significant turning point in the evolution of presidential image-making (pp. 137–138).

6 Jasinski (1993) maintains that a politics of intimacy entails several negative consequences for the American polity, including the inability to sustain action or community through time, the problem of boredom, and an elimination or reduction of the need for reflection, argumentation, and moral advocacy (pp. 480–481). He suggests instead a "politics of friendship" that maintains distance while affirming community. To posit the two as mutually exclusive alternatives ignores the vastness and fluidity of American political culture. Instead, we would suggest that aspects of American politics are devoted to different styles of interaction and discourse, but that the pluralistic nature of that system allows for its maintenance even with increased "threats" from a politics of intimacy.

7 Our discussion of the masculine and feminine nature of presidential politics is not meant to reify existing gendered categories (women are emotional and intimate; men are analytic and intellectual, etc.). What this discussion highlights is the constructed nature of gendered characteristics and the importance of such constructions for politics and presidential campaigning (Lorber, 1994; Jamieson, 1995; Parry-Giles & Parry-Giles, 1996).

REFERENCES

Ailes, R. (Producer). (1988). *Bush campaign film* [Videotape]. (Available from Public Affairs Video Archives, Purdue University, School of Liberal Arts, West Lafayette, IN, 47907)

Bailey, T. A. (1966). *Presidential greatness.* New York: Appleton-Century-Crofts.

Barilleaux, R. J. (1988). *The post-modern presidency: The office after Ronald Reagan.* New York: Praeger.

Bennett, W. L. (1992). *The governing crisis: Media, money, and marketing in American elections.* New York: St. Martin's.

Bennett, W. L. (1995). The cueless public: Bill Clinton meets the new American voter in campaign '92. In S. A. Renshon (Ed.), *The Clinton presidency:*

Campaigning, governing, and the psychology of leadership (pp. 91–112). Boulder, CO: Westview Press.

Blankenship, J., & Robson, D. C. (1995). A "feminine style" in women's political discourse: An exploratory essay. *Communication Quarterly, 43,* 353–366.

Borch-Jacobsen, M. (1992). *The emotional tie: Psychoanalysis, mimesis, and affect.* Stanford, CA: Stanford University Press.

Brummett, B., & Duncan, M. C. (1990). Theorizing without totalizing: Specularity and televised sports. *Quarterly Journal of Speech, 76,* 227–246.

Campbell, K. K. (1989). *Man cannot speak for her: A critical study of early feminist rhetoric* (Vol. 1). New York: Praeger.

Cha, T. H. K. (Ed.). (1980). *Apparatus.* New York: Tanam Press.

Craib, I. (1990). *Psychoanalysis and social theory.* Amherst: University of Massachusetts Press.

Denton, R. E., Jr. (1982). *The symbolic dimensions of the American presidency: Description and analysis.* Prospect Heights, IL: Waveland Press.

Devlin, L. P. (1989). Contrasts in presidential campaign commercials of 1988. *American Behavioral Scientist, 34,* 389–414.

Dionne, E. J., Jr. (1991). *Why Americans hate politics.* New York: Simon & Schuster.

Dow, B. J., & Tonn, M. B. (1993). "Feminine style" and political judgment in the rhetoric of Ann Richards. *Quarterly Journal of Speech, 79,* 286–302.

Dusenberry, P. (Producer). (1984). *A new beginning.* [Videotape]. (Available from the Political Communication Archives, University of Oklahoma, Norman, OK, 73019)

Edelman, M. (1988). *Constructing the political spectacle.* Chicago: University of Chicago Press.

Ellis, J. (1982). *Visible fictions.* London: Routledge & Kegan Paul.

Fisher, W. R. (1982). Romantic democracy, Ronald Reagan, and presidential heroes. *Western Journal of Speech Communication, 46,* 299–310.

Fiske, J. (1987). *Television culture.* London: Methuen.

Flitterman, S. (1981). Woman, desire and the look: Feminism and the enunciative apparatus in cinema. In J. Caughie (Ed.), *Theories of authorship: A reader* (pp. 242–250). London: Routledge & Kegan Paul. (Originally published in 1978)

Flitterman-Lewis, S. (1987). Psychoanalysis, film, and television. In R. C. Allen (Ed.), *Channels of discourse: Television and contemporary criticism* (pp. 172–210). Chapel Hill: University of North Carolina Press.

Frentz, T. S., & Rushing, J. H. (1993). Integrating ideology and archetype in rhetorical criticism, part II: A case study of *Jaws. Quarterly Journal of Speech, 79,* 61–81.

Freud, S. (1955). Notes upon a case of obsessional neurosis. In J. Strachey (Ed. and Trans.), *The standard edition of the complete psychological works of Sigmund Freud* (Vol. 10, pp. 155–318). London: The Hogarth Press. (Originally published in 1909)

Freud, S. (1955). Group psychology and the analysis of the ego. In J. Strachey (Ed. and Trans.), *The standard edition of the complete psychological works of Sigmund Freud* (Vol. 18, pp. 67–144). London: The Hogarth Press. (Originally published in 1921)

Freud, S. (1957). Three essays on the theory of sexuality. In J. Strachey (Ed. and Trans.), *The standard edition of the complete psychological works of Sigmund Freud* (Vol. 7, pp. 123–246). London: The Hogarth Press. (Originally published in 1905)

Freud, S. (1957). Instincts and their vicissitudes. In J. Strachey (Ed. and Trans.) *The standard edition of the complete psychological works of Sigmund Freud* (Vol. 14, pp. 109–140), London: The Hogarth Press. (Originally published in 1915)

Germond, J. W., & Witcover, J. (1993). *Mad as hell: Revolt at the ballot box, 1992.* New York: Warner Books.

Goldman, P., DeFrank, T. M., Miller, M., Murr, A., & Mathews, T. (1994). *Quest for the presidency 1992.* College Station: Texas A&M University Press.

Hahn, D. F. (1987). The media and the presidency: Ten propositions. *Communication Quarterly, 35,* 254–266.

Hankins, S. R. (1983). Archetypal alloy: Reagan's rhetorical image. *Central States Speech Journal, 34,* 33–43.

Hart, R. P. (1994). *Seducing America: How television charms the modern voter.* New York: Oxford University Press.

Hinckley, B. (1990). *The symbolic presidency: How presidents portray themselves.* New York: Routledge.

Hyde, M. J. (1980). Jacques Lacan's psychoanalytic theory of speech and language. *Quarterly Journal of Speech, 66,* 96–118.

Jamieson, K. H. (1988). *Eloquence in an electronic age: The transformation of political speechmaking.* New York: Oxford University Press.

Jamieson, K. H. (1992a). *Dirty politics: Deception, distraction, and democracy.* New York: Oxford University Press.

Jamieson, K. H. (1992b). *Packaging the presidency: A history and criticism of presidential campaign advertising* (2nd ed.). New York: Oxford University Press.

Jamieson, K. H. (1995). *Beyond the double bind: Women and leadership.* New York: Oxford University Press.

Jasinski, J. (1993). (Re)constituting community through narrative argument: *Eros* and *philia* in *The Big Chill. Quarterly Journal of Speech, 79,* 467–486.

Johnson, H. (1991). *Sleepwalking through history: America in the Reagan years.* New York: W. W. Norton.

Kellner, D. (1990). *Television and the crisis of democracy.* Boulder, CO: Westview Press.

Kuhn, A. (1982). *Women's pictures: Feminism and cinema.* London: Routledge & Kegan Paul.

Lorber, J. (1994). *Paradoxes of gender.* New Haven, CT: Yale University Press.

Luke, T. (1986–1987). Televisual democracy and the politics of charisma. *Telos, 70,* 59–80.

Mackey-Kallis, S. (1991). Spectator desire and narrative closure: The Reagan 18-minute political film. *Southern Speech Communication Journal, 56,* 308–314.

Makay, J. J. (1980). Psychotherapy as a rhetoric for secular grace. *Central States Speech Journal, 37,* 184–196.

McGee, M. C. (1978). "Not men, but measures": The origins and import of an ideological principle. *Quarterly Journal of Speech, 64,* 141–154.

Metz, C. (1975). The imaginary signifier. *Screen, 16*(2), 14–76.

Metz, C. (1981). History/discourse: A note on two voyeurisms. In J. Caughie (Ed.), *Theories of authorship: A reader* (pp. 225–231). London: Routledge & Kegan Paul. (Originally work published in 1976)

Meyrowitz, J. (1985). *No sense of place: The impact of electronic media on social behavior.* New York: Oxford University Press.

Morreale, J. (1991a). *A new beginning: A textual frame analysis of the political campaign film.* Albany: State University of New York Press.

Morreale, J. (1991b). The political campaign film: Epideictic rhetoric in a documentary frame. In F. Biocca (Ed.), *Television and political advertising: Signs, codes, and images* (Vol. 2, pp. 187–201). Hillsdale, NJ: Lawrence Erlbaum Associates.

Morreale, J. (1993). *The presidential campaign film: A critical history.* New York: Praeger.

Mulvey, L. (1975). Visual pleasure and the narrative cinema. *Screen, 16*(3), 6–18.

O'Leary, S. D., & Wright, M. H. (1995). Psychoanalysis and Burkeian rhetorical criticism. *Southern Communication Journal, 67,* 104–121.

Parry-Giles, S. J., & Parry-Giles, T. (1996) Gendered politics and presidential image construction: A reassessment of the "feminine style." *Communication Monographs, 63,* 337–353.

Patterson, T. E. (1993). *Out of order.* New York: Alfred A. Knopf.

Payne, D. (1989). The Wizard of Oz: Therapeutic rhetoric in a contemporary media ritual. *Quarterly Journal of Speech, 75,* 25–39.

Pettigrew, L. (1977). Psychoanalytic theory: A neglected rhetorical dimension. *Philosophy & Rhetoric, 73,* 46–59.

Rabinowitz, P. (1992). Voyeurism and class consciousness: James Agee and Walter Evans, *Let us now praise famous men. Cultural Critique, 27,* 143–170.

Rogin, M. P. (1987). *Ronald Reagan, the movie: And other episodes in political demonology.* Berkeley and Los Angeles: University of California Press.

Rosteck, T. (1994). The intertextuality of "The Man from Hope": Bill Clinton as person, as persona, as star? In S. A. Smith (Ed.), *Bill Clinton on stump, state, and stage: The rhetorical road to the White House* (pp. 223–248). Fayetteville: University of Arkansas Press.

Rushing, J. H., & Frentz, T. S. (1991). Integrating ideology and archetype in rhetorical criticism. *Quarterly Journal of Speech, 77,* 385–406.

Schmuhl, R. (1992). *Statecraft and stagecraft: American political life in the age of personality.* Notre Dame, IN: University of Notre Dame Press.

Schram, S. F. (1991). The post-modern presidency and the grammar of electronic electioneering. *Critical Studies in Mass Communication, 8,* 210–216.

Simons, H. W. (1994). Going meta: Definition and political applications. *Quarterly Journal of Speech, 80,* 468–481.

Simons, H. W., & Stewart, D. J. (1991). Network coverage of video politics: "A new beginning" in the limits of criticism. In F. Biocca (Ed.), *Television and political advertising: Signs, codes, and images* (Vol. 2, pp. 203–228). Hillsdale, NJ: Lawrence Erlbaum Associates.

Spencer, T. (1994). *The rhetorical voice of psychoanalysis.* Cambridge, MA: Harvard University Press.

Terrill, R. E. (1993). Put on a happy face: Batman as schizophrenic savior. *Quarterly Journal of Speech, 79,* 319–335.

Thomason, H., & Bloodworth-Thomason, L. (Producers). (1992). *The man from Hope* [Videotape]. (Available from the Public Affairs Video Archives, Purdue University, School of Liberal Arts, West Lafayette, IN, 47907)

Effects of Political Information in the 2000 Presidential Campaign: Comparing Traditional Television and Internet Exposure

Lynda Lee Kaid

The 2000 presidential campaign brought voters more opportunities for political information than did any campaign in U.S. history. The candidates and their parties spent a record amount of money on political advertising (Devlin, 2001), and the candidates engaged in televised political debates and appeared in numerous other live and taped television formats. Although the mainstream television networks covered the campaign less in their traditional newscasts (Center for Media and Public Affairs, 2000), cable news networks provided additional in-depth coverage. In addition, a new medium, the Internet, provided voters with continuous information directly from candidates; from the traditional news media via newspaper, broadcast and cable Web sites; and from a host of independent and special interest group offerings on the World Wide Web. With so much information available to voters in the 2000 campaign and with so much coming from the new medium of the Internet, the study reported here sought to evaluate the relative impact of traditional television information and Internet information. The study was particularly concerned about the potential of the Internet and traditional media to affect voter evaluations of candidates, levels of political cynicism, and the stimulation of additional information seeking and related political behaviors.

★ THEORETICAL PERSPECTIVES

Because this study derives its major concern from a comparison of different media for conveying political information, a major theoretical underpinning of the research is concentrated in the study of channel variables. Message variables are also important in this research, as the type of information conveyed to the voter may interact with the medium through which it is conveyed. Thus, the research is also concerned with the differing formats used for information in political campaigns, concentrating on the three most important formats for campaign information: advertising, debates, and news.

Communication Channels

Although early models of communication from Laswell (1948) to Berlo (1960) always included the channel as an important ingredient in the communication process, it was Marshall McLuhan (1964) who popularized the notion that the medium or channel should be considered the key element in interpretation of communication meaning. Whereas McLuhan's notion that the "medium is the message" was more speculation than proven prediction, his work argued for the importance of considering the unique contribution that a channel of communication could make to viewers' understanding of a message.

Research on channel variables, however, has produced mixed results. McLuhan's most famous example was a study he cited to show that those who had seen the first 1960 Kennedy-Nixon debate on television thought Kennedy had won the debate, whereas those who heard the debate on the radio judged Nixon the winner (Katz & Feldman, 1962). Although other researchers have disputed this research interpretation from 1960 (Vancil & Pendell, 1987), McKinnon, Tedesco, and Kaid (1993) found similar differences for Clinton and Bush in the third 1992 presidential debate, and McKinnon and Tedesco (1999) verified differences between television and radio exposure to debates in evaluations of Clinton and Dole in 1996.

One reason research on channel variables is so tantalizing for political communication research is the potential, suggested by the previous examples from televised debates, that one candidate may excel at communication via one particular channel, whereas other candidates excel in other media. In fact, other researchers have found such interaction effects between channels and candidates (Andreoli & Worchel, 1978; Cohen, 1976). Such findings lead naturally to the prediction that the Internet channel may make its own unique contribution to perceptions of candidates in the political arena.

Little research has addressed this question directly because research about the Internet as a medium for political communication is in its infancy. However, the growth of this new medium and its use for political information warrants such investigation. More than half of the U.S. population now uses the Internet (National Telecommunications and Information Administration, 1999), and 35% of Americans go online for information on politics and issues (The Democracy On-Line Project, 2000). A Pew Internet and American Life Project (2000) report on young voters also indicated that 43% reported that on-line election news had affected their vote choices in 2000.

One of the important reasons for considering the channel differences between the Web and traditional media is that the unique features of the Web offer users benefits in terms of interactivity and user control. Ha and Lincoln (1998) suggested such interactivity allows the source and receiver of a message to respond to each other's needs via five dimensions: playfulness, choice or navigation, connectedness or hyperlinks, information collection and/or retrieval, and reciprocity. The effects of interactivity and control on media effects are not yet documented or fully understood. Some researchers suggest that the increased interactivity and availability for additional information seeking on the Internet stimulates information seeking (Althaus & Tewksbury, 2000; Cutbirth & Coombs, 1997; Jacques & Ratzan, 1997). Although Eveland and Dunwoody (2001) found no advantage for Web materials over traditional print materials for learning, the political arena has appeared to offer more promising effects for political candidates. The presence of interactivity on a candidate's Web site has been found to heighten perceptions of the candidate's sensitivity and responsiveness, leading to more positive candidate perceptions (Sundar, Hesser, Kalyanaraman, & Brown, 1998). In one of the few studies that made a direct comparison between effects of exposure to the same content through traditional and Internet media,

McKinney and Gaddie (2000) studied the differences in exposure to the New Hampshire presidential primary debate between Al Gore and Bill Bradley in October 1999. They found that the Internet was a superior channel to traditional television in terms of issue learning from the debate. Similarly supportive of channel differences between the Web and traditional television, Kaid (2002) reported that young voters who saw political spots via traditional television media were more likely to vote for George W. Bush, whereas those exposed to the same spots on the Internet were more likely to vote for Al Gore. Differences in information-seeking behavior stimulated by the two different media were also documented.

Format Differences

Research on format differences in political communication has also intrigued political communication scholars and practitioners. Patterson and McClure (1976), in their study of the 1972 presidential campaign, found that voters learned more about campaign issues from political spots than from television news. Martinelli and Chaffee (1995) found a similar advantage for television ads in voter learning in the 1988 election, and the superiority of television ads over news for voter recall was confirmed by Brians and Wattenberg (1996) in the 1992 election.

Television ads as a format for conveying political information have also been shown to produce more voter learning than do presidential debates in experimental studies (Just, Crigler, & Wallach, 1990). It is interesting that most comparisons of formats have been concentrated on the relative impact of debates, ads, and news on voter learning or cognitive effects. Much less is known about the effects of format differences on electoral vote choice or candidate evaluation.

Initial studies of the effects of different formats in the new Internet medium have focused on news content and commercial advertising. For instance, researchers have found that presence of multimedia material hinders learning for news content but improves memory for ads (Sundar, 2000).

Political Cynicism Related to Channel and Format

Low levels of political trust in government and reduced regard for political leaders were defining characteristics of the last half of the 20th century in the United States (Lipset & Schneider, 1987), particularly among women and younger voters (Bennett, 1997; Pearlstein, 1996). Researchers have argued that high levels of political cynicism may also lead to lower voter turnout and to a lessening of information seeking about political issues and candidates (Kaid, McKinney, & Tedesco, 2000). It has been particularly popular to blame these effects on one particular format of political media, political advertising, particularly negative political ads (Ansolabehere & Iyengar, 1995), although not all research supports the finding that voter cynicism or decreased participation results from exposure to negative political advertising (Garramone, Atkin, Pinkleton, & Cole, 1990). Political cynicism is one area of political media effects in which format may make a big difference because Kaid et al. (2000) found that although exposure to political spot ads may cause elevated levels of political distrust, exposure to debates may have the opposite effect.

Specifically related to the Internet medium, however, Tedesco and Kaid (2000) concluded that respondents who interacted with a 2000 presidential candidate Web site were less cynical after the activity than before, regardless of whether they were attuned to informational or entertainment content. However, again possibly pointing to format effect differences, Kaid (2002) found that exposure to political spot ads on the Internet versus via traditional television did not affect levels of political cynicism.

Hypotheses

These theoretical and predictive findings suggest the following hypotheses:

Hypothesis 1: There will be a significant difference in evaluation of candidates viewed on the traditional television medium and on the Internet.

Hypothesis 2: There will be a significant difference in evaluation of candidates based on the format (debates, ads, news) in which they are viewed.

Hypothesis 3: Exposure to information on the Internet will reduce political cynicism significantly more than will exposure via the traditional television medium.

Hypothesis 4: There will be a significant difference in information seeking and political behaviors stimulated by exposure to political information via the traditional television medium and via the Internet.

★ METHOD

The hypotheses were tested experimentally by exposing groups of volunteer participants to versions of advertising, debate, and news messages from the 2000 presidential campaigns of George W. Bush and Al Gore on two different media or channels, traditional television and the Internet. This created a basic 3 (formats) x 2 (media) factorial design. The studies were conducted in experimental settings with small groups of volunteer participants between November 1, 2000, and May 15, 2001. None of the experiments were conducted during the disputed phase of the election following the contest, recount, and court cases related to the Florida vote.

Procedures

The stimulus materials for the three formats were drawn from real campaign materials used during the 2000 election. In the case of the political advertising format, the ads consisted of four spots each for Bush and Gore (a mixture of negative and positive spots),[1] with the order alternated. The spots were selected from those running in various markets nationally during the last weeks of the campaign as determined by postings on the *National Journal*'s Web site, which features current ads (http://www.nationaljournal.com).

The debate format was composed of an edited excerpt from the second presidential debate that provided an approximately equal amount of time for each candidate. The news format was composed of excerpted newscast items from network news that included balanced information on both candidates.

In each segment, the traditional televised versions of each format (ads, debates, and news segments) were identical to the Internet version. The only difference in initial exposure was that viewers were exposed to the items while sitting at individual computer monitors in the Internet version, whereas in the traditional television version, viewers watched on a television in a small group.

Participants were recruited in a variety of ways. A total of 502 participants took part in the experiments. Of these, 314 were students in general communication classes at a large Southwestern U.S. university. The remaining 188 participants were adults recruited either by contact with civic groups or by solicitation of volunteers at a large Southwest shopping mall. When participants arrived for each experimental session, they were randomly distributed into the treatment groups. However, because the capacity of the Internet lab was limited, more respondents were assigned to the traditional groups in some sessions. This process resulted in a final sample composed of 47% men and 53% women. The age of the sample ranged from 18 to 84, with a mean age of 30. Partisan affiliation was distributed as 33% Democratic, 41% Republican, and 16% Independent or other.

In the traditional sessions, respondents filled out printed pretest questionnaires, viewed the stimulus materials (ads, debate excerpt, or news excerpts) on a television monitor in a room with other respondents, and filled out posttest questionnaires. In the Internet session, the respondents were seated at computer terminals where they filled out the same pretest questionnaires and then watched the same stimulus material on the computer monitor. However, following the exposure to one of the formats in the Internet session, respondents were given approximately 20 to 30 minutes to choose to view other information before finishing the experiment. Respondents were allowed to (a) view a set of campaign ads, (b) pick individual ads from the set to view one by one, (c) see written scripts of the ads, (d) choose other political spots by the candidates, (e) view excerpts from the presidential debates between Gore and Bush, (f) view ad watches from newspapers about campaign ads, (g) view poll results about the presidential race, (h) go to the candidate or party Web sites, (i) view more information about the issues in the campaign, or (j) send the candidate an e-mail message. These additional information sources were modeled after popular Web sites running during the campaign on various media channels and political Internet sites and included the type of information Rumbough and Tomlinson (2000) found to be typical of the sample of 257 Congressional Web sites they monitored in 2000. Following the chance to make these choices and engage in any or all of these information activities, the Internet respondents then filled out the same posttest questionnaire as did the traditional group.

The procedures used here are based on the assumption that it was important to simulate the specific type of viewing environment available to real voters during the campaign. Thus, voters who view ads, debates, or news formats in traditional television settings cannot immediately seek additional information or find out more about candidates' views, poll numbers, debate performance, and so forth. In contrast, when exposed to one type of information on the Internet, whether through candidates' Web sites or via other political Web venues, it is an inherent characteristic of the Internet experience that viewers can immediately seek other sources of information about the candidates. These are inherent characteristics of each medium, and this difference in interactivity is presumed in this study to be an essential covariant characteristic of each medium for the purposes of testing.

Measuring Instruments

Each pretest questionnaire for all respondents included demographic information, media exposure measures, attitudes toward candidates, vote choice, and a series of cynicism scales. The posttest measure contained repeat measures of some of these items plus a series of 12 questions designed to measure the respondents' desire to seek additional information about candidates following the sessions. For these questions, respondents were asked to respond on a scale of 1 (*not very likely*) to 7 (*very likely*) if they would like to "see more ads from the candidates," "read more news," "volunteer to work in a candidate's campaign," and other informational and activity items detailed in the results section. These measurement items were developed by the research specifically for this

TABLE I

Candidate Evaluation by Medium and Format

	GORE		BUSH	
	Pre	Post	Pre	Post
Medium				
Traditional (n = 277)	46.5	46.8	56.9	57.3
Internet (n = 223)	43.6	45.6*	56.9	61.3*
Format				
Ads (n = 213)	46.4	46.5	58.7	59.2
Debates (n = 148)	45.7	48.5*	53.0	55.1*
News (n = 141)	42.9	43.5	63.2	63.0

Note: Based on feeling thermometer scores ranging from 0 to 100.

*$p \leq .05$ for t test between pretest and posttest scores.

study and were based on the types of information participants could reasonably explore after examination of other Web sites available during the 2000 campaign.

Attitudes toward candidates were measured by a "feeling thermometer" scale used by the National Election Studies to measure candidate favorability (Rosenstone, Miller, & the National Election Studies, 1997). The thermometer asks respondents to place each candidate on a scale from 0 (*cool*) to 100 (*warm*).

The cynicism scale was a summation of eight items used to determine the level of trust or confidence in government.[2] The scale included efficacy items such as "Whether I vote or not has no influence on what politicians do" and distrust items such as "one cannot always trust what politicians say." These items, which were adapted from earlier studies using similar scales (Kaid et al., 2000; Rosenstone et al., 1997), achieved acceptable Cronbach's alpha levels for reliability (.62 in the pretest and .74 in the posttest) and thus were summed and used as a scale in this analysis.

★ RESULTS

The results from these experiments indicate that there are differences in exposure as a result of the medium through which respondents experience political advertising messages. These differences between Internet and traditional television exposure are much stronger than are any differences between formats of the messages, as seen in analysis of the individual hypothesis.

Effects of Medium and Format on Candidate Evaluation

The first two hypotheses predicted there would be differences in evaluation of the candidates based on the medium (traditional television versus Internet) and on the format (ads, debates, or news) of exposure. An initial ANCOVA (using the pretest measure of candidate evaluation on the feeling thermometer as a covariate) indicated there was no interaction effect for the medium and format on the posttest evaluation of either Bush or Gore. However, as Table 1 shows, there was a difference in the formats based on the medium. Those who experienced the messages through the Internet evaluated both Bush and Gore more highly in the posttest than did those who were exposed via traditional television, providing support for the first hypothesis.

The support for the second hypothesis was less striking, but the results do show that

TABLE 2

Differences in Cynicism by Media and Formats

Format	TRADITIONAL		INTERNET	
	Pre	Post	Pre	Post
Ads	25.2	24.3*	25.1	25.2
Debates	26.9	25.9*	27.9	28.3
News	26.8	26.6	25.1	24.6

*p ≤ .05 for paired sample t test.

exposure through the debate format was helpful to both candidates, regardless of the medium through which it occurred. In other words, only in the debate format did both candidates receive significantly higher ratings on the feeling thermometer in the posttest than in the pretest.

Beyond the main effects analyzed for candidate evaluation on these two hypotheses, it is additionally interesting to note that vote choice was also affected by the interaction of medium and format. Those who viewed the debate excerpt in the traditional format were significantly more likely to vote for Gore (53%) than for Bush (48%), whereas those who viewed the debate on the Internet were significantly more likely to vote for Bush (64%) than for Gore (36%). This difference was significant, $\chi^2(1, N = 132) = 3.64, p = .05$. An earlier analysis of data showed that there was also a positive effect for Bush for viewers of the advertising in the traditional format among young (student) voters (Kaid, 2002).

Effects On Political Cynicism

The third hypothesis suggested that the exposure medium would affect the level of political cynicism experienced by voters. Cynicism was measured by summing a series of scales that asked respondents to agree (or disagree) on a 5-point scale with statements about their confidence in government, in the behavior of political leaders, and in their own political efficacy. An initial ANCOVA, using the pretest cynicism level as a covariate, indicated there was a significant interaction effect between medium and format of exposure, $F(2,500) = 2.98, p = .05$.

The analysis of individual effects according to combined medium and format is shown in Table 2. There were significant differences in cynicism levels between groups who were exposed to traditional television versions of political ads and political debates. Contrary to some prior research results, exposure to political ads on the traditional medium reduced cynicism levels from a pretest score of 35.28 to a posttest score of 24.30, $t(127) = 2.41, p = .02$. Viewers of the debate excerpts on the traditional media also reported less cynical attitudes than they had before the exposure (pretest = 26.89, posttest = 25.93), $t(75) = 2.74, p = .01$. Other treatments did not make any statistically significant differences in cynicism levels.

Information Seeking and Political Behaviors

The last hypothesis concerned the effect of medium on information seeking and political behaviors. After viewing the ad, debate, or news segments on the traditional television or Internet media, respondents were asked to indicate on a scale from 1 to 7 how likely they were to engage in a series of information-seeking and related political behaviors. ANOVA results indicated that most of these items were affected by medium and format in very complex ways, generally indicating the presence of both main effects for medium and format and in most cases an interaction effect between them. The most interesting result from these analyses was the fact that there are clearly advantages for each medium in the political information and behavior stimulation arena. Only one behavior,

TABLE 3

Information Seeking and Political Behaviors: Traditional versus Internet Exposure

	NEWS		ADVERTISING		DEBATES	
	Traditional	Internet	Traditional	Internet	Traditional	Internet
	(n = 73)	(n = 66)	(n = 126)	(n = 85)	(n = 77)	(n = 70)
Watch more ads (I)	3.78	4.44	3.41	4.39*	3.67	4.36*
Watch more television news (I)	4.47	5.03	3.14	4.85*	4.51	4.78
Volunteer to work in a political campaign (television)	2.82	2.50	4.99*	2.27	2.55	2.13
Participate in electronic chat about the campaign (television)	2.34	2.58	4.97*	2.73	2.17	2.24
Talk with friends about campaign (I)	5.03	5.33	3.12	5.20*	4.84	5.10
Read more newspaper stories about campaign (I)	4.71	5.02	3.25	5.21*	4.85	5.01
Contact the candidates (television)	2.81	2.89	5.02*	3.06	2.47	2.65
Use Internet for general info on campaign	3.52	3.91	4.24	4.02	3.37	3.74
Vote in the next election (I)	6.04	6.29	2.73	6.28*	6.17	6.69*
Contribute money (television)	2.53	2.56	5.21*	2.00	2.33	2.15
Use Internet for info on issues (I)	3.52	4.38*	4.25	4.29	3.60	4.17
Visit candidate Web site (I)	3.25	4.06*	4.13	4.11	3.17	3.73

Note: Numbers are mean scores on scale of 1 to 7.

*p ≤ .05 for t test

using the Internet for general information on the campaign, was not significantly affected by exposure to information via either Internet or television. In the case of the other items, 7 of the 11 items were significantly more likely to be stimulated by Internet exposure (marked with an "I" in Table 3). The activities stimulated by Internet exposure were mostly information-seeking behaviors such as the desire to watch more ads and television news, read more newspaper stories, talk with friends about the campaign, and use the Internet for issue and candidate information. Significantly, however, those who were exposed via the Internet were significantly more likely to "vote in the next election" than were their counterparts who were exposed via traditional television. On the other hand, television viewers were stimulated

to more behavior-oriented activities such as contacting candidates, contributing money to campaigns, volunteering to work on campaigns, and participating in electronic chats with candidates.

The interaction between medium and format is shown in more detail in Table 3. Here, it is clear that the striking format and medium interactions almost all relate to political television advertising. Traditional advertising viewers are more likely to volunteer to work in a campaign, to participate in an electronic chat, to contact candidates, and to contribute money than are those who saw the same ads on the Internet, indicating that there may still be some excitement and behavioral stimulation related to the traditional television medium. On the other hand, those who saw the same ads on the

Internet and then had a chance to seek other information were more likely to be stimulated to seek even more information: to watch more ads, to watch more TV news, to read more newspaper stories, and perhaps most important, to vote in the next election.

Those who viewed the debates on the Internet were also more likely to vote in the next election. In fact, all other groups were more likely to do so when compared with those who viewed political ads on traditional television. It is interesting, however that Internet debate viewers also wanted to see more ads than did their traditional television counterparts.

Those who viewed the television news segments were less affected by many of the information-seeking or behavioral items, although Internet news viewers were more likely to use the Internet for issue information and to visit the Candidates' Web sites.

CONCLUSIONS

These results suggest some very important differences between exposure to political campaign information through traditional television and the new technology offered by the Internet. First, the results lend new significance to the study of channel variables for the new technology involved in the Internet. As with earlier research, there seems to be some potential interaction between this medium and the source of a message. Some sources (candidates) emerge with more positive evaluations and higher vote likelihood when the channels and formats vary. In this case, both candidates received higher evaluations on the Internet and in the debate format, but Bush benefited more in terms of vote likelihood.

Surprisingly, the Internet medium did not have the positive effects on political cynicism that have been predicted by many observers. In this study, the opposite was in fact true. Those who experienced both television ads and televised debates in a traditional form were less cynical after exposure than before, a result that did not occur for Internet viewers. It may well be that the ability to seek out additional information, to view other sources and types of information from other sources, may make the

voter even more questioning and skeptical about candidates and the political system.

However, the most encouraging results for the political system come from the findings about different patterns of information seeking and political behaviors stimulated by traditional versus Internet exposures. The Internet was very successful in encouraging voters to seek out additional types and sources of information. The very fact that other choices were offered and provided may have served as a stimulating effect. At the same time, the traditional medium of television, particularly in the advertising format, was successful at heightening voters' involvement and behavior intentions. It is not clear why the much-maligned format of television advertising was so successful on so many levels here, but it is possible that some of the advantage may lie in the drama and excitement of television. The traditional television spot also did not provide opportunities for seeking additional information. The traditional television ad performed well some of the functions for which political practitioners hope; for example, it encouraged voters to volunteer for campaigns, made them more likely to contribute money, and increased their likelihood of contacting candidates. Its striking failure, however, was a serious one: Exposure to the political spot caused voters to say they were less likely to vote in the next election.

On this latter and all-important item, the act of voting itself, of course, the Internet medium and the debate format excelled. There is encouragement here for political participants and observers from all sides. Candidates who can get their message out to voters via the two-sided debate format and who can provide maximum exposure for that message via the Internet have a good chance of persuading voters to vote.

Finally, this study raises many other questions and issues. Its limitations in timing, in stimuli and experimental conditions, and in participant samples should be recognized. Such research needs to be replicated on a larger, national scale and also below the presidential level. In addition, more exploration is needed of the patterns of information choice and behavior of those who are exposed to political information on the Internet. It could be important to know, for instance, what types of information the voter is actually choosing, the sequence in which the information is selected, and the amount of time devoted to each type and format chosen. These and other questions must be answered before a more complete picture can be formed of the information and behavioral effects of mediums and formats in the political system.

NOTES

[1] The ads in the sample, in the order of their appearance, were (a) a positive Bush spot titled "Trust" in which Bush talks about trusting America and renewing America's purpose; (b) a positive Gore ad, "College;" in which Gore's college tuition tax deduction for middle-class families is featured; (c) a negative Bush ad, "Gore-Guantuan;" that attacks Gore's spending plan and says it will wipe out the surplus and increase governmental spending; (d) a Gore ad titled "Down" that uses a graphic of a dissolving dollar bill to attack Bush's tax cut plan, ending with the message that Gore will pay down the debt, protect Social Security, and give a tax deduction for college tuition; (e) a Bush ad titled "Education Recession" that suggests there is a Clinton/Gore education recession and that Bush raised education standards in Texas and that tells viewers how to obtain the "Bush blueprint for education," which features accountability, high standards, and local control; (f) a Gore ad titled "Apron" that attacks Bush on the minimum wage in Texas and promotes the "Al Gore plan" of increasing the minimum wage and investing in education, middle-class tax cuts, and a secure retirement; (g) a Bush ad called "Big Relief vs. Big Spending" that compares Bush's tax cut plan with Gore's spending plan, stating Gore's spending plan threatens America's prosperity; and (h) a negative Gore ad called "Needle" that opens with a foggy Houston skyline, attacks Bush on his environmental policies in Texas, and ends with a foggy Seattle skyline, asking the viewer to "imagine Bush's Texas-style environmental regulations" in Seattle.

[2] The specific items used in the cynicism scale were (a) "Whether I vote or not has no influence on what politicians do," (b) "One never really knows what politicians think;" (c) "People like me don't have any say about what the government does;" (d) "Sometimes politics and government seem so complicated that a person like me can't really understand what's going on;" (e) "One can be confident that politicians will always do the right thing" (reversed in coding); (f) "Politicians

often quickly forget their election promises after a political campaign is over;" (g) "Politicians are more interested in power than in what the people think;" and (h) "One cannot always trust what politicians say."

REFERENCES

Althaus, S. L., & Tewksbury, D. (2000). Patterns of Internet and traditional news media use in a networked community. *Political Communication, 17,* 21–45.

Andreoli, V., & Worchel, S. (1978). Effects of media, communicator and message position on attitude change. *Public Opinion Quarterly, 42,* 59–70.

Ansolabehere, S., & Iyengar, S. (1995). *Going negative: How attack ads shrink and polarize the electorate.* New York: Free Press.

Bennett, S. E. (1997). Why young Americans hate politics and what we should do about it. *PS, 30,* 47–53.

Berlo, D. K. (1960). *The process of communication.* New York: Holt, Rinehart and Winston.

Brians, C. L., & Wattenberg, M. P. (1996). Campaign issue knowledge and salience: Comparing reception from TV commercials, TV news, and newspapers. *American Journal of Political Science, 40,* 172–193.

Center for Media and Public Affairs. (2000). Campaign 2000 final: How TV news covered the general election campaign. *Media Monitor 16(6),* 1–9.

Cohen, A. (1976). Radio vs. TV: The effects of the medium. *Journal of Communication, 26,* 29–35.

Cutbirth, C. W., & Coombs, T. (1997, November). *The coming electronic democracy: The Internet, political communication, and the duties of citizenship.* Paper presented at the National Communication Association Convention, Chicago.

The Democracy Online Project. (2000, December 4). Retrieved from http://www.democracyonline.org/databank/dec2000survey.html

Devlin, L. P. (2001). Contrast in presidential campaign commercials of 2000. *American Behavioral Scientist, 44,* 2338–2369.

Eveland, W. P., & Dunwoody, S. (2001). User control and structural isomorphism or disorientation and cognitive load? Learning from the Web versus print. *Communication Research, 28,* 48–78.

Garramone, G., Atkin, C. K., Pinkleton, B. E., & Cole, R. (1990). Effects of negative political advertising on the political process. *Journal of Broadcasting and Electronic Media, 34,* 299–311.

Ha, L., & Lincoln, J. E. (1998). Interactivity reexamined: A baseline analysis of early business Web sites. *Journal of Broadcasting and Electronic Media 42,* 456–473.

Jacques, W. W., & Ratzan, S. C. (1997). The Internet's World Wide Web and political accountability: New media coverage of the 1996 presidential debates. *American Behavioral Scientist, 40,* 1226–1237.

Just, M., Crigler, A., & Wallach, L. (1990). Thirty seconds or thirty minutes: What viewers learn from spot advertisements and candidate debates. *Journal of Communication, 40,* 120–133.

Kaid, L. L. (2002). Political advertising and information seeking: Comparing the exposure via traditional and Internet media channels. *Journal of Advertising, 31,* 27–35.

Kaid, L. L., McKinney, M. S., & Tedesco, J. C. (2000). *Civic dialogue in the 1996 presidential campaign: Candidate, media, and public voices.* Cresskill, NJ: Hampton.

Katz, E., & Feldman, J. (1962). The debates in light of research: A survey of surveys. In S. Kraus (Ed.), *The great debates* (pp. 173–223). Bloomington: Indiana University Press.

Laswell, H. (1948). The structure and function of communication in society. In L. Bryson (Ed.), *The communication of ideas* (pp. 37–51). New York: Harper.

Lipset, S. M., & Schneider, W. (1987). *The confidence gap* (Rev. ed.). Baltimore: Johns Hopkins University Press.

Martinelli, K. A., & Chaffee, S. H. (1995). Measuring new voter learning via three channels of political information. *Journal and Mass Communication Quarterly, 72,* 18–32.

McKinney, M. S., & Gaddie, K. C. (2000, November). *The medium and the message: TV vs. Internet viewing of a presidential primary debate.* Paper presented at the National Communication Association Convention, Seattle.

McKinnon, L. M., & Tedesco, J. C. (1999). *The influence of medium and media commentary on presidential debate effects.* In L. L. Kaid & D. G. Bystrom (Eds.), *The electronic election* (pp. 191–206). Hillsdale, NJ: Lawrence Erlbaum.

McKinnon, L. M., Tedesco, J. C., & Kaid, L. L. (1993). The third 1992 presidential debate: Channel and commentary effects. *Argumentation and Advocacy, 30,* 106–118.

McLuhan, M. (1964). *Understanding media.* New York: New American Library.

National Telecommunications and Information Administration. (1999, July). Falling through the Net: Defining the digital divide. Retrieved from http://www.ntia.doc.gov/ntiahome/fttn99/contents.html

Patterson, T. E., & McClure, R. D. (1976). *The unseeing eye: Myth of television power in politics.* New York: G. P. Putnam.

Pearlstein, S. (1996, January 30). Angry female voters a growing force. *Washington Post,* p. 1, A5.

Pew Internet and American Life Project. (2000). Youth vote influenced by online information: Internet election news audience seeks convenience, familiar names. Retrieved from http://www.pewinternet.org/reports/toc.asp?Report=27

Rosenstone, S. J., Kinder, D. R., Miller, W. E., & the National Election Studies. (1997). *American National Election Study, 1996: Pre- and post-election survey* (Computer file). Ann Arbor: University of Michigan, Center for Political Studies [Producer]. Ann Arbor: Inter-university Consortium for Political and Social Research [Distributor].

Rumbough, T., & Tomlinson, J. (2000, November). *Internet 2000: Evolution of Internet content and effects.* Paper presented at the National Communication Association Convention, Seattle.

Sundar, S. S. (2000). Multimedia effects on processing and perception of online news: A study of picture, audio, and video downloads. *Journalism & Mass Communication Quarterly, 77,* 480–499.

Sundar, S. S., Hesser, K. M., Kalyanaraman, S., & Brown, J. (1998, July). *The effect of Website interactivity on political persuasion.* Paper presented at the 21st General Assembly & Scientific Conference of the International Association for Media and Communication Research, Glasgow, UK.

Tedesco, J. C., & Kaid, L. L. (2000, November). *Candidate Web sites and voter effects: Investigating uses and gratifications.* Paper presented at the National Communication Association Convention, Seattle.

Vancil, D. L., & Pendell, S. D. (1987). The myth of viewer-listener disagreement in the first Kennedy-Nixon debates. *Central States Speech Journal, 38,* 16–27.

CHAPTER 3
Election Campaign Advertising

Political television

advertising has an immense impact on
elections. Presidential candidates now spend
hundreds of millions of dollars to achieve
office. Senatorial and gubernatorial campaigns
expenditures reach tens of millions. Estimates
from campaign staffs of candidates running for
national office suggest that nearly 75 percent of
these expenditures go to television advertising,
the only medium in which candidates can
control their own image and issue messages
without filtering them through the lens of news
journalism. Soon after the advent of television,
negative advertising became a prominent
subject for political communication scholars.

Michael Pfau, Henry C. Kenski, Michael
Nitz, and John Sorenson, in their 1990 essay,
"Efficacy of Inoculation Strategies in Promoting
Resistance to Political Attack Messages:
Application to Direct Mail," discuss ways to
inoculate audiences against negative political
ads. If a campaign wants to strengthen existing
attitudes, beliefs, and behaviors, inoculation

theory suggests the candidate should present
a weak attack on those attitudes, beliefs, and
behaviors. The attack must be strong enough
to challenge the receiver's defenses without
overwhelming them; but if the attack is too
strong, it will cause the attitude, belief, or
behavior to get weaker or even move to the
opposite position. This study explores distinctions regarding the use of inoculation strategies
and the refutation of negative political attacks.

Lynda Lee Kaid and Anne Johnston's 1991
article, "Negative versus Positive Television
Advertising in U.S. Presidential Campaigns,
1960–1988," examines appeals in negative
advertising over time. The authors find that
negativism in presidential campaigns changed
little from 1976 to 1988, but that there was a
steady growth in negative advertising between
1964 and 1976. Content and approaches of
negative and positive ads also changed during
these decades, as political spots tended to reflect
salient concerns of the electorate. The authors
also indicate that negative spots are more likely

to discuss issues than image, and that emotional appeals are used more often than ethical or logical appeals. Finally, the authors tell us, these negative commercials imply that a candidate is superior to his/her competitor and that that fact is significant to the electorate's general welfare. Kaid and Johnston argue, however, that not all political advertising is harmful; that political ads also provide voters with information about issues and the candidate's character.

Kathleen Hall Jamieson's 1992 book, *Dirty Politics: Deception, Distraction, and Democracy*, highlights the tactics used to gain office. The chapter reproduced here, "Tactics of Attack," points to the degree to which political discourse has been reduced to sound bites in political advertisements. The impact of negative advertising is one of the most debated topics in political communication. Perhaps no other campaign feature evokes more reactions from the electorate. Jamieson argues that the information and rapid pace of television enable the audience to participate in its own manipulation. She suggests that television intertwines the visual with audio to grab the viewer's attention immediately. Finally, she says, the audience easily draws false inferences from political advertising on television. Because the audience believes the communication is informative, there is no expectation that speakers will make false claims. Lacking skepticism, the audience may be persuaded without analyzing claims.

Kim Fridkin Kahn's 1993 essay, "Gender Differences in Campaign Messages: The Political Advertisements of Men and Women Candidates for U.S. Senate" examines the similar and conspicuously different methods in their campaign advertisements that male and female candidates for Senate use. For example, men are more apt to concentrate on economic issues; women tend to concentrate on social issues. Male candidates wage negative campaigns less frequently than female candidates do in mixed gender campaigns. However, Kahn argues that these different types of messages are not represented in media coverage of the candidate's campaigns. The author suggests the failure of the media to report these differences may have an impact on the election.

Stephen Ansolabehere, Shanto Iyengar, Adam Simon, and Nicholas Valentino's 1994 essay "Does Attack Advertising Demobilize the Electorate" reinforces claims that the form of political advertising affects voters on a visual, emotional, and dramatic level. The essay indicates that, among voters who are exposed to attack advertising, 5 percent are less likely to vote. Weeks of sustained negative political advertising might cause even more voters to stay home. Whereas earlier research indicates that politicians use negative ads because they work, this study raises complex questions concerning candidates' legitimate and fair use of broadcast advertising.

Efficacy of Inoculation Strategies in Promoting Resistance to Political Attack Messages: Application to Direct Mail

Michael Pfau, Henry C. Kenski, Michael Nitz, and John Sorenson

American political campaigns have undergone revolutionary changes involving strategies and technology during the past 30 years. This essay focuses on two strategic changes, the steady growth of political attack messages in contemporary campaigns, and the potential of techniques that promote resistance to such attacks, within the context of a technological change involving the explosion of the direct mail communication channel.

★ THE GROWTH OF ATTACK MESSAGES

Current political campaign practices place heavy reliance on three persuasive message strategies. *Bolstering or reinforcement messages* are designed to promote the positive attributes of a candidate's character, positions, and public office performance. *Attack messages,* on the other hand, are negative in focus and are designed to call attention to an opponent's weaknesses. Finally, *refutation messages* are post hoc responses, designed to answer an opponent's attack.

Most contemporary campaigns, and some individual messages, feature various combinations of these three basic strategies. The comparative message, for example, contains bolstering and attack material (Gronbeck, 1985). The comparative message has grown more popular with political consultants, who view it as convincing yet less distasteful to voters (Salmore & Salmore, 1985). Generally, incumbents tend to rely more heavily on reinforcement messages, whereas challengers place more emphasis on attack messages (Kaid & Davidson, 1986; Salmore & Salmore, 1985; Trent & Friedenberg, 1983). This is because incumbents usually enjoy a sizable lead over challengers, with superior name recognition and political favorability ratings. In competitive races, both incumbents and challengers employ a mix of message strategies.

The attack message strategy has been increasingly criticized in various quarters, and when used in political advertising has been popularly termed, "negative advertising" (Taylor, 1986). Still, the use of attack messages has grown in recent years. At the start of this decade, Sabato (1981, p. 166) estimated that nearly one-third of all political commercials were negative, and that the proportion was rising. A study of 175 Senate campaign advertisements for 1984 showed about half the messages were negative or comparative (Feltus, cited in Taylor, 1986). This trend has continued, culminating with extensive use of negative advertising during the 1988 presidential nomination and general election campaigns (Nyhan, 1988; Schneider, 1988).

There is some evidence that strong attack messages can prove counterproductive, resulting in voter backlash against sponsors (Garramone, 1984, 1985; Garramone & Smith, 1984; Guskind & Hagstrom, 1988; Mann & Ornstein, 1983; Merritt, 1984; Stewart, 1975).

Further, the literature suggests some important distinctions involving sponsorship, partisanship, and the nature of attack messages. For example, one study found that attack messages are effective only with certain types of receivers, such as "low-energy information seekers" (Surlin & Gordon, 1977). Another study reported that "independently sponsored" attack messages significantly undermine the image of the targeted politician among members of the opposite political party, and to a lesser degree, among members of the same party (Kaid & Boydston, 1987).

However, most political professionals and commentators maintain that attack messages influence voters (Armstrong, 1988; Ehrenhalt, 1985; Guskind & Hagstrom, 1988; Hickey, 1986; Johnson-Cartee & Copeland, 1989; Louden, 1987; Mann & Ornstein, 1983; Martinez & DeLegal, 1988; Moyers, 1984; Nugent, 1987; Pfau & Burgoon, 1988a; Sabato, 1981, 1983; Schneider, 1988; Surlin & Gordon, 1977; Tarrance, 1980; Taylor, 1986). In reviewing the use of attack message strategies for the *Congressional Quarterly Weekly Report,* Ehrenhalt (1985, p. 2560) concluded that, "There is no argument about their [negative ads] short-term impact: they work, and they win elections." Mellman (cited in Taylor, 1986, p. 7) explains their success as follows: "We know that from years of work in research psychology that people process negative information more deeply than positive information. When we ask people about negative ads, they'll say they don't like them. But that's not the point. The point is that they absorb the information."

Recent electoral outcomes have stimulated a major change in campaign strategy. In 1988 many candidates attacked early, "and in some cases without first doing any positive advertising" (Guskind & Hagstrom, 1988, p. 287). Early campaign attacks can effectively define the public's perception of one's opponent, as the Bush campaign's negative efforts against Dukakis clearly demonstrated (Schneider, 1988).

There is little doubt that negative advertising is now a permanent feature of the American political campaign landscape. Although it occurs in multiple channels, the focus of this investigation will be on one current channel, direct mail.

★ DIRECT MAIL

Targeted or direct mail has a relatively long history dating back to 1914 when Woodrow Wilson sent out more than 300,000 pieces of campaign mail. In the fifties, Dwight Eisenhower used *Reader's Digest* experts to design direct-mail appeals. Despite its past use, direct mail did not become a staple of modern campaigns until the advent of the computer, which resulted in "expanding the methods of identifying groups to target and facilitating a volume of communication virtually impossible using traditional methods" (Frantzich, 1989, pp. 216–217). As a result, Armstrong (1988, p. 28) claims that the direct mail communication channel "has utterly revolutionized American politics in the past thirty-five years." In recent elections, direct mail has been an important channel for both incumbent survival as well as challenger success (Armstrong, 1988; Heller, 1987; Reilley, 1987; Sabato, 1981).

Direct mail, as a persuasive tool, has several advantages. It offers "the ability to pretest political messages and to personalize, concentrate, and encourage an immediate response from the target audience. In addition, direct-mail messages can be as long as necessary to explain fully a cause or a candidate" (Godwin, 1988, pp. 32–33). In doing so, such mailings make greater use of threat and fear than other political communication (Martinez & DeLegal, 1988). Moreover, direct mail is less costly than television and radio, and allows for more specific and tailored messages to voter subgroups (Heller, 1987). Armstrong (1988, p. 66) agrees and stresses that direct mail is especially useful to challengers who can target strong issue attacks on incumbents. "Attack your opponent's record on television, and he will respond in kind. Attack your opponent in the mail, and he will never even know what hit him."

Many people, of course, label direct mail "junk mail" and claim to throw it away unopened. Armstrong (1988) doubts that this is the case, observing: "Research shows that approximately 75 percent of the American people open and glance at every piece of mail they receive. When it comes to fundraising mail, including political, over four of five survey respondents (81 percent) say they open it and at least glance at the contents" (Armstrong, 1988, p. 89). These estimates are undoubtedly high, and Armstrong himself concedes that readership may be down due to an oversaturation of direct mail in recent years. Nobody really knows precisely the percentage of readership, which may vary considerably depending on whether generalized or specialized mailing lists are used. The basic point is, however, that direct mail reaches a large number of people, and is an increasingly important channel of political communication.

Faced with actual or anticipated strong negative advertising through direct mail or other media channels, a candidate has several options. One, of course, is refutation, and the quicker the better. However, refutation messages, which constitute an explicit or implicit rebuttal to an attack, are post hoc. Thus, despite the pervasive use of this response option in the face of political attacks, it is unclear whether refutation messages can significantly contain the damage already done by an opponent's attack message. In addition, refutation messages are useless in response to an opponent's attack that is launched late in a close campaign, thus simply precluding response. This is an important limitation in light of reports of increasing use of such "last minute" attacks in a number of 1988 presidential primary contests (Colford, 1988).

★ THE RESISTANCE PARADIGM

An alternative and more promising option to emerge from current research is the inoculation message strategy (Pfau & Burgoon, 1988b). Instead of seeking to convert receivers, the inoculation strategy seeks to promote resistance to changes in attitudes and behaviors (Miller & Burgoon, 1973), thus minimizing the chance that political attacks may influence receivers. The strategy is based on McGuire's original work on inoculation. The theory posits that refutational pretreatments, which raise the specter of content potentially damaging to the receiver's attitude while simultaneously providing direct refutation of that content in the presence of a supportive environment, threaten the individual. This triggers the motivation to bolster arguments supporting the receiver's attitudes, thus conferring resistance (Papageorgis & McGuire, 1961).

A number of early laboratory studies confirmed the relative superiority of the inoculation approach, in contrast to bolstering, in promoting resistance to subsequent persuasive attacks. In a series of direct comparisons, most investigators reported that inoculation pretreatments were superior to bolstering ones (Anderson & McGuire, 1965; McGuire, 1961a, 1962; McGuire & Papageorgis, 1961, 1962; Papageorgis & McGuire, 1961; Tannenbaum, Macaulay, & Norris, 1966; Tannenbaum & Norris, 1965), although a few studies concluded that the use of both were superior to using either separately (Anatol & Mandel, 1972; Burgoon & Chase, 1973; McGuire, 1961a, 1962; Tannenbaum & Norris, 1965).

In the first application of inoculation in field research in the political campaign context, Pfau and Burgoon (1988b, pp. 105–106) concluded that: "Inoculation deflects the persuasiveness of subsequent political attacks in a number of ways: undermining the potential influence of the source of political attacks, deflecting the specific content of political attacks, and reducing the likelihood that political attacks will influence receiver voter intention."

Although much of the early research on inoculation theory focused on what McGuire termed "cultural truisms," germ-free beliefs uncontaminated by counterarguments, Pfau and Burgoon (1989b) identified a number of more recent studies that apply the basic tenets of the theory to more controversial topics. Hence, Pfau and Burgoon (1988b) argue for the applicability of the inoculation strategy in fostering resistance to political attack messages. This study examines the efficacy of the inoculation strategy using direct mail as a communication channel.

H_1: For people who receive an inoculation pretreatment, as compared to those who do not, inoculation messages confer resistance

to attitude change following exposure to a political attack message.

Political consultants recently have begun to explore refutational preemption as a strategic option. Innocenzi (cited in Ehrenhalt, 1985, p. 2563) claims that, "Inoculation and preemption are what win campaigns." Salmore and Salmore (1985, p. 80) advise incumbents to "anticipate negatives and preempt them." Frantzich (1989, pp. 220–221) adds that, "potential subjects of attack often use 'inoculation letters'. A preemptive letter outlining your position on a sensitive issue protects you from future negative information the voter might receive."

At this point it is important to distinguish the concept of inoculation and refutational preemption. Refutational preemption is a necessary but not sufficient ingredient in inoculation. Inoculation promotes resistance through the use of a warning of impending attack, *employed in conjunction with* refutational preemption. The warning of impending attack is designed to threaten the individual, triggering the motivation to bolster arguments supporting attitudes, thereby conferring resistance to subsequent counterpersuasion (Anderson & McGuire, 1965; McGuire, 1964, 1970; Papageorgis & McGuire, 1961).

It is the two elements in tandem, threat plus refutational preemption, that distinguish inoculation from other message strategies. If inoculation were limited to refutational preemption, as Innocenzi (cited in Ehrenhalt, 1985) and Frantzich (1989) imply, then the concept would afford limited utility since candidates would need to prepare specific preemptive messages that correspond to each potential vulnerability.

Inoculation affords much greater potential. The most useful and interesting finding of the inoculation research is that inoculation promotes resistance to *both same and different* counterarguments (McGuire, 1961a, 1962, 1970; Papageorgis & McGuire, 1961; Pfau & Burgoon, 1988b). This finding suggests that the candidate who is able to inoculate receivers regarding one potential vulnerability simultaneously spreads a blanket of protection against an opponent's attacks that target additional vulnerabilities. This confirms the role of inoculation in motivating receivers as opposed to simply providing answers to specific arguments.

H_2: In comparison with people who receive no inoculation, for those who receive an inoculation pretreatment, both same and different inoculation approaches confer resistance to attitude change following exposure to a persuasive attack message.

Since inoculation theory posits that threat triggers the motivation to resist attacks, the theoretical construct implies that refutation is more effective if it precedes, rather than follows, exposure to an attack message. Ironically, this basic assumption has received scant attention in the extant literature. Tannenbaum and Norris (1965) tested the relative effectiveness of refutation administered before and after an attack. While the differences weren't statistically significant, the authors (1965, p. 157) concluded that, "Immunization allows for the introduction of more defense arousal. ..." A year later, Tannenbaum et al. (1966) conducted a similar experiment, concluding that while both approaches conferred resistance, the refutation-attack sequence was somewhat more effective. This study provides a direct comparison of the efficacy of these approaches in the political campaign context, predicting that:

H_3: The inoculation strategy is more effective than post hoc refutation in conferring resistance to attitude change following exposure to a political attack message.

Although the effect of any message stimulus will decay over time, Pfau and Burgoon (1988b, p. 93) found that "inoculation is an active process that facilitates persistence." It is expected that, in actual use in a political campaign, inoculation would be reinforced over time through the use of multiple exposures to the immunizing messages. Yet, there is very little research on the role of reinforcement in inoculation. McGuire (1961b), in testing the superiority of active and passive inoculation pretreatments, reported that, while "single defenses" were effective with both same and different counterarguments, "double defenses" provided a significant boost, but only with same counterarguments. In another study, Tannenbaum et al. (1966) found that "concept-boost" messages provided

a slight increase in resistance compared to a single message, but the difference fell short of statistical significance. Since the inoculation research offers some support for reinforcement, this study predicts that:

H_4: Inoculation plus follow-up reinforcement is superior to inoculation alone in conferring resistance to attitude change following exposure to a political attack message.

★ POLITICAL PARTY IDENTIFICATION

Of particular interest to this analysis is the prominent role of party identification in the vote (Campbell, Munro, Alford, & Campbell, 1986). Since Campbell, Gurin, and Miller (1954) and Campbell, Converse, Miller, and Stokes (1960) posited the psychological theory of voting in two election studies during the fifties, political scientists have emphasized the substantial influence of party identification on political cognition.

Although recent studies document the weakening of party identification during the last two decades, and its relationship to the vote (Axelrod, 1972, 1974, 1978, 1982, 1986; Beck, 1988; Norpoth, 1987; Petrocik, 1981, 1987; Stanley, Bianco, & Niemi, 1986; Wattenberg, 1986), with this trend most pronounced among Democrats, it is still the most reliable predictor of the vote. Democratic pollster Peter Hart conceded after the 1984 election that party attachment today is less strong and more susceptible to change, but he went on to emphasize that "party identification continues to be the single best predictor of what an individual will do" (Moving Right along? . . . , 1985, p. 63). More recently, Stanga and Sheffield (1987) and Whiteley (1988) have underscored the continual force of party identification in voter decisions.

Party identification affects persuasibility in a number of ways. Chaffee and Choe (1980), for example, report that higher political involvement of identifiers reduces persuasibility. King (1977) observes that affiliated receivers are more inclined to selective perception of their candidate's message, a claim that has received considerable support to date (Atkin, 1971; Blumler & McQuail, 1969; Sherrod,

1971; Weisberg & Rusk, 1970). Nonetheless, in an increasingly volatile electoral environment, more and more partisans occasionally defect, casting a vote for candidates of the opposite political party (Niemi & Weisberg, 1984). Consequently, inoculation, which attempts to minimize defections, is a relevant strategy for party identifiers.

In addition, higher political involvement should render strong party identifiers particularly ripe for inoculation because the use of threat, consisting of a warning of impending attack, acts as a catalyst to receiver motivation. In the first test of inoculation and political party identification, Pfau and Burgoon (1988b) reported that the inoculation strategy provided more resistance to political attack messages among strong political party identifiers in a Senate campaign. Although party identification once was thought to exert more influence in nonpresidential elections (Campbell et al., 1986), Kostroski (1973) reported that the impact of party identification on voting has declined in Senate elections, following the same pattern previously observed in presidential elections. Thus, it is anticipated that Pfau and Burgoon's (1988b) finding, that inoculation fosters more resistance among strong party identifiers, will generalize to a presidential election campaign.

H5: Inoculation pretreatments confer more resistance to subsequent exposure to an attack message among strong political party identifiers than among weak political party identifiers or nonidentifiers.

★ METHOD

Participants

Participants ($N = 314$) were potential voters in a midwestern metropolitan area during the 1988 presidential campaign between Democrat Michael Dukakis and Republican George Bush.

Design and Independent Variables

The independent variables in this study were treatment condition, political party orientation, and attack message approach. In all but one of the analyses, the four treatment conditions included inoculation, inoculation-plus-reinforcement, post hoc refutation, and control. In one case, the treatment condition was trichotomized as same inoculation, different inoculation, and control. Political party orientation was operationalized as strong, weak, and none, based on subjects' responses.

The effectiveness of the treatment conditions in deflecting the persuasive attacks was assessed by comparing the attitudes of receivers who received one of the treatments versus those who received no treatment, following exposure to the attack messages. Hence, the attack message variable served an integral function in the study. The two attack message approaches consisted of issue attacks and character attacks. Both issue and character attack messages were included in the design because of the possibility that the effectiveness of the treatments might vary depending on whether the attack messages contained issue or character content (Pfau & Burgoon, 1988b).

Since the study sought to assess the comparative efficacy of distinct strategies in conferring resistance to political attack messages, it was necessary to prepare a number of messages for administration during the study. After identifying the most salient issue and character concerns on the basis of available polling data, experimenters prepared a total of four attack messages, using the existing pool of Bush and Dukakis campaign messages (position papers, print and electronic commercial messages, and the complete and partial accounts of candidate speeches). The Bush messages attacked Dukakis for being weak on crime and for deception involving his record as Governor of Massachusetts. The Dukakis messages attacked Bush for his support for agricultural and development policies that have hurt rural America and for insensitivity to the plight of the average working person. Sponsorship of the attack messages was attributed to the interest group, Citizens for an Informed Electorate.

Inoculation pretreatment messages were prepared in response to each attack message. A same inoculation message was written for each candidate as an implicit rebuttal to each issue and character attack message. In addition, a different inoculation message was constructed for each candidate. The different inoculation messages consisted of generic defenses of the

TABLE 1

Comparison of Inoculation, Reinforcement, and Attack Messages

Possible Message Combinations	Total Words	Contingency Index
Bush Issue Inoculation	246	7.13
Bush Issue Reinforcement	244	7.77
Dukakis Issue Attack	244	7.31
Bush Character Inoculation	249	6.58
Bush Character Reinforcement	245	8.74
Dukakis Character Attack	247	7.01
Bush Generic Inoculation	246	7.06
Bush Generic Reinforcement	244	9.05
Dukakis Issue Attack	244	7.31
Dukakis Character Attack	247	7.01
Dukakis Issue Inoculation	246	9.04
Dukakis Issue Reinforcement	246	8.98
Bush Issue Attack	244	8.10
Dukakis Character Inoculation	245	6.50
Dukakis Character Reinforcement	244	8.85
Bush Character Attack	245	8.12
Dukakis Generic Inoculation	245	7.47
Dukakis Generic Reinforcement	246	8.11
Bush Issue Attack	244	8.10
Bush Character Attack	245	8.12

Note: The Index of Contingency evaluates the readability of sentences. A low Index of Contingency indicates significant diversity in word use. A high Index of Contingency signifies significant repetition in word use.

candidate, absent any rebuttal of the content of the corresponding attack message.

Since inoculation theory posits that threat triggers the motivation to bolster existing attitudes, thereby making them resistant to subsequent attacks, the first paragraph of each inoculation message was designed to threaten receivers. Threat was operationalized as a warning of impending, and potentially persuasive, attacks against the candidate supported by the receiver. Finally, reinforcement messages were written to bolster the content of each of the six inoculation messages.

Each inoculation and reinforcement message attempted to replicate the written style and design of their corresponding attack message.

Burgoon, Cohen, Miller, and Montgomery (1978, p. 33) have previously stressed the need for influence studies to employ messages that are relatively similar. Each pair of inoculation messages, and their corresponding reinforcement messages, were constructed in such a way as to match as closely as possible the writing style and overall comprehensibility of the respective attack message. Particular attention was paid to the total length, average sentence length, verb tenses, and modifiers used in the inoculation, reinforcement, and attack messages (Burgoon et al., 1978). Total word counts and the Index of Contingency, developed by Becker, Bavelas, and Braden (1961) to assess the comprehensibility of messages, were used to evaluate message equivalence. As Table 1 indicates, the total word counts and the Index of Contingency ratings of the inoculation messages, reinforcement messages, and their corresponding attack messages were similar.

Interviewing Procedures

Ten undergraduate, senior students attached to the Center for the Study of Communication served as interviewers for the study. Prior to the study they received six hours of training, consisting of formal instruction followed by supervised practice sessions. Interviewers were assigned randomly to all conditions.

The metropolitan area is divided into 43 voting precincts. Two adjacent, approximately two-square block, predominantly residential areas were selected at random from each precinct. The first phase of the study was conducted from September 12 to September 24. Using the *City Directory*, which organizes resident telephone numbers according to street address, callers completed interviews with 529 households in the designated areas in each voting precinct (46% completion rate). Interviewers asked one potential voter in each of the households: their preference among the candidates in the presidential race, their political party affiliation, general demographic information, and whether they would be willing to participate in an on-going investigation of candidate political messages during the presidential campaign.

The second phase of the study involved the direct mailing of inoculation and reinforcement messages to a randomly assigned portion of the sample population. On September 28, researchers mailed inoculation pretreatment messages to 95 Bush supporters and 114 Dukakis supporters. On the same day, they mailed attack messages to a separate group of 34 Bush supporters and 33 Dukakis supporters who would constitute the refutation condition in the study. The third phase was completed on October 5. Researchers mailed reinforcement messages to 47 of the 95 inoculated Bush supporters and to 56 of the 114 inoculated Dukakis supporters. On the same day, they mailed refutation messages to the 34 Bush supporters and the 33 Dukakis supporters who had previously received attack messages.

The fourth phase of the study was conducted from October 10 to October 22. This phase consisted of three simultaneous steps, all requiring researchers to interview subjects in their homes. First, researchers administered attack messages and posttreatment instruments to those adults who had received previously either an inoculation or inoculation-plus-reinforcement pretreatment via direct mail. All together, 163 of these participants completed this phase of the study (78%), 11 refused further participation (5%), and 35 could not be reached (17%) despite repeated efforts. Second, the researchers administered attack messages and posttreatment instruments to a separate group of 52 Bush supporters and 55 Dukakis supporters who constituted the control condition in the study. A total of 91 control subjects completed this phase of the study (85%), 4 refused (4%), and 12 could not be reached (11%). Third, researchers administered posttreatment instruments to the 34 Bush supporters and the 33 Dukakis supporters who had previously received both an attack and refutation message via direct mail. Altogether, 60 of these participants completed this phase of the study (90%), 2 refused (3%), and 5 could not be reached (8%) despite repeated efforts.

The remaining 146 phase one participants, all nonpartisans, were a part of a separate analysis involving the immediate and delayed impact of political attack messages. The flow sheet in Figure 1 sequentially depicts the steps involved in the study.

Dependent Measures

Three dependent measures were employed in this study. Attitude toward the candidate supported in the attack message and attitude toward the position advocated in the attack message were evaluated using six bipolar adjective pairs previously used by Pfau and Burgoon (1988a, 1988b), Burgoon et al. (1978) and Miller and Burgoon (1979), including: wise/foolish, good/bad, positive/negative, favorable/unfavorable, right/wrong, and acceptable/unacceptable. The reliabilities of the two attitude scales were high: .94 for attitude toward the candidate supported in the attack message and .96 for attitude toward the position advocated in the attack message. Likelihood of voting for

FIGURE 1

Flow Chart Sequentially Depicting the Steps Involved in the Administration of Each of the Major Components (Inoculation, Post-Hoc Refutation, and Control) of This Investigation

PHASE 1 Sept. 12–24		
Initial Phone Interviews ($n = 529$)		
Inoculation Condition	Post Hoc Refutation	Control Condition
PHASE 2 Sept. 28		
Mail Inoculation Messages to Bush & Dukakis Supporters ($n = 209$)	Mail Attack Messages to Bush & Dukakis Supporters ($n = 67$)	
PHASE 3 Oct. 5		
Mail Reinforcement Messages to Half of Bush & Dukakis Supporters ($n = 103$)	Mail Post-Hoc Refutation Messages to Bush & Dukakis Supporters ($n = 67$)	
PHASE 4 Oct. 10–22		
Administer Attack Messages & Measures to Bush & Dukakis Supporters ($n = 163$)	Administer Measures to Bush & Dukakis Supporters ($n = 60$)	Administer Attack Messages & Measures to Bush & Dukakis Supporters ($n = 91$)

the candidate supported in the attack message was assessed using a 0–100 probability scale. Finally, threat, a manipulation check in the study, was assessed with bipolar adjective pairs: nonthreatening/threatening, not harmful/harmful, unintimidating/intimidating, not risky/risky, and safe/dangerous. The reliability of the threat scale was satisfactory (.83).

★ RESULTS

Manipulation Check

A manipulation check was conducted to confirm the presence of sufficient threat levels among inoculated subjects. A planned comparison was computed to assess the combined inoculation

means against the no inoculation mean. It revealed that the combined inoculation conditions produced significantly greater threat levels than the control condition, $F(1, 279) = 8.56$, $p < .05$; $\hat{W}^2 = .03$. Thus, the manipulation check confirmed the presence of significant threat levels among subjects who received inoculation pretreatments, but not among subjects in the control condition.

Hypotheses

Hypotheses 1, 3, and 4 presuppose specific differences in the treatment condition means. A 4 (treatment condition) x 3 (political party orientation) x 2 (attack message approach) factorial analysis of variance was computed, followed by planned comparisons using Dunn's multiple comparison procedure (Kirk, 1982). If the omnibus ANOVA revealed an unpredicted interaction or main effect, then appropriate tests of simple effects were conducted, and if warranted, the Scheffe post hoc test was used to examine the differences in means.

The omnibus ANOVA produced significant differences in the treatment means on the dependent variables of attitude toward the candidate, $F(3, 289) = 14.32, p < .05; \hat{W}^2 = .11$; attitude toward position, $F(3, 290) = 11.00, p < .05; \hat{W}^2 = .09$; and the likelihood of voting for, $F(3, 287) = 15.15, p < .05; \hat{W}^2 = .11$; with a triple interaction involving treatment condition, political party orientation, and attack message approach, $F(6, 287) = 2.34, p < .05; \hat{W}^2 = .02$, overriding the main effect of treatment condition on likelihood of voting for. The triple interaction is examined later in this section. Hypothesis 1, positing that employing direct mail as communication channel, inoculation messages confer resistance to attitude change following exposure to a political attack message, was largely supported. A planned comparison comparing the inoculation and inoculation-plus-reinforcement means against the no inoculation means on the three dependent variables revealed that the combined inoculation means were significantly lower than the control means on attitude toward candidate, $F(1, 289) = 41.54, p < .05; \hat{W}^2 = .11$, as well as attitude toward position, $F(1, 290) = 28.50, p < .05; \hat{W}^2 = .08$. The results indicated that the political attack messages exerted significantly less influence on the inoculated receivers. The treatment condition means are displayed in Table 2.

Hypothesis 3 predicted that the inoculation strategy is more effective than post hoc refutation in conferring resistance to attitude change following exposure to a political attack message. Planned comparisons indicated marginal support for the prediction. There was a trend toward the combined inoculation means being lower than the refutation means on attitude toward candidate, $F(1, 289) = 2.66, p < .10; \hat{W}^2 = .01$, but there were no clear differences in the means on attitude toward position.

Hypothesis 4 posited that inoculation plus follow-up reinforcement is superior to

inoculation alone in conferring resistance to attitude change following exposure to a political attack message. The planned comparisons indicated no support for this prediction on the dependent measures of attitude toward candidate or attitude toward position.

Hypothesis 2 predicted that both same and different inoculation approaches confer resistance to attitude change following exposure to a political attack message. The treatment condition was reconfigured as inoculation same, inoculation different, and control to test this prediction, and a 3 (treatment condition) x 3 (political party orientation) x 2 (attack message approach) factorial analysis of variance was computed. It revealed a significant main effect for treatment condition on the major dependent variables of attitude toward candidate, $F(1, 235) = 22.13, p < .05; \hat{W}^2 = .14$; attitude toward position, $F(1, 236) = 14.99, p < .05; \hat{W}^2 = .10$; and likelihood of voting for the candidate supported in the attack message, $F(1, 233) = 23.55, p < .05; \hat{W}^2 = .15$. Planned comparisons comparing the same and different inoculation means to the control mean verified that each inoculation approach fosters resistance to subsequent attack messages. The comparisons revealed significant differences between the same inoculation and control conditions on attitude toward candidate, $F(1, 235) = 31.40, p < .05; \hat{W}^2 = .10$; attitude toward position, $F(1, 236) = 18.70, p < .05; \hat{W}^2 = .06$; and likelihood of voting for, $F(1, 233) = 33.98, p < .05; \hat{W}^2 = .11$; and between the different inoculation and control conditions on attitude toward candidate, $F(1, 235) = 29.65, p < .05; \hat{W}^2 = .10$; attitude toward position, $F(1, 236) = 23.67, p < .05; \hat{W}^2 = .08$; and likelihood of voting for, $F(1, 233) = 32.58, p < .05; \hat{W}^2 = .10$. These means are displayed in Table 2.

Hypothesis 5 indicated that inoculation pretreatments confer more resistance to subsequent exposure to an attack message among strong political party identifiers than among weak political party identifiers or nonidentifiers. The omnibus ANOVA approached statistical significance on the measures of attitude toward candidate, $F(2, 289) = 2.46, p < .10; \hat{W}^2 = .01$, and the likelihood of voting for $F(2, 287) = 2.79, p < .10; \hat{W}^2 = .01$, but the triple interaction, reported above, overrode the latter effect. Two

TABLE 2

Summary of the Treatment Condition Means on the Primary Dependent Measures

DEPENDENT MEASURE	TREATMENT CONDITION MEANS			
	Control	Refutation	Inoculation	Inoculation Plus Reinforcement
Attitude toward the Candidate				
Mean	4.26	3.30	2.98	2.97
	(n = 90)	(n = 60)	(n = 89)	(n = 74)
SD	1.60	1.57	1.43	1.22
Attitude toward the Position				
Mean	3.96	2.71	2.75	2.84
	(n = 91)	(n = 60)	(n = 89)	(n = 74)
SD	1.81	1.54	1.48	1.41
Likelihood of Voting for...				
Mean	39.62	22.55	17.50	11.68
	(n = 89)	(n = 60)	(n = 88)	(n = 74)
SD	33.38	32.12	24.89	18.01

DEPENDENT MEASURE	TREATMENT CONDITION MEANS		
		Inoculation Condition	
	Control	Same	Different
Attitude toward the Candidate			
Mean	4.26	2.96	3.00
	(n = 90)	(n = 109)	(n = 54)
SD	1.60	1.30	1.40
Attitude toward the Position			
Mean	3.96	2.84	2.70
	(n = 91)	(n = 109)	(n = 54)
SD	1.81	1.47	1.42
Likelihood of Voting for...			
Mean	39.62	14.67	15.19
	(n = 89)	(n = 108)	(n = 54)
SD	33.38	21.42	23.48

Note. Ratings of receivers' attitude toward the candidate supported in the attack message and the receivers' attitude toward the position taken by the candidate supported in the attack message are based on seven-point scales. Assessment of the likelihood of voting for the candidate supported in the attack message is based on a 100-point probability scale. The higher the rating or assessment, the more persuasive the attack message.

planned comparisons examined differences in political party orientation on the measure of attitude toward candidate. A comparison of strong political party with the combined means of weak identifiers and nonidentifiers indicated that strong identifiers were significantly less influenced by attack messages across all treatment conditions, $F(1, 289) = 5.90$, $p < .05$; $\hat{W}^2 = .01$. There were no significant differences involving weak identifiers and nonidentifiers. However, when the same planned comparisons were computed among inoculation and inoculation-plus-reinforcement subjects on the measure of attitude toward candidate, the direction of means was the same, but the differences were not statistically significant.

The triple interaction, involving each of the independent variables in this study on the

TABLE 3

Summary of the Treatment Condition Means on Issue and Character Attack Messages
for Weak Political Party Identifiers on the Dependent Variable of Likelihood of Voting
for the Candidate Supported in the Attack Message

| ATTACK MESSAGE | TREATMENT CONDITION MEANS | | | |
	Control	Refutation	Inoculation	Inoculation Plus Reinforcement
Issue Attacks				
Mean	36.37 ($n = 19$)	9.44 ($n = 9$)	21.45 ($n = 20$)	14.64 ($n = 11$)
SD	27.05	11.30	27.29	19.22
Character Attacks				
Mean	22.82 ($n = 17$)	42.70 ($n = 10$)	21.14 ($n = 14$)	19.44 ($n = 9$)
SD	24.07	41.47	24.44	20.98

Note: Assessment of the likelihood of voting for the candidate supported in the attack message is based on a 100-point probability scale. The higher the rating or assessment, the more persuasive the attack message.

dependent measure of likelihood of voting for the candidate supported in the attack message, affects the results of Hypotheses 1, 3, 4, and 5 on this particular dependent variable. To further probe this interaction, two-way factorial analyses of variance were computed within each of the three levels of party identification. The analysis for weak political party identifiers indicated a two-way interaction involving treatment condition and attack message approach, $F (3, 101) = 3.40, p < .05; \hat{W}^2 = .06$. In comparison with the control condition, both post hoc refutation, $t(287) = 3.50, p < .05$, and inoculation-plus-reinforcement, $t(287) = 2.82$, $p < .05$, deflected the influence of issue attacks, but inoculation did not. However, refutation was completely ineffective in dealing with character attacks. Compared to the control condition, both inoculation, $t(287) = 2.80$, $p < .05$, and inoculation-plus-reinforcement, $t(287) = 3.02, p < .05$, reduced the impact of character attacks, whereas refutation did not (see Table 3).

The remaining two-way factorials revealed main effects for treatment condition, but no interactions. This was true for both strong party identifiers, $F (3, 143) = 11.98$, $p < .05; \hat{W}^2 = .18$, and for nonidentifiers, $F (3, 143) = 4.49, p < .05; \hat{W}^2 = .16$. Further

analysis of these differences revealed a consistent pattern of results, with inoculation and inoculation-plus-reinforcement proving superior to the refutation approach in deflecting the influence of political attack messages. These results are consistent with Hypothesis 3.

Among strong party identifiers, in contrast to the control condition, inoculation, $t(287) = 6.41, p < .05$, inoculation-plus-reinforcement, $t(287) = 8.40, p < .05$, and post hoc refutation were more effective in suppressing the influence of attack messages, but inoculation-plus-reinforcement also proved superior to post hoc refutation, $t(287) = 2.82$, $p < .05$. Among nonidentifiers, the inoculation, $t(287) = 3.80, p < .05$, and inoculation-plus-reinforcement, $t(287) = 3.27, p < .05$, conditions, but not the post hoc refutation approach, were more effective in deflecting the persuasiveness of attack messages.

★ DISCUSSION

Inoculation Effect

The results of this investigation offer additional support for the position that inoculation is both a viable and promising strategy of resistance against the influence of attack messages in political campaign communication.

The results bolster the previous finding of Pfau and Burgoon (1988b), indicating that inoculation pretreatments, whether same or different, deflect the persuasiveness of subsequent political attacks by undermining the potential influence of the source of such attacks, deflecting the specific content of attacks, and reducing the chance that such attacks will affect receivers' voting intention.

The viability of inoculation in political communication is both useful and important, given the increasing number and impact of attack messages in contemporary campaigns. The practical question is, What can be done to combat attack messages? The more popular and obvious options offer little potential. The call for legislative action to restrict attack messages won't withstand court scrutiny, given the judiciary's disposition to safeguard the unfettered expression of "traditional political speech." In addition, voluntary surrender of the attack option is very unlikely since attack messages are perceived as a very important, and effective, strategic option among political professionals (Ehrenhalt, 1985; Louden, 1987; Sabato, 1981; Taylor, 1986). Inoculation provides a viable strategic vehicle to combat attack messages.

Further, the results extend the scope of inoculation to a new domain, suggesting the viability of this resistance strategy via the direct mail communication channel, an important application in light of the rapid growth of direct mail communication in political campaigns and the most recent use of direct mail as a conduit for strong, targeted political attacks. The combined inoculation and reinforcement conditions produced a significant impact, accounting for sizable variance in receivers' responses to the source and content of subsequent attack messages. These results suggest that Armstrong (1988) is on target with his claim that most people open and at least glance at every piece of mail, at least with regard to personalized, political correspondence. Since inoculated and control subjects in this study were alike *in almost every respect,* including exposure to campaign events (e.g., news, political advertisements, and debates), differing only in that the inoculated subjects had received a direct mail inoculation message and the control subjects had not, the greater resistance shown by inoculated subjects to the persuasive attack messages suggests that many of them read and internalized the inoculative material.

Finally, the results of this investigation provide new and important nuances to inform the use of the inoculation and the post hoc refutation response options to political attacks. The results failed to support the prediction that reinforcement messages increase the effectiveness of inoculation pretreatments. This indicates that the initial inoculative stimulus, which triggers an internal motivational process to bolster arguments supporting attitudes, carries considerable persistence. This outcome is consistent with the findings of Chaiken (1987), Petty (1977), and Petty and Cacioppo (1979, 1984) that message strategies producing higher receiver involvement tend to enhance attitude persistence. Previous laboratory research involving college undergraduates (McGuire, 1961b; Tannenbaum et al., 1966) reported small reinforcement effects, while Pfau and Burgoon's (1988b) field study in a political campaign concluded that inoculation pretreatments experience limited decay over a period of three weeks, at least in terms of receiver voting intention.

However, this investigation failed to rule out one other explanation for the failure of reinforcement messages to enhance the effectiveness of the inoculation pretreatments. It may be that the amount of reinforcement is crucial, and that it requires more than a single reinforcement treatment to significantly boost the effectiveness of inoculation pretreatments.

The pattern of results of this study provides modest support for the position that the inoculation message strategy, which was represented in the treatment condition of the study by both inoculation and inoculation-plus-reinforcement, is more effective than post hoc refutation in inhibiting attitude change following exposure to a political attack message. The planned comparisons indicated some advantage for inoculation over post-hoc refutation on the measure of attitude toward candidate, but no differences on attitude toward position.

However, the triple interaction, involving the independent variables of treatment condition, political party orientation and attack message approach, on the dependent measure of likelihood of voting for the candidate supported in the attack message is particularly revealing with regard to the relative effectiveness of the inoculation approach versus post-hoc refutation. The subsequent analyses indicate consistent superiority of inoculation over post hoc refutation among strong political party identifiers as well as nonidentifiers. Among weak party identifiers, however, the effectiveness of inoculation and post hoc refutation varied somewhat, depending on attack message approach. The results indicated that, while post-hoc refutation and inoculation-plus-reinforcement are more effective than inoculation alone in deflecting issue attack messages, inoculation and inoculation-plus-reinforcement are superior to post hoc refutation in combating character attacks. While there is no theoretical explanation that can account for this finding, the impact of inoculation, inoculation-plus-reinforcement, and post hoc refutation on issue and character attack messages among weak party identifiers should be examined further, since additional support for this pattern of results suggests important nuances for political professionals in their efforts to design and target defenses to political attack messages.

The conclusion that the inoculation strategy is superior to post hoc refutation in attenuating political attacks is both useful and important. On a theoretical level, it adds to the initial work of Tannenbaum and Norris (1965) and Tannenbaum et al. (1966), providing confirmation in a field research setting that the sequence of refutation-attack confers more resistance to persuasion than attack-refutation. In addition, the finding confirms the central role of threat in any strategy designed to militate political attack messages. Threat is the motivational trigger for resistance, as inoculation theory posits (Anderson & McGuire, 1965; McGuire, 1962, 1964, 1970; Papageorgis & McGuire, 1961), and the inoculation approach intrinsically is capable of generating higher threat levels than refutation through the use of a warning of impending attack prior to the actual attack.

On a practical level, this finding informs the practice of political campaign communication. In the first direct comparison of the two alternative strategic responses to political attacks, the inoculation strategy generally proved more effective than post hoc refutation in combating the influence of political attacks, with the one exception involving issue attacks among weak political party identifiers.

Limitations

One potential limitation of this investigation is inherent to field, as opposed to laboratory, research. This investigation examined the use of inoculation as a direct mail strategy during a real political campaign. Obviously the events of a campaign affect subjects, thus serving as potential contaminants. For example, since Bush and Dukakis won their respective party nominations following contested primary contests, receivers had prior exposure to the candidates and their messages. Further, both candidates employed extensive advertising during the general election campaign. Finally, the first Bush and Dukakis debate was broadcast on September 25, one day following completion of the first phase of the study, and three days prior to the start of the second phase of the study.

At first glance, the design of this study seems to rule out campaign events as contaminants for all predictions, with the possible exception of Hypothesis 3. The study measured the effectiveness of the treatments by comparing the persuasiveness of the political attack messages administered during phase three of the study among subjects who had received a pretreatment and those who had not. Since both the treatment and control groups were the product of random assignment, it is reasonable to assume that both groups were the same in every respect, including exposure to the full range of campaign events, except for the pretreatment messages that were administered exclusively to the treatment group. Since the treatment group was less influenced by the political attack messages that were subsequently administered to both groups, the most plausible explanation is that it was the pretreatments that were responsible for this difference.

However, the inoculation construct assumes the presence of threat, which acts as a trigger to motivate receivers to bolster arguments supporting attitudes. This implies that inoculative content, which forewarns receivers about one or more potential attacks, is relatively novel. If an inoculation message warned of a potential attack which receivers had already encountered, the message would be less likely to threaten receivers.

Thus, campaign events remain a possible confound to the results, particularly for Hypothesis 3, which posited the superiority of the inoculation strategy to post hoc refutation. To evaluate this prediction, the order of treatment and attack was altered. Those subjects in the inoculation condition received an inoculation pretreatment during phase two, and received an attack message and measurement in phase four. Subjects in the post hoc refutation condition received an attack during phase two, a post hoc refutation message in phase three, with measurement following in phase four. This change in the order of treatment and attack, while necessary in order to test this prediction, renders the results most vulnerable to the contamination of campaign events.

Fortunately, the *inoculative content was relatively novel*, thus minimizing the confound. Three of the four content areas selected for use in the study, the Dukakis attacks against Bush that Republican farm policy had crippled rural America and that he was insensitive to the plight of the average working person, and the Bush attack against Dukakis that he had deceived the public concerning his record as Governor of Massachusetts, were not employed as the basis of major attacks by the candidates prior to October 10 (phases one, two, and three of the study were completed from middle September to early October, whereas phase four commenced October 10).

One of the content areas, the Bush attack against Dukakis that he was soft on crime, was used as the basis of an attack, receiving considerable emphasis in Bush's advertising and some attention in the September 25 televised debate (Hershey, 1989). Thus, the use of the crime attack by the Bush campaign serves as a potential confound, but there is reason to believe that the impact of this contaminant was small. First, Bush's attack that Dukakis was soft on crime was not a major feature of the first debate. In a content analysis of that debate, Hershey (1989, p. 90) revealed that twelve other issue and image concerns received more attention by Bush and Dukakis than crime. Second, a check of area television station logs affirmed that the first regional appearance of Bush's "furlough" advertisement occurred in this ADI on October 10 (also, Americans for Bush, the independent organization that sponsored a similar attack on Dukakis, made no television buys in this ADI prior to October 10). Third, the manipulation check confirmed that the inoculation messages generated significant threat levels, and the results indicated that all four attack messages administered in the investigation, including the Bush attack that Dukakis was soft on crime, generated significant persuasive impact on receivers.

A second limitation concerns a potential liability of the inoculation strategy. The results of this study demonstrate that inoculation is an effective message strategy in defecting the persuasiveness of subsequent attack messages. However, since inoculation requires candidates to raise their vulnerabilities in advance of an opponent's attack, if an attack does not occur, the strategy could undermine the candidate's standing. This is a potential danger, but only if an opponent initiates no attacks during a campaign, an unlikely prospect given the widespread use of attack messages in contemporary election campaigns. However, since the results of this study indicate that both same and different inoculation pretreatments confer resistance, the use of inoculation involving a potential vulnerability simultaneously provides a blanket of protection against opponents' attacks that target other vulnerabilities.

REFERENCES

Anatol, K. W. E. & Mandel, J. E. (1972). Strategies of resistance to persuasion: New subject matter for the teacher of speech communication. *Central States Speech Journal, 23,* 11–17.

Anderson, L. R. & McGuire, W. J. (1965). Prior reassurance of group consensus as a factor in producing resistance to persuasion. *Sociometry, 28,* 44–56.

Armstrong, R. (1988). *The next hurrah: The communication revolution in American politics.* New York: Beach Tree Books, William Morrow.

Atkin, C. K. (1971). How imbalanced campaign coverage affects audience exposure patterns. *Journalism Quarterly, 48,* 235–244.

Axelrod, R. (1972). Where the voters came from: An analysis of electoral coalitions, 1952–1968. *American Political Science Review, 66,* 11–20.

Axelrod, R. (1974). Communication. *American Political Science Review, 68,* 717–720.

Axelrod, R. (1978). Communication. *American Political Science Review, 72*, 622–624 & 1010–1011.

Axelrod, R. (1982). Communication. *American Political Science Review, 76*, 393–396.

Axelrod, R. (1986). Presidential election coalitions in 1984. *American Political Science Review, 80*, 281–285.

Beck, P. L. (1988). Incomplete realignment. The Reagan legacy for parties and elections. In C. O. Jones (Ed.), *The Reagan legacy: Promise and performance* (pp. 145–171). Chatham, NJ: Chatham House Publishers.

Becker, S. W., Bavelas, A. & Braden, M. (1961). An index to measure contingency of English sentences. *Language and Speech, 4*, 138–145.

Blumler, J. G. & McQuail, D. (1969). *Television and politics: Its uses and influence.* Chicago: University of Chicago Press.

Burgoon, M. & Chase, L. J. (1973). The effects of differential linguistic patterns in messages attempting to induce resistance to persuasion. *Speech Monographs, 40*, 1–7.

Burgoon, M., Cohen, M., Miller, M. D. & Montgomery, C. L. (1978). An empirical test of a model of resistance to persuasion. *Human Communication Research, 5*, 27–39.

Campbell, A., Converse, P. E., Miller, W. E. & Stokes, D. E. (1960). *The American voter.* New York: John Wiley & Sons.

Campbell, A., Gurin, G. & Miller, W. E. (1954). *The voter decides.* Evanston: Row, Peterson and Co.

Campbell, J. E., Munro, M., Alford, J. R. & Campbell, B. A. (1986). Partisanship and voting. *Research in Micropolitics, 7*, 99–126.

Chaffee, S. H. & Choe, S. Y. (1980). Time of decision and media use during the Ford-Carter campaign. *Public Opinion Quarterly, 44*, 53–69.

Chaiken, S. (1987). The heuristic model of persuasion. In M. P. Zanna, J. M. Olson and C. P. Herman (Eds.), *Social Influence: The Ontario symposium* (Vol. 5, pp. 3–39). Hillsdale, NJ: Lawrence Erlbaum.

Colford, S. W. (1988, March 14). Politicos resort to "ambush" ads on TV. *Advertising Age*, p. 3.

Ehrenhalt, A. (1985). Technology, strategy bring new campaign era. *Congressional Quarterly Weekly Report, 43*, 2559–2565.

Frantzich, S. E. (1989). *Political parties in the technological age.* New York: Longman.

Garramone, G. M. (1984). Voter responses to negative political ads. *Journalism Quarterly, 67*, 250–259.

Garramone, G. M. (1985). Effects of negative political advertising: The roles of sponsors and rebuttal. *Journal of Broadcasting & Electronic Media, 29*, 147–159.

Garramone, G. M. & Smith, S. J. (1984). Reactions to political advertising: Clarifying sponsor effects. *Journalism Quarterly, 67*, 771–775.

Godwin, R. K. (1988). *One billion dollars of influence: The direct marketing of politics.* Chatham, NJ: Chatham House Publishers.

Gronbeck, B. E. (1985, November). *The rhetoric of negative political advertising: Thoughts on Senatorial race ads 1984.* Paper presented at the annual meeting of the Speech Communication Association, Denver, CO.

Guskind, R. & Hagstrom, J. (1988). In the gutter. *National Journal, 20*, 2782–2790.

Heller, D. J. (1987). Mail, money, and Machiavelli. *Campaigns & Elections, 8*, 32–45.

Hershey, M. R. (1989). The campaign and the media. In G. M. Pomper (Ed.), *The election of 1988: Reports and interpretations* (pp. 73–102). Chatham, NJ: Chatham House Publishers, Inc.

Hickey, N. (1986, October 18). Smear commercials can work: It's high noon for political mudslingers—let the targets beware. *TV Guide*, pp. 5–6.

Johnson-Cartee, K. S. & Copeland, G. A. (1989, May). *Alabama voters and acceptance of negative political advertising in the 1986 elections: An historical anomaly.* Paper presented at the International Communication Association convention, San Francisco, CA.

Kaid, L. L. & Boydston, J. (1981). An experimental study of the effectiveness of negative political advertisements. *Communication Quarterly, 35*, 193–201.

Kaid, L. L. & Davidson, D. K. (1986). Elements of videostyle: Candidate presentation through television advertising. In L. L. Kaid, D. Nimmo and K. R. Sanders (Eds.), *New perspectives on political advertising* (pp. 184–209). Carbondale: Southern Illinois University Press.

King, M. (1977). Assimilation and contrast of presidential candidates' issue positions. *Public Opinion Quarterly, 47*, 515–522.

Kirk, R. E. (1982). *Experimental design: Procedures for the behavioral sciences* (2nd ed.). Belmont: Brooks/Cole Publishing Company.

Kostroski, W. L. (1973). Party and incumbency in postwar senate elections: Trends, patterns, and models. *American Political Science Review, 68*, 1213–1234.

Louden, A. (1987, May). *Political advertising in the Hunt/Helms race: Pot shots and hot spots.* Paper presented at the International Communication Association convention, Montreal, Canada.

Mann, T. E. & Ornstein, N. (1983). Sending a message: Voters and Congress in

1982. In T. E. Mann and N. Ornstein (Eds.),
The American election of 1982 (pp. 133–152).
Washington, DC: American Enterprise Institute.

Martinez, M. D. & DeLegal, T. (1988, April).
Negative ads and negative attitudes: Effects and non-effects on trust and efficacy. Paper presented at the
Midwest Political Science Association convention,
Chicago, IL.

McGuire, W. J. (1961a). The effectiveness of
supportive and refutational defenses in immunizing
and restoring beliefs against persuasion. *Sociometry,
24,* 184–197.

McGuire, W. J. (1961b). Resistance to persuasion
conferred by active and passive prior refutation of the
same and alternative counterarguments. *Journal of
Abnormal and Social Psychology, 63,* 326–332.

McGuire, W. J. (1962). Persistence of the
resistance to persuasion induced by various types of
prior belief defenses. *Journal of Abnormal and Social
Psychology, 64,* 241–248.

McGuire, W. J. (1964). Inducing resistance
to persuasion. Some contemporary approaches.
In L. Berkowitz (Ed.), *Advances in experimental
social psychology* (Vol. 1) (pp. 191–229). New York:
Academic Press.

McGuire, W. J. (1970, February). A vaccine for
brainwash. *Psychology Today, 3,* 36–39 & 63–64.

McGuire, W. J. & Papageorgis, D. (1961). The
relative efficacy of various types of prior belief-
defense in producing immunity against persuasion.
Journal of Abnormal and Social Psychology, 62,
327–337.

McGuire, W. J. & Papageorgis, D. (1962).
Effectiveness of forewarning in developing
resistance to persuasion. *Public Opinion Quarterly,
26,* 24–34.

Merritt, S. (1984). Negative political advertising:
Some empirical findings. *Journal of Advertising, 13,*
27–38.

Miller, G. R. & Burgoon, M. (1973). *New
techniques of persuasion.* New York: Harper & Row
Publishers.

Miller, M. D. & Burgoon, M. (1979). The
relationship between violations of expectations and
the induction of resistance to persuasion. *Human
Communication Research, 5,* 301–313.

Moving right along? Campaign 1984, lessons
for 1988. An interview with Peter Hart and Richard
Wirthlin (1985). *Public Opinion, 7,* 8–11 & 59–63.

Moyers, B. (1984). Press perspectives. In R. C.
Jeffrey (Ed.), *Election 84: Search for a new coalition*
(pp. 24–40). Austin: University of Texas Press.

Niemi, R. G. & Weisberg, H. F. (1984).
Controversies in voting behavior (2nd ed.).

Washington, DC: Congressional Quarterly
Press.

Norpoth, H. (1987). Under way and here to
stay: Party alignment in the 1980s? *Public Opinion
Quarterly, 51,* 376–391.

Nugent, J. F. (1987, March/April). Positively
negative. *Campaigns & Elections, 7,* 47–49.

Nyhan, D. (1988). *The Duke: The inside story
of a political phenomenon.* New York: Warner
Books.

Papageorgis, D. & McGuire, W. J. (1961). The
generality of immunity to persuasion produced by
pre-exposure to weakened counterarguments.
Journal of Abnormal and Social Psychology, 62,
475–481.

Petrocik, J. R. (1981). *Party coalitions:
Realignment, and the decline of the New Deal
party system.* Chicago: University of Chicago
Press.

Petrocik, J. R. (1987). Realignment: New party
coalitions and the nationalization of the South. *The
Journal of Politics, 49,* 347–373.

Petty, R. E. (1977). The importance of cognitive
responses in persuasion. *Advances in Consumer
Research, 4,* 357–362.

Petty, R. E. & Cacioppo, J. T. (1979). Issue
involvement can increase or decrease persuasion by
enhancing message-relevant cognitive responses.
Journal of Personality and Social Psychology, 37,
1915–1926.

Petty, R. E. & Cacioppo, J. T. (1984). The
effects of involvement in responses to argument
quantity and quality: Central and peripheral routes
to persuasion. *Journal of Personality and Social
Psychology, 46,* 69–81

Pfau, M. & Burgoon, M. (1988a). The efficacy
of issues and character attack message strategies in
political campaign communication. *Communication
Reports,* in press.

Pfau, M. & Burgoon, M. (1988b). Inoculation
in political campaign communication. *Human
Communication 75,* 91–111.

Reilley, C. (1987). Direct mail on target.
Campaigns & Elections, 6, 36–40

Sabato, L. J. (1981). *The rise of political
consultants: New ways of winning elections.* New
York: Basic Books, Inc., Publishers.

Sabato, L. J. (1983). Parties, PACS, and
independent groups. In T. E. Mann and
N. J. Ornstein (Eds.), *The American election of
1982* (pp. 72–110). Washington, DC: American
Enterprise Institute.

Salmore, S. A. & Salmore, B. G. (1985).
Candidates, parties, and campaigns: Electoral

politics in America. Washington, DC: Congressional Quarterly Press.

Schneider, W. (1988). Solidarity's not enough. *National Journal, 20,* 2853–2855.

Sherrod, D. (1971). Selection perceptions of political candidates. *Public Opinion Quarterly, 35,* 354–362.

Stanga, J. T. & Sheffield, J. T. (1987). The myth of zero partisanship: Attitudes toward American political parties, 1964–84. *American Political Science, 31,* 829–855.

Stanley, H. W., Bianco, W. T. & Niemi, R. G. (1986). Partisanship and group support over time: A multivariate analysis. *American Political Science Review, 80,* 969–976.

Stewart, C. J. (1975). Voter perceptions of mudslinging in political communication. *Central States Speech Journal, 26,* 279–286.

Surlin, S. H. & Gordon, T. F. (1977). How values affect attitudes toward direct reference political advertising. *Journalism Quarterly, 54,* 89–98.

Tannenbaum, P. H., Macaulay, J. R. & Norris, E. L. (1966). Principle of congruity and reduction of persuasion. *Journal of Personality and Social Psychology, 2,* 233–238.

Tannenbaum, P. H. & Norris, E. L. (1965). Effects of combining congruity principle strategies for the reduction of persuasion. *Sociometry, 28,* 145–157.

Tarrance, V. L., Jr. (1980). *Negative campaigns and negative votes: The 1980 elections.* Washington, DC: Free Congress Research and Education Foundation.

Taylor, P. (1986). Accentuating the negative: Forget issue; campaign ads this year are heavy on "air pollution." *The Washington Post National Weekly Edition, 3*(51), 6–7.

Trent, J. S. & Friedenberg, R. V. (1983). *Political campaign communication: Principles and practices.* New York: Praeger Publishers.

Wattenberg, M. P. (1986). *The decline of American political parties, 1952–1984.* Cambridge: Harvard University Press.

Weisberg, H. F. (1970). Dimensions of candidate evaluations. *American Political Science Review, 64,* 1167–1185

Whitely, P. F. (1988). The causal relationships between issues, candidate evaluations, party identification, and vote choice—The view from "Rolling Thunder." *Journal of Politics, 50,* 961–984.

Negative versus Positive Television Advertising in U.S. Presidential Campaigns, 1960–1988

Lynda Lee Kaid and Anne Johnston

No aspect of modern political campaigning has received as much attention as the phenomenon of negative advertising. Although most observers acknowledge that political attacks are not unique to recent campaigns (4, 10), television's ability to quickly reach millions of voters has elevated negative advertisements to the level of mediated argumentation (2) whereby candidates exchange positions and views through their campaign ads.

Negative ads and positive ads are generally distinguished by their relative emphasis on the sponsoring candidate and his or her opponent. Negative ads focus on criticisms of the opponent, while positive ads focus on the "good" characteristics, accomplishments, or issue positions of the sponsoring candidate. Negative ads were aired in the first presidential campaign to use television, the 1952 Eisenhower-Stevenson race. Several commercials from the "Eisenhower Answers America" series overtly attack the Democrats, although Stevenson was not usually mentioned by name (10). Most subsequent campaigns have had some standout negative ads, none more famous than the 1964 "Daisy Girl" spot produced for Lyndon Johnson by Tony Schwartz (25).

Beginning in 1980, however, with the successful use of negative ads by independent groups such as NCPAC (1, 9), such ads seemed to become more prevalent. By 1981 Sabato (24) estimated that one-third of all campaign spots were negative, and Joslyn's (11) more systematic analysis of a convenience sample of campaign ads found 23 percent with a blame-placing focus.

Hosts of researchers and political observers consider 1988 the year of the negative ad.

Curtis Gans, director of the Committee for the Study of the American Electorate, has said that mudslinging represented "60–70% of all political ads" in 1988 (27). A *Washington Post* reporter proclaimed that 1988 had more negative television ads than had ever before appeared (28), and a *Newsweek* poll found that 64 percent of voters thought ads in 1988 were more negative than in past races (16). Dukakis's advertising staff estimated that 60 percent of their ads were negative, and Bush's managers suggested a 50/50 split between their positive and negative ads (20). Devlin (3) put the actual percentage of negative ads aired by Bush at 38 percent and by Dukakis at 49 percent.

Many reasons have been suggested for this perceived rise in negative advertising, but the most obvious one is that negative ads appear to work. Political media consultants are virtually unanimous in their belief that negative ads can be successful (28). Some claim that negative ads "inform" the public (2), while others suggest that it is "easier to appeal to emotion than to logic" and that negative appeals are easier for voters to remember because they are over-simplified (19, p. 49).

Kern (14) suggests that negative ads are effective because they elicit voter fear and anxiety. The "Daisy Girl" commercial used by Johnson during the 1964 campaign played on the public's fear that Goldwater was unstable and ready to use atomic force against other countries at the slightest provocation. Twenty years later, many of Mondale's ads played on anxiety and fear about nuclear proliferation and war. One such ad suggested that once computers could deploy nuclear weapons, there would be "no time to wake a president," no chance to pull back and bring reason to bear.

Voters are also affected by ads that engender uncertainty by exposing an opponent's inconsistencies, "flip-flops" on issues, or policy failures. For instance, Patterson and McClure (21) reported that one of the most effective ads from the 1972 presidential campaign was the Democrats-for-Nixon ad in which a representation of McGovern's head flipped from side to side while a voice-over recounted McGovern's inconsistent positions on several major issues. Whether the appeal is to logic or emotion,

negative ads appear to have become indispensable in competitive races, particularly for challengers (14).

Practitioners tend to measure the success of negative ads by pointing vaguely to winning and losing candidates. Scholars who measure effects more precisely on people's perceptions of candidates' positions on issues have tended to confirm the instincts of media consultants about the success of negative ads. Negative ads have been found to directly affect candidate images and evaluations, particularly when the ads are sponsored by independent sources (5, 6, 8, 12, 21). However, Merritt (17) and Garramone (5) have both identified lash effect from negative ads. Roddy and Garramone (23) have also noted that negative ads are more successful when they attack an issue rather than an image. A recent study further noted that negative ads influence voters' evaluations of candidates and perceptions about candidates' image attributes (7).

Little is known about how negative and positive television ads actually differ in content. One distinction offered by Trent and Friedenberg (29) suggest that challengers are more likely than incumbents to use attack strategies; Kaid and Davidson's content analysis (13) verified this finding for several 1986 U.S. Senate races. Kern (14) believes that negative ads, particularly of the "hard-sell" type, rely greatly on fear appeals. A frequent assumption that candidates rarely make negative attacks themselves, instead using independent sources or surrogates (2, 14), is in keeping with the findings that independently sponsored negative ads are the most successful.

The research reported here used content analysis to compare positive and negative television ads produced for presidential campaigns from 1960 through 1988. In addition, the research was guided by five questions suggested by previous research:

1. Has there been a trend toward increased negative advertising in presidential campaigns?
2. Are challengers more likely than incumbents to use negative ads in presidential campaigns?

3. Are candidates less likely to appear in negative ads than in positive ads?

4. Do negative ads focus more on issues than on images?

5. Do negative ads appeal more to emotions and/or fear than positive ads?

Because its negative advertisements received so much attention, we also pay particular attention to the 1988 presidential campaign.

We analyzed 830 television commercials from the eight presidential campaigns of 1960 through 1988, obtained from the Political Commercial Archive at the University of Oklahoma. This set represents the most comprehensive collection of presidential advertisements available.[1] Several criteria were used to select these ads. First, we included only ads that were known to have been produced or sanctioned by the candidate's official campaign. Second, in order to avoid confusion about the nature of the "opposition," we included only those ads used during the general election campaign; ads used solely in primaries were excluded. Third, we attempted to be comprehensive as possible, despite incomplete records on which commercials were aired or were aired only regionally.[2]

Our unit of analysis was the commercial spot. Each spot was classified as positive or negative according to its focus; a negative spot focused on the opposition, and a positive spot focused on the candidate sponsoring the ad. In addition to such categories as candidate name, election year, and sponsorship of the ad, we coded the following five categories:

1. *The speaker in the ad.* These included the candidate, an anonymous announcer, or some surrogate speaking for the candidate.

2. *The type of appeal used*—logical, emotional, or ethical. Logical appeals present facts in order to persuade viewers that the evidence (statistics, logical arguments, examples, etc.) favors a particular position. Emotional appeals are designed to evoke particular feelings or emotions in viewers, such as happiness, good will, pride, patriotism, anger, and hope. Ethical appeals use source credibility to enhance the candidate's appeal by suggesting his or her own qualifications or relying on the ethos of a surrogate speaker's endorsement.

3. *The use of fear appeals.* These are designed to make the voter fear that some negative consequence would occur if the candidate were not elected or if his or her opponent were elected.

4. *The type of ad content*—image and issue. Issue ads emphasize specific policy positions or express the candidate's concerns about particular matters of public concern, such as an ad indicating that a candidate favored Medicare. Image ads, on the other hand, stress the candidate's characteristics, personality, human qualities, etc. Such ads might proclaim a candidate's honesty and integrity or suggest his or her "caring, compassionate nature." An ad could contain both types of information.

5. *The use of special effects.* These included computer graphics, slow motion, freeze frames, montages, and stills.

For negative ads we coded two additional categories:

6. *Strategies used in negative ads.* These included humor and ridicule, linking the opponent with undesirable issues or images, negative labels for the opponent (name calling), and implying guilt by association with undesirable persons or groups.

7. *Purposes of negative ads.* These included attacking the opponent's personal characteristics, issue positions, and group affiliations.

Ads were coded by five graduate students using a codebook we provided. After they had been trained in the use of the content categories and their definitions, coders were given time to individually code a sample of ads and then were reassembled to assess coding problems and retrained before proceeding to the actual coding. Intercoder reliability on a sample of the ads, calculated using the formula suggested by Holsti and modified for the number of coders involved (18), averaged .84.

Our results confirm that the number of negative advertisements has increased since the

TABLE 1

Positive and negative televised presidential advertisements, 1960–1988 (n = 830)

	POSITIVE		NEGATIVE	
	n	%	n	%
1960	90	93	7	7
1964	35	60	23	40
1968	58	78	16	22
1972	42	72	16	28
1976	93	76	29	24
1980	159	64	88	36
1984	60	65	33	35
1988	51	63	30	37
Total	588	71	242	29

(1968, 1972, 1976) were 22, 28, and 24 percent, respectively. However, as can be seen in Figure 1, the percentage of negative ads in 1988 (37 percent) was only slightly higher than in 1980 (36 percent) and 1984 (35 percent). And the highest percentage of negative ads (40 percent) came earlier, in the 1964 Johnson-Goldwater race.

The data in Table 2 indicate that challengers use only slightly more negative ads than incumbents. The top half of the table distinguishes between incumbents and challengers. The former include "assumed incumbents," those whose party occupied the White House at the time of the election. No candidate is in a better position to "assume" incumbency and its attendant advantages (see 22) than a sitting vice-president, as was the case with Nixon in 1960, Humphrey in 1968, and Bush in 1988. Thus they, along with Johnson in 1964, Nixon in 1972, Ford in 1976, Carter in 1980, and Reagan in 1984, were here considered incumbents, while their opponents were classified as challengers. Thirty percent of challengers' ads and 28 percent of incumbents' ads were negative, a difference that was not statistically significant. It is interesting to note that, despite the media's emphasis on Bush's negativism in the 1988 campaign, the challenger in fact made

1970s but has held steady in the last three presidential campaigns. As seen in Table 1, over one-third of all ads sampled from the 1980, 1984, and 1988 presidential campaigns had a negative, opposition focus. The comparable percentages for the three preceding campaigns

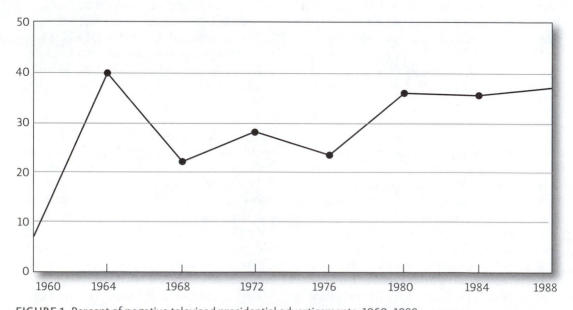

FIGURE 1 Percent of negative televised presidential advertisements, 1960–1988

TABLE 2

Electoral position and party affiliation in positive and negative televised presidential advertisements, 1960–1988

	POSITIVE (n = 588)		NEGATIVE (n = 242)	
	n	%	n	%
Electoral position				
Incumbent	276	72	109	28
Challenger	312	70	133	30
Party affiliation				
Republican	354	72	136	28
Democrat	324	69	106	31

more use of negative ads (41 percent of Dukakis ads compared to only 32 percent of Bush ads), although this difference, too, was not statistically significant.

Table 2 also compares the use of positive and negative ads by the candidate's party. On this dimension there was little difference; 28 percent of Republicans' ads and 31 percent of Democrats' ads were negative. This is very close to the positive/negative breakdown for the sample as a whole.

Do negative ads, as many critics have complained, rely on emotional appeals? Table 3 shows that emotional appeals were used in 89 percent of all negative ads. But 86 percent of the positive ads also used this technique. Most ads relied on a variety of appeals. Negative ads contained logical appeals more often than positive ads (72 percent vs. 66 percent), but positive ads were more likely than negative ads to use ethical appeals (74 percent vs. 56 percent). When only the *dominant* appeal in an ad is considered, these distinctions became clearer. Emotional appeals dominated in negative ads (50 percent), followed by ethical appeals (26 percent) and logical appeals (24 percent). Emotional appeals also dominated in positive ads (45 percent), followed by ethical appeals (39 percent) and logical appeals (15 percent).

The reliance of both negative and positive ads on emotional appeals held up not only in the overall data but also on a campaign-by-campaign basis (see Figure 2). Interestingly, one of the few exceptions was in 1988, when the dominant appeal was logical in negative ads (48 percent) and emotional in positive ads (44 percent). The difference between positive and negative ads in their Use of the three types of appeals in 1988 was statistically significant $\chi^2 = 7.028$, p < .05). This predominance of logical appeals in the negative ads is largely attributable to the Bush campaign's use of logical appeals in 75 percent of its negative ads; the Dukakis campaign used logical appeals in only 29 percent of its negative ads, instead relying chiefly on emotional appeals (47 percent).

Although both positive and negative ads rely on emotional appeals, negative ads more often use fear appeals. As Table 3 indicates, 32 percent of all negative ads use fear appeals. The distinction was most dramatic in 1988, when 75 percent of Dukakis's negative ads and 78 percent of Bush's negative ads contained recognizable fear appeals.

The often-cited distinction between images and issues was used here as a convenient way to characterize the overall content of positive and negative ads. Coders were asked to judge

TABLE 3

Appeals and content of positive and negative televised presidential advertisements, 1960–1988

	POSITIVE (n = 588)		NEGATIVE (n = 242)	
	n	%	n	%
Appeals used				
Logical	391	66	175	72
Emotional	507	86	215	89
Ethical	438	74	135	56
Dominant appeal*				
Logical	90	15	57	24
Emotional	266	45	121	50
Ethical	227	39	63	26
Presence of fear appeal	56	10	78	32
Content				
Issue information	395	67	191	79
Image information	385	65	154	64
Purpose of negative ad				
Attack issue stands/consistency			202	83
Attack personal characteristics			134	55
Attack group affiliations			45	19
Strategy in negative ad				
Humor/ridicule			149	62
Linking with undesirable ideas			110	45
Name calling			29	12
Guilt by association			42	17

*$\chi^2 = 15.1432, p < .001$

whether an ad contained information about an issue, the personal characteristics of the candidate, or both. Table 3 suggests that negative ads are more likely than positive ads to contain information about the political issues (79 percent vs. 67 percent). On the other hand, positive and negative ads used about the same amount of information about the candidate's image (65 percent vs. 64 percent). The emphasis on issues in negative ads is also apparent in the finding that attacking an opponent's positions or consistency on issues was judged an important purpose of 83 percent of all negative ads.

The most popular strategy in negative ads appears to be humor or ridicule, used in 62 percent of the ads. Other strategies used were linking the opponent with undesirable images or issues (45 percent), guilt by association (17 percent), and name calling (12 percent). In 1988, the most used strategy was linking the opponent with undesirable images or issues (90 percent), followed by an unusually heavy use

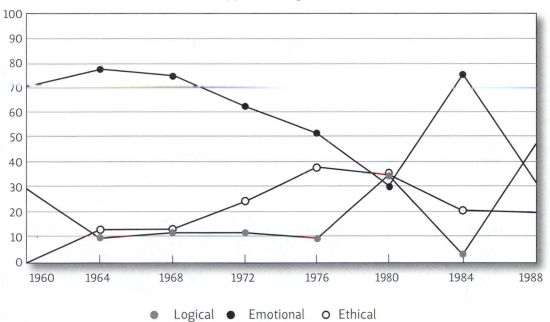

Appeals in Negative Ads

Logical   Emotional   Ethical

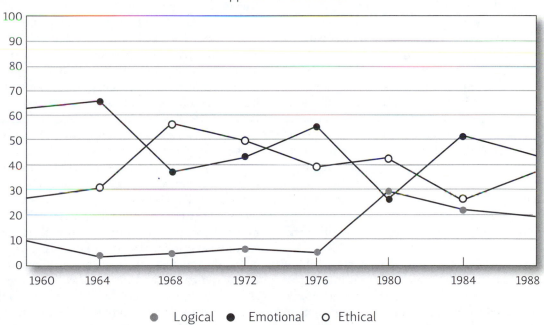

Appeals in Positive Ads

Logical   Emotional   Ethical

FIGURE 2 Percent of logical, emotional, and ethical appeals in positive and negative televised presidential advertisements, 1960–1988

TABLE 4

Speaker Identity and use of special effects in positive and negative televised presidential advertisements, 1960–1988

	POSITIVE (n = 588)		NEGATIVE (n = 242)	
	n	%	n	%
Speaker*				
Candidate	313	53	35	14
Anonymous announcer	148	25	144	60
Surrogate	127	22	63	26
Use of special effects				
Computer graphics	80	14	82	34
Slow motion	11	2	22	9
Freeze frame	54	9	20	8
Montage	89	15	32	13
Stills	228	39	157	65

*$\chi^2 = 120.38$, p < .0001

of guilt by association (60 percent). Humor or ridicule was present in 50 percent of the 1988 ads, and name calling occurred almost twice as often (20 percent) as in the overall sample.

Negative ads are also characterized by their relatively rare inclusion of the candidate himself. Table 4 shows that the candidate is much less likely to be the speaker in a negative ad (14 percent) than in a positive ad (53 percent) ($\chi^2 = 120.38$; p < .0001). This was particularly the case in 1988, when the candidate spoke in only 7 percent of negative ads (relying on an anonymous announcer in 63 percent and on other surrogate speakers in 30 percent).

One final comparison between positive and negative ads involved the extent to which each type relied on various "special effects." Table 4 demonstrates that negative ads were much more likely to use some types of special effects, particularly computer graphics, slow motion, and juxtaposition of stills. Undoubtedly, the use of these techniques has increased with the availability of new technologies. For instance, in 1988, 73 percent of all negative ads used some type of computer graphics.

Our analysis reveals real differences in the content and approaches of negative and positive

television ads for the candidates in eight presidential elections, but no new "watershed of negativism," as some had suggested, in the 1988 ads. However, it is important to note that our method of dichotomizing the sample into positive and negative ads by determining a dominant focus on the candidate or his opponent is useful for analysis but may underestimate the amount of negative information about an opponent present even in a positive ad. Thus, an increasing complexity or mix of information in ads over time or increasing sophistication in graphics or special effects might actually provide more "negativism" in terms of the number of messages or their intensity that would not be captured in this initial sorting of the ads.

In the context of frequent criticisms of recent campaigns as being focused on images at the expense of issues, it is telling that we found negative ads to provide *more* information on issues than positive ads. The reason is suggested in Louden's (15) thorough analysis of the 1984 Hunt-Helms Senate race in North Carolina in which he found that information about the issues had a strong effect on viewers' assessments of a candidate's character and image in negative ads. This was undoubtedly true in the presidential spots analyzed here. For instance, the anti-McGovern "flip-flop" ad was ostensibly about the issues, but its effect was to call into question McGovern's consistency, an image dimension. Consequently, negative ads may contain more issue information than positive ads simply because the issue information provides an effective way of attacking the character of the opponent in a credible, logical, supportable manner.

Other findings overturn similar stereotypes of negative ads while supporting some previous research. For example, we found that challengers do *not* use more negative ads than incumbents. Neither do Republicans use more negative ads than Democrats. While it might be expected that negative ads appeal more than positive ads to voters' fears, they also rely more on logical appeals; both types of ads appeal most to voters' emotions, however. As might be expected, candidates let anonymous announcers and surrogates deliver the message in negative ads.

Since the findings for the 1988 campaign seem to be in keeping with the findings for the rest of the sample, it is worthwhile to focus specifically on the reasons that this particular campaign might have prompted so much press criticism of its "negativism." In particular, why, since Dukakis produced more negative ads than Bush, was the Bush campaign repeatedly labeled as a purveyor of negative ads?

There are several possible reasons. First, as pollster Lou Harris suggests, perhaps Bush's negative ads were simply better than Dukakis's (20). A second possibility is that Bush achieved more effect because he spent more money airing fewer negative ads. Devlin (3) points out that Bush's campaign spent about 40 percent of its advertising budget airing a few of its best ads. Timing may also have been a consideration. Bush's negative ads came early in the campaign; Dukakis delayed airing his negative attacks. Finally, the news media in 1988 gave an extraordinary amount of air time to discussing the candidates' negative ad campaigns (28), leaving viewers with the impression that the campaign was much more negative than in previous years. Our findings suggest that judgments of this phenomenon have been shaped more by the media's emphasis than by the actual ad content.

These findings suggest the need for more detailed analyses of positive and negative ads and of the audiences' reactions to them. Content analysis and audience research data together may help determine if Spero (26) was wise to suggest that political ads be subjected to "truth in advertising" standards similar to those imposed by the Federal Trade Commission on product ads. Such data also may be helpful in evaluating the usefulness of proposed legislation to regulate campaign commercials (30).

NOTES:

[1] The Political Commercial Archive contains only incomplete sets of ads for Eisenhower and Stevenson in 1952 and 1956, making comparisons with other years difficult. For instance, the archive has nine ads featuring Stevenson in 1952, but there is no evidence that his campaign ever sanctioned them. The archive does not have a complete set of Eisenhower ads for 1956. For these reasons, 1952 and 1956 were omitted from the analysis presented here.

[2] For example, several of Kennedy's 1960 spots were made for and aired only in specific regions or states. Five spots were produced by Tony Schwartz for McGovern in 1972, but not all were aired nationally (10). Nonetheless, they were included in this sample because they contributed to an overall, comprehensive view of the campaign.

REFERENCES

1. "Accentuating the Negative." *Time,* November 1, 1982, p. 20.

2. Baukus, R. A., L. G. Payne, and M. C. Reisler. "Negative Polispots." In J. R. Cox, M. O. Sillars, and G. B. Walker (Eds.), *Argumentation and Social Practice.* Annandale, Va.: Speech Communication Association, 1985, pp. 236–252.

3. Devlin, P. L. "Contrasts in Presidential Campaign Commercials of 1988." *American Behavioral Scientist* 32(4), March–April 1989, pp. 389–414.

4. Diamond, E. and S. Bates. *The Spot: The Rise of Political Advertising on Television.* Cambridge, Mass.: MIT Press, 1984.

5. Garramone, G. M. "Voter Responses to Negative Political Ads." *Journalism Quarterly* 61(2), Summer 1984, pp. 250–259.

6. Garramone, G. M. "Effects of Negative Political Advertising: The Role of Sponsor and Rebuttal." *Journal of Broadcasting and Electronic Media* 29(2), Spring 1985, pp. 147–159.

7. Garramone, G. M., C. K. Atkin, B. E. Pinkleton, and R. T. Cole. "Effects of Negative Political Advertising on the Political Process." *Journal of Broadcasting and Electronic Media* 34(3), Summer 1990, pp. 299–311.

8. Garramone, G. M. and S. J. Smith. "Reactions to Political Advertising: Clarifying Sponsor Effects." *Journalism Quarterly* 61(4), Winter 1984, pp. 771–775.

9. Grove, L. "Attack Ads Trickled Up from State Races." *Washington Post,* November 13, 1988, pp. A1, 18–19.

10. Jamieson, K. H. *Packaging the Presidency.* New York: Oxford University Press, 1984.

11. Joslyn, R. A. "Political Advertising and the Meaning of Elections." In L. L. Kaid, D. Nimmo, and K. R. Sanders (Eds.), *New Perspectives on Political Advertising.* Carbondale: Southern Illinois University Press, 1986, pp. 139–183.

12. Kaid, L. L. and J. Boydston. "An Experimental Study of the Effectiveness of Negative Political Advertisements." *Communication Quarterly* 35(2), Spring 1987, pp. 193–201.

13. Kaid, L. L. and D. Davidson. "Elements of Videostyle: A Preliminary Examination of Candidate Presentation through Television Advertising." In L. L. Kaid, D. Nimmo, and K. R. Sanders (Eds.), *New Perspectives on Political Advertising.* Carbondale: Southern Illinois University Press, 1986, p. 209.

14. Kern, M. *30-Second Politics: Political Advertising in the Eighties.* New York: Praeger, 1989.

15. Louden, A. D. "Transformation of Issue to Image Presence: Eliciting Character Evaluations in Negative Spot Advertising." Paper presented to the annual conference of the International Communication Association, Dublin, June 1990.

16. Martz, L., with M. G. Warner, H. Fineman, E. Clift, and M. Staff. "The Smear Campaign." *Newsweek,* October 31, 1988, pp. 16–19.

17. Merritt, S. "Negative Political Advertising: Some Empirical Findings." *Journal of Advertising* 13(3) 1984, pp. 27–38.

18. North, R. C., O. Holsti, M. G. Zaninovich, and D. A. Zinnes. *Content Analysis: A Handbook with Applications for the Study of International Crisis.* Evanston, Ill.: Northwestern University Press, 1963.

19. Nugent, J. F. "Positively Negative." *Campaigns and Elections* 7, March/April 1987, pp. 47–49.

20. Oreskes, M. "TV's Role in 88: The Medium Is the Message." *New York Times,* October 30, 1988, pp. 1, 19.

21. Patterson, T. E. and R. D. McClure. *The Unseeing Eye.* New York: Putnam, 1976.

22. Powell, L. and A. Shelby. "A Strategy of Assumed Incumbency: A Case Study." *Southern Speech Communication Journal* 46(2), Winter 1981, pp. 105–123.

23. Roddy, B. L. and G. M. Garramone. "Appeals and Strategies of Negative Political Advertising." *Journal of Broadcasting and Electronic Media* 32(4), Fall 1988, pp. 415–427.

24. Sabato, L. J. *The Rise of Political Consultants.* New York: Basic Books, 1981.

25. Schwartz, T. *The Responsive Chord.* Garden City, N.Y.: Anchor Press/Doubleday, 1973.

26. Spero, R. *The Duping of the American Voter.* New York: Harper & Row, 1980.

27. Spethmann, B. "Elective Invective." *Advertising Age,* November 7, 1988, p. 60.

28. Taylor, P. "Consultants Rise Via the Low Road." *Washington Post,* January 17, 1989, pp. A1, A14.

29. Trent, J. S. and R. V. Friedenberg. *Political Campaign Communication.* New York: Praeger, 1983.

30. Tucker, L. A. and D. J. Heller. "Putting Ethics into Practice." *Campaigns and Elections* 7, March/April, 1987, pp. 42–46.

Tactics of Attack

Kathleen Hall Jamieson

If Jefferson is elected, proclaimed Yale president Rev. Timothy Dwight, the Bible will be burned, the French "Marseillaise" will be sung in Christian churches, and "We may see our wives and daughters the victims of legal prostitution; soberly dishonored; speciously polluted."[1]

"The whole object of the coalition is to calumniate me, cart loads of coffin hand-bills,

forgeries, and pamphlets of the most base calumnies are circulated by the franking privilege of Members of Congress," wrote Andrew Jackson to a friend in the heat of the

---

This essay originally appeared as a chapter in a book by Kathleen Hall Jamieson, Dirty Politics: Deception, Distraction, and Democracy *(New York: Oxford University Press, 1992).*

election that would put him in the White House. "Mrs. Jackson is not spared, and my pious Mother, nearly fifty years in her tomb, and who, from her cradle to her death, had not a speck upon her character, has been dragged forth by Hammond and held to public scorn as a prostitute who intermarried with a Negro, and [it is alleged that] my eldest brother [was] sold as a slave in California. . . . I am branded with every crime."[2]

To document its claim that Lincoln had been the target of unprecedented mudslinging, in September 1864, *Harper's Weekly* listed some of the terms of endearment applied to the president by his opponents: "Filthy Story-Teller, Despot, Liar, Thief, Braggart, Buffoon, Usurper, Monster, Ignoramus Abe, Old Scoundrel, Perjurer, Robber, Swindler, Tyrant, Fiend, Butcher, Land-Pirate," and "A Long, Lean, Lank, Lantern-Jawed, High Cheek-Boned, Spavined, Rail-Splitting Stallion."[3]

Note the brevity of these charges about Jefferson, Jackson, and Lincoln, their reliance on assertion not argument, the absence of disclosed evidence, and the strong visceral identification with one candidate or rejection of another that they invite. These are not exercises in reasoned, warranted comparison and contrast but in comparison starved down to identification and contrast simmered down to apposition. Such verbal and visual telegraphy has been a mainstay of U.S. politics. And the telegraphed content has been more often naughty than nice. Those who pine for the pristine campaigns of Jefferson, Jackson, or Lincoln remember a halcyon past that never was.

Rather than assuming the heavy burden of defining and defending the controversial, campaigns generally ally the favored candidate with things uncritically accepted, such as flag and freedom, and tie the opponent to such viscerally noxious things as the murder of innocent men, women, and children. Out of the resulting contrasts between and among candidates are borne the simplistic dualities in which campaigns traffic: friend against enemy, saint against satan, the candidate of the people against the candidate of privilege, the patriot against the traitor.

This chapter synopsizes a history of U.S. political discourse built on simplistic dualities

that telegraph messages of exclusion, not inclusion, visceral identification and apposition, not reasoned and warranted comparison and contrast. As critic Kenneth Burke observes, these bodies of identifications "owe their convincingness much more to trivial repetition and dull daily reinforcement than to exceptional rhetorical skill."[4]

★ IDENTIFICATION

Imagine, if you will, Saddam Hussein. Now conjure up Mother Teresa. It would be decidedly unwise to predicate a campaign on the assumption that the former is a saint or the latter a whore. At any moment in the life of a republic, the public can viscerally distinguish those presumed to be villainous from those presumed to be virtuous. Of such assumptions of virtue and villainy political discourse is made. Countering them is difficult—capitalizing on them simple.

Personal Identification

Like the broadcast commercials they prefigure, nineteenth-century campaign songs paired candidates with revered or reviled predecessors. In the process, they created the sense that Washington had fathered both the country and endless generations of political progeny, some legitimate, some bastards. In 1864 voters sang, "We'll have another Washington—McClellan is the man!" In 1916 they chorused, "I think we've got another Washington and Wilson is his name." In 1920 Democrats assured the country that Cox was like Washington: "The man we have has oft been tried/Like Washington, he's never lied."

Assertions of political bloodline survive today. Every Democratic nominee since FDR has claimed him. And every Republican in the 1988 race hinted in one way or another that he and Reagan were ideological twins separated at birth.

While a party claims the sign of Abel for its own, it works mightily to brand the opponent with the mark of Cain. To the tune of "Yankee Doodle," Jeffersonians chorused their conviction that Adams coveted a crown "like Georgy, great." In 1832, an anti-Jackson handbill characterized his cronies in verse: "And Here are the Trio of Cabinet fame, Amos Kendall and

Lewis, and Blair of bad name, the scullions who grovel and revel in shame: Ay—these are the tyrants—the rulers of him, Who, enfeebled by years, is in intellect dim, The dotard of sixty—who 'born to command,' Dishonours himself, and would ruin the land, Ay—these are the minions the People oppose, Apostates, and Tories, and Liberty's foes—The friends of the Traitor, to glory unknown, who would barter his country, and fawn at a throne." And in 1936, Al Smith opposed FDR with the claim that if the "New Deal wanted to don the mask of Lenin and Marx, or even Norman Thomas . . . that was okay 'but what I won't stand for is allowing them to march under the banner of Jefferson, Jackson, and Cleveland.'"[5]

Identification with Policies

Some of the strongest rhetoric of recent memory has tied a candidate to failed policies. Richard Nixon entered the U.S. Senate by allying the voting record of his opponent Helen Gahagan Douglas with that of the leftist New York Congressman Vito Marcantonio. Using pink sheets of paper to carry his message, Nixon labeled Douglas the "pink lady." "Hey, Hey, LBJ. How many kids did you kill today?" was chanted outside the White House by antiwar protestors. In 1980, the Republicans allied Jimmy Carter with pictures of blindfolded U.S. hostages in Iran.

Accuracy has not characterized policy attacks any more than personal ones. The coffin handbills charged that Andrew Jackson had executed Tennessee militiamen without trial and without cause. In 1960, Kennedy tagged the Republicans with responsibility for a missile gap that he could not find once he assumed office. In 1972 the Republicans succeeded in labeling McGovern a champion of acid, amnesty, and abortion. Despite Carter's claim that Reagan would rend North from South and Jew from Gentile, at the end of Reagan's first term no geographical or religious tears were observable in the social fabric. In 1984, Mondale's ad incorrectly prophesied economic collapse for the country in 1985.

Visual Identification

The visual equivalent of these verbal pairs paints the candidate's likeness into a flag banner's stars while overlaying his slogan on the stripes. Flag banners were popular as early as 1840 and prevalent until 1905 when Congress prohibited compromising portraits or marks on a flag. Eight decades later, the Republicans closed their early fall ads with a photo of incumbent president Ronald Reagan wrapped in a flag.

Then as now candidates were idealized by their supporters and vilified by their opponents. The banners carried for Lincoln in 1860 and 1864 show a more handsome man than the one immortalized in Brady's unpublicized photographs.

Similarly, William Jennings Bryan gazing resolutely from his campaign banners in 1908 lacks the wrinkles and the jowls but sports substantially more hair than the portly, balding, jowly, wrinkled Bryan captured in photographs of the day.

Just as their supporters' beautified pictures of them, so too Lincoln's and Bryan's opponents caricatured them. The apelike sketches circulated by Lincoln's enemies seemed to support the Albany *Atlas and Argus*'s claim that he was "the ugliest man in the Union."[6] In his run for the Senate, Lincoln responded to the caricatures with characteristic humor. Parrying Douglas's charge that he was two-faced, Lincoln noted, "I leave it to my audience. If I had another face, do you think I'd wear this one?"

So outraged were California legislators about being pilloried in cartoons that in 1899 they passed an anticartoon law forbidding caricatures that reflected on character. The law was disregarded and unenforced.

The technique survives. No post office wall of wanted posters appeared as menacing as the scowling, unshaven visages of Senators Jenner, McCarthy, and Taft, who, argued a 1952 Stevenson ad, would run the White House if the electorate endorsed Ike. In 1956, the Democrats tried again, this time using the grammar of police file photos to show "the friends Eisenhower would like to forget." This rogues' gallery included such Eisenhower aides as Sherman Adams, who sent political junkies to their dictionaries to determine what manner of beast produced the corrupting vicuna coat that was Adams's undoing. Nearly forty years later, neither Democratic Senator Paul Simon nor his opponent Representative Lynn Martin was easily recognizable in each other's ads. And in California, Pete Wilson's spots showed an opponent who appeared at least a decade older than she did in her own ads.

The invention of photography in the first half of the nineteenth century provided a powerful form of political evidence. "The everyday viewer began to assume the photographic image was the norm for truthfulness of representation," notes a prominent historian of photography.[7]

The assumption that seeing is believing makes us susceptible to visual deception. Awareness of this susceptibility resulted in new forms of attack. To inflame Southern passions in the 1940s and 1950s a campaign needed only to circulate composite photos of a white candidate with blacks.

Placing a candidate's picture next to that of a known Communist was equally effective. In 1950, Maryland Senator Millard Tydings was done in by his Republican opponent John Butler in the dirtiest campaign of that year. The attacks on Tydings as "soft on communism" culminated in mass distribution of a brochure showing him apparently in intimate conversation with Communist leader Earl Browder. Browder had appeared before a Senate Committee that Tydings chaired. A picture of them did exist. But that picture, which showed Tydings looking tough and challenging, didn't suit Butler's needs. The text accompanying the faked photo noted that it was a composite, but, in a lesson to be relearned in future television campaigns, the words did not override the impressions left by the visual images. When, in a televised election eve address, Tydings attacked the brochure as scurrilous and asked Butler to disavow it, Butler replied that Tydings was trying to smear him "by claiming he has been smeared." Tydings lost.[8]

When the trick was next tried, production of a negative foiled the positive impact of the tactic. Unauthorized by the candidate, in 1962 a group in California published a pamphlet showing incumbent governor Pat Brown bowing deferentially to Soviet leader Nikita Khrushchev. The photo was fake. Before the Republicans had tampered with it, the original had shown Brown bowing to a visiting Laotian child. The Democrats produced the photographic negative.

Republican state chair Caspar Weinberger repudiated the pamphlet and quashed its distribution through Republican headquarters.[9] Over time, a grammar of the visual image developed.

★ APPOSITION

Campaigns try to make their candidate's name a synonym for everything the electorate cherishes and to transform the opponent into an antonym of those treasured values. Decency versus debauchery. Loyalty versus treason. "He cares about the criminals; I care about the victims." Corrupt political insiders against honest citizen outsiders. Tax-and-spend Democrats versus no-new-taxes Republicans. Economic stagnation versus let's get the country moving again.

After associating one's candidate with "good" and the opponent with "evil," all a campaign has left to do is remind voters of the resulting contrasts. From the country's origins, apposition has oiled politics.

Verbal Apposition

Two contrastive moves underlie political attack: contrasting our espoused values and those manifest in the life of the attacked candidate or party, and contrasting the two candidates. In the following litany of claims against Lincoln, for example, we can read the commandments honored by the attackers and their presumed audience. To his enemies the sixteenth president was "'a man of coarse nature, a self-seeking politician, who craved high office . . . to satisfy his own burning desire for distinction. . . . His real name is Abraham Hanks. . . . He is the illegitimate son by an [sic] man named Inlow—from a Negress named Hanna Hanks.' His presumptive parents were immoral, shiftless poor white trash. Unscrupulous as a lawyer, he was unprincipled as a politician. He was a man of low morality, and his 'inordinate love of the lascivious, of smut,' it was whispered, was 'something nearly akin to lunacy.'"[10]

Some of these are the sins catalogued in Sunday School and condemned in *Pilgrim's Progress*. He is Full of Pride ("craved high office . . . self seeking"); Covetous and Lustful ("inordinate love of the lascivious"); and Slothful ("shiftless"). Some are sins against social sensibilities ("coarse by nature," "poor white trash"), others against normalcy ("nearly akin to lunacy"). Hinted throughout is the sin of hypocrisy; by changing his name and feigning proper parentage, he invites us to believe that he is what he is not.

Contrast also was the modus vivendi of the gauze-like slogan-bearing transparencies held aloft in nineteenth-century parades. Mottoes on the transparencies "were various," noted *Harper's Weekly* on 11 October 1884, "but the majority referred in some way to the admitted honesty of Governor Cleveland and the bad reputation of Mr. Blaine."

Slogans buttressed support for one candidate or blasted his opponent. Implicit in both were contrasts. The claim that Blaine was "The Continental Liar from the State of Maine" makes political sense only if his opponent is presumed honest. And those who chanted "Rum-soaked Romanist" against Al Smith in 1928 presupposed that Herbert Hoover was a temperate Protestant. Some slogans imply that, if in charge, the supported candidate would have acted differently than the incumbent. Why else recall the use of the military to quell the Bonus March with the chant "Billions for Bankers, Bullets for Vets" or "Down with Hoover, Slayer of Veterans" in 1942?

Contrasting a candidate's past and present positions is effective because it raises doubts about what one can believe about the candidate. Accordingly, in 1802 the *Boston Gazette* juxtaposed the views Jefferson had expressed on slavery in his "Notes on Virginia" and in a letter to Benjamin Banneker.[11] In the Lincoln-Douglas debates, the little giant argued that Old Abe was tailoring his views on slavery to his audiences. "Last year. This year. What about next year?" asked an ad attacking McGovern's inconsistencies in 1972.

In 1976, Jimmy Carter invented the misery index, a figure obtained by summing the negative economic indicators. Four years later the misery index had worsened instead of improved. Predictably, Republican ads pointed that out. Where the Republicans focused that year on high inflation and interest rates, Carter concentrated on his successful negotiation of the Camp David Accords.

Simplifying identification and apposition do not invite rebuttal. There is an assumed uncontestability in their absolutism, a sense that the espoused tenets are credal, their identity fixed with unchallengeable cultural certainty. So, for example, after being accused by Fiorello La Guardia of having a "fixed obsession on Anglo-Saxon superiority," Kansas Congressman J. N. Tincher ended the discussion by stating, "I think the issue is fairly well drawn. On the one side is beer, bolshevism, unassimilating settlements and perhaps many flags—on the other side is constitutional government, one flag, stars and stripes; a government of, by and for the people; America our country."[12] The phrases that close Lincoln's conciliatory Gettysburg Address here have been suborned by chauvinism.

Visual Apposition

There is nothing new about the political impulse to visualize. An observer of the campaign of 1840 recalled that "Great processions showed the barrel of cider, the coonskin, and the log cabin with the latchstring hanging out, which typified Harrison's democracy, while in a carriage rode an image of the aristocratic Van Buren, seated on English cushions and holding the golden teaspoons which he had purchased for the White House. . . . Long banners declared that the Whigs would 'teach the palace slave to respect the log cabin.'"[13]

In the contest between Benjamin Harrison and Grover Cleveland, a poster for Harrison portrayed him as a war hero, a champion of workers, and a hard worker. Drawings on the opposite half of the poster showed Cleveland ducking the war, destroying a factory, and wasting time.

Television added the cueing power of sound and the attention-grabbing impulse of movement. Rifle fire is heard. Dead bodies appear in the still photo. "This is what they do," says the announcer. "Death squads in El Salvador. Innocent men, women, and children murdered in cold blood. This is the man accused of directing those death squads. Roberto D'Aubuisson [picture appears]. And [picture of Jesse Helms appears] this is the man whose aides helped Roberto D'Aubuisson set up his political party in El Salvador. This is Roberto D'Aubuisson's best friend in Washington, maybe his only friend. Now Jesse Helms may be a crusader. But that's not what our senator should be crusading for." The ad was aired by Jim Hunt against Jesse Helms in the 1984 North Carolina Senate race.

Televised Identification and Apposition

If the country has survived two centuries of politicking by telegraphic identification and apposition, why worry about them now? The answer is simple. Television has capacities that stump speakers, print barrages, and radio appeals lacked. When skillfully used, television's multiple modes of communication and powerful ability to orient attention can invite strong, unthinking negative responses in low-involvement viewers. And, by overloading our information-processing capacity with rapidly paced information, televised political ads can short circuit the normal defenses that more educated, more highly involved viewers ordinarily marshal against suspect claims.

Broadsides and radio broadcasts each used a single channel or mode of communication; by contrast, television is multimodal. What makes possible the false inference that 268 first-degree murderers escaped while on furlough is the presence of the print claim "268 escaped," the announcer's spoken claim "many first-degree murderers," the visual image of circling convicts, and the music that cues us to respond apprehensively.

Because it is multimodal, television is more easily comprehended than print. We don't think we need to be taught to "read" television. Additionally, because visuals reinforce and contextualize what we hear, making sense of televised news is easier than deciphering the meaning of a newspaper article.[14] By speaking to us in our native language, television eliminates the decoding required to turn C A T into a furry, purring beast.[15]

Some of the audio and visual cues that are part of television's grammar automatically grab our attention. We can't control our subconscious response to television's cuts, edits, lighting changes, camera changes, shifts in the implied distance of the object that we are watching on the screen (e.g., zooms), changing visual images, or introduction of a new voice.[16] These features affect not only attention but recall of messages[17] and can interfere with the performance of some cognitive tasks.[18]

Television's capacity to use both an audio and a visual channel simultaneously can increase the redundancy and hence the memorability of the message.[19] Alternatively, the amount of content available for cognitive processing can be multiplied by putting complementary information in the two channels. Or, as in Nixon's still-montage ads in 1968, the visual channel showing antiwar protesters and the effects of rioting and looting particularized the meaning of an otherwise platitudinous speech.

Over time, the ways in which television's features have been combined has created a grammar of mood. In political ads, for example, a soft focus, long shots, slow motion, color, use of film, the voice of a reassuring announcer, and lyrical or patriotic music are the grammar of the self-promotional biographical spot. In films, tender romantic scenes and nostalgic moments are shot in soft focus. When slow motion is added, we are invited to move into the domain of wistful memory.

Quick cuts, use of black and white, dark colors, shadowed lighting, stark contrasts, videotape, the voice of a seemingly "neutral" announcer and ominous music are the techniques associated with "oppositional" production spots. The conventional practices of television lead us to associate videotape with news and film with documentary forms.

Established also is music's ability to increase attention, act as a mnemonic aid, cue retrieval of a message, and invite a specific emotional response.[20] Just as McDonald's added "You Deserve a Break Today" to the repertoire of most preschoolers in the United States, so too did the 1976 Ford campaign invite would-be voters to hum along to "I'm feeling good about America, I'm feeling good about me." In 1984, the Reagan campaign took the power of music one step beyond past uses by making a song on the country charts the Republican theme. Lee Greenwood's "I'm Proud to Be an American" bedded the visuals of many of the feel-good ads of the 1984 campaign. It was revived in the

1988 Bush ads and did for the Gulf War what the "Battle Hymn of the Republic" did for the Civil War.

The evocative power of television's visual grammar couples with its use of music to invite strong emotional reactions to what is seen in ads. Because our judgment of information is influenced by the emotional reactions we experience as we process it,[21] these cues can shade and shape our response to a candidate, issues, or both. The Bush furlough ad enwraps us in an alien world of menace, in which isolated individuals move in mechanical rhythm toward our living rooms as the announcer seems to forecast murder and kidnapping as our lot if Dukakis is elected. This is not an informational context eagerly inviting a dispassionate, rational response.

Some wordless images are powerfully telegraphic in their own right. A torn Social Security card functions iconically in Democratic ads against Goldwater in 1964 to make visual the spoken claim, "By making participation in it voluntary, Goldwater would destroy your social security." By tearing a Social Security card to one-eighth its original size, a Dukakis ad in 1988 invited the same inference. Bush, said the image, wanted to cut Social Security substantially. That visually invited inference was false.

Our evolutionary past increases the power of some images. Scholars tell us, for example, that young kittens cower reflexively when a cutout of a hawk appears overhead. Our self-protective instincts are aroused by any large, dark shape that moves toward us. Some images invoke non-cognitive emotional states designed to help us recognize and respond to danger.[22] Because processing pictures does not require immediate cognition, visuals can transmit emotionally powerful information quickly.[23] Television's close-ups also provide viewers with a complex range of verbal and nonverbal material that elicit sometimes unexpected emotional responses.[24]

Finally, television has given political discourse and the low-involvement viewer access to each other. When getting political information required the effort of reading or traveling to a place at which the candidate was speaking, those with minimal interest in politics simply opted out of exposure. Those with a high interest sought out political information; in other words, each group engaged in "selective attention."

"Low involvement" viewers of politics do not seek out political information in broadcast or print news; instead they get most of their political information from inadvertent exposure to political ads.[25] The primary indicator of whether a person will be exposed to political ads is simply how often they are aired and how much television the viewer watches. So, for example, the Times Mirror poll on the 1988 campaign found that those under thirty-five who were less informed about politics and less likely than their parents to read newspapers were nonetheless equally able to recall such Republican ad themes as "Willie Horton" and "Boston Harbor." In 1987, of those under thirty 60 percent reported that "they often did not become aware of candidates until they saw advertisements on television."[26]

By opening low-involvement viewers to the persuasion of ads, television made it possible for political campaigns to address individuals who are more likely than the highly involved to be persuaded by such "peripheral cues" as presumed expertise or attractiveness of the communicator,[27] and are less likely to be persuaded by the quality of the arguments.[28] When individuals are not focused on analyzing the arguments of a message, the number of arguments itself rather than their cogency can serve to persuade.[29]

Indeed, some argue that most of us watch television "passively, without any particular goal." As a result, the information television offers "may be encoded at a relatively low level of abstractness, without thinking about it extensively in relation to previously acquired information. Moreover, the sort of counter-arguing that often occurs when we have a goal of evaluating the candidate and his or her stands on the issues may not be performed."[30]

So, the telegraphic power of television's appositions and identifications is greater than that of print or radio. Moreover, the multimodal capacity of television provides its producers with a greater variety of ways to invite and evoke viewer response. How these features of television have worked and what can be done to counter them when they invite false conclusions are the questions residing at the core of this chapter.

★ GUILT OR GILT BY ASSOCIATION AND APPOSITION

Television can pair previously disconnected images with a speed and seamlessness that defies the scrutiny of the suspicious. Inviting us to impute a causal link to things only associatively tied is such a stock-in-trade of product advertising that over time we have lost our awareness of how strange some of the paired associations are. From 1952 through 1972 this technique was used with increasing sophistication. One of the by-products of Watergate was dispatch of this mode of assertion from political television. In 1984 it was revived and in 1988 was used in one of the presidential campaign's most controversial ads.

The nation's first presidential campaign spot utilized this editing capacity when Eisenhower and citizen questioners were edited together to form the Eisenhower Answers America spots of 1952. Although the viewer had no way of knowing it, the questioners could not actually see Ike, nor he they. His answers had been recorded before their questions had been asked!

The intercutting in a 1960 ad was less benign. From the first Kennedy-Nixon debate, the Democrats lifted moments showing Nixon nodding agreement to the goals he and Kennedy shared. By the wonders of editing, the Democrats injected that scene into a section of the debates in which Kennedy outlined specific controversial proposals.

Had Kennedy proclaimed at the moment before or after the edited insert, "Nixon agrees with me," he would have been lying. Yet there was the Republican Vice President appearing to agree. The false inference prompted by this ad demonstrates the danger harbored by television's ability to reconfigure reality.

But the Democrats weren't through. They also lifted from the debate unflattering reaction shots of Nixon scowling, biting his lip, glancing nervously from side to side, and sweating perceptibly. These too were edited into the Democratic ad. The visual contrasts between

Kennedy and Nixon were striking in the debate and strikingly magnified in the ad. This is the first use of negative nonverbal contrast in a televised presidential ad. When, in 1988, the Republicans juxtaposed a darkened picture of the disheveled Democratic nominee with a brightened angelic photo of the Republican nominee, they were employing an amply precedented tactic.

In 1964, the Democrats and Republicans demonstrated that they understood television's power to use visual association to evoke audience inferences. The Democrats juxtaposed a child plucking the petals from a daisy with the explosion of a bomb as Lyndon Johnson extolled the value of loving one another. A young girl is picking daisies in a field. "Four, five, six, seven," she says. An announcer's voice (actually the voice used to count down the space launches at Cape Canaveral) begins an ominous count. "Ten, nine, eight . . ." At zero the camera has closed on the child's eye. A nuclear bomb explodes. Lyndon Johnson's voice is heard: "These are the stakes. To make a world in which all of God's children can live. Or to go into the darkness. We must either love each other. Or we must die." Until the tag line appears, that ad has no explicit partisan content. "Vote for President Johnson on November 3. The stakes are too high for you to stay at home."

While the Democrats were bonding children to bombs, the Republicans were associating riots, looting, influence peddlers Bobby Baker and Billie Sol Estes and LBJ. In each case, the visual intercutting prompts inferences more effectively than a verbal argument could.

The 1964 Republican film *Choice* was less successful. The reasons for its failure are instructive. The film contrasts Democrat Lyndon Johnson's "decadent" and Goldwater's "decent, God-fearing, peace-loving" America. Johnson's America featured racial violence, topless and bottomless bathing suits, actors impersonating members of the Kennedy family throwing each other into swimming pools, and a car, supposedly Lyndon Johnson's, racing through a ranch while "Johnson" dispatched beer cans through its opened window.

By contrast, Goldwater's America surfeits with God-fearing, peace-loving pioneers, loyal to the Declaration of Independence, Christianity, and the traditions of the founders. So overdrawn was the contrast that it didn't even seem plausible to some Goldwater supporters. The Democrats actually used a pirated copy to raise funds for Johnson's re-election.

In 1968, argument by visual association reached a new level of complexity and potential duplicity when patterns of images were created and repeated by the Republicans using still photos. As "A Hot Time in the Old Town Tonight" alternated with discordant sounds, still photos of the war in Vietnam, of poverty in Appalachia, and of the rioting outside the Democratic convention were rapidly intercut with pictures of Democratic nominee Hubert Humphrey. No such argument is made on the audio track of the ad. To phrase the argument verbally is to reveal its ridiculousness. Even Humphrey's most rabid opponent was unready to argue that he had caused the war, poverty, and social unrest or that he approved of them or was indifferent to them—the three most plausible readings of the visual juxtaposition. The images move with a speed that allows little or no reflection. When the first airing evoked public protests to Republican headquarters and television stations, the Republican high command withdrew the ad.

Unlike ads from 1964 and 1968, the associative ads of 1976 are for a candidate, not against an opponent. The public revulsion at the disclosures of Watergate transformed the ads of 1976. In its wake, no candidate wanted to whisper the possibility that he or she was another Nixon. The guilt by visual association embedded in the Billie Sol Estes ad against LBJ and the anti-Humphrey ad bespoke a willingness if not to overstep the truth, then at least to lure the electorate into false inferences. After the light at the end of the tunnel in Vietnam had proven to be that of the advancing enemy and after the Watergate cover-up revealed a second president had lied, the candidate who would be president was required to quell the fears raised by these tactics.

Consequently, positive associative ads of the sort that characterized the 1976 Ford and Carter campaigns persevered while ads arguing from negative associations disappeared. By intercutting pictures of the Statue of Liberty, tall sailing ships, and picnics with smiling adults and children, and finally by infusing Ford into the rush of pleasant and patriotic images, the 1976 Republican campaign argued that America was feeling good about itself and about Ford. As E. G. Marshall pointed out that a good man can make a great president, Carter's ad dissolved from a picture of FDR to a picture of Truman, from Truman to JFK, and from JFK to Carter. Notably absent was Lyndon Johnson.

It was the Democrats who in 1984 resurrected attack by visual association. In the closing days of the campaign, predictions of a Reagan landslide created the climate in which the Democrats risked revival of this negative technique. To the tune of "Teach Your Children Well," youngsters were juxtaposed with missiles. Mondale's indictments of Reagan in the ad were as oblique as those Johnson used against Goldwater in 1964. If the prediction of war under Reagan existed in the ad, it was in the inferences invited by the intercut visuals.

By 1988 visual association was back with a vengeance. Beginning in September, the National Security Political Action Committee's "crime quiz" ad allied the Democratic nominee with the mug shot of a black murderer who had jumped furlough in Massachusetts and gone on to terrorize a Maryland couple (as described in Chapter 1). The Democrats tried their hand at linking Bush with damaging pictures as well. Among them were drug-dealing dictator Manuel Noriega and an Hispanic drug dealer who murdered the pregnant mother of two. (Use of unflattering pictures plays on our unrecognized bias toward the physically attractive. In Canada in 1974, the "attractive" candidates for federal office received two and a half times more votes than those deemed "unattractive." Almost three-quarters of those interviewed said that attractiveness had played no part in their vote.)

The Republican ads of 1988 allied Bush with world leaders including Gorbachev and Lech Walesa and situated him in an idyllic world of children and picnics. In a parallel move, the Republican ads placed Dukakis in a world of pollution and waste and menacing criminals.

As controversial was an ad aired in 1991 in Virginia. In fall 1991 a special election was called to replace a retiring Republican in the 7th congressional district. In the resulting race

Republican George Allen faced Democrat Kay Slaughter. Allen was a State Delegate, Slaughter a Charlottesville City Councilmember. In the race, the Republican outspent the Democrat two to one.

The National Republican Congressional Committee prepared an ad for Allen showing a rally against the Gulf War held in Washington, D.C. In the scene a protester is holding a sign reading "Victory to Iraq! Defeat US Imperialists." A still photo of Slaughter is then superimposed on the scene. "Kay Slaughter and the liberals in Congress opposed fighting Saddam Hussein," says the narrator as the picture dissolves into a headline reading "City Councilmember Kay Slaughter joined the coalition's December 7 rally . . . [.]" By overlaying a picture of Slaughter on the rally as the announcer describes her opposition to the Gulf War and attendance at a specific rally, the ad invites the false inference that the rally shown was the rally Slaughter attended.

The announcer then states, "Slaughter opposed President Bush and jointed anti-war protesters while our troops were at risk in the Persian Gulf." Troops in the Gulf are shown with a picture of Allen superimposed over them. The ad closes with Allen meeting with Bush in the White House. "George Allen and George Bush. Judgment and leadership we can trust." Slaughter, who had said that she would have voted against movement of U.S. troops against Saddam had she been in Congress at the time of the January 1991 vote, noted, "I am the mother of a National Guardsman, and to imply that I did anything other than give my wholehearted support to our troops is beneath contempt."[31]

Slaughter had attended a peace rally held in Charlottesville, not the rally shown in the ad. The *Charlottesville Daily Progress* editorialized that Allen's ad "is wrong, wrong, wrong. Wrong because it drops the tone of the campaign to a new low. Wrong because it oversimplifies a complicated issue. Wrong because it twists facts and video images to deliberately mislead voters."[32] The ad was aired because the Democrat was closing on the Republican in a traditional Republican stronghold. Some pundits saw it as a forecast of ads to come in 1992. National Republican Congressional Committee Chairman Guy Vander Jagt (R. Mich.)

"warned that such ads may await Democrats who opposed the president on the Persian Gulf vote."[33] In what is known as a traditionally Republican district, Republican Allen won with 62 percent of the vote.

In these spots the evidence required to legitimately link the images is absent. It is absent as well in product ads that associate use of the product with beauty, youth, fame, fortune, and friendship. In that they both rely on assertion by visual association, this type of ad sells politicians the way soap is usually peddled.

★ HOW DOES ASSOCIATION/APPOSITION INVITE FALSE INFERENCES?

Because we assume that communication is intended to be informative, we don't expect speakers to make claims they believe false or for which they lack evidence.[34] We also bring to communication the belief that those who communicate with us don't offer irrelevant, nonsensical, or implausible information.[35] The underlying presupposition that communication is a cooperative act would be violated if irrelevant information was its stock-in-trade. This premise yields what psychologists call "innuendo effects." A headline reading "Is Kathleen Hall Jamieson a criminal?" followed by an article that answers "No" will nonetheless sway readers toward the conclusion of criminality for the hapless person tagged in the headline.[36]

We don't all respond to any message the same way. Psychologists have gone so far as to differentiate cognitive and behavior styles.[37] But there is emerging evidence to indicate the circumstances, message cues, and attitudinal states that minimize our ability to process messages analytically, to counter-argue against suspect messages, or to process some content at all.[38]

Cognitive psychologists tell us that there are two modes of cognitive processing: central and peripheral. The first is analytic; it tests evidence and frames and evaluates propositions. The second is less conscious and more accepting of the visual cues.

Some believe that visuals are always processed peripherally, on the edges of consciousness, where critical acuity does not come into play. Increasingly, cognitive psychologists are arguing that much of what we absorb from the world around us is peripherally processed. We're influenced by things that don't go through evidence testing. Testing requires time for reflection and demands that we have not been distracted from this process by information overload or alternatively deflected from it by our own fears. To the extent that we have time to deal with visual association, we are able to process it as argument. By giving audiences time to think, Choice made a strategic error. Its blatant manipulation and the slow pace of its identifications and appositions invited central processing from its audience. A backlash resulted. It's not an often-made mistake after 1964.

Soon symbols became more subtle. We can be persuaded by communication that we have not carefully evaluated.[39] Indeed, some message characteristics make it *more* difficult to process information systematically. Two of these—rapidly paced information and use of fear appeal—typify many oppositional ads.

The speed with which pictures can now be intercut to identify or contrast two images renders us less able to scrutinize the information coming at us. By flooding us with words, sounds, and images, these stimuli reduce the time that we have to respond and overload our analytic capacity. With that reduction comes a lessened ability to dispute the offered material, a lessened ability to counter-argue. Once these defenses are gone, a persuasive message that might otherwise have been challenged or rejected can slip by.[40] Persuasion without benefit of analytic scrutiny of the message is the result.

★ THE COMPLICITOUS AUDIENCE

Television's amalgamation of information in different channels and rapid pacing enable the audience to be a partner in its own persuasion. Two campaign examples illustrate how this is done.

In a 1964 Democratic ad, a red phone is ringing on a desk, the hotline from Moscow to Washington. This phone only "rings in a serious crisis," says the announcer. Let's "keep it in the hands of a man who's proven himself responsible." In a campaign in which Goldwater has been portrayed as trigger-happy, the ad encourages the audience to insert the message that the phone should be kept out of his hands, even though there is no mention of Goldwater in the ad.

The technique reappeared in the primaries of 1980. Incumbent Jimmy Carter faced a strong challenge from within his own party. The youngest brother of former president John Kennedy was the challenger whose unremitting attacks on Carter's handling of the economy were laying the groundwork on which the Reagan campaign would build its fall victory. But Edward Kennedy was shadowed by the public's memory of "Chappaquiddick," shorthand for the death of a young woman under unexplained circumstances that implicated Kennedy. The Carter campaign evoked Chappaquiddick without ever mentioning the late night ride across the narrow bridge. "Husband, father, president," said a Carter ad. "He's done these three jobs with distinction."

Another Carter ad invited voters to recall their doubts about Kennedy's explanation of Chappaquiddick. Again there was no direct reference to the fatal accident. The ad simply laid in place the premise that truth telling was important with the expectation that focus would prompt an unfavorable comparison to the Democratic Senator from Massachusetts. "You may not always agree with President Carter," said the announcer. "But you'll never have to wonder whether he's telling the truth. It's hard to think of a more useful quality in a president than telling the simple truth. President Carter—for the truth."

On the face of it, neither of these is an attack ad. If one relies on the content of the ad itself, it is not even clear that the Carter and Johnson ads are oppositional. Unmentioned in both is the name of the opponent or any facet of his record. The audience is free to fill in whatever message it prefers.

In the fourth century B.C. Aristotle wrote that the "enthymeme is the soul of persuasion." This powerful idea explains that persuasion requires audience cooperation. By investing messages with suppressed premises, we become accomplices in our own persuasion. We create enthymemes.

In the classic example, "All men are mortal; therefore Socrates is mortal," the enthymeme suppresses the premise "Socrates is a man." If I assume that Socrates is a gummy bear, I will frustrate the arguer's attempt to forge the enthymeme.

Some of the classics in political advertising function enthymematically. The daisy ad of 1964 shows only a child and an exploding nuclear bomb. Goldwater is nowhere to be found in the ad. But in the context of the 1964 campaign, the ad invited viewers to recall Goldwater's statements on use of nuclear weapons and the attacks his fellow Republicans had made on him for those statements. The audience can supply the premise "Goldwater could lead us into a nuclear war." In fact, viewers asked to recall the ad "remembered" seeing Goldwater's face and hearing the announcer explicitly indict the Republican.

All of this might matter less if we held the notions *implied* in one cognitive warehouse and those observed in another. But we don't. Those who study how we comprehend language report that we recode what we hear into a form that doesn't distinguish what was actually said from what was implied.[41]

Enthymematic ads often ask rhetorical questions whose answers have already been revealed to the ad makers by the polls. This encourages the audience to reinforce existing predispositions and to act on them in deciding how to vote. A 1968 ad asked, "What has Richard Nixon ever done for you?" It then listed a series of accomplishments attributable to Humphrey and the Democrats. The ad closed by asking viewers to "Think about it." Here the inability of the audience to fill in information about Nixon's accomplishments fueled the anti-Nixon premise. If the audience could list dozens of ways Nixon had helped it, the ad would have failed.

Some ads circumscribe the evidence they offer in such a way that they actively imply a false conclusion. An anti-Johnson ad in 1964 did this by showing pictures of Johnson cronies under investigation (i.e., Billie Sol Estes and Bobby Baker) before asking how Lyndon Johnson managed to build a fortune. The ad is trying to steer the audience to the conclusion that Johnson was on the take. Those who defied the powerful visuals and thought about it

realized that there was another possible answer. His wife owned a broadcasting station.

Television has the added power to invite false inferences by amalgamating information in different channels. In the process it allows us to create a whole that is greater than the sum of its parts. The Bush furlough ad of 1988, which I discussed in an earlier chapter, assumes that we will ally material found in one channel (visual: 268 escaped) or within one track of communication with that found in another (audio: many first-degree murderers escaped). The Dukakis ad that says that Bush voted to "cut" Social Security, as it shows a Social Security card being torn down to a small part of its former self, makes the same move. At the end of the ad, only a small part remains. The powerful visual deflects us from questioning what "cut" means. What Bush did was vote to freeze a cost-of-living adjustment. Whether that constitutes a vote to cut is open to debate. What is not debatable is the inference suggested by the shredded Social Security card. If one believes the visual, Bush tried to cut seven-eighths of Social Security. The announcer, of course, never said that. But associating the word "cut" with the rapidly diminishing card invites that inference.

We tend to amalgamate all the information we have available—what we see, what we hear, what we read—into one coherent message. In a rapidly paced ad saturated with evocative fear-inducing claims, the likelihood that we will systematically process the information to ask if we should forge a conclusion is minimized. In short, television has changed the techniques and perhaps the effectiveness, if not the basic tactics, of attack.

NOTES

[1] Quoted in David Cushman Coyle, *Ordeal of The Presidency* (Washington, D.C.: Public Affairs Press, 1960), 67.

[2] *Correspondence . . . Jackson,* III, 426.

[3] Coyle, 199.

[4] *A Rhetoric of Motives* (Berkeley: University of California Press, 1950; 1969), 26.

[5] Thomas Kessner, *Fiorello H. La Guardia* (New York: Penguin Books, 1989), 407.

[6] Washburn, 181.

[7] Donald English, *Political Uses of Photography in the Third French Republic 1871–1914*

(Ann Arbor: University of Michigan Research Press, 1984), 12.

8 Stanley Kelley, Jr., *Professional Public Relations and Political Power* (Baltimore: Johns Hopkins University Press, 1956), 135.

9 Felknor, 115.

10 David Donald, "The Folklore Lincoln," in Nicholas Cords and Patrick Gerster, *Myth and the American Experience* (Beverly Hills, Calif.: Glencoe Press, 1973), 45.

11 November 11, 1802.

12 In Kessner, *La Guardia,* 122.

13 Hone, 493.

14 G. Salomon, "Television is 'Easy' and Print Is 'Tough': The Differential Investment of Mental Effort in Learning as a Function of Perceptions and Attributions," *Journal of Educational Psychology* 76 (1984), 647–58.

15 R. Hurwitz and S. J. Samuels, "Reading and Listening to Expository Text," *Journal of Reading Behavior* 3 (1985), 185–98.

16 E. Thorson, B. Reeves, and J. Schleuder, "Message Complexity and Attention to Television," *Communication Research* 12 (1985), 427–54; B. Reeves, E. Thorson, and J. Schleuder, "Attention to Television: Psychological Theories and Chronometric Measures," in *Perspectives on Media Effects,* J. Bryant and D. Zillmann, eds. (Hillsdale, N.J.: Lawrence Erlbaum, 1986); A. Lang, "Involuntary Attention and Physiological Arousal Evoked by Structural Features and Emotional Content in TV Commercials," *Communication Research* 17 (1990), 275–99.

Evidence from EEGs indicates that our response to some of these formal features is involuntary. Indeed, Reeves et al. (1986) suggest that these features "derive their attentional value through the evolutionary significance of detecting movement."

17 Thorson et al., 1985; M. L. Rothschild, E. Thorson, B. Reeves, J. L. Hirsch, and R. Goldstein, "EEG Activity and the Processing of Television Commercials," *Communication Research* 13 (1986), 182–220.

18 G. B. Armstrong and B. S. Greenberg, "Background Television as an Inhibitor of Cognitive Processing," *Human Communication Research* 16 (1990), 355–86.

19 D. Drew and T. Grimes, "Audio-Visual Redundancy and TV News Recall," *Communication Research* 14 (1987), 452–61.

20 M. Clynes and N. Nettheim, "The Living Quality of Music: Neurobiologic Basis of Communicating Feeling," in *Music, Mind, and Brain, The Neuropsychology of Music,* M. Clynes, ed. (New York: Plenum Press, 1982); S. Hecker, "Music for Advertising Effect," *Psychology and Marketing* 1

(1984), 3–8; A. Mitchell, "Current Perspectives and Issues Concerning the Explanation of 'Feeling' Advertising Effects," in *Nonverbal Communication in Advertising,* S. Hecker and D. Stewart, eds. (Lexington, Mass.: Lexington Books, 1988); E. Thorson and M. Friestad, "The Effects of Emotion on Episodic Memory for Television Commercials," in *Cognitive and Affective Responses to Advertising,* P. Cafferata and A. Tybout, eds. (Lexington, Mass.: Lexington Books, 1989); J. Edell and K. L. Keller, "The Information Processing of Coordinated Media Campaigns," *Journal of Marketing Research* 26 (1988), 149–63.

21 V. C. Ottati and R. S. Wyer, Jr., "The Cognitive Mediators of Political Choice: Toward a Comprehensive Model of Political Information Processing," in *Information and Democratic Processes,* J. A. Ferejohn and J. H. Kuklinski, eds. (Urbana and Chicago: University of Illinois Press, 1990), 186–216.

22 P. Lang, "The Cognitive Psychophysiology of Emotion: Fear and Anxiety," in *Anxiety and the Anxiety Disorders,* eds. A. Tuma and J. Maser (Hillsdale, N.J.: Lawrence Erlbaum, 1985).

23 R. B. Zajonc, "On the Primacy of Affect," *American Psychologist* 39 (1984), 117–23. See also R. Batra and M. L. Ray, "Advertising Situations: Implications of Differential Involvement and Accompanying Affect Responses," in *Information Processing Research on Advertising,* R. J. Harris, ed. (Hillsdale, N.J.: Lawrence Erlbaum, 1983).

24 Roger D. Masters, *The Nature of Politics* (New Haven, Conn.: Yale University Press, 1989), 61–68.

25 C. K. Atkin, L. Bowen, O. B. Nayman, and K. G. Sheinkopf, "Quality versus Quantity in Televised Political Ads," *Public Opinion Quarterly* 40 (1973), 209–24; C. K. Atkin and G. Heald, "Effects of Political Advertising," *Public Opinion Quarterly* 40 (1976), 216–28; S. H. Surlin and T. F. Gordon, "How Values Affect Attitudes Toward Direct Reference Political Advertising," *Journalism Quarterly* 54 (1977), 89–98.

26 Times Mirror Center for the People and the Press, "The Age of Indifference: A Study of Young Americans and How They View the News," June 28, 1990, 28.

27 S. Chaiken, "Communicator Physical Attractiveness and Persuasion," *Journal of Personality and Social Psychology* 38 (1979), 1387–97; R. E. Petty, J. T. Cacioppo, and D. Schumann, "Central and Peripheral Routes to Advertising Effectiveness: The Moderating Role of Involvement," *Journal of Consumer Research* 10 (1983), 135–46.

28 R. E. Petty, J. T. Cacioppo, and M. Heesacker, "The Use of Rhetorical Questions in Persuasion,"

Journal of Personality and Social Psychology 40 (1981), 432–40.

29 R. E. Petty and J. T. Cacioppo, "The Effects of Involvement on Responses to Argument Quantity and Quality: Central and Peripheral Routes to Persuasion," *Journal of Personality and Social Psychology* 46 (1984), 69–81.

30 Ottati and Wyer, op. cit., 214.

31 Tim Curran, "'Attack' Ad May Preview '92 GOP Tactics," *Roll Call,* November 4, 1991, 35.

32 October 31, quoted by *Campaign Hotline,* November 1, 1991, 15.

33 Tim Curran, "Allen Clobbers Slaughter in Virginia Special, 62–35%," *Roll Call,* November 7, 1991, 13.

34 H. P. Grice, "Logic and Conversation," in P. Cole and J. L. Morgan eds., *Syntax and Semantics,* Vol. 3: Speech Acts (New York: Seminar Press, 1975), 41–58; D. A. Norman and D. E. Remelhart, eds. *Explorations in Cognition* (San Francisco: Freeman, 1975).

35 R. J. Harris and G. E. Monaco, "Psychology of Pragmatic Implication: Information Processing Between the Lines," *Journal of Experimental Psychology, General* 107, (1978), 1–27.

36 Daniel M. Wegner, Richard Wenzlaff, R. Michael Kerker, and Ann E. Beattie, "Incrimination Through Innuendo: Can Media Questions Become Public Answers?" *Journal of Personality and Social Psychology* 40:5 (1981), 822–32.

37 S. M. Miller, "Monitoring and Blunting: Validation of a Questionnaire to Assess Styles of Information Seeking Under Threat," *Journal of Personality and Social Psychology* 52 (1987), 345–53; M. P. Zanna and J. M. Olson, "Individual Differences in Attitudinal Relations," in *Consistency*

in Social Behavior: The Ontario Symposium, Vol. 1 (Hillsdale, N.J.: Lawrence Erlbaum, 1982), 75–103.

38 A major focus of the studies of processing has asked when people would process messages systematically or centrally, a mode of processing that requires attention, understanding, and elaboration upon the content of the message. Central processing is likely to occur "as a result of a person's careful and thoughtful advocacy." Peripheral processing is likely to occur "as a result of some simple cue in the persuasion context (e.g., an attractive source) that induced [attitude] change without necessitating scrutiny of the central merits of the issue-relevant information presented" (Richard E. Petty and John T. Cacioppo, *Communication and Persuasion: Central and Peripheral Routes to Attitude Change* [London: Springer-Verlag, 1986], p. 3). This model of persuasion presupposes that as our motivation or ability to process an argument decreases, peripheral cues become more powerful in effecting persuasion; correlatively, under argumentative scrutiny, peripheral cues are less powerful. Motivation, interest, and involvement determine how we will process information.

39 D. Axsom, S. Yates, and S. Chaiken, "Audience Response as a Heuristic Cue in Persuasion," *Journal of Personality and Social Psychology* 53 (1987), 30–40; S. Chaiken, "The Heuristic Model of Persuasion," in *Social Influence: The Ontario Symposium,* M. P. Zanna, J. M. Olson, and C. P. Herman, eds., Vol. 5 (Hillsdale, N.J.: Lawrence Erlbaum, 1987), 3–39.

40 R. E. Petty, T. M. Ostrom, and T. C. Brock, eds., *Cognitive Responses in Persuasion* (Hillsdale, N.J.: Lawrence Erlbaum, 1981).

41 Clark and Clark.

Gender Differences in Campaign Messages: The Political Advertisements of Men and Women Candidates for U.S. Senate

Kim Fridkin Kahn

Women are less likely than men to run successfully for high political office. Of the twenty-five women who ran for the U.S. Senate between 1984 and 1990, only two won. One candidate, Nancy Kassebaum of Kansas, was an incumbent, and the other, Barbara Mikulski of Maryland, won election by defeating another woman. Several reasons have been offered to explain women's lack of success in the electoral arena, including inadequate access to political

resources and sex stereotyping by voters (e.g., Bernstein 1986; Boles and Durio 1981; Gertzog 1979; Hedlund et al. 1979). While these explanations are important, I introduce and test another potentially important explanation: differences in the media presentations of men and women candidates.

In this paper I examine televised political advertisements to see whether men and women candidates emphasize different messages in their campaigns. If they do, these alternative messages may differ in their electoral effectiveness. In addition, I examine patterns of campaign coverage to see whether the press distinguish between male and female candidates in their coverage. Since a candidate's message will be most persuasive if that message is echoed by the press, gender differences in press treatment can have electoral consequences.

Both paid and unpaid media attention play a central role in today's electoral campaigns. Candidates try to cultivate good press during their campaigns and they devote considerable resources to campaign advertising (Clarke and Evans 1983; Goldenberg and Traugott 1984; Joslyn 1984). Paid media, such as televised political advertisements, are critical in campaigns because these commercials present the candidate's message directly to the public. In addition, political advertisements have the power to influence voters' perceptions of candidates, thereby influencing the electoral fortunes of these candidates (e.g., Joslyn 1984; Kern 1989; Patterson and McClure 1976).

The unpaid media—the news media—are also crucial in electoral campaigns, because voters receive the bulk of their campaign information from these sources. The news media's coverage of campaigns can affect voters' recognition of candidates by conferring press attention on certain candidates while ignoring others (Aldrich 1980; Banels 1987; Patterson 1980). In addition, the substance of news coverage often influences evaluations of candidates by altering the criteria voters use to judge candidates (Iyengar and Kinder 1987; Iyengar, Peters, and Kinder 1982), while the tone of campaign coverage sometimes alters voters' reactions to candidates (Goldenberg and Traugott 1987; Joslyn 1984; Patterson 1980).

In this paper I examine gender differences in paid and unpaid media messages in U.S. Senate campaigns. I chose Senate races because of the relative abundance of women candidates and because of the demonstrated importance of the media in statewide campaigns (Goldenberg and Traugott 1987). First, I analyzed the candidates' political advertisements to see whether male and female candidates adopt different media appeals. Since the substance of spot ads is controlled by the candidate, these ads can be considered the candidate's "presentation of self" (Kaid and Davidson 1986); a close examination of these ads can help determine whether men and women characterize their candidacies differently.

Another reason to look at gender differences in campaign commercials is that they may lead to gender differences in the effectiveness of these ads. By adopting different types of campaign appeals, male and female candidates may adopt appeals that differ in their impact on voters. Recent experimental work suggests that certain commercials—issue ads and positive ads—are more likely to create positive impressions of candidates (e.g., Garramone 1986; Kahn and Geer 1991; Kaid and Sander 1978). In addition, Ansolabehere and Iyengar's (1991) experimental study of television advertising in the 1990 California gubernatorial campaign suggests that certain appeals are more convincing for women candidates, while others are more profitable for male candidates. Ansolabehere and Iyengar find, for example, that "attack" ads were more effective for Peter Wilson than for Diane Feinstein.

Along with the substance of the candidates' political advertisements, I examine media coverage of the candidates' campaigns. Comparing the content of spot advertisements with the coverage of the candidates in the news can help determine whether the candidates' messages are being mirrored by the news media. The campaign messages that the candidates present in their ads will be most coherent if those messages are then echoed by the press. If the agendas of the candidate and the news media do not correspond, then the impact of the candidate's message may be blunted. A comparison between the content of the candidates' ads and press coverage of the candidates can show whether and to what extent the news media's emphasis is different for male and female candidates.

★ EXPECTATIONS ABOUT GENDER DIFFERENCES IN CAMPAIGN APPEALS

Men and women face different constraints in the electoral arena, and these differences may influence the strategies they adopt in their U.S. Senate campaigns. In particular, people's preconceptions about male and female candidates may influence the campaign appeals that candidates employ. Candidates often have a choice: they may adopt strategies that exploit voters' stereotypes about male and female candidates, or they may try to dispel stereotypes by acting in ways inconsistent with their traditional strengths.

People's stereotypes about male and female candidates may influence the types of issues that candidates choose to emphasize in their campaign messages. Since voters generally believe that men are better at dealing with foreign policy and economic issues, while women are better at handling social issues (e.g., Gallup 1984; National Women's Political Caucus 1987; Rosenwasser et al. 1987; Sapiro 1982), male and female candidates may emphasize these alternative issue domains in their campaign ads.

Voters' priorities about issues are often responsive to the media's emphasis (e.g., Iyengar and Kinder 1987; MacKuen 1981), so candidates can influence these priorities during their campaigns. Candidates who stress their stereotypical strengths in their campaigns can make these issues salient to voters and voters may consider these issues when evaluating the competing candidates. Women candidates may choose to concentrate on education, a stereotypically strong issue for women, thereby leading voters to believe that education is an important issue. Voters may then think about the education issue when evaluating the competing candidates.

Of course, men and women may articulate alternative agendas for other than strategic reasons. More specifically, gender differences in issue emphasis may reflect real differences in the issue priorities of male and female candidates. Research examining the political attitudes of women candidates and women officeholders suggests that women are more supportive of social issues such as abortion and the ERA, even controlling for party affiliation (Carroll 1985; Darcy, Welch, and Clark 1987; Poole and Zeigler 1985).

In addition to stressing their policy priorities during their Senate campaigns, candidates

also emphasize their personal strengths. Again, voters' sex stereotypes often influence the types of personal characteristics that candidates choose to highlight in their campaign appeals. Since voters consider women candidates to be more compassionate and honest, while they consider men to be stronger leaders and more knowledgeable (Ashmore and Del Boca 1979; Boles and Durio 1981; Gallup 1984; National Women's Political Caucus 1987), candidates may develop campaign strategies to respond to these stereotypes.

While candidates are likely to stress their stereotypical strengths when discussing issues, such may not be the case for traits. Although the public's issue agenda is susceptible to media influence (e.g., Iyengar, Peters, and Kinder 1982; Iyengar and Kinder 1987; MacKuen 1981), people's perceptions of important personality traits may be less flexible. Research at the presidential level suggests that voters consistently consider competence and leadership when evaluating competing candidates (e.g., Markus 1982; Miller, Wattenberg, and Malanchuk 1986). In addition, since people evaluate candidates based on prototypes of incumbent officeholders (Kinder et al. 1980), people's images of the prototypical senator may be masculine. Voters may therefore be more likely to consider masculine traits—like strength and leadership ability—when evaluating senatorial candidates. Given the importance of these masculine traits, both male and female candidates may emphasize these traits in their campaign appeals. Men may highlight their stereotypical strengths, while women may try to eradicate stereotypes through "unstereotypical" campaign appeals.

In addition to specific differences in trait and issue agendas, a candidate's gender often influences more general differences in campaign appeals. In particular, candidate's sex may determine whether a candidate makes a personal or a policy-oriented appeal to the electorate. Because people believe that women are less competent than men (e.g., Ashmore and Del Boca 1979; Boles and Durio 1981; Gallup 1984; National Women's Political Caucus 1987), female candidates need to emphasize their policy concerns in their campaign commercials. By talking about their issue priorities, women candidates may dispel voters' doubts about their ability. Male candidates, on the other hand, can be more flexible in their appeals since voters are more confident about their candidacies.

★ METHODOLOGY

Sample of Political Advertisements

To explore gender differences in paid and unpaid media messages in U.S. Senate campaigns, I examined televised political advertisements and press coverage for a sample of Senate candidates. In 1984 and 1986, sixteen women ran for the U.S. Senate. Political commercials were obtained for ten of these women, accounting for a total of 81 spot ads.[1] By stratifying the population of male Senate candidates by status (incumbent, challenger, open-race candidate) and strength of candidacy based on pre-election assessments, I selected a sample of twenty-eight male candidates and 324 corresponding political commercials.[2] With this sample of 405 spot ads, I can compare the media presentations of men and women Senate candidates to see whether there are differences in the way men and women present themselves to the electorate.[3]

Coding of Political Ads

One researcher coded all commercials in the sample.[4] To ensure the reliability of the coding, two checks were performed. First, I coded a sample of articles twice—once at the start of the coding process and once near the end. This reliability check revealed that coding remained stable, with 98 percent agreement on most measures. Second, I assessed intercoder reliability. A coder unfamiliar with the objectives of the study coded a random sample of the political advertisements. The intercoder reliability agreement for this sample of ads was 96 percent, with agreement ranging from 100 percent for some coding categories to a minimum of 90 percent for other categories.

Coding of Newspaper Content

In addition to the data on political advertisement, I analyzed newspaper coverage of male and female candidates for the U.S. Senate. With the addition of the newspaper analysis, we can examine the relationship between the candidates' own messages and the messages communicated by the press. By comparing these two media, we can see whether the correspondence between the candidates' emphasis and the news media's emphasis is the same for male and female candidates.

I chose to analyze newspaper coverage, instead of television coverage, for both substantive and practical reasons. On the substantive side, there is considerable evidence that newspapers cover state-level campaigns more extensively than local television news (Goldenberg and Traugott 1987; Westlye 1991) and that people receive more of their information about statewide races from newspapers than from television (Clarke and Fredin 1978). Furthermore Westlye explains that "newspapers present an amount of information that more closely approximates what campaigns are issuing" as compared with local broadcast news (1991: 45). On the practical side, newspapers are routinely saved on microfilm, making them easily accessible for analysis. In contrast, tapes of local television news are seldom available after a campaign, making the examination of television news more difficult.

I analyzed campaign coverage for thirty-two of the thirty-eight candidates included in the political advertising analysis. Given that the newspaper sample and the advertising sample do not include all the same races, differences in the correspondence between these two media may reflect differences in the samples. Therefore, when comparing the two media, the analysis is limited to those races where both news and advertising data are available.

The newspapers I chose for analysis were, whenever possible, those with the largest circulation in the state, because of their potential impact on large numbers of people in the state.[5] I analyzed any item that mentioned either candidate, including news articles, columns, editorials, and "news analysis" articles every day from September 1 through the day of the elections.[6] The coding categories for the newspaper analysis mirror those categories used in the content analysis of the political advertisements. This coding procedure yielded a sample of 2,538 articles.

★ RESULTS AND DISCUSSION

Gender Differences in the Substance of Political Commercials

An examination of the content of spot ads is important because it will give us clues regarding what voters learn during campaigns. For instance, if women emphasize only issues in their advertisements and virtually ignore their personal characteristics, voters will have little opportunity to learn about the female candidates' traits via their political commercials. Another reason that the substance of political commercials is so important is that it represents the candidate's own campaign message. The substance of the spot ads gives us a sense of what candidates want to emphasize and can illustrate whether men and women differ in how they represent their candidacies. In the analysis of political advertisements, I treat the candidate—not the ad—as the unit of analysis and weigh the ads accordingly. By using the candidate as the unit of analysis, we avoid giving more weight to candidates who have more ads.

Candidates either emphasize their own strengths in their political ads, or they discuss their opponent's weaknesses. Candidate-oriented commercials paint a positive portrait of the candidate by discussing the candidate's qualifications, personality traits, or issue positions. Opponent-oriented commercials, on the other hand, are negative or "attack" ads that emphasize negative aspects of the opponent's candidacy.

Although experimental research suggests that candidate-oriented ads will be more effective than opponent-oriented appeals (Kahn and Geer 1991), candidates and campaign consultants believe the negative ads "work" (Kern 1989). While acknowledging that negative ads can create a "backlash" against the candidate, consultants view these ads as effective tools for "long-shot" candidates (Kern 1989). Given the advantages and disadvantages outlined by campaign strategists; challengers may be more likely to use attack ads in their campaigns. Similarly, women candidates, who may view themselves a[s] perennial "underdogs," may be more likely to use negative appeals in their campaigns.

In this sample of ads, 65 percent of all the ads are candidate-oriented, while 35 percent are classified as opponent-oriented. As expected, incumbents are more likely than challengers to use these positive ads in their campaigns. Incumbents use positive ads 67 percent of the time, while challengers use these appeals less than half of the time (47 percent).[7] Similarly, men are more likely than women to air candidate-oriented appeals: 68 percent of the male candidates' ads and 53 percent of the female candidates' ads are candidate-oriented ($p < .05$).[8] This gender difference in campaign appeals is not merely a reflection of status differences for male and female candidates. Even when we control for status of the candidates and the competitiveness of the race, we find that male candidates continue to use positive appeals more frequency than their female counterparts. For example, male candidates in noncompetitive races use candidate-oriented ads 75 percent of the time, while noncompetitive female candidates use these appeals 52 percent of the time ($p < .01$).

Issue Discussion in Candidate-Oriented Ads

When Senate candidates promote their candidacies in their positive ads they discuss issues more frequently than any other topic; more than half of the candidate-oriented commercials mention the candidates' issue concerns. Women, who may be trying to increase voters' views of their competence, are somewhat more likely to emphasize policy concerns in their commercials. Although the differences are not statistically significant, women discuss issues in 69 percent of their ads, while male candidates talk about issues 59 percent of the time. These differences persist when we control for the status and party of the candidates and the competitiveness of the race.

Although issues are discussed frequently, candidates rarely take controversial policy stands in their spot ads. Instead, candidates typically talk in general terms about the issues that they think are important. This type of issue discussion is not trivial. On the contrary, by paying attention to campaign ads, voters can learn about a candidate's issue agenda. Political

TABLE 1

Issue Discussion in Political Spot Ads

	Male Candidates	Female Candidates	P-Value*
Foreign Affairs†	11%	7%	n.s.
Economic Issues	48	27	p < .01
Farm Issues	4	0	p < .01
Social Programs	7	33	p < .01
Social Issues	11	20	p < .05
Fair Share for the State	15	7	p < .05
Other	4	7	n.s.
	(332:28)‡	(94:10)	

*P-values are based on the difference in proportions test.

†The "foreign affairs" category includes discussion of the following: U.S.S.R-U.S. relations, arms control, Central America, South Africa, Middle East and Europe. The "economic issues" category includes discussion of the following: taxes, the federal budget, and discussion of the economy generally. The "farm" category includes any discussion of farm-related issues. The "social issue" category includes the discussion of gay rights, abortion, school prayer, women's rights, civil rights, the environment, and drugs. The "social program" category includes discussion of education, health programs, employment, welfare programs, and programs for the elderly. The "Fair Share for State" includes discussion of programs and initiatives for the good of the state. All other issues are included in the "other" category.

‡Entries are the number of issue mentions in the spot ads followed by the number of candidates.

advertisements can thereby play an agenda-setting role in Senate campaigns (Erbing, Goldenberg, and Miller 1980; Iyengar and Kinder 1987; Iyengar, Peters, and Kinder 1982). In other words, if certain issues are the focus of a candidate's campaign, men voters who pay attention to these ads will come to think these issues are important and, consequently will think about these particular issues when evaluating the candidates and making their selections (Iyengar and Kinder 1987; Iyengar, Peters, and Kinder 1982).[9]

Even though the quantity of issue discussion does not differ significantly for male and female candidates, male and female candidates discuss different sorts of issues in their campaign appeals. As hypothesized, these differences in the issue agendas correspond to commonly held sex stereotypes (e.g., Gallup 1984; National Women's Political Caucus 1987; Rosenwasser et al. 1987; Sapiro 1982). As the data in Table 1 show, men are more likely to discuss economic issues such as taxes and the federal budget, in their spot ads, while women spend more time talking about social issues and social policy, such as education and health policy. These results suggest that men and women do have distinct issue priorities that they pursue in their quest for election to the U.S. Senate. These alternative issue agendas correspond to the candidates' "stereotypical" strengths.

Traits in Candidate-Oriented Ads

Candidates also emphasize their personality strengths in their campaign commercials. This concentration on personal characteristics can have electoral significance because voters' trait assessments often influence their overall evaluations of candidates (Abelson et al. 1982; Goldenberg, Traugott, and Kahn 1988; Markus 1982). As with issue discussion, women stress their personal strengths in their ads somewhat more often than men (40 percent v. 30 percent), although the difference is not statistically significant.

People not only have sex stereotypes regarding issues, they also have stereotypes regarding personality traits: those that best characterize male candidates—independent, objective, strong leader, tough—those that best describe female candidates—compassionate, honest, gentle—(Ashmore and Del Boca 1979, Boles and Durio 1981, Gallup 1984, National Women's Political Caucus 1987). As hypothesized, when traits are divided into "male" and "female" traits based on the sex stereotype literature, we find that men and women both discuss "male" traits far more extensively than "female" traits. Over 70 percent of all trait discussion is devoted to such "male" traits as competence and leadership, while such "female" traits as compassion and honesty are discussed less than 30 percent of the time. The candidates may emphasize "male" traits in their campaign ads for two reasons: they believe that these traits are most relevant for selecting potential U.S. senators, and they believe that voters will consider these traits when evaluating competing candidates.

Overall, women stress "male" traits in their campaign appeals somewhat more often than men, although the difference is not statistically significant. Women discuss "male" traits 80 percent of the time, while men focus on "male" traits in 73 percent of their campaign commercials. This gender difference in trait emphasis is most dramatic for female incumbents and female challengers.[10] Women challengers, for example, discuss "male" traits in 89 percent of their advertisements, while male challengers mention "male" traits 70 percent of the time (p < .05). These results suggest that women, by stressing their stereotypical weaknesses and talking almost exclusively about "male" traits, try to dispel voters' preconceptions about the "typical" female candidate (e.g., women are weak leaders).

Opponent-Oriented Ads

In campaigns for elective office, candidates try to create negative images of their opponents as well as create favorable images of their own candidacies. Although recent experimental work suggests that "attack" ads are less effective than candidate-oriented ads, these findings conflict with the conventional wisdom expressed by campaign consultants (Kern 1989). Given that candidates and their consultants believe that

negative ads work, it is not surprising that more than one-third (35 percent) of all ads in this sample can be characterized as "attack ads."

As discussed earlier, challengers and women candidates are more likely to use negative ads in their election campaigns. In addition, a candidate's propensity to use negative ads may be related to the gender of the candidate's opponent. Lake (1984), in her interviews with male and female congressional candidates, finds that men feel uncomfortable about attacking female opponents in their campaigns. Male candidates believe that if they engage in a negative campaign, they will be perceived as "beating up on" a woman. Although the number of cases is small, the advertising data show that male candidates are less likely to criticize female opponents in their commercials. Male candidates use negative ads only 17 percent of the time when facing a female opponent, as compared with 36 percent of the time when facing a male opponent (p < .01). These results complement Lake's (1984) findings, suggesting that men adopt different strategies depending on the gender of their opponent.

In addition to using attack ads more frequently than their male counterparts, women may emphasize different topics. Given people's stereotypes about men and women, male and female candidates face different constraints in the electoral arena, and these constraints often influence the type of negative campaign strategy adopted by candidates. In particular, since voters consider men to be more knowledgeable than women (e.g., Kahn 1992; Rosenwasser et al. 1987; Sapiro 1982), women have a greater need to demonstrate their competence in their campaign appeals. To help establish their expertise, women often choose to emphasize policy over personal attacks in their negative commercials.

The data in Table 2 display the primary emphasis of the candidates' negative commercials. These findings demonstrate that women are much more likely than their male counterparts to focus on substantive issues in their attack ads. Male candidates, on the other hand, are more likely to adopt more general appeals that include both trait and issue attacks. When we control for the incumbency of the candidates,

TABLE 2

The Primary Emphasis of Negative Spot Ads*

	Male Candidates	Female Candidates	P-Value
Traits	8%	10%	n.s.
Issues	20	53	p < .01
Mixed†	28	13	p < .05
Comparison of Candidates	43	23	p < .05
	(110:28)‡	(32:10)	

*P-values are based on the difference in proportions test.

†The "mixed" and "comparison of candidates" advertisements do not focus primarily on either traits or issues. The "mixed" advertisement includes a discussion of the opponent's personal traits and issue positions while the "comparison of candidates" advertisement compare[s] the opposing candidates along trait and issue dimensions.

‡Entries are the number of negative ads followed by the number of candidates for each cell.

we continue to find that women candidates emphasize policy more frequently than their male counterparts. Women challengers, for example, emphasize issues in 61 percent of their negative advertisements, while male challengers focus on issues 31 percent of the time (p < .01). Similarly, female Republicans and female Democrats are more likely than their male counterparts to discuss policy in their opponent-oriented ads (p < .05).[11]

The types of issues emphasized in the candidates' opponent-oriented ads are very similar to those emphasized in candidate-oriented ads. Again, as with candidate-oriented ads, men emphasize economic issues most frequently, while women spend most of their time discussing social issues and social programs.

While women are likely to emphasize issues exclusively in their attack ads, men and women do not differ in their use of personal attacks. Male candidates mention their opponents' personality traits in 17 percent of their ads, while women mention their opponents' traits 11 percent of the time.[12] Overall, trait discussion is less pervasive in opponent-oriented ads than in candidate-oriented ads. While men and women mention their own personality traits in 32 percent of these ads, the opponents' personality traits are mentioned in only about 16 percent of the candidates' spot ads. These findings suggest that senatorial candidates largely refrain from using purely personal attacks in their campaign messages. Instead, candidates are more comfortable with policy criticisms, attacking their opponents' policy stands in 31 percent of their spot ads.

The examination of campaign commercials reveals clear differences in the campaign strategies of male and female candidates. Female candidates concentrate more heavily on policy issues—especially in their negative ads. In addition, men and women emphasize different issues; women discuss social issues more frequently, while men largely concentrate on economic policy. These commercials represent what the candidates choose to emphasize in their campaigns. Men and women may emphasize these alternative strategies because they believe that these distinct strategies will be effective in garnering votes. Yet these strategies will be most influential when the candidates' messages are reinforced and echoed by the news media. Voters are more likely to learn about a specific campaign message if they are exposed to this message both through controlled *and* uncontrolled media sources. If the candidate's agenda is ignored by the news media, then voters are unlikely to adopt the agenda.

The Correspondence between Campaign Ads and News Coverage of Candidates

To examine the correspondence between the agendas adopted by male and female candidates and the agendas discussed in the news,

I analyzed campaign coverage for thirty-two of the thirty-eight candidates included in this study.[13] With this content analysis, we can see whether the media are equally effective in representing the candidacies of male and female candidates.[14] If there are gender differences in the press coverage of candidates, this difference may (1) reflect a bias of the news media, or (2) reflect real differences in the campaigns of men and women candidates.

While men and women stress different campaign themes, the news media may not be equally responsive to their messages. Reporters, like voters, are likely to hold sex stereotypes; these stereotypical beliefs may lead reporters to emphasize certain traits (e.g., compassion, honesty) when covering female candidates and other traits (competence, leadership) when covering male candidates, regardless of the candidates' own emphases. Similarly, stereotypes may lead reporters to consider male candidates more "legitimate"; consequently, reporters may echo male candidates' campaign rhetoric more faithfully.

On the other hand, differences in the correspondence between the press's and the candidates' messages may reflect real differences in the campaigns of men and women candidates. If male candidates, for example, are more effective campaigners than their female counterparts, then this difference can explain differences in media coverage of their campaigns. In addition, gender differences in news coverage may reflect differences in the newsworthiness of the campaigns. For instance, by focusing on economic issues, male candidates may be reflecting the concerns of voters more accurately than female candidates. The press may therefore cover the male candidates' agenda more faithfully, deeming this agenda more relevant to voters.

Yet, regardless of the cause, gender differences in the correspondence between the press's agenda and the candidates' agendas can have important electoral consequences. Since voters' priorities are flexible and susceptible to media influence (e.g., Iyengar and Kinder 1987; MacKuen 1981), candidates who can dominate the media's agenda will be more successful in influencing the public's agenda. These candidates, who will presumably emphasize their strengths in their campaign appeals, may have an easier time winning elections.

The Discussion of Issues in Political Ads and in News Coverage

The analysis of political advertisements shows that women are somewhat more likely to discuss policy matters in their political advertisements. This is most striking in the candidates' attack ads, where 40 percent of all attack ads by female candidates mention issues, while only 26 percent of male candidates' ads discuss issues (p < .01).[15] Yet in the press coverage of Senate campaigns, female candidates do not receive more issue attention than their male counterparts. In fact, male candidates consistently receive more issue coverage, even controlling for the status of the candidates and the competitiveness of the race. Each day, more than four paragraphs about issues are published about male candidates while only three paragraphs about issues are published about female candidates. These results suggest that even though women candidates are more likely than male candidates to discuss their policy views in their campaign appeals, their issue positions receive less press attention.

Women not only spend more time than men discussing issues in their campaign advertisements, but they also emphasize different issues in these campaign appeals. However, these differences in policy emphasis may not be represented in news coverage of their candidacies. By dividing policy issues into "male" and "female" issues based on sex stereotyping research (Gallup 1984; Kahn and Goldenberg 1991; National Women's Political Caucus 1987; Sapiro 1982; Rosenwasser et al. 1987), I examine the correspondence between the issue emphasis in political advertisements and the press. "Male" issues include those issues where men are viewed as more competent (e.g., foreign policy, defense, economics, and agriculture); "female" issues are those where women are considered more capable (e.g., minority rights, environment, abortion, school prayer, drugs, and discussions of social programs).

When we compare issue discussion in political ads with issue coverage in the news, we find that "male" issues dominate press

TABLE 3

Comparison of "Male" and "Female" Issue Emphasis in Spot Ads and in News Coverage*

	MALE CANDIDATES		FEMALE CANDIDATES	
	News Coverage	Spot Ads	News Coverage	Spot Ads
"Male" Issues†	71%[a]	73%[b]	54%[ac]	41%[bc]
"Female" Issues	29%	27%	46%	59%
	(6624:25)‡	(283:25)	(1303:7)	(69:7)

*Cells sharing superscripts are significantly different from each other at the specified p-value. P-values are based on difference in proportions test.

†"Male" issues include foreign policy, defense spending, arms control, foreign trade, farm issues, and the economy; "female" issues include day care, helping the poor, education, health care, women's rights, drug abuse, and the environment.

‡Entries are the number of "male" and "female" issue mentions coded for each candidate type followed by the number of candidates.

a,b $p < .01$ c $p < .05$

coverage of Senate races. Sixty-eight percent of all issue coverage in the news is devoted to "male" issues, while only 32 percent of issue coverage deals with "female" issues. As the data in Table 3 show, the coverage of issues by the press does vary with the candidate's gender, with "female" issues covered more extensively for female candidates than for male candidates. Yet the results also show that issue coverage in the news mirrors male candidates' agendas far more faithfully than those of their female counterparts. Male candidates talk about "male" issues 73 percent of the time in their ads, and news coverage of their candidacies reflects this devotion to "male" issues. Women candidates, on the other hand, prefer "female" issues, discussing these issues almost 60 percent of the time in their campaign ads. Yet news coverage of their campaigns emphasizes "male" issues over "female" issues.[16]

The imperfect correspondence between the female candidates' own agendas and the media's coverage of the candidates' issues may have electoral consequences. In particular, women are likely to concentrate on "female" issues for strategic reasons. Women may emphasize such issues as education and health in their campaigns because (1) they feel that they can deal with these issues better than other issues, or (2) they feel they can deal with these issues better than their male counterparts, or (3) they feel that voters, because of the stereotypes they hold, will believe that women candidates

can handle these issues better than men. Yet because these types of issues receive less attention in the news, people are unlikely to think about these issues when they cast their votes (Erbring, Godenberg, and Miller 1980; Iyengar and Kinder 1987; MacKuen 1981). Given the existence of sex stereotypes, the emphasis on traditional "male" issues by the press may hurt women candidates' chances of election to the U.S. Senate.[17]

The Discussion of Traits in Political Ads and in News Coverage

The candidates' campaign commercials are more likely to emphasize personality traits than the news media. Only about 14 percent of all news coverage mentions the candidates' personalities, while traits are mentioned more than twice as often in the candidates' own campaign ads. These results suggest that voters who get most of their political information from spot ads will be more likely to make trait-based judgments of candidates, as compared with voters who get their political information from the news media (Iyengar and Kinder 1987; Iyengar, Peters and Kinder 1982).

When reporters do discuss the candidates' personalities, they are more likely to emphasize "male" traits when covering men than when covering women. As the data in Table 4 show, "male" traits are emphasized 70 percent of the time when covering male candidates, while only 55 percent of female candidates' trait coverage is

TABLE 4

Comparison of "Male" and "Female" Trait Emphasis In Spot Ads and in News Coverage*

| | MALE CANDIDATES | | FEMALE CANDIDATES | |
	News Coverage	Spot Ads	News Coverage	Spot Ads
"Male" Traits†	70%[a]	71%	55%[ab]	78%[b]
"Female" Traits	30%	29%	45%	22%
	(1090:25)‡	(121:25)	(277:7)	(28:7)

*Cells sharing superscripts are significantly different from each other. P-values are based on the difference in proportions test.
†"Male" traits include the following: independent, objective, strong leader, insensitive, aggressive, ambitious, tough; "female" traits include passive, sensitive, gentle, weak leader, and compassionate, honest.
‡Entries are the number of "male" and "female" trait mentions coded for each candidate type followed by the number of candidates.
a p < .01   b p < .05

devoted to "male" traits. These results suggest that reporters rely on sex stereotypes when covering male and female candidates and largely ignore the candidates' own campaign emphases. Women appear "unstereotypically" in their ads, concentrating almost exclusively on "male" traits, but coverage of their campaigns largely ignores this focus. Just as with issues, male candidates can expect a greater correspondence between the message presented in their ads and the coverage provided in the news.[18] While there is no difference between the trait emphasis by male candidates and the trait emphasis by the press, this is clearly not the case for women candidates.

These results suggest that the news media are more receptive to the messages sent by male candidates. When covering male candidates, reporters emphasize the same personality traits and the same policy areas as the candidates. News coverage of female candidates is much less responsive. Women candidates emphasize "female" issues, but the press prefer to discuss "male" issues, such as foreign policy and economics. Similarly, even though women candidates concentrate almost exclusively on "male" traits in their appeals, the press largely ignore this emphasis.

CONCLUSION

Based on this sample of thirty-eight campaigns, I conclude that male and female candidates for the U.S. Senate adopt campaign strategies that are remarkably similar on certain dimensions and strikingly different on others. First, male and female candidates both prefer to focus on policy matters in their candidate-oriented appeals, yet they rarely take specific stands on issues. Similarly, men and women highlight their own personality strengths in their ads instead of criticizing their opponents on personal grounds.

Yet there are important differences in the campaign appeals of male and female senatorial candidates. These differences range from the candidates' propensity to use "attack" ads to the types of topics emphasized in ads. Men, for example, wage negative campaigns less frequently than women candidates, especially when facing female opponents. Men and women also emphasize different sorts of issues in their campaigns for the U.S. Senate. Men concentrate on economic issues, while women are much more likely to discuss social issues such as education and health policy.

Although men and women stress distinct agendas in their campaign appeals, news coverage of their campaigns does not represent these differences. Women discuss issues more frequently than men, and they also discuss "female" issues in the majority of their ads. Yet news coverage of women's campaigns does not reflect these concerns. Similarly, women stress their leadership and competence in their campaign ads, perhaps as a way of revising voters' images of the "typical" woman candidate. Yet reporters largely ignore this emphasis and choose to describe women candidates in stereotypical terms. This unresponsiveness of the news media, by potentially muting the effectiveness of female candidates' strategies, may hamper the electoral prospects of women candidates for the U.S. Senate.

Appendix: Sample of Senate Candidates

MALE CANDIDATES[19]	FEMALE CANDIDATES
Incumbents	**Incumbents**
Bill Bradley (D) of New Jersey	Paula Hawkins (R) of Florida
Rudy Boshwitz (R) of Minnesota	
William Cohen (R) of Maine	**Challengers**
Alan Cranston (D) of California	
Mark Hatfield (R) of Oregon	Nancy Dick (D) of Colorado
Gordon Humphrey (R) of New Hampshire	Joan A. Growe (D) of Minnesota
Roger Jepsen (R) of Iowa	Margie Hendriksen (D) of Oregon
Carl Levin (D) of Michigan	Judy Koehler (R) of Illinois
Charles Percy (R) of Illinois	Elizabeth Mitchell (D) of Maine
Arlen Specter (R) of Pennsylvania	Mary Mochary (R) of New Jersey
Challengers	**Candidates in Open Races**
Nonnan D'Amours (D) of New Hampshire	Linda Chavez (R) of Maryland
Tom Harkin (D) of Iowa	Millicent Fenwick (R) of New Jersey[19]
Bob Edgar (D) of Pennsylvania	Barbara Mikulski (D) of Maryland
Jack Lousma (R) of Michigan	
Paul Simon (D) of Illinois	
Candidates in Open Races	
Victor Asche (R) of Tennessee	
Christopher Bond (R) of Missouri	
Lloyd Doggett (D) of Texas	
Albert Gore (D) of Tennessee	
Phil Gramm (R) of Texas	
John Kerry (D) of Massachusetts	
Richard Kimball (D) of Arizona	
Ken Kramer (R) of Colorado	
Frank Lautenberg (D) of New Jersey[19]	
John McCain (R) of Arizona	
Harry Reid (D) of Nevada	
Jim Santini (R) of Nevada	
Raymond Shamie (R) of Massachusetts	

ENDNOTES

[1] Political commercials were unavailable for the other women Senate candidates. In order to bolster the number of women candidates in the sample, I included New Jersey's 1982 senatorial candidate, Millicent Fenwick, in the sample. Fenwick was the only woman candidate in 1982 for which advertisements were available. Although the number of female candidates included in the sample is necessarily small, the states included do vary in size and by region.

[2] See the appendix for a list of the Senate candidates included in the sample.

[3] All the political ads used in the analysis were obtained from the Political Commercial Archive at the University of Oklahoma.

[4] A copy of the complete codesheet is available from the author upon request.

[5] The largest circulating newspapers in Texas and Colorado could not be obtained so the state papers with the second largest circulation (the *Houston Post* and the *Denver Post*) were analyzed.

[6] Intercoder reliability was measured throughout the newspaper coding process. Three researchers coded the newspaper content and reliability among the coders was high, never falling below 85 percent agreement and reaching as high as 100 percent agreement for some content categories.

[7] This difference is statistically significant at $p < .01$. All p-values are based on the difference in proportions test unless otherwise noted.

[8] Since women candidates tend to be challengers (between 1984 and 1986, 67 percent of the women who ran for the U.S. Senate were challengers while 39 percent of the male candidates were challengers), some of the differences in campaign appeals may reflect status differences and not gender differences. I check for this possibility throughout the analysis by looking at whether gender differences in campaign appeals remain when we look within status categories (e.g., incumbents, challengers, candidates in open races). In making these comparisons, we can be most confident about comparisons between male and female challengers since the number of cases is greatest here. In contrast, we need to be cautious when drawing comparisons between male and female incumbents since only one female incumbent is included in the sample. Similarly, since women are much more likely than men to run in noncompetitive contests (87 percent of the women senate candidates between 1984 and 1986 ran in non-competitive races while 48 percent of the male candidates ran in noncompetitive races), gender differences in campaign appeals may reflect differences due to the competitiveness of the race. I check for this possibility throughout the analysis.

[9] Of course, the agenda-setting role of political commercials will be most influential if the messages presented in the ads are reiterated in other sources of political communication like the news media. I compare issue discussion in political ads to newspaper coverage later in this paper.

[10] When we control for the competitiveness of the race, we continue to find that women candidates emphasize "male" traits somewhat more often than their male counterparts.

[11] When we control for the competitiveness of the race, we find that women continue to emphasize policy more frequently than male candidates. In noncompetitive races, for example, women emphasize issues in 57 percent of their negative ads while men discuss issues 19 percent of the time ($p < .01$).

[12] Men are somewhat less willing to use personal attacks when running against women. When facing a male opponent, male candidates use personal attacks 18 percent of the time. Yet, when facing female opponents, negative traits are only mentioned 8 percent of the time. This difference is statistically significant ($p < .05$).

[13] To insure comparability, I compare advertising and news content for the thirty-two candidates where both types of media content are available.

[14] An earlier study examining news coverage of U.S. Senate campaigns found that the press cover male and female candidates differently (Kahn and Goldenberg 1991). The results of this study suggest that women candidates receive less coverage and the coverage they do receive concentrates more on their viability and less on their issue positions.

[15] Here we are comparing the percentage of times that candidates mention issues in their attack ads. In Table 2, in contrast, we are comparing the *primary* emphasis of the candidates' attack ads.

[16] Even when we control for the status of the candidates and the competitiveness of the race, we continue to find that the correspondence between the media's message and the candidate's message is greater for male candidates.

[17] The press may concentrate on "male" issues because the public is more concerned with these issues. Yet, studies of agenda-setting show that the public's issue priorities are quite malleable. The research suggests that if the press chose to emphasize issues like health and education policy, these issues would become more important to the public (e.g., Iyengar, Peters, and Kinder 1982; Iyengar and Kinder 1987; MacKuen 1981).

[18] Again, when we control for the competitiveness of the race and the status of the candidates, we continue to find that the correspondence between the media's message and the candidate's message is greater for male candidates. For example, female challengers stress "male" traits in 95 percent of their campaign ads, yet the press discuss "male" traits only 56 percent of the time when covering women challengers. In contrast, male challengers talk about "male" traits 70 percent of the time and the media largely echo this emphasis; the press discuss "male" traits 67 percent of the time when covering male challengers.

[19] The New Jersey Senate race from 1982 was included in the sample to bolster the number of races with female candidates.

REFERENCES

Abelson, R. P., D. R. Kinder, M. D. Peters, and S. T. Fiske. 1982. "Affective and Semantic Components in Political Person Perception."*Journal of Personality and Social Psychology* 42: 619–30.

Aldrich, J. H. 1980: "A Dynamic Model of Presidential Nomination Campaigns." *American Political Science Review* 74: 651–69.

Ansolabehere, S., and S. Iyengar. 1991. "Why Candidates Attack: Effects of Television Advertising in the 1990 California Gubernatorial Campaign." Paper presented at the Annual Meeting of the Western Political Science Association.

Ashmore, R., and F. Del Boca. 1979. "Sex Stereotypes and Implicit Personality Theory: Toward a Cognitive-Social Psychological Conceptualization." *Sex Roles* 5: 219–48.

Barone, M., and G. Ujifusa. 1986. *The Almanac of American Politics.* New York: Dutton.

———. 1988. *The Almanac of American Politics.* New York: Dutton.

Bartels, L. M. 1987. "Candidate Choice and the Dynamics of the Presidential Nominating Process." *American Journal of Political Science* 31: 1–30.

Bernstein, R. 1986. "Why Are There So Few Women in the House?" *Western Political Quarterly* 39: 155–64.

Boles, J., and H. Durio. 1981. "Political Woman and Superwoman: Sex Stereotyping of Females in Elected Office." Paper presented at the Midwest Political Science Association Meeting, Chicago, IL.

Broverman, I. K., S. Vogel, D. Broverman, F. Clarkson, and P. Rosenkrantz. 1974. "Sex Role Stereotypes: A Current Appraisal." *Journal of Social Issues* 28: 59–78.

Carroll, S. J. 1985. *Women as Candidates in American Politics.* Bloomington: Indiana University Press.

Clarke, P., and E. Fredin. 1978. "Newspapers, Television, and Political Reasoning." *Public Opinion Quarterly* 42: 143–60.

Darcy, R., S. Welch, and J. Clark. 1987. *Women, Elections, and Representation.* New York: Longman.

Erbring, L., E. N. Goldenberg, and A. H. Miller. 1980. "Front Page News and Real World Cues: A New Look at Agenda-Setting by the Media." *American Journal of Political Science* 24: 16–49.

Gallup Report. 1984. Vol. 276: 3–4.

Garramone, G. 1986. "Candidate Image Formation: The Role of Information Processing." In Lynda Lee Kaid, Dan Nimmo, and Keith R. Sander[s], eds., *New Perspectives on Political Advertising.* Carbondale: Southern Illinois University Press.

Gertzog, I. 1979. "Changing Patterns of Female Recruitment to the U.S. House of Representatives." *Legislative Studies Quarterly* 4: 429–45.

Goldenberg, E. N., and M. W. Traugott. 1984. *Campaigning for Congress.* Washington, DC: Congressional Quarterly Press.

———. 1987. "Mass Media Effects on Recognizing and Rating Candidates in U.S. Senate Elections." In J. P. Vermeer, ed., *Campaigns in the News: Mass Media and Congressional Elections.* New York: Greenwood Press.

Goldenberg, E. N., M. W. Traugott, and K. F. Kahn. 1988. "Voter Assessments of Presidential and Senatorial Candidates." Paper presented at the Midwest Political Science Association Annual Meeting Chicago, IL.

Graber, D. A. 1989. *Mass Media and American Politics.* Washington, DC: Congressional Quarterly Press.

Hedlund, R. D., P. I. Freeman, K. Hamm, and R. Stein. 1979. "The Electability of Women Candidates: The Effects of Sex Role Stereotypes." *Journal of Politics* 41: 513–24.

Iyengar, S., and D. R. Kinder. 1978. *News That Matters.* Chicago, IL: University of Chicago Press.

Iyengar, S., M. D. Peters, and D. R. Kinder. 1982. "Experimental Demonstrations of the 'Not So Minimal' Consequences of Television News Programs." *American Political Science Review* 76: 848–58.

Joslyn, R. 1984. *Mass Media and Elections.* Reading, MA: Addison-Wesley.

Kahn, K. F. 1992. "Does Being Male Help: An Investigation of Gender and Media Effects in U.S. Senate Races." *Journal of Politics* 54: 2.

Kahn, K. F., and J. G. Geer. 1991. "Putting First Things First: An Investigation of the Impact of Political Advertising." Paper presented at the annual meeting of the Midwest Political Science Association, Chicago, IL.

Kahn, K. F., and E. N. Goldenberg. 1991. "Women Candidates in the News: An Examination of Gender Differences in U.S. Senate Campaign Coverage." *Public Opinion Quarterly* 55: 180–99.

Kaid, L. L., and D. K. Davidson. 1986. "Elements of Videostyle: Candidate Presentations Through Television Advertising." In L. L. Kaid, D. Nimmo, and K. R. Sanders, eds., *New Perspectives on Political Advertising.* Carbondale: Southern Illinois University Press.

Kaid, L. L., and K. R. Sanders. 1978. "Political Television Commercials: An Experimental Study of Type and Length." *Communication Research* 5: 57–70.

Kern, M. 1989. *30-Second Politics: Political Advertising in the 80s.* New York: Praeger.

Kinder, D. R., M. D. Peters, R. P. Abelson, and S. T. Fiske. 1980. "Presidential Prototypes." *Political Behavior* 2: 315–37.

Lake, C. 1984. "Impact of Gender on Campaigns: A Study of Men and Women Candidates in 1982." Prepared for the National Women's Political Caucus, Washington, DC.

MacKuen, M. 1981. "Social Communication and the Mass Policy Agenda." In *More than News*, Beverly Hills: Sage.

Markus, Gregory G. 1982. "Political Attitudes During an Election Year: A Report on the 1980 NES Panel Study." *American Political Science Review* 76: 538–60.

Markus, G. B., and P. E. Converse. 1979. "A Dynamic Simultaneous Equation Model of Electoral Choice." *American Political Science Review* 73: 1055–70.

Miller, Arthur, Martin Wattenberg, [and] Oksana Malanchuk. 1986. "Schematic Assessments of Presidential Candidates." *American Political Science Review* 79: 359–72.

National Women's Political Caucus Survey (NWPC). 1987. Washington, DC.

Patterson, T. E. 1980. *The Mass Media Election*. New York: Praeger.

Patterson, T. E., and R. D. McClure. 1976. *The Unseeing Eye: The Myth of Television Power in National Politics*. New York: Putnam.

Poole, K. T.[,] and L. H. Zeigler. 1985. *Women, Public Opinion, and Politics*. New York: Longman.

Rosenwasser, S. M., R. Rogers, S. Fling, K. Silver-Pickens, and J. Butemeyer. 1987. "Attitudes Toward Women and Men in Politics: Perceived Male and Female Candidate Competencies and Participant Personality Characteristics." *Political Psychology* 8: 191–200.

Sapiro, V. 1982. "If U.S. Senator Baker were a Woman: An Experimental Study of Candidate Images." *Political Psychology* 61–83.

Westlye, M. C. 1991. *Senate Elections and Campaign Intensity*. Baltimore, MD: Johns Hopkins University Press.

Does Attack Advertising Demobilize the Electorate?

Stephen Ansolabehere, Shanto Iyengar, Adam Simon, and Nicholas Valentino

It is generally taken for granted that political campaigns boost citizen's involvement—their interest in the election, awareness of and information about current issues, and sense that individual opinions matter. Since Lazarsfeld's pioneering work (Berelson, Lazarsfeld, and McPhee 1954; Lazarsfeld, Berelson, and Gaudet 1948), it has been thought that campaign activity in connection with recurring elections enables parties and candidates to mobilize their likely constituents and "recharge" their partisan sentiments. Voter turnout is thus considered to increase directly with "the level of political stimulation to which the electorate is subjected" (Campbell et al. 1966, 42; Patterson and Caldeira 1983).

The argument that campaigns are inherently "stimulating" experiences can be questioned on a variety of grounds. American campaigns have changed dramatically since the 1940s and 1950s (see Ansolabehere et al. 1993). It is generally accepted that television has undermined the traditional importance of party organizations, because it permits "direct" communication between candidates and the voters (see Bartels

1988; Polsby 1983; Wattenberg 1984, 1991). All forms of broadcasting, from network newscasts to talk show programs, have become potent tools in the hands of campaign operatives, consultants, and fund-raisers. In particular, paid political advertisements have become an essential form of campaign communication. In 1990, for example, candidates spent more on televised advertising than any other form of campaign communication (Ansolabehere and Gerber 1993).

We are now beginning to realize that the advent of television has also radically changed the nature and tone of campaign discourse. Today more than ever, the entire electoral process rewards candidates whose skills are rhetorical, rather than substantive (Jamieson 1992) and whose private lives and electoral viability, rather than party ties, policy positions, and governmental experience, can withstand media scrutiny (see Brady and Johnston 1987; Lichter, Amundson, and Noyes 1988; Sabato 1991). Campaigns have also turned increasingly hostile and ugly. More often than not, candidates criticize, discredit, or belittle their opponents rather than promoting their own ideas and programs. In the 1988 and 1990 campaigns, a survey of campaign advertising carried out by the *National Journal* found that attack advertisements had become the norm rather than the exception (Hagstrom and Guskind 1988, 1992).

Given the considerable changes in electoral strategy and the emergence of negative advertising as a staple of contemporary campaigns, it is certainly time to question whether campaigns are bound to stimulate citizen involvement in the electoral process. To be sure, there has been no shortage of hand wringing and outrage over the depths to which candidates have sunk, the viciousness and stridency of their rhetoric, and the lack of any systematic accountability for the accuracy of the claims made by the candidates (see Bode 1992; Dionne 1991; Rosen and Taylor 1992). However, as noted by a recent Congressional Research Service survey, there is little evidence concerning the effects of attack advertising on voters and the electoral process (see Neale 1991).

A handful of studies have considered the relationship between campaign advertising and political participation, with inconsistent results. Garramone and her colleagues (1990) found that exposure to negative advertisements did not depress measures of political participation. This study, however, utilized student participants and the candidates featured in the advertisements were fictitious. In addition, participants watched the advertisements in a classroom setting. In contrast to this study, an experiment reported by Basil, Schooler, and Reeves (1991) found that negative advertisements reduced positive attitudes toward both candidates in the race, thereby indirectly reducing political involvement. This study, however, was not conducted during an ongoing campaign and utilized a tiny sample, and the participants could not vote for the target candidates. Finally, Thorson, Christ, and Caywood (1991) reported no differences in voting intention between college students exposed to positive and negative advertisements.

We assert that campaigns can be either mobilizing or demobilizing events, *depending upon the nature of the messages they generate.* Using an experimental design that manipulates advertising tone while holding all other features of the advertisements constant, we demonstrate that exposure to attack advertising in and of itself significantly decreases voter engagement and participation. We then reproduce this result by demonstrating that turnout in the 1992 Senate campaigns was significantly reduced in states where the tone of the campaign was relatively negative. Finally, we address three possible explanations for the demobilizing effects of negative campaigns.

★ EXPERIMENTAL DESIGN

There is a vast literature, both correlational and experimental, concerning the effects of televised advertisements (though not specifically negative advertisements) on public opinion (for a detailed review, see Kosterman 1991). This literature, however, is plagued by significant methodological shortcomings. The limitations of the opinion survey as a basis for identifying the effects of mass communications have been well documented (see Bartels 1993; Hovland 1959). Most importantly, surveys cannot reliably assess exposure to campaign advertising. Nor is most of the existing experimental work fully valid. The typical experimental study, by relying on fictitious candidates as the "target" stimuli, becomes divorced from the real world of campaigns. Previous experimental studies thus shed little evidence on the interplay between voters' existing information and preferences and their reception of campaign advertisements. When experimental work has focused on real candidates and their advertisements, it is difficult to capture the effects of particular characteristics of advertising because the manipulation confounds several such characteristics (Ansolabehere and Iyengar 1991; Garramone 1985; Pfau and Kenski 1989). That is, a Clinton spot and Bush spot differ in any number of features (the accompanying visuals, background sound, the voice of the announcer, etc.) in addition to the content of the message. Thus there are many possible explanations for differences in voters' reactions to these spots.

To overcome the limitations of previous research, we developed a rigorous but realistic experimental design for assessing the effects of advertising tone or valence[1] on public opinion and voting. Our studies all took place during ongoing political campaigns (the 1990 California gubernatorial race, the 1992 California Senate races, and the 1993 Los Angeles mayoral race) and featured "real" candidates who were in fact advertising heavily on television and "real" voters (rather than college sophomores) who on election day would have to choose between the candidates whose advertisements they watched. Our experimental manipulations were professionally produced and could not (unless the viewer were a political consultant) be distinguished from the flurry of advertisements confronting the typical voter. In addition, our manipulation was unobtrusive; we embedded the experimental advertisement into a 15-minute local newscast.

The most distinctive feature of our design is its ability to capture the casual effects of a particular feature of campaign advertisement—in this case, advertising tone or valence. The advertisements that we produced were identical in all respects but tone and the candidate sponsoring the advertisement. In the 1992 California Senate primaries, for example, viewers watched a 30-second advertisement that either promoted or attacked on the general trait of "integrity." The visuals featured a panoramic view of the Capitol Building, the camera then zooming in to a close-up of an unoccupied desk inside a Senate office. In the "positive" treatments (using the example of candidate Dianne Feinstein), the text read by the announcer was as follows:

> For over 200 years the United States Senate has shaped the future of America and the world. Today, California needs honesty, compassion, and a voice for all the people in the U.S. Senate. As mayor of San Francisco, Dianne Feinstein proposed new government ethics rules. She *rejected* large campaign contributions from special interests. And Dianne Feinstein *supported* tougher penalties on savings-and-loan crooks.
>
> California *needs* Dianne Feinstein in the U.S. Senate.

In the "negative" version of this Feinstein spot, the text was modified as follows:

> For over 200 years the United States Senate has shaped the future of America and the world. Today, California needs honesty, compassion, and a voice for all the people in the U.S. Senate. As state controller, Gray Davis *opposed* new government ethics rules. He *accepted* large campaign contributions from special interests. And Gray Davis opposed tougher penalties on savings-and-loan crooks.
>
> California *can't afford a politician* like Gray Davis in the U.S. Senate.

By holding the visual elements constant and by using the same announcer, we were able to limit differences between the conditions to differences in tone.[2] With appropriate modifications to the wording, the identical pair of advertisements was also shown on behalf of Feinstein's primary opponent, Controller Gray Davis, and for the various candidates contesting the other Senate primaries.

In short, our experimental manipulation enabled us to establish a much tighter degree of control over the tone of campaign advertising than had been possible in previous research. Since the advertisements watched by viewers were identical in all other respects and because we randomly assigned participants to experimental conditions, any differences between conditions may be attributed only to the tone of the political advertisement (see Rubin 1974).

The Campaign Context

Our experiments spanned a variety of campaigns, including the 1990 California gubernatorial election, both of the state's 1992 U.S. Senate races, and the 1993 mayoral election in Los Angeles. In the case of the senatorial campaigns, we examined three of the four primaries and both general election campaigns. The campaigns we examined were all characterized by extensive broadcast advertising and, in most cases, by frequent use of negative or attack advertising.

We used the same design for all of the campaigns under investigation. That is, we manipulated advertising valence within the identical audiovisual framework. The content of the experimental advertisement, however, varied across campaigns. In general, the experimental advertisements focused on issues or themes that were particularly salient in the various campaigns. In the 1990 gubernatorial race, we created advertisements that dealt with the issues of crime and pollution. In the positive conditions, the sponsoring candidate was presented as "tough" on crime and a protector of the environment. In the negative versions, the opponent was depicted as "soft" on crime and indifferent to the quality of the environment. (Samples of the text and accompanying visuals of the experimental manipulations are provided in Appendix A.)

The experimental advertisements for the 1992 senate primaries dealt with either the candidates' personal integrity or competence. In the case of integrity (discussed in the given examples), the advertisement described the candidate as either honest and a supporter of campaign reform or as dishonest and an opponent of reform. In the case of competence, the advertisement asked voters to consider the sponsor's "ability, determination, and leadership" (or the absence of these characteristics in the opponent).

During the Senate general election campaign, we shifted the focus of the advertisements to the issue of unemployment. The condition of the state's economy and the significant loss of jobs (unemployment had reached 10% in September) were the overriding issues in both races. All four candidates aired advertisements promising to reverse the state's economic decline. Our treatment advertisements depicted the sponsor or opponent as an advocate or critic of government-subsidized job training and industrial modernization programs.

Finally, one of our studies concerned the nonpartisan election for mayor of Los Angeles between Richard Riordan and Michael Woo. Here, the manipulation dealt with the candidates' integrity and discussed the degree to which the candidates' campaign promises to increase job opportunities and reform city government were consistent with their past actions.

In summary, our experimental advertisements dealt with a variety of campaigns and themes. In all cases, however, the advertisements corresponded to the actual focus of campaigns. In their content, the experimental advertisements closely reflected the advertisements aired by the candidates.

Subjects and Procedure

We recruited subjects by multiple methods including advertisements placed in local newspapers, flyers distributed in shopping malls and other public venues, announcements in employer newsletters, and by calling names from voter registration lists. Subjects were promised payment of $15 for participation in an hour-long study of "selective perception" of local news programs.

Although the "sample" was obviously nonrandom, our participants resembled the composition of the greater Los Angeles area. Across all the experiments, 56% of the participants were male, 53% were white, 26% were black, 12% were Hispanic, and 10% were Asian. The median age was 34. Forty-nine percent of the participants claimed affiliation with the Democratic party, 24% were Republicans, and 21% were independents. Forty-four percent were college graduates, with the balance being evenly divided between high school graduates and individuals with some college.[3]

The experiments were conducted at two separate locations: West Los Angeles and Costa Mesa (Orange County). The former is a heavily Democratic area, while the latter, an affluent suburb of Los Angeles, is predominantly Republican. The experimental facilities in both locations were identical—a three-room office suite consisting of two viewing rooms and a separate room for completion of questionnaires (in addition to a reception area). The viewing rooms were furnished casually with sofas and easy chairs. Participants could browse through newspapers and magazines and snack on cookies and coffee.

When participants telephoned the facility they were scheduled for a particular time period of their choice. Experimental sessions were available from 10:00 A.M. to 8:00 P.M., Monday through Saturday. The typical session consisted of two to three participants.

On arrival, subjects were given an instruction sheet informing them that the study concerned selective perception of local newscasts.

They then completed a short pretest questionnaire concerning their social background, media activities, and political interest. Following completion of the pretest, participants were taken to a viewing room, where, depending upon the condition to which they had been assigned.[4] They watched a 15-minute (complete with commercials) videotape recording of a recent local newscast (described to participants as having been selected at random).

The experimental or "treatment" advertisement was inserted into the first commercial break midway through the tape. The political spot was shown always in the middle position in a three-advertisement break. As described, the advertisements in the various conditions were identical in all respects except for the factors of valence and source.

Following completion of the videotape, participants completed a lengthy posttest questionnaire tapping their beliefs and opinions on a wide range of campaign issues. Of course, we also ascertained participants' voting intentions and general level of involvement in the campaign. On completion of the posttest, participants were debriefed and paid.

★ ANALYSIS AND RESULTS

We shall limit our analyses to the effects of negative advertising on intention to vote. In our posttest questionnaire, we ascertained whether participants were registered to vote. Using registration as a filter, we then asked, "Looking forward to the November election, do you intend to vote?" (In the case of the primary election study, the question was worded accordingly.) We identified "likely voters" as those who were both registered and who stated their intention of voting.[5]

In analyzing our experimental data, we pooled the gubernatorial study, the various senatorial studies, and the mayoral study into a single data set. While the effects of attack advertising are tempered by campaign-specific constraints, including the background of the candidates and the specific content of their advertising, we are especially interested in the average effect, if any, of advertising valence.[6] Moreover, pooling the separate studies makes it possible to obtain reliable estimates of the demobilizing effects of attack advertising.

After pooling, we compared the percentage of viewers classified as likely voters among participants who watched the positive and negative versions of the experimental advertisements. The demobilization hypothesis predicts that exposure to negative advertising will lower the percentage of likely voters. Among those who watched a positive advertisement, 64% intended to vote. Among participants who saw a product advertisement instead of a political one, 61% intended to vote. Among participants who were exposed to the negative versions of the campaign advertisement, only 58% were likely to vote. A one-way analysis of variance yielded an F-statistic of 2.2, significant at the .11 level.[7]

The decision to vote depends upon aspects of the campaign other than advertising valence. In addition, some people are more likely to vote than others, regardless of the nature of the campaign. To capture these contextual and dispositional effects on turnout, we regressed intention to vote (using a logistic regression) on advertising tone and a set of dummy variables corresponding to specific elections, as well as various indicators of individual differences. Because the positive and negative advertisements exerted symmetric effects on voting intention, we specified advertising tone as a trichotomy corresponding to positive advertisement (+1), no political advertisement (0), and negative advertisement (-1). The individual difference variables included the frequency with which people said they followed public affairs, prior voting history, the "match" between viewers' and the candidates' gender and party identification, age, race, and education. This multivariate analysis, in essence, estimates the independent effects of the campaign advertising stimulus on voting intention above and beyond campaign-specific influences and personal predispositions.

Table 1 presents the results of two logistic regressions corresponding to a full model (with all control variables included) and a restricted model (with non-significant controls excluded). The baseline (constant) in this specification represents the 1993 Los Angeles mayoral race. Off-year local elections tend to be characterized

TABLE 1

Logistic Regression Estimates of the Effect
of Tone on Intentions to Vote
in the 1990, 1992, and 1993 Experiments

VARIABLE	MODEL	
	Full	Restricted
Constant	-.212 (.331)	-.230 (.331)
Advertising tone[a]	.110 (.055)	.114 (.036)
Experiments		
1990 gubernatorial	.434 (.203)	.477 (.195)
1992 primary	.404 (.179)	.335 (.168)
1992 general election	1.221 (.208)	.778 (.138)
1988 turnout	1.746 (.141)	1.614 (.128)
Follow gov't. affairs	.497 (.059)	.501 (.058)
Independent	-1.112 (.108)	-1.122 (.108)
Same party	-.028 (.087)	—
Same gender	-.033 (.117)	—
Age	.002 (.004)	—
Education	.100 (.068)	.129 (.058)
Female	.034 (.119)	—
White	.346 (.131)	.353 (.128)
Log likelihood	-905.5	-906.7
% correctly predicted	78.2	78.1

Note: Entries are logit coefficients with standard errors
in parentheses.
N = 1,655.
[a]Coded 1 for positive ad, 0 for control ad, -1 for negative ad.

by low levels of citizen involvement. Not surprisingly, the 1990 gubernatorial, the 1992 Senate primary, and the 1992 Senate general elections all registered higher turnout.

The individual difference factor with the greatest ability to discriminate between likely and unlikely voters, as expected, was prior voting history. Participants who reported voting in the 1988 election were much more likely to be classified as likely voters in 1992–93 than those who reported not having voted. Partisans, those with higher levels of political interest, the more educated, and whites were also characterized by significantly higher levels of voting intention.

From our perspective, the most important result in Table 1 is the effect of advertising tone on voting intentions. In both equations, a one-sided t-test showed that advertising tone significantly (at the .05 level) affected turnout. Converting the logistic coefficient on advertising tone into a linear probability shows that those participants exposed to the negative version of the advertisement were 2.5% less likely to vote than those exposed to no political advertisement. Conversely, the positive version of the advertisement increased voting intention by 2.5 percentage points. In short, the initial estimate of the demobilization effect survived the multiple controls.

Overall, the experimental results demonstrate that exposure to negative (as opposed to positive) advertising depresses intention to vote by 5%. Considering the scope of our experimental manipulation (a single 30-second advertisement embedded in a 15-minute newscast) and the variety of campaigns examined, these effects seem remarkable. Despite our best efforts at experimental realism, it is possible that the effect has been magnified by some aspect of the research design. It is important, therefore, to place the experimental findings in the context of the world of actual campaigns.

Replicating the Experimental Results

To reconstruct our experimental framework in the real world, we measured the tone of the campaign in each of the 34 states holding a Senate election in 1992. Senate campaigns are especially appropriate for our purposes because the candidates rely heavily on advertising

(Ansolabehere and Gerber 1993). Moreover, four of our seven experiments focused on Senate campaigns.

Our indicator of campaign tone was based on a systematic content analysis of news coverage of the various Senate races. We searched through the NEXIS and DATATIMES data bases for all newspaper and newsmagazine articles bearing on the Senate campaigns in general and the candidates' advertisements in particular. This search yielded a total of over 2,500 articles ranging from a high of 1,000 on the Feinstein-Seymour contest in California to a low of 28 in the case of the Idaho race. Based on a reading of the news coverage, campaigns were classified into one of three categories: generally positive in tone (scored 1); mixed (scored 0); and generally negative in tone (scored -1). The classification scheme is described in Appendix B, along with each state's tone score.

As our indicator of turnout, we simply computed the votes cast for U.S. Senate and divided by the state's voting-age population. In addition to turnout, we also examined ballot *roll-off* in the Senate elections. For each relevant state, we subtracted the total number of votes cast for senator from the total cast for president and divided by the latter. The roll-off indicator has two distinct advantages. First, roll-off is a campaign-specific effect indicating the degree to which people who were sufficiently motivated to vote in the presidential election chose to abstain in the Senate race. Second, because roll-off uses the presidential vote as a baseline, it adjusts for a variety of state-related differences (e.g., demographic factors, political culture and party competition), which affect the level of voting turnout.[8]

Turnout in senatorial elections depends upon a variety of influences in addition to the tone of the campaign. These include the competitiveness of the race, the volume (or "decibel level") of the campaign, and the electorate's sense of civic duty. (For a thorough discussion, see Rosenstone and Hansen 1993). Our measure of the volume of the campaign was the level of campaign spending by incumbents and challengers (measured in logarithms). Competitiveness or closeness was measured by the squared difference between the Republican and Democratic shares of the total vote. Lastly,

to incorporate differences in civic duty and other relevant orientations, we also controlled for per capita income, turnout in the 1988 presidential election, percentage college-educated, region (South, non-South), and the census form mail-back rate.[9]

Having compiled the turnout, roll-off, and campaign tone indicators, we proceeded to replicate the experimental results. Table 2 presents the results from the full and restricted multiple regression analyses of turnout and roll-off. Following the analysis of the experimental data, the tone variable was specified as a trichotomy (negative tone = -1, mixed = 0, positive tone = 1). This specification measures the deviation in turnout and roll-off of the positive and negative campaign tone categories from the mixed-tone category.[10]

Do Senate races characterized by relatively negative campaigns have lower turnout and higher roll-off rates than races in which the campaign is more positive in tone? For both turnout and roll-off, we found significant effects of campaign tone. Negative campaigns decreased turnout by 2%. (This also means that positive campaigns boosted turnout by 2%, for a total difference of 4%.) Negative campaigns also increased ballot roll-off by 1.2% and vice-versa. Since the demobilization hypothesis is directional, we resorted to one-tailed tests (i.e., negative campaigns decrease turnout and increase roll-off, while positive campaigns increase turnout and decrease roll-off). The t-statistics for this hypothesis were 3.64 for turnout and -2.26 for roll-off, both significant at the .05 level.[11]

The use of both experimental and nonexperimental methods to measure the very same naturally occurring phenomena is highly unusual in the social sciences. It is even more unusual if both methods yield equivalent results. In our study, the aggregate-level analysis of turnout and roll-out in the 1992 Senate elections and the experimental studies of negative advertising converge: negative campaigns tend to demobilize the electorate.

Psychological Correlates

That attack advertisements discourage people from voting raises questions about the

TABLE 2

Regression Estimates of the Effect of Tone on Turnout and Roll-off in the 1992 Senate Elections

INDEPENDENT VARIABLE	TURNOUT[a]		ROLL-OFF[b]	
	Full Model	Restricted	Full Model	Restricted
Constant	-.294 (.171)	-.295 (.124)	.157 (.173)	.150 (.040)
Campaign tone[c]	.020 (.006)	.021 (.006)	-.011 (.006)	-.012 (.005)
1988 turnout	.550 (.101)	.571 (.090)	.046 (.102)	—
Per capita income	.010 (.027)	—	.048 (.027)	.049 (.019)
Mail-back rate	.337 (.149)	.340 (.125)	-.058 (.151)	—
Southern state	.048 (.015)	.047 (.013)	-.014 (.015)	-.016 (.013)
% College-educated	.120 (.099)	.172 (.076)	-.215 (.100)	-.247 -(.067)
Log challenger $	.001 (.005)	—	-.011 (.005)	-.010 (.004)
Log incumbent $	.013 (.007)	.011 (.006)	-.004 (.007)	—
Open seat	.011 (.012)	—	-.009 (.012)	—
(Non)closeness	-.053 (.046)	-.068 (.039)	.058 (.046)	.069 (.037)
R²	.94	.94	.67	.64
SS residuals	.0099	.0102	.101	.0112

Note: Entries are multiple regression coefficients with standard errors in parentheses. N = 34.
[a]Total Votes for Senate Voting-age Population.
[b](Total Votes for President – Total Votes for Senate)/(Total Votes for President).
[c]1 = positive tone, 0 = mixed tone, -1 = negative tone.

psychological underpinnings of this effect. One possibility is that partisanship mediates the effects of attack advertisements on turnout. It is generally thought that campaign messages resonate especially strongly among supporters or proponents of the source of the message. Campaigns thus have the effect of reinforcing or crystallizing existing partisan loyalties. Extending this argument to attack advertising implies the obverse. That is, the intention to vote among supporters of the candidate airing the negative advertisement will be unchanged, since the message provides no reasons to vote for their candidate. On the other hand, voting intention should be weakened among supporters of the candidate who is attacked, since the message provides these partisans with reasons not to vote for their candidate.

If attack advertisements demobilize on a partisan basis, we should find a significant interaction effect between advertising valence and viewers' party identification. We thus reestimated the logistic regression presented in Table 1, this time including the appropriate interaction (valence x same party). The results revealed that the interaction term was nonsignificant and had the wrong sign.[12] Partisanship does not mediate the demobilizing effects of attack advertising; supporters of the source and target candidates are not affected differently.

An alternative account of the demobilization effect is that attack advertising generates blanket negativity toward both candidates. According to this "plague-on-both-your-houses" explanation, voters not only become more critical of the target of the attack but turn against the sponsor as well (for some evidence of this effect, see Basil, Schooler, and Reeves 1991). We investigated this possibility by examining participants' evaluations of the personal traits of both the sponsor and the target of the attack advertisements.[13] Our results indicated that attack advertisements generally "work." That is, ratings of the target were generally less positive after participants watched the attack. Ratings of the sponsor, however, were generally unaffected, suggesting that participants did not penalize candidates for airing negative messages.[14]

The fact that attack advertisements do not demobilize on a partisan basis and do not induce negativity towards both candidates suggests a third explanation for demobilization. Negative advertising may affect voting intent by conveying cues not about the candidates but about the nature of political campaigns and the political influence of ordinary citizens. Perhaps the act of attacking another candidate in a 30-second advertisement denigrates the entire process.

To explore this possibility, we measured our participants' sense of political efficacy—their beliefs in the responsiveness of public officials and electoral institutions to popular will. We used four questions, coded the responses to each as either efficacious (1) or inefficacious (0) and computed the average response to all four items.[15] Among viewers who were exposed to the positive versions of the campaign advertisement, the mean efficacy score was .24. The mean was no different (.23) among participants in the control group. In the case of viewers

who were exposed to the negative versions of the advertisement, the mean dropped to .19. The F-statistic from the one-way analysis of variance was significant at the .02 level.[16] In short, exposure to campaign attacks makes voters disenchanted with the business of politics as usual.

In summary, we have considered three possible explanations for the demobilizing effects of attack advertisements: partisan demobilization, a plague-on-both-houses effect, and general cynicism. Our evidence points toward the third. Among our experimental participants, exposure to attack advertising significantly weakened confidence in the responsiveness of electoral institutions and public officials. As campaigns become more negative and cynical, so does the electorate.

CONCLUSION

Taken together, our studies demonstrate that attack advertising extracts a toll on electoral participation. In the experiments, voting intention dropped by 5% when participants were shown an attack advertisement in place of a positive advertisement. Our aggregate-level replication of the experimental results suggests that Senate turnout in 1992 was roughly 4% lower when the candidates waged relatively negative campaigns. Since the scope of the experimental manipulations never exceeded a single advertisement, our estimates of the demobilizing effects of campaign attacks may be conservative. Over the course of two or three weeks of sustained negative advertising, the flight of voters can be more substantial.

The effects of attack advertising on the decision to vote have significant implications for our understanding of the impact of campaigns on electoral outcomes. Voter withdrawal in response to negative advertising also raises questions concerning the legitimate and fair uses of broadcast advertising.[17]

The most important implication of these results is that in the era of media campaigns, *both* surges and declines in turnout can be generated by high-intensity campaigns. Candidates with sufficient resources can, through the use of negative messages, keep voters away from the polls. Campaigns are not inherently mobilizing forces, and the secular decline in presidential and midterm voter turnout since 1960 (for evidence, see Rosenstone and Hansen 1993) may be attributed, in part, to the increasingly negative tone of national campaigns.

Finally, this research raises normative questions concerning the trade-off between the right to political expression and the right to vote. Should candidates be free to use advertising techniques that have the effect of reducing levels of voter turnout? In the case of publicly financed presidential campaigns, is it legitimate for candidates to use public funds in ways that are likely to discourage voting? How do we weigh the public interest in free political expression against the competing public interest in widespread public participation? When, if ever, should politicians' expression be restrained or subjected to incentives to modify its form or content?

In other areas of public communication, allegations of "antisocial" effects have prompted extensive analysis and debate. In some areas, the outcome has been governmental regulation. Thus the tobacco companies have been banned from using the airwaves for certain forms of commercial speech and are required to include mandated health warnings in their print advertisements. Direct regulation of political speech, which is at the core of the values protected by the First Amendment, is probably both impossible as a matter of law and undesirable as a matter of policy. The classic remedy in this society for injurious speech is simply "more speech." However, there is precedent in the law governing the broadcast media requiring that "equal time" be given to the targets of certain "personal attacks" (see Ferris and Leahy 1990). Possibly, new regulations governing the broadcast media ensuring that the targets of attack advertisements have reasonable opportunity to respond (regardless of their own financial resources) should be considered. Ohio and other states are currently experimenting with "truth in political advertising" guidelines designed to make candidates think twice before resorting to false or misleading advertising. However, approaches that simply ensure that there will be "more speech" miss the essential point raised by

this research, which is that negative advertising impacts adversely on voting; remedies that can only multiply the number of negative advertisements will exacerbate, rather than address, the essential problem.

The more realistic approach to influencing the tone of campaign advertising rests on voluntary or incentive-based restraints. There have been several instances in which public controversy over the content of entertainment programming has prodded the networks, local stations, or record companies to withdraw the program in question. Similar reasoning is embodied in legislation pending in Congress that seeks to reform campaign advertising. (For a discussion of recent legislative efforts, see O'Neill 1992.) One bill would impose a double standard on advertising rates under which only "positive" advertisements would be entitled to the "lowest unit rate" rule. Other suggestions include the so-called in-person rule, under which the candidates would be required to deliver their attack statements in person (on camera).

A third set of suggestions for reform addresses the use of media "monitoring." In the aftermath of the 1988 campaign, the press decided to scrutinize the candidates' paid messages (in the form of "ad watches," "truth boxes," and the like). Anticipation of critical news coverage may deter candidates from relying heavily on attack messages. To this point, however, there is no reliable evidence concerning the effects of these monitoring effects on voter response to advertising.

We do not yet understand the implications of these various approaches. Some would certainly raise objections from civil libertarians, others would be objectionable to those concerned with political competitiveness. As in the case of campaign finance reform, broadcast advertising reform may work to benefit those in office at the expense of challengers. Although providing incentives for campaigns to air "positive" messages provides no assurance that these messages will be more substantive, verifiable, or honest, they would, at least, be less likely to deter voting. While the case for broadcast advertising reform has yet to be made, the relationship between negative advertising and voting suggests that these issues are worth further research and discussion.

★ APPENDIX A:
SAMPLES OF EXPERIMENTAL ADVERTISEMENTS

The wording and visuals used in two of our studies appear below. The changes associated with the negative versions of the advertisements are given in parentheses.

1990 Gubernatorial Study: Crime

Text. It's happening right now in your neighborhood. A generation of youth slowly dying. _____ is (is not) the candidate who intends to stop this tragedy and preserve California's future. As mayor of _____, _____ added (reduced the number of) police officers, constructed (blocked) new jails, and fought hard against drugs (opposed drug education programs). The result: major crime rates fell (increased) by 12%. His (her) record won the endorsement (was condemned by) the California Association of Police Chiefs. They know _____ will push for (will oppose) tougher sentencing and strengthen (weaken) our state's justice system.

Visuals. Schoolchildren on playground; addict injecting heroin; body bag being removed from crime scene; police officers outside courthouse; interior of prison cell; candidate logo.

1992 Senate Study: Unemployment

Text. Since 1990, California has lost two-and-a-half million jobs. The state now has the highest unemployment rate in the nation. California needs elected officials who will end the recession. _____ will work (has done nothing) to bring jobs back to our state. As a U.S. Senator, _____ will introduce legislation (_____ opposes legislation) to increase funding for job training programs and to give California companies incentives to modernize and expand their factories and plants. California needs _____ (can't afford) _____ in the U.S. Senate.

Visuals. Closed factory; graph showing state's unemployment rate; lines at unemployment office; picture of candidate (opponent); factory workers assembling planes; workers on construction site; candidate logo.

★ APPENDIX B:
CLASSIFICATION OF 1992 SENATE CAMPAIGNS ACCORDING TO ADVERTISING TONE

We examined a subset of the NEXIS and DATATIMES data bases that contained full-text reproductions of articles from more than 30 major daily newspapers and five politically oriented magazines (e.g., the *Cook Political Report*, the *Roll Call*, and the *Hotline*). A separate search was conducted for all 34 senatorial campaigns. The search was designed to access all articles about the campaign printed after the primary and before the general election. When the search produced more than 150 articles (as was the case for seven races), then a further search command focusing on campaign advertising was added. This procedure elicited a total of 2,573 articles.

Each article was read by a graduate student coder who specifically looked for discussion of campaign tone. The coder followed a strict scheme in order to place each race into one of the three campaign-tone categories. If a majority of the tone-related references to a campaign were negative (e.g., it was characterized as being nasty, dirty, or vicious and provided specific examples of negative attacks from each of the race's candidates), the race was coded as negative. If at least three articles specifically mentioned that one of the Senate candidates was deliberately refraining from making a negative response to the opponent's attacks and no later article contradicted this information, then the race was coded as mixed. Finally, when the news coverage yielded no discernible information about negative campaign tone, the race was coded as positive.

We validated our news-based classification scheme by asking two major political consultants (David Hill, Republican, and Mark Mellman, Democrat) to rate each of the Senate campaigns on the same three-point scale. The consultants disagreed with our classification in only one instance (Kentucky), and we deferred to their expertise. (The analysis is unchanged if Kentucky is eliminated from the analysis.) Each state's tone score is shown in the following list:

Negative Tone	Mixed Tone	Positive Tone
Arkansas	Alabama	Alaska
California	Arizona	Hawaii
(6-yr. seat)	Florida	Idaho
California	Illinois	Iowa
(2-yr. seat)	Missouri	Kansas
Colorado	Oklahoma	Maryland
Connecticut		Nevada
Georgia		North Dakota
Indiana		South Dakota
Kentucky		Utah
Louisiana		Vermont
New Hampshire		Wisconsin
New York		
North Carolina		
Ohio		
Oregon		
Pennsylvania		
South Carolina		
Washington		

(Note that the California 6-year seat was contested between Boxer and Herschenson and the 2-year seat, between Feinstein and Seymour, and that the Louisiana general election was uncontested.)

NOTES

[1] We use these terms interchangeably to describe whether the advertisement, or the campaign as a whole, focuses on a candidate's positive aspects or on the opponent's liabilities and faults.

[2] In addition to minimizing the visual differences in the advertisement, we also used identical logos, in which the sponsoring candidate's name appeared in large red letters against a brown backdrop.

[3] Using a weighted average of Los Angeles and Orange counties as the baseline, the demographics for our sample match closely for age (median of 34 versus 31), gender (44% vs. 51% male), race (52% vs. 47% white), and partisanship (49% identifying Democratic vs. 47% registration). Our participants deviated in the local area in two respects: 26% of our participants were African-American (compared to 10% in Los Angeles and Orange counties), and 44% were college graduates (compared to 24% for the local area).

[4] Random assignment of participants to experimental conditions was used throughout. The use of random assignment assures (subject to the rules of probability) that differences in the dependent variable can be attributed only to the experimental manipulation (see Campbell and Stanley 1969, 25). We took the additional precaution of controlling for a number of background variables considered predictive of participation, including partisanship, prior voting history, age, and education.

[5] Responses to the two questions were generally cumulative; that is, few people who said they were not registered indicated an intention to vote. These respondents were classified as unlikely voters.

[6] For a more detailed analysis of the effects of advertising valence in specific campaigns, see Ansolabehere, Iyengar, and Valentino 1993.

[7] The number of cases was 1,716. Since the F-statistic is nondirectional, that is a conservative test of the demobilization hypothesis.

[8] The average roll-off in the 1992 Senate elections (rounded to the nearest thousand) was 127,000, with a maximum of 609,000 and a minimum of -13,000. In percentage terms, roll-off averaged 4.9% with a range of -1.8% to 11.6%.

[9] The Bureau of the Census mails forms to every resident in each state. The mail-back rate is the fraction of forms that are completed and returned.

[10] A simple F-test revealed that the symmetry restriction was justified.

[11] There are a variety of other interesting results in this analysis, but since we are especially interested in the effects of campaign tone, we set them aside for future consideration.

[12] These results are available from the authors.

[13] Participants rated the candidates' intelligence, honesty, compassion, leadership, toughness, arrogance, weakness, and deviousness. We formed an index by subtracting the number of negative ratings from the number of positive ratings.

[14] These results are available from the authors.

[15] The questions asked participants to agree or disagree with the following statements: (1) "Generally speaking, those who get elected to pubic office keep in touch with the people in their constituencies"; (2) "In this country, politics works for the benefits of a few special interests, rather than the public good;" (3) "Most politicians are willing to tackle the real problems facing America;"

(4) "Having elections makes government responsive to the views of the people."

[16] The F-statistic was 4.0, with 1,716 cases.

[17] It is possible, of course, that negative advertising also exerts prosocial effects not tapped by our studies. For instance, there is some evidence: that negative advertisements allow voters to differentiate more readily between candidates' issue positions, thus facilitating "issue voting" (see Garramone et al. 1990; Patterson and McClure 1976).

REFERENCES

Ansolabehere, Stephen, and Alan Gerber. N.d. "The Mismeasure of Campaign Spending." *Journal of Politics*. Forthcoming.

Ansolabehere, Stephen, and Shanto Iyengar. 1991. "The Electoral Effects of Issues and Attacks in Campaign Advertising." Presented at the annual meeting of the American Political Science Association, Washington.

Ansolabehere, Stephen, Shanto Iyengar, and Nick Valentino. 1993. "The Effects of Campaign Advertising on Voter Turnout." University of California, Los Angeles. Typescript.

Bartels, Larry M. 1988. *Presidential Primaries and the Dynamics of Public Choice*. Princeton: Princeton University Press.

Bartels, Larry M. 1993. "Messages Received: The Political Impact of Media Exposure." *American Political Science Review* 87: 267–85.

Basil, Michael, Caroline Schooler, and Byron Reeves. 1991. "Positive and Negative Political Advertising: Effectiveness of Advertisements and Perceptions of Candidate." *In Television and Political Advertising*, vol. 1, *Psychological Processes,* ed. Frank Biocca. Hillsdale, NJ: Erlbaum.

Berelson, Bernard, Paul Lazarsfeld, and William McPhee. 1954. *Voting: A Study of Opinion Formation in a Presidential Campaign*. Chicago: University of Chicago Press.

Bode, Kenneth. 1992. "Pull the Plug, Empower the Voters." *Quill* 80; 10–14.

Brady, Henry, and Richard Johnston. 1987. "What's the Primary Message: Horse Race or Issue Journalism?" *In Media and Momentum*, ed. Gary R. Orren and Nelson W. Polsby. Chatham: Chatham House.

Campbell, Angus, et al. 1966. *Elections and the Political Order*. New York; Wiley.

Campbell, Donald T., and Julian C. Stanley. 1969. *Experimental and Quasi-Experimental Designs for Research*. Chicago: Rand-McNally.

Dionne, E. J., Jr. 1991. *Why Americans Hate Politics*. New York: Simon & Schuster.

Ferris, Charles, and Terrance Leahy. 1990. "Red Lions, Tigers, and Bears: Broadcast Contest Regulation and the First Amendment." *Catholic University Law Review* 38:309.

Garramone, Gina M. 1985. "Effects of Negative Political Advertising: The Roles of Sponsor and Rebuttal." *Journal of Broadcasting and Electronic Media* 29:147–59.

Garramone, Gina M., Charles K. Atkin, Bruce E. Pinkleton, and Richard T. Cole. 1990. "Effects of Negative Advertising on the Political Process." *Journal of Broadcasting and Electronic Media* 34:299–311.

Hagstrom, Jerry, and Robert Guskind. 1988. "In the Gutter." *National Journal,* 5 November, 2782–90.

Hagstrom, Jerry, and Robert Guskind. 1992. "Airborne Attacks." *National Journal,* 31 October, 2477–82.

Hovland, Carl. 1959. "Reconciling Conflicting Results from Survey and Experimental Studies of Attitude Change." *American Psychologist* 14:8–17.

Jamieson, Kathleen H. 1992. *Dirty Politics: Deception, Distraction, and Democracy*. New York: Oxford University Press.

Kosterman, Richard J. 1991. "Political Spot Advertising and Routes to Persuasion: The Role of Symbolic Content." Ph.D. diss., University of California, Los Angeles.

Lazarsfeld, Paul, Bernard Berelson, and Hazel Gaudet. 1948. *The People's Choice*. 2d ed. New York: Columbia University Press.

Lichter, S. Robert, Daniel Amundson, and Richard Noyes. 1988. *The Video Campaign*. Washington: American Enterprise Institute.

Neale, Thomas. 1991. *Negative Campaigning in National Politics: An Overview*. Report No. 91-775 GOV. Washington: Congressional Research Service.

O'Neill, Robert M. 1992. "Regulating Speech to Cleanse Political Campaigns." *Capitol University Law Review* 21:575–91.

Patterson, Samuel, and Gregory Caldeira. 1993. "Getting Out the Vote: Participation in Gubernatorial Campaigns." *American Political Science Review* 77:675–89.

Patterson, Thomas, and Robert McClure. 1976. *The Unseeing Eye: The Myth of Television Power in National Politics*. New York: Putnam.

Pfau, Michael, and Henry C. Kenski, 1990. *Attack Politics: Strategy and Defense*. New York: Praeger.

Polsby, Nelson W. 1983. *Consequences of Party Reform*. New York: Oxford University Press.

Rosen, J., and Paul Taylor. 1992. *The New News and the Old News: The Press and Politics in the 1990's*. New York: Brookings Institution.

Rosenstone, Steven, and Mark Hansen. 1993. *Mobilization, Participation, and Democracy in America*. New York: Macmillan.

Rubin, Donald. 1974. "Estimating Causal Effects in Randomized and Non-Randomized Studies." *Journal of Educational Psychology* 66:688–701.

Sabato, Larry. 1991. *Feeding Frenzy: How Attack Journalism Has Transformed American Politics*. New York: Free Press.

Thorson, Esther, William G. Christ, and Clarke Caywood. 1991. "Effects of Issue-Image Strategies, Attack and Support Appeals, Music, and Visual Content in Political Commercials." *Journal of Broadcasting and Electronic Media* 35:465–86.

Wattenberg, Martin P. 1984. *Decline of American Political Parties, 1952–1980*. Cambridge: Harvard University Press.

Wattenberg, Martin P. 1991. *The Rise of Candidate-Centered Politics: Presidential Elections of the 1980's*. Cambridge: Harvard University Press.

CHAPTER 4
Election Campaign Debates

Looking at presidential

elections in the twenty-first century, one might assume that debates have always been part of the mix, just as primaries and conventions have. The reality, however, is that all the landmarks along the "road to the White House"—including the debates—have a history. The first presidential debate was in 1960, between Vice President Richard M. Nixon and Massachusetts Senator John F. Kennedy, but there were no debates in 1964, 1968, and 1972. Until 1976, when President Gerald R. Ford agreed to debate Governor Jimmy Carter, the Democratic challenger, incumbents were reluctant to debate. It was thought that standing side-by-side with a challenger would visually present the challenger and the incumbent as equals and, therefore, surrender the advantage incumbents have in an election. After incumbents Ford (1976), Carter (1980), and Ronald Reagan (1984) agreed to debate, however, it became increasingly difficult for any candidate to refuse. Since then, debates are

likely to be a fixture in presidential campaigns and be treated by the news media as major campaign events.

From the beginning, scholars and media commentators have viewed these debates with some skepticism. Are they no more than joint press conferences? Do they really focus on the issues?

Diana Prentice Carlin, Charles Howard, Susan Stanfield, and Larry Reynolds's 1991 essay, "The Effects of Presidential Debate Formats on Clash: A Comparative Analysis," highlights how candidates differ, or clash, on issues. The authors' conclusion contradicts the negative commentary about the debates. The essay also examines how the choice of debate format might affect the amount or type of clash that occurs, as well as how debates might best be conducted.

John T. Morello's 1992 essay, "The 'Look' and Language of Clash: Visual Structuring of Argument in the 1988 Bush-Dukakis Debates," treats the visual dimensions of the

1988 Bush-Dukakis debates. Morello suggests that how voters experience and interpret a televised news event can be affected by how the television coverage is edited. Morello looks at how reaction shots and cutaway shots in the telecast of the 1988 debates benefitted Vice President George H. W. Bush to Michael Dukakis's disadvantage. Morello's essay is rare among studies of the presidential debates in that it deals with the effect of television editing on how viewers see and interpret the events.

William P. Eveland, Jr., Douglas M. McLeod, and Amy I. Nathanson's 1994 essay, "Reporters vs. Undecided Voters: An Analysis of the Questions Asked During the 1992 Presidential Debates" examines the questions to which the debating candidates respond. In 1992, citizens who were not journalists participated in the debates for the first time. The study shows that neither journalists nor citizens ask markedly superior questions. Although the subject matter of the questions varies between journalists and citizens, both groups ask questions about matters that have been independently shown to be of concern to the electorate.

"White Paper on Televised Political Campaign Debates," is a 2002 essay by a group of scholars who gathered in Racine, Wisconsin, to discuss what should be known about presidential debates. This essay, with numerous selected references to the existing research, outlines several items that matter in debates: format; number of candidates; their gender; what debaters say (especially the mistakes); their presentational style; media coverage; whether viewers watch alone or in a group; and how debates get diffused into everyday conversations, late-night comedy, and other venues. The essay indicates that researchers need to know what specific elements in the debates cause what specific effects. For example, nonverbal communication was important in the 1960 Kennedy-Nixon debates and again in the 2000 Bush-Gore debates. Yet, scholars know very little about precisely *how* candidates' nonverbal communication affects viewers.

The final selection, William L. Benoit, Kevin A. Stein, and Glenn J. Hansen's 2004 essay, "Newspaper Coverage of Presidential Debates," focuses on media coverage of presidential debates. The researchers find that newspapers offer the public a distorted viewpoint. Newspapers over-report the attacks that may have occurred. They also focus on candidates' characters, whereas the debates themselves deal much more heavily with the candidates' positions on various issues.

The Effects of Presidential Debate Formats on Clash: A Comparative Analysis

Diana Prentice Carlin, Charles Howard, Susan Stanfield, and Larry Reynolds

In each of the five presidential election years in which debates were held—1960, 1976, 1980, 1984, and 1988—a common complaint surfaced: the formats prevented confrontation, rebuttal, clash or "real debate." Scholars and journalists have launched attacks on the structure and subsequent quality of arguments produced by the candidate encounters.[1] Since these criticisms are well documented in the literature on presidential debates, the specifics are omitted from this essay but can be summarized into four main categories: (1) there is inadequate time for substantive responses by the candidates; (2) the question-answer format is not conducive to substantive debate; (3) panelists play an overly intrusive role; and (4) panelists do not reflect the public's interests. The most frequently suggested antidote for the clash-deficient presidential debates revolves around changes in format.

While we accept that format and use of panelists influence the level of clash, we suggest throughout the remainder of this essay that the charges that the debates' shortcomings result from format are overstated and that clash and "real debate" do in fact occur. Analyzing the levels and types of clash in presidential debates is important because it is the existence of clash which is used to determine the debates' authenticity.

We support our two claims through a content analysis of the 1988 presidential debates and a comparison of those results with the findings of content analyses conducted on previous debates. Additionally, we suggest reasons for the perceptions of presidential debates as "counterfeit" and argue that changes in format alone will not produce the improvements many critics of presidential debate seek.

★ METHOD

The transcripts of the Bush-Dukakis debates serve as the text for analysis.[2] The transcripts of both presidential debates were first divided into units with each unit consisting of a single predominant topic. In addition, the moderator's interruptions; reporters' questions; candidates' interruptions; and the beginning of a response, rebuttal, or closing statement were considered as dividing points for units. As a result, a unit could be as short as a word or phrase or as long as a four or five sentence paragraph.

Within each unit, clash and non-clash strategies were coded. Strategy categories were used to identify debate techniques employed by the candidates. Given the method of unitizing, it was possible for discussion of a single topic to include more than one strategy. In other words, a candidate might begin a statement on the topic of drugs by presenting his solution to the problem and then conclude by comparing it to his opponent's proposed solution.

Strategy categories were based on a broad definition of political debate as a presentation and examination of opposing views on policies. This definition acknowledges that some debate strategies involve direct clash with the opponent's arguments while others are used to explain a candidate's own position or to answer a question. Specific strategy categories were derived from a content analysis of the Kennedy-Nixon debates (Ellsworth, 1965). These categories were chosen because they were consistent with the definition of political debate and were the basis for content analyses of the 1976 (Riley, Hollihan, & Cooley, 1980) and the 1980 debates (Riley & Hollihan, 1981; Prentice, Larsen, & Sobnosky, 1981). Since the levels of clash discovered in the 1988 debates were compared with those found in previous debates, the use of these categories allowed for better comparisons of results.

Clash categories included:

- *Analysis of opponent's position—offensive:* An analysis of a position held by the opposing candidate that represents an attack on that position, e.g., "George Bush a few years ago said that the Social Security was basically a welfare system" ("Bush and Dukakis: Few Sparks," 1988, p. 3011).

- *Analysis of opponent's position—defensive:* An analysis of a position held by the opposing candidate that represents a defense of one's own position, e.g., "Yes, we shouldn't trade arms for hostages, but we have made vast improvements in our anti-terrorism. Now, it's fine to say that sometimes you have to hit base camps, but when the President saw state-sponsored fingerprints of Moamar Quaddafi on the loss of American life, he hit Libya. And my opponent was unwilling to support that action" ("Bush and Dukakis, Face to Face," 1988, p. 2751).

- *Extension of position—offensive:* An elaboration or further explanation of a position already stated or alluded to in the debate that can include an attack on the other candidate, e.g., "All I'm trying to do is put it in focus. And I hope people don't think that I'm questioning his patriotism when I say he—[when I] use his words to describe his participation in that organization [ACLU]" ("Bush and Dukakis, Face to Face," 1988, p. 2746).

- *Extension of position—defensive:* An elaboration or further explanation of a position already stated or alluded to in the debate that defends one's stand on that position, e.g., ". . . he goes around ranting about Noriega. Now, I've told you what the intelligence briefing he received said about that" ("Bush and Dukakis, Face to Face," 1988, p. 2752).

- *Comparison of positions:* A statement of one's own position accompanied by a statement of the opposing candidate's position which may or may not include analysis, extension, and evidence, e.g., ". . . my answer is: do not make these unilateral cuts. And everybody now realizes that peace through strength works. And so this is where I have a big difference" ("Bush and Dukakis, Face to Face," 1988, p. 2750).
- *Statement to opponent:* Any interruption of one candidate's speech by another or give and take between candidates that was not in direct response to a question, e.g., "I just said . . ."—Bush. "No, let me finish"—Dukakis ("Bush and Dukakis, Face to Face," 1988, p. 2748).

Non-clash categories consisted of strategies that were important in establishing a position or answering a question, but did not acknowledge an opponent's arguments or the debate context. Non-clash categories included:

- *Analysis:* Consideration of the consequences of an action or the causes of a problem, e.g., ". . . we've got to invest in economic growth in this country, in every part of this country. Building that kind of growth expands revenues and helps to bring down that deficit" ("Bush and Dukakis, Face to Face," 1988, p. 2744).
- *Policy statement:* A statement that presents or advances a desired future course or a past position, e.g., "[W]e've got to go out there and collect billions and billions of dollars in taxes owed that aren't being paid in this country" ("Bush and Dukakis, Face to Face," 1988, p. 2744).

Three coders worked independently to determine units and strategies. Coders were trained using the first Reagan-Mondale debate. Practice coding revealed strategies that were confusing to the coders and allowed for further clarification of the category system before coding of the 1988 debates was undertaken. When all three coders did not agree on the presence of a strategy category, agreement was reached,

TABLE 1

Percent of Units Containing Clash:
1998 Presidential Debates

	1st Debate	2nd Debate	Total
Bush	41.0% (48/117)	40.2% (31/77)	40.7% (79/194)
Dukakis	48.5% (49/101)	45.2% (43/95)	46.9% (92/196)
Combined	44.4% (97/218)	43.0% (74/172)	43.8% (171/390)

for purposes of data entry, through discussion and re-examination of the unit. Reliability was determined by calculating agreements for each category identified within a unit. Reliability for treatment categories was .89 using Holsti's (1969) formula (p. 137).

The data from both debates yielded a total of 437 units. The first debate included 241 total units, 117 for Bush, 101 for Dukakis, and 23 for the questioners. The second debate yielded 196 total units, 77 for Bush, 95 for Dukakis, and 24 for the questioners. Chi square tests of significant differences were used to compare each candidate's use of clash and non-clash categories. Each candidate's first and second debate performances were also compared. Significance was set at the .05 level. For purposes of comparing levels of clash in the 1988 debates with those identified through analyses of the 1960, 1976, 1980, and the 1984 debates, the current authors identified the categories within each earlier study that corresponded most closely with definitions of clash and non-clash categories in this study.[3]

★ RESULTS

Content Analysis of the 1988 Debates

Of the 218 candidate units in the first debate, 97 or 44.4 percent contained clash strategies. In the second debate, the percentage dropped slightly to 43 percent (74 of 172 units).

George Bush employed clash strategies in 41 percent (48/117) of his units in the first debate and in 40.2 percent (31/77) in the second. Dukakis' incidence of clash strategies

TABLE 2

Individual Clash Strategies as a Percent of Total Units: *1988 Presidential Debates*

	No. of Units	Analysis Opponent Offensive	Analysis Opponent Defensive	Extension Offensive	Extension Defensive	Comparison	Statement to Opponent
Bush							
1st Debate	117	16.2% (19)	15.3% (18)	<1.0% (1)	2.5% (3)	12.8% (15)	9.4% (11)
2nd Debate	77	14.2% (11)	12.9% (10)	1.2% (1)	2.5% (2)	20.7% (16)	1.2% (1)
Dukakis							
1st Debate	101	28.7% (29)	3.9% (4)	4.9% (5)	<1.0% (1)	12.8% (13)	12.8% (13)
2nd Debate	95	24.2% (23)	3.1% (3)	(0)	(0)	17.8% (17)	9.4% (9)

was higher than Bush's in both debates. In the first debate, 48.5 percent (49/101) of his units revealed clash strategies, and like Bush, his level of clash declined in the second debate to 45.2 percent (43/95). Bush's total for the two debates was 40.7 percent (79/194), and Dukakis' was 46.9 percent (92/196). The total combined percentage was 43.8 percent for both candidates for both debates.

Two additional levels of analysis provide insight into the candidates' debate techniques. Percentages were calculated for each of the clash and non-clash categories and for the presence of clash strategies in each type of speech— response, rebuttal, and close.

Table 2 compares Bush and Dukakis on the basis of clash categories. Percentages are given in terms of the total number of units per debate. Table 3 shows the percentages for each candidate in relationship to the total number of units containing clash. Since a single unit could contain more than one strategy, the combined totals of the individual treatments are greater than are those for the total units of clash.

Dukakis used more analysis of the opponent from an offensive position than did Bush. The

TABLE 3

Individual Clash Strategies as a Percent of Clash Units: *1988 Presidential Debates*

	No. of Units	Analysis Opponent Offensive	Analysis Opponent Defensive	Extension Offensive	Extension Defensive	Comparison	Statement to Opponent
Bush							
1st Debate	48	39.5%	37.5%	2.0%	6.2%	31.2%	22.9%
2nd Debate	31	35.4%	32.2%	3.2%	6.4%	51.6%	3.2%
Dukakis							
1st Debate	49	59.1%	8.1%	10.2%	2.0%	26.5%	26.5%
2nd Debate	43	53.4%	6.9%			39.5%	20.9%

TABLE 4

Non-Clash Treatments: *1988 Presidential Debates*

| | PERCENT OF TOTAL UNITS | | PERCENT OF NON-CLASH UNITS | |
	Analysis	Policy	Analysis	Policy
Bush				
1st Debate	59.8% (70/117)	36.7% (43/117)	78.6% (70/89)	48.3% (43/89)
2nd Debate	77.9% (60/77)	46.7% (36/77)	92.3% (60/65)	55.3% (36/65)
Dukakis				
1st Debate	79.2% (80/101)	31.6% (32/101)	98.7% (80/81)	39.5% (32/81)
2nd Debate	85.2% (81/95)	33.6% (32/95)	98.7% (81/82)	39.0% (32/82)

difference was significant ($df = 1$, $\chi^2 = 6.23$, $p < .025$). This was Dukakis' most common clash strategy in both debates. Both candidates were consistent in the degree to which they used this strategy in both debates. Consequently, Bush exhibited more analysis of the opponent from a defensive position than did Dukakis. The difference was significant at the .001 level ($df = 1$, $\chi^2 = 15.18$).

Bush's most commonly used clash strategy in the first debate was analysis of opposition from an offensive position, but it was comparison in the second. Neither candidate exhibited much use of extension; however, as will be explained in discussion of Table 5, this is one effect of the format. One type of clash that was added to the category system for this analysis that was not included in previous content analyses was "statement to the opponent." In the first debate, Bush interrupted or responded directly to Dukakis eleven times. This constituted 9.4 percent of his total units and 22.9 percent of his total clash units. Dukakis used this technique thirteen times or in 12.8 percent of his total units and in 26.5 percent of his total clash units. In the second debate, Bush's use of direct statements to Dukakis declined significantly to only one incident ($df = 1$, $\chi^2 = 5.84$, $p < .025$). Dukakis continued to employ direct statements

at almost the same level as he did in the first debate (9.4 percent of all units and 20.9 percent of the clash units). The difference between the two candidates' use of the strategy in the second debate was significant at the .05 level ($df = 1$, $\chi^2 = 3.97$).

Table 4 is a summary of non-clash strategies. In examining these statistics, it is important to understand that a unit could contain both a clash and a non-clash statement. Thus, totals for clash and non-clash units combined may be greater than the total number of units per candidate per debate.

In the first debate Bush used non-clash treatments in 76 percent of his units (89/117), and Dukakis employed non-clash in 80.1 percent of his (81/101). Of the two non-clash categories, analysis was used extensively by both candidates. Of Bush's 117 units, 59.8 percent (70) included analysis, and of the 89 units with non-clash treatments, 78.6 percent contained analysis. Dukakis relied more heavily on analysis than did Bush with 79.2 percent (80/101) of his total units including it and 98.7 percent (80/81) of his non-clash units having it. The difference between the candidates was significant at the .001 level ($df = 1$, $\chi^2 = 12.18$).

Policy statements were in evidence in 36.7 percent (43/117) of Bush's total units and in

TABLE 5

Clash Comparison by Speech Types:
1988 Presidential Debates

	Response	Rebuttal	Close
Bush			
1st Debate	25.5% (14/62)	60.0% (30/50)	40.0% (2/5)
2nd Debate	39.4% (15/38)	54.2% (19/35)	50.0% (2/4)
Dukakis			
1st Debate	38.5% (22/57)	67.5% (27/40)	50.0% (2/4)
2nd Debate	32.2% (20/62)	73.3% (22/30)	33.3% (1/3)
Combined			
1st Debate	30.2% (36/119)	63.3% (57/90)	44.4% (4/9)
2nd Debate	35.0% (35/100)	63.0% (41/65)	42.8% (3/7)

both candidates used more clash in rebuttals and in closing speeches than they did in responses to questions. Sixty percent (30/50) of Bush's rebuttal units and 40 percent (2/5) of his closing statement included clash treatments as compared to only 22.5 percent (14/62) of his responses. For Dukakis, 67.5 percent (27/40) of his rebuttal units revealed clash and 50 percent (2/4) of his closing statements included clash while 38.5 percent (22/57) of his response units had clash treatments.

The second debate produced similar results. Bush utilized clash in 54.2 percent (19/35) of his rebuttal statements, in 39.4 percent (15/38) of his responses, and 50 percent (2/4) of his closing statement. The results showed an increase in clash for responses and a decrease for rebuttals. Dukakis also used a higher percentage of clash in rebuttal speeches (73.3%) than in responses (32.2%) or in his close (33.3%). Unlike Bush, Dukakis clashed less in his responses in the second debate than he did in the first and clashed more in rebuttals in the second debate than he had in the first.

To better test the effect of format on clash, clash occurrences for responses and for rebuttals were combined for both debates for each candidate and a chi square test was performed. A significant difference was found at the .001 level (df = 1, χ^2 = 34.8).

Comparison with Content Analyses of Earlier Debates

Since formats varied among the debates and since the category schemes were not consistent among the analyses conducted on the 1960, 1976, 1980, and 1988 debates, comparisons between the levels of clash were imperfect. However, there are sufficient similarities in content analysis techniques to allow for reasonable comparisons. Each of the studies is summarized by Table 6 which included the findings relative to levels of clash in the debates.

Ellsworth (1965) compared the content of the four Kennedy-Nixon debates with that of representative candidate speeches. His system included six categories that constitute clash: analytical criticism, critical evidence, declarative criticism, analytical defense, evidential defense, and declarative defense (p. 797). Riley, Hollihan, and Cooley (1980) and Riley and

48.3 percent (43/89) of his non-clash units. Dukakis used policy statements in 31.6 percent (32/101) of his total number of units and in 39.5 percent (32/81) of his non-clash units.

In the second debate both candidates used more analysis than policy treatments. Of Bush's total units, 77.9 percent (60/77) contained analysis and 46.7 percent (36/77) had policy statements. Analysis was included in 92.3 percent of the non-clash units (60/65). Bush's increased use of analysis in the second debate was significant (df = 1, χ^2 = 6.18, p = .025). Policy statements were found in 55.3 percent (36/65) of the non-clash units. For Dukakis, the results yielded analysis statements in 81 of his total 95 units (85.2%) and in 81 of his 82 non-clash units (98.7%). Policy statements were recorded in 33.6 percent (32/95) of the total units and in 39 percent (32/82) of the non-clash units. As in the first debate, Bush used more policy statements than did Dukakis.

A summary of the levels of clash per speech-type is presented in Table 5. In the first debate

TABLE 6

Comparison of Clash: *1960, 1976, 1980, and 1988 Presidential Debates*

	1st debate	2nd debate	3rd debate	4th debate
1960				
Kennedy-Nixon	34.8%	31.6%	34.8%	49.0%
1976				
Carter	48.9%	62.3%	45.7%	
Ford	37.7%	45.0%	20.7%	
1980 (Riley & Hollihan)				
Reagan	22.4%	61.1%		
Anderson	31.8%			
Carter		34.9%		
1980 (Prentice et al.)				
Reagan		56.0%		
Carter		45.0%		
1988				
Bush	41.0%	40.2%		
Dukakis	48.5%	45.2%		

Figures represent the percent of all statements which were categorized as fitting clash categories in relationship to the total number of statements per debate.

Hollihan (1981) used Ellsworth's categories to analyze the 1976 and 1980 debates respectively. Unlike Ellsworth, their findings are reported by candidate rather than by debate.

Prentice, et al. (1981) analyzed the Reagan-Carter debate using an adaptation of Ellsworth's (1965) system. They included five clash categories: analysis of opponent-offensive, analysis of opponent-defensive, extension-offensive, extension-defensive, and comparison.

Morello (1988) analyzed the 1984 debates but did not report his results in percentage terms as did the others. He simply reported the number of incidents of clash which occurred in the debates. Morello identified instances of clash when a candidate "attacked his opponent's ideas, positions, statements, or proposed programs and policies, or defended against or replied to an attack expressed by the opponent." He identified "55 statements (41 attacks, 14 refutations)" in the first debate and "42 clash statements (32 attacks, 10 refutations)" in the second (p. 279).

Excluding Morello's (1988) results, a comparative table appears in Table 6.

★ DISCUSSION

The Effects of Format on Clash

Despite their detractors, presidential debates do produce clash. While no one has established a clash threshold necessary for there to be a "real" debate, when the unique aspects of presidential debates are considered—among them the necessity for candidates to present both constructive and rebuttal arguments within a single speech—the results suggest a high percentage of clash overall.

In 1988, both Bush and Dukakis included clash strategies in over 40 percent of their remarks. Given the 1988 format which limited rebuttal and did not require both candidates to answer the same or similar questions, this figure takes on added importance. It should also be noted that the content analysis did not include policy statements as clash strategies even though analysis is considered an area for evaluation for debate skills on American Forensic Association debate ballots.

Specifically, the content analysis of the 1988 debates demonstrated that other factors joined format in affecting the level of clash, and that candidates can clash by arguing outside the constraints of formats.

Trent and Friedenberg (1983) suggest that incumbency is one such factor (p. 246). As Vice President, George Bush took on an incumbency role; an analysis of his clash strategies suggests he debated as an incumbent. The breakdown for the categories of opponent analysis from both offensive and defensive positions indicate[s] Bush used far more defensive strategies and fewer offensive ones than Dukakis. Bush's use of comparison suggests that he also played to his strengths as an incumbent and differentiated his experiences and policies from those of Dukakis.

Dukakis was perceived as the better debater going into the debate because of his extensive primary debate schedule and his role on the Public Broadcasting System program, "The Advocates" ("Lectern," 1988; Germond & Witcover, 1989, p. 426). The higher percentage of clash compared to Bush indicates that he was more aggressive in both debates. The attacks Dukakis made on Bush as a result of his incumbency role could also account for the difference.

In addition to incumbency and skill factors as determinants of clash, the content analysis also reveals that strategies changed in the second debate although the format was the same. Such changes could have resulted from events occurring between debates or from an analysis of previous debate performances.

Although it can be argued that format alone does not necessarily hinder debate, the content analysis of the 1988 debate suggests that format can affect the type of clash strategies. Both candidates had very few extension statements. With a format that followed a pattern of question, response, rebuttal, question to opposite candidate, it is not surprising that there was limited extension. Prentice, et al. (1981) found that the second half of the Reagan-Carter debate produced more extension when additional rebuttal time was added (p. 10). The 1988 content analysis revealed that speech type

affects levels of clash with significantly more occurring in rebuttals.

The frequent occurrence in the first debate of statements to the opponent[,] which were primarily interruptions of the other candidate, suggests that candidates can circumvent the format to produce more clash. It is interesting to note that an examination of transcripts from previous debates revealed few such incidents including none in 1960 and 1976. The fact that this type of clash occurred regularly in the first debate and was used nine times by Dukakis in the second suggests one of two things: either the format was so restrictive that the candidates felt compelled to circumvent it to have clash, and/or the 1988 campaign was characterized as being highly personal and negative with the interruptions being a manifestation of those traits.[4]

The comparison of the 1988 debates to the previous four sets suggests no clear-cut pattern of format affecting clash. The first and last Kennedy-Nixon debates were closer to a Lincoln-Douglas debate with extended opening statements. However, the level of clash was significantly higher in the last debate than in the first, and the level in the first was not higher than in the other two which were closer to the press conference format. The level of clash in the fourth was also not as high as that displayed by some individuals in other debates. For instance, Reagan's 1980 totals from both content analyses of the Reagan-Carter debate and Carter's second debate total in 1976 were higher.

The fact that two candidates using the same format have very different degrees of clash, as was the case in the Carter-Ford and Reagan-Carter debates, also gives credence to the arguments that incumbency and individual traits have an influence as well as does format. Other mediating factors such as subject matter, campaign events, and standing in the polls could be considered in explaining the variation in Carter's and Ford's use of clash over three debates in 1976 and Bush's shifts in 1988. However, the bottom line problem with any approach that assumes format changes will improve debates is best expressed by columnist Meg Greenfield (1988): "But no rule change will make any difference to the candidates who are trying to achieve something other than a true, direct engagement and who are following some professional's advice about hitting the same note again and again" (p. 28).

Misperceptions about Clash in Presidential Debates

A presidential debate format which satisfies the needs and interests of scholars, journalists, candidates, and the public may never be devised. However, content analyses of debates since 1960 indicate that the perception of presidential debates as lacking clash is inaccurate. If clash does occur, then what explains the perception that presidential debates are "pseudo-debates"? Three explanations can begin to answer that question.

First presidential and other political debates are often judged by the academic model of stated resolutions, clear affirmative and negative positions, and direct cross examination. Adherents of such a model may be inclined to dismiss much "real world" debate as it is practiced in legislatures, court rooms, and of course, presidential campaigns. The presence of third party panelists, the use of multiple questions and short response time further contribute to the perception that what takes place between presidential candidates is not true debate.

Such a narrow view of debating seems unjustified. Carlin (1989) argued that, in practice, presidential debates meet the three requisites of a debate as identified in argumentation texts: "(1) participants are on opposing sides of a conflict; (2) participants adhere to a formalized set of rules to present their ideas; and (3) a third party is the target of candidate's messages" (p. 209). Content analyses conducted on every presidential debate provide quantitative measures of clash in the candidate exchanges to further support the definitional ones.

The second explanation for misperceptions is found in the nature of the clash itself. The category systems described here for the content analyses of presidential debates allow for clash to be defined as something more than refutation and rebuttal. Because presidential debates differ from the academic model in the ways noted above, traditional debate standards about clash do not always apply. More sophisticated

category systems allow for a more precise understanding of the nature of clash that takes place in presidential debates.

Morello's (1988) verbal and visual analysis of the 1984 debates provides a third factor worth considering when trying to understand why debates are perceived as lacking in clash. He found that visual depictions of clash occurred in only half the situations in which there was verbal clash (p. 280). Research by Tiemens, Hellweg, Kipper, and Phillips (1985) on the Carter-Reagan debate also found the medium failing to display clash to the extent it actually took place. Since most critics form their perceptions while viewing the debates on television, the mediated effects must be considered in explaining the criticisms regarding clash.

CONCLUSIONS

The argument that the label "counterfeit debates" is not supported by content analyses should not be construed to mean that scholars, journalists, candidates, and the public should not seek better formats for future debates. The research presented in this essay can generate guidelines for the types of format choices that might influence debate. This information and other research on political debates should be disseminated more broadly among those who influence debate formats. However, the comparison of content analyses also suggests that there is a strong human element which is not easily controlled by formats. Given that reality as well as political realities which indicate that debates will occur only if candidates feel some control over their form, those of us interested in political debates should be less concerned with the form of debates and should perhaps take a more active role in commenting on them in ways which reach the public and enhance their understanding of the events they have witnessed.

NOTES

[1] For scholarly response see Auer (1962); Bitzer and Rueter (1980); Frana (1989); Hellweg and Phillips (1981); Hogan (1989); Jamieson and Birdsell (1988); Kraus (1964); McClain (1989); Meadow and Jackson-Beeck (1978); Pfau (1981, 1983); Swanson

and Swanson (1978); Weiler (1989). Journalists offering this opinion include: Cater (1980); Goodman (1988); Hewitt (1988); McCarthy (1984); Rosenblatt (1976); and Stern (1960).

2 We used the texts printed in the *Congressional Quarterly Weekly Reports* for analysis.

3 Earlier studies used for comparison included: Ellsworth (1965); Morello (1988); Prentice, et al. (1981); Riley and Hollihan (1981); Riley, Hollihan, and Cooley (1980).

4 The candidates of course have considerable influence on the format through staff negotiations held prior to the debates. This does not mean, however, that a candidate will always feel comfortable with format once a given debate has started. For a discussion of pre-debate negotiation, see Karayn (1979).

REFERENCES

Auer, J. J. (1962). The counterfeit debates. In S. Kraus (Ed.), *The great debates: Background, perspective, effects* (pp. 142–150). Bloomington: Indiana Univ. Press.

Bitzer, L., & Rueter, T. (1980). *Carter v. Ford: The counterfeit debates of 1976.* Madison: The Univ. of Wisconsin Press.

Bush and Dukakis, face to face on key issues. (1988, Oct. 1). *Congressional Quarterly Weekly Report,* pp. 2743–2753

Bush and Dukakis: Few sparks in final clash. (1988, Oct. 15). *Congressional Quarterly Weekly Report,* pp. 3005–3015.

Carlin, D. P. (1989). A defense of the "debate" in presidential debates. *Argumentation and Advocacy, 25,* 208–213.

Cater, D. (1980, November 4). Semi-requiem for semi-debates. *Washington Post,* sec. A, p. 21.

Ellsworth, J. H. (1965). Rationality and campaigning: A content analysis of the 1960 presidential campaign debates. *Western Political Quarterly, 18,* 794–802.

Frana, A. (1989). Characteristics of effective argumentation. *Argumentation and Advocacy, 25,* 200–202.

Germond, J. W., & Witcover, J. (1989). *Whose broad stripes and bright stars?: The trivial pursuit of the presidency 1988.* New York: Warner Books.

Goodman, W. (1988, September 25). Why debates fizzle instead of sizzle. *New York Times,* sec. 2, p. 31.

Greenfield, M. (1988, October 3). Throw away the scripts. *Newsweek,* p. 28.

Hellweg, S. A., & Phillips, S. L. (1981). Form and substance: A comparative analysis of live formats used in the 1980 presidential debates. *Speaker and Gavel, 18,* 67–76.

Hewitt, D. (1988, September 23). The debates: Dead on arrival. *New York Times,* p. 27.

Hogan, J. M. (1989). Media nihilism and the presidential debates. *Argumentation and Advocacy, 25,* 220–225.

Holsti, O. (1969). *Content Analysis for the social sciences and humanities.* Reading, MA: Addison-Wesley.

Jamieson, K. H., & Birdsell, D. (1988). *Presidential debates.* New York: Oxford University Press.

Karayn, J. (1979). The case for permanent presidential debates. In A. Ranney (Ed.). *The past and future of presidential debates* (pp. 155–174). Washington: American Enterprise Institute.

Kraus, S. (1964). Presidential debates in 1964. *Quarterly Journal of Speech, 50,* 19–23.

Lectern to lectern. (1988, November 21). *Newsweek,* p. 123.

McCarthy, C. (1984, October 28). The art of vagueness. *Washington Post,* sec. K, p. 2.

McClain, T. B. (1989). Secondary school debate pedagogy. *Argumentation and Advocacy, 25,* 203–204.

Meadow, R. G., & Jackson-Beeck, M. (1978). A comparative perspective on presidential debates: Issue evolution in 1960 and 1976. In G. F. Bishop, R. G. Meadow, & M. Jackson-Beeck (Eds.). *The presidential debates: Media, electoral, and policy perspectives* (pp. 33–58). New York: Praeger.

Morello, J. T. (1988). Argument and visual structuring in the 1984 Mondale-Reagan debates: The medium's influence on the perception of clash. *Western Journal of Speech Communication, 52,* 277–290.

Pfau, M. (1981, November). *Political debate formats: The next step.* Paper presented at the meeting of the Speech Communication Association, Washington, DC.

Pfau, M. (1983). Criteria and format to optimize political debates: An analysis of South Dakota's "election '80" series. *Journal of the American Forensic Association, 19,* 205–214.

Prentice, D. B., Larsen, J. K., & Sobnosky, M. J. (1981, November). *The Carter-Reagan debate: A comparison of clash in the dual format.* Paper presented at the meeting of the Speech Communication Association, Anaheim, CA.

Riley, P., & Hollihan, T. (1981). The 1980 presidential debate: A content analysis of the issues and arguments. *Speaker and Gavel, 18,* 47–59.

Riley, P., Hollihan, T., & Cooley, D. (1980, April). *The 1976 presidential debate: An analysis of the issues and arguments.* Paper presented at the meeting of the Central States Speech Association Chicago, IL.

Rosenblatt, R. (1976, October 9). Two for the show. *New Republic,* p. 42.

Stern, P. M. (1960, November 11). The debates in retrospect. *New Republic,* pp. 18–19.

Swanson, L. L., & Swanson, D. L. (1978). The agenda-setting function of the Ford-Carter debate. *Communication Monographs, 45,* 347–353.

Tiemens, R. K., Hellweg, S. A., Kipper, P., & Phillips, S. L. (1985). An integrative verbal and visual analysis of the Reagan-Carter debate. *Communication Quarterly, 33,* 34–42.

Trent, J. S., & Friedenberg, R. V. (1983). *Political campaign communication: Principles and practices.* New York: Praeger.

Weiler, M. (1989). The 1988 electoral debates and debate theory. *Argumentation and Advocacy, 25,* 214–219.

The "Look" and Language of Clash:
Visual Structuring of Argument in the 1988 Bush-Dukakis Debates

John T. Morello

One review of the first presidential debate in 1960 hailed the encounter a considerable success "as a device for illuminating issues and personalities in the political campaign" ("The Debate: Chapter I," 1960, p. A-16). While the intervening years have made observers more cynical about the contributions televised debating offers to the democratic process, many remain confident that placing candidates on the same stage has merit if for no other reason than that mentioned by *The Christian Science Monitor* 30 years ago when it commented that ". . . never before have so many Americans had a chance to judge at first hand—and in relation to his opponent—the man they will be choosing for their nation's highest office" ("That Great Debate," 1960, p. 18).

Contending that televised debates offer viewers an "uninterrupted 90-minute shot at the candidates" ("The Second Debate," 1984, p. 28) overlooks, however, the influence exerted by television. While it has been noted before that television shapes a message, and is ". . . an integral part of the total communication process, not just the channel by which the communication is sent" (Hellweg and Phillips, 1981, p. 26), few studies have explored how televised depictions of the candidates alter verbal aspects of a presidential debate. To justify the examination of the visual structures of television debates we need only recall "that through television the visual image, embedded in a variety of dramatic formats, has now emerged as our basic unit of political conversation" (Postman, 1988, p. 13).

If pictures of the debates altered their verbal dimension, then the 1988 debates may stand as a disturbing example of the triumph of visual images over language in politics.

The temptation to substitute visual messages for reasoned judgment in political discussions stems partly from the absence of a grammar to test whether visual assertion can function as argument (Jamieson, 1988, p. 116). While certain dimensions of the televisual image may result from a candidate's management of a variety of nonverbal cues, the selection of camera shots shapes the perspective through which audiences see these nonverbal displays. Even though negotiations by candidates and their staffs set some restrictions, many "visualizing" decisions remain under the control of the broadcast crew (Hellweg and Phillips, 1981). The frequencies and patterns of camera shots employed create a visual text imparting a structure to the debate unlike that perceived by those observing the event in person (Messaris, Eckman and Gumpert, 1979; Tiemens, 1978; Tiemens, Hellweg, Kipper and Phillips, 1981).

Television strives, whenever possible, to achieve a relatively quick visual pace through changes in camera shots. The absence of physical action in televised debates complicates that objective leaving the television director with few options for creating visual interest. The most frequently used change from the "talking head," the cut to a reaction shot, has provoked conflicting opinions. Advocates of cutaways argue that reactions are part of the "story"

(Kraus, 1988, p. 49). Political candidates and their advisers, worried about their lack of control over which reactions are shown and when, have often requested that cutaways be disallowed (Kraus, 1988, p. 48). Protests notwithstanding, reaction shots continue during telecasts of presidential debates.

As presidential campaigning comes to rely increasingly on visual images, the degree of correspondence between a candidate's verbal and visual messages increases in importance (Leuthold). Reaction shots can conceivably alter a candidate's words by introducing discrepant, contradictory, or even supportive visual information, thus affecting the consonance between the verbal and visual messages. One oft-repeated principle of nonverbal communication holds that whenever verbal and visual messages contradict, receivers typically believe the non-verbal message (Richmond, McCroskey, and Payne, 1991, p. 11). Because television's natural grammar is associative, the tendency for visual "claims" to overwhelm verbal ones is magni-fied. As Jamieson reminds us, "When the visual and the verbal dance in step, the power of each is magnified. But while the visual message is a flamenco dancer, its verbal partner is a wall-flower" (1988, p. 60). If viewers respond to visual messages which misrepresent the verbal content, evaluation is replaced by emotional response, thus undermining political discourse.

This study examined the visual structuring of the 1988 debates between George Bush and Michael Dukakis, focusing on moments of clash in which the opposing advocates engaged in statements of attack and defense. The central question examined whether the televised depic-tion of the debate presented an uninterrupted look at the candidates or a process of argument transmuted by the changes in camera shots that punctuated the event. Three conclusions were reached: the shot sequences employed to visu-alize clash in the debates (1) misrepresented the incidence of verbalized clash, (2) gave prefer-ence to the *ad hominem* attack as a verbal cue for the cut to a reaction shot, and (3) offered oppor-tunities for nonverbal refutation of opposing arguments, which one candidate employed more effectively.

Examination of the visual and verbal records of these debates began with the selection of appropriate texts. Off-the-air videotapes of the two 1988 debates were used, with shots clas-sified in accord with the conventional video production terminology used to characterize field of view (Wurtzel, 1983, p. 95–97). Tapes were viewed twice and coded independently.[1] Identifying camera shots requires no judgment on meaning (Bowers and Courtright, 1984, p. 85), so the procedure is efficient and reliable (Krippendorf[f], 1980).

Verbal texts examined were the transcripts of the debates as printed in *The New York Times*.[2] Instances of clash were identified as themes in which a candidate attacked his opponent's stated positions on policy proposals or replied to an attack advanced by the opponent.[3] The debaters routinely prefaced statements of clash with unambiguous referential cues (e.g., "He said," "the Vice President stated," "the Governor said"), making identification of verbal clash relatively uncomplicated. The study of the verbal and visual aspects of the debates focused on those portions of the encounters in which candidates replied to panelists' questions and rebutted one another's statements.

★ MISREPRESENTING THE INCIDENCE OF VERBALIZED CLASH

A total of 99 statements of attack and defense occurred in the two debates: 63 in debate one (47 attacks, 16 refutations) and 36 (28 attacks, 8 replies) in debate two.

Dukakis initiated more arguments than Bush.[4] In debate one, Dukakis attacked Bush 30 times; he offered 17 attacks in debate two. Bush, by contrast, initiated 28 attacks (17 in debate one, 11 in debate two). Bush was, however, responsible for more statements of refuta-tion. He replied to an argument expressed by Dukakis on 17 occasions (12 in debate one, 5 in debate two) whereas Dukakis defended himself against Bush's attacks 7 times (4 in debate one, 3 in debate two). Summing these figures pro-duces a clear portrait of which debater took the lead in providing statements of clash. Dukakis expressed 54 utterances of clash (34 in debate one, 20 in debate two) compared to Bush's 45 (29 in debate one, 16 in debate two).

"Good television," in the case of presidential debates, creates a sense of confrontation (Drucker, 1990). While the task of visualizing clash in debates presents the television director with limited options, the cutaway to a reaction shot (a close-up of the opponent or a two-shot of the speaker and the opponent) offers the best choice for showing the combative nature of the debate (Messaris, Eckman, and Gumpert, 1979, p. 361). The cut to a close-up of the non-speaking candidate would, of course, present the most unambiguous cue that reaction to the speaker mattered. No such shots occurred. There were, however, 92 two-shots depicting the speaker and his opponent: 55 shots in debate one, 37 in debate two. Before examining the relationship between these cutaway shots and the verbal cues that prompted them, we should first examine what the aggregate figures reveal.

Whether as a cause or an effect of the perceived negativity of the 1988 campaign, visual cues that the candidates were engaged in direct debate increased greatly even though the debates included about the same number of verbalized attacks and replies as the debates from four years earlier. In 1984, 68 cutaway shots occurred in the two debates (Morello, 1988a, p. 280); but the frequency of articulated clash in those debates (97 instances of attack and defense) nearly matched the number of arguments occurring in 1988. While the number of times the candidates actually argued against each other remained virtually the same (a mere 2.1% increase from 1984 to 1988), use of reaction shots increased sizably (35.3%). An even clearer depiction of the increased use of reaction shots results from a comparison to the 1976 debates where three debates produced 89 cutaways to the opponent (Messaris, Eckman and Gumpert, 1979, p. 365).

The visual structures of the first debates in 1984 and 1988 deserve particular attention. In 1988, the candidates traded 63 arguments of attack and defense, 16.7% more than the 54 instances of clash noted in the first Mondale-Reagan debate in 1984 (Morello, 1988a). But visual depiction of clash rose at a much greater rate: debate one in 1984 employed 34 reaction shots compared to the first 1988 debate which used 55—an increase of 61.8%. But these two debates are more similar than different in the number of attacks and replies occurring, even though the visual record conveys the impression that the debate in 1988 was more combative.

Perceptions of the debates as expressed in mediated accounts correspond to the differences in visual structuring. Press accounts said that Bush and Dukakis clashed angrily and sharply in snappish exchanges (Perry and Seib, 1988, p. 48; Dionne, 1988, p. A-1), a conclusion in line with the frequency of the reaction shots. On the other hand, press reports called the exchanges in Mondale-Reagan debate, with almost as many arguments but far fewer cutaways from reactions, "more substantive than heated, more insightful than dramatic" ("The Great Debate," 1984, p. 30).

Another difficulty presented by the aggregate visual record of clash concerns the impression of which debater initiated more of the clash. Conventional wisdom holds that cuts from one shot to another should be motivated by the action taking place. As one candidate speaks, the motivation for the cut to a two-shot is that the speaking candidate said something impelling a reaction. In a debate context, a debater's verbal challenge to the opponent invites a reply. Throughout the 1988 debates, moderators introduced candidate statements with language reinforcing the burden of the reply to the opponent: "Mr. Vice President, your one-minute rebuttal" and "Governor, you have one minute to respond." As noted earlier, reaction shots constitute the primary means for visualizing the verbal give and take of a debate. While the utterance of an attack might not be the only motivation to a reaction shot, it is necessarily an important impetus for such cutaways in a debate.

Following that action/reaction principle, we might expect that Dukakis should appear as the speaker in more of the reaction shots since he verbalized more clash. Bush, then, would be seen more often as silent reactor. Yet the opposite occurs: Bush speaks during more of the reaction shots than does Dukakis (51 to 41), visually suggesting he is the more active debater. While the number of cutaways to two-shots approximates the total number of instances of articulated clash (92 total two-shots/99 instances of verbal clash), the visual record of the debate misleads us as to which debater was initiating more of the clash. Given the news media's penchant for judging debates on the basis of who looked to be in charge, or seemed more in command, visually altering the verbal evidence of "control" is indeed problematic.

Along with misstating which debater was in charge of the clash in the 1988 debates, the visual record provided an unequal depiction of the candidates at work in the debates. As has been true of every presidential debate held so far, a panel of journalists initiated each round of debate by posing a question to one of the candidates. Overlooked in the controversy about the utility of this format, and the literature condemning it is vast,[5] is the impact the presence of a panel of questioners has on the direction of debate. Candidates not only clash with one another but also with the panel of reporters. In the 1988 debates, antagonism between panelist and candidate ran high as media personalities unleashed a "variety of techniques designed to embarrass and belittle those who aspire to lead us" (Hogan, 1989, p. 222). The "questions" from the panelists often served not as neutral openers for debate but as pointed critiques to which the candidate had to reply. Virtually "every question was preceded by a mini-speech—always argumentative and often belligerent—either expressing the 'media personalities' pessimistic assessment of some state of affairs or, in some fashion, refuting or belittling the candidate" (Hogan, 1989, p. 221). Bush, more often than Dukakis, was shown interacting with the panelists as he replied to their questions.

Pictures of the candidate responding to the panel involved a combination of reaction shot compositions: the candidate and some or all of the panel were shown together in a long shot, the panelist who asked the question was shown in a close-up as the candidate answered, or the candidate responded while the panel and the opponent were shown in the same long shot listening to the reply. Unlike the two-shots with the opponent, where the size of the reactor's face is large enough for us to detect nonverbal expressions of reply to the argument, shots including the panel (except for close-ups of the panelist) happen at a distance that made it hard to detect reactions. The visual message conveys the impression of a candidate "talking" to the panel.

Cutaways to the panel may, thus, have created an impression that Bush was more involved with the journalists than was Dukakis. In the two debates, Bush speaks in 27 shots involving the panel (15 in debate one, 12 in debate two) while Dukakis appeared in only 7 such shots (5 in debate one, two in debate two). By more frequently showing Bush addressing his answers "to" the panel, the visual text again depicts Bush as the more active debater by showing him speaking to the reporters on stage. Visual underemphasis of the interactions between debaters and panelists has been noted before (Messaris, Eckman, and Gumpert, 1979, p. 362). The visual record of the 1988 debates underemphasizes and misrepresents the extent of those interactions by showing Bush more often than Dukakis when they engaged the panel more or less equally. The paucity (in comparison to his opponent's) of Dukakis' appearance in shots including the panel as reactor thus inadvertently reinforces the aloof demeanor that many debate analysts said was a problem for him.

The frequency of cutaways to the panel during Bush's speeches has the added effect of distorting the pace at which the candidates were shot during the debate. Maintaining visual interest on television depends on a quick pace achieved through frequent changes in shots (Fiske, 1987, p. 27). The problem for presidential debates is that the "action" does not lend itself to such quick cutting. The slow visual pace of a debate makes comparative pace important, with shot discrepancies in the sequences when candidates speak having the potential to make a debater shot at a quicker pace seem more interesting. Televised "talking heads" are notoriously boring (Postman, 1988, p. 74) and faster-paced segments do typically appear more active (Wurtzel, 1983, p. 510).

With respect to pace, past presidential debates have treated candidates more or less equally. While the average duration of shots of Carter in the 1976 debates plodded along at 41.14 seconds, Ford's segments clocked-in at a roughly equal 43.41 (Messaris, Eckman and Gumpert, 1979, p. 364). In 1984, with its substantially quicker overall pace, the candidates again received virtually equal timing. Shots of Reagan speaking averaged

20.44 seconds; Mondale's shots averaged 22.36 (Morello, l988b, p. 235). The 1988 debates, owing to the lopsided advantage Bush received in all reaction shots (78 to 48), produced a distinct imbalance pace. Bush segments averaged 17.64 seconds while Dukakis shots had a mean duration of 24.56 seconds.

The inequality of visual treatment illustrated here is not trivial given the importance television places on the movement and sequencing of images. A television camera creates a limited two-dimensional visual field, thereby making all elements of that space potentially meaningful for viewers (Tiemens, 1978). Perception of a candidate's personality as revealed in a debate performance, an influential factor for some members of the audience (Shields and MacDowell, 1987), may be, at least partially, affected by how the selection of camera shots visualizes the candidates in action. In an election contest where Dukakis' perceived lack of emotion and warmth was one of the stumbling blocks he had to overcome in the debates (Oreskes, 1988, p. A-24), the slower visual pace of his speaking segments was no help.

★ GIVING PREFERENCE TO THE *AD HOMINEM* ATTACK

Integrating the verbal and visual messages during the moments of clash involves discovering patterns in the cues that motivate the cut to a reaction shot of the candidate. As noted earlier, the cut to a two-shot (absent the close-up of the non-speaking candidate) is the most direct signal that the audience should attend to how the other party responds to the verbalized statement. But which statements prompt reactions? With alarming frequency, personal attacks motivate the cut.

Defining the *ad hominem* fallacy as it applies to political campaigns requires special care. Standard definitions of *ad hominem*, attacking the person rather than the idea (Browne and Keeley, 1986, p. 129), lack precision because, in an election campaign, the person often *is* the issue (McDonald, 1989, p. 107). But when candidates resort to name-calling, without discussing the merits of the "labeled" group or idea, the resulting utterance does constitute an *ad hominem* attack. The snarl-words

thus employed tempt listeners to react without logically examining the validity of guilt-by-association remarks.

Twenty-four of the cuts to a two-shot (26.1%) followed a statement in which the speaking candidate tried to associate his opponent with a group, a point of view, or a behavior fraught with negative connotations. These pseudo-arguments functioned solely to remind the audience that they should oppose the candidate who stood in allegiance with these groups, people, or ideas. Over one-quarter of the arguments given visual emphasis in the debate are fallacies when evaluated by traditional criteria.

Bush, once again, received better treatment than his rival. On 16 occasions, Bush names a "despised" group and a two-shot of Bush and Dukakis follows. This camera pattern magnifies the impact of the *ad hominem*: as the speaker reminds the audience of the negative associations of his opponent, we see the person accused of allegiance to that which the speaker brands unfavorable. For a fleeting but important moment, the speaker's opponent becomes a visual anchor for the name-calling.

A few examples detailing how this process of visual reinforcement aided Bush's use of *ad hominem* should clarify the practice. In debate one, Dukakis pops into a two-shot as Bush says "call off all those pickets out there." Dukakis is thus implicated as the leader of the discordant and vocal agitators. Later, Bush argues that "this is the problem I have with big-spending liberals," and the camera cuts to Dukakis. When the Vice-President reminds us that the Reagan administration didn't listen to the freeze advocates, whose face do you suppose flashes into the picture? Along with these negatively-laden symbols, Dukakis appears when Bush mentions the Carter administration (twice), "marvelous phony Boston adjectives," the fact that the educator adviser in Massachusetts is in jail, and, of course, the ACLU (twice). On each occasion, Bush simply mentions the name of a group with negative connotations for his followers and offers no reasons to support the negative attributions. The reaction shots complete the name-calling by visually linking Dukakis with these groups.

The pattern continues in the second debate. "These people over here were talking about a freeze," says Bush. The camera cuts to Dukakis. Bush asserts that, after the Wall Street collapse in 1987, "I wasn't out there wringing my hands as some political leaders were." The camera cuts to a two-shot with Dukakis. Three times, Bush intones the words "left" or "liberal" and Dukakis appears in a two-shot.

The visual weight given Bush's *ad hominem* overwhelms Dukakis' modest efforts at tit-for-tat. Eight times in the two debates, Dukakis names a person, group, or idea with negative connotations and the camera visually associates Bush with the label. In debate one, Dukakis argues that people in the Reagan administration were dealing with Noriega and we see Bush. Once in each debate, Bush is shown after Dukakis talks about favoritism for the rich. Terrorists, Robert Bork, and "godfather" are other negative terms preceding a cut to a Bush reaction shot.

Thus, the visual structure of the debate adds impact to Bush's logically flawed arguments because the camera invites us to look at Dukakis while he is associated with unsavory groups and ideas. This name-calling succeeds because the reaction shot completes the attack, creating a verbal/visual enthymeme. The major premise, a verbally-conveyed identification of an unsavory group (like freeze advocates), is completed by the reaction shot, which functions as the minor premise (Dukakis is one of them).

A typical view of the rhetorical importance of the enthymeme holds that the "process, whether visual or verbal, is at the heart of the way we think and communicate . . ." (Leuthold, 1990, p. 6) because it "motivates the receiver to inferentially supply the premises which help alleviate ambiguity" (Leuthold, 1990, p. 7). But a new argumentative form is created when the camera supplies the premise missing from a verbally constructed argument. The television director, not the receiver, has resolved the gap in the reasoning process and the visual information that completes the argument serves as independent support for it. An ambiguous verbal statement is made more specific through the introduction of a visual anchor. Verbal attacks do not "play" well on television, and Bush avoids resorting to invective because the pattern of reaction shots makes his abstract personal attacks more concrete.

Thus, Bush slings mud without getting his hands dirty.

Dukakis resorts to a strategy of direct accusation of the Vice President's motives that does not play as well visually. In the first debate, Dukakis charges that there is no doubt but that Bush is questioning his patriotism. And, he adds, "I resent it." Later in the same debate, Dukakis says that "when it comes to ridicule, George, you win a gold medal." Both times, following the charge, Bush appears in a two-shot looking like the innocent victim of a verbal low-blow. Dukakis' verbal attacks against Bush are unfitting in a medium that has accustomed us to expect an indirect, more conversational style, where candidates speak softly and "avoid the appearance of carrying a big stick" (Jamieson, 1988, p. 44).

By emphasizing *ad hominem* attacks, the visual structure of the 1988 debates further de-emphasized reasoning as a mode of political persuasion. Television has altered not only the shape of presidential election campaigns but the form of political communication as well. Postman noted with alarm the all-encompassing effect television has had on the style of American discourse. The entertainment values that dominate television have worked their way into all forms of human contact, politics included, thus reshaping the way we communicate. As a result, "Americans no longer talk to each other, they entertain each other. They do not exchange ideas; they exchange images. They do not argue with propositions; they argue with good looks" (Postman, 1985, p. 92–93).

If a television debate provides a forum for the communication of political smears, it similarly affords candidates the opportunity to reply and to even advance arguments one's opponent might more easily duck under less adversarial circumstances. But the experience of the 1988 debates again illustrates how cutaway reaction shots undermine even this potential benefit.

★ OPPORTUNITIES FOR NONVERBAL REFUTATION

In an age when nonverbal cues have become increasingly central to voting decisions (Oreskes, 1988, p. A-24), it is not surprising to find that presidential debates are often reduced to, and remembered by, some distinguishing visual moment. As a communication system, television relies on pictorial symbols that elevate visual information to a position of significance over language (Pfau and Kang, 1989). On at least two occasions, the moment to remember in past television debates emerged during an episode of clash. In each case, the sequence of reaction shots intensified the moment and gave added weight to one candidate's reply to an opposing point.

Enduring an onslaught of criticisms about his stated policy positions, candidate Ronald Reagan needed but four words in his 1980 debate against President Carter to refute the charges lodged against him. "With that familiar crooked grin, with an unbelieving shake of the head, he began an answer with, 'There you go again.' With body English and a familiar phrase, he portrayed the President as an incorrigible distorter of the facts" (Safire, 1980, p. A-27). The remark was the verbal equivalent of a smile and a shrug (Jamieson, 1988, p. 51). The pattern of camera shots visually heightened the impact of the moment. In the only sequence of the debate with juxtaposed close-ups, viewers receive a direct cue that the candidates are engaged in debate (Tiemens, Hellweg, Kipper, and Phillips, 1985, p. 38). Reagan gets the better of Carter at this moment, and the reaction shots punctuate his triumph. In the process, Reagan dramatically differentiates ". . . himself from Carter . . . without projecting him(self) as unduly strident or defensive" (Martel, 1983, p. 44). In 1984, the most dramatic moment of the first debate occurred when Reagan attempted to reprise his hit moment from four years earlier (Cohen, 1984, p. A-19). But Mondale, ready for just such a development, launches into a memorable rebuttal initiated with the words, "Now, Mr. President, you said: 'There you go again.' Remember the last time you said that?"

The ensuing verbal attack argued that Reagan had made his earlier remark in reply to a charge that he would cut Medicare if elected which, Mondale alleged, Reagan actually tried to do. The point was incorrect ("Who's Right on Social Security," 1984, p. A-18), but the exchange was visualized with a combination of close-ups and two-shots of Reagan while

Mondale spoke which served to add tension and visual interest to the incident (Morello, 1988a).

Even though there was more to these debates than the "there you go again" incidents (Jamieson and Birdsell, 1988, p. 170–171), those episodes are most often recalled. While instances of verbalized clash in the 1988 debates produced no such signature visual moments, the cutaways nonetheless had an impact on the debate. Examination of the pattern of camera shots during some of the key exchanges reveals that reaction shots often worked to Dukakis' disadvantage.

"There You Go Again, Again"

Early in debate one, Dukakis tries to reenact the moment that served Mondale so well in the first 1984 debate. Arguing that Bush, or one of his spokespersons, had called the Massachusetts health care plan "socialized medicine," Dukakis claimed that "the last time the Vice President used that phrase, I suspect he remembers it. Don't you?" Dukakis continues the assault: "It was in 1964 and that's what he called Medicare. He was wrong then and he's wrong now."

Unlike the 1984 incident Dukakis apparently seeks to mirror, the pattern of camera shots does not intensify the verbalized point.[6] Unlike Reagan, whose head down, muttered "Um hmm" reply to Mondale's question was captured in two-shot, Bush refuses to take the bait and stoically gazes straight ahead in the two-shot following Dukakis' direct question. In 1984, as Mondale speaks the brunt of his charge against Reagan, the camera has cut to a close-up of Reagan listening to the attack. In a familiar visual sequence reminiscent of a myriad of television dramas, we are cued to pay attention to his facial reaction to the charge. But in 1988, the camera shows Dukakis in a chest-shot as he expresses the attack. Then, when he delivers the "he was wrong then and he's wrong now" punch line, the camera cuts to a long-shot taken from behind Dukakis and showing panelists Peter Jennings and Anne Groer. Bush escapes the pressure of a spotlighted reaction shot. While Dukakis tries verbally to reenact the 1984 incident, the pattern of camera shots depicting it fails to add the visual weight conferred when Mondale had his big moment.

Subsequent events further diluted the potential effect this moment might have had for Dukakis. The audience applauded Dukakis, and moderator Jim Leh[r]er interrupted the debate to scold the crowd for their outbreak of enthusiasm. Suddenly, the focus had shifted from Bush's position on government medical care programs to a discussion of the rules for debate. When the moderator signals the resumption of the debate, Dukakis starts talking about AIDS. The attempt to catch Bush in the same kind of a trap that snared Reagan four years earlier was over, and the moment was verbally and visually inconclusive. Bush never replied to the charge that he opposed Medicare or the Massachusetts health plan, and Dukakis failed to argue why such opposition was a significant issue in the present campaign. In 1984, the pattern of reaction shots employed as Mondale attacked Reagan had the effect of putting Reagan on the spot visually. In 1988, Bush refused to answer Dukakis "on cue" and was not shown close-up as the supposedly telling indictment is expressed.

"I Haven't Sorted Out the Penalties"

According to press accounts, the closest contender for the dreaded "great gaffe" label was Bush's reply to a question about his position on penalties for women and their doctors who would defy a constitutional ban on abortions if one were ratified (Perry and Shribman, 1988, p. 58). The Vice President said: "I haven't sorted out the penalties." After the debate, the Bush campaign issued several "clarifications," and within a few days, the modest furor subsided.

That such a flip answer failed to create a bigger problem for Bush may be in part explained by the visual structuring of Dukakis' attack on Bush's statement. Dukakis argues that "I think what the Vice President is saying is that he's prepared to brand a woman a criminal for making this decision. It's as simple as that." A reaction shot of Bush during that moment might have visually intensified the conflict over this point. But no shot occurred. Later, Dukakis contends that "I don't think it's enough to come before the American people who are watching us tonight and say, 'Well, I haven't sorted it out.'["] A cut to the reaction shot here might

have further dramatized the point. But there was none.

No change from the singular shot on Dukakis happens until Bush interrupted him to say, "I just said if the law is changed." In this two-shot, we see Bush seizing momentary control by interrupting his opponent in mid-statement. Dukakis, shown in the same two-shot says, "No, let me finish." Bush smiles, says "Sure" and the camera cuts back to a shot of Dukakis alone as he continues his argument against Bush's position. The next reaction shot, which occurs not as Dukakis criticizes the Vice President's remark but when he says he respects Bush's right to disagree, confers no additional visual drama to the content of Dukakis' argument.

Bush's position on penalties for violations of an abortion ban does not surface again in the debate. Dukakis made a start on this argument, but it was ultimately inconclusive both verbally and visually. He left the point a simple criticism of a lame debate statement instead of turning the tables on the Vice President to show how the difficulty in "sorting out the penalties" actually supported Dukakis position against a proposed constitutional ban on abortion. Visually, the Dukakis rejoinder fails to generate much emotional heat since no reaction shots of Bush appear when the harshest criticisms are spoken.

The story of the reaction shots for Dukakis in debate one, then, is one of unfulfilled opportunities. Bush, on the other hand, makes the most of his moments as reactor.

The Strategy of Shrugging Off an Argument

Cutaways to a reaction shot afford the non-speaking candidate an opportunity to refute his opponent without ever saying a word. In these two shots, Dukakis typically "leveled a deadpan look at [Bush], with a flicker of skepticism" (Dowd, 1988). Bush, however, employed a variety of poses, which nonverbally communicated responses to Dukakis' arguments. Particularly in the second debate, Bush silently counters several of the verbal attacks made against him.[7]

Observers of political debates have previously discussed how greater familiarity with the constraints of television enables a candidate to avoid behaviors that might not "look" confident to the viewing audience. Dukakis' ineffective management of the television space in the reaction shots adds a new wrinkle to that conclusion since he purportedly had the greater experience as a television debater. Bush campaigners called frequent attention to Dukakis' role as host of "The Advocates," a Public Broadcasting System program ("Lectern to Lectern," 1988). While undoubtedly an act aiming to lower performance expectations for Bush, thereby making it easier for "spin doctors" to label his debating a success, the remark alerts us to the kind of television experience Dukakis had and how the nonverbal performance norms for a program host may not transfer well to the role of television debater.

The intimacy of the television medium and the small screen size compel restraint in physical and vocal expression (especially in close-ups) where gestures might extend out of the frame (Blythin and Samovar, 1985, p. 148). Dukakis' less animated behavior reflects a studio television host at work. Bush's active nonverbal responses do not distract visually in the two-shots because he is shot at sufficient distance for his movements to not appear cut-off (as in a close-up). In one earlier debate where the behavior in reaction shots provided a striking contrast between the candidates (Jamieson and Birdsell, 1988, p. 160), the first debate in 1960, Kennedy looked intently at Nixon in many of the reaction shots while Nixon frequently moved his head around when captured in reaction. The composition of cutaways in that debate overwhelmingly favored close-ups and no two-shots were used (Seltz and Yoakam, 1962, p. 96). Whether by accident or design, Kennedy's generally restrained physical behavior fit the television space used to capture his reactions. Dukakis' less animated physical behaviors might have looked better had the reaction shots in his debates favored close-ups rather than two-shots.

Six times in the two debates, reaction shots capture Bush as he laughs during one of Dukakis' arguments. While one of these depicted a reply to a freeze-dried one-liner ("If I had a dollar for every label, I'd qualify for one of those tax breaks the Vice President wants to give away"), in all other cases Bush laughed during an accusation or a claim by his opponent.

Dukakis asserts in debate one that Bush was "in meeting after meeting after meeting listening to Secretary Schultz and Secretary Weinberger oppose that and yet he supported (the sale of arms to the Ayatollah)." In the accompanying two-shot, the Vice President laughs. Again in debate one, Bush laughs during charges that he supported a "failed policy in Latin America," was involved with Noriega and endorsed Ferdinand Marcos. In the second debate, two-shots depict Bush laughing while Dukakis' claims of "having a record of appointing judges" and "cleaning up" Boston harbor. Only once does the camera show Dukakis laughing while Bush speaks.

Beyond the strategic guffaw, Bush resorts to an assortment of other physical refutations. While Bush often stared straight ahead while Dukakis talked in debate one (Dowd, 1988), two-shots twice show him writing furiously as an attack unfurls. The visual message conveyed is that the Vice President has the answer to the point. In debate two, however, Bush employs the posed reply to arguments with greater frequency.

When a clash develops over whether or not Dukakis had raided the pension fund in Massachusetts as a way of balancing the state budget, Dukakis challenged Bush directly. In response to an earlier question, Bush had said "I won't do one other thing he's had to do: took $29 million out of his state pension fund." In response to a question from Margaret Warner of *Newsweek*, asking if a president had to be likeable to be effective, Dukakis rhetorically asked his questioner for permission to "go back and just say to the Vice President that I didn't raid the pension fund of Massachusetts. You're dead wrong, George."

As Dukakis began to explain himself, the two-shot shows Bush first shaking his head in disagreement. Then, the Vice President interrupts Dukakis' answer to say " . . . " [sic] Dukakis resumes his answer, saying "No, we did not. No, we did not." As he does, Bush appears in a two-shot, smirks and tilts his head toward Dukakis in a gesture which appears to suggest the remark "get him." Attempting to peg particular linguistic decodings to nonverbal behaviors is always problematic, but the interpretation of Bush's gesture is justified in this case. Bush was reacting to Dukakis' answer on the pension fund diversion charge; Bush had just interrupted Dukakis in an abbreviated effort to verbally counter his denials. Now, as Dukakis continued to deny Bush's claim, the Vice-President tilts his head toward his opponent and glances upward. The context of the exchange invites us to view Bush's action as an expression of disbelief, one captured by a reaction shot.

At another point in debate two, Bush stares, his mouth agape, as Dukakis says he voted against a National Governor's Conference resolution supporting a freeze in cost of living adjustments on Social Security payments. Later, when Dukakis challenges one of Bush's statements on farm policy, the two-shot shows the Vice President, his hand on his hip, looking directly at his opponent in a combative stance clearly suggesting his disagreement.

Emotional responses communicated by Bush's laughs, smirks, shrugs, and combative poses function to challenge the statements uttered as he appears in reaction shots. Refutation by impression management appears convincing on the television screen, and resists evaluation as a "logical argument" because no verbal statement exists to test. Reaction shots capturing gestural replies to arguments have the power to supplant listener attention to the ideas expressed at the moment the image of reply occurs since visual images are comprehended more quickly and retained more readily than verbal messages (Jamieson, 1988, p. 114). Verbalized arguments, even the truncated form present in televised political debates, involve some complexity especially when compared to the simple, holistic cues contained in nonverbal expressions. When the two conflict, pictures inevitably command greater attention. This risk perhaps explains why representatives of both candidates asked, to no avail, that reaction shots not be shown (Dowd, 1988).

Press reports frequently criticized Bush, especially after debate one, for the jumbled syntax with which he expressed many of his arguments (Will, 1988, p. 11-A). Those observations overlook, however, the visual grammar which succeeded where words may have failed him. As the camera captured simultaneous nonverbal responses to Dukakis' arguments, Bush made his points without running the risk of mangling another sentence. Jamieson and Birdsell's admonition, that "we can be seriously mislead by the nonverbal communication on which television dotes and to which we almost involuntarily gravitate" (1988, p. 183), underscores the logical dangers inherent in those instances where pictures "answer" words.

CONCLUSION

That cutaway shots pose the danger of capturing a candidate's unintentional, yet damaging, physical reactions has been noted before (Tiemens, Hellweg, Kipper and Phillips, 1985, p. 41; Greenfield, 1982, p. 232). This study demonstrates additional alterations these shots introduce to the television debate process. Simultaneous displays of visual and verbal information in the reaction shots of the 1988 presidential debates transformed the content of clash in three ways.

First, shot sequences misrepresented the incidence of verbalized clash. A significant increase in reaction shots (compared to the 1984 debates) occurred, visually suggesting an increase in articulated clash though the number [of] candidate arguments remained virtually the same. Further, the aggregate visual record of clash depicted Bush as the more frequent initiator of clash when Dukakis actually was. Finally, the more frequent cutaways to the panel gave Bush's speeches a significantly faster visual pace.

Second, shot sequences gave preference to *ad hominem* attacks as the verbal cue for the cut to a reaction shot. Over one-quarter of the arguments give visual emphasis to such personal smears. On 16 occasions, Bush named a "despised" group or idea and the next thing seen was a two-shot of Bush and Dukakis. This camera pattern magnified the impact of the *ad hominem* by making the speaker's opponent a visual anchor for the name-calling.

Lastly, shot sequences employed to visualize clash offered opportunities for nonverbal refutation that Bush seized. Dukakis' attempt to reenact another "there you go again" moment fell by the wayside when the visual structuring defused its impact. Dukakis' refutation of Bush's claim that he had not sorted out the penalties on the proposed abortion ban lacked the visual intensity that might have otherwise made the argument appear more compelling. And while most of the two-shots captured Dukakis in a deadpan glance as Bush spoke, several of Dukakis['] arguments were refuted visually by Bush in reaction shots.

The use of cutaway reaction shots as a device for documenting the "news" of the moment and an attempt to break visual monotony has traditionally been a problematic aspect of the debates. Powerful, visceral responses generated by the visual appeals in cutaway reaction shots have the potential to mitigate the language of a candidate's argument. Political argument by visual association thus presents us with juxtaposed words and images which suggest connections between the two that either are not (and often cannot) be proven (Jamieson, 1984, p. 449–451). This questionable form of discourse acquires additional weight through the visual structuring of televised debates in which the pictures accompanying moments when the candidates engage each other can alter the record of verbal clash.

NOTES

[1] A two-week interval separated the two viewings. Holsti's formula (1969, p. 137) for reliability established the percentage of the agreement between viewings. While usually employed to assess interrater reliability, it can determine interrater reliability of codings done at different times (Wimmer and Dominick, 1987, p. 186). For all camera shots in both debates, R= .951. For reaction shots only, R= .981. Discrepancies between the viewings were resolved by reexamination of the segments of the debate in which differences resulted.

[2] Transcripts used were those in *The New York Times*. All quotes used were double-checked against the videotape and corrected if necessary.

[3] Some of the studies to analyze message content of presidential debates include Samovar (1962; 1965) Hellweg and Verhoye (1990), Ellsworth (1965), Weiss (1981), and Riley and Hollihan (1981). In some of these investigations, researchers identified arguments by the theme of a candidate's utterances.

[4] Analysis of the verbal clash in the debate did not follow a content analytic design, so no reliability figures were calculated. Conclusions about the amount of clash in the debates are supported by other studies. Carlin, Howard, Stanfield and Reynolds

(1991, p. 128) determined that a substantial amount of clash occurred in the debates and that Dukakis expressed more statements of clash than did Bush. Our results are not identical because they defined clash differently and counted some expressions of clash multiple times. Hellweg and Verhoye (1990) reached a similar conclusion about which debater engaged in more verbalized clash, although they also used different means to tabulate frequencies of attacks.

[5] For a brief review of the critique of the "Meet the Press" format in its campaign 1988 revival, see "So We Know Them a Little Better Now" (1988), "Standoff" (1988), "Debates Domesticated" (1988), and "Sure Loser in the Debate: The Format" (1988).

[6] Despite Dukakis' attempt to emulate the verbal form of Mondale's "there you go again" return in 1984, his argument visualized in a way that diffuses its impact. A small preliminary empirical test was conducted in an effort to corroborate this claim.

Two groups of randomly selected students (n=57) enrolled in introductory speech courses at a small, Mid-Atlantic College engaged the two action/reaction sequences mentioned here. One group read transcripts of Mondale's "there you go again" retort and Dukakis' attempted reprise. The second group watched a video-tape of the two segments. Each group completed the same questionnaire after interacting with the debate materials.

For the group reading the transcripts, 62.5 percent rated Dukakis' segment as the more interesting argument. Of those watching the debates, only 9.75 percent rated it the more interesting argument. The Mondale-Reagan clash, rated by 25 percent of the readers as more interesting, was picked the more interesting argument by 68.29 percent of the viewers. (The remaining subjects in each treatment rated the two arguments as equal in interest.)

When subjects rated the importance of the arguments, 87.5 percent of the readers rated Dukakis' argument as more important than Mondale's; only 6.25 percent rated Mondale's attack as the more important one. Viewers, however, rated the segments differently: only 9.75 percent found the Dukakis segment more important while 68.85 percent judged Mondale's remarks the more important argument.

Finally, viewers perceived Dukakis' attack as less damaging to Bush than readers did: 37.5 percent of the readers thought Dukakis' attack the more damaging one and 12.19 percent of the viewers rated it that way.

Of course, the focus of this study as a critical interpretation clash necessitates qualification of the significance of the empirical findings which are, at this point, only suggestive. Additional experimental research, employing a more elaborate design, is required in order to learn whether viewers reacted more to candidate behaviors or how those behaviors were "shot." But this pilot study validates one point of my criticism—that visual structuring of clash in television debates can influence the perception of clash.

[7] In the same study, subjects watched two segments of the second debate in which Bush (who never spoke) engaged in a variety of nonverbal actions which I have interpreted as refutations to Dukakis' attacks. In the first segment, Dukakis says Bush was "dead wrong" in claiming that Dukakis had raided the Massachusetts pension fund to balance his state's budget. The charge is punctuated by reaction shots in which Bush gestures toward Dukakis and later flicks his head in Dukakis' direction; 60.97 percent interpreted his behaviors as disagreement or that Bush was "denying" Dukakis' point.

In the second segment, Dukakis accuses Bush of having made a factual error about the existence of agricultural supply maintenance programs followed by the claim that Bush's "Boston Harbor" television ads were misrepresenting what Dukakis did to clean up the harbor. In reaction shots, Bush first places his hand on his hip, later nods, and finally laughs when Dukakis says, "no thanks to you, George." 70.73 percent of the responses described Bush's actions as disagreeing or "making light of" the attack; 19.5 percent reported that Bush looked uncomfortable or as if Dukakis' point had hurt him. Subjects were asked to freely respond to an open-ended question, asking them to describe what they saw Bush do and to write what this behavior meant to them.

REFERENCES

A Welcome Debate. (1988, September 27). *Christian Science Monitor*, p. 13.

Blythin, E. & Samovar, L. (1985). *Communicating effectively on television*. Belmont, CA: Wadsworth.

Bowers, N. M. & Courtright, J. A. (1984). *Communication research methods*. Glenview, IL: Scott Foresman.

Browne, N. M. & Kelley, S. M. (1986). *Asking the right questions*. 2nd ed. Englewood Cliffs, NJ: Prentice-Hall.

Carlin, D. P., Howard, C., Stanfield, S., & Reynolds, L. (1991). Effects of presidential debate formats on clash: a comparative analysis. *Argumentation and Advocacy, 27*, 126–136.

Cohen, R. (1984, October 9). A failure to communicate. *Washington Post*, p. A-19.

Debates, domesticated. (1988, September 27). *New York Times*, p. A-34.

Dionne, E. J. (1988, September 26). Derisive exchange. *New York Times*, p. A-1.

Dowd, M. (1988, September 26). Two rivals in red ties speak softly. *The New York Times*, p. A-19.

Drucker, S. J. (1990). The impact of mediation on argumentation in presidential debates. Paper presented at the annual convention of the Speech Communication Association, Chicago.

Drucker, S. J. & Hunold, J. P. (1987). The debating game. *Critical Studies in Mass Communication, 4*, 202–207.

Ellsworth, J. P. (1965). Rationality and campaigning: a content analysis of the 1960 presidential campaign debates. *Western Political Quarterly, 18*, 794–802.

Fiske, J. (1987). *Television culture*. London: Methuen.

George Bush's race. (1988, October 17). *Christian Science Monitor*, p. 15.

Gov. Dukakis: trapped. (1988, October 16). *Washington Post*, p. C-6.

Greenfield, J. (1982). *The real campaign*. New York: Summit Books.

Hellweg, S. A. and Phillips, S. L. (1989). A verbal and visual analysis of the 1980 Houston republican presidential primary debate. *Southern Speech Communication Journal, 27*, 32–38.

Hellweg, S. A. & Verhoye, A. H. (1989). A comparative verbal analysis of the two 1988 Bush-Dukakis presidential debates. Paper presented at the Speech Communication Association Convention, San Francisco.

Hogan, J. M. (1989). Media nihilism and the presidential debates. *Journal of the American Forensic Association, 25*, 220–225.

Holsti, O. (1969). *Content Analysis for the Social Sciences and Humanities*. Reading, MA: Addison-Wesley.

Jamieson, K. H. (1988). *Eloquence in an electronic age*. New York: Oxford University Press.

Jamieson, K. H. (1984). *Packaging the presidency*. New York: Oxford University Press.

Jamieson, K. H. & Birdsell, D. S. (1988). *Presidential debates*. New York: Oxford University Press.

Kraus, S. (1988). *Televised presidential debates and public policy*. Hillsdale, NJ: Lawrence Erlbaum.

Krippendorf[f], K. (1980). *Content analysts: an introduction to its methodology*. Beverly Hills: Sage.

Lectern to lectern. (1988, November 21). *Newsweek*, p. 123.

Leuthold, S. M. (1990). Consonance of visual and verbal enthymemes in political communication with examples from the first 1988 presidential debate. Paper presented at the Speech Communication Association Convention, Chicago.

McDonald, D. (1989). *The language of argument.* 6th ed. New York: Harper and Row.

Martel, M. (1983). *Political campaign debates.* New York: Longmans.

Messaris, P.[,] Eckman, B. and Gumpert, G. (1979). Editing structure in the televised versions of the 1976 presidential debates. *Journal of Broadcasting, 23,* 359–369.

Morello, J. T. (1988a). Argument and visual structuring in the 1984 Mondale-Reagan debates: the medium's influence on the perception of clash. *Western Journal of Speech Communication, 52,* 277–290.

Morello, J. T. (1988b). Visual structuring of the 1976 and 1984 nationally televised presidential debates: implications. *Central States Speech Journal, 39,* 233–243.

Oreskes, M. (1988, September 25). Nominees battle tonight to emerge most presidential. *The New York Times,* A-24.

Perry, J. M. and Seib, G. F. (1988, September 26). Bush, Dukakis trade charges on national security. *Wall Street Journal,* p. 48.

Perry, J. M. and Shribman, D. (1988, September 26). Dukakis debate performance may have halted Bush advance. *Wall Street Journal,* p. 48.

Pfau, M. and Kang, J. G. (1989). The impact of relational and nonverbal communication in political debate influence. Paper presented at the Speech Communication Association Convention, San Francisco.

Postman, N. (1985). *Amusing ourselves to death.* New York: Elisabeth Sifton Books.

Postman, N. (1988a). *Conscientious objections.* New York: Alfred Knopf.

Postman, N. (1988b). Critical thinking in an electronic era. In Trudy Govier (Ed.), *Selected Issues in Logic and Communication* (11–19) Belmont, Calif.: Wadsworth.

Richmond, V. P., McCroskey, J. C., and Payne, S. K. (1991). *Nonverbal Behavior in Interpersonal Interactions.* 2nd ed. Englewood Cliffs: Prentice-Hall.

Riley, P. and Hollihan, T. (1981). The 1980 presidential debates: a content analysis of the issues and arguments. *Speaker and Gavel, 18,* 47–59.

Safire, W. (1980, October 30). "There You Go Again." *New York Times,* A-27.

Samovar, L. A. (1962). Ambiguity and unequivocation in the Kennedy-Nixon television debates. *Quarterly Journal of Speech, 43,* 277–279.

Samovar, L. A. (1965). Ambiguity and unequivocation in the Kennedy-Nixon debates: a rhetorical analysis. *Western Speech, 29,* 211–218.

Seltz, H. A. and Yoakam, R. D. (1962). Production Diary of the Debates. In Sidney Kraus (Ed.), *The great debates: background, perspective, effects* (73–126). Bloomington, IN: Indiana University Press.

Shields, S. A. and MacDowell, K. A. (1987). "Appropriate" emotion in politics: judgments of a television debate. *Journal of Communication, 37,* 78–89.

So We Know Them a Little Better Now. (1988, September 27). *Chicago Tribune,* p. 14.

Standoff. (1988, September 26). *Washington Post,* A-14.

Sure Loser in the Debate: The Format. (1988, October 15). *New York Times,* p. 30.

That Great Debate. (1960, September 27). *Christian Science Monitor,* p. 18.

The Debate: Chapter I. (1960, September 28). *Washington Post,* A-16.

The Great Debate. (1984, October 15). *Newsweek,* pp. 30–34.

The Second Debate. (1984, October 23). *Wall Street Journal,* p. 28.

The Voters Won. (1988, September 27). *Wall Street Journal,* p. 32.

There's Still Time. (1988, September 27). *Los Angeles Times,* sec. II, p. 6.

Tiemens, R. (1978). Television's portrayal of the 1976 presidential debates: an analysis of visual content. *Communication Monographs, 45,* 362–370.

Tiemens, R., Hellweg, S., Kipper, P. and Phillips, S. (1985). An integrative verbal and visual analysis of the Carter-Reagan debate. *Communication Quarterly, 33,* 34–42.

Transcript of the TV Debate Between Bush and Dukakis. (1988, September 26). *New York Times,* A-16–19.

Transcript of the Second Debate Between Bush and Dukakis. (1988, October 14). *New York Times,* A-14–16.

Trent, J. S. and Friedenberg, R. (1983). *Political campaign communication.* New York: Praeger.

Weiss, R. O. (1981). The presidential debates in their political context: the issue-image interface in the 1980 campaign. *Speaker and Gavel, 18,* 22–27.

Who's Right on Social Security. (1984, October 9). *Washington Post,* A-18.

Will, G. (1988, September 27). The debate was a national embarrassment. *Des Moines Register,* 11-A.

Wimmer, R. D. & Dominick, J. R. (1987). *Mass media research.* Belmont, CA: Wadsworth.

Wurtzel, A. (1983) *Television production* (2nd ed.). New York: McGraw Hill.

Reporters vs. Undecided Voters: An Analysis of the Questions Asked during the 1992 Presidential Debates

William P. Eveland, Jr., Douglas M. McLeod, and Amy I. Nathanson

Presidential elections inevitably draw the attention of media pundits and researchers to the quality of campaign discourse. As a primary vehicle for this discourse, the presidential debates have not escaped the scrutiny of media commentators and researchers. However, most post-debate commentary has focused on who won, while most research has examined the debates' impact on voting, learning and interest in the campaign (for summaries of the major debate research, see Jamieson and Birdsell, 1988). By comparison, relatively less attention has been paid to the quality of the discourse in the debates (see Friedenberg, 1994 for analyses of each televised presidential and vice-presidential debate).

Experienced journalists have traditionally been entrusted with the important role of asking the questions for the debates. Presumably, this practice has been guided by the assumption that journalists, by virtue of their professional training, would ask questions that would enhance discourse quality. The 1992 presidential debates, however, introduced a new twist to the standard procedure—the use of "undecided voters" selected by the Gallup organization to ask questions during one of the three debates.

This study compares the 1992 reporter panelist debates with the undecided voter debate to determine whether the questions differed in type, composition, clarity, style, and topic. In addition, question topics from both populations are also compared to Harris poll data which assessed critical campaign issues for likely voters.

★ DEBATE QUESTION RESEARCH

Televised presidential debates, held every presidential election year since 1976, are the most watched political messages during any campaign (Jamieson and Birdsell, 1988), drawing audiences between 60 and 100 million viewers in most cases (Trent and Friedenberg, 1991). For many, the debates serve as a primary source of information about candidates' images (Pfau and Eveland, 1994; Pfau and Kang, 1991) and their stands on issues (Drew and Weaver, 1991; Pfau and Eveland, 1994). For this reason, it is important to ensure that the debates provide pertinent information for the general voting public. The decision to use undecided voters as questioners for the second presidential debate in 1992 raises an important issue for future debates: How did the untrained, undecided voters perform relative to the standard panel of journalists?

Media scholars have argued that the quality of questions is an important determinant of the quality of the candidates' responses:

> Overall, the members of the press who have served as panelists must share some of the responsibility with the candidates for the nature of argument in presidential debates. While the format severely limits issue discussion, trivial, unfocused, and loaded questions further diminish the capability of these debates to discuss the issues of the day. (Hellweg, Pfau, & Brydon, 1992, p. 54)

As these authors have noted, however, the full responsibility for candidate answers is not on the shoulders of the questioners—it is shared by the candidates themselves. Even perfect questions may be answered imperfectly if the candidates so choose.

Previous research has typically found that questions asked by reporter panels were deficient in several respects. Bitzer and Rueter (1980) offer a description of what a debate question should and should not be:

> A debate requires starting points consisting of issue statements, questions, or propositions selected and phrased to elicit informative exchanges and arguments between candidates. A good debate question should not be vague, meandering, ambiguous, cosmic, or cluttered. It should not include so many independent questions that the possibility of a cogent response in the allotted time is foreclosed. (pp. 53–54)

Question Type

Multiple questions within a single question round have been one major drawback in the questions of candidates (McCall, 1984; Milic, 1979). Bitzer and Rueter (1980) noted that the frequent use of multiple questions during the 1976 debates contributed to the low quality of answers. For instance, only 16% of the multiple questions were fully answered, compared to 59% of single questions. Multiple questions can both cloud the issue and allow the candidate to focus on only one facet of the question.

Milic's (1979) analysis of the 1976 debates found that alternatives questions, reference questions, and what/which/who questions were likely to be ineffective, producing unsatisfactory answers. Yes/no questions, how questions, and why questions were more likely to elicit satisfactory answers from the candidates. Milic defined a satisfactory answer as one which "reveals the position of a candidate on a given issue, so that the voter may determine whether he wishes to support a candidate with such a view" (p. 189). We adopt this definition in the current study as well. Therefore, an effective question is one which is most likely to produce a satisfactory answer. It should be noted, however, that a candidate can respond to even the best question with an unsatisfactory answer. Candidates at times wish to avoid revealing their true stance on an issue for fear that it may cost them votes, or to conceal the fact that they have not considered the issue at all. Therefore, a good question does not guarantee a good answer. However, a good, precise question makes it more difficult for the candidate to avoid answering without making the audience fully aware that this is exactly what is taking place.

Question Composition

Critics often complain that the questions asked by journalists are unnecessarily wordy. For example, McCall (1984) found that panelists often exceeded time limits for asking questions in the 1980 Reagan-Anderson debate. Lengthy questions inappropriately elevate the prominence of the panelists and detract from the quality of the responses (Hellweg et al., 1992; McCall, 1984). The inclusion of unnecessary introductions and statements confuse rather than enhance questions. Hogan (1989) found that "not once in the 270 minutes of the 1988 debates did a journalist simply ask a candidate: 'What is your position on such and such an issue?' Instead, each and every question was preceded by a mini-speech" (p. 221).

Question Clarity

According to Bitzer and Rueter (1980), poorly stated and vague questions led to less than adequate answers from the candidates in the Ford-Carter debates. They noted that at least some of the questions were "cluttered" or "ambiguous." Hellweg et al. (1992) have referred to some of the past questions as "unfocused." Clearly, one problem with past debate questions has been an inability to discern the true question from the excess verbiage included by the questioner.

Question Style

Several scholars have criticized the tone of questions asked by reporter panelists. Researchers have noted that questions are often accusatory (Bitzer & Rueter, 1980), argumentative (Bitzer & Rueter, 1980; Hellweg et al., 1992; Hogan, 1989), leading (Milic, 1979), and loaded (Hogan, 1989). McCall (1984) asserts that tone is an important criteri[on] for judging question quality, and argues that questions "should reflect a tone of goodwill rather than hostility" (p. 102). Milic (1979) noted that although leading questions were good at preventing Carter and Ford from evading the actual question, they still produced satisfactory answers only about half of the time.

Bitzer and Rueter (1980) found that accusatory questions diverted the candidates away from answering the questions by forcing them to address the implicit accusation instead of the explicit question. Also, McCall (1984) argues that questions challenging a candidate's policy are not necessarily biased, but that bias can result if the questioners do not provide similar challenges to the other candidate(s). According to McCall, John Anderson benefited from this type of bias in his 1980 debate against Ronald Reagan. Similarly, Gravlee, Irvine, & Vancil (1976) found this form of bias in some of the questions in the 1976 Ford-Carter debates.

Question Topic

Finally, reporters have also been criticized for asking questions that are essentially irrelevant to the viewers, focusing instead on campaign issues and new developments of candidate issue stances (Jamieson and Birdsell, 1988). This is not the most useful strategy for conveying information to voters, however, who have been paying less than strict attention to the candidates' issue positions. As Jamieson and Birdsell (1988) lament: "Questions designed to elicit news do not invite the level of basic information on candidate positions and differences that the less educated viewer would find most useful" (p. 169).

Research Questions

In order to determine whether the undecided voters or the reporter panelists asked the more effective questions (those that past research has shown to be more likely to elicit satisfactory answers and address the topics of concern to the electorate), five research questions were posed.

RQ$_1$. Did journalists or undecided voters ask the type of questions that typically produce satisfactory answers?

RQ$_2$. Did journalists or undecided voters ask lengthier questions?

RQ$_3$. Were journalists' or undecided voters' questions less clearly constructed?

RQ$_4$. Did journalists or undecided voters ask more argumentative, accusatory, and leading questions?

RQ$_5$. Did journalists or undecided voters ask questions that reflect more closely the deciding issues for American voters?

★ METHODOLOGY

This study examined all of the 1992 presidential debate question periods from the debates that utilized either undecided voters or reporter panelists to ask questions (N = 44). The questions were classified into one of two groups: reporter panel questions (n = 27) or undecided voter debate questions (n = 17). The first debate, on October 11, used a panel of three journalists and a single moderator to pose questions to the three major presidential candidates.

The October 15 debate in Richmond (VA) used Gallup-designated undecided voters and a moderator. Finally, the second half of the October 19 debate used a three journalist panel similar to the first debate.[1]

The results of this study were based on a quantitative content analysis to describe question characteristics and a qualitative analysis to provide illustrative comparisons. The unit of analysis was the "question period." The question period consisted of the time from when the questioner began to speak until the candidate began to answer. Questioners' attempts at clarification were considered part of the question period, but follow-ups to the original question were not.

A transcript of the questions asked during the debates (created by one of the authors) was used instead of a videotape of the debates in order to remove any indication of the identity of the person asking the question (voter or reporter)—each question was identified to the coders by a random number only. The order of the questions was rearranged so that questions from any one debate were not all grouped together. Then, every question period was coded twice on a number of variables (once each by two independent coders who were trained in the use of the instrument). Intercoder reliability was assessed using Krippendorff's alpha, which takes into account agreement due to chance alone and is therefore a more conservative measure than percent agreement (Table 1). All variables used in the analysis achieved an alpha of at least .73 and 20 out of 23 exceeded .80. According to Krippendorff (1980), alphas greater than .80 are normally considered acceptable, while alphas between .67 and .80 are "marginally" acceptable. The quantitative analysis stressed four primary areas of concern: question type, composition, style and topic. In addition to these areas, general descriptive information about the question periods was collected.

The categories for question type were based on those used by Milic (1979) in his study of the 1976 debates. After identifying several question types, Milic determined which types yield more satisfactory answers. The present study measured seven question types as separate variables; thus the classification of question type was

TABLE 1

Reliability Estimates for Quantitative Analysis

VARIABLE	Alpha
Question type:	
Yes/No question	1.00
Why question	.90
How question	.89
What/Which/Who question	.86
Alternatives question	1.00
Reference question	.83
Multiple questions	.73
Question composition:	
Number of words	.99
Prologue statement	.91
Mesologue statement	1.00
Epilogue statement	.78
Question style:	
Argumentative	.80
Accusatory	.88
Leading	.76
Question topics:	
Economy	.92
Foreign policy	.99
Domestic programs	.99
Domestic problems	1.00
Domestic issues	.90
Character issues	1.00
Leadership	1.00
Government policy	.80
Campaign	.90

Note: N = 44.

not restricted by a mutually exclusive coding system. "Yes/no" questions were defined as questions that are possible to answer with a simple yes or no response. "What-which-who," "why," and "how" questions were identified by whether they used one of these words as a key part of the question. "Multiple" questions pose two or more questions within a single question period. "Reference" questions were defined by Milic (1979) as "a long statement followed by a

question in itself without meaning except by reference" (p. 195) to the preceding statement.[2] "Alternatives" questions require candidates to choose between statements, options, or electives specified within the question. The results of Milic's research indicate that the question types most likely to elicit satisfactory answers are yes/no questions, how, and why questions. The most ineffective question types are reference questions, what-which-who questions, alternatives questions and multiple questions. Our assumptions about the effectiveness of question types were based on this research.

Quantitative measures of question composition included the number of words, questions, and reference statements in the question period. The number of words in the question period included non-essential verbiage such as repeated words and "ums." The number of questions was measured by the number of distinct questions within the question period; hence, if the same question was repeated during the same question period, it was counted as a single question. The presence of reference statements was noted by counting the number of prologues (statements prior to the question), mesologues (statements made between questions), and epilogues (statements after the question). If a question period contained one or more of any of these three types of statements, the question period was categorized as having a reference statement.

Question style variables were measured on 3-point semantic differential scales. They included argumentative versus non-argumentative, accusatory versus non-accusatory, and leading versus non-leading questions. Argumentative questions provoke the candidate or invite dispute. Accusatory questions either explicitly or implicitly accuse a candidate of being involved in or responsible for something undesirable or distasteful. Leading questions contain an implicit assumption(s) that the candidate answering may or may not accept, such as an implication that a candidate holds a certain stand on an issue, or that one event would necessarily follow from another.

Finally, question topics were derived from categories used by the Harris poll. Topics included the economy, foreign policy, domestic social programs (e.g., education, welfare, health care), domestic social problems (e.g., crime, drugs, the environment), domestic social issues (e.g., abortion, gun control, civil rights),[3] character issues, leadership qualities, governance policy (e.g., term limits, line-item veto) and issues related to the campaign itself. Question periods were assigned a value of 0 to 2 for each topic (0 for "not a focus," 1 for a "minor focus," or 2 for a "major focus"). As a result, some questions had more than one topic.

Question topics were then compared to results averaged from two Harris polls asking "likely voters" what they considered the deciding issues of the campaign. The Harris polls were conducted over a period of 45 days prior to the first debate. Comparisons with Harris data were done to determine whether journalists or undecided voters were more likely to ask questions that focused on the deciding issues of the campaign—an important consideration if the purpose of the debates is to educate voters about the candidates so that they can make an informed decision.

In order to compare question topics to the Harris poll results, questions ranked as a major focus were considered two "votes" for the topic. A minor focus ranking was considered a single vote. The number of votes cast for each topic was summed across all question periods for each debate format. Percentages for each topic were then computed and compared to the percentages of mentions in the Harris poll. These percentages were ranked so that Spearman rank order correlations between the two debate formats and the Harris data could be calculated. These correlations allow us to specify which group of questioners was more likely to inquire about issues important to the American public.[4]

★ ANALYSIS RESULTS

Question Type

Analysis of the 1992 presidential debates indicates that journalists generally used question types found by Milic (1979) to be more effective in eliciting satisfactory answers (Table 2). Journalists were almost twice as likely to ask yes/no and why questions than their undecided voter counterparts. The only effective question type that was more likely to be asked by voters than journalists was how questions.

TABLE 2

Percentages of Question Types and Topics for Questions Asked by Journalists and Undecided Voters

	Journalists (n = 27)	Undecided Voters (n = 17)
Question type:		
Yes/ No question	40.7%	23.5%
Why question	14.8	5.9
How question	29.6	35.3
What/Which/Who question	33.3	58.8
Alternatives question	7.4	5.9
Reference question	37.0	11.8
Multiple questions	37.0	64.7
Question composition:		
Reference statements	70.4%	64.7%
Question topics:		
Economy	21.0%	17.0%
Foreign policy	22.0	12.0
Domestic programs	11.0	21.0
Domestic problems	6.0	4.0
Domestic issues	10.0	12.0
Character issues	10.0	4.0
Leadership	13.0	6.0
Government policy	3.0	13.0
Campaign	5.0	12.0

Note: N = 44.

In terms of the less effective question types, journalists were about three times as likely to ask reference questions, but undecided voters asked nearly twice as many what/which/who and multiple questions. There were only minimal differences between the two groups in terms of the percentage of alternatives questions.

In general, these findings indicate that journalists tended to use the types of questions that past research has found to lead to clear statements by the candidates about their policy positions relative to the question being asked—that

TABLE 3

Means (and Standard Deviations) for Question Composition and Style for Questions Asked by Journalists and Undecided Voters

	Journalists (n = 27)	Undecided Voters (n = 17)
Question Composition:		
Number of Words	55.22 (22.15) Median: 50	75.00 (53.06) Median: 56
Question Style: (range = 0 to 2)		
Argumentative	1.07 (.83)	.59 (.87)
Accusatory	.93 (.83)	.53 (.80)
Leading	.96 (.71)	.65 (.61)

Note: N = 44

is, satisfactory answers. This may be due to the fact that journalists are trained to ask questions as part of their profession, and therefore should have learned to use question types that would produce responsive answers. This pattern, however, is not evident across all question types, and thus the conclusion that journalists are more likely to use effective question types is mixed.

Question Composition

Question composition variables included question length and the use of reference questions (those with prologues, epilogues, or mesologues). Table 3 illustrates that, overall, voters' questions contained more words ($\bar{x} = 75.00$) than the journalists' ($\bar{x} = 55.22$). However, when median question lengths were examined, the difference was not so dramatic (median for voters = 56; median for journalists = 50).

While several undecided voters asked extremely long, rambling questions that inflated the mean differences, the qualitative analysis revealed that reporters did seem to be more concise. For example, ABC News correspondent Ann Compton's question on the economy was phrased more directly than a comparable economic question asked by a voter. Compton asked:

Governor Clinton, can you lock in a level, here tonight, on where middle income families can

be guaranteed a tax cut, or at the very least, at what income level they can be guaranteed no tax increase?

Clinton's response to Compton's question was concise and to the point. His first statement was, "The tax increase I have proposed triggers in at family incomes $200,000 and above." Clinton then continued with a brief explanation of his rationale behind this tax policy. In essence, this question was fairly successful at getting the candidate to articulate specific policy information.

The first half of the voter's question, on the other hand, contained extraneous statements that distracted from the question that follows:

This is for Governor Clinton. Um, in the real world, that is outside of, uh, Washington D.C., compensation and achievement are based on goals defined and achieved. The deficit is my, uh, my question is about the deficit. Would you define in specific dollar goals how much you would reduce the deficit in each of the four years of a Clinton Administration, and then enter into a legally binding contract with the American people that if you did not achieve those goals that you would not seek a second term? Answer yes or no and then comment on your answer please.

Once the voter got beyond the extraneous statements, he essentially posed two yes/no questions, but asks Clinton to respond with one simple yes or no, creating a double-barreled question. Clinton responds by saying "No, and here's why." It is difficult to determine which of the two questions Clinton is answering. Ultimately, the question produces a fairly informative response, but could have done so much more efficiently. Compton's question was both more effective and more concise—37 words as opposed to the 101 words used by the undecided voter.

Although journalists generally required fewer words than voters to ask their questions, Table 2 reveals that the percentage of reference statements used by each group were similar (64.7% for undecided voters, 70.4% for journalists). However, the reference statements used by journalists were more likely to be an important part of the question, as opposed to simply adding the unnecessary information. In 59% of the cases, the prologues used by journalists were necessary to understand the question; however, voters' prologues were necessary only 22% of the time. For example, the following question posed by journalist John Mashek included a prologue that was necessary to the interpretation of the question:

> Mr. Perot, racial division continues to tear apart our great cities, the last episode being this spring in Los Angeles. Why is this still happening in America, and what would you do to end it?

On the other hand, voters' prologues tended to be unnecessary, sometimes nearly irrelevant to the question itself, as illustrated in the following example:

Uh, my question was originally for Governor Clinton, but I think I would welcome a response from all three candidates. As you are aware, crime is rampant in our cities. Uh, and in the Richmond area, and I am sure it has happened elsewhere, twelve-year-olds are carrying guns to school. And I am sure when our Founding Fathers wrote the Constitution, they did not mean for the right to bear arms to apply to twelve year olds. So I am asking, where do you stand on gun control, and what do you plan to do about it?

In this example, the last sentence in the question period could have adequately addressed the voter's interest in knowing the candidates' positions on gun control without including introductory remarks. Instead of providing context for the issue of gun control, the prologue of this question period distracted responses toward other crime related issues.

In his response, Clinton proclaimed support for the right to bear arms and then stated support for the Brady Bill mandating waiting periods, a ban on "assault weapons," and putting more police officers on the street. Bush focused more generally on a variety of issues including policies dealing with criminal sentencing, procedural violations by police officers, the death penalty and drug enforcement, only briefly stating his opposition to firearm registration, ownership limitations and the Brady Bill. Before the question was passed to Perot, the moderator reframed the question back to the issue of gun control. Perot characterized the Brady Bill as a "timid step in the right direction." He then stated that American society "has become so preoccupied with the rights of the criminal that we've forgotten the rights of the innocent." He then proceeded to argue that millions of poor people in the inner cities are living in the equivalent of prison because they've been forced "to put bars on their windows and bars on their doors" to protect themselves against crime.

While brevity is not always a direct indicator of question quality, and some questions may require reference statements to properly communicate ideas, many of the longer questions contained unnecessary words and repetitious references that obscured question content. Consider, for example, the following question asked by an undecided voter:

> If I may, um, and forgive the notes here, but I am shy on camera. Um, the focus of my work is [sic] a domestic mediator is meeting the needs of the children that I work with by way of their parents and not the wants of their parents. And I ask of the three of you, how can we as symbolically the children of the future president expect the two of you, the three of you, to meet our needs. The needs in housing, and and and and and and crime and

and you name it as opposed to the wants of your political spin doctors and your political parties. . . . Can we focus on the issues and not the personalities and the mud? I think there is a need, if we can take a poll here, with the folks from Gallup perhaps, I think there is a real need here to focus at this point on the needs. Could I ask one other thing? Could we cross our hearts, it sounds silly here, but could we make a commitment, you know we are not under oath at this point, but could you make a commitment to the, to the citizens of the United States to meet our needs. And we have many. And and not yours, again, I echo you know I repeat that that it's a real need I think that we all have.

This question period, containing 225 words and requiring 47 seconds of debate time to ask, illustrates how excessive verbosity obfuscates the question as the speaker digresses into a lengthy monologue containing substantial amounts of irrelevant information. In this example, the speaker not only included a series of irrelevant reference statements, but also uses an excessive number of words to express a fairly simple set of ideas. Furthermore, the complexity of this question period is increased by the speaker's inclusion of multiple questions. That is, the speaker posed three distinct questions, further blurring the focus.

Bush interpreted the question as asking why the campaign was focusing on the candidates' personal images instead of issues. He answered by defending the importance of a candidate's personal characteristics in terms of suitability for leadership. He finished by stating his willingness to address issues. Perot unequivocally stated that he would "take the pledge to stay on the issues." He then made light of the fact that he didn't have any spin doctors or speechwriters by stating that, "It probably shows." Clinton picked up on this point by saying that, "The ideas I express are mine" and have their basis in 12 years experience as the governor of Arkansas. Perot then made a statement that his campaign did not accept "foreign money," "foreign lobbyists," or "PAC money" and pledged to cut the deficit in half. Clearly this response period lacked focus, which may be in large part attributable to the lack of focus in the question.

Question Clarity

The previously cited question asked by the domestic mediator exhibits several clarity problems that extend beyond lack of conciseness; its vague questions are embedded in a maze of dangling phrases and poorly chosen words. Despite the aforementioned difference in the length of questions asked by journalists and voters, clarity was about equally problematic for both. Indeed, journalists were to blame for producing three of what were arguably the six most unclear questions asked during the debates.

Many of the questions from journalists and undecided voters were obscured by disjointed phrases and halting deliveries. Several examples can be found in the following preface used by one voter to ask each candidate when their party would nominate a woman and an African-American for president:

> What I'd like to know, and this is to any of the three of you is, aside from the recent accomplishments of your party, aside from those accomplishments, in uh, racial representation, and without citing any of your current appointments or successful elections. . . .

Ultimately, this question produced less than satisfactory information. Clinton began by delivering platitudes about the importance of electing women and minorities. Bush responded with the flippant remark that if his wife Barbara were running, she would probably be elected. He then cited Colin Powell as an example of a successful African-American. Perot responded by predicting that Powell would be on a ticket in 1996.

Somewhat surprisingly, some of the journalists' questions were equally disjointed.

For example, in the first debate, PBS anchor Jim Lehrer asked:

> Governor Clinton, how do you respond, on, on, to the president, on the question, you have two minutes, on the question of experience. He says that that is what distinguishes him from the other two of the candidates.

Poor word choice also caused problems. For instance, one of the undecided voters mistakenly used the term "national debt" instead of "recession," thereby derailing her attempt to get the candidates to empathize with the common person. After she asked how the national debt had affected the candidates on a personal level, Perot gave a largely irrelevant answer about his own rags-to-riches story. After Bush began to respond, the questioner and the moderator both interjected twice to clarify the question. At this point, Bush seemed confused and asked for further clarification. Again, the questioner rephrased her question:

> What I am saying is . . . Well, I have personal, uh, problems with the national debt. But how has it affected you? And if you have no experience in it, how can you help us if you don't know what we are feeling?

Finally, the moderator refocused the question on the recession. Bush ended up making the point that it's not fair to say "you haven't had cancer, therefore you don't know what it's like." Clinton then asked the questioner to "tell me how it[']s affected you again?" He paraphrased her earlier response before beginning to address the impact of the deficit, the recession and Republican policies on the problems that he saw as governor of Arkansas. Shortly thereafter, Clinton reverted to a discussion of larger economic issues, losing the issue of personal impact in the process. In summary, the undecided voter raised a potentially interesting question, but used a total of 61 seconds in the various attempts to ask it. The result was a set of answers that were neither coherent nor illuminating.

Some pundits have claimed that Bush's answer to this question sealed his fate in the 1992 election. Although this interpretation is debatable, it is clear that much was made of the candidates' answers to this question by the news media. That is unfortunate, considering the question's lack of clarity and the seeming inability of any of the candidates to truly discern the real question this voter was trying to ask. A better choice of words by the questioner, or a clearer focus to the question, may have allowed the candidates to provide better answers, which is important if such great weight is to be placed on responses to a single question.

Non-sequiturs were another cause of unclear questions. Surprisingly, the journalists were the worst offenders. The most glaring example of this offense is contained in former NBC correspondent Sander Vanocur's question to Bush:

> Mr. President, there's been a lot of talk about Harry Truman in this campaign, so much so that I think tomorrow I'll wake up and see him named as the next commissioner of baseball. The thing that Mr. Truman didn't have to deal with is drugs. Americans are increasingly alarmed about drug-related crimes in cities and suburbs, and your administration is not the first to have grappled with this. And are you at all of a mind that maybe it ought to go to another level, if not to what's advocated by William F. Buckley, Jr. and Milton Friedman, legalization, somewhere between there and where we are now?

The presence of non-sequiturs and vague question wording make it difficult to identify the exact nature of Vanocur's question. He seems to be asking Bush about new or non-traditional approaches to tackling the drug problem, but does not seem to be asking for a position statement on drug legalization per se. Bush misinterprets the question by responding, "No. I don't think that's the right answer. I just don't believe that's the answer." After briefly summarizing the effectiveness of his administration's approach to drug policy, Bush returns to the issue of legalization to conclude by restating his opposition. In the process, the audience receives no information about the candidate's ideas about alternative approaches to the drug problem.

In another glaring example, Helen Thomas of UPI asked two completely unrelated questions in the same question period. The first concerned Perot's allegation that Saddam Hussein had been told of the United States' refusal to intervene in Iraq's border dispute. She then went on to ask:

> And also, uh, I, I really came in with another question. What is this penchant you have to investigate everyone? I, are those accusations correct, investigating your staff, investigating the leaders of the grassroots movement, investigating associates of your family?

Perot's response to these two very dissimilar questions was limited because he needed to address each one separately. He first addressed the second question, attempting to defend his use of these investigators by arguing that it is common for business people to use them when involved in law suits. He then briefly addressed Thomas' first question about Iraq with the time he had remaining. Instead of devoting time to the primary question in their responses, Clinton and Bush both focused on the topic of Saddam Hussein, dropping the topic of Perot's penchant for investigation.

By including irrelevant information, non-sequiturs distract both the candidate and the audience from the issue in question. To some degree, then, such questions reduce the potential for both quality answers and audience learning from the debates.

The reasons for poor execution may differ between journalists and voters. The poor quality of some voters' questions may reflect inexperience with televised debates. Many of the undecided voters did appear somewhat less at ease on camera than the journalists. In fact, one undecided voter admitted to being shy on camera and apologized for using notes.

In the case of the journalists, non-sequiturs and vague referents seemed to be the consequence of attempts to appear literate and knowledgeable. Sander Vanocur dropped the names of current and past political players in four of the five questions he asked (including Army Secretary Michael Stone, Treasury Secretary "James" Brady,[5] Congressman Lee Hamilton, President Harry Truman, William F. Buckley, Jr., Milton Friedman and Wilbur Mills). Vanocur also interjected the titles of specific government legislation and agencies into his questions. This made the questions sound more technically sophisticated, but actually distracted from the meaning of the question. Vague referents and gratuitous name dropping are exemplified by Vanocur's question on health care rationing:

> Governor Clinton, Ann Compton has brought up Medicare. I remember in 1965 when Wilbur Mills, of Arkansas, the Chairman of Ways and Means, was pushing it through Congress. The charge against

it was it was socialized medicine, one you never . . . [Clinton interjects 'Mr. Bush made the charge'] . . . Well, he served with him two, two years later in 1967 where I first met him. The second point though is, that it is now skyrocketing out of control. People want it, we say it is going bonkers. Is not the Oregon plan applied to Medicaid, rationing, the proper way to go, even though the Federal Government last August ruled that it violated the Americans With Disabilities Act of 1990?

Although Vanocur's question is difficult to decipher from the excess verbiage, he seems to be asking for Clinton's response to charges that the Clinton health care program is essentially socialized medicine and for Clinton's opinion of the Oregon health plan. The references to Wilbur Mills and the 1965 Medicare legislation function only as an attempt to enhance Vanocur's credibility. After a brief endorsement of the Oregon plan, Clinton then strays from the topics in question by addressing issues related to Medicare. He then goes on to discuss the Clinton health care plan, but doesn't address the socialized medicine charge.

Another explanation of journalists' use of vague references is that their proximity to the campaign breeds a familiarity with events, issues, and policies that may not be shared by the larger audience (Jamieson and Birdsell, 1988). For instance, many audience members may not have been familiar with the Oregon health insurance plan cited above. By employing vague referents, journalists reduce the value of their questions by rendering them incomprehensible to the general public.

Question Style

The fourth research question addressed stylistic differences between questions asked by journalists and voters; specifically, which group asked more argumentative, accusatory, and leading questions?

Analysis suggests that the greatest stylistic difference was in the use of argumentative questions (Table 3). Specifically, journalists' questions were more argumentative than those of the voters ($\bar{x} = 1.07$, $\bar{x} = .59$, respectively). For example, CNN anchor Susan Rook attempted to provoke Perot by pointing out an inconsistency between his presidential intentions and the traditional presidential role, thereby inviting argument as opposed to simply asking for his opinion or stance on the issue:

> Mr. Perot, you've talked about going to Washington to do what the people who run this country want you to do. But, it is the president's duty to lead, and often lead alone. How can you lead if you are forever seeking consensus before you act?

Perot answered this question by briefly referring to leadership through using the office of president as a bully pulpit, but spent the remaining time discussing the importance of seeking consensus, in effect ignoring the question of leadership and focusing on the topic of consensus building. Bush and Clinton fared no better, with Clinton touting his use of town hall meetings and Bush discussing his role in building a consensus among nations during Desert Storm. The true focus of the question, leadership without seeking consensus, was lost on the candidates in part because Perot needed to defend his tactic of consensus building, and then Bush and Clinton felt it necessary to follow his lead.

Journalists['] questions were also more accusatory than those of the undecided voters ($\bar{x} = .93$, $\bar{x} = .53$). For instance, Ann Compton criticized Bush in a way that implied he was heartless:

> Mr. President, how can you watch the killing in Bosnia, and the ethnic cleansing, or the starvation and anarchy in Somalia, and not want to use America's might, if not America's military, to try to end that kind of suffering?

Framed in this manner, the question goes beyond asking about a foreign policy issue, and becomes an accusation of callousness for allowing a terrible situation to endure.

This question prompted an emotional, defensive response from Bush. Most of his response time was devoted to a general defense of restraint rather than an explanation of past actions or a policy agenda for the future.

Finally, journalists' questions were more leading than those asked by voters ($\bar{x} = .96$, $\bar{x} = .65$). For example, Sander Vanocur asked a leading question to Clinton: "Is not the Oregon plan applied to Medicaid, rationing, the proper way to go, even though the Federal Government last August ruled that it violated the Americans with Disabilities Act of 1990?" In this instance, the journalist did not merely ask the candidate to offer his position on a certain issue, but instead alluded to his own views and merely asked the candidate to validate them. In his answer to this question, Clinton did agree with Vanocur's assertion, but then went on to discuss his own plan rather than focusing on the Oregon plan.

Given that journalists and voters may approach the debates from different perspectives, it makes sense that their questions would be marked by qualitatively different styles. For example, journalists traditionally see themselves in an adversarial role and, as such, their questions often require candidates not only to address specific issues, but also defend their integrity and commitment. Professional ideology, then, may make journalists more likely to pose their questions in an argumentative, accusatory, and leading fashion.

Furthermore, journalists may have asked more challenging questions with the hope of inciting candidates and thereby creating a particularly interesting media event. Argumentative, accusatory, and leading questions may produce more volatile responses than those asked in a neutral manner. Thus, while straightforward, issue-oriented questions usually produce more informative responses (Milic, 1979; Bitzer and Rueter, 1980), hostile and leading questions may be more likely to elicit responses which satisfy journalistic requisites of providing interesting sound-bites.

Finally, stylistic differences between journalists' and voters' questions may be related to the fact that journalists are experienced in asking questions of political figures (Jamieson and Birdsell, 1988). Journalists may be less intimidated by the status of the candidates and thus more comfortable asking argumentative, accusatory, and leading questions.

Question Topics

The final research question asked whether reporters or voters would be more likely to ask questions on the topics considered by Harris poll respondents (and by generalization

TABLE 4

Percentages and Rank-Order of Debate Question Topics and Mentions
as Important Campaign Issues in Harris Polls

QUESTION TOPIC	Harris Poll		Journalists		Undecided Voters	
Economy	57.2%	(1)	21.0%	(2)	17.0%	(2)
Foreign policy	6.1	(4)	22.0	(1)	12.0	(5)
Domestic programs	19.2	(2)	11.0	(4)	21.0	(1)
Domestic problems	3.2	(6)	6.0	(7)	4.0	(8.5)
Domestic issues	10.9	(3)	10.0	(5.5)	12.0	(5)
Character issues	3.5	(5)	10.0	(5.5)	4.9	(8.5)
Leadership	0.0	(8)	13.0	(3)	6.0	(7)
Government policy	0.0	(8)	3.0	(9)	13.0	(3)
Campaign	0.0	(8)	5.0	(8)	12.0	(5)
Spearman's rho						
Harris poll with Journalists	.60					
Harris poll with Undecided voters	.50					
Journalists with Undecided voters	.19					

Note: Harris poll data is based on the average of two polls, one conducted from August 26–September 1, 1992 and the other conducted from October 2–4, 1992. The categories presented in this table in some cases represent combinations of more specific Harris categories (The Harris Poll 1992 #63).

Americans as a whole) to be highly relevant for making voting decisions (Table 4).

To precisely assess the relationship between the topics covered during the debates and the topics considered very important by Harris respondents, each topic was rank ordered according to the frequency of mention by Harris respondents, journalists and voter questioners. Spearman rank order correlations were then calculated to determine the relationship between the Harris data, the topics of questions asked by journalists, and the topics of questions asked by the undecided voters.

The correlation between the Harris issues and the journalists' questions (rho = .60) was similar to the correlation between the Harris data and the undecided voters (rho = .50), revealing that both groups of questioners did a fair job addressing issues deemed important by the Harris respondents. Although the rankings from both groups of debate questioners were similar to the Harris rankings (as evidenced by the similar correlations), they were quite dissimilar with respect to each other. The

correlation between topics addressed by voters and topics addressed by reporters was only .19. These apparent differences between the two groups did not manifest themselves in the way that might have been expected, however. For instance, the voters paid considerable attention to campaign-related issues (which journalists have traditionally been accused of) and governance policy in their questions; by contrast, the journalists placed relatively more emphasis on foreign policy and character issues.

CONCLUSION

The results of this study indicate that differences do indeed exist between the questions asked by journalists and undecided voters. However, neither the questions of journalists nor undecided voters were very good compared to an ideal standard, which would be expected from a review of the extant debate question research (Bitzer and Rueter, 1980; Hellweg et al., 1992). The overall quality of debate questions needs to be improved regardless of who may be asking the questions in future debates. Our results, though, indicate some areas in which each of the two groups of questioners in 1992 outperformed the other.

Journalists were more likely to ask questions of the type that are typically effective in eliciting satisfactory answers from candidates. However, the differences between the two groups were not as strong as might have been expected considering the journalists' tremendous experience advantage in asking questions of political figures.

Journalists were more likely than the voters to ask concise questions. This was in part due to the voters' tendency to make more unnecessary reference statements during their question periods.

Interestingly, the clarity of questions asked by the two groups did not differ substantially. Both journalists and undecided voters asked unclear questions caused in part by poor word choice, non-sequiturs, and disjointed phrases.

Overall, journalists' questions were more argumentative, accusatory, and leading than questions posed by undecided voters, perhaps due to the fact that they were less intimidated by the candidates. Past research has found such questions to be ineffective because they put the candidate on the defensive, so that they often fail to address the question directly.

Finally, the topics of questions asked by journalists and voters reflected, for the most part, the issues that Harris poll respondents deemed important. However, despite their similarity to the Harris poll data, there were apparent differences in topics asked by journalists and undecided voters.

The implications of this study for the future use of undecided voters in presidential debates are mixed. The undecided voters were just as capable as the journalists in asking questions about the important campaign topics. Many of their questions did lack clarity, but this was true of the journalists as well. On a positive note, the undecided voters seemed less likely to ask argumentative, accusatory and leading questions.

If debate organizers decide to use undecided voters again in the future, they should provide additional guidance to reduce the use of ineffective question types and long, rambling questions with irrelevant statements. If reporter panelists are used in the future, they too should be instructed to ask questions that would stimulate debate among the candidates on issues of importance to voters, as opposed to trying to get the candidates to say something "new" or attacking candidates in order to elicit an emotional response from them.

In addition to further experimentation with undecided voters, debate organizers should consider further departures from the standard reporter panelist debates in search of a more successful means of providing information to the electorate. Finally, varying questioners and debate formats would have the additional benefit of facilitating future field experiments to determine the most successful debate questioners and formats, the results of which could be used to further improve televised presidential debates.

NOTES

[1] The first half of the third debate used a third type of format, the single moderator. This debate segment was not analyzed because only three distinct questions were asked.

[2] Reference questions necessarily contain at least one reference statement: a prologue, mesologue or epilogue. But a question period with a reference statement does not necessarily constitute a reference question. To qualify as a reference question, the question would not stand by itself without the presence of a reference statement.

[3] The distinction between social programs, social problems, and social issues is as follows: social programs are essentially large, government funded programs, such as Social Security, public schools, unemployment compensation, etc.; social problems are those things that, although people may disagree on how to deal with them, most agree are things that need to be addressed, such as health care, crime, poverty, etc.; social issues are those things that divide the nation in terms of opinion, such as abortion, gun control, euthanasia, etc.

[4] Due to the small number of question periods in the 1992 debates, formal statistical significance tests of our hypotheses would have a high probability of Type II error as indicated by power computations. Power levels for small (delta = .20), medium (delta = .50), and large (delta = .80) effect sizes were computed (Cohen, 1988). The power assessments of .10 (for small effect size), .38 (medium effect size), and .76 (large effect size) indicate that the power

level is sufficient to find only large effects (which were not expected) without a high probability of Type II error. As such, formal statistical significance tests are inappropriate. Hence, the quantitative data collected for this study was used to provide precise descriptions to enhance the qualitative analysis. More important, however, is that since all reporter panelist and undecided voter question periods from the 1992 debates were coded, our data represents a census as opposed to a sample from a larger population. As such, parametric tests designed to allow generalization to a larger population are unnecessary to conclude that real differences existed between reporters and undecided voters. We therefore discuss how meaningful the differences were between the two groups.

[5] In fact, the name that Vanocur meant to drop was that of Treasury Secretary Nicholas Brady. By instead confusing him with James Brady (President Reagan's press secretary who was wounded in the assassination attempt by John Hinckley in 1981), Vanocur may have further confused the candidates.

REFERENCES

Bitzer, L., & Rueter, T. (1980). *Carter vs. Ford: The counterfeit debates of 1976*. Madison, WI: University of Wisconsin Press.

Cohen, J. (1988). *Statistical power analysis for the behavioral sciences*. Hillsdale, NJ: Erlbaum Associates.

Drew, D., & Weaver, D. (1991). Voter learning in the 1988 presidential election: Did the debates and the media matter? *Journalism Quarterly, 68,* 27–37.

Friedenberg, R. V. (1994). *Rhetorical studies of national political debates: 1960–1992* (2nd ed.). Westport, CT: Praeger.

Gravlee, G. J., Irvine, J. R., & Vancil, D. L. (1976). The final Ford-Carter debate: A rhetoric of rescue. *Exetasis, 3,* 24–32.

The Harris poll 1992 #63, (1992). p. 3.

Hellweg, S. A., Pfau, M., & Brydon, S. R. (1992). *Televised presidential debates: Advocacy in contemporary America.* New York: Praeger.

Hogan, J. M. (1989). Media nihilism and the presidential debates. *Journal of the American Forensic Association, 25,* 220–225.

Jamieson, K. H. & Birdsell, D. S. (1988). *Presidential debates: The challenge of creating an informed electorate.* New York: Oxford University Press.

Krippendorff, K. (1980). *Content analysis: An introduction to its methodology.* Beverly Hills, CA: Sage.

McCall, J. M. (1984). The panelists as pseudo-debaters: An evaluation of the questions and questioners in the presidential debates of 1980. *Journal of the American Forensic Association, 21,* 97–104.

Milic, L. T. (1979). Grilling the pols: Q & A at the debates. In S. Kraus (Ed.), *The great debates: Carter vs. Ford, 1976* (pp. 187–208). Bloomington, IN: Indiana University Press.

Pfau, M. & Eveland, W. P., Jr. (1994). Debates versus other communication sources: The pattern of information and influence. In D. Carlin & M. S. McKinney (Eds.), *The 1992 Presidential Debates in Focus* (pp. 155–174). New York: Praeger.

Pfau, M. & Kang, J. G. (1991). The impact of relational messages on candidate influence in televised political debates. *Communication Studies, 42,* 114–128.

Trent, J. S. & Friedenberg, R. V. (1991). *Political campaign communication: Principles and practices* (2nd ed.). New York: Praeger.

White Paper on Televised Political Campaign Debates

The Racine Group*

★ PREFACE

In the Fall of 2000, with the Bush-Gore debates freshly in memory, the American Forensic Association's Publications Committee and the National Communication Association's Research Board launched a collaborative initiative to facilitate greater cooperation in research on televised presidential campaign debates and to promote and make more usable the diverse range of existing Communication research on the subject. The project convened a select group of Communication scholars representing both the humanities and social sciences. Their research interests ran the gamut from critical

---
**The Racine Group includes the following communication scholars: David S. Birdsell, Diana B. Carlin, Jennifer R. Considine, Edward A. Hinck, Kathleen E. Kendall, Michael Leff, Kathryn M. Olson, Shawn Parry-Giles, Michael Pfau, and David Zarefsky.*

analyses of rhetorical strategies in specific debates to the trans-campaign effects of debates on such matters as voting behavior, image formation, and attitude change, and from the role that the media play in shaping the debates and their interpretations to the way that the debates, beyond their function in campaigns, influence general conceptions of democratic norms, cultural practices, and perceptions of leadership.

During the summer, participants circulated position papers concerning the state, implications, and resource needs of Communication scholarship on presidential debates, and, in September of 2001, they arrived in southeastern Wisconsin and northeastern Illinois. Approximately half of the group contributed to a public program held at the University of Wisconsin-Milwaukee. This program was endorsed by the Wisconsin Humanities Council, the local League of Women Voters, and the Edison Initiative, as well as UWM's College of Letters and Science and Communication Department; it subsequently was broadcast on public radio station WUWM. Approximately half of the participating scholars gave presentations at a colloquium at Northwestern University sponsored by the Department of Communication Studies. On September 21, the two sub-groups converged at the Racine Marriott, halfway between Milwaukee and Evanston, for two days of intensive work. The goal was to produce a White Paper that surveyed the current state of Communication research on televised presidential campaign debates, secured a foundation for coordinating and promoting the discipline's underappreciated, but wide-ranging contributions, and suggested means of expanding the scope and enhancing the quality of this body of scholarship. Primary audiences anticipated for this White Paper were those outside our discipline who have a stake in better understanding the communicative dimensions of such debates and those inside the field who are interested in developing new research or teaching projects.

Preliminary results of the Racine conference were presented at a public panel at the 2001 NCA convention in Atlanta. Revisions were made in light of the ensuing discussion with the audience, and further editing and discussion produced the final product printed below. This White Paper is not definitive but is a first attempt at codifying, encouraging, and stressing the importance of Communication research—and particularly cooperative, multi-methodological Communication research—on televised campaign debates. We intend to follow this paper with a presentation/reaction session at the 2002 NCA Convention in New Orleans.

★ INTRODUCTION

Because they command the attention of the public, the media, and the candidates, televised political campaign debates have become a permanent aspect of America's political landscape. The first nationally broadcast debate, the Kennedy-Nixon encounter of 1960, attracted an audience nearly equivalent to the final game of the 1959 World Series, which to that point had been the most watched event in television history.[1] The debates between Carter and Ford in 1976, the next set of televised debates, were viewed by well over eighty percent of the television audience,[2] and presidential debates invariably command the largest audience for any campaign event.[3] Moreover, the news media make presidential debates a centerpiece of their campaign coverage. For example, in 1996, two-thirds of television news stories during the debate period mentioned the debates and almost one fourth of network news lead stories featured them.[4] Especially in close elections, debates may stimulate interest in the campaign generally and in the debates themselves, with the audience growing in size and interest as the sequence of encounters continues.[5] According to Jamieson and Birdsell, "when debates are announced, movement in the polls slows; in anticipation, the electorate suspends its willingness to be swayed by ads and news. Here is the opportunity to see the candidates side by side, unfiltered and unedited."[6] We may be skeptical whether the debates are really "unfiltered," given the painstaking briefings of the candidates and the tendency to adhere to prefabricated scripts, but these exchanges certainly are more spontaneous and revealing than the spot commercials and stump speeches that, for most voters, provide the only other direct opportunity to observe the candidates.[7] Thus, while journalists and scholars display varying degrees of cynicism about the debates, few deny that viewers find them useful, and almost no one doubts that they play an important role in national campaigns.

Although there was some doubt about this point because of the hiatus in presidential debates between 1960 and 1976, televised campaign debates now seem destined to continue.[8] The revival of the debates in 1976 and 1980 established expectations strongly reinforced in 1984 when incumbent Ronald Reagan agreed to debate Walter Mondale, even though Mondale trailed in the polls and Reagan seemed to gain no strategic advantage and indeed to place himself at some risk in making this decision.[9] In all campaigns since 1984, debates have occurred, and they have become firmly established as a part of the cycle of election events. A candidate now could not refuse to debate without disappointing public expectations and paying a heavy political cost.

Owing to the durability and importance they have achieved in our political culture, televised campaign debates demand and deserve careful scholarly inquiry, and the discipline of Communication is ideally situated philosophically, historically, and methodologically to play a leading role in such scholarship. The discipline traces its origins back to the theory and practice of debate in classical civilization; it includes argumentation as a major element in its teaching and research and has long served as the chief sponsor of intercollegiate debate. Campaign debates have interest for scholars in almost every sub-field of the discipline, and at the same time, the range of interests and expertise that the discipline can bring to bear on the debates provides an appropriately broad and diverse ground for scholarly work. In fact, as this report demonstrates, the discipline already has produced an impressive body of solid research. Unfortunately, however, the significance of this work is not adequately recognized, and the scholarship lacks the systematic, long-term coordination needed to do full justice to the subject.

Although it is not widely recognized or cited outside of our own literature, the discipline has produced an impressive body of diverse and substantial scholarship on televised debates. This scholarship nicely demonstrates how the breadth of the field—its incorporation of several approaches to research—can function constructively when different research protocols are directed toward a single, relatively clear object of study. Thus, the disciplinary literature encompasses traditional studies of rhetoric and argumentation as well as social scientific work grounded in both quantitative and qualitative methodologies. We have produced studies of the strategic dynamics of debates in relationship to their historical contexts,[10] studies that compare local and national contests or national primary and general campaign debates,[11] studies of measurable audience effects (including the learning of information, image formation, and voting choices),[12] and studies of how viewers make use of televised debates.[13] Other recent Communication research focuses on visual or nonverbal aspects of the debates,[14] on the debates' relational dimensions,[15] on the ways that the debates reaffirm or subvert norms and assumptions about democracy and how they socialize auditors to democratic values (independently of the outcome of any particular debate),[16] on how lay viewers interpret the debates within specific cultural and gender expectations,[17] on viewers' perceptions of relative importance of various issues, the relative desirability of candidates' issue positions, and the confidence in their projected voting choice,[18] and on the media's ability to affect interpretation and evaluation of debates.[19]

In addition to theoretical inquiry, research in the discipline also has led to important practical applications. For example, Myles Martel's groundbreaking book, *Political Campaign Debates: Images, Strategies, and Tactics*, offers a comprehensive, research-based strategic guide for political campaigns involving debates.[20] And, with respect to policy studies, we have made a notable contribution through studies of debate format. At the request of the Commission on Presidential Debates, Communication scholars conducted an extensive focus group study that produced a number of interesting conclusions and that strongly influenced the Commission in its decision to use a single moderator format for the presidential debates in 1996 and 2000.[21] Future studies that bear both on practice and policy seem natural projects for scholars in our discipline and also present opportunities for us to put our research to good use.

Participants in political debates long have recognized the expertise available in the discipline, but they sometimes tend to narrow and compartmentalize it. Candidates tap us for strategic advice about how to make and defend arguments as they seek to win partisan advantage through their performances. Media coverage of the debates encourages both debaters and auditors to focus simply on the "knock-out" punch or major gaffe, and this perspective tends to occlude a more thoughtful consideration of the debates. The news media and lay auditors look to us for simple, straightforward expert judgments that reveal who "won" or "lost," but they often have little interest in the reasoning behind our opinions or about the nuances of judgment in these matters. For example, David Zarefsky, the nation's leading scholar on the debates between Lincoln and Douglas,[22] observes that at election time news commentators religiously compare televised campaign debates, always unfavorably and usually unfairly, to the Lincoln-Douglas contests.[23] Idealizing these historic debates without closely examining them and ignoring the significant differences in political context, commentators persist both in holding contemporary campaign debaters to inappropriate evaluative standards and in failing to identify the argumentative features of the Lincoln-Douglas debates that actually could serve as standards for enhancing current debates (e.g., skills in analysis and refutation, in-depth development of arguments in speeches of sufficient length, well-focused subjects for debate).

Any review of the discipline's scholarship on campaign debates reveals that the diversity of research methods and goals has strengthened our understanding of the subject. We strongly believe that this diversity is our primary asset, and this White Paper itself is both a model of cooperative effort among Communication scholars who come from different research communities and an argument for broader, better coordinated, and more systematic scholarship based upon complementary

methodologies. We first survey the existing research, then identify areas for future research, and finally consider the resources needed for improving and expanding research. Throughout the paper we draw mainly from research published in Communication journals and/or by researchers who publish in other venues but have a clear link with the discipline (e.g., departmental affiliation or membership in the National Communication Association or the American Forensic Association). We also must note that the published research cited in this paper is illustrative rather than comprehensive. Consistent with our earlier claim about the sheer volume of research produced in the discipline, we found many more studies of televised campaign debates than space allows us to cite.

★ WHAT WE KNOW

Format Matters

Debate formats have been a subject of discussion at least since Lincoln and Douglas negotiated their famous encounters in 1858. Issues such as the length of the debate, length and types of speeches or responses, topics, questions and questioners, and who participates, all influence formats and subsequent content and argument structure. The format and the questions asked have an influence on the degree of interaction and the clash between or among candidates.

Research since the 1960 Kennedy-Nixon debates[24] indicates that format is one factor influencing the types of arguments and the levels of clash that exist in debates. In the 1980 debates, for example, the format changed at the mid-point and candidates had more rebuttal opportunity. The levels and types of clash were affected by the change in format.[25] Further content analyses of the 1988[26] and the 2000 debates[27] also demonstrated the influence of format on levels and types of arguments. The 1988 study compared the levels and types of clash used in the Bush-Dukakis debates to levels found in studies of previous debates and concluded that format is a factor, but not the only factor influencing what takes place. Other variables such as position in the polls, debate skills, and overall campaign strategy also affect argument and style choices.

The study of the 2000 debates examined changes in strategy by Bush and Gore across three unique formats and also concluded that format was a factor influencing argument strategies as was the form of questions asked by journalists and citizens. The issue of question type as a format factor was explored in other studies that also concluded that citizens ask different types of questions than professionals and that the questions influence the type of argument as well as the language choice used by the debaters.[28]

Length of response or the amount of time devoted to a single issue not only affects how much depth a topic is given but also influences viewer learning and satisfaction with the debate.[29] For example, the formats used in the first half of the third presidential debate in 1992 and in the first and second debates in 2000 enabled the moderator to ask a series of follow-up questions and to build the follow-ups on responses to previous questions. The result was a longer period of time spent on an issue and a more positive response for the format and for the information received by the viewers.[30]

Format also can influence how well a candidate performs. In 1992 viewer reactions and polls taken after the debates indicated that Ross Perot performed best with the traditional format, Bill Clinton "ruled" the town hall meeting format, and George Bush performed best with a free-flowing single moderator structure.

Participants Matter

Who participates in debates naturally affects all elements of the debate. The term "who" includes the number of candidates as well as who is invited and who is an incumbent or a challenger. The presence of a third or minor party candidate such as Ross Perot can influence the issues discussed if that candidate has an agenda that differs from those of the major candidates. It also can influence whether a major party candidate chooses to debate, as was the case with Jimmy Carter who, in 1980, refused to debate against independent candidate John Anderson. The debate that occurred between Ronald Reagan and Anderson resulted less in clash between the two debaters than in attacks on the absent Carter.

Multiple candidate debates reduce the amount of time each candidate has to respond, the number of topics covered, depth of analysis, opportunities for defense as well as attack, and the direction of candidates' address. Primary debate formats often provide no opportunity for candidates answering at the beginning of a sequence to respond to the candidates who follow. Sometimes this problem leads candidates to address previous questions (as a rebuttal tactic) rather than to focus on the immediate question being asked of them. Follow-up questions often are sacrificed in multi-candidate debates.

The gender of the debaters is a final "who" factor that has potential for influence. Debate style issues as well as how a male attacks a female candidate are subjects for analysis in male-female encounters. Rick Lazzio's violation of Hillary Clinton's personal space in the 2000 New York Senate race was a topic that received considerable media attention. Additionally, research has indicated that men and women react differently to contestants in a mixed gender contest. Findings from the 1984 Bush-Ferraro encounter showed that women favored Ferraro more than men did.[31]

Context Matters

Debates do not occur in a vacuum nor are they watched and interpreted in one.[32] Several contextual elements influence debate formats, content, strategies, and outcomes. Contextual elements such as the point in the campaign—primary versus general election or timing and number of general election debates—influence content and strategies as much, if not more, than format or question type. The presence of an incumbent or a member of the party in office also affects attack and defense strategies.[33] Other contextual elements include factors related to the debate itself: where it takes place, whether a live audience is present, who is in the audience, how the stage is arranged, or where the cameras are placed.

Debates reflect what has been said on the campaign trail and covered in the media. Conversely, candidates adapt what they are saying in the campaign based on what occurs in the debate, and debates influence what is said in the media about the candidates. In the 2000 debates, Al Gore scored well in immediate post-debate polls. However, after references to his nonverbal reactions to his opponent (sighing and facial expressions) and to his exaggerated claims occurred in news coverage and opponent's spin, perceptions of Gore changed, and Gore adapted his style so as to appear less confrontational in the second debate.

As debates have spread to emerging democracies, cultural and governmental factors also affect debates. For example, debates in parliamentary systems differ from those in the United States. Candidates represent a party, and according to Stephen Coleman of the British Hansard Society for Parliamentary Government, "it is the manifesto of the party which matters rather more than the character of an aspirant Prime Minister."[34] Thus the types of questions and format that best serve an audience within a parliamentary system are more likely to focus directly on issues than on personalities. Coleman also noted that in emerging democracies formats "adapted to distinct political cultures"[35] during the 1990s. An example of such adaptation would be the concern expressed during discussions in Benin, West Africa, between members of an election team from the National Democratic Institute and a debate advisory team appointed within the country that candidates not be asked any questions that would create direct confrontations among the candidates—even at the level of policy comparisons. Members of the government election tribunal feared that direct attacks by one candidate on another might result in aggressive actions among one candidate's supporters directed at supporters of other candidates.[36]

What Candidates Say Matters

What candidates say in debates matters. Indeed, many of the most memorable moments from past televised presidential debates consist of the words uttered by the candidates. Gerald Ford's misstatement that Poland was not under Soviet domination in the second 1976 debate received significant media attention. In the 1980 debate, Ronald Reagan's "There you go again" response, in conjunction with his warm demeanor, served to blunt incumbent President

Jimmy Carter's charge that he was too reckless to be President. And a classic blow was struck by Lloyd Bentsen in the 1988 vice-presidential debate in response to Dan Quayle's attempt to compare himself to another young senator seeking high office: "Senator, I served with Jack Kennedy, I knew Jack Kennedy, Jack Kennedy was a friend of mine. Senator, you are no Jack Kennedy."

Studies that compared candidate verbal discourse in debates and other communication forums indicate that televised debates provide an advantage in terms of substance. For example, John Ellsworth compared the 1960 debates against candidate stump speeches and concluded that in debates, candidates "made clearer statements of their positions and offered more reasoning and evidence to support their positions."[37] Other early studies reached similar conclusions.[38] Since these studies, researchers have focused more on examining the content of specific debates, often critically, instead of comparing televised debates to other communication forms.

Research reveals that debate content is overwhelmingly about issues. Issue content is the principal focus of the questions posed by moderators and panelists and, therefore, of candidates' responses.[39] Thus, one of the effects of televised debates should be viewer learning about the issues that are covered in debates and the candidates' positions on these issues.

There is strong empirical support for the contribution of televised debates to viewer learning. Studies of intra-party[40] and inter-party[41] presidential debates in 1960, 1976, 1980, 1984, 1992, and 1996 indicate that televised debates enhanced learning. Two caveats temper this judgment, however. First, the political context dictates the potential for learning effects. If voters are unsure about candidates, either because they lack sufficient information or because they are conflicted about the electoral choice, the potential for debates and other communication forms to impact learning is greater. This is most likely to occur with campaigns which do not feature a popular incumbent, during the nomination phase of a campaign (particularly with the out-party), and early in the general election phase of a campaign. Second, although viewers do learn from televised debates, the level of learning tends to fall short of most viewers' expectations,[42] perhaps owing to shortcomings in debate format.

The Candidates' Presentation Matters

Although televised debates are conducted on issue content, what candidates say and how they say it contributes to viewers' impressions of them and, in this way, candidate presentational style often overpowers candidate discourse. Golden and Berquist describe debates as "electronic media events" where candidates' persona, as manifested in their delivery and demeanor, exercise more weight on viewers than substance.[43] A number of scholars have argued that the television medium intrinsically shapes the fundamental nature of political debates, placing a premium on source factors in the process of influence.[44] Gladys Lang notes that "what matters most in them is not the substance of what the candidates say in these debates but how well they say it and whether the candidate projects the image he strives to project."[45]

Do televised debates influence voters? The answer is yes, although debates reinforce far more viewer perceptions than they change. This is not to say that all studies concur. Many of the early experimental studies, which were grounded in the limited-effects gestalt that persisted into the 1960s and 1970s, failed to find significant persuasive effects of the 1960 Kennedy/Nixon or the 1970 Ford/Carter televised debates. What these studies revealed is that debates seldom convert viewers,[46] although they may produce other effects. Relying more heavily on survey data, other studies of these and subsequent presidential debates, found that debates do influence viewer perceptions and, as a consequence, influence voting disposition.[47]

More often televised debates elicit incremental changes in perception, reinforcing most, while shifting the preferences of some viewers who fall in the undecided and conflicted pool of prospective voters. Obviously, the caveat that we posited about learning also applies to the influence of debates: namely, that context dictates the potential for influence. The potential for debates and other types of communication is greater when significant numbers of prospective voters are uninformed or conflicted about the candidates. This is most likely in campaigns that lack a popular incumbent, during the early phase of a campaign, and/or with the out-party during the nomination phase of a political campaign.

When it comes to the actual influence of televised debates on perceptions, attitudes, and behaviors of prospective voters, candidate presentation matters, often even more than what it is that candidates say during debates. Most of the studies that detected effects in past presidential debates attributed these effects more to presentational style than to specific content.[48] Presentational style is embodied in viewers' judgments about the candidate as a person. These judgments about candidates are interchangeably characterized as ethos, image, and/or persona.

Presentational style embodies both obvious as well as more subtle elements. An obvious component is the way presentational style affects viewer judgments about candidate competence, which concerns qualifications for the office in question. Judgments about candidate competence are important, especially with regard to challengers of an incumbent regime and those candidates who have not held the office and who have not served in an apprenticeship role (e.g., in presidential campaigns, Kennedy in 1960, Carter in 1976, Clinton in 1992, and Bush in 2000).[49]

A more subtle element is the way that presentational style affects viewer judgments about candidates' relational messages. Relational messages are intrinsic to all communication, but are most pronounced whenever the communication form makes possible either real (e.g., interpersonal exchanges) or perceived (e.g., television viewing) contact between communicator and receiver. Relational messages, which can be expressed verbally but are usually communicated nonverbally via television, embody softer persona dimensions such as: immediacy/affection (consisting of warmth, involvement, enthusiasm, and a sense of personal interest in the receiver), similarity/depth (comprising friendliness and caring), receptivity/trust (embodying sincerity, honesty, an interest in communicating, and a willingness to listen), and other less influential dimensions.[50]

Exploratory research suggests that candidate presentational style is important to success in televised debates. Presidential debate scholars report that political candidates who in their personal styles are able to reveal to viewers their likeability, trust, and similarity are viewed as more persuasive.[51] The only experimental study of the role and impact of relational messages in televised debates indicated that such relational messages as immediacy/affection, similarity/ depth, receptivity/ trust, and equality contributed significantly to candidate influence in the first 1988 Presidential debate, accounting for sizable variance in dependent measures.[52]

Although there have been no follow-up studies on the influence of relational messages in debates, there is evidence to infer that Gore's relational communication hurt him in 2000 presidential debates. Polls suggest that, substantively, Gore dominated the first and third debate. Members of focus groups, however, criticized his relational style—in the first and third debates, his verbal and nonverbal aggressiveness and in the first debate, his loud sighing as Bush spoke. The media zeroed in on these relational gaffes, and Gore's substantive edge slipped away.[53]

Media Coverage Matters

Subsequent news media coverage of televised debates matters. It can influence the perceptions of those people who actually viewed a debate and the many more who did not. Post-debate news coverage "can define public opinion about and perceptions of candidates' debate performances."[54] Researchers detected the potential impact of post-debate news coverage on debate viewers during the 1976 Ford-Carter debates. Immediate and delayed measures during the first and third debates revealed that subsequent coverage of the debates produced modest changes in attitudes about which candidate performed best, changes that had an impact upon attitudes about the candidates.[55] However, coverage of the second debate produced enormous impact. Immediately following the debate, by a 44–35% margin, more viewers thought that Ford outperformed Carter in the debate and, by a 54–36% margin, most viewers preferred Ford. This was the debate in which Ford stated that Eastern Europe was not under Soviet domination, a claim that news analysts fixated on in post-debate coverage. Twenty-five

hours later public opinion was transformed. The same viewers were polled again. By a 61–19% margin, they believed that Carter had won the debate and, by a 54–37% margin, they expressed a preference for Carter over Ford. Frederick Steeper concluded that "this publicity (about the misstatement) caused the change."[56]

Following the 1976 debates, now aware of the potential influence of their post-debate comments, network television news sought to objectify coverage. Television journalists initially turned to "instant" polls, and later to focus groups, in order to determine debate "winners" and relied increasingly on campaign surrogates to provide analysis of debates. Campaigns responded strategically in order to win the battle over the interpretation of what took place during the debate. Martel refers to the post-debate effort as "meta-debating," or "debate about debates."[57] Others refer to these efforts as "spin control." Whatever it is called, the "debate" about the debate is an integral element in today's debates and exerts considerable influence on post-debate public opinion.[58]

Diffusion (Media and Face-to-Face) Matters

In addition to the direct influence of post-debate news coverage of debates, indirect influence via diffusion of televised debate content through non-traditional media outlets and interpersonal communication matters. Diana Owen refers to "the interwoven nature" of today's campaign communications environment.[59] In an "interwoven" communications environment, candidate communication that is initiated in one forum, such as a televised debate, matriculates to other forums, including non-traditional outlets, such as late night talk shows (e.g., Jay Leno or David Letterman) and comedy (e.g., "Saturday Night Live" or "Politically Incorrect.") For example, influence of the 2000 presidential debates was not confined to the debates themselves or post-debate news analyses. It also showed up in the effects of other communication forms that featured substantive and/or relational content initially raised in the debates (for example, the parodies of the candidates' debate performances on Leno, Letterman, and "Saturday Night Live.") One study of the relative influence of 13 distinct communication forms during the 2000 presidential campaign (both traditional and non-traditional communication outlets) found that debates and "new media," such as political talk radio, TV entertainment shows, TV talk shows and TV news magazines, exerted the greatest influence on prospective voters' perceptions of candidates.[60] This finding is consistent with the results surveys that revealed that 9% of Americans got most of their news about the 2000 presidential campaign primarily from television entertainment talk shows and another 6% got most of their news from television prime-time comedy programs.[61]

People's conversations with others about televised debates also influence perceptions. Research indicates that the sheer volume of political conversations during campaigns is considerable[62] and that such talk can prove influential in people's perceptions of candidates, especially when conversations occur outside the realm of family.[63] Interviews of prospective Cedar Rapids, Iowa, voters conducted two days after the first 1976 Ford and Carter debate revealed that two-thirds of respondents talked to others about the debate (11% talked to three or more people) and that these conversations affected respondents' attitudes toward the Democratic challenger. However, these effects tended to cancel each other out (Ford supporters became less apprehensive about Carter whereas Carter supporters became less enthusiastic toward Carter).[64]

★ WHAT WE NEED TO KNOW

As noted above, Communication scholarship has yielded significant knowledge about presidential debates. Yet the subject hardly has been exhausted as a field of research; indeed, much more remains to be known. In this section we highlight four examples of significant questions on which additional scholarship is vital.

A first question: How do debates achieve their effects? We know that debates matter because they have effects—sometimes overt, sometimes subtle—on candidates, campaigns, and citizens. We need, however, to know much more about how debates achieve these effects. This information would enable scholars to theorize the cognitive processes by which observers

incorporate debates into their world-view, and it would enable candidates and their staffs to plan debate strategies and tactics on the basis of far more sophisticated audience analysis.

Exploring how debates achieve effects requires micro-level investigation of specific debate components or dimensions. For example, we need to know more about framing, the process by which debates contextualize rationales for policies and candidates. How issues get characterized (for example, as threats or as opportunities) and how viewers internalize these characterizations are important questions to consider. How different argument strategies lead audiences to perceive that a candidate is immune from attack, to make refutation easy or difficult, or to minimize the opponent's ground is another important dimension on which more needs to be known. Yet another dimension is the nonverbal message of debates. What messages are conveyed by verbal images, what valence is given to the visual relative to the verbal (when they conflict), and how audiences generalize from visual image to the candidate's underlying personality are matters about which we know far too little and that may prove decisive to viewers of presidential debates.

Beyond the strategic dimension, arguments also need to be studied for their content. They may encapsulate significant cultural truths, social knowledge, presumptions, or hierarchies of value, and these all evolve over time. For this reason, longitudinal studies of particular argument forms or patterns are needed in order to explain the "deep structure" underlying the often very brief references made by candidates.

A final example of a micro-level question is just what counts as the "debate." We know that the controversy includes more than the exchanges among moderator, questioners, and candidates; it is shaped by pre-debate attempts to raise or lower expectations, by post-debate "spinning," and by media analysis and commentary over the days following the debate. Which of these components, singly or jointly, shape audiences' perceptions of the debate, and why, is important to know in order to account for the effects that debates can be shown to produce.

These examples of micro-level questions are illustrative, hardly exhaustive. What they suggest is the need to go beyond treating the debates like the psychologist's "black box" whose dynamics are unknown and to proceed to more detailed study of how they produce the effects that research so consistently has demonstrated.

A second question on which more study is needed: What are the characteristics of the best campaign debates? This question reflects the normative aspect of debate research. Scholars seek not just to describe and explain debates but also to help improve them. Addressing this question requires identifying and justifying the values that debates should serve—whether, for instance, they should aim to inform voters about issues, to arouse interest in the campaign, to differentiate the candidates, to model leadership styles, or to enact democratic values. Then the goal should be to identify those debates that most closely approximate the desired values, so that more detailed analysis could probe what their characteristics are and how these characteristics are conducive to achieving the goals.

We suspect that, in order to answer this question, scholars will need to broaden their focus beyond the general election presidential debates that now preoccupy them. Debates during the primary season and at the state and local level, with their multiplicity of candidates, diversity of formats, and varying levels of citizen involvement, may well offer models of "best practices" that would be worthy of emulation. And the growing interest in studying debates in other nations and different cultures should help us to identify which of our normative standards are culture-specific and which have more general application.

A third, closely related, question needing further research: How can we optimize the potential of debates? In light of the evidence suggesting the contributions that debates make to the campaign and to voters' understanding of issues and candidates, under what conditions will citizens be most likely to learn from them and to use them effectively in making choices?

Several questions come under this rubric. One is what format is optimal. Over the past decade, especially, we have experimented with formats including the single moderator, the town hall, and the talk show. Research is needed on the differential effects of these and other possible formats. On the other hand, we

have not experimented to a significant degree with such format variables as length of statements, opportunity for follow-up questions and answers, and specificity of topics for debate. In the abstract, we can imagine changes in each of these variables that would seem to facilitate more focused clash, more probing discussions, and more sustained interaction. Whether these results actually occur and whether they correlate with improved voter learning and satisfaction are questions needing to be tested. Likewise, there has been only slight variation in the number (between one and four) and frequency of debates; these too are format issues about which we need to know more. Finally, as mentioned above, there may be growing pressure to include more than the two major-party candidates. If so, then we need to know more about what formats most easily will adapt the benefits of debates to multiple-candidate situations.

The literature cited above suggests that debates have an anticipation phase before the formal meeting of the candidates takes place. We are learning of the "debate about the debates" that characterizes this period from the perspective of the campaigns, but we need to know more about how the anticipation phase can be used to most efficiently prepare voters for the debate experience. We need to know how viewers develop expectations for the debates, what background knowledge and perspective they bring to the debates, what sources they consult for advance information about issues, how they decide whether even to watch the debates—and what opportunities for intervention might benefit the public on each of these dimensions.

Likewise, we know that the debate is not really over when the allotted time ends. We know that those who turn off the television immediately have a different experience compared to those who stay and watch the post-debate "spin." We know from the cases of 1976 and 2000 that judgments of who won or lost the debate are affected by subsequent media coverage. And we know that those who watch the debates alone process them differently from those who participate in Debate-Watch or other post-debate discussion groups. What we do not know is whether these differences match differences in the quality of the debate experience and, if so, what sorts of debriefing strategies will be most likely to produce the desired results.

This category of questions—related to formats, preparation, and debriefing—is frankly normative. Based on the research cited above, we assume desirable characteristics of debates and wish to know how to design an environment for debates that will be most conducive to these characteristics.

Our fourth major question is methodological: How can we best study debates? Whereas the first three questions consider the debate itself, this one deals with the relationship between researchers and the debates. Again, there are several sub-questions. For instance, much of the extant research examines debates in a single campaign long after the campaign is over. By the time the results are known, few people care, because a new campaign is underway. We must move our understanding beyond always replaying the last campaign. To do so, we need sustained programmatic research on topics or puzzles that recur across debates. Such studies need to move beyond simple category systems to identify the underlying logic of debates. For similar reasons, we need more comparative studies in which the operation of a particular variable can be examined in different debates.

Probably the most basic product of the debates is the verbal text, the transcript of what was said. Yet we have surprisingly little understanding of the dynamics of the text—of how it works—even though close textual analysis has been shown to illumine texts in other fields of study. Scholars' skill at probing texts to discover meaning needs to be applied to the texts of presidential debates. Equally important is a careful analysis of the relational and nonverbal elements of the debate. We know that they convey significant meaning but we do not know enough about how they work. For that matter, we do not have anything approaching consensus on what all the basic communicative components of a debate are.

What these methodological needs have in common is a call for more ambitious research projects than have yet been undertaken. This requires that there be team projects involving members with different approaches, methods, and theories of knowing. It also will require

extending the scope of our studies to include primary debates and state and local campaign debates. With debates now having become a fixture of the campaign season, addressing these questions will permit the public to maximize their benefits and possibly even to reconcile their goals with the candidates' obvious interest in winning the election.

★ RESOURCES NEEDED

The changes in research and analytical practices recommended here will require scholars to make regular use of large datasets spanning several campaigns. While some of the requisite resources are readily available—for example, the Commission on Presidential Debates has transcripts of all debates posted to its website—others will have to be assembled, often at considerable expense and effort on the part of the research team. Many individual researchers and research teams in several disciplines have made this kind of investment over some subset of the eight presidential debates cycles completed to date, producing much of the scholarship underpinning the recommendations in this paper. But the field as a whole suffers from incompleteness and fragmentation of primary data sources. Rather than approaching these very basic research needs case-by-case, scholarly organizations and consortia should consider developing and disseminating the necessary resources to improve research in the field overall.

The two most compelling needs are for a) comprehensive records of media coverage of debates, and b) a longitudinal dataset on citizen responses to debates similar to (or even a part of) the National Election Studies. Each would be time-consuming and costly, but would dramatically limit the investment required by any single researcher or research team.

A) Comprehensive records of national media coverage of debates. Throughout this paper we have argued that debates are more than their transcripts. They are inextricably bound up in press framing, visual presentation, surrogate spin, and post-debate news analyses. Some of the resources that scholars would ideally examine, such as radio broadcasts and informal conversations, with rare exceptions, are ephemeral and out of reach. Other resources, such as nightly news broadcasts and newspaper coverage, are available but dispersed. Every scholar who wants to assemble editorial responses to presidential debates has to collect the dataset *de novo*, a substantial undertaking even in the days of digital archives. Every scholar who wants to examine news programs bracketing the debate itself will have to travel to a video repository such as Vanderbilt's or the Museum of Television and Radio (or both). The sheer effort involved in this kind of research is a profound disincentive to do it.

The investment-to-results equation looks considerably different, however, if the effort to gather such material were distributed across the products of many scholars. For example, national media coverage of the 2000 general election debates could be assembled once—arbitrarily, a week on either side of each debate pulling televised reports on ABC, CBS, and NBC as well as CNN, Fox, MSNBC, and PBS, and written reports from a fixed number of newspapers and national magazines—and used by any scholar interested in analyzing materials outside of the debates themselves. Assembly would be an onerous task. Using the model suggested here, it would require viewing, coding, and excerpting at least 3.5 hours of broadcast television and 1,008 hours of round-the-clock cable coverage. Before editing or even analyzing the relevant video, this would require more than half a year's effort, not counting the time required to locate and travel to the source materials. Were such a resource widely available and distributed on a reasonably inexpensive and durable medium such as DVD, any scholar interested in the visual dimensions of debates, in press coverage, in the role of commentary, or anything else, could gain ready access to source materials for whatever interpretive agenda he or she desires. This is an approach particularly well suited to historical debates and, once established, could be continued for subsequent election cycles.

The point here is not to specify a collection protocol, much less to argue that no one has performed this sort of collection in the past. The central thrust of this recommendation is that the cost of such efforts will be much better rewarded if they are conducted on a scale sufficient to make them reasonably comprehensive—including the capture of available historical data—with the resulting edited collection made widely available to interested scholars.

B) A longitudinal-dataset on citizen/viewer responses to debates. The National Election Studies, the premier longitudinal survey involving responses of citizens to elections, has a very limited question-set directed to debates. Respondents are asked to say whether they watched debates, whether they watched whole debates, whether anything about the debates impressed them, and whether the debates helped shape their choices, but there are no questions about visuals per se, about reactions to post-debate commentary, nor to many of the issues raised throughout this paper.[65]

Mounting a multi-cycle election survey is an enormous and expensive undertaking, out of reach of any single researcher or research team. Debate scholars can and should, however, organize to ensure that the long-term studies that do exist contain questions that allow an assessment of citizen/viewer reactions to debates consistent with the research goals outlined in this paper. The NES solicits recommendations[66] and may be a suitable vehicle; other projects, most notably the Annenberg Survey[,][67] have attempted to redress the shortcomings of the NES in this area and should be considered as well.

Surveys are, of course, only one means of discovering how viewers responded to debates. Results from focus groups and other qualitative tools can also be pooled and their research protocols extended over multiple election cycles. Extant focus group projects could serve as a model and baseline.[68]

Other than assembling extant work to make it more widely accessible to the scholarly community, this is very much a recommendation for 2004 and beyond; there is little that can be done to gather data from witnesses to elections past. In the manner of the archive described above it would be possible to create a widely accessible concordance of surveys dealing with debates in past election cycles from Roper, Harris, Gallup, as well as other survey firms and academic researchers, but online survey research tools make that a far less compelling project than the two main points described here.

Investments of the sort described here could stimulate an outpouring of the kind of scholarship sought in this paper. Comprehensive video records would be essential to answer questions about the influence of framing and spin. Longitudinal datasets cannot answer these questions by themselves, but they would contribute significantly to our understanding of how debates achieve their effects. Some researchers, of course, would want to reach beyond the boundaries of this kind of collective effort, but the focus of scholarly activity overall could turn from the arduous process of assembling the materials for study to concentrate on the study itself.

These techniques can and should be extended to cover not only presidential debates, but political debates for other offices as well. Though the research could not itself be conducted nationally—other offices are by definition state or local affairs with state or local audiences and news coverage—establishment of national models would allow for much more effective data collection in sub-presidential races and consequently, much richer comparisons across elections and election districts. In the case of a longitudinal dataset, for example, it would be reasonably simple to establish a core question set for House, Senate, and gubernatorial races that could apply equally well to any such election in the nation. Local research teams would include those questions but would be free to add whatever questions they felt necessary to capture the unique dynamics of the race(s) under study. Researchers from other jurisdictions could then use those data to facilitate direct comparisons of responses to debating (and perhaps to other aspects of political culture) from state to state and region to region. Inclusion of the national standards—whether for creating a comprehensive video archive or a longitudinal dataset—would be a powerful review criterion for potential funding agencies and could foreground dramatic improvements in our understanding of the evolving role of debates at every level of American politics.

NOTES

[1] Theodore H. White, *The Making of the President 1960* (New York: Mentor, 1961) 321. On the origin of the moniker "Great Debates" and the unusual broadcast law situation that made televised debates possible in 1960, see Theodore Otto Windt, Jr., "The 1960 Kennedy-Nixon Presidential Debates," *Rhetorical Studies of National Political Debates 1960–1992*, ed. Robert V. Friedenberg, 2nd ed. (Westport, CT: Praeger, 1994) 1–27.

[2] Susan A. Hellweg, Michael Pfau, and Steven R. Brydon, *Televised Presidential Debates: Advocacy in Contemporary America* (New York: Praeger, 1992) 101; David Sears and Steven Chaffee, "Uses and Effects of the 1976 Debates: An Overview of Empirical Studies," *The Great Debates: Carter vs. Ford, 1976*, ed. Sidney Kraus (Bloomington: Indiana UP, 1978) 230.

[3] William L. Benoit, Mitchell S. McKinney, and R. Lance Holbert, "Beyond Learning and Persona: Extending the Scope of Presidential Debate Effects," *Communication Monographs* 68 (2001): 259–260; Diana B. Carlin, "A Rationale for a Focus Group Study," *The 1992 Presidential Debates in Focus*, eds. Diana B. Carlin and Mitchell S. McKinney (Westport, CT: Praeger, 1994) 6–7.

[4] Kathleen E. Kendall, "Presidential Debates Through Media Eyes," *American Behavioral Scientist* 40 (1997): 1193–1207.

[5] William L. Benoit and William T. Wells, *Candidates in Conflict: Persuasive Attack and Defense in the 1992 Presidential Debates* (Tuscaloosa: U. of Alabama P, 1996) 12; Robert E. Denton and Gary C. Woodward, *Political Communication in America*, 2nd ed. (New York: Praeger, 1990), 102; Thomas Patterson on PBS's *News Hour* during the 1996 campaign, qtd. in Alan Schroeder, *Presidential Debates: Forty Years of High-Risk TV* (New York: Columbia UP, 2000) 207.

[6] Kathleen Hall Jamieson and David S. Birdsell, *Presidential Debates: The Challenge of Creating an Informed Electorate* (New York: Oxford UP, 1988) 6.

[7] Benoit, McKinney, and Holbert 259; Myles Martel, *Political Campaign Debates: Images, Strategies, and Tactics* (New York: Longman, 1983) 1.

[8] See Austin J. Freeley, "The Presidential Debates and the Speech Profession," *Quarterly*

Journal of Speech 47 (1961): 60–64; Robert V. Friedenberg, "'We Are Present Here Today for the Purpose of Having a Joint Discussion': The Conditions Requisite for Political Debates," *Journal of the American Forensic Association* 16 (1979): 1–9. A second question that occupied much early Communication research on presidential debates was whether these televised performances actually fit the definition and purview of "debate," as understood by members of the field. (J. Jeffrey Auer, "The Counterfeit Debates," *The Great Debates: Kennedy vs. Nixon 1960,* ed. Sidney Kraus (Bloomington: Indiana UP, 1962) 142–150; Lloyd F. Bitzer and Theodore Rueter, *Carter vs. Ford: The Counterfeit Debates of 1976* (Madison: U of Wisconsin P, 1980)). More recently scholars have argued that, while political debates differ from academic debates in predictable ways, they are a unique form of debate that can be evaluated productively from a Communication perspective (Diana Prentice Carlin, "A Defense of the 'Debate' in Presidential Debates," *Argumentation and Advocacy* 25 (1989): 208–213; Diana Prentice Carlin, Charles Howard, Susan Stanfield, and Larry Reynolds, "The Effect of Presidential Debate Formats on Clash: A Comparative Analysis," *Argumentation and Advocacy* 27 (1991): 126–136; John M. Murphy, "Presidential Debates and Campaign Rhetoric: Text Within Context," *Southern Communication Journal* 57 (1992): 219–228).

9 Roderick P. Hart, *Campaign Talk* (Princeton, NJ: Princeton UP, 2000), 116.

10 William L. Benoit, Joseph R. Blaney, and P. M. Pier, *Campaign '96: A Functional Analysis of Acclaiming, Attacking, and Defending* (Westport, CT: Praeger, 1998) 178–186; Benoit and Wells; Bitzer and Rueter; Robert V. Friedenberg, ed., *Rhetorical Studies of National Political Debate, 1960–1992* (Westport, CT: Praeger, 1994); Jamieson and Birdsell; Martel; Patricia Riley and Thomas A. Hollihan, "The 1980 Presidential Debates: A Content Analysis of the Issues and Arguments," *Speaker and Gavel* 18 (1981): 47–59.

11 James B. Lemert, William R. Elliot, Karl J. Nestvold, and Galen R. Rarick, "Effects of Viewing a Presidential Primary Debate: An Experiment," *Communication Research* 10 (1983): 155–173; Allen Lichtenstein, "Differences in Impact between Local and National Televised Political Candidates' Debates," *Western Journal of Speech Communication* 46 (1982): 291–298.

12 William L. Benoit, David J. Webber, and Julie Berman, "Effects of Presidential Debate Watching and Ideology on Attitudes and Knowledge," *Argumentation and Advocacy* 34 (1998): 163–172;

Goodwin F. Berquist and James L. Golden, "Media Rhetoric, Criticism and the Public Perception of the 1980 Presidential Debates," *Quarterly Journal of Speech* 67 (1981): 125–137; Steven E. Clayman, "Caveat Orator: Audience Disaffiliation in the 1988 Presidential Debates," *Quarterly Journal of Speech* 72 (1992): 33–60; Roderick P. Hart and Sharon E. Jarvis, "Political Debate: Form, Styles, and Media," *American Behavioral Scientist* 40 (1997): 1095–1123; Hellweg, Pfau, and Brydon; Mary Ann Leon, "Revealing Character and Addressing Voters' Needs in the 1992 Presidential Debates: A Content Analysis," *Argumentation and Advocacy* 30 (1993): 88–105; Robert G. Meadow and Marilyn Jackson-Beeck, "A Comparative Perspective on Presidential Debates: Issue Evolution in 1960 and 1976," *The Presidential Debates: Media, Electoral, and Policy Perspectives,* George F. Bishop, Robert G. Meadow, and Marilyn Jackson-Beeck, eds. (New York: Praeger, 1978) 33–58; Robert G. Meadow and Marilyn Jackson-Beeck, "Issue Evolution: A New Perspective on Presidential Debates," *Journal of Communication,* 28 (1978): 84–92; Jian-Hua Zhu, J. Ronald Milavsky, and Rahul Biswas, "Do Televised Debates Affect Image Perception More Than Issue Knowledge? A Study of the First 1992 Presidential Debate," *Human Communication Research* 20 (1994): 302–333.

13 Steven H. Chaffee, "Presidential Debates— Are They Helpful to Voters?" *Communication Monographs* 45 (1978): 330–346; Kathleen H. Jamieson, "Television, Presidential Campaigns, and Debates," *Presidential Debates: 1988 and Beyond,* Joel L. Swerdlow, ed. (Washington, DC: Congressional Quarterly, Inc., 1987) 27–33; Kathleen Hall Jamieson and Christopher Adasiewicz, "What Can Voters Learn from Election Debates?" *Televised Election Debates: International Perspectives,* Stephen Coleman, ed. (New York: St. Martin's, 2000) 25–42; Michael A. Mayer and Diana B. Carlin, "Debates as a Voter Education Tool," *The 1992 Presidential Debates in Focus,* ed. Carlin and McKinney 127–138; David L. Vancil and Sue D. Pendell, "Winning Presidential Debates: An Analysis of Criteria Influencing Audience Response," *Western Journal of Speech Communication* 48 (1984): 62–74.

14 John T. Morello, "Argument and Visual Structuring in the 1984 Mondale-Reagan Debates: The Medium's Influence on the Perception of Clash," *Western Journal of Speech Communication* 52 (1988): 277–290; John T. Morello, "The 'Look' and Language of Clash: Visual Structuring of Argument in the 1988 Bush-Dukakis Debates," *Southern Communication Journal* 57 (1992): 205–218;

John T. Morello, "Visual Structuring of the 1976 and 1984 Nationally Televised Presidential Debates: Implication," *Central States Speech Journal* 39 (1988): 233–243; Robert K. Tiemens, "Television's Portrayal of the 1976 Presidential Debates: An Analysis of Visual Content," *Communication Monographs* 45 (1978): 362–370.

[15] Michael Pfau and Jong Guen Kang, "The Impact of Relational Messages on Candidate Influence in Televised Presidential Debates," *Communication Studies* 42 (1991): 114–128.

[16] Roger Jon Desmond and Thomas R. Donahue, "The Role of the 1976 Televised Presidential Debates in the Political Socialization of Adolescents," *Communication Quarterly* 29 (1981): 302–308; Edward A. Hinck, *Enacting the Presidency: Political Argument, Presidential Debates, and Presidential Character* (Westport, CT: Praeger, 1993); John Louis Lucaites, "Rhetorical Legitimacy, Public Trust and the Presidential Debates," *Journal of the American Forensic Association* 25 (1989): 231–238.

[17] Benoit, McKinney, and Holbert; Linda L. Swanson and David L. Swanson, "The Agenda-Setting Functions of the First Ford-Carter Debate," *Communication Monographs* 45 (1978): 347–353.

[18] Carlin and McKinney; Lynda Lee Kaid, Jacques Gerstle, and Keith R. Sanders, eds., *Mediated Politics in Two Cultures: Presidential Campaigning in the United States and France* (New York: Praeger, 1991); Patricia A. Sullivan, "The 1984 Vice-Presidential Debate: A Case Study of Female and Male Framing in Political Campaigns," *Communication Quarterly* 37 (1989): 329–342.

[19] William K. Benoit and Heather Currie, "Inaccuracies in Media Coverage of the 1996 and 2000 Presidential Debates," *Argumentation and Advocacy* 38 (2001): 28–39; William P. Eveland, Jr., Douglas M. McLeod, and Amy I. Nathanson, "Reporters vs. Undecided Voters: An Analysis of the Questions Asked During the 1992 Presidential Debates," *Communication Quarterly* 42 (1994): 390–406; J. Michael Hogan, "Media Nihilism and the Presidential Debates," *Argumentation and Advocacy* 25 (1989): 220–225; John T. Morello, "'Who Won?': A Critical Examination of Newspaper Editorials Evaluating Nationally Televised Presidential Debates," *Argumentation and Advocacy* 27 (1991): 114–125; David L. Swanson, "And That's the Way It Was?: Television Covers the 1976 Presidential Campaign," *Quarterly Journal of Speech* 63 (1977): 239–248.

[20] Martel.

[21] Carlin and McKinney.

[22] David Zarefsky, *Lincoln, Douglas, and Slavery: In the Crucible of Public Debate* (Chicago: U of Chicago P, 1990).

[23] See also Sidney Kraus, *Televised Presidential Debates and Public Policy,* 2nd ed. (Mahwah, NJ: Lawrence Erlbaum Associates, 2000) 147–180.

[24] Numerous studies of format at presidential primary and general election levels as well as in state contests have examined the issue of format and its effect on variables such as levels of clash, types of arguments, variance across multiple debates in a series, question type according to who asks questions, and subjects addressed.

[25] Diana B. Prentice, Janet K. Larsen, and Matthew J. Sobnosky, "A Comparison of Clash in the Dual Format," paper presented at the Speech Communication Association Convention, Anaheim, CA, November 1981; Michael Pfau, "A Comparative Assessment of Intra-Party Political Debate Formats," *Political Communication Review* 9 (1984): 1–23.

[26] Carlin, Howard, Stanfield, and Reynolds.

[27] Diana B. Carlin, Eric Morris, and Shawna Smith, "The Influence of Format and Questions on Candidates' Strategic Argument Choices in the 2000 Presidential Debates," *American Behavioral Scientist* 44 (2001): 2196–2218.

[28] See Eveland, McLeod, and Nathanson; Hart and Jarvis; and Benoit and Wells for a discussion of the differences in question types of the type of argument produced. Hart and Jarvis discuss the types of language used and concluded that "debates add sobriety to campaigns, ground political discourse, make candidates introspective, and restrain political overstatement" (1095).

[29] Data collected from focus groups conducted after the 1992, 1996, and 2000 presidential debates revealed that viewers want longer responses to reduce the number of commonplaces occurring in debates and to get beyond a statement of position into a discussion of how the candidate would influence policy passage in Congress. The shorter-than-average responses and lack of follow-up questions in the 1996 Clinton-Dole debates left voters especially dissatisfied with the format since little depth of analysis occurred.

[30] See Carlin, Morris, and Smith. Reactions to the format were made in focus groups conducted by Carlin and others after the debates.

[31] J. Gregory Payne, James L. Golden, John Marlier, and Scott C. Ratzan, "Perceptions of the 1988 Presidential and Vice Presidential Debates," *American Behavioral Scientist* 32 (1989): 426.

[32] See Diana B. Carlin, "Presidential Debates as Focal Points for Campaign Arguments," *Political*

Communication 9 (1992): 251–265; Edward Hinck, "The Role of the 1984 Vice Presidential Debate in the Presidential Campaign," paper presented at the Speech Communication Association Convention, Chicago, November 1990; Murphy.

33 See Benoit and Wells.

34 Stephen Coleman, "Meaningful Political Debate in the Age of the Soundbite," in *Televised Election Debates: International Perspectives*, ed. Stephen Coleman (London: Macmillan, 2000) 8.

35 Coleman 7.

36 In February 2001, Diana Carlin was part of a team of election consultants sent to Benin to work with local election officials to develop a plan for debates and political advertising. The concern related here resulted in a wide variety of format offerings for a multi-party debate to all[a]y election officials['] concerns.

37 John W. Ellsworth, "Rationality and Campaigning: A Content Analysis of the 1960 Presidential Campaign Debates," *The Western Political Quarterly* 43 (1965): 794.

38 For example, see Stanley Kelly, Jr., "Campaign Debates: Some Facts and Issues," *Public Opinion Quarterly* 26 (1962): 351–366; and C. David Mortensen, "The Influence of Television on Public Discussion," *Quarterly Journal of Speech* 54 (1968): 277–281.

39 Sears and Chaffee's content analysis of the 1976 Ford and Carter debates revealed that 92% of reporters' questions dealt with issues and nearly 80% of candidates' responses contained issue content. See Sears and Chaffee 223–261.

40 Lemert, Elliot, Nestvold, and Rarick; Michael Pfau, "Intraparty Political Debates and Issue Learning," *Journal of Applied Communication Research* 16 (1988): 99–112.

41 Elihu Katz and Jacob J. Feldman, "The Debates in Light of Research: A Survey of Surveys," *The Great Debates: Kennedy vs. Nixon 1960*, ed. Sidney S. Kraus (Bloomington: Indiana UP, 1962) 173–233; Kelly, Jr. 351–366; Garrett J. O'Keefe and Harold H. Mendelsohn, "Media Influences and Their Anticipation," *The Great Debates*, ed. Kraus (1979) 405–417; Twentieth Century Fund Task Force on Televised Presidential Debates, *With the Nation Watching: Report of the Twentieth Century Task Force on Televised Presidential Debates* (Lexington, MA: D. C. Heath & Company, 1979); Arthur H. Miller and Michael MacKuen, "Informing the Electorate: A National Study," *The Great Debates*, ed. Kraus (1979) 269–297; Chaffee; Jack Dennis, Steven H. Chaffee, and Sun Yuel Choe, "Impact on Partisan, Image, and Issue Voting," *The Great Debates*, ed. Kraus (1979) 314–330;

Steven H. Chaffee and Jack Dennis, "Presidential Debates: An Empirical Assessment," *The Future and Present of Presidential Debates*, ed. Austin Ranney (Washington, DC: American Enterprise Institute for Public Policy Research, 1979) 75–101; Alan I. Abramowitz, "The Impact of a Presidential Debate on Voter Rationality," *American Journal of Political Science* 22 (1978): 680–690; Lee B. Becker, Idowa A. Sobowale, Robin E. Cobbey, and Chaim H. Eyal, "Debates' Effects on Voters' Understandings of Candidates and Issues," *The Presidential Debates: Media, Electoral, and Policy Perspectives*, ed. Bishop, Meadow, and Jackson-Beeck 126–139; Sears and Chaffee; Lichtenstein; David L. Lanoue, "One That Made a Difference: Cognitive Consistency, Political Knowledge, and the 1980 Presidential Debate," *Public Opinion Quarterly* 56 (1992): 168–184; Zhu, Milavsky, and Biswas; Mayer and Carlin; Michael Pfau and William P. Eveland, Jr., "Debates versus Other Communication Sources: The Pattern of Information and Influence," *The 1992 Presidential Debates in Focus*, ed. Carlin and McKinney (1994) 155–173; Jamieson and Adasiewicz; Benoit, Webber, [and] Berman.

42 O'Keefe and Mendelsohn; Doris Graber and Young Kim, "Why John Q. Voter Did Not Learn Much from the 1976 Presidential Debates," *Communication Yearbook 2*, ed. Brent D. Rubin (New Brunswick, NJ: Transaction Books, 1978) 407–421.

43 Berquist and Golden 132.

44 See Kathleen Hall Jamieson, *Eloquence in an Electronic Age: The Transformation of Political Speechmaking* (New York: Oxford UP, 1988); Jamieson and Birdsell; Hellweg, Pfau, and Brydon; Kurt Lang and Gladys E. Lang, *Politics and Television* (Chicago: Quadrangle Books, 1968).

45 Gladys E. Lang, "Still Seeking Answers," *Critical Studies in Mass Communication* 4 (1987): 211–214 (213).

46 For a review of 31 studies of the 1960 debates, see Katz and Feldman. Studies of the 1976 presidential debates finding limited effects include: Kenneth D. Wald and Michael B. Lupfer, "The Presidential Debate as a Civics Lesson," *Public Opinion Quarterly* 42 (1978): 342–353; Ronald D. Mulder, "The Political Effects of the Carter-Ford Debate: An Experimental Analysis," *Sociological Focus* 11 (1978): 33–45; Paul R. Hagner and Leroy N. Rieselbach, "The Impact of the 1976 Presidential Debates: Conversion or Reinforcement," *The Presidential Debates*, ed. Bishop, Meadow, and Jackson-Beeck 157–178; Arthur H. Miller and Michael MacKuen, "Informing the Electorate: A National Study," *The Great Debates*, ed. Kraus (1979) 269–297;

Jack M. McLeod, Jean A. Durall, Dean A. Ziemke, and Carl A. Bybee, "Reactions of Young and Old Voters: Expanding the Context of Effects," *The Great Debates*, ed. Kraus (1979) 348–367; Dennis K. Davis, "Influence on Vote Decisions," *The Great Debates*, ed. Kraus (1979) 331–347; Herbert W. Simons and Kenneth Liebowitz, "Shifts in Candidate Images," *The Great Debates*, ed. Kraus (1979) 398–404; Abramowitz; Douglas D. Rose, "Citizen Uses of the Ford-Carter Debates," *Journal of Politics* 41 (1979): 214–221; Raymond G. Smith, "The Ford-Carter Debates: Some Perceptions from Academe," *Central States Speech Journal* 28 (1977): 250–257; Lee Sigelman and Carol K. Sigelman, "Judgments of the Carter-Reagan Debate: The Eye of the Beholder," *Public Opinion Quarterly* 48 (1984): 624–628; George F. Bishop, Robert W. Oldendick, and Alfred J. Tuchfarber, "The Presidential Debates as a Device for Increasing the 'Rationality' of Electoral Behavior," *The Presidential Debates*, ed. Bishop, Meadow, and Jackson-Beeck (1980) 179–196. Finally, studies of subsequent debates indicating limited effects include: Vancil and Pendell; Payne, Golden, Marlier, and Ratzan.

[47] Significant debate effects were reported in the following reports: Saul Ben-Zeev & Irving S. White, "Effects and Implications," *The Great Debates*, ed. Kraus (1962) 331–337; Russell Middleton, "National Television Debates and Presidential Voting Decisions," *Public Opinion Quarterly* 16 (1962): 426–428; Paul Irving Rosenthal, *Ethos in the Presidential Campaign of 1960: A Study of the Basic Persuasive Process of the Nixon Kennedy Television Debates*, diss., University of California at Los Angeles, 1963; Percy H. Tannenbaum, Bradley S. Greenberg, and Fred R. Silverman, "Candidate Images," in *The Great Debates*, ed. Kraus (1962) 271–288; Elmo Roper, "Polling Post-Mortem," *Saturday Review* (1960): 10–13; George A. Barnett, "A Multidimensional Analysis of the 1976 Presidential Campaign," *Communication Quarterly* 29 (1981): 156–165; Paul D. Krivonos, "The First Debate: Ford versus Carter—A Behavioral Criticism," *Exetasis* 3 (1976): 3–9; Gregory Casey and Michael Fitzgerald, "Candidate Images and the 1976 Presidential Debates," paper presented at Midwest Association for Public Opinion Research, Chicago, October 1977; Samuel L. Becker, Robert Pepper, Lawrence A. Wenner, and Jin Keon Kim, "Information Flow and the Shaping of Meanings," *The Great Debates*, ed. Kraus (1979) 384–397; Steven H. Chaffee and Sun Yuel Choe, "Time of Decision and Media Use during the Ford-Carter Campaign," *Public Opinion Quarterly* 44 (1978): 53–69; Davis 331–347; John P. Robinson, "The Polls," *The Great Debates*, ed. Kraus (1979) 262–268; Stanley Kelley, Jr., *Interpreting Elections* (Princeton, NJ: Princeton UP, 1983); Louis Harris, "Reagan Won Debate, Poll Shows," *St. Paul Pioneer Press* (1980): 1, 6; Everett C. Ladd and G. Donald Ferree, "Were the Pollsters Really Wrong," *Public Opinion* (1981): 13–20; Steven R. Brydon, "The Two Faces of Jimmy Carter: The Transformation of a Presidential Debater, 1976 and 1980," *Central States Speech Journal* 36 (1985): 138–151; Mark H. Davis, "Voting Intentions and the Carter-Reagan Debate," *Journal of Applied Social Psychology* 12 (1982): 481–492; Jay L. Swerdlow, *Beyond Debate: A Paper on Televised Presidential Debates* (New York: Twentieth Century Fund, 1984); J. Leonard Reinsch, *Getting Elected: From Radio and Roosevelt to Television and Reagan* (New York: Hippocrene Books, 1988); John G. Geer, "The Effects of Presidential Debates on the Electorate's Preference for Candidates," *American Political Quarterly* 16 (1988): 486–501; Pfau and Kang; Pfau and Eveland.

[48] For example, see Katz and Feldman 173–223; Lang and Lang 313–330; Samuel Lubell, "Personalities versus Issues," *The Great Debates*, ed. Kraus (1962) 151–162; Rosenthal; Becker, Pepper, Wenner, and Kim; John E. Bowes and Herbert Strentz, "Candidate Images: Stereotyping in the 1976 Debates," *Communication Yearbook 2*, ed. Brent D. Rubin (New Brunswick, NJ: Transaction Books, 1979) 391–406; Casey and Fitzgerald; Davis 331–347; Glenn R. Morrow, "Changes in Perceptions of Ford and Carter Following the First Presidential Debate," *Perceptual and Motor Skills* 45 (1977): 423–429; Smith 250–257; Berquist and Golden 125–137; Brydon; Davis 481–492; Vancil and Pendell 62–74; Michael Pfau, "The Influence of Intraparty Political Debates on Candidate Preference," *Communication Research* 14 (1987): 687–697; Reinsch; David J. Lanoue and Peter R. Schrott, "The Effect of Primary Season Debates on Public Opinion," *Political Behavior* 11 (1989): 289–306; Pfau and Eveland 155–173; Benoit, Webber, and Berman.

[49] For example, see John P. Keating and Bibb Latane, "Politicians on TV: The Image is the Message," *Journal of Social Issues* 32 (1976): 116–132; Doris A. Graber, "Press and TV as Opinion Resources in Presidential Campaigns," *Public Opinion Quarterly* 40 (1976): 285–303; John H. Aldrich, "A Dynamic Model of Presidential Nomination Campaigns," *American Political Science Review* 74 (1980): 651–669; Chaffee and Choe 53–69; Thomas E. Patterson, *The Mass Media Election: How Americans Choose Their President* (New York: Praeger, 1980); Hagner and Rieselback, *The Presidential Debates*, ed. Bishop,

Meadow, and Jackson-Beeck (1978) 157–178; J. David Gopoian, "Issue Preference in Presidential Primaries," *American Journal of Political Science* 26 (1982): 524–546; William C. Adams, "Media Power in Presidential Elections: An Exploratory Analysis, 1960–1980," *Television Coverage of the 1980 Presidential Campaign,* ed. William C. Adams (Norwood, NJ: Ablex, 1983) 161–187; James E. Campbell, "Candidate Image Evaluations: Influence and Rationalization in Presidential Primaries," *American Politics Quarterly* 11 (1983): 293–313; Barry Norrander, "Selective Participation: Presidential Primary Voters as a Subset of General Election Voters," *American Politics Quarterly* 14 (1986): 35–53; Martin Schram, *The Great American Video Game: Presidential Politics in the Television Age* (New York: William Morrow, 1987) 35–53; Larry M. Bartels, *Presidential Primaries and the Dynamics of Public Choice* (Princeton, NJ: Princeton UP, 1988); J. David Kennamer, "Comparing Predictors of the Likelihood of Voting in a Primary and a General Election," *Journalism Quarterly* 67 (1990): 777–784; Samuel L. Popkin, *The Reasoning Voter: Communication and Persuasion in Presidential Campaigns* (Chicago: U of Chicago P, 1991).

50 For initial theorizing about relational communication, see Jurgen Ruesch and Gregory Bateson, *Communication: The Social Matrix of Psychiatry* (New York: W. W. Norton & Company, 1951), and Paul Watzalawick, Janet Beavin, and Don Jackson, *Pragmatics of Human Communication: A Study of Interactional Patterns, Pathologies, and Paradoxes* (New York: W. W. Norton, 1967). For research identifying the dimensions of relational communication, see Judee K. Burgoon and Jerold L. Hale, "The Fundamental Topoi of Relational Communication," *Communication Monographs* 51 (1984): 193–214. For research reporting measures of the specific dimensions of relational communication, see Judee K. Burgoon and Jerold L. Hale, "Validation and Measurement of the Fundamental Themes in Relational Communication," *Communication Monographs* 54 (1987): 19–41.

51 Martel; Kathleen Hall Jamieson, *Eloquence in an Electronic Age: The Transformation of Political Speech Making* (New York: Oxford UP, 1988; Nancy Oft-Rose, "The Importance of Ethos," *Argumentation and Advocacy* 25 (1989): 197–199.

52 Pfau and Kang 114–128.

53 Four national public opinion polls using probability samples were conducted immediately following the first Bush and Gore debate. All four indicated that Gore out-performed Bush in the debate, with margins ranging from a low of 3 percent in an ABC poll (where debate watchers were a bit more supportive of Bush prior to the debate) to 14 percent in a CBS poll (where debate watchers were a bit more supportive of Gore prior to the debate). Michael Traugott, "Assessing Poll Performance in the 2000 Campaign," *Public Opinion Quarterly* 65 (2001): 389–419.

54 Kathleen E. Kendall, ed., *Presidential Campaign Discourse: Strategic Communication Problems* (Albany: State U of New York P, 1995) 149.

55 Gladys Engel Lang and Kurt Lang, "Immediate and Mediated Responses: First Debate," in *The Great Debates,* ed. Kraus (1979) 298–313; Charles Atkin, John Hocking, and Steven McDermott, "Home State Voter Response and Secondary Media Coverage," *The Great Debates,* ed. Kraus (1979) 429–445.

56 Frederick T. Steeper, "Public Response to Gerald Ford's Statements on Eastern Europe in the Second Debate," *The Presidential Debates,* ed. Bishop, Meadow, and Jackson-Beeck 81–101.

57 Martel 169–170.

58 Patterson; Steeper 81–101; Gladys E. Lang and Kurt Lang, *Politics and Television Reviewed* (Beverly Hills, CA: Sage, 1984); Jane Blankenship and Jong Guen Kang, "The 1984 Presidential and Vice Presidential Debates: The Printed Press and 'Construction' by Metaphor," *Presidential Studies Quarterly* 21 (1991): 307–318; James B. Lemert, William R. Elliot, William L. Rosenberg, *The Politics of Disenchantment: Bush, Clinton, Perot, and the Press* (Cresskill, NJ: Hampton, 1996).

59 Diana Owen, *Media Messages in American Presidential Elections* (New York: Greenwood, 1991).

60 Michael Pfau, Jaeho Cho, and Kirsten Chong, "Impact of Communication Forms in Presidential Campaigns: Influences on Candidate Perception and Democratic Process," *Press/Politics* 6 (2001): 88–105.

61 Pew Research Center for the People and the Press, *Audiences Fragmented and Skeptical: The Tough Job of Communicating with Voters,* January 2000 (http://www.peoplepress.org/questionnaires.jan00que.htm).

62 Saadia R. Greenberg, "Conversations as Units of Analysis in the Study of Personal Influence," *Journalism Quarterly* 62 (1975): 128–131; Patterson; Garrett J. O'Keefe, "The Changing Context of Interpersonal Communication in Political Campaigns," *Communication Yearbook,* Michael Burgoon, ed. (New Brunswick, NJ: Transaction, 1982) 667–681; Paul A. Beck, "Voters' Intermediation Environments in the 1988 Presidential Contest," *Public Opinion Quarterly* 55 (1991): 371–394; Robert R. Huckfeldt and John Sprague, "Social Order and Political Chaos: The

Structural Meaning of Political Information," *Information and Democratic Processes,* John A. Ferejohn and James H. Kuklinski, eds. (Urbana: U of Illinois P, 1990) 23–58; June O. Yum and Kathleen E. Kendall, "Sex Differences in Political Communication during Presidential Campaigns," *Communication Quarterly* 43 (1995): 131–141.

63 Greenberg 128–131; Lynda Lee Kaid, "The Neglected Candidate: Interpersonal Communication in Political Campaigns," *Western Journal of Speech Communication* 41 (1977): 245–252; Steven H. Chaffee, "Mass Media in Political Campaigns: An Expanding Role," *Public Communication Campaigns,* Ronald E. Rice and William J. Paisley, eds. (Beverly Hills, CA: Sage, 1981) 95–120; Robert R. Huckfeldt and John Sprague, "Discussant Effects on Vote Choice: The Political Interdependence of Discussion Partners," paper presented at the annual meeting of the American Political Science Association, Washington, DC (September 1988); Michael MacKuen, "Speaking of Politics: Individual Conversational Choice, Public Opinion, and the Prospects for Deliberative Democracy," *Information and Democratic Processes,* Ferejohn and Kuklinski, eds. (1990) 59–99; Harwood Group, *Meaningful*

Chaos: How People Form Relationships with Public Concerns (Bethesda, MD: Kettering Foundation, 1983); Silvo Lenart, *Shaping Political Attitudes: The Impact of Interpersonal Communication and Mass Media* (Thousand Oaks, CA: Sage, 1994); Michael Pfau, Tracy Diedrich, Karla M. Larson, and Kim M. Van Winkle, "Influence of Communication Modalities on Voters' Perceptions of Candidates during Presidential Primary Campaigns," *Journal of Communication* 45 (1995): 122–133.

64 Becker, Pepper, Wenner, and Kim 384–404.

65 NES, "Continuity Guide, Chapter Five: Participation, Involvement, Media," available online at http://www.umich.edu/~nes/resources/conguide/93cgch5.htm See also the pre- and post-election 2000 questionnaires, available online at http://www.appcpenn.org/political/campaign2000/.

66 E.g., NES, "Call for Recommendations for the 1998 Pilot Study," available online at http://www.umich.edu/~nes/studyres/nespil98/98contcall.htm.

67 Information about the Annenberg Survey is available at http://www.appcpenn.org/political/campaign2000/.

68 See Carlin and McKinney; Carlin, Morris, and Smith.

Newspaper Coverage of Presidential Debates

William L. Benoit, Kevin A. Stein, and Glenn J. Hansen

Since their re-introduction in 1976, televised debates have become an integral part of presidential campaigns. Political debates have several important advantages over other kinds of campaign messages. First, they give voters a chance to see and contrast the major candidates face to face, addressing the same topics at the same time. Second, their length is noteworthy: "As messages running an hour or longer, debates offer a level of contact with candidates clearly unmatched in spot ads and news segments. . . . the debates offer the most extensive and serious view of the candidates available to the electorate" (Jamieson, 1987, p. 28). Third, although candidates prepare extensively for these encounters, unanticipated questions or comments from an opponent may elicit spontaneous remarks that can give voters a more accurate view of the candidates than do highly scripted speeches or television spots. Fourth, debates afford candidates the opportunity to refute false or misleading statements from

opponents at the time those statements occur, rather than later.

Scholars have studied presidential debates extensively (books include Benoit & Wells, 1996; Bishop, Meadow, & Jackson-Beeck, 1978; Bitzer & Rueter, 1980; Carlin & McKinney, 1994; Coleman, 2000; Friedenberg, 1994, 1997; Hellweg, Pfau, & Brydon, 1992; Hinck, 1993; Jamieson & Birdsell, 1988; Kraus, 1962, 1979, 2000; Lanoue & Schrott, 1991; Martel, 1983; Schroeder, 2000). However, news coverage of these events has received relatively little scholarly attention. This is unfortunate because "news commentary does influence viewers' perceptions about debates" (Hellweg, Pfau, & Brydon, 1992, p. 99).

One exception is Kendall (1997), who investigated television network news coverage of the 1996 presidential debates:

Media interpretations have been found to follow a pattern: They devote little time to the content of the debates, and much time to the personalities of the candidates and the process by which they make the decision to debate, prepare to debate, and spin the stories about expectations for and effects of the debate. (p. 1)

Kendall found that 9 of 31 lead stories concerned the campaign and 7 more were about the debates. She also reported that these stories tended to discuss the relationship of the debates to the campaign and that "the candidates' own words in the debates" were "seldom shown" (p. 5). Thus, some research indicates that television news coverage of debates offers little of substance. Benoit and Currie (2001) explain that timing is probably a factor:

> Presidential debates are always held in the evening after the network news. By the time the evening news has the opportunity to discuss the debates—on the day after the debate—the debates are now roughly 20 hours old and hardly news. Thus, television news has already moved on to discussion of reactions to the debates. It is unfortunate that this means that the evening news rarely reports on what transpired in the debates. (p. 37)

Hence, it may be more fruitful to focus on newspaper rather than television coverage.

Although debate viewership has tended to decline over the years (Commission on Presidential Debates, 2003), neither candidates nor scholars can afford to ignore a message that has been seen by at least 36 million voters in every campaign (and by as many as 80 million in 1980). The Racine Group (2002) concluded that "while journalists and scholars display varying degrees of cynicism about the debates, few deny that viewers find them useful and almost no one doubts that they play an important role in national campaigns" (p. 201). Benoit, Hansen, and Verser's (2003) meta-analysis found that watching debates can increase issue knowledge and issue salience, have an agenda-setting effect, alter perceptions of the candidates' personality, and affect vote preference. Clearly this message form merits scholarly attention.

Although millions of voters watch these messages, millions more do not. Nonetheless, even nonviewers can learn about debates, and the

participating candidates, from news coverage. Considerable research investigates whether media coverage is ideologically balanced (see, e.g., the meta-analysis by D'Alessio & Allen, 2000, or the recent review by Niven, 2003). We are more concerned with the accuracy of news reports. Can voters rely on newspapers to provide an accurate picture of this important campaign message? This study addresses this question by investigating the relationship between the content of presidential debates (1980–2000) and newspaper coverage of those debates.

★ LITERATURE REVIEW

Analysis of political messages often employs two key categories: functions (positive or negative [attack] messages) and topics (issue-oriented [policy]) or image-oriented [character]). We will elucidate these two categories in turn.

Functions: Acclaims, Attacks, and Defenses

Most research on political campaign messages studies two functions: positive and negative. Functional theory adds a third, less common function: refutation of negative messages (Benoit, 1999, 2001; Benoit, Blaney, & Pier, 1998). Benoit and Harthcock (1999) define these three functions as follows: "Themes that portray the candidate in a favorable light are *acclaims*. Themes that portray the opposing candidate in an unfavorable light are *attacks*. Themes that attempt to repair the candidate's reputation (from attacks by the opposition) are *defenses*" (p. 346). For example, in the first debate of 2000, Governor George W. Bush provided this acclaim:

> I want to take one half of the surplus and dedicate it to Social Security, one quarter of [the] surplus for important projects. And I want to send one quarter of the surplus back to the people who pay the bills. I want everybody who pays taxes to have their tax rates cut.

Protecting Social Security and cutting taxes clearly would be viewed as desirable by many in his audience. In the same debate, Vice President Al Gore attacked thusly:

Under Governor Bush's tax cut proposal, he would spend more money on tax cuts for the wealthiest 1 percent than all of the new spending that he proposes for education, health care, prescription drugs and national defense all combined. Now, I think those are the wrong priorities.

Because many in the audience would not favor tax cuts for the wealthy, this comment is an attack. Gore also claimed that his plan would cover prescription drugs for all senior citizens, whereas Bush's plan covered only 5% of seniors. Bush responded to this attack by saying:

Wait a minute, that's just totally false for him to stand up there and say that. Let me make sure the seniors hear me loud and clear. . . . All seniors will be covered. All poor seniors will have their prescription drugs paid for. In the meantime, we're going to have a plan to help poor seniors.

This is a defense because it identifies ("that's just totally false") and rejects ("All seniors will be covered") an attack. These three functions work together as an informal form of cost-benefit analysis. Acclaims emphasize a candidate's benefits, attacks reveal an opponent's costs, and defenses minimize or dissipate a candidate's alleged costs.

Studies investigating presidential TV advertisements often analyze the functions of these messages (see Benoit, 1999, 2001; Johnston & Kaid, 2002; Kaid & Johnston, 2001; West, 1997). However, research on presidential debates often asks different questions and rarely utilizes functional theory (see Carlin & McKinney, 1994; Coleman, 2000; Friedenberg, 1994, 1997; Hellweg, Pfau, & Brydon, 1992; Hinck, 1993; Jamieson & Birdsell, 1988; Kraus, 1962, 1979, 2000; Lanoue & Schrott, 1991). Bitzer and Rueter (1980) counted attacks in the Carter-Ford debates, but did not compare them with positive comments (or with defenses). Of course, the functional approach cannot answer every important question about debates or other campaign messages. But it can help us determine whether news coverage of debates is reasonably accurate.

Two studies have investigated news coverage of presidential debates from the functional

perspective. Benoit and Currie (2001) compared the functions and news coverage of the 1996 and 2000 general election debates. In both years, the news covered attacks and defenses more often, and acclaims less often, than they occurred in the debates. In 1996, attacks accounted for 54% of news coverage of the debates but represented only 33% of the utterances in the debates. Defenses accounted for 7% of debate utterances but constituted 11% of news coverage. Acclaims, the most common function of debates (59%), represented only about one third of news story comments (35%). In 2000, the same pattern occurred. Attacks were over-represented in news coverage (41% to 24%), as were defenses (11% to 2%). Acclaims were slighted (74% of debates, 48% of news).

Reber and Benoit (2001) compared a Republican and a Democratic primary debate from 2000 with newspaper reports of those debates. Newspaper coverage again accentuated the attacks: criticisms constituted 45% of news but only 31% of debate utterances. Defenses also were over-represented (16% of the newspaper accounts, 12% of the debates). Acclaims again were under-represented (40% in stories but 58% of the debates). So research suggests that, in comparison with their actual occurrence in debates, newspaper coverage over-represents attacks and defenses and under-emphasizes acclaims.

Topics: Policy versus Character

Studies of political advertising frequently compare policy (issue) and character (image) oriented themes (Benoit, 1999, 2001; Johnston & Kaid, 2002; Joslyn, 1980; Kaid & Johnston, 2001; West, 1997). Again, most research on presidential debates takes up other questions (Carlin & McKinney, 1994; Coleman, 2000; Friedenberg, 1994, 1997; Hellweg, Pfau, & Brydon, 1992; Hinck, 1993; Jamieson & Birdsell, 1988; Kraus, 1962, 1979, 2000; Lanoue & Schrott, 1991) and typically does not content analyze these messages for policy and character themes. Bitzer and Rueter (1980) discuss issues raised by the candidates, but do not contrast this with displays of image or character.

Functional theory posits that the three functions of political campaign discourse can occur on two kinds of topics: policy (issues) and image (character). According to Benoit and Harthcock (1999): "Themes that concern governmental action (past, current, or future) and problems amenable to governmental action were considered policy utterances. Themes that address characteristics, traits, abilities, or attributes of the candidates (or parties) were considered character utterances" (p. 346). For example, in the second debate of 2000, Gore outlined his approach to education:

> I think that we should require states to test all students, test schools and school districts. And I think that we should go further and require teacher testing for new teachers, also . . . I want to give new choices to parents to send their kids to college with a $10,000 tax deduction for college tuition per child, per year. I want to reduce the size of the classrooms in this country for one basic reason, so that students can get more one-on-one time with teachers. And the way to do that is, first, to recruit more teachers. I have a plan in my budget to recruit 100,000 new, highly qualified teachers.

Testing in schools, tuition tax deductions, classroom size, and number of teachers all concern education policy. In contrast, Bush's observation in the same debate that "people know that I'm a . . . compassionate person" concerns character rather than policy.

Benoit and Currie (2001) also studied the distribution of topics in the 1996 and 2000 general election debates and in news coverage of those events. They found that, in 1996, news coverage over-emphasized character. Policy comprised 72% of the candidates' remarks but only 55% of coverage. Conversely, character comprised 28% of the debates but 45% of news coverage. However, this finding did not replicate in 2000, when both debates and news coverage devoted 76% of comments to policy and 24% to character. Similarly, Reber and Benoit (2001) found no significant differences between the proportion of policy and character utterances in the two 2000 primary debates and in the newspaper coverage of those debates.

We acknowledge that policy and character topics in political messages are not completely distinct (Zakahi & Hacker, 1995). Benoit and Wells (1996) argue that a candidate's stance on issues shapes that candidate's image, and that a candidate's image probably influences perceptions of his or her issue stances. Similarly, policy positions can influence perceptions of a candidate's character, or image (Louden, 1994). Johnson (1989) suggests that some voters may he more attuned to issues and others to character. Nevertheless, we believe that the two concepts can be distinguished reliably in content analysis and that doing so yields valuable insights.

★ PURPOSE

While day-to-day coverage of presidential campaigns has been studied extensively (e.g., Farnsworth & Lichter, 2003; Lichter & Noyes, 1995; Lichter, Noyes, & Kaid, 1999), relatively little scholarship has compared newspaper coverage of presidential debates with the debates themselves. Extending research by Benoit and Currie (2001), this essay examines whether newspaper coverage of presidential debates accurately reflects the content of those debates.

Hypothesis

As noted above, news coverage of presidential primary and general election debates differed significantly from the debates themselves, with more attacks and defenses but fewer acclaims. Accordingly we predict:

H[1].   The proportion of attacks will be higher (and the proportion of acclaims lower) in newspaper stories about presidential debates than in the debates themselves.

Research Questions

Also as noted above, the findings regarding news coverage of issue and image topics have not been consistent. Given these mixed results, we pose a research question:

RQ[1]. Is the proportion of policy and character comments in newspaper stories about debates different from the proportion of those topics in the debates?

Finally, Benoit and Currie (2001) found that newspaper stories varied in the amount of debate content reported (in 1996 the average story reported 3% of the debate's content;

in 2000 the typical story reported 7% of the debates' content). Thus, we pose a second research question:

RQ$_2$. What percentage of total themes in the debates is reported in newspaper stories?

★ METHOD

We analyzed presidential debates from 1980 to 1992 (we also include the results for previous research on the 1996 and 2000 general election debates from Benoit & Currie, 2001). Lexis-Nexis was used to locate newspaper stories about each of these debates. Articles were located by searching for the names of the candidates participating in each debate and the word "debate" (e.g., for the 1988 presidential debates we searched for "Bush," "Dukakis," and "debate"). Articles were excluded from the sample if they did not focus on the debate, were very short, or were transcripts of the debates. For each debate we included one *New York Times* and one *Washington Post* article, and randomly selected three additional articles from other newspapers.[1] These procedures obtained a sample of five articles about each of the debates in our sample.

The content of these debates is known from previous research (e.g., Benoit & Brazeal, 2002; Benoit & Wells, 1996; Benoit, Blaney, & Pier, 1998; Benoit et al., 2003; Wells, 1999). Following the procedures employed to analyze the debates themselves, the analytic procedure employed here to analyze the content of newspaper reports consisted of three steps. First, we identified statements in these news articles that described the candidates' comments in the debate. Descriptions of other events or other messages and evaluative statements were excluded from the analysis. Second, these statements were unitized into themes or utterances that address a coherent idea (our discussion uses "utterances," "comments," and "remarks" synonymously with "themes"). Berelson (1952) explained that a theme is "an assertion about a subject" (p. 138). Similarly, Holsti (1969) defined a theme as "a single assertion about some subject" (p. 116). Basically, a theme is an argument (argument; see O'Keefe,

1977) about the candidates. Because rhetoric is enthymematic, themes vary in length from a phrase to several sentences. Third, each theme in the articles was coded for the two variables under investigation here: functions (acclaims, attacks, defenses) and topics (policy, character).

We then compared the data produced by these content analyses with those of the presidential debates. In other words, we began with the content analysis of the debates already available in the literature, replicated those procedures to content analyze newspaper stories about the debates, and then compared the two sets of results. The data regarding debates and newspaper coverage of those debates are comparable because they were generated by identical procedures.

Two coders performed the content analysis. Reliability was assessed with a subset of approximately 10% of the texts. We employed Cohen's (1960) κ, which accounts for agreement by chance. κ for function (acclaim, attack, defend) in coding the debates ranged from .80–.95; κ for topic (policy, character) ranged from .69–.98. In the analysis of newspaper stories κ for functions was .88 and for topic was .67. Landis and Koch (1977) indicate that κs of .61–.80 reflect "substantial" agreement and κs of .81–1.0 represent "almost perfect" inter-coder reliability (p. 165). Thus, our data are acceptably reliable.

★ RESULTS

The hypothesis that newspapers would under-represent acclaims and over-represent attacks and defenses was supported. Overall, the debates had significantly more acclaims than newspaper accounts of the debates: 61% of utterances in these debates were acclaims but only 41% of statements in newspaper coverage were acclaims. Conversely, newspaper reports over-represented attacks compared to the debates (50% to 31%). Defenses were reported at roughly the same frequency with which they occurred in the debates (9% to 8%). Statistical analysis reveals that these differences are significant ($\chi^2[df = 2] = 254.55$, $p < .0001$, $V = .19$). Table 1 reveals that this effect is significant, and in the predicted direction, for every campaign

TABLE 1

Functions of General Debates and Newspaper Coverage

	Acclaims	Attacks	Defenses	χ^2 (df = 2)
1980				
Debates	114 (50%)	89 (39%)	23 (10%)	18.58
Newspapers	61 (32%)	114 (61%)	13 (7%)	p < .0001, V = .21
1984				
Debates	229 (51%)	168 (38%)	51 (11%)	6.51
Newspapers	26 (36%)	38 (53%)	8 (11%)	p < .05, V = .11
1988				
Debates	535 (59%)	298 (33%)	75 (8%)	94.63
Newspapers	164 (33%)	291 (59%)	37 (8%)	p < .0001, V = .26
1992				
Debates	331 (56%)	180 (30%)	85 (14%)	47.05
Newspapers	221 (44%)	248 (49%)	34 (7%)	p < .0001, V = .21
1996				
Debates	621 (59%)	347 (33%)	78 (7%)	34.01
Newspapers	59 (35%)	90 (54%)	18 (11%)	p < .0001, V = .17
2000				
Debates	860 (74%)	281 (24%)	24 (2%)	175.61
Newspapers	438 (48%)	379 (41%)	104 (11%)	p < .0001, V = .29
Total				
Debates	2690 (61%)	1363 (31%)	336 (8%)	254.55
Newspapers	969 (41%)	1160 (50%)	214 (9%)	p < .0001, V = .19

in the sample. Thus, there is a significant and consistent distortion of function in newspaper reports of presidential general election debates; the effect size (Kramer's V = .19) is also noteworthy.

The first research question asked if the proportion of policy and character topics is consistent between debates and newspaper coverage of those debates. Overall, stories reported on character (31%) more often than this topic occurred in debates (26%); because policy and character sum to 100%, this means that stories reported policy less frequently (69%) than occurred in the debates (74%). Statistical analysis indicated that these differences were significant (χ^2 [df = 1] = 22.45, p < .0001, V = .06). However, closer examination (see Table 2) revealed that this effect did not occur in every campaign, but was significant only in

1992 and 1996. Clearly, the effect for topics is not as consistent as the effect for functions in newspaper coverage; not surprisingly, the overall effect size is modest (.06).

The final research question asked how much of debate content was reported in an average article. The average number of themes in these debates was 338.3 (ranging from 198.7 to 423); the average number of themes in these newspaper articles was 37 (ranging from 7.2 to 78.9). Thus, the typical newspaper story reports about 11% of the themes in a presidential debate (this figure ranged from 3.2–30.3; see Table 3).

★ DISCUSSION

Millions watch presidential debates; however, millions more learn about them from campaign reporting. Content analysis of presidential

TABLE 2

Topics of General Debates and Newspaper Coverage

	Policy	Character	χ^2 (df = 1)
1980			
Debates	185 (77%)	55 (23%)	.03
Newspapers	145 (76%)	46 (24%)	*ns*
1984			
Debates	315 (81%)	72 (19%)	1.07
Newspapers	62 (87%)	9 (13%)	*ns*
1988			
Debates	561 (66%)	290 (34%)	1.33
Newspapers	305 (63%)	182 (37%)	*ns*
1992			
Debates	**372 (73%)**	139 (27%)	20.69
Newspapers	284 (59%)	**198 (41%)**	*p* < .0001, *V* = .15
1996			
Debates	**620 (78%)**	174 (22%)	26.04
Newspapers	62 (55%)	**50 (45%)**	*p* < .0001, *V* = .17
2000			
Debates	865 (76%)	276 (24%)	0
Newspapers	684 (76%)	217 (24%)	*ns*
Total			
Debates	**2918 (74%)**	1006 (26%)	22.45
Newspapers	1542 (69%)	**702 (31%)**	*p* < .0001, *V* = .06

debates from 1980 to 2000 and newspaper coverage of these debates reveals that those who rely on newspaper coverage do not receive an accurate picture of the content of the debates: newspaper stories consistently and significantly over-represent attacks while under-reporting acclaims. This result is consistent with research on two primary debates from 2000 (Reber & Benoit, 2001).

One implication is that newspaper coverage may foster an unfair perception that candidates are waging negative campaigns. Others have found a negative emphasis in campaign reporting. Hart (2000) observed that "political news is reliably negative" (p. 173; see also Lichter, Noyes, & Kaid, 1999). Jamieson, Waldman, and Devitt (1998) wrote: "In every presidential general election since 1960 reliance on news reports for information about the campaign would lead one to conclude that it contained a far higher level of attack than was the case" (p. 325). Because newspaper coverage of presidential debates is significantly more negative than the debates themselves, voters could be led to believe that these debates, and the campaign generally, are more negative than they actually are. It is important to realize that the information available to voters who *watch* debates is significantly different from the information available to voters who *read about debates in newspapers*. In short, it matters where voters learn about candidates.

The emphases of newspaper coverage are understandable. Attacks by nature foster conflict and therefore might be expected to be more interesting to readers than acclaims. Further, attacks arguably differentiate candidates better than acclaims and thereby provide

TABLE 3

Percentage of General Debate Utterances Reported in Newspaper Articles

	DEBATES			NEWSPAPER ARTICLES			
	Themes	Debates	M	Themes	Articles	M	Percent of Debate
1980	226	1	226	188	5	37.6	10.0
1984	448	2	224	72	10	7.2	3.2
1988	908	2	454	492	10	49.2	10.8
1992	596	3	198.7	304	15	20.3	10.2
1996	1046	2	523	167	10	16.7	3.2
2000	1165	3	388.3	1184	15	78.9	30.3
Total	4398	13	338.3	2407	65	37	10.9

voters with valuable information that better enables them to choose among candidates.

Nonetheless, these findings are troubling because the effect to which they point could be deleterious to democracy. Although some important reservations have been raised about their conclusions (e.g., Finkel & Geer, 1999), Ansolabehere and Iyengar (1995) have argued that attacks in political advertising reduce voter turnout (Ansolabehere & Iyengar 1995; Ansolabehere, Iyengar, & Simon, 1999). Conceivably, a negative tone in campaign coverage could have the same effect. In fact, as Finkel and Geer (1998) note, in one analysis Ansolabehere and Iyengar analyzed *news stories* rather than television advertising in order to assess a campaign's level of negativity. In other words, Ansolabehere and Iyengar unintentionally demonstrated that negative newspaper coverage reduced voter turnout. It is possible that newspaper coverage of debates similarly could discourage turnout among voters who read, rather than watch, debates.[2] As Just, Crigler, and Buhr (1999) observe:

> If candidates spend most of their time attacking each other, journalists should not be blamed for reporting that they do. On the other hand, if reporters distort the candidates' messages, they may heighten the cynicism or negativity of the campaign. (p. 35)

Our data also reveal a tendency for newspaper accounts to discuss policy less, and

character more, than occurred in the debates themselves. However, this effect was significant in only two campaigns (1992, 1996). Reber and Benoit (2001) did not find a significant difference between the 2000 primary debates and newspaper coverage thereof. Hence, the distortion effect for topic is less consistent than it is for function.

It is probably no coincidence that the two campaigns in which this effect was significant involved Bill Clinton. Both of Clinton's Republican opponents, George Bush in 1992 and Bob Dole in 1996, attacked Clinton's character. Yet newspaper stories about the debates focused on character even more than did the candidates. Just as attacks in general may be believed to heighten reader interest by promoting conflict, salacious character attacks in particular may be thought to be more interesting than comparatively dull policy questions.

Other research suggests that news coverage may emphasize character more than do the candidates. Sears and Chaffee (1979) concluded that in 1976, "the debates themselves were heavily issue-oriented, but the subsequent coverage of them decidedly less so" (p. 228). Lichter and Noyes (1995), who analyzed news reports about presidential speeches, found that the news in 1992 focused more on character than did campaign speeches (they did not report whether this difference was statistically significant). Just, Crigler, and Buhr (1999) concluded that, in 1992, "journalists bear most of the responsibility for the negative tone of the campaign" (p. 37). However, although the media may tend to over-represent character, this is not always the case. Emphasis on character may reflect simply a more general media bias in favor of personality. Further, in some years an issue or issues may be believed to be so important to voters (that is, so interesting to newspaper readers) that coverage will focus accordingly.

Our results also suggest that different media may cover debates differently. Despite over-representing character in comparison to debates, these data show that newspapers clearly feature policy over personality (69% to 31%). This contrasts sharply with Kendall's (1997) finding that televised coverage featured candidate personality. This is not to say that Kendall was wrong: It is entirely possible that television news focuses more on character than do newspapers. This discrepancy emphasizes the importance of studying multiple kinds of news media: The content available in one medium (or source) may differ in important ways from content in others.

Finally, the results reveal that newspapers convey relatively little of the content of debates. Overall, the typical newspaper article reports about 10.9% of candidates' remarks (see Table 3). The most ever reported was 30.3% in 1984. Clearly, newspapers serve a gate-keeping function, reporting only a small part of what is actually said in debates. Non-viewers who rely on newspaper accounts of debates receive a highly filtered version of events.

CONCLUSION

Debates are an important and well-established part of presidential campaigns. They impart information, influence voters' perceptions of the candidates, and can change voting behavior. However, many voters do not watch these contests and learn about them from the news media. Even viewers may be influenced by media discussion of these events (Hellweg, Pfau, & Brydon, 1992). Hence, it is important to learn whether media coverage accurately reflects the content of debates.

Future research might investigate news coverage of other messages (e.g., important speeches such as nominating convention acceptance addresses or important political television spots), or might contrast newspaper and television coverage. Coverage of topic (policy and character) also could be studied in more detail. For example, scholars should investigate which issues (e.g., taxation, education, health care, national defense) are featured in campaign messages and in news coverage. Similarly, scholars might examine whether candidates and the media equally emphasize particular character traits such as honesty, compassion, or morality.

Evidence from campaigns from 1980 to 2000 indicates that newspapers do not provide voters with an accurate depiction of presidential debates. News reports potentially may foster inaccurate impressions that these debates are highly negative and that the campaign is largely about character. Of course, voters need to assess a candidate's drawbacks and character. However, voters also need to know a candidate's strengths and his or her position on policy matters. Newspaper coverage consistently under-reports candidates' acclaims. Sometimes it erroneously portrays debates as a clash of personalities. These tendencies are particularly worrisome given that the average article also is so selective, reporting only about 11% of candidates' remarks. Of course, we cannot reasonably expect a newspaper article to report everything in a 90-minute debate. But it is reasonable to expect that news coverage not be unduly selective or inaccurate in reporting on political debates. Moreover, if negative campaigning depresses voter turn-out (Ansolabehere & Iyengar, 1995), the proclivity of newspapers to accentuate the negative in political debates could do a disservice to democracy.

NOTES

[1] *Atlanta Journal and Constitution, Boston Globe, Boston Herald, Buffalo News, Chicago Sun-Times, Columbus Dispatch, New York Daily News, Denver Post, Houston Chronicle, Miami Herald, Omaha World Herald, Cleveland Plain-Dealer, San Diego Union Tribune, San Francisco Chronicle, Seattle Times, St. Louis Post-Dispatch, St. Petersburg Times,*

Minneapolis Star Tribune, Tampa Tribune, New Orleans Time-Picayune, USA Today.

[2] We ran correlations between turnout (using Federal Election Commission data), and (1) percentage of attacks in debates and (2) percentage of attacks in newspaper coverage of debates. Given that our n is only 6, we did not expect to find significant differences, but we wanted to contrast the two rs. For debates, the correlation between attacks and turnout is slightly positive ($r = 0.097$): as attacks increase, turnout increases a little. For news coverage of debates, the correlation between attacks and turnout is negative and larger ($r = -0.177$): the more attacks reported in the newspapers, the less turnout. Thus, unlike attacks in debates, the over-represented attacks in newspaper coverage of debates are associated with lower turnout (although, again, the n is so small that these correlations are not significant).

REFERENCES

Ansolabehere, S., & Iyengar, S. (1995). *Going negative: How attack ads shrink and polarize the electorate.* New York: Free Press.

Ansolabehere, S. D., Iyengar, S., & Simon, A. (1999). Replicating experiments using aggregate and survey data: The case of negative advertising and turnout. *American Political Science Review, 93,* 901–909.

Benoit, W. L. (1999). *Seeing spots: A functional analysis of presidential television advertisements, 1952–1996.* Westport, CT: Praeger.

Benoit, W. L. (2001). The functional approach to presidential television spots: Acclaiming, attacking, and defending 1952–2000. *Communication Studies, 52,* 109–126.

Benoit, W. L., Blaney, J. R., & Pier, P. M. (1998). *Campaign '96: A functional analysis of acclaiming, attacking, and defending.* Westport, CT: Praeger.

Benoit, W. L., & Brazeal, L. M. (2002). A functional analysis of the 1988 Bush-Dukakis presidential debates. *Argumentation and Advocacy, 38,* 219–223.

Benoit, W. L., & Currie, H. (2001). Inaccuracies in media coverage of presidential debates. *Argumentation and Advocacy, 38,* 28–39.

Benoit, W. L., Hansen, G. J., & Verser, R. T. (2003). A meta-analysis of the effects of viewing presidential debates. *Communication Monographs, 70,* 335–350.

Benoit, W. L., & Harthcock, A. (1999). Functions of the Great Debates: Acclaims, attacks, and defense in the 1960 presidential debates. *Communication Monographs, 66,* 341–357.

Benoit, W. L., Pier, P. M., McHale, J. P., Hansen, G. J., & McGuire, J. P. (2003). *Campaign 2000: A functional analysis of acclaiming, attacking, and defending.* Lanham, MD: Rowan & Littlefield.

Benoit, W. L., & Wells, W. T. (1996). *Candidates in conflict: Persuasive attack and defense in the 1992 presidential debates.* Tuscaloosa, AL: University of Alabama Press.

Berelson, B. (1952). *Content analysis for the social sciences and humanities.* Reading, MA: Addison-Wesley.

Bishop, C. F., Meadow, R. G., & Jackson-Beeck, M. (Eds.). (1978). *The presidential debates: Media, electoral, and policy perspectives.* New York: Praeger.

Bitzer, L., & Rueter, T. (1980). *Carter vs. Ford: The counterfeit debates of 1976.* Madison, WI: University of Wisconsin Press.

Carlin, D. B., & McKinney, M. S. (1994). *The 1992 presidential debates in focus.* Westport, CT: Praeger.

Cohen, J. (1960). A coefficient of agreement for nominal scales. *Educational and Psychological Measurement, 20,* 37–46.

Coleman, S. (2000). *Televised election debates: International perspectives.* London: Macmillan Press.

Commission on Presidential Debates. (2003). Accessed 10/3/03: http://www.debates.org.

D'Alessio, D., & Allen, M. (2000). Media bias in presidential elections: A meta-analysis. *Journal of Communication, 50,* 133–156.

Farnsworth, S. J., & Lichter, S. R. (2003). *The nightly news nightmare: Network television's coverage of U.S. presidential elections, 1988–2000.* Lanham, MD: Rowman & Littlefield.

Finkel, S. E., & Geer, J. G. (1998). A spot check: Casting doubt on the demobilizing effect of attack advertising. *American Journal of Political Science, 42,* 573–595.

Friedenberg, R. V. (1994). *Rhetorical studies of national political debates—1960–1992* (2nd ed.). Westport, CT: Praeger.

Friedenberg, R. V. (1997). *Rhetorical studies of national political debates—1996.* Westport, CT: Praeger.

Hart, R. P. (2000). *Campaign talk: why elections are good for us.* Princeton, NJ: Princeton University Press, 2000.

Hellweg, S. A., Pfau, M., & Brydon, S. R. (1992). *Televised presidential debates: Advocacy in contemporary America.* Westport, CT: Praeger.

Hinck, E. A. (1993). *Enacting the presidency: Political argument, presidential debates, and presidential character.* Westport, CT: Praeger.

Holsti, O. (1952). *Content analysis in communication research.* New York: Free Press.

Jamieson, K. H. (1987). Television, presidential campaigns, and debates. In J. L. Swerdlow (Ed.), *Presidential debates 1988 and beyond* (pp. 27–33). Washington, DC: Congressional Quarterly Inc.

Jamieson, K. H., & Birdsell, D. S. (1988). *Presidential debates: The challenge of creating an informed electorate.* New York: Oxford University Press.

Jamieson, K. H., Waldman, P., & Devitt, J. (1998). Mapping the discourse of the 1996 US presidential general election. *Media, Culture, & Society, 20,* 323–328.

Johnson, D. D. (1989). Image and issue information: Message content or interpretation. *Journalism Quarterly, 66,* 379–382.

Johnston, A., and Kaid, L. L. (2002). Image ads and issue ads in U.S. presidential advertising: Using videostyle to explore stylistic differences in televised political ads from 1952–2000. *Journal of Communication, 52,* 281–300.

Joslyn, R. A. (1980). The content of political spot ads. *Journalism Quarterly, 57,* 92–98.

Just, M., Crigler, A., & Bohr, T. (1999). Voice, substance, and cynicism in presidential campaign media. *Political Communication, 76,* 25–44.

Kaid, L. L., & Johnston, A. (2001). *Videostyle in presidential campaigns: Style and content of televised political advertising.* Westport, CT. Praeger.

Kendall, K. E. (1997). The 1996 Clinton-Dole presidential debates: Through media eyes. In R. V. Friedenberg (Ed.), *Rhetorical studies of national political debates—1996* (pp. 1–29). Westport, CT: Praeger.

Kraus, S. (Ed.). (1962). *The great debates: Kennedy vs. Nixon, 1960.* Bloomington, IN: Indiana University Press.

Kraus, S. (Ed.). (1979). *The great debate: Carter vs. Ford, 1976.* Bloomington: Indiana University Press.

Kraus, S. (2000). *Televised presidential debates and public policy* (2nd ed.). Mahwah, NJ: Lawrence Erlbaum.

Landis, J. R., & Koch, G. G. (1977). The measurement of observer agreement for categorical data. *Biometrica, 33,*159–174.

Lanoue, D. J., & Schrott, P. R. (1991). *The joint press conference: The history, impact, and prospects of American presidential debates.* New York: Greenwood Press.

Lau, R. R., Sigelman, L., Heldman, C., & Babbitt, P. R. (1999). The effectiveness of negative political advertising: A meta-analytic assessment. *American Political Science Review, 93,* 851–876.

Lichter, S. R., & Noyes, R. E. (1995). *Good intentions make bad news: why Americans hate campaign journalism.* Lanham, MD: Rowman and Littlefield.

Lichter, S. R., Noyes, R. E., & Kaid, L. L. (1999). No news or negative news: How the networks nixed the '96 campaign. In L. L. Kaid & D. G. Bystrom (Eds.), *The electronic election: Perspectives on the 1996 campaign communication* (pp. 3–13). Mahwah, NJ: Lawrence Erlbaum.

Louden, A. (1994). Voter rationality and media excess: Image in the 1992 presidential campaign. In R. Denton (Ed.), *The 1992 presidential campaign: Communication perspectives* (pp. 169–187). Westport, CT: Praeger.

Martel, M. (1983). *Political campaign debates: Issues, strategies, and tactics.* New York: Longman.

Niven, D. (2003). Objective evidence on media bias: Newspaper coverage of congressional party switchers. *Journalism and Mass Communication Quarterly, 80,* 311–326.

O'Keefe, D. J. (1977). Two concepts of argument. *Journal of the American Forensic Association, 73,* 121–128.

Racine Group. (2002). White paper on televised political campaign debates. *Argumentation and Advocacy, 38,* 199–218.

Reber, B. H., & Benoit, W. L. (2001). Presidential debate stories accentuate the negative. *Newspaper Research Journal, 22,* 30–43.

Schroeder, A. (2000). *Presidential debates: Forty years of high-risk TV.* New York: Columbia University Press.

Sears, D. O., & Chaffee, S. H. (1979). Uses and effects of the 1976 debates: An overview of empirical studies. In S. Kraus (Ed.), *The great debates: Carter vs. Ford, 1976* (pp. 223–261). Bloomington: Indiana University Press.

Wells, W. T. (1999). *An analysis of attacking, acclaiming, and defending strategies in the 1976–1984 presidential debates.* Ph.D. Dissertation University of Missouri, Columbia.

West, D. M. (1997). *Air wars: Television advertising in election campaigns 1952–1995* (2nd ed.). Washington, DC: Congressional Quarterly Press.

Zakahi, W. R., & Hacker, K. L. (1995). Televised presidential debates and candidate images. In K. L. Hacker, (Ed.), *Candidate images in presidential elections* (pp. 99–122). Westport, CT: Praeger.

CHAPTER 5
The Presidency

Speeches by presidents

are among the most important speeches in the United States. More than a third of the "Top 100" twentieth-century public addresses, according to a nationwide survey of communication scholars, were delivered by presidents.[1] Presidents set the nation's agenda, lead us in and out of armed conflict, and try to send the people important messages about the American character. Early in the nation's history, presidential speeches were relatively rare and had a distanced quality—as if the president were speaking almost from "on high." During the twentieth century, the quality of presidential speeches gradually changed; presidents now speak more often and directly to the American people through televised addresses.[2] Recent scholars have taken a variety of approaches in studying how presidential rhetoric now works.[3]

William F. Lewis's 1987 essay, "Telling America's Story: Narrative Form and the Reagan Presidency" focuses on a masterful rhetorician, President Ronald Reagan, and on

one striking characteristic of this new style, the heavy use of narrative. Influenced by Walter R. Fisher's work on narrative as argument, Lewis analyzes Reagan's individual and over-arching narratives, finding them empowering for both the nation and the president[4]—so much so, in fact, that they obscured flaws in Reagan's policies and presidency. Lewis argues that Reagan's use of narrative was also dangerous insofar as it resisted necessary change and isolated those who embraced it from important material conditions and social commentary.

Karlyn Kohrs Campbell and Kathleen Hall Jamieson's "Inaugural Addresses," a chapter from their 1990 book *Deeds Done in Words: Presidential Rhetoric and the Genres of Governance*, focuses on genre rather than narrative. Recognizing that certain kinds of speeches recur, they consider speeches such as inaugurals, state of the union addresses, requests for declarations of war, pardons, and farewells as rhetorical genres. They look back through history to define the genres, noting instances when presidents offered truly exceptional speeches that redefined the genres or defied generic expectations in interesting ways. This chapter discusses the opportunity American presidents have to redefine the American people and reunite them after a divisive election.

Martin J. Medhurst's 1994 essay, "Reconceptualizing Rhetorical History: Eisenhower's Farewell Address," explores another way that the rhetorical study of genre can uncover the riches of particular presidential addresses. Many scholars in communication and political science specialize in particular presidencies, contextualizing a particular speech within that presidency and studying all of the related public records to gain a full picture of that speech. Medhurst presents Eisenhower's farewell not as a philosophical, prophetic warning—in the tradition of the farewell genre— against "the military industrial complex," but as a refutation of what Eisenhower anticipated would be incoming President John F. Kennedy's foreign and budget policies. Medhurst uses archival research to situate the speech as part of Eisenhower's administration-long call for "balance" and to offer a new "reading" of Eisenhower's famous address that exemplifies how a president's words should be considered historically as well as generically.

Amos Kiewe's 1999 essay, "The Body as Proof: Franklin D. Roosevelt's Preparations for the 1932 Presidential Campaign," considers how a president can get lost in discussions of narrative, genre, and history—the president himself, not his words but his physical being. Aware of the nation's prejudice against the disabled, FDR used a variety of rhetorical strategies to refute the suspicion that he, as a weakened man, would be a weakened leader. Kiewe discusses how FDR displayed his active body, used metaphors suggesting health and mobility, attacked prejudice, and worked with journalist friend Earl Looker to get an article and a biography attesting to his health published in a popular magazine. Kiewe's approach

reflects scholars' recent interest in the material dimensions of rhetoric.

John M. Murphy's 2003 essay, "'Our Mission and Our Moment': George W. Bush and September 11th," reflects concerns raised in the previous essays. Situating Bush's public addresses in a time of crisis for the nation, the essay points out that Bush uses epideictic rhetoric appropriate for emotional expression at times when the deliberative rhetoric appropriate for policy-making would be more appropriate. Murphy also claims that the consistent visual imagery and definition of the American people that characterize these speeches are highly effective but also frightening because they insist on a univocal public interpretation of the events of September 11, 2001, and on a single appropriate response, without offering much rational argumentation. As Murphy predicts Bush's popularity ultimately fell as we learned there are no simple answers to national policy decisions.

Notes

[1] Stephen E. Lucas and Martin J. Medhurst, eds., *Words of a Century: The Top 100 American Speeches, 1900–1999* (New York: Oxford University Press, in press).

[2] Roderick P. Hart, *The Sound of Leadership* (Chicago: University of Chicago Press, 1987) does an excellent job examining how often the "new" president speaks, on what occasion, and on what subjects.

[3] James W. Ceaser, Glen E. Thurow, Jeffrey Tullis, and Joseph M. Bessette called this style "the rhetorical presidency" in their essay "The Rise of the Rhetorical Presidency," *Presidential Studies Quarterly* 11 (1981): 158–71. Other scholars in communication and political science have questioned and refined this concept of "the rhetorical presidency." None, however, have denied that presidential public address in recent decades has a different quality. See, for example, David Lewis, "The Two Rhetorical Presidencies: An Analysis of Televised Presidential Speeches, 1947–1991," *American Politics Quarterly* 25, no. 3 (1997): 380–95.

[4] See Walter Fisher, *Human Communication as Narration: Toward a Philosophy of Reason, Value, and Action* (Columbia: University of South Carolina Press, 1987).

Telling America's Story:
Narrative Form and the Reagan Presidency

William F. Lewis

By 1980, America had lost its sense of direction. Economic troubles, a series of foreign policy failures, and corruption in its government had created a national malaise. Then Ronald Reagan came onto the scene with a vision of America that reinvigorated the nation. His great skills as a communicator and his commitment to fundamental ideals were just what the nation needed. We were once again proud to be Americans.

This familiar and well accepted story follows the pattern of many political success stories in which the hero rescues the country from a time of great trouble. This story is special, however, in that Reagan is said to have accomplished the feat through the power of his speaking and, eventually, to have been brought down when that power failed him. After more than five years in office, Reagan was still referred to as "the Western world's most gifted communicator."[1]

Objection to Ronald Reagan did not originate with the discovery of the Iran arms deal, however. Despite Reagan's consistent popularity and continuing praise for his speaking,[2] there has been a substantial segment of a critical public who not only remained unpersuaded by the President, but were offended by his persuasive manner. What is seen by his supporters as clear direction has been attacked by opponents as "ideology without ideas."[3] While it has been noted often that Reagan has provided a renewed sense of confidence and security in the country, expressions of fear about his ineptitude or his willingness to risk war have been frequent. Despite his continuing high levels of approval, a whole genre of literature against Reagan has developed.[4] What makes these books a genre is not just that they share a common opposition to Reagan and his policies, but also that they share a common approach to their criticisms. Reagan is accused repeatedly of being unrealistic, simplistic, and misinformed. Ronald Dallek, for example, claims that Reagan's anti-Communist foreign policy is "a simplistic and ineffective way to meet a complex problem."[5] He explains Reagan's repeated policy mistakes as a manifestation of his psychological make-up

and concludes that his ideology and policy-making are "nonrational."[6] The sense of these criticisms is epitomized in the mocking tone of a *New Republic* editorial that, in the course of bemoaning Reagan's historical ignorance, comments that: "Ronald Reagan has never let the facts get in the way of a good story."[7]

Similar themes recur frequently in the scholarly evaluation of Reagan's rhetoric. His effectiveness is widely recognized, but while Reagan is praised by some for his strategic prowess and for his ability to inspire the American public,[8] others find his success problematic. How, it is asked, can he be so popular when he is uninformed, irrational, and inconsistent?[9] The dominant explanation has been that Reagan manipulates his language, his strategy, or his style to make himself and his policies appear to be attractive.[10] While the power of rhetoric to affect appearances has been demonstrated amply, this insight provides only a partial explanation for the nature of Reagan's rhetoric and the response to it. It does not account satisfactorily for the differences in perception and judgment among Reagan's various audiences, for the difference between support for Reagan and support for his policies, or for the fact that journalistic and scholarly analysis debunking his competence and sincerity was largely irrelevant through most of his presidency.

The purpose of this essay is to account for the distinctive reputation, style, and effect of Ronald Reagan's discourse by providing a consistent and sufficiently comprehensive explanation for the contradictory perceptions of his speaking and for the related paradoxes of this "Great Communicator's" presidency. To construct this account in terms of his discourse requires an explicit awareness of the distinction between a "rational" and a narrative perspective.[11] Narrative theory can provide a powerful account of political discourse, and it is essential for explaining Ronald Reagan's rhetoric, for it is the predominance of the narrative form in Reagan's rhetoric that has established the climate of interpretation within which he is seen and judged.

The frequency of Reagan's story-telling has been widely noted[12] and some perceptive commentaries have demonstrated his consistency with dominant American myths,[13] but what remains to be emphasized is that story-telling is fundamental to the relationship between Reagan and his audience. Stories are not just a rhetorical device that Reagan uses to embellish his ideas; Reagan's message is a story. Reagan uses story-telling to direct his policies, ground his explanations, and inspire his audiences, and the dominance of narrative helps to account for the variety of reactions to his rhetoric.

There is general agreement about the course of the Reagan presidency—the story of his ascendancy has now become the story of his rise and fall—but explanations differ. Those who have criticized Reagan using the standards of technical reasoning and policy-making are likely to contend that his rhetoric is simplistic, untrue, or irrational and to lament the lack of public response to his patent deficiencies.[14] They are likely to explain Reagan's successes as being the result of rhetorical manipulation and to explain the Iran/contra crisis as being the inevitable result of his continuing lack of realism.[15] Those who listen to Ronald Reagan as a story-teller are likely to emphasize Reagan's character and to praise him for providing vision, reassurance, and inspiration to the American public.[16] They are likely to see Reagan as having struck a responsive chord and to explain the Iranian crisis as a weakening of Reagan's previously strong grasp on public leadership.[17] Reactions diverge because listeners perceive Reagan and his speeches differently, and because they apply different standards of judgment to what they perceive.

This essay will (1) explicate the varieties of narrative form active in Reagan's discourse to help explain his presidency and the reactions to it; and (2) discuss some of the moral and epistemic consequences of Reagan's use of narrative, and of the narrative form itself.

★ NARRATIVE FORM IN REAGAN'S RHETORIC

Reagan tells two kinds of stories that differ in scale and purpose, but that work together to establish the dominance of narrative form in the creation and in the interpretation of his rhetoric. *Anecdotes* define the character of an issue at the same time that they illustrate, reinforce, and make his policies and ideas more vivid. Myth structures his message.

Anecdotes are the quick stories, jokes, or incidents that are the verbal counterpart of the visual image. The anecdote is intended to spark interest, and its meaning is established in reference to some larger frame of understanding that is either specified within a discourse or assumed in an audience. In this way, the story of Albert Einstein's difficulty in understanding the 1040 form[18] defines a relationship to the tax code—given a belief that complexity is likely to be the reflection of excessive bureaucracy and that government ought to be accessible to all citizens without requiring special expertise. Similarly, Reagan's story of the Supreme Court decision that, he says, prevented New York children from praying in their cafeteria[19] defines a relationship to the issue of school prayer—given a belief that religious belief is a necessary part of moral order and that people ought to be able to act in private without governmental restriction. In both these instances, a simple story carries a clear message to those whose experience leads them to accept the story as either true or as true-to-life and whose values lead them to accept the moral. As one would expect, Reagan uses anecdotes more often when speaking to audiences that are expected to be uniformly Republican or conservative.

Myth informs all of Reagan's rhetoric. In the broad sense in which it is used here, myth refers to "any anonymously composed story telling of origins and destinies: the explanations a society offers its young of why the world is and why we do as we do, its pedagogic images of the nature and destiny of man."[20] Reagan's myth applies not to the origin of the world, but to the origin of America; not to the destiny of humanity, but to the destiny of Americans. It is a simple and familiar story that is widely taught and widely believed. It is not exactly a true story in the sense that academic historians would want their descriptions and explanations to be true, but it is not exactly fiction either. As Jerome Bruner wrote of myth in general, "its power is that it lives on the feather line between fantasy and reality. It must be neither too good nor too bad to be true, nor must it be too true."[21] Myth provides a sense of importance and direction and it provides a communal focus for individual identity.

America in the Story

Reagan never tells the whole of his American story at any one time, but the myth that emerges in his speeches is familiar and easily stated:

> America is a chosen nation, grounded in its families and neighborhoods, and driven inevitably forward by its heroic working people toward a world of freedom and economic progress unless blocked by moral or military weakness.

Reagan portrays American history as a continuing struggle for progress against great obstacles imposed by economic adversity, barbaric enemies, or Big Government. It is a story with great heroes—Washington, Jefferson, Lincoln, Roosevelt—with great villains—the monarchs of pre-Revolutionary Europe, the Depression, the Communists, the Democrats—and with a great theme—the rise of freedom and economic progress. It is a story that is sanctified by God[22] and validated by the American experience.[23] All the themes of Reagan's rhetoric are contained in this mythic history—America's greatness, its commitment to freedom, the heroism of the American people, the moral imperative of work, the priority of economic advancement, the domestic evil of taxes and government regulation, and the necessity of maintaining military strength. The story fulfills all the requirements of myth—it is widely believed, generally unquestioned, and clearly pedagogical. And Reagan tells the story extremely well. His message is always clear, his examples are chosen well, and his consistent tone of buoyant optimism and unyielding faith in progress complements the picture of continuing success that is proclaimed in the myth. Finally, it provides a focus for identification by his audience. Reagan repeatedly tells his audiences that if they choose to participate in the story, they will become a part of America's greatness.

Reagan's version of the course and direction of American history pervades all of his rhetoric, but he tells his story most clearly on those occasions when he intends to be most inspirational. The character of the myth and the moral implications that he draws from it can be seen clearly in Reagan's Second Inaugural Address.[24]

The key to understanding the Second Inaugural is to see it as a story. Like all of Reagan's rhetoric, the logic of the speech is a narrative logic that emphasizes the connection between character and action, not a rational logic that emphasizes the connections between problems and solutions. In this speech, Reagan establishes the identity of America and the American people, that identity establishes the direction for America's story, and the direction implies the actions that should be taken. By making intelligible the public identity of the audience members (as Americans), the narrative makes those who accept this identity accountable to a system of values and virtues that are used as standards against which to judge policies.

The center of the speech is itself a story. Reagan describes "two of our Founding Fathers, a Boston lawyer named Adams and a Virginia planter named Jefferson." Though they had been "bitter political rivals," Reagan told of how "age had softened their anger" as they exchanged letters and finally came together to the extent that "in 1826, the 50th anniversary of the Declaration of Independence, they both died. They died on the same day, within a few hours of each other. And that day was the Fourth of July." The cosmic harmony of this story is perfectly in keeping with the mythic frame of the speech, and the "important lesson" that Reagan draws from the story is perfectly in keeping with the dominant theme. Reagan concludes his story with a quotation from one of Jefferson's letters to Adams recalling their mutual struggle "for what is most valuable to man, his right of self government." In this story, America represents a single message for all time and for all people. History has been transformed into a lesson that transcends the contingencies of circumstance.

For Reagan, America's meaning is to be found as much in the future as it has been in the past. Seeking to perfect the ultimate American goal of individual freedom, he says, will guarantee peace and prosperity: "There are no limits to growth and human progress, when men and women are free to follow their dreams"; "Every victory for human freedom will be a victory for world peace." Progress toward freedom is tied directly to economic progress by linking unrestrained individual action to economic productivity: "At the heart of our efforts is one idea vindicated by 25 straight months of economic growth: freedom and incentives unleash the drive and entrepreneurial genius that are the core of human progress." The powerfully future-oriented, forward-looking perspective is summed up in his conclusion: America is "one people under God, dedicated to the dream of freedom he has placed in the human heart, called upon now to pass that dream on to a waiting and a hopeful world."

The only impediments to the fulfillment of this dream that Reagan identifies are those that America imposes on itself.[25] For a time, said Reagan, "we failed the system." We suffered through times of economic and social stress because "we yielded authority to the national government that properly belonged to the states or to local governments or to the people themselves." These were temporary difficulties, however. By renewing our faith in freedom "we are creating a nation once again vibrant, robust, and alive." The other great risk that Reagan identifies is military weakness. "History has shown," he states, "that peace does not come, nor will our freedom be preserved, by good will alone."

Reagan's Second Inaugural is based upon a story of America's origins and its quest for freedom. In it, Reagan shows the dire consequences of being distracted from the quest and the rewards and potential glory of regaining faith and direction. He defines the values that are needed (unity, freedom, strength) and he outlines the policies that will aid in pursuit of the goal. Finally, he ties together the past and the future and calls upon Americans to dedicate themselves to living this story.

The Audience in the Story

In the same way in which Reagan's stories give meaning to America, they define what it means to be an American. The narrative form offers a special kind of identification to Reagan's audience because each auditor is encouraged to see himself or herself as a central actor in America's quest for freedom. To accept Reagan's story is not just to understand the course of an American history that is enacted in other places by other people, it is to know that the direction and outcome of the story depends upon you. Proper action makes the audience member into a hero; inaction or improper action makes the listener responsible for America's decline. The narrative logic that defines the nature of heroism in Reagan's rhetoric was the central theme of his First Inaugural Address.[26]

America is defined as the greatest country in the world. It "guarantees individual liberty to a greater degree than any other," it is the "last and greatest bastion of freedom," and, consequently, it has "the world's strongest economy." To be heroes, the audience members must act in ways that will contribute to America's goals. The narrative defines their virtues—determination, courage, strength, faith, hope, work, compassion—and Reagan identifies their character.

In his most explicit and extensive consideration of heroism, Reagan makes it clear that America's real heroes are its ordinary people—the factory workers and the farmers, those who market goods and those who consume them, those who produce ("entrepreneurs" are given special mention here as elsewhere), and those who give to others.[27]

The idea of the American hero is epitomized in the story of Martin Treptow, "a young man . . . who left his job in a small town barbershop in 1917" to serve in WWI. "We're told," said Reagan, "that on his body was found a diary" in which he had written: "America must win this war. Therefore I will work, I will save, I will sacrifice, I will endure, I will fight cheerfully and do my utmost, as if the issue of the whole struggle depended on me alone." The character of the individual and the values that he holds are defined by their contribution to America's struggle. If the audience accepts Reagan's description of the nature of that continuing struggle, then they will be encouraged to accept the same kind of values, actions, and commitments that Treptow accepted in his struggle. In this case, Reagan's use of anecdote defines the character that best fits his story of

America. World War I is taken to exemplify America's struggle for freedom against hostile forces; Treptow exemplifies the common man; the dedication of the soldier exemplifies the dedication to country and the fighting spirit that are necessary to prevail in the struggle; and the diary entry exemplifies the commitment to act upon these principles (work, save, sacrifice, endure) and the attitude that is appropriate to the fight ("cheerfully"). Significantly, the story is presented as true, but the primary sense of its accuracy is that it represents a larger truth. "We're told" is a weak claim to factuality, but the application of the story in a Presidential Inaugural is a strong claim to moral legitimacy.

Reagan's definition of American heroism is primarily, but not exclusively, economic. The key to heroism is effective action in the ongoing struggle to achieve freedom and prosperity. Reagan encourages identification on the ground of a general commitment to the America of his story and discourages distinctions based on differences in politics or interests.[28] The stories he tells as President feature the audience members as Americans rather than as members of different political parties, and *Time* magazine supports the sharing of this perception when it cites as typical the comment by "a retired brewery worker from San Antonio" that: "He really isn't like a Republican. He's more like an American, which is what we really need."[29]

Reagan in the Story

Some of Reagan's critics have attempted to portray him as a dangerous man, seeing him either as a demagogue[30] or a warmonger.[31] Other critics have marveled at his ability to retain his role as a critic of government even after he became its symbolic head and have worried about his detachment from the policies of his own administration[32] or about his lack of accountability.[33] Such criticisms, however, fail to take account of the nature of the public perception that is encouraged by the narrative form.

To understand the response to Reagan it is necessary to see and understand Reagan-in-the-story, not Reagan-the-policy-maker or even Reagan-the-speaker. Since the story is the dominant mode through which the political situation is interpreted, Reagan will not be perceived or judged as a politician or a policy-maker or an ideologue unless that is the role that is defined for Reagan as part of the story. In the story that emerges through his speeches, however, Reagan plays two roles that have succeeded in encompassing the perspective of his critics. As a character in the story, Reagan is a mythic hero. He embodies the role of the compassionate, committed political outsider; he is the active force that has arrived to help right the prevailing wrongs and to get things moving again. As the narrator of the story, Reagan is portrayed as simply presenting the nature of the situation. There is no artifice and no threat in this style of realistic narration; Reagan-as-narrator just presents things as they are.

Reagan's character has been a dominant focus among those who attempt to explain the impact of his rhetoric. One explanation for Reagan's success is that he has "character"— that is, he projects an image of "manly effectiveness."[34] Reagan is said to be "the political embodiment of the heroic westerner,"[35] both in his appearance ("tall, lank, rugged"[36]) and in his character traits ("honesty and sincerity, innocence, optimism and certainty"[37]). He is compared with other Presidential heroes such as Thomas Jefferson, Theodore Roosevelt, and Franklin Roosevelt, whose virtues were those of the visionary and the man of action.[38] In this respect, he is said to contrast with the "softer" Democratic candidates who have opposed him. Reagan has been able to establish the perception of his competence through "tough talk, vigorous promises, and his emphasis on immediate solutions."[39] Reagan's opponents are said to have been pushed by the contrast into appearing "impractical, ineffectual, and effete."[40] Such descriptions reveal Reagan's success establishing himself as a variation on a dominant type of American myth hero— strong, aggressive, distant, in control, and in Reagan's case, able to see the situation clearly and to explain it to a confused public.[41]

The most familiar form of attack on Reagan's character attempts to reveal a true Reagan behind a constructed mask. "Character" becomes a criticism of Reagan when he is accused of playing a role as he did during his movie career. The criticism appears in a number of related forms—he is said to be a "performer," a "host," an "image," to be playing a "game of cultural make-believe," or to be "using" his role to manipulate the public and to more effectively pursue his political or ideological personal goals.[42] This use of "character" as artifice will succeed as a criticism only if Reagan is perceived as constructing a fictional persona. It cannot succeed if the persona is seen as matching or expressing his "real" character. The criticism of Reagan as an artificial creation, however, neglects his role as narrator of the story. Reagan's story, and his role in the story, are presented as a realistic and sensible portrayal of the normal and ordinary course of events. The combination of Reagan's calm demeanor,[43] his frequent reference to familiar situations to explain complex threatening events,[44] and his reliance on American commonplaces[45] combine to create an air of reassuring certainty that has suggested to some commentators that Reagan would be more aptly compared with Harding or Eisenhower than with Theodore or Franklin Roosevelt.[46]

If criticisms of Reagan's character are not adjusted to fit the story, they are likely either to be dismissed or to be reinterpreted—sometimes with unexpected results. The charge that to elect Reagan was to risk war, for example, was unsuccessful for Carter in the 1980 presidential election and for Gerald Ford in the 1976 California primary because these attempts at criticism were perfectly consistent with the strong character that Reagan had established in his story and with the story's assumption that strength is a necessary precondition of peace. From the point of view of the story, Reagan's emphasis on increases in weapons, his assertion of the need to stand up to the Soviets, and his willingness to risk war in pursuit of the higher goals of freedom and democracy reinforced his repeated declaration that "peace is the highest aspiration of the American people," and that he, personally, wanted nothing so much as a peaceful world.[47] The result was that, in both of these elections, the charge made against Reagan did more harm to the accuser than to Reagan. In 1976, Ford's ads were even used by the Reagan campaign.[48] Similarly, Reagan can continue to use "government" as a character in his stories and to oppose himself and his audience to the Federal government after being President for more than one full term because Reagan's role in the narrative situation is to give meaning to the country and government; he and his vision may inspire and shape policy, but he is not held responsible because designing the particulars of policy will not be seen as his role from within this perspective.

The dominance of the story is also revealed by those occasions in which Reagan's character has been called into question. In the first debate with Walter Mondale during the 1984 presidential campaign, his advisors attempted to prepare him with sufficient information and detail, but this tactic was unsuccessful because it did not accord with the character of Reagan in his own story. In the second debate, his advisors resolved to "let Reagan be Reagan."[49] The failure of this attempt to alter Reagan's "character" to meet the demands of his critics and the success of his return to his "normal" style in the second debate confirms the acceptance of Reagan's story and of his role in it. In the Iran/contra affair, Reagan's apparent willingness to deal with an archetypal enemy and to compromise his previously firm stance against terrorism seemed completely inconsistent with the character he had established. There seemed to be only two "rational" explanations (from the point of view of the story): either that Reagan was not responsible for the actions or that his character had changed. Hence, one response to the crisis has been to question Reagan's control over his subordinates and another has been to inquire into his mental and physical health. Neither of these explanations, however, is consistent with the story's image of presidential leadership. The story can encompass Reagan's critics, but it is vulnerable to his own inconsistencies.

Reagan's story encourages his audience to see America as a chosen nation leading the world to freedom and economic progress, to see Reagan as a friendly, well-motivated leader and as a narrator of the American story, and to see themselves as heroes in the unfolding drama of American greatness. In Reagan's rhetoric, the nature of the world, his policies, his values, his character, and the character of his audience are defined together by the story that he tells. The consequences of this reliance on narrative form need to be considered carefully.

★ CONSEQUENCES OF REAGAN'S USE OF NARRATIVE FORM

In a 1984 review essay on "Narrative Theory and Communication Research," Robert L. Scott observed that despite the suggestive correspondences between narrative forms and rhetorical functions, "no rhetorical critic . . . has pressed along the lines suggested thus far by narrative theorists."[50] At the same time, Walter Fisher proposed a theory of human communication based on narrative. Fisher argued that traditional investigation of communication was regulated by the "rational world paradigm," which presumed that rational communicators managed a world that "is a set of logical puzzles which can be resolved through appropriate analysis and application of reason conceived as an argumentative construct."[51] Fisher found this approach to be more incomplete than wrong. Specifically, he objected to its inability to grasp the manner in which symbolization is a universal though non-rational characteristic of human nature, and to its imposition of ideological restrictions upon the process of moral choice. In contrast, Fisher offered the "narrative paradigm," which presumes that humans are essentially story-tellers who act on the basis of good reasons derived from their experience in a world that is "a set of stories which must be chosen among to live the good life in a process of continual recreation."[52]

The distinction between narrative and "rational" forms of consciousness is well grounded in the literature of narrative theory. Drawing from the texts of history, literature, and anthropology, these theorists have shown that narrative is a distinctive and distinctively important means of giving meaning to events. The important question for political discourse parallels Hayden White's inquiry into historic narrative: "With *what kind of meaning* does storying endow" political events?[53] The answers provided by narrative theorists suggest that narrative is a fundamental form of human understanding that directs perception, judgment, and knowledge. Narrative form shapes ontology by making meaningfulness a product of consistent relationships between situations, subjects, and events and by making truth a property that refers primarily to narratives and only secondarily to propositions; narrative form shapes morality by placing characters and events within a context where moral judgment is a necessary part of making sense of the action; and narrative form shapes epistemology by suggesting that all important events are open to common sense understanding.

These characteristics of narrative suggest an explanation for the apparent incongruity of a President with high levels of personal support despite opposition to his policies, and it explains the particular way in which support and opposition Reagan has been expressed—*Reagan's exclusive and explicit reliance on a single story has dominated the realm of political judgment.* The story is the primary basis for defining the situation, morality is the primary basis for justifying public policy, and common sense is the primary basis for analyzing political issues.

Narrative Truth

Reagan's stories are sometimes presented as fictional, sometimes as fact. In either case, their appropriateness to political discourse depends upon their consistency with the historical world of the audience. If the story is not true, it must be true-to-life; if it did not actually happen, it must be evident that it could have happened or that, given the way things are, it should have happened. When narrative dominates, epistemological standards move away from empiricism. History is more likely to be seen as literary artifact, fiction is more likely to be seen as a mimetic representation of reality, and the two forms "cross" in the historicity of the narrative form.[54] Understanding this shift in perspective is essential to understanding Reagan's rhetoric and the reactions to it.

As Bennett and Feldman found in their examination of story-telling in jury trials, "judgments based on story construction are, in many important respects, unverifiable in terms of the reality of the situation that the story represents."[55] The story becomes increasingly dominant as the empirically defined context for the story becomes increasingly distant from confirmation by either experience or consensus. Bennett and Feldman identify two situations in which "structural characteristics of stories become more central to judgment": (1) if "facts or documentary evidence are absent" or (2) if "a collection of facts or evidence is subject to competing interpretations."[56] Both of these conditions are typically present in major political disputes.

Even the most obviously fantastic stories make a claim to truth for the order that they impose on a chaotic world. To support the claim that fairy tales give meaning to a child's life, for example, Bruno Bettelheim quotes the German poet Schiller saying that, "deeper meaning resides in the fairy tales told to me in my childhood than in the truth that is taught by life."[57] Events become meaningful in stories and meaning depends upon the significance of the events within the context of the story. As a consequence, the perception of truth depends upon the story as a whole rather than upon the accuracy of its individual statements. Louis O. Mink argues that a historical narrative "claims truth not merely for each of its individual statements taken distributively, but for the complex form of the narrative itself."[58] The "complex form" of a narrative makes isolated events and individual statements meaningful. Mink concludes that "the significance of past occurrences is understandable only as they are locatable in the ensemble of interrelationships that can be grasped only in the construction of narrative form."[59]

The variety of technical terms developed here all lead to a single basic conclusion: somehow we must recognize that stories admit to a dual evaluation. Alasdair MacIntyre studies moral discourse in terms of *verisimilitude* and *dramatic probability*.[60] Fisher uses *narrative fidelity* and *narrative probability* to express a parallel distinction.[61] In other words, each theorist sees narrative credibility (and narrative power) as having both substantive and formal properties.

An examination of the reaction to Reagan's dominant narrative suggests that the two properties are interdependent, and recognizing the reflexive quality of his narrative suggests an explanation for the difference in claims about the truth of his rhetoric: the kind of "narrative probability" established in Reagan's explicitly narrative and mythic rhetoric has affected judgments of "narrative fidelity." Because his story is so dominant, so explicit, and so consistent, political claims are likely to be measured against the standard of Reagan's mythic American history rather that against other possible standards such as technical competence or ideological dogma. In this way, the story's dominance has diminished the significance of claims about Reagan's factual inaccuracies. For example, in the 1984 campaign Reagan claimed that the tax proposal being advanced by the Democrats would be equivalent to adding $1800 to the tax bill of every American household.[62] The figure was questioned widely, but the charge of inaccuracy never affected Reagan's credibility or popularity. The meaning of the general story was more important than the particular figure. If Reagan's estimate erred by 10% or by 100% that would not affect the meaning of his story— that the Democrats were, once again, offering a "massive tax and spending scheme" that threatened American economic progress—so the error could be dismissed as trivial.

In addition, relying on the internal relationships established in stories to determine the truth discourages direct denial or refutation and encourages the audience to discover their own place in the story. One reason for the lack of success of many of Reagan's critics has been their tendency to attempt to refute Reagan's assertions.[63] Those most successful in confronting Reagan, such as Mario Cuomo, have been those few politicians who offer alternative stories. The argument must be adjusted to the narrative paradigm—for example, by making the "city on a hill" a "tale of two cities"—or it is likely to be seen as trivial or irrelevant.

The stories that have caused the most trouble for Reagan are those which are least in accord with the generally accepted understanding. In a speech to the VFW during the 1980 campaign, for example, Reagan referred to the Vietnam War as "a noble cause." Despite the approval of the immediate audience, the story complicated his national campaign because of its inconsistency with the general understanding of Vietnam as an unjust war in which America played an ignoble role.[64] Similarly Reagan's difficulties with the Bitburg ceremony stemmed from his account contradicting the received understanding of America waging war to destroy the evils of Nazi conquest. Neither of these cases resulted in lasting damage to Reagan's popularity or credibility, however, because he was able to show that his actions were consistent with his story of America.[65] The distinctiveness of the Iran/*contra* affair is that Reagan's actions have been interpreted as being inconsistent with Reagan's own story. Trading arms for hostages was not seen as consistent with standing up to terrorism; providing arms to Iran was not seen as consistent with strong opposition to America's enemies. Because it was perceived as being inconsistent with the established story of the Reagan presidency, the effects of the Iranian arms deal have been general and severe.[66] Even a story that is powerfully resistant to outside criticism cannot survive inconsistency with itself.

Reagan's stories are not completely self-contained—if they could not be interpreted as representing real events in the real world they would be vulnerable to charges that they are merely fantasies conjured up by the conservative imagination[67]—but this is a special kind of reality. The basis for accepting the referential value of Reagan's stories is not empirical justification, but consistency with the moral standards and common sense of his audience.

Moral Argument

Narrative form shapes interpretation by emphasizing the moral dimension of understanding. As Hayden White says of historical narrative, "story forms not only permit us to judge the moral significance of human projects, they also provide the means by which to judge them, even while we pretend to be merely describing them."[68] White takes the "moral impulse" to be a defining characteristic of narrativity,[69] Fisher uses *moral* argument to distinguish that form of public argument most suited to narrative,[70] and Alasdair MacIntyre makes the connection between narrative, personal identity, intelligibility, and accountability fundamental to his

attempt to rescue ethical judgment from what he sees as the sterile standards of enlightenment thinkers.[71] The nature of the narrative form is said to be moral because stories make events intelligible by imposing a temporal order that leads to some end that defines the moral frame of the story and because the nature of the characters and events in the story will be defined with reference to that purpose.

Ronald Beiner explains and exemplifies the moral impulse of narrative in political discourse. "In attempting to define a conception of the human good," he writes, "*we tell a story.*"[72] Not all stories work equally well, but rich and penetrating stories are what we look for in the work of political theorists and in the statements of politicians. The quality of the story will make it more or less effective in disclosing some truth about the human condition. And different stories will suggest different truths, not all of which will be consistent with each other. "For instance," Beiner continues, "if we wish to expound the necessary place of political freedom in a meaningfully human life, we may wish to tell a story about how the union organizers of Solidarity Poland, against all odds, forced a remote party machine to listen to the voice of the Polish people."[73] Or we may recall the heroic acts and noble sentiments of the American Revolution as conservative spokesmen like Reagan often do. Or we may reverse the focus and tell of the horrors of repression and segregation in South Africa. The significant point here is that whatever story is told will provide a moral direction and that this is especially true for narratives that are presented as historical fact.

The heavily moral orientation of Reagan's rhetoric helps to account both for the character of his rhetoric and for the character of the response to it. Reagan characteristically justifies his policies by citing their goals, while critics of his policies characteristically cite problems of conception or implementation. Reagan's moral focus has worked well because the shift of emphasis to ends rather than means pre-empts arguments about practicality and because it provides Reagan with a ready response by transforming opposition to policy into opposition to principle. The difficulties of reaching the goal are not ignored, but in this idealistic framework they take on the status of technicalities—potentially bothersome, but not really fundamental to judging policies or people.

The focus on goals has also led to two sorts of criticisms. Reagan is accused of overlooking the impact that means can have on ends,[74] and of assuming that stating the goal is equivalent to its achievement.[75] These tendencies can be seen clearly in the justification and defense that Reagan provides for his policies.

Reagan's justification for the Strategic Defense Initiative in the 1985 State of the Union Address provides a good example of the ways in which a moral emphasis can influence public argument. There is, said Reagan, "a better way of eliminating the threat of nuclear war" than deterrence:

> It is a Strategic Defense Initiative aimed at finding a non-nuclear defense against ballistic missiles. It is the most hopeful possibility of the nuclear age. But it is not well understood.
>
> Some say it will bring war to the heavens—but its purpose is to deter war, in the heavens and on earth. Some say the research would be expensive. Perhaps, but it could save millions of lives, indeed humanity itself. Some say if we build such a system, the Soviets will build a defense system of their own. They already have strategic defenses that surpass ours; a civil defense system, where we have almost none; and a research program covering roughly the same areas of technology we're exploring. And finally, some say the research will take a long time. The answer to that is: "Let's get started."[76]

The pattern of response is revealing. While the objections cited by Reagan are primarily pragmatic (expense, Soviet response, time), Reagan's justifications are made in terms of the goals of the program. Reagan does not deny that this program might "bring war to the heavens," he cites the goal of the program as sufficient justification; he does not deny its expense, he invokes the goal of saving lives. The relationship between means and ends is skewed to an exclusive focus on goals as means of judgment. If the move from practicality to principle is accepted, it makes the policy immune from most objections. From this point of view, the only reasonable explanation for opposition is the one that Reagan cites, the policy must not be "well understood."[77]

The same combination of an exclusive focus upon ends defined within a particular historical narrative has resulted in charges that Reagan "has been pushing his civil-rights policies with a campaign of 'astonishing misrepresentation.'"[78] Reagan's response to such criticisms is that they are the result of "misperceptions" and "misunderstandings."[79] While his critics cite his factual errors and what they see as inconsistencies between his statements and the actions of his administration, Reagan relies on the story of his life and his story of America to counter the accusation. When questioned about his negative image among black leaders, for example, Reagan responded with a reference to his character (that is, to the character Reagan-in-the-story): "it's very disturbing to me, because anyone who knows my life story knows that long before there was a thing called the civil-rights movement, I was busy on that side."[80] In his Second Inaugural, he again used reference to the past to make racial equality a part of America's story: "As an older American, I remember a time when people of different race, creed, or ethnic origin in our land found hatred and prejudice installed in social custom and, yes, in law. There is no story more heartening in our history than the progress that we've made toward the 'brotherhood of man' that God intended for us." From the narrative point of view, it is sufficient to have the appropriate character, and to believe in the appropriate goals. The proper results are the consequence of the story's progression.

Common Sense

Narrative truth assumes a type of knowledge that differs from the knowledge produced within and sanctioned by rational argument. Both Mink and White claim that narrative is the basic medium of common sense.[81] MacIntyre and Fisher identify narrative with the received wisdom of the community and contrast that to the "elitist" and "technical" knowledge of the academic and political establishment.[82] Since narrative makes sense of experience, the sense that is made will be grounded in the presuppositions of those who accept the narrative, and those presuppositions are common sense. Persuasive narratives, then, both express and assume a knowledge that is shared by the community.

The emphasis on common sense is significant for, as Clifford Geertz in anthropology and Alasdair MacIntyre in philosophy have shown, "common sense" is a culturally defined set of rules and expectations.[83] Just as reliance on a common morality de-emphasizes practical and technical concerns, reliance on a common understanding de-emphasizes objections based on claims to special knowledge or expertise. Common sense is so obvious to those who accept it that disagreement with its implications will often seem irrelevant, impractical, or unintelligible. Hayden White notes approvingly that "one of its virtues is the conviction that informs it; agreement with its dicta is the very mark of goodwill."[84] In this way, common sense insulates its claims from alternative conceptions; it consists of an unreflective, self-evidently "true" set of beliefs that are used to make sense out of situations and events. Common sense establishes a transparent realism—a common sense statement is what everyone knows; a common sense judgment is what any sensible person would do.

Reagan's reliance upon common sense as a standard for understanding and judgment has been noted both by commentators and by Reagan himself,[85] and the consequences of the emphasis on common sense on his expression and his analysis are evident in the style, the logic, and the attitude of his rhetoric. In brief, the common sense grounding that is an element of Reagan's dominant narrative suggests a pattern of understanding that parallels Geertz's informal categorization of the "stylistic features, marks of attitude" of common sense.[86] Reagan's rhetoric employs a simple, familiar, and personal style; a logic grounded in practical analogy; and an attitude that offers a singular perspective, unquestioned assumptions, and definitive portrayals.

Reagan's style encourages the perception that political problems are accessible to solution by the common action of ordinary people. Since common sense is "thin," political understanding requires no mysterious or arcane perceptiveness; things are as they appear.[87] The simplicity of apparently complex issues has been a continuing theme in Reagan's rhetoric. In the so-called Reaganomics speech, he declined to present "a jumble of charts, figures, and economic jargon"; his Strategic Defense Initiative was "not about spending arithmetic"; his proposal for Tax Reform was "a simple, straightforward message"; on Nicaragua "the question the Congress of the United States will now answer is a simple one"; and on arms control, "the answer, my friends, is simple."[88]

One consequence of Reagan's simple style of common sense rhetoric is that he has been subject to charges of being simplistic throughout his political career. In a revealing response to that claim in his Inaugural Address as governor of California, Reagan said: "For many years, you and I have been shushed like children and told there are no simple answers to complex problems that are beyond our comprehension. Well, the truth is there *are* simple answers—just not easy ones."[89] Much of Reagan's relationship to his audience is contained in this "common sense" observation. The reference to "you and I" places Reagan and the audience together against the unspecified forces that oppose the participation of the people in political decision-making and the reference to "simple answers" opens up the political process. Character and style combine to reinforce the presumption that will and courage, not intelligence or expertise, are required to solve difficult political problems.

Aristotle noted that comparison with the familiar allows us to understand the unfamiliar[90] and the assumptions of common sense move that observation farther: unfamiliar events and complex situations are seen to be "really" like the simple and familiar understandings and beliefs of the group.[91] Reagan often uses a common sense logic of practical analogies to explain and to justify his policy choices. In his Acceptance Address at the 1980 Republican Convention, for example, Reagan said: "I believe it is clear our federal government is overgrown and overweight. Indeed, it is time for our government to go on a diet."[92] And in his first speech on "Reaganomics," he met his opposition with common sense: "There were always those who told us that taxes couldn't be cut until spending was reduced. Well, you know, we can lecture our children against extravagance until we run out of voice and breath. Or we can cure their extravagance by simply reducing their allowance."[93] In Reagan's 1986 address on Nicaragua, the Nicaraguan government is referred to as "a second Cuba, a second Libya," while the *contras* are said to be "freedom fighters" who are "like the French Resistance that fought the Nazis."[94] By using the daily dilemmas of diets and allowances and the widely accepted evils of the Nazis and Cuba as parallels to current American policy-making, Reagan suggests that what might have been seen as complex and distant problems are amenable to simple and familiar (if not always pleasant) solutions. As he concluded later in the "Reaganomics" speech, "All it takes is a little common sense and recognition of our own ability."[95]

Since common sense is assumed to be "natural," the correctness and universality of the perceptions and judgments that Reagan propounds is also assumed.[96] His is not a carefully weighed reflection involving doubts and reservations; Reagan presents the picture clearly and incontestably and the actions follow naturally from his descriptions. In his Address to the Nation on Defense and National Security (the so-called "Star Wars" speech), for example, Reagan began by stating that further defense cuts "cannot be made" and that there is "no logical way" to reduce the defense budget without reducing security. In his description of Soviet power he stated that "the . . . militarization of Grenada . . . can only be seen as a power projection into that region" and that "the Soviet Union is acquiring what can only be considered an offensive military force." The appropriate actions are just as clear: "it was obvious that we had to begin a major modernization program," "we must continue to restore our military strength"; and with regard to his proposal: "Are we not capable of demonstrating our peaceful intentions by applying all our abilities and our ingenuity to achieving truly lasting stability? I think we are. Indeed we must."[97]

This sense of unquestioned truth explains why the observations of theorists about common sense in general apply so smoothly to Reagan's rhetoric—a "maddening air of simple wisdom" exercises Reagan's critics and "comfortable certainties" reassure his supporters.[98] Since common sense justification relies on doing what any sensible person would do based on what everyone knows to be true, a narrative frame may encourage those within it to see intelligence in practical terms and to emphasize sensibility over intellectual analysis. The differing perspectives help to explain why his supporters can recognize that Reagan is "no rocket scientist" and still respect his intelligence,[99] at the same time that his opponents lament what seems to them to his obvious intellectual weakness. Technical accomplishment has its place in a common sense perspective—expertise is useful, even essential, in making applications and in completing the details of policy—but one need not be a nuclear engineer or a tax accountant to know that nuclear strength ensures peace or that simplicity brings fairness.[100]

Consequences for Policy: Incommensurable Frames

Fisher's description of the rational and narrative paradigms neatly summarizes major difference in perspective. From the point of view of the rational world paradigm, a story should be substantively true so that it can be used as evidence by example or analogy, or it should be vivid enough to illustrate the problem or possible solution. In either case, stories are not considered likely to be able to carry the knowledge one needs to analyze and solve a problem. From the point of view of the narrative paradigm, a story should be a good story judged by internal aesthetic criteria and by external criteria of "fit" with the audiences' experience and morality. In any case, it is likely to best express what one really needs to know to get by in the world. The two perspectives clash over standards for evidence and the appropriate basis for judgment.

The rhetorical critic should consider that any discourse can be described differently according to these competing though not contradictory accounts. Furthermore, the critic should consider that different auditors may respond differently to the same message because they are applying these different standards of apprehension.

The incommensurability of these two frames of reference is illustrated neatly in Walter Mondale's attack on Reagan's fiscal policy in the 1984 presidential campaign. In his acceptance address at the Democratic Convention, Mondale called for "a new realism." He challenged Reagan to "put his plan on the table next to mine" and then to "debate it on national television before the American people," and he contrasted Reagan's approach with "the truth" five times including his memorable promise to raise taxes: "Let's tell the truth. Mr. Reagan will raise taxes, and so will I. He won't tell you. I just did."[101] Calls for realism, debate, and truth are fundamental to rational analysis, but they take on a different meaning from within the narrative paradigm.

In the Second Inaugural and in the related speeches that followed,[102] Reagan offered two directions for reducing budget deficits. First, "a dynamic economy, with more citizens working and paying taxes," and second, an amendment that would "make it unconstitutional for the federal government to spend more than the federal government takes in." Both these strategies are grounded in the *telos* of Reagan's narrative. Working individuals tend naturally toward economic success unless blocked by barriers constructed by government. The federal government, on the other hand, will tend naturally toward expansion and will increase taxes and spending unless blocked by a permanent control that is beyond its power to change.[103] From the point of view of the rational paradigm, tax increases are the logical solution because adding revenue would correct the imbalance between income and expenditure. From the point of view of Reagan's story, tax increases are illogical because they would frustrate the individual initiative that is the basis for economic growth and they are immoral because they would violate the natural order by restraining individuals to benefit government. From the rational point of view, a Balanced Budget Amendment is irrelevant because it addresses a principle without dealing with the underlying problem. From the point of view of Reagan's narrative, the amendment is logical because the

federal government will never act contrary to its natural character without some outside restraint and it is moral because it is directed toward the quest for individual freedom.

The dispute over tax policy reveals different structures of perception that lead to different policy conclusions. The distinctive character of these differences is that they are defined by Reagan's reliance on narrative form. It is not just the nature of the particular story, but the reliance on story-telling that defines the relationship of those who accept Reagan's rhetoric to a complex of significant issues. A narrative perspective uses consistency with the story as the primary measure of truth, emphasizes moral standards for judgment, and features common sense as the basis for making political decisions.

CONCLUSIONS

When Reagan is seen as a story-teller and his message is seen as a story, it becomes evident why he was so successful in "re-invigorating" the country—his story gave a clear, powerful, reassuring, and self-justifying meaning to America's public life. And it is evident why Reagan's personal popularity consistently exceeds support for his policies—to accept the story is to see Reagan both as a hero exemplifying the virtues of manly efficacy and as a realistic narrator telling things as they are; it makes sense to rely on Reagan-in-the-story. The reason that charges against Reagan's lack of compassion or his militarism have been ineffectual is that the nature of social justice and peace, and the appropriate means for their achievement, are defined from within his story. The reason that repeated charges of ignorance and factual error have not affected either Reagan's popularity or his credibility is that truth is judged in the context of the story and the story is judged for its fit with popular morality and common sense. In short, Reagan demonstrates the enormous appeal of a narrative form handled with artistry by a major public figure.

Reagan also demonstrates how limiting reliance on a single, unquestioned narrative structure can be when applied to the range of national and international concerns that comprise American political discourse. The effectiveness of Reagan's transcendent narrative depends upon establishing the story as the primary context for understanding people and events. Such a self-contained communication form is effective because it is clear, complete, and (therefore) reassuring. In addition to its evident effectiveness, however, such a narrative is also fragile and dangerous.

A dominant narrative structure is fragile because the requirement of internal consistency is permanent, while the ability of people responding to events to maintain that consistency is inevitably partial and temporary. The fragility of Reagan's story became evident in the public response to the Iran/*contra* affair. Since Reagan's character and his actions were perceived as a part of his story and were judged on the basis of their consistency with that story, his credibility was intact as long as he remained consistent. Perceived inconsistency with the standards that he had established, however, was devastating and the effects were immediate and (apparently) lasting.[104]

Reagan's dominant narrative is dangerous because its assertion of permanence assumes both insularity from material conditions and isolation from social commentary. His mythic rhetoric appeals to a tradition of belief and action that lends credence to the virtues and actions that are justified by his historical sense, but the justification is limited by Reagan's limited notion of history. An essential part of Alasdair MacIntyre's consideration of the ethical role of narrative thinking is that "a living tradition . . . is an historically extended, socially embodied argument, and an argument precisely in part about the goods which constitute that tradition."[105] When Reagan treats American history as a clearly defined set of actions with a clear and constant set of lessons to be applied to present action and future policy direction, he isolates his vision from historical reinterpretation and from current controversy. Reagan's consistency provides his audiences with a clear, simple, and familiar framework within which to encompass complex or unfamiliar problems. Yielding to this enticing vision can be dangerous, however, because the assumption of the story's truth hides its contingent nature and its implicit ideology. Adherence to a single story

with a single point of view can make good judgment more difficult by reinforcing the legitimacy of a single set of social stereotypes and by promoting an exclusively American point of view on international problems.[106]

A related danger concerns the role of the public in Reagan's version of America's story. Relying on the (presumably) established moral code and the (presumably) accepted common sense of the American people to establish the legitimacy of the story implicitly denies the legitimacy of either change or challenge with the result that the story's participants are driven to a posture of passive acceptance.[107] Ironically, Reagan's story of an actively heroic American public forces those who accept it into the position of being listeners rather than creators. At most, the individual becomes a participant in a pre-established historical frame.

The application of narrative theory to Reagan's rhetoric also raises some broader questions regarding narrative and political judgment. Fisher's assertion of the moral superiority of the narrative paradigm[108] is not confirmed. Reagan's story-telling does emphasize moral argument and it does act as an explicit counter to technical elitism, but, as just noted, it may also damage public morality. This examination of Reagan's rhetoric suggests that Fisher's reliance on the Aristotelian dictum that "the 'people' have a natural tendency to prefer the true and the just"[109] may be a mystification that requires a more careful examination of the ways in which stories are accepted or rejected. Reagan has shown that powerful appeals can be made to popular belief and popular morality through the narrative form, but the acceptance of his story and the durability of his popularity also seem to show that there is a preference for clarity over complexity, for consistency over aberration, for positive direction over acceptance of limitations, and for self-justification by the derogation of one's enemies. Goods internal to the story need to be consistent with the moral judgment of the audience, and truths that are accepted within the story need to be consistent with the common sense of the audience, but it is not clear from examining this case in which narrative form is dominant that narrative is likely to provide a morality or truth that is superior to other forms of discourse or to combinations of other forms.

There are other disturbing problems as well. Despite identifying two "paradigms," Fisher assumes that rational and narrative modes of thinking are fundamentally compatible.[110] He argues that considerations of narrative fidelity can subsume the skills and requirements of logic. But this examination of Reagan's rhetoric and the responses to it suggests that the narrative and the rational perspectives can be distinctive and incommensurable. One need not claim that narrative is irrational to distinguish its characteristic form of rationality from that of the "rational world" paradigm. Having made the distinction between these two modes of thought clear, it becomes difficult to accept Fisher's conclusion that narrative offers a superior and fully encompassing alternative.[111]

Americans have listened to Ronald Reagan as President for almost a decade, usually with admiration, but often without agreement. Some have heard poor arguments and marveled at his ability to delude his audiences; others have heard good stories and dismissed his errors as trivial. And while the Iran/contra crisis has diminished the credibility of Reagan's presidency, it has not altered the forms of understanding through which he is heard. Until the differences in judgment are identified as differences in perspective, there will be little ground for common discussion and little motivation for self-analysis.

NOTES

[1] Mary McGrory, " . . . and growls from the training camp," Des Moines Register, 6 September 1985, 12A. Paul Erickson begins his book on Reagan with the judgment that, "Ronald Reagan is by far the most persuasive political speaker of our time." Reagan Speaks (New York: New York University Press, 1985), 1.

[2] "More Popular Than Ever," Time, 12 August 1985, 17.

[3] Sidney Blumenthal, "The Reagan Millennium," New Republic, 19 November 1984, 12.

[4] The books cover a range of policies and perspectives; some are explicitly political and were designed to influence election campaigns: Edmund G. Brown, Reagan and Reality (New

York: Praeger, 1976); Brown and Bill Brown, Reagan; The Political Chameleon (New York: Praeger, 1976); Mark Green and Gail MacColl, There He Goes Again: Ronald Reagan's Reign of Error (New York: Pantheon Books, 1983). Others respond to specific issues: Robert Scheer, With Enough Shovels: Reagan, Bush, and Nuclear War (New York: Random House, 1982); Strobe Talbott, Deadly Gambits: The Reagan Administration and the Stalemate in Nuclear Arms (New York: Knopf, 1984). Fred Ackerman, Reaganomics: Rhetoric vs. Reality (Boston: South End Press, 1982). Joan Claybrook, Retreat From Safety: Reagan's Attack on America's Health (New York: Pantheon, 1984). Others attempt more thorough or scholarly appraisals of Reagan's statements and policies: Ronald Dallek, Reagan: The Politics of Symbolism (Cambridge: Harvard University Press, 1984); Ronnie Dugger, On Reagan: The Man and his Presidency (New York: McGraw-Hill, 1983).

[5] Dallek, 178.

[6] Dallek, viii.

[7] "Innocence Abroad," The New Republic, 3 June 1983, 7.

[8] Martin Medhurst, "Postponing the Social Agenda: Reagan's Strategy and Tactics," Western Journal of Speech Communication 48 (1984) 262–76; Henry Z. Scheele, "Ronald Reagan's 1980 Acceptance Address: A Focus on American Values," Western Journal of Speech Communication 48 (1984): 51–61; Bert E. Bradley, "Jefferson and Reagan: The Rhetoric of The Two Inaugurals," Southern Speech Communication Journal 48 (1983): 119–36; Walter Fisher, "Romantic Democracy, Ronald Reagan, and Presidential Heroes," Western Journal of Speech Communication, 46 (1982): 299–310.

[9] Richard L. Johannesen, "An Ethical Assessment of the Reagan Rhetoric, 1981–82," Political Communication Yearbook 1984, eds. Keith R. Sanders, Lynda Lee Kaid, and Dan Nimmo (Carbondale: Southern Illinois University Press, 1985), 226–41; Thomas Preston, Jr., "Reagan's 'New Beginning': Is it the 'New Deal' of the Eighties?" Southern Speech Communication Journal 49 (1984): 198–211; Gregg Phifer, "Two Inaugurals: A Second Look," Southern Speech Communication Journal, 48 (1983): 378–85.

[10] David Zarefsky, Carol Miller-Tutzauer, and Frank E. Tutzauer, "Reagan's Safety Net for the Truly Needy: The Rhetorical Uses of Definition," Central States Speech Journal 35 (1984): 113–19; Richard E. Crable and Steven L. Vibbert, "Argumentative Stance and Political Faith Healing: 'The Dream Will Come True,'" Quarterly Journal

of Speech 69 (1983): 290–301. In his explanation of Reagan's approach to Soviet-American relations Robert L. Ivie found that "a flawed policy is being perceived as successful because of how it is symbolized." "Speaking 'Common Sense' About the Soviet Threat: Reagan's Rhetorical Stance," *Western Journal of Speech Communication* 48 (1984): 40. Sarah Russell Hankins concluded that "the presidential choice in 1980 was an attempt to align the human with the illusion of the heroic." "Archetypal Alloy: Reagan's Rhetorical Image," *Central States Speech Journal* 34 (1983): 34. Similarly, Martha Anna Martin wrote that "the cumulative language, if not the reality, suggested that Carter was an 'unfit' leader." "Ideologues, Ideographs, and 'The Best Men': From Carter to Reagan," *Southern Speech Communication Journal* 49 (1983): 19. Gary C. Woodward makes a parallel claim about Reagan's populist appeal: "Populism has taken on a cosmetic and ironic purpose . . . pretending to serve the 'public interest,' but serving what may be very private interests indeed." "Reagan as Roosevelt: The Elasticity of Pseudo-Populist Appeals," *Central States Speech Journal* 34 (1983): 57–8.

11 Walter R. Fisher, "Narration as a Human Communication Paradigm: The Case of Public Moral Argument," *Communication Monographs* 51 (1984): 1–22.

12 See, Erickson, esp. chapter 3, "Analogies, Allegories, and Homilies," 32–50; David Stockman, *The Triumph of Politics* (New York: Harper & Row, 1986), 90.

13 Martin Medhurst demonstrates the way in which Reagan employs the theme of America as a nation that was set apart, by God. As he notes, "the theme of a people set apart is . . . a standard topos of civil-religious discourse in America." Medhurst, 270. Both Erickson and Johannesen suggest that Reagan's rhetoric uses the form of the jeremiad and the substance of American civil religion. *Reagan Speaks*, 86–93; Richard Johannesen, "Ronald Reagan's Economic Jeremiad," *Central States Speech Journal*, forthcoming. Janice Hocker Rushing argues that "the mythic milieu of the ['Star Wars'] speech is the transformation of the Old West into the New Frontier." "Ronald Reagan's 'Star Wars' Address: Mythic Containment of Technical Reasoning," *Quarterly Journal of Speech* 72 (1986): 417. Perhaps the most notable development of this idea is Gary Wills, *Reagan's America* (New York: Doubleday, 1987).

14 For example, in commenting on Reagan's arms negotiations in Iceland, Anthony Lewis wrote: "Ronald Reagan has never been more breathtaking as a politician than in the weeks since Reykjavik.

He has pictured failure as success, black as white, incompetence as standing up to the Russians. And according to the polls, Americans love the performance." Quoted in Thomas Griffith, "Being Too Easy on Reagan," *Time,* 29 December 1986, 57.

15 This has been evident particularly in the response of the press. A *Time* magazine editorial, for example, offered the following explanation: "A frustrated Washington press corps had felt itself ignored by a public that did not want to hear criticism of a popular President. But the sudden and steep decline in Reagan's popularity suggests that all along the public had recognized, in a man it admired, how casually he minded the store, and how willfully he could deny facts or distort them." Thomas Griffith, "Watergate: A Poor Parallel," *Time,* 29 December 1986, 57.

16 As even the *Washington Post* conceded, "this president has given tens of millions of people in this country a feeling that safe, stable times are returned and that fundamental values they hold dear are back in vogue and unashamedly so" (January 22, 1985).

17 Since the narrative logic of Reagan's story makes his actions on the arms deal difficult to explain, the dominant response has been to remove Reagan from the story either by suggesting that he had no control over the actions of his subordinates or by suggesting that Reagan himself had changed and questioning his mental or physical health.

18 In his campaign speeches, Reagan told the story as a humorous example. In Milwaukee, for example, he said, "Our pledge is for tax simplification, to make the system more fair, to make it easier to understand. Do you know that Einstein has admitted he cannot understand the Form 1040? [*Laughter*]." *Weekly Compilation of Presidential Documents* (hereafter, *WCPD*), 8 October 1985, 1381. In his speech to the nation he told the story in slightly different form: "We call it America's tax plan because it will reduce tax burdens on the working people of this country, close loopholes that benefit a privileged few, simplify a code so complex even Albert Einstein reportedly needed help on his 1040 Form, and lead us into a future of greater growth and opportunity for all." "Tax Reform," 28 May 1985, *WCPD*, 704.

19 "A Debate on Religious Freedom," *Harper's*, October 1984, 15, 18.

20 Rene Wellek and Austin Warren, *Theory of Literature* (New York: Harcourt, Brace, & World, 1956), 119.

21 "Myth and Identity," in *Myth and Mythology* ed. Gilbert Murray (1959; rpt. Boston: Beacon, 1968), 279.

22 Reagan frequently refers to America as a nation "chosen by God." In the 1987 State of the Union

Address, for example, Reagan said that "our nation could not have been conceived without divine help" and that "The United States Constitution . . . grew out of the most fundamental inspiration of our existence: that we are here to serve Him by living free." "The State of the Union," *WCPD*, 27 January 1987, 63, 64.

23 In the 1985 State of the Union Address, for example, Reagan supports his confidence in American abilities by saying, "Two hundred years of American history should have taught us that nothing is impossible." "The State of the Union" *WCPD*, 6 February 1985, 146. Reagan's conception of the American experience closely parallels the "American monomyth" that Robert Jewett and John Shelton Lawrence have found pervading the productions of popular culture. *The American Monomyth* (Garden City, NY: Anchor Press/Doubleday, 1977), xx.

24 All quotations from Reagan's Second Inaugural Address are from the "50th American Presidential Inaugural." *WCPD*, 21 January 1985, 67–70.

25 In the 1985 State of the Union Address. Reagan said, "There are no constraints on the human mind, no walls around the human spirit, no barriers to our progress except those we ourselves erect." "The State of the Union," 141.

26 All quotations are from "Inaugural Address," *Public Papers of the Presidents: Ronald Reagan, 1981,* (Washington. D.C.: GPO, 1982), 1–4.

27 Reagan's language features particular actions and concrete situations that will be familiar to all Americans and that encourage most to see themselves in his description: "Those who say that we're in a time when there are no heroes, they just don't know where to look. You can see heroes every day going in and out of factory gates. Others, a handful in number, produce enough food to feed all of us and then the world beyond. You meet heroes across a counter, and they're on both sides of that counter. There are entrepreneurs with faith in themselves and faith in an idea who create new jobs, new wealth and opportunity. They're individuals and families whose taxes support the government and whose voluntary gifts support church, charity, culture, art, and education. Their patriotism is quiet, but deep. Their values sustain our national life." "Inaugural Address," 2.

28 Unity of interests and goals is a major and continuing theme in Reagan's rhetoric. In welcoming the debate on tax reform, for example, he also stated that "it should not be a partisan debate for the authors of tax reform come from both parties, and all of us want greater fairness, incentives, and simplicity in taxation." "Tax Reforms," *WCPD*, 28 May 1985, 707. In urging support for the *contras* in Nicaragua

he quoted "Senator Scoop Jackson" as saying: "On matters of national security, the best politics is no politics." "Nicaragua," *WCPD*, 16 March 1986, 374. The quotation was also used in the 1986 State of the Union Address, *WCPD*, 4 February 1986, 139.

29 "Every Region, Every Age Group, Almost Every Voting Bloc," *Time*, 19 November 1984, 45.

30 For example, Edmund G. Brown classes Reagan's speeches with "the unreasoned attacks of simplistic self-servers who pander [to] the lowest urges that plague our troubled people," in Brown and Bill Brown, *Reagan: The Political Chameleon*, 8.

31 Dugger, for example, charges that, "[Reagan] has long been allied with the most bellicose elements in the American military establishment; now he is using the power and glory the White House gives him to bring about . . . a mortally dangerous shift in U.S. nuclear strategy." *On Reagan*, xiv.

32 Stanley Hoffman, "Semidetached Politics," *New York Review of Books*, 8 November 1984, 34–6.

33 Reporters have repeatedly expressed their frustration with Reagan's "Teflon Presidency." For example, Tom Wicker, "A smile, a quip and no mud on his shoes . . ." *Kansas City Times*, 31 May 1984, A-18; Sidney Blumenthal, "Reagan the Unassailable," *New Republic*, 12 September 1983, 11–16.

34 Martin, 22. She uses the phrase in a comparison of Reagan with Theodore Roosevelt.

35 Hankins, 41.

36 Fisher, "Romantic Democracy," 302.

37 Fisher, "Romantic Democracy," 302.

38 See, Bradley, "Jefferson and Reagan: The Rhetoric of Two Inaugurals"; Martin, 18–23; Woodward, 44–58.

39 Martin, 22. Fisher reached an almost identical conclusion about Reagan's "manly" character: "Reagan's tough stands on America's military posture and his decisive views on domestic problems gave substance to the perception." "Romantic Democracy," 302.

40 Martin, 15.

41 This role matches the recurring character of the American hero in popular culture identified by Jewett and Lawrence in *The American Monomyth*, xx, 195–6.

42 Christopher J. Matthews, "Your Host, Ronald Reagan," *New Republic*, 26 March 1984, 15–18. Robert J. Kaiser, "Your Host of Hosts," *New York Review of Books*, 28 June 1984, 38–41. Hankins, 42: Reagan is "one step removed . . . we are content to have him play the part." Martin, 24: "Ironically, the media age had no Teddy Roosevelt to offer. Instead, the 1980's offered an actor whose identification was with pseudo-heroism as filtered through film of his

ranch, his horses, possibly even his ability as a 'nice' guy to defeat the guy in the black hat (the Ayatollah and the Communists), Hollywood version."

43 Illustrated most vividly in his reaction to the assassination attempt. Reactions of critics and admirers converge in an appreciation of Reagan's response after being shot. Fisher, "Romantic Democracy," 307–8; Kaiser, 39.

44 For examples, see below in the discussion of common sense.

45 See Ivie for a discussion of Reagan's appeal to American "common sense" about the Soviet Union. Scheele documents Reagan's reliance on American values.

46 Kaiser, 41. French sociologist Michael Crozier believes that Reagan's "soothing style" is a perfect fit for the country's "craving for normalcy." *The Trouble with America* (Berkeley: University of California Press, 1984), 57–60.

47 "Inaugural Address," 20 January 1981, 3. For examples of Reagan's emphasis on the value of "peace" in his Acceptance Address at the 1980 Republican Convention, see Scheele, 56.

48 Lou Cannon, Reagan (New York: G. P. Putnam's Sons, 1982), 281–2; Jack W. Germond and Jules Witcover, *Blue Smoke and Mirrors* (New York: Viking Press, 1981), 243, 224–5.

49 See, Rushing, n. 62.

50 Robert L. Scott, "Narrative Theory and Communication Research," *Quarterly Journal of Speech* 70 (1984): 200.

51 Fisher, "Narration," 4.

52 Fisher, "Narration," 8.

53 "The Narrativization of Real Events," *On Narrative*, ed. W. J. T. Mitchell (Chicago: University of Chicago Press, 1981), 251.

54 Paul Ricoeur, "The Narrative Function," *Hermeneutics and the Human Sciences*, ed. and trans. by John B. Thompson (Cambridge: Cambridge University Press, 1981), 289–96.

55 W. Lance Bennett and Martha S. Feldman, *Reconstructing Reality in the Courtroom* (New Brunswick: Rutgers University Press, 1981), 33.

56 Bennett and Feldman, 89.

57 *The Uses of Enchantment* (New York: Vintage Books, 1976), 5.

58 "Narrative Form as a Cognitive Instrument," in *The Writing of History*, ed. by Robert H. Canary and Henry Kozicki (Madison: University of Wisconsin Press, 1978), 144.

59 Mink, 148.

60 Alasdair MacIntyre, *After Virtue*, 2nd ed. (Notre Dame: University of Notre Dame Press, 1981), 200.

61 Fisher, 8.

62 Reagan made the claim repeatedly in his campaign speeches, often adapting the particulars to the place where he was speaking. In one week, for example, he gave the Democrat's version of Vince Lombardi's famous statement about winning to an audience in Milwaukee ("They're saying, 'Tax increases aren't everything. They're the only thing.'") and he re-defined "shrimp" for an audience in Gulfport, Mississippi ("To you, it's a livelihood; to them, it's your paycheck after they get their hands on it."). *WCPD*, 8 October 1984, 1380, 1405.

63 Sidney Blumenthal suggests that attempts by the press to refute Reagan's errors have been largely ineffectual because Reagan's world view is based on a "unifying vision" which facts "can never fatally undermine." "Reagan the Unassailable," 14.

64 Cannon, *Reagan*, 271–2.

65 William Safire's assessment of Reagan's speeches at Bitburg and Bergen-Belsen demonstrates how the message of Reagan's general story was able to dominate doubts about the propriety of his particular actions: "In driving home the lessons of history, his incredible series of blunders turned out to be a blessing. . . . [H]e drew the central lesson clearly: 'that freedom must always be stronger than totalitarianism, that good must always be stronger than evil.'" "'I am a Jew . . .'" in *Bitburg in Moral and Political Perspective,* ed. Geoffrey H. Hartman (Bloomington: Indiana University Press, 1986), 212–13.

66 Time emphasized the damage to Reagan's credibility: "it seems almost certain that whatever comes out of the many investigations now in progress, Reagan will emerge as a diminished President, his aura of invincibility shattered, his fabled luck vanished, his every policy regarded with new suspicion." "Who Was Betrayed," *Time*, 8 December 1986, 19.

67 Significantly, exactly these charges were made about Reagan. See, for example, Benjamin Barber, "Celluloid Vistas: What the President's Dreams are Made of," *Harper's*, July 1985, 74–5; Sidney Blumenthal, "The Reagan Millennium," *New Republic*, 19 November 1984, 12–14; Green and MacColl, 8–15.

68 "The Narrativization of Real Events," 253.

69 "Where, in any account of reality, narrative is present, we can be sure that morality or a moral impulse is present too." "The Value of Narrativity in the Representation of Reality," in Mitchell, 22. (Quoted approvingly by Fisher, "Narration," 10.)

70 Fisher, "Narration," 12.

71 *After Virtue*, chapter 15, "The Virtues, the Unity of a Human Life and the Concept of a Tradition," esp., 218.

72 *Political Judgment* (Chicago: University of Chicago Press, 1983), 126.

73 Beiner, 126.

74 Jonathan Jacky, "The 'Star Wars' Defense Won't Compute," *Atlantic,* June 1985, 18–30.

75 John Kessel notes that Reagan's aides are sensitive to these problems because his "optimism . . . often leads Reagan to overlook difficulties that bar the path to achievement." "The Structures of the Reagan White House," *American Journal of Political Science* 28 (1984): 233.

76 "The State of the Union," 6 February 1985, 145.

77 Reagan had used a similar strategy in dealing with the opposition to other issues as well. Theodore Windt and Kathleen Farrell, for example, came to the following conclusion about Reagan's support for his 1981 tax cut: "If the rhetoric took hold in the public consciousness, then anyone opposing him would be perceived as being unfair or as one willing to perpetuate waste and fraud to save some special interest program." "Presidential Rhetoric and Presidential Power: The Reagan Initiatives," *Essays in Presidential Rhetoric* (Dubuque, IA: Kendall/Hunt, 1983), 316.

78 James Nathan Miller, "Ronald Reagan and the Techniques of Deception," *Atlantic,* February 1984, 64.

79 Miller, 62.

80 Quoted in Miller, 68.

81 Mink emphasizes the cognitive element of the common understanding. White adds that the meaning of historical narrative also presumes a common base of moral legitimacy. "The Narrativization of Real Events" in Mitchell, 253.

82 MacIntyre, "Epistemological Crises, Dramatic Narrative and the Philosophy of Science," *Monist* 60 (1977): 453–73; Fisher, 9–10.

83 Clifford Geertz, "Common Sense as a Cultural System" in *Local Knowledge* (New York: Basic Books, 1983): 73–93; and MacIntyre, "Epistemological Crises," 453–54.

84 "The Narrativization of Real Events" in Mitchell, 254.

85 Ivie, "Speaking Common Sense"; Reagan's reliance on common sense has also been noted outside of the United States. In a conversation about Reagan between Francois Mitterand and Marguerite Duras, Mitterand says "He is a man of common sense" (10), and Duras says later "He governs less with his intellect than with common sense" (12). In "Mitterand and Duras on Reagan's America" *Harper's,* August 1986, 10–14.

86 Geertz identifies five "quasi-qualities" of common sense: naturalness, practicalness, thinness, immethodicalness, and accessibleness. "Common Sense as a Cultural System," 84–92.

87 Some critics have taken this implication of his style to be a quality of Reagan's rhetoric. Edward Chester observed that, "when one encounters an address by Ronald Reagan, the appearance coincides with the reality." "Shadow or Substance?: Critiquing Reagan's Inaugural Address," in *Essays in Presidential Rhetoric,* 303.

88 "Address to the Nation on the Economy," 5 February 1981, *Public Papers,* 79; "Address to the Nation on Defense and National Security," *WCPD,* 23 March 1983, 437; "Tax Reform," 705; "Meeting with Soviet General Secretary Gorbachev in Reykjavik, Iceland," *WCPD,* 13 October 1986, 1377.

89 Inaugural Message. Governor of California, January 5, 1967. Quoted in "Reagan" by Lou Cannon, *The Pursuit of the Presidency,* 1980, ed. Richard Harwood (New York: Berkeley Books, 1980), 253.

90 *Rhetoric,* 1410b.

91 For example, Reagan concluded a major address on Soviet-American relations with a story that began as follows: "Just suppose with me for a minute that an Ivan and an Anya could find themselves, oh, say, in a waiting room or sharing shelter from the rain or a storm with a Jim and Sally." "Soviet-American Relations," *WCPD,* 16 January 1984, 44–5. International relations between two superpowers are represented by (reduced to?) the familiar circumstances of a chance meeting between two couples and we discover (as common sense always confirms) that people are pretty much the same everywhere.

92 "Acceptance Speech by Governor Ronald Reagan, Republican National Convention, Detroit, Michigan, July 7, 1980," in *The Pursuit of the Presidency,* 1980, 419–20.

93 "Address to the Nation on the Economy," 5 February 1981, 81.

94 "Nicaragua," *WCPD,* 16 March 1986, 371, 373.

95 "Address to the Nation on the Economy," 83.

96 This assumption is so clear that the beliefs often need not even be stated. As Richard Allen, Reagan's former national security advisor, wrote: "Ronald Reagan may no longer say that communists lie and cheat, but he believes that they do—and so does the rest of informed mankind." Quoted in "Damage-Control Diplomacy," *Newsweek,* 7 February 1983, 27.

97 *WCPD,* 23 March 1983, 437, 438, 440, 442.

98 Geertz, 85; Mink, 129.

99 Cannon, "Reagan," *Pursuit,* 270. "Reagan consistently has confounded those who have

underestimated him. There is a kind of small-town common sense about him that serves him well and shows in moments when it is least expected" (270).

100 In the 1980 campaign, Carter's "intelligence" was subordinated to Reagan's "good sense." The fact that he knew more than Reagan became a liability when the perception grew that "his particular brand of 'intelligence' was more suitable to the world of academic test-taking than to the pragmatic world of presidential decision-making." Martin, 15.

101 "Mondale Accepts Presidential Nomination," *Congressional Quarterly,* 21 July 1984, 12–14.

102 "Fiscal Year 1986 Budget," *WCPD,* 2 February 1985, 117–8; "Overhauling the Tax System," *WCPD,* 21 May 1985, 703–707; "The State of the Union," *WCPD,* 4 February 1986, 136–7; "The State of the Union," 1987.

103 " . . . we must take further steps to permanently control government's power to tax and spend. We must act now to protect future generations from government's desire to spend its citizens' money and tax them into servitude when the bills come due." "50th Presidential Inaugural," 21 January 1985, 68. The natural tendency of government expansion is a continuing theme in Reagan's rhetoric. See, for example, his "Address to the Nation on the Economy" delivered in his last year as President: " . . . government—any government—has a built-in tendency to grow." 5 February 1981, *Public Papers,* 80.

104 Just one month after the initial revelations, *Time* reported: "A *New York Times*/CBS poll last week showed the President's approval rating plunging 21 points in the past four weeks, from 67% to 46%. That is the most dramatic one-month drop since presidential opinion polls began 50 years ago. The survey found that 53% of the voters think Reagan knew 'money from the Iranian arms sale was going to help the contras, even though the President insists that he did not.[']" "Under Heavy Fire," *Time,* 1 December 1986, 21–22. A *Newsweek* report on Reagan's 1987 State of the Union speech, for example, offered the following general (and typical) assessment of the effect of the Iran/contra affair on public perception: "It didn't add up to a sudden crisis, but somehow he seemed on the edge of irrelevance." "Going Nowhere Fast," *Newsweek,* 9 February 1987, 24. See, James Reston, "Reagan administration already being spoken of in the past tense." *Des Moines Register,* 24 February 1987, 6A.

105 *After Virtue,* 222.

106 Stanley Hoffman, for example, worries that national pride may be manifest in "self-righteousness and a sense of moral superiority" and that Reagan's rhetoric may have encouraged "a desire not to be

bothered or battered by data." "Semidetached Politics," 36. Similarly, George Ball has expressed concerns about the lack of consideration of the effects of "Star Wars" program in other parts of the world. "The War for Star Wars," *New York Reviews of Books,* 11 April 1983, 41.

107 Janet Rushing found a similar result in her examination of Reagan's "Star Wars" address: "Reagan's 'Star Wars' address cuts off its auditors as effectively and completely as if it were couched in the most convoluted esoterica." Rushing, 428. Our explanations differ, however. While she attributes the audience's acquiescence to the important role of "technoscience" in that issue, this analysis suggests that the passivity of Reagan's auditors is a concomitant of his narrative form and is not a reaction to technical discourse or limited to technical issues.

108 See Fisher's discussion of the responses to Jonathon Schell's *The Fate of the Earth,* "Narration," 11–15.

109 Fisher, "Narration," 9.

110 The assumption is expressed repeatedly in Fisher's first article on the narrative paradigm: "The narrative paradigm does not deny reason and rationality; it reconstitutes them, making them amenable to all forms of human communication" (2); "In truth, . . . the narrative paradigm . . . does not so much deny what has gone before as it subsumes it" (3); "when narration is taken as the master metaphor, it subsumes the others" (6); "Both forms . . . are modes for expressing good reasons—given the narrative paradigm—so the differences between them are structural rather than substantive" (15).

111 Fisher's assertion of the universality of the narrative paradigm is clearest in "The Narrative Paradigm: An Elaboration," *Communication Monographs* 52 (1985): 347–67. Fisher's reading of the contemporary social scientific and humanistic literature confirms his opening observation that "there is no genre, including technical communication, that is not an episode in the story of life (a part of the 'conversation') and is not constituted by *logos* and *mythos.* . . . Put another way: Technical discourse is imbued with myth and metaphor, and aesthetic discourse has cognitive capacity and import" (347). All of the theorists and philosophers that he considers are found to be helpful (in greater or lesser measure) in confirming Fisher's thesis. The extent to which important differences in background, perspective, and assumptions are glossed, however, suggests that Fisher may be demonstrating how these approaches can be viewed from within the narrative perspective rather than establishing the dominance or universality of this "metaparadigm" (347).

Inaugural Addresses

Karlyn Kohrs Campbell and Kathleen Hall Jamieson

The presidential inaugural address is a discourse whose significance all recognize but few praise. Arthur Schlesinger, Jr., for example, acknowledges that, during inaugural addresses, "the nation listens for a moment as one people to the words of the man [sic] they have chosen for the highest office in the land," but he finds little merit in them:

> Even in the field of political oratory, the inaugural address is an inferior art form. It is rarely an occasion for original thought or stimulating reflection. The platitude quotient tends to be high, the rhetoric stately and self-serving, the ritual obsessive, and the surprises few.[1]

Conceivably, inaugurals mirror the alleged mediocrity of American presidents. In our view, inaugural addresses are maligned because their symbolic function is misunderstood. As we shall show, they are an essential element in a ritual of transition in which the covenant between the citizenry and their leaders is renewed. Conventional wisdom and ordinary language treat inaugural addresses as a class. Likewise, critics have taken them to be a distinct rhetorical type, but generalizing about them has been difficult. Despite their apparent dissimilarities, we shall approach these addresses as a group, illuminating their common symbolic functions and identifying the qualities that make them distinctive. In that process, we shall account for the recurrent and the variable in these speeches, describe the unique functions of the presidential inaugural, and seek to explain the power of those inaugural addresses widely regarded as eloquent.

Presidential inaugurals are a subspecies of the kind of discourse that Aristotle called epideictic, a form of rhetoric that praises or blames on ceremonial occasions, invites the audience to evaluate the speaker's performance, recalls the past and speculates about the future while focusing on the present, employs a noble, dignified literary style, and amplifies or rehearses admitted facts.[2]

In a recent work on rhetoric in the Catholic church, John O'Malley notes that epideictic rhetoric presents speakers with a unique problem of invention—a problem in discovering and developing appropriate lines of argument. Unlike forensic (courtroom) or deliberative (legislative) speeches that deal "with more immediate and pressing issues" for which "classical theory proposed *topoi* or commonplaces, . . . [t]he occasional or ceremonial nature of epideictic often deprived it of obviously immediate issues."[3] As a result, *memoria,* or recollection of a shared past, becomes an exceptionally important resource for epideictic speeches. O'Malley also calls attention to the distinctively contemplative character of this genre. He comments that "epideictic wants as far as possible to present us with works and deeds, . . . not for metaphysical analysis but quite literally for viewing. . . . 'to look,' to 'view,' to 'gaze upon,' and to 'contemplate.'"[4] Harry Caplan adds that in epideictic discourse a speaker tries, by means of artistry, "to impress his [sic] ideas upon them [the audience], without action as a goal."[5]

If these criteria are applied, presidential inaugurals are epideictic rhetoric because they are delivered on ceremonial occasions, link past and future in present contemplation, affirm or praise the shared principles that will guide the incoming administration, ask the audience to "gaze upon" traditional values, employ elegant, literary language, and rely on "heightening of effect" by amplification and reaffirmation of what is already known and believed.

The special character of presidential inaugural addresses is defined by these general epideictic features and by the nature of the inauguration ceremony. Inauguration is a rite of passage, a ritual of transition in which a newly elected president is invested with the office of the presidency.[6] The general qualities of epideictic rhetoric, modified by the nature of presidential investiture, generate four

This essay originally appeared as a chapter in a book by Karlyn Kohrs Campbell and Kathleen Hall Jamieson, Deeds Done in Words: Presidential Rhetoric and the Genres of Governance *(Albany: State University of New York Press, 1995)*

interrelated elements that define the essential presidential inaugural address and differentiate it from other types of epideictic rhetoric.[7]

The presidential inaugural (1) unifies the audience by reconstituting its members as the people, who can witness and ratify the ceremony; (2) rehearses communal values drawn from the past; (3) sets forth the political principles that will govern the new administration; and (4) demonstrates through enactment that the president appreciates the requirements and limitations of executive function. Finally, (5) each of these ends must be achieved through means appropriate to epideictic address, that is, while urging contemplation not action, focusing on the present while incorporating past and future, and praising the institution of the presidency and the values and form of the government of which it is a part, a process through which the covenant between the president and the people is renewed.

First, unification of the audience.[8] Before the citizenry or their representatives can witness and ratify an ascent to power, the audience must be unified and reconstituted as "the people." John Adams illustrated the reconstituting power of historical reenactment when he rehearsed the founding of the nation in 1797:

> In this dangerous crisis [under the Articles of Confederation] the people of America were not abandoned by their usual good sense, presence of mind, resolution, or integrity. Measures were pursued to concern a plan to form a more perfect union.[9]

Jefferson sought to create a single people out of partisan division when he said: "We have called by different names brethren of the same principles. We are all republicans. We are all federalists" (8).[10] More recently, after a close election and a divisive campaign, in 1961, Kennedy began: "We observe today not a victory of party, but a celebration of freedom" (165). As one would expect, explicit appeals for unity are most common in addresses that follow divisive campaigns or contested electoral outcomes.[11]

Partisan politicking is not the only source of division. Occasionally a major crisis or a war creates disharmony that must be set aside if the president is to govern all the people.

Acknowledging the disunity created by the Civil War, in 1901 William McKinley declared: "We are reunited. Sectionalism has disappeared. Division on public questions can no longer be traced by the war maps of 1861" (110). In 1917, in the face of the U.S.'s entry into World War I, Woodrow Wilson affirmed the importance of unity: "It is imperative that we should stand together. We are being forged into a new unity amidst the fires that now blaze throughout the world" (127). In 1989, George Bush said: "The final lesson of Vietnam is that no great nation can long afford to be sundered by a memory."[12]

Once the audience has been united and reconstituted as the people, it can perform its role in the inaugural ceremony. Inaugural addresses themselves attest to the witnessing role of the people. For example, in 1889, Benjamin Harrison said:

> There is no constitutional or legal requirement that the president shall take the oath of office in the presence of the people, but there is so manifest an appropriateness in the public induction to office of the chief executive of the nation that from the beginning of the Government the people, to whose service the official oath consecrates the officer, have been called to witness the solemn ceremonial. (94)

Similar statements appear in many others. John Quincy Adams said: "I appear, my fellow citizens, in your presence and in that of heaven to bind myself . . . " (29). "In the presence of this vast assemblage of my countrymen," said Cleveland, "I am about to supplement and seal by the oath which I have taken the manifestation of the will of a great and free people" (91). "I, too, am a witness," noted Eisenhower, "today testifying in your name to the principles and purposes to which we, as a people, are pledged" (162). Lincoln and McKinley made similar comments (72, 103).

Without the presence of the people, the rite of presidential investiture cannot be completed. The people ratify the president's formal ascent to power by acknowledging the oath taking, witnessing the enactment of the presidential role, and accepting the principles laid down to guide an administration. Benjamin Harrison recognized the interdependence of the president and the people in his inaugural:

The oath taken in the presence of the people becomes a mutual covenant. . . . My promise is spoken; yours unspoken, but not the less real and solemn. The people of every State have here their representatives. Surely I do not misinterpret the spirit of the occasion when I assume that the whole body of the people covenant with me and with each other today to support and defend the Constitution of the Union of the States, to yield willing obedience to all the laws and each to every other citizen his [sic] equal civil and political rights. (94)

Great inaugurals reenact the original process by which the people and their leaders "form a more perfect union."[13] In recreating this mutual covenant, great inaugurals both reconstitute the audience as the people and constitute the citizenry as a people in some new way: as those entrusted with the success or failure of the democratic experiment (Washington's first), as members of a perpetual Union (Lincoln's first), as a people whose spiritual strength can overcome material difficulties (Franklin Roosevelt's first), as a people willing to sacrifice for an ideal (Kennedy's), as members of an international community (Wilson's second), as a people able to transcend political differences (Washington's first, Jefferson's first). In 1865, for instance, Lincoln reconstituted the people as limited by the purposes of the Almighty and urged the audience to consider God's view of the conflict between North and South: "Both read the same Bible and pray to the same God, and each invokes His aid against the other. . . . The prayers of both could not be answered. Those of neither have been answered fully. The Almighty has His own purposes" (77).[14] In 1913, in his first inaugural, Wilson reconstituted the citizenry as a people capable of counting the costs of industrial development: "We have been proud of our industrial achievement, but we have not hitherto stopped thoughtfully enough to count the human cost. . . . We have come now to the sober second thought" (123–24). In 1961, Kennedy went beyond a call for sacrifice to speak of "a call to bear the burden of a long twilight struggle, year in, and year out" (166), a call that suggested Götterdämmerung and denied easy victory or inevitable triumph.[15] Notably, the great inaugurals dramatically illustrate the processes of change within a continuous tradition. In them, the resources of epideictic ritual are yoked to political renewal.

Ceremonially, the inaugural address is an adjunct to or an extension of the oath of office, a relationship demonstrated dramatically in the shortest address, Washington's second. After describing himself as "called upon by the voice of my country" to "this distinguished honor," Washington intensified the constitutional oath with a second pledge:

Previous to the execution of any official act of the President, the Constitution requires an oath of office. This oath I am now about to take, and in your presence: That if it shall be found during my administration of the Government I have in any instance violated willingly or knowingly the injunctions thereof, I may (besides incurring constitutional punishment) be subject to the upbraidings of all who are now witnesses of the present solemn ceremony. (3)

Although it consists entirely of an avowal of his personal commitment to the constitutional oath, this inaugural also recognized the witnessing role of the audience in the rite of investiture.

That an inaugural address is an extension of the oath of office is certified by many of these speeches. Cleveland, for example, referred to his speech as a supplement to the oath of office (91). Lyndon Johnson said: "The oath I have taken before you and before God is not mine alone, but ours together" (167). One of the more eloquent inaugurals derived its power in part from its construction as an extension of the oath of office and as an invitation to participate in a mutual covenant. In 1961, each assertion or promise articulated by Kennedy was phrased as a pledge jointly made by leader and people. His litany of mutual pledges culminated in the claim: "In your hands, my fellow citizens, more than mine, will rest the final success or failure of our course." Finally, he explicitly invited audience participation by asking: "Will you join in that historic effort?" (166). By casting his speech as an extension of the oath of office and by inviting the audience to join him in these avowals, Kennedy underscored the ritualistic nature of the occasion.

The force of Lincoln's first inaugural, discussed in more detail below, also derived, in part, from his call for audience participation. In 1881, James Garfield made an appeal that echoed the famous words of Lincoln's first inaugural:

> My countrymen [sic], we do not now differ in our judgment concerning the controversies of past generations, and fifty years hence our children will not be divided in their opinions concerning our controversies. They will surely bless their fathers and their fathers' God that the Union was preserved, that slavery was overthrown, and that both races were made equal before the law. We may hasten or we may retard, but we can not prevent, the final reconciliation. Is it not possible for us now to make a truce with time by anticipating and accepting its inevitable verdict? (88)

The next task the new president faces is that of reaffirming traditional values. Because each of the elements forming a presidential inaugural ought to facilitate the president's task of unifying the audience as the people, the traditional values rehearsed by the president need to be selected and framed in ways that unify the audience. Thus, for example, following a campaign replete with charges that he was an atheist, Jefferson's speech assured former adversaries that he recognized the power of the deity, by "acknowledging and adoring an overruling Providence, . . . that Infinite Power which rules the destinies of the universe" (9–10). Similarly, the founders were eulogized in early inaugurals, but such encomia disappeared as the Civil War approached. Because William Lloyd Garrison and other abolitionists had widely publicized the founders' slaveholding, public veneration of them would ally a president with those who favored slavery and invite the enmity of its opponents.[16] Van Buren's exceptional reference in 1837 to Washington and the other founders can be explained by his continuing need to reassure southerners about what had been the central issue of the campaign, whether he was secretly an abolitionist (37).[17] The point to be noted is that when an appeal that was once a unifying recollection of past heroes interferes with the process of reconstituting the audience as a unified people, it is abandoned.

In order to be invested, presidents must demonstrate their qualifications for office by venerating the past and showing that the traditions of the institution continue unbroken in them. They must affirm that they will transmit the institution intact to their successors. Consequently, the language of conservation, preservation, maintenance, and renewal pervades these speeches. What we conserve and renew is often sanctified as our "creed," our "faith," or our "sacred trust." Cleveland's statement in 1885 is illustrative:

> On this auspicious occasion we may well renew the pledge of our devotion to the Constitution, which, launched by the founders of the republic and consecrated by their prayers and patriotic devotion, has for almost a century borne the hopes and aspirations of a great people through prosperity and peace and through the shock of foreign conflicts and the perils of domestic strife and vicissitudes. (91)

Presidential use of the principles, policies, and presidencies of the past suggests that, in the inaugural address, *memoria,* or shared recollection, is a key source of *inventio,* the development of lines of argument. The final appeal in Lincoln's first inaugural to "the mystic chords of memory" illustrates the symbolic force of a shared past. Coolidge put it more simply: "We can not continue these brilliant successes in the future, unless we continue to learn from the past" (133). Such use of the past is also consistent with the ritualistic process of re-presenting beginnings, origins, and universal relationships.

The past is conserved by honoring past presidents. Washington was praised by John and John Quincy Adams, Jefferson, Taylor, and Van Buren; Monroe and Jackson referred to their illustrious predecessors; Lincoln spoke of the distinguished citizens who had administered the executive branch. The past is also conserved by reaffirming the wisdom of past policies. Cleveland, for example, praised policies of Washington, Jefferson, and Monroe (92). McKinley praised the policy, "wisely inaugurated by Washington," of "keeping ourselves free from entanglement, either as allies or foes" (106).

In 1809, in the sixth inaugural, Madison said: "Unwilling to depart from examples of the most revered authority, I avail myself of the occasion now presented to express the profound impression made on me by the call of my country" (14). Eight years later, James Monroe said:

> In commencing the duties of the chief executive office it has been the practice of the distinguished men who have gone before me to explain the principles which would govern them in their respective Administrations. In following their venerated example . . . . (18)

Over time, earlier presidential inaugurals have frequently been quoted, especially those of Washington, Jefferson, Lincoln, and Franklin Roosevelt. This process of rhetorical introversion illuminates some remarkable coincidences. Harding and Carter, for example, quoted the same verse from Micah. Franklin Roosevelt and Carter each quoted a former teacher, Franklin Roosevelt and Kennedy had rendezvous with destiny, Reagan paraphrased Jefferson, Nixon paraphrased Kennedy, Kennedy echoed Lincoln, Polk rephrased Jackson, and Reagan echoed Kennedy. In other words, presidents recognize, capitalize on, and are constrained by the inaugurals of their predecessors, which, taken together, form a tradition.

The past is also used analogically to affirm that as we overcame difficulties in the past, so will we now; the venerated past assures us that the nation has a future. Thus, in 1933, in the face of severe economic problems, Franklin Roosevelt said: "Compared with the perils which our forefathers conquered because they believed and were not afraid, we have still much to be thankful for" (145). In 1941, with another crisis looming, he reminded his audience of the difficult tasks that confronted Washington and Lincoln (151).

In the world of inaugural addresses, we have inherited our character as a people; accordingly, veneration of the past not only unifies the audience but also warrants present and future action, as recurring references to avoiding "entangling alliances" have illustrated. A more recent example is found in the 1981 inaugural, in which Reagan paraphrased a statement Jefferson made in 1801.[18] Jefferson said: "Sometimes it is said that man [sic] can not be trusted with the government of himself. Can he, then, be trusted with the government of others?" (8). Reagan said: "Well, if no one among us is capable of governing himself [sic], then who among us has the capacity to govern someone else?" (180).

The third job of each president is to set forth the principles that will guide the new administration. The incoming president must go beyond the rehearsal of traditional values and veneration of the past to enunciate a political philosophy. Because rhetorical scholars have focused on the specific political principles laid down in individual inaugurals, they often have failed to note that, although these principles vary from inaugural to inaugural, all inaugurals not only lay down political principles but also present and develop such principles in predictable ways.

In many inaugurals, presidents indicate that they feel obliged to set forth the principles that will govern their tenures in office. Jefferson's explicit 1801 statement exemplified this:

> About to enter, my fellow-citizens, on the exercise of duties which comprehend everything dear and valuable to you, it is proper you should understand what I deem the essential principles of our Government, and consequently those which ought to shape its Administration. (9)

In keeping with the epideictic character of inaugurals, however, specific policies are proposed for contemplation, not action. Proposals are not an end in themselves but illustrations of the political philosophy of the speaker. This contemplative, expository function differentiates policy proposals embedded in inaugurals from those in State of the Union addresses, where such proposals are presented for congressional action.

So, for instance, in a relatively detailed statement of his political views, James Polk discussed "our revenue laws and the levy of taxes," but this discussion illustrated the political axiom that "no more money shall be collected than the necessities of an economical administration shall require" (57). Similarly, he aired his position on the national debt to illustrate the principle that

> melancholy is the condition of that people whose government can be sustained only by a system which periodically transfers large amounts from the labor of the many

to the coffers of the few. Such a system is incompatible with the ends for which our Republican Government was instituted. (56–57)

Because William Howard Taft conceived the inaugural address as a vehicle for articulating relatively specific policy, his speech provides a rigorous test of the claim that inaugurals deal with principles rather than practices. He said: "The office of an inaugural address is to give a summary outline of the main policies of the new administration, so far as they can be anticipated" (115), but his tedious list of recommendations functioned not as a call for specific, immediate action, but as evidence of continuity and of loyalty to the Constitution. He said, for example: "I have had the honor to be one of the advisers of my distinguished predecessor, and as such, to hold up his hands in the reforms he has initiated. . . . To render such reforms lasting, however, . . . further legislative and executive action are needed" [sic] (115). Such reforms ("the suppression of the lawlessness and abuses of power of the great combinations of capital invested in railroads and in industrial enterprises carrying on interstate commerce") were defined as means of maintaining the democratic character of the government. Again, they became illustrations that he would follow broad principles.[19]

Just as recollection of the past and rehearsal of traditional values need to be noncontroversial and unifying, so recommitment to constitutional principles unifies by assuring those who did not vote for a candidate that the president will, nonetheless, scrupulously protect their rights. The same needs to unify the audience and to speak in the epideictic present also influence the language in which presidents articulate the principles that will govern their administrations.

The rite of investiture demands that presidents do more than rehearse traditional values and enunciate a political philosophy. Their fourth task is to enact the presidential role and in so doing demonstrate an appreciation of the requirements and limitations of the executive in our system of government. The audience, unified as the people, witnesses the investiture, but to complete and ratify the president's ascent to power, the inaugural address demonstrates rhetorically that this person can function as a leader within the constitutionally established limits of executive power and can perform the public, symbolic role of president of all the people.

As president, the speaker appropriates the country's history and assumes the right to say what that history means; as president, the speaker asserts that some principles are more salient than others at that moment; as president, the speaker constitutes hearers as the people; and as president, the speaker asks the people to join in a mutual covenant to commit themselves to the political philosophy enunciated in the address.

If an inaugural address is to function as part of a rite of investiture, presidents must speak in the public role of president. An inaugural would not fulfill this function if the address pressed forward the personality or personal history of the incoming president.[20] When evidence is drawn from a president's personal past, it must reveal something about the presidency or about the people or the nation. Personal narrative is inappropriate in a rhetorical genre designed for the formal display of the president as president. The functions of personal material in an inaugural are clearly different from the functions of like material in campaign oratory, where a high level of self-disclosure and self-aggrandizement is both expected and appropriate. The functions of self-references also distinguish the inaugural address from other presidential rhetoric.[21]

A dramatic example of inappropriate personal material appeared in the final paragraph of Ulysses Grant's second inaugural. He concluded:

Throughout the war, and from my candidacy for my present office in 1868 to the close of the last Presidential campaign, I have been the object of abuse and slander scarcely ever equaled in political history, which to-day I feel that I can afford to disregard in view of your verdict, which I gratefully accept as my vindication. (81)

The statements speak of Grant the person, not of the presidency or of Grant the president. In so doing, the statement called into question

Grant's ability to fulfill the symbolic role of president of all the people.

More recently, Carter's use of a statement by a former teacher illustrates a potential pitfall in using personal material. Immediately after thanking Gerald Ford for all he had done to heal the division in the nation, Carter began his speech by saying:

> In this outward and physical ceremony, we attest once again to the inner and spiritual strength of our Nation. As my high school teacher, Miss Julia Coleman, used to say, "We must adjust to changing times and still hold to unchanging principles." (178)

As we have argued, the first duty of a president in an inaugural is to reconstitute the audience as the people. Carter was attempting to forge an American community out of his listeners. However, only certain people have the standing to do that, and Julia Coleman, however able she may have been as a high school teacher, was not one of them. Later in the inaugural, if Carter had made her the voice of the people expressing a timeless truth, Coleman's aphorism might have been appropriate. Later, despite Coleman's lack of authority, her adage might have served had it been an unusual, penetrating, immediately intelligible, vivid statement of the relationship between change and continuity. However, even such a claim is questionable. In Carter's statement, we have the rhetorical equivalent of what would have occurred had Kennedy begun the second paragraph of his speech, "To paraphrase George St. John, my old headmaster, 'Ask not what your country can do for you . . . .'"[22]

Franklin Roosevelt's first inaugural dramatically asserted presidential leadership and the special importance of executive action. He spoke of "a leadership of frankness and vigor" and said: "I am convinced that you will again give the support to leadership in these critical days" (145). "This Nation asks for action, and action now," and "With this pledge taken, I assume unhesitatingly the leadership of this great army of our people" (146). However, Roosevelt was aware that he was pressing the limits of executive power. He said:

> It is to be hoped that the normal balance of executive and legislative authority may be wholly adequate to meet the unprecedented task before us. But it may be that an unprecedented demand and need for undelayed action may call for temporary departure from that normal balance of public procedure. I am prepared under my constitutional duty to recommend the measures that a stricken nation . . . may require. . . . I shall ask Congress for the one remaining instrument to meet the crisis—broad Executive power to wage a war against the emergency, as great as the power that would be given to me if we were in fact invaded by a foreign foe. (147)

What is crucial here is that Roosevelt portrayed his leadership as constitutional. Special powers would be conferred by Congress, and those powers would be analogous to the extraordinary powers exercised by previous presidents in similarly extreme circumstances.

An abiding fear of the misuse of executive power pervades our national history. Washington's opponents accused him of wanting to be king; Jackson was called King Andrew, and Van Buren King Martin; Teddy Roosevelt was attacked in cartoons captioned "Theodore Roosevelt for ever and ever"; Lincoln's abolition of habeas corpus and Franklin Roosevelt's use of executive power as well as his pursuit of third and fourth terms were damned as monarchical or, worse, as despotic.[23] The American Revolution was fought, the Declaration of Independence reminds the citizenry, in response to "repeated injuries and usurpations, all having in direct object the establishment of an absolute Tyranny over these States." To allay fears of incipient tyranny, incoming presidents must assure the people that they do not covet power for its own sake and that they recognize and respect constitutional limits on executive authority.

There is a paradox in the demand that presidents demonstrate rhetorically a capacity for effective leadership while carefully acknowledging constitutional limitations. To the extent that they promise strong leadership, they risk being seen as incipient tyrants. By contrast, should they emphasize the limits on executive power, they risk being seen as inept or enfeebled leaders. Eloquent presidents have walked this tightrope with agility, as Lincoln did in his first inaugural when he responded to the fear that he would use executive power to abolish slavery: "I have no purpose, directly or indirectly, to interfere with the institution of slavery in the States where it exists" (72). He attested that this was a consistent position for him by citing statements from his campaign speeches and a plank from the Republican party platform. This material he characterized as "the most conclusive evidence of which the case is susceptible" (72). On the other hand, responding to abolitionist revulsion against the fugitive slave laws, he quoted Article 4 of the Constitution and averred that these laws were merely an extension of that article, a part of the Constitution that he shortly would swear an oath to uphold.

In recognizing the limits on presidential power, inaugurals not only affirm the balance of power and locate executive initiatives in the mandate of the people, they also offer evidence of humility. The new president humbly acknowledges deficiencies, humbly accepts the burdens of office, and humbly invokes God's blessings. The precedent for evincing humility was set in the first inaugural when Washington said:

> The magnitude and difficulty of the trust
> to which the voice of my country called me,
> being sufficient to awaken in the wisest and
> most experienced of her citizens a distrustful
> scrutiny into his [sic] qualifications, could not
> but overwhelm with despondence one who
> ought to be peculiarly conscious of his own
> deficiencies. (1)[24]

Washington's attitude was echoed in Carter's less felicitous comment in 1977: "Your strength can compensate for my weakness, and your wisdom can help to minimize my mistakes" (178).

As part of the process of acknowledging the limits of executive power, inaugurals typically place the president and the nation under God. These references to God are not perfunctory, because by calling upon God, presidents subordinate themselves to a higher power. The God of the inaugurals is a personal God who is actively involved in affairs of state, an "Almighty Being whose power regulates the destiny of nations," in the words of Madison (15); a God "who led our fathers," according to Jefferson (13); a God who protects us, according

to Monroe (28); a God revealed in our history, according to Cleveland (93); and a God who punishes us, in the words of Lincoln: "He gives to both North and South this terrible war as the woe due to those by whom the offense came" (77). Presidents enact the presidential role by placing themselves and the nation in God's hands. We should note, however, that it is only after they are fully invested with office that presidents have claimed the authority to place the nation "under God." For this reason, perhaps, prayers or prayerlike statements have usually occurred near or at the end of inaugurals. This can explain why Eisenhower called the prayer he delivered before his first inaugural "a private prayer." Although he had taken the oath of office, he was not yet fully invested as president, and until he had performed further rhetorical acts of acceptance, he sensed that he lacked the authority to represent the nation before God.

The placement of prayers or prayerlike statements is a subtle indication that the inaugural address is an integral part of the rite of investiture. Some inaugurals have articulated the notion that the president becomes "the president" through delivering the inaugural address. For example, William Henry Harrison concluded his 1841 speech this way: "Fellow citizens, being fully invested with that high office to which the partiality of my countrymen has called me, I now take affectionate leave of you" (53).

Fifth, and finally, the four elements described above must be adapted to the character of epideictic rhetoric because the special "timelessness" of epideictic discourse is the key to fusing the elements that symbolically constitute the presidential inaugural. The time of epideictic rhetoric, including inaugurals, is the eternal present, the mythic time that Mircea Eliade calls *illud tempus,* time out of time. Eliade writes: "Every ritual has the character of happening *now,* at this very moment. The time of the event that the ritual commemorates or re-enacts is made *present,* 're-presented' so to speak, however far back it may have been in ordinary reckoning."[25] This time out of time allows one to experience a universe of eternal relationships, in the case of inauguration, the relationship between the ruler and the ruled, and it has the potential to be reenacted, made present once again, at any moment. This special sense of the present is central to the generic character of the inaugural because the address is about an institution and a form of government fashioned to transcend any given historical moment. The timelessness of an inaugural address affirms and ensures the continuity of the constitutional system and the immortality of the presidency as an institution, and timelessness is reflected in its contemplative tone and by the absence of calls to specific and immediate action.

Inaugurals transcend the historical present by reconstituting an existing community, rehearsing the past, affirming traditional values, and articulating timely and timeless principles that will govern the administration of the incoming president. The quality of epideictic timelessness to which inaugurals aspire was captured by Franklin Roosevelt in his 1941 address: "To us there has come a time, in the midst of swift happenings, to pause for a moment and take stock—to recall what our place in history has been, and to rediscover what we are and what we may be" (151).

Great inaugurals achieve timelessness. They articulate a perspective that transcends the situation that produced them, and for this reason they retain their rhetorical force. For instance, although Lincoln's first inaugural addressed a nation poised on the brink of civil war, Lincoln's message speaks to all situations in which the rights of constituent units are seen to clash with the powers of a central body. Similarly, the eloquent conclusion of Lincoln's second inaugural remains applicable to the wounds the nation suffered in the conflict over the war in Vietnam. Although Franklin Roosevelt's first inaugural assured his hearers that they, as a people led by him, could surmount that economic crisis, it also assures audiences through time that Americans can surmount all material problems. Kennedy's inaugural reflected the history of the Cold War, but it also expressed the resoluteness required under any circumstances to sustain a struggle against a menacing ideology. Finally, George Washington's inaugural not only spoke to the immediate crisis but also articulated what Arthur Schlesinger calls "a great strand that binds them [the inaugurals] together."[26]

Washington said: "The preservation of the sacred fire of liberty and the destiny of the republican model of government are justly considered, perhaps, as deeply, as finally staked on the experiment intrusted to the hands of the American people" (2).

Inaugurals bespeak their locus in the eternal present in a high style that heightens experience, invites contemplation, and speaks to the people through time. The language of great inaugurals captures complex, resonant ideas in memorable phrases. Americans still recall Jefferson's "peace, commerce, and honest friendship with all nations, entangling alliances with none" (9). They continue to quote Lincoln's conclusion:

> With malice toward none, with charity for all, with firmness in the right as God gives us to see the right, let us strive to finish the work we are in, to bind up the nation's wounds, to care for him who shall have borne the battle and for his widow and his orphan, to do all which may achieve and cherish a just and lasting peace among ourselves and with all nations. (77)

Franklin Roosevelt's "So, first of all, let me assert my firm belief that the only thing we have to fear is fear itself" (145), and John Kennedy's "And so, my fellow Americans, ask not what your country can do for you: Ask what you can do for your country" (166) remain memorable. Such phrases illustrate special rhetorical skill in reinvigorating traditional values; in them familiar ideas become fresh and take on new meaning.

Stylistically and structurally, great presidential inaugurals are suited to contemplation. Through the use of parallelism, for example, Kennedy revived our traditional commitment to the defense of freedom when he said: "We shall pay any price, bear any burden, meet any hardship, support any friend, oppose any foe, in order to assure the survival and success of liberty" (165). The memorable antithesis "Let us never negotiate out of fear. But let us never fear to negotiate" (166), was a vivid restatement of our modern tradition of relationship to foreign nations. Kennedy's more famous antithesis asked citizens to contemplate a redefinition of who they were as a people, a redefinition based on sacrifice. Through the use of assonance, Kennedy underscored the nuclear peril when he spoke of "the steady spread of the deadly atom" (166). By arresting attention, such literary devices invite listeners and readers to ponder these ideas, ideas less suited to contemplation when stated in more mundane language.[27]

The preceding analysis treats presidential inaugurals as one kind of epideictic, or ceremonial, rhetoric. That perspective can create the impression that these speeches are merely ritualistic, meaning that they are relatively insignificant because their content is limited to *memoria*, the shared past. However, inaugurals in which presidents have reconstituted the people in new terms and have selectively reaffirmed and reinvigorated those communal values consistent with the philosophy and tone of the incoming administration suggest ways in which a ritualistic occasion may be directed toward other ends. In other words, praise and blame, the key strategies in ceremonial discourse, can be used ideologically to lay the groundwork for policy initiatives.

What usually distinguishes ceremonial address from policy advocacy is deliberation, the argumentative form associated with justifying new policy. Deliberative argument pivots on the issue of expediency, specifically, which policy is best able to address identified problems, which policy will produce more beneficial than evil consequences, and which is most practical, given available resources.

Lincoln's first inaugural address is significant not only as a masterpiece of epideictic discourse but also as a vehicle for considering the ways in which epideictic rhetoric is related to policy deliberation. In that unusual address, Lincoln integrated key elements of these two genres. Specifically, in the service of epideictic ends (unifying the nation and reaffirming cherished communal values), Lincoln adopted deliberative means (arguments regarding expediency), and he asked the audience to contemplate whether or not the policy of secession was the best means to resolve sectional disputes, and he attempted to allay the fears of Southern slaveholders about interference in their domestic affairs. Lincoln's speech displays epideictic contemplation as a precursor to deliberative decision.[28]

The early parts of the speech are consistent with the inaugural traditions that have been identified. Lincoln began by noting the ceremonial character of the occasion, "a custom as old as the Government itself," and acknowledging the people's role in the ritual of investiture: "I appear before you to address you briefly and to take in your presence the oath prescribed by the Constitution" (72). While the speech differs from other inaugurals because Lincoln spoke in a situation of crisis, early in the speech, as in other inaugurals, Lincoln reaffirmed the Constitution, including those sections supporting the fugitive slave law, and the limits of executive power. Lincoln also followed precedent in swearing a personal oath: "I take the official oath to-day with no mental reservations and with no purpose to construe the Constitution or laws by any hypercritical rules" (73).

What followed set forth the philosophy and tone of the upcoming administration; in this instance, because there was "substantial division," the focus was on secession. If considered apart from historical precedent, these paragraphs might appear divisively specific. However, when the arguments made here are compared with those laid out a few months earlier in the final annual message of Lincoln's predecessor, James Buchanan, the argument emerges in a different light. Buchanan had strong Southern sympathies, and although Buchanan and Lincoln held differing views of the president's constitutional right to act to hold the Union together, particularly in the absence of congressional enactments, they agreed that secession was unconstitutional, and their arguments for that conclusion were remarkably similar.[29] As a result, this section of the speech can fairly be construed as a general statement of administrative philosophy and tone that was consistent with an attempt to unify the auditors into the people.

In other words, although affected by the unusual historical circumstances, the first half of the speech fulfills traditional expectations for an inaugural address.

The speech becomes exceptional as an inaugural and as epideictic discourse in the paragraphs following Lincoln's question, "To those, however, who really love the Union may I not speak?" (74), which was followed in turn by a series of questions designed to induce the audience to think deeply about secession, the reasons for it, and the consequences it would bring. Lincoln asked: "Would it not be wise to ascertain precisely why we do it? Will you hazard so desperate a step? . . . Will . . . you risk the commission of so fearful a mistake?" (74).

The questions were the opening sally in an effort to provoke contemplation of secession as a policy, but although they were rhetorical questions, they were not adequate to this task. They had to be buttressed by reasoning laid out to show that conclusions previously reached might be erroneous. Lincoln established a basic premise: "All profess to be content in the Union if all constitutional rights can be maintained" (74). He developed his argument by maintaining that, as yet, no constitutional rights of slaveholders had been denied, and he challenged his auditors: "Think, if you can, of a single instance in which a plainly written provision of the Constitution has ever been denied" (74). That was a perilous challenge, dependent entirely on widespread agreement that no violations had occurred. As a result, he quickly noted areas of ambiguity. He said:

> No foresight can anticipate nor any document of reasonable length contain express provisions for all possible questions. Shall fugitives from labor be surrendered by national or by State authority? The Constitution does not expressly say. May Congress prohibit slavery in the Territories? The Constitution does not expressly say. Must Congress protect slavery in the Territories? The Constitution does not expressly say. (74)

These areas of ambiguity, he contended, were the issues that divided the nation, and he did not pretend that resolution of them would be easy. At that moment, they appeared irreconcilable: "If the minority will not acquiesce, the majority must, or the Government must cease. There is no other alternative, for continuing the Government is acquiescence on one side or the other" (74). But he immediately added that, despite such a standoff, secession was no solution: "If a minority in such case will secede rather than acquiesce, they make a precedent which in turn will divide and ruin them" (74). He developed this claim by asserting what he presumed would be a universally accepted principle, that in human affairs "unanimity is

impossible" (75). As a result, he argued, one must choose between majority rule on the one hand and some form of anarchy or despotism on the other.

What must majority rule decide? He narrowed the current dispute to conflict over the rightness of slavery and whether or not it should be extended. Given the intensity of the disagreement, he argued that the fugitive slave laws and the laws suppressing the foreign slave trade "are each as well enforced, perhaps, as any law can ever be in a community where the moral sense of the people imperfectly supports the law itself" (75). Conflicts over these issues, he argued, would only worsen following separation, possibilities suggested by a series of rhetorical questions, each of which indicated why differences would only intensify following division. For instance, he asked: "Can aliens make treaties easier than friends can make laws?" (75).

Lincoln reminded the audience of legal avenues of redress, such as amending the Constitution, but proposed nothing, although he indicated that he would not oppose an amendment making the right to hold slaves in those states where slavery already existed "express and irrevocable" (76). His earlier appeal to have "patient confidence in the ultimate justice of the people" was buttressed by rhetorical questions, such as "Is there any better or equal hope in the world?" and by a reminder of executive limitations: "This same people have wisely given their public servants but little power for mischief" (76).

Although he relied heavily on deliberative arguments in the second half of the speech, the contemplative, epideictic purpose of the entire address was evident in its conclusion, when Lincoln said: "My countrymen, one and all, think calmly and well upon this subject. Nothing valuable can be lost by taking time" (76).

Lincoln's first inaugural subtly invites contemplation of the contrast between the present haste of the secessionists and the timeless truths their hasty action could destroy. On the one hand, there is the "eternal truth and justice" of the Almighty and "perpetual Union" while on the other hand, there are those who would "hurry . . . you in hot haste to a step which you would never take *deliberately*" (76). For Lincoln, secession was "precipitate action." In this interplay between the present moment and timeless truths, even an administration that was wicked, as the South feared that his would be, could not "seriously injure the Government in the short space of four years" (76).

Lincoln offered his audience two frames through which to view this moment. One, constructed by those who would act impetuously, began with the nation's founding but would end with "destruction of the Union." The second, characterized by contemplation and thoughtful consideration, began at the nation's founding but was endless, presupposing that the Union was perpetual and, hence, beyond the ability of a few to destroy. Lincoln's repeated urging of contemplation invited the audience to adopt the second frame. Both were introduced with the inaugural's opening statement, in which Lincoln noted that he stood before the audience "in compliance with a custom as old as government itself" (72). The first ended when Lincoln posited the possibility of "destruction of the Union" (73). The second ended with this affirmation:

> I hold that in contemplation of universal law and of the Constitution the Union of these States is perpetual. Perpetuity is implied, if not expressed, in the fundamental laws of all national governments. It is safe to assert that no government proper ever had a provision in its organic law for its own termination. (73)

Contemplation and perpetuity were repeatedly linked. "Descending from these general principles," he said, "we find the proposition that in legal contemplation the Union is perpetual confirmed by the history of the Union itself" (73).

At the core of the speech is an implied question about the continued life of the Union and the principles for which it was founded. Will secessionists destroy the vital element of perpetuity, making mortal and time bound what should be perpetual and timeless?

It was in this context that Lincoln melded past, present, and future into the timelessly memorable contemplation of his peroration:

> The mystic chords of memory [the timeless past], stretching from every battlefield and

patriot grave [the founding of the nation] to every living heart and hearthstone all over this broad land [the present], will yet swell the chorus of the Union, when again touched, as surely they will be [a confident positing of the future], by the better angels of our nature. (76)

Here is Lincoln's final exhortation to contemplate, an invocation that the hurried, passion-strained tensions of the moment be set aside in favor of the perpetual, timeless Union that is greater than any of them.

Lincoln's speech is a masterpiece because it extends the symbolic function of epideictic discourse, to include the contemplation that precedes action, because inducements to contemplation are fused with invitations to participate in the processes by which he reached his conclusions, and because the concerns of the moment are linked to eternal questions. As such, the discourse enacts a respect for thoughtful deliberation by the citizenry, which is the essence of a democratic system, even at a moment of its most intense division and crisis.

CONCLUSION

Seen as a rhetorical genre, the American presidential inaugural address is constituted by the five major elements that we have identified. Our analysis suggests the processes by which a distinctive genre of epideictic rhetoric comes into being. Its broadest outlines are set by the general characteristics of epideictic discourse. A specific kind of ceremony and occasion refines the genre further. In this case, the presidential inaugural is part of a rite of passage, of investiture, a ritual that establishes a special relationship between speaker and audience. The U.S. presidential investiture requires a mutual covenant, a rehearsal of fundamental political values, an enunciation of political principles, and the enactment of the presidential persona. Also, the conventions of this rhetorical type emerge because presidents are familiar with the tradition and tend to study past inaugurals before formulating their own.

Presidential inaugurals vary, but what makes it illuminating to view the U.S. presidential inaugural as a genre is that the variation is of a certain sort. Circumstances vary, as do the personalities of the presidents, but the variation among inaugurals is predictable.

Inaugural addresses vary substantively because presidents choose to rehearse aspects of our tradition that are consistent with the party or political philosophy they represent. Such selective emphasis is illustrated in Franklin Roosevelt's second inaugural address, in which he said:

> Instinctively we recognize a deeper need—the need to find through government the instrument of our united purpose to solve for the individual the ever-rising problems of a complex civilization. . . . In this we Americans were discovering no wholly new truth; we were writing a new chapter in our book of self-government. . . . The essential democracy of our Nation and the safety of our people depend not upon the absence of power, but upon lodging it with those whom the people can change or continue at stated intervals through an honest and free system of elections. . . . [W]e have made the exercise of all power more democratic; for we have begun to bring private autocratic powers into their proper subordination to the people's government. (148)

Later, he added: "Today we reconsecrate our country to long-cherished ideals in a suddenly changed civilization" (150). Similarly, in 1981, Ronald Reagan chose to emphasize facets of the system in order to affirm values consistent with his conservative political philosophy. He said: "Our government has no power except that granted it by the people. It is time to check and reverse the growth of government which shows signs of having grown beyond the consent of the governed" (181).

A major variation occurs in inaugurals delivered by incumbent presidents. Because a covenant already exists between a reelected president and the people, the need to reconstitute the community is less urgent. Because the country is familiar with a sitting president's political philosophy, the need to preview administrative philosophy and tone is also muted. Reelected presidents tend to recommit themselves to principles articulated in their previous inaugurals or to highlight only those principles relevant to the agenda for the coming terms. In this respect, subsequent inaugurals by the same president tend to be extensions, not replications, of earlier inaugurals.

The inaugural addresses themselves articulate the reason for this generic variation. For instance, although he was president in the midst of the most serious of crises, Lincoln said:

> At this second appearing to take the oath of the Presidential office there is less occasion for an extended address than there was at the first. Then a statement somewhat in detail of the course to be pursued seemed fitting and proper. Now, at the expiration of four years, during which public declarations have been constantly called forth on every point and phase of the great contest which still absorbs the attention and engrosses the energies of the nation, little that is new could be presented. (77)

Similarly, in 1805, Jefferson reported that his conscience told him he had lived up to the principles he had espoused four years earlier (11). In 1821, Monroe noted: "If the person thus elected has served the preceding term, an opportunity is afforded him [sic] to review its principal occurrences and to give the explanation respecting them as in his judgment may be useful to his constituents" (23). Some presidents have used a subsequent inaugural to review the trials and successes of their earlier terms, and in so doing, they have rehearsed the immediate past, a move rarely made in first inaugurals. When subsequent inaugurals develop specific policies, these are usually described as continuations of policies initiated in the previous term, continuations presumably endorsed by the president's reelection.

Special conditions faced by some presidents have caused some subsequent inaugurals to resemble first inaugurals. For example, in 1917, confronting challenges quite different from those that existed in 1913, Wilson said: "This is not the time for retrospect. It is time rather to speak our thoughts and purposes concerning the present and the immediate future" (126). In the face of the events of World War I, he said:

> We are provincials no longer. The tragic events of the thirty months of vital turmoil through which we have just passed have made us citizens of the world. There can be no turning

back. Our own fortunes as a nation are involved whether we would have it so or not. (127)

The war prompted Wilson to constitute the people in a new way, as citizens of the world. Similarly, the events leading to World War II affected Franklin Roosevelt's choices in 1941: "In this day the task of the people is to save the Nation and its institutions from disruptions from without" (151). That statement of the task diverged sharply from the principles emphasized in 1933 and 1937.

Variability in inaugural addresses is evidence of an identifiable cluster of elements that form the essential inaugural act. Each apparent variation is an emphasis on or a development of one or more of the key elements we have described. Washington's second inaugural address underscored the role of the audience as witnesses and the address as an extension of the oath of office. Jefferson's first address was a call to unity through the enunciation of political principles; Lincoln's first inaugural was a dramatic appeal to the audience to participate in reaffirming the mutual covenant between the president and the people; his second was a[n] exploration of what it means to say that this nation is "under God." Theodore Roosevelt explored the meaning of our "sacred trust" as it applies to a people with an international role; Franklin Roosevelt's first address explored the nature of executive leadership and the limits of executive power, whereas his second constituted the audience as a caring people; Wilson's first inaugural explored the meaning of U.S. industrial development. Finally, Kennedy's address exploited the possibilities of the noble, dignified, literary language characteristic of the epideictic to such an extent that his address is sometimes attacked for stylistic excess.[30]

From a generic perspective, then, a presidential inaugural reconstitutes the people as an audience that can witness the rite of investiture. It rehearses communal values from the past, sets forth the political principles that will guide the new administration, and demonstrates that the president can enact the presidential persona appropriately. Still more generally, the presidential inaugural address is an epideictic ritual that is formal, unifying, abstract, and eloquent; at the core of this ritual lies epideictic

timelessness—the fusion of the past and future of the nation in an eternal present in which we reaffirm what Franklin Roosevelt called "our covenant with ourselves" (148), a covenant between the executive and the nation that is the essence of democratic government.

Institutionally, the inaugural address performs two key functions. In and through it, each president is invested with office, and at a moment of transition, the continuity of the institution and of the system of government of which it is a part is affirmed.

Finally, the inaugural address is the first of the rhetorical genres which, taken together, constitute a major part of the presidency as an institution and of individual presidencies.

NOTES

[1] Arthur Schlesinger, Jr., ed., *The Chief Executive: Inaugural Addresses of the Presidents of the United States from George Washington to Lyndon B. Johnson* (New York: Crown Publishers, 1965), vi, vii. Presidential discourse is generally not of high literary quality. In announcing that Thomas Jefferson's autobiographical writings and public papers would be included in the Library of America series, Daniel Aaron, president of the selection committee, commented that the works of only a few other presidents—Lincoln, Grant, Wilson, and both Roosevelts—were likely to be included. The criteria for selection are literary, not political, and, Aaron says, "Some could write well, others were wooden" (Herbert Mitgang, "Jefferson's Prose Joins Library of America Series," *New York Times*, 28 May 1984, 15Y).

[2] The name of this kind of discourse comes from the Greek term *epideixis*, meaning display, suggesting the link between this kind of discourse and the proper, even elegant performance of a ritual. See Aristotle, *Rhetoric*, trans. W. Rhys Roberts (New York: Modern Library, 1954), 1358b12–13, 18–20; 1367b37–38; 1368a27; 1414a17–18.

[3] John W. O'Malley, *Praise and Blame in Renaissance Rome: Rhetoric, Doctrine, and Reform in the Sacred Orators of the Papal Court, c. 1450–1521* (Durham, N.C.: Duke University Press, 1979), 40.

[4] O'Malley, 63.

[5] Harry Caplan, *Rhetorica ad Herennium* (Cambridge, Mass.: Harvard University Press, 1954), 173n.

[6] James L. Hoban, Jr., "Rhetorical Rituals of Rebirth," *Quarterly Journal of Speech* 66

(October 1980): 282–83. Investiture necessitates participation in a formal ceremony in which a duly constituted authority, before appropriate witnesses, confers the right to play a certain role or to take a certain position. The ceremony usually involves a demonstration by the candidate for investiture of her or his suitability for such elevation.

7 Karlyn Kohrs Campbell and Kathleen Hall Jamieson, "Form and Genre in Rhetorical Criticism: An Introduction," in *Form and Genre: Shaping Rhetorical Action,* ed. Karlyn Kohrs Campbell and Kathleen Hall Jamieson (Falls Church, Va.: Speech Communication Association, 1978), 9–32.

8 This unification is almost exclusively of male citizens. In the world of inaugural addresses, women rarely exist. In 1985, for example, Reagan referred to "working men and women," but even such an indirect, casual reference is aberrant.

9 All citations from inaugurals through 1985 are from Michael J. Lax, ed., *The Inaugural Addresses of the Presidents of the United States, 1789–1985* (Atlantic City, N.J.: American Inheritance Press, 1985), 4; page numbers hereafter are in parentheses in the text.

10 Dumas Malone notes that Jefferson did not capitalize these key terms and turn them into party names (*Jefferson the President: First Term, 1801–1805* [Boston: Little, Brown, 1970], 4:20).

11 For example, see Buchanan's 1857 address, which followed an election held during the conflict between pro- and antislavery forces in "bloody Kansas" (68–71); Hayes's 1877 address (82–85) and Cleveland's 1885 and 1893 addresses (91–93, 100–102); Benjamin Harrison's address in 1889 (94–99); and Richard Nixon's 1969 address (170–72). See also George Bush, "Transcript of Bush's Inaugural Address: 'Nation Stands Ready to Push On,'" *New York Times,* 21 January 1989, 10Y.

12 "Transcript of Bush's Inaugural Address," 10Y.

13 Inaugurals frequently praised include Washington's first, Jefferson's first, Lincoln's first and second, Franklin Roosevelt's first, and Kennedy's. Some add Theodore Roosevelt's first, Wilson's first, and Franklin Roosevelt's second (Schlesinger, vii).

14 See Glen E. Thurow, *Abraham Lincoln and American Political Religion* (Albany: State University of New York Press, 1976), esp. 98–104.

15 Others inaugurals contain admonitions, e.g. Eisenhower in 1957 (162–63), Truman (154–57), and Harding (128–32).

16 The extent to which the founders, including George Washington, were identified with proslavery positions is illustrated in a speech by John C. Calhoun in the Senate, March 4, 1850: "Nor can the Union be saved by invoking the name of the illustrious Southerner whose mortal remains repose on the western banks of the Potomac. He was one of us—a slave-holder and a planter. We have studied his history, and find nothing in it to justify submission to wrong" (A. Craig Baird, ed., *American Public Addresses, 1740–1952* [New York: McGraw-Hill, 1956], 83).

17 See John Niven, *Martin Van Buren: The Romantic Age of American Politics* (New York: Oxford University Press, 1983).

18 Bert E. Bradley, "Jefferson and Reagan: The Rhetoric of Two Inaugurals," *Southern Speech Communication Journal* 48 (Winter 1983): 119–36; Gregg Phifer, "Two Inaugurals: A Second Look," *Southern Speech Communication Journal* 48 (Summer 1983): 378–85.

19 The problems created by a transition from a president to a political protégé are also illustrated in the inaugurals of Martin Van Buren and George Bush.

20 In his analysis of Richard Nixon's first inaugural, Robert L. Scott calls attention to Nixon's excessive use of the pronoun "I." Such personal references not only violate the presidential persona intrinsic to the address but also tend to preclude the joint action through which the president and the people covenant together. See "Rhetoric That Postures: An Intrinsic Reading of Richard M. Nixon's Inaugural Address," *Western Speech* 34 (Winter 1970): 47, n. 1.

21 Roderick P. Hart's computerized analysis of 380 modern presidential speeches generated an 8.01 level of self-reference (all first-person pronouns were counted.) By contrast, the nine inaugurals in this sample generated a 1.12 level of self-reference. The levels refer to the number of self-references in the middle-most 500 words of the speeches sampled. See *Verbal Style and the Presidency: A Computer-Based Analysis* (Orlando, Fla.: Academic Press, 1984), 273, 279.

22 The Reverend George St. John, headmaster of Choate, the preparatory school in Wallingford, Conn., attended by Kennedy, used to say to his students: "Ask not what your school can do for you; ask what you can do for your school" (Walter Scott, "Walter Scott's Personality Parade," *Parade* [December 15, 1968]: 2).

23 Marcus Cunliffe, *American Presidents and the Presidency* (New York: American Heritage Press, 1968), 149, 152, 154–55, 158, 163, 172.

24 Grant's lack of humility in confronting the future "without fear" and his failure to ask for God's help were remarked by his contemporaries.

(Lloyd Paul Stryker, *Andrew Johnson: A Study in Courage* [New York: Macmillan, 1929], 346).

[25] Mircea Eliade, *Patterns in Comparative Religion,* trans. Rosemary Sheed (Cleveland: World, 1970), 392.

[26] Schlesinger, vii.

[27] Edward P. J. Corbett, "Analysis of the Style of John F. Kennedy's Inaugural Address," in *Classical Rhetoric for the Modern Student,* 2nd ed., ed. Edward Corbett (New York: Oxford University Press, 1971), 554–65; Sam Meyer, "The John F. Kennedy Inauguration Speech: Function and Importance of Its 'Address System,'" *Rhetoric Society Quarterly* 12 (Fall 1982): 239–50.

[28] Chaim Perelman and Lucie Olbrechts-Tyteca, *The New Rhetoric: A Treatise on Argumentation,* trans. John Wilkinson and Purcell Weaver (Notre Dame, Ind.: University of Notre Dame Press, 1969), 49–51.

[29] James D. Richardson, ed., *A Compilation of the Messages and Papers of the Presidents, 1789–1908,* 11 vols. (Washington, D.C.: National Bureau of Literature and Art, 1909), 5:626–39. Late in his analysis, Buchanan said: "But may I be permitted solemnly to invoke my countrymen to pause and deliberate before they determine to destroy this the grandest temple which has ever been dedicated to human freedom since the world began?" (636–37).

[30] Garry Wills, *The Kennedy Imprisonment: A Meditation on Power* (New York: Pocket Books, 1982), 312

Reconceptualizing Rhetorical History: Eisenhower's Farewell Address

Martin J. Medhurst

In the councils of government, we must guard against the acquisition of unwarranted influence, whether sought or unsought, by the military-industrial complex.

—Dwight D. Eisenhower
January 17, 1961[1]

With this one line, President Dwight D. Eisenhower assured himself a place in rhetorical history. The "military-industrial complex" became one phrase—some would say the only phrase—that would not only live beyond the eight-year incumbency of its utterer but go on to become a standard token of the American political vocabulary. Still, rhetorical history, like all histories, is a product of those who write it—subject to the interests, whims, biases, and fears of writers and, of course, to their talents as rhetorical critics and historians. Those who have, to date, written the history of this famous speech have more often than not failed to illumine its distinctively rhetorical features, failed to reveal the speaker's dominant motives, and failed to understand the authority that the speech appropriates or the audience that it creates. To make such assertions is to problematize history as written.

To begin, I will sketch the dominant interpretations of Eisenhower's Farewell Address, with special reference to the "military-industrial complex." Next, I will introduce an alternative interpretation which, I believe, better accounts for the speech as an artistically and strategically structured whole. Finally, I will offer a close reading of the text using the assumptions of my alternative perspective, a reading that will amount to a complete reconceptualization of the purpose, structure, and function of Eisenhower's Farewell. Before introducing my specific arguments, however, it is necessary to review what others have said about Eisenhower, his famous speech, and the "military-industrial complex."

★ HISTORY AS WRITTEN

Historians of the Eisenhower presidency disagree about the place, importance, and even the main theme of the Farewell Address. Perhaps the dominant interpretive stance, though, is to portray Eisenhower as a man of vision. Biographer Stephen E. Ambrose finds in the Farewell Address the "words of a soldier-prophet."[2] The term "prophetic" recurs throughout his discussion of the speech. Likewise, Herbert York, a physicist and former Director of Defense Research and Engineering under Eisenhower, judges the president's words to be "the product of a remarkable intuition."[3] Such an interpretive stance pictures Eisenhower as a sage old general who, having just discovered in a few short years the existence of a military-industrial complex, thought it wise to warn about its potential dangers sensing, somehow, that the potential would someday become the actual. Although dominant, this strain of interpretation is not without its detractors. One such detractor is economist Seymour Melman.

Melman, author of the 1970 book, *Pentagon Capitalism*, finds Eisenhower anything but sagacious. Disingenuous is perhaps a better descriptor of Melman's interpretive stance toward Eisenhower. To Melman, Eisenhower had known about the military-industrial complex all along and had, in fact, been one of its principal creators and sponsors. Suddenly to decry the existence of the complex at the final hour seems, to Melman and others, disingenuous at best.[4] As historian H. W. Brands observes: "By basing American security on possession of the latest scientific and military technology, Eisenhower delivered enormous power over fundamental policy decisions to an elite of scientists, engineers, and defense bureaucrats. . . . [M]ore than any administration before or after, Eisenhower's promoted the growth of the military-industrial complex he decried."[5]

Prophetic sagacity or sly disingenuousness represent, perhaps, the opposite ends of a continuum of interpretation. Between these extremes lies a vast, undifferentiated middle ground that does not know what to make of Eisenhower or his speech and, in some senses, does not really care. The main concern of this group is not the speaker or speech, per se, but the concept of a military-industrial complex—its dimensions, scope and influence, membership, and how it might be controlled or redirected. Members of this group—if such a motley array of scholars, activists, and

journalists can constitute a group—use the idea of a military-industrial complex as a heuristic tool to explain or interpret certain facts and events. Steven Rosen gives a fair overview of the heuristic potential of the MIC concept when he writes, "The theory [of the military-industrial complex] is employed to explain the high cost of defense, the longevity of the Cold War, the persistence of anticommunist mythology, the 'perverted priorities' of the Federal budget, the interventionist proclivities of American foreign policy, and even the generation of cultural values giving rise to riots and assassinations."[6] Clearly, the concerns of such scholars go far beyond what Eisenhower envisions in his Farewell. Nevertheless, the MIC as heuristic has produced—and continues to produce—scores of analyses, arguments, and debates concerning the economic influences of defense spending,[7] the public policy implications of maintaining a vast defense establishment,[8] and the applicability of the concept to the defense establishments of other nations.[9]

Productive though the MIC heuristic has been, the one common factor in all such studies is the reduction of Eisenhower's Farewell Address to footnote status. None of these books or articles treats the Farewell Address as anything more than a ceremonial precursor to the real business of economic, organizational, strategic, or managerial analysis. In short, while this literature is interesting, it tells us almost nothing about Eisenhower's concept of the military-industrial complex or of the rhetorical functioning of that concept within the context of his Farewell Address. To even begin to understand the MIC's place within the larger rhetorical framework of a strategic response to a set of pragmatic exigencies, one must look elsewhere for guidance, primarily to Eisenhower specialists and scholars of speech communication.

The standard Eisenhower biographies of Ambrose, Lyon, Brendon, and Parmet all treat the Farewell Address, though always in two pages or less. While all read the same speech, they do so in significantly different ways. Ambrose quotes extensively from the speech, claiming that it focuses on "the irony of the Cold War."[10] Lyon devotes only two short paragraphs to the address, concluding that Eisenhower wishes to "be remembered by his contemporaries and by history . . . as the soldier who fought for peace."[11] Brendon, though agreeing that the president "had fought long and hard on several fronts to end the arms race," nevertheless concludes that "no one can be sure how much he meant" his Farewell warnings inasmuch as Eisenhower often used public language to obfuscate the truth.[12] Parmet harbors no such doubts about the president's sincerity, arguing that what Eisenhower "said in the Farewell Address's most widely quoted passage . . . expressed what he felt all along."[13]

Of these four Eisenhower specialists, only Lyon so much as hints at a pragmatic, situation-based rationale for the speech, and this in a single sentence. Other historians of the period—with a few notable exceptions[14]—accept the standard view that Eisenhower, wanting to give a memorable Farewell in the same spirit as his hero, George Washington, passively accepted the military-industrial complex idea as prepared for him by speech writers Malcolm Moos and Ralph Williams. The speech is treated as a vehicle for catching public attention and etching Eisenhower's name into the annals of rhetorical history. There are numerous problems with this view, not the least of which is that it flies in the face of everything we now know about Eisenhower's attitude toward speech making. Eisenhower had no use for mere talk. Public rhetoric was to him a weapon which one used to accomplish a goal. Language was an instrument to be used sparingly, pragmatically, and strategically.[15] Even so, to my knowledge, no historian has investigated the Farewell Address as primarily a strategic response to a contemporary situation, nor has interest in the language or logic of the speech been apparent. For insight into these dimensions, one must turn to scholars of speech and communication studies.

While speech scholars often mention Eisenhower's Farewell Address or use it to illustrate other specialized topics, they have, to date, produced but one extended analysis of the speech and one exploration into its authorship.[16] Consequently, we know relatively little about Eisenhower's Farewell. One of the bright spots in this otherwise sketchy picture is A. Duane Litfin's 1974 study of

Eisenhower on the military-industrial complex. Using techniques of rhetorical criticism, Litfin attempts to reconstruct Eisenhower's answers to three questions: 1) "Must the United States have a military-industrial complex?"; 2) "If we must have a military-industrial complex, what should be its limitations?"; and 3) "Has the military-industrial complex overreached its proper limits?"[17] As the questions suggest, the focus is wholly upon the MIC concept. Not surprisingly, Litfin is unable to provide definitive answers to two of his three questions, though he does an admirable job of weighing the evidence on all sides.

The real contribution of Litfin's study, however, has little to do with the military-industrial complex or the peripheral issue of whether Eisenhower's prestige and authority were being misused by those who, after his death, claimed Ike as one of their allies in the fight against increased defense spending. Litfin, unlike the majority of interpreters, correctly identifies Eisenhower's central theme when he notes that "the main ideas of his Farewell Address all center on the matter of balance." He goes on to note that "Eisenhower's discussion of the potential dangers of the MIC . . . may almost be viewed as an illustration of the point he was seeking to make."[18] Had Litfin followed this insight, he might have produced a much different article, for Eisenhower's Farewell Address, I will argue, has everything to do with balance and very little to do with the military-industrial complex per se.

Another important contribution to the study of Eisenhower's Farewell Address is Charles J. G. Griffin's recent essay that focuses on new evidence concerning the authorship of the phrase "military-industrial complex." Griffin suggests that Eisenhower attempted to achieve several ends with his speech, one of which was to "score a tactical blow against his political adversaries."[19] The present study does not dispute Griffin's findings, but argues that the idea—as opposed to the actual wording—for inclusion of the military-industrial complex came from a different source than that identified by Griffin. The present study also holds that Eisenhower's "tactical blow" was not against his political adversaries generally, but was directed specifically against president-elect John F. Kennedy and his economic proposals.

★ RECONCEPTUALIZING THE SPEECH

To understand Eisenhower's Farewell Address, one must attend to the rhetorical history of which it is a culmination. Such a history would, at minimum, include: a) what Eisenhower had previously said on the subjects of balance and military-industrial relations, b) the structure, arguments, and antecedent patterns that Eisenhower drew upon when putting the speech together, and c) the situational exigencies incumbent upon one delivering a farewell address at this particular point in time. By examining the speech from each of these perspectives, I will demonstrate that Eisenhower's Farewell Address, far from being visionary, prophetic, disingenuous, or merely perfunctory is, instead, a carefully planned piece of strategic discourse intended to accomplish several goals simultaneously.

Three strategic goals stand out: to restate the basic themes and philosophies that had characterized Eisenhower's public life; to link the president historically, conceptually, and attitudinally to the persona of George Washington; and to advance, under the rubric of a warning about the military-industrial complex, an indirect and implicit critique of John F. Kennedy while making a direct and explicit appeal for citizen involvement to thwart the designs of the newly elected administration. Before explicating the ways in which Eisenhower attempts rhetorically to achieve these goals, it is necessary to review some of the situational and personal exigencies that called forth such a strategic response.

Situational Exigencies

That Eisenhower recognized specific situational imperatives and attempted to respond to them there is no doubt. He had become increasingly frustrated by the seeming lack of understanding, both in the public at large and within Congress, concerning America's defense position relative to that of the Soviet Union's. Since the 1957 surprise launching of Sputnik I by the U.S.S.R., Eisenhower had endured talk about a supposed "missile gap" as well as charges that he was sacrificing America's security on the altar of a balanced budget. In later years at least one defense expert would find it a great "historical irony that the administration, which had presided over the buildup of America's decisive military edge, should stand condemned at its close for 'neglecting the national defenses'."[20] Yet that is precisely what Eisenhower was charged with by his Democratic opponents.

Second, and as a direct result of the Sputnik launching, Eisenhower had witnessed an ever-increasing effort to lobby the executive branch on behalf of specific weapons systems each, it seemed, more technologically sophisticated than the one preceding. As one member of his administration has noted: "The people who irritated him were the hard-sell technologists who tried to exploit Sputnik and the missile gap psychosis it engendered. . . . In the months after Sputnik, their claims that they could solve the problem if only someone would unleash them carried a lot of weight with the public and some segments of the Congress and press."[21] Although Eisenhower found it "not at all difficult" to ignore the purveyors of technological wonders or "the generals and admirals clamoring for more money for their services,"[22] he was not so sure of others' abilities to withstand the constant onslaught.

Finally, Eisenhower felt compelled to respond to the situation that the events of November 8, 1960, had occasioned with the election of John F. Kennedy. Not only had Kennedy been an early and vocal proponent of the missile gap theory, but he had continued to use the issue throughout the fall campaign, asserting that the times "demand a man capable of acting as the Commander-in-Chief of the grand alliance, not merely a bookkeeper who feels that his work is done when the numbers on the balance sheet come out even."[23] Offended as he was at Kennedy's implied criticism of his military skills, Eisenhower was most worried about the president-elect's seeming lack of concern or understanding about the national economy and the potentially devastating effects of military spending on that economy.

This was not a new concern for Eisenhower. On August 20, 1956, he had written to his old friend Everett "Swede" Hazlett: "But some day there is going to be a man sitting in my present chair who has not been raised in the military services and who will have little understanding of where slashes in their estimates can be made with little or no damage. If that should happen while we still have the state of tension that now exists in the world, I shudder to think of what could happen in this country."[24] By 1961, that "day" had arrived.

After a personal meeting with the president-elect on December 6, 1960—a meeting at which Eisenhower specifically advised Kennedy that if any "streamlining" was to be done that it should come "in a mechanism such as the defense establishment"[25]—Eisenhower came to the realization that his advice would not be heeded. As Ambrose notes, Eisenhower found "that his views had already been examined and rejected by the Kennedy team, which certainly did intend to spend more than it took in, to cut taxes, and to dramatically increase defense spending."[26] At some point after the December 6 meeting, Eisenhower decided that he must alert the public to the impending danger, not of the military or the industrialists, but of a headstrong executive who, given his beliefs and attitudes, could endanger American security by failing to stand up to the spendthrifts within the military-industrial complex. His vehicle would be the speech then in preparation—the Farewell Address. But a farewell, by its very nature, had to be more than a warning. It had also to be the final summation of a life lived in the public spotlight, the last brushstroke on a canvas of words and actions stretching back to World War II.[27] The speech had to reflect not only Eisenhower the president, but Eisenhower the symbol of freedom and democracy.

Personal Exigencies

This was to be the farewell of a president, but more than that, the last official pronouncement of a national and international hero, a man who had devoted "half a century in the service of our country." During the course of those fifty years—from his appointment to West Point in 1911 until his retirement from the presidency

in 1961—Dwight D. Eisenhower had cultivated the public image of a man to whom duty was all. Few knew Eisenhower the man, but all were familiar with the public persona, a persona characterized by "commonality, dedication, considerateness, humility, and a special sort of moral vision."[28] To many, the very name "Eisenhower" was symbolic of democracy's triumph over the evil of fascism. Only once before in the history of the Republic had a hero-president served for so long or been a living embodiment of the hopes, attributes, and aspirations of an entire people. That president, too, had put his name to a farewell address and it was that example—the example of Eisenhower's personal hero, George Washington—that inspired Eisenhower's own farewell.

According to noted journalist and presidential chronicler Robert J. Donovan, Eisenhower had begun thinking about a farewell speech some years before his retirement from office. Donovan reports: "One day in the fall of 1958 [speechwriter Malcolm] Moos . . . was showing President Eisenhower a book on great presidential decisions and speeches. Included was George Washington's Farewell Address. The President was fascinated to hear Moos say that many historians believed Alexander Hamilton had ghosted the speech for Washington. 'I hope you'll be thinking about this,' Gen. Eisenhower said. . . . He told Moos he hoped that on leaving office two years hence he could . . . 'say something significant'."[29]

Of course, what Washington said of significance, at least to later generations, was his warnings against factions or parties and his admonition to avoid foreign entanglements. But Eisenhower's debt to Washington, I shall argue, goes far beyond the mere inclusion of warnings. Eisenhower seeks to link himself and his service to the country to Washington—historically, conceptually, and even in terms of attitudes about the presidency and public service. Although Washington did not deliver his address to Congress in person, he clearly envisioned the Congress and other political elites as his primary audience. Eisenhower's original intention was also to direct his speech to a joint session of Congress, in part because of the theme he wished to develop, and in part because it would echo his triumphant appearance before that body in April of 1945. That Eisenhower was giving serious consideration to just such a farewell is revealed in a personal letter which he sent to his brother Milton, on May 25, 1959, in which he writes: "I have, as yet, no fixed idea that I should deliver a so-called 'farewell' talk to the Congress, even if that body should invite me to do so. The reason I have been toying with this idea is because of my experience—which by that time will have extended to a full six years—in working with a Congress controlled by the opposite political party. Needless to say, there would be no profit in expressing, in such a setting, anything that was partisan in character. Rather I think the purpose would be to emphasize a few homely truths that apply to the responsibilities and duties of a government that must be responsive to the will of majorities, even when the decisions of those majorities create apparent paradoxes."[30]

One of the paradoxes faced by Eisenhower after November 8, 1960, was what to say to an electorate that seemingly wanted a balanced budget, low inflation, and adequate defenses, but which had, nonetheless, just voted into office a candidate who believed in deficit financing, tax cuts to stimulate the economy, and vastly increased defense spending—far beyond the level that Eisenhower thought either reasonable or safe. The election results therefore brought about a change in Eisenhower's thinking. Even though Moos and others still favored an appearance before Congress, "Eisenhower preferred to speak from his office over television."[31] In so choosing, the president changed both the primary audience for his remarks and the content of what he would say. Although he would still speak about the "responsibilities and duties" of democratic government, he would do so in a way that clearly was "partisan in character," though the attack would be indirect, employing Eisenhower's well-honed skills at argument by implication.[32] The public stance would still be that of Washington's: above party politics, responsive only to the call of duty, a forger of consensus and cooperation, and a dedicated servant of democracy whose sole concern is the survival and welfare of the Republic. Table 1 illustrates the numerous conceptual and attitudinal similarities between the Eisenhower and Washington farewells. But Eisenhower is trying to do more than just link himself historically and conceptually with Washington. He uses Washington to help fashion his self-portrait but supplements that use with ideas and images drawn from his own public career, particularly images of balance and ideas about military, industrial, and economic relationships. The self-portrait and the repetition of standard Eisenhower themes helps to give the appearance of staying above partisanship while reinforcing those qualities and concepts for which the president wishes to be remembered. At the same time, the portrait and themes are handled in such a way as to form a powerful argument by implication, the implication being that Kennedy's approach is wrong and that if the public values its freedom then it should become the kind of audience that a democratic system requires: alert, critical, and active in the defense of freedom.

★ ANALYSIS OF THE TEXT

The speech itself is divided into an introduction, four thematic passages, and a conclusion. The thematic sections deal with 1) congressional relations, 2) peace and progress, 3) balance in the present situation, and 4) balance in future situations. Each section features an implied or explicit balance within the development of the theme. Under congressional relations, for example, the implied balance is that between the legislative and executive branches. Under peace and progress, the balance is between the external threat of communism and the internal threat of unwise, precipitant action. The need for balance in the present situation is a multifaceted subject that Eisenhower reduces to two well-chosen illustrations: the acquisition of unwarranted influence by the military-industrial complex and the increasing power of the scientific-technological elite, both of which are themselves balanced by virtue of their positive and negative aspects. Likewise, the need for balance in future situations has two components that must, themselves, be balanced: the domestic economy and the requirements of international security. The speech thus becomes an artistic exemplar of the

TABLE 1

Eisenhower-Washington Analogs

SERVICE TO THE COUNTRY

Eisenhower: "Three days from now, after half a century in the service of our country, I shall lay down the responsibilities of office."

Washington: "[A]fter forty-five years of my life dedicated to its service with an upright zeal."

DEVOTION TO NATIONAL GOOD

Eisenhower: "May we be ever unswerving in devotion to principle, confident but humble with power, diligent in pursuit of the Nation's great goals."

Washington: "[T]hat the free Constitution, which is the work of your hands, may be sacredly maintained; that this administration in every department may be stamped with wisdom and virtue."

A FREE AND RELIGIOUS PEOPLE

Eisenhower: "[O]ur basic purposes have been to keep the peace; to foster progress in human achievement, and to enhance liberty, dignity and integrity among people and among nations. To strive for less would be unworthy of a free and religious people."

Washington: "Of all the dispositions and habits which lead to political prosperity, religion and morality are indispensable supports. . . . Reason and experience both forbid us to expect that national morality can prevail in exclusion of religious principle."

POTENTIAL FOR MISPLACED POWER

Eisenhower: "In the councils of government, we must guard against the acquisition of unwarranted influence, whether sought or unsought, by the military-industrial complex. The potential for the disastrous rise of misplaced power exists and will persist. We must never let the weight of this combination endanger our liberties or democratic processes."

Washington: "All obstructions to the execution of the laws, all combinations and associations, under whatever plausible character, with the real design to direct, control, counteract, or awe the regular deliberation and action of the constituted authorities, are destructive of this fundamental principle, and of fatal tendency."

AN EDUCATED AND ALERT CITIZENRY

Eisenhower: "Only an alert and knowledgeable citizenry can compel the proper meshing of the huge industrial and military machinery defense with our peaceful methods and goals, so that security and liberty may prosper together."

Washington: "Promote, then, as an object of primary importance, institutions for the general diffusion of knowledge. In proportion as the structure of a government gives force to public opinion, it is essential that public opinion should be enlightened."

---

principle it champions. It is about balance and it is balanced.

Introduction

Eisenhower's first sentence encompasses each of his strategic purposes as he says, "Three days from now, after half a century in the service of our country, I shall lay down the responsibilities of office as, in traditional and solemn ceremony, the authority of the Presidency is vested in my successor." Here is foreshadowed the self-portrait of a hero in the tradition of Washington ("half a century in the service of our country"), the review of Eisenhower's governmental philosophy ("the responsibilities of office"), and his concern about Kennedy's use or misuse of executive authority ("the Presidency is vested in my successor"). He calls his speech a "message of leave-taking and farewell" that he wishes to share with "my countrymen." Throughout the address, Eisenhower identifies himself with the audience, an audience that he will eventually ask to be alert, aware, and critical—just as he is and will remain. But in the introduction,

TABLE 1 - (continued)

Eisenhower-Washington Analogs

WARNING OF DANGERS

Eisenhower: "This conjunction of an immense military establishment and a large arms industry is new in the American experience. The total influence—economic, political, even spiritual—is felt in every city, every State house, every office of the Federal government. We recognize the imperative needs for this development. Yet we must not fail to comprehend its grave implications."

Washington: "Hence, likewise, they will avoid the necessity of those overgrown military establishments which, under any form of government, are inauspicious to liberty, and which are to be regarded as particularly hostile to republican liberty."

FISCAL INTEGRITY

Eisenhower: "[W]e—you and I, and our government—must avoid the impulse to live only for today, plundering, for our own ease and convenience, the precious resources of tomorrow. We cannot mortgage the material assets of our grandchildren without risking the loss also of their political and spiritual heritage."

Washington: "As a very important source of strength and security, cherish public credit . . . avoiding likewise the accumulation of debt . . . not ungenerously throwing upon posterity the burden which we ourselves ought to bear."

MUTUAL TRUST AND RESPECT

Eisenhower: "America knows that this world of ours, ever growing smaller, must avoid becoming a community of dreadful fear and hate, and be, instead, a proud confederation of mutual trust and respect. Such a confederation must be one of equals."

Washington: "Observe good faith and justice toward all nations; cultivate peace and harmony with all. . . . It will be worthy of a free, enlightened, and, at no distant period, a great nation, to give to mankind the magnanimous and too novel example of a people always guided by an exalted justice and benevolence."

TONE OF SELF-DEPRECATION

Eisenhower: "I trust that in that service you find some things worthy; as for the rest of it, I know you will always find ways to improve performance in the future."

Washington: "Though, in reviewing the incidents of my administration, I am unconscious of intentional error, I am nevertheless too sensible of my defects not to think it probable that I have committed many errors."

Eisenhower, "like every other citizen," wishes the new president "Godspeed" and prays that "the coming years will be blessed with peace and prosperity"—just, he implies, as the last eight years have been.

Congressional Relations

Eisenhower moves into the body of the Farewell with a short remembrance of his various relationships with Congress, relationships that he characterizes as having moved from "remote" to "intimate" and, finally, to "mutually interdependent." "In this final relationship," says Eisenhower, "the Congress and the Administration have, on most vital issues, cooperated well, to serve the national good rather than mere partisanship." In one sentence, Eisenhower summarizes what he has learned by working with an opposition Congress. This experience, which he earlier saw as the central focus of what he might say in a farewell, is here reduced to the most general level, picturing the president as above "mere partisanship" and as dedicated only to the "national good." Whereas Washington had warned about the "spirit of encroachment,"[33] whereby one branch of government could be tempted to usurp the powers of another, Eisenhower contents himself with emphasizing the effort "to find essential agreement on issues of great moment." This is a particularly interesting choice inasmuch as Eisenhower had not, in fact, enjoyed much cooperation from Congress over the course of his last three years in office. His second term, like Washington's, had been marked by sharp debates, policy failures, and continual disagreements between the executive and legislative branches. Washington chose to highlight his problems; Eisenhower chooses to speak of the principles in which he believes— balance between the branches and a spirit of cooperation—principles about which he had spoken with fervor throughout his public life.

Peace and Progress

Having established one key component of his belief system, Eisenhower next moves to the theme of peace and progress. "Peace, prosperity and progress" had been the 1956 Republican campaign theme, and Eisenhower had echoed that refrain in various combinations throughout his second term. The Farewell is no exception. Eisenhower fulfills the generic demand of characterizing one's stewardship by proclaiming, "America is today the strongest, the most influential and most productive nation in the world." In so speaking, Eisenhower also provides for himself an indirect defense against recent Democratic charges—that America had grown weak, that her influence abroad was at an all-time low, and that the country was standing still instead of pushing forward. Lest anyone doubt Eisenhower's view of such beliefs, he follows the descriptors "strongest" and "most influential" with reference to America's "pre-eminence" and "unmatched material progress, riches and military strength." During the 1960 campaign, John Kennedy had charged that "our security and leadership are both slipping away from us,"[34] but to Eisenhower such assertions were "a debasement of the truth"[35] and "without foundation."[36] Now, though indirectly, he is once again rebutting Kennedy and in so doing reasserting his standing as a good steward.

But Eisenhower is not content merely to rebut. He also offers an implicit critique of the Kennedy approach to governance by noting that "peace," "progress," and "liberty" are the only goals worthy of "a free and religious people. Any failure traceable to arrogance, or our lack of comprehension or readiness to sacrifice," says Eisenhower, "would inflict upon us grievous hurt both at home and abroad." Here Eisenhower is simultaneously placing himself in the rhetorical shadow of George Washington by linking political freedom with religious sentiment while repeating the same criticisms he had made of Kennedy during the fall campaign. On November 4, 1960, for example, Eisenhower said: "When the push of a button may mean obliteration of countless humans, the President of the United States must be forever on guard against any inclination on his part to impetuosity; to arrogance; to headlong action; to expediency; to facile maneuvers; even to the popularity of an action as opposed to the rightness of an action."[37] The implication is clear: anyone who acts first and thinks later is endangering the peace. Such a person is not only reckless, but arrogant—a term Eisenhower repeatedly applied to the political opposition during the fall campaign, and to which he returns in the Farewell Address.

Having introduced the theme of peace and progress, Eisenhower, again echoing the structure of Washington's farewell, turns to two threats—one external and one internal— that could undermine the peace. The external threat is international communism. "We face a hostile ideology," says the president, "global in scope, atheistic in character, ruthless in purpose, and insidious in method. Unhappily the danger it poses promises to be of indefinite duration. To meet it successfully, there is called for, not so much the emotional and transitory sacrifices of crisis, but rather those which enable us to carry forward steadily, surely, and without complaint the burdens of a prolonged and complex struggle—with liberty the stake." There is nothing new in Eisenhower's characterization of the communist threat. "Hostile," "global," "atheistic," "ruthless," and "insidious" are commonplaces of the Eisenhower lexicon of communist epithets. They can be found in dozens of his speeches from 1946 to 1961 and beyond. This is standard Cold War rhetoric,[38] the basic presuppositions of which were shared, in 1961, by majorities in both the Democratic and Republican parties. What was not common was agreement on the methods by which such an implacable foe ought to be fought. To Eisenhower—in his Farewell Address as in all his presidential speaking—the point of waging Cold War is to avoid conflicts that could flare into physical warfare. His well-known tactics of strategic ambiguity, indirection, delay, and implied threat were specifically designed for the purpose of avoiding certain actions, under the assumption—proven correct some thirty years later—that the longer hot war could be avoided the more likely communism would be to collapse from its own inherent weaknesses.[39] Eisenhower's power politics, like his bridge game, was a matter of waiting, cooperation, and strategic timing. Those who advocated a world view where "crises" were central and individual heroic effort at moments of maximum danger the preferred solution—a world view implicit in a book such as *Profiles in Courage*[40]—struck Eisenhower as dangerous, brash, and lacking in the patience necessary to win the Cold War, a war that was certain to be "a prolonged and complex struggle."

If the external threat of communism is ongoing, so too is the internal threat—what Eisenhower calls the "recurring temptation"— to look to "some spectacular and costly action" as the "miraculous solution to all current difficulties." Here, again, is an implicit criticism of the Kennedy penchant for immediate action. In response to Kennedy's campaign call to get the country moving again, Eisenhower said: "Your President . . . must thoroughly think through the problems of our time. In this he cannot succeed unless he is free of rashness; of arrogance; of headlong action; of the inclination to easy compromise. I hear that one candidate says he will act first and act fast. My friends, America needs a man who will think first, and then act wisely."[41] Though the Farewell's critique is oblique, the code words of "arrogance," "crisis," and "action" are clear indicators to anyone familiar with the Eisenhower rhetorical record—and certainly

to John F. Kennedy—that the target of this criticism is the man who is about to follow Eisenhower into the Oval Office.

Eisenhower offers as examples of such "spectacular and costly action" the following: "A huge increase in newer elements of our defense; development of unrealistic programs to cure every ill in agriculture; a dramatic expansion in basic and applied research"—all of which are positions advocated by John F. Kennedy. Note, also, that in each example cited, greatly increased expenditures—government expenditures—are involved. This is the heart of Eisenhower's criticism—that new programs, "each possibly promising in itself," not be implemented unless the economic effects on the system as a whole are first examined. It is concern for *economic* consequences that leads to the need for balance and that allows Eisenhower to make the transition into the third and central portion of the speech—the need for balance in present programs.

Balance in the Present

"But each proposal," says Eisenhower, "must be weighed in the light of a broader consideration: the need to maintain balance in and among national programs—balance between the private and the public economy, balance between cost and hoped for advantage—balance between the clearly necessary and the comfortably desirable; balance between our essential requirements as a nation and the duties imposed by the nation upon the individual; balance between actions of the moment and the national welfare of the future." If there is any one topic or theme that can be said to be uniquely Eisenhower's, that theme is the need for balance. For as far back as Eisenhower's views can be traced, the theme of balance has been present. In November 1945, for example, the general wrote to his childhood friend and frequent correspondent, Swede Hazlett, asserting that "the whole program of preparation must be a balanced one."[42] The following year, he cautioned that disarmament not be "unbalanced"[43] and, later in 1946, explained to the Veterans of Foreign Wars that "the adjustment of our security forces so that they shall be in balanced effectiveness to meet the nation's needs is a task at once complicated and urgent."[44] Balance was a standard Eisenhower *topos* long before he assumed the presidency and continued to be such throughout his life.

Understanding Eisenhower's concept of balance is crucial to a proper appreciation of the rhetorical structure and functioning of the Farewell Address, for contrary to most commentary on the speech the central idea being expressed is not the military-industrial complex. The MIC is but one of two examples—two warnings—used to illustrate the dangers of imbalance. As Eisenhower says, "Good judgment seeks balance and progress; lack of it eventually finds imbalance and frustration." The president then turns to the discussion of the military-industrial complex and the scientific-technological elite, both of which are offered as examples of what can happen if balance is not maintained.

Before turning to a detailed analysis of these most famous sections of the Farewell, it is important to reiterate their structural import to the speech as a unified whole. Already Eisenhower has defended his stewardship and proclaimed America peaceful, prosperous, and progressive. Already he has criticized, albeit implicitly, those who are arrogant, too reactive to momentary crises, and prone to action before analysis. In short, he has criticized Kennedy. Now, having introduced the theme of balance, the Republican president is about to warn of the two areas in which he believes Kennedy—*the man who is about to upset the balance*—to be potentially most dangerous. Both areas have to do, primarily, with economic dangers—the danger of spending too much on new weapons systems, and the danger of federal contract dollars making the private sector financially dependent on the public purse and, to that extent, in danger of losing its freedom. But notice, too, that both warnings are, themselves, balanced. Danger lies on the extremes. Only the middle of the road—the balanced approach used by Eisenhower himself—is safe.[45]

Unfortunately, many students of the Eisenhower era have been so taken by the concept of a military-industrial complex that they have failed to understand its place in the internal logic of the speech or the evolution of the concept within Eisenhower's own rhetorical practices. While the precise phrase "the military-industrial complex" is apparently unique to the Farewell—a creation of Eisenhower speechwriters Malcolm Moos and Ralph Williams—the topic of military-industrial relations is standard Eisenhower fare. There is no need to turn, as Melman does, to an internal memorandum from 1946, or to report, as Parmet does, the private conversations Eisenhower allegedly held aboard the *Helena* in 1952, to account for the general's views on the topic of military-industrial relations. All one need do is read the public record. Litfin is incorrect when he asserts that "it was not until fifteen years later, however, in his farewell address, that Eisenhower publicly spelled out his views,"[46] on the proper relationship between the military and industry. To the contrary, Eisenhower's views are public record: clear, relatively complete, and highly consistent.

While the internal logic of the Farewell Address suggests that the warnings about the MIC and the STE are part of the ongoing critique of Kennedy, so too does one highly placed external source. This source is the person most probably responsible for the inclusion of the *concept* of military-industrial relations in the Farewell Address; the person whose knowledge of the inner workings and political clout of the complex matched or surpassed Eisenhower's; the person who hired and trained Malcolm Moos and who consulted with Moos during the drafting of the speech; the person whom former Eisenhower ghostwriter William Bragg Ewald, Jr.[,] describes as "a five-foot-four-inch Oklahoma veteran of congressional infighting, who through eight years of the presidency and eight more of the ex-presidency would serve Dwight Eisenhower as son serves father, with more energy, devotion, tirelessness, street-wise counsel, and selflessness than almost anyone else."[47] It is an apt description of Bryce Harlow.

Starting in 1937, Bryce Harlow had been at the center of the governmental debate over military-industrial relations. He had served as Chief of Staff of the House Armed Services Committee, as a staff assistant to General George C. Marshall during World War II, and, during the 1950s, as both head speech writer and chief of congressional relations for Dwight D. Eisenhower. As Harlow put it in a personal interview with the author, "I had to use the lobbying power of the Pentagon extensively. Awesome. I mean awesome. . . . I had passed bills and played with the game. I knew how to play the game. By the time I got out of that, I was pretty good at this stuff."[48]

Harlow, who next to Milton Eisenhower, was Ike's closest confidant when it came to speeches and public messages, consulted closely with Malcolm Moos on the Farewell Address during the final days of the Eisenhower administration. Harlow admitted to being "frightened by the power capabilities of the military after Eisenhower left office." The reason for Harlow's concern was not that he thought the military might deliberately try to subvert American liberties, but rather that he doubted the incoming administration's abilities to withstand the lobbying power of the military and their industrial suppliers. Such a concern had not been salient for Harlow during the 1950s precisely because Eisenhower was in charge. As Harlow observed:

> Eisenhower was the only president since George Washington—possibly U.S. Grant—who could tell the military to go jam it. And they'd respect that because Eisenhower had commanded more military strength than any person in the history of the world. So these military chieftains . . . [would] come in to see him. "Hey boss man. We gotta have this, we gotta have that." [He would] say, "Oh, come off it. Take that back. Start over." Ike did that. He'd laugh at them sometimes [and] say, "I used that same argument fifteen years ago, take it back." And they had to. They couldn't mess with him because they couldn't challenge him in the bar of American opinion.

But Harlow began to worry about what would happen if a chief executive occupied the White House who could not or would not tell the military when enough was enough. "I talked to the president about it a number of times," said Harlow. "Under the national security structure that we had created—the Defense Department, with the Joint Chiefs insulated in there and meeting . . . [and] lobbying in secret

amongst themselves [doing] tradeouts—how to control that in the future? A future president could be put upon by the Joint Chiefs."

Here was the crux of the concern—that a president lacking the intimate knowledge and public credibility of a Dwight Eisenhower might someday find himself at the mercy of forces that he did not fully understand and whose spending requirements he could not refuse. Such a concern was particularly salient with Kennedy about to assume the presidency because the president-elect, even before being subjected to the lobbying power of the Pentagon, was promising huge increases in defense spending. The concern in this section of the Farewell Address is not, therefore, about the military-industrial complex per se, but about the ability of future decision makers to utilize that complex in a balanced way, both to protect individual liberties and to prevent the nation as a whole from becoming a garrison state.

Harlow confirmed this interpretation when he noted that "the thing was to try to protect . . . the presidency against being raped in the future after America's number one military president had retired—and this [speech] was the outcome of that." Harlow discussed his concerns with both Eisenhower and Moos. He recalled that "I had Mac [Moos] change what we first put down because of the way he had originally wrote [sic] it—it sounded like they were deliberately trying to subvert our liberties. They don't do that." While Moos and Williams did most of the actual drafting of the speech, with some crucial assistance from Milton Eisenhower, the ideas with which they were working came from the president and Harlow, and the primary motivation behind those ideas was a concern for what might happen should a new chief executive succumb to the blandishments of the militarists, industrialists, and technologists. Both were worried about maintaining the requisite balance between military preparedness and domestic economy.

Reflecting this belief in the need for balance in defense spending and consciously placing himself in the tradition of America's first military president—a president whose farewell address also warned against "overgrown military establishments"[49]—Eisenhower begins with a thesis: "A vital element in keeping the peace is our military establishment." Throughout the first warning, Eisenhower emphasizes what he had repeatedly preached since the end of World War II—the absolute necessity of a military-industrial complex. Far from calling the need for such a complex into question, Eisenhower explicitly and repeatedly defends its role in national security. He follows his thesis statement by observing: "Until the latest of our world conflicts, the United States had no armaments industry. American makers of plowshares could, with time and as required, make swords as well. But now we can no longer risk emergency improvisation of national defense; we have been compelled to create a permanent armaments industry of vast proportions."

It is important to note that the Eisenhower of January 1961 is, in this portion of the Farewell, saying precisely the same thing that he had said some fifteen years earlier when, in April of 1946, he opined: "National security is a state of organized readiness to meet external aggression by a quick and effective mobilization of public opinion, trained men, proven weapons, and essential industries, integrated into the most efficient instrument of armed defense."[50] Ten months later, in January 1947, Eisenhower warned: "We cannot, however, permit a wall of preoccupation with the pursuits of a still unquiet peace to separate industry from the armed forces. . . . An incontestable conclusion that emerges from WW II is that modern wars are fought with the concerted strength of whole nations, and that the integration of our national economy into an effective security machine must be accomplished—in theory and in plans—before an emergency occurs."[51] From the end of World War II all the way through—and including—his Farewell Address, Eisenhower endorsed military-industrial cooperation and partnership.

The first part of the Farewell's initial warning, then, concerns the crucial role played by the armaments industry. As Eisenhower puts it: "This conjunction of an immense military establishment and a large arms industry is new in the American experience. The total influence—economic, political, even spiritual—is felt in every city, every State house, every office of the Federal government. We recognize

the imperative need for this development." Here, then, is the first half of the equation—the necessity for a military-industrial partnership. But the other half of the equation is equally necessary if America is to maintain the balance that Eisenhower desires. It is not enough to recognize the importance and necessity of this new military-industrial development, we must also, says Eisenhower, "not fail to comprehend its grave implications," implications that involve "the very structure of our society." It is here that Eisenhower makes the transition to the other half of the equation. Just as balance is the main theme of his speech, so the warning about the military-industrial complex is, itself, balanced. First he treats the positive aspect of enhanced security, then he turns to the negative potential of "misplaced power" which, it is important to note, Eisenhower locates "in the councils of government." His concern is that the power of decision making, located "in the councils of government"—and especially in the executive and legislative branches—will somehow become "misplaced." That the people who ought to be making the decisions based on the overall good of the nation will, instead, succumb to the power of the military-industrial lobby.

"In the councils of government," says Eisenhower, "we must guard against the acquisition of unwarranted influence, whether sought or unsought, by the military-industrial complex. The potential for the disastrous rise of misplaced power exists and will persist. We must never let the weight of this combination endanger our liberties or democratic processes. We should take nothing for granted.["] Although the use of the linguistic formulation "military-industrial complex" is unique to this passage, the *general idea* being expressed is not. Indeed, even as he was in the process of helping to build America's military-industrial complex during and immediately following World War II, Eisenhower was pointing to its potential dangers. "The security establishment of our democracy," said Eisenhower in 1946, "must always remain representative of our way of life. It must not be a belligerent and noisy horde, screaming threats of atomic destruction, disrupting world harmony. It must not attempt to build the country into a warehouse or stockpile for war."[52] Eisenhower's concern in 1946, as well as in 1961, was primarily economic in nature. The nation needed a sufficient deterrent, but anything beyond sufficiency was, to Eisenhower, merely wasteful. As he told an audience on February 24, 1947, "Every army activity should be held under a critical eye to determine that satisfaction of national needs does not provide excuse for indulgence in careless spending. There is no risk or danger in such economy. Quite the contrary."[53] So, far from being a turn away from his earlier beliefs, the Farewell Address is a culmination of viewpoints expressed many times throughout Eisenhower's public career. It is consistent, in its entirety, with his previous public rhetoric, though its strategic purposes go far beyond mere repetition.

The MIC warning concludes with Eisenhower's observation that "only an alert and knowledgeable citizenry can compel the proper meshing of the huge industrial and military machinery of defense with our peaceful methods and goals, so that security and liberty may prosper together." In this passage, too, Eisenhower is reiterating what had become a commonplace in his public rhetoric. As early as 1946, he claimed that "intelligent familiarity with our military problems is as essential to good citizenship as is knowledge of public schools or public finance."[54] By 1960, Eisenhower was still sounding the theme: "[T]he citizenry cannot abandon its inherent function of critical, self-examination of performance," said he. "All of us must see that the policy decisions of our government officials are responsive to the needs, objectives, values, and historic tendencies of the American people."[55]

So the balanced warning about the MIC, like the sections that come before it, serves several strategic functions for Eisenhower. It continues to portray him as a rhetorical and conceptual heir of Washington, it restates ideas, including the necessity of a military-industrial complex, upon which Eisenhower had based his public career, and it raises concerns about the ability of those in government to resist the blandishments of the MIC, a concern made especially salient by Kennedy's previously announced positions and imminent elevation to the presidency. Equally strategic is Eisenhower's second warning concerning the scientific-technological elite, which he describes as "akin to, and largely

responsible for the sweeping changes in our industrial-military posture." Like the MIC, this warning, too, has equal and opposite dimensions that require judgment and balance.

On one side is "the prospect of domination of the nation's scholars by Federal employment, project allocations, and the power of money," a domination that Eisenhower describes as "ever present" and "gravely to be regarded." The other part of the equation, though, is "the equal and opposite danger that public policy could itself become the captive of a scientific-technological elite." The first concern—that government money and contracts could lead to loss of independence—is not new to Eisenhower. Indeed, one of his major goals upon assuming the presidency in 1953 was to restore a sense of balance between public and private initiative. In practice this meant not trying very hard to roll back surviving New Deal initiatives, a stance that later led Barry Goldwater to describe Eisenhower's administration as "a dime-store New Deal."[56] But this approach also meant not expanding the domain of government any further than it had already been extended. Eisenhower expressed his view on such matters in a 1954 letter to Hazlett, writing: "[I]f Federal authority should be extended throughout the country, through various subterfuges of corporations, authorities, loans and grants, it would eventually stifle the individual freedom that our government was assigned to protect and preserve."[57] In 1959, Eisenhower applied the same reasoning to scientific research when he said: "We must recognize the possibility that the Federal Government, with its vast resources and its increasing dependence upon science, could largely pre-empt the field or blunt private initiative and individual opportunity. This we must never permit."[58] The key, as Eisenhower repeats in his Farewell Address, is to find a "balance between the private and the public economy." Even though one university president (Milton Eisenhower) and one soon-to-be university president (Malcolm Moos) helped draft the speech, Eisenhower needed no instruction on the dangers of federal largesse to educational institutions or its potential negative effect on the "nation's scholars." Both his experience as president of Columbia University and the belief he shared with Washington about the centrality and importance of "enlightened" public opinion compelled him to recognize the potential imbalance that federal domination of education could bring. But if experience and philosophy calls forth one part of the warning, the immediate political situation calls forth the second part.

Public policy becoming the captive of a scientific-technological elite is, for Eisenhower, merely another outworking of a military-industrial complex acquiring unwarranted influence. Just as the president must guard against one-sided advice from generals and munitions makers, so too must he be on guard against technologists—many in scientific guise—who promise a quick technological fix to the ongoing problems of the Cold War. To Eisenhower, there is no such thing as a quick fix, as he repeatedly told audiences throughout his presidency. Although he believed in making "maximum use of science and technology in order to minimize numbers in men,"[59] he also believed in the "development of sound, long-term security . . . characterized by a stability that is not materially disturbed by every propaganda effort of unfriendly nations."[60] One such propaganda effort, in his estimation, was the launching of Sputnik I in 1957. "Earth satellites, in themselves," he told the American people, "have no direct present effect upon the nation's security."[61] But the propaganda effect was, nevertheless, achieved, with ever-more pressure being brought to bear on the executive to do something about what some members of Congress, the press, and the public perceived to be a shortfall in America's defense structure. Eisenhower responded by noting that "whatever the cost, America will keep itself secure. But in the process we must not, by our own hand, destroy or distort the American system. This we could do," said the president, "by useless overspending."[62]

Since it is the president who, more often than not, must apply the brake to the momentum of ever-greater defense spending, Eisenhower concludes his second warning by returning to the theme of balance. "It is the task of statesmanship," says he, "to mold, to balance, and to integrate these and other forces, new and old, within the principles of our democratic system—ever aiming toward the supreme goals

of our free society." The critique is implicit, to be sure, but Eisenhower always selected his words with care and precision. Is John F. Kennedy a statesman or is he merely a politician? Can he withstand the pressures that will be brought upon him and steer clear of the dangers posed by a military-industrial complex and a scientific-technological elite both of which could, unless checked, sap the country's economic strength, transform her into a garrison state, and thereby substitute security for liberty? These are the questions that Eisenhower poses indirectly and implicatively.

Balance in the Future

Balance, though portrayed as a problem of the present, is not something that can be solved today and forgotten about tomorrow. The fourth thematic section thus projects balance into the future and focuses attention on two resources: the future economy and future security needs. Again, the relationship between the principles of fiscal management and those of national and international security are featured. "As we peer into society's future," says Eisenhower, "we—you and I, and our government—must avoid the impulse to live only for today, plundering, for our own ease and convenience, the precious resources of tomorrow. We cannot mortgage the material assets of our grandchildren without risking the loss also of their political and spiritual heritage." Although the syntax is rough, it is not without purpose. The "we" has two parts: "you and I" on the one hand, and "our government" on the other. Eisenhower identifies himself with the average person's concern for balancing the family budget, using such imagery as "mortgage," "material assets," and "grandchildren." The images are drawn from individual, family finances, but the purpose is to help the television audience relate its own economic behaviors to those of its government. In so speaking, Eisenhower is once again reaching back to echo Washington while simultaneously looking forward to the economic dangers posed by Kennedy. Washington had advised early Americans to "cherish public credit" and had noted that "one method of preserving it is to use it as sparingly as possible, avoiding occasions of expense by cultivating peace."[63]

Eisenhower offers precisely the same advice to the American people as he moves from the need to maintain a balanced economy in the future to the parallel need for balanced disarmament. Like Washington, Eisenhower sees economic strength and military outlays as intimately related. To preserve the economy one has to wage a battle for peace, to pay the price that peace demands. This had been the great theme of Eisenhower's Second Inaugural Address,[64] a speech which he echoes in his Farewell by saying, "Down the long lane of history yet to be written America knows that this world of ours, ever growing smaller, must avoid becoming a community of dreadful fear and hate, and be, instead, a proud confederation of mutual trust and respect. Such a confederation must be one of equals. The weakest must come to the conference table with the same confidence as do we. . . . That table, though scarred by many past frustrations, cannot be abandoned for the certain agony of the battlefield."

As Washington pleaded for national unity in his farewell, so Eisenhower raises the vision of an international community based on mutual respect. Such a community can come about only when "mutual honor and confidence" allows "disarmament" to take place. "Together," says Eisenhower, "we must learn how to compose differences, not with arms, but with intellect and decent purpose. Because this need is so sharp and apparent I confess that I lay down my official responsibilities in this field with a definite sense of disappointment." Even though a cessation of atmospheric testing of atomic weapons had been accomplished during his second administration, Eisenhower finds himself leaving the presidency with a series of setbacks prominent in the public mind: the U-2 affair, the collapse of the Paris Summit, and Khrushchev's increasing belligerency and threats, threats which would, within seven months, lead to Soviet resumption of atmospheric testing of atomic weapons.[65] Having confessed his "disappointment," Eisenhower follows with an appeal from ethos and a simple statement of his greatest accomplishment: "As one who has witnessed the horror and the lingering sadness of war—as one who knows that another war could utterly destroy this civilization which has been so slowly and painfully

built over thousands of years—I wish I could say tonight that a lasting peace is in sight. Happily I can say that war has been avoided." This character portrait of a soldier who fights for peace—a staple of Eisenhower's presentation of self since the end of World War II—thus concludes the section. Here is echoed the Eisenhower of 1945 who proclaimed that "there is no greater pacifist than the regular officer,"[66] the Eisenhower of 1946, who confessed, "I hate war as only a soldier who has lived it can,"[67] and the man who taught that "the soldier's true function is to prevent rather than to wage war."[68] He remains, to the end, a soldier true, having ended a war in Korea and avoided war in such places as Dienbienphu, Quemoy and Matsu, Suez, Lebanon, and Berlin.

Having laid claim to his greatest accomplishment, Eisenhower returns once again to the pattern provided by Washington, thanking the audience "for the many opportunities you have given me for public service in war and peace." Like Washington, the outgoing president trusts that "in that service you find some things worthy; as for the rest of it, I know you will always find ways to improve performance in the future." The tone of self-deprecation, the stance of unworthiness, the supposition that others might do better—all are echoes of Washington's farewell. But to speak of "ways to improve performance in the future" is also to call attention to the judgment that awaits future presidents, especially the new president-elect. Indeed, one of the dominant motives for speaking to the general public rather than to Congress is Eisenhower's desire to create a rhetorical constraint for the new president. The references to arrogance, crisis, action, and the need for mature judgment have put the Kennedy administration on notice that Eisenhower does not intend to slip quietly into retirement. Ike, as a fellow citizen, will be suggesting "ways to improve performance" just as he explicitly calls for the public to do the same through exercise of its citizenship rights and responsibilities.[69] Eisenhower knows that he cannot stop Kennedy from doing what he will with respect to the economy and the national defense. Nevertheless, he can create a public benchmark to which he and others can later refer and about which Kennedy must necessarily be mindful. At the very least, the president-elect will be forced to think before acting.[70]

Conclusion

Eisenhower concludes his Farewell Address precisely as he had begun his First Inaugural some eight years before—with a prayer. But even the words of the prayer call out for an implicative, rhetorical reading.[71] Eisenhower says, "May we be ever unswerving in devotion to principle" (not rushing from one extreme to another to satisfy momentary circumstances); "confident but humble with power" (not rash and arrogant); "diligent in pursuit of the Nation's great goals" (not given to headlong action that could subvert the very foundations of democracy).

Having prayed as one of the citizens for his fellow citizens, Eisenhower then takes on the role of spokesperson for the American dream and prays for "all the peoples of the world." It is a prayer for peace, millennial in tone, prophetic in vision: "We pray that peoples of all faiths, all races, all nations, may have their great human needs satisfied; that those now denied opportunity shall come to enjoy it to the full; that all who yearn for freedom may experience its spiritual blessings; that those who have freedom will understand, also, its heavy responsibilities; that all who are insensitive to the needs of others will learn charity; that the scourges of poverty, disease and ignorance will be made to disappear from the earth, and that, in the goodness of time, all peoples will come to live together in a peace guaranteed by the binding force of mutual respect and love." Thus does Eisenhower end his last address to the nation as president of these United States. Looking up from his prepared text—a text which he seemed to have great difficulty reading from the teleprompter—Eisenhower took off his glasses and, for the first time, flashed the famous Eisenhower grin as he said, "Now, on Friday noon I am to become a private citizen. I am proud to do so. I look forward to it. Thank you, and good night."

CONCLUSION

On January 19, 1961, two days after delivering his Farewell Address and one day before the end of his second term in office, Dwight Eisenhower met one final time with John Kennedy. He "urged Kennedy to hold down the costs of defense, and to strive for a balanced budget."[72] But, of course, if Kennedy was listening on the evening of January 17, he had already received that advice, for Eisenhower had three strategic goals that he wanted to accomplish that night: to restate the basic themes that had characterized his public life; to identify—thematically, structurally, and attitudinally—his life and words with those of George Washington; and to advance an implicit critique of the incoming Kennedy administration, thereby erecting a rhetorical constraint with which the president-elect would have to contend in his efforts to overhaul Eisenhower's priorities and philosophies. In erecting this constraint, Eisenhower identifies himself with the citizenry, then calls upon that citizenry to fulfill the role of a rhetorical public: alert, attentive, curious, skeptical, responsive, and interested always in "improving performance"—precisely the kind of "private citizen" Eisenhower himself intends to be.

This interpretation of Eisenhower's Farewell Address is, of course, revisionist in character. It constitutes a substantial reconceptualization of the motives, structural logic, and antecedent forms that Eisenhower calls upon to characterize his stewardship, remind the viewers of his long-held beliefs, and construct the listening and viewing audience as a public capable of functioning as an ever-present constraint upon public policy initiatives. If there is a public watching the military-industrial complex, then there is, perforce, a public watching the actions of the executive and legislative branches—and that, in itself, is a crucial part of the "way of life" Eisenhower seeks to preserve in his Farewell Address.

In addition to revealing more about the rhetorical structure of the speech itself, this essay illustrates the conceptual consistency of Eisenhower's views on military-industrial relations. From the end of World War II until the final days of his presidency, Eisenhower never failed to understand and articulate the need for an integrated military-industrial policy. Though many critics of the military-industrial complex have counted Eisenhower among their supporters, such critics have, almost without exception, failed to understand Eisenhower's basic stance. Like radical filmmaker Oliver Stone (JFK), such critics have chosen to edit out of the speech Ike's belief that the military-industrial complex is both "an imperative need" and "a vital element in keeping the peace." The Farewell Address must be read in the context not only of the immediate situation, but of a whole career spent thinking and talking about military-industrial cooperation.

Finally, this study points to a view of Eisenhower as a strategic communicator—one who knew exactly what he was doing with language and why he was doing it. Unlike the traditional wisdom of the 1950s, 60s, and 70s that painted Ike as a bumbling speaker who had difficulty making three sentences fit together in a coherent fashion, this essay joins an emerging body of work that finds Eisenhower's communication skills to be not only adequate, but in several instances exemplary.[73] Eisenhower fully understood and appreciated the role of language and persuasion in the process of democratic leadership.[74] He also understood that language could be used to impede and constrain as well as to propose and execute. The Farewell Address is a prime example of Ike's ability to place constraints on one audience by "warning" another. It is a justly celebrated oration, but for reasons substantially different than those traditionally advanced.

NOTES

[1] Dwight D. Eisenhower, "Farewell Radio and Television Address to the American People," January 17, 1961[,] in *Public Papers of the Presidents of the United States, 1953* (Washington, D.C.: Government Printing Office, 1954). This and all subsequent quotations from the Farewell Address are from the version published in the Public Papers, as amended by comparison with a videotape of the speech that is in the author's possession.

[2] Stephen E. Ambrose, *Eisenhower, The President* (New York: Simon and Schuster, 1984) 612.

[3] Herbert F. York, *Making Weapons, Talking Peace: A Physicist's Odyssey from Hiroshima to Geneva* (New York: Basic Books, Inc., 1987) 126.

[4] See Seymour Melman, *Pentagon Capitalism: The Political Economy of War* (New York: McGraw-Hill, 1970) 88–89. See appendixes A and B for the alleged link between a 1946 staff memorandum and the 1961 Farewell Address.

[5] H. W. Brands, "The Age of Vulnerability: Eisenhower and the National Insecurity State," *The American Historical Review 94* (1989): 988–989.

[6] Steven Rosen, "Testing the Theory of the Military-Industrial Complex," in *Testing the Theory of the Military-Industrial Complex,* ed. Steven Rosen (Lexington, MA: D. C. Heath and Co., 1973) 1.

[7] J. R. Kurth, "Political Economy of Weapons Procurement: The Follow-On Imperative," *American Economic Review Papers and Processes 62* (1972): 304–311; Seymour Melman, "Ten Propositions on the War Economy," *American Economic Review Papers and Processes 62* (1972): 312–318; Murray L. Weidenbaum, "Arms and the American Economy: A Domestic Convergence Hypothesis," *American Economic Review Papers and Processes 58* (1968): 428–445; J. L. Clayton, "Impact of the Cold War on the Economies of California and Utah, 1946–1965," *Pacific Historical Review 36* (1967): 449–473.

[8] R. J. Art, "Restructuring the Military-Industrial Complex: Arms Control in Institutional Perspective," *Public Policy 22* (1974): 423–459; S. Cobb, "Defense Spending and Defense Voting in the House: An Empirical Study of an Aspect of the Military-Industrial Complex Thesis," *American Journal of Sociology 82* (1976): 163–182; C. Marfels, "Structure of the Military-Industrial Complex in the United States and Its Impact on Industrial Concentration," *Kyklos 31* (1978): 409–423; W. J. Long, "Expand the Military-Industrial Complex? No—It's Unnecessary and Inefficient," *Orbis 33* (1989): 549–559; M. T. Owens, "Expand the Military-Industrial Complex? Yes—Preparedness Requires It," *Orbis 33* (1989): 539–548.

[9] E. Jahn, "Role of the Armaments Complex in Soviet Society (is there a Soviet Military-Industrial Complex?)," *Journal of Peace Research 12* (1975): 179–194; H. W. Jencks, "Chinese Military-Industrial Complex and Defense Mobilization," *Asian Survey 20* (1980): 965–989; M. Agursky and H. Adomeit, "Soviet Military-Industrial Complex," *Survey 24* (1979): 106–124; A. Mintz, "Military-Industrial Linkages in Israel," *Armed Forces and Society 12* (1985): 9–27; J. P. Gallagher, "China's Military-Industrial Complex: Its Approach to the Acquisition of Modern Military Technology," *Asian Survey 27* (1987): 991–1002.

[10] Ambrose, *Eisenhower* 612.

[11] Peter Lyon, *Eisenhower: Portrait of the Hero* (Boston: Little, Brown & Co., 1974) 882.

12 Piers Brendon, *Ike: His Life and Times* (New York: Harper and Row, 1986) 401–402.

13 Herbert S. Parmet, *Eisenhower and the American Crusades* (New York: Macmillan Co., 1972) 571.

14 Those who explicitly recognize the situational exigence of Kennedy's impending ascension to the presidency as a dominant motive for Eisenhower's speech include: James L. Clayton, ed., *The Economic Impact of the Cold War: Sources and Readings* (New York: Harcourt, Brace & World, 1970). Clayton notes: "Because Eisenhower feared that his successor would not fully understand how the military-industrial complex operated, and hence would be vulnerable to its pressures, he decided to warn the country." (239)

Arthur A. Ekirch, Jr., "Eisenhower and Kennedy: The Rhetoric and the Reality," *Midwest Quarterly* 17 (1975–1976), notes: "In his Farewell Address to the country on January 17, 1961, he challenged the incoming Kennedy administration with his warning that 'America's adventure in free government' was menaced by the rise of a 'military-industrial complex'." (288)

15 See, especially, Fred I. Greenstein, *The Hidden-Hand Presidency: Eisenhower as Leader* (New York: Basic Books, Inc., 1982) 57–72. See also, Martin J. Medhurst, *Dwight D. Eisenhower: Strategic Communicator* (Westport, Conn.: Greenwood Press, 1993) 71–96.

16 The one extended analysis is A. Duane Litfin, "Eisenhower on the Military-Industrial Complex: Critique of a Rhetorical Strategy," *Central States Speech Journal* 25 (1974): 198–209. The exploration into the authorship of the "military-industrial complex" is Charles J. G. Griffin, "New Light on Eisenhower's Farewell Address," *Presidential Studies Quarterly* 22 (1992): 469–480. Scholars who make use of Eisenhower's Farewell Address while investigating other topics include Philip Wander, "The Rhetoric of American Foreign Policy," *Quarterly Journal of Speech* 70 (1984): 339–361; Robert L. Scott, "Eisenhower's Farewell: The Epistemic Function of Argument," in *Perspectives on Argumentation: Essays in Honor of Wayne Brockriede*, ed. Robert Trapp and Janice Schuetz (Prospect Heights, Ill.: Waveland Press, 1990) 151–161. Karlyn Kohrs Campbell and Kathleen Hall Jamieson make several references to Eisenhower's Farewell Address in their chapter on farewells as generic rhetoric. See Campbell and Jamieson, *Deeds Done in Words: Presidential Rhetoric and the Genres of Governance* (Chicago: University of Chicago Press, 1990) 191–212.

17 Liftin 200, 202, 205.

18 Liftin 204–205.

19 Griffin 469.

20 James R. Schlesinger, "Organizational Structures and Planning," in *Issues in Defense Economics,* ed. Roland N. McKean (New York: National Bureau of Economic Research, 1967) 188n.

21 York 126.

22 Stephen E. Ambrose, "The Military Impact on Foreign Policy," in *The Military and American Society: Essays & Readings,* ed. Stephen E. Ambrose and James A. Barber, Jr. (New York: The Free Press, 1972) 132.

23 Kennedy quoted in Robert A. Divine, *Foreign Policy and U.S. Presidential Elections 1952–1960* (New York: New Viewpoints, 1974) 192.

24 Letter from Dwight D. Eisenhower to Swede Hazlett, 20 August 1956, in *Ike's Letters to a Friend 1941–1958,* ed. Robert W. Griffith (Lawrence, KS: University Press of Kansas, 1984) 29.

25 Eisenhower Diary, 6 December 1960, in *The Eisenhower Diaries,* ed. Robert H. Ferrell (New York: W. W. Norton, 1981) 380.

26 Ambrose, *Eisenhower* 606.

27 On the generic requirements for a presidential farewell see Campbell and Jamieson, *Deeds Done in Words* 191–212.

28 Medhurst, *Dwight D. Eisenhower* 5.

29 Robert J. Donovan, "Moos Recalls Idea for Eisenhower's Militarism Phrase," *Washington Post* (1 April 1969): A14, col. 1.

30 Letter from Dwight D. Eisenhower to Milton S. Eisenhower, 25 May 1959. Whitman File, Name Series, Box 13, Eisenhower, Milton 1959 (2). Dwight D. Eisenhower Library, Abilene, Kansas.

31 Donovan A14, col. 2.

32 On Eisenhower and argument by implication see Martin J. Medhurst, "Eisenhower's 'Atoms for Peace' Speech: A Case Study in the Strategic Use of Language," *Communication Monographs* 54 (1987): 204–220. Also Medhurst, *Dwight D. Eisenhower* 75–78.

33 George Washington, "Farewell Address," in *Famous American Statesmen & Orators,* ed. Alexander K. McClure and Byron Andrews (New York: F. E. Lovell Publishing Co., 1902) 77.

34 Kennedy quoted in Divine 241.

35 Dwight D. Eisenhower, "Address in San Francisco to the Commonwealth Club of California," October 20, 1960, in *Public Papers, 1960,* 332.

36 Dwight D. Eisenhower, "Radio and Television Report to the American People: Security in the Free World," March 16, 1959, in *Public Papers, 1959* 57.

37 Dwight D. Eisenhower, "Address in Pittsburgh at a Dinner Sponsored by the Allegheny

County Republican Executive Committee," November 4, 1960, in *Public Papers, 1960–61* 354.

38 For a more detailed description of Cold War discourse see Martin J. Medhurst, Robert L. Ivie, Philip Wander, and Robert L. Scott, *Cold War Rhetoric: Strategy, Metaphor, and Ideology* (Westport, Conn: Greenwood Press, 1990); also, Wayne Brockriede and Robert L. Scott, *Moments in the Rhetoric of the Cold War* (New York: Random House, 1970).

39 On Eisenhower's strategic tactics see Medhurst, *Dwight D. Eisenhower* 71–96. On the ultimate success of those tactics see David Lauter, "Ike Still Casts Long Shadow over the Continent," *New York Times* (8 May 1990): A8–A9.

40 Even during the 1960 campaign, Eisenhower had ridiculed Kennedy's experience by saying: "My friends, in their preparation for high office, the experience of Cabot Lodge and Dick Nixon has never been equaled. These men didn't learn their lessons merely out of books—not even by writing books." See "Address at a Republican Rally in the New York Coliseum," November 2, 1960, in *Public Papers, 1960–61* 833–834.

41 Dwight D. Eisenhower, "Address in Philadelphia at a Rally of the Nixon for President Committee of Pennsylvania," October 28, 1960, in *Public Papers, 1960–61* 341.

42 Letter from Dwight D. Eisenhower to Swede Hazlett, 27 November 1945, in *Ike's Letters to a Friend* 29.

43 Dwight D. Eisenhower, "Address before Bureau of Advertising of the American Newspaper Publishers' Association," New York City, New York, April 25, 1946, in *Eisenhower Speaks: Dwight D. Eisenhower in his Messages and Speeches*, ed. Rudolph L. Treuenfels (New York: Farrar, Straus & Co., 1948) 87.

44 Dwight D. Eisenhower, "Address before Convention of Veterans of Foreign Wars," Boston, Massachusetts, September 3, 1946, in *Eisenhower Speaks* 129.

45 Concerning Eisenhower's political philosophy, Robert Wright notes: "Eisenhower called it 'middle of the road', not 'golden mean', but he meant it in an almost Aristotelian sense; his faith in ideological moderation had an almost metaphysical grounding. He believed that the extremes of opinion at either end of any spectrum were bound to be mistaken." See "Eisenhower's Fifties," *Antioch Review 38* (1980): 281.

46 Liftin 201.

47 William Bragg Ewald, Jr., *Eisenhower the President: Crucial Days, 1951–1960* (Englewood Cliffs: Prentice-Hall, 1981) 145.

48 Personal interview with Bryce Harlow, Arlington, Virginia, 21 March 1984. All quotations from this source. This interview is one in a series of interviews with former presidential speech writers that forms part of the data base for a forthcoming book on the subject by Thomas W. Benson and the author.

49 Washington, "Farewell Address" 71.

50 "Bureau of Advertising," *Eisenhower Speaks* 88.

51 Dwight D. Eisenhower, "Address before Industrial Association," January 1947, in *Eisenhower Speaks* 173–174.

52 Eisenhower, "Bureau of Advertising," *Eisenhower Speaks* 88.

53 Dwight D. Eisenhower, "Address at Civic Reception," St. Louis, Missouri, 24 February 1947, in *Eisenhower Speaks* 180.

54 Eisenhower, "Bureau of Advertising," *Eisenhower Speaks* 85.

55 Eisenhower, "Address to the Commonwealth Club of California," *Public Papers, 1960–61* 790.

56 Goldwater quoted in Brendon 409.

57 Letter from Dwight D. Eisenhower to Swede Hazlett, 20 July 1954, in *Ike's Letters to a Friend* 132–133.

58 Dwight D. Eisenhower, "Address 'Science: Handmaiden of Freedom'," New York City, New York, 14 May 1959, *Public Papers, 1959* 400.

59 Dwight D. Eisenhower, "Letter to the Secretary of Defense on National Security Requirements," 5 January 1955, *Public Papers, 1955* 3.

60 Eisenhower, "Letter to the Secretary of Defense," *Public Papers, 1955* 2–3.

61 Dwight D. Eisenhower, "Radio and Television Address to the American People on Science in National Security," 7 November 1957, *Public Papers, 1957* 230. For an analysis of Eisenhower's speaking during the Sputnik crisis see David Henry, "Eisenhower and Sputnik: The Irony of Failed Leadership," in *Eisenhower's War of Words: Rhetoric and Leadership*, ed. Martin J. Medhurst (East Lansing: Michigan State University Press, 1994) 223–250.

62 Dwight D. Eisenhower, "Address to the American Society of Newspaper Editors and the International Press Institute['']," 17 April 1958, *Public Papers, 1958* 80.

63 Washington, "Farewell Address" 79.

64 In his Second Inaugural Eisenhower said: "Yet this peace we seek cannot be born of fear alone: it must be rooted in the lives of nations. There must be justice, sensed and shared by all peoples, for, without justice the world can know only a tense and unstable truce. There must be law, steadily invoked

and respected by all nations, for without law, the world promises only such meager justice as the pity of the strong upon the weak. But the law of which we speak, comprehending the values of freedom, affirms the equality of all nations, great and small. Splendid as can be the blessings of such a peace, high will be its cost, in toil patiently sustained, in help honorably given, in sacrifice calmly borne. We are called to meet the price of this peace." See *Inaugural Addresses of the Presidents of the United States* (Washington, D.C.: Government Printing Office, 1969) 264–265. See Martin J. Medhurst, "Dwight D. Eisenhower's Second Inaugural Address, 1957," in *The Inaugural Addresses of Twentieth-Century American Presidents*, ed. Halford Ryan (New York: Praeger, 1993) 167–179.

65 On the aftermath of these threats and Kennedy's response to them see Martin J. Medhurst, "Rhetorical Portraiture: John F. Kennedy's March 2, 1962, Speech on the Resumption of Atmospheric Tests," in *Cold War Rhetoric* 51–68.

66 Dwight D. Eisenhower, "Speech at Dinner at Waldorf-Astoria," New York City, New York, 19 June 1945, *Eisenhower Speaks* 42.

67 Dwight D. Eisenhower, "Address at the Canadian Club Luncheon," Ottawa, Canada, 10 January 1946, *Eisenhower Speaks* 64

68 Dwight D. Eisenhower, "Art in Peace and War," Metropolitan Museum of Art, New York City, New York, 2 April 1946, *Eisenhower Speaks* 81.

69 Ike followed through on his promise to remain critically involved, but, as usual, did so through indirect means. He asked his brother Milton to form the Republican Critical Issues Council to serve as a countervoice to the incumbent administration. Milton Eisenhower recalls: "And you realize that the military forces, to achieve their purposes, have contracts with most of the leading industries of this country, and thus the military permeates the whole industrial enterprise. . . . In late 1963 and early 1964, he [former President Eisenhower] became quite concerned that the facts and proposals being put before the American people emanated almost exclusively from the administration. Now the administration has vast research resources at its disposal, and therefore is in a position constantly to propagandize the American people with ideas and proposals based upon the studies made for the President. At that time, no constructive alternative proposals were being made. . . . And so he asked me to establish what was called the Republican Critical Issues Council, to carry on research and to come out with constructive proposals based upon valid research findings. He suggested, and I most

surely agreed, that if these proposals were to achieve widespread publicity, and to merit the attention and perhaps respect of the American people, the studies back of them should be made by recognized authorities. And so I brought some eminent people together and formed the Council, and then mustered into the service of the Council leading Americans in various fields who obviously would merit the attention of the people." Milton S. Eisenhower Papers, Box 16, "MSE Oral History Interview (Columbia)." Eisenhower Library, Abilene, Kansas, 53–54.

70 Whether Kennedy did, in fact, consider Eisenhower's remarks to be constraining is not clear. What is known is that Kennedy followed through with his plans to increase dramatically the defense budget and Eisenhower continued to criticize Kennedy's moves, moves which Eisenhower considered "a threat to our liberties." (Eisenhower quoted in Lyon 888). With each passing year, Eisenhower's critiques became more pointed. See, for example, "How Eisenhower Sizes Up the World Today," *U.S. News & World Report* (21 August 1961): 63–65; Dwight D. Eisenhower, "Are We Headed in the Wrong Direction?" *Saturday Evening Post* (11–18 August 1962): 19–25; Dwight D. Eisenhower, "Danger from Within," *Saturday Evening Post* (26 January 1963): 15–18.

71 On public prayer as a form of rhetoric see Martin J. Medhurst, "'God Bless the President': The Rhetoric of Inaugural Prayer," Unpublished Diss. The Pennsylvania State University, 1980; Martin J. Medhurst, "American Cosmology and the Rhetoric of Inaugural Prayer," *Central States Speech Journal* 28 (1977): 272–282; Martin J. Medhurst, "The Politics of Prayer: A Case Study in Configurational Interplay," in *American Rhetoric: Context and Criticism*, ed. Thomas W. Benson (Carbondale: Southern Illinois University Press, 1989) 267–292.

72 Ambrose, *Eisenhower* 615.

73 Such work would include Greenstein, *The Hidden-Hand Presidency;* Medhurst, *Dwight D. Eisenhower;* Medhurst, "Eisenhower's 'Atoms for Peace' Speech"; Robert L. Ivie, "Eisenhower as Cold Warrior" and J. Michael Hogan, "Eisenhower and Open Skies: A Case Study in 'Psychological Warfare'," both in *Eisenhower's War of Words* 7–25, 137–155; and Robert L. Ivie, "Dwight D. Eisenhower's 'Chance for Peace': Quest or Crusade?" Paper presented at the Speech Communication Association Annual Convention, November 3, 1991.

74 See Martin J. Medhurst, "Eisenhower's Rhetorical Leadership: An Interpretation," in *Eisenhower's War of Words* 285–296.

The Body as Proof: Franklin D. Roosevelt's Preparations for the 1932 Presidential Campaign

Amos Kiewe

★ INTRODUCTION

The polio affliction Franklin D. Roosevelt suffered in 1921 was a major setback to the ambitious politician. By then, Roosevelt had accumulated an impressive resume that included being New York State Senator, Under Secretary of the Navy under Woodrow Wilson, and Vice-presidential candidate in 1920. Becoming president was his ultimate objective but a disabled person, then and perhaps even now, could not be conceived as the holder of the highest office in the land. Roosevelt's disability was only part of the story though. Equally deleterious to Roosevelt's electoral ambition was the social stigma attached to infantile paralysis. Since the outset of polio in 1921, Roosevelt made tremendous efforts to improve his physical ability, to hide his disability and to modify his walking ability. The 1928 gubernatorial campaign already proved to Roosevelt the rewards of modifying his appearance (Kiewe, 1999). But the successes on a state level had a limited effect. Roosevelt was still concerned that his disability would be a major issue his opponents would use to defeat him. On the eve of the presidential campaign (1930–31), Roosevelt and his closest advisers sought to lay to rest the health issue for once and for all. The plan called for medical professionals to publicize medical reports of a clean bill of health as definitive proof that Roosevelt was physically fit to be president. This is the focus of this essay.

In addressing Roosevelt's efforts to prove his fitness on the eve of the presidential campaign, I begin by discussing polio as a disability that precluded political office and Roosevelt's attempts to overcome this prejudice by casting his body as a rhetorical site. Next, I discuss the issuance of life insurance as proof of a healthy body. Following I move to the primary focus of this essay—a secret arrangement Roosevelt had with Earle Looker to publicize medical examination as the proof that he was fit for political office.

★ BODY AND DISABILITY AS RHETORICAL SITES

Polio was taken to be the disease of the lower class. Its sufferers were often doomed to seclusion and neglect due [to] the misperception regarding the causes of the disease. Rogers (1992) claims that many associated polio with the lower class and lower moral standing, and that this belief brought many to assign guilt and responsibility of attracting polio to the victims (p. 29). Similarly, Susan Sontag argues that for many, the association between the disease and the diseased "invariably extended to assert that the character causes the disease" (1991, p. 47). This dialectic of terms is a convenient one for those who look for a way to justify marginalizing the sick and the disabled instead of offering special care and alternative ways of managing daily tasks. Any unwillingness to carry the burden of care is likely to be justified rhetorically by turning victims into victimizers. Given this logic, the sick and the disabled are often disadvantaged socially in addition to their physical suffering.

The body is "the most visible marker of difference," and it functions as a potent evidence of differences between individuals (Shome, 1996, p. 510). The body is easily an object of examination through difference. Given the "marker" of a healthy body, a deformed or disabled body transgresses "the boundaries of the 'civilized' body" (Shome, p. 510). A healthy body is thus a representation of the "normal," whereas a disabled body is visually marked. Yet, infantile paralysis deforms the body but not the extent that other serious ailments do. Polio victims are visible in their difficult mobility. However, their upper body is "normal" and their face, the ultimate body mark of health and vitality, is unaffected. Roosevelt would find his potential in making his upper body the mark of health and fitness.

Yet, a disabled politician was, and still is, anathema given the long-standing perception of the body politic as an extension of masculinity and a healthy body (Houck, 1997, pp. 22–23; Jamieson, 1992, p. 82). Politics has been, and to a significant degree, is still conceived as a masculine occupation. This hierarchy assumes the symbolism of a healthy and viral body at the top of a political system. This order, Sontag contends, "is the oldest concern of political philosophy," and thus it is plausible to compare the polis to an organism (Sontag, 1991, p. 77). The polity, then, assumes human characteristics and its symbolic embodiment is that of perfection and power while illness is symbolic of an unhealthy body politic.

Roosevelt's fate could have been similar to that of many polio victims, except for his political ambition and his inherent optimism. Roosevelt understood very well the fate of a disabled person, not to speak of a disabled person with political ambitions. Physical disability "was an automatic disqualification for public life, let alone for the highest political office" (Poore, 1998, p. 244). His chances lay in his ability to hide his disability. Yet, these very efforts reflected "a view of the disabled body as stigmatizing, shameful, and as a physical marker of weakness of intellect and character" (Poore, 1998, p. 244).

Roosevelt's initial years as a polio sufferer were difficult, both physically and mentally. From the outset, Roosevelt and his closest family members and associates began a public relations campaign, the objective of which was to hide the true extent of his illness. No matter how difficult it was for Roosevelt to move his lower body, public statements about his conditions were positive and encouraging (Freidel, 1954, pp. 102–106; Gunther, 1950, pp. 225–227).

Roosevelt did his utmost to avoid "the stigma of being seen in public in a wheel-chair, with all its associations of invalidism and incompetence" (Poore, 1998, p. 241). He invested time and energy in studying methods for improving the conditions of polio victims. His efforts culminated in making a substantial financial investment in a run-down Georgia resort, Warm Springs, and turning it into a rehabilitation center for polio victims. It was here that he learned to create the semblance of walking. With a powerful upper body, Roosevelt learned

to appear to be walking slowly first by using crutches, and later by pulling his legs locked in metal braces, holding a cane in one hand and the arm of a son or an aide in the other. Roosevelt's efforts to present himself as non-disabled was based on a two-pronged strategy: projecting self-confidence and authority, and maintaining the visual expectations of a healthy body (Poore, 1998, p. 242).

Roosevelt's first political comeback began in 1924, when New York governor Alfred E. Smith asked him to give the nominating speech at the Democratic National Convention. Roosevelt was hailed as he slowly walked on crutches to the podium. Though standing was an arduous effort, the crowd saw a smiling and cheerful speaker. What the crowd did not see was Roosevelt being carried in a wheelchair into the convention arena and that he "walked" only [a] few paces, from behind a curtain to the podium. He gained much respect and adulation for his forceful delivery. The 1924 Democratic convention was a major success for Roosevelt who was considered by many as the only bright light in a fractious and dismal convention (Davis, 1974, pp. 30–31; FDR: Campaign of 1924 Scrapbook, FDRPL).

Al Smith repeated his request four years later and Roosevelt again gave the nominating speech during the 1928 Democratic National Convention. Four more years of exercise had improved his walking ability. Now Roosevelt was "determined to show himself . . . as a man merely lame, not crippled" (Davis, 1974, p. 80). Smith had other plans for Roosevelt. Seeking to avoid the deadlock of 1924, Smith asked Roosevelt to run for New York Governor in order to secure the 45 New York delegates. What Smith had in mind was Roosevelt as a titular governor and an able lieutenant governor as the acting governor. This Roosevelt rejected altogether. Once he decided to run for governor of New York in 1928, he engaged in an active and vibrant campaign whose objective it was to deflect suspicions of being physically unfit. Roosevelt mounted a campaign that dispelled rumors of physical disability (Kiewe, 1999).

The strategies Roosevelt used in 1928 during his first run for political office as a disabled person was premised on displaying his body as a rhetorical site. As such, Roosevelt's body became proof for the implied argument that he was healthy and fit for political office. Roosevelt constructed this argument with the following tactics: he traveled throughout the state and in each campaign stop he made allusions to his walking and traveling. The sheer sight of the candidate, smiling, standing in his car (which was only possible by holding a metal bar), and speaking in an affable and jovial way was enough to convince many that regardless of all the talk about his health, there was nothing wrong with Franklin Roosevelt. He used sarcasm to refute comments about his physical condition, scoffing at his opponents for suggesting that he was too sick to be governor. With humor and irony he listed the many campaign stops he already passed only to ask his auditors whether this was the itinerary of a sick man.

Roosevelt also addressed his recovery and improved physical condition since he contracted polio. Thus, he was able to argue that he was on the mend and preempted those who sought to attack him for hiding his disability. To a lesser degree, he attacked religious bigotry displayed during the previous and current presidential campaign (1924 and 1928 respectively) against the Democratic presidential candidate Al Smith who was Catholic. In so doing, Roosevelt challenged bigotry and prejudices in general including those voiced against the disabled (Kiewe, 1999). The 1928 gubernatorial campaign was successful but the success was limited to one state. For the presidential campaign, Roosevelt would have to mount an aggressive national campaign to dispel rumors of being physically unfit.

As New York's Governor, Roosevelt thrust himself into the national scene as a viable presidential contender. When he became governor for a second term in 1930, friends and foes recognized his presidential timber. Though he was an able and active governor who could present a progressive record to be highlighted during the presidential campaign, Roosevelt suspected that his health would be exploited by Democrat challengers as well as by the incumbent president and the Republican party. Roosevelt was concerned with "a deliberative attempt to create the impression that my health

is such as would make it impossible for me to fulfill the duties of President," and in stark contrast to his public statements he added that "those who know how strenuous have been the three years I have passed as Governor of this State, this is taken with great seriousness in the southern states particularly. I shall appreciate whatever my friends may have to say in their personal correspondence to dispel this perfectly silly piece of propaganda" (FDR to Hamilton Mills, May 4, 1931, Governor Papers, quoted in Freidel, 1956, p. 210).

Roosevelt's fear was not unfounded. The *New York Times* reported on April 29, 1930, that "Some Democrats at Washington, obviously with other candidates in mind, have hastened to express fear that Mr. Roosevelt may not be in good enough health to make the race in 1932" (p. 26). The *New York Daily News* reported that Governor Albert Ritchie of Maryland was considered "better fitted than Mr. Roosevelt to bear the physical burdens of the presidency" (*The Literary Digest*, November 15, 1930, p. 7). Anonymous letters spread throughout the country whispering about Roosevelt's poor health, some even suggesting that Roosevelt was incapable of governing not because of his polio but because he suffered from syphilis (in W. M. Odell to [James J. Mahoney], October 1, 1930, DNC 1932, FDRPL; quoted in Freidel, 1956, p. 157). To squelch the growing concerns about the health issue, a risky campaign was put into motion to "prove" Roosevelt's fitness with expert medical reports (Freidel, 1956, p. 210). Roosevelt was now closer than ever before to his dream of becoming president and he was not willing to lose this chance due to the health issue. Once again, he had to develop a strategy that would allay any concern the nation had regarding his health.

On the eve of the presidential campaign, Roosevelt and his closest aides developed a focused public relations campaign designed to preempt potential attacks on his health. This campaign was premised on the need to present medical reports and life insurance policies as "objective" evidence and proof of Roosevelt's health and fitness. This campaign needs to be understood in the larger context of Roosevelt's eleven-year struggle of proving his fitness by displaying his body—both physically and rhetorically. Physically, Roosevelt displayed his body by traveling extensively and showing himself to crowds. Rhetorically, Roosevelt displayed his fitness by resorting to metaphors and arguments whose objective it was to project health, vibrancy, and mobility. Both approaches proved productive in the 1928 gubernatorial campaign. The body was both the means and the end for the argument about physical fitness. Now Roosevelt sought a new approach—publicizing medical records of good health as proof of his physical fitness. Thus, while in 1928, the body itself served as a discursive agency and site, in 1930–31, the strategy was principally that of a discourse about the body.

★ MEDICAL PROOF AS ARGUMENT

To fend off any potential damage that might arise out of the health issue, Louis M. Howe, Roosevelt's closest political aide, began in 1930 a campaign that presented Roosevelt as enjoying excellent health. A well-publicized $500,000 life insurance policy was issued as proof that Roosevelt did not incur high risk for insurers. Dr. Edgar W. Beckwith, the Medical Director of the Equitable Life Assurance Society, the underwriter of the policy, also issued a public report attesting to Roosevelt's excellent health ("Newspaper Interview on Governor Roosevelt Accepting Delivery of $500,000 Life Insurance, October 18, 1930," FDR: Family, Business and Personal Papers, FDRPL). The Life Insurance and the sum of money advertised were meant to project high confidence and low risks underwriters took in considering Roosevelt's conditions. In this sense, the Life Insurance was to put Roosevelt's claim to health and fitness in the hands of others that are not prone to taking unnecessary risks.

The press interviewed both Roosevelt and Dr. Beckwith on October 18, 1930, on the occasion of issuing the life insurance. With Roosevelt next to him, Dr. Beckwith stated that he was pleased "to see such a splendid physical specimen as yourself, and I trust that your remarkable vitality will stand you in good stead throughout your arduous campaign." Though the campaign (the gubernatorial campaign of 1930) put the governor "under very great strain," Dr. Beckwith stated that Roosevelt "passed a better examination than the average individual." Dr. Beckwith also opined that "The moral hazard in the thing counts for a tremendous amount in getting a large amount of insurance. A man who doesn't lead a clean, decent life, even though he passes the examination physically, will be turned down. The moral hazard enters into it almost as important as the physical" (FDR: Family, Business and Personal Papers, FDRPL).

Roosevelt may not have been completely healthy or cured of his illness, implied the medical expert, but he was a moral person. This is a significant point in Roosevelt's attempts to "prove" his fitness. After all, Roosevelt was not cured of polio but only appeared cured. For Roosevelt, "cure" of polio equaled standing and walking. This he managed to accomplish on his own as he proved time and again. But now, with the presidential campaign only a year away, Roosevelt needed a medical cover to seal his own claim to fitness. Since medical reports had to be both qualified and creative, the report also argued a moral stand that sought to counter the prevailing perceptions of the time that polio was the disease of the poor, the unhygienic, and the downtrodden (Rogers, 1992, p. 29). Implied in this understanding is the assumption that sickness and disease are associated with the moral/immoral character of the person who carries them (Sontag, 1991, p. 47).

Roosevelt contributed to the same press interview his personal involvement with Warm Springs. He enthusiastically elaborated on the healing power of warm water and of his initiative to bring polio victims to Warm Springs. Roosevelt's narrative took an active form:

> I took these people and we fixed up a cottage for them. I got the local doctor . . . I put them in the pool . . . I went down there and discovered that the American Orthopedic Association was holding its annual meeting in Atlanta. I went up to the association meeting . . . I took a year's lease, an option on the property. I came up to Albany . . . (FDR: Family, Business and Personal Papers, FDRPL).

With seven first-person references and nine active verbs, Roosevelt constructed the argument that he was a common person who willingly helped others, especially those who suffered. The implication was that a person who helped others was himself cured. In the midst of the Great Depression, such an account was a significant political asset.

★ PREEMPTING FUTURE ATTACKS ON HIS HEALTH

This concentrated effort to publicize Roosevelt's fitness to be president was carefully and delicately arranged with one Earl Looker, a writer, a journalist, a Republican, and a friend of the Oyster Bay Roosevelts. His mission was to present a thorough medical examination as the definitive proof that Roosevelt was healthy and physically fit to be president. Historian and biographer Rollins suggests that Howe may have been the one to mastermind this plot (1962, p. 313), and Gallagher considers the entire arrangement as "cooked up" (1985, p. 84). The primary sources in the Franklin D. Roosevelt Presidential Library do not contradict such suspicions. The documents this author uncovered do suggest that Roosevelt was directly involved in this public relations campaign to publicize a medical report that gave him a clean bill of health.

The preparations for such a project are most interesting. In a letter to Eleanor Roosevelt on December 16, 1930, Earle Looker wrote the following:

Since my trip West, where I have been doing considerable sounding—and the sounds are quite vibrant enough, plans for the story have taken a great step forward, . . . I have been quietly looking about to find the best possible publisher for the particular thing we have in mind, one who is most likely to create the sort of organization we will need for fast and effective distribution of the book . . .

I am writing a story now to be published in the Spring, and probably serially by Collier's, . . . My backers understand exactly what I have in mind and why. Since they are so practically and enthusiastically for you and with me, assuring me I may have just as long as I need to do the very best work I can and insure my peace of mind in many ways, I feel

less embarrassment than I otherwise might, in making one request of you in their behalf: That is that, while the Governor can at no time release information about himself and that he should of course not do so, that, however, until I am well underway with my story, it would be much appreciated if he would find it possible to discourage any extended work of which his personality—not policies—is subject.

As I read this last paragraph back, my dear Mrs. Roosevelt, I suddenly understand why diplomatic language seems so utterly impossible! The request, however, is simple enough; I have merely complicated it because of my intense desire not to make one false step in a matter that seems really very important (FDR: Governor Papers, Series 1, Earle Looker folder, FDRPL).

Though the referent is vague and the backers are not identified, subsequent events would reveal that the subject matter is an article and also a book about Roosevelt's sound health, written for quick publication and distribution. Looker's advice to Roosevelt to refrain from dwelling on his "personality" or character is most likely a reference to his health. It is also clear that Looker appears ill at ease with his project.

The article Looker planned was to be published in *Liberty* magazine. He even wrote as much to Roosevelt. A letter dated July 16, 1931, begins with "Well sir, we got away with the 'Liberty' article despite all obstacles." Looker also described to Roosevelt the excellent circulation of this magazine of approximately two and a half million copies. "Our story," he continues "is the lead article in the magazine and is featured upon the cover. I think we can be sure that at least seven and a half million readers are sure you are physically fit!" (FDR: Governor Papers, Series 1, Earle Looker File, FDRPL). The strategy was clear—an extensive national distribution of an article Looker wrote testifying to Roosevelt's health and fitness.

Once the article in *Liberty* magazine was published, Looker himself became the focal point of press coverage. *The Springfield Republican*, presumably not a fan of Franklin D. Roosevelt, covered the story with the title: "Article on Gov Roosevelt's Health Brings Northampton Writer Bricks and Bouquets."

The newspaper interviewed Looker and suggested that Looker was "hired by politicians to hush a whispering campaign, advised to spike the political ambition of a leader." It summarized the *Liberty* magazine article as claiming "an impartial study of the physical fitness of New York state executive and clean bill is given the man as a result of an examination by three of New York's leading specialists."

The Springfield Republican reported that "Mr. Looker is sticking to his guns. He reiterates that he is in no one's employ, that writing is his business and the topic was dug up by him and by no one else." It also reported that "Mr. Looker himself paid for the medical examination," and for balance, the newspaper described Looker's connection with Theodore Roosevelt and his family. The newspapers discussed the upcoming book Looker was writing on Franklin D. Roosevelt, a book which Looker described not as "a pure biography . . . but . . . a study of the man and his traits." The newspaper interview ended with Looker emphatically denying "that there was any financial compensation from Roosevelt, the Democratic party or anyone else" (FDR: Governor Papers, Series 1, Earle Looker File, FDRPL).

Looker must have pleased with the way he handled the interview as he sent Roosevelt a letter on July 20, 1931, enclosing the article from *The Springfield Republican,* "which may amuse you." The next sentence is most revealing: "The question of who paid for the physical examination was, and still is between us, frightfully embarrassing . . . but it had to be answered as I answered it" (The ellipses are in the original). In other words, Looker did not pay for the medical examination, Roosevelt did.

Looker also indicated to Roosevelt that "The story itself gives the sort of an interpretation we all most desire." He lamented that "while we can dramatize some things we really have nothing of a smashing kind that does not need to have the pumps working to keep it afloat. Those things, undoubtedly, you are reserving for the actual campaign after the convention." Looker advised Roosevelt that "this is the time to go into a prayerful silence to create something of dramatic importance which will provide grand copy before the Convention" (FDR: Governor Papers, Series 1, Earle Looker File, FDRPL).

On September 5, 1931, Looker wrote Roosevelt a short note and attached a cartoon to make a point about their secret arrangement. The cartoon depicted a king identified as Hoover holding a document titled "cause of crime." A criminal is sitting next to him with a gun pointed at King-Hoover and a little Alice standing in front of the impressively elevated seat. The girl is identified as Wickersham with several "reports" spread on the floor. The caption reads as follows:

> "What do you know about this business?" the King said to Alice.
> "Nothing," said Alice.
> "Nothing WHATEVER?" persisted the King.
> "Nothing whatever," said Alice.
> "That's very important," the King said . . . "
> (FDR: Governor Papers, Series 1, Earle Looker File, FDRPL).[1]

The purpose of this letter and the cartoon was to make it clear to Roosevelt that it was very important to state, if necessary, that he knew nothing of any arrangement made between the two of them. Behind the constant advice Looker gave Roosevelt stood a frightened Looker, fearful of having his stunt exposed and his reputation ruined.

The very idea of Looker giving Roosevelt advice indicates that he did not know Roosevelt very well. This was crucial for a writer who claimed to write a special biography. Whatever arrangement Roosevelt had with Looker, it seems that Looker was quite taken by this contact with the presidential contender and felt that the secret deal allowed him both access and the privilege of advice. It also appears that the additional syndicated articles Looker had in mind did not materialize. Roosevelt had only one use for Looker—to publish information that would "prove" his fitness to be president.

In 1932, Earle Looker published his biography titled *This Man Roosevelt*. "The object of this study," writes Looker at the outset,

> is to isolate the truth from the propaganda piled up about this potent name, and to represent the man as he really works and relaxes, thinks and lives. Disregarding controversial political documents and the usual political-life narrative, politics plays no part

in this report except where essential to give a clear view and an unprejudiced expression of his intimate traits of character, his mental and physical abilities and disabilities (p. 1).

Thus begins what purports to be an objective account of a person many wished to see as the next President. Though the real objective of the book centered on the candidate's health, his disability appears at the end of the list of objectives and with "abilities" for balance.

This book, however, has no footnotes or citations for sources. It is essentially a public relations tract designed to promote Roosevelt's presidential potential and to dispel any notion of physical limitations. The book is heavy with claims of impartiality, objectivity, and truthfulness. Looker begins with Roosevelt's illness on August 28, 1921, ten days after the fateful day at Campobello. He accurately states that the initial newspaper reports that Roosevelt caught a heavy cold and that he was threatened with a bad pneumonia were misleading (Looker, 1932, p. 112). He describes at length Roosevelt's impatient character and its importance in forcing him to quickly resume work and get well again.

The first year of struggling with the paralysis already portrayed a heroic Roosevelt and the admiration his friends had for his persistent efforts at a recovery.[2] Looker also writes that in 1922, the medical profession considered the first twelve months after the polio attack as crucial for some improvement, admitting that no further recovery was possible (1932, p. 115). Indeed, he indicates that Roosevelt made no improvement in the first two years and that this lack of progress motivated him to begin swimming exercises, first in Florida and later at Warm Springs. The net effect of this early physical exercise days [sic] was not an improvement in his leg movements but in building his chest and upper-body strength.

★ EXPERT OPINION AS MEDICAL PROOF

The heart of Looker's biographical project was a challenge to Roosevelt to submit himself to a lengthy medical examination by prominent physicians. Roosevelt took the challenge and invited Looker to spend time in the governor's mansion and observe him for several days as he went through his daily routines. This arrangement was made, claims Looker, with no political underhandedness and that [said] Roosevelt was engagingly frank about his infantile paralysis experience (1932, pp. 116–117).

For greater objectivity, Looker writes that he wanted to hear about Roosevelt's health from others as well. "I want," Looker states, "the real evidence which was created before there was the slightest possibility of its having political implication. I want to see your own personal letter files of the time. There must be correspondence there that will give me the opportunity to dig the facts out independently" (1932, p. 118). Roosevelt, Looker reports, was very willing to give him any evidence requested. Thus, Looker was given permission to review all of Roosevelt's personal files, with no selection and without any record being removed (1932, p. 118).

The book is inherently a lengthy argument designed to prove Roosevelt's physical fitness. The author's documentation is selective. For example, Looker quotes from a letter Roosevelt wrote George Peabody (a friend, and the owner of Warm Springs) on October 14, 1924, that "Nothing finer nor more useful to humanity could be done than to establish a 'cure' where the best of treatment along the lines of the accepted treatment could be given." Now (1931–32), Looker reports, Roosevelt considered the word "cure" "misleading," telling him that he used it in the said letter in the sense of "place for treatment." Looker claims that now Roosevelt wanted to "avoid the word [cure] as far as possible," in order "not to spread the false impression that there are miraculous medicinal qualities in the pool or a guarantee of cure in the treatment" (1932, p. 122). Roosevelt sought to reinforce the belief that he was not completely cured but fit nonetheless. Such a statement was advantageous since this way no one could accuse Roosevelt of hiding his disability or falsely arguing that he was completely cured.

Looker documents an early syndicated newspaper story that described Roosevelt as "Swimming Back to Health" (1932, p. 123), depicting him swimming together with Annette Kellerman, the famous swimmer, who also was afflicted with infantile paralysis earlier in her life (see also Gallagher, 1985, pp. 37–38). In those early days, Roosevelt, motivated by his own plan for recovery, pushed polio victims to try exercise. This was manifested in Roosevelt's enthusiasm with investing in the dilapidated Warm Springs, his push to have the American Orthopedic Association recognize the value of underwater treatment, as well as his own efforts to help other polio victims without any scientific or professional knowledge. All these efforts at a cure reinforced the perception that Roosevelt was on the mend. This was Looker and Roosevelt's objective.

In his first run for political office since contracting polio, his gubernatorial campaign of 1928, he faced the health issue head on, claims Looker. He was referred to as "that man on crutches they [Smith and his people] have put up for Governor!" (Looker, 1932, p. 133). Yet, Roosevelt won by more than 25,000 votes and that some [sic] voted out of sympathy (Looker, 1932, p. 133). To strengthen his book's argument that Roosevelt was physically fit to be president, Looker pointed to presidents Wilson and Harding who "cracked physically under the strain of the Presidency. As a nation we have come to accept as an axiom that a sound mind in a sound body is demanded for the Presidency" (Looker, 1932, p. 133). Indeed, voices of concern were heard. When the Women's Democratic Law Enforcement League met in Washington in April 1931, Mrs. Jesse W. Nicholson stated that "This candidate [Franklin D. Roosevelt], while mentally qualified for the Presidency, is utterly unfit physically" (quoted in Looker, 1932, p. 134).

For his final challenge, Looker cites from the letter he sent Roosevelt on February 23, 1931: "Even though you have recovered from your attack of infantile paralysis, the strain of the Presidency will be such as to seriously raise the question as to whether or not you are physically fit to be President . . . I am writing to ask that you make a frank avowal as to whether or not, in the event of your nomination, you are sufficiently recovered to assure your supporters that you could stand the strain of the Presidency" (1932, pp. 134–135).

Roosevelt quickly replied on February 28, 1931:

Of course no statement from me as to my physical fitness should really be acceptable to you. Your question, however, is very distinctly a personal challenge to me, no matter what my present or future position as a public servant may be—even in the humblest of positions. . . . Being assured of your integrity, I am therefore prepared to permit you to make an investigation of my physical fitness, to give you every facility for thoroughly making it, and authority for you to publish its results without censorship from me (Looker, 1932, p. 135).

To add credibility to the seemingly innocent arrangement, Looker writes that "The challenge had been caught and thrown back within four days. My letter to him had been almost brutal in tone. It had in no way expressed a personally sincere anxiety to see fair play. I had shown I belonged to the opposition" (Looker, 1932, p. 136). In other words, Roosevelt was willing to trust a Republican because he had nothing to hide. Contrast this account with that of Thelma Kleinhous, Roosevelt's swim therapist and friend who agreed with Roosevelt's decision not to publicize his disability while running for office (*The Syracuse Post-Standard,* 1998, p. B5).

Looker planted questions that were meant to preempt future attacks on Roosevelt's physical fitness to be president. For example, he asked Roosevelt, "But Governor, I am not questioning your mental fitness as a result of infantile paralysis, because I understand that the disease is not connected with the brain." "You're quite right," answered Roosevelt, "but the fact is not generally understood, and in fairness to myself as well as to all others who have been touched by it, you must not only make this clear but use my own case as proof" (1932, p. 137). The naïveté of the scripted question and answer is striking but understandable in light of the unwarranted fear and misinformation many had of polio and its victims.

Roosevelt used Looker's account to project humility and reluctance to run for the presidency despite his personal ambition: "Was I personally anxious to be Governor? I was not! But I accepted that nomination in order to accept an opportunity for service. You must understand [talking to Looker] I have to use the old words, and that one particularly—service—because no other word exactly fits. I feel the same way about the Presidency" (1932, p. 138). In other words, Roosevelt was willing to sacrifice his body, again, for the service of the people (The reluctant Roosevelt used the word "sacrifice" in 1928 when he finally agreed to run for governor).

Looker forwards several observations regarding Roosevelt's health and passes them on as if they are made by an expert:

His [Roosevelt] walk is slow but steady and in no sense halting. His legs, being locked in their braces, swing forward like a pendulum set in motion from the hips. The moment his foot is firmly planted he swings his other foot forward. The only reason for his braces is to insure his knees locking. This is necessarily awkward but it does not result in fatigue. The Governor's son, James, gave the best demonstration of how the braces work. He put the braces on himself. He found he could walk easily, once he had mastered the motion. But, despite the fact that he was an athlete, he could not climb stairs with them but collapsed again and again while his father shouted with laughter (1932, p. 146).

Looker significantly minimizes the role of the leg braces. The father laughing at his son's inability to walk with the braces "proved" that father Roosevelt had no such difficulties with his mobility.

Looker writes that he had "walked with him [Roosevelt] many times from the entrance hall into the Capitol (Albany), some fifty paces, to the elevator running up to the Executive Chamber. Walking some twenty paces more from the desk, he eases himself into his big Governor's chair and flexes his leg braces so that his knees bend under the edge of his desk. He seems unfatigued" (1932, p. 147). Looker notes that "It is worth recording, since all the details are essential if his physical condition is discussed, that he has not lost any feeling in any part of his legs or feet." For proof, Looker recounts hearing the governor being highly amused one day saying: "The soles of my feet are so ticklish that I was having a terrible time getting my socks on!" (1932, p. 148). In other words, if Roosevelt could feel some sensation in his feet, then this was proof that he was no longer paralyzed.

Looker describes the agreement among press correspondents and photographers not to comment on Roosevelt's disability, and [said] that those photos that were taken were destroyed later by the photographers themselves (see also Poore, 1998, p. 241). "The behavior of the news and the camera men is a real tribute to Roosevelt's personality. But even a gentleman's conspiracy of silence at this moment is hardly fair to Roosevelt. Mystery with regard to his condition would breed all sorts of unfounded rumors" (1932, p. 147). Looker, being Roosevelt's mouthpiece, forwards two arguments: he encourages the press to respect Roosevelt's disability as a private matter and not a public one. He also asks the press to report 'accurately' on Roosevelt's physical fitness, as long as such accuracy means reporting on Roosevelt's active political life and physical ability, and not dwelling on his disability. Indirectly, Looker also sought allies for his own "conspiracy."

The committee of specialists Looker arranged as part of his challenge to Roosevelt to examine his health was selected by Dr. Linsly R. Williams, Director of the New York Academy of Medicine. Credibility and authority were essential to this book project. The specialists selected were Dr. Samuel W. Lambert, a physician, Dr. Russell A. Hibbs, an orthopedist, and Dr. Foster Kennedy, a neurologist (Looker, 1932, p. 150). The medical examination took place on April 29, 1931, in Roosevelt's Manhattan residence. Looker was present in the house but did not witness the actual examination.

Two reports were issued thereafter. The first report, dated April 29, 1931, was short and testified that Roosevelt's "health and powers of endurance are such as to allow him to meet any demand of private and public life" (Looker, 1932, p. 155). A longer report, also dated April 29, 1931, attested to Roosevelt's healthy organs and functions, his normal spinal column, its perfect alignment and the freedom from disease. The report concluded that "There has been progressive recovery of power in the legs" since contracting polio in 1921, and that "this restoration continues and will continue." The final statement was most reassuring: "Governor Roosevelt can walk all necessary distances and can maintain a standing position without fatigue" (Looker, 1932, pp. 155–156). Looker added his own observation: "Roosevelt's improvement has been distinctly discernible even in the period of my observation" (1932, p. 156). Finally, Looker stated the conclusion to which his book-project was undertaken: "Infantile paralysis is no detriment to Franklin Roosevelt. He is physically fit to be President." (1932, p. 158).

CONCLUSION

This concentrated effort to publicize Roosevelt's fitness to be president in the most credible and evidential way was successful. Publicizing the life insurance policy and the article in *Liberty* magazine did bring many skeptical Democrats to see Roosevelt as a viable candidate after all. As a matter of fact, both Howe and Jim Farley, Roosevelt's key campaign advisers, considered the medical reports highly influential. Howe even sent a copy of the *Liberty* article to every county Democratic chairperson in the country and to any correspondent who questioned Roosevelt's fitness (Freidel, 1954, p. 211). Yet, Roosevelt and his aids were still baffled by the continuous concern with his health and the growing "whispering campaign" about his disability and poor health. To counter the continued suspicion about his health, especially among Republicans, Roosevelt resorted to an earlier successful strategy—the 1928 gubernatorial campaign with its emphases on travel, mobility and rhetorical activity upgraded to the national scale in 1932.

For the upcoming Democratic convention a plane was chartered to fly Roosevelt to Chicago to accept the party nomination if offered (Freidel, 1956, p. 312). No winning candidate had ever traveled to the respective party convention. Instead, key convention delegates would travel to the nominee's home to present the nomination. Roosevelt would break that tradition and resort to a mode of transportation not yet associated with politics (Houck,

1997, p. 28). On May 16, 1932, the *New York Times* reported that the Roosevelt camp was contemplating a post-convention train trip from Albany to the West Coast, and that such a trip could help allay further concerns about the candidate's health (p. 8).

The principal thought behind these travel efforts was to display Roosevelt's body in as many locations as possible as "proof" of his physical strength, mobility, and agility. Both the flight to Chicago to accept the presidential nomination, and the subsequent train trips were very successful. These travels, though enacted prior to the television age, did exemplify the very essence of modern presidential travel images that substitute "speech-act performatives for leadership initiatives" (Erickson, 1998, p. 141). Such travels were successful because they afforded the political operative to blur the distinction between the symbolic and the real (Erickson, 1998, p. 141). In Roosevelt's case this blurring of the real with the symbolic was key to his ability to project the image of a healthy, vibrant and enthusiastic politician. His body became symbolic of his fitness.

But Roosevelt was still concerned that the health issue would be used against him. To preempt one more time any last minute doubt about his health, Roosevelt would resort again to the report of a medical expert as evidence of his health and fitness. Two weeks before Election Day, he arranged for the wide publication of a "personal" letter he received from Dr. Beckwith, congratulating him "on the excellence of your physical condition." Dr. Beckwith told his patient how impressed he was with his muscular condition and how impressed he was to see that "your heart action and blood pressure both of which were entirely normal according to the standards for a man of your age." Dr. Beckwith concluded: "I have never before observed such complete degree of recovery in organic function and such a remarkable degree of recovery of muscles and limbs in an individual who had passed through an attack of infantile paralysis such as yours" (Howe's Papers, 1928–1932, FDRPL).

On November 8, 1932, eleven years after contracting polio, and after years of "proving" his fitness, Roosevelt was elected president. The methods of "proving" his physical fitness were unconventional but understandable. Roosevelt did his best to hide the true extent of his disability. He did so with rhetorical strategy of appearance and body presence. He projected the appearance of high energy and mobility, visited many places, and spoke often about his extensive travel and action. From about a year prior to the presidential election until Election Day Roosevelt added a well focused and concentrated campaign meant to publicize medical proof and the opinion of medical experts attesting to his fitness. This campaign, too, was about the appearance of objectivity and credibility. Though the arrangements Looker made were suspect, the medical experts forwarded a fair assessment of Roosevelt's health given their focus on the candidate's ability and not his disability. Neither did stereotypes or prejudices regarding the disabled affect the medical experts.

What distinguishes this focused effort to forward medical proof from other strategies is Roosevelt's pro-active argument that he was fit and medically certified as such. Before and after 1930–31, Roosevelt's main objective was to display his body through physical and rhetorical activities. Roosevelt let his body serve a discursive agency that communicated vibrancy to be complemented with rhetorical allusions to fitness and mobility. A change of strategy is clearly discerned with his arrangement with Earle Looker. This strategy was more in line with traditional argumentation—strong and direct evidence uttered by perceived credible experts from the medical profession. The overall strategy was that of forwarding strong evidence to preempt counter arguments. With this strategy Roosevelt sought a definitive solution to the health issue, especially with Democrats prior to the Democratic convention. Once Roosevelt was nominated the Democratic presidential candidate in July 1932, and the presidential campaign was underway, he reverted back to using his body as a rhetorical agency and proof of his physical stamina.

Roosevelt had no chance of becoming president if he were known as the disabled candidate. He thus decided to modify the public impression of his disability given the prejudices against people with disability. Though Roosevelt considered direct refutation of rumors about his health a necessary objective during a crucial phase in his pursuit of the White House, displaying his body was the more successful approach. While direct refutation is often constrained by the very defensive posture, displaying the body is a subtle form of refutation not prone to the same constraint. By displaying his body, Roosevelt engaged in a visual argument that was more immediate and more convincing. It was difficult for his opponents to argue that Roosevelt was unfit when a vibrant and enthusiastic body was displayed in many local[e]s around the country. The proof of the body was stronger than the proof about the body.

NOTES

[1] George W. Wickersham was Hoover's head of the National Commission on Law Observance and Enforcement, focusing primarily on Prohibition (He was also Taft's attorney general).

[2] The most pertaining chapters in Looker's biography are titled progressively: Fate strikes a blow (chapter XI); Fighting back (chapter XII); Fit to be president (chapter XIII); and, Doctors agree (chapter XIV).

WORKS CITED

Davis, K. S. (1974). *Invincible summer: An intimate portrait of the Roosevelts based on the recollection of Marion Dickerman.* New York: Atheneum.

The Democratic landslide. (1930, November 15). *The Literacy Digest,* pp. 7–9.

Erickson, K. V. (1998). "Presidential Spectacles: Political Illusionism and the Rhetoric of Travel." *Communication Monographs, 65,* 141–153.

Exposed to frost. (1930, April 29). *New York Times,* p. 26.

FDR's Therapist dead at age 94. (1998, June 19). *The Syracuse Post-Standard,* p. B5.

Freidel, F. (1956). *Franklin D. Roosevelt: The triumph.* Boston: Little, Brown and Co.

———. (1954). *Franklin D. Roosevelt: The ordeal.* Boston: Little, Brown and Co.

Gallagher, H. (1985). *FDR's splendid deception.* New York Dodd, Mead.

Gunther, J. (1950). *Roosevelt in retrospect: A profile in history.* New York: Harper & Brothers.

Houck, D. W. (1997). "Reading the body in the text: FDR's 1932 speech to the Democratic National Convention." *Southern Communication Journal, 62,* 20–36.

Jamieson, K. H. (1992). *Dirty politics: Deception, distraction and democracy.* New York: Oxford University Press.

Kiewe, A. (1999). A Dress Rehearsal for a Presidential Campaign: FDR's Embodied "Run" for the 1928 New York Governorship. *The Southern Communication Journal, 64,* 155–167.

Looker, E. (1932). *This man Roosevelt.* New York: Brewer & Putnam.

Poore, C. (1998). "'But Roosevelt could walk': Envisioning disability in Germany and the United States." *Michigan Quarterly Review, 37,* 239–266.

Rogers, N. (1992). *Dirt and disease: Polio before FDR.* New Brunswick, NJ: Rutgers University Press.

Rollins, N. (1962). *Roosevelt and Howe.* New York: Alfred A. Knopf.

Roosevelt hears of whispering plot. (1932, May 16). *New York Times,* p. 8.

Roosevelt, F. D. Presidential Library, Hyde Park, New York. Public papers file: Family, business, and personal papers; Campaign of 1924 scrapbook; Governor Papers, Series 1, Earle Looker folder; Presidential secretary file, Looker-Joseph folder; Howe papers, 1928–1932.

Shome, R. (1996). "Race and popular cinema: The rhetorical strategies of whiteness in *City of Joy,*" *Communication Quarterly, 44,* 502–518.

Sontag, S. (1991). *Illness as metaphor and AIDS and its metaphors.* London: Penguin Books.

"Our Mission and Our Moment": George W. Bush and September 11th

John M. Murphy

On January 20, 2001, President George W. Bush inherited a peaceful and prosperous nation. In less than a year, he found himself mired in war and recession. Nearly three thousand Americans died in the bloodiest terrorist attacks to occur on U.S. soil. It was an extraordinary intelligence failure on the part of the United States.[1] Osama bin Laden, the leader of al-Qaeda, the group said to have carried out the attacks, and Mullah Omar, the leader of the Afghan Taliban, the group said to have supported Al Qaeda, are still at large.[2] The nation is still at war in Afghanistan. In the name of preemptive war, the nation fights in Iraq. Americans now measure their daily safety by the color of the new Department of Homeland Security's terrorist alert scale. The world, in short, has grown significantly less peaceful since George W. Bush took office.[3]

Meanwhile, the nation slid into recession even as Bush pronounced the oath. So far, better than two million jobs have disappeared and one million workers have dropped out of the labor force. For the first time in six years, wage increases fell below the inflation rate for most Americans.[4] The stock market lost nearly $5 trillion in value during the president's first two years in office, the largest real and percentage loss suffered by any president in that period, including Herbert Hoover. In 2001, the budget surplus projected out at $5.6 trillion from fiscal 2002 through fiscal 2011. That same time now yields a $1.8 trillion deficit, a figure that is constantly growing. In other words, the Bush administration has lost a minimum of $7.4 trillion in projected budget surpluses. In 2011, baby boomers begin to retire, a very expensive event for which we are now not prepared. The dollar's value has dropped 13 percent since 2001.[5] The trade deficit hit $435.2 billion in 2002, the largest in history.[6] The nation, in short, has grown significantly less prosperous since George W. Bush took office.

As a result of his performance, George W. Bush has seen his popularity ratings rival those of the most beloved chief executives in memory. Of course, many citizens understand that events from Israeli/Palestinian violence to increasing income inequality to rising crime rates may not be the president's fault. Yet Americans have generally held presidents responsible for events on their watches and rewarded or punished them accordingly. Generosity alone cannot explain Bush's popularity. Of course, Americans tend to rally around the president during a crisis. Yet Jimmy Carter failed to win reelection during the Iran hostage crisis and Abraham Lincoln faced severe criticism for his policies during the Civil War. Crisis alone cannot explain Bush's popularity. We could also attribute his popularity to his intrinsic leadership ability; little of that, however, was apparent before 9/11, and a plurality of the people, whose wisdom he lauds, chose his opponent on Election Day 2000.[7] If we are so smart, why did we not see his leadership qualities then?

Such explanations are useful but not sufficient. I believe that President Bush has done a remarkable job of defining the attacks of September 11 to his advantage and that his rhetoric is a key factor in his success. In the remainder of this essay, I examine his discourse. I explore three strategies—choice of genre, use of visual imagery, and creation of self and audience—that animate his 9/11 rhetoric, primarily his famous speech on September 20, 2001. My major claim is simple: These rhetorical strategies crafted the authority President George W. Bush needed to dominate public interpretation of the events of September 11. This is a speculative essay, an effort to explore a fascinating set of speeches. I invite responses in the hope that critics will begin to grapple with the rhetoric that infuses our increasingly bellicose and divided public sphere.

★ GENRE

Genre means type or sort. Generic critics assume that regularities in rhetorical life matter. If the same sorts of speeches recur, it is likely because they do something important for the community. Critics who employ a generic perspective seek to explain the strategies typically used by rhetors and audiences to encompass similar situations. That is, critics care about the ends sought by a community and the means used to achieve those ends, the ways in which form follows function. A type emerges from this rhetorical action, a constellation of form and argument that facilitates a community's efforts to do the social tasks, such as religious instruction (a sermon), that regularly need doing.[8]

Given the emphasis on routine, a generic perspective is particularly useful when dealing with institutions. An institution such as the presidency must accomplish recurrent rhetorical tasks, including committing the nation to military action. War or crisis rhetoric, in fact, infuses the U.S. presidency. Despite our professed desire for peace, this nation has risen to greatness through war, about once each generation: the Revolution, the War of 1812, the Mexican War, the Civil War, the Plains Indian wars, the Spanish American War, World War I, World War II, the Korean War, the Vietnam War, the First Persian Gulf War, the Afghan or Terror War, and the Second Persian Gulf War. In between have come a series of military actions too numerous to mention.[9] On nearly every one of these occasions, the president must rally the nation to pay any price or bear any burden in the pursuit of victory. Recurrent type, indeed.

Karlyn Kohrs Campbell and Kathleen Hall Jamieson have detailed five appeals common to presidential war rhetoric, Robert L. Ivie has explored the *topos* of savagery that runs through this discourse, and Richard A. Cherwitz, Kenneth S. Zagacki, Bonnie J. Dow, and others have examined crisis rhetoric—that discourse which stops short of a full-fledged war.[10] Through the research runs a common thread: war rhetoric is a rhetorical hybrid, combining the qualities of what Aristotle termed deliberative discourse, arguments to justify the expediency or practicality of an action, and epideictic rhetoric, appeals that unify the community and amplify its virtues. We go to war because it is a practical act and an honorable choice.[11] Depending on situation, presidential preference, communal need, or other factors, presidents emphasize one of the Aristotelian genres over another when taking the United States to war.[12] Remarkably, President Bush has spoken almost solely through the medium of epideictic rhetoric when it comes to his war on terror.

Much to the chagrin of rhetoricians, Aristotle failed to provide a coherent explanation of epideictic rhetoric and that has led to proliferating perspectives. Celeste M. Condit notes that various definitions of epideictic rhetoric focus on the message, the speaker, or the audience.[13]

Particularly troublesome to scholars has been the audience. In the other Aristotelean genres, deliberative and forensic rhetoric, the audience makes clear decisions: we should or should not adopt a particular policy, we should or should not regard a particular act as just. In those cases, Aristotle calls the audience "judges."[14]

Unfortunately, the role accorded to the audience for an epideictic speech is less clear. Translations differ, but the terms used are generally "spectators" or "observers." They come from the Greek *theoros* (spectator) or *theoria* (observation). Interestingly, Aristotle uses the latter term in his famous definition of rhetoric. He calls it the "ability, in each [particular] case, to see the available means of persuasion," or "the faculty of observing in any given case the available means of persuasion." In doing so, he grants rhetoric the power of theoretical reflection through inclusion of *theoria* or observation or spectatorship.[15] As Thomas Farrell notes, rhetoric "retains the concrete emphasis of techne while attempting to include the reflective capacity to identify the possible materials of rhetoric in real settings."[16] The *theoria* that makes up rhetoric, the means we observe, constitute the art in that they give the art, in theory, potential for existence, but it can only be brought to life at a specific time and place by particular people—that is, Aristotle also views rhetoric as a *dynamis,* "a potential for doing, a power in its nascent state."[17]

What is true for rhetoric as a whole is likely to be true for the epideictic genre. When an epideictic audience observes, it reflects on the means of honor or dishonor, unity or disunity, community or chaos in public life; the epideictic performance then brings particular values to life. Indeed, Takis Poulakos sees epideictic rhetoric as a "creative and productive process, an act through which nothing is being copied but something novel comes to be—a new world is disclosed."[18] Yun Lee Too says that it "exemplifies rhetoric as a language of transformations—of old to new, of great to lowly, of familiar to unfamiliar, and vice versa."[19] Poulakos, reading Isocrates, emphasizes epideictic's potential: varied worlds come into being. But it is possible that, for the probabilistically inclined Aristotle, one world is made "real"

or probable in performance, a collaborative creation of speaker and audience as they establish the appropriate relationships between each other in a new world. Each judges the other as a partner in the enterprise, reflecting on the tactics used to create a world (*ethos, pathos, logos,* and so forth) and the world itself. Epideictic rhetoric, then, shapes the world that provides the backdrop of values and beliefs, heroes and villains, triumphs and tragedies against which and through which deliberative and forensic judgments are made in a ceaseless swirl of discourse.

At least, that is the potential for epideictic that I plan to explore. I suspect that I do so partly because I am dealing with a president during a crisis. If ever a new world is brought into being in U.S. society, it is made by a "rhetorical president" in a troubled time. Several studies have explored the ways in which epideictic rhetoric asserts itself during a crisis. Citizens need to understand what has happened and who they are in light of a communal rupture.[20] Epideictic speech addresses such concerns. In addition, studies of the rhetorical presidency emphasize its ability, particularly in comparison to other political institutions, and its power, implicit in the role of head of state, to speak to epideictic concerns and through ceremonial speech.[21] Ronald Reagan, for example, understood this power very well. Jamieson argues that epideictic rhetoric was his "stock in trade," and Campbell and Jamieson note his tendency to transform State of the Union addresses, a genre that traditionally balances deliberative and epideictic concerns, into a purely ceremonial speech.[22] For practical politicians like Reagan and Bush, epideictic rhetoric is appealing. The president speaks synecdochically as the voice of the people, making their world and the amplification strategies inherent in the genre mesh nicely with the display and entertainment functions of a contemporary televisual culture. Amplification makes this new world a vivid creation.

President Bush spoke about the 9/11 terrorist attacks and the Afghan war in almost purely epideictic terms. Initially, such a choice was appropriate. Like Ronald Reagan after the explosion of the space shuttle *Challenger,*

George Bush felt the need to define the meaning of 9/11 and we felt the need to understand this horrific event.[23] Bush's poor speech on the evening of September 11 and his eloquent meditation at a memorial service on September 14 crafted our interpretation of the attacks. He began the former: "our way of life, our very freedom came under attack in a series of deliberate and deadly terrorist attacks."[24] The words "deliberate and deadly" were likely meant to evoke FDR's famous war address to Congress, but the awkward repetition of "attacks" undermined the flow.[25] Bush also placed our experiences in a biblical context through quotation of the opening of the 23rd Psalm, shaping the meaning of 9/11 as a passage through the valley of the shadow of death yet simultaneously assuring us that the Lord was with us (2). This was a nice, if cliché[d], choice. Unfortunately, he turned to a modern translation, disdaining the traditional and comforting language of the King James Bible.[26] He concluded with an awkward lesson for the future: we "unite in our resolve for justice and peace" (2). Given the fact, as he put it, of a terrorist attack on the United States, those two resolves appeared to be mutually exclusive on the evening of September 11. This speech was not helpful.

The prayer service speech was better and explicit in its epideictic purpose: "We are here in the middle hour of our grief. So many have suffered so great a loss, and today we express our nation's sorrow" (5). His deft management of time ("middle hour") crafted the response of the audience; we mourned the past and looked to the future as we stood in the present, an appropriate strategic move for an epideictic address. In this speech, the president shaped our understanding of an inexplicable event, taking as his goal to explain, to express, to comfort. Drawing on the deepest wellspring of the American tradition, Bush interpreted the attacks much as a Puritan would have done. They were seemingly unbelievable, but the "world He created is of moral design" (6). Why, then, did tragedies occur? The president explained that "adversity introduces us to ourselves" (6). He then recounted acts of sacrifice and courage that, in their individual parts, came together to display the whole of the nation's character in the midst

of terrible trauma. "In this trial, we have been reminded," the president said (6), of our character. Framing the attacks as a biblical test of a chosen people made them comprehensible. "God's signs are not always the ones we look for," but they brought out, as God must have intended, the best in the nation (6).

Although focused on character past, the frame permitted him to hint at character tests to come—the war that faced the nation. Bush would not violate the occasion with policy argument, but he would unveil the policy that the national character demanded. Much as Reagan pledged that space flights would continue after the *Challenger* explosion and Clinton claimed that justice would prevail after the Oklahoma City bombing, Bush promised, "This conflict was begun on the timing and terms of others; it will end in a way and at an hour of our choosing" (6).[27] Real Americans could hardly believe differently, any more than they could abandon the New Frontier. The president ended the speech with comfort and policy, put in the language of Christian love and Christian soldiers. He turned to Paul's Letter to the Romans 8:38, assuring us that "neither death nor life, nor angels nor principalities nor powers, nor things present nor things to come, nor height nor depth can separate us from God's love. May he bless the souls of the departed. May he comfort our own. And may He always guide our country" (7). Paul's Letter to the Romans detailed the rebellion of humanity against God's Lordship, a terrible sin for which Jesus Christ redeemed all those who accepted his sacrifice. For the community of belief who embraced Jesus, "We know that in everything God works for good with those who love him. . . . If God is for us, who is against us?" (Revised Standard Version, Romans 8:28, 31).[28] The chosen people who stood by God understood that nothing could separate us from his love. God would, in Bush's words, "comfort our own." As for the others? Neither principalities nor powers could stand against the God of battles. As Bush concluded, "a military choir burst into 'The Battle Hymn of the Republic'— and not one of the soulful renditions that had become popular in the 1990's, but the full-throated anthem of Protestant righteousness militant."[29] He has loosed the fateful lightning of his terrible swift sword in a new world made old by a new war.

Nor did Bush waver in his choice to speak through the epideictic genre in the succeeding weeks. He offered a series of short radio broadcasts, on one occasion noting, "Good morning. I want to report to you on the progress being made on many fronts in our war on terrorism" (18). If not an epideictic speech, it was, at best, a report. Yet that purpose disappeared as the president launched into an encomium for the "many members of our military [who] have left their homes and families" (18). Mixed in with such appeals were deliberative claims, but they were again not developed. For instance, he said, "I'm working with Congress to put federal law enforcement in charge of all bag and passenger screening at our airports" (19). No argument was presented as to the policy's practicality, nor did he engage the then-competing plans for increased air safety.

On October 7, the president announced the start of military action against Afghanistan. Again, objectives and actions were announced, not justified. In contrast to other speeches, there were some reasons given. He said that by "destroying camps and disrupting communications, we will make it more difficult for the terror network to train new recruits and coordinate their evil plans" (20). Unlike his father at the commencement of the First Persian Gulf War, however, this President Bush did not use the occasion to develop a full rationale for war. Rather, the final third of a short speech was, again, an encomium to members of the armed services. In none of these speeches did the president justify the expediency of his policy in terms of the common *topoi* of deliberative address: the harm we faced, the choices available, the time and resources his choice would take, the advantages and disadvantages of his policy and various alternatives, or the long-term effects of the policy on the world community. These speeches focused almost entirely on national *ethos*. In Bush's view, we acted for reasons of character, not expediency. We chose the right way, not the easy way.

The most famous speech of this period, indeed of the Bush presidency, occurred before a joint session of the Congress on September 20. Bush began by appropriating the ritual, and thus the symbolic charge, of the State of the Union address: "In the normal course of events, Presidents come to this chamber to report on the state of the Union. Tonight, no such report is needed. It has already been delivered by the American people" (10). After several vignettes amplifying national unity, a tactic reminiscent of his September 14 address, Bush concluded his opening: "My fellow citizens, for the last nine days, the entire world has seen for itself the state of our Union—and it is strong" (10). The latter line contradicted the former and revealed the first movement of the text. The "report" of the people could only be seen in action; the world observed them, but they could not speak. Bush took for himself, through invocation of the genre of the State of the Union, the authority to speak on behalf of the people. After all, the Constitution mandated that the president report from time to time, not necessarily annually, on the state of the union and that was what he was doing. He thereby invoked the authority of the founders and the Constitution, a legitimacy rarely available outside of the State of the Union genre.[30] He, as the president, interpreted the actions of the people and offered them up for contemplation. The people were mute. He also delivered the report—"it is strong"—he had initially termed unnecessary. Clearly, his voice was needed to supplement the people's actions.

This opening set the genre. He did not preview policies for the union's betterment nor did he suggest expediency arguments. Rather, he was representative of the people; he stood as a part for their whole. He spoke as their voice, expressing their feelings, as, it seemed, the Constitution mandated. Kenneth Burke tells us that synecdoche is the trope of "political representation, where some part of the social body (either traditionally established, or elected, or coming into authority by revolution) is held to be 'representative' of the society as a whole." Burke also reminds us that all "such conversions [part for the whole, whole for the part, container for the contained, and so forth] imply an integral relationship, a relationship of convertibility, between the two terms."[31] Oddly, Bush came to power in all of the ways specified by Burke: as the son of a president, he inherited the throne; as Republican nominee, he was elected by the Electoral College; and, as the president on 9/11, he became authoritative because a new world seemingly revolved into existence on that revolutionary day. Given this role, Bush sought to become the people's voice and to represent their whole in his part. He would be the container for their contained.

But first he needed to make the new world, an imagined creation that would justify his authority to act in the material world. The crucial paragraph occurred early, immediately after the president had thanked the nations that responded with sympathy and fury to the attacks, an enumeration that built momentum for the proclamation to come. He deployed definition: "On September 11th, the enemies of freedom committed an act of war against our country." Three choices were critical. First, those who attacked did so for ideological and not expedient reasons; they were "enemies of freedom," not those who, because of self-interest, "would end American occupation of Saudi Arabia" or some such. This Manichaean frame, almost offhandedly slipped in as fact and not argued as proposition, was valuable to the president later in the speech. Second, this was an act of war, not an act of terror or a crime against humanity. That meant that military strategy, not criminal justice, should inform the nation's actions in this new world. Third, these two reasons meant that we *were now* at war against an implacable foe. Bush brought to bear the sort of orientation that had served the nation (and presidential powers) so well in World War II and the Cold War.[32] An ideological enemy deceitfully began a war against the United States (or might do so), and the president felt compelled (or felt compelled to have to hand) extraordinary powers to respond to that assault (or possible assault).

He followed definition with dialysis—a series of disjunctive propositions that lead to a conclusion.[33] In this case, Bush linked the old with the new to create the unprecedented present: "Americans have known wars—but for the past 136 years, they have been wars on foreign soil, except for one Sunday in 1941. Americans have known casualties of war—but not at the center of a great city on a peaceful morning. Americans have known surprise attacks—but never before on thousands of civilians" (11). The disjunctions asserted in form and content that a break had occurred and that the world was born again. Yet they also enacted in form the claim that the new world had emerged from the cocoon of the old, exploiting the fact that epideictic is a rhetoric of transformation. We had fought wars, but not recently a domestic war; we had suffered surprise attacks, but not in a peaceful city. The past informed the present, but the present was not the past. The present was new. Consistent with the demands of his genre, he disclosed a new world. Note also the realism; the attacks created a world and Bush only told us of it. But once unveiled, this new world demanded of the people new behavior.

The rest of the speech shaped behavior by returning to the synecdoche. He structured the address through four rhetorical queries beginning with "Americans have many questions tonight. Americans are asking: Who attacked our country?" (11). Again, he spoke as the people's voice. He asked the questions and asserted the right to know what we would say were we able to speak. Three were epideictic in nature; who attacked our country and why they hated us developed into ad hominem arguments, nicely illustrating the amplification strategies available in a speech of blame. The Manichaean frame enabled and constrained the character attacks. Within its purview, no subtlety was possible, but amplification of evil was easy. So, for instance, when the president answered the first question, he used grammatically balanced statements to polarize our world and amplify al-Qaeda's evil: "Al Qaeda is to terror what the mafia is to crime. But its goal is not making money; its goal is remaking the world" (11). Comparison and amplification likened al-Qaeda to a familiar marker yet lifted it to the levels of Nazi Germany or the Soviet Union; John Gotti, after all, did not wish to remake the world. The rhythmic balance iconically enacted the newly polarized globe. The Manichaean frame charged these words and, in turn, became more "real" as a result of them. Given all of this, it was easy to accept al-Qaeda as a "Soviet" threat, despite the fact that, unlike the Soviets, it did not possess tens of thousands of nuclear weapons, capable delivery systems, and millions of troops. Within this textual world, however, al-Qaeda seemed an extraordinary menace, comparable to the worst in American history.

Description amplified the threat. Al-Qaeda was a "fringe movement that perverts the peaceful teachings of Islam." It sought to "kill Christians and Jews, kill all Americans," kill "women and children," "plot evil and destruction," and commit "murder" (12). Isocrates writes of amplification that people who blame exaggerate the poor qualities displayed by their subjects and people who praise do the opposite.[34] It was unlikely that the al-Qaeda would, could, or even wanted to kill "all" Americans. Such a threat, however, divided the world and united Americans. That was the goal. The threat seemed realistic and the president believable partly because of the synecdoche. He spoke in our voice. He was a part for the whole of the social body and so he was only saying what we already "knew" if we could only speak. That is the power of synecdoche.

If the first question were devoted to blame, then the second turned initially to praise of the United States: "Americans are asking, why do they hate us? They hate what we see right here in this chamber—a democratically elected government" (13). They also hated our freedoms, which the president recited in a way that strongly resembled Franklin D. Roosevelt's four freedoms.[35] These two sentences, however, constituted the whole of the praise and even that operated through indirection. Bush stated our fine qualities not in a positive fashion, but as a negative contrast—these qualities were what they hated and, as a result, these freedoms were to be treasured.

Bush returned quickly to an attack on al-Qaeda. The audience then received the only hint of pragmatism to color al-Qaeda's motivation: "They stand against us because we stand in their way" (13). But assertion of a practical reason for the hate, to get the United States out of the way, was preceded by extravagant descriptions of their aims. The avowals implied the terrorists could reach such ends (unlikely) or provided clues as to their character (likely).[36] If

they wanted to kill and destroy, then they were the sort of people who liked to do so. Bush said al-Qaeda sought to "overthrow existing governments," "drive Israel out of the Middle East" and "Christians and Jews out of vast regions of Asia and Africa" (13). Al-Qaeda kills "not merely to end lives, but to disrupt and end a way of life" (13). The claim of expedient motivation was followed by analogy. They were "heirs to all the murderous ideologies of the 20th century," including "fascism, and Nazism, and totalitarianism" (13). The implication of blood relations (heirs) solidified the connections. Any idea that al-Qaeda acted out of expediency died under this framing barrage. They were crazed murderers. In Burkean terms, an agent/act ratio crafted the characterization, partly because the who and why questions came first and framed the others. Terrorists did what they did because character (blood) drove them. They could not be reasoned with or rehabilitated. They attacked us because that was what rabid murderers did.

The final question, "What is expected of us" in the face of these murderers, seemed likely to address policy (15). After all, future action is the province of deliberation. But the president implicitly distinguished between public and private action, relegating the citizenry to the private sphere and avoiding deliberation. We should live our lives, hug our children, cooperate with the investigation, have confidence in government, and say prayers for victims. In short, Americans should "uphold the values of America" (15) in daily life, an epideictic act because it solicited performance of national principles. Note that his requests concerned only the private sphere; we were not asked to debate policy, volunteer for the armed services, contribute to bond drives, or perform other public acts. Instead, the government would act in the public sphere and make policy. The citizens would act in the private sphere structured by that policy. Implicit in the speech was praise for such behavior, praise that became explicit in the models provided, an issue I address later. The people's duty rested in private use of what Bush identified as American values.

Only the third question—"How will we fight and win this war?"—concerned policy (13). In this area, he announced his actions. They included financial and military moves, overt and covert war. None was justified in the traditional sense. No arguments were presented as to their practicality. In fact, the audience shifted between the people of the United States and foreign governments. It was here that he issued his warning to those who might harbor terrorists. That warning made the Manichaean shape of the new world as clear as it was possible to be: "Either you are with us, or you are with the terrorists" (14). The shift in addressee, however, relieved him of any need to justify the policy's expediency to an American audience concerned with our future acts because he was not now speaking to that audience; he was threatening others. As a result, he did not have to address issues such as the size of the Special Forces vis-à-vis the tasks he set out for them, the cooperation of financial institutions around the globe and especially in "allies" such as Saudi Arabia, the money needed for defense, or the utility of creating an office of homeland security rather than a cabinet department, a stance Bush insisted on until the 2002 election loomed. This section was more a warning to others than a rationale for his policy and a discussion of the resources needed for its enactment.

Bush's preference for epideictic rhetoric defined the problem we faced not as one of policy, but rather as one of unity. Not a single section of this address, nor of the others he made during this period, moved much beyond the memorialization of the dead, the amplification of al-Qaeda's evil, and the promise of retribution. His two other major statements, the 2002 State of the Union address and the memorial speech on the six-month anniversary of 9/11, took place on ceremonial occasions and used the epideictic genre. Not once did he address us concerning the expediency of his policies—the practical steps we would need to take, the resources we would need to invest, and the consequences of his choices.

We also have evidence from beyond the text. To a degree that was remarkable, the White House revealed almost everything about the composition of the September 20 address. That in itself was noteworthy because, as numerous sources agree, the Bush team, since his first run for governor, was very disciplined.[37] They controlled leaks. Massive leaks regarding this speech and the surrounding events suggested that this was the version of history that they wanted people to know. The sources, primarily Bob Woodward in Bush at War and D. T. Max in the New York Times Magazine, agreed: its goal was, in Max's words, "to reassure Americans."[38]

In addition, there was no sense that Bush sought to initiate a debate about or to justify his policies. When Woodward asked Bush about his relationship to cabinet members, for instance, Bush provocatively explained his view of the presidency: "I'm the commander—see, I don't need to explain—I do not need to explain why I say things. That's the interesting thing about being the president. Maybe somebody needs to explain to me why they say something, but I don't feel like I owe anybody an explanation."[39] In specific reference to his public communication strategy, the president said, "I had to show the American people the resolve of a commander in chief that was going to do whatever it took to win. No yielding. No equivocation. No, you know, lawyering this thing to death." He said of his discussions with other world leaders: "These guys were watching my every move. And it's very important for them to come into this Oval Office, which they do, on a regular basis, and me look them in the eye and say, 'You're either with us or you're against us.'"[40] The president spoke. Others obeyed. This was not a mind that regarded the slow and messy processes of democratic deliberation, diplomacy, and compromise as useful tasks. In his private view, as in his public address, character made policy and there was no need to lawyer the thing to death.

★ VISUALS

In her thoughts on the speech, presidential counselor Karen Hughes noted, "I felt strongly the need for new images to replace the horrible images we'd all seen."[41] Her words eerily recalled Kathleen Hall Jamieson's analysis of Reagan's Challenger speech. Jamieson said that Reagan, to succeed in a televisual age, needed to replace one horrible image—the contrails blowing apart in the sky—with something reassuring. He spoke of "the last time we saw them—this morning—as they prepared for their journey and waved goodbye, and slipped the surly bonds of Earth to touch the face of God."[42] The imagery first substituted the picture of the astronauts walking and waving for the image of the explosion and then, should that move fail, romantically recontextualized the explosion—those contrails were reaching for the face of God.

It has become a truism in U.S. culture to assert that, since the Kennedy funeral, the nation experiences its most traumatic moments through the medium of television. I hesitate to subscribe fully to that notion. If my personal experience is any guide, people not only watched television on 9/11, they also called friends and family and talked through the day. Nonetheless, the assertion possesses validity. We know these events partly from television. It follows, then, that rhetors who dominate the interpretation of common televisual experience are powerful speakers. Presidents, as the leaders we look to for reassurance and direction in a national crisis, are ideally situated to exploit such opportunities. Ronald Reagan understood this and so did George Walker Bush. Like Reagan, Bush used personification of central themes and evocation of televisual experience to dominate the high ground of politics—the pictures that are our window on the world.

Such strategies are nearly required of presidents in a televisual age. Drawing on the work of Michael Warner and W. J. T. Mitchell, Robert Hariman and John Louis Lucaites argue that a public "can only acquire self-awareness and historical agency if individual auditors 'see themselves' in the collective representations that are the materials of public culture. Visual practices in the public media play an important role at precisely this point."[43] Hariman and Lucaites, as well as other scholars in this field of study, emphasize the polysemic, even subversive potentialities, of the visual image.[44] Cori E. Dauber, however, reminds us of two important aspects to the process of visual interpretation. First, in the context of photojournalism and news coverage, "the point of the image is to suppress the fact of its constructedness. . . . visual images offered as news are presented as

authentic and objective pieces of evidence—not as representations of reality, but in a sense, as reality itself." Second, "images are interpreted within an already existing context. Images come with words. . . . They come with historical baggage, both in terms of the particular event and in terms of previous events."[45] These factors have particular salience for presidential crisis address because the visuals, when they appear, are nested in an argument or narrative and that interpretation carries with it the authority of the institution in times of trouble.

Ronald Reagan demonstrated the use of personification with his display of Lenny Skutnick in the 1982 State of the Union address. Skutnick was a government worker who dove into the Potomac River to rescue plane crash survivors. Reagan introduced Skutnick to personify a favorite theme: heroism lived in ordinary Americans. Simultaneously, a visual, associative logic flowed through the story: Skutnick did not need government to do this. If Americans were heroes, then of what use were the government programs that Reagan sought to cut? Heroes did not need food stamps. There was no logical link between said programs and the "evidence" proffered by Skutnick's swim. Yet we "saw" the argument and were more likely to accept the claim. Equally important to this "logic" was the evocation of televisual experience. As Jamieson says, Reagan often argued "that his actions are justified not by what we have read or heard but by what we have seen. The visual evidence conveyed by television eliminates the need for additional words. . . . In such a world, words contextualize pictures."[46] The pictures, rather than traditional modes of argument or evidence, justified policy. Display of persons and pictures, of course, is facilitated by the epideictic genre. Amplification, Aristotle notes, is the key strategy in epideictic address, and the president's words amplified the always already experienced visual aids.

Bush consistently displayed the heroes of 9/11, deploying associative logic, particularly when it came to the Flight 93 passengers who stormed the cockpit and crashed the plane. On September 20, for instance, Bush featured the heroism of ordinary Americans. After Bush asserted that the people had reported on the state of the union, he painted the pictures: "We have seen it [the state of the union] in the courage of passengers, who rushed terrorists to save others on the ground—passengers like an exceptional man named Todd Beamer. And would you please help me to welcome his wife, Lisa Beamer, here tonight" (10). This visual vignette was followed by more pictures, shaped into a parallel structure in which each image was preceded by "We have seen . . ." The images were common from that day and the following ones on television—we saw the unfurling of flags, the giving of blood, the endurance of rescuers, and so forth (10). The verbal repetition amplified the previous *good* televisual experience. President Bush sought to replace images of the planes crashing into the towers, again and again and again, with pictures of rescue workers digging, flags waving, and Americans offering up their blood.

The president fashioned these images into what Burke terms a qualitative progression in form—a movement in mood.[47] Bush not only reported on the Union, he crafted our feelings about it. The sight of Lisa Beamer, the applause, followed by the amplification of common televisual experience, called forth our feelings, feelings Bush then shaped before unveiling the next step: "Our grief has turned to anger, and anger to resolution." No verbs needed in that last phrase; the feelings were there and he channeled them. He continued: "Whether we bring our enemies to justice or bring justice to our enemies, justice will be done" (10). The pictures and feelings did not support the claim nor, in fact, did the claim make sense; what was the difference between bringing enemies to justice or justice to enemies? Yet through the associative logic, the action the nation should take was clear, acts compelled by the pictures we saw and by the pregnant grieving widow whom the president displayed. A western sheriff, in the tradition of Ronald Reagan, knew what justice meant for men who made pregnant wives widows.[48]

Again, this was not deliberative argument. The president shaped experiences, amplified visible qualities, and, in effect, insisted that his war policy was the natural result of those scenes and traits; the speech suppressed the "constructedness" of those images and the policy was,

as Dauber might say, "an authentic and objective" reaction. It needed no more justification. He concluded the speech by displaying the "police shield of a man named George Howard who died at the World Trade Center trying to save others" (17). Bush promised to carry the badge, the part for the whole of those who died, as "my reminder of lives that ended, and a task that does not end." The two were associated, but there was no logical link between the victim of a terrorist attack and a war that did not end. It could have been a link between a horrific crime and a conviction in an international court of law. His connection was an associative relation, one visually displayed for the audience, and his policy relied on visual performance rather than practical wisdom for its persuasive appeal. Bush claimed that his policy (endless war) grew out of Howard's character (visible in the badge) and so the policy was not open to debate, lest one violate the memory and, generically speaking, the epideictic rules of decorum. Support for Bush became a test of character and decorum. If we honored those who died on 9/11, we supported the president. If we understood common decency in moments of grief, we supported the president. To attack Bush's policy was to attack George Howard, Todd Beamer, Lisa Beamer, and the rest.

★ WE THE PEOPLE

Not many Americans made the "wrong" choice. Bush's decision to speak through the epideictic genre positioned him as the voice of America, and his masterful use of visual imagery, a practice that extended beyond September 20, made it difficult to dispute his policies. To stand against Bush was to stand against Lisa Beamer, and we were not likely to do that. The visual images, as Hariman and Lucaites might note, worked well to constitute a public in support of Bush's policies. The president, however, would not rest there. Bush created an audience, endowing it with the qualities needed to support the war on terror.

For centuries, rhetoricians shared the predilection of philosophers for a rational audience member, for the "transcendental subject," a man (and it was a man) who lived prior to and apart from the speech to be judged. As Maurice Charland notes, however, Kenneth Burke's emphasis on identification rather than persuasion as the key term in rhetoric changes things.[49] To identify with someone is to transform identity; we become different as a result of sharing our substance, sharing identity, with another. If discourse enters into identity, then the audience is a rhetorical effect. Who we are as a collective evolves from the discourses we commonly experience. From Edwin Black's "second persona" to Michael C. McGee's "people" to Charland's adaptation of "interpellation," critics have realized that the audience cannot be taken as a given.[50] Charland says, "If it is easier to praise Athens before Athenians than before Laecedemonians [as Aristotle said], then we should ask how those in Athens come to experience themselves as Athenians."[51] If it was easier for Bush to gain support from "Americans" than from others, then we should ask how we came to experience "American" in his discourse.[52]

Three "American" strategies animated the September 20 address, as well as the other speeches during this period. Initially, the praise and blame polarized the world, as I argued above, and crafted a Manichaean frame through which the audience was to interpret its identity. Simply put, we were good and they were evil. In addition to the passages cited earlier, note how Bush brought in the world: "This is not just America's fight. And what is at stake is not just America's freedom. This is the world's fight. This is civilization's fight. This is the fight of all who believe in progress and pluralism, tolerance and freedom" (15). World War II was much on everyone's mind during this time. FDR's voice echoed through the speeches, amplifying the present with the heroic past. A plaque quoting Winston Churchill ("I was not the lion, but it fell to me to give the lion's roar") inspired those in Karen Hughes's office. As they drafted the September 20 speech with few facts, "knowing little increased their natural tendency to sound like Churchill, whose writing they all liked.... The computer screen filled with rolling triads."[53] Their hero appeared, disdaining surrender amidst unremitting defeat. In his "finest hour," he saw a war for civilization: "Upon this battle depends the survival of Christian civilization.... if we fail, then the whole world, including the United States, and all that we have known and cared for, will sink into the abyss of a new dark age made more sinister, and perhaps more prolonged, by the lights of a perverted science."[54] Bush said that al-Qaeda "pervert [ed]" Islam; they were "heirs" to "fascism" and "Nazism"; people feared "an age of terror" (12, 13, 16). This language was not accidental. Like Churchill, Bush framed the conflict as a war between citizens and barbarians, between American values and those of a horde rushing the gates of civilization from the Middle East and Afghanistan. The identity was, shall we say, familiar to the Western mind. To be American was to be civilized; to be al-Qaeda was to be barbaric.[55]

To be American was also to imitate true Americans. These speeches were saturated with models for good conduct, examples that taught us how to be American in the days after 9/11. Chaim Perelman and Lucie Olbrechts-Tyteca say rhetors cite models in order to "incite to an action." Good rhetors use those "whose prestige confers added value on their acts.... One does not imitate just anybody; the person chosen as model must enjoy some measure of prestige."[56] On September 11, Bush praised those "who responded with the best of America—with the daring of our rescue workers, with the caring for strangers and neighbors who came to give blood and help in any way that they could" (1).[57] On September 14 he called forth the "names, the list of casualties we are only beginning to read." Given the popularity of "naming" memorials since the Vietnam monument, the use of "names" was a good strategy for a eulogy. Interestingly, Bush kept them anonymous; he cited "names" but he did not name names. We could fill in the names from the profiles we saw on the news, yet the "names," in their anonymity, were us. They resembled us in our daily activities, "busy with life." But the terrorists came. So, as we might hope of ourselves, "in their last moments [they] called home to say, be brave, and I love you." They were "passengers who defied their murderers, and prevented the murder of others on the ground.... [they] wore the uniform of the United States, and died at their posts" (5). Even when the president cited specific acts, he avoided proper names. He presented the models as typically American, as possessing qualities that we saw and would imitate:

> And we have seen our national character in eloquent acts of sacrifice. Inside the World Trade Center, one man who could have saved himself stayed until the end at the side of his quadriplegic friend. A beloved priest died giving last rites to a firefighter. Two office workers, finding a disabled stranger, carried her down sixty-eight floors to safety. A group of men drove through the night from Dallas to Washington to bring skin grafts for burn victims. (6–7)

These Americans provided models for emulation, as did those I cited from the September 20 speech, the people who "reported" on the state of the union. They, too, displayed truly American acts: waving flags, giving blood, rescuing victims, and, in the persons of Flight 93, fighting evil. To be American in Bush's texts was to do these things, not the least of which was the last. No action involved crafting or debating the U.S. response to terror. No person spoke.

Finally, Bush completed the trope. In his September 20 peroration, the president established a synecdochal relationship with the people. He represented our experiences, feelings, and actions and spoke of those actions in our voice. Karl Rove, his chief political aide, saw this, the creation of "a sense of national unity," as a "huge political opportunity." In his view, "Bush's first eight months had been middling. To many, he seemed a little slight for the job." The attacks fortuitously offered him "a second chance to define himself, an accidental shot at rebirth. . . . A strong speech could revive Bush's presidency."[58] The president sensed the opportunity. For instance, he wanted the conclusion of the September 20 address to be about him: "The speech shouldn't end reflectively, he said. It should end with him leading. . . . The president didn't want to quote anyone else. He'd said this to them in emphatic terms at a meeting the day before, explaining that he saw this as a chance to lead."[59] He took full advantage of the "huge political opportunity" offered by the 9/11 attacks by becoming the one voice of the nation.

President Bush eased into the conclusion with the display of two more models, Governor George Pataki and Mayor Rudolph Giuliani. Bush claimed that the two leaders "embod[ied] the extraordinary spirit of all New Yorkers," foreshadowing the relationship Bush wanted with the American people. If such embodiment were possible on the state level, then it should be possible on the national level. He also addressed one of his nagging problems. While he fluttered about the nation on 9/11, Giuliani strode directly into battle. Sharing Giuliani's substance was useful for President Bush.

If Bush had failed to capture the public's imagination on 9/11, he was determined to grab it here. After the applause for the New Yorkers, Bush became ruminative, a change in mood that signaled the conclusion. He said, "it is natural to wonder if America's future is one of fear." He answered that it was not: "this country will define our times, not be defined by them" (16). The power to define seemed critical to Bush during these days. On September 14, he claimed that we would define the end of the conflict, "an hour of our choosing." Here, he made a larger claim, asserting that time itself, our era, was amenable to American definition. This contrasted to the experience of 9/11 because the terrorist attacks struck at the power of definition. We thought we controlled our lives, but death improbably flew out of the sky on airliners. So, how could the president say that we defined our lives in light of such random destruction?

In Bush's view, we controlled our fate because of our character. Character drove scene, a relationship he had established on the opposite side in his discussion of al-Qaeda. With character, one rode events. Calling on the biblical frame from September 14 and recalling the mood of his introduction, he said, "And in our grief and anger we have found our mission and our moment" (16). Three levels of meaning potentially percolated through this phrase. To say that we were found was to imply with amazing grace that once we were lost. In 2000, he said that the nation had lost its moral compass and wasted the opportunity afforded by prosperity.[60] On a smaller level, Bush also believed that his generation had lost its way. He agreed with conservatives such as Marvin Olasky, David Horowitz, and Myron Magnet who derided the 1960s "as a period of moral decay and knee-jerk northeastern liberal policies that the nation was still paying for."[61] The boomers had embraced bad values, a process that culminated in Bill Clinton, and George Bush offered redemption. On a yet smaller level, the theme of lost and found echoed in him; every biography and many interviews told the story of his redemption, the frat-boy drinker turned born-again president.[62] The current assertion, then, tied the president's interpretation of terrorism to his past and reminded us of his wisdom. In other words, he knew that as a nation, as a generation, and as individuals, we once were lost and now were found. That was, perhaps, why God allowed these terrible events. We needed to find ourselves, as Bush had found himself. In this speech, we found a part for our whole in George W. Bush. Given the redemption story that he had lived and now offered to the nation, no other man was so fitted to be America at this time. We had indeed finally found our mission and our moment—and our man.

But only a man aware of history and the place of this challenge in history could stand for America. Bush interpreted this war as the sort of fight that had shaped his father. "Mission" in fact, echoed the key lines from his father's 1988 nomination acceptance address. Like the father, the son was now defining his life in terms of missions accepted and missions accomplished. In this time and text, the boomers finally became Private Ryan—they could live up to their fathers. Bush's character, now synchronized with the American character, authorized him to define yet again the fight his generation was destined to wage: "Freedom and fear are at war" (17). This definition, however, implied a new scene for the struggle. Bush had termed the fight between the United States and terror as a war between good and evil. Evil could cause fear, but it was not the same as fear. So, if this fight was not that fight, who did it involve and where did it occur?

The battle was to be fought, I suggest, for the nation's soul. Bush continued, reinforcing the generational theme, "Our nation—this generation—will lift the dark threat of violence from our people and our future. We will rally the world to this cause by our efforts, by our courage. We will not tire, we will not falter, and we will not fail" (17). Bush here orchestrated the titans of World War II. The allusion to fear echoed FDR's voice and claim that "this generation" had a rendezvous with destiny. Roosevelt dismissed fear in his first inaugural address, an effort that imbued people with his jaunty confidence. The light/dark metaphor, a favorite of Roosevelt and Churchill, eased us into the Englishman's voice. We were to meet destiny with Churchillian verve, determined, in the master's words, that "we shall not flag or fail. We shall go on to the end. . . . We shall fight on the beaches, we shall fight on the landing grounds, we shall fight in the fields and in the streets, we shall fight in the hills; we shall never surrender."[63] Each leader addressed the people's determination. Before the material fight could be won, the spiritual fight demanded attention. Each sought to assure the people that they were strong. But as Derrida or Mencken might observe, when the president repeatedly told us not to flag nor fail, then he was probably worried that we were about to flag and fail.

If that were the case, the president, in the manner of a Christian witness, was determined to share his faith and strength with us. He expressed "my hope" that "life will return almost to normal" (17). He spoke of memories of 9/11 and turned to the tale of George Howard. His badge, as I said, compelled Bush to fight the endless war. It also led him to share that compulsion with the audience, a resolve that replicated the will of his Churchillian people: "I will not forget this wound to our country or those who inflicted it. I will not yield; I will not rest; I will not relent in waging this struggle for freedom and security for the American people" (17). This rolling triad repeated almost exactly the earlier rolling triad. People and leader became one in the conclusion. Each matched the other and, as it turned out, found strength in the Lord God Almighty. The president proclaimed, "Freedom and fear, justice and cruelty, have always been at war, and we know that God is not neutral between them" (17). The first pair defined the spiritual struggle for our soul and the second defined the military struggle for global hegemony. The enthymeme (he only implied the Lord would smite Osama) led us to come to our own conclusion, one that he then felt the need to say for us: "assured of the rightness of our cause and confident in victories to come," we would go forward certain that God "watch[ed] over the United States of America" (17).

Read in conjunction with the president's earlier interpretation of 9/11 as God's test of his chosen people, the conclusion imbued the struggle against al-Qaeda and for America's soul with religious, even apocalyptic, significance. The paired sets "have always been at war." The current struggle, as the allusions to World War II indicated, was, in the old meaning of "revolution," yet another turn in the fight documented so ably by John Milton. The chosen people and the citizenry and the long civic generation and the baby boomers became a textual symphony, lines weaving together, always already making the same fight and believing in the same values. It was, and was always to be, an eternal struggle. From within the purview of this text, you were either with the president or with Satan.

All presidents seek to shape the national character. Reagan saw us as a special people placed between two great oceans for God's purpose, the elder Bush saw us as a thousand points of light, and Bill Clinton saw us as the restless avatars of a new information age. This Bush, however, became the national character. Polarization divided the world, modeling displayed appropriate conduct in that world, and synecdoche represented the "right" of the world in the person of the president. In this final strategy, George W. Bush became America made flesh. It was hard to argue with the Word incarnate. Karl Rove was undoubtedly pleased.

CONCLUSION

I am filled with admiration for the political results of this strategy and filled with doubts about the policy ramifications. There have been few presidents of recent vintage who have so successfully weathered their first several years in office. Despite economic reverses, President George W. Bush maintains high levels of popularity. Despite the world's disapproval, he creates domestic support for the invasion of another nation. Despite a reputation for a troublesome tongue, he turns rhetoric into a useful asset.

In various venues, his supporters have argued that his rhetorical success results not from traditional eloquence, but rather from a clear and compelling vision of the world. I find no reason to disagree with that assessment. Bush tends, in these speeches and in others, to define the world in which we live. The attacks of September 11th offered him a potent occasion to indulge in that tendency, and he took advantage of the opportunity. As many scholars note, the epideictic genre provides extraordinary inventional resources for the definition of a new world or, perhaps more accurately, it offers a little rhetorical engine that can take the old world and make of it a bright and new creation. President Bush fills that world with heroes and villains, offering as evidence the things we have seen and the people we have watched. The people and the president who has sketched them, in turn, embody the qualities we should possess and the faith we should carry as we move forward to do God's will—which is the president's policy.

The instrumental power of these strategies is self-evident, although I cannot resist the chance to amplify on them. As Kathleen Jamieson says of Ronald Reagan, the marriage of the rhetorical presidency and the epideictic genre is a robust one.[64] The rhetorical president is in the most commanding political and social position to make a world. Epideictic rhetoric is in the most commanding political and social position to amplify in words a world in a televisual age. For a people that seemingly endorses the notion that seeing is believing, presidential epideictic rhetoric strongly encourages us to believe in the world the president's text imagines.

It is here that the power of contemporary epideictic rhetoric asserts itself. President Bush "justifies" his policies through the use of televisual definition. He shows us an unchanging and essential world, performing and displaying the actions and attitudes we should take in that world. Celeste Condit says that epideictic speakers gain "power through the power to define."[65] Richard Weaver argues, "Definition is an attempt to capture essence. When we speak of the nature of a thing, we speak of something we expect to persist. Definitions accordingly deal with fundamental and unchanging properties."[66] For President Bush, the world is, as it ever was, divided between good and evil. People of character oppose evil. Policy is justified not by expediency arguments, but by metaphysical ends—by character and by faith. Definition, Weaver says, "ascribes to the highest reality qualities of stasis, immutability, eternal perdurance—qualities that in Western civilization are usually expressed in the language of theism. . . . The realm of essence is the realm above the flux of phenomena, and definitions are of essences and genera."[67] This president's epideictic argument creates a kind of hermetically sealed system in which the world is as it is, people are as they are, and real Americans act accordingly.

Equally important, such epideictic rhetoric provides powerful disciplinary mechanisms. In this discourse, public judgments are rendered through the prism of honor or dishonor. Pierre Bourdieu writes of a culture bound by such discourses: "The point of honor is the basis of the moral code of an individual who sees himself always through the eyes of others, who has need of others for his existence, because the image he has of himself is indistinguishable from that presented to him by other people. . . . Hence it is that the dynamics of honor are based essentially on the pressure of opinion."[68] In a televisual time, an era in which we see the world displayed before us and observe the relevant actions, the nation begins to resemble such a culture. Although I do not believe we fully inhabit that world, Bourdieu describes the dynamic of authority offered by contemporary epideictic rhetoric. If the world is the way that it is, and good people act accordingly, then we may observe those who act and judge the honor or dishonor of that deed based on the values the president has made visible. Extraordinary public pressure is brought to bear on those who oppose the president because opposition based on practicality and expediency makes no sense in a world governed by theistic essence. If the president's policy is not justified through reference to expediency, then it is not appropriate to judge the policy on its practicality.

Disagreement can be based only on opposition to the values that the president expresses as the synecdochical voice of the people. To oppose him is to oppose the voice and, not coincidentally, the will of the people—and not just any people, but a people of theistic essence, a people of the Book, of the Battle Hymn, of John Milton, Winston Churchill, Franklin Roosevelt, and Private Ryan. In this discourse, President Bush, as the voice of "eternal perdurance," exists above the flux of phenomena.

Although that may be a nice place for presidents to visit, it is not a good idea for them to live there. Democracy is based on the premise that many heads, no matter that some may be silly, come up with better policies than few heads. I believe that is because it is not given to us to exist in a world above the flux of phenomena, and the more people we involve, the greater the chances we can comprehend the flux. The world moves, people alter, character changes, and, as Gerry Adams and Menachem Begin might suggest, one occasionally ends up negotiating with and finding some good in terrorists because it is expedient to do so, as improbable as that may now seem to Americans. To posit essence is to live outside of such contingencies. It is, therefore, to live without deliberation and rhetoric. I doubt that President Bush wishes to live in that world, although in the dark of night I entertain doubts about Attorney General Ashcroft. More serious, perhaps, is the fact that such a world is fragile. As John Adams said, facts are stubborn things. Notwithstanding the cries of Fox News and other supporters of the president, the world may well be somewhat more complex than is suggested in these speeches and it will undoubtedly change over time—in fact, it already has done so. Sooner or later, President Bush will discover the world's resistance to simple answers.

NOTES

[1] For powerful accounts of that failure, see Michael Elliot, "The Secret History," *Time*, August 12, 2002, 28–43; Michael Isikoff and Daniel Klaidman, "A Matter of Missed Signals," *Newsweek*, December 24, 2001, 30–32; David Johnston and Neil A. Lewis, "Whistle-Blower Recounts Faults

Inside the F.B.I.," *New York Times,* June 7, 2002, A1, A21; Jason Vest, "Why Warnings Fell on Deaf Ears," *The American Prospect,* June 17, 2002, 18.

2 Joanna McCreary and Douglas Waller, "Why Can't We Find Bin Laden?" *Time,* November 25, 2002, 28–35.

3 For general assessments of the ongoing wars and Bush foreign policy issues, see Anthony Lewis, "Bush and Iraq," *The New York Review of Books,* November 7, 2002, 4–6; Frances Fitzgerald, "George Bush and the World," *The New York Review of Books,* September 26, 2002, 80–86; Stanley Hoffmann, "America Alone in the World," *The American Prospect,* September 23, 2002, 20–25; Harold Myerson, "Axis of Incompetence," *The American Prospect,* May 20, 2002, 18–19; Gary Hart, "The Other War," *The American Prospect,* December 16, 2002, 10–11; Richard Wolfe and Michael Hirsh, "War and Consequences," *Newsweek,* February 3, 2003, 22–28; John Lewis Gaddis, "Bush's Security Strategy," *Foreign Policy,* November/December 2002, 50–57; Robert Kagan, *Of Paradise and Power: America and Europe in the New World Order* (New York: Alfred A. Knopf, 2003); Fareed Zakaria, "Why America Scares the World and What to Do About It," *Newsweek,* March 24, 2003, 18–33.

4 Not, of course, for the wealthiest quintile. See David Leonhart, "Hiring in Nation Hits Worst Slump in Nearly Twenty Years," *New York Times,* February 6, 2003, A1, C6.

5 The deficit figures come from Paul Krugman, "A Fiscal Train Wreck," *New York Times,* March 11, 2003, A29. The rest of the figures come from Allen Sloan, "Bush's Depressing Economy," *Newsweek,* February 10, 2003, 56–58. For a powerful critique of Bush's economics, see Paul Krugman, *Fuzzy Math* (New York: W. W. Norton, 2001).

6 Martin Crutsinger, "2002 Deficit Hit Record 435.2B," February 20, 2003, http://www.washingtonpost.com.

7 The first "inside" memoir of the administration, in fact, makes surprise at Bush's success its central theme: David Frum, *The Right Man: The Surprise Presidency of George W. Bush* (New York: Random House, 2003).

8 My perspective on genre is shaped by Karlyn Kohrs Campbell and Kathleen Hall Jamieson, *Deeds Done in Words: Presidential Rhetoric and the Genres of Governance* (Chicago: University of Chicago Press, 1990); Karlyn Kohrs Campbell and Kathleen Hall Jamieson, "Form and Genre in Rhetorical Criticism: An Introduction," in *Form and Genre: Shaping Rhetorical Action,* ed. Karlyn Kohrs Campbell and Kathleen Hall Jamieson (Falls Church, Va.: Speech Communication Association, 1978), 9–32; Carolyn R. Miller, "Genre as Social Action," *Quarterly Journal of Speech* 70 (1984): 151–67.

9 For an argument that the United States relied on military prowess for national development, see Geoffrey Ferret, *A Country Made by War* (New York: Random House, 1989).

10 Campbell and Jamieson, *Deeds,* 101–26; Robert L. Ivie, "Images of Savagery in American Justifications for War," *Communication Monographs* 47 (1980): 279–94; Richard A. Cherwitz and Kenneth S. Zagacki, "Consummatory versus Justificatory Crisis Rhetoric," *Western Journal of Speech Communication* 50 (1986): 307–24; Bonnie J. Dow, "The Function of Epideictic and Deliberative Strategies in Presidential Crisis Rhetoric," *Western Journal of Speech Communication* 53 (1989); 294–310.

11 See David S. Birdsell, "Ronald Reagan on Lebanon and Grenada: Flexibility and Interpretation in the Application of Kenneth Burke's Pentad," *Quarterly Journal of Speech* 73 (1987): 267–79.

12 See also John M. Murphy, "Epideictic and Deliberative Strategies in Opposition to War: The Paradox of Honor and Expediency," *Communication Studies* (1992): 65–78.

13 Celeste M. Condit, "The Function of Epideictic: The Boston Massacre Orations as Exemplar," *Communication Quarterly* 33 (1985): 284–99.

14 Aristotle, *Rhetoric,* trans. W. Rhys Roberts (New York: Modern Library, 1954), 32; Aristotle, *On Rhetoric,* trans. George A. Kennedy (New York: Oxford University Press, 1991), 47.

15 Aristotle, *On Rhetoric,* 36–37; Aristotle, *Rhetoric,* 24.

16 Thomas Farrell, *Norms of Rhetorical Culture* (New Haven: Yale University Press, 1993), 65.

17 Farrell, *Norms,* 63.

18 Takis Poulakos, "Isocrates's Use of Narrative in the Evagoras: Epideictic Rhetoric and Moral Action," *Quarterly Journal of Speech* 73 (1987), 323.

19 Yun Lee Too, "Epideictic Genre," in *Encyclopedia of Rhetoric,* ed. Thomas O. Sloane (New York: Oxford University Press, 2001), 252.

20 Condit, "Epideictic"; John M. Murphy, "'A Time of Shame and Sorrow': Robert F. Kennedy and the American Jeremiad," *Quarterly Journal of Speech* 76 (1990): 401–14.

21 For a fine review of scholarship on the rhetorical presidency, see Mary E. Stuckey and Fred Antczak, "The Rhetorical Presidency: Deepening Vision, Widening Exchange," in *Communication Yearbook* 21, ed. Michael E. Roloff (Thousand Oaks, Calif.: Sage), 405–41.

22 Kathleen Hall Jamieson, *Eloquence in an Electronic Age* (New York: Oxford University Press, 1988), 147; Campbell and Jamieson, *Deeds,* 68–71. For another example, see Michael Waldman's brief discussion of President Clinton's Oklahoma City Memorial Address. Michael Waldman, *POTUS Speaks* (New York: Simon and Schuster, 2000), 81–83.

23 Sadly, as I wrote these lines, George W. Bush found himself faced with the same task.

24 My texts for this project come from a commemorative book I found at my local Border's. That says something about the reach of these speeches. I checked them against my personal videotapes. They are accurate. George W. Bush, *United We Stand: A Message for All Americans* (Ann Arbor, Mich.: Mundus, 2001), 1. Subsequent references for speeches in this edition will be by page number in the text.

25 The White House staff, with the possible exception of author Karen Hughes, uniformly regarded this address as a terrible speech. David Frum reports that it even earned the nickname "Awful Oval Office Address." Frum, *Right Man,* 133. It also seems to have convinced everyone that Bush cannot give the standard Oval Office address. After the Columbia disaster, for instance, he spoke first from the Treaty Room and then at the memorial service for the astronauts. For Bush in the Oval Office, see Frum, *Right Man,* 135.

26 I owe this observation to the students in my fall 2001 presidential rhetoric class. Despite their emotional state during our September 12 meeting, they were coolly disdainful of this speech as a whole and of this translation in particular.

27 Bush used the same phrase when he abandoned diplomacy and committed the nation to war in Iraq: George W. Bush, "'This Is Not a Question of Authority; It Is a Question of Will,'" *Washington Post,* March 18, 2003, A12.

28 The King James Version puts this phrase in the conditional, making it more unlikely that anyone could oppose the chosen: "If God be for us, who can be against us?" Satan, perhaps, but the grammar itself diminishes the evil one's powers. Paul is rewriting Psalm 118 here, which is yet more militant: "Out of my distress I called on the Lord; The Lord answered me and set me free. With the Lord on my side I do not fear. What can man do to me? The Lord is on my side to help me; I shall look in triumph on those who hate me. . . . All nations surrounded me; in the name of the Lord, I cut them off!" (RSV, Psalm 118: 5–7, 10).

29 Frum, *Right Man,* 138.

30 The State of the Union has become an increasingly important speech in the contemporary era. Campbell and Jamieson note the traditional salience of the address, given that the Constitution orders the president to report and gives the chief executive the opportunity to act as the "national historian." In addition, "No one else is charged with this specific responsibility. . . . By the sheer fact of its delivery, the address reminds the country that presidents have a unique function in our system of government. They are to view questions in the aggregate and as they pertain to the whole, to the Union." I also believe that, in our media-saturated era, this is a speech that invokes nonpartisan authority. Certainly, the media interprets the address partly through a political frame, but, after all, the Constitution requires it, the networks carry it, and everyone else (most of the time) shows up for it, including the generals, the ambassadors, and the Supreme Court. This speech appears to be an act of government, not an act of politics, in the eyes of many people. That matters. That makes it a very useful genre for Bush to appropriate on this occasion. As national historian, he can unveil this new world. Campbell and Jamieson, *Deeds,* 52.

31 Kenneth Burke, *A Grammar of Motives* (Berkeley: University of California Press, 1969), 508.

32 For a discussion of the orientations available to U.S. foreign policy, see Mary E. Stuckey, "Competing Foreign Policy Visions: Rhetorical Hybrids after the Cold War," *Western Journal of Communication* 59 (1995): 214–27.

33 Richard Lanham, *A Handlist of Rhetorical Terms* (Berkeley: University of California Press, 1991), 52.

34 Sloane, "Epideictic Genre," 252.

35 The editing is telling. The first two are the same. FDR then turned to "freedom from want" and "freedom from fear—which, translated into world terms, means a world-wide reduction of armaments." President Bush was not interested in defending those freedoms. Roosevelt is quoted in James MacGregor Burns, *Roosevelt: The Soldier of Freedom* (New York: Harcourt, Brace Jovanovich, 1970), 34.

36 It was also likely that the president built up al-Qaeda for the same, probably unconscious, reason that conspiracy theorists see much more at work in John Kennedy's assassination than a deranged Lee Harvey Oswald. If one loser could kill our president, then how important were we really in the grand scheme of things? If life is that arbitrary, then we face the uncomfortable (and existential) fact that it makes no sense at all. Similarly, if one small group of suicidal nuts could bring down the World Trade

Center, then where was the rationality in the world? There had to be more here to put America at risk.

37 Bill Minutaglio, *First Son: George W. Bush and the Bush Family Dynasty* (New York: Three Rivers Press, 1999); Molly Ivins and Lou Dubose, *Shrub: The Short but Happy Political Life of George W. Bush* (New York: Vintage Books, 2000); Frank Bruni, *Ambling into History: The Unlikely Odyssey of George W. Bush* (New York: HarperCollins, 2002); Frum, *Right Man.*

38 Bob Woodward, *Bush at War* (New York: Simon and Schuster, 2002); D. T. Max, "The Making of the Speech: The 2,988 Words That Changed a Presidency: An Etymology," *New York Times Magazine,* October 7, 2001, 32–37. The prestige of the two outlets also supports my contention. If you want to write the first draft of history, turning to Bob Woodward and the *New York Times* is a pretty good strategy.

39 Woodward, *Bush,* 145–46.

40 Woodward, *Bush,* 96.

41 Max, "Speech," 35.

42 Quoted in and analysis from Jamieson, *Eloquence,* 128–33.

43 Robert Hariman and John Louis Lucaites, "Public Identity and Collective Memory in U.S. Iconic Photography: The Image of 'Accidental Napalm,'" *Critical Studies in Media Communication* 20 (2003): 36. See also W. J. T. Mitchell, *Picture Theory* (Chicago: University of Chicago Press, 1994); Michael Warner, *Publics and Counterpublics* (New York: Zone Books, 2002).

44 For other examples, see Kevin M. DeLuca, *Image Politics: The New Rhetoric of Environmental Activism* (New York: Guilford Press, 1999); Kevin M. DeLuca and Jennifer Peeples, "From Public Sphere to Public Screen: Democracy, Activism, and the Violence of Seattle," *Critical Studies in Media Communication* 19 (2002): 125–51; Cara Finnegan, "Social Engineering, Visual Politics, and the New Deal: FSA Photography in Survey Graphic," *Rhetoric & Public Affairs* 3 (2000): 333–62; Robert Hariman and John Louis Lucaites, "Dissent and Emotional Management in a Liberal-Democratic Society: The Kent State Iconic Photograph," *Rhetoric Society Quarterly* 31 (2001): 5–32; Robert Hariman and John Louis Lucaites, "Performing Civic Identity: The Iconic Photograph of the Flag Raising on Iwo Jima," *Quarterly Journal of Speech* 88 (2002): 363–92.

45 Cori E. Dauber, "The Shot Seen 'Round the World: The Impact of the Images of Mogadishu on American Military Operations," *Rhetoric & Public Affairs* 4 (2001): 656–57.

46 Jamieson, *Eloquence,* 126.

47 Kenneth Burke, *Counter-Statement* (Berkeley: University of California Press, 1968), 124–25.

48 In lines that became famous, Bush also said that he wanted bin Laden "dead or alive" and declared that we would "smoke out" the "killers" and "git 'em." See Frum, *Right Man,* 141. For an analysis of Reagan as a sheriff, and of this sort of romantic appeal generally, see Walter R. Fisher, "Romantic Democracy, Ronald Reagan, and Presidential Heroes," *Western Journal of Speech Communication* 46 (1982): 299–310.

49 Maurice Charland, "Constitutive Rhetoric: The Case of the *Peuple Quebeçois,*" *Quarterly Journal of Speech* 73 (1987): 133.

50 Edwin Black, "The Second Persona," *Quarterly Journal of Speech* 56 (1970): 109–19; Michael C. McGee, "In Search of 'The People': A Rhetorical Alternative," *Quarterly Journal of Speech* 61 (1975): 235–49; Charland, "Constitutive."

51 Charland, "Constitutive," 134. I would also suggest that our material experience provides the inventional resources to construct a people. The "American" George W. Bush created was not *mandated* by 9/11, but it was certainly made possible by the attacks. Absent those planes, it is difficult to imagine Bush giving this speech or any similar sort of speech.

52 I do not mean to suggest that Bush was the only source for cultural definitions. This is a study of his speeches, however, and it is to those texts I limit myself. Certainly, cultural productions such as the telethon to raise money for the victims and Alan Jackson's "Where were you when the world stopped turning?" contributed to national identity. I still believe, however, that, even in post-modernity, presidents matter more than most cultural or political actors.

53 Max, "Speech," 36, 34. One of the phrases that Max identifies as Churchillian is the civilization quotation I discuss below.

54 Quoted in Roy Jenkins, *Churchill: A Biography* (New York: A Plume Book), 21.

55 "Civil" was a god term for the Bush administration before September 11. It was one of the four god terms that structured his inaugural address, for instance.

56 Chaim Perelman and Lucie Olbrechts-Tyteca, *The New Rhetoric: A Treatise on Argumentation,* trans. John Wilkinson and Purcell Weaver (Notre Dame, Ind.: University of Notre Dame Press, 1969), 362–63.

57 This quotation is typical of that messy speech. The internal rhyme is excellent and the sentence

flows, so the immediate impression is a good one. But the second phrase is confusing. Bush lauded "the caring for strangers and neighbors who came to give blood and help in any way they could." So, speaking in grammatical terms, what he ended up praising was the caring people offered to the stranger and neighbor who came to give blood. I am not at all sure he meant to do that. I suspect he meant to laud those who gave blood and help. That is not, however, what he said.

58 Max, "Speech," 34.

59 Max, "Speech," 35, 36.

60 R. W. Apple Jr., "Bush, Accepting G.O.P. Nomination, Pledges To 'Use These Good Times for Great Goals,'" *New York Times*, August 4, 2000, A1, A18. Apple quotes the key line on the first page: "Our current president embodied the potential of a generation. So many talents. So much charm. Such great skill. But in the end, to what end? So much promise, to no great purpose."

61 Minutaglio, *First Son*, 290.

62 This stock story is present in the biographies cited above. Another fine example is Nicholas

Lemann, "The Redemption," *The New Yorker*, January 31, 2000, 48–63.

63 Quoted in Jenkins, *Churchill*, 611. Jenkins notes that this is, perhaps, the most parodied speech in history and its echoes are here unmistakable, even apart from the fact that the writers admitted that they borrowed from Churchill. It is also worth noting that the generational imagery could bring John Kennedy to mind. Given how often Kennedy cribbed from Roosevelt and Churchill, the three are probably all tangled up in public memory.

64 Jamieson, *Eloquence*.

65 Condit, "Epideictic," 288.

66 Richard Weaver, "Language Is Sermonic," in *The Rhetorical Tradition*, ed. Patricia Bizzell and Bruce Herzberg, 2d ed. (New York: St. Martin's Press, 2001), 1354.

67 Weaver, "Language Is Sermonic," 1355.

68 Pierre Bourdieu, "The Sentiment of Honor in Kabyle Society," trans. by Philip Sheridan, in *Honor and Shame*, ed. by J. G. Peristany (Chicago: The University of Chicago Press, 1966), 211.

CHAPTER 6
The Legislature and the Judiciary

Congressional support

for increased military funding, legislative discussions about welfare reform and social security, Senate filibusters of judicial nominees, proposed constitutional amendments to define marriage, and Supreme Court decisions frequently appear in media headlines. Cornerstones of the American political system, the legislature and judiciary are often subjects of political communication inquiry. Indeed, communication scholars have had a sustained and lively interest in law and public policy since early Greek society and the birth of democracy. Aristotle, for example, advised public speakers that "an understanding of legislation is of special importance, for it is on the laws that the safety of the State is based."[1]

Demonstrating a variety of theories, methodologies, and subject matter, the essays in this chapter provide a representative sample of political communication scholarship on the legislature and judiciary. To varying degrees, each essay accomplishes two goals. First, the work responds to contemporary communication and public policy scholars' calls to use communication research to influence public policy. The essays all explicitly or implicitly outline implications of the research for political actors such as lobbyists, representatives, special interest groups, and scholars. Second, each essay contributes to theories of political institutions, from state and federal courts and legislatures to local education boards.

Michael Halloran's 1978 essay, "Doing Public Business in Public," outlines a rhetorically based theory of political institutions. The author examines the House Judiciary Committee's televised debate on the impeachment of Richard Nixon. A major contribution of this work is its theoretical sketch of public proceedings as rhetorical genres. In this sense, Halloran's essay is groundbreaking, distinct from early legislative studies, which largely focused on particular speeches, individuals, or cases; political controversies; and legal reasoning. This essay, with its attention to the political process as a whole, represents the beginning of a growing trend in political communication scholarship—proposing communication-based theories of the political process and political institutional decision-making.

In "The Rhetorical Boundaries of 'the Law': A Consideration of the Rhetorical Culture of Legal Practice and the Case of the 'Separate but Equal' Doctrine," (1996) Marouf Hasian, Jr., Celeste Michelle Condit, and John Louis Lucaites move toward a rhetorically based theory of legal practice. This article provides a concise historical overview of popular approaches to legal study and sketches an alternative method for understanding the judicial system. The authors argue that the law is dependent on the public vocabulary of the culture; that the very language we use to discuss public issues imposes limits on how judges may interpret cases. For example, prior to the creation of terms such as "domestic violence," "same-sex marriage," or "affirmative action," it would have been difficult to express such ideas in a public or legal context. But as the authors also note, culture and its vocabulary change over time. As a result, legal actors at various points in history interpret the law differently. Shifts in public discourse may provide resources for legal change; innovative metaphors and new words such as "affirmative action," for example, may make new interpretations of the law possible.

In his 1998 essay, "The Contested Space of Prudence in the 1874–1875 Civil Rights Debate," Kirt H. Wilson explores politicians' struggles to reconcile conflicting views of civil rights during the post–Civil War Reconstruction Era. The author discusses how proponents and opponents of civil rights, with differing views of equality, developed criteria for making decisions about race relations and rights that ultimately gave rise to the "separate but equal" doctrine. Using the 1874 and 1875 civil rights debates as a case study, Wilson questions traditional understandings of prudence as a fixed concept, inviting rhetorical scholars to view it instead as a dynamic, fluid concept that political actors attempt to control through language and that fluctuates over time. In other words, congressional actors differ about what constitutes a prudent course of action and use language to justify their own positions as the most judicious and sensible.

Theodore F. Sheckels's "Carol Moseley-Braun Defies the Confederate Flag," a chapter in his 2000 book, *When Congress Debates: A Bakhtinian Paradigm*, focuses on the Senate debates surrounding the Daughters of the Confederacy's request to renew the patent that guaranteed their right to use the Confederate flag. The author illuminates a variety of rhetorical strategies used in the debate. For example, some senators relied on "prosopopeia" to speak on behalf of constituents not present in the room. Others told powerful stories depicting slavery and racism. Senator Carol Moseley-Braun, he argues, engaged in "carnivalesque subversion": challenging Senate rules and procedure, invoking stories of slavery, and calling attention to the lack of diversity in the Senate through her physical appearance. The essay provides insight into how the traditionally disempowered can challenge institutional norms.

Lisa M. Gring-Pemble, in a 2001 essay "'Are We Going to Now Govern By Anecdote?' Rhetorical Constructions of Welfare Recipients in Congressional Hearings, Debates, and Legislation, 1992–1996," examines the welfare reform hearings and debates that led to the 1996 Personal Responsibility and Work Opportunity Reconciliation Act. A case study of how policymakers craft legislation, the essay examines witnesses' stories about welfare recipients and the actions, motives, and goals attributed to those on public assistance. Gring-Pemble shows how stereotypical views of welfare recipients as immoral, incompetent, and immature encourage legislators to ignore and exclude welfare recipient's testimony and rely instead on the testimony of experts, such as scholars and researchers, to form welfare legislation.

Notes

[1] Aristotle, *The Art of Rhetoric*, trans. John Henry Freese (Cambridge, Mass.: Harvard University Press, 1991), 1.4:12–13.

Doing Public Business in Public

Michael Halloran

Consider the following public events:

- A trial with important social or political implications is held, and a few dozen spectators crowd into the courtroom.
- A local board of education conducts its monthly meeting in the high school auditorium. As required by law, the meeting is open to the public, and approximately one hundred taxpayers attend.
- A state legislative body meets in regular session to debate and vote on a controversial piece of legislation. The session is carried live on educational television, and several thousand citizens watch the proceeding.
- A major political party conducts its convention to adopt a platform and nominate presidential and vice-presidential candidates. Several million people watch the "gavel-to-gavel" coverage on network television.

Any one of these events might interest a rhetorician, since it is evident that rhetoric is occurring in all of them. The attorneys in the courtroom, the members of the school board, the legislators, and the participants in the convention will all make speeches and argue with each other. Each proceeding is a series of persuasive messages addressed by participants to other participants whose agreement they hope to win. What may not be so immediately evident is that in each case the series of messages is also an ensemble, a single message addressed to the spectators by the body conducting the proceeding.

In some ways, proceedings of the sort I am talking about are like plays. Just as a play combines a series of interactions among its characters to form an aesthetic unity for contemplation by the audience, the proceeding combines a series of interactions among its participants to form a rhetorical unity addressed to the spectators. Each is a structure having a beginning, a middle, and an end. While it is possible to lift individual parts out of the whole and look at them as if they were structures complete in themselves, the full significance of each part can only be grasped in relation to the structure of the whole. Hamlet's "To be or not to be" soliloquy can be examined as a philosophical essay, but it becomes far more interesting when viewed as a part of the aesthetic whole that is *Hamlet*. Likewise, Barry Goldwater's 1964 address accepting the presidential nomination of the Republican Party can be viewed as simply a ceremonial speech, but it has considerably more significance as the climax of a convention at which Nelson Rockefeller had been loudly boo'd.

The analogy between a political convention, a trial, or a meeting of a legislative body and a play is useful, but by itself cannot satisfactorily account for the rhetorical nature of these events. For one thing, the proceedings have immediate practical consequences, whereas a play does not.

This essay originally appeared in Form and Genre: Shaping Rhetorical Action, *edited by Karlyn Kohrs Campbell (Annandale, Va.: Speech Communication Association, 1975).*

For another, the unity of a play derives from the creativity of a single person, the playwright, whereas that of a proceeding must emerge from the dedication of many people to a common purpose.

It is my belief that the events in question are rooted in rhetorical situations that are similar in important ways, and that as discourses they exhibit important formal similarities. I believe that these similarities are sufficiently relevant to the critic for the events to be regarded as instances of a rhetorical genre, which can be called the *public proceeding*. In the remainder of this essay I shall develop a conception of the genre in terms of both situation and form, and then illustrate its critical utility by examining the televised debate of the House Judiciary Committee on the impeachment of Richard Nixon as an example of the public proceeding.[1]

 I

By a public proceeding, I mean an official business session of a representative body, including debate and decision on specific issues, conducted before an audience made up of members of the body's constituency. The body may be representative in a strict elective sense, as in the cases of the legislature and the schoolboard, or in some wider sense, as in the cases of the court of law and the political convention. In any event, the members of the audience have a real interest in the outcome of the body's deliberations. Because matters of consequence to them are at stake, they are rhetorically *available*. The public proceeding thus serves a dual purpose: it settles whatever matters are before the body, just as a similar proceeding held in closed session would; it shapes the views of the audience directly, as a proceeding held in private could not.

This preliminary definition of the genre distinguishes the public proceeding from other sorts of rhetorical events that bear superficial resemblances to it. A hearing meant to inform the public or to elicit information as a basis for future action may on the surface look very similar to a public proceeding. For example, the Senate Watergate hearings of 1973 bore certain resemblances to the Judiciary Committee debate of 1974, and many people confuse the

two, using the name of one while meaning the other. There is an important difference in that the hearing, unlike a true public proceeding, cannot include official action by the body. There is no sense of closure in the hearing, no need for the body to resolve issues and declare itself as a body on this or that side of the question before it. This means that the form of the hearing will be determined primarily by the need to inform or to elicit information. In a public proceeding, by contrast, there is business to conduct, a decision to be made. Even in a case in which the business is nothing more than a formality, for example a political convention that has only to renominate an unopposed incumbent, the business nonetheless must be conducted and the basic form of the event will be determined by the nature of that business.

The primary role of the audience in a public proceeding is to witness. Indeed, the generic concept I am attempting to develop is intended to focus attention on precisely those modulations that occur when an audience is present at an event whose primary rationale does not call for an audience. To return to the play analogy, a public proceeding is comparable to the traditional sort of play in which the audience is expected to sit quietly through the performance, in contrast to the theater in the participatory idiom which calls on the audience to take an active part in the dramatic event. Within that broad category of non-participatory theater there are many dramatic styles, each demanding a different mode of aesthetic involvement. For example, Brechtian theater calls for a critical and emotionally detached audience, whereas Artaud's "theater of cruelty" calls for an intense emotional engagement.[2] In a similar manner, different modes of rhetorical involvement are called for by different kinds of public proceedings. A limiting case would be the ordinary courtroom trial, in which the audience is expected merely to witness the event. Aside from admonitions by the judge to observe the proper decorum, the form of a trial will normally show little if any adaptation to the audience. (I am speaking here of the audience of spectators as distinct from a jury.) Since under ordinary circumstances the audience has no power to influence the outcome of the proceeding, neither side is likely to exert any effort to win the agreement of the audience, or for that matter even to make its case comprehensible to them. Yet exerting themselves to "overhear" the arguments not addressed to them, the spectators become a rhetorical audience. At the opposite extreme would be the political convention, in which the business at hand is merely an essential prelude to another proceeding—the election—in which the audience will play a decisive role. Consequently, the convention delegates will be wooing the audience rhetorically at the same time that they are discharging the business at hand.

Aristotle says that a rhetorical audience must be composed of either judges (those who decide) or spectators (critics), and he classifies speeches in part according to which of these two roles the audience is called upon to perform.[3] Speeches requiring the audience to judge are either deliberative or forensic, depending on whether the audience is to judge proposals for future action or actions already completed. Speeches that call upon the audience to be spectators are epideictic. Lloyd Bitzer makes a related point when he says that a rhetorical audience is composed of those who are capable of effecting change with regard to the exigence at the base of a rhetorical situation.[4] Viewed in this light, the distinctive character of the public proceeding becomes clearer. The immediate issue before the body holding the proceeding is in every case one calling for judgment in the Aristotelian sense: the body conducting the proceeding must decide and make a binding pronouncement upon either the quality of something that has happened or the advisability of some proposed course of action. Yet the audience that gathers to witness the proceeding cannot judge in that sense; in Bitzer's terms, they are powerless to modify the exigence. They can only approve or disapprove. They are *spectators*—mere observers, as Aristotle would have it. The proceeding that is, in the first instance, either deliberative or judicial thus takes on the character of epideictic rhetoric as well.

The exigence at issue in the deliberative or judicial arguments in a public proceeding is never a matter of private business. The members of the body conducting the proceeding

act in the name of a larger community. They are empowered by specific social arrangements—customs, laws, and procedures of appointment or election—to represent the community in doing specific kinds of public business. Justice is done, laws are passed, policy is established, candidates are nominated—always in the name of the people.[5] The fact that the body is being observed at work by an audience of those people who see themselves represented in that body gives rise to another exigence, considerably broader and in most instances much more significant than the first: the body conducting the proceeding must legitimate itself. Opening the proceeding to the public in effect poses a question about the quality of the body's representation. Will the court act according to the community's standard of justice? Will the party conduct itself in keeping with the American political tradition as the people understand it? Will the school board act responsibly, in the best interests of both taxpayers and children?

There are, in other words, two issues or sets of issues at stake in any public proceeding: (1) whatever the specific questions or proposals before the body, and (2) the legitimacy of the body as representative of the community. The first issue is either deliberative or judicial; the second is epideictic. The relationship between these two issues, or exigences, is complex. The authority of the body conducting the proceeding to deal with the first issue rests on an implicit agreement in the community, an agreement formalized in the customs, laws, and procedures of election or appointment that constitute the body's mandate.[6] While at a given moment the agreement might seem solid and enduring, history suggests that it really is quite fragile. Moreover, it is not difficult to exploit the fragility of that agreement in a public proceeding. Political activists of the late 60's and early 70's, for example, learned that it is possible to turn a trial into an attack on the judicial system. A public proceeding can thus transcend the immediate issues at hand, raising questions that touch the very nature of the community in which it takes place.

An important concept here is *representation*. The body holding a public proceeding is representative in the obvious political sense that it acts for the community in disposing of the immediate issues before it; it is an agent of the community. At the same time, the proceeding is a representation in something like the aesthetic sense of that term: It expresses, stands for, or articulates an image of something—in this case, the community itself. In conducting public business before the public, a representative body presents an image of the community to the community, "holds the mirror up . . .". not to nature but to the people. As with a work of art, the "mirror" is actually more like the lens of a magic lantern. What is presented is one of many possible images of a reality that is itself ultimately more fiction than empirical fact. The proceeding constitutes an image of a community and the audience can either identify with that image as a model of their own common life or reject it. To the degree that the audience identifies with the image, the body achieves credibility.

I am talking about fictions—powerful imaginings that shape the lives of people. Empirically the "body" that conducts a public proceeding is not one thing but many; it is a collection of individuals with certain interests in common and many more that conflict. The "community" is likewise simply a vast number of people whose lives overlap in certain ways, but whose sense of fellowship with each other is tenuous at best. Belonging to a community is a matter of implicitly giving one's consent to a great fiction, of agreeing to pretend together with a mass of others, and for the most part to deny even to oneself that the community is ultimately pretense.[7] Membership in a representative body is likewise consenting to a fiction, though to the degree that one chooses membership in such a body the consent is more consciously granted, and therefore more readily subject to qualification or withdrawal. The body exists as a figment of the imaginations of its members, who choose to enact their conflicts according to established procedures, thereby affirming common interests that transcend immediate conflicts. When a representative body conducts its business behind closed doors, the individual members are free to lay their private and conflicting interests out and bargain their way toward resolution of the issues before them; "the common

interest" may become a very remote abstraction, to be weighed by each member against whatever individual needs or special interests he sees at stake. Much of this bargaining would appear unseemly in public proceedings.[8] Some degree of "staging" is therefore virtually inevitable in a public proceeding, which thus becomes a fiction in the sense of a falsehood as well as in the more powerful sense suggested above.

The practical significance of this perspective becomes apparent if one considers the dilemma of the individual member of a body who opposes the majority view of how an issue should be resolved. To the degree that the proceeding articulates an image of community with which the audience can identify, the force of its decisions in shaping public opinion will be underlined by strong *ethos*. Assuming that there is some means of reversing the body's decision after the proceeding (e.g., appeal, veto, repeal, referendum), the member who opposes the majority view can press his own case by undermining that *ethos* in the forum which holds the power of reversal. He might, for example, level charges of unfairness against members of the majority or try to provoke them into shouting matches or other unseemly displays. If he can succeed in generating an image of mean contentiousness within the proceeding, this may undermine public confidence in its outcome, as the Republican convention of 1964 and the Democratic convention of 1968 both demonstrate. But if a member of the opposition chooses to undermine the *ethos* of the majority position in this way, his tactics will have the further effect of undermining the legitimacy of the body. Yes, it he does not follow such tactics, if instead he argues in the manner of "the loyal opposition," he is, in effect, cooperating in a rhetorical strategy favoring the majority by contributing to the *ethos* that supports their position. To the degree that he identifies with the body, he may undermine his own position on the issue before the body. A member of the opposition is therefore confronted with a hard choice between the immediate issues before the body and the broader issues of its legitimacy. In certain types of proceedings, there are strict rules governing the conduct of those who support a minority position; in the judicial system, for example, an attorney or a witness who attempts to undermine the *ethos* of the court will be cited for contempt. In proceedings in which there are no such rules, one can expect to see the majority dealing very carefully with the minority to prevent them from engaging in divisive tactics.

So far I have used the term *ethos* as a rough synonym for "source credibility," which is the sense in which most contemporary rhetoricians seem to use it. In this sense the term is quite neutral and scientific, but the term has a larger meaning as well. *Ethos* is the spirit of a culture or people, the spirit that enables persons to transcend immediate problems and experiences, thereby giving meaning to the immediate and transforming an aggregation of individuals into a community.[9] *Ethos* in this sense is the meaning of the fictions I spoke of earlier. *Ethos* as a source credibility is rooted in this larger sense of the word in that a speaker achieves credibility to the degree that he makes present to his audience something of the spirit that binds him in community with them. The rhetor therefore becomes the preserver and shaper of culture. Isocrates recognized this point and consequently set a high value on epideictic rhetoric, which is in this sense an exercise in pure *ethos*.

It is in this context that the epideictic character of the public proceeding must be understood. The proceeding dramatizes a model of community, including conflict between members who differ over how the immediate issues are to be resolved and the more fundamental agreements that enable them to transcend the issues at hand and enact their conflicts in an orderly way. If the model presented has validity, if it rings true and seems to touch a living tradition, it can articulate a spirit that enlivens the sense of community. If the model seems invalid—false, "staged," unfair—the proceeding can demoralize its audience by saying that their common life is likewise invalid. What may ultimately be at stake in a public proceeding is the communion that makes community possible.

In summary, then a public proceeding must be viewed under two aspects. It is: (1) a forum in which questions of immediate concern to a community are discussed and decided according to procedures rooted in tradition and law; (2) a ritual of communion, celebrating the identity of the community. There is a tension between these two aspects, and in a given instance one or the other may become fully dominant. Under ordinary circumstances, a courtroom proceeding would be dominated by the need to dispose of specific and immediate issues, and the ritual aspect would be fully subordinated to this need to "do business." At the other extreme, a political convention in which the platform and candidates had been decided beforehand would become pure ritual, with the agenda serving merely to set the pattern of the ritual: the 1972 Republican convention would be a good example. More often both aspects are, or at least appear to be, realized simultaneously in a mutually constraining fashion: the ritual celebration of identity proceeds according to the form prescribed for the conduct of business in the forum; business in the forum is conducted under the substantial added weight of its ritual significance.

The overall form of the proceeding is, as I suggested at the outset, dramatic. Members of the body conducting the proceeding are *dramatis personae* who act out a conflict centering on how the issues before them are to be resolved. As in a play, the action will tend naturally to be unified, sometimes in defiance of the nature of the business at hand. The conflict will fall into a pattern of rising action, the exchanges between the actors moving climactically toward a single moment of resolution—the jury's verdict, the nominee's acceptance address, the vote on the central issue. If there are several issues before the body, lesser issues will be dealt with as means of defining the conflict and furthering the movement of action toward the resolution of the major issue. If there are other matters to be disposed of after the resolution of the conflict, they will function either as a denouement or an anticlimax.

 II

As an example of the public proceeding, I will consider the televised debate of the House Judiciary Committee from July 24 through 30,

1974, on the proposed impeachment of Richard Nixon. I choose this example because the fact that the debate was held as a public proceeding rather than in closed session contributed materially to the weight of an issue of indubitable historical significance.

The impeachment debate was the culmination of a long and arduous process. As early as July 31, 1973, committee member Robert Drinan had placed an impeachment resolution before the full House of Representatives.[10] By October 10, 1973, the committee had produced a 718-page study of the concept of impeachment.[11] In February 1974, the committee received formal authorization for its investigation by a vote of 410–4 in the full House,[12] and full-scale closed sessions were underway. During the closed sessions, 38 volumes of "evidentiary material" were accumulated as the basis for the final deliberations and the vote on five proposed articles of impeachment.

To be more precise, the debate was not the culmination of the process, but rather one step on the road leading toward an impeachment trial in the Senate. The process was truncated by Nixon's revelation of the June 23, 1972[,] conversation in which he and H. R. Haldeman had committed a casual obstruction of justice amid talk of Mrs. Nixon's hairdo, and by his subsequent resignation. It would have been possible to press on with the impeachment process, and there was some support in Congress and the general public for doing so.[13] The overwhelming consensus, however, was that to continue the impeachment process would serve no end. On the purely practical level, this was obviously true; removal from office is the only punishment an impeachment trial can impose, and Nixon had already removed himself from office. Yet impeachment serves a symbolic as well as practical end. It clarifies the values of the society—articulates *ethos,* if you will—by pronouncing judgment on the conduct of public officials. On this symbolic level, however, I would argue that it was unnecessary to continue the impeachment process precisely because the Judiciary Committee elected to conduct their debate as a public proceeding before the nation. Because it was a public proceeding—a ritual celebration of identity as well as a practical

decision-making forum—the impeachment debate fulfilled that symbolic end.

During the long, publicly excruciating chain of events that led up to the impeachment debate, impeachment had been transformed in the public mind from a left-wing fantasy into a real and, for many people, a frightening possibility. Jimmy Breslin reports that Drinan's original impeachment resolution had been tabled because House Majority Leader Tip O'Neill and Speaker Carl Albert agreed that the time was not yet politically ripe: "At this time the most votes an impeachment resolution could possibly get would have been twenty-five. Such a vote would appear in the newspapers as a vindication of Nixon by Congress."[14] Impeachment was not simply a matter of legal business in the Congress, and proponents and opponents alike knew it. A decision to impeach would have to be rooted in public understanding and acceptance of the basis for such a drastic action. To impeach and remove from office the highest elected official in the country would touch in a fundamental way the American people's understanding of themselves as a people. By the time of the televised debate, the people had read or heard about the tape transcripts; created a "firestorm" over the dismissal of Archibald Cox and the resignations of Elliot Richardson and William Ruckelshaus; and puzzled over who was responsible for the mysterious 18 1/2-minute gap in one of the tapes, and what damning evidence had been destroyed. These and other events had, in the words of political scientist Charles Hamilton, *impugned* Nixon, thus making impeachment possible.[15] During the same period, the methodical and circumspect work of the Judiciary Committee had made it credible as an instrument for removing Nixon from office. When on July 19, just five days before the opening of the televised debate, Presidential news secretary Ronald Zeigler referred to the committee as a "kangaroo court," his remark provoked considerable public outrage.

But while impeachment was not *simply* a matter of legal business in Congress, it was that too. The question that loomed so large in the press and in public opinion—Should Nixon be impeached?—tended to overshadow the more esoteric and involved legal questions that had occupied the committee during its closed sessions—questions of precedent, evidence, and procedure, questions of what precisely constitutes an impeachable offense and how such an offense must be proven. Yet these were the questions that formed the agenda for the televised debate. There was not one broad question before the committee but rather five articles of impeachment alleging five particular offenses: 1) obstruction of justice in the Watergate cover-up, 2) abuse of power through misuse of such agencies as the FBI and IRS, 3) failure to honor the lawful subpoenas of the Judiciary Committee, 4) unlawful bombing of Cambodia, and 5) tax evasion and acceptance of unlawful emoluments.

This distinction is simply an application of the general point made above that a public proceeding has two aspects. On one level, the impeachment debate was a forum in which a problem of immediate and practical concern to the nation was discussed and decided according to national procedures rooted in law and tradition. From this perspective, the power of the Judiciary Committee was severely delimited: it could merely recommend to the full House of Representatives, which in turn would decide whether or not to impeach.[16] And impeachment would be merely a prelude to trial in the Senate. The debate was a legal proceeding in which it would be necessary to decide such evidentiary questions as whether a "policy" can be implicit in a pattern of actions or must be stated explicitly.[17] Yet on another level, the debate was a ritual of communion articulating an image of the United States as a political unit—a community. At this level, the single question at issues was whether the American *ethos* could tolerate Richard Nixon's conduct as President. In this case, the precise content of the debate would matter less than whether it was conducted with appropriate solemnity.

The form of the debate reflected the inevitable tension between these two aspects in a number of ways. Most obvious was the allocation of time. From the viewpoint of the debate as a forum for doing business, each of the five articles was as important as each of the others, and one would therefore expect roughly the same amount of time to be devoted to consideration of each. Instead, the debate proceeded according to the following schedule:

> Wednesday, July 24—Opening remarks by individual members
> Thursday, July 25—Opening remarks, continued
> Friday, July 26—Debate on article I
> Saturday, July 27—Debate on article I, continued; vote on article I
> Sunday, July 28—Recess
> Monday, July 29—Debate and vote on article II
> Tuesday, July 30—Debate and vote on articles III, IV, and V.

Thus while the agenda did cover each of the five articles, only one-third of the total debate was devoted to consideration of articles II through V. Even assuming that the need to settle procedural matters would naturally slow down debate on the first article, the disproportion remains striking. However, if one views the debate as a ritual of communion, the discussion of articles II through V was extraneous, perhaps even anticlimactic. Once Nixon's conduct had been considered and formally condemned, the ritual was, for all practical purposes, complete. While the agenda of the debate reflected its function as a working forum and a single step in the larger process of impeachment, the allocation of time to items in the agenda tended to emphasize its ritualistic function, and therefore to lend additional weight to its decisions.

The timing of the debate gave further emphasis to its ritualistic aspect. As indicated, the final debate and balloting on article I took place on Saturday and was followed by a full day of recess. A very strong sense of closure at the end of this portion of the debate underlined the significance of the vote on article I. From the viewpoint of dramatic structure, the climax of the proceeding was the Saturday evening vote, Chairman Peter Rodino's voice cracking audibly as he cast the final ballot and called the recess. The weekly news magazines tended to underscore further the impression that the debate was fully resolved in this one vote, since they went to press too soon for the Monday and Tuesday sessions to be reported.

The issues of *Time* and *Newsweek* that were on the newsstands and in people's mailboxes as the debate was ending carried cover stories on what happened up to the Sunday recess. Both magazines had headlines referring to the balloting on article I as "the fateful vote,"[18] and both placed some emphasis on the emotional responses of individual members after casting "the most momentous vote of their political lives, or of any representative of the American people in a century."[19] *Newsweek* carried a page of photographs of individual committee members at their desks, all in poses of high seriousness, Charles Wiggins of California apparently weeping.[20] All of this tended to minimize the fact that the committee was considering a series of particular issues to make recommendations to the full House, and to emphasize instead the one great issue before the committee.

The language of the debate illustrates the mutually constraining effect of the dual aspects of the public proceeding as working forum and ritual. The most obvious examples are the formulaic courtesies and parliamentary jargon that run through the transcript. On the level of the debate as forum, these exchanges were merely the linguistic conventions of Congressional debate, with no more rhetorical significance than the casual greetings exchanged by acquaintances or colleagues. Yet for the television audience, these recurrent verbal formulae took on the character of incantations and helped to establish the ritual solemnity of the debate.[21] Insofar as the formulae prescribed for Congressional debate were linguistically unfamiliar to the audience, this incantatory effect was further emphasized, just as the Latin of the old Roman Catholic liturgy emphasized its ritual character. Recurrent phrases from the debate—"I thank the gentleman for yielding." "The chair recognizes the gentleman from California." "The amendment is/is not agreed to"—were thus in a certain sense equivalent to the "Dominus vobiscum" of the old Roman mass. In both cases, the rhythm and solemnity of the ritual is enhanced by the recurrence of stylized verbal refrains.

A similar point can be made about the recitations of evidence offered by members of the pro-impeachment bloc in the committee. For the most part, these were the dullest sort of narrative, with frequent and tedious references to dates and times, painstaking cross-references to related events, and passages of direct quotation from transcripts of conversations that were dull at best and opaque at worst. They were usually offered in response to legalistic questions that went beyond the interest and understanding of the vast majority of viewers, which is to say that they had very specific technical meanings for the participants in the debate as a forum. Yet for the audience that watched on televisions, these recitations tended to take on less specific but far weightier meanings—ritualistic meanings. A particular piece of narrative might be offered in support of an allegation that Nixon had withheld "relevant and material evidence" or whether the President was legally justified in withholding it, the tale would become part of a litany of voices, a demonic myth recited by priests of the cult of law. From this viewpoint the significance of such recitations was less in their particular details than in their overall weight. While in the debate as forum they served argument, in the debate as ritual they became incantations.

This effect was particularly noticeable on Saturday, the second day of debate on article I. On the previous day, the opponents of impeachment had made much of the issue of "specificity," arguing that the language of the proposed article was so general as not to provide the President with due notice of exactly what he was charged with having done, thus denying him the opportunity to prepare a defense. The merits of this abstruse legal argument were impossible for the audience to evaluate, since it rested on the concept of "due notice" and the conventional procedures for drawing indictments. The real force of the argument was not, however, in its legal merits, but in the suggestion it offered that the proponents of impeachment were not being fair to Nixon. On Saturday, the proponents of impeachment came up with a nice parliamentary tactic to answer this argument without narrowing the language of the article as the anti-impeachment members had wanted. Walter Flowers (D, Alabama) offered a series of motions to strike the various subparagraphs of the article: these motions were not made in earnest, as was demonstrated by Flowers voting 'present' on each of them. Rather, they gave other members of the pro-impeachment bloc an opportunity to read lengthy narrative summaries of the evidence as "specifics" in support of the general charges made by the subparagraphs.[22] On the level of the debate as forum, these recitations were entirely irrelevant to the claim that specific allegations should be made in the language of the article of impeachment itself. Yet they satisfied the audience's need for a story, told with due ritual solemnity, to support the general claim that Nixon's conduct was so unworthy as to merit his removal from office. The ritual character of the recitations was enhanced by the frequent repetition of the word "specifically" to introduce episodes of the story.[23] This had the further effect of emphasizing for the anti-impeachment members the fact that they were being hoist with their own rhetorical petard: Charles Sandman (R, New Jersey), who on Friday had argued as strenuously as anyone for "specificity," was obviously angry and frustrated by Saturday's turn of events.

From the viewpoint of the dramatic form of the debate, it is worth pausing over the fact that it was Flowers who took on the role of establishing the platform from which the "specifics" could be read to the audience without being written into the impeachment articles. Had it been one of the long-time Nixon foes, such as Conyers or Drinan, the series of motions to strike would probably have appeared to be what it in fact was—a parliamentary tactic to sidestep the issue of whether the articles should or shouldn't include specific allegations. And such an appearance would have undermined somewhat the impression of scrupulous fairness and thoroughness the committee had so far given. Flowers was a Democrat, but a southern conservative Democrat who had supported George Wallace and whose congressional district had gone solidly for Nixon in 1972. His established political loyalties seemed to place him closer to the pro-Nixon forces than to the known proponents of impeachment. He had been depicted in the popular press as so deeply anguished over the evils brought to light in the committee's investigation that he had developed an ulcer

as a result. He was thus the right person to lead the pro-impeachment bloc as they moved toward the climactic vote because he of all the supporters of impeachment was least likely to seem a man after Nixon's scalp. His willingness to assume the role would itself be a kind of reluctant evidence of the essential rightness of their cause. In return for taking on this role—at some political risk, given the nature of his constituency—Flowers was granted five minutes to speak between the completion of debate on all amendments and the calling of the roll on the first article, the most pregnant moment of the entire proceeding. His speech, one of the most eloquent of the debate, was for the most part a justification of his vote for impeachment.[24]

I have already argued the general point that the performance of those members who oppose the majority view in a body holding a public proceeding is especially important, since they can exploit conflict within the body as a means of reducing its ethos and thereby narrowing public support for the majority view. The danger of such exploitation of conflict in the impeachment debate was particularly acute, since as the debate opened it was really the only tactic left to those who opposed impeachment. In their opening statements, exactly half of the committee's 38 members in one way or another indicated that they would vote for impeachment, and another eight suggested that they were leaning very strongly in that direction.[25] It was thus certain that the committee would recommend at least one article of impeachment to the House of Representatives, though it was as yet not certain that the full House would follow the Committee's recommendation, or that the Senate was prepared to convict Nixon in an impeachment trial. Which way the full House and the Senate would come down on the issue would be largely determined by which way the political wind seemed to be blowing. The one likely way to avoid impeachment was therefore to undermine the Judiciary Committee's *ethos* and thus blunt the effect of its inevitable report in shaping public opinion. According to Jimmy Breslin, the White House had already gone to some trouble in a futile attempt to discredit the committee by smearing its chairman, Peter Rodino.[26] Ronald Zeigler's "kangaroo court" remark might well have been intended as a signal to the pro-Nixon committee members, suggesting that they do what the White House had been unable to. In order to minimize the public impact of the impeachment vote, they should strive to damage the committee's *ethos* by making it appear that it was unfair and/or incompetent.

Certain anti-impeachment members—most notably Sandman of New Jersey—followed just such a strategy. Yet surprisingly, the committee member who came to be regarded as the ablest and most outspoken opponent of impeachment refused to follow the strategy. Charles Wiggins (R, California) chose instead to mount a legalistic attack on the sufficiency of admissible evidence supporting the charges. While Sandman attacked the pro-impeachment members, in effect trying to prevent the debate from becoming a valid ritual of communion, Wiggins identified with them as "my colleagues," thus validating the legitimacy of the proceeding and contributing to its ritual force. Consider, for example, the ways in which Sandman and Wiggins argued in support of one of the Flowers motions to strike a subparagraph of article I:

Sandman—
The thing that amuses me the most today, what a difference 24 hours makes. Yesterday they had so much testimony they were afraid to put in nine simple sentences. Now today every other word they breathe is the word "specify." Isn't that unusual! So unusual. Everything is so specific. But they have not changed one word in the articles, have they, not a word. There has got to be a reason. You know what the reason is. When you tame it down to a time and a place and an activity, they do not have it. All they have is conjecture. They can tell you all about what Dean told somebody, Ehrlichman told somebody, what somebody else told somebody. This is going to be the most unusual case in the history of man. They are going to prove the whole case against the President of the United States over in the Senate with tapes and no witnesses. Won't that be unusual? And this is what it all amounts to.

Now, if I went through this thing paragraph by paragraph I could cite with great detail no Presidential involvement. They know it, you know it, I know it.[27]

Wiggins—
Now, I want to refresh the recollection of the members as to whether or not the President's concern about CIA was justified under all of the circumstances. We remember that McCord was in fact arrested and a former CIA agent. We remember that Barker was in fact arrested and a former CIA agent, perhaps an active CIA agent. Martinez was arrested and he was an active CIA agent. [Continues offering particulars on the Watergate burglary].

Given those facts, ladies and gentlemen, we are asked to conclude that the President corruptly instructed his aid[e]s to request that there be coordination between the CIA and the FBI so as not to reveal unrelated CIA covert activities.

Now, ladies and gentlemen, that is all the evidence there is in between the 23rd of June and the 6th of July. There is no question that John Dean acted improperly. I am willing to stipulate to that. But that does not execute the President's instructions which were given on the 23rd of June. On that issue, ladies and gentlemen, the question really is not all that close. I would think that the weight, if not the preponderance, of the evidence in favor of the President is that he acted in the public interest as distinguished from corruptly. Surely, however, there is not a clear and convincing showing that the President acted corruptly given the facts and the knowledge that he had at the time he issued the instructions.[28]

These two passages illustrate a number of contrasts that are fairly typical of the argumentative styles consistently followed by the two men: 1) Wiggins argues substantively, whereas Sandman concentrates on attacking the motives of the pro-impeachment members; 2) Wiggins is formal and polite toward the other members, whereas Sandman is more casual and at times even disdainful; 3) Wiggins addresses his remarks to the other members, whereas

Sandman seems to be speaking to the television audience; 4) Wiggins finds the arguments he opposes weighty enough to merit serious rebuttal, whereas Sandman dismisses them with contemptuous sarcasm. In general, one can say that Wiggins argued as "the loyal opposition"; he identified with the committee, thus implicitly acknowledging the validity of its proceeding. Sandman attempted to bring his case to the community represented by the committee and undermine the validity of the proceeding in that larger forum.

The contrast between Sandman and Wiggins poses a nice critical problem. If one considers only the issue of impeachment, Sandman would have to be judged the better speaker. Given the rhetorical situation within which the debate was conducted, his means were reasonably well-chosen for pursuing the end of preventing impeachment, whereas Wiggins' tactics were bound to fail. In fact, Wiggins can actually be seen as having contributed to building public support *for* impeachment in at least three ways: 1) He undermined the effectiveness of Sandman's tactics by not cooperating with them; 2) Wiggins contributed to the committee's *ethos* by identifying with the other members and their procedures; 3) By offering a narrowly legalistic defense of Nixon, Wiggins implied that the best one could say of him was that one couldn't be absolutely certain he was guilty of particular crimes. Far from being "the point man for the defense"[29] that many commentators took him to be, Wiggins was in many ways the best ally the pro-impeachment members had.

But there is always the larger issue of "legitimacy" in a public proceeding, and in the case of the impeachment debate that issue was of enormous importance. The shabby dealings we know as "Watergate" had cast a shadow on American politics generally. Public confidence in the institutions of government had been severely shaken. Insofar as the institutions of government represent the people, are indeed a representation of the people insofar as they share a common life, it can rightly be said that the people's confidence in themselves had been shaken.[30] The means indicated for avoiding impeachment by the full House—the Sandman strategy of undermining the committee's

ethos—would have further eroded public confidence in the institutions of government, and would thus have been demoralizing to a nation whose morale was already low. Wiggins' rhetorical tactics must therefore be seen not as a series of bad choices in dealing with a particular issue before the committee, but as the expression of a judgment on the larger implications of how that issue was to be resolved. In acting the role he did, he set the nation's confidence in itself above the immediate issue. One might pronounce Sandman the abler speaker, but one would have to find Wiggins the wiser man.

A cynic might claim that the wisdom of Wiggins was in the end nothing more than the survival instinct. Nixon's cause turned out to be a sinking ship that would take down many who clung fast to the wreckage. It might be argued that, by defending Nixon in the way he did, Wiggins was simply fulfilling the requirements of party loyalty while protecting his own credibility with the electorate. It is certainly worth noting that Wiggins was reelected to Congress in November 1974, while Sandman was defeated. Wiggins' manner of arguing the case against impeachment may have been just the work of a clever rat sneaking unnoticed off a ship he knew to be doomed, though I am not inclined to think so. Impeachment was such an unprecedented issue that no one could tell just where in it political advantage was to be found, which is why the rest of Congress was happy to see Nixon resign and let impeachment rest where the Judiciary Committee had left it.

But whatever his personal motives, Wiggins' manner of arguing the case for Nixon helped make the impeachment debate a model of public life that the American people could and evidently did take as valid representation of themselves.[31] Even those members of the television audience who could not approve the committee's recommendation could at least identify with a voice in the committee, a voice that confirmed the validity or the proceeding even as it disputed the outcome. In a similar manner, citizens from diverse backgrounds and with diverse ideological commitments could hear voices in the committee speaking for them. Barbara Jordan (D, Texas) spoke of herself as having been included in the "We the people" of the Constitution only by the process of amendment and interpretation, thus identifying herself as a representative of blacks and women.[32] Tom Railsback (R, Illinois) expressed particular concern for the effect of Watergate and of the committee's proceeding on the minds of young people.[33] Edward Mezvinski (D, Iowa) spoke of his parents having emigrated from czarist Russia, thus identifying himself with the concerns of "hyphenated Americans."[34] Charles Rangel (D, New York) made himself a spokesperson for war veterans by referring to the men "who died next to me in Korea."[35] William Hungate (D, Missouri) spoke for those who were more outraged by Nixon's humorless and self-righteous pomposity than his specific violations of law and public trust.[36] Conyers (D, Michigan), Waldie (D, California) and other long-time Nixon foes spoke for various elements of the left and the anti-war movement. Flowers (D, Alabama) spoke as a representative of a Wallace-Democrat constituency. Even on the level of phonetics, the committee contained a diversity of voices, from Drinan's flat Bostonian and Rangel's gravelly New York east-side to Hungate's sharp Missourian and James Mann's genteel South Carolina tidewater.

The diversity of voices in the committee could very easily have produced a cacophony, which of course would have served the ends of the Nixon White House quite well. But thanks to the good sense and good will of the great majority of the committee members, and to the skillful leadership of Rodino, the committee remained unified in its diversity. The members spoke to each other and to the nation in mutual respect and a conscious awareness of a fundamental agreement that transcended their regional and ideological differences. Many of them alluded to that agreement by referring to "the founding fathers" or to specific passages from the Constitution; Barbara Jordan's reference to the phrase "We the People" in the preamble was an especially lucid instance. Rodino expressed his own sense of that agreement with simple eloquence: "I am proud," he said to his colleagues, "to be a part of you, to be among you, to be of you."[37] On the level of rhetoric, these references to the agreement underlying the diversity of the committee suggest

the importance of Kenneth Burke's observation that "Identification is affirmed with earnestness precisely because there is division."[38] On the level of politics, and of *ethos* in its larger cultural sense, they recall the motto "*E pluribus unum.*"

★ III

What I have presented in this paper is neither a full analysis of the impeachment debate nor a complete theory of the public proceeding as a rhetorical genre. Neither would be possible in such a brief space, if indeed a "full analysis" or a "complete theory" of any rhetorical phenomenon would he possible in any amount of space. Rather, I have made an essay, in the old sense of a tentative effort or a probing. Assuming that the effort has seemed interesting enough to warrant further exploration, it might be appropriate to conclude by suggesting some directions.

1. I have tried to conceptualize the genre broadly enough to accommodate very different sorts of proceedings, but in the absence of analyses of public trials, political conventions, legislative sessions, and the like, it remains possible that the genre has been drawn too narrowly. And, if it is broad enough as it stands the differences between sub-classes within the genre could be delineated. A televised political convention may be sufficiently like the impeachment debate to be regarded as belonging to the same rhetorical genre, but it surely is more like another political convention, which suggests that sub-genres or species of public proceedings could he described. Other events should be examined from the critical perspective of this essay, not only to come to an understanding of those events, but also as a means of developing a fuller understanding of public proceedings in general. Perhaps something like the model of documentary film genres presented in Bruce Gronbeck's essay in this volume could be developed for public proceedings.

2. Certain aspects of the critical perspective developed in this paper suggest hypotheses that could be submitted to empirical testing, either in field studies or in experimental settings. One might, for instance, try to discover what sorts of people take the trouble to attend school-board or city council meetings, or to tune in the

state legislature rather than *All in the Family*. The effect of various interactive styles and argumentative strategies on the attitude changes a public proceeding brings about in its audience could be measured. Whether such empirical research should or could lead to a predictive theory that could be used to control public attitudes toward representative bodies and the policies they espouse is a question for others to answer. It could, however, help refine the critical tools available for analyzing and evaluating public proceedings.

3. With respect to the impeachment debate, any number of alternative critical perspectives might be brought to bear on the event. One could, for example, analyze politically the behind-the-scenes bargaining among members of the committee; perform a Toulmin-based analysis of the argumentative structure of the debate; examine audience response as evidenced in press accounts, correspondence with congressmen, public opinion polls, and the like; or do a fantasy-theme analysis of the discussions of Nixon's conduct in the debate.[39] The general point to be made here is that criticism is and ought to be pluralistic. There is no one correct perspective on the impeachment debate, or for that matter on any public proceeding or any other rhetorical event.

NOTES

[1] This paper owes much to Lloyd Bitzer's "The Rhetorical Situation," *Philosophy and Rhetoric* 1 (January 1968), 1–14. However, insofar as Bitzer suggests that discourse arises directly from situation and need only be "fitting" in terms of prior situational constraints, I disagree with him. The public proceeding is defined as a rhetorical genre by a complex interaction between situation and the form of discourse. In the case of the impeachment debate, for example, no antecedent situational constraints demanded that the debate be conducted on national television; rather, the decision to televise the debate helped establish a rhetorical situation that was further articulated by the particular form of the debate as it was being conducted, as well as by many extrinsic factors.

[2] See Antonin Artaud, *The Theater and its Double* (New York, 1958) and John Willett (ed.), Brecht on Theater (New York, 1964).

[3] *Rhetoric*, I, 3; see Lane Cooper (trans.), *The Rhetoric of Aristotle* (New York, 1932), 16–17.

[4] Bitzer, 8.

[5] The impeachment resolution recommended by the House Judiciary Committee contains the following preamble: "Articles of impeachment exhibited by the House of Representatives of the United States of America in the name of itself *and of all the people of the United States of America,* against Richard M. Nixon, President of the United States of America, in maintenance and support of its impeachment against him for high crimes and misdemeanors." (emphasis added) *Impeachment of Richard M. Nixon, President of the United States: The Final Report of the Committee on the Judiciary, House of Representatives* (New York, 1975), 1.

[6] The notion of agreement I take from Ch. Perelman and L. Olbrechts-Tyteca. *The New Rhetoric* (Notre Dame, Ind.: Univ. of Notre Dame Press, 1969), 65–114.

[7] The fictionality of social structures and the consequences of recognizing them as fictions is an important theme in modern literature. See, for example, Jean-Paul Sartre's *Nausea,* Samuel Beckett's *Watt,* Thomas Pynchon's *The Crying of Lot 49,* and Robert Coover's *The Universal Baseball Association.*

[8] This distinction between how politics works behind closed doors and the face politicians present to the public is one of the central themes of Murray Edelman's *The Symbolic Uses of Politics* (Urbana, Ill.: Univ. of Ill. Press, 1964). The public proceeding might in fact be regarded as a subcategory of the form of political communication Edelman calls "hortatory language" (pp. 134–8).

[9] This concept of ethos is developed at greater length in my "On the End of Rhetoric, Classical and Modern," *College English* XXXVI (February 1975), 621–31, and "Tradition and Theory in Rhetoric," *Quarterly Journal of Speech* LXII (Oct. 1976), 234–41. *The Oxford English Dictionary* gives as the first definition of *ethos* "the characteristic spirit, prevalent tone of sentiment, of a people or community; the 'genius' of an institution or system"; as authority for this meaning the OED cites Aristotle's *Rhetoric*, II, 12–14.

[10] The Staff of the New York Times, *The End of a Presidency* (New York: 1974), 221.

[11] Jimmy Breslin, *How the Good Guys Finally Won* (New York: Viking, 1975), 70.

[12] *The End of a Presidency*, 241; this resolution, H.R. 803, was in effect merely the ratification of a process that had begun months before at the direction of the House leadership.

13 For example, Jerome Waldie urged continuation of the impeachment process in his "Separate Comments" appended to the Judiciary Committee's final report. *The Final Report of the Committee on the Judiciary,* 410–13.

14 Breslin, 44.

15 In Demetrios Caraley *et al.,* "American Political Institutions after Watergate—a Discussion," *Political Science Quarterly* LXXXIX (Winter, 1974–75), 729.

16 H.R. 803 directed the committee "to investigate fully and completely whether sufficient grounds exist for the House of Representatives to exercise its constitutional power to impeach Richard Nixon, President of the United States of America." Barry Sussman, *The Great Cover-Up: Nixon and the Scandal of Watergate* (New York: Signet, 1974), 289.

17 This issue produced some of the most pointless and confusing interchanges of the entire proceeding. See, for example, the discussion of an amendment to article I in which Tom Railsback (R, Illinois) substituted the words "course of conduct or plan" for the word "policy." When asked to explicate the change, Railsback replied in part ". . . I am not sure that I can answer that there is that much difference between the word 'plan' and 'policy' except there seems to be a feeling on the part of the counsel that I dealt with in drafting that 'policy' seems to give more of an impression of an affirmative, orchestrated, and declarative decision." *Debate on Articles of Impeachment: Hearings of the Committee of the Judiciary, House of Representatives, Ninety-Third Congress, Second Session, Pursuant to H. Res. 803* (Washington, D.C.: U.S. Gov't. Printing Office, 1974), 265.

18 *Newsweek,* Aug. 5, 1974, 18; *Time,* Aug. 5, 1974, 10.

19 *Time,* 10: note that this evaluation seems to draw an equivalence between the committee's decision to *recommend* impeachment and the Senate's decision on whether to *convict* Andrew Johnson in an impeachment trial.

20 *Newsweek,* 19.

21 Karlyn Kohrs Campbell makes a related point about the conventional courtesies of the debate: "Because congressional debate is relatively inaccessible, these conventions have special rhetorical impact for the public—after an era of confrontation, this is civilized disagreement. When times are good, congressional courtesy can be considered frivolous, simply manners, mere decor. But when times are bad, this decor becomes the vital matter of decorum. And decorum is sorely needed in a situation in which the President of the Nation is being judged for deeply indecorous behavior." "The Judicial Context: The House Judiciary Committee Debates Over Articles

of Impeachment," paper presented at the 1975 convention of Speech Communication Association.

22 The discussion of these amendments runs from page 251 through page 325 of *Debate on Articles of Impeachment.*

23 See, for example, the recitation by William Cohen (R, Maine), *Debate on Articles of Impeachment,* 272–3.

24 *Debate on Articles of Impeachment,* 326–7.

25 As I read their opening statements, the following members declared for impeachment: Donohue, Kastenmeier, Edwards, Hungate, Conyers, Eilberg, Waldie, Hogan, Butler, Danielson, Sieberling, Drinan, Rangel, Jordan, Thornton, Holtzman, Owens, Mezvinski, and Rodino. Leaning were McClory, Brooks, Railsback, Fish, Flowers, Sarbanes, Cohen, and Froehlich. In addition to these 27 members, James Mann, whose opening statement expressed no commitment one way or the other (but who was known to favor impeachment), eventually voted for impeachment.

26 The story of how pressure was applied to former Congressman Neil Gallagher of New Jersey, then in federal prison for tax evasion, to cooperate in a smear attempt is told in *How the Good Guys Finally Won,* 146ff.

27 *Debate on Articles of Impeachment,* 296–7.

28 *Ibid.,* 299–300.

29 R. W. Apple Jr., "Introduction" to *The Final Report of the Committee on the Judiciary,* xv.

30 In concluding their "Statement of Evidence on Article I," the committee stated that "President Nixon's actions resulted in *manifest injury to the confidence of the nation* and great prejudice to the cause of law and justice" (emphasis added). *The Final Report of the Committee on the Judiciary,* 198.

31 A story in the August 28, 1974 *New York Times* (11.4) reported that the Gallup Poll recorded an 18% increase in public confidence in Congress over the figures for April 1974, and that the increase was directly attributable to the televised impeachment debate.

32 *Debate on Articles of Impeachment,* 111.

33 *Ibid.,* 28.

34 *Ibid.,* 129.

35 *Ibid.,* 107.

36 *Ibid.,* 28–32 and *passim.*

37 *Ibid.,* 136.

38 Kenneth Burke, *A Rhetoric of Motives* (Berkeley and Los Angeles: Univ. of Calif. Press, 1969), 22.

39 On the method of fantasy-theme analysis, see Ernest G. Bormann. "Fantasy and Rhetorical Vision: The Rhetorical Criticism of Social Reality," *Quarterly Journal of Speech* 58 (December 1972), 396–407.

The Rhetorical Boundaries of "the Law":
A Consideration of the Rhetorical Culture of Legal Practice and the Case of the "Separate but Equal" Doctrine

Marouf Hasian, Jr., Celeste Michelle Condit, and John Louis Lucaites

I am not a lawyer, but I have never believed that a layman who thought soberly was incompetent to express a judgment upon the Constitution.

—Theodore Roosevelt[1]

In the lexicon of contemporary liberal-democratic legal practice, to "think like a lawyer" is to have mastered the fundamental, rational principles of "the law," a mastery that confers a technical, professional understanding of legal practices unavailable to ordinary, untrained people.[2] From this perspective, while social actors not trained in the ways of legal thinking clearly experience the short term and localized influence of legal edicts, their passions and self-interests preclude them from balancing long term rights and duties. In the words of Glendon A. Shubert, the law has evolved as a form of judicial policy-making that depends on having a "legitimized elitism" in which judges operate in closer proximity to the "music of the heavenly spheres" than to "the people and their raucous marketplaces."[3]

Although this professionalist perspective on the rationality of the law is an article of faith among contemporary legal practitioners, as well as among many legal educators, it is not the only theoretical framework within which to understand the scope and function of everyday legal practices. Legal realists attacked the traditional perspective thoroughly in the middle part of our century, but the most recent challenges to the professionalist view have emerged from the work of a variety of critical theorists, including feminist scholars, race theorists, law and society analysts, and in greatest profusion, Critical Legal Studies (CLS).[4] These groups draw heavily from poststructural and postmodern paradigms that advocate the interrogation of professionalist privileging of legal discourse as a scientifically measured, neutral and objective rational standard of social and political conduct. Often times these communities employ critical techniques that illustrate the internal contradictions in the liberal-democratic commitment to the "rule of law." Frequently, CLS writers seek to demonstrate that the law is a dominant ideology that represents a narrow and exclusive range of sociopolitical and economic interests.[5]

In what follows we review the debate between the professionalist and CLS perspectives on legal practice as a prelude to the consideration of a third possibility which seeks to transcend the opposition between these two views. We focus on CLS because it is the largest and most thoroughly articulated of these contemporary critical legal programs.[6] We will argue that, in practice, the law is neither a rationally constructed discourse nor simply a dominant ideology, but rather an active and protean component of a hegemonically crafted rhetorical culture. Through legal argumentation and debate, various partisan communities make compromises that function as the boundaries within which the law takes on public meaning. We illustrate our conception of the rhetorical boundaries of legal practice by examining the emergence and subsequent demise of the "separate but equal" doctrine in American law. Through this case study we hypothesize a set of characteristics that demarcate the rhetorical substance of legal practices within American rhetorical culture.

★ THREE PERSPECTIVES ON THE SUBSTANCE OF THE LAW

Historically, the power to identify the substance of our laws has been a recurrent point of dispute. Indeed, one of the most famous debates in legal folklore involves the controversy between Sir Edward Coke and King James I of England on the legal meaning of the term "reason." Coke argued that the "common law," based on fundamental and centuries old principles, contained a form of legal reason that limited even the power of English monarchs. In an attempt to defend the absolute rights of the monarchy, King James maintained that the royal prerogative automatically granted him the power of reason. In a response that the American colonists would later echo, Coke explained that "true it was, that God had endowed His Majesty with excellent science, and great endowments of nature; but His Majesty was not learned in the laws of his realm of England, and causes . . . are not to be decided by natural reason but by artificial reason and judgment of law, which law is an act which requires long study and experience, before that a man can attain to the cognizance of it."[7] King James would neither be the first nor the last to criticize the existence and authority of the technical or professional domain of the law.

The intensive professionalization of the law has become a significant marker of modern legal theory and practice. Classical theorists work under the assumption that the law is an independent discursive field, occupied by trained specialists who participate in, apart from, and above the body politic.[8] Contemporary legal discourse is defined accordingly in terms of firmly established exclusionary rules that designate who will and who will not legitimately be allowed to speak the language of the law.[9] Thus, it is assumed that the U.S. Constitution assigns the sole responsibility for "political" decision-making to the executive and legislative branches of government, who alone are publicly accountable to the politically and economically interested constituencies that they represent. At the same time, however, the responsibility for applying the law, which is supposed to operate somehow outside of the boundaries of politics, is assigned to the judicial branch of government, whose public accountability is limited to providing legal reasons for their decisions.

The intended effect of professionalizing the law is to separate those whose task it is to interpret the meaning of the law from those involved in the domain of politics.[10] Perhaps no better illustration of this segregation exists than in the taken-for-granted assumptions operating in Justice Antonin Scalia's concurring opinion in *Webster v. Reproductive Health Services* (1989):

> . . . our retaining control, through *Roe*, of what I believe to be, and many of our citizens recognize to be, a political issue, continuously

distorts the public perception of the role of this Court. We can now look forward to at least another term with cars full of mail from the public, and streets full of demonstrators, urging us—their un-elected and life-tenured judges who have been awarded those extraordinary, undemocratic characteristics precisely in order that we might follow the law despite the popular will—to follow the popular will.[11]

To create the image of an apolitical legal forum, judges, lawyers, and legal scholars constantly emphasize the need for an independent judiciary capable of withstanding the public pressures that special interest groups bring to bear upon it. The law thus becomes a process of containment, wherein legal practices are confined to a judicial system, complete with the regalia of office and elaborate technical vocabularies that typically invoke their Latinate origins. To "think like a lawyer" is thus to participate in and reproduce a professional consciousness that avoids actively engaging in the full range of possible alternative social relationships.[12] Because of the complexity of many legal cases and the density of the vocabulary of legal discourse, only those anointed with the proper professional credentials, i.e., a law degree from an accredited law school, are allowed to practice law; fewer still, of course, achieve the opportunity to sit in judgment on state and federal courts.

The authority to define the parameters of the law has been achieved in part by the dominance of a judicial perspective that we call "scientific."[13] Viewed through this prism, jurisprudence is a process of textual exegesis through which empowered individuals engage in a hermeneutic enterprise that seeks the correct meanings of fixed Constitutional dicta, administrative rules, and general legal principles. As long as the Constitution is not amended and statutes are not revised or repealed, the assumption is that there are clear, truthful, settled guidelines that constrain interpreters from making arbitrary and "unreasonable" choices. Over time, a community of legal specialists supposedly "discover[s]" the correct legal decisions in complex cases because they are guided by non-political rules and logics that operate outside of the context of individual interests and human discretion. As Lief Carter observes:

Our culture encourages some misunderstanding about legal reasoning. Perhaps because, starting in the Renaissance, a streak of discoveries about the physical world has continuously bombarded Western civilization, we too often assume that legal reasoning is good when it discovers the law's "right answer," the correct legal solution to a problem. The idea that we live under a government of laws, not men, seems based on the assumption that correct legal results exist, like undiscovered planets or subatomic particles, quite independent of man's knowledge.[14]

As a set of rules, the law is thus said to become increasingly accurate and precise as time and experience allow us to uncover its latent structures and implicit wisdom—at least, that is, so long as a profane "politics" can be kept out of the judicial equation. For the law to progress, it must remain wholly impartial, clearly based on neutral principles of governance, i.e., "laws, not men."

In recent years, academic legal theorists operating under the rubric of the CLS movement have loudly expressed disenchantment with the exclusivity of scientific and objectivist interpretations of the law.[15] Borrowing heavily from a variety of poststructuralist and deconstructionist logics, they have argued for a radical reconceptualization of the commonplace assumptions that underlie the relationship between law and politics in ordinary, contemporary legal practices.[16] As John Louis Lucaites recently noted, the CLS perspective views the boundary between law and rhetoric as a political space that may be used to "repress and undermine the possibilities for radical social change."[17]

The proponents of CLS typically "trash" the claims of classical legal theorists that characterize particular and historically specific discursive interpretations of the law as if they represented the universal premises of judicial thinking.[18] The significant result for CLS advocates is that such theories—and the legal practices they warrant—hide both the politics and the mutability of the law by incorrectly and unjustly depicting legal institutions and judicial processes as "necessary" components of the normal/natural social order.[19] Functioning as a "legitimating ideology," such depictions cut off "access to genuine possibilities of transformation."[20] Indeed, for many of those operating under the CLS banner, the traditional rhetoric of the law prohibits even visualizing alternatives to existing legal institutions.[21] By constantly critiquing the hegemonic, discursive structures or legal practices that perpetuate the dominance of specific legal institutions, and by pointing out the plethora of plausible judicial options that the legal system frequently ignores, CLS advocates conclude that they can begin to open up political spaces in which the disempowered may gain a legitimate voice. Unlike the professionalized model of legal communication, this perspective assumes that critics have an obligation to highlight the politics and contradictions that permeate our system of governance. By pointing out the created and institutionalized judicial antinomies, CLS writers are satisfied that they have helped to transform the law without engaging in an essentializing "rights" talk.[22]

The power of the CLS critique comes from the recognition that it is not the "abuse" *of* our legal system that perpetuates social inequities, but that the judiciary itself is a rhetorical construction that systematically silences some voices, while it grants presumptive authority to others. Employing a variant of the dominant ideology thesis, CLS writers frequently conclude that the law is merely an ideology, and as such it represents an illegitimate exercise of coercive power.[23] Put in more concrete terms, they argue that "the rule of law" is little more than a means of hiding and legitimizing the maldistributions of wealth and power in society.

We are sympathetic to the CLS project and its critique of the presumed objectivity and neutrality of the law. However, we believe ultimately that this perspective on legal rhetoric is both theoretically and pragmatically insufficient.[24] Part of the problem stems from concentrating on uncovering contradictions in the mandarin texts of judicial elites, a focus which reinforces the perception that substantive social change in the judicial process can only occur within the halls of the legal academy.[25] By replacing traditional legal jargon with the equally complex language of literary and philosophical poststructuralism, CLS advocates have merely shifted the locus of power and control from one elite to another.[26] The end result is that the CLS critique of classical liberal legal theory remains fundamentally an instrumentalist interpretation of legal discourse that places the construction of the "rule of law" outside of the range of ordinary political actors who cannot lay claim to being members of the legal fraternity. While attacking the reproduction of hierarchies within technical discourse, the CLS movement has typically neglected the production of judicial relationships in traditionally extra-judicial contexts, i.e., the vibrant social and political culture made up of audiences and speakers who share collective, lived experiences of the law.[27] Ironically, then, even as CLS proponents argue for such an instrumentally derived, emancipatory moment, they absolutely deny any consensual and rational component to the law. In sum, the CLS movement provides a compelling, immanent critique of elite legal discourse, but it fails to provide either thoroughly articulated alternative outcomes or concrete strategies for dealing with the substantive issues of political change outside of the rigidly defined structure of the legal educational system.[28] As such, it reduces the law to an overdetermined system of rules and regulations created beyond the boundaries of human discretion.

In place of both the traditional classical liberal theories of law and the CLS critique, we offer a third alternative that seeks to transcend the tension between these two perspectives by positing that the law exists as part of an evolving rhetorical culture. By "rhetorical culture" we mean to draw attention to the range of linguistic usages available to those who would address a historically particular audience as a public. In this rhetorical culture we find the full complement of commonly used allusions, aphorisms, analogies, characterizations, ideographs, images, myths, narratives, and commonplace argumentative forms that demarcate the symbolic boundaries within which public advocates find themselves flexibly constrained to operate.[29] Rhetorical cultures evolve by adapting to changing social, political, and economic exigencies, and the law is an inevitable branch of such a culture.[30] From this perspective, then, the law is neither an immutable, foundational principle,

nor a relentlessly overdetermined dominant ideology, but one component in the organic evolution of a social order that continually (re)constitutes itself through public discourse.

Unlike those orientations that treat the law as pristine procedure free of external coercion or the product of "mere" ideology, the concept of a "rhetorical culture" encourages us to examine the argumentative postures of ordinary humans as they actively negotiate the social boundaries of both their domination and liberation. Contained by this perspective is the recognition that legal hegemony entails more than the efforts of a homogeneous ruling class to impose its worldview on some subordinate, subject class. Instead, legal hegemony refers to "government by consent," a social and political order in which a set of ruling relationships represents a temporary "stand-off" among competing groups seeking to achieve the most they can under the prevailing circumstances.[31] Such relationships might not be fair and equal in the best of all possible worlds, but they nonetheless possess a certain cultural authenticity insofar as they are forged in the fires of controversy where prudential concerns often necessitate the acceptance of less than perfect public arrangements.

Scholars operating from a variety of perspectives have long recognized that public discourse controls individual and collective behavior by establishing motivational norms.[32] The public vocabularies in which such norms emerge also set the boundaries within which the law functions. A number of studies have recently shown that specific legal pronouncements assume specific charactertypes drawn from the public vocabulary.[33] To the extent that a judge adopts a particular worldview, peopled with particular kinds of human agents, he or she will find some judicial choices logical and others irrational. In *Williams v. Mississippi* (1898), for example, the justices of the Supreme Court assumed the accuracy of the public vocabulary's portrayal of black Americans as wanting in those traits necessary for responsible citizenship. The Court thus ruled that laws restricting the vote on the basis of the length of residency or petty criminal records were constitutional.[34] Similarly, Celeste Condit has shown that in *Roe v. Wade* (1973), those justices who characterized females as "mothers" rather than as "liberty-bearing persons" dissented from the majority view and sought to restrict a woman's right to abortion.[35]

Although the point we are driving at would seem to be obvious, it bears emphasis: the law cannot exist apart from the public vocabulary of a rhetorical culture. It is virtually impossible to conceive of a law apart from the agents who enact it and the actions it governs. But how are we to describe such agents and actions? In the absence of a neutral vocabulary, legal actors must rely upon the common discourse of a culture to derive a vocabulary that will effectively depict such agents and actions and locate them in legally significant contexts. Were the legal system to be divorced entirely from such a public vocabulary it would be very difficult, if not impossible, to craft a meaningful law that could be communicated to the polity. No one except for specially trained jurists would know who was subject to the mandates of a particular law, or which actions it permitted or prohibited. In its inability to communicate, the law would thus be powerless to act upon the public it was meant to protect and control.

A rhetorical culture is therefore power-in-action, and the meaning of the law necessarily derives from the forms available in the rhetorical culture. From this perspective we can begin to see that the law is not the simple result of deductive reasoning, scientific discovery, or even the arbitrary imposition of the private interests of powerful legal elites; rather, like the public vocabulary itself, the distinctive form of the law is hegemonic. To effect an influential "rule of law" requires winning the consent of a substantial number of different individuals and groups. The relevant standard of justice is therefore contingent probability, not certainty.[36] Classical legal scholars have tended to decry contingent probability as lacking substance, preferring instead to cast their lot with either scientific or philosophical standards of certainty. We believe, however, that the historical record definitively denies the existence of permanent and universal rules; or if that seems too extreme, then at least the record dramatically limits the number of rules that can claim the status of certainty to a number far fewer than those necessary to govern a society. Consequently, the persistent touting of certainty as the standard of justice does little more than to

warrant the CLS critique that such legal claims are efforts at ill-intended misuniversalizations, tailored to generate an inevitably oppressive false consciousness, precisely because they seek to reify contingent and negotiable relationships as permanent and unavoidable.

Indirectly, however, CLS can be tarred with the same brush. Their critiques of the traditionalists' focus on the law implicitly identify universality as the only acceptable standard of truth. The CLS perspective argues that because the traditionalists' claim to universal truth is false, only false consciousness remains. This disjunctive argument—positing as it does either certainty or groundlessness—errs in ignoring the alternatives of probability and contingency as the sources of the reasonable foundations of governance. Ordinary human actors do not routinely make this error. Knowing through human experience that achieving certainty is impossible in the vast majority of human decision making contexts, most human actors commonly choose their actions on the basis of what the available information indicates is most likely to produce a positive or desired outcome. Put simply, when operating in the "realm of the contingent," choices and standards of decision making may be substantive and reasonable without being certain.[37]

Not surprisingly, this rhetorical approach to the law shares much with the juridical rhetoric offered by Chaim Perelman. Perelman presupposes a "universal audience" constructed of "all reasonable and competent men."[38] By contrast, our perspective presumes a heterogeneous audience (including both men and women) that is linked to a pre-existing community. This audience is specific to a particular time and place, and though it is capable of reason, it does not focus on ideally universal perspectives so much as highly self-interested ends. Our perspective also presumes a somewhat broader understanding of what is "reasonable."

The legal actors operating within a rhetorical culture arrive at probable and substantively reasonable conclusions by engaging in the practice of public debate. In this context, arriving at the "truth" of a matter relies not solely on analytical, rational, or scientific demonstration, or even solely upon what Perelman identifies as "quasi-logical" forms. Instead, it includes the broad human activity of "giving proof" to an audience in the Aristotelian sense, of *entekhnoi pisteis* or artistic proofs, i.e., the integration of *logos, ethos,* and *pathos* in support of a probability statement that relies upon the *koinoi topoi,* or common knowledge of the audience.[39] The incorporation of *ethos* and *pathos* insures that *logos* is not formulary, but integrated with the relationships of the community (through *ethos*) and with the community's values (through *pathos*).

As a consequence of the fullness and particularity of rhetoric as a way of forming law, the legal system that emerges from a rhetorical culture seldom produces specific laws that meet any idealistic or *a priori* standard of fairness. Because a rhetorical culture is necessarily responsive to the inputs from the social system that it interprets, it does not provide an externally certifiable, permanent, or universal code. Instead it produces a "compromise," "standoff," or "concordance" among social actors motivated by competing interests, which allows for a modicum of stability and predictability in social, political, and economic relationships. On this view, the law is more like a treaty bound to mutual assured destruction than like a scientific principle bound to an immutable and inexorable truth. Its virtue is therefore best judged by the willingness of competing actors to acquiesce reluctantly, and for the time being, to its ministrations. If this leaves the disconcerting feeling that the law is impermanent, it has the advantage of allowing openness to needed change; and in point of fact, it assumes that publicly warranted changes will be made.

An example of how this process works in American jurisprudence is found in the case of the strange career of the "separate but equal" doctrine. We choose this case to illustrate our theoretical perspective because the public meanings assigned to the term "equality" have varied starkly across the past two hundred years, and because the law regarding the place of "equality" in American governance has exhibited the most notorious of shifts. Opponents of the foundationalist approach to the law find these shifts from post–Civil War egalitarianism, to *Plessy v. Ferguson* (1896), and back again to *Brown v. Bd. of Education* (1954), to be the most condemning example of the instability and irrationality of the American judicial system. If we can offer an interpretation of this case that explains this strange history, we will have demonstrated the potency of the rhetorical approach in answering the CLS challenge without resorting either to a reductionistic dominant ideology thesis or an *ad hoc* exceptionalism. To give a full account of this history, however, would require more space than is available. Therefore, we offer here an interpretation, rather than a fully evidenced argument, referring the reader to Condit and Lucaites's *Crafting Equality: America's Anglo-African Word* for the fuller data upon which this interpretation is built.

★ EQUALITY IN AMERICA'S SECOND CENTURY

The Civil War marks the most serious and significant legitimation crisis in America's political history. It was in the context of justifying the war through Northern eyes that President Lincoln dedicated the blood shed in that gory conflict to the rebirth of American liberty and the establishment of "equality" as a fundamental principle of the nation's Constitution. The term "equality" held a special place in the developing rhetorical culture of nineteenth-century America, but its precise meaning was by no means clear and its usage varied widely in public debates concerning the nation's future. In the judicial, legislative, and executive branches of government, public officials debated the extent to which the coercive power of a postwar Congress could be used in enforcing the newly minted Thirteenth, Fourteenth, and Fifteenth Amendments. At the same time, many American citizens used the power of the press and pulpit to voice their opinions on the issue of legal equality and the meaning of Reconstruction. While traditional analyses have characterized the policies of the era primarily in terms of the success or failure of radical Republicans, we contend that the new constitutional codes that emerged at this critical juncture were the product of more complex and varied voices, and that the law and policies that emerged functioned as a compromise among at least three different and competing voices.

Between 1865 and 1896, white anti-egalitarians, African-Americans, and white

Republican egalitarians articulated competing conceptions of "political," "civil," and "social" equality, all of which interacted to influence the ways in which Americans discussed enfranchisement, access to public accommodations, segregated schools, and interracial marriages. These public discourses were transformed into "law" via both the legislature and the judiciary, and these two law-producing venues were themselves often in tension. During much of the first decade following the Civil War, radical egalitarians dominated the national legislature, but they were not in a position to impose their own usages of "equality" single-handedly onto the new amendments to the constitution. At the same time, many federal court judges disappointed their radical counterparts when they provided rulings that narrowly construed the meaning of the "privileges and immunities" clause or denied the constitutionality of much of the postwar legislation.[40]

In Congress, white radical egalitarians preferred usages of "equality" summed up most frequently by the ideograph "equal rights." For example, Charles Sumner claimed that after slavery, freemen had "Equality of Rights" as their "foremost" right, and he included more than the right to testify or the right to vote. Sumner claimed that the law of "Equality" was a general rule that also protected citizens in the areas of travel, health, pleasure, public conveyances, and common schools.[41] The phrase "equal rights" sanctioned a legal structure in which all men (not women) would have the same privileges to vote, to use public facilities (except perhaps schools), and to act generally as citizens. The number of radical egalitarians in Congress did not constitute a two-thirds majority, however, and so while the egalitarians were largely in control of drafting the Civil War Amendments, they had to craft them as a compromise of competing interests that would allow those who favored a more narrow range of usages of equality to authorize their ratification. The moderates were also influenced by the vocal group of anti-egalitarians, who cast all usages of "equality" in the most threatening terms possible.[42] In order to head off this rhetorical attack on the viability of "equality" as a principle of governance, egalitarian Republicans labored to make their version of equality less

vivid and more non-threatening. Their ability to do this, however, was influenced also by the presence of a fairly large group of vocal African-Americans who favored an even more thoroughgoing vision of "equality" than that promoted by most congressional egalitarians, a vision that included both "equal access" to public schools and "equal opportunities."[43]

One consequent of the lack of unanimity on what constituted an appropriate version of "equal rights" was that the drafters of the new amendments chose ambiguous language that could later easily be subjected to either broadened or narrowed interpretations. Hence, the Fourteenth Amendment enshrined "equal citizenship" without actually specifying those rights which citizenship entailed or without explicitly granting "equal access" to all public facilities. Similarly, the Fifteenth Amendment did not guarantee the "equal right to vote," but rather outlawed voter discrimination on the basis of "race, color or previous condition of servitude" (thereby permitting discrimination on auxiliary characteristics that might be correlated with race). Such strategic obscurities meant that some new provisions expanding equality could be successfully ratified, but it also meant that the constitutional doctrine of equality was broad enough to allow a diverse range of interpretations. As the Civil War and slavery grew dimmer through the passage of time, significant changes in the public culture led to extremely narrow interpretations of these ambiguously egalitarian amendments.

From 1865 to about 1875, the Republican congressional majority, combined with the presence of Federalist troops in Southern states, mandated a fairly broad usage of "citizenship" and "equal rights." So, for example, the Civil Rights Bill of 1874 guaranteed equal access to all public facilities, and a variety of other legislation functioned to protect equal voting rights for black Americans.[44] By 1877, however, white Southerners managed to wrestle a significant modicum of power away from Southern egalitarian blacks and Northern egalitarian whites.[45] In so doing, they substantially increased their influence in dictating and interpreting the legal code, and their primary task in this regard was to narrow the scope and meaning of legal equality.

As the public debate unfolded in these years, white Southern advocates and their Northern supporters began to argue that the Thirteenth, Fourteenth, and Fifteenth Amendments should be interpreted separate from the context of the end of slavery, and thus with disregard for any intent to protect the "privileges" of the former slaves. Anti-egalitarians argued that the drafters of these amendments never meant to interfere with states' rights, and they argued that radicals were tyrannizing Americans by defining "equality" as "identity."[46] Claiming that egalitarians were conflating civic with social rights, white Southerners began to argue that the nation needed to consider the adoption of the phrase "Equal, but Separate" as a way of characterizing "legal" rights. So, for example, Henry W. Grady promoted "Equal, but Separate" as a means of characterizing appropriate legal access in a number of public facilities cases, including most specifically public transportation.[47] His argument was that if facilities "equal in comfort" could be provided to blacks, then the rhetorical mandate for "equality" could be fulfilled without resorting to integration. White Southerners like Grady thus claimed that nature and/or social conditioning had produced feelings of antipathy between the races that could not be remedied by legislation; accordingly, they concluded that separation was the best approach, and that it could be provided without violating the sacred principle of equality.

Simultaneously, Southern representatives on the bench declared the Civil Rights Act to be illegitimate, thus assigning the narrowest possible interpretation to the Civil War Amendments.[48] Northern white egalitarians acquiesced to this redefinition of "equality," in which social equality was denied and public equality was restricted. The reasons were many and varied, and have been amply chronicled by historians. The case was somewhat different with black spokespersons. They generally wanted to maintain access to public facilities without separation, because they knew that separate facilities would be neither symbolically nor materially equal. However, the way in which they made these arguments unintentionally conceded important ground to white racists. Congressman John Lynch's statement in Congress was the most thorough articulation of the black leadership's position on the restriction of public access under the "Equal, but Separate" rubric. He argued for public access, but defined the relevant issues quite narrowly: "No, Mr. Speaker, it is not social rights that we desire. We have enough of that already. What we ask is protection in the enjoyment of *public* rights." Lynch here conceded a "social sphere" where the government should not mandate equality. He also conceded the importance of separation by promising that when those public rights were enacted, "[You] will find that there is no more social equality than before. That whites and blacks do not intermarry any more than they did before the passage of the bill."[49] Thus, though he disagreed with white anti-egalitarians about how far the "public" and "social" spheres stretched, the rhetoric of Lynch and most prominent black leaders accepted the underlying premises of the "Equal, but Separate" doctrine, even while arguing against the practical application of that doctrine to public facilities. Furthermore, during this era blacks were divided about the concrete issue of which facilities fell within the shared public sphere and which did not. Most importantly, there was a decided absence of consensus among black Americans on the propriety and value of separate schools. Black newspapers such as the *Washington Bee* and the San Francisco *Elevator* covered the dispute, noting that separate schools provided the best employment opportunities for black teachers and administrators, as well as an education more free from taunts by white youth.[50] Because it conceded the possibility of separation between the races in some realms, black rhetoric of the era acquiesced to the "Equal, but Separate" doctrine, as long as that rhetoric promised "equality."

This concession was bolstered by the general tendency in the black community to emphasize economic over political issues—a focus generated by intense pragmatic considerations. In part, black leaders of the era were responding to the brutal violence inflicted upon them by Southern whites seeking to prevent them from exercising their vote. Many blacks hoped that a narrowing of the scope of political equality would cause such violence to abate. Furthermore, in this period black poverty and illiteracy were enormous, and the success of a tiny black middle-class gave hope that action in the economic sphere could alleviate these economic problems. The leadership saw attention to economic survival and growth as a pressing priority, perhaps one more immediately substantive than an abstract right to vote that did not seem to be having an effect on economic well-being. Hence Booker T. Washington was simply the most widely heard voice arguing for economic rather than political endeavors.[51] He was joined by black newspapers all over the country, including the *Colored Citizen*, the *New York Globe*, the *Washington Bee*, the San Francisco *Elevator*, and the Indianapolis *Freeman*. The *Colored Citizen* put it this way: "they are tired of risking their fortunes upon the uncertainties of politics. They recognize the fact that their only salvation lies in work. The right to franchise alone cannot elevate us to respectability among men. If we would win a name and a fame among nations, we must hew out our own fortunes.["][52]

Black egalitarians in the era, therefore, had other priorities than fighting for the elimination of "Separate" from the "Equal, but Separate" doctrine. It is not clear to what extent their acquiescence mattered in the ultimate compromise. Some would argue that even had they fought intensively and absolutely against this doctrine, it would have been enacted anyway. We suspect that even in this era, the black community had somewhat more power and influence than that. However, it is the nature of hegemonic compromises that leaders of the era recognize the limitations of their own power and seek to lead in those areas that promise the greatest success. This leads to *de facto* compromise for the policies with which one does not agree, but which cannot be fought, or which can be fought only at too great a cost. In any case, the implicit support for separation and the relative preference for economic over political advancement within the black community during this era matched the public compromise in ways that made it relatively easy for the new, more restrictive, doctrine of equality to be legitimated.

In 1896 the Supreme Court legitimated the emerging shift from a constitutional commitment to "equal rights" to the "separate but equal" doctrine in *Plessy v. Ferguson*[53] When

located in its rhetorical historical context, the Court's finding clearly was not simply the logical conclusion of a group of wise men, schooled to "think like lawyers," whose vigilance led them to discover one of the timeless verities of the law. Writing in the rhetorical culture of the 1990s, and filtering the *Plessy* decision through the lens of its 1954 reversal in *Brown v. Bd. of Education,* it seems all too obvious that the "separate but equal" doctrine did not fairly and equitably represent the interests of all of the parties involved.[54] White Southerners in particular gained disproportionate advantage from the compromise.

Neither, however, was *Plessy* simply the top-down imposition of a singular and oppressive interpretation by a politically isolated Court. A doctrine that reflected only the dominant white racist interests would have dispensed with the commitment to "equality" altogether. That would have closed the discursive opening that allowed for future advancements in America's commitment to equality via the gradual development of black power that eventually would force elimination of the "separate" doctrine in the 1950s and 1960s. Thus it is in legal action that while hegemonic arrangements reflect the interests of all active parties to a limited extent, the interests of some are nevertheless reflected more extensively than those of others. It is precisely this imbalance that helps us to understand that the Court's ruling in *Plessy* was not simply an error that can be written off as an aberration in the legal system.

It seems altogether implausible to assume that judicial decisions are tainted by political interests only in those cases in which "errors" have been discovered. When the Court overturned *Plessy* in the *Brown* decision, it did so precisely because the changing racial and political dynamics in American society had led to a significant alteration in the rhetorical culture. From the 1890s forward, American-American rhetors worked hard in a mutually enhancing interactive spiral of public discourse and economic gain. Their heightened power culminated in the 1950s and 1960s in their ability to force a new compromise over the constitutionally mandated definition of "equality" through a series of planned legal appeals. The usage they promoted was even broader than the nineteenth-century notion of "equal rights" had been, because *Brown* insisted on equal access in every arena—including schools. *Brown,* however, is clearly a decision no less political than *Plessy,* a point made evident by the current debate over the sufficiency of *Brown,* in which conservatives now defend the previously "progressive" decision and progressives attack it.[55]

This account, focused as it is upon the broad sweep of American rhetorical culture, does not require a view of the individual justices on the Court as merely passive transmitters of the waves of cultural history. An enormous literature in political science has taken pains to highlight the relationship between the attitudes of individual justices and the outcomes of their decisions.[56] With regard to the *Brown* decision, in particular, scholars have described the ways in which Justice Earl Warren actively courted and constructed a unanimous opinion repudiating segregation. Warren had just joined the Court, and many writers contend that if the *Brown* decision had been made even two years earlier, the Court would have been equally divided on the issue. Justice Douglas would argue years later that in December of 1952 only four justices—Douglas, Minton, Burton, and Black—felt that segregation was unconstitutional.[57] Justice Warren was thus clearly an active agent of change whose efforts not only drew from the rhetorical culture to craft a new legal doctrine, but subsequently and immediately altered the rhetorical culture itself in significant ways.

Moreover, Warren and the other justices were acutely conscious of the active and significant role they were playing in history. For many years following the decision, Warren would tell audiences that he had purposely written a short decision (thirteen pages) so that any "layman interested in the problem could read the entire opinion."[58] The persuasiveness of this decision to the lay audience seems to have been uneven. In many ways, of course, *Brown* was a successful decision, effectively legitimating a shift from "separate but equal," to integrated equality. Within an hour after Warren's public reading of the decision, the Voice of America broadcast to the world that "racial segregation has no place in American public education."[59]

Much empirical research also shows high levels of support for the *Brown* decision nationally.[60] And for listeners such as Martin Luther King, Jr., the decision had a symbolic importance because it "brought hope to millions of disinherited" blacks who had been denied the "dream of freedom."[61] That said, many scholars have more recently questioned the effectiveness of the *Brown* decision, pointing to the resistance both from lower courts and from local school districts, especially in the South.[62]

The divided character of the response to the *Brown* decision reflects the nature of hegemonic decision-making processes. It is precisely the point of a hegemonic theory that public doctrines represent no one group's preferred principles. Because the Court must craft or endorse compromises among competing public vocabularies that represent world views hostile to each other, one can expect rejection of important Supreme Court rulings by many groups. The Court acts not when unanimity has been achieved within the rhetorical culture, but when a decision must be crafted where disagreement reigns. It is the rhetorical boundaries within which it makes these decisions that change through time, not necessarily the degree of public consensus.

Because both *Plessy* and *Brown* represented new compromises among hostile and self-interested parties, rather than universally and objectively self-evident truths, they had, inherently, to act as persuasive documents that sought to convince those of varying and competing positions to accept them as the most reasonable (i.e., fair, under the circumstances) resolutions. But they also had to be drawn from the shifting values, norms, and characterizations of the public discourse. In the era in which *Plessy* was decided, a relatively weak black community succumbed to stereotypes that depicted undesirable "Negroes" from whom whites could be separated as long as there were "equal" facilities.[63] By the time *Brown* was decided, not only had it become obvious that "separate" would never produce "equal," but the advent of World War II made it virtually necessary for black and white Americans to work side-by-side on the home front, a condition that led national newspapers and magazines to recharacterize black Americans as hard-working, intelligent, and able.[64] The range of what might reasonably be called "equal" within those two different discursive sets was different, and so the Court's doctrines on "equality" were different as well.

The complexity of attitudes postulated by an hegemonic model is ultimately the crucial ingredient in reconciling individualistic, justice-centered perspectives toward the law with a perspective focused on the broad history of rhetorical cultures. Justices must craft their decisions from extant rhetorical vocabularies. However, because these vocabularies are contested and not monolithic, the precise character and the particular persuasiveness of the decisions shaped by the justices retain an important distinctiveness. The creative human agency of the Supreme Court justices in crafting a legal doctrine that is concordant to many disparate interests is clearly bounded by the limits of an historically particular rhetorical culture, but it is not determined in its particular form and effectiveness by that rhetorical culture. In this way, therefore, the activity of such justices and their responsiveness to the broad currents of their rhetorical culture are symbiotic.

★ CHARACTERISTICS OF THE RHETORICAL ACTION OF THE LAW

This case study of "equality" in American law illustrates the kinds of interpretations opened up by taking a rhetorical perspective on the law, a perspective that highlights the ways in which the law is shaped within the public discourse. Based on that theoretical orientation and this case study, we offer a series of characterizations of the law as rhetoric which might replace the traditionalist's perspectives on the law and fill in for missing characterizations that are not generated by a CLS perspective alone.

1. *Law is bounded by public culture.* In a representative form of government, the law can only function effectively within the rhetorical boundaries set by a public vocabulary. The law flows from the public discourse. It is therefore at least partially dependent upon the political action of the community in which it operates.

2. *The law is polysemic.* Legal actors rely upon the public vocabulary as a paradigm from which to choose characterizations of legal action. Legal statutes specify a range of acceptable and unacceptable behaviors by characterizing human action through a terminology that evaluatively colors the motives for such action. The terminology employed to this end typically presumes a technical, legal meaning, but because it generally derives at least in part from the public vocabulary of common, everyday discourse, the meaning of the legal statutes so constructed is inherently ambiguous. When legal actors, such as Supreme Court justices, attempt to interpret the meaning of such statutes, they are forced to confront the polysemic and indeterminate quality of the law.[65] The result is that different legal actors, operating at different points in time or from different sociopolitical locations, make different selections from among the options available in the public vocabulary.[66] It is, of course, always possible to describe any particular situation from a number of different terminological perspectives. In the technical discourse of the law the doctrine of *stare decisis* seeks to contain the selection process and to avoid utter chaos by demanding judicial obeisance to the principle of precedent. The question always remains, however, as to when the appropriate conditions have been met to overturn precedent. And indeed, even without the doctrinal proviso of precedent, the characteristic interpretations made by legal actors are stabilized to some degree by the prevailing rhetorical culture, which restricts the *range* of meaningful vocabulary choices available to those who would effectively communicate with the members of a particular community.

3. *The law is hegemonic.* Legal actors typically employ legal characterizations that are consonant with the prevailing social alignments. This can be accounted for in two different ways. First, the individual agents of the Court are selected through a political process that insures some degree of hegemonic representation in the legal system.[67] This is more a systemic tendency than a constitutional guarantee, but to the extent that it is actualized—historical anomalies to the contrary—those selected to serve will typically work to reproduce and legitimize the process that empowered them in the first place. Second, the courts are so concerned to appear "apolitical," that they generally avoid the appearance

of controversy whenever possible. Significantly, the posture that appears to be the least political is almost always that which appears the most natural to the largest audience, and it is precisely this hegemonic position that the courts tend to reiterate and legitimate. In times of social and political quiescence this is easily achieved; when social and political stability is disrupted, however, the courts face manifest difficulties for they are forced to predict, to articulate, or to lead the development of new hegemonic alliances.

4. *The law is vulnerable to social change.* Major shifts in the rhetorical culture produce significant tensions in the legal system. One of the defining characteristics of Western society is its linear, temporal orientation to development, progress, and change.[68] The range of factors contributing to such change consists of demographic considerations, economic shifts, technological innovations, and even the evolution of self-consciousness resulting from artistic, intellectual, and religious thought. Taken together and combined with a plethora of other relevant socio-political elements, such factors effect temporal movement in the public vocabulary of a rhetorical culture. Sometimes these shifts represent a rejection of prior vocabularies, as in the seventeenth century when "popular sovereignty" was substituted for the "divine right of kings." At other times, they simply consist of new terminologies previously uncontemplated in public discourse, such as "birth control technologies" or "homosexual marriages." In either case, when a significant change in the rhetorical culture occurs, the legal system faces a serious problem. To the extent that the law claims to operate on the basis of presumably timeless principles, it must adhere to old vocabularies that inadequately encompass new situations.

In many cases, the legislature comes to the rescue with new statutes that enable the judicial system to resolve its tension through a period of rhetorical realignment. During this period, the older, technical/legal vocabulary is adapted simultaneously to the new legislation, to the new public vocabulary, and to the new rhetorical culture that public interpretations of such statutory changes produce. In this context, the production of "newness" is assigned to the legislature, and so the apolitical integrity of the judiciary is apparently preserved, even as the

courts lend their authority to the new political alignment by the ways in which they legitimize its "reason" and "meaningfulness" in practice.

In other cases, the situation faced by the court system is far more difficult. Consider, for example, those instances where momentous social and political changes produce significant hegemonic realignments, but interest groups that prefer to preserve older vocabularies retain substantial power. One solution to such problems is to amend the constitution so as to legitimize the new vocabulary as a rhetorical foundation of the social and political order. Of course, constitutional amendments require overwhelming consent from the polity, and given the partisan alignments in most hegemonic situations, such consent is seldom achieved. As a result, constitutions are almost never amended. Accordingly, in such cases the Court is faced with the stark and unavoidable choice of maintaining the old hegemonic order or legitimating the new. Either choice will be self-evidently "political," for the Court must eventually align itself with the partisan interests of one vocabulary or the other. While it will thus typically respond to such situations by maintaining that its actions are politically neutral, guided either by the doctrine of *stare decisis* (if it aligned itself with the old order) or with regard to the "original principles" of a "living Constitution" (if it aligns itself with a new order), few outside the legal profession are taken in by such posturing.[69]

We do not mean to suggest here that the judiciary acts politically only in the contexts of crisis and division. As we have seen, insofar as the courts are forced to select their characterizations of legal action from among the public vocabularies of a rhetorical culture, it will always be an inherently political action. Rather, we suggest that because the primary political effect of court action in stable, quiescent times is the reenactment of a widely accepted hegemonic order, such an effect is not widely perceived as politically consequential. In times of crisis, however, the courts must be not only political, but evidently partisan, actively choosing to legitimate either the prevailing hegemonic order or its competitor. Such visible partisanship, enacted at a critical moment in the life of a community, is often labeled as undesirable political action by strict legal constructionists, but it is a partisanship made inevitable by particular historical circumstances. We believe, therefore, that the judiciary would be served better if it gave up the attempt to present the courts as outside of time and "above politics"—based as that claim is in a debilitating dichotomy opposing "reasonableness" to "politics." Instead of promoting itself as a body outside politics, we believe that the judiciary should promote itself as an institution that attempts to generate reasonable decisions, often entailing reasonable compromises, about important political issues. It is further a body charged with estimating when old principles must be supplanted or supplemented with new. This self-portrait would not necessarily be more convincing to those who now chastise the Court as partisan when they disagree with any given decision, but it would more accurately portray the Court's activity without conceding the claim to the reasonableness of its goals and procedures.

5. *The law is usually not FAIR.* Although this characterization sounds both pessimistic and provocative, we only mean to suggest that the law is unfair in precisely those ways that life in society is inherently unfair. That is, the law is incapable of producing scientifically measured (or critically idealized) principles of justice in the same way that it is impossible to enact the ideals enshrined in Plato's *Republic*. A hegemonic order is not an ideal world. Rather, it is a pragmatic and material world organized around a consensus between and among the various interested parties participating in a common rhetorical culture. Because the public practice of the law is bounded by this hegemonic rhetorical culture, it serves as an agent of that hegemony.

This characteristic of the law constitutes a key difference between a rhetorical approach to the law and the approach offered by CLS. Those who favor the CLS perspective seek a legal system that guarantees that "those whose interests are most at stake" (read: the most oppressed and beleaguered individuals or groups) will be protected and best represented by the law. A rhetorical perspective sees the quest for such a guarantee as either futile or quite dangerous. Such a quest is futile as long as human societies are subject to both change and diversity. In a stable, homogeneous society,

a system that is permanently fair to all persons (and fair in the view of all persons) might perhaps be devised. In a changing, diverse society, it is virtually impossible to lay down permanent legal principles which will not eventually generate unforeseen inequities that lead to the charge of being "unfair." Additionally, in a diverse society, agreement on what legal principles are most fair is not a given. The claim that "those whose interests are most at stake" is always and exclusively equivalent to "the most oppressed and beleaguered" is a notion popular in the academy, but less so outside these ivory walls, where every group believes its own interests worth defending. Moreover, conflict among various minority ethnic and gender groups suggests that deciding "who is the most oppressed and beleaguered" is not itself always self-evident. A rhetorical perspective views the CLS desire to impose principles that it believes would guarantee fairness as dangerous because it seems to entail granting a small elite group (albeit of leftist academics) the power to determine totalistically and permanently what the definition of "fair" might be. For all its serious failings, the rhetorical perspective prefers to vest judgment in a popular representative system, encouraging more open debate forms, but seeing such debate as superior to all *a priori* systems that presume they have certain knowledge of what is most just for all.

CONCLUSION

If law is bounded by the rhetorical culture of a society, and if the rhetorical culture is a hegemonic product of multiple voices within the society, then we encounter a fundamentally different account of the legal process than is offered by either legal professionalists or the CLS movement. From the rhetorical perspective, the law is neither a series of timeless rules and principles to be stamped upon human action through a disembodied and apolitical deductive rationality, nor is it an illegitimate, false ideology lacking in moral substance or fidelity to lived, human experience. Instead, it is the consensual product of the rhetorical efforts of a variety of public agents acting in concert and contest with one another in an uneven dialectic of unity and division. By this account, the law is simultaneously a more optimistic and less revolutionary social phenomenon than the advocates of CLS would lead us to believe. From the CLS perspective, the only way to eradicate the law's role in enforcing oppressive social and political relationships is to eradicate the prevailing legal structures. But what structures would guarantee absolute and indisputable fairness, CLS has not told us.[70]

To refuse the viability of a truly revolutionary reconstruction of the legal system is not to concede the impossibility of meaningful change. In a social order where the law is constrained by a rhetorical culture, any interest group dissatisfied with the public arrangement may work to change either the legal system or the rhetorical culture in which it operates. Oppressive laws are not fixed in concrete, and disempowered groups are not permanently locked out by an all-powerful dominant elite. Chattel slavery was eliminated. Segregation of public facilities has been largely eliminated. A black middle class has developed. Segregated schools, wage differentials, and the travails of the inner city remain, but the means for changing the power relations in such cases is neither simple pronouncement of timeless truths nor erudite critique of false universals. Rather such change is best achieved through public efforts to alter social relationships, in part by changing values, characterizations, metaphors, and the full range of the public vocabulary. The struggle to increase one's share of justice and equality has never been an easy one, and it is never a task that will be completed. This is unfortunate, and more, unfair, but the opportunities for change provided by such a system in a representative form of government are superior to those available in a social or political system in which the prevailing order is enshrined as permanently just by either a jealous Creator, a heartless Nature, or a vanguard party certain of its own infallibility. Moreover, we believe that the self-reflexivity of the rhetorical perspective, which calls attention to the inherently political and argumentative nature of legal decisions, serves the same emancipatory function as does the CLS critique of the courts as enforcers of a dominant ideology.

Finally, an understanding of the rhetorical boundaries of the law has serious implications for the professionalism of the legal system. It suggests first that if lawyers and justices are to understand the full scope of the law, they must not be trained merely as effective technicians, capable of mechanically applying an elite vocabulary to exigent situations; they must also be wise and prudent individuals, trained to interpret the rhetorical culture of their society with creativity, fairness, and decency. It suggests likewise that the discourse of the law must be opened up to the full range of citizens who own it, shape its contours, and live by the discretion of its rules. There is a need for investigating and implementing procedures that would democratize the legal system, giving better access to the voices of those whose interests are disproportionately underrepresented in both the public rhetoric and the translation of that rhetoric into law (and we think these include both those who are "the most beleaguered and oppressed" and the broader working class). The responsibility of the full citizenry for the form and substance of the laws must be heightened and highlighted, so that eventually, judgments about our constitutions, even those made by ordinary individuals who are not trained to "think like lawyers," may be taken as competent contributions to the crafting of that law.

NOTES

[1] Theodore Roosevelt, letter to Frederick G. Fincke, 7 June 1901, *The Letters of Theodore Roosevelt*, ed. Elting E. Morison, vol. 3 (Cambridge, MA: Harvard University Press, 1951), 89.

[2] For a discussion of the traditional ideals of "legal reasoning" that reflects a government of "laws, not of men" see Gerald B. Wetlaufer, "Rhetoric and Its Denial in Legal Discourse," *Virginia Law Review* 76 (1990): 1545–97.

[3] Glendon A. Shubert, *Judicial Policy Making* (Glenview, IL: Scott, Foresman and Co., 1974) i; William Lewis, "Of Innocence, Exclusion, and the Burning of Flags: The Romantic Realism of the Law," *Southern Communication Journal* 60 (1994): 4–5.

[4] Legal realism became something of a consensus position among political scientists studying the law, but not necessarily among judges and teachers of law. See David W. Adamany, "The Party Variable in Judges' Voting: Conceptual Notes and a Case Study," *American Political Science Review* 63 (1969): 58. On more contemporary perspectives

see Katharine T. Bartlett and Rosanne Kennedy, *Feminist Legal Theory: Readings in Law and Gender* (Boulder, CO: Westview Press, 1991); Jerry D. Leonard, ed., *Legal Studies as Cultural Studies: A Reader in (Post) Modern Critical Theory* (Albany: State University of New York Press, 1995); Austin Sarat and Thomas R. Kearns, eds., *The Rhetoric of Law* (Ann Arbor: The University of Michigan Press, 1994); Mari J. Matsuda, Charles R. Lawrence III, Richard Delgado, and Kimberle Williams Crenshaw, eds., *Words That Wound: Critical Race Theory, Assaultive Speech, and the First Amendment* (Boulder: Westview Press, 1993).

5 For a critique of the strengths and limitations of many of these early CLS approaches, see Costas Douzinas, Peter Goodrich and Yifat Hachamovitch, eds. *Politics, Postmodernity, and Critical Legal Studies: The Legality of the Continent* (London: Routledge, 1994).

6 The issues raised by feminists, race theorists, and law and society perspectives overlap with CLS in important ways, but to treat their distinctiveness fairly would require a book-length manuscript.

7 Edward Coke, *Prohibitions Del Roy*, 12 *Coke Reports* 63 (1607).

8 Duncan Kennedy, *Legal Education and the Reproduction of Hierarchy: A Polemic Against the System* (Cambridge, MA: AFAR, 1983).

9 For a historical discussion of the exclusionary practices of the American legal profession, see Jerold S. Auerbach, *Unequal Justice: Lawyers and Social Change in Modern America* (New York: Oxford University Press, 1976); Lawrence M. Friedman, *A History of American Law* (New York: Simon and Schuster, 1973) 396–97, 550–51.

10 Robert H. Bork, "The Case Against Political Judging," *National Review* 8 December 1989: 24.

11 *Webster v. Reproductive Health Services* 109 S. Ct. 3040, 3065–66 (1989) (Scalia, J., concurring).

12 John Louis Lucaites, "Between Rhetoric and 'The Law': Power, Legitimacy, and Social Change," *Quarterly Journal of Speech* 76 (1990): 435–49.

13 As Makau explains, analytic and scientific reasoning models leave little room for "the interpretive process fundamental to all legal reasoning." Josina M. Makau, "The Supreme Court and Reasonableness," *Quarterly Journal of Speech* 70 (1984): 379.

14 Lief Carter, *Reason in Law*, 3rd ed. (Glenview, IL: Scott, Foresman, and Co., 1989) 2 [Authors note: We acknowledge, but do not endorse, the sexist usage of "man" in this and other quoted passages appearing in this essay. Nevertheless, we allow the authors cited to speak in their own voices and do not identify each such sexist usage.]

15 Even before the advent of CLS, there were some who viewed the law from an artistic perspective. See e.g. Milner S. Ball, "The Play's the Thing: An Unscientific Reflection on Courts Under the Rubric of Theater," *Stanford Law Review* 28 (1975): 81–115. Prior to that legal realists advocated a move away from metaphysical interpretations of the law. Morton White, *Social Thought in America: The Revolt Against Formalism* (Boston: Beacon Press, 1961); Morton J. Horwitz, *The Transformation of American Law, 1870–1960: The Crisis of Legal Orthodoxy* (New York: Oxford University Press, 1992) 9–64.

16 Manza, however, notes an important distinction between the "first generation" of CLS writers whose work was guided by an agenda designed to "trash" the prevailing legal order and the "second wave" who seem more concerned to exploit the emancipatory aspects of liberal legal thought. Jeff Manza, "Critical Legal Studies," *Berkeley Journal of Sociology* 35 (1990): 138–39, fn 5. We here participate in a "second generation" critique of the first wave of CLS.

17 Lucaites, "Between Rhetoric and 'The Law'" 436.

18 Mark G. Kelman, "Trashing," *Stanford Law Review* 36 (1984): 293–348; Thomas Streeter, "Beyond Freedom of Speech and the Public Interest: The Relevance of Critical Legal Studies to Communication Policy," *Journal of Communication* 40 (1990): 43–63.

19 Lucaites, "Between Rhetoric and 'The Law'" 438–39; Robert M. Unger, *The Critical Legal Studies Movement* (Cambridge: Harvard University Press, 1986).

20 Alan D. Freeman, "Truth and Mystification in Legal Scholarship," *Yale Law Journal* 90 (1981): 1235.

21 Karl Klare contends that classical legal theories render "radical, nonliberal visions of freedom literally inconceivable," quoted by Louis Menard, "What is 'Critical Legal Studies'?: Radicalism for Yuppies," *The New Republic*, 17 March 1986: 21.

22 See Kelman, "Trashing" 299, and Mark Tushnet, "Critical Legal Studies and Constitutional Law: An Essay in Deconstruction," *Stanford Law Review* 36 (1984): 623–47.

23 See Freeman's discussion of the difference between "ideological change" and "real change" in "Truth and Mystification in Legal Scholarship" 1234.

24 Wendy Raudenbush Olmsted, "The Uses of Rhetoric: Indeterminacy in Legal Reasoning, Practical Thinking and the Interpretation of Literary Figures," *Philosophy and Rhetoric* 24 (1991): 1–24.

25 Anthony E. Cook, "Beyond Critical Legal Studies: The Reconstructive Theology of Dr. Martin Luther King, Jr.," *Harvard Law Review* 103 (1990): 992.

26 For an opposing view on this, see Streeter, "Beyond Freedom and Speech and the Public Interest" 55.

27 Lucaites, "Between Rhetoric and 'The Law'" 440, 446.

28 Victoria Kahn, "Rhetoric and the Law," *Diacritics* 19 (1989): 33.

29 For an elaboration of these units and their role in the public vocabulary see Celeste Michelle Condit and John Louis Lucaites, *Crafting Equality: America's Anglo-African Word* (Chicago: University of Chicago Press, 1993) ix–xviii.

30 On the role of constitutive rhetoric in law, see James Boyd White, *Justice as Translation: An Essay in Culture and Legal Criticism* (Chicago: University of Chicago Press, 1991).

31 For an elaboration of the nature of such compromises, see Celeste M. Condit, "Hegemony in a Mass Mediated Society: Concordance About 'Reproductive Technologies'" *Critical Studies in Mass Communication* 11 (1994): 205–230.

32 See Kenneth Burke, *Attitudes Toward History* (1937; Berkeley, CA: University of California Press, 1984), esp. 3–110; Jose Ortega y Gassett, *Man and People,* trans. Willard R. Trask (New York: W. W. Norton, 1957) 176–272; Frederic Jameson, *The Prison-House of Language: A Critical Account of Structuralism and Russian Formalism* (Princeton, NJ: Princeton University Press, 1972); Murray Edelman, *Political Language: Words That Succeed and Policies that Fail* (New York: Academic Press, 1977); W. Lance Bennett, *Public Opinion in American Politics* (New York: Harcourt Brace Jovanovich, 1980), esp. 133–344, 366–400.

33 We have in mind here, for example, the feminist deconstruction of the "rational man" standard and the CLS critique of the "legitimate force" standard.

34 *Williams v. Mississippi,* 170 U.S. 213 (1898). For a more detailed analysis of this case see Condit and Lucaites, *Crafting Equality* 162–63. During this same period, appellate courts legitimated the use of protective legislation for women by creating symbolic constructions of "women" that denied them agent status. Carrie Crenshaw, "The 'Protection' of 'Women': A History of Legal Attitudes Towards Women's Workplace Freedom," *Quarterly Journal of Speech* 81 (1995): 63–82.

35 This is not to say that this characterization of women was the only rationale functioning in the decision, but it would seem to be a significant one. *Roe v. Wade* 410 US 113 (1973); and Celeste Michelle Condit, *Decoding Abortion Rhetoric: Communicating Social Change* (Urbana, IL: University of Illinois Press, 1990) 96–122.

36 Cf. the Aristotelian tradition of "contingency" with the Cartesian tradition of scientific "certainty." See Aristotle's *Rhetoric,* Bk. 1: 12 [1357a] in George A. Kennedy, trans., *Aristotle on Rhetoric: A Theory of Civic Discourse* (New York: Oxford, 1991), 41–43, and Rene Descartes, "Rules for the Direction of the Mind," in *The Philosophical Works of Descartes,* trans. Elizabeth S. Haldane and G. R. T. Ross (Cambridge: The University Press, 1967) 3, 22, 45.

37 See Karl Wallace, "The Substance of Rhetoric: Good Reasons," *Quarterly Journal of Speech* 29 (1964): 279–87; Chaim Perelman and L. Olbrechts-Tyteca, *The New Rhetoric: A Treatise on Argumentation,* trans. John Wilkinson and Purcell Weaver (1958; Notre Dame, IN: University of Notre Dame Press, 1969) 1–62.

38 Chaim Perelman, *The New Rhetoric and the Humanities: Essays on Rhetoric and Its Applications* (Boston: D. Reidel Publishing, 1979) 14.

39 See Makau, "The Supreme Court and Reasonableness"; Aristotle, *Rhetoric,* 37 [1357a]; and Donald N. McCloskey, *The Rhetoric of Economics* (Madison, WI: University of Wisconsin Press, 1985) 27–30.

40 Perhaps the most notorious of these decisions were the *Slaughter-House Cases,* 83 U.S. (16 Wall.) 36 (1873), and the *Civil Rights Cases,* 109 U.S. 3 (1883).

41 *Cong. Globe,* 42nd Cong. 2nd sess. 1872: 382.

42 Representative Blount, for example, claimed that giving blacks "equal rights" would alter "social intercourse" and would lead to "amalgamation" and the "degradation" of the white race. 2 *Cong. Rec.* pt 1, 6 January 1874; 411.

43 Black congressional leader Alonzo Ransier defined "equal opportunity" as an "equal chance" for African Americans in the "race of life, and same privileges and protection meted out to other classes. . . ." 2 *Cong. Rec.* part 2, 5 January 1874: 382.

44 As one writer for the *New York Times* reported in June of 1874, since the passage of the Civil Rights bill, blacks had rushed "to the courts for the recovery of damages to which they consider themselves entitled for a denial of equal privileges with the Caucasian race in the entertainments, at salons, and other public places." "Suits Under the Civil Rights Bill," *New York Times,* 2 June 1974: 1.

45 A brief but cogent explanation of the 1877 compromise can be found in Thomas H. O'Connor, *The Disunited States: The Era of Civil War and*

Reconstruction (New York: Harper and Row, 1978) 268–72.

46 In *Logwood v. Memphis & C. R. Co*, 23 F. 318 (1885), Judge Hammond claimed that races and nationalities could be "reasonably separated" because "equal accommodations" did not mean "identical accommodations" (319).

47 Henry W. Grady, "In Plain Black and White," *Century* April 1885: 909–17.

48 The *Civil Rights Cases* 109 U.S. 3 (1883).

49 Rep. John Lynch, *Cong. Rec.* 3 February 1875: 944–47. See also Rep. Joseph H. Rainey, *Cong. Rec.* 3 February 1875: 960; Rep. James T. Rapier, *Cong. Rec.* 4 February 1875: 1001.

50 See for example, San Francisco *Elevator*, 29 December 1871; 27 April 1872; 23 August 1873.

51 August Meier, *Negro Thought in America, 1880–1915; Racial Ideologies in the Age of Booker T. Washington* (Ann Arbor: University of Michigan Press, 1963) 85.

52 *Colored Citizen*, 2 August 1878: 4; *New York Globe*, 29 March 1884.

53 *Plessy v. Ferguson*, 163 U.S. 537 (1896).

54 *Brown v. Bd. of Education*, 347 U.S. 483 (1954).

55 For the conservative view, see Meese's claim that *Brown* was the "restoring of the original principle" as opposed to the attack on *Brown* as an oppressive "perpetrator's" decision by Freeman. Edwin Meese III, "Address before the D.C. Chapter of the Federalist Society Lawyers Division," in *Interpreting Law and Literature: A Hermeneutic Reader*, ed. Sanford Levinson and Steve Mailloux (Evanston, IL: Northwestern University Press, 1988): 25–33; Alan David Freeman, "Legitimizing Racial Discrimination Through Antidiscrimination Law: A Critical Review of Supreme Court Doctrine," *Minnesota Law Review* 62 (1978): 1049–1119.

56 See for example, David J. Danelski, "Values as Variables in Judicial Decision Making: Notes Toward a Theory," *Vanderbilt Law Review* 19 (1966); 721–40; J. A. Segal, "Supreme Court Justices as Human Decision Makers," *The Journal of Politics* 48 (1986): 938–55; Bradley C. Canon, "Courts and Policy: Compliance, Implementation, and Impact," *The American Courts: A Critical Assessment*, eds. J. B. Gates and C. A. Johnson (Washington, D.C.: Congressional Quarterly, 1991) 435–66; David W. Adamany, "The Party Variable in Judges' Voting: Conceptual Notes and a Case Study," *The American Political Science Review* 63 (1969): 57–73; J. L. Gibson, "Social Backgrounds and Judicial Decision-Making," *Harvard Law Review* 79 (1966): 1551–1564; J. W. Howard, Jr. "Judicial Biography

and the Behavioral Persuasion," *The American Political Science Review* 65 (1971): 704–715.

57 William O. Douglas, *The Court Years: 1939–1975: The Autobiography of William O. Douglas* (New York: Random House, 1980) 113. For some excellent accounts of how Warren helped achieve this unanimity, see Richard Kluger, *Simple Justice* (New York: Alfred A. Knopf, 1976) 693–99; S. Sidney Ulmer, "Earl Warren and the Brown Decision," *The Journal of Politics*, 33 (1971): 689–702; Dennis J. Hutchinson, "Unanimity and Desegregation: Decisionmaking in the Supreme Court, 1948–1958," *The Georgetown Law Journal* (1979): 1–96.

58 Henry J. Abraham, *Freedom and the Court: Civil Rights and Liberties in the United States*, 3rd ed. (New York: Oxford University Press, 1977) 372, n. 90.

59 "'Voice' Speaks in 34 Languages to Flash Court Ruling to World," *New York Times* 18 May 1954: 1.

60 Roger Handberg, "Public Opinion and the United States Supreme Court, 1935–1981," *International Social Science Review* 59 (1984): 3–13; Francine Sanders, "*Brown v. Board of Education*: An Empirical Reexamination of Its Effects on Federal District Courts," *Law and Society Review* 29 (1995): 731–75.

61 Martin Luther King Jr., *Stride Toward Freedom: The Montgomery Story* (New York: Harper and Row, 1958) 191.

62 Gerald N. Rosenberg, *The Hollow Hope: Can Courts Bring About Social Change?* (Chicago: University of Chicago Press, 1991).

63 See Condit and Lucaites, *Crafting Equality*, chapters 5 and 6 for evidence that demonstrates that black newspapers in the era focused their attention on "uplifting" the race. This included a rhetoric that castigated the black population of the era for their failings, in order to get them to strive and achieve intellectually, artistically, and economically. This exhortation, however, also appeared congruent with white negative stereotypes of blacks.

64 See Celeste M. Condit, "Democracy and Civil Rights: The Universalizing Influence of Public Argumentation," *Communication Monographs* 54 (1987): 1–18.

65 John Fiske, "Television: Polysemy and Popularity," *Critical Studies in Mass Communication* 3 (1987): 391–408.

66 It is here that our analysis interfaces with the political science literature which emphasizes the determinative influence of the political orientations of individual justices in arriving at legal decisions. From our perspective, it is important to recognize that individual justices operate from within the

larger flow of social and political history. Thus, while they indeed make choices based on their own individual politics and ideology, we must not lose sight of the recursive relationship between such politics and ideologies and the larger flows of history and rhetorical culture that we describe. This does not deny individual agency, but contextualizes it. Justices do not merely or mechanically execute the rhetorical culture, but rather make specific, and often quite creative, choices concerning how to articulate the various elements and options made generally available by the rhetorical culture. Of course, the rhetorical culture does close off many options and increases the likelihood of others by influencing who gets selected to serve on the court. L. Baum, "Membership Change and Collective Voting Change in the United States Supreme Court," *The Journal of Politics* 54 (1992): 3–24.

67 For a review of these issues, see David Adamany, "Legitimacy, Realigning Elections and the Supreme Court," *Wisconsin Law Review* 790 (1973): 791–846.

68 Randall Lake, "Between Myth and History: Enacting Time in Native-American Protest Rhetoric," *Quarterly Journal of Speech* 77 (1991): 123–51.

69 See Adamany, "Legitimacy, Realigning Elections and the Supreme Court."

70 Their problem in providing concrete visions of such structures rests in the conflict between democratic majoritarianism and the desire to protect the rights of minorities—the same conflict experienced in the current structure. Such a conflict is sometimes the result of a fiat effected by the claim that "true" democracy would protect the rights of minorities via majority vote, but we have encountered little evidence to suggest that human majorities under other structures would be less short-term and self-interested in their perspectives than human majorities as presently constituted in a variety of large-scale social systems around the globe.

The Contested Space of Prudence in the 1874–1875 Civil Rights Debate

Kirt H. Wilson

During the Reconstruction era in the United States, Congress experienced a political conflict that paralleled the Civil War. From 1865 to 1877, factions clashed as they rebuilt a nation that had collapsed almost completely. Sections of the South lay in ruin, increasing class conflict. Death and injury had devastated families and communities. An expanded federal government threatened the system of American Federalism, and the status of the seceding states remained uncertain, as did the future of Southern representation in Congress.[1] Among these problems one question was always at the edge and often at the center of debate: What shall we do with the former slaves? For the politicians who framed this question, several answers came quickly. The Thirteenth Amendment guaranteed freedom for all African Americans. The 1866 Civil Rights Act and the Fourteenth Amendment (1868) established that those of color were national citizens with constitutional rights. The Fifteenth Amendment (1870) gave black citizens the right to vote. In short, "racial equality, equal rights, and the use of national authority to secure both were living ideas in the Reconstruction era" much as they are today.[2] In this spirit in 1870, Senator Charles Sumner proposed a civil rights bill that desegregated public accommodations.

The national politicians of 1870 struggled with more than the reconstruction of a war-worn nation. Their efforts to define equality with respect to African Americans reflect a deeper uncertainty about the appropriate standards for political judgment. This essay examines how the rhetoric of congressional actors reconstructed a viable prudence for decisions about race and rights. To accomplish this goal, I argue that prudence is not a fixed concept. What is prudent for a rhetorical culture shifts with time; moreover, prudence may have multiple meanings within the same historical moment, because it is a contested sensibility that obtains meaning only through discursive practice and negotiation. Based on these theoretical claims, I contend that the national politicians of late Reconstruction articulated two visions of the United States, and I interpret the 1874 and 1875 civil rights debate as a conflict between two forms of prudence. Proponents and opponents of civil rights enacted adverse norms of discursive practice and competing conceptions of equality; subsequently, the results of this conflict helped to bring about the separate but equal doctrine that guided race relations into the next century.

Analysis of the debate over the 1875 Civil Rights Act begins to fill a troubling gap in our literature. Although works by Bert Bradley, Cal M. Logue, Thurmon Garner, Waldo W. Braden, and Harold Mixon are notable exceptions, few have studied U.S. public address between 1865 and 1877.[3] Our field has paid even less attention to the period's national political discourse; indeed, Braden argues that Reconstruction's political rhetoric is unimportant given the Radical Republicans' hegemony. Taking issue with that perspective, I perceive Reconstruction rhetoric as setting the trajectory for race relations into the next century. Its debates over African American civil rights are a rich resource to understand the U.S. struggle over ethnic diversity and social power. In addition, this study refines our understanding about the relationship between social change and prudence. Social change, I conclude, has links to the variability of prudence. Because rhetoric refashions prudence in every moment of practice, a progressive articulation may rework the norms that inform that practice. From this perspective, political judgment theory becomes a useful perspective to illuminate the evolution of a rhetorical culture and community.

★ PRUDENCE AS A CONSTRUCT OF DISCURSIVE PRACTICE

Scholars of public discourse have moved toward theories that perceive political judgment as the outgrowth of reasoned calculation and rhetorical performance. Characterized by a renewed interest in Aristotle, Isocrates, Cicero, and Machiavelli, this intellectual project examines specific moments of discursive action and rhetoric's cultural functions. The efforts of Robert Hariman and Thomas Farrell provide a rhetorical alternative to the troubled project of modern rationality.[4] Michael C. Leff facilitates these goals by reconstructing the sensibilities that regulated Latin and Renaissance rhetoric.[5] James Jasinski demonstrates how

textual analysis reveals modes of judgment and prudential practices.[6] In distinct ways these scholars detail the relations between reason and aesthetic performance.[7] At the same time they gain unity through the critical implementation of one assumption: political judgments not only result from discursive practice, but they are constructed by the dynamic processes of rhetoric. Hariman, for example, recovers prudence as a point of entry into deliberation which, in his words, "requires [an] implicit understanding of the possible, the probable, and the appropriate within a specific community, and is not reducible to categorical imperatives, deontologies, or universal laws."[8] For Leff, decorum is a similar "principle of action that accounts for the adaptive power of persuasive discourse."[9] Thus, prudence and decorum provide a vocabulary and set of meanings for criticism, and although each involves a distinct heritage, both terms illumine the negotiation of policy, discursive expectations, circumstances, and culture.

Whether the 1874–1875 civil rights bill constituted prudent policy was at issue within the debate; consequently, Congress's rhetoric reveals explicit standards of judgment, and it enacts implicit norms for future discursive practice. My critical purpose here is to interpret and trace the consequences of these rival standards, but I also advocate a specific approach to the study of prudence. It is accepted generally that speakers perform different forms of prudence to direct political judgment. Prudence's variability is important, because our literature appreciates the concept in relation to rhetoric's dynamic nature; nevertheless, despite the instructive exception of John Lucaites and Charles Taylor,[10] critics typically approach prudence as a stable even *a priori* reflection of cultural expectations. David Levasseur's recent essay, for example, contrasts the prudential functions of Edmund Burke's rhetoric against its heroic functions.[11] I do not dispute Levasseur's reading per se, but I do question his dichotomy that implies a settled and widely accepted notion of what is prudent. When critics draw sharp boundaries between prudent and imprudent rhetoric or when our work only catalogues various kinds of prudence, we underrate the dynamic elements that make the concept an important window into rhetorical theory and practice.

But what if the critic approaches prudence as a contested space that political actors struggle to control through discourse? Seen in this light, its "dialectical tension between adaptation and constancy" receives new meaning. Not only does it demand a balance between the ideal good and the practically possible, political rhetoric remakes prudence so that it coincides with the speaker's position.[12] Few politicians would accept the conclusion that their position or rhetoric was imprudent; instead, they are quick to claim prudence as their own. Prudence, then, is a coveted space of legitimacy that they attempt to occupy by discursively controlling its meaning.[13] To emphasize that fact is to expand the possibilities for criticism. The study of prudence can become a search for potentially disruptive articulations that may mark the evolution of a rhetorical culture and a particular community. This assumption guides my analysis of the Reconstruction civil rights debate. I begin with the question, how do the texts of debate participants create an internal context or "textual context" that encompasses the past, present and future?[14] I then interpret the forms of prudence implicated by these textual contexts. Finally, I consider how the interaction between divergent forms altered nineteenth-century rhetorical culture where it concerned race and rights.

★ ALTERNATIVE CONCEPTIONS OF PRUDENCE IN THE 1870s CIVIL RIGHTS DEBATE

On May 13, 1870, Sumner introduced a "Supplementary Civil Rights Bill" that prohibited public discrimination against African Americans. The measure called for federal authority to eliminate racial segregation in hotels, trains, restaurants, churches, and schools.[15] Sumner's Republican colleagues thought the proposal too radical, which was not surprising since Lincoln's party had sustained a conflict between egalitarianism and prejudice from its inception.[16] Before the war most European Americans regarded African Americans as biologically inferior; consequently, many who opposed slavery did so for economic rather than moral reasons.[17] After the

conflict, Republicans hesitated to grant African Americans full legal equality for political reasons; furthermore, they maintained the racist sentiments of the general population.[18] Speaking of the United States generally, William Gillette writes, "the majority regarded America as a white man's country, with a government and a society run by and for the benefit of the whites. They excluded the blacks by denying them power, wealth, and position, and mistreated them by perpetrating racial violence, riots, and lynchings."[19] Within this context, the measure represented a radical interpretation of the Thirteenth, Fourteenth, and Fifteenth amendments, and it embodied a public revolution that Abolitionists and African Americans long had sought.[20]

Several events led to a widespread interest in black civil rights after the summer of 1873. Sumner's ill health and eventual death garnered support as a memorial to his political service. Mississippi, Louisiana, Arkansas, Florida, and Alabama desegregated their public accommodations and transportation facilities giving the policy added legitimacy.[21] Several African Americans obtained seats in the House, and they dedicated themselves to passing the civil rights bill.[22] Most important, the "redeemed" South endangered Republican power, and many of Lincoln's party came to believe that unity was necessary to retain control. By using desegregation to recapture the moral authority of the previous decade, Republicans hoped to sustain their power and secure black votes. But, in response to and in conjunction with their improved position, Democrats vocally opposed all civil rights efforts. In January of 1874, a sustained debate over the wisdom of racial desegregation began.[23]

The Textual Context of Civil Rights' Opponents

Prudence requires an apprehension of circumstances and an anticipation of potential futures.[24] Thus, to appreciate the prudence articulated by the Democrats and conservative Republicans who opposed desegregation, it is necessary to recover the reality that their discourse created—that is, their rhetoric's textual context. A May 22, 1874, speech by Augustus Merrimon exemplifies the opponents' perception of the past. As he narrated a chronology of U.S. history, Merrimon declared, "From the foundation of our Government, as I have shown, the negro race in this country were [sic] held in a state of bondage, in a state of servitude; they were slaves." Eventually, a good portion of the country came to "dislike" this institution, because "they believed that no human being had a right to hold another human being in bondage." Nevertheless, the South insisted that slavery was moral. According to him, when the North "made war" on the South, the Southern states defended slavery, and, as a result, "these two aggressive spirits came together, first in moral, then in political conflict, and finally conflict of arms. That conflict resulted in the absolute destruction of that institution by force . . . that civil war resulted in its abolition, in its destruction, in its absolute overthrow."[25] A fellow Democrat agreed with Merrimon's characterization. Once the vice-president of the Confederacy, then a representative from Georgia, Alexander Stephens declared, "this thorn in the flesh, so long the cause of irritation between the States, is now out for all time to come."[26]

Several aspects of this discourse are significant. Merrimon's depiction of slavery assumed a tone of detachment and objectivity. He presented himself as uninfluenced by the old slavery system, which is remarkable when one considers that the myth of the Old South, a rhetoric that valorized the ante-bellum, was gaining strength among Southern communities.[27] A detached observer, Merrimon stood in the present and observed events in the distant past. Stephens's metaphor is also instructive, because it adds an important dimension to Merrimon's tone. A corporeal metaphor, it entailed an organic vision of national politics. Prior to the war, Southern politicians characterized the nation as a set of sovereign states joined by *contractual* relationships.[28] In 1874, Stephens chose to portray the United States as a single organic whole, a significant choice that constructed a context in which the States were interdependent and unified. Performatively, it illustrated the spirit of compromise and accommodation that Celeste Condit and John Lucaites attribute to late Reconstruction rhetoric.[29] In addition, the metaphor established a

temporal disjunction: the United States as an injured body and the United States as a healing organism. These images existed in a "then" and "now" frame. Then, before the war, the nation suffered from the "thorn" of slavery, but, now Stephens assures his audience, "the passions and prejudices which attended the conflict are fast subsiding and passing away, the period has now come for the descendants of a common ancestry, in all the States and sections of the country, to return to the original principles of their fathers. . . ."[30]

The bill's critics articulated a temporal perspective marked by four distinct stages. In the beginning was the mythic period of the founders. Democrats constructed this time as an idyllic moment in U.S. history. Subsequently, the benign institution of slavery turned malignant, resulting in geographic and ideological division. Critics of the bill failed to explain why or how this transpired but argued instead that strife and conflict marked this period. Eventually the conflict escalated into the Civil War, which, in Stephens's terms, removed the thorn of slavery from the national body. For opponents, the war became an epochal rupture that divided time and *situational realities*. This disruption was crucial to the context that their rhetoric portrayed. It facilitated their detached attitude with respect to the slavery era; the rupture of the war provided new surroundings. In their "now," the geographical animosity that had existed previously was irrelevant, and because new circumstances existed, Southern Democrats could speak of reconciliation without betraying their pre-war position. Furthermore, their "now" suggested that a new sensibility guided their behavior. Not only had they abandoned their principled defense of slavery as no longer relevant, they had embraced a new perspective illustrated by a desire to see the former slaves excel. According to Senator John Johnson of Virginia,

> Some Senators seem to think that the southern whites are inflamed with hatred of the colored people, that they desire nothing so much as to destroy them, deprive them of every right, impose upon them every burden. Mr. President, there can be no greater mistake than that. . . . The southern people have every desire

to treat them with the last degree of justice, and to give them every opportunity of attaining the highest civilization possible for them to reach.[31]

On January 7, 1874, Hiram P. Bell emphasized the "good feeling and harmony now existing between the races" throughout the South.[32] These feelings extended to *actions* of good will. Congressman Durham declared, "[African Americans] are protected in their lives, liberties, and in the pursuit of happiness at the expense of the white people. They are protected in all of their political rights without the payment of one farthing to secure that protection."[33] According to the Democrats, the most important privilege that African Americans enjoyed in the reconstructed South was an education. Senator John Johnson affirmed that:

> [Virginia's] system provides that the schools of the white and colored people shall be kept separate; but except in that particular they are the same. They employ good teachers in both. They give the same proportion of public money to each. They build the same sort of school-houses for both, and the colored people are provided to the same degree precisely by this common-school system that the white people are.[34]

Allen Thurman, a former gubernatorial candidate who had promised to save Ohio from "the thralldom of niggerism," declared that everyone in his state wanted to see those of color educated.[35]

These assurances represent an important dimension of the opponents' textual context— their present time was a period of recovery and harmony, and white behavior toward African Americans was guided by the substantial realities of the Southern context. With slavery abolished, they pledged themselves to those they had owned. Alexander Stephens proclaimed, "there is not a colored man in Georgia who knows me (and my acquaintance with that class is not very limited) who would not come to me for a personal favor, or personal counsel, or in case of real grievance for a redress of personal wrongs, with more confidence in my having justice secured him, than to any 'carpet-bagger' in the State."[36] Thomas Whitehead argued

that he was a good example of the people in his state, yet he was willing to have Congress judge whether his character was not equal to the bill's House sponsor, Benjamin Butler.[37] He assured Congress that he would protect and defend the former slaves just as well. Stephens and Whitehead used themselves as examples, and their enlightened positions came to represent a new Southern sensibility altogether consistent with the "now" of their situational realities.

The Textual Context of Civil Rights' Proponents

The textual context constructed by Republican radicals and a few moderates contrasted sharply with that created by opponents. The advocates of desegregation claimed that African Americans encountered unwarranted prejudice daily. Examples were plentiful; however, the testimonies of black Representatives provided a special exigency.[38] Joseph Rainey of South Carolina recounted two instances from a trip to Richmond, Virginia.[39] In the first case, a city streetcar conductor expelled him from the car despite a city ordinance that prohibited racial segregation.[40] Officials also had decided to build a street through a burial ground dedicated to Richmond's ante-bellum slaves. Although the workers had removed a few bodies, they had used some remains to fill in the low places and "mudholes." To Rainey this act symbolized the reality of race relations, and he contrasted the meaning of that action against the claims of his congressional opponents. He declared:

> Yet you talk about humanity; your kindly feeling for the colored race. Gracious Heaven! If you have no feelings for the ashes of the dead; if you have no regard for the dust of the dead slave who served you all the days of his life faithfully, honestly, well, we may have apprehensions as to the manner in which we will be treated, now that we are free and struggling for equal rights, unless we are protected by the strong arms of the law.[41]

Still, if the antagonists in this debate had differed only in characterizing the present, some accommodation might have been possible. Instead, supporters of black civil rights situated these individual moments within a historical pattern of inequity. Simply stated, they defended the civil rights bill as the only solution to circumstances that were simultaneously immediate and historical. A January 10, 1874[,] speech by the black Representative Richard Cain illustrates this point. He said:

> I propose to state just this: that we have been identified with the interests of this country from its very foundation. The cotton crop of this country has been raised and its rice-fields have been tilled by the hands of our race. All along the march of progress, as the march of commerce, as the development of your resources has been widening and expanding and spreading, as your vessels have gone on every sea, with the stars and stripes waving over them, and carried your commerce everywhere, there the black man's labor has gone to enrich your country and to augment the grandeur of your nationality.[42]

Cain's labor history affirmed black equality, elevated black behavior and character, and it testified that African Americans had helped build the country's prosperity. Concurrently, his narrative established the relevance of slavery to the post-bellum context. He associated the slavery past and the civil rights present first through his verb tense. The passage's present perfect tense described a context in which the contributions of African Americans had no definitive conclusion. He said, "We have been identified," the cotton crop "has been raised" by Blacks, and our labor "has gone to enrich your country." Cain could have said, "we had been identified," or that the cotton crop "had been raised by Blacks." The past perfect tense would have suggested a clear conclusion to black action, and it would have affirmed a disjunction between the past and present. Instead, Cain's articulation gave the passage a sense of openness and possibility. It allowed for additional claims such as, "Blacks continue to grow the nation's cotton," and "our labor continues to enrich your country." The present perfect tense, which other Republicans also employed, rejected any clear separation between the past and the present.[43] Subsequently, Cain declared, "Inasmuch as we have toiled with you in building up this nation; inasmuch as we have suffered side by side with you in the war; inasmuch as we have together passed

through affliction and pestilence, let there be now a fulfillment of the sublime thought of our fathers—let all men enjoy equal liberty and equal rights."[44] This present perfect verb tense and the Republicans' explicit statements reflected a common thesis. African Americans had been an integral part of the nation, and their service demanded the fulfillment of a historical transaction. Past circumstances combined with the present to demand action—desegregation.

Because the past and the present merged for the advocates of civil rights, they were able to argue that individual acts of discrimination were really systemic failures. Put another way, their "now" was defined by their "then." The white Representative William Lawrence noted that the House's black librarian had been expelled from a railroad car.[45] Richard Cain described how a restaurant had refused to serve his colleague, Robert Elliott, when he traveled between Washington, D.C., and his home.[46] Riding together, Cain and Elliott had their meals brought aboard the train, but even this attempt to avoid trouble caused resentment among the porters who believed that they were putting on airs.[47] According to George Edmunds, these incidents resulted from the belief system of slavery that Southerners maintained despite their "honeyed phrases."[48] The texts of Republicans suggest that these present problems had meaning only as the result of past practices and beliefs. They implied that certain cultural norms began in the ante-bellum era, flowed through the Civil War and continued to the present. On February 3, 1875, Cain said, "No, Mr. Speaker, it [the problem of segregation] is a damnable prejudice, the result of the old cursed system of slavery. It is that which brought about this prejudice and has caused it to overshadow the whole land. Slavery has left the poison still in their minds."[49]

Two Visions, Two Forms of Prudence

The distinct textual contexts created by opponents and proponents implied divergent norms for political judgment and discursive practice. Where the opponents located a temporal rupture that divided the slavery past and the harmonious present, bill advocates argued for continuity. Where the Democrats emphasized the good will of the Southern people, Radical

Republicans pointed to systemic prejudice sustained by slavery's beliefs. Each side articulated a different vision of the then and the now, and these expressions led to opposing ideas about the wisdom of desegregation.

Recall the testimony of Alexander Stephens and Thomas Whitehead. When they compared themselves to carpet-baggers and Radical Republicans, they did more than promise to help African Americans. Their rhetoric implied that good race relations resulted from good relationships; moreover, their arguments suggest that positive interaction between European and African Americans resulted from personal virtue. Stephens and Whitehead became synecdoches, visible illustrations of the integrity of the Southern populace. These implicit claims reveal an important feature of their prudence. Key to the opponents' position was the notion that Congress should judge racial policy on the basis of substantial relationships and concrete realities. In their discourse, individuals controlled the quality of interracial activities. Only the individual was responsible for her or his actions toward the other race. Only the individual could know the character of his or her acquaintances, and only the individual could appreciate the complexities of each community and relationship. According to this sensibility, desegregation was imprudent, because it was a formal response to the substantial issues of character and association. It was unwise, because it tried to legislate an interaction best controlled by people in their own locality. With a discursive emphasis on the circumstances of racial interaction, the Democrats concluded that desegregation was inexpedient.

Sometimes translated as expediency and sometimes as the advantageous or beneficial, *sympheron,* as explained by Aristotle, is important to political judgment and thus deliberative rhetoric.[50] The performance of expediency involves explicit comparisons between current conditions and the expected consequences of action. Expediency arguments are marked by a kind of pragmatism in which discursive strategies sublimate idealized truth, abstract values, and moral righteousness to concrete realities.[51] The opponents of desegregation enacted the principle of expediency most obviously by contrasting the harmonious present

to an unstable future. To use a metaphor, they portrayed the South as a tranquil pond and the civil rights bill as a large rock hurled at its center. According to Hiram P. Bell, "the great mass of the colored people in the South are quiet and contented; they neither know nor care anything about the provisions of this bill. . . . It is unfortunate and unwise in the extreme, by this agitation, to disturb the good feeling and harmony now existing between the races."[52] Critics repeatedly used vivid images of destruction to describe the bill's consequences. On May 22, 1874, John Stockton said of the Republicans' efforts to desegregate cemeteries: "You invade every social principle without regard to distinctions of race or color; you tear away all that is worth living for in this blessed land."[53] That same day Senator Saulsbury declared, "you have no right to afflict the white people of this country in order to make party capital and secure forever the negro vote."[54] Even the rhetorically moderate Merrimon characterized desegregation as an act of "aggression."[55] The terms "aggression," "afflict," and "disturb" were meant to conflict with the opponents' accommodating tones and testimonies of good will. Democrats extended this disjunction with warnings about "oppression or violence."[56] The Senator T. F. Bayard declared in 1875, "I can see only new and increased heart-burnings and unkindnesses between those races whom every good man must wish to see at peace with each other in their relative spheres of life and usefulness. . . . I fear this bill will create causes of collision, of unkindness, and misunderstanding, in which pecuniary loss must occur to the white, with no benefit whatever to the black."[57] Senator John Stockton of New Jersey claimed that the South would not allow Congress to enact this legislation,[58] and John Harris threatened the return of the Civil War.[59]

A second war was impossible, but these threats were a powerful symbolic performance. They stipulated boundaries of acceptable policy based not on abstract principles but on the reality of personal interracial relationships. According to Merrimon, "there is this natural antipathy between the races. Whatever you may say about the corruption of man, there is still something that lingers and lives within his bosom and whispers to him of that law of his nature which he shall not contravene. . . ." He said, further, "I believe [prejudice] is inherent in the nature of the white man; I believe it is inherent in the nature of the black man everywhere. Naturally, those of one race like their own best, until they are corrupted and brought in close contact with another, when the evil consequences I adverted to a while ago are brought on."[60] Once again, the opponents of desegregation had emphasized substantial criteria for judging policy. Individual virtue would lead European Americans to help African Americans, but only if Congress allowed these persons to act as their nature required. Prejudice was not the result of slavery; rather, it was a necessary attitude that informed appropriate interracial behavior. Accordingly, positive race relations resulted from good relationships, personal virtue, *and* a deep respect for the substantial feelings of each race. If Congress violated these realities, it would disrupt the social order; furthermore, it would bear all the blame, because it had ignored the dictates of nature. There was only one option. Aaron Sargent explained, "we ought to legislate here as statesmen, having in view not merely abstract ideas or theoretical principles or sublimated ideas, but to observe the condition of the times and know whether by any law which we may pass here we inflict an injury upon the country. . . . We may insist that we are led in a certain direction by our principles and should disregard all prudence in order to follow them; but that is not wise statesmanship."[61]

The Republicans' textual context gave rise to different political principles. They argued that prudence required a formal standard of judgment that encompassed the country's systemic failures, its long-term future, and a critique of its cultural norms. Proponents believed they stood at an epochal crossroads between continued trouble and future glory.[62] Ellis H. Roberts said, "It seems to me that we have again reached a critical point in the politics of this country. Step by step a great party has insisted that the *Declaration of Independence* instead of being a glittering generality shall be made a practical verity. This is another step in that march."[63] A new application of traditional principles was required. On December 19, 1873, Benjamin Butler proclaimed:

Every man has a right to go into a public inn. Every man has a right to go into any place of public amusement or entertainment for which a license by legal authority is required. He has a right to ride in "any line of stage-coaches, railroad, or other means of public carriage of passengers or freight," and to be buried in any public cemetery; or he has a right in any "other benevolent institutions or any public school supported in whole or in part at public expense or by endowment for public use." . . . Now, then, we propose simply to give to whoever has this right taken away from him the means of overriding that state of hostile legislation, and of punishing the man who takes that right away from him. This is the whole of that bill.[64]

According to proponents, if Congress evaluated desegregation against the standard of human rights, it would pass the bill. This decision was wise because only desegregation could resolve the nation's moral stasis. Several advocates claimed that it would resolve the present social conflict in a higher form of civilization.[65] Lawrence Williams even warned that if Congress failed in its duty, the question of color would return to haunt the Republic.[66] Thus, those who defended desegregation argued that the bill was prudent, because it would forestall deterioration and legitimate the nation's founding doctrine—the *Declaration of Independence*. This notion reached its most eloquent expression in the speeches of African American Representatives. On June 9, 1874, James Rapier confronted his white colleagues with the following conclusion: "This question resolves itself to this: either I am a man or I am not a man. If one, I am entitled to all the rights, privileges, and immunities common to any other class in this country; if not a man, I have no right to vote, no right to a seat here."[67]

Just as the concept of expediency reflects the opponents' rhetoric, the ideal of justice characterizes the political judgment of those who defended desegregation. Aristotle argues that justice involves using formal criteria to divide material goods and abstract advantages. He states in *Nicomachean Ethics*, "And justice is that in virtue of which the just man is said to be a doer, by choice, of that which is just, and one who will distribute either between himself and another or between two others not so as to give more of what is desirable to himself and less to his neighbour . . . but so as to give what is equal in accordance with proportion."[68] Of course, Aristotle's justice is not egalitarian, especially with respect to political resources.[69] Guthrie explains that it connotes the regulating force of a "rational principle," facilitating judgments that are uninfluenced by individual interest. Using justice to manage interracial relationships and to enact transcendent values became the driving force of the proponents' rhetoric. Once they had clarified the social context—slavery continues through public segregation—they demanded the *just* application of human right—desegregation.

The most dramatic appeal to justice in this debate stemmed from a narrative of military sacrifice. Benjamin Butler explained that he had led a column of 3,000 black soldiers across the James River to attack New Market Heights on September 29, 1864. Not permitted to fire their guns and stopped by a wooden blockade, the column came under heavy fire. But, said Butler, "a brave black hand seizes the colors; they are up again and wave their starry light over the storm of battle; again the ax—men fall, but strong hands and willing hearts seize the heavy, sharpened trees and drag them away, and the column rushes forward, and with a shout which now rings in my ear, go over that redoubt like a flash, and the enemy never stop running [sic] for four miles." Butler concludes:

> It became my painful duty, sir, to follow in the track of that charging column, and there . . . lay the dead bodies of five hundred and forty-three of my colored comrades . . . and as I rode along among them, guiding my horse this way and that way lest he should profane with his hoofs what seemed to me the sacred dead, and as I looked on their bronzed faces upturned in the shining sun to heaven as if in mute appeal against the wrongs of the country for which they had given their lives . . . I swore to myself a solemn oath, "my right hand forget its cunning and my tongue cleave to the roof of my mouth if I ever fail to defend the rights of these men who have given their blood for me and my country this day and for their race

forever;" and, God helping me, I will keep that oath.[70]

The narrative's imagery is startling, and its appeal to the regulating force of justice is significant. The "black hands," "dead bodies," and "bronze faces" reinforce the claim that black soldiers suffered the same pain and death as white soldiers. Their blood stained the soil with the same red color. But, more important, Butler's historical narrative demanded present action. To warrant the sacrifice of these African Americans, he and Congress had a responsibility to establish procedures that ensured their children's rights. As one Republican proclaimed, "I am in favor of this bill in a modified form, because I believe it is just and right, and is therefore of the highest expediency."[71]

I have refrained from labeling the prudence constructed by either side in this debate. To use phrases like a "prudence of justice" or a "prudence of expediency" reifies what I believe to be two dynamic sensibilities that simultaneously directed and legitimized the participants' political judgments. Instead, I have interpreted the key characteristics that comprised each side's articulation: substantial relationships, individual character/nature, and expediency for opponents and formal procedures, human rights, and justice for proponents. In what remains, I consider the implications of this debate for the nineteenth-century's systems of power and rhetorical culture.

★ ESTABLISHING THE TRAJECTORY OF U.S. RACE RELATIONS

Although the civil rights bill became law in 1875, most believe that it was a failure. The *New York Times* reported that "there is nothing left in the bill passed which is of very great consequence to the Negro or the white race."[72] Although it gave broad power to federal courts, the bill required that the offended party first file a lawsuit. With little political power, scarce economic resources and no social authority, most African Americans were ill prepared to seek redress; consequently, the 1875 Civil Rights Act had little effect on Southern racial practices.[73] When the Supreme Court ruled it unconstitutional in the 1883 *Civil Rights Cases,* it nullified a dead law.[74] Wyatt-Brown states, "Northerners and Southerners had come to agree, as they had in the 1830's, that basically the Negroes were undeserving of first class citizenship."[75] He concludes, "if the bill could claim any significance, it lay in its demonstration of the bankruptcy of Republican Reconstruction principles. Rather than being a true memorial to Charles Sumner and his cause, it was a travesty of racial justice, because neither the white public nor its representatives expected or wanted the Act's enforcement."[76]

While these comments are accurate, they reflect too narrowly on the measure's political consequence, missing its symbolic significance. Prudence is never without a cultural context; it requires common practices for substance. But because speakers construct prudence within discursive practice, particular norms, standards, or expectations do not determine it. Prudence does, however, influence the norms that guide its articulation; consequently, it has the potential to unsettle or even remake its discursive context. This reciprocal relationship is significant because, as Hariman has observed, the "rules" of appropriate behavior "are primary determinants of power, and . . . power becomes a by product of successful performance."[77] What scholars have not considered is that the prudence constructed by *both* sides in this debate challenged discursive norms as they existed before Reconstruction's amendments. That challenge is significant, because it marks the evolution of a rhetorical culture.[78] One particular exchange evinces this claim particularly well.

On January 5, 1874, John T. Harris said that the civil rights bill was dangerous, because "it is based upon the purpose, the theory, of the absolute equality of the races. It seeks to enforce by law a doctrine which is not accepted by the minds nor received in the hearts of the people of the United States—that the Negro in all things is the equal of the white man."[79] This statement angered the African Americans present, and when he declared, "I say there is not one gentleman upon this floor who can honestly say he really believes that the colored man is created his equal," Representative Alonzo Ransier

responded, "I can." To this interruption Harris replied, "Of course you can; but I am speaking to the white men of the House; and, Mr. Speaker, I do not wish to be interrupted again by him."[80] Harris then extended his claims about natural prejudice with the argument that Southern white children were born with the knowledge of their supremacy. Ransier again interjected saying, "I deny that," to which Harris replied, "I do not allow you to interrupt me. Sit down; I am talking to white men; I am talking to gentlemen."[81] In that moment, the discursive practice of racial exclusion—a foundation of nineteenth-century rhetorical culture and power—was exposed to new sensibilities.

Prior to Reconstruction, African Americans, like Women and Native Americans, were excluded from congressional communication. Their absence maintained a silence that resulted from legal statute and discursive norms about who could participate in the public and political spheres. Harris remained situated within the ante-bellum rhetorical culture, and he exhibited its sense of prudence and decorum. Unfortunately for him, he had failed to recognize two issues. First, the physical constitution of Congress had changed, and his audience contained representatives of a formerly excluded group. He had tried to silence not only an African American but also a member of the House. Although the equality of the black voice was uncertain for his white colleagues, its congressional status was clear. Second, Harris's performance clashed with the forms of prudence articulated by debate participants. His attempt to silence Ransier was neither expedient nor consistent with the situational reality created by his Southern colleagues. His display actually strengthened the proponents' claims about systemic prejudice and a temporal continuity between the slavery past and the present. (The *Chicago Times* called his comments an ill-tempered display of plantation manners.)[82] Harris's behavior was imprudent, not because it violated a fixed cultural standard, but because it challenged the farms articulated by his peers. When it came to race relations, the discourse of either side departed from past norms; subsequently, change was a given. What remained at risk was the nature of that change, and that would depend, in part, on who successfully occupied the space of prudence.

The proponents' rhetoric was surprisingly egalitarian. For example, the white Republican Daniel Pratt declared that if his colleagues would only "forget the color of his skin, the difference between him and you would disappear."[83] His statement was remarkable given our knowledge of nineteenth-century racism. According to Peggy Lamsan, the distinctively African features of Representative Robert Elliott shocked white Republicans.[84] Gillette writes that though the bill was seen as politically necessary, it was widely unpopular, and moderate Republicans were particularly uncomfortable with its implications.[85] Why would individuals who maintained the prejudices of their era employ such progressive language to defend a civil rights bill that they personally disliked? The answer lies in their need to justify desegregation as a prudent policy. To distinguish themselves from their opponents and legitimate their position, Republicans combined the ideals of human unity and universal rights with immediate demands far justice. Eighteenth and nineteenth-century Abolitionists had used this discourse against slavery, as early feminists had against misogyny.[86] The Republican politicians who defended desegregation employed it to argue that the slaves' freedom was nominal unless Congress protected their public rights.[87] The Enlightenment ideal expressed in the *Declaration* became, paradoxically, an expedient discourse to support the Republicans' emphasis on justice. Equality reinforced the wisdom of their policy, it secured the political support of African Americans, and it resisted the nineteenth century's systems of power.

By 1875, a specific set of communal beliefs structured the power relationships between African and European Americans. Most European Americans believed that a person's physical attributes were sufficient criteria for determining his or her race, that races differed in intellectual and moral capacity, that physical difference determined one's position on a hierarchical scale, and that individuals of European de[s]cent occupied the scale's highest point. With the growth of anthropology and Darwinian sociology, scientists inscribed

inequality into the physical bodies of African Americans.[88] Based on mid-century investigations of crania, facial angles, and brain mass, late nineteenth-century social scientists concluded that nature had confined people of color to an inferior status. John Haller writes, "under the guise of finding general laws of nature operating in both the social and biological organism, they were really engaged in an effort to prescribe what America ought to be—an idea that incorporated the subjective prejudices and assumptions about themselves and others, and a belief that science was an objective tool engaged in an 'uninvolved' diagnosis of empirical reality."[89] The Republicans' prudence countered the inequities maintained by this knowledge. If it had prevailed, it might have influenced congressional rhetorical culture in at least two ways. First, the abstract ideal of human unity might have played a more central role in political judgments about race. So long as African Americans were human, this prudence implied that racial difference was irrelevant to discursive interaction. The rules of communication it stipulated required the equal participation of all. Second, congressional rhetorical culture might have made room for an interventionist government to ensure the just application of equal rights. The procedural emphasis in the Republicans' prudence implied that law was a legitimate tool to direct communal knowledge. In Sumner's words, "Prompted by the law, leaning on the law, they will recognize the equal rights of all. . . . Thus will the law be an instrument of improvement, necessary in proportion to existing prejudice."[90]

African Americans would wait until the next century for this sensibility to alter the discursive landscape. Condit's essay, "Democracy and Civil Rights," describes this process within the mass media, and many are familiar with the arguments of the NAACP in such cases as *Sweatt v. Painter, McLaurin v. Oklahoma,* and eventually *Oliver Brown et al. v. Board of Education of Topeka[,] Kansas.*[91] E. Culpepper Clark and Raymie McKerrow argue that Gunnar Myrdal's seminal study helped to shift academic communities towards a more egalitarian rhetoric.[92] As the nation moved towards a formal sensibility that embraced African

Americans as humans and citizens, "it became virtually impossible in national public dialogue to speak racist characterizations."[93] This shift did not begin in the political sphere but in the legal, academic, and public spheres. One reason is that the prudence of bill opponents had the greatest influence on political judgments into the twentieth century.

Most of those who opposed the civil rights bill understood the need to leave behind the discursive practices of the ante-bellum era. Lucius Q. C. Lamar warned his colleagues, "a few inflammatory speeches from our side would do their work for them."[94] Instead, Democrats and some conservative Republicans enacted the principle of expediency as they reinforced the necessity of that regulating principle. First, they acknowledged that African Americans were equal to European Americans. Henry Cooper, once a strong advocate for slavery, declared, "whatever may have been my education, whatever may have been my feelings, whatever may have been my actions in regard to the colored race, I trust I am prepared to accept as a verdict from which there can be no appeal that they are citizens, and as citizens I propose to treat them, and to treat them as equals before the law, for my equals they are before the law."[95] At the same time, opponents added an important qualification. In the words of Stephens, not all "men were created equal in all respects, either in physical, mental, or moral development." The *Declaration of Independence* was never meant to affirm a natural sameness; it only invoked the truth that all have the right to stand equally before the law, he said.[96]

These comments were consistent with the situational reality and prudence of bill critics. On the one hand, opponents termed the measure inexpedient, but they coupled that criticism with what seemed to be a sign of political conversion. Only a decade earlier, Stephens and his colleagues had chosen war rather than relinquish slavery or acknowledge any equality with African Americans. Even Harris was at least partially cognizant of the shift within the Democrat's rhetoric, and he quoted Lincoln at length to demonstrate the harmony between Lincoln and himself.[97] By quoting the President, former Confederates demonstrated the novelty of their present and their commitment to the *Declaration*. Performing the central principle of their prudence, they expediently acknowledged black legal and political equality, but they also emphasized individual difference and the need to maintain that difference in the social sphere. To do otherwise would be an assault on the South's social system.[98]

When scholars discuss "separate but equal", they tend to focus on *Plessy v. Ferguson* and the period after 1896; however, the discursive strains of this ideology are evident in late Reconstruction. The prudence constructed by bill critics approached policy decisions with an emphasis on substantial relations and individual character; simultaneously, it legitimized personal prejudice as an important component of social behavior. In the years after 1875, Southern then Northern politicians imitated these arguments. Equality rarely surfaced as an important consideration for policy, because it was unnecessary for prudent judgments. Personal character remained the most important factor for good race relations, and the national government possessed no real role, because the discursive heritage of the 1875 Civil Rights Act was an over-arching emphasis on individual authority and the need to accommodate prejudice for the sake of social stability. As speakers refined this prudence in later discursive moments, it led to the separate but equal doctrine. Myrdal's *An American Dilemma* illustrates how violence and Jim Crow legislation defused the public power of African Americans. He argues further that these actions were at odds with the "American Creed," a philosophy that entailed the precept of universal equality. To justify social inequity and circumvent a confrontation with the United States' principles, segregationists argued for the supremacy of personal liberty in all that was social.[99] The Jim Crow rhetoric of personal liberty is, I believe, the discursive consequence of the Democrats' rhetoric. Out of the civil rights debate came a discourse of materiality that eschewed abstract ideals for immediate circumstances and the practical consequence of action. This rhetoric informed the later period's prejudices and political philosophies. America's rhetorical culture, influenced by the prudence of Reconstruction segregationists and the unchallenged beliefs of scientific racism, maintained inequity for years to come.

★ THE POLITICAL TRAJECTORY OF PRUDENCE

This essay has pursued several issues. It examined a period and rhetoric that has not received deserved attention. It illumined a discursive sensibility that led to the separate but equal doctrine. In the process, it demonstrated that the study of prudence as a contested space of legitimacy can reveal shifts within a rhetorical culture. I conclude with an observation about the relationship between prudence and social change. In 1969, Robert L. Scott and Donald K. Smith argued that "civility and decorum serve as masks for the preservation of injustice...they become the instrumentalities of power for those who 'have.'"[100] Also citing "reason" and the "good," Scott and Smith imply that classical rhetorical concepts like prudence may work against the rhetoric of confrontation. Subsequent scholars have furthered the characterization that prudence is inherently conservative, viewing its use as "a means for maintaining the community's traditional alignment of its social practices."[101] To the extent that one understands prudence as the determined exercise of communal codes, this characterization has merit. This essay suggests a different vision, however. Because speakers construct prudence to justify any number of political judgments, it does not have an inherent trajectory. In every communicative act, prudence may be a conservative or progressive influence on the norms that guide its articulation. This debate demonstrates that sometimes a "successful" prudence—i.e., the form that determines political judgment and is imitated afterward—merely reinscribes prior practices in a slightly altered form. At other moments the outcome differs. Perhaps scholars have viewed prudence as a conservative force because the forms that typically dominate public debate sustain the status quo. In other words, we have mistaken prudence for the conservative result of most political judgments. Those who speak from a privileged position have the upper hand,

and they work quickly to secure prudence for themselves. Whoever controls prudence directs the standards of political judgment and discursive performance, and when privileged speakers occupy prudence's space, they reinforce their often conservative position. What we need now are studies that consider the conditions in which marginal voices disrupt the pattern I just described. The civil rights debate studied here is little help, because the Republicans eventually surrendered their position and adopted the opponents' prudence.

In February 1875, the issue of desegregation came to a climax in Congress. The previous fall elections had given the Democrats a major victory. Among the losers were Benjamin Butler and several other prominent Republicans. But, more significantly, the Republican House majority would soon become a seventy-vote deficit. In this climate, the desegregation measure obtained a second purpose. Lame-duck Republicans used it to gain enough support to break a Democratic filibuster. Once the filibuster was broken, Republican leaders intended to pass a new Enforcement Act, a bill designed to expand federal jurisdiction, and various appropriation measures that would enhance the stature of departing members.[102] Fifteen Republicans refused to support Butler's plan, because they disliked the major rules change that he proposed. To gain their votes, Butler removed the bill's provision to desegregate public schools. This compromise sent a clear signal that the Republicans were willing to sacrifice their formal standards when they became inconvenient. Perhaps one reason why later politicians would imitate the Democrats' rhetoric is because Republicans failed to maintain the consistency of their own position. Wyatt-Brown correctly argues that the 1875 Civil Rights Act demonstrated the bankruptcy of Republican principles, but he is wrong to claim that it was inconsequential. With the tacit approval of their opponents' position, Republicans helped to bury black civil rights for almost a century.

NOTES

[1] For a general overview of the Reconstruction era see Eric Foner, *Reconstruction: America's Unfinished*

Revolution (New York: Harper & Row, 1988); Morgan Kousser and James M. McPherson, eds., *Region, Race, and Reconstruction: Essays in Honor of C. Vann Woodward* (New York: Oxford UP, 1982); W. E. B. Du Bois, *Black Reconstruction in America, 1860–1880* (1935; New York: Atheneum, 1992); Michael Perman, *The Road to Redemption: Southern Politics, 1869–1879* (Chapel Hill: U of North Carolina P, 1984). For a description of Reconstruction's early years and the effects of the Civil War see David Herbert Donald, *The Politics of Reconstruction, 1863–1867* (Baton Rouge: Louisiana State UP, 1965); Eric L. McKitrick, *Andrew Johnson and Reconstruction* (Chicago: U of Chicago P, 1960); Joel Williamson, *After Slavery: The Negro in South Carolina During Reconstruction, 1861–1877* (1965; Hanover: UP of New England, 1990). For issues relating to the Constitution, the Reconstruction Amendments and federalism see Robert J. Kaczorowski, *The Politics of Judicial Interpretation: The Federal Courts, Department of Justice and Civil Rights, 1866–1876* (New York: Oceana Publicans Inc., 1985); Robert J. Kaczorowski, "The Enforcement Provisions of the Civil Rights Act of 1866: A Legislative History in Light of *Runyon v. McCrary*," *Yale Law Journal* (1989): 565–595; Earl M. Maltz, "Reconstruction Without Revolution: Republican Civil Rights Theory in the Era of the Fourteenth Amendment," *Houston Law Review* (1987): 221–279.

2 W. R. Brock, "The Waning of Radicalism," *Reconstruction: An Anthology of Revisionist Writings,* ed. Kenneth M. Stampp and Leon F. Litwack (Baton Rouge: Louisiana State UP, 1969) 497.

3 Bert Bradley, "Negro Speakers in Congress: 1869–1875," *Southern Communication Journal* 18 (1953): 216–225; Cal M. Logue, "The Rhetorical Appeals of Whites to Blacks During Reconstruction," *Communication Monographs* 44 (1977): 241–251; Cal M. Logue; "Restoration Strategies in Georgia, 1865–1880," *Oratory in the New South,* ed. Waldo W. Braden (Baton Rouge: Louisiana State UP, 1979) 38–73; Cal M. Logue and Thurmon Garner, "Shift in Rhetorical Status of Blacks after Freedom," *Southern Communication Journal* 54 (1988): 1–39; Waldo W. Braden and Harold Mixon, "Epideictic Speaking in the Post–Civil War South and the Southern Experience," *Southern Communication Journal* 54 (1988): 40–57; Waldo W. Braden "Repining over an Irrevocable Past: The Ceremonial Orator in a Defeated Society, 1865–1900," *Oratory in the New South,* ed. Waldo W. Braden (Baton Rouge: Louisiana State UP, 1979) 9–37.

4 Robert Hariman, "Relocating the Art of Public Address," *Rhetoric and Political Culture in Nineteenth-Century America,* ed. Thomas W. Benson (East Lansing: Michigan State UP, 1997) 222–248; Robert Hariman, *Political Style: The Artistry of Power* (Chicago: U of Chicago P, 1995); Robert Hariman, "Decorum, Power, and the Courtly Style," *Quarterly Journal of Speech* 78 (1992): 149–172; Robert Hariman, "Prudence/Performance," *Rhetoric Society Quarterly* 21 (1991): 26–35; Thomas B. Farrell, *Norms of Rhetorical Culture* (New Haven: Yale UP, 1993); Thomas B. Farrell, "Rhetorical Resemblance: Paradoxes of a Practical Art," *Quarterly Journal of Speech* 72 (1986): 1–19.

5 Michael C. Leff, "The Habitation of Rhetoric," *Argument and Critical Practices,* ed. Joseph W. Wenzel (Annandale: Speech Communication Association, 1987) 1–8; Michael C. Leff, "Textual Criticism: The Legacy of G. P. Mohrmann," *Quarterly Journal of Speech* 72 (1986): 377–389; Michael C. Leff, "Things Made By Words: Reflections on Textual Criticism," *Quarterly Journal of Speech* 78 (1992): 223–231.

6 James Jasinski, "Rhetoric and Judgment in the Constitutional Ratification Debate of 1787–1788: An Exploration of the Relationship Between Theory and Critical Practice," *Quarterly Journal of Speech* 78 (1992): 197–218; James Jasinski, "The Forms and Limits of Prudence in Henry Clay's (1850) Defense of the Compromise Measures," *Quarterly Journal of Speech* 81 (1995): 454–478.

7 Much of this work is indebted to Victoria Kahn, *Rhetoric, Prudence, and Skepticism in the Renaissance* (Ithaca: Cornell UP, 1985) and Eugene Garver, *Machiavelli and the History of Prudence* (Madison: U of Wisconsin P, 1987).

8 Hariman, "Prudence/Performance" 26.

9 Leff, "The Habitation of Rhetoric" 7.

10 John Louis Lucaites and Charles A. Taylor, "Theorizing the Grounds of Rhetorical Judgment," *Informal Logic* 15 (1993): 29–40.

11 David G. Levasseur, "A Reexamination of Edmund Burke's Rhetorical Art: A Rhetorical Struggle Between Prudence and Heroism," *Quarterly Journal of Speech* 83 (1997): 332–350.

12 Levasseur 335.

13 Lucaites and Taylor (p. 30) claim that in U.S. politics "prudence has functioned less as an idealized or reified theoretical construct, than as an ideological token . . . From this perspective, 'prudence' represents the recursive interaction between a rhetoric of judgment and the grounds on which that rhetoric is evaluated . . . its meaning at any given point in time negotiated by competing interests in the crucible of discursive controversy."

14 My use of the term "textual context" stems from Stephen E. Lucas, "The Renaissance of American Public Address: Text and Context in Rhetorical Criticism" *Quarterly Journal of Speech* 74 (1988): 249. A textual context is not the same as a rhetorical situation; rather, it is a context created by a text, containing circumstances, temporality, characters, and norms of action. I expand Lucas's term beyond the context created by a single text, and I maintain that each side in this debate worked collectively to construct a common textual context.

15 Edward L. Pierce, *Memoir and Letters of Charles Sumner*, vol. 4 (Boston: Roberts Brothers, 1893) 499.

16 See Eric Foner, *Free Soil, Free Labor, Free Men: The Ideology of the Republican Party Before the Civil War* (New York: Oxford UP, 1970).

17 David Zarefsky, *Lincoln, Douglas, and Slavery: In the Crucible of Public Debate* (Chicago: U of Chicago P, 1990) 19.

18 Earl M. Maltz, "Fourteenth Amendment Concepts in the Antebellum Era" *The American Journal of Legal History* 32 (1988): 305–309.

19 William Gillette, *Retreat From Reconstruction, 1869–1879* (Baton Rouge: Louisiana State UP, 1979) 191.

20 See James M. McPherson, *The Struggle for Equality: Abolitionists and the Negro in the Civil War and Reconstruction* (Princeton: Princeton UP, 1964); Celeste Michelle Condit and John Louis Lucaites, *Crafting Equality: America's Anglo-African Word* (Chicago: U of Chicago P, 1993).

21 Michael Perman, *The Road to Redemption: Southern Politics, 1869–1879* (Chapel Hill: U of North Carolina P, 1984).

22 Howard N. Rabinowitz, ed., *Southern Black Leaders of the Reconstruction Era* (Urbana: U of Illinois P, 1982); Annjennette Sophie McFarlin, *Black Congressional Reconstruction Orators and Their Orations, 1869–1879* (Metuchen: Scarecrow Press Inc., 1976).

23 See Bertram Wyatt-Brown, "The Civil Rights Act of 1875," *Western Political Quarterly* 18 (1965): 765–767; Gillette 191–203. See also Michael Les Benedict, *A Compromise of Principle: Congressional Republicans and Reconstruction 1863–1869* (New York: Norton, 1974).

24 Nathan Rotenstreich, "Prudence and Folly," *American Philosophical Quarterly* 22 (1985): 95.

25 *Congressional Record* 22 May 1874: appendix, 310.

26 *Congressional Record* 5 January 1874: 381. Note also that William Robbins, an extreme Democrat or "fire-eater" from North Carolina, said on January 24, 1874, "The old system of negro slavery, as once

existing in all the States, is forever dead and buried, and I have no tears to shed over its grave." See *Congressional Record* 24 January 1874: 899.

27 See Braden, "Repining Over an Irrevocable Past: The Ceremonial Orator in a Defeated Society, 1865–1900."

28 See David Zarefsky and Victoria J. Gallagher, "From 'Conflict' to 'Constitutional Question': Transformation in Early American Public Discourse," *Quarterly Journal of Speech* 76 (1990): 245–254.

29 Condit and Lucaites 116–119.

30 *Congressional Record* 5 January 1874: 381.

31 *Congressional Record* 21 May 1874: 4114.

32 *Congressional Record* 7 January 1874: appendix, 3.

33 *Congressional Record* 6 January 1874: 406.

34 *Congressional Record* 21 May 1874: 4115.

35 See Foner, *Reconstruction* 313; *Congressional Record* 20 May 1874: 4089.

36 *Congressional Record* 5 January 1874: 381.

37 *Congressional Record* 3 February 1875: 953.

38 Seven African Americans represented their districts in December of 1873. Joseph Rainey (South Carolina), John R. Lynch (Mississippi), Richard H. Cain (South Carolina), Robert B. Elliott (South Carolina), James Rapier (Alabama), Alonzo J. Ransier (South Carolina), and Josiah Walls (Florida) brought a new urgency to black civil rights. For a brief biographical summary of these and other black Congressmen see Annjennette Sophie McFarlin.

39 Rainey was the first African American to sit in the House, arriving to fill a vacancy on December 12, 1870. Known as a strong advocate of desegregation, he once refused to leave a segregated restaurant causing the management to evict him physically. See Peggy Lamson, *The Glorious Failure: Black Congressman Robert Brown Elliott and the Reconstruction in South Carolina* (New York: W. W. Norton & Co., 1973) 68, 188, 121.

40 *Congressional Record* 3 February 1875: 955–957.

41 *Congressional Record* 3 February 1875: 959.

42 *Congressional Record* 10 January 1874: 565–566.

43 For example, Ransier used the present perfect tense to describe black labor, *Congressional Record* 5 January 1874: 382. Robert Elliott used it to describe the Civil War, *Congressional Record* 6 January 1874: 410.

44 *Congressional Record* 10 January 1874: 566.

45 *Congressional Record* 19 December 1874: 341.

46 Historians suggest that Richard "Daddy" Cain was familiar with the South and racial tension. Once a Methodist preacher and the editor of the *South*

Carolina Leader, he and his family lived in "constant fear" and had their home guarded by armed men. See Lamson 284; Foner, *Reconstruction* 426.

[47] *Congressional Record* 10 January 1874: 565.

[48] *Congressional Record* 27 February 1875: 1869.

[49] *Congressional Record* 3 February 1875: 957.

[50] Aristotle, *The Rhetoric* trans. W. Rhys Roberts (New York: Random House, 1984) 1358b. See also George A. Kennedy's comments in footnote 81 of his translation of Aristotle's *The Rhetoric* (New York: Oxford UP, 1991) 49.

[51] The relationship among particular circumstances, political discourse, and expediency is an enduring concern for rhetorical theorists. Although vocabularies differ, similar principles are evident in Chaim Perelman and L. Olbrechts-Tyteca, *The New Rhetoric: A Treatise on Argumentation,* trans. John Wilkinson and Purcell Weaver (Notre Dame: U of Notre Dame P, 1969) 266–270; in Richard Weaver, *The Ethics of Rhetoric* (1953; Davis: Hermagoras Press, 1985); and John M. Murphy, "Epideictic and Deliberative Strategies in Opposition to War: The Paradox of Honor and Expediency," *Communication Studies* 43 (1992): 65–78.

[52] *Congressional Record* 7 January 1874: appendix, 3.

[53] *Congressional Record* 22 May 1874: 4146.

[54] *Congressional Record* 22 May 1874: 4160.

[55] *Congressional Record* 22 May 1874: 4164.

[56] See Allen G. Thurman, *Congressional Record* 20 May 1874: 4088.

[57] *Congressional Record* 26 February, 1875: appendix, 105.

[58] *Congressional Record* 22 May 1874: 4146.

[59] *Congressional Record* 5 January 1874: 378.

[60] *Congressional Record* 22 May 1874: appendix, 317.

[61] *Congressional Record* 22 May 1874: 4172.

[62] See Richard Cain, *Congressional Record* 10 January 1874: 565.

[63] *Congressional Record* 4 February 1875: 981.

[64] *Congressional Record* 19 December 1873: 340.

[65] See the speech of Josiah Walls, *Congressional Record* 8 January 1874: 416–417.

[66] *Congressional Record* 4 February 1875: 1002.

[67] *Congressional Record* 9 June 1874: 4784.

[68] Aristotle, "Nicomachean Ethics," *The Complete Works of Aristotle,* ed. Jonathan Barnes, trans. W. D. Ross revised by J. O. Urmson, vol. 2 (Princeton: Princeton UP, 1984) 1134a.

[69] W. K. C. Guthrie, *A History of Greek Philosophy* vol. 6 (1981; Cambridge: Cambridge UP, 1990) 371–374.

[70] *Congressional Record* 7 January 1874: 458.

[71] Barbour Lewis, *Congressional Record* 4 February 1875: 998.

[72] "Passage of the Civil Rights Bill in the House," *New York Times* 6 February 1875: A1.

[73] McPherson, "Abolitionists and the Civil Rights Act" 509.

[74] See *Civil Rights Cases,* 109 US 3, United States Supreme Ct., 1883.

[75] Wyatt-Brown 774. See also Gillette 218.

[76] Wyatt-Brown 775.

[77] Hariman, "Prudence/Performance" 34.

[78] For an extended consideration of rhetorical culture see Farrell's *Norms of Rhetorical Culture.* Based largely on Farrell's treatment, I use the term to mean the assumptions, expectations, norms, and traditions of communicative practice that unify and sustain a community of individuals.

[79] *Congressional Record* 5 January 1874: 376.

[80] *Congressional Record* 5 January 1874: 376.

[81] *Congressional Record* 5 January 1874: 377.

[82] "Civil Rights Debate," *Chicago Times* 8 January 1874: 3.

[83] *Congressional Record* May 1874: 4083, 4081–4083.

[84] Until Elliott entered the House, most of the black representatives had been biracial. See Lamson 119.

[85] Gillette 202–203.

[86] See Herbert Aptheker, *Anti-Racism in U.S. History: The First Two Hundred Years* (Westport: Praeger, 1993) 71–81; Martha Solomon Watson, "The Dynamics of Intertextuality: Re-reading the Declaration of Independence," *Rhetoric and Political Culture in Nineteenth-Century America,* ed. Thomas W. Benson, (East Lansing: Michigan State University Press, 1997) 91–111; Karlyn Kohrs Campbell, "Style and Content in the Rhetoric of Early Afro-American Feminists," *Quarterly Journal of Speech* 72 (1986): 434–455.

[87] See Robert Elliott, *Congressional Record* 6 January 1874: 408 and Charles Sumner, *Congressional Globe* 15 January: 1872: 381.

[88] Oscar Handlin, *Race and Nationality in American Life,* 3rd ed. (Boston: Little, Brown and Co., 1957). See also Thomas F. Gossett, *Race: The History of an Idea in America* (Dallas: Southern Methodist UP, 1968) chapters 4 and 7.

[89] John S. Haller, Jr., *Outcasts from Evolution: Scientific Attitudes of Racial Inferiority, 1859–1900* (Carbondale: Southern Illinois UP, 1995) 140.

[90] Charles Sumner, *Congressional Globe* 15 January 1872: 383.

[91] See Celeste Michelle Condit, "Democracy and Civil Rights: The Universalizing Influence of Public Argumentation," *Communication Monographs*

54 (1987): 1–18; Jack Greenberg, *Crusaders in the Courts: How a Dedicated Band of Lawyers Fought for the Civil Rights Revolution* (New York: Basic Books, 1994).

92 E. Culpepper Clark and Raymie E. McKerrow. "The Historiographical Dilemma in Myrdal's American Creed: Rhetoric's Role in Rescuing a Historical Moment," *Quarterly Journal of Speech* 73 (1987): 303–316; Gunnar Myrdal, *American Dilemma: The Negro Problem and Modern Democracy* (New York: Harper & Brothers, 1944).

93 Condit 15.

94 As quoted by Wirt Armistead Cate, *Lucius Q. C. Lamar: Secession and Reunion* (1935; New York: Russell & Russell, 1969) 183.

95 *Congressional Record* 22 May 1874: 4154.

96 *Congressional Record* 5 January 1874: 379.

97 *Congressional Record* 5 January 1874: 376. See Abraham Lincoln, "The Charleston Debate," *The Complete Lincoln-Douglas Debates 1858*, ed. Paul M. Angle (1858; Chicago: U of Chicago P, 1991) 235.

98 See William Herndon, *Congressional Record* 6 January 1874: 421.

99 Myrdal 573–586.

100 Robert L. Scott and Donald K. Smith, "The Rhetoric of Confrontation," *Quarterly Journal of Speech* 55 (1969): 1–8.

101 Hariman, "Prudence/Performance" 29.

102 Foner, *Reconstruction* 553–555; Gillette 260–267; Wyatt-Brown 772.

Carol Moseley-Braun Defies the Confederate Flag

Theodore F. Sheckels

On July 22, 1993, Senator Carol Moseley-Braun of Illinois hurried to the Senate Chamber to, as she put it, kill Dracula again (S 9258). She had thought that she (and others) had put to rest the Daughters of the Confederacy's request for a renewal of their patented use of the Confederate Flag during Judiciary Committee hearings. However, Senators Jesse Helms and Strom Thurmond, believing that the Committee's action was a slap in the face of the Daughters of the Confederacy, brought the issue to the floor via an amendment to an unrelated piece of education legislation (S 9251–71).

★ VOICES

Helms and Thurmond spoke; Moseley-Braun (joined briefly by Senators Howard Metzenbaum and Patty Murray) spoke. Then, there was a vote, against tabling the motion granting the patent. Moseley-Braun, upset by this vote, refused to yield the floor until the Senate changed its mind. Several rallied to her side, including members who had voted against tabling. So, after what Butler correctly discusses as an unusually emotional sharing of personal histories by members of the Senate, the Senate reconsidered the matter and tabled the motion, in essence denying the patent. Before and after that vote, many thanked Moseley-Braun for what she had brought, as an African American,

to the Senate that day. Only Helms refused to join in the celebration, characterizing the comments against the patent as "political rhetoric and partisan oratory," the racism issue as "a political ploy," and his colleagues as "pious, self-satisfied Senators" and "turncoats who ran for cover for political reasons" (S 9271). Thus, conflict led to a defeat, which created tension. The tension then led to a catharsis, which then led to victory and celebration—a dramatic structure reminiscent of Shakespearean comedy—except for one Jacques-like bitter voice, one who, in this case, responded to events by saying, "I felt that I was going to throw up" (S 9271).

★ INTER-VOICES

This drama, as Butler notes, is compelling. What is perhaps more interesting is the change in the use of inter-voices that occurs as one moves through the drama. Helms and Thurmond mixed references to authorities with stories of the service the Daughters of the Confederacy have performed. In telling his colleagues the history of the organization, Helms evoked the authority of past presidents:

This essay originally appeared as a chapter in a book by Theodore F. Sheckels, When Congress Debates: A Bakhtinian Paradigm *(Westport, Conn: Greenwood, 2000).*

In the years following the War Between the States, thousands of men and women came together in reunions across the country. They buried the sword, and they paid honor to each other. It was in this spirit that Congress and Presidents Arthur, Cleveland, Harrison, and McKinley—the last two being former Union soldiers—encouraged the formation of groups such as the United Daughters of the Confederacy, not to refight the battles long since lost, but to preserve the memory of courageous men who fought and died for the [cause] they believed in. (S 9251)

Helms cited authorities from the previous century; Thurmond, on the other hand, focused on what Congress has "said" by its actions in the twentieth century:

> This amendment is essentially the same language which we approved last year to extend and renew the design patent for the insignia of the United Daughters of the Confederacy. This design patent was originally issued on November 8, 1898[,] and has been extended on numerous occasions since then. It was extended in 1926, 1941, 1963, and 1977. In November of last year the patent expired. In order to ensure continued protection for the insignia, Congress must extend design patent protection for the UDC. (S 9252)

Thurmond later noted how Congress had honored similar groups, again bringing the voice of previous Congressional action to bear on the amendment he had cosponsored:

> Mr. President, for the record, I want to note recognition granted by the Congress to several other groups whose origin can be traced to the Civil War. The Congress has granted Federal Charters to the Ladies of the Grand Army of the Republic, the Sons of Union Veterans of the Civil War, the National Women's Relief Groups, Auxiliary to the Grand Army of the Republic, and the Daughters of Union Veterans of the Civil War. Additionally, most of these groups have been granted by the Congress exclusive rights to the use of their name, emblem, seals, and badges. (S 9253)

Together with citations of what previous Presidents and previous Congresses did and thereby "said," Thurmond and Helms talked about the United Daughters of the Confederacy (UDC). Helms talked about the group's service during World War II:

> During World War II, the United Daughters of the Confederacy continued to offer its services to the U.S. Government for war relief. They provided financial support, donated ambulances, established a blood plasma unit, sold millions of dollars in war bonds and were ultimately recognized by the War Department and the Red Cross for its outstanding work and contributions. (S 9252)

Helms zeroed in on the story of Oveta Culp Hobby:

> In World War II, the UDC answered Franklin Roosevelt's summons by sponsoring the Nurse Cadet Corps, by raising money for war bonds, and by organizing blood plasma drives. The head of the Texas chapter, Oveta Culp Hobby, was asked by the Chief of Staff of the Army, Gen. George C. Marshall, to draw up the plans for the establishment of the Women's Army Corps, known to history as the WAC's. And this same Oveta Culp Hobby was the first Secretary of Health, Education, and Welfare under President Eisenhower. This lady, as I said, was president of the Texas chapter of the UDC. (S 9252)

Helms and Thurmond offered a mixture of evidence types—authorities and narratives, which evoked the persona of the folksy Southern lawyer. Helms' sole use of prosopopoeia had this same flavor: "It [a rejection of the patent renewal] will be rewriting history to say to them, 'you no longer count, and you no longer are going to have a recognition that so many other organizations have had since the turn of the century—including the UDC'" (S 9252).

Moseley-Braun used a style she herself termed "lawyerly" (S 9257). It lacked the folksiness of Helms' and Thurmond's in its mixture of common knowledge and cited and quoted authorities. It is very legalistic, very rational. She talked about the symbolism of the Confederate flag in a restrained tone:

> The fact of the matter is the emblems of the Confederacy have meaning to Americans

even 100 years after the end of the Civil War. Everybody knows what the Confederacy stands for. Everybody knows what the insignia means. That matter of common knowledge is not a surprise to any of us. When a former Governor stood and raised the Confederate battle flag over the Alabama State Capitol to protest the Federal Government support for civil rights and a visit by the Attorney General at the time in 1963, everybody knew what that meant. (S 9254)

One can "feel" Senator Moseley-Braun holding back. Similarly, as she introduced and then discussed a letter she received from Michael K. Kirk, Acting Assistant Secretary of the U.S. Commerce Department and Acting Commissioner of Patents and Trademarks, one can hear the lawyer in her. The following quotations are excerpts from the words she used while presenting her evidence:

> Mr. President, I will have printed in the RECORD a letter to me dated April 30, 1993, from Mr. Kirk, of the U.S. Department of Commerce, Patents and Trademarks Office.
>
> Mr. President, he answered this question: Is it common practice for nonprofit groups to obtain design patents for their insignia and logos?
>
> In other words, what he is saying is that most organizations have other kinds of protections and do not have this design patent, which is sought today by the United Daughters of the Confederacy.
>
> The next question asked in the letter is: Are design patents typically renewed?
>
> This is more than a second renewal for this organization. It is not necessary to begin with. They can continue to use their insignia. It does not interfere with their charitable activities. (S 9254)

After the initial vote, Moseley-Braun's intervoices and her tone changed. She "announced" that change:

> Madam President, I really had not wanted to have to do this because in my remarks I believe that I was restrained and tempered. I talked about the committee procedure. I talked about the lack of germaneness of this amendment. I talked about how it was not

necessary for this organization to receive the design patent designation, which was an extraordinary extension of an extraordinary act to begin with. What I did not talk about and what I am constrained now to talk about with no small degree of emotion is the symbolism. (S 9256–57)

She described her earlier tone as "dispassionate" and "lawyering about" (S 9257); now, she will, with emotions that she occasionally feels obliged to apologize for, tell how the Confederate flag symbolizes "the single most painful episode in American history" (S 9257) from the perspective of African Americans. She speaks, in personal terms, of how African Americans see the flag and the vote that just occurred:

> I am sorry, Madam President. I will lower my voice. I am getting excited, because, quite frankly, that is the very issue. The issue is whether or not Americans, such as myself, who believe in the promise of this country, who feel strongly and who are patriots in this country, will have to suffer the indignity of being reminded time and time again, that at one point in this country's history we were human chattel. We were property. We could be traded, bought, and sold.
>
> It is an outrage. It is an insult. It is absolutely unacceptable to me and to millions of Americans, black or white, that we would put the imprimatur of the United States Senate on a symbol of this kind of idea. (S 9257)

She very emotionally tried to tell her colleagues what it is like to be an African American and what it is like to be an (the only) African American in the Senate. She also evoked popular culture, personifying the patent design request several times as Dracula. She also heavily used prosopopoeia. She gave voice to how the American voters responded to the 1992 Republican National Convention: "Folks took a look at the convention and said, my God, what are these people standing for? This is not America" (S 9257). She imagined the voice of those who voted against tabling the Helms amendment: "'Well, we are just going to do this, you know, because it is no big deal'" (S 9258).

As others joined her, we heard more prosopopoeia, more stories, and many networking references to Moseley-Braun and the others who were joining her cause. Both the stories and the affiliative references to Moseley-Braun are worth examining closely.

As Butler notes, the stories—and the emotional way they are told—are quite striking because they are atypical of discourse in the usually staid Senate. After she told her story and that of her ancestors, Native American Senator Ben Lighthorse Campbell told his. He first identified himself as "the only other so-called person of color" in the Senate. He then spoke about places in the United States where his Native American people are "called prairie niggers" and of how one VFW representative tried to block a chapter's endorsement of Campbell, a veteran of the Korean War, because he was an Indian. He noted how Southern Senators were citing "tradition" in defense of the UDC and the Confederate flag and stated that, "slavery was once a tradition, like killing Indians like animals was once a tradition. That did not make them right" (S 9261).

Then, Senator Howell Heflin of Alabama offered his story. He talked about his Southern roots:

I come from a family background that is deeply rooted in the Confederacy. My great-grandfather on my mother's side was one of the signers of the Ordinance of Secession by which the State of Alabama seceded from the Union. My grandfather on my father's side was a surgeon in the Confederate Army.

I have many connections through my family with the Daughters of the Confederacy organization and the Children of the Confederacy, and I have a deep feeling, relative to my family's background, that what they did at the time they thought was right. (S 9262)

He then noted that "we live today in a different world," "in a Nation that everyday is trying to heal the scars of racism" (S 9262). He cited a conversation that he had with his Black legislative director: they, somewhat jokingly, compared notes on how their buried ancestors would react to the stands the Senator might take. Heflin concluded that his ancestors would, if alive in 1993, "stand for what is right and honorable"; therefore, Heflin decided to change his vote and, when the matter was reconsidered, voted to table the Helms amendment.

Campbell and Heflin shared their personal stories in announcing their support for the position Moseley-Braun had staked out. Senator Mitch McConnell from Kentucky shared his story to explain his vote against Moseley-Braun:

My roots, like the senior Senator from Alabama, run deep in the South. . . . My great grandmother's first husband was killed in the Civil War. I have learned that he was not a slaveholder, but he, like others in Alabama, viewed that conflict through the lenses of those days. And his view was that it was a fight for his region. My grandmother belonged to the United Daughters of the Confederacy. I know she did not support slavery. So it has been my view in growing up that the UDC largely was a group not about the purpose of glorifying slavery, but a group that very much revered the lives of those who were lost during that great conflict. (S 9264)

McConnell, "out of respect for [his] ancestors," (S 9264) decided to vote to support the UDC's request. He did, however, very much want his colleagues to understand how his personal story had led him to his vote.

References to Moseley-Braun's words are understandably numerous in the speeches Senators made while she is defiantly maintaining control of the floor in the wake of the 48-52 vote not to table the Helms amendment. Let me quote some of these references:

Feinstein: So I would like to submit to you, Madam President, that Senator Carol Moseley-Braun is correct. Carol, I think you said it the way it had to be said. You said it eloquently. You said it beautifully. (S 9258)

Bradley: I appeal to people who voted for this amendment to understand not just the wisdom, but the passion and the depth of feeling from which Senator Moseley-Braun spoke. (S 9258)

Moynihan: May I say to the distinguished Senator from Illinois that in my 17 years in this body, I have been not so moved as by her statement. (S 9260)

Biden: [M]y whole purpose here in going through this charade is to compliment the Senator. (S 9261)

Simon: Mr. President, I simply want to tell my colleague from Illinois how proud I am of her at this moment. (S 9264)

Riegle: First of all, I want to say to the Senator from Illinois how I appreciate her extraordinary leadership today. (S 9264)

Boxer: To the Senator from Illinois, I thank her for guiding us, for teaching us, for reminding us, for being insistent, for standing on her feet, for appealing to what is best in us. (S 9266)

Conrad: Mr. President, the statement of the Senator from Illinois, Carol Moseley-Braun, I think, was perhaps the most powerful, most moving statement I have heard on the floor of the Senate since I came here 7 years ago. (S 9266)

Metzenbaum: Mr. President, I rise because I have seen something here today that I have not seen since I have been in the Senate. I saw one person, who was able to make a difference, stand up and fight for what she believes in, and she gave a message to this body that electrified the body. (S 9266)

Kennedy: Mr. President, the Senator from Illinois, like another great leader from Illinois, President Lincoln, appealed to the better angels in us this afternoon. She reminded us in a most eloquent way about the wounds, worn in the fabric of our society as a result of the Civil War and racism, that still exist. (S 9266)

Mitchell: The eloquence, the conviction, the power of the remarks made by the Senator from Illinois, the persuasiveness as seen in the subsequent remarks, is something rarely seen in the Senate. (S 9267)

Lautenberg: Madam President, I have been here 10 years now, and there have been few, if any, occasions in which the remarks of a U.S. Senator left the kind of impression that the comments made by Senator Moseley-Braun, of Illinois, have made because she touched the nerve of everybody who had the opportunity to hear what she was saying. (S 9270)

Dodd: I just want to join with others in commending the distinguished junior Senator from Illinois. This was a truly remarkable moment. She gave a wonderful speech. (S 9270)

★ DOUBLE-VOICING AND CARNIVALESQUE

Moseley-Braun's words created a network on July 22, 1993. She wove together an affiliation of Senators who wished not only to share her commitment to racial justice but also the emotion and the honesty with which she expressed herself. Her creating such an affiliation centered on not just an idea but on a manner of speaking contrary to the somewhat somber tradition of the Senate. This manner set the stage for the carnivalesque.

Eventually joined by these many others, Moseley-Braun effects carnivalesque subversion. The Senate is a place wrapped in its rules and its courtesies. After the initial vote, the two clashed. Although Moseley-Braun had no right to the floor, she took it and refused to yield it. Her peers, out of courtesy, did not try to have her declared out of order; rather, they—after some prodding by Moynihan—listened to what she had to say. As she held the floor (speaking to business already concluded), her allies gathered, and, working with some Senators who had initially voted against Moseley-Braun, they constructed a motion to reconsider. That motion eventually is introduced: all the while, Moseley-Braun is speaking, yielding time she had no right to have to others for questions that were really statements.

If it were not for the seriousness of the issue under discussion, the way the procedure unfolded would be almost comic. Moseley-Braun declared, "I will do everything I can to see to it that this body does not disgrace itself by giving its imprimatur to a symbol of a flag that was defeated in the Civil War" (S 9260). Determined "to take this floor and not give it up forever" (S 9269) and committed to "stand[ing] here until this room freezes over" (S 9258), Moseley-Braun yielded to a succession of colleagues. Bradley, after his statement, said, "So I am getting to my question" (S 9259). Exon began his statement by saying, "I will ask a question in just a moment" (S 9259). Campbell referred to the unusual "convention" that was being practiced and said "I will be getting around to my question in a short time" (S 9261). Biden, when it was finally time for a question after his long statement, said, "So my question to the Senator is one I cannot think of because my whole purpose here in going through this charade is to compliment the Senator" (S 9261). He did eventually think of a question, but, like the previous questions, it was part of a veil that allowed colleagues to speak—usually in support—while Moseley-Braun maintained control of the floor, something she really had no right to do. As this serious, emotional, but nonetheless comic "debate" ensued, Moseley-Braun stood in the well—conducting what amounted to a single-handed filibuster.

The discussion did not proceed as it should have. Moseley-Braun subverted procedures, and, in the carnivalesque energy her subversion created, the Senate regrouped, increasingly showing solidarity around her. During the regrouping, the Senators spoke differently, and, after it, they voted differently. During the carnivalesque moment, Moseley-Braun brought the body into the discourse in two ways that were subversive. First, she brought in the bodies of her slave ancestors—bodies that were bought and sold like livestock. Second, she kept her body—the only African American body in the U.S. Senate—before her peers by refusing to yield the floor. No matter who spoke, Senator Moseley-Braun physically was center stage. I emphasize the body at this point for a reason. Bakhtin's discussion of the carnivalesque in Rabelais stresses the role the human body plays in the satirist's attempts to level hierarchies by reducing all humans to the same plane. Once naked—once the fact that we all share certain bodily functions is undeniable, humans cannot array themselves by ranks based on birth or wealth or power as readily. Moseley-Braun's foregrounding of black bodies—including her own—served a similar function, for, once the bodily fact of slavery is made visible, politicians cannot escape what bondage meant for her ancestors by using abstractions.

The central argument in the debate was, of course, different, depending on the side you were on. One group wanted to honor the UDC, the symbolic significance of the Confederate flag notwithstanding because, if the flag had that message for some, it did not have that message to many in the South and did not have that message to the UDC. The other group saw the symbolic significance of the flag for African Americans (and others) as the issue and, although willing perhaps to honor the UDC, was not willing to honor the organization with a design patent for that symbol. On both sides, there was a high degree of emotion. Moseley-Braun's physical presence before the debating Senators, however, may be a clue to another argument that those opposed to the patent were offering.

Passive varidirectional double-voiced discourse does not always involve arguments opposed to one another. In this case, the second argument simply goes in another direction. It is a message many in the Senate wanted to send about the Senate: that the Senate does not contain enough diversity to truly understand or represent the people of the United States.

The argument is offered by several in the course of the debate. Referring to Moseley-Braun, Senator Murray, early in the debate, said

> I know her sense of frustration, I recognize her outrage. As a woman, I share some understanding of her situation. But I cannot know her sense of isolation being the only African American in this body. (S 9256)

Later in the debate, Delaware Senator Joseph Biden notes that he "and others have been saying for so long that there is a need for diversity in this body, not need for diversity to have a numerical representation representing the country, but need for diversity" in order to produce "civility and a sense of understanding of the other person's point of view" (S 9260). Senator Boxer made essentially the same point still later in the debate, saying "We are enriched as an institution because the American people made this a more diverse body" by electing Senators such as Moseley-Braun and Campbell (S 9266). Senator John Kerry of Massachusetts put the argument a slightly different way. He noted that "there is a real discomfort as I think about the fact that we are 96 white men and women debating whether or not we ought to be sensitive to the expression of one African American and one Native American. If that," Kerry added, "does not tell us what the problem is, then nothing will" (S 9265). Senator Metzenbaum sounds an "Amen" when he says, "It was long past due that we have a woman of color in the U.S. Senate" (S 9266).

Note how this example of double-voiced discourse and the carnivalesque work together. They both push the point of view of the historically and still disempowered to the fore. They challenge the way the Senate has traditionally done its business, just as the highly personal, highly emotional style of almost all the rhetors does. This challenging of the traditional perhaps brings the debate into something like a circle, for Southern Senators, defending the Confederate flag had insisted that it stood for a Southern tradition that somehow excluded slavery. The rhetoric of those opposed to giving the design patent to the UDC are in essence saying, by their arguments and their ways of arguing, that tradition is often a curtain to hide behind, a curtain that must be ripped aside.

★ LACK OF FINALIZABILITY

The debate on July 22, 1993, did not begin or end that afternoon. Butler does a good job tracing earlier events of the day—that is, Moseley-Braun's objections to the serious discussion of the *Dred Scott* decision during confirmation hearings for Ruth Bader Ginsburg as Supreme Court Associate Justice—that culminated in this debate. His analysis overcomes the tendency to assign the debate too neat a beginning. Perhaps his analysis should have extended even farther back—beyond Senator Moseley-Braun's arrival in Washington, beyond George Wallace's flying of the Confederate flag in Montgomery to protest federal government action and Robert Kennedy's visit to the Alabama capital city to the Civil War itself and its aftermath in the South. The issue of slavery—and how the Confederate flag symbolized it for many citizens—is not a twentieth-century one.

On the other end of the debate, one needs to read the debate itself for positive and negative hints of how questions of racism will be discussed and understood in the future. Several Senators, most notably Paul Simon of Illinois and Daniel Patrick Moynihan of New York, suggested that the Senate will never be the same—that Moseley-Braun's personal, emotional remarks had jarred the Senate and made it no longer possible to hide behind abstractions such as "patents," devalue matters because they were "history," or fail to see what might be lurking behind matters labeled routine or business-as-usual or honorific or traditional. It was an "epiphany," Moynihan declared (S 9260). Even Senators who in the end still voted against Moseley-Braun voiced their appreciation for her willingness to abandon the "lawyerly" and truly humanize the chamber's discourse.

But then there was Senator Helms' closing remarks, in which he attacked those who "contrived" to bring "the spectre of race" into the debate for "political" and "partisan" reasons (S 9271). In a comment that rushes the Senate back into the abstract, Moseley-Braun's heartfelt comments on racism are labeled "a political ploy to escape responsibility for false pretense that should not have happened in the first place" (S 9271). The conflict between what the many Senators said and what Helms said (or tried to say in the obscure phrase I just quoted) suggested that the nation's confrontation with its racism is not yet over. The debate on July 22 did not reach an end; it was, rather, an important chapter in discourse ultimately not finalizable.

The debate was in the summer of 1993. I am writing this analysis in the summer of 1999—six years later. Just this week, the NAACP has begun "calling for a national boycott of vacation spots in th[e] tourism-dependent state" of South Carolina (Pressley: A3). Why? Because South Carolina is flying the Confederate flag from the top of its statehouse in Columbia. "Just this week, a state Supreme Court justice in Mississippi began hearing a challenge to the Mississippi flag brought by the state NAACP" (Pressley: A3). Why? The Mississippi flag—like that of Georgia—incorporates the Confederate flag within it. As NAACP national director of field operations Nelson Rivers III notes, the flag "is a symbol of oppression and slavery, and it represents probably the biggest symbol of the abuse of African American people." The fact that it is still flown sends the following message: "We've told you for years it offends us, yet you continue to fly it, and that shows you hold us in disregard and much disdain" (Pressley: A3).

The same day this story was featured in the pages of the *Washington Post,* columnist William Raspberry chose to link the flying of the Confederate flag with the city of Richmond's displaying a picture of Robert E. Lee and Supreme Court Chief Justice Rehnquist's leading a 4th Circuit Judicial Conference in the singing of "Dixie." Raspberry is not as upset at the symbolism as Rivers. But the coincidence of these events in the summer of 1999 and the fact that they occurred six years after

Carol Moseley-Braun made her stand before the Senate reveals that debates are not finalized by votes or by the sounding of a gavel.

And, as I revise this chapter in the fall of 1999, Helms is threatening to block President Clinton's nomination of Moseley-Braun as United States ambassador to New Zealand. Although "Helms made no mention of Moseley-Braun's successful opposition in 1993 to a Helms proposal that would have renewed the United Daughters of the Confederacy's design patent," the reporter—the *Washington Post*'s Helen Dewar—did. In fact, she cited Helms' comment to another reporter that "At a very minimum she [Moseley-Braun] has got to apologize for the display that she provoked over a little symbol for a wonderful group of little old ladies" or "look for another line of work" (Dewar: A17).

[Editors' note: this essay appeared as a chapter in a book, which had a single list of works cited. The author has provided a list below for this excerpted chapter.]

WORKS CITED

Butler, John. "Carol Moseley-Braun's Day to Talk about Race: A Study of Forum in the United States Senate," *Argumentation and Advocacy* 32 (1995): 62–74.

Dewer, Helen. "Helms vs. Moseley-Braun Again." *Washington Post,* October 19, 1999: A17.

Presley, Sue Anne. "Boycott Aims to Bring Flag Down." *Washington Post,* August 2, 1999: A3.

The S references (e.g. S 9258) are to the *Congressional Record,* published by the U.S. Government Printing Office and available online through Lexis-Nexis's *Congressional Universe. S* indicates the U.S. Senate portion of that daily record.

"Are We Going to Now Govern By Anecdote?":[1]
Rhetorical Constructions of Welfare Recipients
in Congressional Hearings, Debates, and Legislation, 1992–1996

Lisa M. Gring-Pemble

Today we begin our first hearing on the important issues of overhauling America's welfare system. The American people know our current system is broken. They want it fixed. We are here to fix it. . . . Welfare in America today does not give people a sense of personal responsibility. Welfare in America today does not give people economic incentives to get a job and keep a job. Welfare in America today does not create moral values that unite families as they move up the ladder of opportunity.

—House Committee on Ways and Means,
13 January 1995, 7

With these words, chairman of the House Subcommittee on Human Resources, E. Clay Shaw (R-FL), initiated one in a series of hearings on welfare reform legislation that eventually culminated in the 1996 Personal Responsibility and Work Opportunity Reconciliation Act, P.L. 104–193, one of the most controversial social policy reforms in recent history. The congressional hearings and subsequent proposals attracted widespread attention from both critics and supporters, initiating heated debates, editorials, opinion polls, protest marches, and policy arguments. *New York Times* reporter Jerry Gray explained in an August 1, 1996 article that many groups, like the United States Chamber of Commerce, "hailed the legislation as a reaffirmation of 'America's work ethic'" (1996, A23). "Republican presidential nominee Robert J. Dole praised the bill and said it would be remembered as a Republican victory," reported *Washington Post* correspondent Barbara Vobejda in an August 23, 1996 article (A17). In contrast, reporter Francis X. Clines observed in an August 22, 1996 *New York Times* article that many individuals and groups such as the nation's Roman Catholic bishops, Children's Defense Fund, National Organization of Women, and Feminist Majority decried the President's historic signing as a "moment of shame" (A1). In an Act that "illustrated the deep divisions in the Administration over Mr. Clinton's decision to approve the Republican welfare legislation," *New York Times* reporter Alison Mitchell explained in a September 11, 1996 article that two of the Clinton Administration's top welfare policy officials, Peter Edelman and Mary Jo Bane, resigned in protest of PRWORA's passage (A1). Lauded as "historic welfare legislation . . . that . . . rewrites six decades of social policy," and "the most radical overhaul" in welfare policy since the New Deal, the 1996 welfare reform bill officially ended the cash assistance, entitlement based program, Aid to Families With Dependent Children (Harris and Yang 1996, A1; Vobejda 1996, A1).

As a series of discursive practices that eventually became codified into law, the congressional hearings and debates over welfare reform merit careful consideration by communication scholars because they provide insight into the policy formation process. As Cynthia Cooper notes in her study of congressional hearings over television violence: "Congressional hearings may be a window into legislative policy making. Ever since the first hearing was held in 1792, . . . subcommittee hearings have been an important tool for information-gathering essential to informed decision making" (1995, 11). Indeed, over several centuries, communication scholars have developed a sustained and lively interest in the relationship between rhetoric and public policy. Early accounts of oratory reflect an emphasis on public speaking in the deliberative arena (Kennedy 1980, 3–40). In his *Art of Rhetoric,* Aristotle claims that legislation is one of "the most important questions upon which the would-be deliberative orator must be well informed" (1.4:13). In more recent years, communication scholars have refined and expanded policy-making studies, investigating the specific role of rhetoric in public policy formation. A clear example of this sustained commitment is the 1998 inauguration of a new journal in the discipline, *Rhetoric & Public Affairs,* whose mission statement calls for rhetorical investigation into "executive

leadership, diplomacy, political campaigns, judicial and legislative deliberations, and public policy debate."

Despite several studies on public policy debates and legislation, communication scholars have not yet examined the negotiation and construction of public policy *as a rhetorical process* beginning with bill proposals, congressional hearings, and congressional debates. Making a similar point, Janice Schuetz notes in her study of legislative argumentation that research in the communication discipline "seldom examines a large segment of the political process or the development of one argument through the hierarchy of the decisional process" (1986, 223). Going further, Craig Allen Smith and Kathy B. Smith contend that "Scholars have rarely studied the rhetoric of political institutions. . . . It should, therefore, come as no surprise that there is, as yet, no theory of . . . congressional rhetoric" (1990, 251). More recently, in a *Quarterly Journal of Speech* article on legislative debates, Linda Miller concludes that despite a few empirical studies of public controversies[2] in legislative contexts, "the relationship between public argument and policy change remains unclear." Consequently, she calls for "further analysis of the formation of a variety of public policies at the municipal, state or federal legislative levels" (1999, 375).

Such observations clearly point to the importance of studies which seek to understand the rhetorical construction of public policies. My goal in this essay is to add to our developing knowledge of deliberative hearings as a precursor to legislation through a case study of a significant piece of recent legislation, the Personal Responsibility and Work Opportunity Reconciliation Act of 1996, P.L. 104–193 (PRWORA). Because public policy legislation is largely the result of discussions that occur within the context of committee meetings and hearings, I confine my analysis to the hearings and debates from the 102nd, 103rd, and 104th Congresses surrounding welfare reform, all of which led to President Clinton's historic August 22, 1996 signing of PRWORA. I analyze these records as a means of gaining insight into the rhetorical processes by which social policy is formulated. Interested in the discursive practices by which policymakers negotiate and create a given social reality, a powerful construction on which future legislative action is premised, I examine how welfare recipients are depicted and what actions, motives, and goals are attributed to them. In so doing, I provide insight into the construction of a timely, highly controversial, and influential piece of legislation.

Ultimately, I show in this essay how depictions of welfare recipients and their families form the basis of the enacted welfare legislation. Although communication theorist Walter Fisher would contend that legislator reliance on depictions frees policymakers to evaluate the validity of the stories in an environment "inimical to elitist politics," this case study suggests otherwise (1984, 9). In contrast, I argue that the depictive forms facilitate elite discourse, discourage the inclusion of alternative public views, and delegitimize particular public voices. In making this argument, I first outline the theoretical approaches that inform this study. Next, I describe the historical context in which the welfare reform hearings and debates occurred. This background provides the framework within which I analyze representations of welfare recipients. I conclude with a discussion of the rhetorical implications of this study.

★ DEPICTION AND NARRATIVE: THEORETICAL CONTEXT

This paper's goal and textual evidence suggest the utility of depictive and narrative rhetoric as methodological approaches that provide an excellent framework for identifying significant depictions emergent in welfare reform history and contemporary legislative hearings and debates. Michael Osborn's (1986) work on rhetorical depiction seeks to shift the traditional focus of rhetorical studies from what he terms "primarily rational calculations" where scholars study how speakers devise complex arguments and proofs to defend well-considered positions. Instead, Osborn's focus on depictions "seeks those moments in which audiences encounter significant presentations of reality, and it strives to illuminate the rhetorical implications of such encounters" (97). Throughout this essay, I analyze "significant presentations of reality" concerning welfare recipients and their attitudes, values, and behaviors as constructed in hearings and debates.

Defined as "strategic pictures, verbal or nonverbal visualizations that linger in the collective memory of audiences as representative of their subjects," rhetorical depictions perform a vital role in the formation and maintenance of community life, chiefly by embodying accepted cultural values and goals (Osborn 1986, 79, 80). These depictions assume a variety of forms including extended anecdotes, metaphors, allegories, and empirical evidence. Taken together, these depictive forms function as brush strokes in painting a vivid portrait of the typical welfare recipient and welfare family that serves as the basis for policy formation in the context of a public moral argument.

Another central feature of depictive rhetoric for the purposes of this project is that depictions imply narratives. Osborn contends that depiction is "more a compression than a reflection. The portrait it offers may express implicitly and simultaneously an assertion concerning the origins of a subject, a prediction of that subject's fate, and the moral stance of the speaker" (1986, 79–80). W. Lance Bennett and Murray Edelman make a related point in their study of political narratives. They write: "Just as any narrative is likely to imply a wider set of related stories and an ideology, so a term or a simple reference in any political text may evoke a full-fledged story.... Political communications, then, ... are always seedbeds of stories" (1985, 164, 165). Similarly, in the context of the welfare reform hearings and debates, the demographic and character attributes ascribed to welfare recipients in the hearings and debates implicate a more comprehensive story about the past and future behaviors, lifestyles, and aspirations of welfare recipients. Ultimately, these depictions of welfare recipients serve as evidence to support legislative proposals and policies designed to enforce values and desirable behaviors.

Rhetorical theorist Walter Fisher (1984, 1985) explores how audiences evaluate one form of depictive rhetoric—narratives—in his work on the narrative paradigm. The narrative paradigm holds that humans are essentially storytellers who create and communicate stories that form understanding, guide collective reasoning, and shape behavior. Fisher explains that "symbols are created and communicated ultimately as stories meant to give order to human experience and to induce others to dwell in them to establish ways of living in common, in communities in which there is sanction for the story that constitutes one's life" (1984, 6). According to Fisher, narration is the dominant mode of human communication, and is particularly well-suited to evaluating public moral argument such as welfare reform deliberations. Fisher writes: "No matter how rigorously a case is argued . . . it will always be a story, an interpretation of some aspect of the world which is historically and culturally grounded and shaped by human personality" (1987, 17). Consequently, Fisher believes that the narrative paradigm is the best way to account for how and why people adopt particular stories to create meaning and guide collective action.

Fisher contrasts this narrative approach with what he terms "the rational world paradigm," or traditional logic associated with public deliberation. According to Fisher, reliance on technical expertise and formal logic excludes the general public from actively participating in the decision-making process. He explains: "Traditional rationality implies some sort of hierarchical system, a community in which some persons are qualified to judge and to lead and some other persons are to follow" (1984, 9). Instead, Fisher proposes the concept of narrative rationality to capture the role of the general public in making and assessing public moral arguments without the aid of technical experts and training in formal logic. Because all humans have an innate ability for narrative rationality, Fisher claims that the narrative paradigm is "inimical to elitist politics," because it insists that the "'people' do judge the stories that are told for and about them" (1984, 9). While Fisher does not claim that such rationality guarantees that audiences will not adopt "bad" stories, he does argue that narrative rationality "does mitigate this tendency" (1985, 349). Moreover, Fisher claims that the narrative paradigm allows for the "natural tendency" of "the people" to "prefer the true and the just" (1984, 9), and he claims that narrative rationality "engenders critical self-awareness and conscious choice" (1985, 349).

Fisher offers two ways people evaluate stories: narrative probability (what constitutes a coherent story) and narrative fidelity (whether or not the story "rings true" to experience). In particular, Fisher believes that character is essential to evaluating the narrative probability of a story: "Central to all stories is character. Whether or not a story is believable depends on the reliability of the characters, both as narrators and as actors. Determination of one's character is made by interpretations of a person's decisions and actions that reflect values" (1987, 16). People judge fidelity, according to Fisher, by assessing the merits of the "good reasons" that all narratives contain. Defined as "elements that give warrants for believing or acting in accord with the message fostered by that text," these value-laden reasons are expressed in a variety of forms including argument, metaphor, and myth (1985, 357).

In essence, as this case study demonstrates, depictions serve as evidence for audiences to determine both narrative probability and narrative fidelity. Because they assess character, depictions provide insight into the attitudes, values, and behaviors of welfare recipients and their families. The consistency and volume of the repetitive depictions encourage legislators to judge them as coherent. Because legislators use the depictions to warrant policy reforms, the depictions also serve as the "good reasons" legislators use to make decisions and assess the fidelity of welfare narratives. In contrast to Fisher's theory, however, this case study questions the liberatory and participatory nature of narratives, arguing that some narrative forms foster elitism and discourage critical, self-reflexive analysis.

★ THE PERSONAL RESPONSIBILITY AND WORK OPPORTUNITY RECONCILIATION ACT OF 1996: POLITICAL CONTEXT

A brief review of the context in which the welfare reform hearings and debates occurred provides the background necessary to understand the force of the depictions in the hearings and debates. Political interests were perhaps the largest factor in instigating welfare reform efforts in the 1990s, reforms that culminated in PRWORA. In an interview with the author on March 19, 1999, Ron Haskins, Staff Director for the Subcommittee on Human Resources of the House Committee on Ways and Means, revealed that Republican leaders were mindful of welfare's paramount importance as a key political issue and they carefully planned a strategy to ensure a conservative policy victory. The seeds for the Republican position can be found in what Haskins referred to as the first central Republican educational document on welfare, a paper entitled "Moving Ahead: How America Can Reduce Poverty Through Work." Produced in July 1992 by Republican members of the Human Resources Subcommittee including representatives E. Clay Shaw (FL), Nancy L. Johnson (CT), and Fred Grandy (IA), this document served as the basis for a systematic education campaign to inform key legislators about welfare reform issues and concerns. Haskins explained that a major key to winning the welfare reform debate was to ensure that a core "A-team" of Republicans knew the arguments and research that informed the Republican welfare philosophy. In addition to the authors of "Moving Ahead," key Republican leaders included, among others, Missouri Representative James Talent, Pennsylvania Senator Rick Santorum, Texas Representative Tom DeLay, and Arkansas Representative Y. Tim Hutchinson.

As they prepared to control the House of Representatives, Republicans organized several welfare reform task forces and devised several welfare reform proposals grounded in the 1992 "Moving Ahead" document. Similar in many respects, all of the proposals continued a trend of decreased federal involvement in welfare policy and increased state control over public welfare. Reflecting growing public hostility toward welfare, the proposals further stressed work requirements (rather than social services or education) as the principal vehicle for leaving welfare and instituted strict regulatory measures designed to reform welfare recipients. What was significant about these proposals and task force efforts, noted Haskins, was that they allowed the Republican party to build solid relationships with various constituencies and to test the conservative and moderate limits of welfare

policy carefully, thereby ensuring support from the greatest number of both Democrats and Republicans.

Meanwhile, in an attempt to keep his campaign promise to "end welfare as we know it," President Clinton introduced the "Work and Responsibility Act of 1994" consisting of four main goals: 1) limit welfare receipt to two years, after which time recipients would be required to work; 2) increase child support enforcement; 3) reduce teenage pregnancy; and 4) assist welfare recipients in finding employment through provision of education, child care, and job training (Abramovitz 1996, 361; Cammisa 1998, 64–65, 72).[3] When Clinton's proposal reached the Republican dominated Congress, it was rejected. Instead, Congress offered another proposal that extended and incorporated some elements from Clinton's plan. Republicans outlined this proposal in their *Contract with America*, promising to balance the budget, reduce taxes, and cut social welfare programs (Axinn and Levin 1997, 305; Cammisa 1998, 65). The Republican's proposals, both vetoed by President Clinton on December 6, 1995[,] and January 9, 1996, called for a number of controversial work and family regulations.[4] These requirements included a ban on the use of federal funds for unmarried mothers under age 18, strict paternity penalties, and a family cap (i.e., cutting off AFDC benefits to families who had more children while on welfare) (Abramovitz 1996, 363; Axinn and Levin 1997, 314; Cammisa 1998, 73). A key difference between the Republican bills and Clinton's 1994 proposal was that the Republican versions ended entitlements through a block grant. Under AFDC, any family that met eligibility requirements was entitled to receive benefits. In contrast, block grants capped federal spending and allowed states to deny aid to individuals who otherwise met eligibility requirements.

The National Governor's Association (NGA), an interest group comprised of the 50 state governors, also offered suggestions on welfare reform. The NGA convened in February of 1996, endorsed block grants, and proposed welfare reforms including cuts in the food stamp, child nutrition, and job programs. The NGA proposal was highly influential because it represented a bipartisan effort, a compromise between both Democratic and Republican governors. In addition, the NGA proposal reflected the views of the governors who would be responsible for running any state controlled welfare block grant.

Legislators debated each of these proposals to varying degrees in a series of hearings and debates held from 1992 to 1996, the majority of which occurred during the Republican dominated 104th Congress. Haskins explained that several benefits accrued to the Republicans during the hearings because of their majority status. For example, Republican leaders were able to hand select the majority of witnesses and determine the order and structure of the hearings panels. Not surprisingly then, a large number of witnesses within the hearings and debates affiliated with groups supportive of the Republican platform including religious organizations and conservative institutions such as the American Enterprise Institute (Douglas Besharov, Marvin H. Kosters, Charles Murray), Heritage Foundation (Robert Rector, Kate Walsh O'Beirne), Christian Coalition (Heidi Stirrup), Traditional Values Coalition (Andrea Sheldon), American Fathers Coalition (David Burgess, Bill Harrington, Murray Steinberg), and Hudson Institute (Anna Kondratas, Michael Horowitz).[5] Commenting on the force of conservative scholars in the hearings process, Michigan Representative Dave Camp (R) observed:

> With the help of prominent conservative thinkers, several of whom will testify today, Republicans have succeeded in drawing the Nation's attention to the magnitude of the illegitimacy crisis. Millions of Americans now understand that out-of-wedlock births are at the center of a tangle of social pathologies, including school dropout, welfare use, unemployment, drug addictions and crime. (House Committee on Ways and Means, 20 January 1995, 134)

Three important consequences resulted from Republican structuring of the hearings. First, in selecting witnesses whom they knew would support the Republican welfare reforms, Republicans created a group of texts with constitutive force (Charland 1987). Specifically,

these texts invited legislators to act on evidence presented in the hearings and debates in ways that benefited both the legislators' and the party's public record. Second, Republicans were also able to mitigate the force of opposing testimony that threatened to damage the Republican position. As Haskins pointed out, Republicans could "bury" strong Democratic witnesses in panels with less significant testimony and during unfavorable times. Third, witness selection and panel structuring clearly facilitated Republican leaderships' use of the hearings as a critical venue for presenting their views and educating other Republican members on the party policy platform.

The result of the hearings and debates over the governors' proposals, state initiatives, the *Contract with America,* and Clinton's 1994 proposal was the Personal Responsibility and Work Opportunity Reconciliation Act of 1996 (Axinn and Levin 1997, 315–16; Cammisa 1998, 61–122). Essentially, PRWORA promised to decrease welfare spending by $55 billion over five years, limit welfare receipt to two years after which time recipients must work, establish a lifetime limit of five years on welfare, and allocate a lump-sum payment (block grant) to states to create state-based welfare programs. This block grant became known as Temporary Assistance to Needy Families (TANF) and replaced Aid to Families with Dependent Children (AFDC).

★ DEPICTIONS OF WELFARE RECIPIENTS IN THE HEARINGS AND DEBATES

With this historical context in mind, I now turn to an examination of three rhetorical depictions of welfare recipients emergent in the hearings and debates: the misfortunate, the feckless, and the young. Ultimately, these depictions formed the basis upon which legislators constructed the Personal Responsibility and Work Opportunity Reconciliation Act of 1996.

The Misfortunate

The typical narrative of the misfortunate welfare recipient constructed in the hearings and debates is of a competent, able-bodied individual who expresses a strong desire to work, but who is unable to achieve the American dream of working for wages, largely due to the lack of living-wage job opportunities. The misfortunate poor, then, are those individuals who experience an unexpected misfortune or circumstance and require short-term assistance to stabilize their lives.

Many legislators and witnesses praise the abilities and talents of the misfortunate welfare recipient. For example, Robert Friedman, Chair and Founder of the Corporation for Enterprise Development, argues that "Among the poor are people of considerable talent and energy whose futures are limited by lack of opportunity not lack of capacity" (Senate Finance Committee, 20 March 1995, 47; House Committee on Ways and Means, 2 February 1995, 1191). Attesting to the hardworking entrepreneurial spirit of welfare recipients, John Else, President of the Institute for Social and Economic Development, explains: "Welfare recipients have demonstrated their ability to achieve what everybody considers the American dream, owning a business, sustaining their own lives through that business." As support for his claim, Else offers several powerful anecdotes, one about a welfare recipient who could do profit and loss statements that an MBA graduate could not do (Senate Committee on Appropriations, 9 December 1994, 36–38). As these passages demonstrate, many participants in the hearings and debates believe that some welfare recipients are intelligent, industrious, responsible individuals capable of professional achievements.

Acknowledging the existence of a capable class of people who share mainstream American values of family and work and who still need welfare requires an external explanation for the source of failure. In the hearings and debates, witnesses and legislators account for any difficulties misfortunate welfare recipients face in terms of unanticipated circumstances outside of their control such as personal disasters or poor economic conditions (e.g., job lay-offs, unemployment rates, unequal job distribution). For example, Vermont Senator and Chair of the Committee on Agriculture, Nutrition and Forestry Patrick G. Leahy (D) explains: "There are too many Americans today that are just a step away from government assistance. You are suddenly unemployed; you have a serious illness; or you are faced with a natural disaster, as we saw in California. That is all it takes. Americans cannot anticipate the emergency situations where their families will suddenly be in need" (Senate Committee on Agriculture, Nutrition, and Forestry, 2 February 1994, 2). Former South Carolina Governor Carroll Campbell adds later in the hearing process:

> My mother grew up in Youngstown, Ohio, which for generations was a thriving community. People had good jobs in the steel mills. Then in the early 1980's, the auto industry went through terrible circumstances. There is now no functioning steel mill in Youngstown, Ohio. There are families who, for a couple of generations, relied on those steel mills for their livelihood and could have good jobs without college education, sometimes without even a high school education, and could support their families. Those kind of folks need our help, as well, when we are looking at a welfare reform measure. (Senate Committee on Governmental Affairs, 25 January 1995, 53–54)

Here legislators note that all American families, even hardworking, law-abiding families are subject to adverse circumstances and may require temporary aid. Because these passages all blame unanticipated circumstances for the welfare recipient's current poverty state, the statements preserve faith in the power of the American dream. In other words, all able-bodied people who work hard can succeed with limited temporary public assistance to alleviate short-term need.

The legislators' emphasis on equal opportunity and the similarities between all Americans frequently overlooks the importance of racial, ethnic, class, or gender differences. For example, in one hearing, Vermont Governor Howard Dean concludes his remarks by claiming that: "The colors of peoples' skins may be a little bit different, but poverty is poverty wherever it is and we have the same kinds of problems that everybody else does" (Senate Committee on Finance, 18 January 1994, 22). Representative John Ensign (R-NV) adds later in the hearing process: "We have to eliminate looking at race or religion, for example, and provide for all people that are economically disadvantaged, the incentives for getting off welfare. . . . You know, poverty knows no creed or race" (House Committee on Ways and Means, 2 February 1995, 985–86). Given all of the evidence that suggests that welfare recipients are just like other hardworking Americans, it would be easy to conclude along with Representative E. Clay Shaw (R-FL) that: "the problem with welfare is not the people who are in it. . . . The problem is a failed system that we risk leaving in place" (House Committee on Ways and Means, 20 February 1996, 5).

Despite acknowledgment of misfortune, however, most witnesses and legislators adamantly maintain that in the United States, self-improvement is possible through initiative, perseverance, and hard work without any public assistance. No one captures this enduring faith in the American dream better than Lawrence E. Townsend, Jr., Director of the Riverside County Department of Public Social Services in California, who testifies that "The old-fashioned work ethic that made America great was if you work hard, show your stuff, be reliable, eventually you will prosper. In our country we have found this still to be true" (House Committee on Ways and Means, 23 January 1995, 303). An exchange between Louisiana Representative Jim McCrery (R) and welfare recipient Cheri Honkala, Executive Director of the Pennsylvania Welfare Rights Union, suggests how powerful the belief in hard effort as a solution to misfortune is. Honkala explains her plight in plaintive terms to critique welfare reform proposals that include a time limit: "But what about people like me that have been on and off of public assistance and would be slated to be cut off, even though I have tried to look everywhere possible for employment? What would I do with my child?" Mr. McCrery replies "we are counting on you finding a job." More forcefully invoking this notion of the misfortunate welfare recipient who actively seeks employment and cannot acquire living-wage labor, Honkala retorts: "But I have been on national television saying I need a job, and I would think by now, if there was a job out there, that I would have gotten it by now." In one of the most glaring examples of faith in the power of the individual to rise about poverty through

self-help, Mr. McCrery ends the discussion by resolutely insisting "Well, I submit to you that there are jobs out there and I am hopeful that you will find another job" (House Committee on Ways and Means, 2 February 1995, 1115). Such testimony seemingly contradicts the notion that some people may require aid to succeed.

Clearly, legislators and witnesses craft an image of the misfortunate poor as an individual who is committed to the family and work ethic and suffers a short-lived calamity. Despite the recognition that some people are temporarily poor, faith in the power of individuals to overcome adversity through hard work leads most legislators and witnesses to express strong reservations about the misfortunate poor. As a result, legislators become increasingly skeptical of the misfortunate welfare recipient paradigm and turn to other depictions of welfare recipients as feckless and young to account for persistent poverty.

The Feckless

A second depiction of welfare recipients as feckless acquires a dominant voice throughout the hearings and debates. Whereas structural and systemic challenges impede the misfortunate welfare recipient from achieving success, poor values and choices prevent the feckless welfare recipient from rising out of poverty. In direct contrast to the misfortunate paradigm where some legislators perceive the system as broken and in need of repair, in the feckless welfare recipient framework, the recipients themselves are broken and need to be "made whole." Typically then, legislators and witnesses characterize what I am labeling the feckless welfare recipient as an able-bodied female who is undeserving of public assistance because she refuses to work, engages in criminal activities (e.g., drug abuse, illegal food stamp trade), and makes poor choices with regard to her personal life (e.g., relationships and parenting). As a result, the feckless welfare recipient relies on public assistance for years and bears children who follow suit, thereby perpetuating multi-generational welfare dependency. Two central features mark the depiction of the feckless welfare recipient: (1) failure to accept and practice key values and (2) inability to make sound choices.

According to legislators and witnesses, welfare recipients' lack of values accounts for their welfare dependence. Former welfare recipient Pam Harris White explains that "a lack of values and the decline in the morals and religious beliefs" are linked to welfare receipt at "high cost to both the person and to society" (House Committee on Ways and Means, 20 January 1995, 179). Kay Coles James, Secretary for the Virginia Department of Health and Human Resources, explains: "Poverty is more than the lack of material things. It is the lack of personal fortitude and in many cases social stability" (House Committee on Ways and Means, 9 August 1994, 983). Perhaps the most damning evidence comes from Robert Rector, Senior Policy Analyst at the Heritage Foundation, who categorizes welfare recipients as behaviorally poor charging that their poverty "essentially stem(s) from moral character": "The plight of the underclass is rooted in behavior. . . . It is a chasm of values and behavior which today separates the underclass and the chronically poor from the American middle class" (House Committee on Economic and Educational Opportunities, 18 January 1995, 17, 27; Senate Committee on Finance, 9 March 1995, 15). Relying on witness testimony in the debates, Senator Dan Coats (R-IN) elaborates: "the basic problem lies in the realm of values and character, and those values are shaped, particularly in early childhood, by increasing cultural standards. . . . People are not pure economic beings analyzing costs and benefits. We are moral beings. We make choices that reflect our values. Incentives are not irrelevant but it is ultimately our beliefs and habits I think that determine our future" ("Family Self-Sufficiency Act," *Congressional Record*, 13 September 1995, S13498). According to this testimony, any decision a welfare recipient makes (to remain a single parent, to decline a job offer, to buy non-nutritious foods) is merely a reflection of her lack of values and therefore at base, a poor choice.

A second characterization of welfare recipients in the hearings and debates is of welfare recipients as making poor life choices concerning issues as varied as education, training, and alcohol use. Representative Bill Emerson (R-MO) asserts: "I'm not sure that a lot of these folks . . . know what the right choices for them are. I think they need some counseling and advice to go after the right choices" (House Select Committee on Hunger, 9 April 1992, 31). These poor choices, legislators explain, lead welfare recipients to indulge in a whole host of intergenerational social ills including crime, illiteracy, disease, substance abuse, and sexual promiscuity. Ultimately, by linking welfare receipt to social pathologies, welfare recipients, like pathological diseases, are subject to annihilation (House Committee on Ways and Means, 13 January 1995, 84). As Senator Byron L. Dorgan (D-ND) expresses in a September 7, 1995 debate: "We must eliminate those people for whom welfare has become an institutionalized way of life" ("Family Self-Sufficiency Act," *Congressional Record*, 7 September 1995, S12759). Statements linking welfare recipients with a variety of social pathologies also call into question the ability of welfare recipients to make sound choices. As a result of making poor choices, welfare recipients, legislators argue, possess poor education and skill levels, abuse illegal substances, and participate in criminal activities.

Unskilled and Uneducated. For a variety of reasons, many welfare recipients are described as unable to obtain the educational competence and skills necessary for success in life. Oftentimes, welfare recipients are depicted as lacking basic employment life skills. Lawrence Townsend, Jr., Director of the Riverside County Department of Public Social Services in California explains that welfare recipients have trouble with "basic" skills such as "setting the alarm clock; getting to work on time; accepting supervision; learning to complete tasks reliably; getting along with coworkers; and, dressing appropriately for work" (Senate Committee on Finance, 20 March 1995, 83). Representative Michael Castle (R-DE) remarks that many recipients "don't have transportation, they don't know how to go about it, they don't show up on time, you have to work with them" (House Committee on Agriculture, 8 February 1995, 129).

In addition to lacking basic skills, according to depictions, most welfare recipients have less than an eighth grade education so they are often functionally illiterate. For example, Sheri Hernandez, Case Manager with Promise Jobs in Davenport, Iowa[,] describes a typical welfare recipient as a woman with "five children, all under the age of 5," "no driver's license," and an eighth grade education (Senate Committee on Appropriations, 9 December 1994, 30–32). Similarly, Nancy Ebb, Senior Staff Attorney for the Children's Defense Fund, states that "the average young AFDC mother has reading skills at or below the sixth grade level" (House Committee on Ways and Means, 11 March 1993, 88). Testimony by welfare recipients occasionally reinforces these depictions of the illiterate, uneducated, unskilled welfare mother. For example, in one hearing, Irma Alvarado, an El Salvadoran participant in California Greater Avenues to Independence (GAIN), relates: "I have three children, my husband left me and I had to apply for welfare. . . . When I left El Salvador, I . . . spoke very little English." Alvarado adds that in the United States she "finished the sixth level of study" but was unable to complete high school courses because her welfare benefits expired (House Committee on Education and Labor, 28 October 1994, 9–11). These and other statements create an image of welfare recipients as uneducated and incapable of enacting basic behaviors necessary to find and keep a job.

Welfare Recipients as Substance Abusers.
According to witnesses and legislators, another example of how welfare recipients demonstrate poor choices is by abusing drugs and alcohol. William J. Bennett, Co-Director of Empower America, surmises that "You will not get ahold of the welfare problem unless you get ahold of the open air drug markets and crackhouses" (House Committee on Ways and Means, 20 January 1995, 156). Resident Scholar at the American Enterprise Institute for Public Policy Research, Douglas Besharov, explains that the increase in the African American out-of-wedlock birth rate from 1985 to 1990 may be associated with drug use: "There are many explanations for that increase. My own, by the way, is that this is the effect of crack cocaine on our inner cities. If you look at where those babies are being born, you see a real connection there" (Senate Committee on Finance,

14 March 1995, 3). Representative Barbara B. Kennelly (D-CT) makes a strikingly similar statement when she asserts: "Out to the street when those drug dealers are there. That is when impregnation often happens, when those people are around" (House Committee on Ways and Means, 20 January 1995, 170). These statements create an image of welfare recipients as drug dealers and users who are ignorant and incompetent. Moreover, the passages cast doubt on the ability of welfare recipients to make sound judgments.

Welfare Recipients as Criminals.
A final way the hearings and debates construct welfare recipients as making poor personal choices is to portray these recipients as fraudulent criminals. This perception of welfare recipients as taking advantage of the welfare system results in referring to welfare recipients as "training junkies" and "welfare cheats" who "are just playing the system" and are "scamming us" through "padded" claims and "double dip[ping]" (House Committee on Ways and Means, 9 August 1994, 970; House Committee on Agriculture, 14 February 1995, 525; House Committee on Ways and Means, 2 February 1995, 1294; Senate Committee on Agriculture, Nutrition, and Forestry, 2 February 1994, 11).

The congressional hearings and debates carefully describe the various types of fraud in which welfare recipients engage including lying about their circumstances, trafficking food stamps, bearing children to gain additional welfare benefits, and claiming benefits in two states simultaneously. In all cases the individuals depicted are deceiving the system either intentionally or unintentionally to receive higher payments. Representative E. de la Garza (D-TX) expresses this viewpoint when he notes that over the past year, AFDC overpayments that were the result of caseworker errors were $763 million, recipient unintentional errors were $637 million, and recipient intentional errors were $424 million (House Committee on Agriculture, 8 February 1995, 149). Many legislators also charge welfare recipients with food stamp fraud. Representative Ron Wyden (D-OR) speaks about how welfare recipients frequently trade food stamps for illegal items. "Food stamps," he notes, "are used as an underground currency. They are traded for drugs. They are traded for weapons. All kinds of illegal activity is essentially fueled with food stamps" (House Committee on Agriculture, 14 February 1995, 477).

Others who testify accuse welfare mothers of having many children to increase their monthly welfare payments. Representative E. Clay Shaw (R-FL) explains that "these people that are on welfare aren't stupid. They certainly can understand that there is going to be a certain amount paid for them, paid to them once they have children out of wedlock" (House Committee on Ways and Means, 26 July 1994, 397). Representative Jim Talent (R-MO) concludes: "I think that the fact that the out-of-wedlock birth rate is so much greater among lower-income Americans . . . that it [welfare] is a financial incentive, because they mean more to somebody coming from a lower-income background" (House Committee on Ways and Means, 27 July 1994, 553). In these examples, those who testify highlight how women on welfare use payments to fuel illegal activity and simply bear one child after another in order to receive higher monthly checks.

Many of the depictions also accuse welfare recipients of claiming benefits in multiple states at the same time or of "shopping" around to locate a home in a high paying welfare state. Representative Dick Zimmer (R-NJ) reports that claiming benefits in more than one state is a serious national problem. He notes that the some welfare recipients "were collecting welfare in New Jersey, going to New York, establishing themselves as homeless in New York, and collecting benefits from both States" ("Personal Responsibility Act of 1995," *Congressional Record*, 22 March 1995, H3502). In a closely related version of the multiple-state claiming scheme, some representatives suggest that welfare recipients desire to avoid work so desperately that they identify states with the highest benefit ratios and then relocate to those regions. Representative Michael N. Castle (R-DE) expresses such a fear when he notes that a problem with raising benefit levels in some states and not others will result in a "migration of welfare recipients from one State to another" (House Committee on Agriculture, 8 February 1995, 128). Such depictions create an image of

undeserving welfare recipients unjustifiably receiving welfare benefits, sometimes not just once but twice, at the expense of hardworking taxpaying citizens.

Throughout the hearings and debates, witnesses and legislators explicitly and implicitly link the feckless welfare recipient paradigm to poor women and minority groups, chiefly African-Americans and Hispanics, an historically consistent and powerful linkage of minorities to undeserving welfare status. In contrast to the misfortunate welfare recipient paradigm, where legislators and witnesses de-emphasize differences associated with race, ethnicity, gender, and class in order to highlight the similarities between welfare recipients and non-welfare hardworking American families, the feckless welfare recipient paradigm fuels stereotypes of poor minority women who cannot achieve the American dream without assistance, frequently take advantage of the welfare system, and violate mainstream middle-class American values. For example, Representative Floyd Flake (D-NY) clarifies: "I am saying that at some point, we as African-American people are going to have to deal with the reality that there are some problems endemic to our communities and to our people. . . . Our minorities, and principally African Americans often need extra help" (House Committee on Ways and Means, 27 July 1994, 569). Missouri Senator John C. Danforth (R) explains why African American welfare recipients may need this assistance: "I have worried about the problem of welfare, . . . most particularly, the problem of black Americans who are disproportionately among the poor, among the unemployed who disproportionately go to schools that are not very good, that are from families that are dysfunctional, that have very few activities, other than just to pour into the street at the end of the school day" (Senate Committee on Finance, 25 February 1994, 72). Frustrated by the persistent and what he terms "false" link between welfare and race, Dr. Ronald Walters, Chairman of the Department of Political Science at Howard University, comments that "with the juxtaposition of RACE and welfare dependency in the public imagination, there has been a return to the value system of the 'undeserving poor' and images of the laggard, lazy dull welfare recipient on the 'dole' who deserves the punitive attitude of the elite visited upon them because they constitute a drag upon the economy and a blot upon the moral image of the nation" (House Committee on Government Operations, 10 March 1994, 83). By linking welfare to lower-income minority women as well as to major social pathologies including crime, drug abuse, and violence, legislators encourage people to view these groups with suspicion. In addition, because the depictions link welfare to problems surrounding the poor choices of lower-income and minority individuals, the depictions stratify and cleave society along racial, gender, and class lines.

The Young

The final major depiction of welfare recipients centers on welfare mothers as predominantly immature youth. Expressing ambivalence about the category of young welfare recipients, representatives are unsure whether these teenagers are deserving or undeserving of aid. Neither completely deserving or undeserving, the juvenile welfare recipient is constructed as somewhere in between the misfortunate and feckless welfare recipient categories. Clearly legislators and witnesses are sympathetic to young welfare recipients and affirm their status of welfare mothers under the age of eighteen as children who are unable, as legal minors, to make adult decisions. Calling attention to the immaturity of young welfare recipients, Wisconsin Representative Peter W. Barca (D) notes that "many of these kids still need parenting themselves" (House Committee on Ways and Means, 28 July 1994, 615). Eloise Anderson, Director of California's Department of Social Services, explains: "But we don't consider them [welfare mothers] women. We consider them girls" (House Committee on Ways and Means, 12 January 1995, 674). In fact, many legislative participants refer to welfare recipients as teenagers and girls. For example, Representative Jim Ramstad (R-MN) suggests legislators discuss how to "reverse this alarming trend in teenage girls having babies?" (House Committee on Ways and Means, 10 January 1995, 103). One indication of the power of the construction of welfare recipients as youth is the fact that Congress held several special welfare

hearings solely dedicated to the issue of teenage pregnancy.

In addition to being young, these welfare recipients are also depicted as victims of their upbringing. As Representative Eva M. Clayton (D-NC) explains: "Teenage pregnancy is just one marker of growing up poor and poorly nurtured, both physically and emotionally, I would say" (House Committee on Ways and Means, 12 March 1996, 17). Senator David Pryor (D-AR) reinforces in the debates that "teens from poor and educationally disadvantaged families are more likely to become pregnant than those from more affluent and highly educated parents" ("Family Self-Sufficiency Act," *Congressional Record*, 14 September 1995, S13601). Thus, according to those who testify, some welfare teen mothers are predisposed to bearing out-of-wedlock children due to insufficient parental guidance and instability at home.

Teenagers are also depicted in the congressional proceedings as victims of rape and incest. For example, Christopher Shays (R-CT), Chair of the Subcommittee on Human Resources and Intergovernmental Relations, explains: "[A]dolescent girls need our protection and our guidance. Their cry for help is made even more poignant by recent studies concluding that adult men father more than half the children born to 15- to 17-year-old mothers" (House Government Reform and Oversight Committee, 30 April 1996, 1). Senator Joseph Lieberman (D-CT) adds: "A 1992 sampling of 500 teen mothers revealed that two-thirds had histories of sexual abuse with adult men averaging age 27" ("Personal Responsibility, Work Opportunity, and Medicaid Restructuring Act of 1996," *Congressional Record*, 19 July 1996, S8368). These statements capture legislator sympathy for young recipients who bear children as a result of circumstances beyond their control.

Despite acknowledgment of the immaturity of young welfare recipients growing up in undesirable and abusive circumstances, qualities that seem to warrant public assistance, witnesses and legislators also note that young welfare recipients frequently share some characteristics with the feckless welfare recipient. More specifically, legislators fault the young welfare recipient with making poor choices. For example, Professor

Rebecca A. Maynard explains that teens are susceptible to out of wedlock pregnancies and subsequent welfare dependence because of the "disorganization and impulsiveness that characterizes the lives of many of these young, largely poor, teenagers," "poor counseling regarding the side effects of various contraceptives," and "unwillingness on the part of many of the males to cooperate with contraceptive use, at least to do so consistently" (Senate Committee on Finance, 14 March 1995, 7). Michael D. Tanner, Director of Health and Welfare Studies at the Cato Institute in Washington[,] D.C., adds that the fact that teenagers do not find bearing children out-of-wedlock problematic indicates poor values: "[T]here was a study in Philadelphia where they asked inner city teenagers, would having a baby be a major crisis in YOUR life, and found 60 percent saying, no. . . . As long as that is the predominant attitude among poor inner city teenagers, you are going to have an explosion in illegitimacy" (Senate Committee on Finance, 9 March 1995, 17). Further, like feckless welfare recipients, young welfare recipients also become associated with a variety of social ills including gangs, drugs, crime, and violence. Representative Jim Talent (R-MO) explains: "These teen moms are children themselves, often living in drug- and gang-infested neighborhoods with no family to speak of" (House Committee on Ways and Means, 30 January 1995, 532). Many of these depictions liken the young and feckless welfare recipient as individuals who make poor choices that have profound consequences for themselves and for society.

★ THE INFLUENCE OF DEPICTIONS ON WELFARE POLICY

Depictions of welfare recipients as misfortunate, feckless, and young clearly influence policy proposals and the Personal Responsibility and Work Opportunity Reconciliation Act of 1996. As discussed earlier, factors such as partisan politics and negotiations among legislators and special interest groups influenced legislative outcomes. Nevertheless, as is evident in the following section, the link between the depictions and corresponding legislation also underscores the significance of language in shaping policy change.

Policy Initiatives Based on the Misfortunate Welfare Recipient Depiction

Reflecting the construction of the misfortunate welfare recipient as a capable, talented, able-bodied individual who is committed to hard work and family and prevented from achieving her full potential due to temporary misfortune beyond her control, PRWORA contains a provision for Individual Development Accounts (IDAs). Essentially, IDAs are incentive-based funds designed to help recipients save money for homes, education, and businesses. Throughout the hearings and debates several witnesses attest to the merits of IDAs. For example, Senator Dan Coats (R-IN) discusses the Assets for Independence Amendment, claiming "In some respects, IDA's are like IRA's for the working poor. . . . The individual or family deposits whatever they can save—typically $5 to $20 a month—in the account. The sponsoring organization matches that deposit with funds provided by local churches and service organizations" ("Personal Responsibility, Work Opportunity, and Medicaid Restructuring Act of 1996," *Congressional Record,* 19 July 1996, S8368–S8369). Under the Temporary Assistance for Need Families Block Grant, STATES may use a portion of their grant to establish IDAs for individuals to accumulate funds for any qualified purpose such as post-secondary educational expenses, first home purchase, and business capitalization (*Personal Responsibility and Work Opportunity Reconciliation Act, Statutes at Large* 110 (1996): 2125–27; "Family Self-Sufficiency Act," *Congressional Record,* 6 September 1995, S126730).

The inclusion of asset-building provision in the 1996 welfare reform bill attests to the relative power of the construction of the misfortunate welfare recipient as a capable and responsible individual. By encouraging ownership of property, IDAs reinforce capitalist and work ethic ideologies and affirm the historical importance of property in America as a precursor to participation in American socio-political life. Still, the fact that IDAs are the only major misfortunate welfare recipient driven solution apparent in

PRWORA may reflect legislator skepticism of this paradigm. Legislators instead endorse numerous policy initiatives consistent with feckless and young conceptions of welfare recipients, perhaps indicating legislator preference for these accounts of welfare dependence.

Policy Initiatives Arising from the Feckless Welfare Recipient Paradigm

The force of the feckless welfare recipient constructions is clearly manifest in PRWORA. For example, constructions of welfare recipients as lacking in values and morals and proposals designed to reinforce those values encourage legislators to view religious organizations as a main solution to the welfare problem. Basically, the Act authorizes STATES to contract with religious, charitable, and private organizations to supply social services to welfare recipients (*Personal Responsibility and Work Opportunity Reconciliation Act. Statutes at Large* 110 (1996): 2161–62). In addition, PRWORA continues to reflect the construction of an unskilled, feckless welfare recipient, providing for work activities that include "job search and job readiness assistance," "vocational educational training (not to exceed 12 months)," and "job skills training directly related to employment" (*Personal Responsibility and Work Opportunity Reconciliation Act, Statutes at Large* 110 (1996): 2133). While the thrust of the Act is to encourage work activities, the legislation nevertheless reflects constructions of the feckless and young welfare recipients who may not be equipped to work due to lack of skills and training.

PRWORA also validates the construction of welfare recipients as drug users by containing provisions that allow states to require individuals to undergo substance abuse treatment. A statement by Representative Gary A. Franks (R-CT) powerfully illustrates the influence of depictions emergent in the hearings and debates on the resulting legislation. Franks testifies:

> Today I would like to talk about one bill that would deal with a debit card, H.R. 4764. Mr. Chairman, I strongly believe that we should take cash out of our welfare system and replace welfare checks with a debit card. This would give us as taxpayers an accounting of all dollars spent by a welfare recipient. However, I do recognize that there may be a need to allow a small amount of cash for incidental items but I would hope that the vast majority of welfare funds would be dispensed via a debit card. . . . I believe that billions of taxpayers' dollars intended for families with dependent children are ending up in the hands of drug dealers via the purchase of drugs by some welfare recipients. . . . In Chicago, we all read how 20 people were living in a 2-bedroom apartment with the 4 adults receiving approximately $4,500 in welfare cash. It was alleged that all four adults were drug users. Part of their $4,500 was going to support their alleged drug habits, not going to supporting their children. . . . but we cannot have a card system that would allow welfare recipients to draw out their funds in the form of cash. That defeats the purpose of having an accounting of the taxpayers' funds and, thus, under the administration's plan, recipients would still be able to buy illegal drugs with their welfare money. (House Committee on Ways and Means, 28 July 1994, 596; House Committee on Ways and Means, 2 February 1995, 795)

The reference to the Chicago incident, which occurs in several places in the hearings and debates,[6] provides a clear image of welfare recipients, a construction that obviously warrants Franks' support of an amendment directed toward drug addicted welfare recipients (House Committee on Ways and Means, 30 January 1995, 534). Following this lead, a section in PRWORA entitled "Sanctioning for Testing Positive for Controlled Substances," allows STATES to condition welfare receipt on testing negative for controlled substances (*Personal Responsibility and Work Opportunity Reconciliation Act, Statutes at Large* 110 (1996): 2141, 2278). Other PRWORA provisions deny assistance to individuals convicted of "any offense which is classified as a felony by the law of the jurisdictions involved and which has [as] an element the possession, use, or distribution of a controlled substance" (*Personal Responsibility and Work Opportunity Reconciliation Act, Statutes at Large* 110 (1996): 2180).

Further reflecting the construction of welfare recipients as criminals, PRWORA contains many provisions that deny assistance to felons, parole violators, and others engaged in criminal behaviors such as trafficking food stamps, bearing children to gain additional welfare funds, and claiming benefits in multiple states simultaneously. For instance, the Act doubles penalties for violating food stamp requirements (*Personal Responsibility and Work Opportunity Reconciliation Act, Statutes at Large* 110 (1996), 2314). PRWORA also requires that States must demonstrate "Certification of standards and procedures to ensure against program fraud and abuse," and that states must deny "assistance for fugitive felons and probation and parole violators" (*Personal Responsibility and Work Opportunity Reconciliation Act, Statutes at Large* 110 (1996): 2115, 2138, 2185). Indeed, entire sections of PRWORA deal with the "Treatment of Prisoners," "Expanded Criminal Forfeiture for Violations," "Elimination of Housing Assistance with Respect to Fugitive Felons and Probation and Parole Violators" (*Personal Responsibility and Work Opportunity Reconciliation Act, Statutes at Large* 110 (1996): 2186–87, 2334, 2348–49).

The construction of welfare mothers as bearing additional children to increase their welfare benefits also influences the Act in a subtle but important way. Previous bill proposals included a highly contentious and publicized family cap designed to limit payments to women who bear children while on welfare. Although the family cap does not appear in the 1996 Personal Responsibility and Work Opportunity Reconciliation Act by specific reference, the TANF block grant contains two significant sections that implicitly encourage States to implement a family cap or child exclusion provision in their welfare bills. First, under TANF, STATES do not need to apply for a waiver in order to implement a family cap. As a result, the fourteen STATES that enforced a family cap at the time of TANF's passage can continue to implement this cap and receive federal funding (*Personal Responsibility and Work Opportunity Reconciliation Act, Statutes at Large* 110 (1996): 2157). Moreover, TANF may actually encourage STATES to continue such waivers with a provision for "Secretarial Encouragement of Current Waivers," which says that "The Secretary shall encourage any State operating a waiver described in

subsection (a) to continue the waiver and to evaluate, using random sampling and other characteristics of accepted scientific evaluations, the result or effect of the waiver" (*Personal Responsibility and Work Opportunity Reconciliation Act, Statutes at Large 110* (1996): 2158). In addition, TANF makes the family cap attractive by promising five eligible states a share of $20,000,000 ($25 million if fewer than five eligible) for reducing out-of-wedlock births without a corresponding increase in abortion for fiscal years 1999, 2000, 2001, and 2002. (*Personal Responsibility and Work Opportunity Reconciliation Act, Statutes at Large 110* (1996): 2121–22. Although the exclusion waivers are more strict than prior policies, they respond to a growing social perception that the number of welfare mothers having many "illegitimate" children is a significant and costly problem.

Finally, perhaps in response to stories that welfare recipients migrate to higher benefit states, that PRWORA contains a provision expressly designed to discourage welfare recipients from migrating to STATES in order to claim higher benefits. For example, the Act asserts that states can deny "assistance for 10 years to a person found to have fraudulently misrepresented residence in order to obtain assistance in 2 or more states" (*Personal Responsibility and Work Opportunity Reconciliation Act, Statutes at Large 110* (1996): 2139, 2321; "Personal Responsibility Act of 1995," *Congressional Record,* 22 March 1995, H3453, H3497). In addition, PRWORA requires STATES to indicate whether and how the State intends to treat families who move from one state to another differently from families who currently reside in the state (*Personal Responsibility and Work Opportunity Reconciliation Act, Statutes at Large* 110 (1996): 2114, 2124).

Policy Initiatives Arising from the Young Welfare Recipient Paradigm

The depictions of the young welfare recipient and corresponding proposals also clearly influence PRWORA. Specifically, many provisions respond to the construction of welfare recipients as young, poorly nurtured, and victims of sexual abuse. For example, in the case of unmarried mothers under the age of eighteen, PRWORA includes a provision for second chance homes defined as programs that provide individuals "with a supportive and supervised living arrangement in which such individuals are required to learn parenting skills, including child development, family budgeting, health and nutrition, and other skills to promote their long-term economic independence and the well-being of their children" (*Personal Responsibility and Work Opportunity Reconciliation Act, Statutes at Large* 110 (1996): 2137). PRWORA also denies assistance to all teenage parents who are not living in an adult-supervised setting excepting those who have been "subjected to serious physical or emotional harm, sexual abuse, or exploitation" (*Personal Responsibility and Work Opportunity Reconciliation Act, Statutes at Large* 110 (1996): 2136). In the case of those exceptions, the states must "provide or assist the individual in locating, a second chance home, maternity home, or other appropriate adult-supervised supportive living arrangement" (*Personal Responsibility and Work Opportunity Reconciliation Act, Statutes at Large* 110 (1996): 2136). Finally, PRWORA also allows states to use funds provided to support a voucher system rather than to give cash aid to recipients (*Personal Responsibility and Work Opportunity Reconciliation Act, Statutes at Large* 110 (1996): 2351). The legislation responds to legislator uncertainty about whether youth are deserving or undeserving of aid. Provisions such as second chance homes are sympathetic to the needs of young teens for adult guidance while others such as denial of cash assistance reflect legislator skepticism of the young welfare recipient's tendency to act like feckless welfare recipients and misuse public assistance.

Further, PRWORA reads that STATES must provide evidence of how they are going to "prevent and reduce the incidence of out-of-wedlock pregnancies, with special emphasis on teenage pregnancies" (*Personal Responsibility and Work Opportunity Reconciliation Act, Statutes at Large* 110 (1996): 2113–14). To that end, PRWORA provides for the allocation of money to STATES for abstinence education. The law specifies that the purpose of such education is to teach people "that a mutually faithful monogamous relationship in context of marriage is the expected standard of human sexual activity," and that "sexual activity outside of the context of marriage is likely to have harmful psychological and physical effects," and "harmful consequences for the child, the child's parents, and society" (*Personal Responsibility and Work Opportunity Reconciliation Act, Statutes at Large* 110 (1996): 2354). The underlying rationale that informs these changes is that welfare parents are unable to provide their children with moral instruction. Because feckless welfare recipients are depicted as incompetent parents, ensuring that all children learn about when sexual activity, childbearing, and marriage are appropriate requires nationally supervised school programs.

Finally, depictions of young welfare recipients as victims of rape and abuse by older men rationalize legislation designed to reduce statutory rape and prosecute offenders more harshly. Specifically, in PRWORA, the Congress notes that "An effective strategy to combat teenage pregnancy must address the issues of male responsibility, including statutory rape culpability and prevention" (*Personal Responsibility and Work Opportunity Reconciliation Act, Statutes at Large* 110 (1996): 2111, 2349–50). Consequently, Sec. 402 dictates that STATES must include education and training on the problem of statutory rape as part of their family assistance plan (*Personal Responsibility and Work Opportunity Reconciliation Act, Statutes at Large* 110 (1996): 2114).

★ RHETORICAL IMPLICATIONS

As I have demonstrated throughout this paper, legislators and witnesses rhetorically construct three distinct depictions of welfare recipients—the misfortunate, the feckless, and the young—to account for the existence of poverty and welfare dependence in America. On a larger scale, this case study makes four important contributions to rhetorical theory and public policy.

First, this study challenges the liberatory and participatory functions of the narrative paradigm as conceived by Walter Fisher. Implying that audiences have the power to interpret and assess narratives, Fisher's narrative paradigm endows audiences with significant control in the creation of meaning. Fisher's insistence upon audiences' ability to judge a text critically based on its narrative rationality, however, discounts the power of discourse to shape and position audiences' understanding of their world in particular ways. Thus, while Fisher claims that "The sort of hierarchy condemned by the narrative praxis is the sort that is marked by the will to power, the kind of system in which elites struggle to dominate and to use the people for their own ends," this study suggests otherwise (1984, 9). An analysis of the congressional hearings and debates that led to the passage of PRWORA points to the power of some depictions to facilitate elite discourse and to exclude and delegitimize particular public voices.

Interestingly, the hearings appear to solicit a variety of opinions from interested citizens including clerics, social scientists, policy experts, and occasionally, former welfare recipients. Some hearings announcements also invite interested citizens to submit statements for inclusion in the public record. And, some hearings do include the testimony of unsolicited witnesses. This evidence seems to confirm Lloyd F. Bitzer's conclusion that "legislative bodies provide explicitly for the active participation of interested parties" (1987, 426).

Despite an apparent openness to the hearings, however, the legislative process possesses an elitist tenor. Because legislators exercise considerable control in selecting witnesses, most panels are comprised of invited witnesses. The written statements of other unsolicited individuals are appended to the printed public record, and rarely invoked in the actual proceedings. While witnesses who testify in the hearings represent a diverse demographic and professional group, almost all share similar views on welfare reform. Indeed, according to Human Resources Subcommittee Staff Director Ron Haskins, Republican staff invite people to testify because they know these witnesses hold similar beliefs. In so doing, they can promote Republican welfare strategies, educate their constituency, and lessen the force of oppositional testimony. Rather than bypassing elite audiences as Fisher would hope, this form of public moral argument thus privileges the interpretations of the elite audience of legislators who are able to invite witnesses, structure the hearings, evaluate the "narrative rationality"

of testimony, and develop policies in line with their agendas. As highly controlled, disciplined public conversations, the hearings and debates assume a Foucaultian (1972) quality. The Republican party largely determines who will speak and on what topic, and a select audience of legislators applies the tests of fidelity and coherence to the testimony.

Further, the hearings and debates can be considered elitist because they relegate welfare recipients to what Philip Wander terms the "Third Persona," or the audience negated by the discourse. Wander writes:

> 'being negated' includes not only being alienated through language—the 'it' that is the summation of all that you and I are told to avoid becoming, but also being negated in history, a being whose presence, though relevant to what is said, is negated through silence. The moral significance of being negated through what is and is not said reveals itself in all its anguish and confusion in context, in the world of affairs wherein certain individuals and groups are, through law, tradition, or prejudice, denied rights accorded to being commended or, measured against an ideal, to human beings. The objectification of certain individuals and groups discloses itself through what is and is not said about them and through actual conditions affecting their ability to speak for themselves. Operating through existing social, political, and economic arrangements, negation extends beyond the 'text' to include the ability to produce texts, to engage in discourse, to be heard in the public space. (210)

As I have demonstrated, throughout the hearings and debates, legislators and witnesses depict welfare recipients as enacting values antithetical to social ideals. Constructions of the feckless welfare recipient as immoral and incompetent and the young welfare recipient as immature and inexperienced create an image of welfare recipients as incapable of speaking wisely on the subject of welfare reform. These depictions in turn largely warrant the exclusion of welfare recipient testimony. In other words legislators construct welfare recipients as forfeiting their right to speak authoritatively on welfare, precisely because they are on welfare.

The introduction of any welfare recipient testimony on March 10, 1994, a full two years after the incipience of welfare reform hearings on March 25, 1992, provides some indication of the relative unimportance of welfare recipient testimony in the eyes of legislators. The few welfare recipient stories included in the hearings are largely those of the misfortunate welfare recipient, the individual who conforms to the family and work ethics and eventually succeeds. Importantly, in this case, the people who testify are typically *former* welfare recipients. Former welfare recipient testimony and legislator stories about welfare recipients whom they know give the illusion that welfare recipient voices are being heard in the hearings, when in fact others are speaking on behalf of recipient interests.

A second contribution of this study is that it provides insight into a process currently overlooked in studies of public moral argument and policymaking, and that is the role of depictions in policy formation. In so doing, this study contributes to a clearer understanding of the role and function of depictions in public moral argument. In his study of American views on welfare reform, Martin Gilens demonstrates that the public's perceptions "are influenced more by vivid examples than by statistical information, even if the evidentiary value of the statistical information is far higher" (1999, 206). Similarly, as this study on welfare reform suggests, social policy deliberations are anecdotal in nature because the depictions vivify problems that are difficult to quantify. Although they warn against the dangers inherent in basing public policy on depictions,[7] legislators prefer the depictions as evidence to warrant public policy changes because the depictions tap into deep cultural reservoirs.[8]

A third contribution of this study is that it responds to calls by communication and public policy scholars to use communication research as a vehicle for influencing public policy. For instance, noting that communication scholars have had little to say to public policy makers, David Docherty et al., in "Scholarship as Silence," urges communication scholars to become involved in policymaking, examine policy debates, and in general, investigate the relationship between an "institutionally based articulation of particular symbol systems and

the formation of public consciousness" (1993, 237, 233; Mueller 1995, 459; Noam 1993, 199–200). Understanding how policy develops from public discussion is a crucial step in being able to influence policymaking. Because this study views policy as emergent from congressional hearings and debates, it contributes to our understanding of the policy formation process.

Fourth, if as this case study suggests, representations of welfare recipients ultimately impact public policy decision-making, then on a practical level, public policy practitioners need to learn how to construct rhetorically attractive messages (narratives, arguments, depictions) that influence policymaking. This study implies that an understanding of rules and assumptions that currently guide welfare reform deliberations and reforms is a necessary precursor to informed and effective policymaking. Rhetorical critical methods are especially suited to uncovering the tensions inherent in discourse and how discourse works to sustain, challenge, and reform structural and power relations in various socio-historical contexts. Communication theorist Raymie McKerrow refers to this process as "critical rhetoric," and he outlines a strategy for unmasking the discourse rules and processes that govern who speaks, which topics are appropriate to address, and what counts as authoritative evidence (1989, 93). Using a similar approach, policy advocates can expose how the rules and assumptions that govern social policymaking influence legislative outcomes. Adopting a critical approach to the evidence and data that support depictions in legislative hearings and debates, prepares legislators, public policy advocates, and citizens to evaluate the arguments that warrant policy changes better.

Once policy advocates understand the complex discursive and social practices that inform current legislation, they can create compelling narratives and depictions to influence policy. For policymakers who desire to perpetuate the status quo, creating powerful depictions means constructing representations that reinforce dominant societal beliefs, complement historical "truths," and uphold socially sanctioned values. In other words, as narrative theory suggests, some stories are better than others because they cohere and resonate with their audiences. Policymakers who tell the best stories and paint a vivid picture of problems and solutions that is consistent with their audiences' experiences are more likely to achieve their desired goals.

In contrast, policy advocates who wish to counter current welfare reform legislation need to construct alternative rhetorical contexts favorable to their arguments. Two communication theories offer promising methods for constructing effective narratives and depictions that challenge dominant political frames. In an article entitled "'Going Meta': Definition and Political Applications," communication theorist Herbert W. Simons outlines a strategy of "Going Meta," a process by which people critique dominant ideological "taken for granted" frames by engaging in frame altering responses (1994, 471). Using this technique in the public moral argument over welfare, policy advocates may offer self-reflexive narratives—new interpretive paradigms—that expose the hidden assumptions currently governing welfare debates and suggest alternative premises to guide deliberations. Maurice Charland's theory of constitutive rhetoric also implies auspicious possibilities for constructing discourse that provides policymakers with "new perspectives and motives" for action (1987, 142). One way to influence the policymaking process is by "providing stories that . . . shift and re-work the subject and its motives" (Charland 1987, 148). In addition to stories, social policymakers may also draw on other rhetorical forms that compete with the persuasive force of depictions. For instance, Charland suggests that different aesthetic practices such as "music, drama, architecture, and fashion" can also "elicit new modes of experience and being" and therefore promote changes in social meaning (1987, 148). Introducing new stories and aesthetic practices into the legislative arena can position (or constitute) policymakers to think and act in different ways.

Legislators have already demonstrated a willingness to participate in innovative aesthetic practices. For instance, in one welfare hearing, Chair of the House Committee on Human Resources and Intergovernmental Relations, Christopher Shays (R-CT), overruled his staff and invited teenagers who participate in a teenage pregnancy prevention program to sing their theme song. Shays proclaimed: "I would love to end [the hearing] with a nice theme song. . . . I am taking tremendous glee in the fact that I am overruling my staff. I feel like I am exerting myself. You are allowed to clap. You are allowed to do whatever you want" (House Committee on Government Reform and Oversight, 30 April 1996, 147). While some may dispute the efficacy of singing songs in Congress, Shays' enthusiasm is indicative of some legislator interest in alternative forms of testimony. In addition, a March 27, 1995, "Simulation Hearing on Obtaining Federal and State Assistance" before the House Committee on Economic and Educational Opportunities gave legislators first-hand knowledge of the difficulties welfare recipients face in applying for federal programs. During this hearing, legislators formed teams, assumed the role of a typical welfare family, and tried to apply for the federal and state welfare programs for which this fictional family was eligible. While only three members attended the hearing, this creative role-playing exercise dramatically exposed participants to the complex bureaucracy that governs welfare and the scarce resources available to needy families. By introducing new stories and aesthetic experiences such as these into the legislative arena, policymakers can establish a new framework within which to debate a given social policy, thereby providing a context that gives presence (Perelman 1971) to alternative depictions and alternative solutions.

NOTES

1 Frustrated by the use of anecdotes in the hearings and debates, Senator Paul Wellstone (D-MN) remarks: "I have heard my colleagues come to the floor and give examples. Are we going to now govern by anecdote?" ("Family Self-Sufficiency Act," *Congressional Record*, 7 August 1995, S11749).

2 See for example, Condit's (1984) ideographic study of the abortion debate, Duffy's (1997) fantasy theme analysis of the riverboat gambling controversy in Iowa, and Hogan and Dorsey's (1991) study of the relationship between public opinion and policymaking through an analysis of the nuclear freeze debates.

3 In retaining support services and job skills training, Clinton's Work and Responsibility Act was actually a logical extension of the Family Support

Act of 1988 (FSA), which Clinton had helped negotiate during his tenure as Arkansas Governor and head of the National Governors' Association (Cammisa 1998, 57). The main difference between Clinton's proposal and FSA was that in addition to the reform goals characteristic of FSA, the "Work and Responsibility Act" included a deterrent in the form of a welfare time limit.

4 The *Contract with America,* the group of proposals endorsed by the Republican party prior to the 1995 November congressional elections, was just one in a series of welfare reform proposals that informed PRWORA. Following Clinton's proposed time limit, the *Contract with America* proposed a five year lifetime limit of welfare benefits. In addition, the Republican Congress offered states the option of taking welfare as a block grant. Theoretically, a block grant gives states greater control over welfare spending and therefore narrows the role of federal government in public welfare as well as shifts the burden of program administration and responsibility to the states. The first Republican welfare reform bill was tied to budget reconciliation legislation. When Clinton vetoed this bill on December 6, 1995, he justified his opposition on the grounds that the deficit reduction provisions were unsatisfactory. Attempting to get President Clinton to veto welfare reform specifically and thereby renege on his campaign promise to "end welfare as we know it," Republicans separated the welfare reform bill from the budget legislation and sent the welfare bill to the president as a stand-alone bill. President Clinton vetoed this welfare reform bill on January 6, 1996.

5 Haskins indicated African American witness testimony was also important to the Republican case because it highlighted the party's awareness of race and gender issues in welfare. Haskins mentioned, in particular, the importance of testimony from Boston University Economics professor Glenn Loury, University of California Public Policy professor James Q. Wilson, and Kellogg Stress Institute owner Virginia Kellogg.

6 In July 1994, Representative Louise Slaughter (D-NY) describes a compelling instance of abuse in Chicago: "but one of the things that struck me, and I don't think I will ever get over, is the finding of 19 babies in 2 rooms in Chicago who were the children of 4 mothers in their twenties and that they received something like $5,000 a month in welfare payments and what kind of chance do those children have" (House Committee on Ways and Means, 27 July 1994, 521). Relying on the same story in January 1995, Representative James Talent (R-MO) asserts: "Last year, in a drug raid of an apartment in Chicago, police found 19 children—the oldest 14

years old, the youngest one—living in squalor among filth, cockroaches, and broken windows covered with old blankets. When the police entered the apartment, they found five children asleep on the floor in their underwear and others gnawing a bone with a dog" (House Committee on Ways and Means, 30 January 1995, 534). Drawing on the same testimony in February 1995, Patrick T. Murphy, Public Guardian in Cook County, Illinois, narrates: "Perhaps the ultimate example of this was the Keystone case which happened in Chicago just a year ago. In that case, Chicago coppers investigating drug allegations stumbled across nineteen kids living in a hovel with their five moms who were taking in approximately $6,500 a month in welfare and other benefits for the children. Most of the money was going out the door into the hands of drug pushers. Ultimately, we discovered that these five mothers had twenty[-]three children by seventeen fathers, none of whom was a dad to his kid" (House Committee on Ways and Means, House Committee on Economic and Educational Opportunities, 3 February 1995, 119). Later, in a March 1995 debate, California Representative Randy "Duke" Cunningham (R) reports: "I look in Chicago, and police found 19 children living in squalor in a cold, dark apartment. Two children in diapers were sharing a bone with the family dog. Why? Because the parents were living on cocaine and drugs. Child abuse services need to be brought in" ("Personal Responsibility Ad of 1995," *Congressional Record,* 21 March 1995, H3382). One day later, Arizona Representative J.D. Hayworth (R) inquires: "How can we in the name of freedom and decency stand by silently when we see examples just as we saw a couple of years ago in Chicago during the drug raid when police found 19 children living in squalor in a cold, dark apartment, 2 children in diapers sharing a bone with a family dog, the children belonging to 3 mothers and 6 different fathers who were getting $4,000 in cash benefits per month from the Federal Government?" ("Personal Responsibility Act of 1995," *Congressional Record,* 22 March 1995, H3506).

7 Throughout the hearings and debates, congressional leaders disparage non-scientific evidence (i.e. anecdotes, personal opinion) as a basis for policymaking because they believe that such evidence is an unreliable source of data that leads to biased decisions. In particular, legislators fault non-empirical evidence with being ideological, stereotypical, and fictitious in such a way as to cloud important issues. For instance, quoting welfare scholar James Q. Wilson, Senator Daniel Patrick Moynihan (D-NY) states: "The debate that has begun about welfare reform is, in large

measure, based on untested assumptions, ideological posturing, and perverse priorities" (Senate Finance Committee, 10 March 1995, 24). Chair of Howard University's Department of Political Science Ronald Walters urges; "I think, again, we have to get down to facts and not ideology. If we let the ideology rule our approach to this, we are really going to come out at a dead end, in terms of public policy. We cannot make good public policy from mythology" (House Committee on Government Operations, 10 March 1994, 124; 65). Senator Byron L. Dorgan (D-ND) notes that "In public debate we all too often use stereotypes" ("Family Self-Sufficiency Act," *Congressional Record*, 7 September 1995, S12759).

8 In a more extensive analysis, I show how legislators prefer the depictions even when those depictions are contradicted and/or not supported by social science evidence (Gring-Pemble 2000, 302–43).

WORKS CITED

Abramovitz, Mimi. 1996. *Regulating the Lives of Women: Social Welfare Policy from Colonial Times to the Present*. Boston: South End.

Axinn, June and Herman Levin. 1997. *Social Welfare: A History of the American Response to Need*. 4th ed. New York: Longman.

Bennett, W. Lance and Murray Edelman. 1985. Toward a New Political Narrative. *Journal of Communication* 35 (Autumn): 156–71.

Bitzer, Lloyd F. 1987. Rhetorical Public Communication. *Critical Studies in Mass Communication* 4 (December): 425–28.

Cammisa, Anne Marie. 1998. *From Rhetoric to Reform?: Welfare Policy in American Politics*. Dilemmas in American Politics. Boulder, CO: Westview.

Charland, Maurice. 1987. Constitutive Rhetoric: The Case of the *Peuple Québécois*. *Quarterly Journal of Speech* 73 (May): 133–50.

Condit, Celeste. 1990. *Decoding Abortion Rhetoric: Communicating Social Change*. Urbana: University of Illinois Press. *Congressional Record*. 1995–1996. Washington, D.C.

Cooper, Cynthia A. 1996. *Violence on Television: Congressional Inquiry, Public Criticism and Industry Response: A Policy Analysis*. New York: University Press of America.

Docherty, David, David Morrison, and Michael Tracey. 1993. Scholarship as Silence. *Journal of Communication* 43 (Summer): 230–38.

Duffy, Margaret. 1997. High Stakes: A Fantasy Theme Analysis of the Selling of Riverboat Gambling in Iowa. *Southern Communication Journal* 62 (Winter): 117–132.

Fisher, Walter R. 1984. Narration as a Human Communication Paradigm: The Case of Public Moral Argument. *Communication Monographs* 51 (March): 1–22.

Fisher, Walter R. 1985. The Narrative Paradigm: An Elaboration. *Communication Monographs* 52 (December): 347–67.

Fisher, Walter R. 1987. Technical Logic, Rhetorical Logic, and Narrative Rationality. *Argumentation* 1 (I): 3–21.

Foucault, Michel. 1972. *The Archaeology of Knowledge and Discourse on Language*. Translated by A. M. Sheridan Smith. New York: Pantheon.

Gilens, Martin. 1999. *Why Americans Hate Welfare: Race, Media, and the Politics of Antipoverty Policy*. Chicago: University of Chicago Press.

Gring-Pemble, Lisa M. 2000. "Constructing Welfare As We Know It": A Rhetorical Analysis of the Welfare Reform Hearings and Debates Resulting in the 1996 Personal Responsibility and Work Opportunity Reconciliation Act. Ph.D. diss., University of Maryland.

Harris, John F. and John E. Yang. 1996. "Clinton to Sign Bill Overhauling Welfare." *Washington Post* (August 1): A1+.

Hogan, J. Michael and Leroy Dorsey. 1991. Public Opinion and the Nuclear Freeze: The Rhetoric of Popular Sovereignty in Foreign Policy Debate. *Western Journal of Speech Communication* 55 (Fall): 319–38.

Kennedy, George. 1980. *Classical Rhetoric and Its Christian and Secular Tradition from Ancient to Modern Times*. Chapel Hill: University of North Carolina Press.

McKerrow, Raymie E. 1989. Critical Rhetoric: Theory and Praxis. *Communication Monographs* 56 (June): 91–111.

Miller, M. Linda. 1999. Public Argument and Legislative Debate in the Rhetorical Construction of Public Policy: The Case of Florida Midwifery Legislation. *Quarterly Journal of Speech* 85 (November): 361–79.

Mueller, Milton. 1995. Why Communications Policy is Passing "Mass Communication" By: Political Economy as the Missing Link. *Critical Studies in Mass Communication* 12 (December): 455–72.

Noam, Eli. 1993. Reconnecting Communications Studies with Communications Policy. *Journal of Communication* 43 (Summer): 199–206.

Osborn, Michael. 1986. "Rhetorical Depiction." Pp. 79–107 in *Form, Genre, and the Study of Political Rhetoric*, eds. Herbert W. Simons and Aram A. Aghazarian. Columbia, SC: University of South Carolina Press.

Perelman, Ch. and L. Olbrechts-Tyteca. 1971. *The New Rhetoric: A Treatise on Argumentation.* Translated by John Wilkinson and Purcell Weaver. London: University of Notre Dame Press.

Personal Responsibility and Work Opportunity Reconciliation Act of 1996. U.S. Statutes at Large 110: 2105–2354.

Schuetz, Janice. 1986. Overlays of Argument in Legislative Process. *Journal of the American Forensic Association* 22 (Spring): 223–34.

Simons, Herbert W. 1994. "Going Meta": Definition and Political Applications. *Quarterly Journal of Speech* 80 (November): 468–81.

Smith, Craig Allen and Kathy B. Smith. 1990. "The Rhetoric of Political Institutions." Pp. 225–54 in *New Directions in Political Communication: A Resource Book,* eds. David L. Swanson and Dan Nimmo. Newbury Park: Sage.

U.S. House. 1992. *Welfare Reform: Rhetoric, Reality, and Opportunities.* 102nd Cong., 2nd sess. 9 April.

U.S. House. 1993. Committee on Ways and Means, Subcommittee on Human Resources. *Trends in Spending and Caseloads for AFDC and Related Programs.* 103rd Cong., 1st sess. 11 March.

U.S. House. Committee on Education and Labor, Subcommittee on Human Resources. *Field Hearing on Welfare Reform.* 103rd Cong., 2nd sess. 28 October.

U.S. House. Committee on Government Operations, Subcommittee on Human Resources and Intergovernmental Relations. *Ending Welfare As We Know It: Progress or Paralysis?* 103rd Cong., 2nd sess. 10 March 1994.

U.S. House. Committee on Ways and Means, Subcommittee on Human Resources. *Welfare Reform Proposals, Including H.R. 4605, The Work and Responsibility Act of 1994, Part 1.* 103rd Cong., 2nd sess. 14, 26–28 July.

U.S. House. Committee on Ways and Means, Subcommittee on Human Resources. *Welfare Reform Proposals, Including H.R. 4605, The Work and Responsibility Act of 1994, Part 2.* 103rd Cong., 2nd sess. 29 July and 9, 16 August.

U.S. House. 1995. Committee on Agriculture, Subcommittee on Department Operations, Nutrition, and Foreign Agriculture. *Reforming the Present Welfare System.* 104th Cong., 1st sess. 7–9, 14 February.

U.S. House. Committee on Economic and Educational Opportunities. *Contract with America: Hearing on Welfare Reform.* 104th Cong., 1st sess. 18 January.

U.S. House. Committee on Economic and Educational Opportunities, Subcommittee on Oversight and Investigations. *Simulation Hearing on Obtaining Federal and State Assistance.* 104th Cong., 1st sess. 27 March.

U.S. House. Committee on Ways and Means. *Contract With America: Overview.* 104th Cong., 1st sess. 5, 10–12 January.

U.S. House. Committee on Ways and Means. *Contract With America: Welfare Reform, Part 1.* 104th Cong., 1st sess. 13, 20, 23, 27, 30 January.

U.S. House. Committee on Ways and Means. *Contract With America: Welfare Reform, Part 2.* 104th Cong., 1st sess. 2 February.

U.S. House. Committee on Government Reform and Oversight, Subcommittee on Human Resources and Intergovernmental Relations. *Preventing Teen Pregnancy: Coordinating Community Efforts.* 104th Cong., 2nd sess. 30 April.

U.S. House. Committee on Ways and Means, Subcommittee on Human Resources. *National Governors' Association Welfare Reform Proposal* 104th Cong., 2nd sess. 20 February.

U.S. House. Committee on Ways and Means, Subcommittee on Human Resources. *Causes of Poverty with a Focus on Out-of-Wedlock Births.* 104th Cong., 2nd sess. 12 March.

U.S. Senate. 1994. Committee on Agriculture, Nutrition, and Forestry. *Fraud in Federal Nutrition Programs.* 103rd Cong., 2nd sess. 2 February.

U.S. Senate. Committee on Appropriations, Subcommittee on Labor, Health and Human Services, and Education, and Related Agencies. *Welfare Reform: Special Hearing.* 103rd Cong., 2nd sess. 9 December.

U.S. Senate. Committee on Finance, Subcommittee on Social Security and Family Policy. *Welfare Reform.* 103rd Cong., 2nd sess. 18 January and 25 February.

U.S. Senate. 1995. Committee on Finance. *Broad Policy Goals of Welfare Reform.* 104th Cong., 1st sess. 9 March.

U.S. Senate. Committee on Finance. *Administration's Views on Welfare Reform.* 104th Cong., 1st sess. 10 March.

U.S. Senate. Committee on Finance. *Teen Parents and Welfare Reform.* 104th Cong., 1st sess. 14 March.

U.S. Senate. Committee on Finance. *Welfare to Work.* 104th Cong., 1st sess. 20 March.

U.S. Senate. Committee on Governmental Affairs. *Reinventing Government.* 104th Cong., 1st sess. 25 January and 2 February.

Vobejda, Barbara. 1996. Clinton Signs Welfare Bill Amid Division. *Washington Post* (August 23): A1+.

Wander, Philip. 1984. The Third Persona: An Ideological Turn in Rhetorical Theory. *Central States Speech Journal* 35 (Winter): 197–216.

CHAPTER 7
Voices from the Margins

How did Philip A. Randolph and Martin Luther King, Jr., stir thousands to march on Washington for civil rights? How did Lucretia Coffin Mott, Elizabeth Cady Stanton, and Susan B. Anthony mobilize women in the cause for women's rights? Why was Harvey Milk, the first openly gay person to be elected to public office in California, successful in his grassroots political organizing? Advocates for large-scale social change such as civil rights, women's rights, and gay and lesbian liberation struggle to gain media attention and public support. Often considered apart from mainstream politics and institutions, these voices from the margins have used various strategies that have become of increasing interest to rhetorical theorists and critics. Some rhetorical theorists, for example, study how language works to sustain or challenge power relationships that benefit some people at the expense of others.[1] Many critics have also investigated the strategies that marginalized groups use to effect social change.[2]

Studies of marginalized voices frequently challenge prevailing conceptions of political communication. Political communication scholars have tended to focus on presidential rhetoric, election campaigns, advertising, and other traditional forms of communication that purport to capture great historical moments and rhetorical masterpieces, and that typically reflect the rhetorical strategies of privileged, mainstream society. In contrast, scholars who focus on the rhetoric of marginalized voices study how groups that are frequently ignored or excluded from mainstream political discourse develop and exert a public presence, sometimes sufficiently powerful to produce significant social change.

Although diverse in content and perspective, the essays in this chapter share at least two important themes. First, they address obstacles that marginalized groups encounter in their quest for public expression. For example, historically, it has been difficult for women, African Americans, and members of the

427

working class to raise legitimate grievances about their problems and be heard. Often, members of these groups feared that they would be punished or harmed if they spoke out. Even today, misperceptions and stereotypes about groups such as welfare mothers and members of the gay, lesbian, bisexual, and transgendered (GLBT) community limit the ability of these groups to speak out and be taken seriously. Second, the essays all demonstrate the ingenuity of marginalized groups in overcoming these obstacles. Reclaiming the power to define their own identity and challenging the legitimacy of mainstream political, economic, and social institutions are just a few ways these groups exert rhetorical force.

Randall Lake's 1989 essay, "Temporal Metaphors, Religions, and Arguments," reveals how Native Americans have preserved their cultural identities and resisted assimilation into mainstream American culture by challenging traditional European conceptions of time. In the Euro-American worldview time is linear, a chronological progression from an inferior past to a superior present and future. Lake points out that opponents of Native American activists exploit that linear conception to relegate Native American rituals and culture to an irrelevant, inferior past, thereby absolving opponents of culpability for historical injustices to Native Americans. In contrast, Lake observes that Native American activists draw strength from cyclical temporal metaphors in a "rhetoric of the powerless." Native Americans conceive of time as a repetitive, unending cycle of rebirth where distinctions between past, present, and future are meaningless. This view essentially allows Native Americans to preserve their culture and identities, and predict the eventual triumph of their way of life.

Karlyn Kohrs Campbell's 1995 essay, "Gender and Genre: Loci of Invention and Contradiction in the Earliest Speeches by Women," addresses obstacles women speakers faced in their quest for social change. In nineteenth-century United States, women activists who spoke in public were considered improper and unfeminine. As a result, Campbell explains, women faced a powerful double bind: they had to craft innovative ways to speak appropriately and simultaneously affirm their femininity. This essay reveals the early women speakers' ingenuity in accomplishing these two seemingly conflicting goals. Suggesting that later women's rights advocates patterned their arguments after those established by early women speakers, Campbell also underscores the historical importance of marginalized rhetoric in social movements, suggesting that social advocates often exploit the rhetorical resources and strategies of their predecessors to gain public voice and effect change.

In her 1996 essay, "Creating a Discursive Space through a Rhetoric of Difference: Chicana Feminists Craft a Homeland," Lisa A. Flores explores a set of obstacles that Chicana feminists face. As Flores explains, "Chicana traditionally refers to women of Mexican descent who were born in the United States and/or are residing there. . . . while Chicana feminists ally themselves with their Chicano heritage, they also question those aspects of their culture that they find problematic." One such cultural aspect is patriarchy that results in the oppression of women. Flores demonstrates how Chicana feminists overcome their marginalization, which arises from their race and sex, and from living in the United States away from their homeland. This essay shows how Chicana feminists, in the absence of a physical space or homeland, use language to forge their own unique identity, celebrate their rich and complex heritage, and create meaningful relationships with other feminists.

Lester C. Olson's 1997 essay, "On the Margins of Rhetoric: Audre Lorde

Transforming Silence into Language and Action," explores the role of silence in social change. Audre Lorde was a self-proclaimed "Black lesbian feminist socialist mother," who spoke eloquently throughout her life of the multiple layers of oppression she encountered. Speculating on why Lorde's public speeches are often excluded from public address texts even though they are models of rhetorical excellence, Olson says that one reason may be Lorde's membership in a variety of "outgroups." He shows how fear of political, social, or economic reprisal works to silence individuals from expressing alternative viewpoints. Finally, Olson underscores one of Lorde's central arguments—that transforming silence into action is a necessary precursor to liberation from many factors (such as shame, taboos, verbal abuse, and social structures) that suppress subordinated communities.

Gary S. Selby's 2002 essay, "Mocking the Sacred: Frederick Douglass's 'Slaveholder's Sermon' and the Antebellum Debate over Religion and Slavery," reveals Frederick Douglass's strategic use of parody to challenge Biblical justifications for slavery. Throughout history, religion has been used both as a source of support and as an obstacle to social change. In the United States, opponents of racial equality often cited scripture to justify their claims. As an African American and former slave, Douglass also faced serious obstacles to speaking with authority in public even before he attacked biblical support for slavery. This essay demonstrates Douglass's rhetorical skill in using parody as a primary rhetorical strategy to question the "naturalness" of racial superiority, portray powerful arguments for slavery as ridiculous, and challenge stereotypical and disabling images of African Americans. The essay also explains the value of exposing inconsistencies among attitudes, values, behaviors, and beliefs as a catalyst for social change.

Notes

1 See for example, Raymie McKerrow, "Critical Rhetoric: Theory and Praxis," *Communication Monographs* 56 (June 1989): 93.

2 For work on women, consult Karlyn Kohrs Campbell "The Rhetoric of Women's Liberation: An Oxymoron," *Quarterly Journal of Speech* 59 (1973): 75–86; A. Cheree Carlson, "Creative Casuistry and Feminist Consciousness: The Rhetoric of Moral Reform," *Quarterly Journal of Speech* 78 (1992): 16–32; Lisa M. Gring-Pemble, "Writing Themselves into Consciousness: Creating a Rhetorical Bridge between the Public and Private Spheres," *Quarterly Journal of Speech* 84 (1998): 41–61; and Susan Zaeske, "Signatures of Citizenship: The Rhetoric of Women's Antislavery Petitions," *Quarterly Journal of Speech* 88 (May 2002): 147–68. For work on African Americans see John Louis Lucaites and Celeste Michelle Condit, "Reconstructing <Equality>: Culturetypal and Countercultural Rhetorics in the Martyred Black Vision," *Communication Monographs* 57 (1990); 5–24; and Robert E. Terrill, "Colonizing the Borderlands: Shifting Circumference in the Rhetoric of Malcolm X," *Quarterly Journal of Speech* 86 (February 2000): 67–85. For scholarship on American Indians, consult Randall Lake, "Enacting Red Power: The Consummatory Function in Native American Protest Rhetoric," *Quarterly Journal of Speech* 69 (1983): 127–421 and Richard Morris and Philip Wander, "Native American Rhetoric: Dancing in the Shadows of the Ghost Dance," *Quarterly Journal of Speech* 76 (May 1990): 164–91. For work related to the gay, lesbian, bisexual, transgendered and queer communities, see James Darsey, "From 'Gay is Good' to the Scourge of AIDS: The Evolution of Gay Liberation Rhetoric, 1977–1990," *Communication Studies* 42 (Spring 1991): 43–66; Charles E. Morris III, "Pink Herring and the Fourth Persona: J. Edgar Hoover's Sex Crime Panic" *Quarterly Journal of Speech* 88 (May 2002): 228–44; and R. Anthony Slagle, "In Defense of Queer Nation: From *Identity Politics* to a *Politics of Difference*, *Western Journal of Communication* 59, no. (Spring 1995): 85–102. For scholarship related to class, consult Charles Conrad, "Work Songs, Hegemony, and Illusions of Self," *Critical Studies in Mass Communication* 5 (1988): 179–201 and Mari Boor Tonn, "Militant Motherhood: Labor's Mary Harris 'Mother' Jones," *Quarterly Journal of Speech* 82 (1996): 1–21.

Temporal Metaphors, Religions, and Arguments

Randall A. Lake

The experience of temporality is a fundamental aspect of human experience, and the construction of time's shape and meaning is a basic process of human symbolization. Suzanne Langer (1942/1957, 1953) suggests that symbolic forms, both discursive and presentational, seek to articulate thoughts and feelings that spring, originally, from the experience of the rhythms of organic life itself. Such rhythms are manifold, including the daily voyage of the sun, phases of the moon, passage of seasons, and the individual's encounter with birth, maturation, and death. With respect to temporal meaning, the pattern of the days and seasons usually is felt as repetitive, connoting a cosmos in which "there is nothing new under the sun." In contrast, the pattern of life and death, because it confronts humans with their own mortality, is felt as a finite, unidirectional, irreversible time. The root (and perhaps archetypal) metaphor of the former is the circle; of the latter, the line or arrow.

In the Western tradition, philosophical reflection on these patterns dates at least from the pre-Socratic contemplation of cosmic permanence and change. In a fluctuating universe, changes may well be chronological; hence, time is directional or linear, with the present becoming the historical past as life proceeds toward a qualitatively different future. On the other hand, in a stable universe, time, to the extent that it is a relevant category of experience, tends to be cyclical: with events perpetually repeating themselves, often according to a preconceived pattern. Famed historian of religion Mircea Eliade (1954; 1957, esp. 68–113; 1963, esp. 75–91) differentiates these views as "profane" and "sacred" time, respectively.

Through the elaboration of such temporal metaphors, individuals and societies endow their lives and actions with meaning. For "time does not exist independently of human life" but "is always socially constructed" (Lauer, 1981, vii). And, as Japp (1986, 92) notes, language gives "presence to phenomena not in our immediate sensory field," permitting us to "recall and share that which has happened, predict what will happen," and thereby finds continuity and meaning in the panoply of events that, so woven together, comprise our life stories. Different metaphors configure time differently, as for example, progression, repetition, change, or tradition (Japp, 1986, 80), and thereby can both shape and express different communal temporal understandings. In short, "communication is, ultimately, about creating shared time" (Fabian, 1983, 31).

This collaborative articulation of cultural understandings of time is the subject of this essay. More specifically, I examine the ways in which temporal metaphors structure the discourse of the so-called "Red Power" movement and the white establishment's responses thereto. I argue that native activists and their opponents both exploit the resources of temporal metaphors in arguments concerning (1) the relative superiority of "native" and "white" cultures, (2) the meaning and relevance of the "past," i.e., historical events in native/American relations, to the contemporary Native American activist cause, and (3) the inevitability of the triumph of one way of life over the other. However, because each side grounds its arguments in different temporal metaphors, the claims made and the cultural senses of time evoked are diametrically opposed. Drawing principally upon time's arrow, white discourse characterizes Indian activism as an historical anachronism, Indian history as uncorrectable, if regrettable, and Indian cultures as out of step with progress. Activist rhetoric, in contrast, exploits time's circle to characterize the modern movement as the fulfillment of ancient prophecies, Indian "history" as an ongoing tale of injustice, and Indian cultures as the sort to which all human life will turn to survive.

The metaphor of the arrow has come to play a vital part in Western thinking about time over the centuries. Nowhere is this better shown than in Toulmin and Goodfield's well-known and revealingly entitled work, *The Discovery of Time* (1965, 15, 247, 263–265), in which the authors trace the "gradual emergence of a continuing sense of history out of earlier mythological and theological" conceptions of Nature; argue that, by the nineteenth century, all natural sciences save physics and chemistry had rejected the *a priori* categories of Greek thought in favor of a historical consciousness; and conclude that even the "laws of nature" may be discovered to be, not immutable, but subject to evolutionary change over time. And Frentz (1985, 6) has claimed that "temporality has become the Darth Vader for philosophical traditions whose ideological commitments lean toward permanency and universality" (see also Farrell, 1982, 27). As examples, our concept of "history", as the chronological passage of events locatable by dates, and the biological theory of evolution become incomprehensible absent the assumption of sequential, irreversible time. Highly influential in solidifying the position of time's arrow has been Christianity, in which time—one product of the Creation—unfolds unidirectionally the continuous action of God through history, progressing from the past into the future, until the eschatological end of time foretold in Revelation as Christ's second coming (Puech, 1957, 40). Although not universally, Christianity largely rejected the cyclical view of time (Frye, 1980, esp. 38, 40, 61).

Moreover, time's arrow does not simply describe reality, but is normative. The history of the idea of "progress" is not coincident with that of "history" itself, and is in some respects at odds with the Christian story of the Fall. "Progress" is, nonetheless, one ethical extension of the doctrines of history and Darwinism; and, like them, rejects time's cycle (Bury, 1932, esp. xi–xxix, 334–349; relatedly, see Kane, 1983). Such a normative arrow is presupposed in expressions like "time marches on," and in evolution's infamous sociopolitical cousins, Social Darwinism and Manifest Destiny. In time's arrow, anteriority often signifies inferiority while posteriority implies superiority (Brown, 1982, 117).

In contrast, time's cycle is in a sense atemporal. Shorn of chronology, sacred time is static, cosmic. It is not simply a frozen moment of chronological time. The ancient Greeks conceived of time as cyclical, turning perpetually upon itself under the influence of astronomical movements, recapitulating the immutable and *a priori* categories of existence (Puech, 1957, 39–40). Each moment in a turn of the cycle is not simply a recapitulation of previous identical moments; rather, it is all those moments, and all those yet to come. This is to say that sacred time is a kind of eternal nonhistorical present (Eliade, 1957, 70).

Sacred time is eternal because it is mythical time (Cassirer, 1944, 83, 95, 173). It is "a primordial time, not to be found in the historical past, an *original time*, in the sense that it came into existence all at once, that it was not preceded by another time, because no time could exist *before the appearance of the reality narrated in the myth*" (Eliade, 1957, 72). In "primitive" cosmologies, many myths recount how things—the universe, flora and fauna, tribal customs and rites, the tribes themselves—came to be. As creation myths they depict the primordial past. But while they are thus "histories," they are *sacred* histories. That is, the characters and events they recount are not simple stories of the irretrievable past; rather, they are *archetypes*, models of action (Eliade, 1954/1974, 3–48; Highwater, 1981, p. 117). "The myths," Eliade (1954/1974, xiv) says, "preserve and transmit the paradigms, the exemplary models, for all the responsible activities in which men engage."

Consequently, recitation of these myths, frequently in conjunction with the ritual reenactment of events narrated therein, temporarily arrests profane time, permitting participants to pass into the "primordial mythical time made present" (Eliade, 1957, 26). Ritual enacts mythical events, and participants thereby are present at the original occurrence of these events in a cosmic time made present at each enactment, removed from chronological sequence and historicity (Eliade, 1957, 71–72, 1963, 68; see also Cassirer, 1955, esp. 104–118; Eliade, 1984).

This process is neatly synopsized by Tahca Ushte, a.k.a. John Fire Lame Deer (Lame Deer & Erdoes, 1972, 118; see also Underhill, 1965, 125), a Lakota medicine man, as he explains the meaning of Sioux religious symbolism. He spreads some red earth on the floor, flattens it with his palm, and smoothes it with an eagle feather. Then his finger traces a circle in it. The figure of a person is part of this circle, representing both Lame Deer himself and a spirit. The figure's head has four horns, representing the four winds. With his thumb, Lame Deer makes twenty-four marks around the circle, which stand both for the twenty-four new medicine men he dreamt he would have to ordain and for the directions of the universe, "four dots each for the north, the east, the west, the south, the sky above and the earth below." Taking his peace pipe, Lame Deer points it toward all these directions and concludes: "Now we are one with the universe, with all the living things, a link in the circle which has no end. It means we were here long before the first white man came, we are here now, we will still be here at the end of time—Indian Time. We will live!"

Traditional Native American religions are strongly influenced by time's cycle (Brown, 1982, 4, 49–50, 86). Native cultures were closely attuned to the cyclical rhythms of organic life, inextricably interwoven with the pattern of the seasons and the cardinal directions from which their forces come (Witherspoon, 1977, 140–149). The hunting tribes depended on the seasonal migration of game, especially, for the Plains Indians, the sacred buffalo (Brown, 1953, 6; Dary, 1974; Moorehead, 1914, 330, 337). The cultivating tribes were vitally concerned with the seasonal growth of crops, particularly corn and pollen (Underhill, 1965, 207, 230–231).

The cosmos itself often was believed to obey such cycles. Mooney (1896, 785) reports the common belief "that the earth becomes old and decrepit, and requires that its youth be renewed at the end of certain great cycles." Siouan mythology, for example, speaks of the world as repetitively transformed in four phases: the rock, bow, fire, and pipe ages (Brown, 1953, 100). At the beginning of the cycle, a buffalo was placed at the west edge of the universe to hold back pending floodwaters. Every year this buffalo loses a hair, and every age it loses a leg, until all its hair and all four legs are gone, when the waters rush in again and the cycle comes to an end (Brown, 1953, 9).

This temporal orientation often is manifested linguistically. Most native languages are tenseless (Brown, 1982, 50; Cassirer, 1955, 223–224).

The Hopi language, for example, contains no words to represent or designate time, conceived as "a smooth flowing continuum in which everything in the universe proceeds at an equal rate, out of a future, through a present, into a past" (Whorf, 1975, 121). Frequently, native terms for "world" or "cosmos" also mean "year"; thus one might speak of the world having passed and mean that a year had gone by (Eliade, 1957, 73).

In this context, ritual enactment harmonizes personal and tribal life with the cyclical rhythms of nature in sacred time (Witherspoon, 1977, 22; see also Hoban, 1980, 278–279). Indeed, ritual is *necessary* to sustain the cycles and tribal life itself. Among the Pueblo, for example, "Without the seasonal enactment of the rites and ceremonies it is believed that recycling of the sacred world- and life-sustaining powers will cease, the world will die, and the people will be no more" (Brown, 1982, 22). To accomplish this, the symbolism of ritual must recapitulate the archetypes found in nature and rationalized in myth. Thus, as nature is paradigmatically cyclical, the paradigmatic symbol of ritual is the circle. Lame Deer (Lame Deer & Erdoes, 1972, 112) explains:

> To our way of thinking the Indians' symbol is the circle, the hoop . . . . With us the code stands for the togetherness of people who sit with one another around the campfire, relatives and friends united in peace while the pipe passes from hand to hand. The camp in which every tipi had its place was also a ring. The tipi was a ring in which people sat in a circle and all the village were in turn circles within a larger circle, part of the larger hoop which was the seven campfires representing one nation. The nation was only a part of the universe, in itself circular and made of the earth, which is round, of the sun, which is round, of the stars, which are round. The moon, the horizon, the rainbow—circles within circles within circles, with no beginning and no end.

The metaphor of the circle, therefore, which is "symbol and reality at the same time" (Lame Deer & Erdoes, 1972, 112), draws its meaning and power from the temporal principle of the universe, and is the symbol *par excellence* of the unity of all things that adhere to this principle.

Use of the circle in ritual not only unites one with this unchanging, ahistoric cosmos, but also replenishes it. The pipe ceremony, a practice common among tribes throughout North America, takes place in a circle (Brown, 1953, 3–30; Lame Deer & Erdoes, 1972, 250–266; Powers, 1975, 86–88; Underhill, 1965, 163–164, 184, 186, 194–195, 201–202). The pipe itself simultaneously represents the universe, the Indian and individual humans (Brown, 1953, 21; Lame Deer and Erdoes, 1972, 250; Powers, 1975, 86). Prayers are offered to the cardinal directions, each of which represents a virtue such as courage, purity, or wisdom (Neihardt, 1932, 2). The pipe is smoked, with careful attention paid to the smallest details, including the number of puffs. In so doing, participants are unified with the cosmos in "Indian Time."

Similarly, the ritual of the sweat lodge occurs in a small, beehive shaped dwelling that represents the whole universe, with a small pit in the center, into which are placed hot rocks that produce purificatory steam that is the spirit (Lame Deer & Erdoes, 1972, 174–182; Powers, 1975, 49, 89–91, 134–136). "This pit," Lame Deer (Lame Deer & Erdoes, 1972, 178) relates, "is a circle within the circle formed by the hut. This symbol, a circle within a circle, stands for life, for that which has no end. Plants, animals, men are born and die, but the Indian people will live." In this way, ritual overcomes the ravages of linear historicity, exemplified by death, and replenishes the world through the recovery of sacred time.

In enacting primordial archetypes, ritual rejects the historicist notion of "progress." Archetypes are no less valued simply because they are ancient. If anything, the reverse is true: anteriority in time signifies superiority, not inferiority, because the first events become the models for all subsequent events (Brown, 1982, 71). Revealingly, the Lakota word "wakan," which refers, roughly, to the "sacred," also carries connotations of the "old" (Powers, 1975, 47, 205).

These ritual traditions afford native activist rhetors a basis for appeal that is relatively alien to an American society accustomed to temporal representations dominated by time's arrow. But what is the subject of appeal? In the confrontation between movement and establishment rhetors, considerable dispute has centered on the history of native/white relations in the United States, and the status of the contemporary native activist movement.

It is vital, at the outset, to acknowledge the obvious but fundamental fact that, in the United States, Native Americans today possess miniscule political, economic, and other power. The history of European subjugation of the continent and its inhabitants is long and well-chronicled. At issue between contemporary activists and their opponents is the meaning of this history and its relevance roughly a century after the end of the "Indian wars."

Time's arrow treats past events as irretrievably past, as strictly historical, without the potential to be made ritually present. Consequently, it denies the very basis for contemporary militancy that time's cycle provides, and is therefore a powerful way to cast modern activism as an anachronism. Argumentatively, linearity can be used to dissociate the past from the present, treating the latter, while perhaps the product of the former, as nonetheless a qualitatively different stage in evolutionary progress.

In establishment arguments, this dissociation is manifested in a "let bygones be bygones" strategy, wherein past wrongs are regretted without admitting that redress is in order, or even possible. For example, following the 1972 occupation of the Bureau of Indian Affairs offices in Washington, D.C., the Springfield, Massachusetts, *Republican* (*Trail*, 1974, 37) opined: "There's no doubt about it: the American Indians have been badly treated. So have lots of other people, for that matter. From coast to coast, the country is full of folks—red, white, blacks, brown and yellow—who have had some hard knocks or whose ancestors were cruelly misused, by somebody, sometime, somewhere. But most Americans are inclined to accomplish something for themselves right now—never mind what happened yesterday—or three centuries ago." Similarly, during the 1973 occupation of Wounded Knee, South Dakota, then–Secretary of the Interior Rogers Morton (*Voices*, 1974, 114) adopted the negotiating position that past grievances were irrelevant.

"There is no way that I or any other Secretary can undo the events of the past," he argued. "If it was wrong for the European to move on to this continent and settle it by pioneerism and combat, it was wrong. But it happened and here we are." Deloria (1973, 7) bemoans the prevalence of this attitude, contending that most Americans believe the problems of native tribes to be "facts of American history, not problems of the present."

Perversely, arguments grounded in time's arrow have a second effect. Because linear time is sequential and progressive, any "cracks" in the dissociative strategy, i.e.; any lingering associations between past and present, may render current issues as outmoded as the history they echo. The present appears as retrogressive as the past, rather than vice versa. Brooks Atkinson (Forbes, 1964, p. 138) observes this tendency in an editorial concerning Seneca treaty rights and the Kinzua Dam: "Everything about the situation is complex except the moral problem. For no one disputes the fact that the United States is breaking a treaty. But people are tired of the moral problem, which seems to them petty and obsolete. 'Well, now, really, in this day and age,' they say in effect, 'why all this fuss over some Indians?'" In this way, even present wrongs can be admitted but their import banished to the irredeemable past.

In contrast, Native Americans desiring to preserve their traditional ways of life, and withstand the assimilative pressures of white society, have seen their vindication in the cycle of life. Sacred time has been a source of hope for Indians wishing to vanquish white society and reestablish their once preeminent cultures. The best-known example of this understanding is the spread of the Ghost Dance religion in the late nineteenth century, which stimulated the Sioux uprising of 1890 that culminated in the massacre of nearly 300 Indians at Wounded Knee Creek, South Dakota (Bailey, 1957; Lame Deer & Erdoes, 1972, 225–235; Mooney, 1896).

Fundamentally messianic, the Ghost Dance religion taught that, soon, the earth would roll up on itself and bury all of white civilization, while Indians would be lifted up into the air and then set down upon the freshly turned soil, free to live the traditional life again without white interference: "the whole Indian race; living and

dead, will be reunited upon a regenerated earth, to live a life of aboriginal happiness," while the white race, "being alien and secondary and hardly real, . . . will be left behind with the other things of earth that have served their temporary purpose, or else will cease entirely to exist" (Mooney, 1896, 777).

The belief in a cycle of ages with periodic apocalypse that will recreate aboriginal native life was widely accepted among Plains tribes in the 1880's, and is part of the lore of other tribes as well. Both Hopi and Iroquois religions, for example, predict the end of white domination of the continent (Deloria, 1969, 242).

This belief is invoked by the pervasive theme of "rebirth" in contemporary Native American protest discourse. Activists assert their ties to the past, and its repeatability, in three interrelated ways: they consider themselves heirs (1) to traditional tribal metaphysics, (2) to the historical struggle between native and white, and (3) to the resources of "Indian Time."

For activists, too, the symbolism of the circle is the root metaphor of existence. Vernon Bellecourt (1973, July, 62) former national director of the militant American Indian Movement, explains: "We Indians live life within the sacred hoop, the sacred cycle of life, in unity with all living things. . . . When the Indian killed his four-legged brother—to live on, that animal provided itself, that was its role. . . . But when we died, we went back to the earth, so that the ground could be fertilized and the grass and the flowers could grow to pollinate other things and make more living things grow. . . . That was our way, the cycle of life."

Further, activists describe their struggle as a continuation of the historical "Indian wars" (Lake, in press). This was particularly evident during the siege of Wounded Knee. One activist (*Voices*, 1974, 246) observed: "Our revolution never ended. A lot of the old people on the reservations remember the time when they bore arms against white people. This has been passed right down to their children and now their grandchildren." Clyde Bellecourt (*Voices*, 1974, 148), a co-founder of A.I.M., asserted that the 1973 situation was "like 1890."

More specifically, the historical struggle continues in its essential aspects. The conditions in which Indians live are said to have remained essentially unchanged from the days when whites first conquered the continent: the poverty of reservation life continues and the need for a land base and tribal sovereignty remain as pressing as ever. Whites remain fundamentally exploitative and untrustworthy, making the same unfulfilled promises made generations ago while continuing to oppress tribal people. John Trudell ("Interview," 1975, Early Winter, 23) neatly articulates these two concerns: "The Indian elders . . . have heard every promise that the last four generations of politicians have made—they've heard it all. And they know nothing has changed from the day they were born to today. The rhetoric and the promises remain the same, and the way we have to live remains the same."

Finally, activists believe, the resources of sacred time still may be mobilized on Indians' behalf, through the preservation of traditional tribal culture, including ritual enactment. Their efforts to find a spiritual grounding for contemporary activism in ancient religious practice and to revitalize that practice attest to the strength of their desire to make the past present (Deloria, 1974, 1–41; Lake, 1983, 129–132; Ross & Most, 1976, September 2, 10C; Steiner, 1968, 87, 119; Voices, 1974, 60).

More than simple associational strategies that ennoble activists' cause by wrapping it in the mantle of historical injustice, and perhaps thereby exploiting latent white guilt, such discourse can be seen as part of the process through which "Indian Time" is ritually recaptured, and history itself defeated. Just as the seasons and the earth go through periodic stages of birth, growth, decay, death, and rebirth, so, allegedly, does Native American resistance to white oppression. The modern movement is posited as the fulfillment of ancient prophecies (Deloria, 1970, p. 242; Voices, 1974, 247).

Arguments about the currency of native activism tell half the story. Time's arrow and time's cycle also furnish resources with which whites and native activists construct competing accounts of the inexorability of each side's ultimate victory. In linear time, the inexorable march of progress ensures that all events necessarily and certainly must become merely historical, superseded by the superior future (Bury, 1932, 109), while, in cyclical time, the equally inexorable recurrence of the ages ensures that primordial events eventually will triumph. In discourse surrounding native/white relations these determinist metaphors are manifest in opposing arguments concerning the "inevitability" of assimilation or tribalism.

Time's arrow prizes modernity and repudiates longevity because change is thought to be the underlying principle of the universe. Endurance is proof of anachronism because the chronological march of progress dictates that the old pass away, to be supplanted by the new. Among whites, this metaphor is the ground of the familiar theme of the "vanishing red man" (Dippie, 1982). The belief that primitive native societies must and would give way before the tide of Western civilization, to be either absorbed or crushed, has a long history. A century ago, a West Point cadet named Custer (Steiner, 1968, p. x) lamented the passing of the race in a term paper for his ethics class: "The red man is alone in his misery. We behold him now on the verge of extinction, standing on his last foothold . . . and soon, he will be talked of as a noble race who once existed but have passed away." The theme of inevitable doom was common "in song and story," and exemplified by James E. Fraser's equestrian statute, "The End of the Trail," first shown at the San Francisco Exposition in 1915 (McNickle, 1973, 3).

Doomsaying continued into the middle of this century. In the 1932 chronicle, The Passing American, Frank Linderman (Steiner, 1968, xi) observed that even the Indian had forgotten the Indian: "The young Indians know next to nothing about their people . . . and now it is too late to learn." The closing line of Paul Radin's The Story of the American Indian (1927, 371) stressed the finality of the 1890 massacre at Wounded Knee. "The white man had triumphed . . . the Indians were crushed. Their nerve was gone. Broken, disorganized, externally and internally they gave up the fight." In this way, the theme of the "vanishing red man" voices the chronological, evolutionary claim that time, indeed, marches on.

Ironically, many of these pronouncements of the end were sounded by observers acutely sympathetic to the plight of Native Americans. To a degree, the theme of the "vanishing red man," like that of the "noble savage" before it, romanticizes native people, and martyrs them to white greed and racism. Yet, the sense of inevitability of their doom is so strong that it tends to absolve whites of culpability, fixing blame instead on the inexorable march of abstract forces like "progress." Therefore, unsurprisingly, this theme quickly became a self-fulfilling prophecy, legitimizing even greater incursions upon the lands and liberties of native people (McNickle, 1973, 62). As Native Americans survived in an ever-smaller part of the real world, to the general public they increasingly lived on only in the romantic fictions of literature and Hollywood (Forbes, 1964, 13; Friar & Friar, 1972), thereby cementing their consignment to history and irrelevancy.

In sharp contrast to arguments that bespeak the inexorability of assimilation-or-else stands the Native American activists' argument that tribalism is inevitable. The militants' conviction that their movement eventually will, indeed, of necessity must, succeed is grounded in the belief that "time decides." Herbert Blatchford (Steiner, 1968, 120) explains: "When something has to be decided it is good to wait. If you act too quickly then you do not give time a chance to act. We believe that time will help the decision to be made." This is not to say simply that time gives people an opportunity to decide, but that Time itself, as "part of the process of life," decides.

Hence, the capacity to wait is a great virtue. Former Commissioner of Indian Affairs John Collier (Steiner, 1968, 121) once observed that the Indian had such a capacity, "which was of ancient man" and "bestows the power to endure . . . to outlast." The Indian, he noted, still retains "the capacity to wait, to endure, to possess things that seem gone."

This notion trades directly upon the cyclical metaphor. When time decides, longevity rather than modernity indicates that time is favorable. Only that which is worthy lasts. Philip Deere ("IFCO," 1975, Early Winter, 26), an activist Creek medicine man, emphasizes this point: "Our Indian way of life has been tested for thousands of years, and we still have it. What has been given to us since the dawn of Creation we are willing to stand up and die for." Periodic Native American political victories confirm the

validity of traditional ways of life and, thus, are testimonials to longevity. Federal recognition of the Tigua tribe in 1968 confirmed, to many, that time's cycle could overcome time's arrow. "If, many Indian people thought, the Tiguas had survived for three centuries in the middle of El Paso," Deloria (1970, 241) reports, "might not their own tribe also survive somehow? . . . The basic operating assumption of tribes changed from that of preserving the tribal estate for an eventual distribution to the idea that tribes would always manage to survive, that present difficulties were not insurmountable." In this way, the longevity of the tribal group signifies time's favorability.

The longevity of the individual, in contrast, is relatively unimportant; Native Americans recognize that time may take longer than a lifetime—perhaps even generations—to decide. The priority accorded group survival contrasts sharply with the Christian emphasis on personal salvation, both of which can be traced to underlying temporal metaphors. For time's arrow lends to the moment a sharp urgency, in that the present is constantly vanishing into the past, never to recur; in time's cycle, however, the moment is not so urgent, for it will come again. Deloria (1970, 83) argues: "In the scheme of individual salvation, time is of the essence. One has only one lifetime to harvest the goodies of the world. It is therefore imperative that one use the most direct methods to amass wealth, prestige, and power. With a group tribalistic approach to life, time is meaningless. If we do not accomplish the task in our lifetimes, someone else will do so in time."

To the latter way of thinking, therefore, success need not be immediate; indeed, even setbacks are not final, but—quite literally— only momentary. Instead, long-term goals may be set with every confidence that they will be achieved in the indeterminate future. As a participant in the siege of Wounded Knee (*Voices*, 1974, 248) observed: "Everything will have to be a slow and on-going process. And it's going to be a process that most of us won't even be around to see. We will be gone before we're able to live like we want to live, but our children will be able to, or maybe our grandchildren or great-grandchildren, and that's what we're going to be building for." In this way, Native

American activists argue that they will outlast whites, who are "regarded as a temporary aspect of tribal life," and that "the tribe will survive the domination of the white man and once again rule the continent" (Deloria, 1970, 11; see also Means, 1982, esp. 167–168). An elderly Papago (Deloria, 1970, March 8, 56) compared his tribe to "the old mountain in the distance. The Spanish had come and dominated them for 300 years and then left. The Mexicans had come and ruled them for a century, but they also left. 'The Americans,' he said, 'have been here only about 80 years. They, too, will vanish but the Papagos and the mountain will always be here.'"

Deloria's defense of this view is the most sophisticated. Arguing that all forms of social life are shaped and constrained by the land on which social groups live, he (1979, 106–107, 131) suggests that modern technological innovations are effectively retribalizing human societies. "Thus whether the land is developed or not, and whether the people desire it or not," Deloria (1970, 190) contends, "the land determines the forms by which societies are able to live on this continent. An undeveloped land created tribes and a fully developed land is creating tribes." Aliens to the land either must conform to its dictates or be destroyed; just as the Holy Land, "having been periodically conquered and beaten into submission by a multitude of invaders, today remains the land which God gave to Abraham and his descendants," so too "will America return to the red man" (Deloria, 1970, 178). "The only answer will be to adopt Indian ways to survive," he contends elsewhere (Deloria, 1970, 208). "For the white man even to exist, he must adopt a total Indian way of life. That is really what he had to do when he came to this land. It is what he will have to do before he leaves it once again."

Conveniently, such forces render "mere" political and economic clout, which Native Americans lack, unnecessary. "As Indians," Deloria (1970, 221) argues,

we will never have the efficient organization that gains great concessions from society in the marketplace. We will never have a powerful lobby or be a smashing political force. But we will have the intangible unity that has carried us through four centuries of persecution and

we will survive. We will survive because we are a people unified by our humanity; not a pressure group unified for conquest. And from our greater strength we shall wear down the white man and finally outlast him. But above all, and this is our strongest affirmation, we SHALL ENDURE as a people.

Indeed, such forces have already determined the outcome of the cultural battles; all that remains is for the cycle of the ages to manifest the result once again. "In essence," Deloria (1970/1974, p. 190) concludes. "Indians have really won the battle for cultural survival. It remains only for years to go by and the rise of youth to continue, and everyone will be in the real mainstream of American life—the tribe." In this same spirit could Steiner (1976) write coyly of "the vanishing white man."

The pervasive theme of the "vanishing red man" is a patent obstacle to Native American activism. It relegates contemporary native grievances to the perhaps regrettable but certainly unalterable past. It dismisses the entire rationale for activism, that is, traditional tribal worldviews, as a primitive and outmoded way of thinking. Most fundamentally, it confronts activists with their own nonexistence. For if Indians have vanished, how can there be a movement today? As one participant in the 1972 Trail of Broken Treaties caravan (Trail, 1974, 18) noted perceptively: "The myth has been perpetuated that we don't exist anymore—that's the hardest thing we have to fight against." The evolutionary perspective of time's arrow severs the ties between Native American history and contemporary life, while "Indian Time" seeks to restore the primordial grounds of meaning.

Can it succeed? These competing terminologies of the inevitable are self-justifying. Each employs its presuppositions to define the nature of and predict eventual success for itself. As a result, the question of success is in part comparative, a matter of the relative ability of each terminology to account for discontinuities forced upon it by the other.

A discourse grounded in time's cycle, strictly speaking, can postpone indefinitely its ultimate victory without undermining its essential validity. The rejuvenation of tribal entities like the Tiguas, for example, certainly does not constitute final success for the Red Power movement. Yet it is a necessary beginning and a positive sign, holding out the potential for greater future success by empirically contradicting the historicist thesis that the time for tribal existence has passed irretrievably. Every such example reinforces the belief in eventual, albeit indeterminate, native victory by interrupting the march of evolutionary progress. No setback, no matter how horrific, is final.

Further, no deadlines need be met to preserve the integrity of this metaphor, save those imposed on it by impatient individuals. Success may come tomorrow, next year, or generations from now. As a nationally visible force, the American Indian Movement has been moribund for a decade, with much of its energy sapped by legal skirmishes (for two accounts of events since Wounded Knee in 1973, see Matthiessen, 1980, 1984). News coverage of AIM leaders has focused largely on these skirmishes (e.g., "Indian Leader," 1984, September 14, Pt. I, 21); on the controversy surrounding Russell Means' opposition to the Sandinista government in Nicaragua (e.g., "American Indians to Fight," 1985, December 28, Pt. I, 10) and on personality pieces (Stumbo, 1986, June 15, 10–21). However, as other events reveal, tribal localities everywhere perennially confront the issues of land, sovereignty, and cultural integrity (e.g., Chandler, 1985, August 25, Pt. I, 3, 28–29). Thus, conditions are perpetually ripe for activism and, if today represents a downturn in the cycle of resistance, inevitably a resurgence will occur.

In contrast, each discontinuity in a discourse grounded in time's arrow is not simply a delay in the triumph of this metaphor, but a challenge to its very integrity. The terminology of progress necessarily must set deadlines of some kind, to mark the passage of evolutionary ages and, indeed, to differentiate time itself as change in an otherwise static reality. Consequently, this terminology requires that discontinuities be accounted for, normally through the readjustment of deadlines. The rejuvenation of tribal entities like the Tiguas certainly does not disprove the entire historicist thesis. The terminological resources that permit the accommodation of such "anachronistic" events are vast,

and the movement's relative dormancy can lend credence to the evolutionary view. Nonetheless, every anachronism, as an exception to the march of progress, threatens the integrity of the very idea of "progress."

Thus, while time's arrow confronts Native Americans with their own nonexistence, time's cycle confronts whites with a reciprocal dilemma. For if traditional tribal life is in fact undergoing a revival, how can the evolutionary account of history be true? and why cannot the injustices of history be reversed?

This essay has examined what might be termed a rhetoric of the powerless, wherein marginalized people whom, by circumstance or design, the march of progress threatens to leave behind, may preserve their cultural identities and hope of ultimate vindication. The inevitability of time's arrow condemns them, counseling despair, but may be overcome by the inexorability of time's cycle.

In principle, these roles can be reversed. Power elites may invoke time's cycle rescue their privilege (King, 1976, 133–134). And the powerless can (and revolutionaries often do) exploit the resources of time's arrow, claiming to be the vanguard of a historical tide that will sweep away the retrogressive, myopic establishment. But the latter alternative is not available to Native American activists, not simply because the judgment of history is overwhelmingly to the contrary, or even because white audiences, steeped in time's arrow, would find such a claim ludicrous. Rather, this alternative is unavailable because to exploit the resources of time's arrow would be to deny both a central aspect of Native American cultures and the Red Power movement's self-proclaimed *raison d'etre*, i.e., the revitalization of these cultures.

Elsewhere I have explored ritual self-address which enacts Red Power demands and enables the movement to "succeed" in spite of (and, in a very real sense, because of) its alienation of the white power structure (Lake, 1983). However, this success is of a peculiar, qualified kind. Alienation of whites may achieve certain separatist militant goals, but it thereby also perpetuates the conditions of life which white aid might alleviate (Lake, 1983, 142). The genius of the militant theme of inevitability is its ability to compensate for this limitation. The ritual invocation of "Indian Time" enacts a period when life was better, or at least promises that this period will return. Thus, even if whites today will not listen, *some day* time's cycle will reestablish tribal preeminence regardless. The cycle of the ages does not wait for, nor depend upon, such extrinsic efficacy.

This theme is not without its own limitations, however. In its rigid insistence upon the reenactment of past events, its use of patterns of speech and action whose meanings are not only well-established and stable but said to have been specified at the dawn of Creation, ritual employs what Philip Wheelwright (1968, p. 94) has called "steno-symbols," i.e., symbols whose meanings have become standardized and hardened either through stipulation or through human inertia and lack of creativity. Such symbols are perfect exemplars of a cyclical worldview that conceives the present as a recurrence of archaic archetypes. However, to a linear worldview committed to evolutionary progress, steno-symbols represent only the outmoded, inferior past. The Native American theme of inevitability is itself apt to be perceived as anachronistic wishful thinking, as merely a "cliched symbol" (Ochs, 1974, April, 6; Lake, 1983, 127–128), by whites (including rhetorical critics) operating within a predominately linear framework.

Therefore, arguments that invoke "Indian Time" remain principally an instance of activist self-address. Controversial American Indian Movement leader Russell Means (1982, 161) has said, "I don't really care whether my words reach whites or not." The time socially constructed in militant discourse instills patience and offers hope principally to those who voice and ritually enact it. It is simply and supremely ironic that time's arrow of history, thought to have sounded the death knell of universalist philosophies of permanence, itself may have been relied as an equally universal form of understanding, thereby prejudicially condemning discourse that engages other temporal metaphors (e.g., Bass, 1983).

Native activists and the white establishment may contest the historical efficacy of tribalism, its relevance in the modern age, and the likelihood of Red Power's eventual triumph. But on one point they may agree: Time will tell.

REFERENCES

American Indians to fight Sandinista regime. (1985, December 28). *Los Angeles Times,* Pt. I, p. 10.

Bailey, P. (1957). *Wovoka: The Indian messiah.* Los Angeles: Westernlore Press.

Bass, J. D. (1983). Becoming the past: The rationale of renewal and the annulment of history. In D. Zarefsky, M. O. Sillars, & J. Rhodes (Eds.), *Argument in transition: Proceedings of the third summer conference on argumentation.* (pp. 305–318). Annandale, VA: Speech Communication Association.

Bellecourt, Vernon. (1973, July). Penthouse interview (Richard Ballad, Ed). *Penthouse,* pp. 56ff.

Brown, I. E., Ed. (1953/1972). *The sacred pipe: Black Elk's account of the seven rites of the Oglala Sioux.* Baltimore: Penguin Books.

Brown, J. E. (1982). *The spiritual legacy of the American Indian.* New York: Crossroad.

Brummett, B. (1984). Premillenial apocalyptic as a rhetorical genre. *Central States Speech Journal,* 35, 84–93.

Bury, J. B. (1932/1960). *The idea of progress: An inquiry into its origin and growth.* New York: Dover.

Cassirer, E. (1944/1975). *An essay on man: An introduction to a philosophy of human culture.* New Haven: Yale University Press.

Cassirer, E. (1955/1975a). *Language.* Vol. 1 of *The philosophy of symbolic forms* (R. Manheim, Trans.). New Haven: Yale University Press.

Cassirer, E. (1955/1975b). *Mythical thought.* Vol. 2 of *The philosophy of symbolic forms* (R. Manheim, Trans.). New Haven: Yale University Press.

Chandler, R. (1985, August 25). Foresters, Indians clash over fate of sacred ground. *Los Angeles Times,* Pt. I, pp. 3, 28–29.

Collier, J. (1947). *The Indians of the Americas.* New York: W. W. Norton.

Condit, C. M. (1989). Nixon's "fund": Time as ideological resource in the "Checkers" speech. In M. Leff & F. Kauffeld (Eds.). *Texts in context: Critical dialogues on significant episodes in American political rhetoric* (pp. 219–242). Davis, CA: Hermagoras Press.

Cox, J. R. (1982). The die is cast: Topical and ontological dimensions of the locus of the irreparable. *Quarterly Journal of Speech,* 68, 227–239.

Cox, J. R. (1989). The fulfillment of time: King's "I Have a Dream" speech. In M. Leff & F. Kauffeld (Eds.), *Texts in context: Critical dialogues on* significant episodes in American political rhetoric (pp. 181–204). Davis, CA: Hermagoras Press.

Curry, B. (1984, December 10). Alaska's natives fear way of life is doomed. *Los Angeles Times,* Pt. I, pp. 1, 20, 22–23.

Curry, B. (1986, July 6). Relocation deadline arrives but Navajo have won reprieve. *Los Angeles Times,* Pt. I, p. 4.

Curry, B. (1986, August 3). Light is growing dim for Columbia River Indians. *Los Angeles Times,* Pt. I, pp. 1, 16–17.

Dary, D. (1974). *The buffalo book.* Chicago: Swallow Press.

Deloria, V., Jr. (1969/1970). *Custer died for your sins: An Indian manifesto.* New York: Avon Books.

Deloria, V., Jr. (1970, March 8). This country was a lot better off when the Indians were running it. *New York Times Magazine.*

Deloria, V., Jr. (1970/1974). *We Talk. You Listen: New Tribes, New Turf.* New York: Dell.

Deloria, V., Jr. (1973/1975). *God is red.* New York: Dell.

Deloria, V., Jr. (1974). *Behind the trail of broken treaties: An Indian declaration of independence.* New York: Dell.

Deloria, V., Jr. (1979): *The metaphysics of modern existence.* New York: Harper & Row.

Dennis Banks given 3 years. (1984, October 9). *Los Angeles Times,* Pt. I, pp. 1, 25.

Dippie, B. W. (1982). *The vanishing American: White attitudes and U.S. Indian policy.* Middletown, Conn.: Wesleyan University Press.

Drogin, B. (1985, September 3). Poverty still grips newly rich tribes. *Los Angeles Times.* Pt. I, pp. 1, 20.

Eliade, M. (1954/1974). *The myth of the eternal return, or, cosmos and history* (W. R. Trask, Trans.). Bollingen Series XLVI. Princeton: Princeton University Press.

Eliade, M. (1957/1959). *The sacred and the profane: The nature of religion* (W. R. Trask, Trans.). New York: Harcourt, Brace & World.

Eliade, M. (1963/1968). *Myth and reality* (W. R. Trask, Trans.). New York: Harper & Row.

Eliade, M. (1984). Cosmogonic myth and "sacred history." In A. Dundes (Ed.). *Sacred narrative: Readings in the theory of myth* (pp. 137–151). Berkeley: University of California Press.

Fabian, J. (1983). *Time and the other: How anthropology makes its object.* New York: Columbia University Press.

Farrell, T. B. (1982). Knowledge in time: Toward an extension of rhetorical form. In J. R. Cox & C. A. Willard (Eds.), *Advances in argumentation theory and research* (pp. 123–153). Carbondale: Southern Illinois University Press.

Farrell, T. B. (1985). Narrative in natural discourse: On conversation and rhetoric. *Journal of Communication,* 35, 109–127.

Forbes, J. D., Ed. (1964). *The Indian in America's past.* Englewood Cliffs, NJ: Prentice-Hall.

Frentz, T. S. (1985). Rhetorical conversation, time, and moral action. *Quarterly Journal of Speech,* 71, 1–18.

Friar, R., & Friar, N. (1972). *The only good Indian . . . The Hollywood gospel.* New York: Drama Book Specialists.

Frye, N. (1980). *Creation and recreation.* Toronto: University of Toronto Press.

Hager, P. (1986, January 22). Supreme Court limits right to speedy trial. *Los Angeles Times,* Pt. I, pp. 1, 16.

Hariman, R. (1989). Time and the reconstitution of gradualism in King's address: A response to Cox. In M. Leff & F. Kauffeld (Eds.). *Texts in context: Critical dialogues on significant episodes in American political rhetoric* (pp. 205–218). Davis, CA: Hermagoras Press.

Highwater, J. (1981). *The primal mind: Vision and reality in Indian America.* New York: New American Library.

Hillinger, C. (1985, May 5). Mixing old and new in the land of the pueblos. *Los Angeles Times,* Pt. VI, pp. 12–14.

Hoban, J. L., Jr. (1980). Rhetorical rituals of rebirth. *Quarterly Journal of Speech,* 66, 275–288.

The IFCO Native American consultation—A report. (1975, Early Winter). *Akwesasne Notes,* pp. 26–30.

Indian leader Banks surrenders after 9 years, faces sentencing on riot conviction. (1984, September 14). *Los Angeles Times,* Pt. I, p. 21.

An interview with John Trudell. (1975, Early Winter). *Akwesasne Notes,* pp. 22–23.

Japp, P. M. (1986). Rhetoric and time: Dimensions of temporality in theory and criticism (Doctoral dissertation, University of Nebraska).

Kane, T. (1983). The American concept of progress in liberal argument. In D. Zarefsky, M. O. Sillars, & J. Rhodes (Eds.), *Argument in transition: Proceedings of the third summer conference on argumentation* (pp. 352–364). Annandale, VA: Speech Communication Association.

Kennedy, J. M. (1985, April 8). Tribe clings stubbornly to a way of life long past. *Los Angeles Times,* Pt. I, pp. 1, 14–15.

King, A. A. (1976). The rhetoric of power maintenance: Elites at the precipice. *Quarterly Journal of Speech,* 62, 127–134.

Lake, R. A. (1983). Enacting red power: The consummatory function in Native American protest rhetoric. *Quarterly Journal of Speech, 69,* 127–142.

Lake, R. A. (in press). The implied arguer. In D. C. Williams & M. D. Hazen (Eds.), *Argumentation theory and the rhetoric of assent.* University, AL: University of Alabama Press.

Lame Deer, J. F., & Erdoes, R. (1972). *Lame Deer seeker of visions: The life of a Sioux medicine man.* New York: Simon and Schuster.

Langer, S. K. (1942/1957). *Philosophy in a new key: A study in the symbolism of rite, reason, and art.* Princeton, NJ: Princeton University Press.

Langer, S. K. (1953). *Feeling and form.* New York: Charles Scribner's Sons.

Lauer, R. (1981). *Temporal man: The meaning and uses of social time.* New York: Praeger Special Studies.

Leff, M. (1983). Rhetorical timing in Lincoln's "House Divided" speech. Van Zelst Lecture in Communication. Evanston, IL: Northwestern University.

Leff, M. (1986). Textual criticism: The legacy of G. P. Mohrmann. *Quarterly Journal of Speech, 72,* 377–389.

Leff, M. (1988). Dimensions of temporality in Lincoln's second inaugural. *Communication Reports, 1,* 26–31.

Lorch, L. (1982). Human time and the magic of the Carmen: Metamorphosis as an element of rhetoric in Ovid's "Metamorphoses." *Philosophy and Rhetoric, 15,* 262–273.

Matthiessen, P. (1980/1983). *In the spirit of Crazy Horse.* New York: Viking Press.

Matthiessen, P. (1984). *Indian country.* New York: Viking Press.

McManus, D. (1986, January 30). Indian activist Means under fire from Sandinistas. *Los Angeles Times,* Pt. I, p. 17.

McNickle, D. (1974). *Native American tribalism: Indian survivals and renewals.* New York: Oxford University Press.

Means, R. (1982). For the world to live, 'Europe' must die. In W. Linkugel, R. R. Allen, & R. Johannesen (Eds.), *Contemporary American speeches* (pp. 159–170). 5th edition. Dubuque, IA: Kendall/Hunt.

Mooney, J. (1896/1973). *The Ghost Dance religion and the Sioux outbreak of 1890.* 14th Annual Report of the Bureau of Ethnology, Pt. 2. Glorieta, NM: Rio Grande Press.

Moore, B., Jr. (1978). *Injustice: The social bases of obedience and revolt.* White Plains, NY: M. E. Sharpe.

Moorehead, W. K. (1914). *The American Indian in the United States: 1850–1914.* Andover, Mass.: Andover Press.

Neihardt, J. G. (1932/1972). *Black Elk speaks.* New York: Pocket Books.

Ochs, D. J. (1974, April). A fallen fortress: BIA, 1972. Paper presented at the Central States Speech Association Convention, Milwaukee, WI.

O'Leary, S. D. (1987). Reading the signs of the times: Strategies of argument in apocalyptic discourse. In J. Wenzel (Ed.), *Argument and critical practices: Proceedings of the fifth SCA/AFA conference on argumentation* (pp. 522–532). Annandale, VA: Speech Communication Association.

Powers, W. K. (1975/1982). *Oglala religion.* Lincoln: University of Nebraska Press.

Puech, H. (1957/1983). Gnosis and time. In J. Campbell (Ed.), *Man and time: Papers from the Eranos yearbooks* (pp. 38–84). Bollingen Series XXX. Princeton: Princeton University Press.

Radin, P. (1927/1937). *The story of the American Indian* (Rev. ed.). New York: Garden City Publishing.

Reid, R. F. (1983). Apocalypticism and typology: Rhetorical dimensions of a symbolic reality. *Quarterly Journal of Speech, 69,* 229–248.

Ross, A., & Most, S. (1976, September 2). A.I.M. seeking new strength in spiritual roots of the Indians. *Kansas City Times,* p. 10C.

Steiner, S. (1968). *The new Indians.* New York: Dell.

Steiner, S. (1976). *The vanishing white man.* New York: Harper & Row.

Stumbo, B. (1986, June 15). A world apart. *Los Angeles Times Magazine,* pp. 10–21.

Toulmin, S. E. & Goodfield, J. (1965). *The discovery of time.* Chicago: University of Chicago Press.

Trail of Broken Treaties: B.I.A., I'm not your Indian anymore. (1974). 2nd ed. Rooseveltown, NY: Akwesasne Notes.

Underhill, R. M. (1965). *Red man's religion.* Chicago: University of Chicago Press.

Voices from Wounded Knee, 1973. (1974). Rooseveltown, NY: Akwesasne Notes.

Wheelwright, P. (1968). *Metaphor and reality.* Bloomington: Indiana University Press.

Whorf, B. L. (1975). An American Indian model of the universe. In D. Tedlock & B. Tedlock (Eds.), *Teachings from the American earth: Indian religion and philosophy* (pp. 121–129). New York: Liveright.

Witherspoon, G. (1977). *Language and art in the Navajo universe.* Ann Arbor: University of Michigan Press.

Gender and Genre: Loci of Invention and Contradiction in the Earliest Speeches by U.S. Women

Karlyn Kohrs Campbell

Gender is a title identifying the social roles deemed appropriate for persons of both sexes. Like other social roles, gender-related social roles are communicatively useful and significant because they frame behavior in ways that enable others to interpret its meaning and to respond to it appropriately. That women were prohibited from speaking in public or functioning as citizens because of their sex throughout much of human history should alert us to the significance of gender in rhetorical interactions. As Campbell and Jerry have noted, the qualities associated with successful rhetorical action—cogent argument, expertise, and skill in rebuttal—are qualities associated with masculinity, whereas defects in rhetorical presentation—sentimentality, weak logic, and timidity—are traits that have stereotypically been linked to femininity. Put differently, women were deemed ill-suited to the role of rhetor historically, and when they performed well in that role, they were seen as "unsexed," that is, as behaving in masculine ways.

Rhetorical genres are also social constructions. The name of a given genre is the titular term identifying an occasion culturally defined as one on which discourse is appropriate, including some general expectations about what kinds of symbolic action are suitable. Like the social roles implied by gender, genres frame symbolic behavior in ways that enable audiences to understand its meaning and to know what kinds of action to expect and what sorts of responses are appropriate. In some instances, there is no "name" entitling the occasion, but those who form the audience will have had their expectations shaped by their perception of the occasion and by prior experiences that will enable them to recognize *topoi* or styles that typify particular kinds of discourse. As Jamieson and Campbell have shown, generic hybrids emerge out of occasions that embrace more than one purpose.

Traditionally, because women were prohibited from speaking in public, all rhetoric, meaning all rhetorical genres, were gendered masculine. That is, whatever the legal, legislative, or ceremonial rhetorical occasion, it was generally understood that appropriate symbolic action could be produced only by males. Accordingly, when U.S. women began to produce public discourse at the end of the eighteenth and the beginning of the nineteenth century, they faced significant obstacles, and they felt a need to justify their violations of these powerful taboos. The occasions that offered opportunities for speaking, however, often were at odds with discourse defending their entry into the public sphere. Accordingly, the discourse of the earliest women speakers manifests considerable inventional skill as it reflects the double bind such women faced as they attempted to speak ingratiatingly, that is, consistent with audience expectations for the occasion, and to warrant their violations of gender roles.

In the broadest sense, on every occasion when a woman spoke, there was an awareness of taboos being violated and an expectation that the woman would act rhetorically to reaffirm traditional notions of womanhood. Campbell has described the feminine style used by many early woman's rights advocates as made up of strategic elements that reassured audiences about the femininity of speakers (*Man Cannot Speak for Her;* "Style and Content"). To mitigate the violation represented by a woman speaking in public, women advocates often structured their arguments inductively to give audiences the impression that the conclusions were their own, relied on the personal experience thought appropriate to women, and turned to male authorities in support of claims. In addition, women were expected to reaffirm female roles; accordingly, they often argued for enlarged rights in order to be better wives and mothers. In other words, no matter what the occasion, overlaid on any specific expectations was the general expectation that the woman would reaffirm, at least in part, traditional conceptions of womanhood. Obviously, such expectations were most powerful for the first women who broke the sound barrier. In effect, then, they faced two kinds of expectations—generic expectations related to the occasion and an anticipation, indeed, a demand, that, at the least, they overlay their discourse with feminine gestures and, at most, reaffirm the norms of traditional femininity, perhaps even to the extent of deprecating the public role that they were playing.

Two of the earliest discourses by U.S. women vividly illustrate these problems. The earliest, delivered by Priscilla Mason near the end of the eighteenth century, is an instance of a clearly defined and familiar genre—the salutatory oration or welcoming speech made at the beginning of graduation exercises. But such an address was now being delivered by a woman, a fact extraordinary enough to constrain a defense of women's public speaking.

The second speech occurred almost a decade later and is a hybrid of the patriotic oration and the public confession of a repentant sinner. As part of a theatrical entertainment, it is also an early example of what would become another genre, the lecture recital.[1] Deborah Sampson Gannett's lecture was an entr'acte between dramatic performances of scenes from well-known plays. It capitalized on curiosity about the speaker—she was a woman who had fought bravely as a soldier in the Revolutionary War. Her lecture combined characteristics of two genres that would have been familiar to the audience, the patriotic oration celebrating bravery and love of country, which was thought to be the exclusive purview of male speakers, and that form of witnessing in which the public confession of a repentant sinner functions as a moral warning to others, which was a type of discourse in which women had participated for centuries.[2]

In what follows, I use these two speeches as evidence for two claims: (1) the double bind that women faced as speakers was a spur to inventional creativity such that these addresses constitute remarkable efforts at transcendence, and (2) the conflict between justifying their violation of taboos and speaking in ways appropriate to the occasion and to their sex limited their ability to produce coherent works of rhetorical art.

★ PRISCILLA MASON'S SALUTATORY ORATION

As a recognized form of discourse in U.S. culture, the salutatory oration was as old as institutions of higher education;[3] however, women had been excluded from secondary, much less higher, education. When young women began to graduate from the first seminaries or girls high schools, opportunities arose to deliver discourse appropriate to graduation exercises. Thus, Priscilla Mason, the daughter of Dr. Mason of Philadelphia, was called on to deliver a salutatory oration as one of the first graduates of what was probably the first seminary for girls, Poor's Female Seminary in Philadelphia (Goodsell, 8–10).

Priscilla Mason's salutatory oration, at present the earliest extant public speech by a U.S. woman to an audience that included men, was published in 1794 but came to the attention of woman's rights advocates in 1887 when a copy was sent to *The Woman's Journal*. The copy was accompanied by a letter from Frances E. Willard, president of the Woman's Christian Temperance Union, which stated that a Pennsylvania temperance worker had sent her this "most unique and interesting relic" that she, in turn, was forwarding,[4] an indication of the importance of the struggle for the right to speak for early woman's rights advocates.

Mason's welcoming speech is of particular interest because, at the time of its delivery, there were no precedents, no culturally accepted definitions, for what a *woman* might say on such an occasion.[5] She began in ways that were wholly consistent with the occasion and in a manner that evinced no gender distinctions. The introduction was cast in the high style of ceremonial discourse, as in "Suffer us to present the first-fruits of your labors." Her language was suffused with decorum, acknowledging obligations and sensitive to norms for appropriate behavior, referring to "the barbarous custom of offering adulation in such a place as this" and to "language suitable to your feelings," asking pardon for "the defects of an attempt to please . . . arising in some measure from due respect." As a salutatory oration, it included a greeting and welcome, addressing in turn those who played a crucial role on this occasion:

> *Venerable Trustees of this Seminary, Patrons of the Improvement of the Female Mind. . . . Worthy Principal, Tutor, Friend and Parent, all in one, . . . Respected and very respectable audience.* While your presence inspires our tender bosoms with fear and anxiety, your countenances promise indulgence, and encourage us to proceed. In the name of myself and sisters, therefore, I cordially salute you.

Mason early departed from formulaic utterance, however. She recognized that her very presence required comment:

> A female, young and inexperienced, addressing a promiscuous assembly, is a novelty which requires an apology [that is, a statement of self-defense], as some may suppose. I therefore, with submission, beg leave to offer a few thoughts in vindication of female eloquence.

She immediately added a reservation: "I mean not at this early day to become an advocate for that species of female eloquence of which husbands so much and so justly stand in awe—a species of which the famous Grecian orator, Xanthippe, was an illustrious example." "Eloquence" is a term ordinarily reserved for unusually forceful and imaginative discourse; it is not routinely associated with Socrates' wife, whose "peevish scolding and quarrelsome temper may have become proverbial" ("Xanthippe" 2962). Xanthippe's identification as "the famous Grecian orator" strategically conflated private and public persuasion, rejecting the public-private sphere divisions that undergirded gender distinctions at the time. Thus, Mason linked what was a woman's acknowledged right to private influence to "the further right of being heard on more public occasions—of addressing the reason as well as the fears of the other sex." In other words, she claimed the masculine right to argue as well as the feminine right to the protection of males, and she responded to this opportunity by choosing to make what was surely one of the first public defenses by a U.S. woman of a woman's right to speak.

At the outset, Mason argued that if women demonstrated oratorical skills, their right to speak became self-evident. As proof, she cleverly turned negative stereotypes of women into evidence for her claims, which she presented in the novel form of a dialogue with herself that invited audience participation:

> Is a power of speech and volubility of expression one of the talents of the orator? Our sex possess it in an eminent degree. Do personal attractions give charm to eloquence, and force to the orator's arguments? There is some truth mixed with the flattery we receive on this head. Do tender passions enable the orator to speak in a moving and forcible manner? This talent of the orator is confessedly ours. In all these respects the female orator stands on equal, nay, on superior ground, If, therefore, she should fail in the capacity for mathematical studies, or in the metaphysical profundities, she has, on the whole, equal pretensions to the palm of eloquence.

She also responded to the argument that a woman's limited mental capacity rendered her unfit for public advocacy with comments that suggest familiarity with Greco-Roman rhetorical works such as Cicero's *De Oratore*:

> Granted it is that a perfect knowledge of the subject is essential to the accomplished orator. But seldom does it happen that the abstruse sciences become the subject of eloquence. And, as to that knowledge which is popular and practical, that knowledge which alone is useful to the orator, who will say that the female mind is incapable?

In other words, if the common topics are the proper sphere of rhetoric, even the more limited female mind might be capable of understanding them. The speech also evidenced rhetorical training in its adherence to norms for eighteenth-century public address and salutatory orations, although she noted the need to modify these norms in a republic.

The tone then shifted radically. Renouncing any hint of feminine coquetry or humor, Mason attacked what contemporary feminists would call the patriarchy. She said:

Our high and mighty lords (thanks to their arbitrary constitutions) have denied us the means of knowledge, and then reproached us for the want of it. Being the stronger party, they early seized the sceptre and sword; with these they gave laws to society; they denied women the advantages of a liberal education; forbade them to exercise their talents on those great occasions which would serve to improve them. They doomed the sex to servile or frivolous employments, on purpose to degrade their minds, that they themselves might hold unrivalled the power and pre-eminence they had usurped.

No inherent female inferiority was admitted. *Men's* acts were the causes of women's deficiencies; women were denied, forbidden, and doomed in order to ensure male superiority, which originated merely in greater physical strength. This is palliated a little by her added comment, "Happily a more liberal way of thinking begins to prevail." Moreover, Mason pointed out, when women had greater opportunities their achievements were evidence of women's abilities, and she cited examples of "'illustrious female characters' [who] have shown of what the sex are capable under the cultivating hand of science." Despite these exceptions, however, she immediately acknowledged the dilemma that confronted trained and talented women:

But supposing, now, that we possessed all the talents of the orator, where shall we find a theatre for the display of them? The church, the bar, and the senate are shut against us. Who shut them? *Man;* despotic man first made us incapable of the duty, and then forbade us the exercise.

The speech here revealed great frustration, and the attack on males was notably direct and forceful, indeed, masculine in tone; but again the attack was mitigated somewhat by her optimism. To her sisters, she said: "Let us, by suitable education, qualify ourselves for those high departments; they will open before us," then added:

They *will*, did I say? They have done it already. Besides several churches of less importance, a most numerous and respectable society has displayed its impartiality, I had almost said gallantry, in this respect. . . . They regard not the anatomical formation of the body. They look to the soul, and allow all to teach who are capable, be they male or female.

The reference was to the Society of Friends that then predominated in Pennsylvania and permitted women to preach. Many in the audience must have been affiliated with the Friends. The ellipses in the cited material include another shift in tone. In the midst of this praise was a biting contrast: "With others, women, forsooth, are complimented with the wall, the right hand, the head of the table, with a kind of mock pre-eminence in small matters; but on great occasions the sycophant changes his tune and says: 'Sit down at my feet and learn.'" The distinction between small acts of chivalry and fundamental assertions of inferiority is clear, although the final biblical allusion reverses the tenor of the story of Mary and Martha (Luke 10:38) to hint at misogyny even in the behavior of Jesus.

Consistent with that allusion, Mason's attack on the religious grounds for prohibiting speaking by women was the most startling part of the speech.[6] With remarkable temerity, and in an unmistakably masculine manner, she attacked the weightiest authority for silencing women, the apostle Paul:

But Paul forbids it. Contemptible little body! The girls laughed at the deformed creature to be revenged. He declares war against the whole sex, advises men not to marry them, and has the insolence to order them to keep silence in the churches; afraid, I suppose, that they would say something against celibacy, or ridicule the old bachelor.

Her attack was irreverent and startling because it reframed and debunked the Pauline prohibitions. It was powerful because it was cast as a narrative rooted in biblical materials suggesting that Paul was lame and chronically ill as well as celibate.[7]

Mason wove these into an artfully unfeminine story of ridicule of Paul's size and deformity by young girls who resented his treatment of them. His attacks on women as a sex were treated as retaliation, and his injunctions against women teaching or preaching were presented as insolent use of his authority to prevent them from challenging his views of marriage or demonstrating their capacity for religious authority. In the process, Paul was unmasked as a religious authority, and proscriptions against women's speaking were contextualized to a particular time and place as the vendetta of a misogynist against some young women of the early church. Quite probably, the force of this narrative strategy was overshadowed by what some surely heard as blasphemy.

Mason also claimed the forensic sphere for women, saying that "citizens of either sex have an undoubted right to plead their own cause," and asserted that here, too, successful examples could be adduced. In a burst of optimism that would prove unfounded (Chester), she concluded: "I am assured there is nothing in our laws or constitution to prohibit the licensure of female attorneys, and surely our judges have too much gallantry to urge proscription in bar of their claim." Nonetheless, it is noteworthy that, as a woman, she invited the audience to play the "gallant" role she desired.

Finally, displaying her classical learning, highly suitable for the occasion, she asserted woman's right to act in the political sphere. "In regard to the Senate," she said,

> precedent is clearly in our favor. We have one or two cases exactly in point. Heliogabalus, the Roman Emperor of blessed memory, made his grandmother a senator of Rome. He also established a senate of women, appointed his mother president, and committed to them the important business of regulating dress and fashions.[8]

She suggested that "a similar institution, established at our seat of government," might be desirable. The reasons she offered were related to the recent war of independence and to a recognition of women's need for a place in which to exercise their developing skills. She appealed to nascent United States nationalism when she said:

> We cannot be independent while we receive our fashions from other countries. . . . Such a senate composed of women most noted for

wisdom, learning, and taste, delegated from every part of the Union, would give dignity and independence to our manners; uniformity and even authority to our fashions.

Moreover, she argued:

> It would furnish the most noble theatre for the display, the exercise, and the improvement of every faculty. It would call forth all that is human, all that is divine, in the soul of woman; and having proved them equally capable with the other sex, would lead to their equal participation of honor and office.

This "immodest proposal" (Rossi) carved out and institutionalized a sphere for women's action in the new nation that neatly bridged the public political and private domestic spheres, at least as they then were construed. In other words, she sought to enlarge woman's political role but in a limited, appropriately feminine area.

Viewed as a whole, this speech is an attempt to synthesize two conflicting purposes, that is, to deliver an appropriate, hence masculine, salutatory oration while defending a woman's right to speak. The first required deferential greeting, the high style of epideictic discourse, a suitable display of classical learning, and praise for one's school and for those who made one's education possible, ordinarily followed by promises regarding future contributions to society. The second mandates refutation of the prohibitions, logical argument for and evidence of women's abilities, an assertion of the speaker's authority, and the middle style of forensic discourse, all masculine qualities now put to feminist ends. Mason's efforts give evidence of considerable inventional skill, particularly in the earlier sections of the address, but the two purposes and the styles and strategies appropriate to them do not fuse easily. The deferential introduction was undermined by her clever but impudent characterization of Xanthippe as a Greek orator. Her defense of speaking charmingly turns the tables on misogynistic stereotypes, but is followed by a blunt attack on patriarchy. Mason's praise of Quaker practices might have mollified the audience, but her irreverent attack on Paul must have shocked them. In fact, by personalizing this issue, a move often identified as a characteristically feminine, she made her refutation, if anything, more offensive. She channeled wide familiarity with classical sources into a proposal to institutionalize women's political contribution to the nation's development.

To describe the speech this way is to heighten both its originality and its defects; it delights and outrages as it careens between its competing styles and purposes; while evoking praise for its invention, it inevitably fails as an artistic whole. It is a salutatory oration that shocks as it welcomes, and it is a speech justifying a woman's right to speak through means then clearly gendered masculine. Yet its originality and its flaws make it a nearly ideal exemplar of the problems posed by the discourse of early women speakers. Can a critic overlook what is appropriate to the salutatory oration to emphasize the originality of attempts to coopt the genre for feminist purposes? Conversely, can a critic overlook the prohibitions against women speaking to concentrate on the ceremonial qualities of salutatory orations?

Mason's speech allows us to see more clearly the conflict between producing discourse appropriate to an occasion when rhetors are expected to unify the audience and to praise shared values and being a female whose very presence calls traditional assumptions into question. Yet the occasion gave Mason an opportunity to speak and prompted highly creative discourse as she seized the moment to defend a woman's right to enter the public sphere. She cleverly combined the possibilities inherent in the salutatory oration with an apologia for her temerity in fulfilling that typically masculine role that responded to the predominant grounds justifying the silencing of women. Nonetheless, it is the conflict between the speech's salutatory and feminist purposes that gives it rhetorical significance. That conflict, however, is inevitable on similar occasions. Both the speaker and the audience exist in two overlapping and inseparable situations—the opening of the commencement ceremonies calls for a speech of welcoming defined as masculine by precedent; that a woman is delivering it calls for a justification of woman's right to speak, a purpose that evokes strategies and styles gendered masculine. That these purposes are at odds, to say nothing

of the conflict between the gender of the speaker and of the speeches, circumscribes the result in artistic terms.

★ DEBORAH SAMPSON GANNETT'S 1802 LECTURES

Less than a decade later, a remarkable woman traveled to some twenty New England towns to justify publicly her decision to fight for her country as a soldier in the Revolutionary War. Deborah Sampson was born in 1760; at age 5, she was indentured to a farm family; despite very limited formal education, she learned to read and write (Elmes-Crahall 380–392; Friedenberg). She was unusually tall—5' 7"— and unusually strong, probably as a result of rigorous outdoor farm labor. In April of 1781, wearing a uniform she had sewn, she enlisted in the Fourth Massachusetts Regiment of the Continental Army using the name of a distant relative, Robert Shurtleff. Documents attest that she was an able soldier, was wounded in battle at Tarrytown, New York, and was in the army that Washington force-marched from New York to cut off Cornwallis's escape from the peninsula at Yorktown and that stormed the British redoubts there in some of the bloodiest fighting of the Revolutionary War. A wound she received at Yorktown became infected; she was taken to a hospital where a physician discovered her secret and helped her to obtain an honorable discharge. She returned to Massachusetts, settled in Stoughton, and married an impoverished local farmer named Benjamin Gannett with whom she had three children. When Herman Mann, a local publisher, approached her about a lecture tour in 1802,[9] she agreed, probably as much to make money as to attest to the truth of her incredible story and to justify her extraordinary actions;[10] both would be important in her effort to obtain a military pension.[11]

According to the introduction to the text published in 1805, Sampson Gannett's address was "procured"; in all likelihood, Mann helped her to compose it. Charges that early speeches by women were written by others are quite common, however, reflecting the gender-related belief that women were naturally incapable of producing rhetorical arguments.[12] To whatever extent Mann influenced its creation, analysis discloses strong grounds to accept the address as an authentic and unusually powerful expression of the conflicting purposes and voices in early women's rhetoric.

Sampson Gannett's address is a complex hybrid that responded to the occasion, to her purposes, and to gendered expectations. As part of a theatrical event, she needed to entertain the audience. Her value as an attraction was related to her unusual history, which she needed to discuss in ways that would explain and justify her egregious violation of the female role and present her simultaneously as a respectable woman and a patriotic, brave soldier who, if both were true, would merit a pension for her services to her country.[13] In presenting herself as a soldier worthy of a pension, she used elements of high style and lines of argument typical of patriotic orations, and in presenting herself as a respectable and worthy woman, and in justifying her temerity in speaking in public, she presented herself as a repentant sinner whose life was a moral message reaffirming the principles of true womanhood.

Like many women who would follow her to the platform, Sampson Gannett responded to the questions raised by her very presence on the platform by commenting on her motives, but she defended herself by blurring the lines between motives for her past actions as a soldier and her present actions as a speaker; she first described them in ungendered terms that reflected U.S. values: "That genius which is the prompter of *curiosity,* and that spirit which is the support of *enterprise,* early drove, or, rather illured [sic] me, from the corner of humble obscurity" (17). She conceded that her tale as told by others "ought to expel me from the enjoyment of society, from the acknowledgment of my own sex and from the endearing friendship of the other" but rejected that narrative as "saying too much: For as I should thus not respect *myself,* [I] should be entitled to none from *others.*" (16–17). Here as elsewhere in the lecture, she conceded the conflict between the norms guiding evaluation of women's action in general and the criteria by which she believed her own actions should be judged.

Throughout the lecture, she spoke in two distinct voices that reflected two different personae, one masculine, the other feminine. One of them (masculine) voiced the patriotic oration, asserting her heroism and humanity and praised the love of country of all who had fought in the war; the other (feminine) repented of these acts as sins, condemning her trespass of the limits of woman's sphere, and reaffirmed the tenets of True Womanhood (Cott; Welter). These competing voices were apparent from the outset. As a True Woman, she recalled her career as a soldier "as a foible, an error and presumption," but a second, masculine voice added: "And yet I must frankly confess, I recollect it with a kind of satisfaction" (18). The True Woman admitted that soldiering was "a breach in the decorum of my sex, unquestionably; and, perhaps, . . . irreconcilable with the rigid maxims of the moralist," but her alter ego labeled it "a sacrifice," a form of action for which either a soldier or a True Woman could be praised.

Speaking in that second, masculine voice, she described her decision to join the army as occasioned by natural curiosity allied with patriotic agitation, which, her True Woman voice noted, "may be deemed unnatural in my sex," but, her alter ego interjected, was "not a demoralization of human nature" (20). Her actual decision to become a soldier was explained in appropriately high style as the triumph of patriotic zeal over the narrow confines of femininity:

Wrought upon at length, you may say, by an enthusiasm and phrenzy,[14] that could brook no control—I burst the tyrant bands, which *held my sex in awe,* and clandestinely, or by stealth, grasped an opportunity, which custom and the world seemed to deny, as a natural priviledge [sic]. And whilst poverty, hunger, nakedness, cold and disease had dwindled the *American Armies* to a handful—whilst universal terror and dismay ran through our camps, ran through our country—while even WASHINGTON himself, at their head, though like a god, stood, as it were, on a pinacle [sic] tottering over the abyss of destruction, the last prelude to our falling a wretched prey to the yawning jaws of the monster aiming to devour—not merely for the sake of gratifying a fecetious [sic] curiosity, . . . did I throw off the soft habiliments of *my sex,* and assume those of the *warrior,* already prepared for battle. Thus I became an actor in that important drama, with an inflexible resolution to persevere through the last scene; when we might be permitted and acknowledged to enjoy what we had so nobly declared we would possess, or lose with our lives—FREEDOM and INDEPENDENCE! (21–22)

She exploited stylistic resources of the patriotic oration both to enact and to arouse in the audience the feelings that led to her extraordinary decision.

That climax construction was followed by an extremely discreet recounting of her experiences as a soldier. The True Woman confessed to an occasional "tear of repentence [sic]" (22), modestly and strategically asking, "Shall I not stop short, and leave to your imaginations to pourtray [sic] the tragic deeds of war?" In a clever paraleipsis the True Woman added, "And were it not improper, . . . I would appeal to the soft bosom of my own sex to draw a parallel between the perils and sexual inconveniences of a girl in her teens . . . obliged to perform the duties in the field." (23). Shifting her tone quite abruptly, the voice of her masculine alter ego celebrated the terrors and triumphs of the war in a section of the address that took the form of a patriotic paean that praised all who fought for freedom and that culminated in a sonnet saluting "dearest LIBERTY!" For the newly minted Americans she was addressing, this may have been the highest form of ingratiation possible.

An abrupt transition followed in which she acknowledged that the central issue she represented as a woman soldier had not yet been addressed:

But the question again returns—*What particular inducement could she have thus to elope from the soft sphere of her own sex* [said True Woman], *to perform a deed of valor* [said her masculine alter ego] *by way of sacrilege on unhallowed ground* [True Woman added]— *voluntarily to face the storms both of elements and war, in the character of him who is more*

fitly made to brave and endure all danger [noted the alter ego]? (28–28)

In a highly strategic use of ambiguity, she made no attempt to answer these questions directly; instead, once again, she exploited the dramatic context to recast the issue poetically:

And dost thou ask what fairy hand inspired
A *Nymph* to be with martial glory fired?
Or, what from art, or yet from nature's laws,
Has join'd a *Female* to her country's cause?
Why on great Mars's theatre she drew
Her *female* pourtrait [sic], though in soldier's hue?

Poetry and drama transformed questions of motive into the stuff of myth and legend, suggesting extraordinary characters and events, including the interposition of superhuman forces—a "fairy hand"—and the sorts of metamorphoses associated with the beautiful, half-human creatures believed to inhabit trees, mountains, and water and to assist in the rites of Pan and Dionysus. The poem addressed these questions with more questions, each of which alluded to great men doing great deeds:

Then ask—why *Cincinnatus* left his farm?
Why science did old PLATO'S bosom warm?
Why HECTOR in the Trojan war should dare?
Or why should HOMER trace his actions there?
Why NEWTON in philosophy has shown?
Or CHARLES, for solitude, has left his throne?
Why LOCKE in metaphysics should delight—
Precisian [sic] sage, to set false reason right?
Why ALBION'S SONS should kindle up a war?
Why JOVE or VULCAN hurried on the car?
Perhaps the same propensity you use,
Has prompted her a martial course to choose.
Perhaps to gain refinements where she could,
This rare achievement for her country's good.

These questions hint at answers mysterious and heroic. She exonerates herself by likening her motives to those of the male giants of politics, philosophy, combat, and science that she praises. These are the same urges that move great men, citizens of legendary lands (Albion's sons), the gods, and members of the audience, and these comparisons ingratiate by alluding to historical and literary figures likely to be familiar to the audience. Recollecting herself, she quickly added a couplet suggesting a womanly motive,

> Or was some hapless *lover* from her torn—
> As EMMA did her valient [sic] HAMMON
>   mourn?[15]

but her alter ego authored the final lines:

> Else he must tell, who would this truth attain,
> Why one is formed for pleasure—one for pain:
> Or, boldly, why our MAKER made us such—
> Why *here* he gives too *little*—there too *much!*

Exploiting literary ambiguity to the utmost, the poetry was her only answer; next words were: "I would not purposely evade a pertinent answer; and yet I know not, at present, how to give a more particular one than has already been suggested" (28).

As a True Woman, she immediately acknowledged that what she did was "an error and *presumption,* because [she had] swerved from the accustomed flowry [sic] paths of *female delicacy* to walk upon the heroic precipice of feminine perdition!" (28–29). Her masculine alter ego, however, offered a perfect counterpoint that made her actions creditable: "Had all this been achieved by the rougher hand, more properly assigned to wield the sword in duty and danger in a defensive war. . . these thorns might have been converted into wreaths of immortal glory and fame."

In the final paragraphs, True Womanhood appeared to triumph. The constraints of being a woman who had violated prescribed roles demanded ingratiation; similarly, to be acceptable as a woman speaking, her feminine voice had to predominate. Put differently, the patriotic oration had to be subsumed into the public confession.[16] In order to synthesize praise of her patriotic soldiering and her confession of sin, Sampson Gannett presented herself as a moral exemplar from whose errors lessons could be learned. Comparing herself to a prodigal, libertine, or baggage, the worst charges that could have been brought against her, she asked:

> who can behold the effects of the[ir]
> unprincipled conduct . . . without bringing
> into exercise every passion of abhorrence and
> commisseration [sic]? And yet, happy, those,
> who at the same time receive a monitor which

> fixes a resolve never to embark on such a
> sea of perdition; where we see shipwreck of all
> that is enobling [sic] to the dignity of *man*—
> all that is lovely and amiable in the character
> of *woman!* (31).

At this point, she retreated into a more acceptable feminine rhetorical role—addressing only the women in her audience: "But in whatever I may be thought to have been unnatural, unwise and indelicate, it is now my most fervent desire it may have a suitable impression on you—and on me, a penitent for every wrong thought and step" (31). The voice of a masculine patriot had been transmuted into that of a feminine moral exemplar whose sinful ways might show other women the right path.

In the speech's conclusion, she spoke as a True Woman, sharply demarcating the separate spheres of women and men:

> The rank you hold in the scale of beings is,
> in many respects, superior to that of man.
> *Nurses* of his growth, and invariable models
> of his habits, he becomes a suppliant at your
> shrine, emulous [sic] to please, assiduous to
> cherish and support, to live and to die for you!
> *Blossoms* from your very birth, you become his
> admiration, his joy, his eden [sic] companions
> in this world. . . . On the whole, as we readily
> acquiesce in the acknowledgment, that the field
> and *cabinet* are the proper spheres assigned
> to our MASTERS and LORDS; may *we,* also,
> deserve the dignified title and encomium of
> MISTRESS and LADY, in our *kitchens* and in our
> *parlours.* And as an overruling providence may
> succeed our wishes—let us rear an offspring in
> every respect worthy to fill the most illustrious
> stations of their predecessors (31–32).[17]

The tenets of True Womanhood had to be reaffirmed if this woman speaker who had egregiously violated one taboo by soldiering and was now engaged in violating still another by speaking in public was to be accepted and affirmed by her audiences. As a repentant sinner, she played a recognized and permissible public role as a woman. Audience members could salve their consciences for permitting her to speak by reminding themselves that it was in a good cause: moral edification from the example of a reformed sinner.

Ironically, this peroration was not the conclusion. After completing her address, Sampson Gannett would leave the stage briefly to return as the visible embodiment of her masculine alter ego dressed in the buff and blue uniform of a Continental Army infantryman, complete with gun, and finish her rhetorical act by performing the manual of arms, as one observer noted, "briskly and with perfection" (Holbrook 60, cited in Friedenberg).

Imagine her as she stands there: Woman and Warrior at war with herself, embodying and enacting two conflicting selves and speaking in two competing voices. One is masculine—a person, a citizen, a patriot, filled with human curiosity, driven to fight to save her beloved country. The high style of the patriotic oration and the resources she draws from the dramatic context, including her enactment of the manual of arms, make that voice powerful and appealing. The other is feminine—a True Woman who condemns that other self as guilty of the sin of trespass, of violating the fixed limits of woman's proper sphere. In her discretion about detail and in her sometimes demure, sometimes forceful style, her espousal of these views is credible. As a soldier, she was proud of her deeds, of her skill and bravery, and of what she had done for her country. As a woman she had to renounce that self, denounce her deeds, and plead to be readmitted to the narrow compass of the domestic domain as a moral exemplar to warn other women not to transgress fixed feminine boundaries.[18]

CONCLUSION

Post-modern critics have argued that all texts embody contradictory voices, that *aporia*, usually defined as ambiguity or equivocation, is a condition of meaning. For most texts, those claims must be argued because critics traditionally have approached texts as artistic wholes unified by a single overriding purpose. But in the instances adduced here, that is not the case. In Mason's speech, the clash between gender and purpose reverberates on many levels. The salutatory oration has been shaped by at least a half century of masculine precedents; how can a woman feminize it? That a woman is speaking is a circumstance so extraordinary that it demands a vindication of a woman's right to speak, which can only be done with invention and in a manner then gendered masculine—a feminist end can only be defended with masculine means; femininity precludes logical argument, marshaling evidence, offering rebuttal.

In Sampson Gannett's lecture, one hears the voices of two personae—the masculine citizen-soldier and the feminine True Woman. Rhetorically, only the masculine voice can deliver the patriotic oration to authenticate her bravery and patriotism and justify her decision to join the army, but if she is to be accepted by the audience *as a woman*, she must speak in a feminine voice in order to reaffirm her morality, always in doubt whenever a female left the domestic realm, and adopt an acceptable public feminine persona through which to become a moral exemplar by confessing and repenting the sin of soldiering. Neither voice, neither persona, can be suppressed, but each subverts the other.

It is often claimed that early women did not produce rhetorical masterpieces; feminists are prone to respond by producing works that show women's considerable rhetorical skills—as these texts do—and by indicating the obstacles women faced in being barred from education and from the settings in which the arts of eloquence are honed. The rhetorical problems illustrated by these speeches suggest another explanation: early women rhetors failed to produce artistic wholes because they were caught in a double-bind, a Catch-22. If Mason had delivered a salutatory oration "with decency and propriety" (Woody 337), she could not have addressed the issue that she embodied: Should women have the right to speak in public? Yet to address that issue was not only to violate norms for salutatory orations but also to speak in an "unfeminine," indeed, a masculine voice.

Deborah Sampson Gannett's lecture combined a patriotic oration of self-vindication with a confession and abject repentance. Because she was guilty by soldiering of a gross violation of the female role, only certain rhetorical options were available to her. Accordingly, she assumed an acceptable feminine public role, that of a remorseful sinner renouncing her patriotic deeds based on the tenets of True Womanhood. Yet equally, in defiance of True Womanhood, she was proud of having been a soldier in the Continental Army who had fought bravely to bring these United States into being, and so she spoke in and enacted both masculine and feminine personae. The result? A rhetorical act in conflict with itself.

Culturally, every United States woman who broke the sound barrier confronted similar conflicts and struggled toward syntheses that would unify disparate purposes and personae into unifying wholes; few succeeded. Yet like those of Mason and Sampson Gannett, their speeches reveal considerable inventional skill in attempting to transcend these constraints. Accordingly, these works disclose the originality of early women speakers as their flaws explain why the sisters of Madison and Jefferson found it so difficult to produce works of seamless eloquence.

Yet their aesthetic limitations are balanced by their social significance. The very fact of violating sexist prescriptions and of making arguments justifying women's speaking contributed to eroding the prescriptions. In addition, these speeches rehearsed arguments that could be used by other women. The inventional skill with which these speakers found ways to capitalize on contradictions embedded in stereotypes created lines of argument that other women could exploit: Women's volubility became evidence of their suitability for speaking; women's lack of specialized expertise was no barrier to rhetoric, according to the classical masters; women's violations of taboos were evidence of their humanity. Both women's speeches were evidence that (*pace* Freud) women wanted the same things that men did— to use their talents, to develop their skills, and to serve their country. That they were preserved and published and republished enabled these discourses, whatever their internal contradictions, to embolden other women to speak and to seek ways to express their patriotism and their ambition. The ambiguity in these texts may have been a resource as well. The competing voices and conflicting views may have manifested women's divided consciousness, but in that division, one voice articulated the aspirations that are the first stirrings of what would become a movement for woman's rights. In that

sense, these discourses are also the beginnings of contemporary feminism.

NOTES

1 Her lecture was a precursor of the lecture-recital in the sense that her dual purposes led her to combine dramatic entertainment with moral exhortation (Harrison). Harrison cites Moiree Compere (37) as describing lecture recitals as "programs combining a lecture on a subject, motif, or theme with examples of prose, poetry, or both, to illustrate the points developed in the lecture," which, he notes, "makes the mode sound less a poetic form and more an adjunct of some rhetorical purpose" (12). Mary Margaret Robb writes that "Anna Cora Mowatt, the author of *Fashion,* claims the distinction of being the first American Woman to read professionally [in 1841]. . . . Shortly thereafter, there were six women elocutionists who were giving programs throughout the country" (180). The lecture recital is of interest because it is a genre in which women later excelled, perhaps because of their traditional link to educating and civilizing, perhaps because the emotional or poetic element in it was seen as particularly suited to women's nature. On the other hand, actresses were not seen as respectable women, in part because they appeared in public.

2 This is the basic form of Christine de Pizan's great fifteenth century work, *The Treasure of the City of Ladies: or The Book of the Three Virtues.* Ostensibly, such works were addressed only to women.

3 The genre persisted intact well into the twentieth century. An account of Harvard orations in the *Boston Evening Globe,* June 20, 1940, reported that "three 'commencement parts,' one delivered in Latin, by students graduating with exceptionally high honors, opened the ceremonies. First of these was the traditional welcome in Latin, extended by Robert Brooks '40 of Needham. Using profuse gestures to illustrate his meaning, he first welcomed Dr. [James Bryant] Conant [president of Harvard] who was roundly applauded. Next Brooks saluted Governor [Everett] Saltonstall, and the recipients of honorary degrees. The youthful orator then expressed welcome and gratitude to the 'puellae' or young ladies present. Finally he urged them, in spite of the war, to use the principles and lessons of the classroom in the interpretation of all human affairs with a calm and critical mind" (qtd. in Robb 22).

4 According to Willard, the speech was delivered December 3, 1787, in Harrisburg; however, the address as originally published (1794) is dated May 15, 1793. The text in *The Woman's Journal* is the same as the original; accordingly, all citations are from the more accessible text in *The Woman's Journal*. An excerpted version appears in Ruether and Keller.

5 Thomas Woody describes these exercises at the Female Academy at Philadelphia this way;

[After the processional] There followed a prayer, "a salutatory oration" and "selected pieces well adapted to the female character," by several scholars, and more appropriate music. A valedictory was delivered "with decency and propriety." . . . The addresses by young ladies at commencement are interesting for their defense of female education—possibly inspired by Poor [the school's founder] (337–338).

In contrast, however, Woody quotes lines written by a gentleman who attended the commencement of June 20, 1792:

"On the soft accents of the female tongue,
"To rapt attention every nerve was strong:
"While decent confidence, and modest grace,
"Diffus'd a lustre o'er each charming facet
"Delightful task, t'expand the human mind,
"With virtue, knowledge, sentiment, refin'd—
"To teach th'aspiring faculties to soar,
"And the bright realms of science to explore;
"To form the maiden for th'accomplish'd wife,
"And fix the basis of a happy life!" (from a pamphlet on the "Young Ladies Academy" in the State Library at Harrisburg, Pa., 1793, qtd. in Woody 236)

These comments suggest that defenses of female education in commencement speeches may have been exceptional.

Moreover, the salutatory and valedictory speeches in commencement exercises were named for their greeting and farewell functions in Latin. Other kinds of speaking were also part of these exercises, e.g. conferences, essays, literary disquisitions, dissertations, philosophical disquisitions, forensic disputations, and orations (both in Latin and English). In the programs for Harvard's commencement exercises, for example, no topics were listed for the salutatory or valedictory speeches, confirming their predominantly phatic functions. By contrast, the topics of all of the other types were listed. See for example, Cameron (100–101).

6 In her letter to the *Woman's Journal*, Frances E. Willard quotes Mrs. Fanny D. B. Chase, who sent her the speech, as saying: "The paragraph about St. Paul seems a little irreverent. This must have been quite startling to the trustees, and the respected and very respectable audience."

7 According to tradition, Paul was a small man, partially lame. The Acts of Paul and Thecla, an apocryphal document, describes Paul as "a man of little stature, thin-haired upon the head, crooked in the legs . . ." (*Encyclopedia Britannica*, 1966, Vol. 17, p. 472). At Lystra, it is reported that Paul was mistaken for Hermes (Acts 14: 12), a god sometimes described as small and vivacious, but who was also a messenger. One epistle reports that Paul's enemies saw "his bodily presence" as "weak" (2 Cor. 10:10). He also referred to a "thorn in the flesh" (2 Cor. 7:7), apparently a recurring illness that was a matter of discomfort and that sometimes hindered his movements (Gal. 4:13–14). In his letter to the Romans, Paul exhorted Christians to remain celibate, and was himself unmarried, although he conceded that it was "better to marry than to burn." He was also the primary author of injunctions against women's speaking (I Cor. 14:34–35; 1 Tim. 2:11–14).

8 Elagabalus (corrupted to Heliogabalus by some Greek writers), Roman emperor 218–222 C.E., was the son of Julia Soæmias and grandson of Julia Mæsa, sister-in-law of the emperor Septimius Severns, and took his name from the sun-god of Emesa (Horns in Syria), of whom he was the hereditary priest. In his fifteenth year he was saluted by Augustus at Emesa under the name Marcus Aurelius Antoninus, his mother alleging that he was the son of Caracalla. After the defeat of the Prætorian prefect Macrinus, he finally reached Rome in 219. His chief interest was the advancement of his religion. His mother attended debates in the Senate, and also presided over a "female senate," which formulated rules of etiquette. His mother induced him to adopt his cousin Alexander as his son and heir in 221; jealousy and intrigue ensued till an opportune bribe by Alexander's mother induced the Prætorians to murder Elagabalus and his mother (Hammond and Scullard 377).

9 Her lecture preceded the beginnings of the lyceum, founded in 1826 by Yale graduate Josiah Holbrook, to promote "the universal diffusion of knowledge," by many years; the American Lyceum Association was founded in 1831 (Mead 15).

10 The introduction to the text as originally published in 1805 reported: "It is from her naturally ambitious disposition, and taste for a more elevated

style of life, that she is induced . . . to appear in public, to open the eyes of the incredulous, and to wipe off any aspersions, which the whispers of satire, caprice, or malevolence may have wantonly thrown upon her" (Gannett 15). Page numbers of subsequent quotations from this publication are found in parentheses in the text.

Audiences of men and woman paid twenty-five cents admission with children admitted at half-price to attend. Her diary of the fifteen-month tour indicates that she concerned herself with business details—bookings, advance publicity, and accounting. She cleared at least $100, an amount that equals some $3,000 earned today, and was equivalent to more than a year's earnings at a time when a woman schoolteacher typically earned $1 or less a week plus room and board, and a seamstress typically earned twenty-five to forty cents a day (Friedenberg 13–14).

Her tour took her to Holden, the home of Captain George Webb, into whose troop she had enlisted, and she stayed at the Lisle, N.Y., home of her commanding officer, General John Patterson, whom she had served as an orderly, from November 11 to December 11, 1802. Their presence attests to the accuracy of the facts in her lecture, which have never been challenged. Moreover, the lecture contained facts not widely known, e.g. that Cornwallis surrendered his sword to General Lincoln, not General Washington (Friedenberg 9).

11 She applied for and was awarded a pension by the state of Massachusetts in 1792 and by the U.S. Congress in 1805 (National Archives, Military Records Division, pension file #S32722; Deborah Sampson Gannett Collection, Massachusetts State Archives). The latter includes sworn statements by Pvt. Shurtleffs commanding officers taken during 1791–1792. See also Stickley 233–241. I refer to her as Sampson Gannett in order to distinguish her from her husband, Gannett.

12 For example, commenting on Priscilla Mason's speech, which he quotes at length, Woody says: "Another miss (1793) defended oratory for her sex with much more spirit, though the originality of her 'piece' may be doubted" (338).

13 Elmes-Crahall quotes John Hancock's letter to D. Cobb, January 19, 1792, written on her behalf, saying, "it further appears that the said Deborah exhibited an extraordinary instance of female heroism by discharging the duties of a faithful gallant soldier, and at the same time preserving the virtue of Chastity of her Sex unsuspected and unblemished, and was discharged from the service with a fair and honorable character" (1993, 381).

14 "The spelling *phrenzy* is now rare; some writers show a tendency to prefer it when referring to prophetic ecstasy of daemonical possession" ("Phrenzy" 1007). That is the sense of the term as used here.

15 Despite my best efforts, I cannot identify this allusion.

16 As Jamieson and Campbell (1982) point out, in speeches that combine two or more genres, one of them must predominate.

17 This is the limited role Linda Kerber (11–12) identifies as that of Republican Motherhood.

18 In contrast to Joan of Arc, who wore men's clothing while insistently reminding others that she was female and virgin, Sampson Gannett succeeded completely in assuming a masculine identity. Unlike Joan, she was a transvestite, a sexual performance that, as Judith Butler argues, calls into question established notions of gender and problematizes social norms of sexuality. One of my graduate students, Rob Brookey, argues that this lecture is also an example of the narrative form that Marjorie Garber calls "the transvestite's progress" (1993, p. 69), which functions to desexualize cross-dressing by offering an acceptable rationale—in this case, patriotism—for it. Moreover, presenting this lecture on stage, a setting in which cross-dressing has a long history, reduces its threat by suggesting that it is merely a theatrical device. The reappearance of Robert Shurtleff at the end of her lecture, Brookey argues, is a sign that transgendered experience is not so easily explained away. Although Brookey's perspective is intriguing, I see it in a still larger frame. That is because, from my perspective, Sampson Gannett is cross-dressing throughout the lecture as her voice glides smoothly between its masculine and feminine tones in a performance full of swift changes of gender costume. She embodies, if you will, the rhetorical bisexual whose voice links feminist criticism and queer theory.

WORKS CITED

Brookey, Robert A. "Keeping a Good Wo/Man Down: Normalizing Deborah Sampson Gannett." University of Minnesota, 1994.

Butler, Judith. *Gender Trouble: Feminism and the Subversion of Identity*. New York: Routledge, 1990.

Cameron, Kenneth W. *Thoreau and His Harvard Classmates: Henry Williams' Memorials of the Class of 1837 with a Commentary and an Index*. Hartford, CT: Transcendental Books, 1965.

Campbell, Karlyn Kohrs. *Man Cannot Speak for Her: A Critical Study of Early Feminist Speakers*. Westport, CT: Greenwood Press, 1989.

Campbell, Karlyn Kohrs. "Style and Content in the Rhetoric of Early Afro-American Feminists." *Quarterly Journal of Speech* 72 (1986): 434–445.

Campbell, Karlyn Kohrs, and E. Claire Jerry. "Woman and Speaker: A Conflict in Roles." *Seeing Female: Social Roles and Personal Lives.* Ed. Sharon S. Brehm. New York: Greenwood Press, 1988. 123–133.

Chester, Ronald. *Unequal Access: Women Lawyers in a Changing America.* South Hadley, MA: Bergin & Garvey, 1985.

Compere, Moiree Scott. Ed. *Living Literature for Oral Interpretation.* New York: Appleton-Century-Crofts, 1949.

Cott, Nancy. *The Bonds of Womanhood: "Woman's Sphere" in New England, 1780–1835.* New Haven: Yale UP, 1977.

Elmes-Crahall, Jane. "Deborah Sampson Gannett." *Women Public Speakers in the United States, 1800–1925: A Bio-Critical Sourcebook.* Ed. Karlyn Kohrs Campbell. Westport, CT: Greenwood Press, 1993. 380–392.

Friedenberg, Robert. "'I Burst the Tyrant Bands Which Held My Sex': Deborah Sampson Gannett, America's First Feminist Speaker." Paper, National Endowment for the Humanities Symposium on Women in American History, 1976.

Gannett, Deborah Sampson. "An Addrss [sic], delivered with applause, at the *Federal-Street Theatre,* Boston, four successive nights of the different plays, beginning March 22, 1802; and after, at other principal towns, a number of nights successively at each place; by Mrs. Deborah Gannet [sic], the American heroine, who served with reputation (undiscovered as a female) in the late American army. Published at the request of her audiences." Dedham, MA: Printed and sold by H. Mann, for Mrs. Gannet[t], at the Minerva Office,—1802. Reprinted in *Publications of the Sharon Historical Society of Sharon Massachusetts,* No. 2, April 1905, 15. Sampson, Deborah. "Address." *Outspoken Women: Speeches by American Women Reformers, 1635–1935.* Ed. Judith Anderson. Dubuque, IA: Kendall/Hunt, 1984. 135–41.

Garber, Marjorie. *Vested Interests: Cross-Dressing and Cultural Anxiety.* New York: Harper Perennial, 1993.

Goodsell, Willystine. Ed. *Pioneers of Women's Education in the United States: Emma Willard, Catherine Beecher, Mary Lyon.* New York: McGraw-Hill, 1931.

Hammond, N. G. L., and H. H. Scullard, eds. *The Oxford Classical Dictionary.* 2d. ed. Oxford: Clarendon Press, 1970.

Harrison, A. Cleveland. "Basic Lore of the Lecture Recital." *Communication Education* 20 (January, 1971): 10–15.

Holbrook, Stewart H. *Lost Men of American History.* New York: Macmillan, 1947.

Jamieson, Kathleen Hall, and Karlyn Kohrs Campbell, "Rhetorical Hybrids: Fusions of Generic Elements," *Quarterly Journal of Speech* 68 (1982): 146–57.

Kerber, Linda. *Women of the Republic: Intellect and Ideology in Revolutionary America.* Chapel Hill: U of North Carolina P, 1980.

Mason, Miss [Priscilla]. "Salutatory Oration." *The Woman's Journal,* vol. 18, no. 40 (October 1, 1887): I. originally *The Rise and Progress of the Young Ladies' Academy of Philadelphia.* Philadelphia: Stewart and Cochran, 1794. 90–93; excerpted in *Women and Religion in America.* 3 vols. Ed. Rosemary Radford Ruether and Rosemary Skinner Keller. San Francisco: Harper & Row, 1981. 2:406–408.

Mead, David. *Yankee Eloquence in the Middle West: The Ohio Lyceum, 1850–1870.* 1951; rpt. Westport, CT: Greenwood Press, 1977.

"Phrenzy." *Webster's New International Dictionary of the English Language.* 1950 ed.

Pizan, Christine de. *The Treasure of the City of Ladies; or The Book of The Three Virtues.* Trans. Sarah Lawson. 1405. London: Penguin, 1985.

Robb, Mary Margaret. "The Elocutionary Movement and Its Chief Figures." *History of Speech Education in America.* Ed. Karl R. Wallace. New York: Appleton-Century-Crofts, 1954. 178–201.

———. *Oral Interpretation of Literature in American Colleges and Universities.* 1941; New York: Johnson Reprint Co., 1968.

Rossi, Alice. "Equality Between the Sexes: An Immodest Proposal" Daedalus, 93, (1964): 607–652.

[Sampson Gannett, Deborah]. The Deborah Sampson Gannett Collection, Massachusetts State Archives, Boston, Massachusetts.

———. The Deborah Sampson Gannett Collection (also listed under Robert Shirtliff [sic]), National Archives, Washington, D.C., Military Records Division, pension file S32722.

Stickley, Julia Ward. "The Records of Deborah Sampson Gannett, Woman Soldier of the Revolution." *Prologue: The Journal of the National Archives* (Winter 1972): 233–241.

Welter, Barbara. *Dimity Convictions: The American Woman in the Nineteenth Century.* Athens: Ohio UP, 1976.

Woody, Thomas. *A History of Women's Education in the United States.* 2 vols. New York: Science Press, 1929.

"Xanthippe." *Webster's New International Dictionary of the English Language.* 1950 ed.

Creating Discursive Space through a Rhetoric of Difference: Chicana Feminists Craft a Homeland

Lisa A. Flores

In the novel *The House on Mango Street*, Esperanza, the main character, recalls being asked by a nun from school where she lived. She remembers the nun's response:

> There. . . . You live *there*? The way she said it made me feel like nothing. *There*. I lived *there*. I nodded.
>
> I knew then I had to have a home. A real home. One I could point to. (emphasis in original) (Cisneros 5).

As the novel progresses Esperanza grows from a child to a teenager and continues to long for a house. The dream house becomes not only one she can "point to," but one in which she can retain her identity and her culture. "One day I'll own my own house, but I won't forget who I am or where I came from," says Esperanza (Cisneros 87).

Esperanza's longing for a house and a home stems partly from her feelings of inadequacy, manifested in her interaction with her teacher. She also experiences an awareness of her differences, in culture and class, from those around her, and a sense of how her displacement is evident in spatial relations. Whether remembering the fear she sees in those people who find themselves in her neighborhood by mistake or the conspicuousness she feels when the other students stare at her as she eats her rice sandwich, Esperanza knows she does not belong (Cisneros 45). Esperanza also recalls how the women in her community experience space differently from the men, how Rafaela, locked in because her husband is afraid she will leave, watches the world from her window (Cisneros 79). Esperanza remembers the day at the carnival; others were having fun, but she was sexually assaulted (Cisneros 99–100). She finds that in writing and reading she can create a metaphoric house. Her writing ultimately becomes the tool through which she both escapes and returns living *"there"* (109–110). "One day," says Esperanza, "I will pack my bags of books and paper. One day I will say goodbye. . . . I am too strong. . . . One day I will

go away. . . . I have gone away to come back. For the ones I left behind. For the ones who cannot out [sic]" (Cisneros 110). Esperanza's desire for a house of which she can be proud and in which she can feel comfortable mirrors the dream of many Chicana feminists who, feeling alienated and isolated from both Chicano and mainstream culture, long for a space and a home in which they belong.

Chicana feminists are not alone in their discussions of space; indeed, the concept of space in relation to public and private spheres is common in feminist works.[1] Space as it relates to home, however, is a notable theme in the writings of Chicana feminists.[2] Living with the unique experience of being a border culture between Mexico and the Southwest part of the United States, Chicanas/os find themselves with a foot in both worlds. The sense of being neither truly Mexican nor truly American often results in feelings of isolation, where Chicanas/os may find that they do not belong in either land. Such isolationism leads to a struggle for a space and a home of their own that drives much Chicana feminist work.[3]

While confined geographically as a border culture between the United States and Mexico, Chicana feminists can cross rhetorical borders through the construction of a discursive space or home. By employing a rhetoric of difference, in which Chicana feminists construct an identity that runs counter to that created for them by either Anglos or Mexicans, Chicana feminists begin the process of carving out a space for themselves where they can break down constraints imposed by other cultures and groups.[4] In this essay I argue that Chicana feminists use their creative works as a tool in the discursive construction of a space of their own.[5] A critical examination of these works allows us to witness the building of individual and community identity (R. Campbell 327).

The emphasis on identity among Chicanas has roots in the 1960s Chicano movement. Richard Jensen and John Hammerback note that a focus on rebuilding self-worth and community pride was instrumental in advancing the Chicana movement.[6] They contend further that years of oppression had resulted in a weak community spirit. In their study of the poetry of Corky González, Jensen and Hammerback demonstrate that cultural identity was the Chicanos' "one remaining thread of hope" ("'No Revolutions'" 77). The focus on cultural identity was brought about in part through the discourse of Chicano leaders and the use of the terms "Chicano" and "Raza."[7] However, the growth of the Chicano movement saw these ideas expressed via other avenues as well. Poetry, literature, and art were also popular means through which the ideas of Chicano and Raza were stressed (Sedano; Jensen and Hammerback "No Revolutions"). The insights into the use of discourse by the Chicano movement to protest Anglo domination and to create identity and community form the foundation for this study of Chicana feminist works.

While Chicana feminists share much history and political commitment with Chicanos, their discourse also reflects the specific nature of their experiences of multiple oppressions. My purpose in this essay, then, is to illustrate one function of the discourse of Chicana feminists, the creation of a space and ultimately a home.[8] I begin my narrative with an exploration of the nature of the border existence and its influence on the writings of Chicana feminists. A four-part discussion of the use of a rhetoric of difference to build a space follows. This section includes first, the structure of a rhetoric of difference; second, the carving out of a space; third, the move to turn space into home; and fourth, the establishment of bridges from the newly constructed home to surrounding lands. Finally, in the conclusion, I discuss the implications of the concept of discursive space for marginalized groups.

★ LIVING ON THE BORDER

The fight for space of their own is driven in part by geographical influences affecting Chicanas/os. The Rio Grande River stands as a physical representation of the separation and isolation experienced by Chicana feminists, who have lived their lives "on the border." And yet, the associations with the border, especially for those who spent part or all of their lives on it, are powerful. Gloria Anzaldúa recognizes the continued impact of her childhood, "in leaving home I did not lose touch with my origins because *lo mexicano* is in my system. I am a turtle, wherever I go I carry 'home' on my back" (*Borderlands* 21). Their border experience colors the writing of Chicana feminists, illustrating its effects on their lives. In the titles of four well-known Chicana works—*Borderlands, Between Borders, Breaking Boundaries,* and *This Bridge Called My Back*—the pervasiveness of the border influence is apparent.[9] The first three clearly show the prominence of the border experience; while in *This Bridge* we see the concept of crossing from one land to another. These titles and the works of many Chicana feminists stress the difficulty of being a border culture.[10]

The tension of the border experience is evident in the lives of those Chicanas who find themselves unable to negotiate their mixed identity. Cherríe Moraga reflects upon this tension, "I am the daughter of a Chicana and anglo. I think most days I am an embarrassment to both groups" (*Loving* vi). But the struggle between groups is not limited to only that of Mexicana versus Anglo but includes Mexico versus the United States, patriarchy against feminism, and white feminism versus Third World feminism.

The Chicana feminist is often literally between worlds. Frequently made to feel an unwanted presence in the United States, she cannot, and likely does not want to, go to Mexico. Childhood and family also contribute to her multifaceted identity, and her upbringing means many splits that divide her loyalties. The unconditional acceptance of feminism can mean a rejection of the Chicana culture, for it means elevating sex oppression over race oppression and denying ties to Chicano men (N. Alarcón "Chicana's Feminist"). Moraga argues that allegiance to feminism and commitment to women have alienated Chicanas from many Chicanos, "Because heterosexism—the Chicana's sexual commitment to the Chicano male—is proof of her fidelity to her people, the Chicana feminist attempting to critique the sexism in the Chicano community is certainly between a personal rock and a political hard place" (*Loving* 105). As Chicana feminists realize the need for feminism to address issues of race and class and the paucity of such scholarship, they often feel frustrated and further marginalized. Sonia Saldívar-Hull makes this point rather strongly when she says, "Clearly, Chicana feminists cannot look to their Eurocentric 'sister' for discussions of our specific positions" (206). Such feelings of isolation within the women's movement are not unique to Chicana feminists but are shared by many people of color.[11] Constantly asked to choose between groups, the Chicana feminist loses identity.

The numerous borders on which the Chicana feminist finds herself mean that she has no discursive space of her own. Without a land of her own, the Chicana feminist, as evidenced by Tey Diana Rebolledo, must find a space in between; "[W]e have grown up and survived along the edges, along the borders of so many languages, worlds, cultures and social systems that we constantly fix and focus on the spaces in between . . ." (136). Expressing a similar sentiment is Anzaldúa who sees the border feminist as constantly negotiating the spaces between worlds (*Borderlands* 20). By her limitation to the border, the Chicana feminist encounters numerous boundaries that constrain her identity and action. Her stance as a feminist means her acceptance within her culture is decreased, and her identity as a Chicana leads to limited acceptance with the feminist movement. Such multiple allegiances to many groups without complete acceptance by any results in a diminished sense of community.

Following from this feeling of split identity is increased isolation resulting from the inability to mix with either Chicanas/os or Anglos. After years of diligently studying and reading, Olivia Castellaño illustrates the reactions of white teachers, "'But how did you get to be so smart? You are Mexican, aren't you,'" and the anger from Chicana classmates, "'What are you trying to do, be like the whites?'" (378–379). Chicana feminists find they cannot cross over into the Anglo world without facing recriminations from Chicanas/os and encountering ridicule from Anglos. The attempts to retain culture while interacting with nonChicanas/os often mean rejection by both groups. The Chicana feminist finds herself unable to belong in either home and forced to define a space into which she does fit.

The rhetorical implications of the border experience are manifest in several challenges that Chicana feminists face. Perhaps most prominent is the interactive nature of the relationship between form and content. What are the effects of the seemingly purposeful use by Chicana feminists of first person, of multiple languages, of multiple tones, including academic, autobiographical, and poetic? How are arguments for the celebration of multiplicity made? Working oppositionally to challenge imposed dichotomies, many Chicana feminists write in a style that becomes a rhetorical tool allowing them to maintain multiple allegiances as they proclaim self-named identity. As Angie Chabram Dernersesian states, ". . . content as well as form must be transformed, re-created, if Chicana/o subjects are to speak with their own accents and populate language with their own vernacular" (36). The label "Chicana feminist" emerges as an identity separate from Chicanos and feminists but linked to both.

In addition to the need to blend form and content, the border experience also leads to the need to fuse public and private. While much of rhetorical history investigates the influence of discourse that is clearly public, such as speeches, for marginalized groups whose access to the public sphere has been limited, "private" discourse plays a public role. Chicana feminists find poetry and other "private" discourses to be useful rhetorical tools for publicly expressing their private selves.[12] Given the links between the specific border experiences of Chicana feminists and the resulting rhetorical expression, we can turn to a detailed analysis of how such writing enables a negotiation of the border experience through the creation of border spaces.

★ CONSTRUCTING DISCURSIVE SPACE THROUGH A RHETORIC OF DIFFERENCE

Chicana feminist rhetoric is by nature neither "Western" nor nonWestern. It is certainly influenced by Western mores, but it also reveals the "ethnicity" of Chicano/a and Mexican literary traditions. It is partly the border experience of living in two worlds that brings the flavors of both to the writings of Chicana feminists. With goals of increasing the exposure of other Chicana feminists and rewriting history that denies or denigrates Chicanas, Chicana feminist discourse affirms Chicana feminist identity. Through their recognition and subsequent rejection of stereotypes, their reordering of significant experiences to include the daily activities of many Chicanas and Mexican Americans, their celebration of their culture, and their redefinition of family, Chicana feminists proclaim their identity and create for themselves not only a space but a home in which they can overcome feelings of isolation and alienation. It is through their rhetoric, a rhetoric of difference, that Chicana feminists construct their space and build their home.

A Rhetoric of Difference

In its most basic form, a rhetoric of difference includes repudiating mainstream discourse and espousing self- and group-created discourse. Through the rejection of the external and creation of the internal, marginalized groups establish themselves as different from stereotyped perceptions and different from dominant culture (Schwichtenberg 3). Through this struggle with dominant culture, marginalized groups are able to establish self and group autonomy because the individuals and groups name themselves.

The naming that comes about through a rhetoric of difference allows groups to reflect on the uniqueness of their identity. Pride and solidarity within one's group are essential to a group's interaction with other groups. By building group pride and solidarity, marginalized groups can combat their internalization of themselves as subordinate (Pheterson 35–36). Marginalized groups then find security and a sense of home within. Both the rejection of dominant definitions and the affirmation of self identity contribute to feelings of pride and solidarity.

While the generic structure of a rhetoric of difference is constant across groups, the specific strategies used to reject dominant definitions and create internal definitions will reflect the historical circumstances and nature of the oppression of the group. The discourse of Chicana feminists provides one example of the use of a rhetoric of difference to create discursive space.

When Chicana feminists refuse to accept mainstream definitions of themselves and insist that they establish and affirm their own identity, they build a space through discourse. For Chicana feminists, this process is accomplished in three stages. They begin by merely carving out a space within which they can find their own voice. After establishing this space, they begin to turn it into a home where connections to those within their families are made strong. Finally, recognizing their still existing connections to various other groups, Chicana feminists construct bridges or pathways connecting them with others. Such a process allows for the construction of boundaries that establish the Chicana feminist homeland as distinct but are flexible enough to allow for interaction with other homelands.

Living on the borders translates into existing on the margins; however, by constructing their own space, Chicana feminists begin to move from the margins closer to their own center. Such positioning of communities within a larger society affects the status of members of communities, according them either dominant or subordinate rank. Status and power become dependent on one's position within that society. Robert Hariman argues that "inferior status is a condition of social *marginality*, and we empower discourse by imposing a social order upon the world that relegates words, writers, and speakers to zones of centrality or marginality" (emphasis in original) (39). When Chicana feminists accept their border positions, they cooperate in their own lack of power and status. However, as they construct their own space, where they are in the center, they refuse to accept a marginal identity.

Establishing a Space

For Chicana feminists to create their own space, ultimately their own homeland, and thus, their own identity, they must first reject the definitions imposed on them by others. This countering of other-created images is the first step in their rhetoric of difference. In Norma Alarcón's words, Chicana feminism "requires no less than the deconstruction of paternalistic 'communal modes of power'" ("Chicana feminism" 254). Such opposition is the beginning of the breakdown of boundaries constraining Chicana feminists. The result of such actions is that Chicana feminists control their identity. Rosaura Sánchez comments on the role of Chicana literature in this process of self-definition:

> [N]ew discourses which interpellate women and ethnic minorities as discursive subjects have emerged to challenge the dominant discursive practices in history and in academia. These counter-discourses have not only empowered new discursive subjectivities but led as well to a resistance against the subjugation. . . . (1)

One result of being a border inhabitant is that Chicana feminists are often defined by those in the different lands who are calling for allegiance. The Chicana feminist must defuse the existing definitions. The signs created for Chicanas constrain them, taking away their power of agency and making Chicanas into spectacles. The Chicana feminist finds herself being surveyed by those around her. Often, to the white feminist, the Chicana is an interesting oddity. She finds herself asked for her opinion and then brushed aside, or positioned as an exotic to be studied (Anzaldúa "Speaking" 167–168). Jo Carrillo expresses her anger at tokenization, "Our white sisters/radical friends love to own pictures of us" (63). The Chicana feminist finds that she is given the role of object of study.

Not only is she made a spectacle by white feminists, but by white men, Chicanos, and other Chicanas. She finds herself defined, usually negatively, by those around her. To the white man she is a sex object, different from white women (Anzaldúa "Speaking" 167). The Chicano sees her as servant, responsible for taking care of all his desires. Moraga recalls her role as "servant," "[t]o this day in my mother's home, my brother and father are waited on, including by me" (*Loving* 90). Both Chicanos and Chicanas who do not identify with the feminist movement view the Chicana feminist as a traitor (N. Alarcón "Chicana's Feminist" 186). Thus, the Chicana feminist, in straddling different worlds and belonging to none, finds that she is defined by the inhabitants of those different worlds to the point that she is seen as object rather than subject.

As object, the Chicana feminist is disempowered. Knowledge about her has been created by others, and she is forced into roles that do not fit. As she is not allowed involvement in the construction of her identity, she loses control and is given an inferior status in an already unbalanced hierarchy.

While the first step in creating their own identity is becoming aware of existing definitions, Chicanas' awareness must be followed with their own identity constructions. Or, as Alarcón states, Chicana feminism must engage in "the thematization and construction of new models of political agency for women of color" (N. Alarcón "Chicana Feminism" 254). Until they are able to displace those who formerly controlled the definitions, Chicana feminists remain powerless and decentered (R. Campbell and Reeves 34). The creation of their own discursive space means defining themselves independently of the dominant group (Fiske 392), and such a move for Chicana feminists is the second step in creating discursive space. Celebration of their everyday experiences and of their culture allows Chicana feminists to replace negative images with positive ones.

To regain control of her subjectivity and become an active agent involved in the construction of her identity, the Chicana feminist must create the knowledge about herself. Anzaldúa describes the process, "we women of color strip off the mascaras others have imposed on us . . . so that we may become subjects in our own discourses" ("Haciendo Caras" xvi).

Chicana feminist writing includes a focus on the everyday experiences of Chicanas. These experiences are given the same worth as the traditionally white-valued "exceptional" experiences. Understanding Chicanas requires insight into the lives and experiences of the women, and this celebration of the everyday leads to an empowerment of Chicanas (Hill Collins "Learning" S16–S17; Smith 151–153). Vicki Ruiz describes the power of the everyday in the lives of cannery workers in California, "Their day-to-day problems . . . cemented feelings of solidarity among these women, as well as nurturing an 'us against them' mentality in relation to management" (284). This celebration of the everyday is found in the prose and poetry of many writers.[13] It includes memories of the seemingly mundane, such as memories of mothers cooking or of back-breaking manual labor (Viramontes "'Nopalitos'" 291; Zamora 131). As these writers detail their experiences in their homes, on the streets, and with their friends, they announce the importance of their lives and culture. Hank Bromley emphasizes the relationship between identity and materiality:

> Material conditions give rise to one's personal history (or identity) which, when interpreted through some culturally specific mode of discourse, leads to a particular form of (self-)consciousness. The consciousness, in turn, enables an individual understanding of the role material conditions have had in forming one's identity. (211)

Through their focus on their material lives, Chicana feminists begin to carve out their space and their unique circumstances. In her short story, "The Caribou Cafe," Helena María Viramontes describes young Sonya who echoes the call of Virginia Woolf for privacy. However, to Sonya, privacy will come when she has a "toilet of her own" ("Cariboo Cafe" 61). This explicit reminder of the material conditions faced by many Chicanas and other people of color forces readers to see those who might otherwise remain invisible. By elevating the everyday, Chicana feminists empower those who might otherwise go unnoticed (R. Campbell and Reeves 30).

Through their emphasis on day-to-day activities, Chicana feminists engage in a process of translation, whereby they rework existing, and often negative, information into positive portrayals. Jody Freeman defines translation as "forcing traditional discourse to say what it does not want to say by using new language, different evidence, or an innovative strategy.... At a minimum, translation is marked by a crossing of boundaries" (309). This realignment of existing perceptions is a process that is self-empowering and liberating (Francesconi 36). It involves appropriating the definitions created by others and reworking the meaning into an affirmation of Chicana feminism (Gray 377). The very acts that are used to denigrate Chicanas, such as the use of Spanglish, become tributes to the uniqueness of Chicanas. Chicana artist Yolanda Lopez engages in translation through a reclaiming of the Virgin Mary from passive idol to be worshipped to active strong woman. Her series "Our Lady of Guadalupe" includes portraits of herself, her mother, and her grandmother. Her self portrait depicts her running, smiling, and holding a snake (Portrait 325). Her mother, in another piece, works at a sewing machine (Margaret 326–327), while a third portrait has her grandmother sitting and holding a snake (Victoria 326–327). Each of the women is surrounded by rays of light typically shown around the Virgin Mary, and each woman is pictured with or wearing Guadalupe's cape. Commenting on the series, Lopez states:

> I feel living, breathing women also deserve the respect and love lavished on Guadalupe. . . . It is a call to women, hard working, enduring and mundane, as the heroines of our daily routine. . . . We privately agonize and sometimes publicly speak about the representation of us in the majority culture. . . . It is dangerous for us to wait around for the dominant culture to define and validate what role models we should have (qtd. in LaDuke 121).[14]

Through translation, Chicana feminists make real their existence as a unique group able to establish their own identity and space. Linda Steiner recognizes the potential for increasing one's stature by commandeering existing texts: "Reclaiming and sharing insulting texts may have other purposes besides therapy. Most centrally, the activity gives shape and meaning to group experiences, symbolically marking the group's normative boundaries and reconfirming its convictions and commitments" (11).

Through such oppositional readings, Chicana feminists resist the dominant construction of their identity and insert their own creation. Moraga illustrates the empowerment she feels in controlling her identity: ". . . we refuse to make a choice between our cultural identity and sexual identity.... We are not turning our backs on our people nor on ourselves. We even claim lesbianism as an 'act of resistance' . . . against the forces that silence us as people of color" ("Between the Lines" 106). Turning around what their culture and others try to use to constrain them, Chicana feminists proclaim their identity and glory in the power it gives them. By creating their own signs, Chicana lesbian feminists and other Chicana feminists widen their space, giving themselves the power to reclaim their voices.

In the third and final step of creating discursive space, Chicana feminists celebrate their culture. They embrace their Mexican heritage, Indian heritage, and even their white heritage, and it is within their cultural artifacts that their spirit as a people is expressed (Burke 216). For some, embracing the heritage means reformulating the many facets of it:

> What I want is an accounting with all three cultures—white, Mexican, Indian. I want the freedom to carve and chisel my own face. . . . And if going home is denied me then I will have to stand and claim my space, making a new culture—*una cultural mestiza*—with my own lumber, my own bricks and mortar and my own feminist architecture (Anzaldúa *Borderlands* 22).

The need to reevaluate the past and the present and accept the good with the bad allows Chicanas to reject external definitions of the Mexican as dirty or lazy and to revel in their heritage. For Helena María Viramontes, traditions must be passed on to children ("'Nopalitos'" 35). The joy and love of her childhood is what Moraga equates with being Chicana (*Loving* 54). Cultural practices become significant through their effects within and on the culture itself (Peterson 38). The acceptance and celebration of the Chicana culture is an empowering process for Chicana feminists that leads to a spiritual rebirth (Treacy 83). Tejana musicians use their songs to affirm their cultural heritage as well as to challenge cultural constraints (González and Flores 40–41). Steiner explains that turning to one's own background and accepting it on its own terms builds a sense of identity; a social group can "sustain its cultural identity and styles by addressing its own concerns in its own language" (1).

Through a welcoming of their heritage, Chicanas create a definition of themselves that emphasizes those aspects most central to their identity. They move away from patriarchal definitions imposed by Chicanos and racist definitions dictated by nonChicanos, and they move toward the vision of the Chicana that *they* construct (Phelan 59). The redefinition of Chicana gives them the power of being actively involved in the construction of knowledge. They move away from being objects and become subjects who can then begin to establish their own home.

Turning a Space into a Home

Through their celebration of their culture Chicana feminists begin to transform their space into a home. Creating a home is a necessary step in the building of a Chicana feminist community in that the sense of belonging associated with home is often missing from their lives. When Chicanas declare themselves as feminists and become actively involved in the women's movement, they create tension between themselves and their families. Their stance as feminists makes them outsiders. During her early work, Moraga explained, "this is a book [*Loving*] my family will never see. And yet, how I wish I could share this book with them" (*Loving* iv). Similarly, in anticipation of a pending visit to her family, Anzaldúa states, "Because I no longer share their [family] world view, I have become a stranger and an exile in my own home. . . . Though I continue to go home, I no longer fool myself into believing that I am truly 'home'" ("Bridge, Drawbridge" 218). Thus, while Chicana feminists have found a space for themselves, a lingering feeling of isolation persists. The loss of one's family and friends as well as the inability to form bonds with those most like oneself results in feelings of loneliness (Pratt 50). The nagging sense of being alone can make the victory less fulfilling.

The desire to craft a homeland which places Chicana feminists at their own center rather than straddling two cultures was and is shared by Chicanos. From the beginning of the Chicano movement, many Chicanos pronounced the existence of their homeland *Aztlán*.[15] Jensen and Hammerback argue, "[t]o many, Aztlan [sic] was an ideal, to others a physical reality in the future. In either case Aztlan was a powerful image for building solidarity in the community" ("Radical Nationalism" 196). However, as with the label Chicano, the identity linked to *Aztlán* was a static and largely ethnic identity that many Chicana feminists found constraining (Quintana; Fregoso and Chabram; Segura and Pesquera). Daniel Alarcón argues, "the Chicano architects of the Movement reconstructed Aztlán as a monolithic narrative that would inevitably force marginalized Chicanos and Chicanas to break away and bring about its collapse" (53). Thus, many Chicana feminists found themselves needing a home that welcomed differences.

The connotations of home may vary somewhat across cultures, including perhaps the idea that home is linked to one's biological family or, as in the Chicano nationalist conception, home as including the members of one's race. For Chicana feminists, neither race nor biology is sufficient. The Chicana feminist homeland reflects the diversity and multiplicity that is central to Chicana feminists. This rhetorical world encompasses many languages, many cultures, and many commitments. The links to Chicano heritage are evident in the affirmation of mothers and mother figures. Chicana feminists use their writings and their art to honor their mothers (McCracken; Ortega and Sternbach; Treacy). Moraga explains, "(t)he most valuable aspect of Chicana theory thus far has been its re-evaluation of our history from a woman's perspective through unearthing the stories of Mexican/Chicana female figures that early on exhibited a feminist sensibility" (*Loving* 107).

The Chicana feminist homeland allows for the creation of a sisterhood among women that restores a feeling of family and that is women-affirming. The need for connections with women, for relationships equal to those their mothers shared with other women, drives Chicana feminists. Moraga, upon establishing such ties, explains, "*Sí, son mis comadres.* Something my mother had with her women friends and sisters. Coming home. For once, I didn't have to choose between being a lesbian and being Chicana; between being a feminist and having a family" ("Preface" xvii–xviii). Similarly, Emma Pérez remarks that her new sisters fill a need: "I know that with women of color, particularly lesbians of color, I reenact the best times that I had as a child" (65). By finding

other women with whom she can connect, the Chicana feminist establishes what Bromley terms an "ideological home" (209). In this new home the ties to family simultaneously contain and free in that the boundaries of the family are established but permeable, and Chicana feminists can build extended families.

Because they may never have the connections to their biological families that allow them to be whole, Chicana feminists create a home with other Third World feminists: "Surfacing . . . is the genuine sense of loss and pain we feel when we are denied our home because of our desire to free ourselves as specifically female persons. So, we turn to each other for strength and sustenance" (Moraga "Between the Lines" 106). Chicana feminists complete the formation of their identity by constructing themselves as autonomous women and then placing themselves in relation to other women. By turning their space into their home, Chicana feminists find themselves able to accept the contradictions of being both Chicana and feminist. The Chicana feminist comes full circle, first separating herself as a feminist, then rejoicing in her heritage, and finally using her history to establish herself as a feminist.

Chicana feminists, upon creating their own identity and thus their own discursive space, find that they are home, in what Anzaldúa calls, "*El Mundo Zurdo*" ("El Mundo Zurdo" 196). This land, the left-handed world, is the place where the misfits suddenly fit: "The vision of radical Third World Feminism necessitates our willingness to work with those people who would feel at home in *El Mundo Zurdo, the left-handed world*: the colored, the queer, the poor, the female, the physically challenged" (Anzaldúa, "El Mundo Zurdo" 196). When she finally finds her home, the Chicana feminist often realizes how long she has been homeless. For Chávez, it has been since childhood, "I grew up between and in the middle of two languages, Spanish and English, speaking my own as a defense. My mother always said I made up words" (31). The struggle she has been undergoing throughout her life is made easier once her home is found.

In *El Mundo Zurdo*, Chicana feminists are free to speak whatever language they choose.

They are no longer silenced by those who want them to adopt one language and reject others. The emphatic need to deny making the choice of one language over another is seen by Littlebear, "These words are mine because this is now *my* language—13 years of English, 13 years of Spanish" (emphasis in original) ("Earthlover" 158). For many Chicana feminists, there is a sense of peace and of self-love in finding a home (Anzaldúa, "Haciendo Caras" 202).

Creating Bridges: Autonomy, Alliances and Hermanas

Although Chicana feminists have created their own homeland, established their autonomy, and could conceivably stand alone, they do not. Realizing that fighting oppression requires more strength than they alone can provide, Chicana feminists construct bridges that connect their newly gained homeland to those surrounding lands upon which they once stood. This extending of the community to include inter-action with others is essential, for as feminists, they are connected to all oppressed groups, not merely Chicanas (Phelan 168).

The joining together represents the crafting of *hermanas,* sisters, for Chicana feminists welcome nonChicana feminists as their sisters. Addressing her contributors to *This Bridge* Moraga states, "We are a family who first only knew each other in our dreams, who have come together on these pages to make faith a reality and to bring all of our selves to bear down hard on that reality" ("Preface" xix). The sister-hood created by Chicana feminists increases the power for all feminists, for rather than focusing only on why they are different, Chicana femi-nists move beyond differences to find the simi-larities shared by feminists. The listening that is involved when differences are overcome builds understanding, for, as Pratt explains, it ". . . is one way of finding out how to get to the new place where we can all live and speak . . ." (14). The solidarity that is created gives them a strength they would not have if they stood alone.

The process of crafting *hermanas* involves building bridges that connect Chicana femi-nists with other feminists, Third World and white. The bridges are necessary because while ties are important, so is the hard-won autonomy that has been gained by Chicana feminists. Anzaldúa notes the need for "alliances around differences" ("Bridge, Drawbridge" 220), and Littlebear looks for a way to meet between two worlds ("Dreams" 17). By constructing bridges, Chicana feminists break down boundaries that separate them from others, removing any borders that must be straddled. For Anzaldúa, the path to *El Mundo Zurdo* is both a moving within oneself and a journey outward ("Bridge, Drawbridge" 208). The opening up of spaces is part of the action that Chicana feminists demand be a part of the feminist movement.

The breaking down of boundaries calls for great attention, for past divisions are often hard to overcome.[16] However, through their writing style and through their joining with other Third World Feminists, Chicana feminists lay the foundation for the bridges. Chicana feminists use their writing style as a means to connect with others. In their anthologies and their books, Chicana feminists combine a mix of poetry, prose, and stream of conscious-ness. They jump from English to Spanish to Indian to Spanglish, with no warning and no apology.[17] The different styles and languages represent different aspects of their varied heri-tages, and the use of expression of different backgrounds gives voice to previously silenced groups (Freeman 306). Chicana feminists refute the notion that there is one correct style or language, and instead, they use many. Their creative use of form helps Chicana feminists to retain their unique identity as they speak to others (Francesconi 38–39).

CONCLUSION

I have argued that a discursive space can be opened through a rhetoric of difference which allows a marginalized group to reverse existing and external definitions and to create their own definitions. The creation of one's own identity which relies upon the material conditions of the people is more likely to reflect the culture of the people, rather than the dominant culture of the empowered. Such a process is necessary for those groups who experience the decentering associated with a lack of space of their own, as it is a means through which the oppressed can move themselves from the periphery toward their own center.

For Chicana feminists, who carry the baggage of their border existence and who often find themselves straddling different cultures, creating a home is essential. As R. Campbell and Reeves explain, "[b]eing without home transports a person, often violently and unwillingly, from mainstream to margin" (21). Chicana feminists and other marginalized groups who find that their politics put them at odds with their own culture are pushed to the margins of the margin. The creation of discursive space means that the margins are transformed into the center of a new society, and the disempowered find power.

Within the writings of Chicana feminists, we find the processual move from carving one's space, to creating a homeland, and finally to establishing bonds with others, and in this process, the move from other-defined to self-defined is illustrated. Further exploration of the process of creating one's own definitions should be a part of feminist scholarship. The use of the everyday and of one's heritage are available to feminist scholars, especially those studying Third World women. As we become aware of the different ways in which women use the resources available to them to construct their identity, we can continue to build feminist theory that opens spaces and provides voice for women.

NOTES

[1] A discussion of space and gender relations can be found in Karlyn Kohrs Campbell, who responds to spatial inequities by challenging the traditional rhetorical canon and including women in that canon. Other feminist scholars who discuss space and gender include Lana Krakow, Patricia Hill Collins "Learning," Carole Spitzack and Kathryn Carter, Lynn Spigel, and Daphne Spain.

[2] The word Chicana traditionally refers to women of Mexican descent who were born in the United States and/or are residing there. More recently the word has taken on political implications that surfaced in the 1960s when Mexican-Americans stressed their ethnic background and their political involvement in the La Raza movement.

[3] One important distinction that separates Chicana feminists from other Chicanos/as is that while Chicana feminists ally themselves with their Chicano heritage, they also question those aspects of their culture that they find problematic. Static notions of sexuality and gender roles are questioned, and multiplicity is welcomed. A diverse group, Chicana feminists are scholars, writers, students, and workers. They are lesbian and they are straight. They are working class and middle class. They are monolingual and bilingual.

Alma Garcia argues that Chicana feminism grew out of the frustrations many Chicanas felt with the nationalist turn of the Chicano movement that failed to acknowledge sexism within the culture and with Anglo American feminism which was often blinded to the role of racism in the oppression of women (418–419). She, along with others, notes that many Chicana feminists claim allegiances with both the Chicano movement and the women's movement while they place themselves in a unique third position that emphasizes the intersections of gender, race, and class (Garcia; Segura and Pesquera; de la Torre and Pesquera "Introduction").

[4] A rhetoric of difference is that discourse which affirms an identity different from that attributed to Chicana feminists by others and which proclaims the uniqueness of Chicana feminists. Such discourse must come from within the group; in a rhetoric of difference, outsiders cannot speak for a people. A rhetoric of difference glories in difference, especially in response to the attribution of negative connotations to difference.

[5] The role of writing as a means of protest and of self-proclamation is not unique to Chicana feminists, but is shared among Chicanos who used writing as a tool for empowerment throughout the Chicano movement (Hammerback and Jensen "Ethnic Heritage").

[6] As is evident in the works of Richard Jensen and John Hammerback, Chicanos in the Chicano movement, from which the Chicana feminist movement emerged, also relied on discourse to build community identity. Jensen and Hammerback note the political impact brought about by Chicano political leaders César Chávez, Rodolfo 'Corky' González, Reies Tijerina and others. Hammerback and Jensen argue that "Public Address was Tijerina's means to God's ends . . . [while] Chávez relied on public address to change the established order" ("Rhetorical Worlds" 170–171).

7 For a complete discussion of the role of the terms "Chicano" and "Raza" as well as an overall picture of the discourse of early Chicano leaders see Hammerback and Jensen "The Rhetorical Worlds of César Chávez and Reies Tijerina"; Jensen, "An Interview with José Angel Gutiérrez"; Jensen and Hammerback, "No Revolutions without Poets: The Rhetoric of Rodolfo 'Corky' González"; and Jensen and Hammerback, "Radical Nationalism among Chicanos: The Rhetoric of José Angel Gutiérrez."

8 I use space as an extension of the margin/center metaphor in which traditionally underrepresented groups are seen as fringe members of society, defined by those in the center as less relevant. Creating space means rejecting the dichotomy of either at the margins or in the center and replacing that perspective with one that allows for Chicana feminists to be at their own center intellectually, spiritually, emotionally, and ultimately physically. The desire for space is the need for both a physical location and an intellectual one. By creating an intellectual space that redefines centers and margins, Chicana feminists transform the geographic space from one of hostility and displacement to one of home.

9 The complete titles of the books are: Gloria Anzaldúa, *Borderlands: La Frontera* San Francisco: aunt lute, 1987; *Between Borders: Essays on Mexicana/Chicana History* ed. by Adelaida R. Del Castillo, Encino: Floricanto P, 1990; *Breaking Boundaries: Latina Writing and Critical Readings* ed. by Asuncíon Horno-Delgado, Eliana Ortega, Nina M. Scott, and Nancy Saporta Sternbach, Amherst: U of Massachusetts P, 1989; and *This Bridge Called My Back: Writings by Radical Women of Color* ed. by Cherríe Moraga and Gloria Anzaldúa, Watertown, MA: Persephone P, 1981.

10 Other examples of the "border experience" can be found in Gloria Anzaldúa, "Bridge, Drawbridge, Sandbar or Island: Lesbians-of-color Hacienda Alianzas." *Bridges of Power: Women's Multicultural Alliances;* Norma Alarcón, "Chicana's Feminist Literature: A Re-Vision Through Malintzin/or Malintzin: Putting Flesh Back on the Object," *This Bridge;* Eliana Ortega and Nancy Saporta Sternbach, "At the Threshold of the Unnamed: Latina Literary Discourse in the Eighties," *Breaking Boundaries;* Nancy Saporta Sternbach, "'A Deep Racial Memory of Love': The Chicana Feminism of Cherríe Moraga," *Breaking Boundaries;* and Helena María Viramontes, "'Nopalitos': The Making of Fiction," *Breaking Boundaries.*

11 Victoria Chen labels this feeling hyphenated identity and argues that many hyphenated individuals are seen as having split personas and must learn to see through multiple lenses ("De/hyphenated Identity"). Also making this argument is Patricia Hill Collins who maintains that Black women must learn to watch themselves through the lens of the oppressors (Learning). Many people of color discuss their split personalities and their seeming inability to be either "white" enough or "foreign" enough (Chen; Nakayama; Gong; Tanno; Moraga *Loving*; and Takaki).

12 The turn to poetry is not unique to Chicana feminists but is shared by Chicanos. For example, the poem *I Am Joaquín* by Rodolfo Gonzáles, a prominent figure in the Chicano movement, served as one of the movement's declarations of identity (Jensen and Hammerback "No Revolutions" 76–77).

Among Chicana feminists, poetry becomes an important tool for affirming identity. In her analysis of Chicana poetry, Chabram Dernersesian observes that poems by Chicanas "record the passage of an empowered ethnic subject from complacency to action, from social dislocation to political groundedness, and from individual oblivion to collective memory" ("And Yes" 37).

13 For examples of the everyday, see Naomi Littlebear, "Dreams of Violence," *This Bridge;* Jo Carrillo, "And When You Leave, Take Your Pictures With You," *This Bridge;* Gloria Anzaldúa, "Speaking in Tongues: A Letter to 3rd World Women Writers," *This Bridge;* Gloria Anzaldúa, "La Prieta," *This Bridge;* Denise Chávez, "Heat and Rain," *Breaking Boundaries;* and Helena María Viramontes, "'Nopalitos': The Making of Fiction," *Breaking Boundaries.*

14 The quotation from LaDuke is from an interview of Lopez done by Betty LaDuke. LaDuke states in her article on Lopez that she was interviewed both in 1983 and 1991. Beyond that, LaDuke does not specify when the interview from which the quotation comes was done.

15 The land commonly known as the Southwestern United States was claimed by the Chicano movement as *Aztlán,* the Chicano homeland. To many Chicanos, the reclaiming of *Aztlán* serves as a declaration of prior existence. Before the war between Mexico and the United States, much of the land that now makes up the states Arizona, New Mexico, California, and Texas was Mexican territory. After the treaty of Guadalupe-Hidalgo, this land was ceded to the United States. Originally, the treaty was to guarantee, among other things, that those Mexican citizens living in the ceded area would retain ownership of their land and would have the right to choose to remain Mexican

citizens or to become citizens of the United States. However, the United States did not uphold those provisions, and most of the Mexicans living there had their land stolen from them. Chicano leader and rhetor Reies Tijerina centered much of his discourse on the injustices perpetrated against the original land owners and revived anger among Chicanos at the loss of their ancestral land. By renaming the Southwestern United States *Aztlán,* the Chicano movement asserted the existence of their homeland and inscribed themselves as a "bronze people" with Mexican, Indian, and American heritage (Rico and Mano 479–485; Pina 36).

16 The insistence on the label "Chicana feminist" is an important move in the challenging of boundaries. As Jensen and Hammerback have noted, Chicano political leaders used the label "Chicano" as a means of establishing identity and creating solidarity ("Radical Nationalism" 195–196). The emergence of the label "Chicano" helped to change public vocabulary to include the political needs and interests of the Chicano movement. However, as more and more women found themselves still marginalized even within the Chicano movement, the need to identify themselves as Chicana feminists increased. Celeste Condit explains the rhetorical significance of such self labeling: "If some members do not have their interests and experiences expressed in public vocabulary, it is virtually impossible to have their interests protected in the laws of the land" ("Opposites" 212).

17 For examples of the mixtures, see Anzaldúa, *Borderlands;* Anzaldúa, *Making Face, Making Soul: Haciendo Caras;* Moraga and Anzaldúa, *This Bridge;* and Moraga, *Loving.*

WORKS CITED

Alarcón, Daniel Cooper. "The Aztec Palimpsest: Toward a New Understanding of Aztlán, Cultural Identity and History." *Aztlán* 19 (1988): 33–68.

Alarcón, Norma. "Chicana Feminism: In the Tracks of 'The' Native Woman." *Cultural Studies* 4 (1990): 248–256.

Alarcón, Norma. "Chicana's Feminist Literature: A Re-Vision Through Malintzin/or Malintzin: Putting Flesh Back on the Object." Moraga and Anzaldúa 182–190.

Anzaldúa, Gloria. *Borderlands: La Frontera.* San Francisco: aunt lute, 1987.

Anzaldúa, Gloria. "Bridge, Drawbridge, Sandbar or Island: Lesbians-of-color Hacienda Alianzas." *Bridges of Power: Women's Multicultural Alliances.* Ed. Lisa Albrecht and Rose M. Brewer.

Philadelphia: New Society Publishers, 1990. 216–231.

Anzaldúa, Gloria. "El Mundo Zurdo." Moraga and Anzaldúa 195–196.

Anzaldúa, Gloria. "Haciendo Caras, Una Entrada." Anzaldúa *Making Face* xv–xxviii.

Anzaldúa, Gloria. "La Prieta." Moraga and Anzaldúa 198–209.

Anzaldúa, Gloria, ed. *Making Face, Making Soul/Haciendo Caras: Creative and Critical Perspectives by Feminists of Color.* San Francisco: aunt lute books, 1990.

Anzaldúa, Gloria. "Speaking in Tongues: A Letter to Third World Women Writers." Moraga and Anzaldúa 165–174.

Bromley, Hank. "Identity Politics and Critical Pedagogy." *Educational Theory* 39 (1989): 207–223.

Burke, Peter. "The 'Discovery' of Popular Culture." *People's History and Socialist Theory.* Ed. Raphael Samuel. London: Routledge and Kegan Paul, 1981. 216–221.

Campbell, Karlyn Kohrs. *Man Cannot Speak For Her: A Critical Analysis of Early Feminist Rhetoric.* Vol. 1. New York: Praeger Publishers 1989. 2 vols.

Campbell, Richard. "Securing the Middle Ground: Reporter Formulas in 60 Minutes." *Critical Studies in Mass Communication* 4 (1987): 325–350.

Campbell, Richard and Jimmie L. Reeves. "Covering the Homeless: The Joyce Brown Story." *Critical Studies in Mass Communication* 6 (1989): 21–42.

Carrillo, Jo. "And When You Leave, Take Your Pictures With You." Moraga and Anzaldúa 63–64.

Castellaño, Olivia. "Canto, Locura y Poesia." *Race, Class, and Gender: An Anthology.* Ed. Margaret L. Anderson and Patricia Hill Collins. Belmont: Wadsworth, 1992. 376–385.

Chabram Dernersesian, Angie. "And, Yes . . . The Earth Did Split: On the Splitting of Chicana/o Subjectivity." de la Torre and Pesquera *Building* 34–56.

Chávez, Denise. "Heat and Rain." Horno-Delgado, Ortega, Scott, and Sternbach 27–32.

Chen, Victoria. "(De)hyphenated Identity: The Double Voice in The Woman Warrior." González, Houston, and Chen 3–11.

Cisneros, Sandra. *The House on Mango Street.* New York: Vintage Books, 1989.

Condit, Celeste Michelle. "Opposites in an Oppositional Practice: Rhetorical Criticism and Feminism." *Transforming Visions: Feminist Critiques in Communication Studies.* Ed. Sheryl Perlmutter

Bowen and Nancy Wyatt. Cresskill, NJ: Hampton P, 1993.

de la Torre, Adela and Beatríz M. Pesquera, eds. *Building With Our Hands: New Directions in Chicana Studies.* Berkeley: U of California P, 1993.

de la Torre, Adela and Beatríz M. Pesquera. "Introduction." de la Torre and Pesquera *Building* 1–11.

Del Castillo, Adelaida R., ed. *Between Borders: Essays on Mexicana/Chicana History.* Encino, CA: Floricanto P, 1990.

Fiske, John. "Television: Polysemy and Popularity." *Critical Studies in Mass Communication* 3 (1986): 391–408.

Francesconi, Robert. "Free Jazz and Black Nationalism: A Rhetoric of Musical Style." *Critical Studies in Mass Communication* 3 (1986): 36–49.

Freeman, Jody. "Constitutive Rhetoric: Law as a Literary Activity." *Harvard Women's Law Journal* 14 (1991): 305–325.

Fregosa, Rosa Linda and Angie Chabram. "Chicana/o Cultural Representations: Reframing Alternative Critical Discourses." *Cultural Studies* 4 (1990): 203–212.

Garcia, Alma M. "The Development of Chicana Feminist Discourse, 1970–1980." *Unequal Sisters.* Ed. Ellen Carol DuBois and Vicki L. Ruiz. New York: Routledge, 1990. 418–431.

Gong, Gwendolyn. "When Mississippi Chinese Talk." González, Houston, and Chen 92–99.

González, Alberto, Marsha Houston, and Victoria Chen, eds. *Our Voices: Essays in Culture, Ethnicity, and Communication.* Los Angeles: Roxbury, 1994.

González, Alberto and Gloria Flores. "Tejana Music and Cultural Identification." González, Houston, and Chen 37–42.

Gray, Herman. "Television, Black Americans, and the American Dream." *Critical Studies in Mass Communication* 6 (1989): 376–386.

Griswold del Castillo, Richard, Teresa McKenna, and Yvonne Yarbro-Bejarano, eds. *CARA: Chicano Art Resistance and Affirmation, 1965–1985.* Los Angeles: Wight Art Gallery, 1991.

Hammerback, John C. and Richard J. Jensen. "The Ethnic Heritage as Rhetorical Legacy: The Plan of Delano." *Quarterly Journal of Speech* 80 (1994): 53–70.

Hammerback, John C. and Richard J. Jensen. "The Rhetorical Worlds of César Chávez and Reies Tijerina." *Western Journal of Speech Communication* 44 (1980): 166–176.

Hariman, Robert. "Status, Marginality, and Rhetorical Theory." *Quarterly Journal of Speech* 72 (1986): 38–54.

Hill Collins, Patricia. *Black Feminist Thought: Knowledge, Consciousness, and the Politics of Empowerment.* New York: Routledge, 1990.

Hill Collins, Patricia. "Learning from the Outsider Within: The Sociological Significance of Black Feminist Thought." *Social Problems* 33 (1986): S14–S32.

Horno-Delgado, Asunción, Eliana Ortega, Nina M. Scott, and Nancy Saporta Sternbach, eds. *Breaking Boundaries: Latina Writing and Critical Readings.* Amherst: U of Massachusetts P, 1989.

Jensen, Richard J. "An Interview with José Angel Gutiérrez." *Western Journal of Speech Communication* 44 (1980): 203–213.

Jensen, Richard J. and John C. Hammerback. "No Revolutions without Poets: The Rhetoric of Rodolfo 'Corky' González." *Western Journal of Speech Communication* 46 (1982): 72–91.

Jensen, Richard J. and John C. Hammerback. "Radical Nationalism among Chicanos: The Rhetoric of José Angel Gutiérrez." *Western Journal of Speech Communication* 44 (1980): 191–202.

LaDuke, Betty. "Yolanda Lopez: Breaking Chicana Stereotypes." *Feminist Studies* 20 (1994): 117–130.

Littlebear, Naomi. "Dreams of Violence." Moraga and Anzaldúa. 16–17.

Littlebear, Naomi. "Earth-Lover, Survivor, Musician." Moraga and Anzaldúa 157–159.

Lopez, Yolanda M. *Margaret F. Stewart: Our Lady of Guadalupe.* Griswold del Castillo, McKenna, and Yarbro-Bejarano 326–327.

Lopez, Yolanda M. *Portrait of the Artist as the Virgin of Guadalupe.* Griswold del Castillo, McKenna, and Yarbro-Bejarano 323, 325.

Lopez, Yolanda M. *Victoria F. Franco: Our Lady of Guadalupe.* Griswold del Castillo, McKenna, and Yarbro-Bejarano 326–327.

McCracken, Ellen. "Sandra Cisneros' *The House on Mango Street:* Community-Oriented Introspection and the Demystification of Patriarchal Violence." Horno-Delgado, Ortega, Scott, and Sternbach 62–71.

Moraga, Cherríe. "Between the Lines." Moraga and Anzaldúa 105–106.

Moraga, Cherríe. *Loving in the War Years: Lo Que Nunca Pasó Por Sus Lábios.* Boston: South End P, 1983.

Moraga, Cherríe. "Preface." Moraga and Anzaldúa xiii–xix.

Moraga, Cherríe and Gloria Anzaldúa, eds. *This Bridge Called My Back: Writings by Radical Women of Color.* New York: Kitchen Table, 1983.

Nakayama, Thomas. "Dis/orienting Identities: Asian Americans, History, and Intercultural

Communication." González, Houston, and Chen 12–17.

Ortega, Eliana and Nancy Saporta Sternbach. "At the Threshold of the Unnamed: Latina Literary Discourse in the Eighties." Horno-Delgado, Ortega, Scott, and Sternbach 2–23.

Pérez, Emma. "Sexuality and Discourse: Notes from a Chicana Survivor." *Chicana Critical Issues: Mujeres Activas en Letras y Cambia Social.* Ed. Norma Alarcón, Rafaela Castro, Emma Pérez, Beatriz Pesquera, Adaljiza Sosa Riddell, and Patricia Zavella. Berkeley: Third Woman Press, 1993. 45–69.

Peterson, Eric E. "Media Consumption and Girls Who Want to Have Fun." *Critical Studies in Mass Communication* 4 (1987): 37–50.

Phelan, Shane. *Identity Politics: Lesbian Feminism and the Limits of Community.* Philadelphia, Temple UP, 1989.

Pheterson, Gail. "Alliances between Women: Overcoming Internalized Oppression and Internalized Domination." *Bridges of Power: Women's Multicultural Alliances.* Ed. Lisa Albrecht & Rose M. Brewer. Philadelphia: New Society Publishers, 1990. 34–48.

Pina, Michael. "The Archaic, Historical and Mythicized Dimensions of Aztlán." *Aztlán: Essays on the Chicano Homeland.* Ed. Rudolfo A. Anaya and Francisco A. Lomelí. Albuquerque: Academia/El Norte Publications, 1989. 14–48.

Pratt, Minnie Bruce. "Identity: Skin Blood Heart." *Yours in Struggle: Three Feminist Perspectives on Anti-Semitism and Racism.* Elly Bulkin, Minnie Bruce Pratt, and Barbara Smith. Ithaca: Firebrand, 1984. 9–63.

Quintana, Alvina. "Politics, Representation and the Emergence of a Chicana Aesthetic." *Cultural Studies* 4 (1990): 257–280.

Rakow, Lana F. "Gendered Technology, Gendered Practice." *Critical Studies in Mass Communication* 5 (1988): 57–70.

Rebolledo, Tey Diana. "The Politics of Poetics: Or, What Am I, A Critic, Doing in This Text Anyhow?" *Chicana Creativity and Criticism: Charting New Frontiers in American Literature.* Ed. Maria Herrera-Sóbek and Helena María Viramontes. Houston: Arte Publico P, 1988. 129–138.

Rico, Barbara Roche and Sandra Mano. *American Mosaic: Multicultural Readings in Context.* Boston: Houghton Mifflin, 1991.

Ruiz, Vicki L. "A Promise Fulfilled: Mexican Cannery Workers in Southern California." Del Castillo 281–298.

Saldívar-Hull, Sonia. "Feminism on the Border: From Gender Politics to Geopolitics." *Criticism in the Borderlands: Studies in Chicano Literature,*

Culture, and Ideology. Ed. Roberto Trujillo, José David Saldívar, and Héctor Calderón. Durham, NC: Duke UP, 1991. 203–220.

Sánchez, Rosaura. "The History of Chicanas: Proposal for a Materialist Perspective." Del Castillo 1–30.

Schwichtenberg, Cathy. "Introduction: Connections/Intersections." *The Madonna Connection: Representational Politics, Subcultural Identities, and Cultural Theory.* Ed. Cathy Schwichtenberg. Boulder: Westview P, 1993.

Sedano, Michael Victor. "Chicanismo: A Rhetorical Analysis of Themes and Images of Selected Poetry from the Chicano Movement." *Western Journal of Speech Communication* 44 (1980): 177–190.

Segura, Denise A. and Beatríz M. Pesquera. "Beyond Indifference and Antipathy: The Chicana Movement and Chicana Feminist Discourse." *Aztlán* 19 (1992): 69–92.

Smith, Dorothy. *The Everyday World as Problematic.* Boston: Northeastern UP, 1987.

Spain, Daphne. *Gendered Spaces.* Chapel Hill: U of North Carolina P, 1992.

Spigel, Lynn. "The Domestic Economy of Television Viewing in Postwar America." *Critical Studies in Mass Communication* 6 (1989): 337–354.

Spitzack, Carole and Kathryn Carter. "Women in Communication Studies: A Typology for Revision." *Quarterly Journal of Speech* 73 (1987): 401–423.

Steiner, Linda. "Oppositional Decoding as an Act of Resistance." *Critical Studies in Mass Communication* 5 (1988): 1–15.

Sternbach, Nancy Saporta. "'A Deep Racial Memory of Love': The Chicana Feminism of Cherríe Moraga." Horno-Delgado, Ortega, Scott, and Sternbach 48–61.

Takaki, Ronald. "A Different Mirror: Asian Americans in our History." Lecture delivered at DePaul University. 4 April 1994.

Tanno, Dolores. "Names, Narratives, and the Evolution of Ethnic Identity." González, Houston, and Chen 30–33.

Treacy, Mary Jane. "The Ties that Bind: Women and Community in Evangelina Vigil's *Thirty an' Seen a Lot.*" Horno-Delgado, Ortega, Scott, and Sternbach 82–93.

Viramontes, Helena María. "The Cariboo Cafe." *The Moths and Other Stories.* Houston: Arte Publico Press, 1985.

Viramontes, Helena María. "'Nopalitos': The Making of Fiction." Anzaldúa *Making Face* 291–294.

Zamora, Bernice. "Notes from a Chicana 'Coed'." Anzaldúa *Making Face* 131–132.

On the Margins of Rhetoric:
Audre Lorde Transforming Silence into Language and Action

Lester C. Olson

These are not natural silences, that necessary time for renewal, lying fallow, gestation, in the natural cycle of creation. The silences I speak of here are unnatural; the unnatural thwarting of what struggles to come into being, but cannot. In the old, the obvious parallels: when the seed strikes stone; the soil will not sustain; the spring is false; the time is drought or blight or infestation; the frost comes premature.

—Tillie Olsen, *Silences*[1]

What underlying cultural conditions encourage or discourage speaking in public forums? What sociological factors, for example, account for speech and silence: Who speaks to and for the community? With what kinds of power and authority? With access to which public forums? Such questions led me to contemplate Audre Lorde's speech, "The Transformation of Silence into Language and Action," in light of what it reveals about the limits, boundaries, or margins of rhetoric in the sense of the public speech, or oration. By margins, I mean both the parameters employed for defining a practice and the relative place or value of varied activities exemplifying the practice, some of which are considered central, while others are peripheral. As the title of Lorde's speech suggests, her address in 1977 to the Modern Language Association (MLA) provides a glimpse into some margins of rhetoric, because she examines factors that may cause some people to remain silent, while enabling others to speak and act. Her speech reveals some underlying and necessary conditions for the possibility of rhetoric, conditions that may go unnoticed to the extent that we allow ourselves to be habituated to them as natural or inevitable.

Best known as a poet of international stature, the author of such collections as *Coal, The Black Unicorn,* and *Our Dead Behind Us,* Audre Lorde was also an essayist and public speaker, whose oratory focused upon the role of language in communicating differences in ways that construct relations of power among social groups.[2] Her public speeches, some of which were collected in *Sister Outsider: Essays & Speeches by Audre Lorde,* have an aphoristic, expansive quality resulting from her extensive use of metaphors, maxims, proverbs, and stories to affirm her perspective on the relationship among language, self, and society.[3] Her speeches, like her essays and her poems, often examine human differences communicated within a sociocultural system of power, ranging as it does across symbolic oppositions between white and black, male and female, capitalist and socialist, heterosexual and homosexual, master and slave-oppositions which Lorde criticizes as simplistic and as useful to dominant groups for exploiting subordinated communities.[4] Her public speaking is a vital resource for communication scholars engaged in examining the role of language and action in transforming self and society.

Audre Lorde's public speeches merit the attention of communication scholars, not only because they are models of rhetorical excellence, but also because her oratory provides singular access to a point of view about some underlying sociological and political factors entailed in the act of assuming a role as a public speaker. Lorde was keenly aware of these sociological and political factors because, whenever she spoke in public, she explicitly defined her own position as multiply marginal in relationship to dominant groups. "As a forty-nine-year-old Black lesbian feminist socialist mother of two, including one boy, and a member of an interracial couple," Lorde remarked in a speech at Amherst College during April 1980, "I usually find myself a part of some group: defined as other, deviant, inferior, or just plain wrong."[5] In addition to using her public speeches, essays, and poems actively to resist externally imposed and reductive definitions of her differences from dominant groups, Lorde also explicitly resisted the pressure "to pluck out some one aspect of myself and present this as the meaningful whole, eclipsing or denying the other parts of self," because in her view "this is a destructive and fragmenting way to live." She affirmed, "My fullest concentration of energy is available to me only when I integrate all the parts of who I am, openly, allowing power from particular sources of my living to flow back and forth freely through all my different selves, without the restrictions of an externally imposed definition."[6] In a speech at Harvard University during 1982, Lorde commented similarly that "As a Black lesbian mother in an interracial marriage, there was usually some part of me guaranteed to offend everybody's comfortable prejudices of who I should be. That is how I learned that if I didn't define myself for myself, I would be crunched into other people's fantasies for me and eaten alive."[7]

Several recent essays and anthologies have articulated compelling reasons for including diverse voices in critical and theoretical accounts of rhetoric, as did Karlyn Kohrs Campbell in her essay, "Hearing Women's Voices."[8] But even the best contributions to improving the current situation have omitted Lorde's speeches or featured her relatively less controversial or challenging public address.[9] Ironically, in the communication discipline Lorde's speech has been subject to the very silence and invisibility that were the central focus of Lorde's remarks. Regardless of whether this neglect is the result of deliberately devaluing the significance of her rhetoric or the inadvertent product of habitual attention to the speech of politically powerful and economically privileged figures, such an exclusion can be understood as an act of silencing that in this case conceals some political and social conditions that may make possible a definition of a discipline. The very role of legitimate speaker may rest upon varieties of symbolic power and authority that are derived from underlying political and sociological factors such as those mentioned in Lorde's public speeches.

In Lorde's speech to the MLA in 1977, she articulates a deep understanding of some specific ways that underlying sociological and political factors connected to her many differences militate against her public speaking, factors she actively and explicitly engages

through her speech. At the same time, Lorde's speech exemplifies her extraordinary ability to draw upon the diverse aspects of herself as resources in defining her own understanding of silence. The central insights in her speech on transforming silence into language and action were precipitated by her own recent experiences with doctors diagnosing a tumor in her breast, because the doctors had informed her of a 60 to 80 percent likelihood it was malignant. In fact, Lorde's immediate response to experiencing the first biopsy was not to attend the conference. In an interview with Lorde, Adrienne Rich recalled her remarks, "you said there was no way you were going to the MLA—remember? That you couldn't do it, you didn't need to do it, that doing it could not mean anything important to you."[10] At Rich's urging, "Why don't you tell them about what you've just been through," Lorde transformed her initial reaction by developing and delivering an eloquent speech at the MLA about her experiences with cancer.[11] Yet her public meditation on the silence surrounding breast cancer is interwoven with insights drawn from her experiences as a member of several subordinated communities, especially as they relate to the misuse of power to silence those who are different.

There are at least three published versions of Lorde's speech, which was printed initially in *Sinister Wisdom* in 1978, later in *The Cancer Journals* in 1980 and in *Sister Outsider* in 1984.[12] Each of these texts conveyed Lorde's ideas to additional audiences beyond the MLA. Each is a reiteration reaching additional audiences in a broadening range of contexts. The later placement of the speech's text in *The Cancer Journals* significantly alters the context for reading it, however, because in 1977 when Lorde spoke to the MLA the biopsy had been for a benign tumor. The reprinting of the speech in *The Cancer Journals* occurred in 1980 after a diagnosis of a malignant tumor and a mastectomy, relocating the text as a moment in dealing with a disease that ultimately claimed Lorde's life.

"The Transformation of Silence into Language and Action" is a brilliantly designed speech that enacts what it requests of its audiences,[13] Lorde's speech is a powerful and eloquent example of human liberation rhetoric.[14] In this essay, I will comment briefly on the varied perspectives on silence and speech as treated in communication scholarship. Next, I will discuss literature in other disciplines commenting on silence insofar as it sheds light on recurring topics in Lorde's speech about silence: silencing and power, sexism, verbal abuse, violence and sexualized aggression, shame, the taboo, and hostile social environments. Then, because silence is a theme in Lorde's *oeuvre,* I will examine the interrelated metaphors of silence and speech that are so central to understanding Lorde's rhetoric, not only to shed light on this single speech, but also to illuminate a salient aspect of the rest of her speeches, essays, and poems. One result of these inquiries will be a glimpse into the margins of rhetoric in the sense of the public speech. To Lorde, silence as a response to either internalized shame or wrongful deeds is as devastating to an individual's self as cancer is to the body. Because of cancer's associations with the fear of a protracted and painful death resulting from the body's betrayal of itself, a wasting away in a stereotypical narrative with a familiar and ineluctable conclusion, cancer becomes a powerful metaphor for any silent destroyer.

★ PERSPECTIVES ON SILENCE AND SPEECH

Silence recurs as an important topic in scholarship on communication. Recognizing as I do that, as Robert L. Scott puts it, "I cannot truly essay all the motivations for silence,"[15] I should like here to examine scholarly literature on silence that illuminates recurring topics in Lorde's rhetoric, beginning with general treatments of silencing and power. Tillie Olsen's classic book, *Silences,* identified several factors that tend in general to silence literary figures: "work aborted, deferred, denied. . . . Censorship silences. Deletions, omissions, abandonment of the medium . . . paralyzing of capacity. . . . Publisher's censorship, refusing subject matter or treatment as 'not suitable' or 'no market for'. Self censorship. Religious, political censorship . . . 'the knife of the perfectionist attitude in art and life.'"[16] More recently, Charles A. Braithwaite has contributed to our understanding of the relationship between power and silencing in his careful review of most of the literature on silence and speech produced specifically in the communication discipline. Summarizing such literature, he stresses two "warrants" about the nature of silence in relationship to power, mentioning in the first warrant derived from Keith Basso's scholarship that "Silence as a communicative action is associated with social situations in which the relationship of the focal participants is uncertain, unpredictable, or ambiguous."[17] The second warrant that Braithwaite mentions has equally obvious relevance to this essay in light of Lorde's explicit recognition of power differences among the races, sexes, sexualities, and economic classes: "Silence as a communicative action is associated with social situations in which there is a known and unequal distribution of power among focal participants."[18]

Silence is often represented in scholarship as a product of gender socialization, a factor that merits mention in that Lorde defined herself as speaking in her role as a woman, as when she wrote in an essay that "Black feminists speak as women because we are women, and do not need others to speak for us."[19] By drawing upon the extensive literature in women's studies and by focusing specifically on the role of silence and the "voice of authority" of women in American colleges and Universities, the environment within which Lorde worked most extensively, Nadya Aisenberg and Mona Harrington devote a chapter of their book, *Women of Academe: Outsiders in the Sacred Grove,* to "the difficulties women have in developing a voice of authority, despite long training and experience."[20] The authors affirm that "A strong, clear voice is necessary to the practice of the profession, both literally in the classroom and figuratively in written research."[21] They inquire, "Why do women find persistent difficulty with forms of public assertion? Why do they refer to silence, apology, diffidence, hesitancy, as characteristic of their discourse?"[22] In response, the authors answer, "One powerful reason is that a voice of authority is exactly the voice the old norms proscribe."[23] They add to this analysis by stressing that women "encounter resistance to authority in women from the moment they begin to claim it"[24] and by focusing upon double binds: "Thus a conflict is set up early—silence to further social ends, speech to develop intellectual goals."[25] They conclude in general that "women's voice of authority is, to some degree, contingent on a broad redefinition of social responsibility, a redefinition of male and female roles in all spheres of life."[26]

Mary Field Belenky, Blythe McVicker Clinchy, Nancy Rule Goldberger, and Jill Mattuck Tarule have argued in *Women's Ways of Knowing: The Development of Self, Voice, and Mind* that speech and silence are gendered in general in that "women commonly talked about voice and silence: 'speaking up,' 'speaking out,' 'being silenced,' 'not being heard,' 'really listening,' 'really talking,' 'words as weapons,' 'feeling deaf and dumb,' 'having no words,' 'saying what you mean,' 'listening to be heard,' and so on in an endless variety of connotations all having to do with sense of mind, self-worth and feelings of isolation from or connection to others."[27] They add, "One growth metaphor in particular reverberated throughout the women's stories of their intellectual development. Again and again women spoke of 'gaining a voice.'"[28] The authors also contrast metaphors for knowledge employed typically by women and men, emphasizing that "The tendency for women to ground their epistemological premises in metaphors suggesting speaking and listening is at odds with the visual metaphors (such as equating knowledge with illumination, knowing with seeing, and truth with light) that scientists and philosophers most often use to express their sense of mind."[29] Accordingly, speech and silence are rife with gendered implications for epistemology and the development of self in relationship to community.

While silence has a tendency to be gendered in significant respects as a consequence of commonplace patterns of socialization, it also may result from underlying factors such as disproportionate experiences of verbal abuse, violence, and poverty that cut across diverse subordinated communities within a culture, as Lorde often mentions in her essays and speeches. Examples of such communities include children and minority groups organized around such variables as race, sexuality, religion, and economic class. Because the experiences of individuals within such communities are heterogenous, and because individuals also define for themselves in varying ways their

responses to similar experiences, I want to emphasize that these factors point to tendencies in patterns of socialization, not causally determining forces. Lorde herself often stressed this role of self definition explicitly, as I will illustrate later in this essay with reference to her use of the terms "casualty" and "warrior." One difficulty in reviewing scholarly literature on silence, however, is a tendency in much of the literature to treat the experiences of communities as uniform or homogenous in respect to one or another characteristic, even when the authors explicitly affirm awareness of diversity of experiences within communities and the varied definitions of those experiences by oneself and others.

Silence as a product of child abuse, for instance, can be one significant factor in the development of a fundamental way of knowing. Child abuse may contribute to shaping the epistemology of some individuals as a result of a deep distrust of language, the very tool for constructing what one knows. The authors of *Women's Ways of Knowing* comment, "These silent women were among the youngest and the most socially, economically, and educationally deprived of all those we interviewed."[30] They explain the epistemological problem of the silent women: "Words were perceived as weapons. Words were used to separate and diminish people, not to connect and empower them. The silent women worried that they would be punished just for using words—any words."[31] In addition to this use of words to wound children, the English language contains an all too familiar list of terms employed to distance, degrade, and thereby silence the members of subordinated communities. Examples include bitch, cunt, dyke, faggot, queer, sissy, nigger, kike, spic, dago, heathen, and Christ-killer, to name only a few.

Lorde often raised to conscious awareness such abusive uses of language to silence members of subordinated communities. In an essay entitled "Eye to Eye: Black Women, Hatred, and Anger," Lorde mentions several childhood experiences in public contexts in which she was subjected to overt expressions of contempt rooted in racism, sexism, and economic class: "as a child I decided there must be something terribly wrong with me that inspired such contempt."[32] She remarked, "As children we absorbed that hatred, passed it through ourselves, and for the most part, we still live our lives outside of the recognition of what that hatred really is and how it functions."[33] In addition, she often commented in her speeches and essays on the use of the term, "lesbian," to intimidate women into silence, while driving a wedge of distrust and suspicion between women.[34] She remarked in one speech that "A fear of lesbians, or of being accused of being a lesbian, has led many Black women into testifying against themselves."[35] She countered such uses of language by using the term, "lesbian," to define herself for herself and by laying claim to her heritage as a black woman, as when she remarked that such relationships are among "twelve different kinds of marriage" in parts of Africa.[36] In other speeches and essays she comments upon "such filth" used by a black academic to refer to homosexuals,[37] and "nigger bitch" used to refer to a black woman.[38] In "Man Child," an essay about her son, Jonathan's, childhood experiences, she commented, "for years, in the name calling at school, boys shouted at Jonathan not—'your mother's a lesbian'—but rather—'your mother's a nigger.'"[39]

In addition to verbal abuse, the experiences of violence and shame also contribute to silencing members of subordinated communities, and these experiences are often interrelated to the extent that survivors of violence are often blamed for having had the experience, especially in cases of sexualized aggression. Focusing primarily upon the gay and lesbian movement in a way that interweaves considerations of race, sex, and, economic class in the United States, Urvashi Vaid writes in *Virtual Equality* that "Hate crimes against gay people were regarded in much the same way as violence against women had been before the feminist movement shifted the paradigm of patriarchy. Gay people were told we should not go out at night, not be so blatant, that we invited this violence upon ourselves, that we were murdered because we picked up strangers in bars."[40] Vaid stresses that under the Reagan administration "the Justice Department of Edwin Meese issued a report in 1987 that termed lesbians and gay men 'probably the most frequent victims of hate

violence in this country.'"[41] Under such conditions, it is not surprising; as Vaid writes elsewhere in her book, that "Invisibility and silence about homosexuality are two of our oldest enemies."[42]

Violence and sexualized aggression recur often as topics in Lorde's rhetoric in connection with race, sex, religion, class, and sexuality. In an essay, Lorde comments on a pattern in American culture in which it is common "to blame the victim for victimization: Black people are said to invite lynching by not knowing our place; Black women are said to invite rape and murder and abuse by not being submissive enough, or by being too seductive."[43] In one of her speeches, Lorde observes that "Rape is on the increase, reported and unreported, and rape is not aggressive sexuality, it is sexualized aggression."[44] She often commented upon rape, violence, and the threat of violence as pervasive experiences: "Black women and our children know the fabric of our lives is stitched with violence and with hatred, that there is no rest . . . violence weaves through the daily tissue of our living."[45] While Lorde considered acts of intimidation and violence as tools used by dominating groups to silence members of subordinated communities, she laid special stress on such uses of threats and violence by members of some subordinated communities against other minorities.[46] In general, Lorde observed a deep interconnection among diverse subordinated communities' experiences of symbolic and physical aggression, as when she remarked in a speech at Harvard University, "Each one of us here is a link in the connection between anti-poor legislation, gay shootings, the burning of synagogues, street harassment, attacks against women, and resurgent violence against Black people."[47]

Depicting shame, anxiety, and fear as patterns of human response to such experiences as verbal abuse, violence, sexualized aggression, and the misrepresentation of one's difference as deficiency, Gershen Kaufman and Lev Raphael draw extensively upon psychological literature on silence and shame to argue that "The hallmark of shame is silence."[48] They add that the interrelationship of silence and shame has a cyclical quality in that "Silence breeds shame every bit as much as shame breeds further silence. The two are locked in an endless cycle of mutual reactivation."[49] The authors stress that "When silence is systematically imposed on a broad societal plane, it becomes a more powerful form of oppression than is experienced in the family."[50] Generalizing across social groups, they affirm that "The phenomenon of gay bashing that has become even further magnified in response to the AIDS crisis is not unlike lynchings for African Americans and pogroms for Jews who lived in Eastern Europe. These are all magnified expressions of contempt for those who are outcasts."[51] Again generalizing across several subordinated communities, they claim that "You cannot simultaneously belong to a minority group and the wider culture without some measure of conflict. It is that conflict which must be confronted directly if it is to be eventually transformed."[52] As Joan Nestle affirms and reiterates in one of her poems, "Shame is the first betrayer."[53] This role of shame in self-betrayal may shed light on some underlying reasons that Lorde's rhetoric explicitly comments on the necessity of overcoming internalized shame, anxiety, and fear as well as the underlying factors that contribute to these emotions. Lorde's speech to the MLA exemplifies perhaps her most sustained commentary on undertaking such transformation.

While the underlying factors of verbal abuse, physical violence, and internalized shame often contribute to silencing members of subordinated communities, there are also the variations of silence surrounding other taboo topics. Some of these topics, like sexual harassment, often entail a complex intermingling of these factors, while other taboo topics, such as cancer, ordinarily do not. Some of these varieties of silence are overt as when expressions that are superficially about sexual interest are, in fact, vehicles for communicating power, domination, and control that silences victims, sometimes through the explicit threat of a face smashed beyond recognition, or bruised breasts. Such silences have been explored in anonymous narratives about the experience of sexual harassment in the communication discipline. Julia T. Wood affirms in her introduction to the narratives, "these stories do more than break the long and oppressive silence surrounding sexual harassment; they also argue for change."[54] There are subtle variations of silence surrounding various forms of sexualized aggression that may enable it to continue. Sometimes the silence of an entire community enables inappropriate behavior, because the silence is a necessary condition for the behavior, regardless of whether the silence is rooted in self protection, a sense of professional duty, the impositions of gags, or less tolerable factors such as personal convenience, political opportunism, cowardice, fear of legal fees, or a misguided belief that an institution's public relations and fund raising are harmed by acknowledging a problem in the spirit of going to the root of it. Such silence and silencing by those around a perpetrator enables the harassment to continue in the work place.[55] It is sometimes appropriate to recognize and name the willed silence of an entire community as an enabling behavior in the sense that the silence provides a necessary condition for the behavior.

It is possible that Lorde directly addresses the transformation of silence into language and action precisely because she recognizes the role of silence as an enabling behavior, though she never articulates this insight in her speech. Instead, she focuses upon silence as the equivalent of acquiescence, surrender, and even death. Lorde certainly recognized the role of a hostile social environment in making violence and abuse increasingly likely. For example, Lorde remarks in "Scratching the Surface" on one instance when "Phone calls threatening violence were made to those Black women who dared to explore the possibilities of a feminist connection with non-Black women." Lorde adds, "When threats did not prevent the attempted coalition of feminists, the resulting campus-wide hysteria left some Black women beaten and raped." Lorde then identifies a role for a hostile social environment in supporting such deeds: "Whether the threats by Black men actually led to these assaults, or merely encouraged the climate of hostility within which they could occur, the results upon the women attacked were the same."[56]

Silence has many further dimensions, not all of them negative, including, for instance, silence as a means of active, political resistance, as Lisa Delpit has argued.[57] There is a variety of silence in the tranquility of the Quaker's inward light, as discussed by Richard Bauman: "Silence, for the Quakers, was not an end in itself, but a means to the attainment of the defining spiritual experience of early Quakerism, the direct personal experience of the spirit of God within oneself."[58] Bauman explains, "God spoke his Word anew within the soul of every person, doing away with virtually all mediating, agencies in the ultimate exaltation of inner experience. . . . As this most important act of speaking took place inwardly and was spiritual, it required that one refrain from speaking that was outward and carnal."[59] There is the value of silent meditations both spiritual and secular.[60] Silence and speech should not be reduced to a simplistic opposition in which silence is negative and speech is positive, if only because there are liberating deeds done in eloquent silence and talk can conceal a significant silence.

For Audre Lorde, however, silence was almost always negative, as she stressed at length in an interview with Karla Hammond:

> Silence for me is a very negative quality because it's the nameless. As Adrienne (Rich) has said, what remains nameless eventually becomes unspeakable, what remains unspoken becomes unspeakable. That silence is a very negative quality when it's preserved by violence. Some people can't tolerate any silence at all and that's equally bad. But that enforced silence, the inability to speak, the refusal to speak is a very violent silence, where you know there is a great deal happening but it's not spoken.[61]

Lorde's remarks stress her perception of silence as detrimental to the extent that it results from violence, abuse, and shame. Her speech to the MLA in 1977 focuses entirely on harmful aspects of silence as an insidious destroyer.

Lorde's speech, "The Transformation of Silence into Language and Action," adds to our understanding of silence specifically as a response to internalized shame or wrongful deeds by underscoring that such silence is as devastating to a healthy sense of self as cancer is to the body. Delivered as a part of a panel at the MLA during 1977, the speech endeavored to deal in public with what had been a very private issue. As Nancy K. Bereano noted in her editorial introduction to *Sister Outsider:* "Here Lorde grapples with a possible diagnosis of

cancer. . . . She deals in public, at an academic gathering, in front of 700 women."[62] The large size of the audience probably accounts for the declamatory style of the delivery, while its demographics shed light on Lorde's rhetorical strategies. According to an interview between Audre Lorde and Adrienne Rich recorded during August 1979 and printed in part in *Signs* during 1981, the silence surrounding breast cancer was central to Lorde in this speech, though she amplified her treatment of it by interweaving numerous sources of silence.[63] The speech illustrates Lorde's extraordinary ability to draw upon the diverse and multiple aspects of her self to explore and enact the transformation of silence into language and action.

★ A METAPHORIC ANALYSIS OF SILENCE AND SPEECH

Lorde's speech scrutinizes two antithetical topics, silence and speech, which she amplifies through interrelated metaphors to develop her central insight that silence as a response to internalized shame or wrongful deeds is as devastating to the self as cancer is to the body. The first of these metaphors affirms her personal position that speech is ineluctably an act of self-revelation with the attendant possibilities of self-examination and transformation: "I have come to believe over and over that what is most important to me must be spoken, made verbal and shared, even at the risk of having it bruised or misunderstood. That the speaking profits me, beyond any other effect."[64] The speech begins with a highly personal and introspective focus upon the self that is so characteristic of human liberation discourse, while calling conscious awareness to some risks that attend breaking silence. Yet Lorde's opening enacts a course of action that she models for the audiences, whom she later encourages explicitly to collaborate with her in the uses of language to change self and society.

Her next several sentences quickly introduce three taboo topics, each surrounded by silence in contemporary U.S. culture-race, sexuality, and a life-threatening illness, breast cancer:

> I am standing here as a Black lesbian poet, and the meaning of all that waits upon the

fact that I am alive at all, ... Less than two months ago I was told by two doctors, one female and one male, that I would have to have breast surgery, and that there was a 60 to 80 percent chance that the tumor was malignant. Between that telling and the actual surgery, there was a three-week period of the agony of an involuntary reorganization of my entire life. The surgery was completed, and the growth was benign.

Because breast cancer affects all women, without regard for race, class, or ethnicity, Lorde's remarks about her experience of fear articulate a basis for identification across such differences among women, though such cancer does affect biologically childless women disproportionately. Delese Wear comments, "Perhaps no other disease summons the kind of dread in women than that evoked by even the mention of breast cancer." Wear adds, "She is terrified because of the sharp double edge of facing a potentially fatal disease, and of losing a precious part of her body that is deeply tangled in her sexuality/femininity/self."[65]

Lorde's literal confrontation with her own personal mortality provides the foreground in the speech for a series of metaphors about the nature of silence and speech in terms of death and life: "I was forced to look upon myself and my living with a harsh and urgent clarity that has left me even now still shaken but much stronger. . . . Some of what I experienced during that time has helped elucidate for me much of what I feel concerning the transformation of silence into language and action." She adds, "[W]hat I most regretted were my silences." Lorde amplifies the imagery that silence is death, as when she affirms, "Death . . . is the final silence. And that might be coming quickly, now, without regard for whether I had ever spoken what needed to be said, or had only betrayed myself into small silences, while I planned someday to speak, or waited for someone else to say the words for me." Such remarks affirm a need to speak for oneself as an act of personal integrity, courage, and self respect, not to defer responsibility to another. Beyond the deep issues associated with endeavoring to overcome one's own internalized shame through the act of speaking, there is also the matter of regretting one's acts of silent omission in facing one's own death: "priorities and omissions became very strongly etched in a merciless light."

Lorde draws upon personal experience to dispel as an illusion the idea that silence provides protection: "I was going to die, if not sooner then later, whether or not I had ever spoken. My silences had not protected me." This personal insight becomes the basis for a broader claim in a pattern that recurs throughout the speech, moving from personal experience and insight to communal, political ones. She adds, "Your silence will not protect you." To the contrary, the refusal of language amounts to self betrayal and self destruction, if only because language is essential to the process of self definition. Silence is in these respects like an undetected cancer embodying a betrayal of oneself. Her use of direct questions coaxes audience participation in an open-ended, expansive way: "What are the words you do not yet have? What is it that you need to say? What are the tyrannies that you swallow day after day and attempt to make your own, until you will sicken and die of them eventually, still in silence?" The tyrannies that are swallowed become the seed of the "cancer" that grows in silence undetected within the self.

To Lorde, the metaphor that silence provides protection is not only illusory; it also represents a way that one internalizes an enemy with outposts in one's own head: "In the cause of silence, each one of us draws the face of her own fear—of contempt, of censure, of some judgment, of recognition, of challenge, of annihilation. But most of all, I think we fear that very visibility without which we also cannot truly live."[66] In Lorde's analysis silence often results from a complex intermingling of feelings of shame, guilt, and internal anger at oneself, which she conveys through humorous remarks attributed to her daughter: "But my daughter, when I told her of our topic and my difficulty with it, said, 'Why don't you tell them about how you're never really a whole person if you remain silent, because there's always that one little piece inside of you that wants to be spoken out, and if you keep ignoring it, it gets madder and madder and hotter and hotter, and if you don't speak it out one day it will just up and punch you in the mouth.'" In telling this story, Lorde was probably aware that active cancer was described as "hot" in medical circles, yet another resonance between the consequences of silence and cancer for self and body. Speech and other uses of language, by implication, represent freedom, visibility, and life.

These metaphors about speech and silence unfold temporally as antithetical motifs which Lorde brings together through another, more fundamental motif—more fundamental, that is, because to Lorde fear is an underlying cause of both silence and speech. She asks herself in the presence of her audiences: "Of what had I ever been afraid? To question or to speak what I believed could have meant pain, or death." Yet Lorde also articulates an underlying role for fear in choosing to speak, "And of course I am afraid—you can hear it in my voice or not—because the transformation of silence into language and action is an act of self-revelation always, and that very frequently seems fraught with danger." She adds, "The fear is a weapon used to encourage our silence." While silence equals the illusion of protection, an illusion endangering the self as undetected cancer endangers the body, speech equals the real risks attendant on visibility, the risk of having one's ideas "bruised or misunderstood," as she remarked in her opening comments.

While speech, for Lorde, represents risk, it also represents the possibilities of naming oneself for oneself, of transforming oneself and of bridging differences with others entering into community: "[F]or every real word I had ever spoken, for every attempt I had ever made to speak those truths for which I am still seeking, I had made contact with other women . . . , bridging our differences." This contact with others through speech and action provided her with a resource in that it connected her with communal support: "And it was the concern and caring of all those women that gave me strength and enabled me to scrutinize the essentials of my life." Again, Lorde draws upon her personal experience in a way that promotes broad identifications across sociological groups: "The women who sustained me through that period were Black and white, old and young, lesbian, bisexual, [and] heterosexual, and we all shared a war against the tyrannies of silence."

She affirms identification among all women through division in a "war" with silence.[67]

Lorde's speech treats the antithetical metaphors in a candid, highly personal and intimate style that points frankly toward the underlying factors that compel her speech in this instance—factors that provide a glimpse into the limits of rhetoric in what I take to be a tragic way. Her speech asserts bluntly that it was the greater fear of what she took to be her own impending death that led her to reexamine her silences and her own fears of the visibility accompanying her speech, an acknowledgement that she transforms: "And I began to recognize a source of power within myself that comes from the knowledge that while it is, of course, most desirable not to be afraid, learning to put fear into a perspective gave me a great strength." Later, in her conclusion, she encourages the audience members to recognize and confront the sources of their own fears and to put them into perspective, "We can learn to work and speak when we are afraid in the same way we have learned to work and speak when we are tired. For we have been socialized to respect fear far more than our own needs for language and definition, and while we wait in silence for that final luxury, that epiphany, of fearlessness, the silence will choke us to death."

What are the sources of this fear? As indicated in earlier quotations, the fear is, in part, a product of each individual having internalized her own forms of oppression thereby betraying the self as cancer betrays one's own body in initially undetected but ultimately devastating ways. Lorde lists the sources of fear directly when she locates some causes of silence in what Brigid Brophy refers to as "the invisible cage,"[68] for example. This source of fear becomes the locus of powerful opposition from within oneself, as Lorde herself articulated in an essay, "It is easier to deal with the external manifestations of racism and sexism than it is to deal with the results of those distortions internalized within our consciousness of ourselves and one another."[69] In her speech, the fear of the outsider within gives shape to a paradox: "Within those weeks of acute fear came the knowledge that within the war we are all waging with the forces of death, subtle and otherwise, conscious or not—I am not only a casualty, I am a warrior." Lorde repeats her pattern of moving from personal insight to communal political action toward the conclusion, when she urges her audience to take part in the transformation from silence into language and action: "It is not without fear—of visibility, of the harsh light of scrutiny and perhaps judgment, of pain, of death. But we have lived through all of these already, in silence, all except death."

She adds to her analysis of the sources of fear again metaphorically when she alludes to "a war against the tyrannies of silence" and, more specifically, "this dragon we call america [sic]." She describes the activities of the unnamed enemy through a series of passive voice constructions listing evil actions without naming specific actors: "We can sit in our corners mute forever while our sisters and our selves are wasted [by whom?], while our children are distorted and destroyed [by whom?] while our earth is being poisoned [by whom?]; we can sit in our safe corners or our offices or our homes or wherever mute as bottles, and we will still be no less afraid." The lack of specificity allows each member of the audience to name her own oppressors, her own fears, opening and expanding the implicit range of unspoken implications. For instance, the image of "wasting away" alludes to the physiological course of cancer that is analogous to silence wasting away the self. The references to birth defects and environmental poisoning specify personal health concerns resulting from an excessively profit-driven culture, just as silence often results from a hostile and intimidating environment.

In this context, her cryptic references to herself as a "warrior woman" or her statement, "I am not only a casualty, I am a warrior" take on an enigmatic ambiguity that allows the message to open up possible interpretations. Lorde's self-definition as "warrior" against the silent destroyers within, cancer and silence, expands politically and socially to the warrior who breaks silence to combat the community's failure to address women's health concerns, or, for that matter, any wrongful deeds endangering the political health of the entire community. There is also the political concern of alien ideas planted by the dominant culture within the mind[s] of even those who would fight the system. In addition, there is the movement from the passivity of being defined as a "victim" or "casualty" awash in despair, powerlessness, and silence to "battling" such despair through actively resisting the sources responsible for one's wasting away, whether of self or body, as Lorde amplifies explicitly in *The Cancer Journals:* "I have found that battling despair does not mean closing my eyes to the enormity of the tasks of effecting change, nor ignoring the strength and the barbarity of the forces aligned against us."[70] Later in the *Journals,* she adds, "I was also afraid that I was not really in control, that it might already be too late to halt the spread of cancer, that there was simply too much to do that I might not get done, that the pain would be just too great."[71] The feelings of a loss of control, typical of many persons living with cancer and other life threatening illnesses, are rooted in defining oneself as "casualty" without also naming oneself as "warrior." As Lorde also explains in *The Cancer Journals,* "For silence and invisibility go hand in hand with powerlessness."[72] She stresses that "It was very important to me, after my mastectomy, to develop and encourage my own internal sense of power. I needed to rally my energies in such a way as to image myself as a fighter resisting rather than as a passive victim suffering."[73] Members of her audience could have responded to her remarks to the MLA by supplying any of these unspoken implications in response to the paradox of being both "warrior" and "casualty," though drawing upon *The Cancer Journals* to suggest unspoken implications risks revising the rhetorical understandings at the moment of her speech in light of her later experiences as conveyed in her writings. For example, Lorde amplifies in remarks after her mastectomy that the Amazons of Dahomey were one[-]breasted women, alluding to being a "warrior" in a way that also refers to her own body.

At the time of the MLA, Lorde almost certainly conceived of herself as a "warrior" on several fronts. First, she stood in agonistic opposition to dominating groups whose characteristics she outlines in detail in connection with "*a mythical norm*" in another speech: "In america [sic], this norm is usually defined as white, thin, male, young, heterosexual, christian, and financially secure."[74] Second, she engaged in confrontational consciousness raising of potential allies across differences within the women's communities, especially affluent, white, heterosexual women who too often ignore or explicitly distance themselves from considerations of class, race, and sexuality. Finally, of course, she experienced inner conflicts within herself over her priorities for speaking during an abruptly limited lifetime. In fact, in another speech, Lorde questioned the value of speaking to the representatives of the dominating groups beyond the women's community, recognizing as she did that "There is a constant drain of energy which might be better used in redefining ourselves and devising realistic scenarios for altering the present and constructing the future."[75] Lorde's comments in "An Open Letter to Mary Daly" suggest that she even enacted her role as warrior within the women's communities with misgivings. In this letter, Lorde remarks that shortly before the speech to the MLA she had "decided never again to speak to white women about racism. I felt it was wasted energy because of destructive guilt and defensiveness, and because whatever I had to say might better be said by white women to one another at far less emotional cost to the speaker, and probably with a better hearing."[76] Whatever the sources of fear, whether external or internal, to Lorde they will abide as a consequence of silence recognized as a symptom of failing to become a warrior on these many fronts.

Indeed, Lorde's speech enacts her role as warrior engaging audiences whom she regularly experienced as devaluing her contributions, silencing her, or rendering her invisible, as may be discerned in several of her rhetorical strategies. For example, Lorde calls conscious awareness to herself as an embodiment of some audience members' fears with her remark earlier in the speech to the MLA: "Perhaps for some of you here now, I am the face of one of your fears. Because I am woman, because I am black, because I am lesbian, because I am myself—a black woman warrior poet doing her work—come to ask you, 'Are you doing yours?'" The sequence of self-namings is a significant technique in her confrontational consciousness raising, because it moves from the broadest basis of identification with the women at the MLA to

a series of differences within the group. In this connection, an allusion to Winnie Mandela in the introduction, where Lorde dedicates a poem to Mandela and depicts her as "A South African freedom fighter," and a later allusion to Kwanza, an "African American festival of harvest" that Lorde is celebrating during the MLA convention, may take on additional, implicit significance, because of Lorde's presentation of herself as a *Black* lesbian: "Within this country where racial difference creates a constant, if unspoken, distortion of vision, Black women have on one hand always been highly visible, and so, on the other hand, we have been rendered invisible through the depersonalization of racism. And yet even within the women's movement, we have had to fight, and still do, for that very visibility which also renders us most vulnerable, our Blackness." Invisibility is to the eyes what silence is to the ears. To Lorde, it is vital to speak and be visible as both different within and yet intimately related to one's communities as a means of actively constructing one's own sense of self with adequate attention to one's own distinct yet interrelated interests.[77] In *The Cancer Journals*, Lorde amplifies on the underlying dilemma posed by language in defining self as a member of various communities: "I am defined as other in every group I'm a part of. The outsider, both strength and weakness. Yet without community there is certainly no liberation, no future, only the most vulnerable and temporary armistice between me and my oppression."[78]

In her speech to the MLA, Lorde's discussion of Kwanza outlines the general structure of the speech and serves as a transition from a central focus upon self to community, while underscoring ineluctable differences among members of a community: "There are seven principles of Kwanza, one for each day," she remarks. The first principle, which "means unity, the decision to strive for and maintain unity in self and community" is followed by the second principle, "self determination—the decision to define ourselves, name ourselves, and speak for ourselves, instead of being defined and spoken for by others." The third principle corresponds to the final section of the speech: "Today is the third day of Kwanza . . . collective work and responsibility—that decision to build and maintain ourselves and our communities and to recognize and solve those problems that we share together." The speech unfolds in predominant emphasis temporally through these three principles, the only ones she mentions, though they are interwoven without sharp demarcations among them, no emphatic transitions.[79] It could be argued that these organizing principles represent an epistemologically specific conceptualization of rhetoric such as Afrocentrism in that Kwanza embodies the principles of African American cultural nationalism that emerged during the late 1960s and 1970s. By alluding to this social, political, and rhetorical movement, Lorde incorporates and extends those principles to promote forms of identification and differentiation among the women in her audience. To the extent that the audience members respond to her call for collective action, their deeds can be defined and understood as participation in the principles of Kwanza.

The final section of the speech calls upon audience members to reflect upon aspects of personal responsibility for the transformation from silence into language and action, but not in the traditional, directive way characterized by urging one specific plan, or course of action. She calls upon the audiences to engage in self-examination, consciousness raising, and personal transformation as well as communal engagement, because one can only define the self through language in relationship to the community: "Each one of us here is here because in one way or another we share a commitment to language and to the power of language, and to the reclaiming of that language which has been made to work against us. In the transformation of silence into language and action, it is vitally necessary, I believe, for each one of us to establish or examine her function in that transformation and to recognize her role as vital within that transformation." This request opens up the possibilities for active, creative, and unanticipated contributions by her audiences. At the same time, it voices awareness that language as a tool "has been made to work against us," calling attention to another layer of fear in the process of speaking through language, because Lorde recognizes language itself as one of the master's tools in that language tends to represent and reproduce the interests of dominating groups.[80]

For this reason, it becomes important that "we examined the words to fit a world in which we all believed" and it becomes vital "to scrutinize not only the truths of what we speak, but the truth and validity of that language by which we speak it." To Lorde, language as a communal resource enables one to define oneself in relationship to the community through a complex process of identification and differentiation, but not without the inherent risk of language subverting that very sense of self because of any language's history as communal resource.[81]

Mindful of the inherent risks that attend using language, Lorde then treats language as a resource for acknowledging and bridging differences among human beings, developing toward the conclusion of the speech an idea foreshadowed by a single line in the introductory poem dedicated to Mandela: "our spices are separate and particular/but our skins sing in complementary keys." After mentioning as specific examples some possible roles for women who write or who teach literature, she endeavors through confrontational consciousness raising to engage subtle forms of defensiveness among her audiences, what Betty Schmitz refers to as indirect forms of resistance that might enable the audiences to distance themselves from the literature of those who are different.[82] Lorde urges

> That we not hide behind the mockeries of separations that have been imposed upon us and which so often we accept as our own. For instance, "I can't possibly teach Black women's writing—their experience is so different from mine." Yet how many years have you spent teaching Plato and Shakespeare and Proust? Or another, "She's a white woman and what could she possibly have to say to me?" Or, "She's a lesbian, what would my husband think, or my chairman say if he sees my book list?" Or again, "This woman writes of her sons and I have no children." And all the other endless ways in which we rob ourselves of ourselves and each other.

In these remarks, the sequence again proceeds from the broadest identifications with the immediate audience, women, to examine a series of differences within the community across race, sexuality, and parental status. More important,

Lorde endeavors to dispel a form of silence rooted in anxieties about communicating across differences, anxieties that cut in multiple directions. As Lorde's opening poem for Winnie Mandela affirmed and reiterated, "Our labor has become more important than our silence."

Finally, she focuses upon silence as more fundamental than difference among sociological groups, since speech can enable us to identify with one another and act together in diverse respects in the community: "The fact that we are here and that I speak even now these words are an attempt to break that silence and bridge some of those differences between us. For it is not difference that immobilizes us, but silence. And there are so many silences to be broken." While Lorde affirms in these final lines that the breaking of silence is fundamental, not only primarily to constructing and sustaining the health of the self, but also to acknowledging and bridging differences, and so identifies one of the most fundamental causes for the increasing importance of communication in a heterogeneous society, communication also requires *listening*, an activity that complicates the ways in which we engage messages such as Lorde's "The Transformation of Silence into Language and Action," as Lorde herself recognizes when she urges her audience, "Where the words of women are crying to be heard, we, each of us, must recognize our responsibility to seek those words out, to read them and share them and examine them in their pertinence to our living."

The title of one of Karlyn Kohrs Campbell's recent essays is suggestive in this connection, because she stresses "Hearing Women's Voices."[83] As Abena P. A. Busia affirms, "the systematic refusal to hear our speech is not the same thing as our silence."[84] Comments by bell hooks along similar lines raise a question about whether Lorde was adapting her treatment of silence and speech to her audience of predominantly white women:

> Within feminist circles, silence is often seen as the sexist 'right speech of womanhood'—the sign of woman's submission to patriarchal authority. This emphasis on woman's silence may be an accurate remembering of what has taken place in the households of women from WASP backgrounds in the United States, but in black communities (and diverse ethnic communities), women have not been silent. Their voices can be heard. Certainly for black women, our struggle has not been to emerge from silence into speech but to change the nature and direction of our speech, to make a speech that compels listeners, one that is heard.[85]

These remarks complicate our understanding of black women's rhetoric, reminding us of the dangers of essentialism in characterizing the speech of entire communities as though it were uniform or homogeneous. Ultimately, hooks recognizes diversity among black women's experiences with silence explicitly, when hooks comments, "for women within oppressed groups who have contained so many feelings—despair, rage, anguish—who do not speak, as poet Audre Lorde writes, 'for fear our words will not be heard nor welcomed,' coming to voice is an act of resistance." Hooks adds, "Speaking becomes both a way to engage in active self-transformation and a rite of passage where one moves from being object to being subject."[86] Breaking silence is a necessary condition for overcoming internalized shame or for acknowledging and bridging differences in the interest of combating wrongful deeds, but it is not a sufficient condition. We have evidence in the historical record of how well we listen to such voices.[87]

CONCLUSION

But listening is always a difficult activity, especially when the perception of differences is great, especially when differences in underlying cultural experiences may shape our very abilities to listen. Lorde's speech has a haunting quality in that it specifies the tragic circumstances that in her own personal case impelled her to speak. This effect of the speech cannot be ascribed simply to her intentions, or to the prevailing concerns of her immediate audience. The central metaphor of the essay, that silence equals death, Lorde articulated in 1977, several years before the AIDS pandemic that has moved so many to break the silences surrounding sexuality and life threatening illnesses. Today, we cannot possibly hear Lorde's speech in precisely the same terms as when she delivered it, because the underlying cultural conditions that inform its meanings have changed so dramatically, so swiftly and unpredictably. This represents—perhaps ineluctably—an appropriation of Lorde's language and action, but one consistent with Lorde's endeavors to broaden the range of identifications among social groups. Her insights about silence abide.

In closing, I want to underscore that Lorde's treatment of speech and silence through metaphors represents one point of view that should not be categorized simply in terms of sex, race, sexuality, economic class, or health. Her speech is about human liberation in the context of any acts of domination and control over speech, including such acts by the members of one's own community.[88] This essay has by no means exhausted the topic of silence, having only explored a few of its roots in power, domination, verbal abuse, violence and the taboo, as well as resulting emotions such as shame, anxiety, or fear. Several additional dimensions of silence and communication merit further consideration, not only the negative variations of silencing or remaining silent as a response to wrong, but also the positive roles of silence in reflecting on self development in life enhancing ways. Silence has multiple meanings. It is sometimes a product of oppression, a survival skill in dealing with domination and violence, at other times a chosen form of liberation, and on yet other occasions the exercise of a fundamental human right, as in the right to remain silent. Moreover, speaking is not necessarily an act of liberation. In fact, speech about any consequential matters may inherently entail what may be represented as significant silences simply because an individual's speech necessarily entails a progression of ideas expressed one at a time in a finite time and space. But to theorize silence adequately would require the space of an entire book, not an essay, as Adrienne Rich's *On Lies, Secrets, and Silence* or Tillie Olsen's *Silences* may imply.[89]

Although much more remains to be said about silence, Lorde's speech does shed light on the opening questions about the margins of rhetoric. What, then, are the limits of rhetoric? Lorde's oration identifies one limitation in the fear of social, political, or economic sanctions that can result from speech and visibility.[90] This fear can become the source of invisible impositions upon oneself that are more powerful and effective than any external ones. Lorde's speech also amplifies the role of external sources of fear such as physical violence, which can be understood as a symbolic practice that limits the possibilities of rhetoric: from rape and harassment to lynching and fag bashing, a broader, cultural pattern emerges enabling us to recognize the symbolic role of acts of intimidation in keeping some of us in our places while enabling others of us to dominate the public space. Lorde's speech points to yet another limit of rhetoric by underscoring the role of the taboo in demarcating topics surrounded by silence. Her remarks about race, sex, and sexuality underscore sociological factors that shed light on the question, Who gets to speak to and for the community, with what authority and power, with access to what public forums? As a Black lesbian poet, Lorde can draw upon her personal experiences in a way that provides her with a privilege to speak and be heard with a power and authority that others cannot possess, except possibly through imaginative and sympathetic understanding. Yet her access to public forums may be circumscribed by the very aspects of her personhood that give her speech its power and its urgency.

These features of the margins of rhetoric may seem obvious to those who have devoted energy to studying the communicative practices of various subordinated populations. Yet these margins merit mention for those of us who have become so habituated to acts of devaluation and exclusion that the limits of rhetoric are neither noticed nor appreciated. They also enable us to see clearly the enabling conditions of a discipline to the extent that rhetoric is defined as synonymous with oratory or speech. The role of speaker may emerge out of underlying political and social factors that as a matter of habit lend authority, legitimacy, and symbolic power to the speech. If further evidence is necessary to support this claim, perhaps it will be sufficient to mention that every President in U.S. history has been a politically powerful and economically privileged white male, who almost always has a traditional family with a wife and children signifying heterosexuality. To the extent that underlying political and social factors contribute to empowering some while disempowering many, these factors outline a few noteworthy margins of rhetoric in the sense of both boundaries and relative value. Yet a deeper margin of rhetoric may be at the point where words fail us: This may be the silence imposed by child abuse, by grief, by incest, rape and other forms of physical assault, by fear of any kind, and certainly by the confrontation with one's own mortality. Silence may be more decorous than a scream, but silence is unlikely to secure necessary support, assistance, and care from concerned communities, or to bring about social or political change.

Paradoxically, Lorde's speech is as much about the possibilities of rhetoric as its limits. For those who define rhetoric as the study of public speech or oratory, Lorde's message calls for an imaginative re-vision of the range of discourse from which we generalize as well as a revaluing of the varieties of speaking practices, for surely rhetorical techniques vary with the range of personal experiences, types of power and authority, and access to public forums.[91] Lorde's speech enacts at once her roles as both an orator and a critical rhetorician. It articulates a powerful synthesis of these two roles through her use of stylistic eloquence as well as her critical self-reflection and scrutiny of language. While oratory ordinarily reinforces and reproduces the ideology of dominant groups, occasionally rhetors endeavor to employ language to resist domination and to transform self and community.[92] This is in many respects a paradoxical undertaking. Alternatively, because Lorde calls for both language and action, Lorde's speech underscores the value of focusing upon rhetoric defined in terms of symbolic action along the lines articulated by such theorists as Kenneth Burke or, more recently, Pierre Bourdieu, because this sense of rhetoric as symbolic action provides one means of including and respecting the diverse ways in which people communicate their perspectives. Deeds can be done in eloquent silence, and ideas conveyed through a wide range of symbolic means beyond the spoken or written word.

Throughout the centuries, public figures have broken silence in endeavors to transform self and society. Speakers will continue using language, as bell hooks puts it, to choose the margin as the space of radical openness, a site of resistance, a place for freedom of expression and action, despite powerful sanctions for speech, including the loss of life.[93] In this connection, observations by bell hooks in her book, *Talking Back*, are instructive. In an essay bearing the same title, she explains that "In the world of the southern black community I grew up in, 'back talk' and 'talking back' meant speaking as an equal to an authority figure. It meant daring to disagree and sometimes it just meant having an opinion."[94] Although hooks expresses skepticism about typifying all women as silent, she resists the temptation to essentialize the speech of entire communities. She affirms in her conclusion: "Moving from silence into speech is for the oppressed, the colonized, the exploited, and those who stand and struggle side by side a gesture of defiance that heals, that makes new life and new growth possible. It is that act of speech, of 'talking back,' that is no mere gesture of empty words, that is the expression of our movement from object to subject—the liberated voice."[95] As for the audiences of such liberating speech, hooks remarks in another essay, "When we end our silence, when we speak in a liberated voice, our words connect us with anyone, anywhere who lives in silence."[96]

Enacting the breaking of silence can take many forms. For Audre Lorde, the process entails a complex sequence of self-namings through reference to demographic groupings that she evokes sequentially to promote identifications and differentiations: human, but not male; woman, but not white; black, but not straight; lesbian, but not childless; living with cancer, but not a passive victim. The ways of breaking silence can be enacted, through additional forms, as illustrated in this essay when I endeavor to use language to affirm and promote underlying values, such as active and respectful listening across many differences between Lorde and myself in age, race, sex, parental status, health, political commitments, and economic theories, while drawing upon some similarities in sexuality, nationality, and humanity. Jeanne Perreault points out that "academic retreat from the complexities of cross-cultural and cross-racial reading and writing can serve only those who wish to maintain the status quo, to sustain the academy's now precarious grip on an aging world view." Perreault cautions, however, "This self-awareness need not be the naive assumption that if one merely names one's heritage, or sexual orientation, or class background, one will be thus 'positioned,' and thus a known entity. Instead, what readers and writers need to do is to discern from within the critical material . . . what values are held and how they are expressed."[97] Because differences and similarities are inherent in the relationship between any two people, it follows that the challenge becomes reading and speaking and writing across differences, not allowing differences to become an excuse for disengaging from others, but instead exploring the variations among us as welcome resources for creating a more complex understanding of communication practices within and among communities.

NOTES

[1] Tillie Olsen, *Silences* (1965; New York: Dell, 1978) x.

[2] Audre Lorde, *Coal* (New York: Norton, 1976); *The Black Unicorn: Poems* (New York: Norton, 1978); *Our Dead Behind Us: Poems* (New York: Norton, 1986).

[3] Some would argue that these are salient features of African American rhetoric, as in Jack Daniel, Geneva Smitherman-Donaldson, and Milford A. Jeremiah, "Makin' A Way Outa No Way: The Proverb Tradition in the Black Experience," *Journal of Black Studies* 17 (1987): 482–508.

[4] Audre Lorde, *Sister Outsider: Essays and Speeches by Audre Lorde* (Freedom, CA: Crossings, 1984).

[5] Audre Lorde, "Age, Race, Class, & Sex: Women Redefining Difference," *Sister Outsider* 114.

[6] Lorde, "Age, Race, Class, & Sex" 120–121.

[7] Audre Lorde, "Learning from the 60s," *Sister Outsider* 137. Later in the same speech, she makes another similar set of observations about multiple features of her identity and the external pressure to be fragmenting and reductive in her self definition (143).

[8] Karlyn Kohrs Campbell, "Hearing Women's Voices," *Communication Education* 40 (1991): 33–49.

[9] There is no entry for Audre Lorde's public address, for example, in Karlyn Kohrs Campbell, ed., *Women Public Speakers in the United States: A Bio-Critical Sourcebook*, 2 vols. (Westport, CT: Greenwood, 1993–94). Nor is there an entry for her in Richard W. Leeman's forthcoming volume in the same Greenwood series on *African-American Orators: A Bio-Critical Sourcebook* (Richard W. Leeman, letter to author, 9 June 1995). These omissions probably result from the fact that Lorde is best known as a poet and had been included in a volume in a Greenwood series devoted to writers: Sandra Pollack and Denise D. Knight, eds., *Contemporary Lesbian Writers of the United States: A Bio-Bibliographical Critical Sourcebook* (Westport, CT: Greenwood, 1993) 316–324. Lorde is listed, for example, in Ernest Kay, ed., *International Who's Who in Poetry,* 4th ed. (Cambridge, Eng.: Melrose, 1974) 275. One of Lorde's speeches, "Learning from the 60s," was printed in Robbie Jean Walker, ed., *The Rhetoric of Struggle: Public Address by African American Women* (New York: Garland, 1992) 125–140. But because most of Lorde's rhetoric challenged patriarchal authority, it is unfortunate in this respect that her only anthologized speech is a tribute to Malcolm X. One of the selections representing Alice Walker, who gave us the term "Womanist," is likewise a tribute to Martin Luther King (121–124), though the volume does include two additional speeches by Walker. Likewise, Victoria L. Defrancisco and Marvin D. Jensen, eds., *Women's Voices in Our Time: Statements by American Leaders* (Prospect Heights, IL: Waveland, 1994) makes available a wide range of women's rhetoric, but omits any speeches by Lorde, except a collaborative "Statement for Voices Unheard" prepared by Adrienne Rich, Audre Lorde, and Alice Walker in 1974, when Rich refused to accept the National Book Award "as presented" for her poetry collection, *Diving into the Wreck* (271–272). The editors recognize "There are silences amid the voices in this collection" (xiii). Ronald K. Burke, ed., *American Public Discourse: A Multicultural Perspective* (Lanham, MD: UP of America, 1992) omits any texts of Lorde's rhetoric altogether. Lorde's speech, "The Transformation of Silence into Language and Action," has never been cited in any national journals on communication sponsored by the Speech Communication Association (SCA), to judge from the Arts and Humanities Citation Index through 1994. There are, however, references to one of her best known speeches, "Uses of the Erotic," in an essay by Anne Balsamo in *Communication* in 1988 and one of her essays, "An Open Letter to Mary Daly," in articles about feminism by Nancy Fraser and Linda Nicholson in *Communication* in 1988 and about Mary Daly by Cindy Griffin in *Communication Monographs* in 1993 (where it was cited in the version published in 1981 in *This Bridge Called My Back*). Both the essay and the speech by Lorde were reprinted in *Sister Outsider*.

[10] "An Interview: Audre Lorde and Adrienne Rich," *Sister Outsider* 108.

[11] "An Interview: Audre Lorde and Adrienne Rich" 108.

[12] Audre Lorde, "The Transformation of Silence into Language and Action," *Sinister Wisdom* 6 (1978): 11–15; rpt. with revisions in *The Cancer Journals* (San Francisco, CA: Spinsters Ink, 1980): 18–23 and in *Sister Outsider* 40–44. None of these texts exactly transcribe her remarks to the MLA, to judge from the audiotape of her remarks recorded by a panel participant, Judith McDaniel, a copy of which she provided to me. Judith McDaniel, letter to author, 17 February 1995. All quotations ascribed to Lorde are from the audiotape except for one sentence that was not recorded when the tape was turned over. I am grateful to Professor Merrily Swoboda for calling my attention to this speech and to Judith McDaniel for providing me with an audiotape of it.

The text in *Sinister Wisdom* is the most reliable, because it includes several prefatory remarks omitted from the version in *Sister Outsider:* an allusion to Winnie Mandela's struggles as a "South African freedom fighter," the text of a poem entitled "A Song for Many Movements" that Lorde had written and dedicated to Mandela, and a transition alluding to Mary Daly's use of language during her earlier speech on the same MLA panel. *Sinister Wisdom* is especially useful for information about the rhetorical context of the speech, because it published the texts for the rest of the panel presentations. The version of the speech printed in *The Cancer Journals* is also better than the version in *Sister Outsider* in degree of completeness, but it excises a transition alluding to Daly's earlier speech, probably because of the new context for the remarks in the *Journals.* The least reliable version in *Sister Outsider* is the most frequently quoted in published commentary on Lorde's speech, all of which has taken place outside of the national journals of the SCA. Because I discuss this secondary literature in detail in a companion essay, "Other-Wise: Listening Across the Essential Chasm to Audre Lorde's Speech, 'The Transformation of Silence into Language and Action,'" I omit a discussion of it here out of respect for journal space. In addition to the excised lines mentioned above, *Sister Outsider* also omits self-reflexive statements on the quality of Lorde's voice as she speaks to the MLA. In the original speech, for example, Lorde had remarked, "And of course I am afraid—you can hear it in my voice or not—because the transformation of silence into language and action is an act of self-revelation always." The text in *Sister Outsider* omits the reference to the aural qualities of her voice.

The introductory poem, "A Song for Many Movements," was published in Lorde, *The Black Unicorn* 52. At least two other poems in this collection also bear a close relationship to Lorde's speech, because one of them, "Sister Outsider," was also the title for her collection of speeches and essays including one text of the speech (106), and because another of them, "A Litany For Survival," contains several lines that closely resemble remarks in the speech (31–32).

[13] Karlyn Kohrs Campbell and Kathleen Hall Jamieson introduce the concept of enactment and illustrate it in "Introduction to Form and Genre," *Form and Genre: Shaping Rhetorical Action* (Falls Church, VA: SCA, [1978]): 16–32.

[14] Audre Lorde's speech fulfills several of the generic conventions that Karlyn Kohrs Campbell has outlined in her essay, "The Rhetoric of Women's Liberation: An Oxymoron," *Quarterly Journal of Speech* 59 (1973): 74–86, though Lorde was interested more generally in human liberation.

[15] Robert L. Scott, "Rhetoric and Silence," *Western Journal of Speech Communication* 36 (1972): 146.

[16] Olsen 8–9.

[17] For a more detailed review of the literature on silence as discussed in communication journals, see Charles A. Braithwaite, "Communicative Silence: A Cross-Cultural Study of Basso's Hypothesis" and an earlier essay by Keith H. Basso, "'To Give Up on Words': Silence in Western Apache Culture," both in Donal Carbaugh, ed., *Cultural Communication and Intercultural Contact* (Hillsdale, NJ: Erlbaum, 1990). Braithwaite 323.

[18] Braithwaite 324.

[19] Audre Lorde, "Sexism: An American Disease in Blackface," *Sister Outsider* 60.

[20] Nadya Aisenberg and Mona Harrington, "Voice of Authority," *Women of Academe: Outsiders in the Sacred Grove* (Amherst, MA: U of Massachusetts P, 1988) 64. The chapter provides a useful survey of literature on voice and silence in women's studies.

[21] Aisenberg and Harrington 64.

[22] Aisenberg and Harrington 64–65.

[23] Aisenberg and Harrington 65.

[24] Aisenberg and Harrington 66.

[25] Aisenberg and Harrington 68.

[26] Aisenberg and Harrington 82.

[27] Mary Field Belenky, Blythe McVicker Clinchy, Nancy Rule Goldberger, and Jill Mattuck Tarule, *Women's Ways of Knowing: The Development of Self, Voice, and Mind* (New York: Basic, 1986) 18.

[28] Belenky *et al.* 16.

[29] Belenky *et al.* 18

[30] Belenky *et al.* 23–24. For the exploration of child abuse as a factor influencing some women, see the chapter entitled "Silence" 23–35.

[31] Belenky *et al.* 24.

[32] Audre Lorde, "Eye to Eye: Black Women, Hatred, and Anger," *Sister Outsider* 146; for the childhood experiences, see esp. 145–159.

[33] Lorde, "Eye to Eye" 116.

[34] Her most extensive commentary in *Sister Outsider* on the uses of "lesbian" occur[s] in "Scratching the Surface: Some Notes on Barriers to Women and Loving" (esp. 47–50), but the topic recurs in several speeches and essays (e.g. "An Interview: Audre Lorde and Adrienne Rich" 99 and 106, "Age, Race, Class, & Sex" 121, "Learning from the 60s" 143–144). Similarly, Audre Lorde, *I Am Your Sister: Black Women Organizing Across Sexualities* (New York Kitchen Table/Women of Color, 1985) 4–5. Evidently, the communication discipline is not free of such uses of language, as exemplified in an anonymous reviewer's criticisms as quoted in Carole Blair, Julie R. Brown, and Leslie A. Baxter, "Disciplining the Feminine," *Quarterly Journal of Speech* 80 (1994): 399.

[35] Lorde, "Age, Race, Class, and Sex" 121.

[36] Lorde, "Scratching the Surface" 50; similarly, Lorde, "The Master's Tools" 111; Lorde, "Age, Race, Class, & Sex" 120–121 and 122; Audre Lorde, "Uses of Anger: Women Responding to Racism," *Sister Outsider* 132.

[37] Lorde, "Learning from the 60s" 143.

[38] Lorde, "Learning from the 60s" 142; Lorde, "Eye To Eye" 170.

[39] Audre Lorde, "Man Child: A Black Lesbian Feminist's Response," *Sister Outsider* 75.

[40] Urvashi Vaid, *Virtual Equality: The Mainstreaming of Gay & Lesbian Liberation* (New York: Doubleday, 1995) 141.

[41] Vaid 143.

[42] Vaid 79.

[43] Lorde, "Sexism" 61.

[44] Lorde, "Age, Race, Class, & Sex" 120. For examples of additional commentary by Lorde on rape in various essays, Lorde "Scratching the Surface" 47 and 49; Lorde "Sexism" 64; and Lorde, "An Open Letter to Mary Daly," *Sister Outsider* 70.

[45] Lorde, "Age, Race, Class, & Sex" 119.

[46] This idea is well illustrated by one entire essay: Lorde, "Sexism" 60–65, esp. 64; another sustained series of examples can be found in Lorde, "Scratching the Surface" 46–48.

[47] Lorde, "Learning from the 60s" 139.

[48] Gershen Kaufman and Lev Raphael, *Coming Out of Shame: Transforming Gay and Lesbian Lives* (New York: Doubleday, 1996) dust jacket.

[49] Kaufman and Raphael 103.

[50] Kaufman and Raphael 104.

[51] Kaufman and Raphael 82.

[52] Kaufman and Raphael 80.

[53] Joan Nestle, "Stone Butch, Drag Butch, Baby Butch," *A Restricted Country* (Ithaca, NY: Firebrand, 1987) 74–77.

[54] "'Telling Our Stories': Sexual Harassment in the Communication Discipline," *Journal of Applied Communication Research* 20 (1992): 360–361.

[55] The twenty-first narrative in the series points to such a subtle variation of silence surrounding harassment that may enable it to continue. The author comments, "I cannot discuss the details of the charge. I have been gagged." In addition, the author mentions that even though the college administration established the perpetrator's guilt, secured his signature admitting his guilt, and imposed minimal sanctions, the administration also took "no action" after the perpetrator later violated the terms of those sanctions. Further, the author alludes to "the lawyers" who saw to it that "There will be nothing in his permanent record" signalling the misconduct to prospective employers. "'Telling Our Stories'" 379–381.

[56] Lorde, "Scratching the Surface" 47.

[57] Lisa Delpit, "The Silenced Dialogue: Power and Pedagogy in Educating Other People's Children," *Harvard Educational Review* 58 (1988): 280–298

[58] Richard Bauman, "Let Your Words Be Few: Speaking and Silence in Quaker Ideology," *Let Your Words Be Few: Symbolism of Speaking and Silence among Seventeenth-Century Quakers* (Cambridge, Eng.: Cambridge UP, 1983) 23.

[59] Bauman 29–30.

[60] These aspects of silence elude Pierre Bourdieu, for whom silence is always a consequence of domination in his otherwise admirable volume, *Language & Symbolic Power* ed. and intro. John B. Thompson, trans. Gino Raymond and Matthew Adamson (Cambridge, MA: Harvard UP, 1991) 22, 71, 83, 97, 99, 101, 138, and 190.

[61] Karla Hammond, "An Interview with Audre Lorde," *American Poetry Review* 9.2 (1990): 18.

[62] Nancy K. Bereano, "Introduction," *Sister Outsider* 10. An account in *Sinister Wisdom* also mentions that the session was "Attended by 700 women." *Sinister Wisdom* 6 (1978): 4.

[63] "An Interview: Audre Lorde and Adrienne Rich" 108.

[64] The idea that language is important because it enables self-definition and transformations is one that Richard B. Gregg would almost certainly consider an instance of the ego-function in rhetoric,

"The Ego-Function of Protest Rhetoric," *Philosophy and Rhetoric* 4 (1971): 71–91. Lorde's speech, "Age, Race, Class, & Sex" 114–123, provides ample evidence that Gregg's formulation requires re-vision in term of both the assumptions that inform the perspective and the substantive claims.

65 Delese Wear, "'Your breasts/sliced off': Literary Images of Breast Cancer," *Women & Health* 20. 4 (1993): 82.

66 The idea of the enemy with outposts in one's own head was articulated by Sally Kempton in "Cutting Loose," as quoted in Campbell, "The Rhetoric of Women's Liberation" 80.

67 Kenneth Burke, *A Rhetoric of Motives* (Berkeley: U of California P, 1950).

68 Brigid Brophy, "Women: Invisible Cages," in *Don't Never Forget* (New York: Holt, 1963); rpt. in Evelyn Ashton-Jones and Gary A. Olson, eds., *The Gender Reader* (Boston: Allyn and Bacon, 1991) 498–505.

69 Lorde, "Eye to Eye" 147.

70 Lorde, *The Cancer Journals* 17.

71 Lorde, *The Cancer Journals* 33.

72 Lorde, *The Cancer Journals* 61.

73 Lorde, *The Cancer Journals* 73.

74 Lorde, "Age, Race, Class, & Sex" 116.

75 Lorde, "Age, Race, Class, & Sex" 115.

76 Lorde, "An Open Letter" 70.

77 Lorde articulates such concerns about difference and relatedness within communities in her speech, "Age, Race, Class, & Sex," for instance, when she amplifies the insight that "There is a pretense to a homogeneity of experience covered by the word *sisterhood* that does not in fact exist" (116). The idea may also be illustrated by the entirety of "An Open Letter" (66–71).

78 Lorde, *The Cancer Journals* 12–13. Lorde makes an almost identical remark in one of her best-known speeches, "The Master's Tools" 112.

79 I have used the spelling of Kwanza employed by Lorde and her editors in all three printed versions of the text.

80 Lorde, "The Master's Tools" 110–113. She does not mention language as a specific illustration here, but analysis of power relations in this speech and essay apply well to language. For an explicit commentary on language along these lines, see Ossie Davis, "The English Language Is My Enemy," in Arthur L. Smith, ed., *Language, Communication, and Rhetoric in Black America* (New York: Harper, 1972) 49–57.

81 Lorde, *The Cancer Journals* 12–13.

82 On this point, see Betty Schmitz, *Integrating Women's Studies into the Curriculum: A Guide and Bibliography* (Old Westbury, NY: Feminist Press, 1985) esp. 51–55.

83 Campbell, "Hearing Women's Voices" 33–49.

84 Abena P. A. Busia, "Silencing Sycorax: On African Colonial Discourse and the Unvoiced Female," *Critique* 14 (1990): 103.

85 bell hooks, "talking back," *Talking Back* (Boston, MA: South End, 1989) 6.

86 bell hooks, "'when i was a young soldier for the revolution': coming to voice," *Talking Back* 12.

87 Lorde comments, "The history of white women who are unable to hear Black women's words, or to dialogue with us, is long and discouraging." Lorde, "An Open Letter" 66. I treat this activity of listening at length in a companion essay, "Other-Wise."

88 Lorde devoted extensive time and energy to engaging the problems resulting from silencing by members of one's own communities. For example, as a black, she focused upon such activity by black men in "Sexism" 60–65; as a woman, she engaged such activities by white women in "Age, Race, Class, & Sex" 114–123; as a lesbian, she examined such silencing by heterosexual black women in *I Am Your Sister*, 3–8, as well as heterosexual white and black women in "Age, Race, Class, & Sex" 121–122.

89 Olsen, *Silences;* Adrienne Rich, *On Lies, Secrets, and Silence* (New York: Norton, 1979).

90 For another example illustrating this broader cultural pattern, see Thomas Weaver, "The Human Rights of Undocumented Workers in the United States–Mexico Border Region," in Theodore E. Downing et al., eds., *Human Rights and Anthropology* (Cambridge, MA: Cultural Survival, 1988).

91 One recent book that revalues and creatively engages in re-vision of rhetoric is Mark Lawrence McPhail's *Zen in the Art of Rhetoric: An Inquiry into Coherence* (Albany, NY: State U of New York P, 1996). His position on essentialism rejects several premises that inform Audre Lorde's rhetoric, while he imaginatively articulates philosophical alternatives to what he characterizes as binary thinking about language. In order for the analysis to be compelling, however, he would have to engage the history of essentialist language as deeply embedded in the rituals, legal codes, and formal procedures of several institutions. Essentialism looms large, for example, in the current controversy in the United States over various exclusion from marriage acts which have been strategically misnamed as "defense" of marriage acts, since inclusion would not have the effect of dissolving existing marriages or change the rights of those who may now marry.

92 Lorde outlines some salient features of this process of resistance through language in a brief

essay, "Poetry Is Not a Luxury," *Sister Outsider* 36–39. bell hooks also comments on some aspects of this process in an essay, "on self-recovery," *Talking Back* 28–34.

93 bell hooks, "Choosing the Margin as a Space of Radical Openness," *Yearnings: Race, Gender, and Cultural Politics* (Boston, MA: South End, 1990): 145–154.

94 hooks, *Talking Back* 5.

95 hooks, *Talking Back* 9.

96 hooks, *Talking Back* 18; for hooks' skepticism, see 6–7 and 12.

97 Jeanne Perreault, "Notes from the Co-Editors: Contemporary North-American Native Writing," *Ariel—A Review of International English Literature* 25 (1994): 10.

Mocking the Sacred: Frederick Douglass's "Slaveholder's Sermon" and the Antebellum Debate over Religion and Slavery

Gary S. Selby

On November 4, 1841, in an address before the Plymouth County Anti-Slavery Society gathered in Hingham, Massachusetts, to debate a resolution condemning racial prejudice, Frederick Douglass denounced society's fundamental attitude toward blacks:

> [P]eople in general . . . will say they like the colored men as well as any other, *but in their proper place.* Who is to decide what is their proper place? *They* assign us that place; they don't let us do it for ourselves, nor will they allow us a voice in the decision. They will not allow that we have a head to think, and a heart to feel, and a soul to aspire. They treat us not as men, but as dogs—they cry *"Slu-boy!"* and expect us to run and do their bidding. That's the way we are liked.[1]

His critique identified a foundational principle underlying slavery, the pervasive belief that persons of African descent were a race of people fundamentally different from and vastly inferior to whites in the scale of civilization.[2] This hierarchical perspective provided white society with a world view, in the words of Kenneth Burke, a "principle of order,"[3] in which slavery not only was justified but also "natural." Accordingly, to abolish it would have been both immoral and dangerous.

Douglass recognized that religion was a key element sustaining these beliefs. Religion, he told one northern audience, "sanctifies the system under which I suffer, and dooms me to it, and the millions of my brethren in bondage." Although other influences may have helped to sustain slavery, its "main support" was religion

(pp. 24–25). Indeed, Douglas Ambrose concludes, most Evangelical Christians in the South

> understood slavery as a familial relation between unequal members of a hierarchically structured and divinely ordained household. . . . [S]uch a relation, like all relations, carried with it duties and obligations that flowed from God. Ministers continually reminded their flocks that how well individuals fulfilled or failed to fulfill those duties and obligations would bear heavily on the fate of their immortal souls.[4]

In reaction to the rise of radical abolitionism, these beliefs were expressed in explicit arguments that the Bible sanctioned slavery.

In the earliest period of his career as an abolitionist orator, from his initial emergence in 1841 until his departure for England and Ireland in 1845, Douglass was uniquely positioned to challenge these assumptions.[5] As a fugitive slave, he occupied a subhuman place in the social hierarchy as white man's chattel. At the same time, his presence on the abolition platform as an intelligent, articulate, dignified man contested that identity, forcing audiences, in John Blassingame's words, "to confront the shocking contradiction of a fluent black man subject to the lash."[6] In this essay I explore the ways that Douglass exploited this tension to undermine religion's support for slavery, highlighting his use of parody as a crucial element in his response to proslavery religious discourse. I argue that in his speeches on religion and slavery, particularly his famous and oft-repeated "Slaveholder's Sermon," Douglass juxtaposed explicit claims to be a slave with a persona enacted through this rhetorical form.[7] Through his use of parody, he confronted audiences with a "perspective by incongruity" that forcefully undermined proslavery religion's claim to legitimacy.

★ PARODY AND SOCIAL ORDER

Kenneth Burke's writings explore the ways that people use language to impose order ("the sense of what properly goes with what") on their experience and how that impulse toward order is translated into larger social structures. Human beings, he said, are driven to "round things out, to fit experiences together into a unified whole."[8] Such "interpretive networks," Thomas Rosteck and Michael Leff observe, are "stable frames of reference which direct human perception and determine our judgment about what is proper in a given circumstance."[9] The process of "giving things meaning by assigning them to different positions within a classificatory system," Stuart Hall argues, is the basis for "that symbolic order which we call culture."[10]

Burke emphasized that hierarchy is inevitable. The "hierarchic principle . . . is embodied in the mere process of growth, which is synonymous with class divisions of youth and age, stronger and weaker, male and female, or the stages of learning, from apprentice to journeyman to master."[11] As Hall notes, the stability of cultural systems depends on "things . . . [staying] in their appointed place. Symbolic boundaries keep the categories 'pure.' . . . What unsettles culture is 'matter out of place'—the breaking of our unwritten rules and codes."[12]

Stratified social arrangements retain stability by appearing to be "natural," which, Burke said, "rhetorically reinforces the protection of privilege."[13] Hall comments:

> If the differences between black and white
> people are "cultural," then they are open
> to modification and change. But if they are
> "natural"—as the slave-holders believed—then
> they are beyond history, permanent and fixed.
> "Naturalization" is therefore a representational
> strategy designed to *fix* "difference," and thus
> *secure it forever.*[14]

Hierarchical structures become imbued with a sense of sacredness, Burke argued, describing them with such terms as piety, mystery, worship, and guilt. Rosteck and Leff note the incongruity in this usage, that the "clear connection between piety and appropriateness strains against our conventional usage of the two terms. Piety, in our normal way of thinking, describes a profound religious or moral commitment; propriety connotes the artificial conventions of a social elite."[15] Burke pointed to the ways that religious belief reinforces notions of propriety and order and hinted that violations of the social order can appear blasphemous.[16] As Martha Solomon puts it, we become blind "to other views, we develop a 'trained incapacity' and strongly resist attempts to alter our perspective. Indeed, new views seem 'impious' to us because they violate our 'sense of what properly goes with what' and produce guilt in those attracted to them."[17]

Recognizing the potentially oppressive nature of these schemata, Burke offered a strategy to challenge and transform them: perspective by incongruity, which involves "taking a word usually applied to one setting and transferring its use to another setting,"[18] a process resembling the literary figure of oxymoron.[19] Burke saw this as a deliberate "wrenching apart [of] all those molecular combinations of adjective and noun, substantive and verb, which still remain with us," subjecting language "to the same 'cracking' process that chemists now use in their refining of oil."[20] Because dominant ideologies and schemes of orientation are so deeply embedded in human thought and language, confronting them requires discourse that shocks and disturbs in a way that "pries apart existing linkages" and upsets "normal patterns of association."[21]

Parody is such a strategy. As an imitative performance, parody can appropriate identities from across categories within the social hierarchy in ways that violate the rigid distinctions between them. The effect is symbolically to collapse the categories and, in Judith Butler's words, "redeploy and destabilize" them.[22] Parody invites the very condition that Hall envisioned in his analysis of representational practices and social hierarchy: "What really disturbs cultural order is when things turn up in the wrong category."[23] Further, as Butler points out, parody can powerfully undermine the appearance of "naturalness" that surrounds ascribed identities. Identity is socially constructed through a "set of repeated acts within a highly rigid regulatory frame that congeal over time to produce the appearance of substance, of a natural sort of being." As a strategy of "subversive repetition," parody is uniquely suited to challenge that appearance:

It is a production which, in effect—that is, in its effect—postures as an imitation. This perpetual displacement constitutes a fluidity of identities that suggests an openness to resignification and recontextualization; parodic proliferation deprives hegemonic culture . . . of the claims to naturalized or essentialist . . . identities.

In other words, parody is a blatant imitation of what is culturally accepted as an original, but the act of imitation exposes as illusory the very notion that there can be an original, fixed, or "natural" identity. The laughter that parody evokes is a "subversive laughter" because "in the pastiche-effect of parodic practices, . . . the original, the authentic, and the real are themselves constituted as effects."[24]

Because it violates the sense of "what properly goes with what" and unmasks the illusory character of identity as "natural," parody has the potential to create the kind of contradictions that Burke believed could lead to new meanings. In its potential for creating dissonance, Frederick Douglass found a way to address the argument that the Bible sanctioned slavery.

★ THE ANTEBELLUM DEBATE OVER THE BIBLE AND SLAVERY

Although a number of influences conspired in the early decades of the nineteenth century to raise the peculiar institution "to an abstract model of necessary social order,"[25] none was more pervasive or deeply rooted in southern culture than religion. The clergy wielded enormous influence,[26] subjecting slaves and masters alike to a tradition of preaching dating back at least to the turn of the century that focused on "infusing relations between masters and slaves

with Christian notions of duty, obedience, and order."[27] Ambrose concludes that although

other aspects of proslavery thought, such as the critique of free labor and the pseudoscientific racial argument, were only beginning to emerge in the generation after the Revolution and would not figure prominently until the 1830s, the notion of the hierarchical, paternalistic, Christian household that characterized evangelical discussions of slavery by 1810 remained a constant feature of the southern defense of the social order there.[28]

Radical abolitionists challenged that view by claiming that slavery was a sin for which the only appropriate form of repentance was immediate and complete emancipation.[29]

In their attempts to support this cause from Scripture, however, they faced the vexing problem that in numerous passages the Bible appeared to sanction slavery. Radical abolitionists responded by appealing to what they claimed to be the transcendent principles of Christianity. Angelina Grimké, for example, grounded her "Appeal to the Christian Women of the South" in what she called the "precepts" of Jesus:

"*Whatsoever* ye would that men should do to you, do *ye even so to them*[.]" Let every slaveholder apply these queries to his own heart; Am *I* willing to be a slave—Am *I* willing to see *my* wife the slave of another—Am *I* willing to see my mother a slave, or my father, my sister or my brother? If *not,* then in holding others as slaves, I am doing what I would *not* wish to be done to me or any relative I have; and thus have I broken this golden rule which was given *me* to walk by.[30]

Opponents of slavery offered complex arguments demonstrating that the slavery allowed in the Bible was different from the "monstrous system . . . of American *slavery*," going so far as to claim that the word "slave" in English translations of the Bible was, at least in some passages, actually a mistranslation.[31]

Slavery's defenders countered by appealing to Scripture's "plain meaning." One proslavery writer, for example, ridiculed abolitionists' assertions that Abraham "never owned a slave:

that, on the contrary, he was 'a prince,' and the 'men whom he bought with his money' were 'his subjects' merely!" Abolitionists, he chided, reject "all honest arguments and pleas" in their belief that "the plain matter of record 'was all a mistake.'"[32] Turning to the New Testament, another cited passages that prescribed the various duties of slaves and masters, concluding that slavery was the

> state, condition, or relation among the members of the apostolic churches, whether among Gentiles or Jews; which the Holy Ghost, by Paul for the Gentiles and Peter for the Jews, recognizes as lawful; the mutual duties of which he prescribes in the language above.[33]

What made these proslavery biblical arguments so devastating to the abolition cause was their foundation in the common sense epistemology that dominated U.S. culture in the first half of the nineteenth century, which gave rise to the conviction that the Bible was composed of literal "facts" that could be "inductively compiled . . . [and] appealed to for any person of 'common sense' to see."[34] In their attempts to show that the Bible only appeared to sanction slavery, radical abolitionists faced "a double burden of staggering dimensions":

> On the one hand, they had to execute the delicate task of showing that straightforward, proslavery conclusions did not adequately exegete the biblical texts. On the other band, they also were compelled to perform a religious high-wire act by demonstrating why arguments against slavery should not be regarded as infidel attacks on the authority of the Bible itself.[35]

Southerners, by contrast, preached "to a people who knew their Bible well and . . . preferred to take it straight," believing that "those who call themselves Christians" should simply "accept the Bible as God's revealed truth and . . . understand that God, not man, defined sin and virtue."[36] Using the same common sense hermeneutic with which they intuited African Americans' place in the social hierarchy, white slaveholders found a clear scriptural warrant for keeping them there, a warrant against which mere counter-exegesis was woefully inadequate.[37]

In the intellectual climate in which Douglass emerged as an antislavery orator, radical abolitionists had been largely unsuccessful in their attempts to convince others that the Bible condemned slavery. Their arguments failed to win converts in both the North and the South.[38] A different response was needed.

★ DOUGLASS'S EARLY SPEECHES ON RELIGION AND RACE

In his speeches from this early period (1841–1845), Frederick Douglass debated such issues as slavery and the Union, the utility of the abolitionists' petition campaigns and other anti-slavery political action, and he frequently recounted his own experiences of the horrors of slavery. No theme, however, occupied his attention more than religion.[39] He used a variety of arguments to refute pro-slavery religious views. His earliest extant address, "I Have Come To Tell You Something About Slavery" (October, 1841), vehemently condemned religion's complicity with racial oppression. He began by affirming his ability to bring before his hearers the true horrors of slavery, alluding to "a back covered with scars . . . ; for I have felt these wounds; I have suffered under the lash without the power of resisting. Yes, my blood has sprung out as the lash embedded itself in my flesh" (p. 3). Having claimed authority to speak, Douglass immediately turned his attention to the practice of using religion to vindicate cruel treatment of slaves. Citing the reputation of his master, Thomas Auld, as "a pious man and a good Christian" and a "class leader in the Methodist church," Douglass recounted that Auld would quote biblical texts to defend his abuse: "I have seen this pious class leader cross and tie the hands of one of his young female slaves, and lash her on the bare skin and justify the deed by the quotation from the Bible, 'he who knoweth his master's will and doeth it not, shall be beaten with many stripes.'"

On a number of occasions in this early phase of his career, Douglass denounced churches in the North for their failure to condemn slavery. "Your religion," he told one New England audience, "justifies our tyrants, and you are yourselves our enslavers. I see my enslavers here in Concord, and before my eyes—if any are here who countenance the church and the religion of your country" (pp. 24–25). Particularly trenchant were his accounts of racist religious practices among northern Christians, revealing "the inconsistency of the professions of many of the Christian Churches which rail against slavery and uphold it by their practice" (p. 19). One of his common illustrations of such bigotry was a segregated Communion service he had witnessed at a Methodist Episcopal Church in New Bedford, Massachusetts. As Douglass recounted it, the minister first distributed the elements to the whites in attendance, after which he "drew a long breath and looking out toward the door, exclaimed, 'Come up, colored friends, come up! for you know *God is no respecter of persons!'*" (p. 11). He also would relate the story of a revival led by an Elder Knapp in New Bedford who, Douglass said, throwing "his net into the sea, . . . cannot expect to catch all white fish; there will be some black ones, but he culls them out after he draws the net to the shore" (p. 20). At one point during the revival, Douglass reported, a white woman, newly baptized, refused to accept the communion cup after a black woman had used it, a black woman "who entertained the same hope, and had just been baptized in the same water" (p. 20). At this same revival, he recounted on another occasion, one young woman reportedly fell into a trance and, upon waking, "declared that she had been to Heaven" (p. 11). As Douglass described the scene,

> her friends were all anxious to know what and whom she had seen there; so she told the whole story. But there was one good old lady whose curiosity went beyond that of all the others— and she inquired of the girl that had the vision, if she saw any black folks in Heaven? After some hesitation, the reply was, *Oh! I didn't go into the kitchen!*

In this way, Douglass sought to show that "the Church, *so-called,* was an obstacle to the progress of the abolition movement."

Although Douglass's personal testimony was an important element in these early speeches on religion and slavery, what gave them particular persuasive force was the incorporation of parody in the form of what came to be called his "Slaveholder's Sermon." He frequently condemned Southern "priests" who, as he put it, defended "even from their Bibles" the "system that sold my four sisters and my brother in bondage" (p. 12). In response he offered an imitative, parodic performance of pro-slavery preaching. As Blassingame points out, Douglass frequently delivered the "sermon" during his "youthful days as an abolitionist lecturer,"[40] earning it a place, Lampe notes, as "perhaps the most famous aspect of Douglass's rhetorical repertoire in his early abolitionist speeches."[41] At least two speeches that include the "Slaveholder's Sermon" are preserved from this early period of his career,[42] and they are the focus of this analysis.

Douglass delivered the first, entitled "American Prejudice and Southern Religion," at the quarterly convention of the Plymouth County Anti-Slavery Society in Hingham, Massachusetts, on the evening of November 4, 1841, before a predominantly white audience.[43] That evening's session had been called so the convention could consider a series of resolutions postponed from an earlier session, among them one condemning racism as "cruel and malignant, utterly at variance with Christianity, [and] in direct violation of the word of God." The first speaker, Edmund Quincy, urged his hearers to support the resolution, arguing that this "unnatural prejudice,—not implanted by God . . . will not cease while slavery lasts; for men always hate those whom they injure."[44] Quincy then invited Douglass to relate his personal knowledge of prejudice.

Douglass began by describing instances of ill treatment he had received at the hands of whites since coming to the North, including encounters with bigotry among northern churches. He decried the denial of educational and economic opportunity to blacks, noting with irony the way society then puzzled at their ignorance and ineffectuality: "You degrade us, and then ask why we are degraded—you shut our mouths and then ask why we don't speak—you close your colleges and seminaries against us, and then ask why we don't know more!" (p. 12).

These examples of prejudice, Douglass continued, paled in significance when compared to slavery and its defenders, the "slaveholding ministers [who] preach up the divine right of slaveholders to property in their fellow men"

(p. 12). With this, he offered his imitative performance of what the "Southern preachers say to the poor slave":

> Oh! if you wish to be happy in time, happy in eternity, you must be obedient to your masters; their interest is yours; God made one portion of men to do the working, and another to do the thinking; how good God is! How you have no trouble or anxiety; but ah! you can't imagine how perplexing it is to your masters and mistresses to have so much thinking to do in your behalf! You cannot appreciate your blessings; you know not how happy a thing it is for you that you were born of that portion of the human family which has the working instead of the thinking to do!

Douglass mimicked the southern preacher's "evidence" for this hierarchical social arrangement:

> Oh! how grateful and obedient you ought to be to your masters! How beautiful are the arrangements of Providence! Look at your hard, horny hands—see how nicely they are adapted to the labor you have to perform. Look at our delicate fingers, so exactly fitted for our station, and see how manifest it is that God designed us to be the thinkers, and you to be the workers.

The sermon concluded with this mock-rapturous exultation: "Oh! the wisdom of God!"

The most complete surviving account of the "Slaveholder's Sermon" is in an address delivered on January 28, 1842, at the conclusion of a public meeting sponsored by the Massachusetts Anti-Slavery Society. Held in Boston's Faneuil Hall, the event drew an enthusiastic audience of 4000 people, many of them Irish-Americans who strongly supported the abolition cause and who, Blassingame notes, particularly appreciated Douglass's parody of proslavery preaching.[45]

Douglass began by dramatically calling attention to his own status as a fugitive slave. He was interrupted by his audience and quickly fell into a "call and response" dialogue with his hearers:

> I rejoice to be permitted, as well as to be able to speak upon this subject in Faneuil Hall. I will not detain you long, for I stand here as a slave. (No! no! *from the meeting*.) A slave at least in the eye of the Constitution. (No! no! with *emphasis from the meeting*.) It is a slave by the laws of the South, who now addresses you. (That's it! *from the meeting*) (p. 16).

He could, he continued, show them his "back . . . scarred by the lash"; moreover, he could "make visible the wounds of this system upon my soul." Instead, he wished merely to convey on behalf of the slaves his gratitude to the abolition movement, "representing as I do, the two and a half millions remaining in that bondage from which I have escaped." He spoke for them, he said, because they

> are entirely deprived of the privilege of speaking for themselves. They are goods and chattels, not men. They are denied the privileges of the Christian—they are denied the rights of citizens. They are refused the claims of the man. They are not allowed the rights of the husband and the father. They may not name the name of Liberty.

By working to save them from this oppression, he said, the abolitionists would earn God's reward, and their consciences would testify that they had faithfully fulfilled "the demands of the religion of Christ. (Applause.)"

Having mentioned the "demands of the religion of Christ," Douglass turned his attention to what he called the "*mockery* of His religion . . . preached at the South" (p. 16). He told of how southern ministers (trained in the North, he wryly noted), would take a text such as, "Do unto others as you would have others do unto you," and apply it to the slaveholders: "They would explain it to mean, 'slaveholders, do unto *slaveholders* what you would have them do unto you'" (p. 17). Then, to shouts of laughter and applause, Douglass mimicked the voice and gestures of the preacher, who would turn his eyes toward his hearers in the slave gallery and say,

> And you too, my friends, have souls of infinite value—souls that will live through endless happiness or misery in eternity. Oh, *labor diligently* to make your calling and election sure. Oh, receive into your souls these words

of the holy apostle—"Servants, be obedient to your masters."

He mocked the preachers' assertion that God had designed slaves for their station:

Oh, consider the wonderful goodness of God! Look at your hard, horny hands, your strong muscular frames, and see how mercifully he has adapted you to the duties you are to fulfil [sic]! (continued laughter and applause) while to your masters, who have slender frames and long delicate fingers, he has given brilliant intellects, that they may do the *thinking*, while you do the *working*. (Shouts of applause.)

He concluded by dramatically shifting his tone from derisive humor to grave seriousness, noting that it was often said in the North that "slaves have the gospel preached to them." This was the "gospel" slaves received, "a gospel which, more than chains, or whips, or thumb-screws, gives perpetuity to this horrible system."

These examples demonstrate that in his speeches on religion and race, as in his other early addresses, Douglass showed a remarkable facility with various stylistic and argumentative techniques, whether poignantly narrating personal experiences in slavery, deftly using metaphor to move from the scars on his back to what he called "the wounds of this system" upon his soul, or arguing logically that blacks occupied the place in society they did because they were denied economic and educational opportunities offered to whites.[46] Unlike his other early speeches, however, they indicate that when it came to challenging the church's complicity with racial oppression, his characteristic strategy was to parody its racist discourse. Indeed, eyewitnesses often explicitly noted Douglass's use of imitation, as in this quotation from one performance of his "Slaveholder's Sermon": "Looking impudently up to the slaves' gallery, . . . and spreading his hands gracefully abroad, he [the preacher] says, (*mimicking*,) 'And you too, my friends, have souls of infinite value . . .'" [emphasis added] (p. 17). Similarly, an account of his "Slaveholder's Sermon" delivered in Cork, Ireland, at the beginning of his European tour (October 14, 1845) noted the following in reference to Douglass's imitation of a proslavery preacher: "Here the Speaker

[Douglass] assumed the attitude and drawling manner so characteristic of the American preachers, amid the laughter of all present, and continued—Thus do these hypocrites cant" (p. 43). Abolitionist James Monroe, who had heard Douglass give his "Slaveholder's Sermon" on several occasions, described it as

a brilliant example of irony, parody, caricature, and *reductio ad absurdum,* all combined. It abounded in phrases which, though innocent in the original preacher, when delivered by Mr. Douglass with suggestive tone and emphasis to a Northern audience, became irresistibly ludicrous. . . . To do him justice . . . you must imagine his marvelous power of imitation and characterization—the holy tone of the preacher—the pious snuffle—the upturned eye—the funny affectation of profound wisdom . . . and the tearful sympathy with which the speaker dwelt upon the helpless condition of his hearers in case they should cease to be the property of slaveholding masters."[47]

Parody was a central element of Douglass's attacks on proslavery religion as well as one of the features of his oratory that most impressed his hearers. When his use of parody is viewed in light of the debate over the Bible and slavery, however, it becomes clear that it was far more than mere entertainment for abolitionists. Rather, it represented a creative response to what, before Douglass's emergence, had been the proslavery cause's virtually unassailable case, that the Bible sanctioned slavery.

★ REFUTING THE BIBLICAL ARGUMENT

Frederick Douglass's attacks on proslavery religion may be viewed from several perspectives. At the most basic level, they poignantly expressed his visceral outrage that Christianity, which should have been a force propelling society toward justice, had become the tool of his oppression. The connections he frequently made between slaveholders' extreme acts of cruelty and their professions of religious devotion, moreover, reinforced abolitionist claims about the brutality of slavery, supporting the movement's larger agenda. His use of ridicule, particularly his mimicry of proslavery preaching, may also be viewed against the backdrop of both traditional African American discourse and the rhetorical theory to which he was exposed in the *Columbian Orator*.[48] On the one hand, his parodies are examples of "signifying," which Bacon describes as a "uniquely African-American rhetorical form" through which the oppressed, exploiting "the ambiguity and indeterminacy of language, . . . gain power by appropriating the discourse of the oppressor."[49] At the same time, his mockery of proslavery religious discourse accorded with the *Columbian Orator*'s instruction on how to refute an opponent's claims when they were deemed "trifling and unworthy of serious answer." In that case, it advises that

> a facetious manner, both of expression and gesture, may be the most proper way to confute them. For, to attempt to answer, in a grave and serious manner, what is in itself empty and ludicrous, is apt to create a suspicion of having more in it than it really has.[50]

Douglass's parodies were a deft interweaving of traditional African American rhetorical forms with the European tradition of persuasion.

Further, his use of parody was a means to enlist the support of those in his audience already sympathetic to the antislavery cause by creating what Morris describes as a "conspiracy among author and auditors," made possible by parody's capacity to position the audience as "an 'elite group' . . . that gains its air of superiority from the notion that it shares a special wisdom and intelligence with the author."[51] Similarly, Douglass's parodies invited his hearers to conspire with him in unmasking the hypocrisy of proslavery religion, symbolically bringing those sympathetic to the abolition cause into an alliance with him as insiders enlightened about the nature of this false religion. Participating in Douglass's parodies through their laughter and applause had the potential to shift audiences closer to the radical abolitionist position.

Douglass's parodies reveal his genius as a rhetor and are most significant as a response to religion's legitimization of racial oppression. What Kenneth Burke suggested about the role of religious sensibility in sustaining notions of order and propriety, Douglass pointed to as a

blatant fact: religion was the agency that kept the system in place. Douglass's focus on religion shows an acute understanding of the forces conspiring to maintain the nation's oppressive social hierarchy. His parodies of religious discourse violated society's notions of "what properly goes with what."[52] Two features of his anti-religious rhetoric, his claim to be a slave and his use of parody to enact a persona of superiority in relation to his oppressors, created a tension that forcefully challenged that social order.

Although all of his early speeches assume a background in slavery, Douglass's speeches confronting religion deliberately emphasized that status. Even in his earliest extant address, one in which his overall rhetorical strategy is still ill-defined at best, he was careful to refer to his position in slavery as if it were a present fact. Although he began by describing his experiences as events in the past ("When I *came* to the North . . ."), he spoke in the present tense when recounting his master's religious hypocrisy: "My master *has* the reputation of being a pious man and a good Christian." (p. 3). This identification with slavery became more explicit in his later speeches confronting religion, which he typically began by calling attention to his status as a fugitive slave. He began one such speech dramatically with this declaration: "I appear before the immense assembly this evening as a thief and a robber. I stole this head, these limbs, this body from my master, and ran off with them."[53] "I will not detain you long," he began a different address, "for I stand here as a slave" (p. 16). On another occasion, he accentuated his identity as a slave so strongly that a reporter, offering only the briefest mention of Douglass's speech "endeavoring to prove . . . that the Christian Church, 'so called,' is the bulwark of slavery," recalled being "informed that he was a fugitive from slavery" (p. 18).[54] In this way, Douglass began his speeches on religion by ostensibly claiming his "place" in the nation's social hierarchy, a status that traditionally called for a demeanor of deference and respect toward one's "superiors."

Douglass's use of parody strongly challenged that identity, which is underscored by consideration of the rhetorical choices he might have made. Even in the earliest months of his career as an abolitionist orator, Douglass possessed an array of inventional resources.[55] He knew, for example, how to arouse the pity of his hearers with compelling narratives of slave life. He also was able to offer rational arguments in support of particular courses of action in the abolition movement as well as for emancipation in general. Had he simply narrated the cruel wrongs he had endured, however, he would have retained his inferior position in the social hierarchy. His discourse would have enacted the persona of a helpless victim appealing for compassion from those with power over him, an appeal "from below." Had Douglass offered rational arguments refuting the religious claims in support of slavery, he would have accorded them a kind of legitimacy. To do so would have granted his oppressors status as persons engaged in decorous deliberation. Instead, Douglass chose as his principal tactic for dealing with religion the parody, a rhetorical form that symbolically reversed the social hierarchy, placing him in a position of superiority in relation to those who used religion to support slavery. Such arguments and those who made them, his discourse implied, were "beneath" a "serious" response.

In a broad sense, this juxtaposition of identities enabled Douglass to draw his hearers into a dissonance that disturbed their sense of the "natural" social order. By stressing his identity as a slave, Douglass invoked a set of pervasive cultural assumptions about slaves, that they were ignorant and childlike, incapable of learning, dependent on their white masters, and suited only for servitude. Douglass enacted a persona starkly incongruous with those assumptions.[56] To use Hall's language, Douglass turned up "in the wrong category" as one possessed of the insight and power to expose the sophistry of clergy who justified slavery with religious arguments. His discourse violated the representational practices that perpetuated the social construction of slave identity.

His use of imitative rhetoric, set against his claimed status as a slave, also brought a unique voice to the controversy over the Bible and slavery. Unlike those on both sides of the debate who made their cases by constructing serious, systematic, and painstakingly detailed expositions of the Scriptures, in these early speeches Douglass offered little in the way of counter-exegesis. Instead, he simply held proslavery religious discourse up to ridicule. In some cases he would merely enumerate, in a sarcastic and disdainful tone, instances in which people used religion to justify their oppressive treatment of blacks, as when he recounted how his master savagely beat a slave while quoting the words of Jesus. That tone, Blassingame points out, was not lost on his hearers, one of whom, the editor of the Hingham *Patriot,* was particularly struck by his "'forcible' and 'very sarcastic' oratory."[57] More often, Douglass mimicked proslavery preaching, as if the most forceful refutation of such discourse would be for white Christians to hear it from the lips of the slave himself, a tactic with the potential to alter dramatically the debate over the Bible and slavery in at least two ways.

First, parodies challenged the authority of ministers who propounded the proslavery argument. As Douglass portrayed him, for example, the southern preacher who applied the Golden Rule exclusively to slaveholders' dealings with each other obtusely overlooked what was obvious to Douglass's hearers, that he had misconstrued a text clearly intended for universal application. Similarly, Douglass's northern preacher failed to see the glaring inconsistency between his claim that "God is no respecter of persons" and his racially segregated administration of the sacraments, a failure that invited derisive laughter from many in Douglass's audience. The effect was heightened by his habit of imitating their vocal tones and mannerisms in a way that reinforced his caricature, which led one reporter to observe that, when the specific target of Douglass's attack was in his audience, "the tone and manner in which Douglass pronounced this quotation, imitating, apparently, the voice and manner of the Methodist minister, must have cut like a two-edged sword."[58]

Even more important, his rhetoric lent an air of absurdity to the entire debate over the Bible and slavery by creating the "comic incongruity" on which parody as a rhetorical form rests.[59] The *Columbian Orator* had pointed out that answering an opponent's arguments in a "facetious" manner could make them appear "empty and ludicrous."[60] In his parodies of racist discourse generally and particularly in his "Slaveholder's

Sermon," Douglass exploited that potential with extraordinary sophistication and force because by mocking the very arguments used to enslave him, Douglass demonstrated that he had "mastered" his opponents' line of reasoning. Ironically, however, that he, a slave, could demonstrate such mastery over the arguments "proving" the naturalness and divine origin of his supposed ignorance and incapacity was itself a logical contradiction, which seriously undermined their cogency. Indeed, the very idea that white exegetes—even those opposed to slavery—should debate the meaning of biblical texts in order to determine whether one such as Douglass could legitimately be enslaved became ridiculous in the face of the superior intellectual and moral position he occupied by virtue of his rhetoric. Given the milieu in which he spoke, one in which most parties to the debate operated out of a hermeneutic centered in a literal view of Scripture and typically produced complex, technical arguments, the importance of Douglass's contribution cannot be overstated. He did not offer biblical argument; instead, he offered a perspective that transcended the details of biblical exegesis, a perspective driven by the incongruity between his social status and his rhetorical persona. From this new perspective, any approach to the Bible that could justify the enslavement of an individual like Douglass was patently misguided, regardless of any particular biblical text. Whatever the Bible meant when it spoke of slavery, surely it could not have meant that.

Frederick Douglass was able to do what white abolitionists, with their carefully constructed exegetical arguments, had been unable to do—offer a compelling refutation of what was one of the most damaging obstacles to their cause. By mocking the sacred, he challenged white society's view of African Americans even as he undermined the hermeneutic with which it used the Bible to support that view. He did so in a way that exploited his culture's prevailing epistemology in order to deconstruct its own sense of social order. In a cultural milieu that privileged observable facts, Douglass invited his hearers to trust their senses, but in doing so, they risked confronting a disturbing contradiction between experience and belief. They could not experience Douglass's persona while

assigning to African Americans a position of sub-humanity in the social hierarchy, nor could they continue to use Scripture to support a position that common sense said was absurd.

CONCLUSION

Most of the correspondents who preserved Douglass's early speeches also recorded the reactions of those who heard him,[61] reactions that provide insight into the dynamic by which parody could create incongruity. In general, of course, audiences universally were amazed to encounter a slave possessed of eloquence, a response captured in an account of one speech originally published in the Boston *Courier*:

> We have seldom heard a better speech before a popular assembly—better, we mean, as to the language and the manner. Many of the speakers who followed him, and of a lighter complexion, men who boasted that they were ministers, and who had, doubtless, the advantage of education, which the man of color could never have enjoyed, might well be desirous of emulating the appropriateness of his elocution and gesticulation, and the grammatical accuracy of his sentences.[62]

Another hearer commented that in no way did Douglass "manifest any of that deficiency of mental power, which is said, by many, to be characteristic of the African race." Considering that Douglass was a fugitive slave "less than four years from the lands of whips and thumb-screws," his eloquence brought reactions of "absolute astonishment."[63]

For some, the effect of the encounter was dramatic and overwhelmingly positive. An eye-witness to one of Douglass's speeches on religion, writing in the Salem *Observer*, described the impact this way:

> The most wonderful performance of the evening was the address of Frederick Douglass, himself a slave only four years ago! His remarks and his manner created the most indescribable sensation in the minds of those unaccustomed to hear *freemen* of his color speak in public, much more to regard a *slave* as capable of such an effort. He was a living, speaking, *startling* proof of the folly,

absurdity and inconsistency . . . of slavery. Fluent, graceful, eloquent, shrewd, sarcastic, he was without making any allowances, a fine specimen of an orator.[64]

Another hearer, a non-abolitionist who was admittedly a "bundle of prejudices" before hearing Douglass, wrote of attending one of his addresses on religion and slavery for "amusement and recreation," and of finding in Douglass a person "chaste in language, brilliant in thought, and truly eloquent in delivery. His mind seemed to overflow with noble ideas, and they always came forth in suitable garb. He is a remarkable man." This hearer left the hall that day "with a mountainload of prejudice tumbling from his back."[65]

Among many others, however, his speeches, in particular his parodies of religious discourse, appear to have provoked violently negative reactions. Elevina Smith, an abolitionist who heard his "American Prejudice and Southern Religion" address with its rendition of the "Slaveholder's Sermon," although personally impressed with his "great talent," noted that many were "very mad" at Douglass's "impudence."[66] In response to another speech demonstrating "the brutal reality of the connection between the American church and the slave plantations of the South," said one correspondent, members of the audience "gnashed their teeth and howled."[67] Another eyewitness reported on a different occasion that Douglass's address on religion and slavery elicited "hissings" from audience members who found his ideas "insufferable, coming from a 'nigger.'"[68] So great was the outrage he provoked that, on the next day, abolitionists found their rented hall closed to them because the owner refused to "allow his property to be used for the dissemination of such principles as were advanced by DOUGLASS, in a lecture there the night before."[69] At another meeting, Douglass and his fellow abolitionists were "constantly interrupted, in an indecent, profane and mobocratic manner, by a considerable number of rowdies, who piously came to rescue the clergy and the church." The mob swore that they would not "stand such damned nonsense" and such "'rascally charges' to be brought against the divine order."[70]

These extreme reactions, particularly anger and outrage, demonstrate parody's potential to create the kind of "wrenching" process that Burke described in his explanation of perspective by incongruity.[71] They suggest that Douglass successfully forced his audiences to confront the contradiction between his persona and the pervasive cultural assumptions that assigned blacks to subservience in the social hierarchy, evoking what psychologist Leon Festinger, in his classic work on cognitive dissonance, described as the "psychological discomfort" that results when people face information or events that contradict previously held views.[72] In the case of Douglass's hearers, they could not continue to maintain the traditional construction of biblical doctrine in the presence of this one whose persona so forcefully challenged it.

As Festinger also noted, "the difficulty of changing . . . may be too great, or the change, while eliminating some dissonances, may create a whole host of new ones."[73] Because the implications of altering one's orientation may be too costly, people often seek to reduce the tension by eliminating or otherwise counteracting the offending cognition. In the case of Douglass's attacks on religion and slavery, this took the form of outrage and even physical violence. Beyond merely offering a positive, alternative representation of the black slave, Douglass's parodies of white religion violated the boundaries of the social hierarchy, forcefully appropriated revered cultural identities, and undermined the religious authority that legitimized the entire system. In so doing, he destabilized notions of the "naturalness" of slave identity so profoundly that many of his hearers found his discourse blasphemous and his presence threatening. Unable to escape the alarming dissonance that resulted from hearing such language on the lips of a slave, they sought resolution by removing the offense to their familiar orientation, by discrediting Douglass.[74]

For those willing to have their views challenged, Douglass's early addresses on religion and slavery became a compelling force for change. Resolving the incongruity between their cultural assumptions and Douglass's persona demanded that they see African Americans in a radically new way, not as their property, but as fellow human beings. Theirs was a response that one of Douglass's contemporaries, Milo Townsend, poignantly summarized: "The truth flashed its light upon the minds of many . . . and they went away believing."[75]

NOTES

[1] Frederick Douglass, *Frederick Douglass Papers, Series One: Speeches, Debates and interviews*, vol. 1 (1841–46), ed. John W. Blassingame (New Haven: Yale Univ. Press, 1979), 12. Subsequent citations from this collection will be indicated in parentheses in the text.

[2] An example of this hierarchical view is Thomas Roderick Dew, *Review of the Debate in the Virginia Legislature of 1831 and 1832*, (1832; reprint Westport: Negro Universities Press, 1970), 2, 105. For an extensive historical treatment, see Winthrop D. Jordan, *White over Black; American Attitudes toward the Negro, 1550–1812* (Baltimore: Penguin Books, 1969). Douglass's awareness of social hierarchy forms the backdrop to his rhetoric from the beginning of his career as an abolitionist orator. It lay behind his complaint that the slaveowners "ride about in their carriages . . . with the finest of cloth on their backs, with rings upon their fingers, and in enjoyment of every luxury that wealth can buy," all paid for through the labor of "the poor slaves" (p. 7). His outrage at being dragged from railroad passenger cars, "where the *dogs* of his fellow passengers were suffered to remain" (pp. 9–10), was fueled by his sense of the place in the social order to which he had been assigned—beneath white men's dogs. In contrast, he praised those in the abolition movement who chose to treat him "like a man and a brother" (p. 14). He claimed the abolition movement as the place where "the slave sees an exposition of his true position in the scale of being. He finds that he is, indeed, a man" (p. 22).

[3] Kenneth Burke, *A Rhetoric of Motives* (Berkeley: Univ. of California Press, 1969), 307.

[4] Douglas Ambrose, "Of Stations and Relations: Proslavery Christianity in Early National Virginia," in *Religion and the Antebellum Debate over Slavery*, ed. John R. McKivigan and Mitchell Snay (Athens: Univ. of Georgia Press, 1998), 40.

[5] Douglass was able to claim his status as a fugitive slave only early in his career because supporters purchased his freedom shortly before he returned from England in 1847. An excellent rhetorical history of this period is Gregory P. Lampe, *Frederick Douglass: Freedom's Voice, 1818–1845* (East Lansing, MI: Michigan State

Univ. Press, 1998). Other rhetorical studies include Neil Leroux, "Frederick Douglass and the Attention Shift," *Rhetoric Society Quarterly* 21 (1991): 36–46; Gregory Stephen, "Frederick Douglass' Multiracial Abolitionism: 'Antagonistic Cooperation' and 'Redeemable Ideals' in the July 5 Speech," *Communication Studies* 48 (1997): 175–91; David B. Chesebrough, *Frederick Douglass: Oratory from Slavery* (Westport: Greenwood Press, 1998); Jacqueline Bacon, "Taking Liberty, Taking Literacy: Signifying in the Rhetoric of African-American Abolitionists," *Southern Communication Journal* 64 (1999): 271–87; and Gary S. Selby, "The Limits of Accommodation: Frederick Douglass and the Garrisonian Abolitionists," *Southern Communication Journal* 66 (2000): 52–66.

[6] John W. Blassingame, introduction to *Frederick Douglass Papers, Series One: Speeches, Debates and Interviews*, vol. 1 (1841–46), ed. Blassingame (New Haven: Yale Univ. Press, 1979), 1. A number of scholars have noted that Douglass frequently attempted to reveal the incongruities inherent in the nation's treatment of African Americans. See, for example, Philip S. Foner, *Frederick Douglass* (New York: Citadel Press, 1969), 50–51; Henry L. Gates, "Binary Oppositions in Chapter One of Douglass' Narrative," in *Critical Essays on Frederick Douglass*, ed. William L. Andrews (Boston: G. K. Hall, 1991), 79–93; and Lampe, 80.

[7] Although most scholars recognize the presence of parody in Douglass's antislavery rhetoric, his strategic use of it is largely unexplored. See, for example, Blassingame, xxxi; Chesebrough, 92–93; Foner, 50–51; and Lampe, 80–81.

[8] Kenneth Burke, *Permanence and Change: An Anatomy of Purpose*, 3rd ed. (Berkeley: University of California Press, 1984), 74–75.

[9] Thomas Rosteck and Michael Leff, "Piety, Propriety, and Perspective: An Interpretation and Application of Key Terms in Kenneth Burke's *Permanence and Change*," *Western Journal of Speech Communication* 33 (1989): 329.

[10] Stuart Hall, "The Spectacle of the 'Other,'" in *Representation: Cultural Representations and Signifying Practices*, ed. Hall (London: Sage, 1997), 236.

[11] Burke, *Rhetoric of Motives*, 141.

[12] Hall, 236.

[13] Burke, *Rhetoric of Motives*, 141.

[14] Hall, 244.

[15] Rosteck and Leff, 327.

[16] Burke echoes what Mary Douglas discovered in her anthropological study of taboos and social order, that religious or ritual notions of purity "have as their main function to impose system on an inherently

untidy experience." Mary Douglas, *Purity and Danger: An Analysis of Concepts of Pollution and Taboo* (London: Routledge and Kegan Paul, 1966), 15.

17 Martha Solomon, "Ideology as Rhetorical Constraint: The Anarchist Agitation of 'Red Emma' Goldman," *Quarterly Journal of Speech* 74 (1988): 186–87.

18 Burke, *Permanence and Change*, 90.

19 Solomon, 187.

20 Burke, *Permanence and Change*, 90, 119.

21 Rosteck and Leff, 330.

22 Judith Butler, *Gender Trouble: Feminism and the Subversion of Identity* (New York: Routledge, 1990), 122.

23 Hall, 236.

24 Butler, 33, 147, 139, 146.

25 Elizabeth Fox-Genovese and Eugene Genovese, "The Divine Sanction of Social Order: Religious Foundations of the Southern Slaveholders' World View," *Journal of the American Academy of Religion* 55 (1989): 211. One factor was the South's "deepening economic stake in slavery and its pursuit of social cohesion in the face of threatening slave revolts." See Richard J. Carwardine, *Evangelicals and Politics in Antebellum America* (New Haven: Yale University Press, 1993), 154. Another was the rise of free market capitalism in the North, which led southerners, as Fox-Genovese and Genovese argue, to defend slavery as "the best possible bulwark against the corrosive and un-Christian impact of industrial capitalism and its cruel and morally irresponsible market in human labor-power" (pp. 211–13). They note that "the slaveholders never tired of saying that they treated their slaves better than the capitalists treated free workers—that their slaves had better and immeasurably more secure living conditions than most of the world's proletarians and peasants" (pp. 224–25). A third was the emergence of a scientific discourse that, in the view of many, empirically rationalized the "ideology that a person's potential is determined by his or her race." See Kirt H. Wilson, "Towards a Discursive Theory of Racial Identity: *The Souls of Black Folk* as a Response to Nineteenth-Century Biological Determinism," *Western Journal of Communication* 63 (1999): 193. For other discussions of the scientific argument, see George M. Frederickson, *The Black Image in the White Mind: The Debate on Afro-American Character and Destiny, 1817–1914* (New York: Harper and Row, 1971), 71–96; and William Stanton, *The Leopard's Spots: Scientific Attitudes Toward Race in America, 1815–59* (Chicago: University of Chicago Press, 1960). Two accounts of attempts by African Americans to counter these prevailing beliefs are Stephen H. Browne,

"Counter-Science: African American Historians and The Critique of Ethnology in Nineteenth-Century America," *Western Journal of Communication* 64 (2000): 268–284, and Wilson.

26 Larry E. Tise, *Proslavery: A History of the Defense of Slavery in America, 1701–1840* (Athens: University of Georgia Press, 1987), 127.

27 Ambrose, 36.

28 Ambrose, 54. See his analysis of a sermon by a prominent turn of the century Anglican preacher, Devereux Jarrett, entitled "Cure and Conversion of Naaman," which contains language remarkably similar to that parodied in Douglass's "Slaveholder's Sermon."

29 For a discussion of the roots of radical abolitionism in the rise of the Protestant evangelism, see Gilbert H. Barnes, *The Antislavery Impulse, 1830–1844* (New York: Harcourt and World, 1963), and Carwardine. For an overview of the debate on whether the Bible supported slavery, see Susan Zaeske, "Angelina Grimké's 'Appeal to the Christian Women of the South': Characterizing the Female Citizen in Jacksonian America," forthcoming in *Constructing the Citizen in Jacksonian America* (East Lansing, MI: Michigan State University Press).

30 Angelina Grimké, "Appeal to the Christian Women of the South," in *The Public Years of Sarah and Angelina Grimké: Selected Writings, 1835–1839*, ed. Larry Ceplair (New York: Columbia Univ. Press, 1989), 50.

31 Grimké, 51–52. For an overview of Grimké's argument, see Zaeske. Other examples of antislavery exegesis include LaRoy Sunderland, *The Testimony of God against Slavery: A Collection of Passages from the Bible, Which show the sin of Holding and Treating the Human Species as Property*, 2nd ed. (Boston: Isaac Knapp, 1835); Theodore Weld, *The Bible Against Slavery* (New York: American Anti-Slavery Society, 1837); and Albert Barnes, *Inquiry into the Scriptural Views of Slavery* (Philadelphia: Perkins & Purves, 1846).

32 David Christy, "Liberty or Slavery; or, Slavery in the Light of Moral and Political Philosophy," in *Cotton is King, and Pro-Slavery Arguments*, ed. E. N. Elliott (Augusta: Pritchard, Abbott and Loomis, 1860), 339.

33 T. Stringfellow, "Slavery in the light of Social Ethics," in *Cotton is King, and Pro-Slavery Arguments*, ed. E. N. Elliott (Augusta: Pritchard, Abbott and Loomis, 1860), 484.

34 Michael W. Casey, "From British Ciceronianism to American Baconianism: Alexander Campbell as a Case Study of a Shift in Rhetorical Theory," *Southern Communication Journal* 66 (2001): 153. In the early decades of the nineteenth century,

common sense realism "exerted a master influence upon American thought. From the mid-1820's, its preeminence was challenged increasingly by various and mushrooming forms of romantic idealism, but it remained the single most powerful current in general intellectual and academic circles until after the Civil War." Theodore Dwight Bozeman, *Protestants in an Age of Science: The Baconian Ideal and Antebellum Religious Thought* (Chapel Hill: Univ. of North Carolina Press, 1977), 21.

35 Mark A. Noll, "The Bible and Slavery," in *Religion and the Civil War,* ed. Randall M. Miller, Harry S. Stout, and Charles Reagan Wilson (New York: Oxford Univ. Press, 1998), 44.

36 Fox-Genovese and Genovese, 223. Ironically, the same evangelical fervor that gave rise to radical abolitionism in the North led southern Christians to see in the Bible "the natural grounding for the moral obedience of slavery."

37 As Noll points out, the perversity of the proslavery biblical argument was that it failed to distinguish between the Bible's treatment of slavery and its treatment of race: "The precise problem was the indiscriminate mingling of truths delivered by plain, universal, intuitive common sense. Exegetes merged their conclusions from the Bible (derived through intuitive literalism) with their conclusions from common sense intuitions that blacks were an inferior people fit by nature for what Philip Schaff called 'the wholesome discipline of slavery'" (p. 61).

38 Based on his study of published sermons from northern and southern churches, Noll concludes that by the time the war began, "proslavery advocates had largely succeeded in winning the Bible" (p. 45). McKivigan and Snay similarly note that even "a striking number of prominent northern divines— including Nathan Lord, president of Dartmouth College, Moses Stuart, a professor at Andover Seminary, and John Henry Hopkins, Episcopal bishop of Vermont—joined southerners in finding slavery sanctioned by biblical teaching." John R. McKivigan and Mitchell Snay, "Introduction: Religion and the Problem of Slavery in Antebellum America," in *Religion and the Antebellum Debate over Slavery,* ed. McKivigan and Snay (Athens: Univ. of Georgia Press, 1998), 8. See also Fox-Genovese and Genovese, 23.

39 Blassingame includes at least partial texts of nine speeches in his edition of Douglass's speeches from this period. Of those, five deal extensively with religion and slavery.

40 Blassingame, 17, n. 1.

41 Lampe, 19.

42 One of the recorded speeches from early in his European tour entitled "I Am Here to Spread Light on American Slavery" (October 14, 1845) contains a version of the "Slaveholder's Sermon" (Douglass, 43). Remarkably, Douglass also includes a parody of the "ignorant slave's" response to the sermon that is not found in any of his other early speeches on religion and slavery: "Me hear a good sermon to day, de Minister make ebery thing so clear, white man above a Nigger any day."

43 Blassingame states that the audience also included some "New England freeman" and at least "one southern gentleman" (p. 9).

44 Blassingame, 9.

45 Blassingame, 16.

46 For an analysis of other argumentative strategies in these early speeches, see Selby.

47 Quoted in Lampe, 81.

48 Caleb Bingham, *The Columbian Orator: Containing a Variety of Original and Selected Pieces; Together with Rules, Calculated to Improve You and Others in the Ornamental and Useful Art of Eloquence* (Boston: Caleb Bingham and Company, 1817), 26. The pivotal role of this treatise in Douglass's rhetorical development is discussed in Lampe, 9–13.

49 Bacon, 271. See also Henry Louis Gates, Jr., *The Signifying Monkey: A Theory of Afro-American Literary Criticism* (New York: Oxford University Press, 1988), and Hall, 244–46.

50 Bingham, 26.

51 Barry Alan Morris, "The Communal Constraints of Parody: The Symbolic Death of Joe Bob Briggs," *Quarterly Journal of Speech* 73 (1987): 46.5.

52 Burke, *Permanence and Change,* 74.

53 Quoted in Lampe, 103–104.

54 See also the account of his "Southern Slavery and Northern Religion" (p. 24).

55 As Lampe demonstrates, Douglass was remarkably well prepared to begin a career as an abolitionist orator by the time he was "discovered" by Garrison (pp. 1–56).

56 As a number of scholars have observed, enactment can be a compelling form of evidence through which, as Campbell and Jamieson argue, a rhetor "incarnates the truth, *is* the proof of what is said." The power of enactment inheres in the congruity between the enacted persona and the claims about identity being advanced. The speaker embodies irrefutable evidence in support of those claims. Remarkably, for Douglass the opposite was the case. The force of his discourse hinged on the incongruity between the identity he claimed, with the associations it evoked, and the actual persona he enacted, which was incontrovertible refutation of the identity given him by society. Karlyn Kohrs Campbell and Kathleen Hall Jamieson, "Form and

Genre in Rhetorical Action: An Introduction," in *Form and Genre: Shaping Rhetorical Action*, ed. Campbell and Jamieson (Falls Church: Speech Communication Association, 1978), 5.

57 Quoted in Blassingame, 6.

58 Blassingame, 20–21.

59 Margaret A. Rose, *Parody: Ancient, Modern, and Post-Modern* (Cambridge: Cambridge Univ. Press, 1993), 33.

60 Bingham, 26.

61 I am indebted to Lampe's painstaking historical reconstruction of Douglass's early oratorical career.

62 "Anti-Slavery," *Liberator,* 3 June 1842, 86.

63 "Frederick Douglass," *Liberator,* 17 June 1842, 94.

64 "Latimer Meeting," *Liberator,* 9 December 1842, 194.

65 *Liberator,* 8 July 1842, 106.

66 Personal correspondence quoted in Lampe, 82.

67 Milo A. Townsend, "Frederick Douglass— The Clergy and the Church," *Liberator,* 8 December 1843, 94.

68 "Letter from Dr. Hudson," *Liberator,* 8 July 1843, 2.

69 H. Gay, "Disgraceful State of Things in Hartford," *Liberator,* 26 May 1843, 82.

70 "Convention at Dedham," *Liberator,* 22 March 1844, 43.

71 Burke, *Permanence and Change,* 19.

72 Leon Festinger, *A Theory of Cognitive Dissonance* (Stanford: Stanford Univ. Press, 1957), 2.

73 Festinger, 19.

74 This also explains attempts to discredit Douglass by circulating rumors that he had never been a slave. J. M. McKim, reporting in William Lloyd Garrison's *Liberator* about a speech on religion and slavery that Douglass gave in Philadelphia in August 1844, noted that "many persons in the audience seemed unable to credit the statements which he gave of himself, and could not believe that he was actually a slave. How a man, only six years out of bondage, and who had never gone to school a day in his life, could speak with such eloquence—with such precision of language and power of thought— they were utterly at a loss to devise." (J. M. McKim, "Frederick Douglass in Philadelphia," *Liberator,* 31 August 1844, 138.) In his second autobiographical work, *My Bondage and My Freedom,* Douglass reports hearing people challenge his claims to be a slave because he "did not talk like a slave, look like a slave, nor act like a slave." People said of him, "he is educated, and is, in this, a contradiction of all the facts we have concerning the ignorance of the slaves." Frederick Douglass, *My Bondage and My Freedom* (1855; reprint, New York: Arno, 1968), 362.

75 Townsend, 194.

Looking Toward the Future: Additional Readings

Whether we are looking at presidential studies, campaign management strategies, the role of the mass media, communication in the legislative and judicial branches, or the voices from the margins that have only begun to be heard, we can clearly see that political communication scholars have developed a substantial body of work, with much more work to be done in the future. We believe that a few important areas of study will dominate the field in the near future.

As noted earlier in this volume, most early political communication research focused on the presidency. Soon, however, elections drew just as much or more attention. Some of that research was rhetorical, focusing on texts such as speeches and ads, and asking questions about words, images, and their effects on audiences. Other research was empirical, using research tools such as content analysis, focus groups, and statistics to study campaign messages.

The presidency will probably remain a central concern of researchers, who may look not only at particular speeches, but also at the role of the speech writer, the political consultant, and other advisors who surround the presidency. How presidents adapt and incorporate new technologies into their communication strategies is also worthy of attention. Presidential debates will probably also remain a major focus of research; as the Racine Group stresses, many questions still need to be answered. Debates in other races, in the United States and abroad, may also attract attention as scholars try to discern whether communication dynamics vary among political arenas.

Additional research will probably focus on the communication dynamics of state and local elections. As the media used in campaigns change, more research will probably focus on Internet campaigning, less on traditional speeches. Research on the legislature and judicial branches may be even more significant in the future. Despite groundbreaking initial research, political communication scholars are challenged to craft more comprehensive and compelling theories of institutional rhetoric that provide insight into legislative decision-making and jurisprudence. In addition, recent scholarship on the legislature and judiciary suggests that elements of rhetorical culture, social norms, and mediated discourse influence—and are influenced by—public proceedings. Further investigation of the multi-faceted relationship between this broader culture and political institutions is needed.

More exploration of the role of alternative public voices in political institutions is also warranted. While legislative bodies, by their nature, provide a space for active participation, future work should also attend to how complex procedures, rules, and public perceptions work to exclude important, opposing, and minority voices from the legislature and courtroom. Rhetorical critical methods are especially useful in exploring how language works to sustain, challenge, and reform structural and power relations in various contexts. Given the relative absence of work devoted to class issues, further study of other "silenced" voices, such as poor and lower-income citizens, is also needed.

Political communication is a rich, lively field of study, filled with possibilities. There is much to be done. We hope this collection of essays will inspire, guide, and challenge you on to future work in this complex, yet wonderful field.

★ ADDITIONAL READINGS

CHAPTER 1
POLITICAL COMMUNICATION FRAMEWORKS

Hahn, D. F. *Political Communication: Rhetoric, Government and Citizens*. 2 ed. State College, Pa.: Strata, 2003.
This text looks at the role of ideology in political argument. Approaching the study of politics from a rhetorical standpoint, the author presents a framework for understanding how language choices and other strategic devices help shape public discourse. Looking at a variety of historical and contemporary events, Hahn argues that politics is essentially a rhetorical process, an ongoing conversation among and between citizens and their government.

Hart, R. P., Jarvis, S. E., Jennings, W. P., and Smith-Howell, D., eds. *Political Keywords: Using Language That Uses Us*. New York: Oxford University Press, 2005.
The editors look at eleven studies of political language to determine the terms or "keywords" that are important to the study of political communication. They identify dominant words in American political discourse and show how they impact political thinking. Through social science and cultural interpretations, this volume considers how people, the media, politicians, and political parties are portrayed, as well as the importance of language in shaping political reality.

Kaid, L. L., ed. *Handbook of Political Communication Research*. Lawrence Erlbaum Associate Communication Series. Mahwah, N.J.: Erlbaum, 2004.
A collection of essays by political communication scholars, this book explores the current state of political communication research and demonstrates major approaches to political communication. Reflecting the interdisciplinary nature of the scholarship, contributors come from communication, political science, journalism, and other disciplines. Each chapter focuses on major

lines of research and theory for the area under discussion.

Perloff, R. M. "An Introduction to Political Communication," in *Political Communication: Politics, Press, and Public in America*. Mahwah, N.J.: Erlbaum, 1998.
This chapter focuses on the role of the media and how it can affect political communication. It provides useful definitions and an overview of the field, with a special focus on the relationship between the press and the presidency.

Rife, D. M. "History and Political Communication: An Introduction," *Political Communication* 18, no. 4 (October 1, 2001): 407–420.
In this summary of articles about the role of history in political communication, the author observes that many researchers have ignored the importance of history in shaping political communication. He argues that understanding the political process often depends upon reading historical narratives.

Schudson, M. *The Good Citizen: A History of American Civic Life*. Cambridge, Mass.: Harvard University Press, 1998.
This volume describes the evolution of voting both as an idea and as a practice in United States history. The author describes the evolution of the concept of citizenship, from the Colonial period, to the Progressive Era of "informed voters," to the late 1990s. Challenging the conventional wisdom that U.S. civic health is in trouble, Schudson argues that the modern-day focus on individual rights does not harm community values. He also debunks nostalgic myths that reflect on simpler political times.

Stuckey, M. C. *The Theory and Practice of Political Communication Research*. SUNY Series in Speech Communication. Albany: State University of New York Press, 1996.
This edited volume provides a variety of perspectives and research on political communication, from interdisciplinary frameworks in communication and political science. The essays focus on the way meaning is produced by those who hold political power,

those who mediate it, and those who receive the messages. These essays consider the study of political communication in institutional or cultural contexts, and draw conclusions about how those contexts affect the transmission of messages and social change.

CHAPTER 2
ELECTION CAMPAIGNS

Ansolabehere, S., and Iyengar, S. "Riding the Wave and Claiming Ownership over Issues: The Joint Effects of Advertising and News Coverage in Campaigns," *Public Opinion Quarterly* 58 (1994): 335–357.
The authors use an experimental design to test two hypothesis concerning the impact and effectiveness of campaign advertising in relationship to news coverage. Results suggest that candidates gain the most in their advertising when they claim ownership of an issue, but that there is little support for a cause and effect relationship between campaign advertising and news broadcasts.

Benoit, W. L., Wells, W. T., Pier, P. M., and Blaney, J. R. "Acclaiming, Attacking, and Defending in Presidential Nominating Acceptance Addresses, 1960–1996," *Quarterly Journal of Speech* 85 (1999): 247–267.
This essay observes that in order to appear preferable to their opponents, presidential candidates engage in self-praise, attack, or defense in their convention speeches. The authors discovered that Republicans tend to attack more than Democrats do, defense tactics are rarely used, and recent nominees are more apt to make statements about candidates than about the party. The authors also indicate that in both their acclamations and attacks, nominees discuss issues far more often than they discuss character.

Hart, R. "The People's Voice," in *Campaign Talk: Why Elections Are Good for Us.* Princeton, N.J.: Princeton University Press, 2000.
The author attempts a description of the people's voice that looks beyond campaign

polling in the United States. He argues that polling has its place, but it does not allow people to speak in their own words. He studied a large sample of letters to the editor written during presidential elections between 1948 and 1996, concluding that the political elite are more concerned with a snapshot of the moment while letter writers seem much more concerned with enduring matters.

Iyengar, S., and Simon, A. F. "New Perspectives and Evidence on Political Communication and Campaign Effects," *Annual Review of Psychology*, 51 (2000): 149–169.
This essay reviews recent empirical evidence that political campaigns are more potent than is usually thought. It offers an overview of methodologies in political communication that makes the case for the resonance model, which considers the relationship between message content and receiver predispositions, and is a stronger predictor than the traditional hypodermic message-based approach.

Moy, P., Pfau, M., and Kahlor, L. "Media Use and Public Confidence in Democratic Institutions," *Journal of Broadcasting and Electronic Media* 43, no. 2 (1999): 137–158.
This essay challenges the idea that media negativity undermines public confidence in democratic institutions. It examines the impact of various media on elections, the office of the presidency, Congress, the criminal court system, the news media, the police, and the public school system. After accounting for the impact of respondent demographics, knowledge (expertise), and political partisanship, the results reveal limited influence of media on perceptions of these institutions.

Parry-Giles, S. J., and Parry-Giles, T., eds. "Special Issue on the 2004 Presidential Election Campaign," *Rhetoric & Public Affairs* 8, no. 4 (winter 2005).
This issue of the journal looks at the 2004 presidential campaign from several standpoints. Essays consider post-9/11 political topics and leaders, with a focus on how rhetoric reflects a sense of "ideological certainty" or "cultural

amnesia." Collectively, the essays in this volume note a retreat to messages of comfort, rather than creation of a new message of "confronting a global war."

Popkin, S. L. "Going without Data: Information Shortcuts," in *The Reasoning Voter: Communication and Persuasion in Presidential Campaigns.* Chicago: University of Chicago Press, 1994.

The author draws on insights from cognitive psychology to demonstrate that campaigns offer voters a surprising amount of information on candidates' views and skills. He argues that all voters have information gaps, which they tend to address by using information shortcuts to evaluate candidates, and posits that interpersonal relationships, party affiliation, and image creation may all have significant impact on the voting public.

CHAPTER 3
ELECTION CAMPAIGN ADVERTISING

Benoit, W. L., Pier, P. M., and Blaney, J. R. "A Functional Approach to Televised Political Spots: Acclaiming, Attacking, Defending," *Communication Quarterly* 45 (1997): 1–20.

The authors investigate political advertising in the 1980–1996 presidential campaigns, using the functional theory of political campaign discourse. They explore how candidates use strategies of self-praise, attack their opponents, and defend or respond to attack. The study indicates that Democrats and incumbents acclaimed more than they attacked, while Republicans and challengers attacked more than they acclaimed.

Finkel, S. E., and Geer, G. G. "A Spot Check: Casting Doubt on the Demobilizing Effect of Attack Advertising," *American Journal of Political Science* 42 (1998): 573–595.

The authors challenge recent research that contends that campaign attack advertising demobilizes the electorate, arguing that there is little reason to suspect a correlation between the number of attack ads and voter turnout. If attack ads demobilize some voters, the authors argue, they are also likely to increase the

participation of others. Their research found that attack ads did not influence voter turnout in congressional elections between 1960 and 1992.

Gronbeck, B. E. "Mythic Portraiture in the 1988 Iowa Presidential Caucus Bio-Ads," *American Behavior Scientist* 32 (1989): 351–364.

The author illustrates the dramatic evolution of media coverage of the primaries since the advent of television. Specifically, he says, television has led to a new focus on the campaign, characterizing it as drama. He argues that television spotlights candidates' personal traits rather than policy or ideas.

Jamieson, K. H. *Packaging the Presidency: A History and Critique of Presidential Campaign Advertising.* New York: Oxford University Press, 1996.

This work is a powerful critique of the impact of televised political ads upon the United States electorate. The author discusses political advertising as the major means by which contemporary candidates for the presidency communicate their messages to voters. She also demonstrates how candidates, by personalizing issues, assert their relevance to voters' lives.

Johnson-Cartee, K. S., and Copeland, G. A. *Manipulation of the American Voter: Political Campaign Commercials.* Westport, Conn: Praeger, 1997.

This book investigates the theoretical and practical reasons that political advertising is successful. It shows readers how to analyze political commercials by illustrating the motives, advertising strategies, and tactics that political candidates and their surrogates use.

Noggle, G., and Kaid L. L. "The Effects of Visual Images in Political Ads: Experimental Testings of Distortions and Visual Literacy," *Social Science Quarterly* 81 (2000): 913–927.

The article investigates the impact that distortions in visual imagery in televised political advertisements might have on the electorate, an increasing concern as political advertising has become the dominant form of political communication in campaigns. The authors also investigate unethical uses of editing techniques, special effects, and computerized alterations.

Trent, J. S., and Sabourin, T. "Sex Still Counts: Women's Use of Televised Advertising during the Decade of the 80's." *Journal of Applied Communication Research* 33 (1993): 21–40.
This essay explores the role of gender in political campaign advertisements in the United States. The authors compare male and female political candidates' campaign advertising styles, investigate whether female candidates and their male counterparts tend to promote different issues, and discuss the amount of negativity in mixed-gender campaigns.

CHAPTER 4
ELECTION CAMPAIGN DEBATES

Benoit, W. L., and Hansen, G. J. "Presidential Debate Questions and the Public Agenda," *Communication Quarterly* 49, no. 2 (2001): 130–141.
The authors examine the questions journalists have asked during the presidential debates from 1960 to 2000. They found that these questions do not reflect the issues that the voting public is interested in.

Friedenberg, R. V. "Patterns and Trends in National Political Debates: 1960–1992," in *Rhetorical Studies of National Political Debates*. 2 ed. Westport, Conn: Praeger, 1994.
This essay summarizes analyses of the presidential and vice presidential debates from 1960 to 1992. The author considers why candidates have debated, candidates' issue and image goals, candidates' rhetorical styles, and the effects.

Hinck, E. A. "Political Debates and the Enactment of Leadership," in *Enacting the Presidency: Political Argument, Presidential Debates, and Presidential Character*. Westport, Conn.: Praeger, 1993.
The author suggests that debates are more performances than discussions of public

policy issues. What is being performed is the presidency: candidates attempt to show that they possess the desirable elements of the presidential character. Candidates must behave in keeping with the popular image of the presidency: they must exhibit good sense, good moral character, and good will; and they must argue well, responding to opponents' and questioners' challenges.

Jamieson, K. H., and Birdsell, D. S. "The Problem of Broadcast Debates," in *Presidential Debates: The Challenge of Creating an Informed Electorate*. New York: Oxford University Press, 1988.
The authors consider how problems inherent in the debates may prevent them from meeting the needs of the electorate. They consider the compressed answers, the question-and-answer format, and the relevance of journalists' questions, as well as how media coverage fails to aid voters' education and how the debates provide too little information or information that is too complex for the uninformed voter, too contradictory, and irrelevant.

Kraus, S. "Debate Effects: Who Wins," in *Televised Presidential Debates and Public Policy*. 2 ed. Mahwah, N.J.: Erlbaum, 2000.
This chapter reviews the literature from several academic disciplines on the effects of the presidential debates. Post-debate polling focuses on candidate characteristics, effects on voting preference, and the simple win-lose question. Polls and studies show that debates primarily reinforce viewer preferences, sway some undecideds, and educate voters about the candidates' positions on issues. The author also considers the visual dimension of the first Nixon-Kennedy debate.

McKinney, M. S., and Carlin, D. B. "Political Campaign Debates," in *Handbook of Political Communication Research*, ed. Lynda Lee Kaid. Mahwah, N.J.: Erlbaum, 2004.
The authors offer a very readable review of the extensive research on political campaign debates. They introduce the reader to the

several theoretical bases on which the research is premised and point to what this research tells us about the effects of presidential debates and their content.

CHAPTER 5
THE PRESIDENCY

Benson, T. W. "'To Lend a Hand': Gerald R. Ford, Watergate, and the White House Speechwriters," *Rhetoric and Public Affairs* 1, no. 2 (1998): 201–225.
Recent scholarship has made critics more attentive to how much a president's words might be mediated by speechwriters. This essay explains a controversial speech by then–vice president Gerald Ford, arguing that much of it was Richard Nixon's speechwriters' words and that Ford's "normal" editing failed to make the speech anything other than a part of the Nixon administration's antagonistic response to the unfolding Watergate investigation.

Ceaser, J. W., Thurow, G. E., Tulis, J., and Bessette, J. M. "The Rise of the Rhetorical Presidency," *Presidential Studies Quarterly* 11 (1981): 158–171.
The authors pinpoint what they believe to be the crucial change in presidential communication in the twentieth century. In earlier eras, they note, presidents rarely spoke. In recent times, presidential speaking has increased dramatically. Lacking constitutional power to do more than propose in many policy areas, presidents frequently take their case to the people, urging them to push Congress in the direction the president desires.

Hart, R. P. "Speech and Action: Building the Presidential Image," in *The Sound of Leadership: Presidential Communication in the Modern Age.* Chicago: University of Chicago Press, 1987.
The author offers "a sociology" of presidential communication, establishing how often, when, on what occasions, and on what subjects presidents speak. He finds that presidential speechmaking has dramatically increased, although there are interesting variations in how individual presidents enact their expanded rhetorical role. He also finds that presidents sometimes speak at largely staged events simply to signal their leadership.

Jamieson, K. H. "Dramatizing and Storytelling," in *Eloquence in an Electronic Age: The Transformation of Political Speechmaking.* New York: Oxford University Press, 1988.
The author focuses on crucial effects of television on presidential communication, with particular attention to how the potential of that medium was realized especially well during the Reagan presidency. Reagan's speechwriters used striking, compelling visual images, coupled with dramatic storytelling, to create an eloquence quite different from that associated with Franklin Delano Roosevelt or John F. Kennedy.

Parry-Giles, S. J., and Blair, D. M. "The Rise of the Rhetorical First Lady: Politics, Gender, Ideology, and Women's Voices," *Rhetoric & Public Affairs* 5, no. 4 (2002): 565–599.
The authors note that First Ladies have always had a political role to play, but have used the power of public persuasion more explicitly in the last century. From 1789 to 1920, First Ladies engaged in social politicking and benevolent volunteering. After 1920, they assumed "the republican mother pulpit," embracing causes such as drug use by children, and addressing women as citizens by speaking to them about public matters. Despite such changes, the authors find that there still seem to be gendered limits on the First Lady role.

Stuckey, M. E. "Competing Foreign Policy Visions: Rhetorical Hybrids after the Cold War," *Western Journal of Communication* 59 (1995): 214–227.
The author argues that presidents use paradigmatic dramas that the public can readily grasp to speak about foreign policy. The Cold War drama facilitated public understanding of foreign policy issues, but alternative dramas of the New World Order or power politics have proven less engaging.

George H. W. Bush combined the Cold War drama with the New World Order and Bill Clinton combined the Cold War drama with power politics, but neither hybrid proved especially successful.

CHAPTER 6
THE LEGISLATURE
AND THE JUDICIARY

Hasian, Jr., M. "Judicial Rhetoric in a Fragmentary World: 'Character' and Storytelling in the Leo Frank Case," *Communication Monographs* 64, no. 3 (September 1997): 250–269.
Adopting a narrative approach to examine the infamous Leo Frank Case, the author demonstrates the lasting rhetorical appeal of "characters" in society and the law as he explores the construction of jurisprudential norms. The essay also reveals the role of race, class, and gender in shaping public perceptions of trials.

Hogan, J. M., and Dorsey, L. "Public Opinion and the Nuclear Freeze: The Rhetoric of Popular Sovereignty in Foreign Policy Debate," *Western Journal of Speech Communication* 55 (Fall 1991): 319–338.
Studying the relationship between public opinion and policy formation, the authors contend that the public's role in the policy-making process varies situationally. Through an analysis of the 1982–1983 congressional nuclear freeze debate, they argue that public opinion can be ascertained best through examining the will of the people, as mediated by the decision makers in their rhetorical documents.

Lay, M. M. "Midwifery on Trial: Balancing Privacy Rights and Health Concerns after Roe v. Wade," *Quarterly Journal of Speech* 89 (February 2003): 60–77.
This essay examines several court cases surrounding midwifery in the aftermath of *Roe v. Wade*. Capitalizing on *Roe*'s ambiguous language about who could be recognized as a legitimate health care provider, proponents of

midwife care used several strategies in court to resist the medicalization of pregnancy, which had curtailed the authority and roles of midwives. Drawing on Foucault, the author investigates the relative success and failure of resistance strategies.

Miller, M. L. "Public Argument and Legislative Debate in the Rhetorical Construction of Public Policy: The Case of Florida Midwifery Legislation," *Quarterly Journal of Speech* 85 (November 1999): 361–379.
This study of the Florida legislature's debate over lay midwifery and homebirth assesses how legislative debates represent, transform, and omit the public arguments of marginalized constituencies. The author demonstrates the limitations of certain forms of arguments for marginalized groups, concluding that legislative discourse seeks to perpetuate strategic alliances that mirror public opinion.

Sullivan, P. A., and Goldzwig, S. R. "A Relational Approach to Moral Decision-Making: The Majority Opinion in *Planned Parenthood v. Casey*," *Quarterly Journal of Speech* 81 (1995): 167–190.
Drawing in part on feminist theory, the authors analyze the majority opinion in *Planned Parenthood v. Casey* as a case study to develop a relational approach to moral reasoning. They challenge traditional approaches to rhetorical investigation and highlight the role of morals and values in judicial decision-making.

Waddell, C. "The Role of *Pathos* in the Decision-Making Process: A Study in the Rhetoric of Science Policy," *Quarterly Journal of Speech* 76 (November 1990): 381–400.
Concerned about how nonscientists debate complex technical and scientific issues, the author analyzes the public hearings and deliberations of the Cambridge Experimentation Review Board regarding recombinant DNA. This essay highlights the vital role that emotional appeals play in policy making and offers suggestions for critiquing such emotional appeals.

CHAPTER 7
VOICES FROM THE MARGINS

Conrad, C. "Work Songs, Hegemony, and Illusions of Self," *Critical Studies in Mass Communication* 5 (1988): 179–201.
Exploring working class identity through an examination of country work songs, this essay outlines three prevailing themes: a community of working people, the inevitability of hard work, and the virtue of self-sacrifice for family. The author argues that even as country work songs celebrate physical labor as an essential characteristic of working class identity, they naturalize hierarchical power structures and encourage self-defeating and repressive identities for the working class.

Cordova, N. I. "The Constitutive Force of the *Catecismo del Pueblo* in Puerto Rico's Popular Democratic Party Campaign of 1938–1940," *Quarterly Journal of Speech* 90 (May 2004): 212–233.
This essay traces the rise of the Popular Democratic Party (PDP) under the leadership of Luis Muñoz Marin. In particular, and relying on a Burkean approach, Cordova examines the constitutive force of the *Catecismo del Pueblo,* a small PDP booklet intended to cultivate the support of the working classes.

Morris, III, C. "Pink Herring and the Fourth Persona: J. Edgar Hoover's Sex Crime Panic," *Quarterly Journal of Speech* 88 (May 2002): 228–244.
This essay investigates a rhetoric of passing, showing how J. Edgar Hoover adopted the rhetorical strategy of "pink herring" to deflect public attention from questions of his personal sexual identity. By viciously persecuting "sex deviates," Hoover appeared to conform with heterosexual norms and silence using the "fourth persona"—an implied audience that acknowledges and is complicit in the passing.

Tonn, M. B. "Militant Motherhood: Labor's Mary Harris 'Mother' Jones," *Quarterly Journal of Speech* 82 (1996): 1–21.
Using "Mother Jones" as a case study to explore the relationship between the labor movement and symbolic motherhood, this essay argues that maternal personae are especially empowering for severely oppressed groups such as coal miners. The essay reveals how Mother Jones negotiated social expectations of femininity with her goals of agitation and reform, exploiting the power inherent in motherhood.

Wander, P. "The Third Persona: An Ideological Turn in Rhetorical Theory," *Central States Speech Journal* 35 (Winter 1984): 197–216.
The author explains how language works to ignore, devalue, and even negate the views of some groups. In particular, he argues that economic, social, and political structures represent marginalized groups in ways that affect the ability of these groups to speak for themselves and be heard, and that, as a result, hegemonic relationships often warrant the exclusion of outgroups from public debate.

Watson, M. S. "The Issue Is Justice: Martin Luther King Jr.'s Response to the Birmingham Clergy," *Rhetoric & Public Affairs* 7 (Spring 2004): 1–22.
This essay examines Martin Luther King Jr.'s "Letter from Birmingham Jail" within the larger context of two statements by Birmingham clergy, to which King responds. The author argues that, in crafting his rhetorical masterpiece, King shifted the debate to a moral realm where justice prevails as a value over peace. The author also argues that the widespread appeal of the letter is partly due to the audience constituted by the letter.

Zaeske, S. "Signatures of Citizenship: The Rhetoric of Women's Antislavery Petitions," *Quarterly Journal of Speech* 88 (May 2002): 147–168.
This essay investigates the invaluable contribution of women's antislavery petitioning to the success of the abolitionist movement. It also argues that through the very act of petition-signing, women redefined their socio-political status, claiming more widespread access to the public sphere and renegotiating their status as citizens.

Index

About the Editors

Theodore F. Sheckels

Theodore F. Sheckels is Professor of English and Communication at Randolph-Macon College. He received his B.S. from Duquesne University and his M.A. and Ph.D. from Penn State University. He is the author of *Debating: Applied Rhetorical Theory* (1984), *When Congress Debates* (2000), *Maryland Politics and Political Communication, 1950–2005* (2006), and books on South African literature, Australian film, and Canadian women writers. His work has been published in edited collections on Commonwealth literature and film, as well as in *Argumentation & Advocacy, Communication Quarterly, Howard Journal of Communications, Rhetoric and Public Affairs,* and *Southern Journal of Communication.* Randolph Macon College has nominated him twice for the Virginia State Council of Higher Education's Professor of the Year Award.

Janette Kenner Muir

Janette Kenner Muir is Associate Professor of Interdisciplinary and Integrative Studies and an affiliate member of the Communication and Women's Studies Departments at George Mason University, where she has also served as Associate Dean of the New Century College. She received her B.A. from Palm Beach Atlantic College, her M.A. from Wake Forest University and her Ph.D. from the University of Massachusetts Amherst. She is a contributing author on *Inventing A Voice: The Rhetoric of American First Ladies of the Twentieth Century* (2004), *Hate Speech (*1995), and *The Clinton Presidency: Images, Issues and Communication Strategies,* (1993). She has also published several instructional handbooks for communication classes and has served as editor of *Communication Quarterly.* Dr. Muir has received the Distinguished Service Award from the Eastern Communication Association and the Teaching Excellence Award from George Mason University.

Terry Robertson

Terry Robertson is Associate Professor and Chair of the Department of Communication Studies, as well as the Director of the Interdisciplinary Education and Action Program, at the University of South Dakota. He received his B.A. from Drury University, his M.A. from Missouri State University, and his Ph.D. from the University of Oklahoma. His research interests include media coverage of political campaigns, women in the political process, and presidential rhetoric. He is co-author of the book *Gender and Candidate Communication* (2004) and has published articles in *Communication Quarterly, American Behavioral Scientist, The Journal for Critical Education, Policy Studies, Atlantic Journal of Communication,* and *Speaker & Gavel.* Dr. Robertson has received the Outstanding New Teacher Award from the Central States Communication Convention as well as the Belbas Larson Teaching Award and Cutler Research Award from the University of South Dakota.

Lisa M. Gring-Pemble

Lisa M. Gring-Pemble is Associate Professor of Interdisciplinary and Integrative Studies, as well as an affiliate member of the Cultural Studies and Women's Studies Departments, at George Mason University. She received her B.A. from St. Olaf College and her M.A. and Ph.D. from the University of Maryland. She is the author of *Grim Fairy Tales: The Rhetorical Construction of American Welfare Policy* (2003). Her work has appeared in *The Quarterly Journal of Speech, Political Communication,* and *Communication Quarterly.* She has taught in several communication and interdisciplinary learning communities and has written articles in *Inventio* and *Connecting the Classroom to the World: Integrative Studies.* Dr. Gring-Pemble has received the Teaching Excellence Award from George Mason University.